MUSIC THEORY FROM ZARLINO TO SCHENKER

A Bibliography and Guide

Frontispiece from *Gradus ad Parnassum* by Johann Joseph Fux, 1725. Reproduced with permission from Sibley Music Library, Eastman School of Music, University of Rochester

MUSIC THEORY FROM ZARLINO TO SCHENKER

A Bibliography and Guide

by
David Damschroder
The University of Minnesota
and
David Russell Williams
Memphis State University

HARMONOLOGIA No. 4.

Joel Lester, Series Editor

PENDRAGON PRESS
STUYVESANT, NY

OTHER TITLES IN THE HARMONOLOGIA SERIES

No. 1 *Heinrich Schenker: Index to analysis* by Larry Laskowsi (1978) ISBN 0-918728-06-1

No. 2 *Marpurg's* Thoroughbass and Composition Handbook: *A narrative translation and critical study* by David A. Sheldon (1989) ISBN 0-918728-55-x

No. 3 *Between Modes and Keys: German Theory 1592-1802* by Joel Lester (1990) ISBN 0-918728-77-0

No. 5 Musical Time: *The Sense of Order:* by Barbara R. Barry (1990) ISBN 0-945193-01-7

Library of Congress Cataloging-in-Publication Data

Damschroder, David.
    Music theory from Zarlino to Schenker: a
      bibliography and guide / by David Damschroder and
      David Russell Williams.
    p. cm. -- (Harmonologia series : no. 4)
    ISBN 0-918728-99-1 : $54.00
    1. Music--Theory--Bibliography.   I. Williams, David
      Russell.   II. Title.   III. Series.
    ML 128.T5D27   1990
    016.781--dc20   90-6952 CIP MN

TABLE OF CONTENTS

Preface   vii

Acknowledgments   viii

Introduction   ix

Abbreviations

    Periodical, Series, and   xv
      General Abbreviations

    Congress Reports   xxxviii

    Festschriften   xli

Dictionary of Theorists   1

Literature Supplement   397

Topical Index   449

Chronological Index   459

Title Index   471

Name Index   489

PREFACE

Three deceptively plain and workaday adjectives may help to convey the exceptional worth of this book—*useful, reliable, needed*. Students surveying the history of music theory will find here the names of the many early writers who in their treatises have bequeathed a legacy of musical thought distinctive of their time. Each theorist's name is followed by a succinct and informative essay designed to provide an initial acquaintance with his main concerns and most notable contributions. In the event that the reader's interest should focus on a particular historical figure, the authors of this volume have foreseen that he or she will need a complete list of the theorist's known writings, information regarding the location of original manuscripts or prints, and notice about the availability of microfilm reproductions, facsimile or modern editions, and translations. In addition, they have organized the subsequent bibliography of secondary literature in a way that will give a sense of which items would be best to seek first. The nearly exhaustive lists of articles and books offer an opportunity for a broad perspective, even for seasoned scholars, who may specialize in only a few of the theorists represented; and the topical and chronological indices on pages 449 and 459 provide a solid base that can facilitate a teacher's task of planning a course syllabus.

The study of early ideas concerning music has attracted the interest of an increasing number of scholars. Notwithstanding certain obvious precautions, the writings of theorists are surely among the most important sources of context for understanding the music of any period. It will no longer do to attempt an analysis of an eighteenth-century piece without having recourse to the conceptual tradition that surrounded its making. Lately, because of that conviction, whole conferences and whole journals have been organized around the history of music theory as a unifying agendum. This is not a passing trend; it is an inevitable evolution, as some historians and theorists may well be tempted to say. Already one senses the difficulty of keeping abreast of it all. For progress to continue, it must be accompanied by a secure awareness of past undertakings, and this includes not only the grand discoveries and syntheses, but also the wrong turns and the extended debates. The authors of the present work, the series editor, and the publisher deserve sincere thanks and congratulations for producing a valuable record of this field of scholarship, and a catalyst as well for future research. We have waited long for this book.

Benito V. Rivera

ACKNOWLEDGMENTS

A book such as this comes about only through the cooperation and support of a large number of individuals and institutions. For six years we have been the beneficiaries of extraordinary kindness and goodwill from all quarters, and we offer our thanks to every individual who offered help or guidance.

The institutions which supported us and their administrative officers deserve high praise and sincere thanks. The University of Minnesota provided not only two Grants in Aid of Research, Artistry and Scholarship from the Graduate School, but also a Summer Research Fellowship and two McMillan Travel Fund grants. Memphis State University provided a semester sabbatical and in other ways made it possible to combine teaching with vigorous research.

The staffs of libraries whose resources were made available to us are to be commended for their efficient and tireless assistance and access. In particular Katie Holum, Laurie Scholtus, and Marian Kienholz of the University of Minnesota and Ann Viles, Anna Neal, Carol Lowry, Philip Smith, Deborah Brackstone, Ann Denton, and Rita Broadway of Memphis State University have graciously accommodated the fussiest of bibliographers residing in their midst. Our research has been facilitated by staff members at the Library of Congress, Sibley Music Library (Eastman School of Music), New York Public Library, Yale University Library, Harvard University Library, Indiana University Library, University of Michigan Library, Minneapolis Public Library, Boston Public Library, and St. Paul Public Library.

Several experts in foreign languages were of special help: Jan Alboszta, Jennette Mayo, Ludek Miller, Yoshinobu Mizutani, Mariann Tiblin, and Nicolas Van der Sanden. Mark Engebretson was an efficient and industrious research assistant. Charlie Biggers supplied assistance concerning computers. Thomas Dettbarn and Larry Zbikowski read and commented upon everything we had to offer.

Special thanks go to the many scholars in the field who have contributed in one way or another to the undertaking. Your letters, your willingness to share research in progress, your zeal in proofreading entries in your areas of specialization, and your gentle nagging have all been appreciated. Though this list cannot be complete, we would like to acknowledge especially David Bernstein (twentieth-century theory), Allen Cadwallader (Schenker), Ellon Carpenter (Russian theory), James Chenevert (Sechter), Thomas Christensen (French theory and the science of music), Susan Clermont (German theory of the nineteenth and twentieth centuries), Paul Leprade (French theory), Elizabeth West Marvin (Riemann), Gordon McQuere (Russian theory), Severine Neff (Schoenberg and Ziehn), Richard B. Nelson (German theory), Beverly L. Parker (Taneev), Benito Rivera (sixteenth- and seventeenth-century theory), Miguel A. Roig Francolí (Spanish theory), Lee Rothfarb (Kurth), John Rothgeb (Schenker), and Robert Wason (nineteenth- and twentieth-century theory).

The support of Managing Editor Robert Kessler and Series Editor Joel Lester at Pendragon Press in the creation of such a complicated book has been most gratifying, and the six years that Elsa Williams has shared in her husband's project—with everything from umlaut checks to cheerleading—is appreciated by both authors.

INTRODUCTION

Though the centuries during which composers discovered, flourished under, and eventually began to abandon tonal practices continue to recede from our modern world, the music which survives from those times continues to inspire and delight. Efforts to maintain the integrity and power of that vast, great repertoire have increased. In the company of editors, instrument builders, performers, and the musical public, scholars have endeavored to learn from what past generations have left behind so that the fundamental principles of the art live on. Paintings retain their character so long as a congenial physical environment is maintained; music must continually be renewed. Those who commit themselves to the stewardship of our art as it flourished from the late Renaissance through the early twentieth century face an awesome task: to assimilate the stylistic and structural intricacies which the best musicians of those times understood, so that the music comes alive again with undiminished beauty and vitality.

The musical scores are our principal legacy. Yet notes and slurs are no more than instructions—often quite imprecise—by which performers, infused with a grasp of a particular musical idiom, reveal in sound their interpretation of what a composer intended. The responsibility for elucidating all facets of compositional practice, for waging controversies concerning the validity of various compositional choices, for asserting the foundations upon which the musical art was grounded, for revealing the performer's responsibilities in the improvisational aspect of a work's ultimate creation—all this, and more, fell to individuals who pursued what is now labeled "music theory."

Many were performers or composers, a few built instruments, some were scientists, others dilettantes. But what they wrote—addressed most often to their contemporaries, but on occasion with an eye towards posterity—is of incalculable value. We cannot, after all, visit the Thomaskirche and overhear Bach's practice, or join Attwood in his lessons with Mozart. We can, however, read Kirnberger or Marpurg. We can study the volume of Fux upon which Mozart based his teaching and through which countless composers learned their art. While such sources lead us only partway to the essence of past practices, they are—when combined with a careful assessment of the scores themselves—our best companions in the quest for an understanding of our heritage.

The pursuit of the past has been a concern of large numbers of scholars, as this volume amply documents. Yet access to their contributions has never before been organized in a way that is adequate for the multiple purposes to which they are subjected. We have attempted to coordinate these materials so as to appeal to a variety of readers. Whereas we assume that even seasoned scholars will find citations and pathways that lead to further understanding, we are especially eager to be of service to the many individuals for whom theoretical topics are of interest but not a central pursuit. By offering brief, lucid introductions to each theorist's ideas and by assembling a large amount of information in bibliographical format, we hope to improve the prospects for an integration of theoretical investigations and other endeavors (such as developing technical facility on an instrument or exploring music's history) within the perspectives of all musicians. Those who perform might achieve greater fidelity to a composer's conceptions and an era's conventions; those who listen might attain a heightened responsiveness to the beauty and logic of the art. Yet these rewards accrue only after rigorous, devoted work. The introductions can give but a hint of the perspective and awareness that result from further study.

Subdivisions of the text

Though our format is straightforward, there are certain conventions and idiosyncrasies to which readers should be alerted immediately. First, locate the main sections of the volume:

The **ABBREVIATIONS** section contains three parts. The large file of Periodical, Series, and General Abbreviations is followed by similar listings for Congress Reports and for Festschriften.

The **DICTIONARY OF THEORISTS** includes individual chapters for over two hundred authors, arranged alphabetically.

The **LITERATURE SUPPLEMENT** lists articles, books, and dissertations which pertain to several DICTIONARY OF THEORISTS authors and which therefore would be inappropriately placed in any one of those chapters. With very few exceptions, entries in the LITERATURE SUPPLEMENT are indexed in all appropriate DICTIONARY OF THEORISTS chapters.

Various **INDICES** facilitate the effective use of this guide. Included are a topical index; a chronological index of treatise titles; an alphabetical index of treatise titles; and an index of all authors mentioned anywhere in the ABBREVIATIONS, DICTIONARY OF THEORISTS, or LITERATURE SUPPLEMENT.

Cross-reference citations

So that we might expand our listings in future editions without disrupting the existing network of cross-references, we have elected not to undertake sequential numbering of the bibliographical entries. Instead each entry is uniquely addressed by its placement within the volume, the author's last name, and

the year(s) of publication (plus occasionally a word or two of the title when further discrimination is necessary). We trust that references such as "Strunk (1950)" and "Palisca (1985)" will be more useful than mere numbers. Three categories of cross-references are utilized, as follows:

1. Reference to an item in another DICTIONARY OF THEORISTS chapter

Examples: See RIEMANN: (1895-1901).
See RIEMANN: (1898):Haggh (1961/. . . /1974).
See SCHENKER: (1906-35):Vol. III (1935).
See SCHENKER: Jonas (1934/1972): Rothgeb (1982).
See ROUSSEAU, J.-J.: Jansen (1884/1971); ZARLINO: (1558):Cohen (1977/1983).

Explanation: The citation always begins with the last name, in capital letters, of one of the theorists for whom a DICTIONARY OF THEORISTS chapter exists. If a year, enclosed in parentheses, follows the theorist's name, the reference is to the primary item (a treatise or article by that theorist) published first in that year. If instead another name is found, followed by a date, the citation refers to an item from the LITERATURE section of that chapter, written by the named author and published in the given year.

If a specific edition or translation is being referred to, the citation will continue with the name of an editor or translator as well as the date of the edition published under his or her supervision. If a specific volume within a multi-volume work is being referred to, the number of the volume and its date of publication will follow.

Often, as an added service for our readers, the citation will include dates of both the first and the most recent editions (useful in ascertaining at a glance the availability—perhaps in facsimile—of the work cited).

2. Reference to an item in the same DICTION-ARY OF THEORISTS chapter

Examples: (Within the SCHENKER chapter):
See (1925), below.
See Jonas and Salzer (1937-38), below.
See also Beach (1969/1977), above, and
Beach (1985), below.

Explanation: The words "above" and "below" replace the redundant and potentially confusing referral to the very chapter one is consulting. The direction assists in locating the citation. As with other DICTIONARY OF THEORISTS citations, the positioning of dates and names indicates whether the item is among the primary entries or within the LITERATURE section.

3. Reference to an item in the LITERATURE SUPPLEMENT

Examples: See **Cohen (1981)**; Cohen and Miller (1979).
See Mitchell, J. W. (1963).
See **Palisca** (1968/1985), ["Theory"] **(1980)**.
See also ROUSSEAU, J.: (1678); SCHENKER: (1925-30):Kalib (1973); Morgan (1978); LITERATURE SUPPLEMENT: Morgan (1969), (1978).

Explanation: As most cross-references will be made to entries found in the LITERATURE SUPPLEMENT, the absence of either a theorist's name in capital letters at the beginning of a citation or the words "above" or "below" at the end of a citation indicates that the item is found in the LITERATURE SUPPLEMENT. However, when multiple citations are listed within the same paragraph and some are from the DICTIONARY OF THEORISTS chapters and others from the LITERATURE SUPPLEMENT, then the words LITERATURE SUPPLEMENT will precede the appropriate citations. Multiple citations will be ordered so as to proceed from the front to the back of this volume. Thus LITERATURE SUPPLEMENT citations will always follow all DICTIONARY OF THEORISTS citations.

As an aid in using the large LITERATURE SUPPLEMENT file, we have used bold type to call attention to a few books and articles which we regard as particularly informative or authoritative.

We make a careful distinction between commas, semicolons, and colons. Commas may separate two independent citations, both written by the author whose name appears before the first citation. A comma may also follow the last name of an author when his or her initials are included (to distinguish Jean ROUSSEAU from Jean-Jacques ROUSSEAU, for example). Semicolons separate citations of works by different LITERATURE or LITERATURE SUPPLEMENT authors and individual primary citations of works by a DICTIONARY OF THEORISTS author. Colons, when followed by a space, initiate the listing of all citations from the chapter whose title precedes the colon. When followed immediately by a name, date, or volume number (with no space), they separate components within a single citation.

Primary entries in the DICTIONARY OF THEORISTS

We attempt to present a complete and authoritative listing of each theorist's books pertaining to music theory, arranged chronologically. Articles and manuscripts are listed selectively, depending upon their importance. Work in areas other than music theory are neglected without comment.

Publication information is listed selectively. For most older treatises, especially when all editions are available on microfilm or in facsimile, we supply data on each edition. However, for many nineteenth-century works (some of which appeared in dozens of editions) we indicate "later editions" or some similar remark, sometimes specifying the number of editions or the date of the last edition. Words such as "Witwe" (widow) or "Erben" (heirs) are left untranslated, though when the author is also the publisher, we indicate "the author" rather than "Autor" or "Selbstverlag." When a printer other than the official publisher actually produced the book, we often supply his or her name, enclosed in parentheses. Dates are enclosed in brackets if conjecture is involved, while the abbreviation "ca." or a question mark signals a probable lack of precision. For German-language dissertations, we follow Richard Schaal's *Verzeichnis deutschsprachiger musikwissenschaftlicher Dissertationen* in the inclusion of both the date of appearance and the date upon which the degree was awarded (if not identical), the latter being noted within parentheses. When a manuscript is cited, we attempt to supply reliable information on the date of its creation and current whereabouts, though we have sometimes failed in this attempt.

For all pre-1800 materials, references to various distributors of microfilm or microcards are included. Three of these deserve special mention. The most comprehensive is LCPS (Library of Congress Photoduplication Service), which offers for sale most items from the Library of Congress pre-1800 treatise collection on microfilm. A single reel may contain a dozen or more treatises. A similar service, with greater emphasis upon microcards, is SMLMS (Sibley Music Library Microform Service). Finally, Harvard's rare holdings in music theory are available in a single large set of microfilms called HoM (History of Music). The ABBREVIATIONS section (under LCPS, SMLMS, and HoM) should be consulted for further information.

Most facsimile editions and translations of treatises are listed. Those publications which do not alter the language of the original are called Sources (and are highlighted by the symbol "S●" in the left margin). Those which do are called Translations (and are highlighted by the symbol "T●" in the left margin). In some cases segments of a treatise have appeared. They, too, are listed in this format.

Secondary entries in the DICTIONARY OF THEORISTS

The word LITERATURE signals the beginning of the secondary materials. This listing is arranged according to the year in which each item was first published. Later editions and translations are included with the original citation. Items selected for inclusion will generally contain information relating specifically to an author's theoretical work. We have tended to omit items of a biographical nature or those which pertain strictly to another facet of the author's career. After these entries, we present a listing of cross-references to other DICTIONARY OF THEORISTS chapters and to the LITERATURE SUPPLEMENT. The DICTIONARY OF THEORISTS citations are made selectively, whereas those to the LITERATURE SUPPLEMENT are exhaustive.

Entries in the LITERATURE SUPPLEMENT

As the LITERATURE SUPPLEMENT entries are identical in format to those in the LITERATURE sections of the DICTIONARY OF THEORISTS, no special explanations are required. However, since this list is very large and some authors are very prolific, please note the careful arrangement of items both alphabetically and, for a given author's output, chronologically.

Special features

References to book reviews pertaining to works cited are included. Coverage is extensive but not exhaustive.

Those who are not familiar with a given theorist or his work should find items marked with the symbol ●●● to be particularly useful as introductory reading. The symbol is in most cases applied to materials that are both readily available in research libraries and written in English. Remember also that LITERATURE SUPPLEMENT entries which we regard as especially informative are consistently cited using bold type.

As a reminder that further bibliographical information is available in some of the materials listed, the abbreviation "Bibliog." is appended to selected entries.

Whenever mention is made of a theorist for whom a DICTIONARY OF THEORISTS chapter exists, his name is printed in capital letters (except, of course, within direct quotations or titles of books or articles).

Extensive references to *Rilm*, *Rism*, and *DA* are provided. (Here and in all future contexts, the ABBREVIATIONS list supplies complete titles of such works.)

Whenever possible, information on the series in which a volume has been published is included. In the ABBREVIATIONS list, the series editor is often named along with the full title of the series.

Coverage

No issue we have faced in the creation of this volume has warranted more careful consideration than the selection of theorists for inclusion. Our interest in offering our readers maximum access to the information they might seek soon came in conflict with the physical bulk of what we were assembling. We reluctantly accepted the fact that a guide for all Western music theory from Greek times to the modern era (our original intent) would require three hefty volumes, of which we have produced only the second. We hope that someday two companion volumes will emerge, though we do not commit ourselves to that task.

The materials that were assembled for our LITERATURE SUPPLEMENT file helped us in assessing the frequency with which various theorists have been discussed within the secondary literature. This information led to the formation of a roster of some six hundred names, of which approximately two hundred were earmarked for inclusion within our work. The roster was distributed to a number of scholars in the field, many of whom responded with suggestions for changes in the status of individual theorists—some to be included, others to be deleted. Considering their suggestions, we made the choices that are reflected within this volume.

We have purposefully emphasized compositional practice, speculative theory, and the most significant pedagogical works. We have de-emphasized adjunct disciplines such as music criticism, aesthetics, and perception, which would expand our volume beyond a comfortable size were they dealt with comprehensively.

Once a theorist was accepted for inclusion, extensive bibliographical research was undertaken to bring together as much information pertinent to his theoretical contributions as was possible. Our bibliographies are strongest in the scholarship of the past four decades (for which *Music Index* and, for materials published between 1967 and 1983, *Rilm* listings were available). Our files were closed to further expansion on July 1, 1989, so that the production process could commence.

The scale of this undertaking should not be construed as an indication that we have achieved exhaustive coverage of the theorists included. We anticipate that individual readers who possess specialized knowledge in certain areas or who have access to rare library holdings will note some omissions or (inevitably) some errors in our work. We eagerly await the suggestions and criticisms of our readers, so that future editions might more fully realize the goals of this endeavor.

PERIODICAL, SERIES, AND GENERAL
ABBREVIATIONS

With a Selective Listing of Reprint and Microfilm Editions

Aaad	*Annonces, affiches et avis divers*
AAR	Acta Albertina Ratisbonensia
AARov	*Atti della I. R. Accademia di scienze lettere ed arti degli agiati in Rovereto*
AASIB	*Atti della Accademia delle Scienze dell' Istituto de Bologna*
ABAWPpK	*Abhandlungen der Bayerischen Akademie der Wissenschaften: Philosophisch-philologische Klasse*
ABBW	*A B Bookman's Weekly: For the Specialist Book World*
	Antiquarian Bookman through 1967.
ABDS	Anton Bruckner: Dokumente und Studien
AC	*Annales Chopin*
ACM	Auction Catalogues of Music
Acol	Actes et colloques
ACR	*American Choral Review*
AcR	*[Ackermann's] Repository of Arts, Literature and Fashions*
ACRPP	Association pour la Conservation et la Reproduction Photographique de la Press (Marne-La-Vallee)
ADAWB	Abhandlungen der Deutschen Akademie der Wissenschaften zu Berlin: Klasse für Philosophie, Geschichte, Staats-, Rechts- und Wirtschaftswissenschaften
AdB	*Allgemeine deutsche Bibliothek*
AdBiog	*Allgemeine deutsche Biographie* [DunH.]
Adem	*Adem: Tweemaandelijks tijdschrift voor muziekcultuur*
AdM	*Allgemeine deutsche Musik-Zeitung* [Dat.]
AdN	*Annalen der Naturphilosophie*

ADV	Akademie Druck- und Verlagsanstalt (Neufeldweg)
Aeco	*Archivum europae centro-orientalis*
AfGPh	*Archiv für Geschichte der Philosophie*
AfMf	*Archiv für Musikforschung* [DG.] A continuation of *ZfMw.*
AfMw	*Archiv für Musikwissenschaft* [Dat. DG. GO. IDC. LCPS.]
AfSf	*Archiv für Sippenforschung*
AgP	*Archiv für gesamte Psychologie*
AHES	*Archive for History of Exact Sciences*
AHMB	Athlone History of Music in Britain, edited by Ian Spink
AHR	*American Historical Review*
AI	Art and Imagination
Aihi	Archives internationales d'histoire des idées
Aihs	*Archives internationales d'histoire des sciences*
AiM	Aesthetics in Music
AIP	American Institute of Physics (New York)
AJME	*The Australian Journal of Music Education: The Official Journal of the Australian Society for Music Education*
AJO	*American Journal of Ophthalmology*
AJP	*American Journal of Psychology*
AJPh	*American Journal of Physics*
AKMLw	Abhandlungen zur Kunst-, Musik- und Literaturwissenschaft
AKSGW	*Abhandlungen der Königlich Sächsischen Gesellschaft der Wissenschaften: Mathematisch-physische Klasse*

Alash	*Acta litteraria academiae scientiarum hungaricae/A Quarterly of the Hungarian Academy of Science*
Alit	*L'année littéraire*
Am	*Acta musicologica* [DG. BH. JRC.]
AMagS	Abrahams Magazine Service (New York)
AMAWL	*Abhandlungen der Mainzer Akademie der Wissenschaften und der Literatur: Geistes- und sozialwissenschaftliche Klasse*
Ambix	*Ambix: Being the Journal of the Society for the Study of Alchemy and Early Chemistry*
AmCS	Accademia musicale Chigiana, Siena
AmE	*Atti e memorie della real deputazione di storia patria per le province dell'Emilia*
AmM	*American Music* [UMI.]
AMMo	*The American Mathematics Monthly: Official Journal of the Mathematical Association of America*
AmO	*The American Organist* Published through 1970.
AmO:AGO	*The American Organist: Official Journal of The American Guild of Organists and The Royal Canadian College of Organists* [UMI.]
AMoz	*Acta Mozartiana*
AmR	*Atti e memorie della real deputazione di storia patria per le province della Romagna*
AmSc	*American Scientist*
AMSFS	Abrahams Magazine Service Film Service (New York)
AMS/MLARS	American Musicological Society/Music Library Association Reprint Series
AMSNYP	American Musicological Society, Greater New York Chapter Publications
AMSP	Abrahams Magazine Service Press (New York)
AMSSD	American Musicological Society Studies and Documents
AMT	*American Music Teacher: Official Journal of the Music Teachers National Association* [UMI.]
Amus	*Arte musical: Revista de doutrina, noticiário e crítica*

AMuZ	*Allgemeine Musik-Zeitung: Wochenschrift für das Musikleben der Gegenwart* [Dat. KIP. LCPS. SMS.] Title varies.
AmZ	*Allgemeine musikalische Zeitung* [Dat. FK. LCPS. SMLMS. UME.]
AmZ(L)	*Allgemeine musikalische Zeitung* (Leipzig) [FK.]
Anamu	*Analecta musicologica: Veröffentlichungen der Musikabteilung des Deutschen Historischen Instituts in Rom*
Anbruch	*Anbruch: Österreichische Zeitschrift für Musik* [Dat. LCPS. SMS.] The continuation of *MAn.*
Anm	*Annales musicologiques*
Anmon	*Annales monégasques*
Anmu	*Anuario musical*
Annm	*L'année musicale* [Dat. IDC. KIP. MinR.]
ANQ	*American Notes and Queries*
Ao	*Acta organologica*
AÖAW	*Anzeiger der philosophisch-historische Klasse der Österreichischen Akademie der Wissenschaften*
AoM	Anthology of Music
ApA	*Acta physica Austraiaca*
APAWPhK	*Abhandlungen der Preußischen Akademie der Wissenschaften: Philosophisch-historische Klasse*
Apsy	*Année psychologique*
AR	*American Recorder*
ArB	Académie royale de Belgique, classe des beaux-arts, mémoires
ARBA	*American Reference Books Annual*
ArBB	*Académie royale des sciences, des lettres et des beaux-arts de Belgique: Bulletin de la classe des beaux-arts* [Dat.]
ArBBs	*Académie royale des sciences, des lettres et des beaux-arts de Belgique: Bulletin de la classe des sciences*
ARG	*The American Record Guide: An Independent Journal of Opinion*
Armus	*Arti musices: Croatian Musicological Review*
Arphil	*Archives de philosophie*
ArsOr	*Ars Organi: Zeitschrift für das Orgelwesen*
ARTM	Annotated Reference Tools in Music

AS	*Annals of Science: A Quarterly Review of the History of Science Since the Renaissance*
ASch	*The American Scholar*
ASh	Astrologische Studienhefte
ASHPS	Australasian Studies in History and Philosophy of Science, edited by R. W. Home
Asi	Actualités scientifiques et industrielles
ASJJR	*Annales de la Société Jean-Jacques Rousseau*
AST	*American String Teacher: Official Publication of the American String Teachers Association*
ASUCP	*American Society of University Composers: Proceedings*
AUMLA	*AUMLA: Journal of the Australasian Universities Language and Literature Association*
AusJP	*Australasian Journal of Philosophy*
AUU	Acta Universitatis Upsaliensis: Studia musicologica Upsaliensia
Avs	*L'avant scène: Organe de l'Association d'auteurs et compositeurs*
AVZ	*Allgemeine Vermessungsnachrichten: Zeitschrift für alle Zweige des Vermessungs-, Karten- und Liegenschaftswesens*
AWBH	*Akademie der Wissenschaft, Berlin: Histoire de l'Académie royale des sciences et belles-lettres de Berlin*
AWLMA	*Akademie der Wissenschaften und der Literatur im Mainz: Abhandlungen der geistes- und sozialwissenschaftliche Klasse*
AzPG	Abhandlungen zur Philosophie und ihrer Geschichte, edited by Benno Erdmann
Ba	*La belle assemblée; or, Bell's Court and Fashionable Magazine, Addressed Particularly to the Ladies*
Bach	*Bach: The Quarterly Journal of the Riemenschneider Bach Institute*
BachJb	*Bach-Jahrbuch* [Dat. JRC. LCPS. SMS.]
BAfMw	Beihefte zum Archiv für Musikwissenschaft, edited by Hans Heinrich Eggebrecht
BAIMA	*Bollettino dell' AIMA: Archivio per l' informazione sulla musica antica*
BAMS	*Bulletin of the American Musicological Society*

BamZ	*Berliner allgemeine musikalische Zeitung* [SMLMS.]
BB	*Books and Bookmen*
BbA	Bibliotheca bibliographica Aureliana
BbF	*Bulletin des bibliothèques de France, Paris: Direction des bibliothèques de France*
BBN	*British Book News: A Monthly Review of New Books*
BC	*The British Critic: A New Review*
BcÉn	*Bibliothèque choisie; Series 1: Études de la nature*
Bcm	Biblioteca di cultura musicale: Autori e opere
BCol	*The Book Collector*
BD	Bach Dokumente
BdG	Bibliothèque de Graphe
Bdp	*Bibliographie de la philosophie*
BECPS	Bilingual Editions of Classics in Philosophy and Science
Bém	Bibliothèque d'études musicales
BEMag	*Blackwood's Edinburgh Magazine*
Benm	Bibliothèque d'enseignement musical
BFBRS	Burt Franklin Bibliography and Reference Series
Bfk	Biblioteka filozoficzna klasyków
BFWU	*Beiträge zur Freiburger Wissenschafts- und Universitätsgeschichte*
BH	Breitkopf & Härtel (Leipzig)
BhG	Beiträge zur harmonikalen Grundlagenforschung, edited by Rudolf Haase
Bhisp	*Bulletin hispanique*
BHKM	*Blätter für Haus- und Kirchenmusik*
BHM	*Bulletin of the History of Medicine*
BHmH	Breitkopf & Härtels musikalisches Handbibliothek
Bhp	Bibliothèque d'histoire de la philosohie
BibS	Biblos-Schriften
Bibsi	Biblioteca scientifica internazionale
BJA	*British Journal of Aesthetics*
BJECS	*British Journal for Eighteenth-Century Studies*
BJhM	*Basler Jarhbuch für historische Musikpraxis*
BJHS	*British Journal for the History of Science*
BJME	*British Journal of Music Education*

BJP	*British Journal of Psychology*
BJPS	*British Journal for the Philosophy of Science*
Bl	Bibliothèque des lettres
Blph	Biblioteca de la literatura y el pensamiento hispánicos
Bm	Bibliothèque méditations
BmA	Berliner musikwissenschaftliche Arbeiten, edited by Carl Dahlhaus and Rudolf Stephan
BMäh	*Böhmen und Mähren: Blatt des Reichprotektors in Böhmen und Mähren*
BMag	*Burlington Magazine*
BmB	Bibliotheca musica Bononiensis, edited by Giuseppe Vecchi
BMCN	*Book-of-the-Month-Club News*
BMhM	*Bulletin du Musée historique de Mulhouse*
Bmm	Biblioteca manuales musicales
BmrM	Beiträge zur mittelrheinischen Musikgeschichte, edited by the Arbeitsgemeinschaft für mittelrheinische Musikgeschichte
Bmus	*La bibliographe musicale*
BmZ	*Berlinische musikalische Zeitung*, edited by Johann Friedrich Reichardt [GO.]
BnLg	Beiträge zur neueren Literaturgeschichte, Neue Folge, edited by Max Freiherr von Waldberg
Bo	Bibliotheca organologica: Facsimiles of Rare Books on Organ and Organbuilding
Booklist	*The Booklist and Subscription Books Bulletin*
Bouw	*Bouwsteenen: Jaarboek der vereeniging voor Noord-Nederlands muziekgeschiedenis* [LCPS. SZ.]
BP	Bibliothèque de la Pléiade
Bpc	Bibliothèque de philosophie contemporaine
Bph	Bibliothèque de philosophie
BpW	*Berliner philologische Wochenschrift*
BQ	*Brass Quarterly*
BrB	*Brass Bulletin: International Magazine for Brass Players*
Brh	Biblioteca romänica hispanica

Brio	*Brio: Journal of the United Kingdom Branch of the International Association of Music Libraries* [UMI.]
BrM	Beiträge zur rheinischen Musikgeschichte
BrP	Brookhaven Press (La Crosse, Wisconsin)
BS	Bollingen Series
BSAII	Blankenburger Studien zur Aufführungspraxis und Interpretation der Instrumentalmusik der 18. Jahrhunderts
BSAP	*Bibliographical Society of America: Papers*
BSel	*Best Sellers*
BsgrT	Bibliotheca scriptorum graecorum et romanorum Teubneriana
Bsi	Bibliothèque scientific internationale
BSL	Bohn's Standard Library
BSlhB	*Bulletin de la Société littéraire et historique de la Brie*
BSlm	*Bulletin de la Sociéte liégeoise de musicologie*
BSM	*British Studies Monitor*
BSmB	*Bulletin de la Société de mathématique de Belgique*
BSu	Bibliothek Suhrkamp
BsW	*Bibliothek der schönen Wissenschaften und der freyen Künste*
BSzMw	Berliner Studien zur Musikwissenschaft, edited by Adam Adrio
BTNU	*Bulletin of Tokyo National University of Fine Arts and Music*
Btp	Bibliothèque des textes philosophique
BUGJ	*Boston University Graduate Journal*
BUL	Bibliothèque de la Faculte de Philosophie et Lettres de l'Université de Liège
Bulmuz	*Bulgarska muzika*
BV	Biblioteca Villar
BVSAWL	*Bericht über die Verhandlungen des Sächsischen Akademie der Wissenschaften zu Leipzig*
BW	*Book World*
BWQ	*Brass and Woodwind Quarterly*
BYU	*Bulletin of Yamanashi University*
BzD	Beihefte zum Daphnis
BzMf	Beiträge zur Musikforschung, edited by Max Schneider and by Reinhold Hammerstein, Siegfried Hermelink, and Wilhelm Seidel

BzMw	*Beiträge zur Musikwissenschaft* [JRC. KrR.]
BzmwF	Beiträge zur musikwissenschaftlichen Forschung in der DDR, edited by the Zentralinstitut für Musikforschung
Caecilia	*Caecilia: A Review of Catholic Church and School Music*
CanMJ	*Canadian Music Journal*
Canon	*The Canon: Australian Journal of Music*
CathHR	*Catholic Historical Review*
CAY	*Come-All-Ye*
CBioS	Composer Biography Series
CCen	*Christian Century*
CCh	*The Catholic Choirmaster*
Ccm	Collection "Le choeur des muses"
CCMPT	Colorado College Music Press Translations, edited by Albert Seay
CD	*Chord and Discord: A Journal of Modern Musical Progress*
Cdc	Collection "Les documents célèbres"
Cdm	Contributi di musicologia, edited by Lino Bianchi
Cds	Classici della scienza
Centaurus	*Centaurus: International Magazine of the History of Mathematics, Science, and Technology*
CfP	Collano filosofica Principato, edited by C. Augusto Viano
CG	Classiques Garnier
CH	*Computers and the Humanities*
ChaM	*Chamber Music: A Supplement to "The Music Student"*
Chelys	*Chelys: The Journal of the Viola da Gamba Society*
Cher	*Chervonii shliakh* [Dat.]
Ches	*The Chesterian*
ChG	*Choral [and Organ] Guide*
ChH	*Church History*
Chigiana	*Chigiana: Rassegna annuale di studi musicologici*
CHim	Collection Histoire illustrée de la musique, edited by François Vaudou and Dorel Handman
ChJb	*Chopin-Jahrbuch*
Chm	*Collectanea historiae musicae*
ChMJ	*The Choir and Music Journal*
CHmu	*Caecilia en Het muziekcollege*
Chmus	*La chronique musicale: Revue bi-mensuelle de l'art ancien & moderne*
ChR	*Chicago Review*
CHTMB	Colloquia on the History and Theory of Music at the International Musical Festival in Brno
Čhud	*Česká hudba*
ChuM	*Church Music* (Concordia)
ChuMus	*Church Music* (Church Music Association, London)
CI	*Critical Inquiry*
CIfm	*Contributi dell'Istituto de filologia moderne, serie Francese* (Milan: Università Cattolica del Sacro Cuore)
CistC	*Cisterciensen-Chronik*
Civcat	*La civiltà cattolica*
CJ	*Choral Journal*
CJH	*Canadian Journal of History/Annales canadiennes d'histoire*
CJL	*Canadian Journal of Linguistics/La revue canadienne de linguistique*
CK	*Caecilien Kalender: Redigirt zum Besten der kirchlichen Musikschule* [IDC.]
CL	Colección Labor
Clio	*Clio: A Journal of Literature, History and the Philosophy of History*
CLit	*Comparative Literature*
ClPS	Clarendon Press Series
CLRS	California Library Reprint Series
CLSC	Cass Library of Science Classics
CLW	*Catholic Library World*
CM	*Current Musicology*
CME	*Contributions to Music Education*
CMJ	*Computer Music Journal* [UMI.]
CMm	Collection "Musiques et musiciens"
CMS	*College Music Symposium: Journal of the College Music Society*
CMTM	Cambridge Musical Texts and Monographs, edited by Howard Mayer Brown, Peter le Huray, and John Stevens
Cmu	*Le courrier musical* [Dat.]
Cmus	Collection de musicologie, edited by Joseph-François Kremer

CMvm	*Caecilia: Maandblad voor muziek*
Cnv	*Cum notis variorum*
Coda	*Coda: Canada's Jazz Magazine* [MicL.]
Cœplf	Corpus des œuvres de philosophie et langue française
Composer	*Composer: The Journal of the Composers' Guild of Great Britain* [UMI.]
Consort	*Consort: Annual Journal of the Dolmetsch Foundation*
Conv	*Convivium: Rivista di lettere, filosofia e storia*
COKK	*Caecilia: Organ für Katholische Kirchenmusik*
Corlit	*Correspondance littéraire*
	Accessible through *Correspondance littéraire, philosophique et critique (1753-1793) par Grimm, Diderot, Raynal, Meister, etc.*, edited by M. Tourneux. Paris: Garnier, 1877-82.
COSB	*Central Opera Service Bulletin*
Courant	*The Courant: Journal of the Academy of Early Music*
CpaB	Calvary's philologische und archaeologische Bibliothek
CPS	The Century Psychology Series, edited by Richard M. Elliott
CPsy	*Contemporary Psychology*
CQ	*Cambridge Quarterly*
CR	*Centennial Review*
Cresset	*The Cresset: A Review of Literature, the Arts, and Public Affairs*
Crit	*Critique: Revue générale des publications françaises et étrangères*
CRLM	Cambridge Readings in the Literature of Music
CRMEB	*Council for Research in Music Education Bulletin*
CRmms	*Caecilia: Revue mensuelle de musique sacrée*
CrR	*The Critical Review; or, Annals of Literature*
CS	*Common Sense*
Csa	Centro studi antoniani
Csal	La cultura sagga di arte e di letteraturea
CSM	Cambridge Studies in Music, edited by John Stevens and Peter le Huray
CSNCM	California Studies in Nineteenth-Century Music
CSoc	*Contemporary Sociology: An International Journal of Reviews*
CsrmF	Centro studi rinascimento musicale, Firenze: Nuova metodologia
Ctma	Collezione di trattati e musiche antiche edite in fac-simile
CTME	Classic Texts in Music Education, edited by Bernarr Rainbow
CUASM	The Catholic University of America Studies in Music
CUMR	*Canadian University Music Review/Revue de musique des universities canadiennes*
CUSM	Columbia University Studies in Musicology
CVZ	*Central Verein-Zeitung: Blätter für Deutschtum und Judentum; Organ des Central-Vereins deutscher Staatsbürger jüdischen Glaubens e. V.; Allgemeine Zeitung des Judentums*
Cyc	*The Cyclopaedia; or, Universal Dictionary of Arts, Sciences, and Literature*
DA	*Dissertation Abstracts* [*International*]
Dafmf	*Dansk årbog for musikforskning*
DAGb	*Deutsch-Amerikanische Geschichtsblätter* [*Jahrbuch der Deutsch-Amerikanischen Historischen Gesellschaft von Illinois*]
Dat	Datamics, Inc. (New York)
DAWBQS	Deutsche Akademie der Wissenschaften zu Berlin: Quellen und Studien zur Geschichte Osteuropas
DBdM	Der Dom: Bücher deutscher Mystik
DCPMRS	Da Capo Press Music Reprint Series, edited by Frank d'Accone, Roland Jackson, Frederick Freedman, or Bea Friedland
DFB	*Dolmetsch Foundation: Bulletin*
DfMMF	Dokumente früher Musik und Musikliteratur im Faksimile
DG	Dakota Graphics (Lakewood, Colorado)
DH	*Diapason-Harmonie*
Dhs	*Dix-huitième siècle*
Diapason	*The Diapason: An International Monthly Devoted to the Interests of Organists* [AMSFS.]
DIB	*Der deutsche Instrumentenbau* [Dat. LCPS.]

DILBM	Dent's International Library of Books on Music, edited by A. Eaglefield-Hall
Dilmu	Diletto musicale
DJbMw	*Deutsches Jahrbuch der Musikwissenschaft*
Djdgkn	*Doshisha jyoshi diagaku gakujutsu kenkyu nenpo*
DLd	Deutsche Literaturdenkmale des 18. und 19. Jahrhunderts
Dm	Dictionarium musicum
DMb	Deutsche Musikbücherei, edited by Gustav Bosse
DMBA	Die grossen Darstellungen der Musik-geschichte in Baroque und Aufklärung, edited by Othmar Wessely
Dmdp	*De musica disputationes pragensis*
DMM	*A Dictionary of Music and Musicians*, first edition, edited by George Grove (1879-89)
Dmt	*Dansk musiktidsskrift* [SZ.]
DNB	*Dictionary of National Biography*, edited by Sir Leslie Stephen and Sir Sidney Lee
DPàD	De Pétrarque à Descartes
DQTR	*Drama: The Quarterly Theatre Review*
DR	*Dublin Review*
DS	*Diderot Studies*
DSB	*Dictionary of Scientific Biography*, edited by G. C. Gillespie
DSMB	Detroit Studies in Music Bibliography, edited by J. Bunker Clark
Dss	*Dix-septième siècle*
DTB	*Denkmäler der Tonkunst in Bayern* [= *Denkmäler deutscher Tonkunst, Zweite Folge*]
DTh	Das deutsche Theater des 18. Jahrhun-derts, edited by Reinhart Meyer
DTÖ	*Denkmäler der Tonkunst in Österreich* [ADV. Dat. UME.]
DTZ	*Deutsche Tonkunstler-Zeitung*
DunH	Dunker & Humblot (Berlin)
DVLG	*Deutsche Vierteljahrsschrift für Literatur-wissenschaft und Geistesgeschichte*
DZP	*Deutsche Zeitschrift für Philosophie*
DzwMz	*23 [Dreiundzwanzig]: Einer Musikzeitschrift*
Éc	*Les études classiques*

ECCB	*The Eighteenth Century: A Current Bibliog-raphy*
ECenS	*Eighteenth-Century Studies*
Econ	*The Economist*
ECrit	*Essays in Criticism*
ECS	Eighteenth-Century Studies
EdF	Erträge der Forschung
EdR	*Edinburgh Review*
EdS	*Enciclopedia dello Spettacolo*
EE	The English Experience: Its Record in Early Printed Books Published in Fac-simile
ÉEp	*Épiméthée: Essais philosophiques*, edited by Jean-Luc Marion
EFPL	The English and Foreign Philosophical Li-brary
Ég	*Études grégoriennes*
EH	Europäische Hochschulschriften/Publica-tions universitaires européennes/Euro-pean University Studies
EHM	*English Harpsichord Magazine and Early Keyboard Instrument Review*
EHR	*English Historical Review*
ELin	English Linguistics, 1500-1800 (A Collec-tion of Facsimile Reprints), edited by R. C. Alston
ELN	*English Language Notes*
EM	*Early Music*
EMG	*English Musical Gazette*
EMH	*Early Music History: Studies in Medieval and Early Modern Music*, edited by Iain Fenlon
EMI	*The Euterpeiad; or, Musical Intelligencer* [DCPMRS.]
EMLB	*Early Music Laboratory Bulletin*
EMS	Early Music Studies
Éms	*Les éditions du mois suisse*
EMSer	Early Music Series, edited by John M. Thomson
EMTLC	Early Music Theory in the Low Countries, edited by Fritz R. Noske
Endeavour	*Endeavour: A Review of the Progress of Science*
Eng	*English*
Éns	*Édition nationale suisse*

Ép	*Les études philosophiques*
ErArs	Extraits des registres de l'Académie royale des sciences
Eras	*Erasmus, Speculum scientiarum: International Bulletin of Contemporary Scholarship*
Eth	*Ethnomusicology*
Ethics	*Ethics: An International Journal of Social, Political, and Legal Philosophy*
EurM	*The European Magazine and London Review*
Eut	*The Euterpeiad: An Album of Music, Poetry, and Prose*
Examiner	*Examiner: A Weekly Paper on Politics, Literature, Music and Fine Arts* [UMI.]
Fam	*Fontes artis musicae*
FBzMw	Frankfurter Beiträge zur Musikwissenschaft, edited by the Musikwissenschaftliche Institut der Johann Wolfgang Goethe-Universität
FesS	Festschrift Series
FgA	*Frankfurter gelehrten Anziegen*
FK	Fritz Knuf (Buren, The Netherlands)
FLV	Forschen–Lehren–Verantworten, edited by Berthold Sutter
Fm	*Feuilles musicales et Courrier suisse du disques: Revue musicale romande*
FÖM	*Forschung an Österreichs Musikhochschulen*
FR	*Fortnightly Review*
Frm	*La France musicale*
Fronimo	*Il "Fronimo": Rivista trimestrale di chitarra e liuto*
FrR	*French Review*
FrS	*French Studies*
FS	*Die freie Schulgemeinde*
FSMw	*Frieburger Schriften zur Musikwissenschaft*
FSUS	*Florida State University Studies*
FZ	*Frankfurter Zeitung und Handelsblatt*
GBSP	Gordon & Breach Science Publishers (New York)
GBWW	Great Books of the Western World, edited by Robert Maynard Hutchins
Gc	*Le guide du concert et des théâtres lyriques* [Dat. LCPS.]
Gch	*Le glaneur châtelleraudais*
GDMgBA	Die großen Darstellungen der Musikgeschichte in Baroque und Aufklärung, edited by Othmar Wessely
GeoR	*Georgia Review*
GG	*Gestalt und Gedanke*
GitL	*Gitarre + Laute*
GJ	*Gutenberg Jarhbuch*
GK	*Gottesdienst und Kirchenmusik*
GLL	*German Life and Letters: A Quarterly Review*
GLM	*Guitar and Lute Magazine*
Gm	*Le guide musical: Revue internationale de la musique et des théatres* [Dat. IDC. LCPS. MinR.]
GmA	Göttinger musikwissenschaftliche Arbeiten, edited by Hermann Zenck
GMag	*Gentleman's Magazine, and Historical Chronicle*
GmdM	*Gazzetta musicale di Milano* [Dat. LCPS.]
GMfMA	Gesellschaft für Musikforschung: Musikwissenschaftliche Arbeiten
GMPI	Gosudarstvennyi muzykal'no-pedagogicheskii institut imeni Gnesinykh
GMt	Geschichte der Musiktheorie
GN	Große Naturforscher, edited by H. W. Frickhinger
Gnmu	*[Gazette nationale; ou,] Le moniteur universel*
GO	Georg Olms (Hildesheim)
GR	*Guitar Review*
Gram	*Gramophone* [UMI.]
Greg	*Gregoriusblad: Tijdschrift tot bevordering van liturgische muziek uitgave van de nederlandse Sint Gregoriusvereniging*
GrI	*Gregg International (Aldershot, Hampshire, England)*
GrJ	*The Grainger Journal*
GRLH	Garland Reference Library of the Humanities
GSJ	*Galpin Society Journal* [SZ.]
GSLM	*Geschichts-Blätter für Stadt und Land Magdeburg*
Gss	I grandi scrittori stranieri
GuitP	*Guitar Player: The Magazine for Professional and Amateur Guitarists*
GuW	*Guardian Weekly*

GW	*Grenzgebiete der Wissenschaft*
GWDNZ	Geschichte der Wissenschaften in Deutschland: Neuere Zeit
HAR	*The Humanities Association Review/La review de l'Association des humanités*
Harmon	*Harmonicon* [GrI.]
HArs	*Histoire de l'Académie royale des sciences* [Paris]
Haus	*Hausmusik: Zweimonatsschrift für Haus- und Jugendmusik, Chorwesen und Musikerziehung*
HaydnJb	*The Haydn Yearbook/Das Haydn Jahrbuch*
HBgS	*Hamburgische Berichte von gelehrten Sachen*
HbM	Handbücher der Musikerziehung
HBzMw	Hamburger Beiträge zur Musikwissenschaft, edited by Constantin Floros
Het	*Heterofonia*
HFL	Harper's Family Library
HfM	Handbooks for Musicians, edited by Ernest Newman
HFMA	*High Fidelity[/Musical America]* [UMI.]
HFS	*HiFi-Stereophonie*
HibJ	*Hibbert Journal*
Hicl	Histoire des idées et critique littéraire
HiH	Hesses illustrierte Handbücher
HindJb	*Hindemith-Jahrbuch*
Hisp	*Hispania: A Teacher's Journal Devoted to the Interests of the Teaching of Spanish and Portuguese*
HispAmR	*Hispanic American Report*
History	*History: The Journal of the Historical Association*
HJ	*Historical Journal*
HJb	*Händel-Jahrbuch* [JRC.]
HL	Herbert Lang (Berlin and Frankfurt)
HmcB	"Historiae musicae cultores" Biblioteca
HMl	Handbücher der Musiklehre, edited by Xaver Scharwenka
HMYB	*Hinrichsen's Musical Year Book*
HoM	History of Music
	A series of 107 microfilm reels published by Research Publication, Inc. (Woodbridge, Ct.). The set incorporates the collection documented in David A. Wood's *Music in Harvard Libraries: A Catalogue*

	of Early Printed Music and Books on Music in the Houghton Library and the Eda Kuhn Loeb Music Library (Cambridge, Mass.: Houghton Library of the Harvard College Library; Harvard University Department of Music [Harvard University Press], 1980), which serves as the index for the series.
Hos	*Histoire des ouvrages des s[ç]avans*
Hp	Histoire de la pensée
HPON	Hauptwerke der Philosophie in Originalgetreuen Neudrucken
HR	*Hudson Review*
HRNB	*History: Reviews of New Books*
Hroz	*Hudební rozhledy: Časopis Svazu československých skladatelu*
HS	*Haydn-Studien*
HSc	*History of Science*
HSMT	Harmonologia: Studies in Music Theory, edited by Joel Lester
HT	*History and Theory*
HTo	*History Today*
Hv	*Hudební věda*
HwmT	*Handwörterbuch der musikalischen Terminologie*, edited by Hans Heinrich Eggebrecht
IAHI	International Archives of the History of Ideas
IAMR	*Inter-American Music Review*
IBMw	Innsbrucker Beiträge zur Musikwissenschaft
IDC	Inter Documentation Company (Leiden, The Netherlands; Zug, Switzerland)
IGMDm	Internationale Gesellschaft für Musikwissenschaft: Documenta musicologica
IGmis	I Grandi musicisti italiani e strangieri, edited by Carlo Gatti
IJE	*International Journal of Ethics: Devoted to the Advancement of Ethical Knowledge and Practice*
IJMMS	*International Journal of Man-Machine Studies*
IJSLP	*International Journal of Slavic Linguistics and Poetics*
ILPPSM	International Library of Psychology, Philosophy, and Scientific Method
Im	Instituta et monumenta

Imami	Istituzioni e monumenti dell'arte musicale italiana
IME	*International Music Educator: Journal of the International Society for Music Education*
IMus	*International Musician: Official Journal of the American Federation of Musicians of the United States and Canada* [Dat.]
Instr	*Instrument: Zeitschrift für Musiker, Veranstalter und Musikinteressierte*
Int	Les introuvables
Interface	*Interface: Journal of New Music Research*
IntW	*Internationale Wochenschrift für Wissenschaft, Kunst, und Technik*
IPQ	*International Philosophical Quarterly*
IRASM	*International Review of the Aesthetics and Sociology of Music* [SZ.]
IRsi	*Intersezioni: Rivista di storia delle idee*
Isis	*Isis: An International Review Devoted to the History of Science and Its Cultural Influences*
ISM	*Israel Studies in Musicology*
ISOI	*International Society of Organ-Builders Information*
ISP	*International Studies in Philosophy*
ISS	International Scientific Series
ITGN	*International Trumpet Guild Newsletter*
ITO	*In Theory Only* [UMI.]
ITR	*Indiana Theory Review*
IwB	Internationale wissenschaftliche Bibliothek
JAAC	*Journal of Aesthetics and Art Criticism* [AMSP. KrR. UMI.]
JAE	*Journal of Aesthetic Education*
JALS	*Journal of the American Liszt Society* [UMI.]
JAMIS	*Journal of the American Musical Instrument Society*
JAMS	*Journal of the American Musicological Society*
Janus	*Janus: Revue internationale de l'histoire des sciences, de la médicine, de la pharmacie et de la technique*
JASA	*Journal of the Acoustical Society of America* [AIP.]
JASI	*Journal of the Arnold Schoenberg Institute*
JAWG	*Jahrbuch der Akademie der Wissenschaften in Göttingen (Societät der Reichsakademie)*
Jbas	*Journal des beaux-arts et des sciences* [ACRPP.]
JBISM	*Jahres-Bericht der Internationalen Stiftung Mozarteum*
JBzMf	*Jenaer Beiträge zur Musikforschung*, edited by Heinrich Besseler
JCAUSM	*Journal of the Canadian Association of University Schools of Music*
JCM	*Journal of Church Music*
JCP	*Journal für Chemie und Physik*
JCPs	*Journal of Comparative Psychology*
JDB	*Jahrbuch der Dissertationen der Philosophischen Fakultät der Friedrich-Wilhelms-Universität zu Berlin*
Jdm	*Journal de musique, par une société d'amateurs* [*Rism* B/VI/2, p. 944. LCPS: Anon-037. MinR.]
JdP	*Journal de Paris*
Jds	*Journal des savants*
JEGP	*Journal of English and Germanic Philology*
Jenc	*Journal encyclopédique ou universel* [KrR. SlatR.]
JfmW	*Jahrbücher für musikalische Wissenschaft*, edited by Friedrich Chrysander [GO.]
JGMSOSU	*The Journal of the Graduate Music Students at The Ohio State University*
JHA	*Journal of the History of Astronomy*
JHBS	*Journal of the History of the Behavioral Sciences*
JHHS	The Johns Hopkins Humanities Seminars
JHI	*Journal of the History of Ideas*
JHM	*Journal of the History of Medicine and Allied Sciences: A Quarterly*
JHP	*Journal of the History of Philosophy*
JITA	*Journal of the International Trombone Association*
JITG	*Journal of the International Trumpet Guild*
JLH	*Jahrbuch für Liturgik und Hymnologie*
JLSA	*Journal of the Lute Society of America, Inc.*
JM	*The Journal of Musicology: A Quarterly Review of Music History, Criticism, Analysis, and Performance Practice*

JMbP	*Jahrbuch der Musikbibliothek Peters* [BrP. IDC. KrR. Les.]
Jmf	*Journal musical français, musica-disques: Organe des jeunesses musicales de France*
JMH	*Journal of Modern History*
JMR	*Journal of Musicological Research* [GBSP.]
JMT	*Journal of Music Theory* [JRC. UMI.]
JMTP	*Journal of Music Theory Pedagogy*
JMus	*The Journal of Musicology: A Quarterly to Publish Reports of Reseach in the Field of Music*
JMw	*Jahrbuch der Musikwelt/The Yearbook of the Music World/Annuaire du monde musical*
Jœc	*Journal œconomique ou mémoires, notes et avis sur l'agriculture, les arts, le commerce et tout ce qui peut avoir rapport à la santé ainsi qu'à la conservation et à l'augmentation des biens des familles*
JoM	*Jahrbuch des oberösterreichischen Musealvereins*
JpFPUM	*Jahrbuch der philosophischen Fakultät der Philipps-Universität zu Marburg: Philolo-gisch-historische Abteilung*
JPhil	*The Journal of Philosophy, Psychology, and Scientific Methods*
JR	*Juilliard Review* [KIP.]
JRASC	*Journal of the Royal Astronomical Society of Canada*
JRC	Johnson Reprint Corporation (New York)
JRME	*Journal of Research in Music Education* [KrR. UMI.]
JSIM	*Jahrbuch des Staatlichen Instituts für Musik-forschung, Preußischer Kulturbesitz*
JTr	*Journal de Trévoux* See *Mhsba.*
JV	*Jahrbuch für Volksliedforschung*
JVGSA	*Journal of the Viola da Gamba Society of America*
JWCI	*Journal of the Warburg and Courtauld Insti-tutes*
KBzMf	Kölner Beiträge zur Musikforschung, edited by Karl Gustav Fellerer
KenR	*Kenyon Review*
KeyM	*Keyboard Magazine*
KHMG	Kleine Handbücher der Musikgeschichte nach Gattungen, edited by Hermann Kretzschmar
KieBzMw	Kieler Beiträge zur Musikwissenschaft
KieSzMw	Kieler Schriften zur Musikwissenschaft
KIP	Kraus International Publications (White Plains, New York)
KJb	*Kirchenmusikalisches Jahrbuch* [LCPS.]
KL	*Der Klavier-Lehrer: Musikpädagogische Zeitschrift für alle Gebiete der Tonkunst*
Km	*Der Kirchenmusiker: Mitteilungen der Zen-tralstelle für evangelische Kirchenmusik [: Zeitschrift des Verbandes evan-gelischer Kirchenmusiker Deutschlands]*
KMCLBS	Kunitachi Music College Library Bibliog-raphy Series
KNwT	Klassiker der Naturwissenschaft und Tech-nik, edited by Franz Strunz
KOöL	Katalog des Oberösterreichisches Landesmuseum
KR	*Kirkus Reviews*
KrR	Kraus Reprint (Millwood, New York)
KSL	Katalog des Stadtmuseums Linz
KSMBR	*Keats-Shelley Memorial Bulletin: Rome*
KSzMw	Königsberger Studien zur Musikwissen-schaft
KUdMI	Kobenhavns Universitet det Musik-videnskabelige Institut
Kunstwart	*Der Kunstwart: Monatshefte für Kunst, Lit-eratur und Leben*
KZ	*Kolnischen Zeitung*
LATBR	*Los Angeles Times Book Review*
LCPS	Library of Congress Photoduplication Service (Washington, D.C.)
LCPS: x-xxx	Library of Congress Photoduplication Service, Music 5000, Item x-xxx Order from LCPS, Dept. C, Washington, D.C. 20540. The individual Items were filmed in numerical sequence, with as many Items as possible on each reel. Music 5001 (one reel) is a table of con-tents for the Music 5000 series.
LCQJ	*Library of Congress: Quarterly Journal*
Les	Lessing (Wiesbaden)
Lét	*Lettres sur quelques écrits de ce temps*
Libr	*The Library: A Quarterly Review of Bibliog-raphy*

LiS	*Language in Society*
Lital	*Lettere italiana*
LJ	*Library Journal*
LKC	Leipzig Künstler: Carakterskizzen, edited by A. Baresel
LLA	Library of Liberal Arts
LM	*London Magazine*
LME	*London Musical Events: Comprehensive Musical Guide*
LMFI	*Literature, Music, Fine Arts: A Review of German-Language Research Contributions on Literature, Music, and Fine Arts*
LMS	Longman Music Series, edited by Gerald Warfield
Lmus	*Littérature et musique*
LonM	*London Mercury*
LQ	*The Library Quarterly*
LQHR	*London Quarterly and Holborn Review*
LRB	*London Review of Books*
LRes	*Library Research: An International Journal*
LSF	*Lebensbilder aus Schwaben und Franken*
LSJ	*Lute Society Journal*
LSL	The Life of Science Library
LTZ	*Litteratur- und Theater-Zeitung*
Lychnos	*Lychnos: Lärdomshistoriska samfundets årsbok*
LZD	*Literische Zentralblatt für Deutschland*
MA	*Music Analysis* [UMI.]
MAA	Mediaeval Academy of America
MAb	*Masters Abstracts*
MaBo	Musica antiqua Bohemica
MagM	*Magazin der Musik*, edited by Carl Friedrich Cramer [*Rism* B/VI/1, p. 242. BrP. GO. LCPS: C-100. SMLMS.]
Magnus	*Magaleh musighi*
Magyar	*Magyar zene*
MakM	*Making Music*
MAm	*Musical America* [UMI.]
MAmrM	*Mitteilungen der Arbeitsgemeinschaft für mittelrheinische Musikgeschichte*
Mamu	Les maîtres de la musique
MAn	*Musikblätter des Anbruck: Monatsschrift für moderne Musik* Continues as *Anbruch*.

Manu	*Manuscripta*
MArs	*Mémoires [de mathématique et de physique] de l'Académie royale des sciences [Paris]* Numerous editions, some bound with *HArs*. Pagination varies among editions.
MArsB	*Mémoires de l'Academie des sciences de Berlin*
MathR	*Mathematical Reviews*
MB	*Musik und Bildung: Zeitschrift für Musikerziehung*
MBis	*Miscellanea Berolinensia ad incrementum scientiarum . . .*
MBol	La musica a Bologna
MBWl	Manesse Bibliothek der Weltliteratur
MBzMw	Münsterische Beiträge zur Musikwissenschaft, edited by W. Korte, later by Karl Gustav Fellerer
MC	*Musical Courier [and Review of Recorded Music]*
MCM	*Music Clubs Magazine* [UMI.]
Md	*Musica disciplina* Supersedes *Journal of Renaissance and Baroque Music*.
MdFr	*Mercure de France*
MdM	Meisterwerke der Musik: Werkmonographien zur Musikgeschichte, edited by Ernst Ludwig Waeltner
MDMGP	*Mitteilungen der Deutschen Mathematischen Gesellschaft in Prague*
MdST	*Mitteilungen des Steirischen Tonkünstlerbundes*
Me	*Musikerziehung: Zeitschrift der Musikerzieher Österreichs*
MEJ	*Music Educators Journal* [KrR. UMI.] *Music Supervisors Journal* through Vol. 20 (1933-34).
Melos	*Melos: Zeitschrift für [neue] Musik* [Dat. SMS.]
Melos/NZfM	*Melos/Neue Zeitschrift für Musik*
Mén	*Le ménestrel: Journal du monde musical, musique et théatres* [ACRPP. Dat. LCPS. MinR.]
Mens	*Mens en melodie: Algemeen maandblad voor muziek*
Met	*The Metronome*
MEur	*Musical Europe*

MEv	*Musical Events*
Mf	*Die Musikforschung*
MFa	Musica Facsimil
MFhR	Musikalische Formen in historischen Reihen
MFKKH	*Mitteilungen für Freunde der Kirchen-, Kammer- und Hausmusik*
MFl	Meyers Fachlexika
MFm	Musurgiana: Fonti e materiali de storia e teoria della musica
MForsk	*Musik & Forskning*
MFüh	Meisterführer: Einführungen in das Schaffen einzelner Tonmeister
MG	*Musik und Gesellschaft*
MGf	Musikalische Gegenwartsfragen
MGG	*Die Musik in Geschichte und Gegenwart*, edited by Friedrich Blume
Mgil	*Die Musikantengilde: Blätter der Erneuerung aus dem Geiste der Jugend*
MgnJ	Musikgeschichte des 19. Jahrhunderts
MGot	*Musik und Gottesdienst: Zeitschrift für evangelische Kirchenmusik* [UMI.]
MH	Manuali Hoepli
MHHM	Max Hesse's Handbücher der Musik
Mhi	La musique, les hommes et les instruments
MHiK	Max Hesse's illustrierte Katechismen
MHM	*Maryland Historical Magazine*
Mhsba	*Mémoires pour l'histoire des sciences et des beaux-arts* [SlatR.] Known as *Journal de Trevoux.*
Mi	*Das Musikinstrument*
MiB	*Musik in Bayern: Halbjahresschrift der Gesellschaft für Bayerische Musikgeschichte e. V.*
MicL	Micromedia Limited (Toronto)
MiE	*Music in Education*
MilQ	*Milton Quarterly*
MiM	Monographs in Musicology
MinR	Minkoff Reprint (Geneva)
Miscm	*Miscellanea musicologica: Adelaide Studies in Musicology*
MISM	*Mitteilung der Internationalen Stiftung Mozarteum*
MITCT	The MIT Press Series on Cognitive Theory and Mental Representation,
	edited by Joan Bresnan, Lila Gleitman, and Samuel Jay Keyser
MiU	*Musik im Unterricht*
MJ	*Music Journal* [KrR. UMI.]
MJSMA	*Music: Journal of the Schools' Music Association*
MK	*Musik und Kirche* [SMS.]
MKAW	Mededelingen van de Koninklijke Academie voor Wetenschappen, Letteren en Schone Kunsten van België, Klasse der Schone Kunsten
MkB	*Musikalische-kritische Bibliothek*, edited by Johann Nicolaus Forkel [*Rism* B/VI/1, p. 324. GO. LCPS: F-045. SMLMS.]
ML	*Music and Letters* [SZ. UMI.]
Mlav	Musicologica lavaniensia
Mleb	*Das Musikleben*
MLN	*Modern Language Notes*
MLNCF	Musical Life in 19th-Century France/La vie musicale en France au XIXe siècle, edited by H. Robert Cohen and Yves Gérard
MLQ	*Modern Language Quarterly*
MLR	*Modern Language Review*
MM	Musica e Musicisti
Mm	Musique-musicologie, edited by Danièle Pistone
MMag	*The Monthly Magazine; or, British Register* [*of Literature, Sciences, and Belles-Lettres*]
MMC	Manuals of Musical Composition
MMer	*The Musical Mercury*
MMg	*Monatshefte für Musikgeschichte* [Dat. SMS.]
MMMLF	Monuments of Music and Music Literature in Facsimile
MMMw	Das moderne Musikempfinden, Musikwissenschaft
MMR	*Monthly Musical Record* [Dat. LCPS.]
MMS	The Master Musician Series
Mmu	*Le monde musical*
Mmus	*Musiques et musiciens*
MN	*Musical News* [*and Herald*]
MnN	*Münchner neueste Nachrichten*

MO	*Musical Opinion [and Music Trade Review: British, Foreign and Colonial]* [KIP. UMI. WMP.]
ModM	*Modern Music* [AMSP.]
Mog	*Musica d'oggi: Rassegna divita e di cultura musical* [Dat. SMS.]
MonAb	*Monograph Abstracts*
MonR	*The Monthly Review; or, Literary Journal*
MoT	Milestones of Thought
Mozart-Jb	*Mozart-Jahrbuch des Zentralinstituts für Mozartforschung* (Internationale Stiftung Mozarteum Salzburg)
MozJ	*Mozart-Jahrbuch* (Munich)
MP	*Music Perception*
Mp	*Die Musikpflege* [SMS.]
MPar	*Music Parade*
MpB	*Musikpädagogische Blätter* [Dat.]
MpFL	Musikpädagogik: Forschung und Lehre, edited by Sigrid Abel-Struth
MPhil	*Modern Philology*
MpS	*Mathematisch-physikalische Semesterberichte zur Pflege des Zusammenhangs von Schule und Universität*
MPsy	*Musik Psychology: Jarhbuch der Deutschen Gesellschaft für Musikpsychologie*
MPT	Music: Practice and Theory
MQ	*The Musical Quarterly* [AMSP. KR. PMC. UMI.]
MR	*The Music Review* [KrR. UMI.]
MRIG	Music Research and Information Guides
MRz	*Musikalische Realzeitung* [*Rism* B/VI/1, p. 170. GO. LCPS: B-124.]
MS	Musikwissenschaftliche Studien
Ms	Manuscript
Msac	*Musica sacra*
MSch	*Musik in der Schule*
Ms:CVO	*Musica sacra: Cäcilien-Verbands-Organ* [SMS.]
MSD	Musicological Studies and Documents, edited by Armen Carapetyan
MSel	Musikalische Seltenheiten
Msh	*Música sacro-hispana*
MShP	*Mémoires de la Société de l'histoire de Paris et de l'Ile-de-France*
MSisaaL	Mémoires de la Société impériale des sciences, de l'agriculture et des arts, de Lille
MSo	Musical Sources
MSP	Music: Scholarship and Performance, edited by Thomas Binkley
MSS	Musik aus der Stiermark, Sonderdruck
MSt	Musikalische Studien
Msu	*Mois suisse littéraire et politique, revue nationale et européenne*
MSur	*Music Survey*
MSzMw	Mainzer Studien zur Musikwissenschaft, edited by Hellmut Federhofer
MT	*The Musical Times* [UMI. WMP.]
MTBT	Musik-Taschen-Bücher: Theoretica
MTelS	Magdeburger Telemann Studien
MTFSEC	Music and Theatre in France in the Seventeenth and Eighteenth Centuries
MTft	*Musik: Tidskrift for tonekunst*
Mth	*Musiktheorie*
MtKM	Musica per la tastiera: Keyboard Music from the Sixteenth and Seventeenth Century
MTS	*Music Theory Spectrum*
MTT	Musical Theorists in Translation
MTTS	Music Theory Translation Series, edited by Claude V. Palisca
MuA	*Musik und Altar*
Mucél	Les musiciens célèbres
MuF	*The Music Forum*, edited by William J. Mitchell and Felix Salzer
MuG	Musik und Geistesgeschichte, Berliner Studien zur Musikwissenschaft, edited by Arnold Schering
Muh	*Musikhandel: Offizielles Fachblatt für den Handel mit Musikalien, Schallplatten, Musikinstrumenten und Zubehör*
Mujeu	*Musique en jeu*
MuL	*Musical Leader*
MuM	*Music and Man*
MuMM	*Music: A Monthly Magazine Devoted to the Art, Science, Technic and Literature of Music* [UMI.]
MuMus	*Music and Musicians*
MuN	*Musical Newsletter* [UMI.]

Mus	*Musicology* (The Musicological Society of Australia)
Musart	*Musart: Official Publication of The National Catholic Music Educators Association*
MusDisq	*Musica: Disques*
Music	*Music: The A. G. O. and R. C. C. O. Magazine* Original title of *AmO:AGO*.
Musica	*Musica: Zweimonatsschrift [für alle Gebieter des Musiklebens]* [GO. UMI.]
Musikern	*Musikern: Svenska musikerförbundets tidning*
MusMag	*Musikalisches Magazin* [Dat. KIP.]
MusN	*Music News*
MusT	*The Music Teacher [and Piano Student]* [UMI.]
MuWb	*Musikalisches Wochenblatt: Organ für Musiker und Musikfreunde* [BrP. IDC. KIP. SMS.]
Muzl	*Muzykal'nyi listok* [Musical Leaflet]
Muzm	*Muzika – masam* [Music – to the Masses]
Muzo	*Muzykal'noe obrazovanie* [Music Education] [KIP.]
Muzp	*Muzyka i penie* [Music and Singing]
Muzsov	*Muzykal'nyi sovremennik* [The Musical Contemporary] [Dat.]
Muzy	*Muzykoznanie* [Musicology]
Muzyka	*Muzyka: Kwartalnik poświecony historii i teorii muzyki oraz krytyce naukowej i artystycznej*
Muzyka(K)	*Muzyka* (Kiev)
MVM	München Veröffentlichungen zur Musikgeschichte, edited by Thrasybulos G. Georgiades
MW	*The Musical World: A Record of Music, the Drama, Literature, Fine Arts, Foreign Intelligence, etc.* [KIP. UMI. SMS.]
MwBM	Das Musikwerk: Eine Beispielsammlung zur Musikgeschichte
MWM	*Music of the West: A Monthly Report to the Nation on Music and Musicians of Western America*
MwS	Musikwissenschaftliche Schriften
MZ	Musikalische Zeitfragen: Eine Schriftenreihe, edited by Walter Wiora
NACWPIJ	*National Association of College Wind and Percussion Instructors Journal* [UMI.]
NAMIS	*Newsletter of the American Musical Instrument Society*
NAR	*North American Review*
NatR	*National Review*
NATSB	*The NATS Bulletin: The Official Magazine of the National Association of Teachers of Singing, Inc.* [JRC.]
NcasP	*Novi commentarii academiae scientiarum Petropolitanae*
NCM	*Nineteenth-Century Music* [UMI.]
NCS	Norton Critical Scores
Neo	*Neophilologus: A Quarterly Devoted to the Study of Modern Languages and of Classical Languages in Relation thereto*
NF	*National Forum*
NGHM	The Norton/Grove Handbooks of Music
NglI	*Nuovo giornale de' letterati d'Italia*
NGrove	*The New Grove Dictionary of Music and Musicians*, edited by Stanley Sadie
NGroveAm	*The New Grove Dictionary of American Music*, edited by H. Wiley Hitchcock and Stanley Sadie
NHQ	*New Hungarian Quarterly*
NHSzMw	Neue Heidelberger Studien zur Musikwissenschaft, edited by Reinhold Hammerstein
NhV	*Neue hessischen Volksblätter*
NJL	*Niedersächsisches Jahrbuch für Landesgeschichte: Neue Folge der "Zeitschrift des Historischen Vereins für Niedersachsen"*
NLDMK	Novello's Library for the Diffusion of Musical Knowledge
Nlit	*Nouvelles littéraires* Accessible through *Corlit*: Tourneux (1877-82).
NLS	Norton Library Series
NLSCS	Norton Library Seventeenth-Century Series
Nm	*Norsk musikktidsskrift*
NmF	Neue musikgeschichtliche Forschungen, edited by Lothar Hoffmann-Erbrecht
Nmk	*Nordisk musikkultur* [SZ.]

NMPES	Novello's Music Primers and Educational Series, edited by John STAINER
NMQ	*New Mexico Quarterly*
NMR	*The New Music Review and Church Music Review*
Nmu	*Nuestra música*
NMUM	*New Musical and Universal Magazine*
NMZ	*Neue Musik-Zeitung* [Dat. KIP. LCPS. SMS.]
NMZnJD	*Neue Musikzeitung: Die Zeitung der musikalischen Jugend Deutschlands und allgemeine Ausgabe*
NMzs	*Neue Musikzeitschrift: Monatsschrift für Musiker und Musikfreunde*
NN	*News and Notes*
NOHM	New Oxford History of Music
Notes	*Notes: The Quarterly Journal of the Music Library Association* [AMagS.]
NPS	Neue Psychologische Studien
NQ	*Notes and Queries: A Medium of Inter-Communication for Literary Men, General Readers, etc.*
NR	*Naturwissenschaftliche Rundschau: Wöchentliche Berichte über die Fortschritte auf dem Gesammtgebiete der Naturwissenschaften*
NRep	*The New Republic: A Weekly Journal of Opinion*
NRev	*A New Review; with Literary Curiosities, and Literary Intelligence*
Nrf	*Nouvelle revue française*
Nrmi	*Nuova rivista musicale italiana: Bimen-strale di cultura e informazione musicale*
NRRSL	*Notes and Records of the Royal Society of London*
Nrt	*Nouvelle revue théologique*
NS	*New Statesman*
NSc	*New Scientist*
NSR	*Neue Schweizer Rundschau*
Numu	*Nutida musik: Tidskrift för vår tids tonkonst utgiven av Sveriges Radio*
Nuomu	*La nuova musica* [SMS.]
NW	*Numus-West*

NwMPG	*Die Naturwissenschaften: Organ der Max-Planck Gesellschaft zur Förderung der Wissenschaften; Organ der Gesell-schaft deutscher Naturforscher und Ärzte*
Nwr	Noorduijn's wetenschappelijke reeks
NY	*New Yorker*
NYHT	*New York Herald Tribune*
NYRB	*New York Review of Books*
NYT	*The New York Times*
NYTBR	*New York Times Book Review*
NZfM	*Neue Zeitchrift für Musik* [KIP. SMS.]
NZGS	*Neue Zeitungen von Gelehrten Sachen*
NZZ	*Neue Zürcher Zeitung*
NZZB	*Neue Zürcher Zeitung. Beilage: Literatur und Kunst*
OA	Orbis Academicus, Problemgeschichten der Wissenschaft in Dokumenten und Darstellungen
Observatory	*Observatory: A Review of Astronomy*
Occ	*L'occident: Architecture, sculpture, pein-ture, musique, poésie*
ÖB	Österreichische Blasmusik
Oém	*Observations sur les écrits modernes*
ÖM	*Österreichische Musikzeitschrift*
ÖMu	*Österreichische Musikzeitung*
Og	*Ongaku gaku*
OIQ	*Organ Institute Quarterly* [UMI.]
Omér	*Orgues méridionales*
OmSM	*Orbis musicae/Studies in Musicology*
Opmus	*Opus musicum*
OpN	*Opera News* [UMI.]
OPS	Oxford Psychology Series
OpW	*Opern Welt*
OQ	*Opera Quarterly*
Ormus	Orbis musicarum
Orch	*Das Orchester: [Organ der Deutschen Or-chestervereinigung] Zeitschrift für Or-chesterkultur und Rundfunk-Chorwesen*
OrganYb	*The Organ Yearbook: A Journal for the Players and Historians of Keyboard In-struments*
OrR	*Organists Review*
OSC	Oxford Studies of Composers

OSGM	Orpheus-Schriftenreihe zu Grundfragen der Musik, edited by the Gesellschaft zur Förderung der systematischen Musikwissenschaft, later by Martin Vogel
OT	*Offene Tore*
Ovt	*Orgelkunst viermaandelijks tijdschrift*
PAA	*Proceedings of the Australasian Association of History, Philosophy and Social Studies of Science*
Pag	*Pagine: Polsko-włoskie materialy muzyczne/Argomenti musicali polacco-italiani*
PAIM:M	Publications of the American Institute of Musicology: Miscellanea, edited by Armen Carapetyan
PAMS	*Papers [Read by Members of the] American Musicological Society*
PAPS	*Proceedings of the American Philosophical Society*
PaptM	*Publikation aelterer praktischer und theoretischer Musikwerke*, edited by the Gesellschaft für Musikforschung [UME.]
Parabola	*Parabola: Myth and the Quest for Meaning*
Parn	*Parnassus: Poetry in Review*
Pauta	*Pauta: Cuadernos de teoria y critica musical*
PB	Philosophische Bibliothek
PBSHPZ	Philosophische Bibliothek, oder Sammlung der Hauptwerke der Philosophie alter und neuer Zeit
Pbsm	Piccola biblioteca di sciencze moderne
Pc	*Le pour et le contre: Ouvrage périodique a d'un gout nouveau . . .*
PEA	Princeton Essays on the Arts
Pfmi	*Primie fioriture del melodramma italiano*, edited by Francesco Mantica
PharH	*Pharmacy in History*
PhH	*Philosophy and History*
PHHMS	Prentice-Hall History of Music Series
Phil	*Philosophy [Journal of Philosophical Studies]*
Philologus	*Philologus: Zeitschrift für das klassische Alterthums*
PhilQ	*Philological Quarterly*
PHMS	Prentice-Hall Music Series, edited by Douglas Moore
PhP	*Philharmonic Post*
PhQ	*Philosophical Quarterly*
PhR	*Philosophical Review*
PIMg	Publikationen der Internationalen Musikgesellschaft, Beihefte
PISG	Publicationen der Internationalen Schönberg-Gesellschaft
PJLR	*Philomathic Journal and Literary Review*
Pm	*Paléographie musicale: Les principaux manuscrits de chant grégorien, ambrosien, mozarabe, gallican publiés en fac-similés phototypiques par les Bénédictins de Solesmes [Dat. HL.]*
PMA	*Proceedings [Journal] of the [Royal] Musical Association [BrP. KrR.]*
PMC	Princeton Microfilm Corporation
PMLAA	*Publications of the Modern Language Association of America*
PMM	*Penguin Music Magazine*
PMS	*Perceptual and Motion Skills*
Pmuz	*Proletarskii muzykant* [Proletarian Musician]
PNM	*Perspectives of New Music* [JRC.]
PolS	*Political Studies*
PopM	*Popular Music*
PP	*Pan Pipes*
PPR	*Philosophy and Phenomenological Research*
PPrR	*Performance Practice Review*
PQ	*Piano Quarterly*
PR	*Pädagogische Reform*
PRhet	*Philosophy and Rhetoric*
PRund	*Philosophische Rundschau: Eine Vierteljahrsschrift für philosophische Kritik*
PS	*Prairie Schooner*
PSE	Purcell Society Edition, edited by Thurston Dart
PSfm	Publications de la Société française de musicologie
PSM	Princeton Studies in Music
PSMG	Publikationen der Schweïzerischen Musikforschenden Gesellschaft
Psp	Prace specjalne
PSSR	Primary Sources from the Scientific Revolution, edited by Allen G. Debus

PsyR	*Psychological Record*
PT	*Piano Teacher* [UMI.]
PTCI	*Periodical of Theory-Composition, Illinois State Teacher's Association*
PTJ	*Piano Technician's Journal*
PTRS	[Royal Society of London:] *Philosophical Transactions* [JRC. KrR.]
PW	*Publishers' Weekly: The American Book Trade Journal*
PWMa	Publikationen der Wiener Musikakademie
QDGWp	Quellen und Darstellungen zur Geschichte Westpreußens
QdRm	*Quaderni della Rassegna musical*
QFSKV	Quellen und Forschungen zur Sprach- und Kulturgeschichte der germanischen Völker, edited by Hermann Kunisch
QJEP	*Quarterly Journal of Experimental Psychology*
QMMR	*Quarterly Musical Magazine and Review*
QMR	*Quarterly Musical Register*
QMt	Quellenschriften der Musiktheorie, edited by Johannes Wolf
QQ	*Queen's Quarterly*
QRim	Quaderni della Rivista italiana di musicologia, edited by the Società italiana di musicologia
Quad	*Quadrivium*
Rasm	*La rassegna musicale* [SMS.]
RasmC	*Rassegna musicale* [delle Edizioni] *Curci*
RB	*Revue de Bourgogne*
RBBR	*Reprint Bulletin Book Reviews*
Rbdm	*Revue belge de musicologie*
Rbén	*Revue bénédictine: Le messager des fidèles*
RBzMw	Regensburger Beiträge zur Musikwissenschaft, edited by Hermann Beck
RCMM	*The R. C. M. Magazine: A Journal for Past and Present Students and Friends of the Royal College of Music, London, and Official Journal of the R. C. M. Union*
Rcsf	*Rivista critica di storia della filosofia*
Rdm	*Revue de musicologie* [KrR.]
RdS	*Revue de Synthèse*
RecMus	*Recorder and Music*
RenRef	*Renaissance and Reformation/Renaissance et réforme*
RES	*Review of English Studies*
Response	*Response in Worship, Music, the Arts*
Resth	*Revue d'esthétique* [ACRPP.]
Revdm	*Revista de musicología*
Rf	*Res facta*
RG	The Renaissance and the Gods . . ., edited by Stephen Orgel
RgmdP	*Revue et gazette musicale de Paris* [BrP. KIP. LCPS. SMLMS.] The merger of FÉTIS's *Revue musicale* and the *Gazette musicale de Paris*.
Rgspa	*Revue générale des sciences pures et appliquées*
Rh	*Revue historique*
Rhcm	*Revue d'histoire de de critique musicales: Publication mensuelle* [principalement consacrée à la musique française ancienne et moderne] [Dat. KIP. SMS.] Later titled simply *La revue musicale*.
Rhein	*Die Rheinlande: Monatsschrift für deutsche Kunst*
RhlF	*Revue d'histoire littéraire de la France*
Rhphgc	*Revue d'histoire de la philosophie et d'histoire générale de la civilisation*
Rhr	*Revue de l'histoire des religions*
Rhsa	*Revue d'histoire des sciences et de leurs applications*
Ridm	*Rivista italiana di musicologia*
Rilm	*Répertoire international de littérature musicale*
Rim	*Revue internationale de musique* [KIP.]
Rism	*Répertoire international des sources musicales*
RlN	Respublica literaria Neerlandica, edited by F. F. Blok, C. M. Bruehl, C. S. M. Rademaker, and P. Tuynman
Rm	*Revue musicale* (founded 1920) [SZ.]
RMARC	*Royal Musical Association Research Chronicle*
RmC	*Revista musical Chilena*
Rmen	*Revista mensual*
RMet	*Review of Metaphysics*
Rm(F)	*Revue musicale*, edited by François-Joseph FÉTIS [Dat. KIP. SMLMS.]
Rmfc	"Recherches" sur la musique français classique

Rmg	*Russkaia muzykal'naia gazeta* [Russian Musical Newspaper] [Dat.]
Rmi	*Rivista musicale italiana* [Dat. IDC. KIP. LCPS. SMS.]
RMS	Russian Music Studies, edited by Malcolm Hamrick Brown
RmSIM	*Revue musicale S. I. M.* [SMS.] Began as *Le mercure musical* and adopted various other titles over the years.
RmSr	*Revue musicale de Suisse romande*
RMTZ	*Rheinische Musik- und Theater-Zeitung: Allgemeine Zeitschrift für Musik*
Rmus	*Ricerche musicali*
Rmuz	*Ruch muzyczny*
RN	*Renaissance News* Original title of *RQ*.
Rocg	*Rocznik gdański*
RoF	*Romanische Forschungen*
RQ	*Renaissance Quarterly*
RR	*Romanic Review*
RRMBE	Recent Researches in the Music of the Baroque Era
RRMCA	Recent Researches in the Music of the Classical Era
RRSer	*Romantisme: Revue de la Société des études romantiques*
RS	*Recorded Sound: Journal of the British Institute of Recorded Sound*
Rsh	*Revue des sciences humaines*
Rspt	*Revue des sciences philosophique et théologique*
RUB	Reclam Universal-Bibliothek
Rusf	*Russkii fol'klor* [Russian Folklore]
Rusves	*Russkii vestnik* [The Russian Herald]
S	Source
SA	*Sudhoffs Archiv: Zeitschrift für Wissenschaftsgeschichte*
SacM	*Sacred Music*
SAF	The Shakespeare Association Facsimiles
Sagittarius	*Sagittarius: Beiträge zur Erforschung und Praxis alter und neuer Kirchenmusik*
SAII	*Studien zur Aufführungspraxis und Interpretation von Instrumentalmusik des 18. Jahrhunderts*
SAJM	*South African Journal of Musicology*
Sammler	*Der Sammler: Beilage der München-Augsburger Abendzeitung*
SAMT	*The South African Music Teacher/Die Suid-Afrikaanse musiekonderwyser*
SAQ	*South Atlantic Quarterly*
SatR	*Saturday Review* [of Literature]
SBC	*Sounding Brass and The Conductor*
SBF	*Science Books and Films*
SBHF	Sonderhefte der Blätter für Harmonikale Forschung
SC	Schriften der Corona
SCAC	*Studia Cartesiana/Analecta Cartesiana*
ScAm	*Scientific American*
SchüJb	*Schütz-Jahrbuch*
Science	*Science* [American Association for the Advancement of Science]
SchM	*The School Musician*
SCJ	*Sixteenth Century Journal*
SCMC	Studies in Croatian Musical Culture: Collection of Translations
SCN	*Seventeenth-Century News*
Scrut	*Scrutiny: A Quarterly Review*
SCTM	Studies in the Criticism and Theory of Music, edited by Leonard B. Meyer
Sdbe	La Sociedad de bibliófilos españoles
SdG	Die Schweiz im deutschen Geistesleben, edited by Harry Maync
SdM	*Süddeutsche Monatshefte*
SdOB	Süddeutsche Orgelmeister des Baroque
SECC	Studies in Eighteenth-Century Culture
SEL	*Studies in English Literature: 1500-1900*
SewR	*Sewanee Review*
SFG	*Spanische Forschungen der Görresgesellschaft. Erste Reihe: Gesammelte Aufsätze zur Kulturgeschichte Spaniens*
Sfr	*Studi francesi*
SFrR	*Stanford French Review*
Sg	*Die Singgemeinde*
Sgen	*Studium generale*
SGös	Sammlung Göschen
Sh	*Slovenská hudba*
SHA	Study of the History of Aesthetics
ShakS	*Shakespeare Studies: An Annual Gathering of Research, Criticism, and Reviews*

Shdom	*Sentiment d'un harmoniphile sur différens ouvrages de musique* [Rism B/VI/1, p. 466. MinR.]
SHIM	*Studies in the History and Interpretation of Music*
SHM	Studies in the History of Music, edited by Lewis Lockwood and Christoph Wolff
ShMg	Studien zur hessischen Musikgeschichte
Shmpb	Société pour l'histoire musicale de pays-bas: Musique et musiciens au XVIIᵉ siècle
SHMPS	Studies in the History of Mathematics and the Physical Sciences
SHMS	Schriften der Hochschule "Mozarteum" Salzburg
SHR	*Southern Humanities Review*
SHZ	*Schwäbische Heimat: Zeitschrift zur Pflege von Landschaft, Volkstum, Kultur*
Signale	*Signale für die musikalische Welt* [SMS.]
SiM	Studies in Musicology, edited by George J. Buelow
SIMg	*Sammelbände der Internationalen Musikgesellschaft/Quarterly Magazine of the International Musical Society* [DG. GO. IDC. JRC.]
SJIZ	Studien aus dem C. G. Jung-Institut, Zürich
SJMw	*Schweizerisches Jahrbuch für Musikwissenschaft* [SZ.]
SK	*Singende Kirche*
SKir	Studia Kircheriana
Sl	*Le semaine littéraire: Revue hebdomadaire*
SlatR	Slatkine Reprints (Geneva)
SLit	*Soviet Literature*
SLMfK	Schriften des Landinstituts für Musikforschung, Kiel
Sm	*Studi musicali*
SmA	Sammlung musikwissenschaftlicher Abhandlungen/Collection d'études musicologiques
SMB	Schriften des Musikinstrumentenmuseums Brüssels
SMb	Schlesinger'sche Musikbibliothek
SMg	Studien zur Medizingeschichte des neunzehnten Jahrhunderts, edited by W. Artelt, E. Herschkel, and G. Mann
SMLMS	Sibley Music Library Microform Service Distributor of microfiche and microfilm copies of many holdings from the Sibley Music Library, c/o Eastman School of Music, 27 Gibbs Street, Rochester, New York 14604.
Smm	*Studia musico-museologica*
Smn	*Studia musicologica norvegica*
SmpB	*Schweizer musikpädagogische Blätter*
SMS	Schnase Microfilm Systems (Scarsdale, New York)
SmU	Studia musicologica Upsaliensia
SMus	Studies in Music
SMUWO	*Studies in Music from the University of Western Ontario*
Smuz	*Sovetskaia muzyka* [Soviet Music]
SmV	*Sammlung musikalischer Vorträge: Ein Almanach für die musikalische Welt*, edited by Paul Graf Waldersee [KrR.]
Smven	Studi di musica veneta (Centro di cultura e civiltà)
SMw	Studien zur Musikwissenschaft
SmwA	Sammlung musikwissenschaftlicher Abhandlungen
SMz	*Schweizerische Musikzeitung* [und Sänger-blatt]/Revue [Gazette] musicale suisse [KrR. SMS.]
SNQ	*Scottish Notes and Queries*
Sonus	*Sonus: A Journal of Investigations into Global Musical Possibilities*
Sos	*Sonorum speculum: Mirror of Musical Life in the Netherlands*
Soun	*Soundings: A Music Journal*
Spct	*Studi e problemi di critica testuale*
Spec	*Spectator*
Spetm	*Lo spettatore musicale*
SpFfBU	*Sborník prací Filosofické fakulty Brněnské University*
SpfmuP	Scuola di paleografia e filologia musicale dell'università di Pavia: Instituta et Monumenta
SPL	Studien zur Philosophie und Literatur des neunzehnten Jahrhunderts
SPR	*The Small Press Review*
SR	*Schweizer Rundschau: Monatsschrift für Geistesleben und Kultur*

SRis	*"Scientia" [Rivista di scienza]: Rivista internazionale di scientifica/International Review of Scientific Synthesis*
SrzM	Schriftenreihe zur Musik
SS	*Science and Society*
Sslm	Saggi di storia e letteratura musicale, edited by Giovanni da Nova
SSzMw	Saarbrücker Studien zur Musikwissenschaft, edited by Walter Wiora
ST	Source and Translation
St	Sbornik trudov
STel	*Sky and Telescope*
Stfm	*Svensk tidskrift för musikforskning [SZ.]*
StiM	*Studies in Music [KIP.]*
STimes	*Sunday Times*
StL	*Studia Leibnitiana: Zeitschrift für Geschichte der Philosophie und der Wissenschaft*
Stm	*Studia musicologica*
Stmus	Studi e testi musicologia, edited by Oscar Mischiati and Luigi Ferdinando Tagliavini
Stp	*Science et techniques en perspective*
Strad	*The Strad: A Monthly Journal for Professionals and Amateurs of All Stringed Instruments Played with the Bow*
StRev	*Stereo Review [UMI.]*
Studies	*Studies: An Irish Quarterly Review of Letters, Philosophy and Science*
Stusec	*Studi secenteschi*
Suasv	Skrifter utgivna av svenskt visarkiv
SVEC	*Studies on Voltaire and the Eighteenth Century*
SW	*Sterne und Weltraum*
SWI	Studies of the Warburg Institute, edited by J. B. Trapp or F. Saxl
SwM	*The Southwestern Musician*
Syt	Ser y tiempo
SZ	Swets & Zeitlinger (Lisse, The Netherlands)
SZG	*Schweizerische Zetischrift für Geschichte/Revue suisse d'histoire/Rivista storica svizzera*
SzJ	Stimmen des XX. Jahrhunderts
SzM	Schriften zur Musik, edited by Walter Kolneder
SzMg	Studien zur Musikgeschichte des 19. Jahrhunderts
SzMp	Schriften zur Musikpädagogik, edited by Richard Jakoby
SzMw	*Studien zur Musikwissenschaft: Beihefte der Denkmäler der Tonkunst in Österreich* [DG. IDC.]
T	Translation
T&P	*Theory and Practice*
Tablet	*The Tablet: A Weekly Newspaper and Review*
Tatzlil	*Tatzlil (The Chord): Forum for Music Research and Bibliography*
TC	*Twentieth Century*
TCSE	Teachers College Studies in Education
TechR	Technical Report
Tempo	*Tempo: A Quarterly Review of Modern Music* [KrR.]
TES	*Times Educational Supplement*
TG	*Technik Geschichte: Verein Deutscher Ingenieure*
Tgakhn	Trudy gosudarstvennoi akademii khudozhestvennikh nauk, psikho-fizicheskii laboratoriia [Transactions of the State Academy of Artistic Sciences, Psychophysical Laboratory]
ThA	*Theatre Arts*
Theoria	*Theoria: Historical Aspects of Music Theory*
THL	Theory and History of Literature
ThS	*Theoretically Speaking*
Tibia	*Tibia: Magazin für Freunde alter und neuer Bläsermusik*
TLS	*Times Literary Supplement*
Trorg	*Tribune de l'orgue*
TS	*Teyler's Stichting, Haarlem: Museum [Archives du Musée Teyler]*
TTL	Tuning and Temperament Library
TTS	Thurn und Taxis-Studien
TvNm	*Tijdschrift der vereeniging voor Nederlandsche [Noord-Nederlands] muziekgeschiedenis,* currently titled *Tijdschrift van de vereniging voor Nederlandse muziekgeschiedenis*
Tvom	*Tijdschrift voor oude muziek*
TzF	Textes zur Forschung

TzMw	Taschenbücher zur Musikwissenschaft, edited by Richard Schaal
UA	Universitas-Archiv, Eine Sammlung wissenschaftlicher Untersuchungen und Abhandlungen, edited by Siegfried Behn, Gerhard Kallen, Günther Müller, Kurt Perels, Julius Schwering, and Walther Vetter
UH	*Unser Harz: Zeitschrift für den gesamten Harz und seine Vorlande*
UKK	*Unterhaltungen für Kinder und Kinderfreunde*, edited by Johann Joachim Eschenburg and D. Schiebler
UME	University Music Editions
UMI	University Microfilms International (Ann Arbor, Michigan)
URLB	*University of Rochester Library Bulletin*
US	*Universität des Saarlandes: Annales Universitatis Saraviensis, Philosophie*
UT	Urban-Taschenbücher
UWOSPS	University of Western Ontario Series in Philosophy of Science
VAMÖ	Veröffentlichung der Arbeitsgemeinschaft der Musikerzieher Österreichs
VdKfM	Veröffentlichungen der Kommission für Musikforschung, edited by Franz Grasberger
VE	*Vestnik Evropy: Zhurnal' istorii-politiki-literatury* [Bulletin of Europe: Journal of History, Politics, and Literature]
VEGL	Veröffentlichungen der Evangelischen Gesellschaft für Liturgieforschung, edited by Oskar Söhngen and Gerhard Kunze
VhVOR	*Verhandlungen des historischen Vereins für Oberpfalz und Regensburg*
Viet	*Voprosy istorii estestvoznaniia i tekhniki* [Questions on the History of Aesthetics and Technique]
VIHF	Veröffentlichungen des Instituts für Harmonikale Forschung, Sektion Deutschland
VilV	*Village Voice*
VLA	Veröffentlichung des Leibniz-Archivs
Vm	*Vlaams muziektijdschrift*
VMbPH	Veröffentlichungen der Musik-bibliothek Paul Hirsch

VmF	La vie musicale en France sous les rois Bourbons, edited by Norbert Dufourcq
Vmus	*La vie musicale: Bulletin mensuel d'information de la Revue internationale de musique*
VMw	*Vierteljahrsschrift für Musikwissenschaft* [DG. GO. IDC.]
VOBIMg	Veröffentlichungen der Ortsgruppe Berlin der Internationalen Musikgesellschaft
VPMTNA	*Volume of Proceedings of the Music Teachers National Association*
VQR	*Virginia Quarterly Review: A National Journal of Literature and Discussion*
VS	*Victorian Studies*
VSIMPK	Veröffentlichungen des Staatlichen Instituts für Musikforschung, Preussischer Kulturbesitz, edited by Hans-Peter Reinecke and Dagmar Droysen
Vtem	*Voprosy teorii i estetiki muzyki* [Questions on the Theory and Aesthetics of Music]
VV	*Violins and Violinists*
VWS	Veröffentlichungen der Walcker-Stiftung
WAMS	Wissenschaftliche Abhandlungen/Musicological Studies
WdF	Wege der Forschung
WF	*Württembergisch Franken*
WG	Welt des Gesangbuchs
WiKat	Weber's illustrirte Katechismen
WK	*Wissenschaft und Kultur*
WLB	*Wilson Library Bulletin*
WM	*The World of Music* [SZ.]
WMb	Wiener Musikbücher
WMP	World Microfilms Publications
WNAMb	*Wöchentliche Nachrichten und Anmerkungen die Musik betreffend*, edited by Johann Adam Hiller [*Rism* B/VI/1, p. 415. GO. LCPS: H-049. SMLMS.]
WnJ	*Die Wissenschaften im 19. Jahrhundert*
WTFpS	Weisheit und Tat: Eine Folge philosophischer Schriften, edited by Arthur Hoffmann
WUA	Wiener Urtext Ausgabe, edited by Karl Heinz Füssl and H. C. Robbins Landon
WVzMw	Wiener Veröffentlichungen zur Musikwissenschaft, edited by Othmar Wessely
WW	*Wissenschaft und Weltbild*

WWBP	*Woodwind World—Brass and Percussion*
WZKMU	*Wissenschaftliche Zeitschrift der Karl-Marx-Universität Leipzig: Gesellschaft- und sprachwissenschaftliche Reihe*
WZMLU	*Wissenschaftliche Zeitschrift der Martin-Luther-Universität Halle-Wittenberg: Gesellschafts- und sprachwissenschaftliche Reihe*
YIFMC	*Yearbook of the International Folk Music Council*
YMC	*Your Musical Cue*
YR	*Yale Review*
YSHM	Yale Studies in the History of Music, edited by Leo Schrade
ZfbL	*Zeitschrift für bayerische Landesgeschichte*
ZfGf	*Zeitschrift für Ganzheitsforschung*
ZfGNTM	*Zeitschrift für Geschichte der Naturwissenschaften, Technik, und Medizin*
ZfhF	*Zeitschrift für historische Forschung*
ZfM	*Zeitschrift für Musik*

	Truncation of *NZfM.*
ZfMG	*Zentralblatt für Mathematik und ihre Grenzgebiete*
ZfMp	*Zeitschrift für Musikpädagogik*
ZfMt	*Zeitschrift für Musiktheorie*
ZfMw	*Zeitschrift für Musikwissenschaft* [BrP. Dat. DG. JRC. KIP. LCPS.] Continued by *AfMf.*
ZfS	*Zeitschrift für Sinnesphysiologie*
ZfvMw	*Zeitschrift für vergleichende Musikwissenschaft*
ZIMG	*Zeitschrift der Internationalen Musik-Gesellschaft*
Zrvtls	Zwolse reeks van taal- en letterkundige studies
ZTM	*Zeitung für Theater und Musik zur Unterhaltung gebildeter, unbefangener Leser*
ZVhG	*Zeitschrift des Verein für hamburgische Geschichte*
Zvuk	*Zvuk: Jugoslovenski muzički časopis*

CONGRESS REPORTS

Bach-Fest 1975 Bericht über die wissenschaftlich Konferenz zum III. Internationalen Bach-Fest der DDR, Leipzig, 18./19. September 1975, edited by Werner Felix, Winfried Hoffmann, and Armin Schneiderheinze. Leipzig: VEB Deutscher Verlag für Musik, 1977.

Bericht Basel 1924 Bericht über den musikwissenschaftlichen Kongreß in Basel: Veranstaltet anläßlich der Feier des 25jährigen Bestehens der Ortsgruppe Basel der Neuen Schweizerischen Musikgesellschaft, Basel vom 26. bis 29. September 1924. Leipzig: Breitkopf & Härtel, 1925.

Bericht Berlin 1974 Gesellschaft für Musikforschung: Bericht über den internationalen musikwissenschaftlichen Kongress Berlin 1974, edited by Hellmut Kühn and Peter Nitsche. Kassel: Bärenreiter, 1980.

Bericht Bonn 1970 Gesellschaft für Musikforschung: Bericht über den internationalen musikwissenschaftlichen Kongress, Bonn 1970 edited by Carl Dahlhaus, Hans Joachim Marx, Magda Marx-Weber, and Günther Massenkeil. Kassel: Bärenreiter, 1971.

Bericht Hamburg 1956 Gesellschaft für Musikforschung: Bericht über den internationalen musikwissenschaftlichen Kongress Hamburg 1956, edited by Walter Gerstenburg, Heinrich Husmann, and Harald Heckmann. Kassel: Bärenreiter, 1957.

Bericht Kassel 1962 Gesellschaft für Musikforschung: Bericht über den internationalen musikwissenschaftlichen Kongress Kassel 1962, edited by Georg Reichert and Martin Just. Kassel: Bärenreiter, 1963.

Bericht Köln 1958 Internationale Gesellschaft für Musikwissenschaft: Bericht über den siebenten internationalen musikwissenschaftlichen Kongress, Köln 1958, edited by Gerald Abraham, Suzanne Clercx-Lejeune, Hellmut Federhofer, and Wilhelm Pfannkuch. Kassel: Bärenreiter, 1959.

Bericht Leipzig 1925 Deutsche Musikgesellschaft [Deutsche Gesellschaft für Musikwissenschaft]: Bericht über den 1. musikwissenschaftlichen Kongress der Deutschen Musikgesellschaft in Leipzig vom 4. bis 8. Juni 1925. Leipzig: Breitkopf & Härtel, 1926.

Bericht Mozart Mozart und seine Umwelt: Bericht über die Tagung des Zentralinstituts für Mozartforschung der Internationalen Stiftung Mozarteum Salzburg. Kassel: Bärenreiter, 1979.

Bericht Musiktheorie Bericht über den 1. internationalen Kongreß für Musiktheorie, Stuttgart 1971, edited by Peter Rummenhöller, Friedrich Christoph Reininghaus, and Jürgen Habakuk Traber. Stuttgart: Ichthys-Verlag, 1972.

Bericht Walcker-Stiftung 1972 Zur Terminologie der Musik des 20. Jahrhunderts: Bericht über das zweite Colloquium der Walcker-Stiftung 9.-10. März 1972 in Freiburg im Breisgau, edited by Hans Heinrich Eggebrecht. VWS, no. 5. Stuttgart: Musikwissenschaftliche Verlags-Gesellschaft, 1974.

Bericht Wien 1974 Internationale Schönberg-Gesellschaft: Bericht über den 1. Kongreß der Internationalen Schönberg-Gesellschaft, Wien, 4. bis 9. Juni 1974, edited by Rudolf Stephan. PIGS, no. 1. Vienna: Elisabeth Lafite, 1978.

Celebrazioni 1963 Le celebrazioni de 1963 e alcune nuove indagini sulla musica italiana del XVIIIe XIX secolo, edited by Mario Fabbri, Adelmo Damerini, and Gino Roncaglia. AmCS, no. 20. Florence: Leo S. Olschki, 1963.

Colloques Wégimont Les colloques de Wégimont IV— 1957: Le "Baroque" musical; Recueil d'études sur la musique du XVIIᵉ siècle. BUL, no. 171. Paris: Société d'Édition "Les belles lettres", 1963.

Colloquium Janáček *Colloquium Leoš Janáček et Musica Europaea,* edited by Rudolf Pečman. CHTMB, no. 3. Brno: International Music Festival, 1970.

Colloquium Rom 1978 *Die stylistische Entwicklung der italienischen Musik zwischen 1770 und 1830 und ihre Beziehungen zum Norden: Colloquium, Rom, 20.-23. März 1978,* edited by Friedrich Lippmann. Anamu, no. 21. Laaber: Arno Volk & Laaber Verlag, 1982.

Congress Basle 1949 *International Musicological Society: Forth [sic] Congress, Basle June 29 – July 3, 1949, Report.* Basel: Bärenreiter, [1951].

Congress Chopin 1960 *The Book of the First International Musicological Congress Devoted to the Work of Frederick Chopin, Warszawa, 16th-22nd February 1960,* edited by Zofia Lissa. Warsaw: PWN – Polish Scientific Publishers, 1963.

Congress Copenhagen 1972 *International Musicological Society: Report of the Eleventh Congress, Copenhagen 1972,* edited by Henrik Glahn, Søren Sørensen, and Peter Ryom. 2 vols. Copenhagen: Hansen, 1974.

Congresso "Manierismo" 1973 *Atti del Congresso internazionale sul tema "Manierismo in arte e musica" – Roma, Accademia Nazionale di Santa Cecilia, 18-23 ottobre 1973.* Florence: Leo S. Olschki, 1977.

Congresso Monteverdi 1968 *Congresso internazionale sul tema Claudio Monteverdi e il suo tempo: Relazioni e comuniazioni; Venezia-Mantova-Cremona, 3-7 maggio 1968,* edited by Raffaello Monterosso. Verona: Valdonega, 1969.

Convegni rinascimento 1976 *Convegni internazionali di musicologia del Centro studi rinascimento musicale, 3-10 maggio 1976: Poesia e musica nell'estetica del XVI XVII secolo,* edited by Hagop Meyvalian. Florence: Artimino, 1979.

Gasparini convegno 1978 *Comune di Camaiore: Francesco Gasparini (1661– 1727): Atti del primo convegno internazionale (Camaiore, 29 settembre – 1° ottobre 1978),* edited by Fabrizio Della Seta and Franco Piperno. Qrim, no. 6. Florence: Leo S. Olschki, 1981.

Haydn Ausstellung 1982 *Joseph Haydn in seiner Zeit: Eisenstadt, 20. Mai – 26. Okt. 1982: Ausstellung,* edited by Gerda Mraz, Gottfried Mraz, and Gerald Schlag. Eisenstadt: Amt der burgenländischen Landesregierung, 1982.

Huygens Symposium 1979 *Studies on Christiaan Huygens: Invited Papers from the Symposium on the Life and Work of Christiaan Huygens, Amsterdam, 22-25 August 1979,* edited by H. J. M. Bos, M. J. S. Rudwick, H. A. M. Snelders, and R. P. W. Visser. Lisse: Swets & Zeitlinger, 1980.

Josquin Festival 1971 *Josquin des Prez: Proceedings of the International Josquin Festival-Conference Held at The Juilliard School at Lincoln Center in New York City, 21-25 June 1971,* edited by Edward E. Lowinsky with the collaboration of Bonnie J. Blackburn. London: Oxford University Press, 1976.

Kepler-Symposion 1980 *Kepler-Symposion zu J. Keplers 350. Todestag, Linz 1980,* edited by Rudolf Haase. Linz: Linzer Veranstaltungsgesellschaft, 1982.

Kieler Tagung 1963 *Norddeutsche und nordeuropäische Musik: Referate der Kieler Tagung 1963,* edited by Carl Dahlhaus and Walter Wiora. KieSzMw, no. 16. Kassel: Bärenreiter, 1965.

Kieler Tagung 1980 *Gattung und Werk in der Musikgeschichte Norddeutschlands und Skandinaviens: Referate der Kieler Tagung 1980,* edited by Friedheim Krummacher and Heinrich W. Schwab. KieSzMw, no. 26. Kassel: Bärenreiter, 1982.

Konferenzbericht Blankenburg/Harz 1975 *Zu Fragen des Instrumentariums, des Besetzung und der Improvisation in der ersten-Hälfte des 18. Jahrhunderts: Konferenzbericht der 3. wissenschaftlichen Arbeitstagung Blankenburg/Harz 28./29. Juni 1975.* SAII, no. 2/2. [ca. 1975.]

Konferenzbericht Blankenburg/Harz 1976 *Die Blasinstrumente und ihre Verwendung sowie zu Fragen des Tempos in der ersten Hälfte des 18. Jahrhunderts: Konferenzbericht der 4. wissenschaftliche Arbeitstagung Blankenburg/Harz, 26./27. Juni 1976,* edited by Eitelfriedrich Thom. 2 vols. SAII, no. 4/1-2. Magdeburg: Rat des Bezirkes; Leipzig: Zentralhaus für Kulturarbeit, 1977.

Konferenzbericht Blankenburg/Harz 1979 *Zu Fragen der Verzierungskunst in der Instrumentalmusik der ersten Hälfte des 18. Jahrhunderts: Konferenzbericht der 7. wissenschaftliche Arbeitstagung Blankenburg/Harz, 29. Juni bis 1. Juli 1979,* edited by Eitelfriedrich Thom and Renate Bormann, SAII, no. 11. Magdeburg: Rat des Bezirkes, 1980.

Konferenzbericht Blankenburg/Harz 1980 *Die Einflüsse einzelner Interpreten und Komponisten des 18. Jahrhunderts auf das Musikleben ihrer Zeit: Konferenzbericht der VIII. wissenschaftlichen Arbeitstagung Blank- enburg/Harz 27. Juni bis 29. Juni 1980,* edited by Günter Fleischhauer, Walther Siegmund-Schultze, and Eitelfriedrich Thom. SAII, no. 13. Magdeburg: Rat des Bezirkes, n.d.

Kongress Bamberg 1953   *Gesellschaft für Musikforschung: Bericht über den internationalen musikwissenschaftlichen Kongress Bamberg 1953,* edited by Wilfried Brennecke, Willi Kahl, and Rudolf Steglich. Kassel: Bärenreiter, 1954.

Kongress-Bericht Lüneburg 1950   *Gesellschaft für Musikforschung: Kongress-Bericht Lüneburg 1950,* edited by Hans Albrecht, Helmuth Osthoff, and Walter Wiora. Kassel: Bürenreiter, n.d.

Kongress Leipzig 1966   *Gesellschaft für Musikforschung: Bericht über den internationalen musikwissenschaftlichen Kongress, Leipzig 1966,* edited by Carl Dahlhaus, Reiner Kluge, Ernst H. Meyer, and Walter Wiora. Kassel: Bärenreiter; Leipzig: VEB Deutscher Verlag für Musik, 1970.

Kongress Wien 1956   *Gesellschaft zur Herausgabe von Denkmälern der Tonkunst in Österreich: Bericht über den internationalen musikwissenschaftlichen Kongress Wien Mozartjahr 1956,* edited by Erich Schenk. Graz/Cologne: Hermann Böhlaus Nachf., 1958.

Leibniz-Kongress 1972   *Akten des II. internationalen Leibniz-Kongresses, Hannover, 17-22 Juli 1972. StL,* Supplementa, nos. 12-15. Wiesbaden: F. Steiner, 1973-75.

Musica antiqua III   *Musica antiqua III: Acta scientifica,* edited by Jerzy Wiśniowski. Bydgoszcz: Bydgoskie Towarzystwo Naukowe, 1972.

Musica antiqua V   *Musica antiqua V: Acta scientifica.* Bydgoszcz: Bydgoskie Towarzystwo Naukowe, 1978.

Orgelsymposium Innsbruck 1979   *Die süddeutsch-österreichische Orgelmusik im 17. und 18. Jahrhundert; Tagungsbericht: 2. Orgelsymposium, Innsbruck 26.-28.8.1979,* edited by Walter Salmen. IBMw, no. 6. Innsbruck: Musikverlag Helbling, 1980.

Oxford Symposium 1977   *Oxford International Symposium (1977: Christ Church College): Modern Musical Scholarship,* edited by Edward Olleson. Stocksfield [Northumberland] and Boston: Oriel Press, 1980.

Plato Colloque 1976   *Platon et Aristote à la Renaissance: XVIᵉ Colloque international de Tours.* DPàD, no. 32. Paris: J. Vrin, 1976.

Proceedings Haydn 1975   *Haydn Studies: Proceedings of the International Haydn Conference, Washington,*

D.C., 1975, edited by Jens Peter Larsen, Howard Serwer, and James Webster. New York: W. W. Norton, 1981.

Referate Berlin 1970   *Über Musiktheorie: Referate der Arbeitstagung 1970 in Berlin,* edited by Frieder Zaminer. KSIMPK, no. 5. Cologne: Volk, 1970.

Report Berkeley 1977   *International Musicological Society: Report of the Twelfth Congress, Berkeley 1977,* edited by Daniel Heartz and Bonnie Wade. Kassel: Bärenreiter, 1981.

Report New York 1961   *International Musicological Society: Report of the Eighth Congress, New York 1961,* edited by Jan LaRue. Kassel: Bärenreiter, 1961.

Rousseau Colloquium   *Rousseau after Two Hundred Years: Proceedings of the Cambridge Bicentennial Colloquium,* edited by R. A. Leigh. Cambridge: Cambridge University Press, 1982.

Salzburger Musikgespräch 1984   *Musik und Mathematik: Salzburger Musikgespräch 1984 unter Vorsitz von Herbert von Karajan,* edited by Heinz Götze and Rudolf Wille. Berlin: Springer-Verlag, 1985.

Schubert-Kongreß 1978   *Schubert-Kongreß Wien 1978: Bericht,* edited by Otto Brusatti. Graz: Akademische Druck- und Verlagsanstalt, 1979.

Studia musico-museologica   *Studia musico-museologica: Bericht über das Symposium, Die Bedeutung, die optische und akustische Darbeitung und die Aufgaben einer Musikinstrumentensammlung.* Nuremberg: Germanisches Nationalmuseum; Stockholm: Svenskt Musikhistoriskt Arkiv, 1970.

Symposium McGill 1981   *L'orgue à notre époque: Papers and Proceedings of the Symposium Held at McGill University, May 26-28, 1981,* edited by Donald Mackey. Montreal: McGill University, 1981.

Telemann Bericht 1967   *Georg Philipp Telemann: Ein bedeutender Meister der Aufklärungsepoche; Konferenzbericht der 3. Magdeburger Telemann-Festtage vom 22. bis 26. Juni 1967,* edited by Günter Fleischhauer and Walther Siegmund-Schultze. 2 vols. Magdeburg: Rat der Stadt, 1969.

Telemann Festtage 1973   *Telemann und die Musikerziehung: Konferenzbericht der 5. Magdeburger Telemann-Festtage vom 19. bis 27. Mai 1973,* edited by Günter Fleischhauer and Walther Siegmund-Schultze. Magdeburg: [s.n.], 1975.

FESTSCHRIFTEN

AdlerFs   *Studien zur Musikgeschichte: Festschrift für Guido Adler zum 75. Geburtstag*. Vienna: Universal Edition, 1930; reprint edition, 1971.

AlbertFs   *Festschrift zur Ehrung von Heinrich Albert (1604-1651)*, edited by Günther Kraft. Weimar: Buchdruckerei Uschmann, 1954.

AlbrechtFs   *Hans Albrecht in memoriam*, edited by Wilfried Brennecke and Hans Haase. Kassel: Bärenreiter, 1962.

BeckFs   *Gedenkschrift Hermann Beck*, edited by Hermann Dechant and Wolfgang Sieber. Laaber: Laaber-Verlag, 1982.

BeckerFs   *Festschrift Heinz Becker zum 60. Geburtstag am 26. Juni 1982*, edited by Jürgen Schläder and Reinhold Quandt. Laaber: Laaber-Verlag, 1982.

BesselerFs   *Festschrift Heinrich Besseler zum sechzigsten Geburtstag*, edited by the Institute für Musikwissenschaft der Karl-Marx-Universität. Leipzig: VEB Deutscher Verlag für Musik, 1961.

BlumeFs   *Festschrift Friedrich Blume zum 70. Geburtstag*, edited by Anna Amalie Abert and Wilhelm Pfannkuch. Kassel: Bärenreiter, 1963.

BoetticherFs   *Convivium musicorum: Festschrift Wolfgang Boetticher zum sechzigsten Geburtstag am 19. August 1974*, edited by Heinrich Hüschen and Dietz-Rüdiger Moser. Berlin: Verlag Merseburger, 1974.

CuylerFs   *Notations and Editions: A Book in Honor of Louise Cuyler*, edited by Edith Borroff. Dubuque, Iowa: Brown, 1974.

EngelFs   *Festschrift Hans Engel zum siebzigsten Geburtstag*, edited by Horst Heussner. Kassel: Bärenreiter, 1964.

FederhoferFs   *Symbolae historiae musicae: Hellmut Federhofer zum 60. Geburtstag*, edited by Friedrich Wilhelm Riedel and Hubert Unverricht. Mainz: Schott, 1971.

FellererFsI   *Festschrift Karl Gustav Fellerer zum sechzigsten Geburtstag am 7. Juni 1962*, edited by Heinrich Hüschen. Regensburg: G. Boße, 1962.

FellererFsII   *Musicae scientiae collectanea: Festschrift Karl Gustav Fellerer zum siebzigsten Geburtstag am 7. Juli 1972*, edited by Heinrich Hüschen. Cologne: Arno Volk Verlag, 1973.

GakuenFs   [Collected Papers in Honor of the 75th Anniversary of Ueno Gakuen], edited by Hiro Ishibashi. Tokyo: Ueno Gakuen, 1979.

GeeringFs   *Festschrift Arnold Geering zum 70. Geburtstag: Beiträge zur Zeit und zum Begriff des Humanismus vorwiegend aus dem Bereich der Music*, edited by Victor Ravizza. Bern and Stuttgart: Paul Haupt, 1972.

GeiringerFs   *Studies in Eighteenth-Century Music: A Tribute to Karl Geiringer on His Seventieth Birthday*, edited by H. C. Robbins Landon in collaboration with Roger E. Chapman. London: Allen and Unwin, 1970.

GerstenbergFs   *Festschrift Walter Gerstenberg zum 60. Geburtstag*, edited by Georg von Dadelsen and Andreas Holschneider. Wolfenbüttel and Zürich: Möseler Verlag, 1964.

GolffingFs   *Poems and Essays in Honor of Francis Golffing*, edited by W. Clymer. 1977.

GriersonFs   *Seventeenth Century Studies Presented to Sir Herbert Grierson*. Oxford: Clarendon Press, 1938.

GroutFs   *New Looks at Italian Opera: Essays in Honor of Donald J. Grout*, edited by William W. Austin. Ithaca, N.Y.: Cornell University Press, 1968.

GudewillFs   Beiträge zur Musikgeschichte Nordeuropas: Kurt Gudewill zum 65. Geburtstag, edited by Uwe Haensel. Wolfenbüttel and Zürich: Möseler, 1978.

HaberlFs   Festschrift Ferdinand Haberl zum 70. Geburtstag: Sacerdos et cantus gregoriani magister, edited by Franz A. Stein. Regensburg: Boße, 1977.

HaydonFs   Studies in Musicology: Essays in the History, Style, and Bibliography of Music in Memory of Glen Haydon, edited by James W. Pruett, with a Foreword by Charles Seeger. Chapel Hill, N.C.: The University of North Carolina Press, 1969.

HobokenFs   Anthony vaan Hoboken: Festschrift zum 75. Geburtstag, edited by Joseph Schmidt-Görg. Mainz: B. Schott's Söhne, 1962.

Hoelty-NickelFs   Festschrift Theodore Hoelty-Nickel: A Collection of Essays on Church Music, edited by Newman W. Powell. Valparaiso, Ind.: Valparaiso University, 1967.

HüschenFs   Ars musica, musica scientia: Festschrift Heinrich Hüschen zum fünfundsechzigsten Geburtstag am 2. März 1980, edited by Detlef Altenburg. Cologne: Gitarre & Laute, 1980.

HusmannFs   Speculum musicae artis: Festgabe für Heinrich Husmann zum 60. Geburtstag am 16. Dezember 1968, edited by Heinz Becker and Reinhard Gerlach. Munich: Fink, 1970.

KaufmannFs   Music East and West: Essays in Honor of Walter Kaufmann, edited by Thomas Noblitt. FesS, no. 3. New York: Pendragon Press, 1981.

KroyerFs   Theodor Kroyer: Festschrift zum sechzigsten Geburtstage, edited by Hermann Zenck, Helmut Schultz, and Walter Gerstenberg. Regensburg: G. Boße, 1933.

LangFs   Music and Civilization: Essays in Honor of Paul Henry Lang, edited by Edmond Strainchamps and Maria Rika Maniates in collaboration with Christopher Hatch. New York: W. W. Norton, 1984.

LaurencieFs   Mélanges de musicologie offerts à M. Lionel de la Laurencie. PSfm, ser. 2, no. 3-4. Paris: E. Droz, 1933.

LeipzigFs   Festschrift zur 75-jährigen Bestehen des Königl. Konservatoriums der Musik zu Leipzig am 2. April 1918. Leipzig: Kistner & Siegel, 1918.

LenaertsFs   Renaissance-muziek 1400-1600: Donum natalicium René Bernard Lenaerts, edited by Jozef Robijns, Willem Elders, Roelof Lagas, and Guido Persoons. Mlav, no. 1. Leuven: Katholieke Universiteit, Seminarie voor Muziekwetenschap, 1969.

MassonFs   Mélanges d'histoire et d'esthétique musicale offerts à Paul-Marie Masson. Bém. Paris: Richard-Masse-Éditeur, 1955.

MendelFs   Studies in Renaissance and Baroque Music in Honor of Arthur Mendel, edited by Robert L. Marshall. Kassel: Bärenreiter; Hackensack, N.J.: Boonin, 1974.

MerrittFs   Words and Music, the Scholar's View: A Medley of Problems and Solutions Compiled in Honor of A. Tillman Merritt by Sundry Hands, edited by Laurence Berman. Cambridge, Mass.: Department of Music, Harvard University, 1972.

MeyerFs   Festschrift für Ernst Hermann Meyer zum sechzigsten Geburtstag, edited by Georg Knepler. Leipzig: Deutscher Verlag für Musik, 1973.

MoyleFs   Problems & Solutions: Occasional Essays in Musicology Presented to Alice M. Moyle, edited by Jamie C. Kassler and Jill Stubington. Sydney: Hale & Iremonger, 1984.

Müller-BlattauFs   Zum 70. Geburtstag von Joseph Müller-Blattau, edited by Christoph-Hellmut Mahling. Kassel: Bärenreiter, 1966.

MünnichFs   Festschrift Richard Münnich zum achtzigsten Geburtstage: Beiträge zur Musikästhetic, Musikgeschichte, Musikerziehung. Leipzig: Deutscher Verlag für Musik, 1957.

NewlinFs   Dika Newlin, Friend and Mentor: A Birthday Anthology, edited by Theodore Albrecht. Denton, Texas: Jagdhorn Verlag, 1973.

NomuraFs   [Nomura Festschrift: Musical Sound and Philosophic Thoughts], edited by the Committee for the Celebration of the 60th Birthday of Professor Yosio Nomura. Tokyo: Ongaku no tomo sha, 1969.

OrelFs   Festschrift Alfred Orel zum 70. Geburtstag, edited by Hellmut Federhofer. Vienna: Rudolf M. Rohrer, 1960.

PalmFs   Logos musicae: Festschrift für Albert Palm, edited by Rüdiger Görner. Wiesbaden: Franz Steiner, 1982.

ReeseFs   Aspects of Medieval and Renaissance Music: A Birthday Offering to Gustave Reese, edited by Jan LaRue. New York: W. W. Norton, 1966; reprint edition, New York: Pendragon Press, 1978.

RiemannFs   *Riemann-Festschrift: Gesammelte Studien.* Leipzig: Hesse, 1909; reprint edition, Tützing: Schneider, 1965. Bibliog.

RongaFs   *Scritti in onore di Luigi Ronga.* Milan and Naples: Ricciardi, 1973.

RuhnkeFs   *Festschrift Martin Ruhnke zum 65. Geburtstag.* Neuhausen and Stuttgart: Hänssler Verlag, 1986.

SchenkFs   *De ratione in musice: Festschrift Erich Schenk zum 6. Mai 1972*, edited by Theophil Antonicek, Rudolf Flotzinger, and Othmar Wessely. Kassel: Bärenreiter, 1975.

ScheringFs   *Festschrift Arnold Schering zum sechzigsten Geburtstag*, edited by Helmuth Osthoff, Walter Serauky, and Adam Adrio. Berlin: A Glas, 1937.

ScheurleerFs   *In Gedenkboek aangeboden aan Dr. D. F. Scheurleer op zijn 70sten verjaardag*. . . Amsterdam: Martinus Nijhoff, 1925.

Schmidt-GörgFs   *Festschrift Joseph Schmidt-Görg zum 60. Geburtstag*, edited by Dagmar Weise. Bonn: Beethovenhaus, 1957.

Schmidt-GörgFsII   *Colloquium amicorum: Joseph Schmidt-Görg zum 70. Geburtstag*, edited by Siegfried Kross and Hans Schmidt. Bonn: Beethovenhaus, 1967.

SchneiderFs   *Festschrift Max Schneider zum 60. Geburtstag*, edited by Hans Joachim Zingel. Halle: Ernst Schneider, 1935.

SchneiderFsII   *Festschrift Max Schneider zum achtzigsten Geburtstage*, edited by Walther Vetter. Leipzig: Deutscher Verlag für Musik, 1955.

SieversFs   *Heinrich Sievers zum 70. Geburtstag*, edited by Richard Jakoby and Günter Katzenberger. Tützing: Hans Schneider, 1978.

SpohrFs   *Louis Spohr: Festschrift 1959*, edited by the Sektion Musikwissenschaft des Verbandes deutscher Komponisten und Musikwissenschaftler, Arbeits-kreis Thüringen in conjunction with the Rat des Bezirkes Erfurt, Abteilung Kultur. Weimar: 1959.

StäbleinFs   *Festschrift Bruno Stäblein zum 70. Geburtstag*, edited by Martin Ruhnke. Kassel: Bärenreiter, 1967.

SteinFs   *Festschrift Fritz Stein zum 60. Geburtstag*, edited by Hans Hoffmann and Franz Rühlmann. Brunswick: Henry Litolff, 1939.

SteirischerFs   *40 [Vierzig] Jahre Steirischer Tonkünstlerbund: Festschrift.* MSS. Graz: Akademische Druck- und Verlagsanstalt, 1967.

ValentinFs   *Festschrift Erich Valentin zum 70. Geburtstag*, edited by Günter Weiß. Regensburg: Boße, 1976.

VetterFs   *Musa-Mens-Musici: Im Gedenken an Walther Vetter*, edited by the Institut für Musikwissenschaft, Humboldt-Universität (Berlin). Leipzig: VEB Deutscher Verlag für Musik, 1969.

VötterleFs   *Musik und Verlag: Karl Vötterle zum 65. Geburtstag am 12. April 1968*, edited by Richard Baum and Wolfgang Rehm. Kassel: Bärenreiter, 1968.

VolkFs   *Festschrift für Arno Volk*, edited by Carl Dahlhaus and Hans Oesch. Cologne: Gerig, 1974.

WesselyFs   *Festschrift Othmar Wessely zum 60. Geburtstag*, edited by Manfred Angerer, Eva Diettrich, et al. Tützing: Hans Schneider, 1982.

WioraFs   *Festschrift für Walter Wiora zum 30. Dezember 1966*, edited by Ludwig Finscher and Christoph-Hellmut Mahling. Kassel: Bärenreiter, 1967.

WolfFs   *Musikwissenschaftliche Beiträge: Festschrift für Johannes Wolf zu seinem sechzigsten Geburtstag*, edited by Walter Lott, Helmuth Osthoff, and Werner Wolffheim. Berlin: Martin Breslauer, 1929.

WürzburgFs   *Aus der Vergangenheit der Universität Würzburg: Festschrift zum 350-jährigen Bestehen der Universität*, edited by Max Buchner. Berlin: J. Springer, 1932.

DICTIONARY OF THEORISTS

JAKOB ADLUNG

[1699–1762]

In extraordinary detail, Jakob Adlung documented his masterful understanding of all facets of organ construction and design—from the arrangement of pipes within the case to how they should be tuned, from a description of the characteristics of individual registers to the dispositions of over eighty significant instruments. Left in manuscript upon his death, *Musica mechanica organoedi* was published in two handsome volumes in 1768.

With equal ardor, Adlung undertook to assemble comprehensive listings of treatises relating to various historical and practical musical topics for his *Anleitung zu der musikalischen Gelahrtheit* (1758). The historical component is focused particularly upon the organ, though Adlung's general survey of music history, based in part on works by PRINTZ and MATTHESON, is extensive. Within the practical component, the discussion of keyboard playing is divided into four aspects: performance of figured bass, the art of chorale-playing, improvisation, and tablature. Those readers seeking detailed information on these practices and on the arts of singing and composition might be disappointed, however, for Adlung devoted himself more to discussing the problems and issues of the various treatises which he listed than to the actual dissemination of detailed practical information. In fact, the *Anleitung* was published with very few plates of music examples, in sharp contrast to the beautifully illustrated organ treatise.

"Anweisung zur Fantasie und zu den Fuge"

Ms., [ca. 1723-27]. [Lost.]

"Anweisung zur italienischen Tablatur"

Ms., [ca. 1723-27]. [Lost.]

"Vollständige Anweisung zum Generalbaße"

Ms., [ca. 1723-27]. [Lost.]

Musica mechanica organoedi; Das ist, Gründlicher Unterricht von der Struktur, Gebrauch und Erhaltung, etc. der Orgeln, Clavicymbel, Clavichordien und anderer Instrumente . . . [*Rism* B/VI/1, p. 67.]

First draft completed ca. 1726. Edited by Johann Lorenz Albrecht [and Johann Friedrich AGRICOLA].

Berlin: Friedrich Wilhelm Birnstiel, 1768. 2 vols. [LCPS: A-007. HoM: 20. SMLMS.]

S ● Mahrenholz, Christhard, ed. Facsimile edition. Kassel: Bärenreiter, 1931; reprint edition (IGMDm, ser. 1, no. 18), 1961.

T ● Ellison, Ross Wesley, trans. "Baroque Organ Registration: Chapter Eight of Jacob Adlung's *Musica mechanica organoedi* 1768." *Music* 8/1 (1974):25-28, 50-51.

T ● Faulkner, Quentin. "An Annotated Translation of Jacob Adlung's *Musica mechanica organoedi*." Ph.D. dissertation, The University of Nebraska, forthcoming.

Anleitung zu der musikalischen Gelahrtheit: Theils vor alle Gelehrte, so das Band aller Wissenschaften einsehen; Theils vor die Liebhaber der edlen Tonkunst überhaupt; Theils und sonderlich vor die, so das Clavier vorzüglich lieben; Theils vor die Orgel- und Instrumentmacher [*Rism* B/VI/1, p. 67.]

Erfurt: J. D. Jungnicol, 1758. [LCPS: A-006a. HoM: 19. SMLMS.]

Expanded edition, edited by Johann Adam Hiller:

Dresden and Leipzig: Breitkopf, 1783. [LCPS: A-006b. SMLMS.]

S ● Moser, Hans Joachim, ed. Facsimile of the 1758 edition. IGMDm, ser. 1, no. 4. Kassel: Bärenreiter, 1953.

Reviews in *JAMS* 9/1 (1956):40-46 (A. Tillman Merritt), *MK* 24 (1954):219 (Walter Blankenburg), *ML* 37/1 (1956):87-88 (Eric Blom), and *NZfM* 115/5 (1954):294-95 (Erich Valentin).

S ● Aeschbacher, Gerhard. "Zwei aktuelle Probleme in der Sicht Jakob Adlungs, aus dessen Anleitung zur musikalischen Gelahrtheit, 1758." *MGot* 15/1 (1961):3-8.

Musikalisches Siebengestirn; Das ist, Sieben zu der edlen Tonkunst gehörige Fragen . . . [*Rism* B/VI/1, pp. 67-68.]

Edited by Johann Lorenz Albrecht.

Berlin: Friedrich Wilhelm Birnstiel, 1768. [LCPS: A-008.]

LITERATURE:

Valentin, Erich. "Adlung, Jakob." In *MGG* (1949-68).

Buelow, George J. "Adlung, Jakob." In *NGrove* (1980).

See also FÉTIS: (1833-44); HERBST: Allerup (1931); MARPURG: (1759-63):Vol. 2 (1761-63):451-55; WALTHER: (1732); LITERATURE SUPPLEMENT: **Arnold (1931/ . . . /1965)**; **Barbour (1951/ . . ./1972)**; Becker (1836-39/1964); Beiche ["Dux"] (1972-); **Benary (1956/1961)**; Cahn ["Repurcussio"] (1972-); **Coover (1980)**; David and Mendel (1945/ 1966); Dolmetsch (1915/ . . .); Dreyfus (1987); Duckles (1970); Eggebrecht (1955); Eitner (1900-1904/1959-60); Ferand [*Improvisation*] (1956/1961); Flindell (1983-84); Forkel (1792/1962); Gerber (1790-92/1977); Green (1969); Hiller (1768-

69), (1784); Houle (1960), (1987); Jackisch (1966); Jackson (1988); Kelletat ["Tonordnung"] (1960); Kümmerling (1977); **Lester (1989)**; Mendel (1948), (1955), (1978); Müller-Blattau (1923/ . . . /1963); Neumann, Frederick (1978); Ratner (1970), (1980); Reckow (1972-); ● ● ● Reese (1957/ 1970); Sachs (1972-); Schmalzriedt ["Subiectum"] (1972-); Schwartz (1908); Stowell (1985); Ulrich (1931/1932); Vanhulst (1971); Williams, P. (1970); **Zaminer (1985)**; Zimmermann (1976).

AGOSTINO AGAZZARI

[1578–ca. 1640]

The emergence of an alternative to the sixteenth-century church style brought into being the new continuo practice. Accompaniments were more transparent and thus could be improvised rather than laboriously notated in tablature or score, thereby saving paper, ink, and shelf space in the process. Agostino Agazzari commented on these changes in style and supplied, in his *Del sonare sopra'l basso* (1607), a useful set of instructions for the artistic creation of accompaniments using a bass to which numbers and accidentals were affixed. Two categories of instruments are discussed: those which serve as a foundation (such as the organ) and those which create delightful counterpoints or embellishment above (for which the lute is the favored choice). A high degree of skill was required to create the texture which Agazzari advocated, but its capacity to support rather than obscure the projection of the text and the economy of its notation made it indispensable in much of the music written during the remainder of the century and into the next.

Del sonare sopra'l basso con tutti li stromenti e dell'uso loro nel conserto [*Rism* B/VI/1, p. 68.]

>Siena: Domenico Falcini, 1607. [LCPS: A-009.]

>>Incorporated within reprints of his *Sacrarum cantionum . . . liber II . .* [*Rism* A/I/1, p. 19.]:

>Venice: Ricciardo Amadino, 1608.

>>Additional printings in 1609 and 1613.

S ● A related document, "Copia d'una lettera scritta dal Sig. Agostino Agazzari à un virtuoso sanese suo compatriotto, dalla quale si viene in cognitione dello stile, che tener se deue in concertare organo voci et stromenti," dated 25 April 1606, is found in BANCHIERI: (1591):(1609). Translated in MacClintock (1979).

ST ● See PRAETORIUS: (1614-20):Vol. 3 (1618):Part iii, Ch. 6.

S ● See Kinkeldey (1910/1968).

S ● Facsimile edition. Ctma. Milan: Bollettino bibliografico musicale, 1933.

T ● See ● ● ● **Strunk (1950)**:424-31.

S ● Facsimile edition. BmB, ser. 2, no. 37. Bologna: Forni, [1969].

La musica ecclesiastica dove si contiene la vera diffinitione della musica come scienza, non più veduta, e sua nobiltà [*Rism* B/VI/1, p. 69.]

>Siena: Bonetti, 1638.

LITERATURE:

Luciani, S. A. "Agostino Agazzari e l'orchestrazione del seicento." *Mog* 13/3 (1931):103-6.

Adrio, Adam. "Agazzari, Agostino." In *MGG* (1949-68). Bibliog.

Barblan, Guglielmo. "Contributo a una biografia critica di Agostino Agazzari." *Chm* 2 (1957):33-63. Bibliog.

>Review in *Rbdm* 12/1-4 (1958):106 (R. E. Wolf).

Rose, Gloria. "Agazzari and the Improvising Orchestra." *JAMS* 18/3 (1965):382-93.

Materassi, Marco. "Teoria e pratica del *suonare sopra'l basso* nel primo seicento." *Fronimo* 7/29 (1979):24-31. [*Rilm* 79-5579.]

Rose, Gloria. "Agazzari, Agostino." In *NGrove* (1980). Bibliog.

Dixon, Graham. "Agostino Agazzari (1578−after 1640): The Theoretical Writings." *RMARC* 20 (1986-87):39-52.

Reardon, Colleen Ann. "Agostino Agazzari and the Performance of Sacred Music in the Sienese Cathedral during the Baroque." Ph.D. dissertation, The University of California at Los Angeles, 1987. [*DA* 49/02A, pp. 165-66. UMI 88-03641.]

See also FÉTIS: (1833-44); HEINICHEN: (1728):Buelow (1961/ . . . /1986); RIEMANN: (1898); SAINT-LAMBERT: (1707):Burchill (1979); VIADANA: Haack (1964/1974); WALTHER: (1732); LITERATURE SUPPLEMENT: Abraham (1968/ 1969); Ambros (1878/ . . . /1909); **Arnold (1931/ . . . / 1965)**; Badura-Skoda et al. (1980); Becker (1836-39/1964); **Bent, I.** ["Analysis"] **(1980/1987):(1987)**; Borgir (1971/1987); Brown (1973); Brown and McKinnon (1980); Buelow (1972); Burney (1776-89/ . . . /1957); Donington (1963/ . . . /1974); Dupont (1933/ . . . /1986); Eggebrecht (1955); Eitner (1900-

1904/1959-60); Fellerer ["Zur Kontrapunktlehre"] (1972), ["Ausdruck"] (1982), (1983), (1984); Ferand (1937/1938), [*Improvisation*] (1956/1961); Forkel (1792/1962); Gaillard (1971); Gerber (1790-92/1977), (1812-14/1966); Gerboth et al. (1964); Goldschmidt (1901-4/1967); Hein (1954); Hill (1983); Horsley (1977); Hucke (1969); Jackson (1988); Kauko (1958); Kinkeldey (1910/1968); Meier (1974/1988); Neumann, Frederick (1978); Newman (1959/ . . . /1983); North (1987); Oberdoerffer (1949-68), (1967); **Palisca** [*Baroque*] (1968/1981), ["Theory"] **(1980)**; Reimer ["Concerto"] (1972-); Rothgeb (1968); Sachs (1972); Schmitt (1974-75); Schneider (1917/ . . . /1971); Schulenberg (1984); Strizich (1981); Subirá (1947/ . . . /1958); Tagliavini (1975/1983); Tenney (1988); Troeger (1987); Ulrich (1931/1932); Wienpahl (1953); Williams, P. (1970).

JOHANN FRIEDRICH AGRICOLA

[1720–1774]

The prominent singer and organist Johann Friedrich Agricola had the excellent idea of presenting TOSI's *Opinioni de' cantori antichi, e moderni* [1723] to the German public in a much amplified translation, published in 1757. Through it the bel canto style of singing was amply documented. Whereas TOSI had relied on words alone, Agricola supplied a number of music examples which aided him in clarifying the techniques of embellishment. His high regard for the late J. S. Bach (his former teacher) and his willingness to accept the task of translating a work that was then over thirty years old attest to a somewhat conservative stance, which is further documented by his rejection of Gluck's progressive influence and his criticism of MARPURG's support for French music. Another of his projects involved the editing of ADLUNG's monumental treatise on the organ, *Musica mechanica organoedi* (published posthumously in 1768). Agricola also completed a study on melody, "Beleuchtung von der Frage von dem Vorzuge der Melodie vor der Harmonie," which appeared in Cramer's *Magazin der Musik* posthumously in 1787.

"Beleuchtung von der Frage von dem Vorzuge der Melodie vor der Harmonie"

Dated 10 June 1771.

MagM 2/2 (1786-87):809-29.

See also ADLUNG: ([ca. 1726]/1768); TOSI: [1723].

LITERATURE:

Hiller, Johann Adam. *Anweisung zum musikalisch-richtigen Gesang.* [*Rism* B/VI/1, p. 413.] Leipzig: Johann Friedrich Junius, 1774 [LCPS: H-042a. HoM: 744.]; 2nd edition, Leipzig: Johann Gottlieb Feind, 1798. [LCPS: H-042b.]

Hiller, Johann Adam. *Anweisung zum musikalisch-zierlichen Gesang.* [*Rism* B/VI/1, p. 413.] Leipzig: Johann Friedrich Junius, 1780. [LCPS: H-043. HoM: 745.]

Wucherpfennig, Hermann. "Johann Friedrich Agricola." Ph.D. dissertation, The University of Berlin, 1922.

Abstract in *JDB 1921-22* (1926):298-302.

Blume, Friedrich. "Agricola, Joh. Friedrich." In *MGG* (1949-68). Bibliog.

Harriss, Ernest C. "J. F. Agricola's *Anleitung zur Singkunst*: A Rich Source by a Pupil of J. S. Bach." *Bach* 9/3 (1978):2-8.

Helm, Eugene. "Agricola, Johann Friedrich." In *NGrove* (1980). Bibliog.

See also FÉTIS: (1833-44); MARPURG: (1763); TOSI: Celletti (1967); Beicken (1980); LITERATURE SUPPLEMENT: Babitz (1952), (1967/1969); Babitz and Pont (1973); Bauman (1977); Becker (1836-39/1964); **Benary (1956/1961)**; Beyschlag (1907/ 1953); Bircher (1970); Blake (1988); Brown and McKinnon (1980); Bruck (1928); Burney (1776-89/ . . . /1957); **Dahlhaus et al. (1987)**; David and Mendel (1945/1966); Dean (1977); Donington (1963/ . . . /1974), (1980); Eitner (1900-1904/1959-60); Frobenius ["Vollstimmig"] (1972-); Fuller (1977); Geering (1949-68); Gerber (1790-92/1977), (1812-14/1966); Goldschmidt (1890/1892), (1907); Helm (1960); Hiller (1768-69); Hoffmann (1974); Jackson (1988); Jander (1980); Jeppesen (1930/ . . . /1974); Kelletat [*Temperatur*] (1960); Lawrence (1978); List (1976); Mahlert and Sunter (1972-); Mendel (1955); **Neumann** ["Appoggiatura"] (1982), [*Essays*] (1982), (1986); Newman (1985); Palisca ["Rezitativ"] (1972-); Rothschild (1961); Smiles (1978); Swain (1988); Wichmann (1966).

JOHANN GEORG AHLE

[bapt. 1651–1706]

By the end of the seventeenth century, triadic theory had established itself firmly in the minds of practitioners and permeated the writings of music's more articulate spokesmen, such as Johann Georg Ahle. The practice of careful voice-leading was especially revered, as theorists formulated rules for chord connection and concerned themselves with proper doublings, spacing, and the prohibition of various parallel movements. Furthermore, the supremacy of the major and minor modes was, though progressive, an acceptable notion.

Like many of his contemporaries, Ahle promoted a compositional practice which emphasized the rhetorical aspect of music. He was particularly perceptive concerning the setting of texts. His *Musikalisches Sommer-Gespräche* (1697), written as a conversation among Helianus (Ahle) and friends, documents his thoughts on these matters, while works designated by the other three seasons introduce issues such as consonance and dissonance, cadences, intervals, and the modes. Ahle's other writings, which include an extensive commentary on his father's singing manual and some novels, offer further examples of his keen and practical insight.

Unstruhtinne, oder musikalische Gartenlust, welcher beigefügt sind allerhand ergetz- und nützliche Anmerkungen [*Rism* B/VI/1, p. 73.]

> Mühlhausen: the author (Johann Christof Brückners Witwe), 1687.

[Deutsche] kurze doch deutliche Anleitung zu der lieblich- und löblichen Singkunst . . . [*Rism* B/VI/1, p. 73.]

> A revision and enlargement of his father Johann Rudolf Ahle's *Brevis et perspicua introductio in artem musicam . . .* (1673).

> Mühlhausen: Christian Pauli, 1690.
> Mühlhausen: Tobias David Brückner (Michael Keiser), 1704.

> A further expansion.

Musikalisches Frühlings-Gespräche, darinnen fürnehmlich vom grund- und kunstmässigen Komponiren gehandelt wird [*Rism* B/VI/1, p. 72.]

> Mühlhausen: Christian Pauli, 1695.

Musikalisches Sommer-Gespräche, darinnen ferner vom grund- und kunstmässigen Komponiren gehandelt wird [*Rism* B/VI/1, p. 73.]

> Mühlhausen: Christian Pauli, 1697.

Musikalisches Herbst-Gespräche, darinnen weiter vom grund- und kunstmässigen Komponiren gehandelt wird [*Rism* B/VI/1, p. 73.]

> Mühlhausen: Tobias David Brückner, 1699.

Musikalisches Winter-Gespräche, darinnen ferner vom grund- und kunstmässigen Komponiren gehandelt wird [*Rism* B/VI/1, p. 73.]

> Mühlhausen: Tobias David Brückner, 1701.

LITERATURE:

Adrio, Adam. "Ahle, . . . Johann Georg." In *MGG* (1949-68). Bibliog.

Schuhmacher, Gerhard. "Zum Werkverzeichnis von Johann Georg Ahle." *JLH 1971* 16 (1972):174-76. [*Rilm* 75-799.]

Sevier, Zay V. David. "The Theoretical Works and Music of Johann Georg Ahle (1651-1706)." Ph.D. dissertation, The University of North Carolina at Chapel Hill, 1974. [*Rilm* 74-2204. *DA* 35/08A, p. 5452. UMI 75-04869.]

● ● ● Sevier, Zay V. David. "Johann Georg Ahle on Voice Leading and Dissonance." *JMT* 20/1 (1976):93-104. [*Rilm* 76-561.]

Ichikawa, Schinichiro. "Johann Georg Ahle no sakkyoku riron ni okeru 'kotaba to oto no kankei'." *Og* 24/2 (1978):96-114. [*Rilm* 78-2638.]

Buelow, George J. "Ahle, Johann Georg." In *NGrove* (1980). Bibliog.

Krones, Hartmut. "Die Figurenlehre bei Bachs Amtsvorgänger Johann Georg Ahle." *ÖM* 40/2-3 (1985):89-99.

See also FÉTIS: (1833-44); LIPPIUS: Rivera (1974/1980); WALTHER: (1732); Gehrmann (1891); Schmitz (1952); LITERATURE SUPPLEMENT: Bartel (1982/1985); Becker (1836-39/1964); **Benary (1956/1961)**; Braun (1970); Buelow (1972); Dammann (1958/1967); Eitner (1900-1904/1959-60); Feldmann (1958); Flindell (1983-84); Forchert (1986); Forkel (1792/1962); Gerber (1812-14/1966); Krützfeldt (1961); Lange (1899-1900); Leuchtmann (1957/1959); Lindley (1982); Müller-Blattau (1923/ . . . /1963); Neumann, Frederick (1978); Rivera (1978), (1984); Ruhnke (1949-68); Schäfke (1934/1964); Schünemann (1928/1931); Subirá (1947/ . . . /1958); Walker (1987).

JOHANN GEORG ALBRECHTSBERGER

[1736–1809]

At the end of the eighteenth century, Viennese music theory was dominated by Johann Georg Albrechtsberger, whose popular counterpoint and figured-bass manuals were well received both among those who read German and, later, among the French and English, for whom translations were completed. Albrechtsberger continued the conservative tradition of FUX, aiding young composers (including Beethoven) in mastering the foundations of their art. His approach to counterpoint included a variety of species models which accommodated the major/minor system. His published instruction in figured bass shows no trace of inversion theory, though his pupil Ignaz Ritter von Seyfried either contaminated the theory or incorporated unpublished facets of Albrechtsberger's teaching method when he included such material in his influential compilation of his teacher's theoretical works.

Albrechtsberger's *Gründliche Anweisung zur Composition* (1790) offers a comprehensive course in contrapuntal writing, from elementary rudiments through the rigors of species-type contrapuntal exercises to the challenges of fugue, double counterpoint, and canon. His *Kurzgefaßte Methode den Generalbaß zu erlernen* [ca. 1791] and related Generalbaß-Schule develop, in a condensed form, the notions of consonance and dissonance, triads (Albrechtsberger's "perfect" chords), 6/3-position chords (which were considered "imperfect"), and principles of doubling. Despite his conservatism, Albrechtsberger filled an important pedagogical role in the training of musicians. As both teacher and author, he sought to assure a solid foundation for musical composition.

Gründliche Anweisung zur Composition mit deutlichen und ausführlichen Exempeln, zum Selbstunterrichte, erläutert; und mit einem Anhange: Von der Beschaffenheit und Anwendung aller jetzt üblichen musikalischen Instrumente [*Rism* B/VI/1, pp. 76-77.]

> Leipzig: Johann Gottlob Immanuel Brietkopf, 1790. [LCPS: A-021. HoM: 34. SMLMS. IDC.]

>> Review in *AdB* 113/2 (1793):433-43 [Johann Gottlieb PORTMANN]. Enlarged edition, as *Anweisung zur Composition* . . . :

> Leipzig: Breitkopf & Härtel, [ca. 1818].
> Leipzig: Breitkopf & Härtel, [1821].

T ● CHORON, Alexandre-Étienne, trans. and ed. *Méthode élémentaire de composition* . . . 2 vols. Paris: Mme. V[euve] Courcier, 1814.

T ● "Elements of Composition." In *EMG* 1 (1819):61-64, 81-84, 97-100, 113-19.

S ● Seyfried, Ignaz Ritter von, ed. *J. G. Albrechtsberger's sämmtliche Schriften über Generalbaß, Harmonie-Lehre, und Tonsetzkunst; zum Selbstunterrichte* . . . 3 vols. Vienna: Tobias Haslinger, [ca. 1825-26]; Anton Strauß, [ca. 1825-26]; revised edition, Vienna: Tobias Haslinger, 1837 [IDC.]; reprint of the 1837 edition (3 vols. in 1), Kassel: Bärenreiter; Leipzig: Zentralantiquariat der Deutschen Demokratischen Republik, 1975.

> The model for publications by CHORON, Merrick, Duggan, Novello, and Mann, below.

T ● CHORON, Alexandre-Étienne, trans. *Méthodes d'harmonie et de composition, à l'aide des quelles on peut apprendre soi-même à accompagner la basse chiffrée et à composer toute espèce de musique*. 2 vols. Paris: Bachelier et à l'Institution de musique religieuse, 1830; 2nd edition, 1834.

> Based on Seyfried's edition, above. Review in *Rm*(F) [Year 4], Vol. 9 [= Series 2, Vol. 3] (1830):60-63 (François-Joseph FÉTIS).

T ● Merrick, Arnold, trans. *Methods of Harmony, Figured Base and Composition, Adapted for Self-Instruction*. 2 vols. London: Robert Cocks, [ca. 1834]; [1844].

> Based on CHORON's French translation (1830) of Seyfried's edition, above.

T ● Duggan, Joseph F., trans. *Albrechtsberger's Elementary Work on the Science of Music, including Thorough Bass, Harmony, and Composition*. Edited by Edward Wolf. Philadelphia: James G. Osbourne, 1842.

> Based on Seyfried's edition, above.

T ● Novello, Sabilla, trans. *J. G. Albrechtsberger's Collected Writings on Thorough-Bass, Harmony, and Composition, for Self-Instruction* . . . NLDMN, Theoretical Series, no. 6. London: Novello, Ewer, 1855; Boston: Ditson, n.d.

> Based on CHORON's French translation (1830) of Seyfried's edition, above.

T ● See ● ● ● **Mann (1955/ . . . /1987)**.

> Based on CHORON's French translation (1830) of Seyfried's edition, above.

Kurzgefaßte Methode den Generalbaß zu erlernen [*Rism* B/VI/1, p. 77.]

> Vienna: [ca. 1791]. [Lost.]

>> Enlarged edition:

> Vienna and Mainz: Artaria, [ca. 1792]. [LCPS: A-022. SMLMS.]

>> *Rism* lists two other very rare editions published around the same time.

S ● *Generalbaß-Schule*. Leipzig: Kühnel, n.d.; Leipzig: Hoffmeister & Kühnel (Bureau de musique), [1804]; Leipzig: C. F. Peters, [1805]; other editions.

> Basically the same work as *Kurzgefaßte Methode*, but in a revised format. Review in *BmZb* 2/13 (1806):52 (M.).

T ● CHORON, Alexandre-Étienne, trans. *Méthode d'accompagnement selon les principes des écoles d'Allemagne*. Paris: Simon Gaveaux, [1815].

T ● Jousse, John, trans. and ed. *Principles of Accompaniment or Thorough Bass*. London: Chappell, [ca. 1815-22].

S ● Though significantly expanded from the brief instruction Albrechtsberger actually wrote, Volume 1 of (1790):Seyfried [ca. 1825-26], above, is derived loosely from Albrechtsberger's *Methode*.

Kurze Regeln des reinsten Satzes als Anhang zu dessen gründlicher Anweisung zur Composition

> Vienna: Kunst & Ind. Comptoir, [ca. 1804].
> Vienna: Steiner, n.d.
> Vienna: Tobias Haslinger, n.d.

Ausweichungen von C-dur und C-moll in die übrigen Tonarten

Inganni: Trugschlüße, per l'organo o pianoforte

Unterricht über den Gebrauch der verminderten und übermäßigen Intervallen

> A group of related publications derived from a manuscript, dated 1793, housed in the Berliner Stadtbibliothek. The Vienna publishers Haslinger and Cappi, the Leipzig publishers Peters and A. Kühnel, and the Bonn publisher N. Simrock offered one or more of these brief works during the early decades of the nineteenth century.

T ● *Modulations, from C Major & C Minor into All the Keys, for the Piano Forte*. Dublin: I. Willis, [ca. 1820].

T ● Jousse, John. *A Catechism of Music*. Edited by Theodore Baker. New York: Schirmer, 1891; reprinted with Burrowes's *Pianoforte Primer and Guide to Practice*, Boston: Oliver Ditson; New York; C. H. Ditson, 1897.

> Contains an Addendum, "Forty-Six Modulations from C-Major and C-Minor into All the Keys for the Pianoforte or Organ, by Albrechtsberger" (pp. 93-108), derived from (1790):Seyfried [ca. 1825-26], above.

Clavierschule für Anfänger

> Vienna: Artaria, n.d.

> Posthumously published (?). Based upon a manuscript, housed in the Gesellschaft der Musik-freunde in Vienna, titled "Anfangsgründe zur Klavierkunste."

"Generalbass- und Harmonielehre"

> Ms. [Vienna: Gesellschaft der Musikfreunde.]

LITERATURE:

Seyfried, Ignaz Ritter von. *Ludwig van Beethoven's Studien im Generalbaße, Contrapuncte und in der Compositions-Lehre*. Vienna: Tobias Haslinger, 1832; revised edition (edited by Henry Hugh Pierson), Leipzig: Schuberth, 1853; as *Études de Beethoven: Traité d'harmonie et de composition* (translated and edited by François-Joseph FÉTIS; 2 vols.), Paris: Schlesinger, 1833; as *Louis van Beethoven's Studies in Thorough-Bass, Counterpoint and the Art of Scientific Composition . . .* (translated by Henry Hugh Pierson), Leipzig: Schuberth, 1853; facsimile of the 1853 German edition, Hildesheim: Georg Olms, 1967.

> A record of Beethoven's studies under Albrechtsberger. See Nottebohm (1872/ . . . /1970), below.

Nottebohm, Gustav. "Generalbass und Compositionslehre betreffende Handschriften Beethoven's und J. R. v. Seyfried's Buch *Ludwig van Beethoven's Studien im Generalbass, Contrapuncte u.s.w.*" In *Beethoveniana: Aufsätze und Mittheilungen*, pp. 154-203. Leipzig and Winterthur: J. Rieter-Biedermann, 1872; 2nd edition, 1925; facsimile of the 1872 edition (with an Introduction by Paul Henry Lang), New York: Johnson Reprint Corporation, 1970.

Nottebohm, Gustav. *Beethovens Studien*. Vol. 1: *Beethovens Unterricht bei J. Haydn, Albrechtsberger und Salieri*. Leipzig and Winterthur: J. Rieter-Biedermann, 1873; facsimile edition, Niederwalluf (bei Wiesbaden): Martin Sändig, 1971.

Oppel, Reinhard. "Albrechtsberger als Bindeglied zwischen Bach und Beethoven." *NZfM* 78/20 (1911):316-19.

Übele, Gerhard. "Johann Georg Albrechtsberger, der Theoretiker." Ph.D. dissertation, The University of Vienna, 1932.

Tenschert, Roland. "Johann Georg Albrechtsberger." *AMuZ* 63/7 (1936):100-101.

Goos, Herta. "Albrechtsberger, Johann Georg." In *MGG* (1949-68). Bibliog.

Paul, Ernst. *Johann Georg Albrechtsberger: Ein Klosterneuburger Meister der Musik und seine Schule*. Klosterneuburg: Jasomirgott-Verlag, 1976.

> Review in *Me* 30/5 (1976-77):238 (Eberhard Würzl).

Clark, Michael. "The Quest for Johann Georg." *SBC* 9/1 (1980):24-25.

● ● ●Freeman, Robert N. "Albrechtsberger, Johann Georg." In *NGrove* (1980). Bibliog.

Senn, Walter. "Zu Mozarts angeblicher *Kurzgefassten Generalbass-Schule.*" *MISM* 29/3-4 (1981):28-33. [*Rilm* 81-4837.]

Paul, Bernhard. "Johann Georg Albrechtsberger, der Domkapellmeister aus Klosterneuburg." *SK* 33/3 (1986):108-13.

Zanden, Jos van der. "De jonge Beethoven in lichte klaviermuziek, contrapuntoefeningen en orgelfuga's." *Mens* 41/9 (1986):356-66.

Weinmann, Alexander. *Johann Georg Albrechtsberger.* Vienna: Musikverlag L. Krenn, 1987.

See also CHORON: (1810-11); FÉTIS: (1833-44); SCHENKER: (1906-35):Vol. II (1910-22); LITERATURE SUPPLEMENT: **Arnold (1931/ . . . / 1965)**; Babbitt (1987); Bauman (1977); Beach (1967); Becker (1836-39/1964); Beiche ["Inversio"] (1972-); **Benary (1956/1961)**; Bent ["Analysis"] (1980/1987):(1987); Bircher (1970); Bullivant (1980); Burke (1963); Cohen (1873-74); **Dahlhaus (1984); Dahlhaus and Sachs (1980)**; Dziebowska

(1976); Eitner (1900-1904/1959-60); Federhofer (1985); Fellerer (1927/ . . . /1972); Forkel (1792/ 1962); Gerber (1790-92/1977), (1812-14/1966); **Groth (1983)**; Hamilton [1854]; Haydon (1933/ 1970); Horsley [*Fugue: History*] (1966); Jacobi (1957-60/1971); Jeppesen (1922/ . . . /1970), (1930/ . . . /1974), (1935); **Kassler** (1971), **(1979)**; Kirkendale (1979); Kramer (1975), (1987-88); Lawrence (1978); Lindley (1982); **Mann (1955/ . . . /1987)**, (1970/1971), (1981), (1987); McQuere (1983); Müller-Blattau (1923/ . . . /1963); Munkachy (1968); Nelson (1984); Neumann (1986); Newman (1963/ . . . /1983), (1969/ . . . /1983); Oberdörffer (1949-68); Oldroyd (1948); Palisca (1949-68); Ratner (1980); **Ritzel (1967/1968)**; Rosenblum (1988); Rothschild (1961); Rowen (1979); Sachs (1972-); Sanders (1919); Schmalzriedt ["Episode"] (1972-); Sheldon (1982); Shellhous (1988); Subirá (1947/ . . . / 1958); Thomson (1960/1978); Tittel (1959), (1966); Todd (1983); **Wagner (1974); Wason (1981/1985)**; Williams, P. (1970); Wirth (1966); **Zaminer (1985)**.

JEAN LE ROND D'ALEMBERT

[1717–1783]

At a time when considerable attention was being devoted to the science of music, the brilliant young mathematician and philosopher Jean le Rond d'Alembert emerged as a leading voice in the Parisian intellectual scene. The formulation of partial differential equations by which the vibrating string could be analyzed was among his mathematical accomplishments.

D'Alembert was an influential member of the Académie royale des sciences, which sought to guide opinion by offering reports on submitted papers and inventions, including musical instruments. His report on what RAMEAU later published as *Démonstration du principe de l'harmonie* (1750) was particularly favorable. Soon thereafter he completed—in part as a demonstration of his own scientific methodology—a synopsis of RAMEAU's theories, under the title *Élémens de musique, théorique et pratique, suivant les principes de M. Rameau* (1752). MARPURG's German translation of this work, published in 1757, was instrumental in spreading RAMEAU's ideas eastward.

During this time d'Alembert's energies were also being directed towards the huge *Encyclopédie, ou dictionnaire raisonné des sciences, des arts et des métiers* (1751-65), which he edited with Denis Diderot and for which he created a number of articles on music. His celebrated "Discours préliminaire," which heads the first volume, calls particular attention to RAMEAU's achievements. The warmth between the men was soon to disappear, however, for

RAMEAU (who had declined an invitation to write articles on musical topics for the *Encyclopédie)* was displeased with the contributions of his adversary Jean-Jacques ROUSSEAU (whom the editors succeeded in luring and whose articles were, unfortunately, hastily composed). The battle began with RAMEAU's *Erreurs sur la musique dans l'Encyclopédie* (1755) and focused more directly upon d'Alembert in the *Lettre à M. d'Alembert, sur ses opinions en musique, insérées dans les articles "Fondamental" et "Gamme" de l'Encyclopédie* [1760]. D'Alembert responded in letters of 1761 and 1762, as well as in his revisions of the *Élémens* for a new edition in 1762.

"Recherches sur la courbe que forme une corde tendüe mise en vibration"

　　S ● In *AWBH, An 1747* 3 (1749):214-49.

"Rapport sur un mémoire où M. Rameau expose les fondemens de son système de musique théorique et pratique"

　　　　With Jean-Jacques Dortous de Mairan and François Nicole.

　　　　ErArs (December 10, 1749).

　　S ● Paris, Academie des sciences, Archives: Registres des procès-verbaux, vol. 68, pp. 495-506.

　　S ● See RAMEAU: (1750).

Articles in the *Encyclopédie, ou dictionnaire raisonné des sciences, des arts et des métiers*, edited by Denis Diderot and d'Alembert.

> Paris: Briasson, David, Le Breton, Durand, 1751-65. 17 vols.
>
> > D'Alembert wrote the "Discours préliminaire" and was fully or partially responsible for the following articles on music: Acoustique, Apotome, Basse fondamentale, Cadence, Castrati, Chaconne, Clé, Compositeur, Conjoint, Consonnance, Contre-sens, Dissonnance, Dominante, Double emploi, Echelle, Echo, Ecole, Élégiaque, Enharmonique, Fondamental, Gamme, Genre, Gigue, Gôut, Harmonique, Mode, Note sensible, Ondulation, Phonique, Septieme, Son, and Sousdominante. See RAMEAU: (1755); (1756); [*Réponse*] (1757); [*Code*] (1760); [*Lettre*] (1760) and Responses. See SERRE: (1763).

S ● The *Encyclopédie* was a source of material for many reference works published during the latter eighteenth century and beyond. A prominent example is the *Encyclopédie méthodique: Musique* [see MOMIGNY: (1791-1818)]. The "Discours préliminaire" was reprinted frequently.

T ● Schwab, Richard N., trans. and ed. *Preliminary Discourse to the Encyclopedia of Diderot.* With Walter E. Rex. LLA, no. 88. Indianapolis: Bobbs-Merrill, 1963.

S ● *Discours préliminaire de l'Encyclopédie.* Bm, no. 45. Paris: Gonthier, 1966.

T ● See Fubini (1969).

T ● See le Huray and Day (1981).

Élémens de musique, théorique et pratique, suivant les principes de M. Rameau [*Rism* B/VI/1, pp. 77-78.]

> Paris: David l'aîné, Le Breton, Durand, 1752. [LCPS: A-023a. HoM: 37.]
>
> > Reviews in *MdFr* (April 1752):141-46 and *JTr* (July 1752):1721-23. Response by RAMEAU in *MdFr* (May 1752):75-77 (reprinted in La Borde (1780/1978):Vol. 3, pp. 541-43). Review in *Jœc* (July 1752):89-121 (Jean-Laurent de BÉTHIZY). Further interaction between d'Alembert and BÉTHIZY in *Jœc* (November-December 1752):113-27, 85-102; (January, March, June 1753):120-42, 64-95, 97-105. For reprints of these documents, see RAMEAU: Collected Works (1967-72):Vol. 6.
>
> Paris: Charles-Antoine Jombert; Lyon: Jean-Marie Bruyset, 1759. [HoM: 38.]
>
> Expanded edition:
>
> Lyon: Jean-Marie Bruyset, 1762. [LCPS: A-023b. HoM: 39. SMLMS.]

> > Reviews in *Jenc* (March 1762):65-69 and *JTr* (February-March 1762):401-15, 597-611. Reprints of these reviews appear in RAMEAU: Collected Works (1967-72):Vol. 6.
>
> Lyon: Jean-Marie Bruyset, 1766. [LCPS: A-023c.]
> Lyon: Jean-Marie Bruyset, 1772. [LCPS: A-023d. HoM: 40.]
> Lyon: Jean-Marie Bruyset pére & fils, 1779. [LCPS: A-023e. HoM: 41. IDC.]

T ● MARPURG, Friedrich Wilhelm, trans. *Systematische Einleitung in die musicalische Setzkunst, nach den Lehrsätzen des Herrn Rameau.* [*Rism* B/VI/1, p. 78.] Leipzig: Johann Gottlob Immanuel Breitkopf, 1757 [LCPS: A-023f. HoM: 42. SMLMS.]; facsimile edition, Leipzig: Zentralantiquariat der DDR, 1980.

T ● Barattieri, Gian Francesco, trans. "Elementi di musica teorica, e pratica secondo i principii di Mᵘ Rameau." Ms., 1766. [New York: New York Public Library.]

T ● Blacklock, Thomas, trans. and ed. Partial translation of the 1762 edition. In *Encyclopaedia Britannica*, 2nd edition, 1784. S.v. "Music."

> See also 3rd edition, 1797. Reprinted in other British encyclopedias of the era.

T ● A Spanish translation. Ms., [19th century]. [New York: Columbia University Library.]

S ● Facsimile of the 1752 edition. MMMLF, ser. 2, no. 19. New York: Broude Brothers, [1966].

S ● See RAMEAU: Collected Works (1967-72):Vol. 6.

> Reprint of the "Discours préliminaire."

S ● Bardez, Jean-Michel, ed. Facsimile of the 1752 edition. Ressources, no. 77. Geneva: Slatkine, 1980.

S ● Facsimile of the 1779 edition. Int. Sainte-Maxime, France: Éditions d'aujourd'hui, 1984.

T ● Elsberry, Kristie Beverly. "*Élémens de musique, théorique et pratique, suivant les principes de M. Rameau* by Jean le Rond d'Alembert: An Annotated New Translation and a Comparison to Rameau's Theoretical Writings." Ph.D. dissertation, The Florida State University, 1984. [*DA* 45/05A, p. 1234. UMI 84-16700.]

"De la liberté de la musique"

S ● In his *Mélanges de littérature, d'histoire et de philosophie*, new edition, vol. 4, pp. 381-462. Amsterdam: Zacharie Chatelain et fils, 1759; numerous later printings.

> Review in *Jdm* [1/10] (October 1770):3-35.

S ● Frequent reprintings in collected editions of d'Alembert's writings.

"Réflexions sur la théorie de la musique"

Ms., [1777]. [Paris: Institut de France.]

S ● Henry, Charles, ed. *Œuvres et correspondances inédites de d'Alembert*. Paris: Didier, Perrin, 1887; facsimile edition, Geneva: Slatkine Reprint, 1967.

Additional manuscripts are listed in Rushton (1980), below.

LITERATURE:

M. D. * * * de Dijon. *Dissertations en forme de lettres sur différens sujets de littérature et des beaux-arts*. London and Paris: Burnet, 1788. [LCPS: R-089.]

> Contains "Lettre à M. d'Alembert, sur la second édition de ses *Élémens de musique*," pp. 43-61.

Müller, Robert. "D'Alemberts Aesthetik." Ph.D. dissertation, The University of Berlin, 1924 (1925).

> Abstract in *JDB Dekanatsjahr 1923-24* (1925):454-60.

Muller, Maurice. "Essai sur la philosophie de Jean d'Alembert." Ph.D. dissertation, The University of Paris, 1926; published edition, Paris: Payot, 1926.

Serauky, Walter. "Alembert, Jean Lerond d'." In *MGG* (1949-68). Bibliog.

Pappas, John. "Diderot, d'Alembert et l'*Encyclopédie*." *DS* 4 (1963):191-208. Bibliog.

Hankins, Thomas Leroy. "Jean d'Alembert: Scientist and Philosopher." Ph.D. dissertation, Cornell University, 1964; published edition (as *Jean d'Alembert: Science and the Enlightenment*), Oxford: Clarendon Press, 1970. [*DA* 25/08, pp. 4671-72.]

> Reviews in *AfGPh* 53/3 (1971):317-18 (Hans Wagner), *Aihs* 23/92-93 (1970):258-59 (J. Ravetz), *BJHS* 6/3 [23] (1972-73):327-29 (Roger Hahn), *Centaurus* 16/1 (1971):56-59 (C. Truesdell), *FrS* 26/4 (1972):458-60 (Ronald Grimsley), *History* 57/190 (1972):277-78 (Eric G. Forbes), *Isis* 62/2 [212] (1971):255-57 (Robert H. Silliman), *Janus* 57/2-3 (1970):228-31 (E. M. Bruins), *JMH* 44/1 (1972):109-12 (Keith M. Baker), *LJ* 95/19 (1970):3792 (Frank N. Jones), *Lychnos 1971-72* (1973):479-82 (Nils Fröström), *PhQ* 21/84 (1971):268-69 (Arthur Thomson), *Rh* 95/499 [246] (1971):219-22 (Daniel Roche), *Science* 171/3975 (1971):997 (J. Morton Briggs, Jr.), and *TLS* 69/3576 (1970):1000.

Briggs, J. Morton. "Alembert, Jean le Rond d'." In *DSB* (1970-80). Bibliog.

Rushton, Julian. "D'Alembert, Jean le Rond." In *NGrove* (1980). Bibliog.

Escal, Françoise. "Musique et science: D'Alembert contre Rameau." *IRASM* 14/2 (1983):167-90.

Escal, Françoise. "D'Alembert et la théorie harmonique de Rameau." *Dhs* 16 (1984):151-62.

Christensen, Thomas Street. "Science and Music Theory in the Enlightenment: D'Alembert's Critique of Rameau." Ph.D. dissertation, Yale University, 1985. [*DA* 46/11A, p. 3184. UMI 86-00976.]

Christensen, Thomas Street. "Music Theory as Scientific Propaganda: The Case of d'Alembert's *Élémens de musique*." *JHI* 50 (1989).

Isherwood, Robert M. "The Conciliatory Partisan of Musical Liberty: Jean Le Rond d'Alembert, 1717-1783." In Cowart [*French*] (1989):95-119. Bibliog.

Duchez, Marie-Élisabeth. "D'Alembert diffuseur de la théorie harmonique de Rameau: Deduction scientifique et simplification musicale." In a forthcoming report on the Communication au colloque d'Alembert organisé par le Centre International de Synthèse, June 15-18, 1983.

See also BÉTHIZY: Earhart (1985); CATEL: George (1982); CHORON: (1810-11); FÉTIS: (1831); (1833-44); MOMIGNY: (1791-1818):(1791); Görner (1982); RAMEAU: [*Lettre*] (1760); Collected Works (1967-72); Pischner (1961/ . . . /1967); Leipp (1965); Billeter (1973); ● ● ● Bernard (1980); Beaussant [ca. 1983]; Kintzler (1983); Robrieux (1985); Christensen ["Eighteenth-Century"] (1987); RIEMANN: (1898); ROUSSEAU, J.-J.: Heintze (1963); Strauss (1978); SERRE: (1763); LITERATURE SUPPLEMENT: Alekperova (1982); Archibald (1924); Asselin (1981); Atcherson (1960); Becker (1836-39/1964); Bell et al. (1980); Burney (1776-89/ . . . /1957); Cazden (1948), (1980); Chailley (1967); Chevaillier (1925/1931-32); Cohen (1977), (1981); Cohen and Miller (1979); Cohen (1984); **Coover (1980)**; Cotte (1951); **Dahlhaus** ["Relationes"] (1975), ["Harmony"] (1980), **(1984); Dahlhaus et al. (1987)**; Diderot (1748/ . . . /1875-77); Duckles (1970); Eitner (1900-1904/1959-60); Forkel (1792/1962); Fubini (1969), (1971/1983); Gerber (1790-92/1977), (1812-14/1966); **Groth (1983)**; Gut (1972-); Haase (1969); Handschin (1948); Hartmann (1923); Heinlein (1927/1928); Hiller (1768-69); Hosler (1978/1981); Hunt (1978); Jackson (1988); Jacobi (1957-60/1971); Jones (1934); Jorgenson (1957); Jullien (1873); **Kassler ● ● ● (1979)**, (1983-85); Kauko (1958); Kleinman (1971/1974); Krehbiel (1964); La Borde (1780/1978); le Huray (1978-79); Lindley (1982); Lottermoser (1949-68); Mitchell, W. J. (1963); Morche (1974); Newman (1963/ . . . /1983); Oliver (1949/1947); **Palisca** [Baroque] (1968/1981), ["Theory"] **(1980)**; Pole (1879/ . . . /1924); Révész (1946/ . . . /1954); Rex (1981); **Ritzel (1967/1968)**;

Rohwer (1949-68); Rowen (1979); Scher (1975); Schmalzriedt ["Reprise"] (1972-); **Seidel and Cooper (1986)**; Serauky (1929); Sheldon (1981); **Shirlaw (1917/ . . . /1970)**; Strizich (1981); Subirá (1947/ . . . /1958); Taddie (1984); Telesco (forth-coming); Thürlings (1877); Truesdell (1960); Ulrich (1931/1932); Vogel (1955/1954), (1962); Warrack (1945); **Wason (1981/1985)**; Winckel (1949-68); Yates (1947); Zimmermann (1976).

JOHANN HEINRICH ALSTED

[1588–1638]

The state of music theory in early seventeenth-century Germany is reflected in Johann Heinrich Alsted's various encyclopedic works. As a component of both mathematics and physics, music holds a prominent position in Alsted's systemization. Not surprisingly, ZARLINO and LIPPIUS are principal sources for Alsted's perspective, though he borrowed extensively from a large number of disparate authors. Birchensha's belated English translation of one of Alsted's more mature formulations on music provided British readers with easier access to LIPPIUS's conceptions and to various seven-syllable alternatives to the archaic six-syllable system of solmization.

Scientiarum omnium encyclopaediae . . . [*Rism* B/VI/1, p. 82.]

> Herborn: 1610.
> Herborn: 1630.
> Lyon: Jean-Antoine Huguetan fils & Marc-Antoine Ravaud, 1649.

Elementale mathematicum . . . VI. Musica . . . [*Rism* B/VI/1, pp. 81-82.]

> Frankfurt am Main: Johann Bringer (Anton Humm), 1611.

Methodus admirandorum mathematicorum: Complectens novem libros Matheseos universae, in quorum . . . 8. Musica . . [*Rism* B/VI/1, p. 82.]

> Herborn: 1613.
>> Later editions in 1623 and 1641.

Cursus philosophici encyclopaedia libris XXVII complectens universae philosophiae methodum, serie praeceptorum, regularum et commentariorum perpetua . . . [*Rism* B/VI/1, p. 81.]

> Herborn: Christoph Corvin, 1620.

Triumphus bibliorum sacrorum seu encyclopaedia biblica . . , [*Rism* B/VI/1, p. 83.]

> Frankfurt am Main: Bartholomäus Schmidt, 1625.
> Frankfurt am Main: J. D. Zunner, 1642.

Compendium philosophicum, exhibens methodum, definitiones, canones, distinctiones et quaestiones, per universam philosophiam [*Rism* B/VI/1, p. 82.]

> Herborn: Georg Corvin & Johann-Georg Muderspach, 1626.

Encyclopaedia septem tomis distincta . . . [*Rism* B/VI/1, p. 82.]

> Herborn: 1630.
>> The musical portions are found also in (1610):(1649), above.

T ● Birchensha, John, trans. *Templum musicum; or, The Musical Synopsis of the Learned and Famous Johannes Henricus Alstedius, Being a Compendium of the Rudiments both of the Mathematical and Practical Part of Musick . . .* [*Rism* B/VI/1, pp. 82-83]. London: Peter Dring (Will. Godbid), 1664 [LCPS: A-027.]; facsimile edition (MMMLF, ser. 2, no. 35), New York: Broude Brothers, [1968].

T ● Cole, Percival Richard. A Neglected Educator, Johann Heinrich Alsted: Translations, etc., from the Latin of His Encyclopaedia. Sydney: William Applegate Gullick, 1910.

S ● See Schultz (1967), below.

LITERATURE:

Atteln, Horst. "Alsted, Johann Heinrich." In *MGG* (1949-68):Supplement (1973-79). Bibliog.

Schultz, Ingo. "Studien zur Musikanschauung und Musiklehre Johann Heinrich Alsteds (1588–1638)." Ph.D. dissertation, The University of Marburg, 1967. [*Rilm* 69-952.]

Cosma, Viorel. "Alba Iulia: Un centru de înfloritoare cultură muzicală renascentistă." *Muzica* 26/1 (1976):11-24. [*Rilm* 76-9270.]

Schultz, Ingo. "Alsted, Johann Heinrich." In *NGrove* (1980).

See also FÉTIS: (1833-44); HERBST: (1643); LIPPIUS: Rivera (1974/1980); Howard (1985); WALTHER: (1732); LITERATURE SUPPLEMENT: Becker (1836-39/1964); Burton (1956); Chenette (1967); Eitner (1900-1904/1959-60); Frobenius ["Dauer"] (1972-), ["Polyphon"] (1972-); Gerber (1790-92/1977), (1812-14/1966); Hein (1954); Lange (1899-1900); Niemöller (1970); Rivera (1978), (1984); Sachs (1972-); Schäfke (1934/1964); Taddie (1984); Walker (1987); Wienpahl (1953), (1955).

GIOVANNI MARIA ARTUSI

[ca. 1540–1613]

The theoretical tradition established by ZARLINO was carried into the seventeenth century by Giovanni Maria Artusi, whose battles with MONTEVERDI have not enhanced his posthumous reputation. Nevertheless Artusi moderated ZARLINO's rigid rules concerning dissonance treatment and advocated an expanded role for equal temperament in instrumental music. He was not uncomprehending of the motivations of the progressives; he simply took issue with them.

Like GALILEI with his "Compendio" [ca. 1570-72], Artusi, also a student of ZARLINO, formulated a synopsis of portions of his former teacher's *Le istitutioni harmoniche* (1558). In *L'arte del contraponto* (1586) ZARLINO's rules on counterpoint are arranged in a tabular scheme. Perhaps provoked by rumor of GALILEI's work in progress on dissonance, Artusi continued his study of counterpoint with his own treatise devoted to dissonance, published in 1589. His explanation of the suspension is particularly astute, for he clearly distinguished the roles of the pitches involved.

In *L'Artusi* (1600) both BOTTRIGARI and MONTEVERDI are taken to task, the former for his views on tuning for ensemble performances as presented in his *Il desiderio overo de' concerti di varii strumenti musicali* (1594), the latter for his outlandish compositions, excerpts from which were included and discussed. Artusi spoke through the interlocutor Vario and put what he took to be MONTEVERDI's pleas into the mouth of Luca. The match was swayed, however, for Artusi published MONTEVERDI's music *without* text. Further volleys were hurled on both fronts. In Artusi's *Seconda parte dell'Artusi* (1603), a mysterious fourth party who called himself l'Ottuso Accademico became involved as a MONTEVERDI supporter. MONTEVERDI responded with his famous Preface (1605), which was followed by two further pieces by Artusi (1606 and 1608) and the defense by Giulio Cesare MONTEVERDI (1607).

L'arte del contraponto ridotta in tavole . . . [*Rism* B/VI/1, p. 99.]

> Based on ZARLINO's *Le istitutioni harmoniche* (1558), Part 3.

> Venice: Giacomo Vincenti & Ricciardo Amadino, 1586. [LCPS: A-055. HoM: 110. SMLMS.]

>> Revised and merged with the work of 1589, below, to form *L'arte del contraponto . . .* [*Rism* B/VI/1, pp. 99-100.]:

> Venice: Giacomo Vincenti, 1598. [LCPS: A-056.]

> T ● Trost, Johann Caspar, ed. and trans. German translation. Ms.[?], mid seventeenth century. [Lost.]

S ● Facsimile of the 1598 edition. Hildesheim: Georg Olms, 1969.

S ● Facsimile of the 1586 edition. Bologna: Forni.

"Lettera apologetica del Burla academico Burlesco al reverendo D. Vincentio Spada da Faenza"

> Ms., 14 January 1588. [Lost.]

> S ● Excerpts in BOTTRIGARI: (1604).

Seconda parte dell'arte del contraponto; Nella quale si tratta dell' utile et uso delle dissonanze [*Rism* B/VI/1, p. 99.]

> Venice: Giacomo Vincenti, 1589. [HoM: 111. SMLMS.]

>> Incorporated within (1586):(1598), above.

"Trattato apologetico in difesa dell'opera del . . . Zarlino: Giuditio musicale . . intorno alle differenze note frà il dottissimo Zarlino, et . . . Vincenzo Galilei . . ."

> Ms., 8 April 1590. [Lost.]

> S ● Excerpts in BOTTRIGARI: (1604).

L'Artusi overo delle imperfettioni della moderna musica ragionamenti dui . . . [*Rism* B/VI/1, p. 100.]

> Venice: Giacomo Vincenti, 1600. [LCPS: A-057a. HoM: 112. SMLMS.]

> S ● Vecchi, Giuseppe, ed. Facsimile edition. BmB, ser. 2, no. 36. Bologna: Forni, [1968].

>> The volume contains a facsimile reprint of this work as well as those of 1603 and 1608, below.

> T ● See **Strunk (1950)**:393-404.

> T ● See Rowen (1979).

Seconda parte dell'Artusi overo delle imperfettioni della moderna musica . . . [*Rism* B/VI/1, p. 100.]

>> Contains "Considerationi musicali," an attack on BOTTRIGARI's *Il Patricio* (1593), and a response to BOTTRIGARI's *Ant-Artusi* [ca. 1601-3].

> Venice: Giacomo Vincenti, 1603. [LCPS: A-057b. HoM: 113. SMLMS.]

> S ● See (1600):[1968], above.

Impresa del molto rev. Gioseffo Zarlino da Chiogga . . . dichiarata [*Rism* B/VI/1, p. 100.]

> Bologna: Gio. Battista Bellagamba, 1604.

Discorso musicale di Antonio Braccino da Todi

> A response to MONTEVERDI: (1605).

[ca. 1606]. [Lost.]

Discorso secondo musicale di Antonio Braccino da Todi per la dichiaratione della lettera posta ne' Scherzi musicali del sig. Claudio Monteverdi [*Rism* B/VI/1, p. 100.]

    Venice: Giacomo Vincenti, 1608. [LCPS: A-058.]

S ● Facsimile edition. Ctma. Milan: Bollettino bibliografico musicale, 1934.

S ● See (1600):[1968], above.

See also BOTTRIGARI: (1594):(1601).

LITERATURE:

Redlich, Hans F. "Artusi, Giovanni Maria." In *MGG* (1949-68). Bibliog.

Damerini, Adelmo. "Giovanni Maria Artusi e alcune sue opere teoriche." *Celebrazioni 1963* (1963):9-14.

Massera, Giuseppe. *Artusi e la seconda pratica monteverdiana.* Parma: 1966. [?]

Jackson, Roland. "The *Inganni* and the Keyboard Music of Trabaci." *JAMS* 21/2 (1968):204-8. [*Rilm* 68-349.]

● ● ● Palisca, Claude V. "Artusi, Giovanni Maria." In *NGrove* (1980). Bibliog.

See also BOTTRIGARI: (1594):(1924); [ca. 1601-3]; (1602); (1604); CACCINI: Anfuso and Gianuario (1970); FÉTIS: (1833-44); KEPLER: Dickreiter (1971/1973); MARTINI: (1774-75); MERSENNE: (1617-48); MOMIGNY: (1791-1818):(1818); MONTEVERDI: (1605); (1607); Vogel (1887); Schrade (1950/ . . . /1981); Arnold (1963/1975); Claro (1965); Anfuso and Gianuario [1971]; Fabbri (1985); OUSELEY: (1882); PRAETORIUS: (1614-20):Vol. 3 (1618); RIEMANN: (1898); VIADANA: Haack (1964/1974); WALTHER: (1732); LITERATURE SUPPLEMENT: Abraham (1968/ 1969); Ambros (1878/ . . . /1909); Apfel (1981); Arnold (1957); Barbieri (1983); Barbour (1932), (1948), (1949-68), (1951/ . . . /1972); Becker (1836-39/1964); Beiche ["Inversio"] (1972-); ● ● ● **Berger (1975/1980);** Boetticher (1954); Bryant (1981); Buelow (1972); Burney (1776-89/ . . . /1957); Chomiński (1962/1981); Cohen (1971); Dahlhaus ["Zur Theorie"] (1961), ["Untersuchungen"] (1966/ . . . /1988); **Dahlhaus et al. (1987); Dahlhaus and Sachs (1980);** Eitner (1900-1904/1959-60); Fellerer ["Zur Kontrapunktlehre"] (1972), ["Ausdruck"] (1982), (1983); Ferand (1937/1938), [Improvisation] (1956/1961); Forkel (1792/1962); Fubini (1971/ 1983); Gaspari (1876/ . . . /1969); Gerber (1790-92/1977), (1812-14/1966); Goldschmidt (1901-4/1967); Grout (1960/ . . . /1980); Haar (1977), (1986); Harrán (1986); Hawkins (1776/ . . . /1969); Hein (1954); Horsley (1963), ["Fugue and Mode"] (1966/1978), (1972); Hucke (1969); Hüschen (1986); Isgro (1968), (1979); Jackson (1988); Jeppesen (1922/ . . . /1970), (1930/ . . . /1974); Jones (1981); Katz (1985); Kauko (1958); Koenigsberger (1979); Kroyer (1901/ . . . /1970); La Fage (1864/1964); Lang (1941); Levitan (1938); **Lindley** ["Temperaments"] **(1980)**, (1982), (1984); Lowinsky (1946/1967); Mahlert and Sunter (1972-); **Maniates (1979)**; Massera (1969); Meier (1974/1988); **Palisca** (1949-68), (1953), ["Artusi-Monteverdi"] ● ● ● (1968/1985), [*Baroque*] (1968/1981), ["Theory"] (1980); Reese (1954/1959); Robbins (1938); Ruhnke (1949-68); **Seidel and Cooper (1986)**; Sirch (1981); Subirá (1947/ . . . /1958); Vecchi (1969); Vogel (1955/1954); **Walker** (1941-42/ . . . /1985), (1950/1985), **(1978)**; Walker (1987); Yamaguchi (1977); **Zaminer (1985)**.

BORIS VLADIMIROVICH ASAFIEV

[1884–1949]

One of the Soviet Union's most influential music scholars, Boris Vladimirovich Asafiev wrote profusely on many topics, among them articles and reviews for the general public under the name Igor Glebov. Yet his major contributions to theoretical discourse, *Muzykal'naia forma kak protsess* [Musical Form as a Process] (1930) and the later *Intonatsiia* [Intonation] (1947), are as dense and challenging as any work on music, even to those who are fluent in Russian. Asafiev held several prominent positions in the musical life of twentieth-century Russia: after nearly twenty years as a professor at the Leningrad Conservatory, he began a tenure at the Moscow Conservatory in 1943. In addition, he controlled the history of music section of the Russian Institute for the History of the Arts. He wrote seemingly as fluently as he spoke, resulting in a huge literary output which sometimes lacks the refinement and consistency that would have come from better edited work.

Muzykal'naia forma kak protsess is the product of a careful assessment of the relationship between music and its intended society, from a Marxist point of view. An any point in history, certain musical patterning, or intonations, are normative. In stable political times, these norms may crystallize; whereas unstable periods may be foreshadowed or echoed by shifts in the standard intonations. (For example,

Beethoven is a reflection of the French Revolution.) Composers persistently confront the conservative tastes of the public (who accept the existing intonations) while striving to evolve new intonations which may eventually become absorbed into the public consciousness. An intonation may seem viable and meaningful to some, while stale and outmoded to others.

Some forms, including variation or fugue, derive their impetus from processes such as repetition and imitation, which emphasize the identity of a given intonation. Other forms, particularly the sonata-allegro, stem from the notion of contrast. The confrontational character of this latter form is a reflection of the political and social milieu in which it was developed. The minute details of music, including cadences and dissonance treatment, contribute to its overall momentum or closure and are themselves a part of what constitutes the conventions of intonation for a given society. As he stated in *Intonatsiia*, an intonation may have validity for an era, a composer, or even a single work. Composers are ever evolving a musical language which expresses their interpretation of reality. As that reality is constantly changing, so also do the normative intonations of the language.

Kniga o Stravinskom [A Book on Stravinsky]

> Leningrad: Triton, 1929.

> S ● Facsimile edition. Leningrad: Muzyka, 1977. [*Rilm* 78-5233.]

> T ● French, Richard F., trans. *A Book about Stravinsky*. Introduction by Robert Craft. RMS, no. 5. Ann Arbor: UMI Research Press, 1982.

Muzykal'naia forma kak protsess [Musical Form as a Process]

and

Muzykal'naia forma kak protsess kn. 2-aia: Intonatsiia [Musical Form as a Process, Book 2: Intonation]

> Moscow: Muzsektor gosizdata, 1930. Vol 1. Moscow and Leningrad: Muzgig, 1947. Vol. 2.

> S ● See Selected Works (1952-57):Vol. 5 (1957):163-276, below.
>> The Selected Works edition includes Vol. 2, *Intonatsiia*, but omits Vol. 1.

> S ● Orlova, Elena Mikhailovna, ed. Moscow: Gosudarstvennoe muzykal'noe izdatel'stvo, 1963. Both vols.
>> Review in *Sh* 9/8 (1965):396-97 (Oskár Elschek).

> T ● Jičinský, B. *Hudební forma jako proces*. Klasikové hudební vědi kritiky, ser. 2, nos. 5-6. Prague: Státní hudební vydavatelství, 1965.
>> Review in *Sh* 9/8 (1965):396-97 (Oskár Elschek).

> S ● Leningrad: Muzyka, 1971. Both vols.

> T ● Karbusicky, Vladimir, trans. "*Die musikalische Form als Prozeß (Musikalnaja forma kak process)* III. Teil, Kap. 12: Suite und Symphonie." In *Texte zur Musiksoziologie*, edited by Tibor Kneif (Foreword by Carl Dahlhaus), pp. 177-81. Cologne: Arno Volk Verlag, 1975.

> T ● Kuhn, Ernst, trans. *Die musikalische Form als Prozeß*. Edited by Dieter Lehmann and Eberhard Lippold. Berlin: Neue Musik; Kassel: Bärenreiter, 1976.
>> Reviews in *Hv* 15/1 (1978):87-88 (Jaroslav Jiránek), *MG* 28/4 (1978):240-41 (Siegfried Bimberg), *MSch* 30/2-3 (1979):94-95 (Siegfried Bimberg), *Musica* 31/4 (1977):359-60 (Gerhard Wienke), and *NMZ* 28/5 (1979-80):30 (Sabine Schutte).

> S ● Bobrovsky, Viktor. *Funktsional'nye osnovy muzykal'noi formy*. [The Functional Bases of Musical Form.] Moscow: Muzyka, 1977. [*Rilm* 77-5726.]

> T ● Tull, James Robert. "B. V. Asaf'ev's *Musical Form as a Process*: Translation and Commentary." 3 vols. Ph.D. dissertation, The Ohio State University, 1977. Bibliog. [*Rilm* 77-1583. *DA* 38/02A, p. 542. UMI 77-17147.]

Evgenii Onegin, liricheskie stseny P. I. Chaikovskogo: Opyt intonatsionnogo analiza stilia i muzykal'noi dramaturgii [*Eugene Onegin,* Chaikovsky's Lyric Scenes: An Attempt at an Intonation Analysis of the Style and Musical Dramaturgy]

> Moscow and Leningrad: 1944.

> T ● Waldmann, Guido, trans. *Tschaikowskys "Eugen Onegin": Versuch einer Analyse des Stils und der musikalischen Dramaturgie*. Potsdam: Akademische Verlagsgesellschaft Athenaion, 1949.
>> Review in *Mf* 4/1 (1951):95-98 (Willi Kahl).

> S ● See Selected Works (1952-57):Vol. 2 (1954):73-141, below.

Charodeika, opera P. I. Chaikovskovo: Opyt raskrytiia intonatsionnogo soderzhaniia [Chaikovsky's Opera *The Sorceress*: An Attempt to Reveal Its Tonal Content]

> Moscow and Leningrad: Gosudarstvennoe muzykal'noe izdatel'stvo, 1947.

> S ● See Selected Works (1952-57):Vol. 2 (1954):142-68, below.

See also CATEL: ASAFIEV (1947); KURTH: (1917):(1931). See Selected Works (1952-57):Vol. 5 (1957), below, for an exhaustive bibliography of Asafiev's publications.

SELECTED WORKS EDITION:

Kabalevsky, D. B., et al. *B. V. Asafiev: Izbrannye trudy*. [B. V. Asafiev: Selected Works.] 5 vols. Moscow: Izd-vo akademii nauk SSSR, 1952-57. Bibliog.

> Volume 5 includes a comprehensive bibliography of Asafiev's writings, edited by T. P. Dmitrieva-Mei, on pages 293-347.

LITERATURE:

Rimsky-Korsakov, Georgii Mikhailovich. "Akusticheskoe obosnovanie teorii ladovogo ritma." [The Acoustical Basis of the Theory of Modal Rhythm.] *Muzy* 4 (1928):79-92.

Waldmann, Guido. "Glebow, Igor (Pseudonym) = Assafjew, Boris Wladimirowitsch." In *MGG* (1949-68). Bibliog.

Pamiati akademika Borisa Vladimirovicha Asafieva. [In Memory of Boris Vladimirovich Asafiev.] Moscow: 1951.

> Includes "Voprosy melodiki v trudakh B. V. Asafieva" [Questions of Melody in the Works of B. V. Asafiev], by V. Vasina-Grossman, pp. 79-86.

Orlova, Elena Mikhailovna. "Issledovanie B. V. Asafieva *Intonatsiia*." [Asafiev's Study *Intonation*.] In Selected Works (1952-57):Vol. 5 (1957):153-62, above.

Mazel, Lev A. "O muzykal'no-teoreticheskoi kontseptsii B. Asafieva." [Asafiev's Concepts of Music Theory.] *Smuz* /3 (1957):73-82.

Montagu-Nathan, M. "The Strange Case of Professor Asafiev." *ML* 38/4 (1957):335-40.

Fédorov, Vladimir. "B. V. Asafiev et la musicologie russe avant et après 1917." *Rdm* 41 (1958):102-106; see also *Bericht Köln 1958* (1959):99-100.

Kučera, Václav. "Vývoj a obsah Asafjevovy intonační teorie." [Development and Content of Asafiev's Intonation Theory.] *Hv* [early series] 1/4 (1961):7-21.

Skrebkov, Sergei. "Teoriia muzyki i sovremennyi slushatel'." [Theory of Music and the Contemporary Listener.] *Smuz* /1 (1961):56-63; as "Die Musiktheorie und der zeitgenössische Hörer: Bemerkungen zu den theoretischen Arbeiten Boris Asafjews" in *MG* 11/6 (1961):340-47.

Orlova, Elena Mikhailovna. *B. V. Asafiev: Put' issledovatelia i publitsista*. [B. V. Asafiev: The Path of a Researcher and Writer.] Leningrad: Muzyka, 1964.

> Reviews in *BzMw* 10/1-2 (1968):90-93 (Dieter Lehmann) and *Smuz* /12 (1965):135-38 (V. Vasina-Grossman).

Jiránek, Jaroslav. "Nekotorye osnovnye problemy marksistskogo muzykovedeniia v svete teorii intonatsii Asafeva." [Some Basic Problems of Marxist Musi-

cology in Light of Asafiev's Theory of Intonation.] In Yarustovsky (1965):53-94.

Lissa, Zofia. "Problema vremeni v muzykal'nom proizvedenii." [The Problem of Time in a Musical Work.] In Yarustovsky (1965):321-53.

Orlova, Elena Mikhailovna. "Raboty B. V. Asafiev nad teoriei intonatsii." [Works of B. V. Asafiev on the Theory of Intonation.] In Yarustovsky (1965):148-68.

Shakhnazarova, N. G. Intonastionnyi "Slovar'" i problema narodnosti muzyki. [An Intonational "Dictionary" and the Problem of the Folk Quality of Music.] Moscow: 1966.

Jiránek, Jaroslav. *Asafjevova teorie intonace: Její geneze a význam*. [Asafiev's Intonation Theory: Its Origins and Significance.] Prague: Academia, 1967. [*Rilm* 68-1299.]

> Includes a summary in English. Reviews in *Hroz* 22/5 (1969):144-46 (Zdeněk Sádecký), *Hv* 5/4 (1968):613-16 (Jaroslav Zich), *MG* 18/7 (1968):493-94 (Dieter Lehmann), and *Stm* 13/1-4 (1971):399-400 (J. Maróthy).

Jiránek, Jaroslav. "K problému hudebního času – Z raných teoretických prací B. V. Asafjeva." *Hroz* 20/19 (1967):582-85.

Jiránek, Jaroslav. "Příspěvek B. V. Asafjeva k srovnavací teorii umění." [The Contribution of B. V. Asafiev to the Comparative Theory of Art.] *Estetika* 4/4 (1967):305-14. [*Rilm* 68-1301.]

Riza, Bayram. "Die Theorie der Intonation und Gestalt in der Musik: Die Such nach einem Kriterium zur ideologischen Kontrolle der Musik." *Sowjetstudien* 23 (1967):53-69. [*Rilm* 68-4196.]

Střitecký, Jaroslav. "Intonation as a Problem." *SpFfBU*, 17/H3 (1968):99-116. [Rilm 68-4202.]

Farbshtein, Aleksandr. "K poniatiiu muzykal'nogo realizma." [Contribution to the Notion of Musical Realism.] *Smuz* /5 (1969):8-14. [*Rilm* 69-2925.]

Jiránek, Jaroslav. "Statistika jako pomocný nástroj intonační analýzy." [Statistics as an Auxiliary Means to Intonation Analysis.] *Hv* 8/2 (1971):165-82.

Jiránek, Jaroslav. "Assafjews Intonationslehre und ihre Perspektiven." *Dmdp* 1 (1972):13-45.

Pushchin, B. "Eto bylo geroicheskoe vremia . . . " [That Was a Heroic Time!] *Smuz* /5 (1972):50-57. [*Rilm* 72-2176.]

Zemtsovsky, Izalii. "Nuzhna li muzykoznaniiu semasiologiia?" [Does Musicology Need Semasiology?] *Smuz* /1 (1972):28-35. [*Rilm* 72-1206.]

Brown, Malcolm H. "The Soviet Russian Concepts of 'Intonazia' and 'Musical Imagery'." *MQ* 60/4 (1974):557-67. [*Rilm* 74-4095.]

Černý, Miroslav K. "Problém hudebního díla, jeho podstaty, identity a forem existence." [The Problem of the Musical Work: Its Essence, Its Identity, and Its Modes of Existence.] *Estetika* 11/3-4 (1974):164-82, 193-212. [*Rilm* 76-16454.]

Orlova, Elena Mikhailovna. "K istorii stanovleniia teorii muzykal'noi formy." [Contribution to the History of Musical Form.] *Smuz* /8 (1974):91-94. [*Rilm* 74-3929.]

Zemtsovsky, Izalii. "Znachenie teorii intonatsii Borisa Asaf'eva dlia razvitiia metodologii muzykal'noi fol'kloristiki." [The Significance of Boris Asafiev's Theory of Intonation for the Development of the Methodology of Musical Folklore.] In *Sotsialisticheskaia muzykal'naia kul'tura: Traditsii, Problemy, Perspektevy* [The Socialist Musical Culture: Traditions, Problems, Perspectives], edited by Jürgen Elsner and Givi Ordshonikidse. Moscow: Muzyka, 1974; as "Die Bedeutung der Intonationstheorie Boris Assafjews für die Entwicklung der Methodologie der musikalischen Folkloristik" (translated by Dieter Lehmann in *Sozialistische Musikkultur: Traditionen, Probleme, Perspektiven*, pp. 95-109), Berlin: Neue Musik; Moscow: Muzyka, 1977. [*Rilm* 77-1102.]

Jiránek, Jaroslav. "Sémantické moznosti a meze hudby." [Semantic Possibilities and the Limits of Music.] *Estetika* 12/2 (1975):77-105. [*Rilm* 76-16513.]

Ruchevskaia, Ekaterina. "Intonatsionnyi krizisi problema pereintonirovaniia." [The Crisis of Music Theory and the Problems of the Reinterpretation of Dissonance.] *Smuz* /5 (1975):129-34. [*Rilm* 75-1610.]

Černý, Miroslav K. "Historismus a Nejedlého koncepce muzikologie." [Historicism and Nejedly's Concept of Musicology.] *Hv* 14/1 (1977):52-71. [Rilm 77-244.]

Jiránek, Jaroslav. "Houslový koncert Albana Berga." [The Violin Concerto of Alban Berg.] *Hv* 14/1 (1977):3-50. [*Rilm* 77-1603.]

Jiránek, Jaroslav. "Zum gegenwärtigen Stand der semantischen Auffassung der Musik." *AfMw* 34/2 (1977):81-102. [*Rilm* 77-5967.]

Levin, Saul. "Iz istorii stanovleniia sovetskogo muzykoznaniia." [From the History of the Formation of Soviet Musicology.] *Vtem* 15 (1977):16-43.

Luk'ianov, V. [Boris Asafiev's Doctrine of Intonation and Its Elaboration in Soviet Music Literature.] In Farbshtein (1977).

Nazaikinsky, Evgenii, ed. *Muzykal'noe iskusstvo i nauka*. [Musical Art and Science.] Vol. 3. Moscow: Muzyka, 1978. [*Rilm* 78-4249.]

    Includes numerous articles based upon Asafiev's teaching, including "Terminologicheskaia sistema B. V. Asafieva (Na primere issledovaniia *Muzy-*

kal'naia forma kak protsess)" [B. V. Asafiev's System of Terminology: A Study of His *Musical Form as a Process*], by T. Cherednichenko, pp. 215-29.

Jiránek, Jaroslav. *Tajemství hudebního významu*. [The Secret of Musical Meaning.] Prague: Academia, 1979. [*Rilm* 79-1925.]

Shaknazarova, Nonna. "O trekh aspektakh realizma." [Three Aspects of Realism.] *Smuz* /5 (1979):8-15. [*Rilm* 79-3654.]

Lebedeva, Elena. "Kontrast kak muzykal'naia kategoriia (v aspekte muzyki pervoi poloviny XX veka)." [Contrast as a Musical Category: Aspects of Music from the First Half of the 20th Century.] M.A. thesis, Akademii Nauk (Kiev), 1980. [*Rilm* 81-6156.]

Lippold, Eberhard. "Zum Widerspiegelungsproblem in der Musik." *MSch* 31/2-3 (1980):81-88. [*Rilm* 80-2130.]

Medushevsky, Viacheslav. "Chelovek v zerkale intonatsionnoi formy." [Humanity in the Mirror of Intonation Patterns.] *Smuz* /9 (1980):39-48. [*Rilm* 80-5604.]

Norris, Geoffrey. "Asaf'yev, Boris Vladimirovich." In *NGrove* (1980). Bibliog.

Pavlov-Arbenin, A. *B. Asafiev o khorozom iskusstve*. [B. Asafiev on the Choral Art.] Leningrad: Muzyka, 1980.

    Review in *Smuz* /1 (1981):110-11 (M. Galushko).

Vendrova, T. "Muzyka v shkole i intonatsionnoe uchenie B. Asaf'eva." *Smuz* /6 (1980):87-89.

Lippold, Eberhard. "Intonation und Widerspiegelung—Neue Gedanken zu einem alten Problem." In *Musikästhetik in der Diskussion*, edited by Harry Goldschmidt and Georg Knepler, pp. 11-23. Leipzig: VEB Deutscher Verlag für Musik, 1981. [*Rilm* 82-3878.]

Orlova, Elena. "Muzykal'naia zhizn' i protsess intonirovaniia." [Musical Life and the Process of Intoning.] *Smuz* /6 (1981):11-17.

Erzakovich, B. " . . . v nei oshchushchaiut zhivoi otklik na deistvitel'nost . . . " *Smuz* /9 (1982):23-24.

Fujioka, Yumiko. "Russia ongaku no bigaku—Asafiev no intonation ron o megutte." M.A. thesis, Tokyo University of Fine Arts and Music, 1982. [*Rilm* 82-1494.]

Mazel, Lev Abramovich. "O nekotorykh storonakh kontseptsiia B. V. Asaf'eva." [About Several Sides of the Conception of B. V. Asafiev.] In his *Stat'i po teorii i analizu muzyki* [Articles on the Theory and Analysis of Music], pp. 277-306. Moscow: 1982.

    Derived, in part, from Mazel's 1957 article, above.

Zak, Vladimir. "Asafiev's Theory of Intonation and the Analysis of Popular Song." *PopM* 2 (1982):91-111. [*Rilm* 82-3550.]

Nazaikinsky, Evgenii. "Slukh Asafiev." [Asafiev's Ear for Music.] *Smuz* /7 (1983):81-89.

Rozin, Vadim. "Sravnitel'nii metodologicheskii analiz kontseptsii Kurta i Asaf'eva." [A Comparative Methodological Analysis of the Conceptual Systems of Kurth and Asafiev.] In *Voprosy metodologii teoreticheskogo muzykoznaniia* [Methodological Issues in Theoretical Musicology], edited by Jurii Bychkov. Moscow: Gosudarstvennyi Muzykal'no-Pedogogicheskii Inst. imeni Gnesinykh, 1983. [*Rilm* 83-1610.]

Aranovsky, M. "Intonatsiia, otnoshenie, protsess." [Intonation, Relation, Process.] *Smuz* /12 (1984):80-87.

Orlova, Elena Mikhailovna. *Intonatsionnaia teoriia Asafiev.* [The Intonational Theory of Asafiev.] Moscow: 1984.

Orlova, Elena Mikhailovna, and Kriukov, Andrei Nikolaevich. *Akademik Boris Vladimirovich Asafiev.* Leningrad: Sov. kompozitor, 1984.

Nazaikinsky, Evgenii Vladimirovich. "B. V. Asafiev i sovetskoe teoreticheskoe muzykoznanie." [B. V. Asafiev and Soviet Theoretical Musicology.] *Smuz* /3 (1985):88-94.

Iiranek, Ya. "Teoriia intonatsii Asafieva v svete sovremennogo marksistskogo podkhoda k semanticheskomu analizu muzyki." [Asafiev's Theory of Intonation in Light of the Contemporary Marxist Approach to the Semantic Analysis of Music.] In *Metodologicheskie problemy muzykoznaniia* [The Methodological Problems of Musicology], edited by D. V. Zhitomirsky, I. V. Nest'ev, Yu. I. Paisov, and N. G. Shakhnazarova. Moscow: Muzyka, 1987.

Mazel, Lev Abramovich. "Kontseptsiia Asafieva i tselostnyi analiz." [Asafiev's Concepts and Integrated Analysis.] *Smuz* /2 (1987):76-82.

See also LITERATURE SUPPLEMENT: Aranovsky (1980/1983); Barenboim (1970), (1974); Burlas (1974); Carpenter (1988); Černý (1976); Jiránek (1967); Kremlev ["Estetika"] (1967), ["O metodologii"] (1967); La Motte-Haber (1976); Mazel (1940); ● ● ●McQuere (1983); Ryzhkin (1967); Scher (1975); Schmalzriedt ["Durchführen"] (1972-); Sochor (1967); Sydow-Saak (1972-); Vitányi (1968-69); Yarustovsky (1974).

CARL PHILIPP EMANUEL BACH

[1714–1788]

J. S. Bach's most talented son, Carl Philipp Emanuel, spent nearly thirty years as principal keyboardist at the court of Frederick the Great, thus placing himself in the midst of a magnificent assemblage of composers and performers, including QUANTZ. Though the king's tastes were conservative, and though Bach was not treated particularly well, his various interactions in Berlin and the influence of his father's tutelage heightened his considerable natural talents, making him the ideal author for a treatise called *Versuch über die wahre Art das Clavier zu spielen* (1753-62).

A number of keyboardists of the current era have enjoyed tracing their lineage back to J. S. Bach, somehow supposing that each successive teacher handed down the true performance tradition intact. Seemingly less problematical would be the application of Carl Philipp Emanuel's precepts to the music of Johann Sebastian. Yet caution must be advised. The music of the son is remarkably different from that of the father. The once prevalent practice of mapping Carl Philipp Emanuel's stylistic proclivities upon the keyboard repertoire of two centuries does an injustice to earlier traditions of fingering and figured-bass realization. Yet as a guide to keyboard performance in the decades between mature Baroque and mature Classical styles, it is unparalleled.

Bach's division of materials into two books reflects a specific pedagogical directive: one must become proficient in notated keyboard music before proceeding to the arts of figured-bass realization, accompaniment, and improvisation. Thus in the first volume one finds extensive commentary on principles of fingering and embellishment, as well as numerous general hints and strategies for the development of artistry. The second book, which followed after nine years, transmits a more rigorous compositional perspective, for Bach felt that only through the careful study of the mechanics of voice leading could success in accompanying and in improvisation be achieved. His exposition on the principles of figured bass is thorough and masterful. His four decades of active practice in the best musical environments of Europe led to an enormous facility, which he was able to transmit clearly and with excellent organization. Notably absent is any suggestion that chords in positions other than 5/3 be regarded as derivatives generated from a fundamental pitch in one of their upper voices. Given the commotion MARPURG, who also resided in Berlin, was then making about RAMEAU's theories, this omission should be noted carefully, as it was by SCHENKER. The study of Bach's chapters on figured bass and improvisation (including some materials found in the 1797 edition but not included in Mitchell's translation [see Kramer (1985), below]) is regarded, along with the attainment of skill in species counterpoint, as an excellent preparation for the study of SCHENKER's theories.

Correspondence

S ● Suchalla, Ernst, ed. *Briefe von Carl Philipp Emanuel Bach an Johann Gottlob Immanuel Breitkopf und Johann Nikolaus Forkel.* MSzMw, no. 19. Tutzing: Hans Schneider, 1985. Bibliog.

> Review in *JMR* 7/2-3 (1987):294-301.

Versuch über die wahre Art das Clavier zu spielen [Rism B/VI/1, pp. 105-6.]

1) *Mit Exempeln und achtzehn Probe-Stücken in sechs Sonaten*
2) *Zweyter Theil, in welchem die Lehre von dem Accompagnement und der freyen Fantasie abgehandelt wird; nebst einer Kupfertafel*
   Berlin: the author (Christian Friedrich Henning), 1753. Vol. 1. [LCPS: B-001a. HoM: 135 (plus Examples: HoM: 129-30). IDC.]
   Berlin: the author (George Ludewig Winter), 1759. Vol. 1. [LCPS: B-001b. HoM: 136 (plus Examples: HoM: 129-30).]
   Berlin: the author (George Ludewig Winter), 1762. Vol. 2. [LCPS: B-001c. HoM: 137. IDC.]

> Review in *BsW* 10/1-2 (1763-64):50-53.

Leipzig: Schwickert, 1780. Both volumes. [LCPS: B-001d (Vol. 2 only). HoM: 138.]
Leipzig: Schwickert, 1787. Vol. 1. [LCPS: B-001e.]
Leipzig: Schwickert, 1797. Vol. 2.

S ● Schilling, Gustav, ed. Both volumes. Herzberg: Franz Mohr, 1852; Berlin: Stage, 1856.

S ● Niemann, Walter, ed. Abridged edition. Leipzig: Kahnt, 1906; later printings through 1965.

> Review in *MMR* 37/438-39 (1907):122-24, 145-48 (Ebenezer PROUT).

T ● ● ● ● Mitchell, William J., trans. and ed. *Essay on the True Art of Playing Keyboard Instruments.* New York: W. W. Norton; London: Cassell, 1949; London: 1951; London: Eulenburg Books, 1974. Bibliog.

> Reviews in *Econ* 253/6849 (1974): Survey: 19, *JAMS* 2/2 (1949):123-25 (Putnam Aldrich), *Met* 66/1 (1950):32 (Barry Ulanov), *MiE* 39/371 (1975):29 (Peter Craddock), *ML* 31/1 (1950):71-73 (Robert Donington), *MQ* 35/2 (1949):323-29 (Arthur Mendel), *MR* 11/1 (1950):57-58 (Gerald Abraham), *MR* 39/1 (1978):69 (A. F. Leighton Thomas), *MusT* 54/5 (1975):27 (Lionel Salter), and *Notes* 6/2 (1948-49):301-2 (Ralph Kirkpatrick; Willi Apel).

T● See **Strunk (1950)**:609-15.

S● Hoffmann-Erbrecht, Lothar, ed. Facsimile of the 1753 and 1762 editions. Leipzig: Breitkopf & Härtel, 1957; 2nd edition, 1969.

> Review in *Rdm* 41 (1958):131 (Eugène Borrel).

T● See Gerboth et al. (1964).

T● Tokawa, Seiichi, trans. *Tadashii piano soho*. 2 vols. Tokyo: Zenon gakufu, 1968-70.

T● Muller, Jean-Pierre, trans. "Passages théoriques essentiels tirés du traité de C. P. E. Bach *Versuch über die wahre Art das Clavier zu spielen*, Berlin 1753." *Rbdm* 23/1-4 (1969):3-121; 26-27 (1972-73):159-236. [*Rilm* 75-2572; 76-1500.]

T● Verona, Gabriella Gentili, trans. *L'interpretazione della musica barocca: Saggio di metodo della tastiera Carl Philipp Emanuel Bach*. Milan: Edizioni Curci, 1973.

> Review in *Nrmi* 8/3 (1974):462-66 (Francesco A. Répaci).

T● Collins, Dennis. *Essai sur la vraie manière de jouer des instruments à clavier*. Paris: J. C. Lattès, 1979. [*Rilm* 79-1578.]

> Review in *Harmonie* 152 (1979):128.

T● See MacClintock (1979).

"Einfall, einen doppelten Contrapunct in der Octave von sechs Tacten zu machen, ohne die Regeln davon zu wissen"

S● See MARPURG: (1754-78):Vol. 3/2 (1757-58): 167-81.

T● Helm, E. Eugene. "Six Random Measures of C. P. E. Bach." *JMT* 10/1 (1966):139-51.

Gedanken eines Liebhabers der Tonkunst über Herrn Nichelmanns Tractat von der Melodie [*Rism* B/VI/1, p. 498.]

> Under the pseudonym Caspar Dünkelfeind.

> Nordhausen: 1755.

See also Schmid (1949-68), below, and Helm (1980), below, for listings of manuscripts attributed to Bach.

LITERATURE:

Morsch, Anna. "Carl Philipp Emanuel Bach im Kreise seiner Berliner theoretischen Freunde." *MpB* 37/5-7 (1914):91-94, 115-17, 135-39.

Richard, August. "Philipp Emanuel Bach: Zu seinem 200. Geburtstag am 8. März 1914." *NMZ* 35/12 (1914):234-36.

Vrieslander, Otto. *Carl Philipp Emanuel Bach*. Munich: R. Piper, 1923.

Vrieslander, Otto. "Carl Philipp Emanuel Bach als Theoretiker." In *Von neuer Musik: Beiträge zur Erkenntnis der neuzeitlichen Tonkunst*, edited by H. Grues, E. Kruttge, and E. Thalheimer, pp. 222-79. Cologne: Marcan, 1925.

Clercx, Suzanne. "Carl Philipp Emanuel Bach." *Rm* 16/155 (1935):245-55.

Mitchell, William J. "C. P. E. Bach's *Essay*: An Introduction." *MQ* 33/4 (1947):460-80; reprinted in (1753-62): Mitchell (1949/. . ./1974), above.

Plamenac, Dragan. "New Light on the Last Years of Carl Philipp Emanuel Bach." *MQ* 35/4 (1949):565-87.

Schmid, Ernst Fritz. "Bach, Carl Philipp Emanuel." In *MGG* (1949-68). Bibliog.

Barford, Philip. *The Keyboard Music of C. P. E. Bach, Considered in Relation to His Musical Aesthetic and the Rise of the Sonata Principle*. London: Barrie & Rockliff, 1965; New York: October House, 1966.

> Reviews in *ABBW* 39/10 (1967):948, *Choice* 4/4 (1967-68):429, *Composer* 18 (1966):19 (Anthony Milner), *Consort* 23 (1966):189-91 (Richard D. C. Noble), *Mf* 22/1 (1969):120-22 (Lothar Hoffmann-Erbrecht), *MJ* 25/2 (1967):72 (Richard Tetley-Kardos), *ML* 47/1 (1966):66-67 (John Byrt), *MO* 89/1068 (1965-66):735 (B. R.), *MT* 107/1475 (1966):35-37 (Stanley Sadie), *Notes* 23/4 (1966-67):726-27 (David Fuller), *NZfM* 127/7-8 (1966):307-8 (Carl Dahlhaus), *Tempo* 77 (1966):26-27 (R. Donington), and *TLS* 64/3323 (1965):977.

Mitchell, William J. "Modulation in C. P. E. Bach's *Versuch*." In *GeiringerFs* (1970):333-42.

Cohen, Peter. "Theorie und Praxis der Clavierästhetik Carl Philipp Emanuel Bachs." Ph.D. dissertation, The University of Hamburg, 1973; published edition (HBzMw, no. 13), Hamburg: Verlag der Musikhandlung Wagner, 1974. Bibliog. [*Rilm* 75-886.]

> Review in *Mf* 31/2 (1978):221-24 (Siegfried Kross).

●●● Kirkpatrick, Ralph. "C. P. E. Bach's *Versuch* Reconsidered." *EM* 4/4 (1976):384-92.

Helm, Eugene. "Bach, Section III, Part 9: Carl Philipp Emanuel." In *NGrove* (1980). Bibliog.

Ottenberg, Hans-Günter. *Carl Philipp Emanuel Bach*. Leipzig: Reclam, 1982; Munich and Mainz: Piper/Schott, 1988; an English edition (translated by Philip Whitmore), Oxford: Oxford University Press, 1987.

> Reviews in *BachJb 1984* 70 (1984):177-78 (Hans-Joachim Schulze), *EM* 17/2 (1989):248-51 (John Deathridge), *ML* 65/4 (1984):373-76 (Susan Wollenberg), *NZfM* 150/3 (1989):53-54 (Peter Niklas

Wilson), and *ÖM* 38/10 (1983):597 (Manfred Wagner).

Scholz-Michelitsch, Helga. "Der Hofmusiker und Pädagoge Georg Christoph Wagenseil." In *WesselyFs* (1982):495-513. [*Rilm* 82-2481.]

Berg, Darrell M. "C. P. E. Bach's 'Variations' and 'Embellishments' for His Keyboard Sonatas." *JM* 2/2 (1983):151-73.

Ord-Hume, Arthur W. J. G. "Ornamentation in Mechanical Music." *EM* 11/2 (1983):185-93.

Kramer, Richard. "The New Modulation of the 1770s: C. P. E. Bach in Theory, Criticism, and Practice." *JAMS* 38/3 (1985):551-92.

Clark, Stephen L., ed. *C. P. E. Bach Studies*. Oxford: Clarendon Press, 1988. Bibliog.

> Contains numerous articles, including "C. P. E. Bach's Aesthetics as Reflected in His Notation" (Etienne Darbellay), "A Supplement to C. P. E. Bach's *Versuch*: E. W. Wolf's *Anleitung* of 1785" (Christopher Hogwood), and "C. P. E. Bach in Literature: A Bibliography" (Stephen L. Clark). Reviews in *EM* 17/2 (1989):248-51 (John Deathridge) and *NZfM* 150/3 (1989):53-54 (Peter Niklas Wilson).

Romijn, C. "Carl Philipp Emanuel Bach en die wahre Art das Clavier zu spielen." *Tvom* 3/1 (1988):7-10.

Marx, Hans Joachim, ed. *C. P. E. Bach Symposium-Bericht*. Göttingen: Vandenhoeck & Ruprecht, forthcoming.

> Includes "Nichelmann Contra C. P. E. Bach: Harmonic Theory and Musical Politics at the Court of Frederick the Great" (Thomas Christensen).

See also FÉTIS: (1833-44); HEINICHEN: (1728):Buelow (1961/. . ./1986); LÖHLEIN: (1765-81):Wilson (1979); QUANTZ: Eitner (1902); SAINT-LAMBERT: (1707):Burchill (1979); SCHENKER: (1904); ["Kommentar"] Ms.; Slatin (1967); TELEMANN, G. M.: Chrysander (1869); TELEMANN, G. P.: Allihn (1980); VIADANA: Haack (1964/1974); LITERATURE SUPPLEMENT: Ahlgrimm (1973); Alekseev (1974); Allen ["Philosophies"] (1939); **Arnold (1931/. . ./1965)**; Aulabaugh (1958); Babbitt (1967), (1987); Babitz (1952), (1967/1969); Babitz and Pont (1973); Badura-Skoda et al. (1980); Badura-Skoda (1983); Barbour (1947); Beach (1967); Becker (1836-39/1964); **Benary (1956/1961)**, (1963); **Bent** ["Analysis"] **(1980/1987):(1987)**; Beyschlag (1907/ 1953); Blake (1988); Boomgaarden (1985/1987); Borgir (1971/1987); Brown and McKinnon (1980); Broyles (1983); Bruck (1928); **Buelow** ["Rhetoric"] **(1980)**; Burde (1976); Cahn ["Retardatio"] (1972-); Castellani

(1976); Chew (1980), (1983); Chiba (1976); Cole (1988); Collins (1963), (1966), (1969), (1973); Crocker (1966); **Dahlhaus (1984); Dahlhaus et al. (1987)**; David (1956); David and Mendel (1945/1966); Dean (1977); de Zeeuw (1983); Dolmetsch (1915/. . ./1969); Donington (1963/. . ./1974), (1980); Dreyfus (1987); Duckles (1970); Dunsby and Whittall (1988); Dupont (1933/. . ./1986); Eggebrecht (1955); Eitner (1880), (1900-1904/1959-60); Feil (1955); Ferand [*Improvisation*] (1956/1961); Fischer (1957); Flaherty (1989); Forkel (1792/1962); Frobenius ["Isotonos"] (1972-), ["Vollstimmig"] (1972-); Fubini (1971/ 1983); Ganz (1972), (1976); Gerber (1790-92/1977), (1812-14/1966); Gillingham (1981); Grout (1960/. . ./ 1980); Hailparn (1981); Hammel (1977-78); Hansell (1968); Harich-Schneider ([1939]/. . ./1970); Hartig (1982); Hedges (1978); Heimann (1970/ 1973); Helm (1960); Hiller (1768-69); Hoffmann (1974); Hosler (1978/1981); Houle (1987); Ibberson (1984); Jackson (1988); Jeppesen (1930/. . ./1974); **Kassler** (1971), **(1979)**; Kaufmann (1969); Kauko (1958); Keller (1931/. . ./1966), (1955/1965); Kelletat [*Temperatur*] (1960); Kinkeldey (1910/1968); Kretzschmar (1911-12); Kubota (1986); La Motte-Haber (1969); Lawrence (1978); **Lester (1989)**; **Lindley** ["Temperaments"] **(1980)**, (1982); List (1976); Mahlert and Sunter (1972-); Mallard (1978); Mann (1987); McIntyre (1965); Mitchell, W. J. (1963); Moyer (1969); Munkachy (1968); Nelson (1984); **Neumann**, Frederick (1965/. . ./1982), (1967/1982), (1977/1982), (1978), (1979/ 1982), (1981/1982), [*Essays*] **(1982)**, (1986); Newman (1985); Newman (1946), (1963/. . ./1983), (1976); Oberdörffer (1949-68); O'Donnell (1979); Ottenberg (1973/1978); **Palisca** ["Theory"] **(1980)**; Rasch (1981); Ratner (1970), (1980); Reichert (1978); Reimer ["Kenner"] (1972-); **Ritzel (1967/ 1968)**; Robison (1982); Rosenblum (1988); Rothgeb (1968); Rothschild (1953), (1961); Rowen (1979); Schmalzriedt ["Reprise"] (1972-), ["Subiectum"] (1972-); Schulenberg (1982), (1984); Seidel (1971); Serauky (1929); Sheldon (1975), (1981); Shellhous (1988); Sisman (1978); Smiles (1978); Sondheimer (1925); Spitzer and Zaslaw (1986); Stege (1927-28); Stowell (1985), (1988); Subirá (1947/. . ./1958); Swain (1988); Tenney (1988); Thaler (1984); Todd (1983); Troeger (1987); Ulrich (1931/1932); Unger (1941/1969); Vanhulst (1971); Wagner (1981); **Wason (1981/1985)**, (1983); Wessel (1955); Wichmann (1966); Williams, P. ["Harpsichord"] (1968), (1970); Wirth (1966); Yeston (1975).

BÉNIGNE DE BACILLY

[ca. 1625 (?)–1690]

The pervasive Baroque device of melodic ornamentation had its origins in vocal practice, and no theorist of the seventeenth century more thoroughly documented its motivations or described its usage than did Bénigne de Bacilly, whose *Remarques curieuses sur l'art de bien chanter* (1668) refers to the thriving art of the French *air de cour*. Basing his perspective upon the idiomatic usage of the French language, he found justification for *agréments* primarily as a means for reinforcing the weight of long syllables, though also as an expressive device. The second and later verses of the *airs* were particularly susceptible to improvised ornamentation. In their very composition they were already more florid than was the initial verse.

Bacilly insisted that singers understand the principles of French declamation and that they imbue their ornaments with freedom both in terms of their execution and their placement within the melodies. The vocal origin of what eventually spread to keyboard and instrumental music should inspire all performers to appreciate the sensitivity and spontaneity with which the practice ought to be undertaken.

Remarques curieuses sur l'art de bien chanter, et particulièrement pour ce qui regarde le chant françois . . . [*Rism* B/VI/1, pp. 108-9.]

> Paris: the author and Ballard (C. Blageart), 1668. [LCPS: B-005a. HoM: 156. SMLMS.]

>> Later editions under various titles, including *L'art de bien chanter . . .*:

> Paris: the author, 1679. [LCPS: B-005b.]

T ● ● ● Caswell, Austin B., trans. and ed. *A Commentary upon the Art of Proper Singing.* MTT, no. 7. Brooklyn, N.Y.: Institute of Mediaeval Music, 1968. [*Rilm* 69-776.]

> Reviews in *JAMS* 23/2 (1970):353-55 (Owen Jander), *Notes* 26/3 (1969-70):527-28 (Vincent Duckles), *Rdm* 58/1 (1972):118-20 (J. Bran-Ricci), and *YMC* 5/6 (1969):21-22.

S ● Facsimile of the 1679 edition. Geneva: Minkoff Reprints, 1971; 1974.

> Review in *Rdm* 58/2 (1972):271-72 (André Verchaly).

LITERATURE:

Prunières, Henry. "Un maître de chant au XVIIᵉ siècle: Bénigne de Bacilly." *Rdm* 7 [nouvelle série, no. 8] (1923):156-60.

Bridgman, Nanie. "Bacilly, Bénigne de." Translated by Siegfried Schmalzriedt. In *MGG* (1949-68): Supplement (1973-79). Bibliog.

Wolff, Hellmuth Christian. "Gesangs-Improvisationen der Barockzeit." *Mleb* 6/2 (1953):46-49.

Caswell, Austin Baldwin. "The Development of Seventeenth-Century French Vocal Ornamentation and Its Influence upon Late Baroque Ornamentation-Practice." 2 vols. Ph.D. dissertation, The University of Minnesota, 1964. Bibliog. [*DA* 26/12, pp. 7353-54.]

> Includes a preliminary version of (1668): Caswell (1968), above.

Caswell, Austin B. "*Remarques curieuses sur l'art de bien chanter.*" *JAMS* 20/1 (1967):116-20. [*Rilm* 67-141.]

Cohen, Albert. "*L'art de bien chanter* (1666) of Jean Millet." *MQ* 55/2 (1969):170-79. [*Rilm* 69-800.]

Caswell, Austin B. "Bacilly, Bénigne de." In *NGrove* (1980). Bibliog.

Tegen, Martin. "Hur sjöng man på 1600-talet?" *Musikrevy* 36/5 (1981):266-68.

Ryhming, Gudrun Kristina. "Quelques remarques sur l'art vocal français de la seconde moitié du 17ᵉ siècle." *SMz* 122/1 (1982):1-7; expanded version (as "L'art du chant français au XVIIᵉ siècle selon Bénigne de Bacilly") in *RmSr* 35/1 (1982):10-25. Bibliog. [*Rilm* 82-1469.]

Reid, Michael Alan. "Remarks and Reflections on French Recitative: An Inquiry into Performance Practice Based on the Observations of Bénigne de Bacilly, Jean-Leonor de Grimarest, and Jean-Baptiste Dubos." M.M. thesis, North Texas State University, 1985. [*MAb* 24/02, p. 89. UMI 13-26460.]

See also FÉTIS: (1833-44); LITERATURE SUPPLEMENT: Badura-Skoda et al. (1980); Becker (1836-39/1964); Braun (1986); Cohen (1988); Collins (1973); Donington (1963/. . ./1974); Eitner (1900-1904/1959-60); Fuller (1977); Geering (1949-68); Gerber (1812-14/1966); Goldschmidt (1907); Houle (1987); Jackson (1988); Kooiman (1981); **Neumann,** Frederick (1964/1982), (1977/1982), (1978), (1981/1982), [*Essays*] **(1982)**; (1988); North (1987); O'Donnell (1979); Schneider (1985); Troeger (1987); Turner (1974); Wichmann (1966).

JOAN ALBERT BAN

[1597 or 1598–1644]

While MERSENNE was erecting his monumental treatises on music in Paris, Joan Albert Ban (Bannus, Bannius) was at work creating general principles for composition in Haarlem. When the two began a correspondence in 1638, their differences became a source of frustration for MERSENNE, who had found Ban's *Dissertatio* of 1637 trivial and outmoded. To prove his point, MERSENNE set up a competition between Ban and the French composer Antoine Boësset, wherein both were to set the same poem. Though the details were botched (Ban received an imperfect copy of the poem, while Boësset had set it even before the competition began), the verdict, not surprisingly, came down in Boësset's favor. Not one to accept defeat, Ban continued to pester MERSENNE and other correspondents.

Ban's central concern was the development of what he called *musica flexanima*, or music wherein the text was vividly expressed by following strict rules concerning melody, rhythm, and concord. Unfortunately the prescriptions Ban formulated were confusing and contradictory. His suggestions for setting French texts were inadequately attuned to the true character of that language, while his elaborate treatment of each melodic interval, though akin to the prevalent notion that minor intervals were sad while major intervals were robust, suffered too many exceptions during the actual composition of music to be as effective as Ban claimed. Since the exact size of each interval is of great importance in his system, Ban borrowed DESCARTES's notion of an eighteen-note octave and developed a keyboard and other instruments in which the difficulties inherent in just intonation would be minimized. For example, two D keys were supplied—one in tune with G and B, the other with F and A. Despite his persistence, his ideas failed to win the acceptance that he felt they deserved.

Dissertatio epistolica de musicae natura, origine, progressu, et denique studio bene instituendo [*Rism* B/VI/1, p. 113.]

    Leiden: Isaac Commelin, 1637. [LCPS: B-015. IDC.]

    S ● Grotius, Hugo, et al. *Dissertationes de studiis instituendis* [*Rism* B/VI/1, p. 113.]. Amsterdam: Louys Elzevier, 1645.

    S ● VOSSIUS, Gerardus Joannes, et al. *Dissertationes de studiis bene instituendis* [*Rism* B/VI/1, p. 113.]. Utrecht: Theod. Ackersdyck & Gisb. Zylius, 1658.

"Cort beduydsel vant zingen"

    Ms., 1642. [Liège: Université de Liège.]

    S ● Land, J. P. N. "Joan Albert Ban en de theorie der toonkunst." *TvNm* 1/2 (1882-85):95-111; 3/4 (1888-91):204-18.

Zangh-bloemzel . . . [*Rism* A/I/1, p. 203.]

    Amsterdam: Paul Matthysz, 1642.

    S ● Noske, Fritz R., ed. Facsimile edition. EMTLC, no. 1. Amsterdam: Fritz Knuf, 1969. [*Rilm* 69-907.]

        Reviews in *Consort* 28 (1972):120-21 (Lillian M. Ruff), *Mf* 25/2 (1972):240-41 (Alfons Annegarn), *Notes* 27/4 (1970-71):729-30 (Albert Dunning), *l'Organo* 8/1 (1970):109-10 (Luigi Ferdinando Tagliavini), *Sos* 42 (1970):32-36 (Chris Maas), and *TvNm* 21/4 (1970):247-49 (Jan Böhmer).

Kort sangh-bericht van I. A. Ban . . . op zyne ziel-roerende zangen [*Rism* B/VI/1, p. 113.]

    Amsterdam: Louys Elzevier (Paul Mathysz), 1643. [IDC.]

    S ● See (1642): Noske (1969), above.

"Zangh-bericht"

    Ms. [Lost.]

Correspondence

    S ● See DESCARTES: (1619-50):Roth (1926); DONI: Correspondence; MERSENNE: (1617-48); LITERATURE SUPPLEMENT: Jonckbloet and Land (1882).

Miscellanea

    Mss. [Liège: Université de Liège.]

LITERATURE:

Heije, J. P. "Ban." *Bouw* 2 (1872-74):77-88.

Land, J. P. N. "Het volmaeckte klaeuwier van Jo. Alb. Ban." *TvNm* 2/1 (1885-87):57-60.

Kalff, S. "Een Haarlemsche musicus." *De muziek* 5/4 (1930-31):153-63.

Noske, Fritz R. "Ban, Joan Albert." Translated by Gerrit J. Tetenburg. In *MGG* (1949-68): Supplement (1973-79). Bibliog.

Klerk, Jos de. "De 'zinroerende zangh' van Joan Albert Ban." *Mens* 14/12 (1959):370-73.

● ● ● Walker, D. P. "Joan Albert Ban and Mersenne's Musical Competition of 1640." *ML* 57/3 (1976):233-55. Bibliog. [*Rilm* 76-2643.]

    Reprinted in Walker (1978).

Tollefsen, Randall H. "Ban, Joan Albert." In *NGrove* (1980). Bibliog.

Rasch, Rudolf. "Ban's Intonation." *TvNm* 33/1-2 (1983):75-99. [*Rilm* 83-519.]

See also DESCARTES: Pirro (1907/1973); FÉTIS: (1833-44); WALTHER: (1732); LITERATURE SUPPLEMENT: Becker (1836-39/1964); **Dahlhaus**

et al. **(1987)**; Eitner (1900-1904/1959-60); Gerber (1812-14/1966); Keislar (1987); **Lindley ["Just"] (1980)**, **(1984)**; Meer (1988); **Seidel and Cooper (1986)**; Stoll (1978/1981); **Walker (1978)**.

ADRIANO BANCHIERI

[1568–1634]

An articulate spokesman for the trends in early seventeenth-century Italian musical practices, particularly those of the church, Adriano Banchieri wrote prolifically on a variety of subjects, including music theory. Though his tendency to revise and rename works and the rarity of many items create complications for the scholar and bibliographer, several of his major treatises are available in facsimile and offer important information on organs and their uses, solmization, the changing theoretical foundations for church composition, tuning, numbers and accidentals used with a bass to notate keyboard accompaniment, counterpoint, improvisation, and ornamentation.

The 1609 edition of *Conclusioni nel suono dell'organo* and 1611 edition of *L'organo suonarino* deal with the primitive figured-bass practice. But it is the "Dialogo musicale" added to the 1614 edition of the latter work which contains Banchieri's most detailed treatment of the subject. The use of figures is endorsed, and innovations such as accidentals and the figuring of dissonances and their resolutions are applauded. Though Banchieri claimed to be a composer, not an organist, he succinctly captured the essence of the practice and suggested ways to enhance the musical texture.

The ecclesiastical modes of the Renaissance evolved through the incorporation of transpositions (using key signatures) and through a rigorously hierarchical relationship among pitches within a mode to produce the somewhat different system favored during the seventeenth century. Banchieri, in his *Cartella musicale* (1614 edition), systematically explained the new practice and compiled detailed summaries of the characteristics of each of its eight components. In his treatment of counterpoint, Banchieri proffered specific guidelines for composing a subject and answer in each of these modes. He also advocated that composers learn their craft by first attaining a thorough grasp of the older *contrapunto osservato* before proceeding to *contrapunto commune*. To this end, he developed a method involving six species of counterpoint similar to that of DIRUTA. Elsewhere in *Cartella* he advocated the expansion of the solmization system by adding syllables for the seventh step, namely *ba* or *bi* for the flat and natural forms of that scale degree.

Conclusioni nel suono dell'organo . . . [*Rism* B/VI/1, pp. 113, 115.]

Lucca: Silv. Marchetti, 1591.

Bologna: heredi di Giovanni Rossi, 1609.

Edition entitled *Armoniche conclusioni nel suono dell'organo, canto fermo figurato, e contraponto* . . . :

Bologna: Girolamo Mascheroni, 1626.

Latin version, as *Conclusiones de musica in organo modulanda, testimoniis auctorum insignium comprobatae*:

Bologna: Girolamo Mascheroni, 1627.

S ● Facsimile of the 1609 edition. Ctma. Milan: Bollettino bibliografico musicale, 1934.

S ● Facsimile of the 1609 edition. BmB, ser. 2, no. 24. Bologna: Forni, 1968.

Review in *ISOI* 3 (1970):240 (Maarten A. Vente).

S ● Facsimile edition. MMMLF, ser. 2, no. 101. New York: Broude Brothers.

Review in *OrganYb 1983* 14 (1983):124-25 (Peter Williams).

T ● See MacClintock (1979).

T ● Garrett, Lee Raymond. "Adriano Banchieri's *Conclusioni nel suono dell'organo* of 1609: A Translation and Commentary." D.M.A. dissertation, The University of Oregon, 1972; published edition (as *Conclusions for Playing the Organ (1609)*, CCMPT, no. 13), Colorado Springs, Colo.: Colorado College Music Press, 1982. [*Rilm* 73-1772. *DA* 33/09A, p. 5224.]

Review in *ML* 64/3-4 (1983):286-87 (Peter Williams).

Cartella, overo regole utilissime à quelli che desiderano imparare il canto figurato . . . [*Rism* B/VI/1, pp. 114-15.]

Venice: Giacomo Vincenti, 1601.

Edition entitled *La cartella . . . utile à gli figliuoli et principianti che desiderano con facilità imparare sicuramente il canto figurato*:

Venice: Giacomo Vincenti, 1610.

Edition entitled *Cartella musicale nel canto figurato, fermo, et contrapunto*:

Venice: Giacomo Vincenti, 1614. [LCPS: B-016. SMLMS.]

> Edition entitled *La cartellina musicale che in documenti facili ridotti dall'antico allo istile moderno introduce i principianti à sicuro posesso del canto figurato*:

Venice: Giacomo Vincenti, 1615.

> Edition entitled *La Banchierina, overo cartella picciola del canto figurato . . .*:

Venice: Alessandro Vincenti, 1623.

S ● See HERBST: (1642).

> A printing of the vocal ornaments from the *Cartella musicale*.

S ● Vecchi, Giuseppe, ed. Facsimile of the 1614 edition. BmB, ser. 2, no. 26. Bologna: Forni, 1968.

T ● Cranna, Clifford Alan, Jr. "Adriano Banchieri's *Cartella musicale* (1614): Translation and Commentary." Ph.D. dissertation, Stanford University, 1981. Bibliog. [*Rilm* 81-4605. *DA* 42/05A, p. 1843. UMI 81-24050.]

L'organo suonarino . . . [*Rism* B/VI/1, pp. 115-16.]

Venice: Ricciardo Amadino, 1605. [IDC.]
Venice: Ricciardo Amadino, 1611.

> Contains "Dialogo musicale del . . . Banchieri Bolognese con un amico suo, che desidera suonare sicuramente sopra un basso continuo in tutte le maniere."

Venice: Alessandro Vincenti, 1622.

> Reprinted in 1627 [?].

Venice: Alessandro Vincenti, 1638. [LCPS: B-018. SMLMS.]

S ● Capaccioli, Enrico., ed. "Dialogo musicale di A. Banchieri con un amico suo che desidera sonare sicuramente sopra un basso continuo nell'organo in tutte le maniere." *Msac* 90 (ser. 2, no. 11)/4-5 (1966):121-26.

S ● Cattin, Giulio, ed. Facsimile of the 1605 edition, with portions of the 1611 and 1638 editions. Bo, no. 27; BmB, ser. 2, no. 31. Amsterdam: Knuf; Bologna: Forni, 1969.

> Review in *ISOI* 3 (1970):240 (Maarten A. Vente).

T ● Marcase, Donald Earl. "Adriano Banchieri, *L'organo suonarino*: Translation, Transcription and Commentary." Ph.D. dissertation, Indiana University, 1970. [*Rilm* 70-1714. *DA* 31/07A, p. 3585. UMI 70-26938.]

La mano, et documenti sicuri prodotti d'autori gravi, et cantici ecclesiastici

Milan: heredi di Simon Tini & Filippo Lomazzo, 1611.

Cartellina del canto fermo gregoriano . . . [*Rism* B/VI/1, p. 115.]

Bologna: heredi di Gio. Rossi, 1614.

> Incorporated within (1601):(1614), above.

Frutto salutifero alli R. P. Sacerdoti per prepararsi alla celebratione della S. Messa privata e cantata [*Rism* B/VI/1, p. 115.]

Bologna: heredi di Gio. Rossi, 1614.

> Incorporated within the 1622 and later editions of (1605), above.

Al direttorio monastico di canto fermo . . . [*Rism* B/VI/1, pp. 113-14.]

Bologna: heredi di Gio. Rossi, 1615-16. [SMLMS.]

> As *Progressi politici e christiani . . .*:

Bologna: heredi di Gio. Rossi, 1616.

> A partial reprint.

> Thoroughly revised, as *Cantorino utile a novizze e chierici secolari e regolari, principianti del canto fermo . . .*:

Bologna: heredi di Bartol. Cochi, 1622.

Il principiante fanciullo . . ., che . . . impara solfizare note e mutationi, e parole solo . . . [*Rism* A/I/1, p. 207.]

Venice: Gardano (Bartolomeo Magni), 1625.

Lettere armoniche [*Rism* B/VI/1, p. 115.]

Bologna: Girolamo Mascheroni, 1628. [LCPS: B-017.]

> Continued as *Lettere scritte à diversi patroni, & amici*:

Bologna: Nicolò Tebaldini, 1630.

S ● Vecchi, Giuseppe, ed. Facsimile of the 1628 and 1630 volumes. BmB, ser. 5, no. 21. Bologna: Forni: 1968.

La sampogna musicale . . .

Bologna: Girolamo Mascheroni, 1628.

LITERATURE:

Redlich, Hans F. "Banchieri, Adriano." In *MGG* (1949-68). Bibliog.

Capaccioli, Enrico. "Precisazioni biografiche su Adriano Banchieri." *Rmi* 56/4 (1954):340-41.

Vecchi, Giuseppe. "Una seduta dei Filomusi a Bologna e il *Virtuoso Ritrovo Accademico* di A. Banchieri (1626)." *Chigiana* 25 [5] (1968):39-52.

Vecchi, Giuseppe. "L'opera didattico-teorica di Adriano Banchieri in rapporto alla 'nuova prattica'." In *Congresso Monteverdi 1968* (1969):385-95.

Mischiati, Oscar. "Adriano Banchieri (1568-1634): Profilo biografico e bibliografia della opera." In *Annuario 1965-1970 del Conservatorio di musica "G. B. Martini" di Bologna* 1 (1971):38-201; reprinted separately, Bologna: Pàtron, 1972. Bibliog. [*Rilm* 73-279.]

> Reviews in *Civcat* 125/1 [2968] (1974):414 (F. M. Bauducco) and *OrganJb* 6 (1975):160 (Peter Williams).

Marcase, Donald E. "Adriano Banchieri's *L'organo suonarino*." *Diapason* 64/8-9, 11 [764-65, 767] (1973):6-7, 4-5, 6-8.

Bernick, Thomas. "Heinrich Schütz on Modality." Ph.D. dissertation, The University of Chicago, 1979. [*Rilm* 79-2497. *DA* 40/06A, p. 2966.]

May, William S. "Banchieri, Adriano." In *NGrove* (1980). Bibliog.

Wernli, Andreas. *Studien zum literarischen und musikalischen Werk Adriano Banchieris (1568-1634)*. PSMG, ser. 2, no. 31. Bern and Stuttgart: Paul Haupt, 1981. Bibliog.

> Reviews in *JMT* 27/2 (1983):282-90 (Clara Marvin), *Mf* 37/1 (1984):55-56 (Martin Seelkopf), and *NZfM* 143/2 (1982):67 (Elmar Budde).

See also DIRUTA: (1593-1609):Soehnlein (1975); FÉTIS: (1833-44); HERBST: (1643); MERSENNE: (1617-48); MOMIGNY: (1791-1818):(1818); MONTEVERDI: Fabbri (1985); RIEMANN: (1898); VIADANA: Haack (1964/1974); WALTHER: (1732); LITERATURE SUPPLEMENT: Ambros (1878/. . ./1909); Apfel (1962), (1981); ● ● ● Arnold (1931/. . ./1965); Atcherson (1973); Becker (1836-39/1964); Borgir (1971/1987); Brown and McKinnon (1980); Buelow (1972); Bukofzer (1947); Chew (1980); Collins (1963), (1964); Dahlhaus ["Zur Entstehung"] (1961), ["Untersuchungen"] (1966/. . ./1988); (1981); **Dahlhaus et al. (1987)**; **Dahlhaus and Sachs (1980)**; Donington (1963/. . ./1974); Dürr (1964); Eitner (1900-1904/1959-60); Fellerer ["Ausdruck"] (1982), (1983), (1984); Ferand (1937/1938); Ferand (1951), ["Improvised"] (1956), [*Improvisation*] (1956/1961); Flindell (1983-84); Forkel (1792/1962); Gaillard (1971); Gaspari (1876/. . ./1969), Geering (1949-1968); Gerber (1790-92/1977), (1812-14/1966); Haar (1986); Harrán (1986); Hein (1954); Hill (1983); Horsley (1963), [*Fugue: History*] (1966), (1972), (1977); Houle (1987); Hucke (1969); Hüschen (1986); Jackson (1988); Jeppesen (1922/. . ./1970), (1930/. . ./1974); Kauko (1958); Kinkeldey (1910/1968); Kirkendale (1979); Kleinman (1971/1974); Kuhn (1902); Lange (1899-1900); **Lester** (1978), **(1989)**; Lewis (1975/1978); Mahlert and Sunter (1972-); **Maniates (1979)**; Mendel (1978); Neumann, Frederick (1978), (1987); Newman (1959/. . ./1983); Oberdoerffer (1967); Pacchioni (1983); **Palisca** (1949-68), ["Artusi- Monteverdi"] (1968/1985), [*Baroque*] (1968/1981), ["Theory"] **(1980)**; Powers (1974), ["Mode"] ● ● ● (1980), (1981); Reese (1957/1970); Reimer ["Concerto"] (1972-); Robbins (1938); Roberts (1967); Rowen (1979); Sachs (1972-); Schneider (1917/. . ./1971); Schulenberg (1984); Subirá (1947/. . ./1958); Taddie (1984); Tirabassi (1925); Tittel (1959), (1966); Vecchi (1969); Walker (1987); Wienpahl (1953); Williams, P. (1970).

HENRICUS [PIPEGROP] BARYPHONUS

[1581–1655]

According to PRAETORIUS, Henricus Baryphonus was a prolific author on music theory. Unfortunately only one of his works is extant, although three others were published. His *Pleiades musicae* exists in two distinct editions: one issued in 1615, before he had absorbed the incipient triadic theory of LIPPIUS; the other afterwards, in 1630. By that time harmony was beginning to usurp the role which counterpoint had played in controlling compositional structure, and Baryphonus responded with the concept of *triga harmonica* (the triad) and with a consideration of how triads could be connected. In this context the bass assumes a central role, while the positioning of the root in either the bass or in another voice contributes to each chord's character.

Isagoge musica

> Magdeburg: 1609. [Lost.]

Pleiades musicae, quae in certas sectiones distributae praecipuas quaestiones musicas discutiunt . . . [*Rism* B/VI/1, pp. 121-22.]

> Halberstadt: Jacob-Arnold Kothe, 1615. [LCPS: B-034. HoM: 177.]

>> Expanded edition, edited by Heinrich GRIMM, as *Pleiades musicae, quae fundamenta musicae theoricae ex principiis mathematicis eruta . . .*, and bound with CALVISIUS's Μελοποιια:

Magdeburg: haeredes Johann. Franc., 1630. [IDC.]

Institutiones musico-theoricae ex fundamentis mathematicis exstructae

    Leipzig: 1620. [Lost.]

Ars canendi . . .

    Leipzig: 1620. [Lost.]

Letter to Heinrich Schütz

    S ● See WERCKMEISTER: (1700).

    T ● See Moser (1936/. . ./1959).

Numerous manuscript treatises, now lost, are listed in PRAETORIUS: (1614-20):Vol. 3 (1618) and in Buelow (1980), below.

LITERATURE:

Jacobs, Eduard. "Zwei harzische Musiktheoretiker des sechzehnten und siebzehnten Jahrhunderts: . . . II. Heinrich Baryphonus, 1581-1655." *VMw* 6 (1890):111-22.

See also *VMw* 7 (1891):459-63 and 8 (1892):145-47.

Adrio, Adam. "Baryphonus, Henricus." In *MGG* (1949-68). Bibliog.

● ● ● Buelow, George J. "Baryphonus, Henricus." In *NGrove* (1980). Bibliog.

See also CALVISIUS: Benndorf (1894):421, 441, 444; FÉTIS: (1833-44); HERBST: (1643); LIPPIUS: Rivera (1974/1980); PRAETORIUS: (1614-20): Vol. 3 (1618); RIEMANN: (1898); WALTHER: (1708); (1732); Gehrmann (1891):478-80; LITERATURE SUPPLEMENT: **Apfel (1981)**; Becker (1836-39/1964); Bukofzer (1947); Burney (1776-89/. . ./1957); Chomiński (1962/1981); Dahlhaus ["Untersuchungen"] (1966/. . ./1988), ["Harmony"] (1980); Eitner (1900-1904/1959-60); Forkel (1792/1962); Kauko (1958); Gerber (1812-14/1966); Lester (1977); Moser (1967); Müller-Blattau (1923/. . ./1963); Preußner (1924), (1939); Rivera (1984); Robbins (1938); Rogers (1955); Ruhnke (1949-68); Taddie (1984).

JOHANN BEER

[1655–1700]

A colorful figure of the mid-Baroque, Johann Beer (Bähr) possessed a versatility which led him to prominence as a vocalist, as an author of satirical novels, and as a sometimes teacher of composition pupils, for whom he created, in 1690, his posthumously published *Musicalische Discurse* (1719). Beer's *Ursus murmurat* and *Ursus vulpinatur* (1697) resulted from a disagreement with Gottfried Vockerodt, whose Pietist views concerning the worship service had led him to condemn the improvisational and operatic elements which had become a prominent aspect of German church music. Beer's more practical and tolerant attitude permeates not only his response to Vockerodt, but his other writings as well.

Ursus murmurat: Das ist, Klar und deutlicher Beweiss, welcher gestalten Herr Gottfried Vockerod . . . in seinem den 10. Aug. des abgewichenen 1696ten Jahres herausgegebenen (nunmehr verteutscht beigefügten) Programmate der Music, und per consequens denen von derselben dependirenden zu viel gethan . . . [*Rism* B/VI/1, p. 110.]

    Wießenfels: 1697.
    Weimar: Johann Andreas Müller, 1697.

Ursus vulpinatur: List wieder List oder musicalische Fuchs-Jagdt, darinnen Gottfried Vockerodens . . . Apologie, der Balg abgejagt, ausgestreifft, auch ohne eintzige Vulpi-

nationirung oder Fuchsschwäntzerey . . . vorgestellet wird [*Rism* B/VI/1, p. 110.]

    Weißenfels: the author, 1697.

Bellum musicum; oder, Musicalischer Krieg, in welchem umbständlich erzehlet wird, wie die Königen Compositio nebst ihrer Tochter Harmonia mit denen Hümpern und Stümpern zerfallen . . . [*Rism* B/VI/1, pp. 109-10.]

    N.p., 1701. Edited by Peter Wenig.

      See also (1719), below.

Musicalische Discurse, durch die Principia der Philosophie deducirt, und in gewisse Capitel eingetheilt, deren Innhalt nach der Vorrede zu finden. Nebst einem Anhang von eben diesem Autore, genannt der musicalische Krieg zwischen der Composition und der Harmonie [*Rism* B/VI/1, p. 110.]

    Nuremberg: Peter Conrad Monath, 1719. Edited by Peter Wenig. [LCPS: B-008. IDC.]

    S ● "Johann Beerens . . . *Musicalische Discurse* . . ." *CK* 10 (1885):61-75; *KJb* 1 (1886):66-74; 2 (1887):82-88; 3 (1888):56-61; and 4 (1889):72-83.

S ● Krause-Graumnitz, Heinz, ed. Facsimile edition. Leipzig: VEB Deutscher Verlag für Musik, 1982.

> Reviews in *MG* 33/10 (1983):624-25 (Karl-Heinz Viertel) and *ML* 64/3-4 (1983):261-62 (George J. Buelow).

"Schola phonologica sive tractatus doctrinalis de compositione harmonica: Dass ist, Aussführliche Lehrstücke, welche zu der musicalischen Composition nöthig erfordert werden"

> Ms. [Leipzig: Musikbibliothek der Stadt.] Schnellroda: M. C. Seifert, 1732. [?] [*Rism* B/VI/1, p. 110.]

LITERATURE:

Alewyn, Richard "Johann Beer: Studien zum Roman des 17. Jahrhundert." Habilitationsschrift; published edi-

tion (Palaestra, no. 181), Leipzig: Mayer & Müller, 1932.

Krause, Heinz. "Johann Beer 1655 – 1700: Zur Musikauffassung im 17. Jahrhundert." Ph.D. dissertation, The University of Leipzig, 1935.

Werner, Arno. "Beer, Johann." In *MGG* (1949-68). Bibliog.

Schmiedecke, Adolf. "Johann Beer und die Musik." *Mf* 18/1 (1965):4-11.

Buelow, George J. "Beer, Johann." In *NGrove* (1980). Bibliog.

See also FÉTIS: (1833-44); MATTHESON: (1722-25); (1740); WALTHER: (1732); LITERATURE SUPPLEMENT: Ahlgrimm (1969-70); **Barbour (1951/.../1972)**; Becker (1836-39/1964); Buelow (1972); Cahn ["Transitus"] (1972-); Dreyfus (1987); Eitner (1900-1904/1959-60); Forkel (1792/1962); Gerber (1790-92/1977); Gurlitt (1954/1966); Menck (1931); Neumann, Frederick (1978); Riedel (1956/1959); Schäfke (1934/1964); Walker (1987); Wessely (1971-72).

(JOHANN GOTTFRIED) HEINRICH BELLERMANN

[1832–1903]

The nineteenth century's successor to FUX was Heinrich Bellermann, whose several books and numerous articles focus upon Renaissance practices of notation, meter, mode, and counterpoint. Vocal music is championed as the most perfect genre, with compositions by Isaac, Ockeghem, Josquin, Lassus, and Palestrina serving as models.

First published when he was only twenty-six years old, Bellermann's *Die Mensuralnoten und Taktzeichen des XV. und XVI. Jahrhunderts* (1858) offers a thorough examination of earlier notational practices and metrical conventions. Its fourth edition was published as recently as 1963. *Der Contrapunct* (1862) follows FUX's formulation of five species, each of which is undertaken in two, three, four, and more voices. One also finds therein a formulation of rules for text underlay and an introduction to fugal procedures, all in a strictly modal idiom. Bellermann was also responsible for the publication of passages from several early theoretical treatises, including works by Franco of Cologne and Tinctoris.

Die Mensuralnoten und Taktzeichen des XV. und XVI. Jahrhunderts

> Berlin: Georg Reimer, 1858.
> Berlin: Georg Reimer, 1906. Foreword by Ludwig Bellermann.

> > Review in *Rmi* 13/2 (1906):359-60 (Luigi Torchi).

> Berlin: Walter de Gruyter, 1930.

Berlin: Walter de Gruyter, 1963. Edited by Heinrich Husmann.

> Reviews in *MK* 33/6 (1963):274, *Msac* 64/3 (1963):149, *MT* 104/1450 (1963):870 (Denis Stevens).

Der Contrapunct; oder, Anleitung zur Stimmführung in der musikalischen Composition

> Berlin: Julius Springer, 1862.

> > Later editions through 1922. Review in *Rmi* 8/4 (1901):1048-52 (Luigi Torchi).

"Joannis Tinctoris: *Terminorum musicae diffinitorium*, lateinisch und deutsch mit erläuternden Anmerkungen"

> *JfmW* 1 (1863):55-114.

> S ● Gülke, Peter, ed. IGMDm, ser. 1, no. 37. Kassel: Bärenreiter, 1983.

"Das Locheimer Liederbuch nebst der Ars Organisandi von Conrad Paumann, als Documente des deutschen Liedes sowie des frühesten geregelten Contrapunktes und der ältesten Instrumentalmusik"

> With Friedrich Wilhelm Arnold.

> *JfmW* 2 (1867):1-234.

Über die Entwicklung der mehrstimmigen Musik

> Berlin: A. Sacco, 1867.

"Das eilfte Kapitel der Ars cantus mensurabilis des Franco von Köln, namentlich in Bezug auf die Eintheilung der Intervalle in Konsonanzen und Dissonanzen"

> *AmZ* (L) 3/43-44 (1868):337-40, 346-48.

"Einige Bemerkungen über Hucbald'schen Notationen"

> *AmZ* (L) 3/37 (1868):289-91.

"Bemerkungen über den melodischen Gebrauch der Intervalle"

> *AmZ* (L) 4/27 (1869):209-11.

"Die Wechselnote oder Cambiata bei den Componisten des sechszehnten Jahrhunderts"

> *AmZ* (L) 4/49-50 (1869):385-87, 393-95.

"Einige Bemerkungen über die consonirende Quarte bei den Componisten des 16. Jahrhunderts"

> *AmZ* (L) 5/35 (1870):273-75.

"Die Schlüssel im ersten Buche der vierstimmigen Motetten von Palestrina"

> *AmŻ* (L) 5/49-50 (1870):388-90, 395-97.

"Über die Eintheilung der Intervalle in Consonanzen und Dissonanzen bei den ältesten Mensuralisten"

> *AmZ* (L) 5/11-13 (1870):81-83, 89-92, 97-98.

"Zur Quintenfrage"

> *AmZ* (L) 5/36, 42, 43 (1870):281-83, 329-32, 337-39.

"Bemerkungen über den Gesangunterricht"

> *AmZ* (L) 7/10-11 (1872):158-62, 174-77.

"Notker Labeo, von der Musik"

> *AmZ* (L) 7/35-37 (1872):553-57, 569-74, 585-90.

Die Größe der musikalischen Intervalle als Grundlage der Harmonie

> Berlin: Julius Springer, 1873.

"Franconis de Colonia Artis cantus mensurabilis caput XI, De discantu et eius speciebus: Text, Übersetzung und Erklärung"

> In *Festschrift zu der dritten Säcularfeier des Berlinischen Gymnasiums zum grauen Kloster*, pp. 383-413. Berlin: Weidmannsche Buchhandlung (J. Reimer), 1874.

> S ● Offprint edition. Berlin: Weidmannsche Buchhandlung (J. Reimer), 1874.

See also KIRNBERGER: (1779-83):BELLERMANN (1871-72).

LITERATURE:

Schneider, Otto. *Heinrich Bellermann: Gedächtnisrede*. Berlin: Julius Springer, 1903.

Sasse, Dietrich. "Bellermann." In *MGG* (1949-68). Bibliog.

Drabkin, William. "Bellermann; (Johann Gottfried) Heinrich Bellermann." In *NGrove* (1980). Bibliog.

See also RIEMANN: (1898); SCHENKER: (1906-35):Vol. II (1910-22); LITERATURE SUPPLEMENT: Cazden (1948); Chomiński (1962/1981); Dahlhaus ["Zur Theorie"] (1961), ● ● ●["Geschichte"] (1980); (1984); Dahlhaus et al. (1987); Dahlhaus and Sachs (1980); Dreyfus (1987); Dunsby and Whittall (1988); Federhofer (1944/1950); Fellerer (1927/. . ./1972); Ferand (1937/1938); Frobenius ["Homophonus"] (1972-), ["Polyphon"] (1972-), ["Vollstimmig"] (1972-); Harrán (1986); Haydon (1933/1970); Jeppesen (1922/. . ./1970), (1930/. . ./1974), (1935); Kinkeldey (1910/1968); Lindley (1982); Mann (1987); McQuere (1983); Mendel (1948), (1978); Müller-Blattau (1923/ . . ./1963), (1949-68); Palisca (1949-68); Sachs (1972-); Schmalzriedt ["Durchführen"] (1972-), ["Exposition"] (1972-); Schmidt (1979); Subirá (1947/ . . ./1958); Tuksar (1978/1980); Wirth (1966).

ANGELO BERARDI

[ca. 1636–1694]

Towards the end of the seventeenth century, the innovations forged by the Camerata and by MONTEVERDI had become part of the musical mainstream. Though two practices continued to exist, the validity of the second was generally accepted, while practitioners of the first felt obliged to remind their public that the two practices could indeed coexist—that the second was not intended to *replace* the first. Angelo Berardi clearly understood the differences between the two systems and, as early as his *Ragionamenti* *musicali* (1681), proposed further distinctions based upon characteristics which made music appropriate for church, chamber, or theatre settings, each utilizing its own set of stylistic devices. Though derived in part from the formulation of his teacher SCACCHI, Berardi's perspective brought the classification of style up to date and fostered a clearer insight among other writers on music.

Though less widely circulated than the *Gradus* of FUX a generation later, Berardi's several works on the contrapuntal art are of great importance in the development of a pedagogy for composition. Nearly a century after Palestrina's death, his music was serving as the primary model in the quest for mastery over the art. The fact that several leading theorists of the time, including Berardi, were also churchmen certainly contributed to this choice of model. More pervasively than had his predecessors, Berardi divided compositional practice into various component parts, each of which was reinforced through exercises with strict limitations on certain parameters (such as allowing only stepwise motion in the counterpoint or only quarter-half-quarter rhythm). Though the resulting pieces were not to be construed as ideal compositions, their very uniformity forced upon the student a lively interaction with specific problems of composition. The skills derived from these components were, when combined, the makings of a solid compositional craft.

In the *Documenti armonici* (1687) one finds a thorough account of fugue (including double counterpoint and double fugue), canon at various intervals, and the appropriate use of dissonances (now somewhat relaxed from ZARLINO's norms). Here also Berardi introduced notions which link fugal writing with various practices of logic. The remaining practical works, the *Miscellanea musicale* (1689) and *Arcani musicali* (1690), offer further refinements in the contrapuntal art (some more elementary than those of the *Documenti armonici*) and an assessment of the relationship between the construction of a fugue and of an oration.

Dicerie musicali

Before 1681. [Lost.]

Ragionamenti musicali [*Rism* B/VI/1, p. 138.]

Bologna: Giacomo Monti, 1681. [LCPS: B-066a. SMLMS.]

To which was added *Aggiunta . . . alli suoi ragionamenti musicali . . .*:

Bologna: Giacomo Monti, 1681. [LCPS: B-066b.]

Documenti armonici . . . [*Rism* B/VI/1, pp. 137-38.]

Bologna: Giacomo Monti, 1687. [LCPS: B-063. SMLMS.]

S ● Facsimile edition. BmB, ser. 2, no. 40a. Bologna: Forni, 1970.

T ● See Larsen (1979), below.

T ● See Rowen (1979).

Miscellanea musicale . . . [*Rism* B/VI/1, p. 138.]

Bologna: Giacomo Monti (Marino Silvani), 1689. [LCPS: B-064. SMLMS.]

S ● Facsimile edition. BmB, ser. 2, no. 40b. Bologna: Forni, 1970.

T ● See Larsen (1979), below.

T ● See Rowen (1979).

Arcani musicali . . . [*Rism* B/VI/1, p. 137.]

Bologna: Pier-Maria Monti, 1690. [LCPS: B-062. SMLMS.]

Bologna: Marino Silvani, 1706.

Il perché musicale, overo staffetta armonica . . . [*Rism* B/VI/1, p. 138.]

Bologna: Pier-Maria Monti (Marino Silvani), 1693. [LCPS: B-065. SMLMS.]

LITERATURE:

Blume, Friedrich. "Berardi, Angelo." In *MGG* (1949-68).

Waack, Karl-Friedrich. "Angelo Berardi als Musiktheoretiker." Ph.D. dissertation, The University of Kiel, 1955.

Spena, Rosa. "Analisi di alcuni trattati musicali di Angelo Berardi." Thesis, The University of Messina, 1973-74. Bibliog.

Larsen, Arved Martin, III. "Angelo Berardi (1636-1694) as Theorist: A Seventeenth-Century View of Counterpoint." Ph.D. dissertation, The Catholic University of America, 1979. [*DA* 40/03A, p. 1516. UMI 79-21065.]

● ● ● Larsen, Arved M., III. "Berardi, Angelo." In *NGrove* (1980). Bibliog.

See also FÉTIS: (1833-44); KIRNBERGER: (1782); MOMIGNY: (1791-1818):(1818); OUSELEY: (1882); RIEMANN: (1898); SCACCHI: (1649): Palisca (1972); WALTHER: (1732); LITERATURE SUPPLEMENT: Abraham (1968/1969); **Apfel** (1977), **(1981)**; Becker (1836-39/1964); **Bent** ["Analysis"] **(1980/1987):(1987)**; Buelow (1972); Bukofzer (1947); Bullivant (1980); Butler (1977); **Dahlhaus and Sachs (1980)**; Dammann (1958/1967); David and Mendel (1945/1966); Eitner (1900-1904/1959-60); Falck (1965); Federhofer (1969); Fellerer (1927/. . ./1972), (1969), ["Zur Kontrapunktlehre"] (1973), (1983); Forkel (1792/ 1962); Frobenius ["Vollstimmig"] (1972-); Gaillard (1971); Gerber (1812-14/1966); Gerboth et al. (1964); Ghislanzoni (1949-51); Hawkins (1776/ . . ./1969); Hein (1954); Horsley [*Fugue: History*] (1966), (1972); Isgro (1968); Jeppesen (1922/ . . ./1970), (1930/. . ./1974); Katz (1926); La Fage (1864/1964); **Mann (1955/. . ./1965)**; Oberdoerffer (1967); Ortigue (1853/. . ./1971); Pacchioni (1983); **Palisca** (1949-68), [*Baroque*] (1968/1981), ["Theory"] **(1980)**; Reimer ["Concerto"] (1972-), ["Kammermusik"] (1972-); Sachs (1972-); Schmalzriedt (1972-); Tittel (1966); Walker (1987).

JUAN BERMUDO

[ca. 1510–ca. 1565]

Well versed in the theoretical literature of his day and supportive of new developments in the art of composition, Juan Bermudo set out to erect a lucid and thorough foundation for the art of music in Spain. The result, after two preliminary works which were incorporated within his magnum opus, was *Comiença el libro llamado declaración de instrumentos musicales* (1555). Bermudo addressed a wide variety of materials, including a discussion of rudiments and of more advanced aspects of melodic and polyphonic composition, a numerical system of notation for polyphony, information for performers (especially concerning Spanish stringed instruments), some original organ music, and a serviceable modification of Pythagorean tuning.

Comiença el libro primero de la declaración de instrumentos . . . [*Rism* B/VI/1, p. 140.]

Osuna: Juan de Léon, [1549]. [IDC.]

S ● Tapia, Martín de. *Vergel de música spiritual speculativa y activa . . .* [*Rism* B/VI/2, pp. 818-19.] Burgo de Osma: Diego Fernández de Córdova, 1570. [LCPS: T-006.]

An unacknowledged reworking of Bermudo's treatise.

Comiença el arte tripharia . . . [*Rism* B/VI/1, p. 140.]

[Osuna: Juan de Léon, 1550.]

Comiença el libro llamado declaración de instrumentos musicales . . . [*Rism* B/VI/1, p. 140.]

Derived, in part, from the two preceding works.

Osuna: Juan de Léon, 1555. [LCPS: B-068. HoM: 201.]

S ● Kastner, Macario Santiago, ed. Facsimile edition. IGMDm, ser. 1, no. 11. Kassel: Bärenreiter, 1957.

Reviews in *Mf* 11/1 (1958):109-10 (Margarete Reimann), *ML* 39/4 (1958):392-94 (Thurston Dart), *MR* 19/4 (1958):345-46 (J. A. Westrup), and *Stfm* 39 (1957):171 (Bengt Hambræus).

T ● Bushnell, Vinson Clair. "The *Declaración de instrumentos musicales* of Fray Juan Bermudo." M.A. thesis, The University of Rochester, 1960.

Contains a translation of Book 5, "Of Composition."

T ● Kinney, Gordon J. Translation. Lexington, Ky.: M. I. King Library, The University of Kentucky, 1977.

T ● Hermosillo, Carmen. "Juan Bermudo's *Statement on Musical Instruments*: A Translation with Commentary on Pedagogical Significance." M.A. thesis, San Jose State University, 1985.

LITERATURE:

Anglès, Higino. "Bermudo, Fray Juan." Translated by Christel Blume. In *MGG* (1949-68). Bibliog.

● ● ● Stevenson, Robert. *Juan Bermudo*. The Hague: Martinus Nijhoff, 1960. Bibliog.

Reviews in *JAMS* 16/1 (1963):86-88 (Isabel Pope), ● ● ● *JMT* 6/1 (1962):156-58 (John William Woldt), *Mf* 16/3 (1963):297-99 (Margarete Reimann), *ML* 42/4 (1961):375-76 (Peter E. Peacock), *MR* 23/1 (1962):71, *Notes* 18/3 (1960-61):417-18 (Gilbert Chase), and *NZfM* 123/10 (1962):481 (G. A. Trumpff).

Stevenson, Robert. "Juan Bermudo." [Music Review.] *Notes* 20/3 (1962-63):397-98.

Frol'kin, Viktor. ["Juan Bermudo and His Music-Pedagogical Viewpoint."] In *Istoriko-teoreticheskie problemy zapadnoevropeiskoi muzyki (ot vozrozhdeniia do romantizma)* [Historical Theoretical Problems of West-European Music (from the Renaissance to Romanticism)], edited by Ruzanna K. Shirinian, pp. 118-41. St, no. 40. Moscow: Gosudarstvennyi muzykal'no-pedagogicheskii institut imeni Gnesinykh, 1978. Bibliog.

Stevenson, Robert. "Bermudo, Juan." In *NGrove* (1980).

Meeùs, Nicolas. "Juan Bermudo et le clavier enharmonique." *BSlm* 8 (1984):1-16. [*Rilm* 74-3673.]

See also DIRUTA: Soehnlein (1975); FÉTIS: (1833-44); LIPPIUS: Rivera (1974/1980); SANTA MARÍA: Roig-Francolí ["Compositional"] (forthcoming); VIADANA: Haack (1964/1974); WALTHER: (1732); LITERATURE SUPPLEMENT: Abraham (1968/1969); Anglés and Subirá (1946-51); Apel (1942/. . ./1961); **Barbour** (1932), (1948), **(1951/. . ./1972)**; Becker (1836-39/1964); Beebe (1976); Berger (1987); Brown (1973), (1976); Chew (1980); Chomiński (1962/1981); Collet (1912); Crocker (1966); Dahlhaus et al. (1987); Dupont (1933/. . ./1986); Eggebrecht (1955); Eitner (1900-1904/1959-60); Ferand (1937/1938); Forkel (1792/1962); Gable (1979); Gerber (1812-14/1966); Gleason (1981); Haar (1977); Hannas (1934); Harrán (1986); Haydon (1933/1970); Hoag (1976); Howell (1972); Hüschen (1986); Jackson (1988); Jacobi (1957-60/1971); Jacobs (1968); Johnson (1973), (1978); Kastner (1973-74/1987); Kinkeldey (1910/1968); Krantz (1989); León Tello (1962); Lindley ["Temperaments"] (1980), (1984); Lowinsky

(1946/1967); Mendel (1948), (1978); Müller-Blattau (1923/. . ./1963); Parkins (1983); Powers ["Mode"] (1980); ● ● ● Reese (1957/1970); Rodgers (1971); Rogers (1955); Sachs (1972-); Soderlund (1980);

Stevenson (1960), (1976); Subirá (1947/. . ./1958), (1953); Taddie (1984); Tyler (1975); Vellekoop (1959); Wagner (1981); Wienpahl (1953).

CHRISTOPH BERNHARD

[1628–1692]

Christoph Bernhard, one of the more illuminating authors of the seventeenth century, wrote several treatises which remained unpublished during his lifetime. Fortunately his manuscripts were copied and circulated, though certainly not as widely as published volumes would have been. As a subordinate of Schütz at Dresden and visitor to Italy, Bernhard was exposed to the best of contemporary composition. Though scholars today doubt that Schütz had Bernhard in mind when he endorsed (in his *Geistliche Chormusik* of 1648) an unnamed forthcoming treatise, Müller-Blattau's provocative title for his edition of Bernhard's works – "The Composition Manual of Heinrich Schütz in the Formulation of His Student Christoph Bernhard" – conveys the sense that Bernhard was describing procedures that had only recently been developed.

In the wake of MONTEVERDI's bold departure from accepted practice, theorists began to accommodate more diverse stylistic possibilities. Bernhard's synthesis in "Tractatus compositionis augmentatus" [ca. 1657-64] is particularly elegant, though perhaps dependent in part upon SCACCHI. The older practice (MONTEVERDI's *prima prattica*) is called *stylus gravis* and contains only time-honored means of incorporating dissonance (what we now would call unaccented and accented passing and neighboring notes, as well as suspensions, both tied and rearticulated). Second is the *stylus luxurians communis*, wherein a wide variety of devices acceptable in contemporary sacred and secular music, both vocal and instrumental, is to be found. The incomplete neighbor, anticipation, more varied uses of suspensions, and more daring leaps are among the fifteen figures which Bernhard treated and labeled with terms such as *superjectio*, *subsumtio*, and *consonantiae impropriae*. The final category, *stylus theatralis*, contains the most progressive handling of dissonance, resulting from the complete reversal of the music/words dichotomy found in *stylus gravis*. Appropriate primarily for the stage, where words are in command, it incorporates Bernhard's final eight figures. Only here would a composer prolong a dissonance, omit or alter a resolution, or use a melodic augmented second. All of the figures described by Bernhard are illustrated with clear and interesting examples.

In addition, the "Tractatus" covers standard procedures of counterpoint (including canon and double counterpoint) and modal theory. Some of its contents appeared in an abbreviated form in his "Ausführlicher Bericht vom Gebrauch der Con- und Dissonantien" [ca. 1664-74]. The brief

"Von der Singe-Kunst oder Maniera" [ca. 1649] is a guide to stylistic performance for singers, modeled heavily upon Italian practice. Three categories are designated: *cantar soda* (basic singing), *cantar d'affetto* (wherein the affect of the text is emphasized), and *cantar passagiato* (incorporating diminution).

"Von der Singe-Kunst oder Maniera"

Mss., [ca. 1649]. Title varies.

S ● See Collected Works, below.

T ● See Falck (1965).

T ● See Collected Works, below.

T ● See **Katz and Dahlhaus (1987-)**: Vol. 3.

"Tractatus compositionis augmentatus"

Mss., [ca. 1657-64]. Title varies.

S ● See Collected Works, below.

T ● See Falck (1965).

T ● See Collected Works, below.

"Ausführlicher Bericht vom Gebrauch der Con- und Dissonantien"

Mss., [ca. 1664-74]. Title varies.

S ● See Collected Works, below.

T ● See Falck (1965).

T ● See Collected Works, below.

COLLECTED WORKS EDITIONS:

Müller-Blattau, Josef Maria, ed. "Die Kompositionslehre Heinrich Schützens in der Fassung seines Schülers Christoph Bernhard." Habilitationsschrift, The University of Königsberg, 1922; published edition, Leipzig: Breitkopf & Härtel, 1926; reprint edition (updated), Kassel: Bärenreiter, 1963.

Reviews in *Mf* 18/4 (1965):452 (Peter Benary), *MK* 36/1 (1966):31 (Martin Geck), *OrganYb* 4 (1973):134 (Peter Williams), *QdRm* 3 (1965):269-70 (Alfredo Bonaccorsi), *Rdm* 50/128 (1964):135-36 (D. Launay), and *Rmi* 34/3 (1927):441-43 (G. Pannain).

Streetman, Richard David. "Christoph Bernhard." Ph.D. dissertation, North Texas State University, 1967. [*DA* 28/09A, p. 3709. UMI 67-15022.]

● ● ● Hilse, Walter, trans. "The Treatises of Christoph Bernhard." In *MuF* 3 (1973):1-196. [*Rilm* 73-1750.]

LITERATURE:

Grusnick, Bruno. "Bernhard, Christoph." In *MGG* (1949-68). Bibliog.

Dahlhaus, Carl. "Die Figurae superficiales in den Traktaten Christoph Bernhards." In Osthoff (1954):135-38. Bibliog.

Federhofer, Hellmut. "Die Figurenlehre nach Christoph Bernhard und die Dissonanzhandlung in werken von Heinrich Schütz." In Osthoff (1954):132-35.

Dahlhaus, Carl. "Christoph Bernhard und die Theorie der modalen Imitation." *AfMw* 21/1 (1964):45-59.

Federhofer, Hellmut. "Marco Scacchis *Cribrum musicum* (1643) und die Kompositionslehre von Christoph Bernhard." In *EngelFs* (1964):76-90.

Stockmann, Bernhard. "Zur Kritik der barocken Musiktheorie." *NZfM* 127/2 (1966):56-60. Bibliog.

Braun, Werner. "Zwei Quellen für Christoph Bernhards und Johann Theiles Satzlehren." *Mf* 21/4 (1968):459-66. [*Rilm* 68-3198.]

Rifkin, Joshua. "Schütz and Musical Logic." *MT* 113/1557 (1972):1067-70. [*Rilm* 72-3181.]

Fiebig, Folkert. "Christoph Bernhard und der stile moderno: Untersuchungen zu Leben und Werk." Ph.D. dissertation, The University of Hamburg, 1979; published edition (HBzMw, no. 22), Hamburg: Karl Dieter Wagner, 1980. [*Rilm* 80-442; 80-4506.]

>Review in *Mf* 35/4 (1982):374 (Siegfried Schmalzriedt).

Snyder, Kerala Johnson. "Bernhard, Christoph." In *NGrove* (1980). Bibliog.

Stockmann, Bernhard. "Zum Stilwandel in der Musik des später 17. Jahrhunderts." In *Bericht Berlin 1974* (1980):285-86. [*Rilm* 80-500.]

Steinbeck, Wolfram. "Sprachvertonung bei Heinrich Schütz als analytisches Problem." *SchüJb 1981* 3 (1981):61-63. [*Rilm* 81-6247.]

Bernick, Thomas. "Modal Digressions in the *Musicalische Exequien* of Heinrich Schütz." *MTS* 4 (1982):51-65. [*Rilm* 82-4493.]

Ruhnke, Martin. "Gattungsbedingte Unterschiede bei der Anwendung musikalisch-rhetorischer Figuren." In *Kieler Tagung 1980* (1982):51-61. [*Rilm* 82-2360.]

Braun, Werner. "Schütz als Kompositionslehrer: Die "Geistlichen Madrigale" (1619) von Gabriel Mölich." *SchüJb 1985/86* 7-8 (1986):69-92.

See also BONONCINI: Holler (1955/1963); FÉTIS: (1833-44); FUX: Federhofer (1957-58); MATTHESON: (1739); (1740); SCACCHI: (1649):Palisca (1972); SCHENKER: Slatin (1967); Morgan (1978); SWEELINCK: Walker (1986); VIADANA: Haack (1964/1974); WALTHER: (1732); LITERATURE SUPPLEMENT: Abraham (1968/1969); **Apfel** (1962), [*Beiträge*] (1964), ["Wandlungen"] (1964), **(1981)**; Audbourg-Popin (1984); Babitz (1952); Babitz and Pont (1973); Bartel (1982/1985); Becker (1836-39/1964); Beiche ["Inversio"] (1972-); **Benary (1956/1961)**; Brandes (1935); Braun (1986); Brown and McKinnon (1980); **Buelow** (1972), ["Rhetoric"] **(1980)**, (1982); Bukofzer (1947); Cahn ["Repercussio"] (1972-), ["Retardatio"] (1972-), ["Transitus"] (1972-); Collins (1967); Constantini (1975); **Dahlhaus** ["Konsonanz"] (1949-68), ["Untersuchungen"] (1966/. . ./1988), ["Harmony"] **(1980)**, ["Hindemiths"] (1983), (1986); **Dahlhaus and Sachs (1980)**; Dammann (1958/1967); Dunsby and Whittall (1988); Eggebrecht (1957), (1959); Eitner (1900-1904/1959-60); Federhofer (1944/1950), (1958), (1964), (1969), (1980), (1981); Feldmann (1958); Flindell (1983-84); Forchert (1986); Forkel (1792/1962); Frobenius ["Isotonos"] (1972-), ["Vollstimmig"] (1972-); Fürstenau (1861-62); Geering (1949-68); Gerber (1812-14/1966); Ghislanzoni (1949-51); Grusnick (1964-66); Gut (1972-); Heimann (1970/1973); Hein (1954); Henderson (1969); Horsley (1963), [*Fugue: History*] (1966); Hucke (1969); Isgro (1968); Jackson (1988); Katz (1926); Kinkeldey (1910/1968); Kirkendale (1979); Kooiman (1981); Krantz (1989); Krützfeldt (1961); Krummacher (1979), (1986); Kunze (1979-83); Lawrence (1978); **Lester** (1977), (1978), **(1989)**; Lindley (1982); **Mann (1955/. . ./1987)**; Massenkeil (1963); Moser (1936/. . ./1959); Müller-Blattau (1923/. . ./1963); **Neumann**, Frederick (1978), [*Essays*] **(1982)**; Newman (1985); Oberdörffer (1949-68); **Palisca** (1949-68), [*Baroque*] (1968/ 1981), ["Theory"] **(1980)**; Rauhe (1959-60); Reckow (1972-); Reese (1957/1970); Reilly (1984-85); **Ritzel (1967/1968)**; Rivera (1984); Robbins (1938); Sachs (1972-); Schmalzriedt ["Subiectum"] (1972-); Schmitz (1950); Schulenberg (1984); Sheldon (1982); Snyder (1980); Stoll (1978/1981); Subirá (1947/. . ./1958); Tittel (1966); Unger (1941/1969); Walker (1987); Wessely (1971-72); Wichmann (1966); Williams (1979); Wolff (1972-); **Zaminer (1985)**; Zenck (1942); Ziebler (1933).

JEAN LAURENT DE BÉTHIZY

[1709–1781]

Jean Laurent de Béthizy shared d'ALEMBERT's goal of creating a straightforward summary of RAMEAU's basic tenets. D'ALEMBERT's *Élémens de musique, théorique et pratique* (1752) preceded Béthizy's *Exposition de la théorie et de la pratique de la musique* (1754) by two years, during which time Béthizy took d'ALEMBERT to task in two extended reviews published in the *Journal œconomique*.

The *Exposition* is divided into sections on melody and harmony. The latter treats fundamental bass, chromaticism, cadences, basso continuo, and basic principles of fugue. Some of the examples contain both an unfigured basso continuo line and a rendering of the fundamental bass, while several examples containing figured bass conclude the work.

Exposition de la théorie et de la pratique de la musique, suivant les nouvelles découvertes [*Rism* B/VI/1, p. 145.]

> Paris: Michel Lambert, 1754. [LCPS: B-081a. SMLMS. IDC.]
>
>> Review in *JTr* (July 1754):1575-92. A partial German translation of this review and further commentary appear in MATTHESON: (1754-56): Vol. 3 (1755):465-71. Facsimiles are provided in RAMEAU: Collected Works (1967-72): Vol. 6.
>
> Paris: F. G. Deschamps, 1764. Enlarged edition. [LCPS: B-081b. HoM: 209.]
>
> S ● Facsimile of the 1764 edition. Geneva: Minkoff Reprint, 1972.

Effets de l'air sur le corps humain considérés dans le son, ou discours sur la nature du chant [*Rism* B/VI/1, p. 145.]

>> Attributed to Béthizy, though published under the name Eugène-Eléonor de Béthisy de Mézières.

Amsterdam and Paris: Lambert & Duchesne, 1760. [LCPS: B-080.]

See also d'ALEMBERT: (1752): Reviews.

LITERATURE:

Paquette, Daniel. "Béthizy, Jean Laurent de." Translated by Susanne Diederich. In *MGG* (1949-68): Supplement (1973-79). Bibliog.

Cohen, Albert. "Béthizy, Jean Laurent de." In *NGrove* (1980). Bibliog.

Earhart, A. Louise Hall. "The Musical Theories of Jean-Laurent de Béthizy and Their Relationship to Those of Rameau and d'Alembert." Ph.D. dissertation, The Ohio State University, 1985. [*DA* 46/03A, p. 549. UMI 85-10567.]

See also d'ALEMBERT: (1752):Elsberry (1984); FÉTIS: (1833-44); RAMEAU: Collected Works (1967-72): Vols. 3, 4, 6; Pischner (1961/. . ./1967); SERRE: (1763); LITERATURE SUPPLEMENT: Asselin (1981); Atcherson (1960); Becker (1836-39/1964); Burney (1776-89/. . ./1957); Cazden (1948), (1980); Chevaillier (1925/1931-32); **Dahlhaus et al. (1987)**; Donington (1963/. . ./1974); Eitner (1900-1904/1959-60); Forkel (1792/1962); Gerber (1790-92/1977); Groth (1983); Horsley [*Fugue: History*] (1966); **Kassler (1979)**; Krehbiel (1964); **Ritzel (1967/1968)**; Shellhous (1988).

ELWAY BEVIN

[ca. 1554–1638]

Elway Bevin's *Briefe and Short Introduction to the Art of Musicke* (1631) addresses the issue of canonic writing with great thoroughness. Although little instruction is given, many examples are supplied. SIMPSON, PLAYFORD, and PURCELL all praised this treatise and referred to it with respect. It may be coincidental that fewer canons were published after Bevin revealed so many secrets about their construction.

A Briefe and Short Instruction of the Art of Musicke, to Teach How to Make Discant, of All Proportions That Are in Use . . . [*Rism* B/VI/1, p. 146.]

> London: R. Young, 1631. [LCPS: B-085.]

LITERATURE:

Fludd, W. H. Grattan. "New Light on Late Tudor Composers: Elway Bevin." *MT* 68/1015 (1927):796.

Young, Percy M. "Bevin, Elway." Translated by Thomas M. Höpfner. In *MGG* (1949-68): Supplement (1973-79). Bibliog.

Hooper, Joseph Graham. *The Life and Works of Elway Bevin*. Bristol: 1971. [?]

Hooper, Graham. "Bevin, Elway." In *NGrove* (1980).

See also FÉTIS: (1833-44); KOLLMANN: (1799); LITERATURE SUPPLEMENT: Becker (1836-39/1964);

Bridges (1984); Burke (1963); Burney (1776-89/. . ./ 1957); Burton (1956); Chenette (1967); Collins (1963); Dolmetsch (1915/. . ./1969); Eitner (1900-1904/1959-60); Forkel (1792/1962); Gerber (1790-92/1977), (1812-14/1966); Hawkins (1776/. . ./ 1969); Horsley [*Fugue: History*] (1966); Miller (1960); Pulver (1927/. . ./1973); **Seidel and Cooper (1986)**; Wienpahl (1953).

FRANCESCO BIANCIARDI

[ca. 1571–1607]

An early formulation for the realization of unfigured bass appeared on a single large sheet in 1607, soon after the death of its author, Francesco Bianciardi. *Breve regola*, as it was called, specifies suitable intervals to be added above a bass pitch for a variety of ascending and descending bass progressions. For example, in the bass succession of an ascending fourth, the first note would typically support a major third, even if an accidental was required. Though Bianciardi mentions the system of indicating the intervals to be used with figures, he does not endorse it.

Readers are offered advice on the use of doubling to create richer chordal textures. In particular, added octaves are encouraged, while too complex an interval structure in the lower register is to be avoided. Though his instructions are inadequate for the more fully developed practice which later emerged, they provide some of the earliest documentation on specific characteristics of improvised keyboard accompaniment.

Breve regola per imparar' a sonare sopra il basso con ogni sorte d'istrumento [*Rism* B/VI/1, p. 148.]

Siena: Domenico Falcini, 1607.

ST● Haas, Robert, trans. and ed. "Das Generalbassflugblatt Francesco Bianciardis." In *WolfFs* (1929):48-56.

LITERATURE:

Billeter, Bernhard. "Bianciardi, Francesco." In *MGG* (1949-68): Supplement (1973-79). Bibliog.

Lonardi, Massimo. " 'Del sonare sopra 'l basso' ovvero la realizzazione liutistica del basso continuo." *Fronimo* 5/21 (1977):7-15. [*Rilm* 77-5585.]

Lederer, Josef-Horst. "Bianciardi, Francesco." In *NGrove* (1980). Bibliog.

See also AGAZZARI: Rose (1965); FÉTIS: (1833-44); HEINICHEN: (1728):Buelow (1961/. . ./1986); RIEMANN: (1898):Mickelsen (1977); WALTHER: (1732); LITERATURE SUPPLEMENT: ● ● ●**Arnold (1931/. . ./1965)**; Eitner (1900-1904/1959-60); Fellerer (1984); Gaillard (1971); Gerber (1812-14/1966); Mitchell, J. W. (1963); Rothgeb (1968); Strizich (1981); Wienpahl (1953); Williams, P. (1970).

SEVERO BONINI

[1582–1663]

Approaching old age, Severo Bonini reflected upon the changes he had witnessed in Italian musical practices over the past half century. Having observed the Florentine musical culture firsthand (and probably having himself studied under CACCINI), his report, a manuscript called "Discorsi e regole sopra la musica" (left unfinished in about 1650), is of considerable interest. A monk who had enjoyed a brief success as a composer but who spent his later years in somewhat bitter obscurity, Bonini created a dialogue in which a fictitious student named Filareto conveniently asks the very questions Bonini wishes to address. In addition to supplying a rich assortment of cultural and biographical information, Bonini defended the modern *stile recitativo* against the purported superiority of ancient music and considered what music might be presented appropriately in church. His explanations of music's origins and basic characteristics stem directly from ZARLINO, while GALILEI and CACCINI are consulted for their perspectives on the changes which they had formulated. In a scheme similar to that of SCACCHI, Bonini divided music into three broad classifications, the first of which, the *stile antico*, was antecedent to Palestrina. What MONTEVERDI would have called the *prima* and *seconda prattica* form Bonini's second and third categories, which together comprised the *stile moderno*. This softening of the contrast between the two surviving styles reflects Bonini's allegiance both to the church that he had served and to the glorious period of his youth, when he had played an active role in progressive Florentine circles. Though the inner title page promises rules for counterpoint, none appear in the surviving manuscript. Likewise one searches in vain for a treatment of the controversial issues of tuning and mode. Filareto apparently lacked curiosity in these areas.

"Prima parte de' discorsi e regole so[p]ra la musica [et il contrappunto]"

>Ms., [ca. 1649-50]. [Florence: Biblioteca Riccardiana e Moreniana.]

S ● See Solerti (1903/1969).

>An extract.

S ● Luisi, Leila Galleni, ed. Im, ser. 2, no. 5. Cremona: Fondazione Claudio Monteverdi, 1975.

>Reviews in *JMT* 22/1 (1978):111-15 (Barbara Russano Hanning), *KJb* 60 (1976):121-22 (Karl Gustav Fellerer), and *Nrmi* 10/4 (1976):683-85 (Francesco Luisi).

ST ● ● ● Bonino, MaryAnn Teresa. "Don Severo Bonini (1582–1663): His 'Discorsi e regole'." 2 vols. Ph.D. dissertation, The University of

Southern California, 1971; published edition (incomplete), Provo, Utah: Brigham Young University Press, 1979. Bibliog. [*Rilm* 79-2500. *DA* 33/09A, pp. 5220-21.]

LITERATURE:

Palisca, Claude V. "Bonini, Don Severo." Translated by Herta Goos. In *MGG* (1949-68). Bibliog.

Bonino, MaryAnn. "Bonini, Severo." In *NGrove* (1980). Bibliog.

See also FÉTIS: (1833-44); MONTEVERDI: Fabbri (1985); WALTHER: (1732); LITERATURE SUPPLEMENT: Abraham (1968/1969); Eitner (1900-1904/1959-60); Fellerer ["Ausdruck"] (1982); Gerber (1812-14/1966); La Fage (1864/1964); Martin (1932-33); Williams, P. (1970).

GIOVANNI MARIA BONONCINI

[bapt. 1642–1678]

Less comprehensive than PENNA's musical treatise of about the same time, but containing more penetrating commentary on the countrapuntal art, Giovanni Maria Bononcini's *Musico prattico* (1673) was among the late seventeenth century's most popular practical manuals. Its second part, on counterpoint, appeared in a German translation (1701), whose influence was felt in the works of WALTHER (1708) and MATTHESON (1739).

A brief primer on the fundamentals of music constitutes the first part. Then, in the second part, the reader's skills in writing are honed through a detailed exposition on strict counterpoint. Using a methodology common among several writers of the time, Bononcini proceeded from exercises consisting entirely of whole notes through the incorporation of half notes to quarter notes and suspensions. His remarks on various sorts of imitative writing are particularly striking, as they reveal that the strict intervallic correspondence between subject and answer which ZARLINO had advocated well over a century earlier was beginning to break down in response to the developing sense of tonality, for which an inexact imitation would often yield a more suitable result. In addition, double counterpoint and canon are discussed and demonstrated. Bononcini offered a traditional explanation of the twelve modes but asserted that only seven of them remained in common use.

Musico prattico che brevemente dimostra il modo di giungere alla perfetta cognizione di tutte quelle cose, che concorrono alla composizione de i canti, e di ciò ch'all' arte del contrapunto si ricerca [*Rism* B/VI/1, p. 166.]

Bologna: Giacomo Monti, 1673. [LCPS: B-116a. SMLMS.]
Venice: Giuseppe Sala, 1678.
Bologna: Giacomo Monti (Marino Silvani), 1688. [LCPS: B-116b. SMLMS.]

T ● *Musicus practicus, welcher in kürtze weiset die Art, wie man zu vollkommener Erkäntniß aller derjenigen Sachen . . . gelangen kan.* Stuttgart: Paul Treu, 1701. [*Rism* B/VI/1, p. 166. LCPS: B-116c.]

>A German translation of the second part of *Musico prattico*.

S ● Facsimile of the 1673 edition. Hildesheim: Georg Olms, 1969.

S ● Facsimile of the 1673 edition. MMMLF, ser. 2, no. 78. New York: Broude Brothers, [1969].

LITERATURE:

Bollert, Werner. "Bononcini." In *MGG* (1949-68).

Holler, Karl Heinz. "Giovanni Maria Bononcini's *Musico prattico* in seiner Bedeutung für die musikalische Satzlehre des 17. Jahrhunderts." Ph.D. dissertation, The University of Mainz, 1955 (1956); published edition (SmA, no. 44), Strasbourg: P. H. Heitz, 1963. Bibliog.

>Reviews in *Me* 17/4 (1963-64):173-75 ("Bononcini und Fux," by Ernst Tittel), *Musikrevy* 19/6

(1964):234-35 (Bengt Hambræus), *QdRm* 3 (1965):263-65 (Alfredo Bonaccorsi), and *Stfm* 47 (1965):106-8 (Ingmar Bengtsson).

Klenz, William. "Giovanni Maria Bononcini of Modena: A Chapter in Baroque Instrumental Music." Ph.D. dissertation, The University of North Carolina, 1958; published edition, Durham, N.C.: Duke University Press, 1962; reprint edition, Westport, Ct.: Greenwood Press, 1987. Bibliog. [*DA* 19/11, p. 2972.]

> Reviews in *Eras* 17/3-4 (1965):111 (K. G. Fellerer), *JAMS* 17/2 (1964):218-21 (John G.Suess), *LJ* 87/20 (1962):4194 (Catharine K. Miller), *MJ* 21/2 (1963):70 (Owen Anderson), *ML* 44/4 (1963):399-400 (Arthur Hutchings), *MT* 104/1445 (1963):485 (Denis Stevens), *Notes* 20/3 (1962-63):464-65 (Thomas Warner), *QdRm* 3 (1965):208-9 (Alfredo Bonaccorsi), *RQ* 17/1 (1964):30-31 (Newell Jenkins), and *Stfm* 48 (1966):235-37 (Ingmar Bengtsson).

Bennett, Lawrence E. "Bononcini; (1) Giovanni Maria Bononcini." In *NGrove* (1980). Bibliog.

See also BONTEMPI: (1695); FÉTIS: (1833-44); KIRN-BERGER: (1782); MATTHESON: (1717); (1739); MOMIGNY: (1791-1818):(1818); PENNA: Lederer (1970); RIEMANN: (1898); WALTHER: (1732); Gehrmann (1891); LITERATURE SUPPLEMENT: **Apfel** ["Wandlungen"] (1964), **(1981)**; Becker (1836-39/1964); Beiche ["Inversio"]

(1972-); **Benary (1956/1961)**; Borgir (1971/1987); Buelow (1972); Bukofzer (1947); Burney (1776-89/. . ./1957); Carse (1925/1964); Chew (1980), (1983); Cohen (1981); Collins (1963), (1966); Crocker (1966); Dahlhaus ["Zur Entstehung"] (1961), ["Untersuchungen"] (1966/ . . ./1988); **Dahlhaus et al. (1987)**; David and Mendel (1945/1966); Donington (1963/. . ./1974); Eitner (1900-1904/1959-60); Falck (1965); Federhofer (1964); Fellerer (1927/. . ./1972); Ferand [*Improvisation*] (1956/1961); Forkel (1792/1962); Geering (1949-68); Gerber (1790-92/1977), (1812-14/1966); Ghislanzoni (1949-51); Hawkins (1776/. . ./1969); Heimann (1970/1973); Hein (1954); Horsley [*Fugue: History*] (1966), (1972); Houle (1960), (1987); Hucke (1969); Jeppesen (1922/. . ./1970), (1930/. . ./1974); Kauko (1958); Lawrence (1978); Lippman (1986); ● ● ● Mann (1955/. . ./1987); Meier (1974/1988); Müller-Blattau (1923/. . ./1963); Neumann, Frederick (1978); Newman (1959/. . ./1983); Palisca (1949-68), [*Baroque*] (1968/1981); Pole (1879/. . ./1924); Powers ["Mode"] (1980); Reimer ["Concerto"] (1972-); Rogers (1955); **Seidel and Cooper (1986)**; **Shirlaw (1917/. . ./1970)**; Subirá (1947/. . ./1958); Tittel (1966); Todd (1983); Walker (1987); Wichmann (1966).

GIOVANNI ANDREA BONTEMPI

[ca. 1624–1705]

With few models and no particular proclivity towards presenting a balanced account, Giovanni Andrea Bontempi (originally named Angelini) set out to assemble an assortment of facts into what he called *Historia musica* (1695). The ancient Greeks and modern Italians occupied most of his attention, and since both of these groups contributed to music theory (in either its speculative or practical branch), his work deserves our attention.

The account of Greek musical thought is extensive, occupying over half of the volume. It is not a reliable guide for the modern scholar, though in its time it must have seemed quite impressive. Of greater interest, however, is the material which focuses upon contemporary practice, particularly the contrapuntal art. Bontempi's instructions anticipate the classic formulation by FUX a few decades later and produce similarly conservative results. At first the discussion is limited to consonances. Numerous rules of voice leading develop an artful coordination between the perfect and imperfect consonances. Later, dissonances are introduced, and the means by which their use is coordinated with surround-

ing consonances is emphasized. The work also contains material on cadences and on canon.

Bontempi's observations regarding motivic development within fugal writing have been lauded by modern commentators. [See especially Butler (1977) and Mann (1955/. . ./1987).] With greater insight than did his contemporaries, he explained how components derived from a contrapuntal theme could be incorporated in those sections of the work wherein the theme itself was not present, so as to create a strong unifying force.

Nova quatuor vocibus componendi methodus, quâ musicae artis plane nescius ad compositionem accedere potest [*Rism* B/VI/1, p. 167.]

> Dresden: Seyffert, 1660.

Tractatus in quo demonstrantur occultae convenientiae sonorum systematis participati

> Bologna: 1690. [Lost.]

Historia musica, nella quale si ha piena cognitione della teorica, e della pratica antica della musica harmonica . . . [*Rism* B/VI/1, p. 167.]

Perugia: L. Costantini, 1695. [LCPS: B-117. SMLMS. IDC.]

S ● Facsimile edition. BmB, ser. 2, no. 48. Bologna: Forni, [1971].

S ● Facsimile edition. Geneva: Minkoff Reprint, 1975.

LITERATURE:

Fürstenau, Moritz. *Zur Geschichte der Musik und des Theaters am Hofe zu Dresden*, vol. 1. Dresden: 1861; reprint edition (edited by Wolfgang Reich), Leipzig: Edition Peters, 1971.

> Reviews in *Melos/NZfM* 134/3 (1973):191 (Hubert Unverricht), *MG* 23/3 (1973):180-82 (Karl-Heinz Viertel), and *Rdm* 62/1 (1976):161-62 (M. C. Marion).

Zanetti, Emilia. "Bontempi (Angelini), Giovanni Andrea." Translated by Anna Amalie Abert. In *MGG* (1949-68). Bibliog.

Briganti, Francesco. *Gio. Andrea Angelini-Bontempi (1624-1705): Musicista-letterato-architetto, Perugia-Dresda*. HmcB, no. 4. Florence: Leo S. Olschki, 1956. Bibliog.

Timms, Colin. "Bontempi, Giovanni Andrea." In *NGrove* (1980). Bibliog.

See also FÉTIS: (1833-44); MATTHESON: (1722-25); MOMIGNY: (1791-1818):(1818); WALTHER: (1732); LITERATURE SUPPLEMENT: Allen ["Philosophies"] (1939); **Apfel (1981)**; Becker (1836-39/1964); Beiche ["Inversio"] (1972-); Bukofzer (1947); Burney (1776-89/. . ./1957); Butler (1977); Collins (1963); Eitner (1900-1904/1959-60); Fellerer ["Zur Kontrapunktlehre"] (1973), (1983); Fischer (1978); Forkel (1792/1962); Fürstenau (1861-62); Gerber (1812-14/1966); Grusnick (1964-66); Hawkins (1776/. . ./1969); Hein (1954); **Kassler (1979)**; Lippman (1986); Mahlert and Sunter (1972-); **Mann (1955/. . ./1987)**; Mendel (1955); Palisca (1949-68); Sachs (1972-); **Seidel and Cooper (1986)**; Subirá (1947/. . ./1958); Tittel (1966).

ERCOLE BOTTRIGARI

[1531–1612]

The musical environment of Bologna, where Ercole Bottrigari spent his first forty-five years, was conservative and church-dominated. Fortunately circumstances allowed him to spend over a decade (1576-87) at nearby Ferrara, where the musical life was far more vibrant, and where he developed a sense of allegiance to the progressive cause. Much better equipped linguistically than most music scholars, Bottrigari undertook numerous translations from the ancient treatises and completed several original works which inspired the venomous pen of his fellow Bolognese, ARTUSI.

Discussions of the Greek tonal system were still regarded as necessary at the century's end, as witnessed by Bottrigari's criticism, in *Il Patricio* (1593), of Francesco Patrizi's account of tetrachord division and his support for and elaboration upon VICENTINO's views regarding the three genera in *Il Melone* (two parts; 1602). A more practical orientation is evident in *Il desiderio* (1594), which contains a vivid description of the musical life in Ferrara and offers sensible advice concerning the combination of instruments in ensemble performance. Since three types of instruments existed—namely, those with absolutely fixed tuning (such as keyboard instruments), those for which subtle adjustments could be made during performance (such as fretted instruments), and those with free alterability (such as the trombone)—care was to be taken in the formation of an ensemble. In general, the combination of instruments from different categories was to be minimized.

ARTUSI's *L'Artusi* (1600 and 1603) was an attack upon Bottrigari. The exchange involved both the published works of 1593 and 1594 and Bottrigari's assertion that ARTUSI had stolen material from his manuscript treatise "Il Trimerone" for *L'Artusi*. An edition of *Il desiderio* was published under ARTUSI's editorship in 1601 in an attempt to establish that Bottrigari's friend Annibale Melone, and not Bottrigari, had written the work. Unlike MONTEVERDI, whose reaction to ARTUSI's criticisms was prominently displayed and remains an important document in the history of music, Bottrigari's responses, though much more substantial, remain in manuscript or have been lost.

Il Patricio, overo de' tetracordi armonici di Aristosseno, parere, et vera dimostratione [*Rism* B/VI/1, p. 171.]

> Bologna: Vittorio Benacci, 1593. [LCPS: B-127.]

> > A response to Francesco Patrizi's *Della poetica: La deca istoriale; La deca disputata* (1586).

S ● Vecchi, Giuseppe, ed. Facsimile edition. BmB, ser. 2, no. 27. Bologna: Forni, 1969. Bibliog.

Il desiderio, overo de' concerti di varij strumenti musicali . . . [*Rism* B/VI/1, p. 171.]

> Venice: Ricciardo Amadino, 1594. [LCPS: B-126. SMLMS.]

> > Under the name Alemanno Benelli [anagram of Annibale Melone].

Bologna: Gioambattista Bellagamba, 1599.

> Under Bottrigari's name.

Milan: Stampatori archiepiscopali, 1601.

> Under Annibale Melone's name. Letter of dedication and Preface by ARTUSI.

S ● Meyer, Kathi, ed. Facsimile of the 1599 edition. VMbPH, no. 5. Berlin: Martin Breslauer, 1924. Bibliog.

> Reviews in *AfMw* 7/1 (1925):147-48 (H. Abert) and *Rmi* 32/3 (1925):469-70 (G. C.).

T ● MacClintock, Carol, trans. *Il desiderio; or, Concerning the Playing Together of Various Musical Instruments . . .* MSD, no. 9. [Rome]: American Institute of Musicology, 1962.

S ● Facsimile of the 1594 edition. BmB, ser. 2, no. 28. Bologna: Forni, 1969.

> Review in *Nrmi* 4/1 (1970):149-52 (Remo Giazotto).

"Il Trimerone de' fondamenti armonici, overo lo essercitio musicale: Dialoghi . . . ne' quali si ragiona de' tuoni antichi e moderni, e de' caratteri diversi usati da' musici in tutti i tempi"

> Ms., 1599. [Bologna: Civico museo bibliografico musicale.]

Ant-Artusi

> A response to ARTUSI's *L'Artusi* (1600).

> [ca. 1601-3]. [Lost.]

"Lettera di Federico Verdicelli a' benigni, e sinceri lettori in defesa del . . . Bottrigari contra . . . Artusi"

> Ms., 1602. [Bologna: Civico museo bibliografico musicale.]

Il Melone: Discorso armonico . . . et il Melone secondo: Considerationi musicali del medesimo sopra un discorso di M. Gandolfo Sigonio intorno à' madrigali et à' libri dell'Antica musica riduta alla moderna prattica di D. Nicola Vicentino; e nel fine esso Discorso del Sigonio [*Rism* B/VI/1, p. 171.]

Ferrara: Vittorio Baldini, 1602.

S ● Vecchi, Giuseppe, ed. Facsimile edition. BmB, ser. 2, no. 29. Bologna: Forni, 1969.

"Aletelogia di Leonardo Gallucio à' benigni, e sinceri lettori; lettera apologetica"

> A response to ARTUSI's "Consideratione musicali" (1603).

Ms., 1604. [Bologna: Civico museo bibliografico musicale.]

LITERATURE:

Anonymous. "Del libro chiamato il Patricio, overo de' tetracordi d'Hercole Butrigario." Ms. [Milan: Biblioteca Ambrosiana.]

Bottrigari, Enrico. *Notizie biografiche intorno agli studi ed alla vita del cavaliere Ercole Bottrigari.* Bologna: 1842.

Manzoni, G. "Della sconosciuta tipografia bolognese aperta nel 1547 nelle case del cav. . . . Bottrigari . . ." *AmR* 3/1 (1883):121-39.

Sesini, Ugo. "Studi sull'umanesimo musicale: Ercole Bottrigari." *Conv* 13 (1941):1-25; reprinted in his *Momenti di teoria musicale tra Medioevo e Rinascimento* (MBol; Bologna: Tamari, 1966), pp. 41ff.

Walker, D. P. "Bottrigari, Hercole." Translated by Theodora Holm. In *MGG* (1949-68). Bibliog.

Giazotti, Remo. "*Il Patricio* di Hercole Bottrigari dimostrato praticamente da un anonimo cinquecentista." In *Chm* 1 (1953):97-112 (HmcB, no. 2); reprinted in his *Musurgia nova*, pp. 121-33 (Milan: G. Ricordi, 1959).

Newman, Joel. "Over-Ornamentation." *AR* 8/1 (1967):12.

● ● ● MacClintock, Carol. "Bottrigari, Ercole." In *NGrove* (1980). Bibliog.

See also ARTUSI: (1603); Palisca (1980); FÉTIS: (1833-44); MONTEVERDI: (1607); WALTHER: (1732); LITERATURE SUPPLEMENT: Abraham (1968/1969); Barbour (1932), (1951/. . ./1972); Becker (1836-39/1964); ● ● ● Berger (1975/1980); Brown (1976); Brown and McKinnon (1980); Burney (1776-89/. . ./1957); **Dahlhaus et al. (1987)**; Eitner (1900-1904/1959-60); Fellerer ["Ausdruck"] (1982), (1983); Ferand (1937/1938); Gable (1979); Gaspari (1876/. . ./1969); Gerber (1790-92/1977), (1812-14/1966); Haar (1983); Harrán (1986); Hüschen (1986); Isgro (1968); Jackson (1988); Kinkeldey (1910/1968); Kroyer (1901/. . ./1970); Levitan (1938); **Lindley (1984)**; Lowinsky (1946/1967); **Maniates (1979)**; Mendel (1978); Palisca (1953), ["Artusi-Monteverdi"] (1968/1985), [*Baroque*] (1968/1981), (1985); Reese (1954/1959), (1957/1970); Reimer ["Concerto"] (1972-); Sachs (1972-); Tuksar (1978/1980); Vecchi (1969); Vogel (1976).

SÉBASTIEN DE BROSSARD

[bapt. 1655–1730]

Sébastien de Brossard undertook the modest task of assembling a brief list of Italian terms and their French equivalents as a preface to one of his collections of vocal works, hoping thereby to bring his fellow Frenchmen in line with the other European nations in the uniform adoption of Italian terms for score markings. While preparing a new edition of his compositions, his enormous erudition (stimulated, to be sure, by what was probably the largest personal collection of music books then in existence) led him to expand his dictionary to the point that it warranted separate publication, first in a very rare octavo printing (1701), and soon thereafter as *Dictionaire de musique* (1703). It ranks as one of the seminal works of music lexicography. The dictionaries of WALTHER, Grassineau, and J.-J. ROUSSEAU, among others, display an indebtedness to Brossard's pioneering efforts—both for his concise and generally reliable definitions and for the model provided by his organizational plan and his high scholarly standards.

Especially among the earlier entries, Brossard was extraordinarily compact in his definitions. This fact perhaps results from a lack of communication between author and publisher, as a manuscript for an expanded version of these opening pages exists. None of Brossard's entries extend for more than a few pages, in contrast to the procedure of JANOVKA, whose dictionary, published in Prague in 1701, was not known to Brossard. Among the entries (numbering over seven hundred in all) one finds a wide assortment of Greek, Latin, Italian, and French terms pertaining not only to performance, but also to Greek musical practices and the theories and genres developed by Brossard's contemporaries. He himself was apparently not active in the generation of new theories.

Brossard intended to complement his dictionary of terms with an annotated catalogue of music books. A manuscript of over six hundred pages was created, but Brossard was unable to bring it to a reasonable conclusion. An interesting substitute was appended to the dictionary: an acknowledgment of the authors whom Brossard had studied in creating his definitions, as well as a very thorough listing of other authors he recognized but had not consulted. MATTHESON, not to be outdone, supplemented this list with an additional four hundred names in his *Critica musica* (1725).

Élévations et motets à voix seule, avec la basse continue [*Prodromus musicalis*] [*Rism A/I/1, p. 427.*]

> Contains a brief Italian-French lexicon from which the *Dictionaire* (below) evolved.

Paris: Christophe Ballard, 1695.

Dictionaire des termes grecs, latins et italiens, dont on se sert fréquemment dans toutes sortes de musique, et particulierement dans l'italienne . . . [*Rism B/VI/1, p. 180-81.*]

Paris: Christophe Ballard, 1701.

> Later editions, under the title: *Dictionaire de musique, contenant une explication des termes grecs, latins, italiens, & françois les plus usitez dans la musique . . .*:

Paris: Christophe Ballard, 1703. [LCPS: B-139a. SMLMS.]
Paris: Christophe Ballard, 1705. Seconde édition. [LCPS: B-139b.]
Amsterdam: Estienne Roger, [ca. 1708]. Troisième édition. [LCPS: B-139c. HoM: 266.]
Amsterdam: Pierre Mortier, [ca. 1710]. Sixtième édition.

S ● Facsimile of the 1703 edition. Amsterdam: Antiqua, 1964.

> Review in ●●●*Notes* 24/4 (1967-68):700-701 (Vincent Duckles).

S ● Heckmann, Harald, ed. Facsimile of the 1705 edition. Dm, no. 1. Hilversum: Fritz Knuf, [1966].

> Review in *Sos* 42 (1970):31-32 (Frans Brüggen).

S ● Facsimile of the [ca. 1708] edition. Geneva: Minkoff Reprint.

T ● See Rowen (1979).

T ● ● ● ● Gruber, Albion, trans. and ed. *Dictionary of Music (Dictionnaire de musique), Paris 1703.* MTT, no. 12. Henryville, Pa.: Institute of Mediaeval Music, 1982. [*Rilm* 82-14.]

"Catalogue des livres de musique théorique et prattique, vocalle et instrumentalle . . ."

> Ms., 1724. [Paris: Bibliothèque nationale.]

Lettre en forme de dissertation à Monsieur Demoz, sur sa nouvelle méthode d'écrire le plain-chant et la musique [*Rism B/VI/1, p. 181.*]

Paris: J. B. C. Ballard, 1729.

"Fragments d'une méthode de violin"

> Ms. [Paris: Bibliothèque nationale.]

"Meslanges et extraits relatifs à l'histoire de la musique"

> Includes revisions intended for the *Dictionaire.*

Ms. [Paris: Bibliothèque nationale.]

"Recueil d'extraits d'ouvrages imprimés sur la musique"

> Ms. [Paris: Bibliothèque nationale.]

LITERATURE:

Grassineau, James. *A Musical Dictionary* . . . [*Rism* B/VI/1, p. 375.] London: J. Wilcox, 1740 [LCPS: B-139d and G-064a. HoM: 267.]; London: J. Robson, 1769 [LCPS: B-139e and G-064b.]; 1784; reprint edition, Amsterdam: Antiqua, 1964; reprint edition (MMMLF, ser. 2, no. 40), New York: Broude Brothers, 1966.

> Dependent upon Brossard's dictionary, though not an exact translation. An "Appendix Selected from the *Dictionnaire de musique* of M. Rousseau" was added to the 1769 edition. Reviews in *Consort* 26 (1970):459-60 (Lillian M. Ruff) and *MT* 109/1505 (1968):637 (Stanley Sadie).

Bobillier, Marie [Brenet, Michel]. "Sébastien de Brossard: Prêtre, compositeur, écrivain et bibliophile (165... — 1730) d'après ses papiers inédits." *Mhi*, no. LF1. Paris: Coderg, 1982. Bibliog.

> Extract from *MShP* 23 (1896).

Bourreau, Louis. *Un musicien bibliophile: Sébastien de Brossard, maître de musique de la cathédrale de Meaux.* Meaux: Imprimerie André-Pouyé, 1936. Bibliog.

> Extract from *BSlhB* 15 (1936).

Lebeau, Elisabeth. "Brossard, Sébastien de." Translated by Hans Albrecht. In *MGG* (1949-68). Bibliog.

Lebeau, Elisabeth. "L'entrée de la collection musicale de Sébastien de Brossard à la Bibliothèque du Roi, d'après des documents inédits." *Rdm* 32 [29] (1950):77-93; 33/97-98 (1951):20-43.

Goehlinger, F.-A. "Sébastien de Brossard." *CRmms* 64-65 (1956-57).

Winzenburger, Janet, and Barber, Elinore. "Riemenschneider Bach Library Vault Holdings (*Dictionnaire de musique*)." *Bach* 3/1 (1972):31. [*Rilm* 72-7.]

Sajak, Rainer. "Sébastien de Brossard als Lexikograph, Bibliograph und Bearbeiter." Ph.D. dissertation, The University of Bonn, 1973; published edition, Bonn: 1974. [*Rilm* 74-2195.]

Anthony, James R. "Brossard, Sébastien de." In *NGrove* (1980). Bibliog.

See also FÉTIS: (1831), (1833-44); MATTHESON: Buelow and Marx (1983): Palisca; MERSENNE: (1617-48); MOMIGNY: (1791-1818):(1818); RIEMANN: (1898); WALTHER: (1732); LITERATURE SUPPLEMENT: Allen ["Philosophies"] (1939); Atcherson (1973); Audbourg-Popin (1986); Auhagen (1987); Becker (1836-39/1964); Beiche ["Dux"] (1972-), ["Inversio"] (1972-); Beyschlag (1907/ 1953); Blumröder (1972-); Burney (1776-89/. . ./ 1957); Butler (1977); Cohen (1966/1978), (1971), ["Symposium"] (1972), (1981); ● ● ● **Coover (1980); Dahlhaus et al. (1987);** David (1956); Dolmetsch (1915/. . ./1969); Donington (1963/ . . ./1974), (1980); Dreyfus (1987); Duchez (1979); Eitner (1900-1904/1959-60); Eggebrecht (1955); Fellerer (1983); Fischer (1978); Forkel (1792/1962); Frobenius ["Cantus"] (1972-); Gerber (1790-92/1977), (1812-14/1966); Green (1969); Gut (1972-); Harrán (1986); Hawkins (1776/. . ./1969); Hoshino (1979); Houle (1960), (1987); Irving (1986); Jackson (1988); Jacobi (1957-60/1971); Jones (1934); Kassler (1979); Katz (1926); Kauko (1958); Kirkendale (1979); Kramer (1978); La Borde (1780/1978); Lang (1941); Lange (1899-1900); Launay (1982); **Lester** (1977), **(1989); Lindley** ["Temperaments"] **(1980);** Mahlert and Sunter (1972-); Maier (1984); Mann (1955/ . . ./1987); McIntyre (1965); Mendel (1978); Müller-Blattau (1923/. . ./1963); **Neumann,** Frederick (1978), (1981/**1982**); Newman (1985); Newman (1959/. . ./1983), (1963/. . ./1983); O'Donnell (1979); Ratner (1970), (1980); Reckow (1972-); Reimer ["Concerto"] (1972-), ["Kammermusik"] (1972-); **Ritzel (1967/1968);** Rothschild (1953) ; Sachs (1972-); Schmalzriedt ["Coda"] (1972-), ["Reprise"] (1972-), ["Subiectum"] (1972-); Seidel (1972-); **Seidel and Cooper (1986); Shirlaw (1917/. . ./1970);** Sisman (1978); Subirá (1947/ . . ./1958); Taddie (1984); Tenney (1988); Tolkoff (1973); Walker (1987); Wienpahl (1953); Williams, P. (1970), (1979); Wolff (1972-); **Zaminer (1985).**

(JOSEPH) ANTON BRUCKNER

[1824–1896]

The long period of theoretical education which Anton Bruckner completed during the 1840s and 50s led to a thorough grounding in a conservative nineteenth-century tradition. His interactions with Johann August Dürrnberger (author of *Elementar-Lehrbuch der Harmonie- und Generalbaß-Lehre*, 1841) and correspondence with SECHTER fostered a rigor which well matched his personality and in-troduced him to some notions of harmonic and contrapuntal procedures which became lifelong preoccupations of his teaching. Unfortunately, few bridges can be built to connect the scattered legacy of student notes taken during his lectures at the Vienna Conservatory and University to his monumental symphonic and choral works. It appears that he never discussed his own music (other than to excoriate his critics) during lecture hours, probably in part because the theory doled out to beginning students had little to do with the full-blown richness of his own compositional style.

The careful piecing together of whatever remnants of Bruckner's lectures could be gathered has resulted in a substantial and more or less consistent body of harmonic theory of an elementary nature. It is not at all speculative and largely derivative of SECHTER. An innovation was the acceptance of the ninth chord as a fundamental harmony; a retrogression (in the eyes of many present-day scholars) was the crystallization of the 6/4-position chord before the cadential dominant as a representative of the tonic's fundamental. Though the system holds little utility today for any insight into music of the nineteenth century, it is of considerable historical interest as a link between SECHTER's theory and the new modes of thought developed a few decades later by another radical Viennese composer, Arnold SCHOENBERG.

Teaching Materials Concerning Music Theory

> Mss. [Vienna: Österreichische Nationalbibliothek, Musiksammlung; New York: New York Public Library.]

S ● Schwanzara, Ernst, ed. *Vorlesungen über Harmonielehre und Kontrapunkt an der Universität Wien*. Vienna: Österreichischer Bundesverlag für Unterricht, Wissenschaft und Kunst, 1950. Bibliog.

> Derived from Bruckner's lectures of 1891-94. Reviews in *Mf* 6/3 (1953):286 (Hermann Erpf), and *MusN* 43/4 (1951):22.

S ● Eckstein, Friedrich. Manuscripts concerning Bruckner. [Vienna: Österreichische Nationalbibliothek, Musiksammlung.]

> Includes "6 Notenhefte zum Theorieunterricht bei Anton Bruckner," "Anton Bruckner System der Musiktheorie," "Universitäts Vorlesungen und Nachträge zur Harmonielehre/Notizen zum doppelten Kontrapunkt," "Studien über Harmonielehre, gemacht bei Anton Bruckner. 5 Notenhefte," and "Anton Bruckners Universitäts Vorlesungen über Harmonie-Lehre, gehalten 1884-86 zu Wien."

LITERATURE:

Decsey, E. "Anton Bruckner als Lehrer der Sechterschen Theorie: Erinnerungen und Beiträge." *Musik* 6/22 (1906-7):191-204.

> Contains "Die Lehre Sechters im Unterricht bei Bruckner," pp. 27-93.

Decsey, Ernst. *Bruckner, Versuch eines Lebens*. Berlin: Schuster & Löffler, [1919].

Eckstein, Friedrich. *Erinnerungen an Anton Bruckner*. Vienna: Universal-Edition, 1923.

Klose, Friedrich. *Meine Lehrjahre bei Bruckner: Erinnerungen und Betrachtungen*. DMb, no. 61. Regensburg: Gustav Boße Verlag, 1927.

Stefan, Paul. "Pupils of Bruckner Preserve the Composer's Theory." *MAm* 59/18 (1939):38.

Orel, Alfred. *Ein Harmonielehrekolleg bei Anton Bruckner*. WMb, no. 1. Berlin: Verlag für Wirtschaft und Kultur (Payer), 1940.

Blume, Friedrich. "Bruckner, Josef Anton." In *MGG* (1949-68). Bibliog.

Schwanzara, Ernst. "Anton Bruckner als Lektor für Harmonielehre und Kontrapunkt an der Universität in Wien." *Me* 3/1 (1949-50):7-11.

Schwanzara, Ernst. "Anton Bruckner und die reine Stimmung." *ÖM* 4/9 (1949):260-63.

Waters, Edward N. "Variations on a Theme: Recent Acquisitions of the Music Division." *LCQJ* 27/1 (1970):51-83. [*Rilm* 70-53.]

Fiechtner, H. A. "Anton Bruckner als Lehrer." *ÖM* 6/4-5 (1951):130-32; reprinted in *MiU* 42 (1951):215-16.

Bieri, Georg. "Bruckner als Lehrer für Musiktheorie." *SmpB* 43/4 (1956):164-74.

Newlin, Dika. "Bruckner the Teacher." *CD* 2/9 (1960):35-38.

Grasberger, Franz, ed. *Bruckner-Studien: Leopold Nowak zum 60. Geburtstag*. Vienna: Musikwissenschaftlicher Verlag, 1964.

> Includes "Bruckners musikalischer Ausbildungsgang," pp. 105-11 (Ernst Tittel) and "Bruckner als Lehrer," pp. 113-20 (Wilhelm Waldstein).

Nowak, Leopold. "Ein Doppelautograph Sechter-Bruckner." In *FederhoferFs* (1971):252-59. [*Rilm* 73-638.]

Wessely, Othmar, ed. *Bruckner-Studien: Festgabe der Österreichischen Akademie der Wissenschaften zum 150. Geburtstag von Anton Bruckner*. VdKfM, no. 16. Vienna: Verlag der Österreichischen Akademie der Wissenschaften, 1975.

> Includes "Rafael Loidols Theoriekolleg bei Bruckner 1879/80, " pp. 379-431 (Rudolf Flotzinger) and " 'Die ganzen Studien': Zu Josef Vockners Theorieunterricht bei Anton Bruckner," pp. 349-77 (Erich Schenk and Gernot Gruber). Reviews in *Me* 29/4 (1976):190-91, *Mf* 31/3 (1978):338-39 (Walter Wiora), *ML* 57/2 (1976):192-95 (Richard Evidon), *Nrmi* 11/3 (1977):493-96 (Vito Levi), *ÖM* 31/3 (1976):178-79 (Friedrich C. Heller), and *Orch* 24/4 (1976):272-73 (Kurt Westphal).

Anton Bruckner in Lehre und Forschung: Symposion zu Bruckners 150. Geburtstag, Linz a. d. Donau, September 1974. VAMÖ, no. 7. Regensburg: Gustav Boße, 1976.

> Includes "Bruckner als Theorielehrer an der Universität," pp. 39-46 (Rudolf Flotzinger) and "Anton Bruckner als Didaktiker: Zur Problem

der Lehrbarkeit in der Kunst," pp. 79-91 (Josef Sulz). Reviews in *Mf* 30/4 (1977):525 (Manfred Wagner) and *Musica* 31/2 (1977):164-65 (Karl Grebe).

Cooke, Deryck, and Nowak, Leopold. "Bruckner, (Joseph) Anton." In *NGrove* (1980). Bibliog.

Maier, Elisabeth, and Zamazal, Franz. *Anton Bruckner und Leopold von Zenetti*. ABDS, no. 3. Graz: Akademische Druck- und Verlagsanstalt, 1980. [*Rilm* 80-752.]

Kirsch, Winfried. "Die Bruckner-Forschung seit 1945: Eine kommentierte Bibliographie." *Am* 53/2 (1981):157-70; 54/1-2 (1982):208-61; 55/2 (1983):201-44; 56/1 (1984):1-29. Bibliog.

Grasberger, Renate. *Bruckner-Bibliographie (bis 1974)*. ABDS, no. 4. Graz, Austria: Akademische Druck- und Verlagsanstalt, 1985. Bibliog.

Reviews in *Me* 40/1 (1986-87):43 (Herwig Knaus), *Mf* 40/4 (1987):373-76 (Isolde Vetter), *ML* 69/1 (1988):95 (Paul Banks), and *ÖM* 41/12 (1986):674-75.

Nowak, Leopold. *Über Anton Bruckner: Gesammelte Aufsätze 1936-1984*. Vienna: Musikwissenschaftlicher Verlag, 1985.

Reviews in *Me* 38/5 (1984-85):230 (Herwig Knaus), *Me* 40/2 (1986-87):85 (Gerold W. Gruber), *NZfM* 146/9 (1985):58-59 (Manfred Wagner), and *ÖM* 40/10 (1985):560 (Manfred Wagner).

See also HALM: [1914]; KURTH: (1925); LITERATURE SUPPLEMENT: Auhagen (1982/1983); **Dahlhaus (1984)**; Kerman (1980-81); Mann (1987); Neumann (1939); Parncutt (1988-89); Smith (1974); Tittel (1959), (1966); Vogel (1976); **Wason ● ● ● (1981/ 1985)**, (1983), (1988); **Zaminer (1985)**.

JOACHIM BURMEISTER

[1564–1629]

Joachim Burmeister's *Hypomnematum musicae poeticae synopsis* (1599) and its two revisions (1601 and 1606) inaugurated a new and important direction for theoretical inquiry, one in which the relationship between rhetoric and music was treated systematically. Though the numerous terms which Burmeister borrowed from rhetorical theory (mainly from Lucas Lossius's *Erotemata dialecticae et rhetoricae Philippi Melanchtonis* of 1562) do not always seem to fit their new musical connotations, the very fact that a musical device (such as a suspension, melodic sequence, or repeated pattern) is given a rhetorical name reinforces the association which Burmeister was attempting to draw. Numerous musical examples, particularly from the work of Lassus, were included, especially in *Musica αυτοσχεδιαστικη*. By 1606 a list of twenty-seven rhetorical devices had been assembled. In an unprecedented and not soon surpassed example of analysis, Burmeister used the motet *In me transierunt* of Lassus to demonstrate the typical division into three segments (introduction, body, and conclusion) and to exemplify a variety of rhetorical devices. The use of rhetorical figures was regarded as a means for more powerfully expressing the meaning of the text and thus responded to a central aesthetic concern of the era.

Burmeister understood that the most useful sounds of polyphony fell into four basic groups: those with a perfect fifth and minor third, a perfect fifth and major third, a minor sixth and minor third, and a major sixth and major third above the bass. He did not, however, make an association between a six-three chord and a five-three chord with bass a third lower.

Hypomnematum musicae poeticae . . . synopsis [*Rism* B/VI/1, p. 189.]

Rostock: Stephan Myliander, 1599. [IDC.]

Musica αυτοσχεδιαστικη, quae per aliquot accessiones in gratiam philomusorum quorundam ad tractatum de hypomnematibus musicae poëticae ejusdem auctoris σποραδην quondam exaratas, in unum corpusculum concrevit, in quâ redditur ratio [*Rism* B/VI/1, p. 189.]

Derived from *Hypomnematum musicae poeticae . . . synopsis*, above.

Rostock: Christoph Reusner, 1601. [LCPS: B-154. IDC.]

Musicae practicae sive artis canendi ratio [*Rism* B/VI/1, p. 189.]

A segment of *Musica αυτοσχεδιαστικη*, above.

Rostock: 1601. [IDC.]

Musica poetica . . . [*Rism* B/VI/1, p. 190.]

Derived from *Musica αυτοσχεδιαστικη*, above.

Rostock: Stephan Myliander, 1606. [LCPS: B-155.]

41

S ● Ruhnke, Martin, ed. Facsimile edition. IGMDm, ser. 1, no. 10. Kassel: Bärenreiter, 1955.

> Reviews in *JAMS* 9/1 (1956):40-46 (A. Tillman Merritt), *Mf* 9/2 (1956):227-29 (Carl Dahlhaus), and *ML* 37/1 (1956):88 (Eric Blom).

T ● See ● ● ● Palisca [*"Ut oratoria musica"*] (1972).

> Contains a translation of and commentary on Burmeister's analysis of the Lassus motet *In me transierunt*.

T ● Rivera, Benito V., trans. MTTS. New Haven, Ct.: Yale University Press, forthcoming.

Musica theorica Henrici Brucaei [*Rism* B/VI/1, p. 183.]

> Edited by Burmeister.

> Rostock: Reusner, 1609.

LITERATURE:

Blume, Friedrich. "Burmeister, Joachim." In *MGG* (1949-68). Bibliog.

Wille, Günther. "Quintilian." In *MGG* (1949-68).

Ruhnke, Martin. "Das musiktheoretische Werk des Magisters Joachim Burmeister." Ph.D. dissertation, The University of Kiel, 1954; published edition (as *Joachim Burmeister: Ein Beitrag zur Musiklehre um 1600*, SLMfK, no. 5), Kassel: Bärenreiter, 1955.

> Reviews in *Mf* 9/2 (1956):227-29 (Carl Dahlhaus), *Notes* 13/3 (1955-56):437-38 (Egon F. Kenton), and *Rdm* 38/2 (1956):184-86 (Simone Wallon).

● ● ● Ruhnke, Martin. "Burmeister, Joachim." In *NGrove* (1980).

See also DRESSLER: Luther (1936/1942); FÉTIS: (1833-44); KEPLER: Dickreiter (1971/1973); LIPPIUS: Rivera (1974/1980); SCHENKER: Morgan (1978); VIADANA: Haack (1964/1974); WALTHER: (1732); LITERATURE SUPPLEMENT: ● ● ● **Apfel (1981)**; Atcherson (1960); Audbourg-Popin (1984); Auhagen (1982/1983); Bartel (1982/1985); Beck (1973), (1974); Becker (1836-39/1964); Beebe (1976); **Bent** ["Analysis"] **(1980/1987)**; Boetticher (1954); Brandes (1935); **Buelow** (1972), ["Figures"] **(1980)**, ["Rhetoric"] (1980); Butler (1977), (1980); Cahn ["Transitus"] (1972-); Cohen (1981); Crane (1960); Dahlhaus ["Untersuchungen"] (1966/. . ./1988), (1986); Dammann (1958/1967); Derksen (1982); Dunsby and Whittall (1988); Eggebrecht (1959); Eitner (1900-1904/1959-60); Federhofer (1985); Feldmann (1958); Fellerer (1983); Flindell (1983-84); Forchert (1986); Forkel (1792/1962); Frobenius ["Homophonus"] (1972-); Gerber (1812-14/1966); Gissel (1980/1983), (1986); Gurlitt (1942/1966), (1944/ 1966); Harrán (1986); Horsley ["Fugue and Mode"] (1966/1978); Hüschen (1986); Kirkendale (1979), (1984); Kleinman (1971/1974); Krützfeldt (1961); Krummacher (1986); Kunze (1979-83); Lange (1899-1900); **Lester** (1974), (1977), **(1989)**; Leuchtmann (1957/1959); Lindley (1982); Luoma (1977); Mahlert and Sunter (1972-); **Maniates (1979)**; Meier (1963/1988), (1974); Niemöller (1964/1969); Palisca (1959) [*Baroque*] (1968/1981), ● ● ● (1974/1977), ["Theory"] (1980); Pietzsch (1936-42/1971); **Powers** (1974), ["Language"] (1980), ["Mode"] **(1980)**; Preußner (1924), (1939); Rauhe (1959-60); Rivera (1978); Ruhnke (1949-68), (1973), (1974); Sachs (1972-); Schmalzriedt ["Coda"] (1972-); Schmitt (1974-75); Schmitz (1950); Stoll (1978/1981); Taddie (1984); Unger (1941/1969); Walker (1987); Williams (1979); Wiora (1962); Ziebler (1933).

CHARLES BUTLER

[ca. 1560–1647]

Charles Butler, an amateur musician knowledgeable in the history, theory, and performance of music, published *The Principles of Musik* (1636), a thorough, scholarly textbook codifying earlier practice. Butler was an English priest who had received an education in general history, philosophy, languages, and literature at Oxford. Treatises on beekeeping and the English language were among his projects. His orthography includes some characters which never attained general acceptance. Many were incorporated within the *Principles*.

Much of the musical substance of Butler's treatise was garnered from Boethius, GLAREAN, CALVISIUS, and MORLEY. Each section contains annotations as well as notes upon these annotations. Butler drew a distinction between major and minor modes and suggested that the fourth be classified as a secondary concord, similar to the minor third and both sixths. The continued use of the hexachord was endorsed. Butler also included materials on dissonance treatment and information on invertible counterpoint, as well as examples of 4-3, 2-3, 7-6, 7-8, and 9-8 suspensions.

The Principles of Musik, in Singing and Setting: With the Two-fold Use Thereof, Ecclesiasticall and Civil [*Rism* B/VI/1, p. 194.]

> In Latin and Butler's "phonetic" script.

London: the author (John Haviland), 1636. [LCPS: B-163. HoM: 290. SMLMS.]

S ● Facsimile edition. EE, no. 284. Amsterdam: Theatrum Orbis Terrarum, 1970; with a Preface by Gilbert Reaney (DCPMRS), New York: Da Capo, 1970.

Reviews in *ML* 52/2 (1971):207-8 (Jack A. Westrup) and *MT* 112/1537 (1971):241 (Ian Spink).

T ● Smith, Arthur Timothy. "Charles Butler's *The Principles of Music in Singing and Setting, with the Twofold Use Thereof, Ecclesiastical and Civil* (1636): A Computer-Assisted Transliteration of Book I and the First Chapter of Book II, with Introduction, Supplementary Notes, Commentary, and Appendices." Ph.D. dissertation, The Ohio State University, 1974. [*DA* 35/08A, p. 5453. UMI 75-03198.]

LITERATURE:

Pruett, James W. "Butler, Charles." Translated by Thomas M. Höpfner. In *MGG* (1949-68): Supplement (1973-79). Bibliog.

● ● ● Pruett, James. "Charles Butler—Musician, Grammarian, Apiarist." *MQ* 49/4 (1963):498-509.

Baker, David, and Baker, Jennifer. "A 17th-Century Dial-Song." *MT* 119/1625 (1978):590-93. [*Rilm* 78-2610.]

Pruett, James W. "Butler, Charles." In *NGrove* (1980). Bibliog.

See also FÉTIS: (1833-44); WALTHER: (1732); LITERATURE SUPPLEMENT: Abraham (1968/1969); Allen ["Philosophies"] (1939); **Apfel (1981)**; Atcherson (1972); Becker (1836-39/1964); **Buelow** ["Rhetoric"] **(1980)**; Burke (1963); Burney (1776-89/. . ./1957); Burton (1956); Butler (1977), (1980); Carpenter (1955); ● ● ● Chenette (1967); Colles (1928-29); Collins (1963); **Dahlhaus et al. (1987)**; Donington (1963/. . ./1974); Eitner (1900-1904/1959-60); Forkel (1792/1962); Gerber (1812-14/1966); Gouk (1980); Grashel (1981); Hancock (1977); Hannas (1934); Hawkins (1776/. . ./1969); Henderson (1969); Houle (1960), (1987); Jackson (1988); **Kassler (1979)**, (1983-85); Kassler and Oldroyd (1983); Lange (1899-1900); Lawrence (1978); Lewis (1981); Miller (1960); Rogers (1955); Ruf (1972-); Ruff (1970); **Seidel and Cooper (1986)**; Shute (1972); Taddie (1984).

JOHANN HEINRICH BUTTSTETT

[1666–1727]

When the young Johann MATTHESON completed *Das neu-eröffnete Orchestre* (1713), his first published work on theory, he must have realized that within the German lands there resided numerous musicians who would not appreciate his cosmopolitan, modern, and secular attitude towards music. Johann Heinrich Buttstett, fifteen years MATTHESON's senior and an adherent of WERCKMEISTER's theological-theoretical system, was one such musician, and a vocal one: his *Ut, mi, sol, re, fa, la, tota musica et harmonia aeterna*, published within a few years of the *Orchestre*, took MATTHESON to task on almost every issue that was raised, and at the same time advocated a return to centuries-old traditions regarding the church modes and Guidonian solmization. Yet MATTHESON ably met this challenge, in *Das beschützte Orchestre* (1717), wherein his superior intellectual capabilities and more realistic perception of contemporary practices served him well in countering Buttstett's assault. Buttstett continued the dispute with *Der wieder das beschützte Orchestre ergangenen öffentlichen Erklärung* (1718), while MATTHESON went on to become one of the era's most thorough and eloquent musical spokesmen.

*Ut, mi, sol, re, fa, la, tota musica et harmonia aeterna; oder, Neu-eröffnetes, altes, wahres, eintziges und ewiges Funda-*mentum musices, entgegen gesetzt dem neu-eröffneten Orchestre . . . [*Rism* B/VI/1, pp. 194-95.]

Erfurt: Otto Friedrich Werther; Leipzig: Johann Herbord Kloß, [ca. 1715-17]. [LCPS: B-164. HoM: 291. SMLMS.]

Der wieder [sic] das beschützte Orchestre ergangenen öffentlichen Erklärung . . . [*Rism* B/VI/1, p. 195.]

[Erfurt: 1718.] [Lost.]
[Erfurt: 1718.] 2nd edition. [LCPS: B-165.]

LITERATURE:

Ziller, Ernst. "Johann Heinrich Buttstädt (1666-1727)." Ph.D. dissertation, The University of Halle, 1934; published edition, Halle/Saale: Buchdruckerei der Hallischen Nachrichten, 1934; as *Der Erfurter Organist Johann Heinrich Buttstädt [1666-1727]*, (BzMf, no. 3), Halle/Saale and Berlin: Buchhandlung des Waisenhauses G.m.b.H., 1935; reprint edition, Hildesheim: Georg Olms, 1971.

Blume, Friedrich. "Buttstett, Johann Heinrich." In *MGG* (1949-68). Bibliog.

Blankenburg, Walter. "Der Titel und das Titelbild von Johann Heinrich Buttstedts Schrift *Ut, mi, sol, re, fa, la—tota musica et harmonia aeterna oder Neueröffnetes altes, wahres, einziges und ewiges Fundamentum musices* (1717)." *Mf* 3/1 (1950):64-66.

Blankenburg, Walter. "Zum Titelbild von Johann Heinrich Buttstedts Schrift *Ut-mi-sol-re-fa-la, tota musica et harmonia aeterna* (1716)." In *SieversFs* (1978):21-28. [*Rilm* 78-4840.]

Buelow, George J. "Buttstett, Johann Heinrich." In *NGrove* (1980). Bibliog.

See also FÉTIS: (1833-44); KEPLER: Dickreiter (1971/1973); LIPPIUS: Rivera (1974/1980); MATTHESON: (1717); (1722-25):(1725); Meinardus (1879); Cannon (1947/1968); Buelow and Marx (1983): Pa-lisca; WALTHER: (1732); LITERATURE SUPPLEMENT: Auhagen (1982/1983); Becker (1836-39/1964); **Benary (1956/1961)**; Blankenburg ["Harmonie"] (1959); Dammann (1958/ 1967); Duparcq (1977); Eitner (1900-1904/1959-60); Forkel (1792/1962); Gerber (1812-14/1966); Henderson (1969); Hiller (1768-69); Katz (1926); Kleinman (1971/1974); Krummacher (1979); Lange (1899-1900); **Lester** (1977), (1978), **(1989)**; Neumann, Frederick (1978); Reimer ["Kammermusik"] (1972-); Ruhnke (1949-68); Seidel (1972-); Schenkman (1976); Sheldon (1975); Schünemann (1928/1931); Walker (1987); Wessely (1967).

GIULIO CACCINI

[ca. 1545–1618]

Giulio Caccini, called Giulio Romano, was a prominent member of Bardi's Camerata in Florence and later served as music director at the Medici court. To preserve the novel madrigals and airs which he had composed according to the Camerata's Neoplatonic ideals, Caccini assembled *Le nuove musiche* (1601). The preface to this important collection of solo songs contains an early defense of the monodic style, an explanation of vocal ornamentation, and a description of the emerging continuo practice. The music itself abounds with simple and compound figures above the bass and well represents the monodic writing of the period.

Le nuove musiche [*Rism* A/I/2, p. 1; B/VI/1, p. 196.]

> Florence: Marescotti, 1601 [Colophon: 1602].
> [LCPS: C-002.]
> Venice: Raverii, 1607.
> Venice: Vincenti, 1615.

T ● See PLAYFORD: (1654/. . ./1730):4th through 12th editions (1664-94).

> Erroneously attributed to an Englishman under the following or a similar title: "A Brief Discourse of, and Directions for Singing after the Italian Manner: Wherein is set down those Excellent Graces in Singing now used by the Italians: Written some time since by an English Gentleman who lived many years in Italy, and Taught the same here in England; intending to publish the same, but prevented by Death." The translation is incomplete and defective.

T ● Kiesewetter, Raphael Georg. *Schicksale und Beschaffenheit des weltlichen Gesanges vom frühen Mittelalter bis zu der Erfindung des dramatischen Styles und den Anfängen der Oper.* Leipzig: Breitkopf & Härtel, 1841; reprint edition, Osnabrück: Biblio-Verlag, 1970.

> Contains "Beilage. Die Gesanglehre von Giulio Caccini, genannt Romano, vom Jahre 1601. Ein Auszug aus der Vorrede desselben zu den *Nuove musiche*," pp. 61-66. Translation (incomplete) into German.

T ● GEVAERT, François-Auguste, trans. "L'art du chant vers 1600: Préface de *Nuove musiche* de Caccini." *Mén* 40/7, 8, 9 (1873-74):53-54, 59-60, 66-67.

ST ● See Goldschmidt (1890/1892):14-22.

> The text of the preface and a translation into German.

S ● Solerti, Angelo. *Le origini del melodramma: Testimonianze dei contemporanei.* Pbsm, no. 70. Turin: Bocca, 1903; reprint edition (BmB, ser. 3, no. 3), Bologna: Forni, 1969; reprint edition (Pbsm, no. 70), Hildesheim: Georg Olms, 1969.

T ● See Dolmetsch (1915/. . ./1969):2-3.

> Extracts from the translation printed by PLAYFORD, above.

S ● Mantica, Francesco, ed., with Giorgio Barini. Facsimile of the 1601 edition. Pfmi, no. 2. Rome: Raccolte Claudio Monteverdi, 1930.

> Review in *Rmi* 38/3 (1931):462-63 (L. R.).

S ● Vatielli, Francesco, ed. Facsimile of the 1601 edition. Rome: Reale accademia d'Italia, 1934.

T ● See **Strunk (1950)**:377-92.

> Adapted from the translation printed by PLAYFORD, above.

S ● Maragliano Mori, Rachele, ed. *I maestri del bel canto: La prefazione alle "Nuove musiche" di Giulio Caccini (1550-1615) . . . riduzione in lingua moderna.* Rome: De Santis, 1953.

T ● Newton, George, trans. "*Le nuove musiche*—Caccini: A New Translation of the Preface Made from the Facsimile Reprint of the First Edition, Firenze, 1601." *NATSB* 19/2 (1962-63):14-18.

T ● ● ● ● Hitchcock, H. Wiley, trans. and ed. *Le nuove musiche.* RRMBE, no. 9. Madison, Wisc.: A-R Editions, 1970. Bibliog. [*Rilm* 70-1666.]

> Reviews in *JAMS* 25/3 (1972):483-86 (William V. Porter) and *Notes* 28/4 (1971-72):757-58 (Howard E. Smither).

S ● Facsimile of the 1601 edition. MMMLF, ser. 1, no. 29. New York: Broude Brothers, 1973.

T ● See Rowen (1979).

LITERATURE:

Ehrichs, Alfred. "Giulio Caccini." Ph.D. dissertation, The University of Leipzig, 1908.

Schmitz, Eugen. "Caccinis *Nuove musiche*." *BHKM* 15/6 (1910-11):91-95.

Ghisi, Federico. "Caccini, Giulio." Translated by Anna Amalie Abert. In *MGG* (1949-68). Bibliog.

Maze, Nancy. "Tenbury Ms. 1018: A Key to Caccini's Art of Embellishment." *JAMS* 9/1 (1956):61-63.

Feller, Marilyn. "The New Style of Giulio Caccini, Member of the Florentine Camerata." In *Bericht Köln 1958* (1959):102-4.

Spink, Ian. "Playford's 'Directions for Singing after the Italian Manner'." *MMR* 89/994 (1959):130-35.

Feerst, Robin Nan. "*Le nuove musiche* by Giulio Caccini: Musical Analysis and Historical Significance." Master's thesis, Hunter College, 1967.

Galliver, David. " 'Favolare in armonia' — A Speculation into Aspects of 17th-Century Singing." *Miscm* 4 (1969):128-46. [*Rilm* 69-834.]

Anfuso, Nella, and Gianuario, Annibale. *La problematica delle alterazioni nelle "Nuove musiche" di Giulio Caccini*. CsrmF, no. 2. Florence: OTOS, 1970.

Hitchcock, H. Wiley. "Vocal Ornamentation in Caccini's *Nuove musiche*." *MQ* 56/3 (1970):389-404; reprinted in Rosand (1985):Vol. 5, pp. 131-46. [*Rilm* 70-1697.]

Stark, James Arthur. "The Rise of Virtuoso Singing." Ph.D. dissertation, The University of Toronto, 1973. [*Rilm* 75-2352.]

Galliver, David. "Vocal Colour in Singing in Seventeenth-Century Italy: The Contribution of Caccini." In *Congress Copenhagen 1972* (1974):385-88.

MacClintock, Carol. "Caccini's *Trillo* — A Re-examination." *NATSB* 33/1 (1976-77):38-44.

Galliver, David. "Giulio Caccini — *per canto famoso*." *Miscm* 10 (1979):38-46. [*Rilm* 79-4588.]

Galliver, David. "The Vocal Technique of Caccini." In *Convegni rinascimento 1976* (1979):7-12.

● ● ● Hitchcock, H. Wiley. "Caccini, Giulio." In *NGrove* (1980). Bibliog.

● ● ● Brown, Howard Mayer. "The Geography of Florentine Monody: Caccini at Home and Abroad." *EM* 9/2 (1981):147-68. Bibliog. [*Rilm* 81-396.]

Willier, Stephen. "Rhythmic Variants in Early Manuscript Versions of Caccini's Monodies." *JAMS* 36/3 (1983):481-97.

Carter, Tim. "On the Composition and Performance of Caccini's *Le nuove musiche*." *EM* 12/2 (1984):208-17.

Szweykowski, Zygmunt M. "Giulio Caccini wobec teorii Cameraty Florenckiej." *Muzyka* 31/1 [120] (1986):51-65.

See also FÉTIS: (1833-44); GALILEI: Fano (1934); MONTEVERDI: Schrade (1950/. . ./1981); Anfuso and Gianuario [1971]; Fabbri (1985); RIEMANN: (1898); VIADANA: Haack (1964/1974); WALTHER: (1732); LITERATURE SUPPLEMENT: Abraham (1968/1969); Arnold (1957); Arnold (1931/. . ./1965); Babitz (1952), (1967/1969); Badura-Skoda et al. (1980); ● ● ● Baron (1968); Beyschlag (1907/1953); Borgir (1971/1987); Brown (1976); Brown and McKinnon (1980); Burney (1776-89/. . ./1957); Cahn ["Transitus"] (1972-); Cohen (1984); Colles (1928-29); Crocker (1966); Dahlhaus ["Untersuchungen"] (1966/. . ./1988), (1986); Dammann (1958/1967); Dolmetsch (1915/. . ./1969); Donà (1967); Donington (1963/. . ./1974), (1980); Eitner (1900-1904/1959-60); Fellerer ["Wesen"] (1982), (1983); Ferand (1937/1938), [*Improvisation*] (1956/1961); Frobenius ["Monodie"] (1972-); Geering (1949-68); Gerber (1790-92/1977), (1812-14/1966); Goldschmidt (1890/1892), (1901-4/1967); (1907); Haar (1986); Hanning (1969/1980); Hawkins (1776/. . ./1969); Hill (1983); Horsley (1963); Houle (1960), (1987); Jackson (1988); Kahl (1953); Katz (1985); Kauko (1958); Kinkeldey (1910/1968); Kirkendale (1979); Koenigsberger (1979); Kivy (1980); Kooiman (1981); Kuhn (1902); La Fage (1864/1964); Lang (1941); Lawrence (1978); **Lindley** (1982), **(1984)**; **Maniates (1979)**; Martin (1932-33); Neumann, Frederick (1978), [*Essays*] (1982), (1988); Newman (1985); North (1987); Norton (1984); Oberdörffer (1949-68); Pacchioni (1983); **Palisca** (1959), ["Alterati"] (1968), ["Artusi-Monteverdi"] (1968/1985), [*Baroque*] (1968/1981), ["Rezitativ"] (1972-), ["Camerata"] (1972), (1979), ["Camerata"] (1980), ["Theory"] **(1980)**, **(1985)**, [*Florentine*] (1989); Pirrotta (1953/. . ./1984); Reese (1954/1959); Robison (1982); Schavernoch (1981); Schneider (1917/. . ./1971); Schulenberg (1984); Seidel (1976); **Seidel and Cooper (1986)**; Solerti (1903/. . ./1969); Subirá (1947/. . ./1958); Szweykowski (1985); Tenney (1988); Troeger (1987); Wichmann (1966); Wienpahl (1953); Williams, P. (1970); Wolff (1972-); Yeston (1975).

SETHUS CALVISIUS

[1556–1615]

The transmission of ZARLINO's theory was a critical step in the development of a *musica poetica* tradition in the German lands. Sethus Calvisius took what was most practical in ZARLINO's *Istitutioni harmoniche* (1558) and, with some additions and modifications, forged Μελοποιια, which may have appeared as early as 1582. Included among its progressive features was a comparison between the segmentations which occur in a musical work and the punctuation points of poetry. Calvisius also formulated the first summary of the history of music theory ["De initio et progressu musices" in *Exercitationes musicae duae* (1600)] and championed and defended a system of solmization, attributed to Hubert Waelrant, in which the syllables *bo ce di ga lo ma ni* were utilized. In England Calvisius was a major source for the absorption of ZARLINO's ideas, as can be verified by examining the theoretical writings of BUTLER and Thomas CAMPION.

Correspondence with KEPLER

      See KEPLER: Collected Works: von Dyck et al., Vols. 15, 16, 18.

Μελοποιια [*Melopoiia*] *sive melodiae condendae ratio, quam volgo musicam poeticam vocant* . . . [*Rism* B/VI/1, pp. 122 and 198.]

      A 1582 edition might have existed. The first extant edition:

  Erfurt: Georg Baumann, 1592.

      Edited by Heinrich GRIMM, with BARYPHONUS's *Pleiades musicae*:

  Magdeburg: haeredes Johann. Franc., 1630.

  ST ● Benndorf, Kurt. "Calvisiana." *MMg* 33/6 (1901):85-93.

Compendium musicae [*practicae*] *pro incipientibus conscriptum* [*Rism* B/VI/1, p. 198.]

  [Leipzig: Voigt, 1594.] [Lost.]
  Leipzig: Franz Schnellboltz Erben (Bartholomaeus Voigt), 1602.

Exercitationes musicae duae: Quarum prior est, de modis musicis, quos vulgò tonos vocant, rectè cognoscendis, & dijudicandis; Posterior, de initio et progressu musices, aliis quibusdam ad eam rem spectantibus [*Rism* B/VI/1, p. 198.]

  Leipzig: Jacob Apel, 1600. [LCPS: C-007.]

  S ● Facsimile edition. Hildesheim: Georg Olms, 1973.

Exercitatio musica tertia . . . De praecipuis quibusdam in arte musicâ quaestionibus, quibus praecipua ejus theoremata continentur [*Rism* B/VI/1, p. 198.]

  Leipzig: Thomas Schürer (Michael Lantzenberger), 1611. [LCPS: C-008.]

  S ● Facsimile edition. Hildesheim: Georg Olms, 1973.

Musicae artis praecepta nova et facilima . . . [*Rism* B/VI/p. 198.]

      Derived from *Compendium musicae*, above.

  Jena: Weidner, 1612. [IDC.]

LITERATURE:

Benndorf, Kurt. "Sethus Calvisius als Musiktheoretiker." Ph.D. dissertation, The University of Leipzig, 1894 (1895); published edition, in *VMw* 10 (1894):411-70; published separately, Leipzig: Breitkopf & Härtel, 1894.

Pietzsch, Gerhard. "Seth Calvisius und Johannes Kepler: Ein Beitrag zur Musikanschauung in Deutschland um 1600." *Mp* 1 (1930-31):388-96.

Riemer, Otto. "Seth Calvisius, der Musiker und Pädagoge." *Mp* 3 (1932-33):449-55.

Adrio, Adam. "Calvisius, Sethus." In *MGG* (1949-68).

Dahlhaus, Carl. "Musiktheoretisches aus dem Nachlaß des Sethus Calvisius." *Mf* 9/2 (1956):129-39.

● ● ● Adrio, Adam. "Calvisius, Sethus." In *NGrove* (1980). Bibliog.

Rivera, Benito V. "Zarlino's Approach to Counterpoint Modified and Transmitted by Seth Calvisius." *Theoria* 4 (1989).

Wilkinson, Cathryn. "Seth Calvisius: A Rising Star in Seventeenth-Century German Theory." Ph.D. dissertation, The University of Iowa, forthcoming.

See also BURMEISTER: Ruhnke (1955); CRÜGER: Fischer-Krückeberg (1929-30); DRESSLER: Luther (1941); FÉTIS: (1833-44); HERBST: (1643); Allerup (1931); KEPLER: Dickreiter (1971/1973); KOCH: Dahlhaus (1978); LIPPIUS: Rivera (1974/1980); MATTHESON: (1721); (1740); MERSENNE: (1617-48); MORLEY: Stevenson (1952); RIEMANN: (1898); WALTHER: (1732); Gehrmann (1891); LITERATURE SUPPLEMENT: Allen ["Baroque"] (1939), ["Philosophies"] (1939); **Apfel (1981)**; Atcherson (1960); Bartel (1982/1985); Becker (1836-39/1964); Beiche ["Dux"] (1972-), ["Inversio"] (1972-); **Benary (1956/1961)**; Beyschlag (1907/1953); Blankenburg ["Kanonimprovisationen"] (1959); Boetticher (1954); Brandes (1935); Buelow (1972), (1982); Bukofzer (1947); **Bullivant (1980)**; Burney (1776-89/. . ./1957); Butler (1980); Cahn ["Transitus"] (1972-); Cazden (1948); Chomiński (1962/1981); Dahlhaus ["Termini"] (1955), ["Zur Theorie"] (1961), ["Untersuchungen"] (1966/. . ./1988); Dahlhaus et al. (1987); Dammann (1958/1967); Dupont (1933/. . ./1986); Eitner (1900-1904/1959-60); Feldmann (1958); Fellerer (1983); Ferand (1937/1938), ["Improvised"] (1956), [*Improvisation*] (1956/1961); Fischer (1978); Flindell (1983-84); Forchert (1986); Forkel (1792/1962); Frobenius ["Vollstimmig"] (1972-); Gerber (1790-92/1977), (1812-14/1966); Gissel (1980/1983), (1986); Gurlitt (1942/1966); Haase (1972); Hannas (1934); Harrán (1986); Hawkins (1776/. . ./1969); Horsley ["Fugue and Mode"] (1966/1978); Houle (1987); Hüschen

(1986); Isgro (1968); Jacobi (1957-60/1971); Kauko (1958); Krantz (1989); Lange (1899-1900); Lawrence (1978); Lester ● ● ● (1977), (1989); Leuchtmann (1957/1959); Livingstone (1971); Luoma (1977); Mahlert and Sunter (1972-); Mann (1955/. . ./1987); McKinnon (1978); Meier (1963), (1966), (1969), (1974/1988); Mendel (1978); Moser (1967); Müller-Blattau (1923/. . ./1963); Neumann (1987); Niemöller (1964/1969); Norton (1984); Palisca (1949-68); Powers ["Mode"] (1980); Preußner (1924), (1939); Rauhe (1959-60); Reese (1954/1959); Reilly (1984-85); Reimer ["Kammermusik"] (1972-); Robbins (1938); Ruhnke (1949-68), (1973); Sachs (1972-); Sannemann (1903/1904); Schäfke (1934/1964); Schmalzriedt ["Reprise"] (1972-), ["Subiectum"] (1972-); Schünemann (1928/1931); Seidel and Cooper (1986); Snyder (1980); Subirá (1947/. . ./1958); Taddie (1984); Tilmouth (1980); Unger (1941/1969); Vogel (1955/1954); Walker (1978); Walker (1987); Wessely (1971-72); Wienpahl (1953), (1955); Wiora (1962); Zenck (1942).

FRANÇOIS CAMPION

[ca. 1686–1748]

The virtuoso guitarist François Campion ventured to publish, in his *Traité d'accompagnement et de composition* (1716), a scheme which he had found helpful in his own accompanying and composing. He called it *la règle des octaves* (later, *la règle de l'octave*). Using a limited palette of chordal possibilities, he demonstrated that a bass octave scale could be navigated according to a set pattern, as follows:

> Scale degree 1: 5/3; scale degree 2: 6/4/3; scale degree 3: 6/3; scale degree 4: 6/5/3; scale degree 5: 5/3; scale degree 6: 6/3; scale degree 7: 6/5/3; scale degree 8: 5/3; scale degree 7: 6/3; scale degree 6: 6/4/3; scale degree 5: 5/3; scale degree 4: 6/4/2; scale degree 3: 6/3; scale degree 2: 6/4/3; and scale degree 1: 5/3.

Though this plan had found favor in Italy, Campion helped expand its popularity in France. Over a decade later, he compiled information of a more technical nature (relating primarily to fingering for players of fretted stringed instruments), published under the title *Addition au traité d'accompagnement et de composition* in 1730.

Traité d'accompagnement et de composition, selon la règle des octaves de musique: Ouvrage généralement utile pour la transposition, à ceux qui se meslent du chant et des instrumens d'accord, ou d'une partie seule, et pour apprendre à chiffrer la basse continue (Op. 2) [*Rism* B/VI/1, pp. 199-200.]

> Paris: veuve G. Adam and the author, 1716.
> Amsterdam: Estienne Roger, [ca. 1717].

> S ● Facsimile of the 1716 edition. Geneva: Minkoff Reprint, 1976.
>
>> Includes also a facsimile of [1729] and (1730), below.

Lettre . . . à un philosophe disciple de la règle de l'octave [*Rism* B/VI/1, p. 199.]

[Paris: 1729.]

> S ● See (1716):(1976), above.

Addition au traité d'accompagnement et de composition par la règle de l'octave; Où est compris particulièrement le secret de l'accompagnement du théorbe, de la guitare et du luth avec la manière de transposer instrumentalement, et de solfier facilement la musique vocale sans l'usage de la gâme (Op. 4) [*Rism* B/VI/1, p. 200.]

> Paris: veuve Ribou, Boivin, Le Clerc, and the author, 1730.

> S ● See (1716):(1976), above.

*Lettre . . . à Monsieur de *** [Voltaire], auteur du Temple du goust, sur la mode des instrumens de musique, ouvrage curieux et interressant pour les amateurs de l'harmonie* [*Rism* B/VI/1, p. 199.]

> Published under the pseudonym Abbé Carbasus.

> Paris: veuve Allouel, 1739. [LCPS: C-010.]

LITERATURE:

Brenet, Michel. "La règle de l'octave et ses inventeurs." In *Gm* 34/39-40 (1888):235-37, 243-44.

Borrel, Eugène. "Campion, François." Translated by Hans Albrecht. In *MGG* (1949-68). Bibliog.

Charnassé, Hélène. "Sur l'accord de la guitare." *Rmfc* 7 (1967):25-37. Bibliog.

Bourligueux, Guy. "Campion, François." In *NGrove* (1980). Bibliog.

Mason, Kevin. "François Campion's Secret of Accompaniment for the Theorbo, Guitar, and Lute." *JLSA* 14 (1981):69-94. [*Rilm* 81-455.]

Russell, Craig H. "Santiago de Murcia: The French Connection in Baroque Spain." *JLSA* 15 (1982):40-51. [*Rilm* 82-417.]

See also FÉTIS: (1833-44); MOMIGNY: (1791-1818): (1791); RIEMANN: (1898); WALTHER: (1732); LITERATURE SUPPLEMENT: Becker (1836-39/1964); Chevaillier (1925/1931-32); Eitner (1900-1904/1959-60); Gerber (1790-92/1977), (1812-14/

1966); Gut (1972-); North (1987); Oberdörffer (1949-68); **Shirlaw (1917/. . ./1970)**; Strizich (1981); Williams, P. (1970).

THOMAS CAMPION

[bapt. 1567–1620]

Thomas Campion's *A New Way of Making Fowre Parts in Counter-point*, first printed around 1612, is striking in its recognition of the bass as the foundation for part-writing. Campion specifically stated that when sixths are used over the bass, such basses are not true basses. He told his readers to keep common tones and move other voices to the nearest chord tones; if no common tone exists, move the upper three voices in the direction opposite the bass. This treatise reappeared in 1654, issued by PLAYFORD with annotations by SIMPSON as part of his *Introduction to the Skill of Musick*. The work was published separately as *The Art of Setting or Composing of Musick in Parts* in 1655 and was then included in all editions of PLAYFORD through 1683 except the 1658 edition. PURCELL withdrew it to insert his own treatise on composition for the 1694 edition.

Campion viewed the scale as a complete octave rather than as a combination of hexachordal overlappings. He also offered a discussion of the ambiguity of musical terms—in particular, various meanings of 'tone' and 'note'.

A New Way of Making Fowre Parts in Counter-point, by a Most Familiar, and Infallible Rule . . . [*Rism* B/VI/1, p. 200.]

    London: John Browne (Thomas S[nodham]), [ca. 1612-14].

S● See PLAYFORD: (1654):edition of 1655 and those of 1660 through 1679.

    With annotations by SIMPSON.

S● As *The Art of Setting or Composing of Musick in Parts*. London: John Playford, 1655. [*Rism* B/VI/1, p. 200.]

S● Vivian, Percival, ed. *Campion's Works*. Oxford: Clarendon Press, 1909; reprint edition, 1966.

    Review in *Nation* 91/2356 (1910):161-64 (Stuart P. Sherman).

S● Davis, Walter R., ed. *The Works of Thomas Campion: Complete Songs, Masques, and Treatises, with a Selection of the Latin Verse*. Garden City, N.Y.: Doubleday, 1967; London: Faber, 1969; (NLSCS), New York: W. W. Norton, 1970. [*Rilm* 67-626.]

    Reviews in *ABBW* 40/3 (1967):116, *Choice* 4/11 (1968):1238, *JEGP* 67/2 (1968):306-8 (Lloyd E.

Berry), *KR* 35 (1967):555, *LJ* 92/8 (1967):1624-25 (H. H. Bernt), *ML* 51/2 (1970):169-71 (David C. Greer), *MR* 32/2 (1971):191-92 (David C. Brown), *Notes* 24/4 (1967-68):707-9 (Bertrand H. Bronson), *PhilQ* 47/4 (1968):601-5 (Rhodes Dunlap), *RQ* 21/3 (1968):362-63 (Peter J. Seng), *SEL* 8/1 (1968):164-65 (Kathleen Williams), *Spectator* 224/7389 (1970):179-80 (Anthony Burgess), and *TLS* 69/3566 (1970):725-26.

LITERATURE:

Pulver, Jeffrey. "The English Theorists: XI—Thomas Campian." *MT* 75/1102 (1934):1080-82.

Dart, Thurston. "Campion, Thomas." Translated by Theodora Holm. In *MGG* (1949-68). Bibliog.

Gibbons, Henry. "Observations on *A New Way of Making Fowre Parts in Counter-point* by Thomas Campion." M.A. thesis, Harvard University, 1964.

●●●Lowbury, Edward Joseph Lister; Salter, Timothy; and Young, Alison. *Thomas Campion: Poet, Composer, Physician*. New York: Barnes & Noble; London: Chatto & Windus, 1970. [*Rilm* 74-244.]

    Reviews in *Choice* 8/3 (1971-72):370, *MiE* 35/348 (1971):447 (Michael Hurd), *MR* 32/2 (1971):191-92 (David C. Brown), *Notes* 29/1 (1972-73):32-34 (Barbara Rosecrance), *RQ* 24/3 (1971):404-5 (John P. Cutts), *Tablet* 224/6802 (1970):978 (Gerard Meath), and *TLS* 69/3581 (1970):1187.

Finney, Oliver John. "Thomas Campion, Music, and Metrics." Ph.D. dissertation, The University of Kansas, 1975. [*DA* 36/07A, p. 4506. UMI 75-30029.]

Poulton, Diana. "Campion, Thomas." In *NGrove* (1980). Bibliog.

Ratcliffe, Stephen. *Campion: On Song*. Boston: Routledge & Kegan Paul, 1981.

    Reviews in *ECrit* 34/3 (1984):244-48 (Leslie Dunn), *ML* 64/3-4 (1983):264-66 (Christopher Wilson), *RQ* 35/4 (1982):655 (Elise Bickford Jorgens), *SHR* 18/1 (1984):78 (Mark Booth), and *TLS* 80/4009 (1981):1243 (Wilfrid Mellers).

Wilson, Christopher Robert. "Words and Notes Coupled Lovingly Together: Thomas Campion, a Critical

Study." Ph.D. dissertation, Oxford University, 1982. [*Rilm* 82-2283.]

Davis, Walter R. *Thomas Campion*. Boston: Twayne, 1987.

> Review in *ML* 69/4 (1988):509-10 (Robin Headlam Wells).

Feldman, Martha. "In Defense of Campion: A New Look at His Ayres and Observations." *JM* 5/2 (1987):226-56.

See also FÉTIS: (1833-44); LIPPIUS: Rivera (1974/1980); PLAYFORD: Kidson (1918); Munstedt (1983); LITERATURE SUPPLEMENT: **Apfel (1981)**; Atcherson (1972); Burton (1956); Colles (1928-29);

Dahlhaus ["Untersuchungen"] (1966/. . ./1988), ["Harmony"] **(1980)**; Eitner (1900-1904/1959-60); Forkel (1792/1962); Hancock (1977); Hawkins (1776/. . ./1969); Heckmann (1953); Hein (1954); Henderson (1969); Jacobi (1957-60/1971); Lawrence (1978); **Lester** (1974), **(1989)**; Lewis (1981); Miller (1960); Mitchell, J. W. (1963); Mitchell, W. J. (1963); Pulver (1927/. . ./1973); Reese (1954/1959); Rogers (1955); Ruf (1972-); Ruff (1970); Sachs (1972-); Scholes (1947); **Seidel and Cooper (1986)**; Wienpahl (1953), (1955).

CHARLES-SIMON CATEL

[1773–1830]

When Paris's Conservatoire de musique first opened in 1795, each professor of harmony taught in accordance with his own specific predilection. Within a few years, however, a committee was formed to shape a more specific set of instructional materials. Charles-Simon Catel's *Traité d'harmonie* (1802) was selected as the most appropriate book to put into the hands of those beginning a serious study of harmony, and its acceptance in Paris generated, not surprisingly, a number of French editions, as well as translations into German, English, and Italian. It served a generation of French musicians and profoundly influenced later French writers on harmony.

In contrast to RAMEAU's complex, speculative formulations, Catel offered a set of eight basic chords which constituted *harmonie simple ou naturelle*. The single chord G-B-D-F-A (wherein the A might be modified to A-flat) contained all eight chords, as follows: G B D, D F A, B D F, G B D F, B D F A, B D F A-flat, G B D F A, and G B D F A-flat. All other combinations of pitches constituted *harmonie composée ou artificielle* and were regarded as modifications (employing the technique of suspension, for example) of the eight simple harmonies.

Catel's treatise contains abundant music examples arranged in a logical format. Figures indicating interval content accompany most of these examples, whereas neither Roman numerals nor any sort of fundamental bass notation is included. The chapter on cadences offers a particularly rich variety of options, while his chapter on modulation shows a full panorama of possible key relationships. Though many of the examples are straightforward, a few—such as the ascent of an octave using parallel 6/3 chords—offer interesting glimpses of the outer fringes of acceptable chord succession. Though the Conservatoire took a new path upon CHERUBINI's arrival, Catel's work was still circulating past the middle of the century.

Traité d'harmonie . . . adopté par le Conservatoire pour servir à l'étude dans cet établissement

> Paris: à l'imprimerie du Conservatoire de musique (Mme Le Roy), *An* X [1802].
>
>> Review in *Gnmu* (*An* X [1802]):546 (Luigi CHERUBINI), excerpted in Hellouin and Picard (1910), below.
>>
>> As *Traité complet d'harmonie*, enlarged by Ambroise Leborne:
>
> Paris: Brandus, 1847.
>
>> Numerous other printings under various titles, including *L'harmonie à la portée de tous: Traité complet d'harmonie* and *Méthode ou traité d'harmonie*, with various degrees of editorial revision.

ST ● *Traité d'harmonie . . . /Abhandlung über die Harmonie (Generalbasslehre) . . .* Leipzig: C. F. Peters, [1816?]; other editions.

T ● *A Treatise on Harmony*. London: Chappell, [ca. 1825]; an American edition (edited by Lowell Mason), Boston: James Loring, 1832; a revision by Josiah Pittman of a translation by Mrs. Cowden Clarke, London: J. A. Novello, 1854; other editions.

T ● Alfieri, Pietro, trans. *Trattato di armonia di Catel*. Rome: Pliserio, 1840.

T ● *Trattato completo di armonia*. Milan: Ricordi, n.d.

See also LANGLÉ: (*An* VIII); (*An* X).

LITERATURE:

Carlez, Jules Alexis. *Catel: Étude biographique et critique*. Caen: H. Delesques, 1894.

Hellouin, Frédéric, and Picard, Joseph. *Un musicien oublié: Catel de l'Institut royal de France, 1773-1830.* Preface by Julien Tiersot. Paris: Fischbacher, 1910.

Douel, Martial. "Un autre centenaire oublié: Charles-Simon Catel (1773-1830)." *Gc* 17/5-6 (1930-31):135-37, 167-68.

Favre, Georges. "Catel, Charles-Simon." Translated by Hans Albrecht. In *MGG* (1949-68). Bibliog.

ASAFIEV, Boris. *M. I. Glinka.* Moscow: 1947; 1950; reprint edition, Leningrad: "Muzyka," Leningradskoe otdnie, 1978. [*Rilm* 78-2838.]

> See especially "K voprosu o putiakh, sviazuiushchikh tvorcheskii metod Glinki s metodom muzykal'nykh kompozitsii, sozdannykh na grani XVIII-XIX vekov Parizhskoi konservatorei sredi intonatsionnoi praktiki resoliutsionnoi epokhi" [To the Question of Threads, Connecting the Creative Method of Glinka with the Method of Musical Composition, Created in the Limits of 18th-19th Centuries of the Paris Conservatory among the Intonational Practice of the Revolutionary Epoch], pp. 287-302 of the 1950 edition. Review in *SLit* 4/4 (1949):147-48.

Suskin, Sylvan. "Catel, Charles-Simon." In *NGrove* (1980). Bibliog.

George, David Neal. "The *Traité d'harmonie* of Charles-Simon Catel." Ph.D. dissertation, North Texas State University, 1982. [*Rilm* 82-5763. *DA* 43/11A, p. 3451. UMI 83-07926.]

See also CHORON: [1809]:Review [*QMMR*] (1820); Simms (1975); FÉTIS: (1833-44); (1840); [*Traité*] [1844]; RIEMANN: (1898); LITERATURE SUPPLEMENT: Becker (1836-39/1964); Blumröder (1972-); Burke (1963); Cavallini (1949); Cazden (1948); **Dahlhaus (1984)**; Eitner (1900-1904/1959-60); Gerber (1812-14/1966); ● ● ● **Groth (1983)**; Jacobi (1957-60/1971); Jones (1934); Jorgenson (1957); **Kassler** (1971), ● ● ● **(1979)**; Konecne (1984); Mitchell, J. W. (1963); Packard (1952); Rothschild (1961); Ryzhkin (1933), (1934-39); Subirá (1947/. . ./1958); Vertrees (1974); **Wagner (1974)**; **Wason (1981/1985)**; Wirth (1966); **Zaminer (1985)**.

SALOMON DE CAUS

[ca. 1576–1626]

Salomon de Caus, French theorist and mathematician, devoted himself to Greek theory and described the intervals of that period and of his time in terms of their mathematical relationships. He also provided, in his *Institution harmonique* (1615), a thorough review of contrapuntal rules, derived from ZARLINO. De Caus may have been the first theorist to liken musical sound propagation to the concentric circles generated when an object is thrown into standing water.

ZARLINO's *senario* is expanded to include the number 8, which is used to accommodate the ratio of the minor 6th. As with ZARLINO, however, the number 7 is not accepted. The modes on C and D serve as models for the remaining modes, creating categories characterized as either happy or sad. One also finds information on organ building, prolation, consonance and dissonance, and composition in two through six parts, as well as a discussion of just intonation.

Institution harmonique divisée en deux parties. En la première sont monstrées les proportions des intervalles harmoniques, et en la deuxiesme les compositions d'icelles [*Rism* B/VI/1, p. 213.]

> Frankfurt am Main: Jan Norton, 1615. [LCPS: C-033.]

T ● Trost, Johann Caspar, ed. and trans. German translation. [Ms., mid seventeenth century.] [Lost.]

T ● Gruber, Albion, trans. "Salomon de Caus: Institution Harmonique — A Translation [of Book Two]." Ms., 1968. [Rochester, N.Y.: Sibley Music Library, Eastman School of Music.]

S ● Facsimile edition. MMMLF, ser. 2, no. 81. New York: Broude Brothers, [1969].

S ● Féruselle, Pierre, ed. Facsimile edition. Geneva: Minkoff Reprint, 1980.

Les raisons des forces mouvantes avec diverses machines tant utiles que plaisantes aus quelles sont adjoints plusieurs desseings de grotes et fontaines . . . Livre troisiesme traitant de la fabrique des orgues [*Rism* B/VI/1, p. 213.]

> Frankfurt am Main: Jan Norton, 1615. [LCPS: C-034. IDC.]
> Paris: Hierosme Drouart, 1624.
> Paris: Charles Sevestre, 1624.

T ● *Von gewaltsamen Bewegungen* . . . Frankfurt am Main: Abraham Pacquart (Parts 1 and 2); Johann Norton (Part 3), 1615; facsimile of the Pacquart edition (Part 1 only), Hannover: Curt R. Vincentz Verlag (Th. Schäfer), 1977. [*Rism* B/VI/1, p. 213.]

S ● Caus, Isaac de. *Nouvelle invention de lever l'eau* . . . London: [Moxon], 1644; T. Davies, 1667; English translation (as *New and Rare Inventions of Water-Works* . . ., translated by John Leak), London: Joseph Moxon, 1659; later editions.

> Based, in part, on Salomon de Caus's work.

S ● Sumner, W. L., ed. Facsimile of the 1615 edition. Bo, no. 21. Amsterdam: Fritz Knuf, 1973.

> Reviews in *ArsOr* 22/44 (1974):1970-71 (Wolfgang Adelung) and *Trorg* 27/2 (1975):11-12.

LITERATURE:

Maks, Christina Sandrina. "Salomon de Caus: 1576-1626." Ph.D. dissertation, The University of Leiden, 1935; published edition, Paris: Jouve, 1935. Bibliog.

Cohen, Albert. "Caus, Salomon de." In *NGrove* (1980). Bibliog.

See also FÉTIS: (1833-44); FLUDD: Yates (1972); OUVRARD: (1658):Boulay (1984); RIEMANN: (1898); LITERATURE SUPPLEMENT: **Apfel (1981)**; **Barbour (1951/. . ./1972)**; Becker (1836-39/1964); Beiche ["Dux"] (1972-); Chomiński (1962/1981); Cohen (1966/1978), ["Symposium"] (1972), (1988); Dekker (1979); Eitner (1900-1904/1959-60); Fellerer ["Zur Kontrapunktlehre"] (1973); Forkel (1792/1962); Gerber (1812-14/1966); Gruber (1969); Hawkins (1776/. . ./1969); Horsley [*Fugue: History*] (1966); Hüschen (1986); Kauko (1958); Launay (1972); Mann (1955/. . ./1987); Mendel (1948), (1978); Reese (1954/1959); Ruhnke (1949-68); Schneider (1972); Seidel and Cooper (1986); Taddie (1984); Tolkoff (1973).

PIETRO CERONE

(1561–1625)

The controversial "Spanish" theorist Pietro Cerone was Italian, and though he spent around a dozen years in Spain, he was not entirely conversant in the language of his hosts. His concern for preserving and developing the musical art in Spain and the fact that Naples was then under Spanish dominion prompted him to compile a massive summation of sixteenth-century theory in Castilian. Modern scholars have revealed that *El melopeo y maestro* (1613) is a patchwork of several treatises—in part translation and amplification of Italians such as ZARLINO and PONTIO; in part reworking of BERMUDO, MONTANOS, and SANTA MARÍA. Little credence is given nowadays to FÉTIS's assertion that Cerone may have had access to a now lost manuscript of ZARLINO. The extent of Cerone's borrowings and the persistence of his meanderings into topics such as the prudent use of wine have given the work a notoriety which belies its enormous utility and substantial influence on the admittedly conservative musical culture of seventeenth-century Spain.

Cerone's appreciation of Palestrina's music strongly influenced the writing of *El melopeo y maestro*. One segment of the work is devoted to an analysis of his mass *L'homme armé*. Much of the remainder contains related contrapuntal and compositional instruction. Cerone's virtuous tone does not prevent the inclusion of some entertaining fare, such as puzzle canons. Yet the eyes of the Church Fathers are never far away.

Le regole più necessarie per l'introduttione del canto fermo . . . [*Rism* B/VI/1, p. 216.]

> Naples: Gio. Battista Gargano & Lucretio Nucci, 1609.

S ● Baroffio, Bonifacio, ed. Facsimile edition. MFm, no. 4. Lucca: Libreria musicale italiana editrice, 1988.

El melopeo y maestro: Tractado de música theórica y prática . . . [*Rism* B/VI/1, p. 216.]

> Naples: Juan Bautista Gargano & Lucrecio Nucci, 1613. [LCPS: C-043. SMLMS. IDC.]

S ● Guzmán, Jorge de. *Curiosidades del canto llano, sacadas de las obras del reverendo Don Pedro Cerone de Bérgamo, y de otros autores*. Madrid: en la Imprenta de música, 1709. [*Rism* B/VI/1, p. 390. LCPS: G-085.]

T ● See **Strunk (1950)**:262-73.

S ● Gallo, F. Alberto, ed. Facsimile edition. 2 vols. BmB, ser. 2, no. 25. Bologna: Forni, 1969.

> Review in ● ● ●*JAMS* 24/3 (1971):477-85 (Robert Stevenson).

LITERATURE:

Reiff, Alfred. "Pedro Cerone, der größte Musiktheoretiker des 16. Jahrhunderts." *NMZ* 44/1 (1922):5-6.

Hannas, Ruth. "Cerone, Philosopher and Teacher." *MQ* 21/4 (1935):408-22.

Hannas, Ruth. "Cerone's Approach to the Teaching of Counterpoint." *PAMS 1937* [1939]:75-80.

Hannas, Ruth. "Cerone's Exposition of Mensural Notation, Including Proportions." *BAMS* 3 (1939):8-9.

Anglès, Higino. "Cerone, Domenico Pietro." Translated by Christel Blume. In *MGG* (1949-68). Bibliog.

Fellerer, Karl Gustav. "Zur Cerones musiktheoretischen Quellen." In *SFG*, ser. 1, no. 11 (1955):171-78.

Pollin, Alice M. "Towards an Understanding of Cerone's *El melopeo y maestro*." *RR* 53/2 (1962):79-95. Bibliog.

Gallo, Franco Alberto. "Il *Melopeo* di Pietro Cerone." *Quad* 9 (1968):111-26. Bibliog.

Poch Blasco, Serafina. "Conceptos musicoterapéuticos de autores españoles del pasado, válidos en la actualidad." *Anmu* 26 (1971):147-71.

García, Francisco. "Pietro Cerone's *El melopeo y maestro*: A Synthesis of Sixteenth-Century Musical Theory." Ph.D. dissertation, Northwestern University, 1978. [*Rilm* 78-5951. *DA* 39/08A, p. 4580. UMI 79-03263.]

● ● ● Hudson, Barton. "Cerone, Pietro." In *NGrove* (1980).

See also EXIMENO: [1802-6]; Pedrell (1920); FÉTIS: (1833-44); d'INDY: (1903-50):Montgomery (1946); MERSENNE: (1617-48); MOMIGNY: (1791-1818):(1818); OUSELEY: (1879); SOLER: (1765); WALTHER: (1732); LITERATURE SUPPLEMENT: Abraham (1968/1969); Allen ["Baroque"] (1939), ["Philosophies"] (1939); Anglés and Subirá; ● ● ●**Apfel (1981)**; Armstrong (1978); Becker (1836-39/1964); Beiche ["Dux"] (1972-), ["Inversio"] (1972-); **Bent** ["Analysis"] **(1980/1987)**; Blumröder (1972-); Borgir (1971/1987); Bruck (1928); Burney (1776-89/. . ./1957); Cahn ["Retardatio"] (1972-); Chomiński (1962/1981); Dahlhaus ["Untersuchungen"] (1966/. . ./1988); **Dahlhaus et al. (1987)**; Eggebrecht (1955); Eitner (1900-1904/1959-60); Fellerer (1969), ["Zur Kontrapunktlehre"] (1973), (1983); Ferand (1937/1938), [*Improvisation*] (1956/1961); Forkel (1792/1962); Forrester (1973); Frobenius ["Vollstimmig"] (1972-); Gerber (1790-92/1977), (1812-14/1966); Ghislanzoni (1949-51); Haar (1977); Hannas (1934); Harrán (1986); Hawkins (1776/. . ./1969); Hein (1954); Hoag (1976); Houle (1960); Howell (1972); Hucke (1969); Hüschen (1986); Jackson (1988); Jacobs (1968); Jander (1980); Jeppesen (1922/. . ./1970), (1930/. . ./1974), (1935); Katz (1985); Kauko (1958); Kinkeldey (1910/1968); Kuhn (1902); La Fage (1864/1964); Launay (1972); **Lindley** ["Temperaments"] (1980), (1982); Lockwood (1966/1978); Lowinsky (1948):(1949); Luoma (1976), (1977); Luper (1938); Mahlert and Sunter (1972-); **Mann (1955/. . ./1987)**; Mendel (1948), (1978); Moyer (1969); Müller-Blattau (1923/. . ./1963); **Neumann** [*Essays*] **(1982); Palisca** (1949-68), ["Theory"] **(1980)**; Pedrell (1888); Reese (1954/1959), (1957/1970); Reimer ["Concerto"] (1972-); Rogers (1955); Ruhnke (1949-68); Sachs (1972-); Stevenson (1960), (1976); Strizich (1981); Subirá (1947/. . ./1958); (1953); Taddie (1984); Tilmouth (1980); Tittel (1959); Walker (1941-42/. . ./1985); Walker (1987); Wolff (1972-).

SCIPIONE CERRETO

[ca. 1551–ca. 1633]

For Scipione Cerreto even the absorption of four additional modes (nine through twelve) into the theoretical system was too innovative. The eight ecclesiastical modes were sufficient, he felt, so long as one could transpose them using at most two sharps or flats. His *Della prattica musica* (1601) contains a detailed account of contrapuntal procedures and their theoretical underpinnings. Like other treatises of the time, improvised counterpoint is emphasized, as are various types of canons and invertible counterpoint. ZACCONI paid Cerreto a compliment by borrowing some of his examples for his *Prattica di musica seconda parte* (1622).

Della prattica musica vocale et strumentale, opera necessaria a coloro, che di musica si dilettano . . . [*Rism* B/VI/1, p. 216.]

Naples: Giovanni Jacomo Carlino, 1601. [LCPS: C-044. HoM: 322. SMLMS.]

Reprinted in 1611.

S ● Facsimile of the 1601 edition. BmB, ser. 2, no. 30. Bologna: Forni, 1969.

Dell'arbore musicale . . . espositione dodici [*Rism* B/VI/1, p. 216.]

Naples: Gio. Battista Sottile (Scipione Bonino), 1608.

S ● Luisi, Francesco, ed. Facsimile edition. MFm, no. 12. Lucca: Libreria musicale italiana editrice, 1989.

"Dialoghi armonici pel contrapunto e per la compositione"

Ms., 1626. [Naples: Conservatorio di musica S. Pietro a Majella.]

"Dialogo harmonico, ove si tratta con un sol raggionamento di tutte le regole del contrappunto che si fa sopra canto fermo et sopra canto figurato, et anco della compositione di più voci, de' canoni, delle proportioni, et d'altre cose essenziali ad essa prattica"

A revision of "Dialoghi armonici" (1626).

Ms., 1631. [Bologna: Civico museo bibliografico musicale.]

LITERATURE:

Palisca, Claude V. "Cerreto, Scipione." Translated by Theodora Holm. In *MGG* (1949-68).

Kataoka, Gido. "Die musiktheoretischen Schriften des Scipione Cerreto." Ph.D. dissertation, The University of Kiel, 1956.

● ● ● Horsley, Imogene. "Cerreto, Scipione." In *NGrove* (1980).

Tacconi, Massimo. "Scipioni Cerreto e il contrappunto improvisato." Thesis, The University of Rome, 1987-88. Bibliog.

See also FÉTIS: (1833-44); MARTINI: (1757-81); LITERATURE SUPPLEMENT: Abraham (1968/1969); Ambros (1878/. . ./1909); **Apfel (1981)**; Atcherson (1973); Becker (1836-39/1964); Eitner (1900-1904/1959-60); Fellerer ["Zur Kontrapunktlehre"] (1972), ["Zur Kontrapunktlehre"] (1973), ["Ausdruck"] (1982), (1983); Forkel (1792/1962); Gerber (1790-92/1977), (1812-14/1966); Ghislanzoni (1949-51); Harrán (1986); Hawkins (1776/. . ./1969); Hein (1954); Hüschen (1986); Jackson (1988); **Maniates (1979)**; Pacchioni (1983); Palisca (1949-68); Reimer ["Concerto"] (1972-); Robbins (1938); Ruhnke (1949-68); Tyler (1975); Walker (1987).

PETR IL'ICH CHAIKOVSKY

[1840–1893]

In 1866 the young Petr Il'ich Chaikovsky accepted a post as a teacher of harmony at what soon became the Moscow Conservatory. During the next twelve years this appointment supplied a part of his income and led him to publish several works of a pedagogical nature, including translations of treatises by GEVAERT and LOBE and two textbooks of his own. Through his efforts, Russian theory gained a degree of autonomy from the mainstream of European harmonic theory. His precepts permeate the contributions on tonal theory of later Russian authors.

Chaikovsky completed two textbooks on harmony: *Rukovodstvo k prakticheskomu izucheniiu garmonii* (1872) and a derivative and less complicated *Kratkii uchebnik garmonii* (1875). He advocated a solid command of voice-leading techniques, acquired both through the careful harmonization of melodies (wherein each voice was expected to possess an independent character) and through contrapuntal exercises (in a species format). He also expected his students to develop fluency in moving from one tonal center to another, for which he specified two types of modulation: one proceeded swiftly through the presentation of the new key's dominant; the other fostered a more gradual transition through a more varied succession of chords. In some ways Chaikovsky's independence led him astray, as in his assertion that augmented-sixth chords typically resolved on tonic (a technique which is found in his own music but which does not reflect the normative context for such sonorities). Yet he approached his subject with humility: rather than postulating boldly and abstractly, he wrote straightforwardly and with many examples, as if by default he had been called upon to clarify and codify the basic foundations of music until some later author offered a more refined synthesis.

Rukovodstvo k prakticheskomu izucheniiu garmonii [A Guide to the Practical Study of Harmony]

Moscow: 1872.

Numerous later editions.

T ● Juon, Paul, trans. *Leitfaden zum praktischen Erlernen der Harmonie*. Leipzig et al.: Petr Jurgenson, [1899]; facsimile edition, Bonn/Bad Godesberg: Forberg-Jurgenson, 1976.

S ● See Collected Works (1957):1-162, below.

T ● Krall, Emil, and Liebling, James, trans. (from the German). *Guide to the Practical Study of Harmony*. Leipzig et al.: Petr Jurgenson, 1900; facsimile edition (Introduction by Byron Cantrell), Canoga Park, Calif.: Summit, [1970]; facsimile edition, Bonn-Bad Godesberg: Forberg-Jurgenson, 1976; facsimile edition, Brighton, Mass.: Carousel, 1983.

Reviews in *MT* 118/1617 (1977):917 (Geoffrey Norris), *MT* 125/1699 (1984):503 (Patric Standford), and *Notes* 27/4 (1970-71):707-8 (Walter Piston).

Kratkii uchebnik garmonii, prisposoblennyi k chteniu dukhovnomuzykal'nykh sochinenii v Rossii [A Short Textbook of Harmony, Adapted to the Reading of Church Music Composition in Russia]

Moscow: 1875.

Later editions.

S ● See Collected Works (1957):163-216, below.

See also GEVAERT: (1863):(1866); LOBE: (1851): (1870); RIMSKY-KORSAKOV: CHAIKOVSKY: (1885).

COLLECTED WORKS EDITION:

Protopopov, Vladimir, ed. *P. I. Chaikovskya i perepiska* [P. I. Chaikovsky: Complete Collected Works: Literary Works and Correspondence], Vol. 3-A. Moscow: Gosudarstvennoe muzykal'noe izdatal'stvo, 1957.

LITERATURE:

Juon, Paul. *Anhang zur Harmonielehre von P. Tschaikowsky: Praktisches Übungsbuch/Prilozhenie k uchebniky garmonii P. Chaikovskogo: Sbornik prakticheskikh uprazhnenii.* 2 vols. Moscow, St. Petersburg, and Leipzig: Petr Jurgenson, 1900.

> Captions in Russian and German.

Ogolevets, Aleksei Stepanovich. "Chaikovskii: Avtor uchebnika garmonii." [Chaikovsky: The Author of a Textbook of Harmony.] *Smuz* /5-6 (1940):124-29.

Lloyd-Jones, David. "Tschaikowsky, Pjotr Iljitch." Translated by Margarete Hoffmann-Erbrecht. In *MGG* (1949-68). Bibliog.

Boganova, Tat'iana Vasil'evna. "Teoreticheskie raboty P. I. Chaikovskogo." [The Theoretical Work of P. I. Chaikovsky.] *Smuz* /10 (1958):143.

Miasoedov, Andrei Nikolaevich. *Traditsii Chaikovskogo v prepodavanii garmonii.* [The Tradition of Chaikovsky in the Teaching of Harmony.] Moscow: Muzyka, 1972.

Stepanov, Aleksei Alekseevich. "Voprosy garmonicheskoi struktury i funktsional'nosti v *Rukovodstve k prakticheskomu izucheniyu garmonii* P. I. Chaikovskogo." [Questions of Harmonic Structure and Functionality in *The Guide to the Practical Study of Harmony* of P. I. Chaikovsky.] In Rags (1972):152-77.

Stepanov, Aleksei Alekseevich. "Traditsii russkoi muzykal'no-teoreticheskoi pedagogiki i nekotorye zadachi sovremennogo uchebnogo kursa garmonii." [The Traditions of Russian Music Theory Pedagogy and Several Problems of the Contemporary Textbook Course of Harmony.] In *Metodika prepodavaniia istoriki-teoreticheskikh distsiplini* [Methods of the Teaching of History and Theory Disciplines], edited by Yury Bychkov, pp. 102-15. St, no. 26. Moscow: Gosudarstvennyi muzykal'no-pedagogicheskii institut imeni Gnesinykh, 1976.

Brown, David. "Tchaikovsky, Pyotr Il'yich." In *NGrove* (1980). Bibliog.

Nemirovskaya, I. "O printsipe simfonicheskogo kontrdeystviya." *Smuz* /8 (1983):105-7.

See also OUSELEY: (1882); LITERATURE SUPPLEMENT: Carpenter (1988); Larosh (1873/1913); Lawrence (1978); ● ● ● McQuere (1983); Ryzhkin (1933), (1934-39).

LUIGI CHERUBINI

[1760–1842]

Among his many other distinctions, Luigi Cherubini became director of the Paris Conservatoire in 1822, having previously served that institution as one of its professors of composition, counterpoint, and fugue. His colleagues there included CATEL, REICHA, and FÉTIS. Through Cherubini's instigation, FÉTIS was induced to write his counterpoint manual [1824] as a counteroffensive to REICHA's system. Later, through the diligence of his student Fromental Halévy (who joined the faculty in 1833), the *Cours de contre-point et de fugue* [1835] was published under Cherubini's name. Founded upon the species approach, the work is divided into sections on counterpoint, imitation, double counterpoint, and fugue, followed by a number of examples in which the subjects, answers, countersubjects, stretti, and so forth, are labeled. Unfortunately the rigidity of Cherubini's formulations contributed to the development of a sterile, "academic" style of fugue writing, one of the less salutary legacies of nineteenth-century theory pedagogy. Its dissemination was promoted by a number of translations, including two into German and two into English.

Cours de contre-point et de fugue

> With the collaboration of Fromental Halévy.

> Paris: Maurice Schlesinger, [1835].

>> List of errors in *RgmdP* 3/23 (1836):190-91 plus inserts (Fromental Halévy).

> Paris: Heugel (au Ménestrel), [between 1842 and 1851].

ST ● Stöpel, Franz, trans. *Theorie des Contrapunktes und der Fuge/Cours de contre-point et de fugue.* Leipzig: Kistner, [ca. 1835-36].

T ● Hamilton, James Alexander, trans. *A Course of Counterpoint and Fugue*. 2 vols. London: Robert Cocks, 1837; 2nd edition, 1841.

T ● Clarke, Mary Cowden, trans. *A Treatise on Counterpoint and Fugue*. NLDMK, Theoretical Series, no. 1. London: Novello; New York: J. L. Peters; Boston: O. Ditson, 1854; numerous later editions (revised by Joseph Bennett).

T ● Jensen, Gustav [and Klauwell, O.], trans. and ed. *Theorie des Kontrapunktes und der Fugue*. Cologne and Leipzig: H. vom Ende, [1896]; revised edition (edited by Richard Henberger), Leipzig: F. E. C. Leuckart, 1911.

> Notice in *MMg* 28/12 (1896):170.

T ● Rossi, Luigi Felice, trans. Milan: Lucca, n.d.

T ● See OUSELEY: (1869).

Marches d'harmonie pratiquées dans la composition, produisant des suites regulières de consonnances et de dissonnances

> Paris: Heugel; Troupenas, n.d.

T ● *Andamenti d'armonia praticati nella composizione i quali producono successioni regolari di consonanze e di dissonanze*. Milan: Giovanni Ricordi, n.d.

See also CATEL: [1802]:Review; LANGLÉ: (*An* VIII); (*An* X). Cherubini also wrote numerous didactic exercises for use at the Paris Conservatoire.

LITERATURE:

Bellasis, Edward. *Cherubini: Memorials Illustrative of His Life and Work*. London: Burns & Oates, 1874; Birmingham, G.B.: Cornish Brothers, 1905; 1912; reprint of the 1912 edition, New York: Da Capo, 1971; German edition (as *Luigi Cherubini: Leben und Werk in Zeugnissen seiner Zeitgenossen*, translated by Josef Rheinberger), 1876; German edition (edited by Hans-Josef Irmen; MgnJ, no. 30), Regensburg: Boße, 1972.

> Reviews in *DR* 74 [New series: 22] (1874):497-98, *KJb* 56 (1972):109 (Karl Gustav Fellerer), *MT* 113/1551 (1972):459-60 (Basil Deane), *Musica* 28/1 (1974):60, and *NZfM* 135/8 (1974):529-30 (Carl Dahlhaus).

Vidal, Paul. *52 leçons d'harmonie*. Paris: Enoch, [1904].

Hohenemser, Richard Heinrich. *Luigi Cherubini: Sein Leben und seine Werke*. Leipzig: Breitkopf & Härtel, 1913; reprint edition, Wiesbaden: Martin Sändig, 1969. Bibliog.

Schemann, Ludwig. *Cherubini*. Stuttgart: Deutsche Verlags-Anstalt, 1925.

Confalonieri, Giulio. *Prigionia di un artista: Il romanzo di Luigi Cherubini*. 2 vols. Sslm. [Milan: Genio, 1948]; as *Cherubini: Prigonia di un artista*, Milan: Accademia, 1978.

Cotte, Roger. "Cherubini, Luigi Carlo Zanobi Salvadore Maria." Translated by Hans Albrecht. In *MGG* (1949-68). Bibliog.

Bronarski, Ludwik. "Chopin, Cherubini et la contrepoint." *AC* 2 (1958):238-42.

Damerini, Adelmo, ed. *Luigi Cherubini nel II centenario della nascita: Contributo alla conoscenza della vita e dell'opera*. HmcB, no. 19. Florence: Olschki, 1962. Bibliog.

> Contains a "Bibliografia critica Cherubiniana," edited by Mariangela Donà. Reviews in *Consort* 22 (1965):66-67 (Richard D. C. Noble) and *Eras* 19/9-10 (1967):288-89 (Karl Gustav Fellerer).

Deane, Basil. *Cherubini*. OSC, no. 3. London: Oxford University Press, 1965.

> Reviews in *ABBW* 37/5 (1966):410, *Composer* 22 (1966-67):29 (William Wordsworth), *Listener* 74/1914 (1965):928-29 (Edward Lockspeiser), *ML* 47/2 (1966):170 (Michael Tilmouth), *MO* 89/1066 (1965-66):607 (B. R.), *MR* 33/2 (1972):150-51 (A. F. Leighton Thomas), *MT* 107/1484 (1966):871-72 (Winton Dean), *MuMus* 14 (1965-66):64 (Stanley Sadie), *ÖM* 22/11 (1967):674 (H. M.-S.), *PP* 59/1 (1966):33 (Melva Peterson), *RS* 21 (1966):31 (A. H.), *Tablet* 219/6550 (1965):1360 (Rosemary Hughes), *Tempo* 75 (1965-66):34-35 (Gerald Abraham), and *TLS* 65/3339 (1966):136.

Deane, Basil. "Cherubini, Luigi (Carlo Zanobi Salvadore Maria)." In *NGrove* (1980). Bibliog.

See also FÉTIS: (1833-44); SCHENKER: (1906-35):Vol. II (1910-22); LITERATURE SUPPLEMENT: Becker (1836-39/1964); Beiche ["Dux"] (1972-); **Bullivant (1980)**; Cohen (1873-74); **Dahlhaus (1984)**; **Dahlhaus and Sachs (1980)**; Eitner (1900-1904/1959-60); Federhofer (1985); Gerber (1790-92/1977), (1812-14/1966); Ghislanzoni (1949-51); **Groth (1983)**; Horsley [*Fugue: History*] (1966); Jacobi (1957-60/1971); Jeppesen (1922/. . ./1970), (1930/. . ./1974), (1935); La Fage (1864/1964); Lawrence (1978); Lindley (1982); **Mann (1955/. . ./1987)**, (1987); McQuere (1983); Müller-Blattau (1923/. . ./1963), (1949-68); Newman (1963/. . ./1983); Oldroyd (1948); Palisca (1949-68); Rothschild (1961); Rowen (1979); Sachs (1972-); Sanders (1919); Schmalzriedt ["Coda"] (1972-), ["Episode"] (1972-), ["Exposition"] (1972-), ["Subiectum"] (1972-); Scholes (1947); Tittel (1959); Vertrees (1974); **Wagner (1974)**; Whatley (1981); Wirth (1966).

ALEXANDRE-ÉTIENNE CHORON

[1771–1834]

A unique voice among nineteenth-century French musical thinkers, Alexandre-Étienne Choron devoted himself wholeheartedly to disseminating information about and models of earlier musical practices. He was an influential administrator of musical institutions, an editor of significant repertoire, a translator of major eighteenth- and early nineteenth-century treatises by authors such as ALBRECHTSBERGER, MARPURG, and KOCH, and an original creative theorist with a decidedly anti-RAMEAU perspective. Fortunately he possessed sufficient personal wealth to undertake the publication of sumptuous volumes for which there was no assured readership. His efforts made a significant impression upon many of his contemporaries, including FÉTIS, who found in Choron and Fayolle's *Dictionnaire historique des musiciens* (1810-11) a model for his more comprehensive *Biographie universelle des musiciens* (1833-44), and in Choron's historical perspective a framework for his own formulation regarding the progress of the musical art.

Choron published, with Vincenzo Fiocchi, *Principes d'accompagnement des écoles d'Italie* around 1804. Though the work is an amalgam of the writings of numerous authors then little known in France, the introductory materials by Choron are decidedly not the work of a skilled composer. Suspensions clash with their resolutions; voice-leading errors abound; leading tones are left dangling; etc. Much better as an introduction to harmony and accompaniment is the first part of his later *Principes de composition des écoles d'Italie* [1809], a remarkable work printed in three hefty volumes, each of which contains hundreds of pages of music in score. The second through fifth parts of this work—derived from the writings of MARPURG, with music examples borrowed from MARTINI's *Esemplare* (1774-75) and other sources—are devoted to counterpoint, fugue, and canon. The final part, which occupies the entire third volume, is devoted to a discussion of various styles and genres and includes a massive anthology of music examples.

Choron's prolific output was only selectively published. Numerous manuscripts await the diligent scholar at the Bibliothèque nationale. One project which Choron did see to its completion was a French edition of ALBRECHTSBERGER's major writings, including the synopsis by Seyfried. At the end of his life he was immersed in an ambitious series, the *Manuel complet de musique vocale et instrumentale* (1836-38), which, through the painstaking efforts of Juste Adrien de La Fage, was published posthumously. The work is derived in part from the theoretical writings of KOCH, MARPURG, and FUX. The topics of its twelve segments give an indication of Choron's careful pedagogical plan: fundamentals; composition, especially of melody; harmony; counterpoint; imitation; instrumentation; text-music relationships; genres; physical-mathematical theory; musical institutions; the history of music; and bibliography.

Principes d'accompagnement des écoles d'Italie, extraits des meilleurs auteurs: Leo, Durante, Fenaroli, Sala, Azopardi, Sabbatini, le père Martini, et autres; Ouvrage classique, servant d'introduction à l'étude de la composition . . .

> With Vincenzo Fiocchi.

> Paris: Imbault, [1804].

Principes de composition des écoles d'Italie, adoptés par le gouvernement français pour servir à l'instruction des élèves des maîtrises de cathédrales; Ouvrage classique formé de la réunion des modèles les plus parfaits en tout genre, enrichi d'un texte méthodique rédigé selon l'enseignement des écoles les plus célèbres et des écrivains didactiques les plus estimés

> Paris: Auguste Le Duc, [1809]. 6 books in 3 vols.

> > Reprinted in 1816 and perhaps again between 1818 and 1820. Review in *QMMR* 2/6 (1820): 200-212, including an English translation of much of the preface. Offprints of individual segments of this set were issued separately, as *Abrégé des principes de composition des écoles d'Italie* (2 vols.); *Niccolò Sala: Règles de contrepoint pratique* (2 vols.); and *Traité de la fugue et du contrepoint par Marpurg.*

> T ● "On Composition and Counterpoint in General." *QMMR* 2/8 (1820):425-34.

> > From Book 2 of the *Principes de composition.*

Dictionnaire historique des musiciens . . .

> > With François Joseph Fayolle. Includes Choron's "Sommaire de l'histoire de la musique." Thirty-five of the articles (including those on ALBRECHTSBERGER, d'ALEMBERT, FINCK, FUX, GLAREAN, RAMEAU, ROUSSIER, and L. A. SABBATINI, as well as an autobiographical article) are by Choron.

> Paris: Valade & Lenormant, 1810-11. 2 vols.

> > Review in *AmZ* 14/14 (1812):217-21.

> Paris: Chimot, 1817. 2 vols.

> > Perhaps reprinted in 1819.

> T ● Translation of an excerpt from the "Sommaire de l'histoire de la musique," as "Allgemeine historische Übersichten der Musik," in *AmZ* 15/5, 6 (1813):73-79, 89-97.

> T ● "On the Different Schools." *QMMR* 2/7 (1820):273-95.

T ● *A Dictionary of Musicians* . . . 2 vols. London: Sainsbury, 1825; 1827; reprint edition (edited by Henry G. Farmer), New York: Da Capo Press, 1966.

S ● Facsimile of the 1810-11 edition. Hildesheim: Georg Olms, 1970.

"Méthode pratique d'harmonie et d'accompagnement"

Proof sheets with Choron's corrections; never published. [Paris: Bibliothèque nationale.]

An extract was published as "Essai d'une nouvelle théorie des intervalles de musique" in *Rm*(F) 6/12/11, 13 (1832):85-87, 100-103.

"Harmonie. — Systèmes."

Rm(F) 6/12/40 (1832):313-16.

"Sur la composition musicale"

Rm(F) 7/13/12 (1833):91-93.

[*Nouveau*] *manuel complet de musique vocale et instrumentale, ou encyclopédie musicale*

Posthumously published. With Juste Adrien de La Fage.

Paris: Roret, 1836-39. 6 vols. of text; 5 vols. of examples.

"Introduction à l'étude générale et raisonnée de la musique"

Ms. [Paris: Bibliothèque nationale.]

See also ALBRECHTSBERGER: (1790):(1814); (1790):(1830); [ca. 1791]:[1815]; SABBATINI, L. A.: (1789-90):(1810). More comprehensive coverage of Choron's numerous manuscript and published works, including those on pedagogy, is found in Simms (1971), below.

LITERATURE:

Catalogue de livres et œuvres de musique — autographes, manuscrits, imprimés ou gravés — provenant du cabinet de M. Bêche . . .; et de celui de M. Choron . . . dont la vente aura lieu le lundi, 4 janvier 1836, et jours suivans, à midi. Paris: Martinon; Le Blanc, 1835.

La Fage, Juste Adrien Lenoir de. *Éloge de Choron*. Paris: Comptoir des imprimeurs unis, 1843.

Gauthier, L.-E. *Éloge d'Alexandre Choron*. Paris: Derache; Caen: A. Hardel, 1845. Bibliog.

Réty, Hippolyte. *Notice historique sur Choron et son école*. Paris: C. Douniol, 1873.

Carlez, Jules [Alexis]. *Choron: Sa vie et ses travaux*. Caen: F. Le Blanc-Hardel, 1882. Bibliog.

Vauthier, Gabriel. "Un chorége moderne: Alexandre Choron, d'après des documents inédits." *Rhcm* 8/13, 15 (1908):376-89, 436-42.

Vauthier, Gabriel. "L'école de Choron: 1817-1834." *Rhcm* 8/23-24 (1908):613-24, 664-70; 9/2 (1909):54-58. Bibliog.

Vauthier, Gabriel. "Lettres inédites de Choron." *Rhcm* 9/7, 8, 10 (1909):195-201, 223-29, 275-79.

Vauthier, Gabriel. *Choron sous l'Empire*. Poitiers: Société française d'imprimeries, n.d.

Borrel, Eugène. "Choron, Etienne Alexandre." Translated by Hans Albrecht. In *MGG* (1949-68). Bibliog.

Kahl, Willi. "Zur musikalischen Renaissancebewegung in Frankreich während der ersten Hälfte des 19. Jahrhunderts." In *Schmidt-GörgFs* (1957):156-74.

Simms, Bryan Randolph. "Alexandre Choron (1771-1834) as a Historian and Theorist of Music." Ph.D. dissertation, Yale University, 1971. Bibliog. [*Rilm* 71-624. *DA* 32/12A, p. 7034. UMI 72-17175.]

● ● ● Simms, Bryan R. "Choron, Fétis, and the Theory of Tonality." *JMT* 19/1 (1975):112-38. [*Rilm* 75-2658.]

Hutchings, Arthur. "Choron, Alexandre(-Etienne)." In *NGrove* (1980). Bibliog.

Simms, Bryan R. "The Historical Editions of Alexandre-Étienne Choron." *Fam* 27/2 (1980):71-77. [*Rilm* 80-4097.]

Féderoff, Yvette, and Wallon, Simone. "Choron et ses essais de réforme musicale à l'Église de la Sorbonne." In *PalmFs* (1982):63-70. [*Rilm* 82-2556.]

See also FÉTIS: (1833-44); (1840); Wangermée (1951); KOCH: Baker (1976); MOMIGNY: Chailley (1982); ROUSSEAU, J.-J.: Blum (1985); LITERATURE SUPPLEMENT: Bartenstein (1971); Becker (1836-39/1964); Bronfin (1974); Cazden (1980); Cole (1969); Cohen (1873-74); **Coover (1980)**; **Dahlhaus (1984)**; Eitner (1900-1904/1959-60); Fellerer (1927/. . ./1972); **Groth (1983)**; Horsley [*Fugue: History*] (1966); **Kassler (1971), (1979)**; La Fage (1864/1964); Levenson (1981); Lindley (1982); Newman (1946), (1963/. . ./1983); Norton (1984); Pinsart (1980-81); Ratner (1949); Reese (1954/1959); **Ritzel (1967/1968)**; Schmalzriedt ["Durchführen"] (1972-), ["Episode"] (1972-), ["Reprise"] (1972-); Schneider (1985); Seidel (1972-); Stevens (1974); Vogel (1955/1954); **Wagner (1974)**; **Wason (1981/1985)**; Williams, P. (1970); Wirth (1966).

ADRIANUS PETIT COCLICO

[ca. 1500–ca. 1562]

A curious figure in the history of music, Adrianus Petit Coclico habitually exaggerated his credentials. Whether he indeed spent time as a student of Josquin, as he wanted potential employers to believe, or merely acquired insights on that style (perhaps from reading Lampadius), his text, *Compendium musicae* (1552), equipped youths of the mid sixteenth century with a concise introduction to vocal embellishment and improvised counterpoint, as well as to the more routine topic of written counterpoint, and anticipated more thorough treatments of these subjects by authors such as FINCK and ZACCONI.

Some of Coclico's prescriptions, such as his encouragement to embellish individual lines of polyphonic compositions, kept older traditions alive, despite the general opposition to these practices by contemporaries such as ZARLINO and BERMUDO. Yet his remarks on and examples of solo vocal ornamentation confirm similar information supplied by ORTIZ and document this aspect of performance practice. References to *musica reservata*, both in the *Compendium* and in connection with a set of motets (his *Musica reservata: Consolationes piae ex psalmis Davidiciis* of 1552), offer interesting yet confusing hints about that elusive practice. His perspective emphasizes the careful setting of text (imperfectly realized in his motets) and fosters a refined style of singing.

Compendium musices . . . in quo praeter caetera tractantur haec: De modo ornate canendi; De regula contrapuncti; De compositione . . . [*Rism* B/VI/1, p. 227.]

> Nuremberg: Johann Berg [Montanus] and Ulrich Neuber, 1552. [SMLMS.]

T ● Sholund, Edgar Roy. "The *Compendium musices* by Adrianus Petit Coclico." 2 vols. Ph.D. dissertation, Harvard University, 1952.

S ● Bukofzer, Manfred F., ed. Facsimile edition. IGMDm, ser. 1, no. 9. Kassel: Bärenreiter, 1954.

> Reviews in *JAMS* 9/1 (1956):40-46 (A. Tillman Merritt), *Mf* 9/4 (1956):479-81 (Martin Ruhnke), and *ML* 39/4 (1958):392 (Denis W. Stevens).

T ● Seay, Albert, trans. *Musical Compendium (Compendium musices).* CCMPT, no. 5. Colorado Springs, Colo.: Colorado College, 1973.

> Review in *ML* 55/3 (1974):344 (Roger Bray).

LITERATURE:

Kade, O. "Adrianus petit [*sic*] Coclicus (1500 – 1555/56): Ein Beitrag zur Musikgeschichte im XVI. Jahrhundert." *MMg* 29/1-2 (1897):1-16, 17-29.

Federmann, Maria. *Musik und Musikpflege zur Zeit Herzog Albrechts: Zur Geschichte der Königsberger Hofkapelle in den Jahren 1525 – 1578.* KSzMw, no. 14. Kassel: Bärenreiter, 1932.

Crevel, Marcus van. *Adrianus Petit Coclico: Leben und Beziehungen eines nach Deutschland emigrierten Josquinschülers.* The Hague: Martinus Nijhoff, 1940. Bibliog.

> Review in *AfMf* 7/3 (1942):170-74 (Hermann Zenck).

Crevel, Marcus van. "Coclico, Adrianus Petit." In *MGG* (1949-68). Bibliog.

Meier, Bernhard. "The Musica Reservata of Adrianus Petit Coclico and Its Relationship to Josquin." Translated by L. A. Dittmer. *Md* 10 (1956):67-105. Bibliog.

Meier, Bernhard. "Reservata-Probleme: Ein Bericht." *Am* 30/1-2 (1958):77-89. Bibliog.

Kneif, Tibor. "Der prädikative Mensch: Bemerkungen zum musikalischen Snobismus." In *Über das Musikleben der Gegenwart*, pp. 52-60. Berlin: Merseburger, 1968. [*Rilm* 68-4269.]

Dunning, Albert. "Coclico, Adrianus Petit." In *NGrove* (1980). Bibliog.

See also FÉTIS: (1833-44); LIPPIUS: Rivera (1974/1980); WALTHER: (1732); LITERATURE SUPPLEMENT: Alette (1951); **Apfel (1981)**; Atcherson (1970); Babitz (1967); Becker (1836-39/1964); Beebe (1976); Berger (1987); Boetticher (1954); Brennecke (1953); Brown (1976); Bush (1939), (1946); Cahn ["Repercussio"] (1972-); Chomiński (1962/1981); Dunning (1980); Eitner (1900-1904/1959-60); Fellerer (1983); Ferand (1951); Frobenius ["Tactus"] (1972-); Geering (1949-68); Gerber (1790-92/1977), (1812-14/1966); Ghislanzoni (1949-51); Gurlitt (1942/1966); Harrán (1986); Horsley (1951); Jackson (1988); Kuhn (1902); Lindley (1982); Lowinsky (1946/1967), (1948):(1949); Luoma (1976), (1977); ● ● ● Maniates (1979); McKinnon (1978); Meier (1949-68), (1974/1988); Niemöller (1964/1969); Palisca (1949-68), ● ● ● (1959); Reese (1954/1959); Sachs (1972-); Sovík (1985); Straková (1975); Taddie (1984); Wichmann (1966); Zenck (1942).

JOHN COPRARIO

[ca. 1570-80?–ca. 1626]

Giovanni Coprario, as John Cooper wished to be known, was an Englishman who had journeyed to Italy for instruction and experience. He was highly regarded in his time. If MORLEY clutched desperately to the Renaissance and its musical traditions, Coprario eagerly embraced the newer currents in the English musical air. His work treats of imitation and decorative tones in four-part music. One of the earliest to write about what we now call root progressions, he advocated relating the other parts to the bass voice rather than to the tenor and maintained a clear distinction between inner and outer parts. Coprario offered information on melodic progressions, accidentals, the six-five chord, and cadences. In some sources one finds his name spelled Coperario.

"Rules How to Compose"

> Ms., [before 1617?]. [San Marino, Calif.: Henry E. Huntington Library and Art Gallery.]

> S ● ● ● ● Bukofzer, Manfred F., ed. Facsimile edition. Los Angeles: Ernest E. Gottlieb, 1952.
>
> > Reviews in ● ● ● *JAMS* 6/2 (1953):173-76 (Glen Haydon), *MQ* 39/1 (1953):130-31 (Paul Henry Lang), *Notes* 10/1 (1952-53):99-100 (Hans T. David), and *RN* 5/4 (1952):79-80 (Thurston Dart).

LITERATURE:

Pulver, Jeffrey. "Giovanni Coperario alias John Cooper." *MMR* 57/676 (1927):101-2.

Dart, Thurston. "Coperario, John." Translated by Theodora Holm. In *MGG* (1949-68). Bibliog.

Ruff, Lillian M. "Dr. Blow's *Rules for Composition*." *MT* 104/1441 (1963):184-85.

Field, Christopher D. S. "Coprario, John." In *NGrove* (1980). Bibliog.

See also FÉTIS: (1833-44); PLAYFORD: (1654); WALTHER: (1732); LITERATURE SUPPLEMENT: **Apfel (1981)**; Atcherson (1972); Beiche ["Dux"] (1972); Bukofzer (1947); Bullivant (1980); Dahlhaus ["Untersuchungen"] (1966/. . ./1988); Eitner (1900-1904/1959-60); Fellerer ["Zur Kontrapunktlehre"] (1973); Gerber (1790-92/1977); Hancock (1977); Hawkins (1776/. . ./1969); Heckmann (1953); Henderson (1969); Jacobi (1957-60/1971); Lawrence (1978); Lester (1974); Lewis (1981); **Mann (1955/. . ./1965)**; Miller (1960); Mitchell, J. W. (1963); Palisca (1949-68), [*Baroque*] (1968/1981); Pulver (1927/. . ./1973); Ruff (1962); **Seidel and Cooper (1986)**; Shute (1972); Wienpahl (1953), (1955); Williams, P. (1970).

JOHANNES CRÜGER

[1598–1662]

Through disinclination and an untimely death at age twenty-seven, LIPPIUS did not himself provide the means whereby his conception of the triad could be popularized. Johannes Crüger, both in works for beginning students and in his more rigorous *Synopsis musica* (1630), served as executant of this important task, bringing to the general musical public and to later generations the essence of LIPPIUS's thought. Yet he did not serve blindly or devote himself exclusively to LIPPIUS: Crüger's works show numerous influences, including those of CALVISIUS and SWEELINCK. His treatment of triadic theory is neither as fully articulated nor as consistent as is LIPPIUS's own *Synopsis musicae novae* (1612).

Crüger, who is also remembered for his compilations of chorales, maintained a practical orientation. His perspective includes discussions of solmization, beginning instruction in composition, and extensive examples of ornamentation. His explanation of the modes in the 1630 edition of *Synopsis musica* includes LIPPIUS's important categorization according to the quality of the third above the final,

while the revision of 1654 confuses the situation by reverting to more conservative formulations.

Praecepta musicae practicae figuralis . . . [*Rism* B/VI/1, p. 245.]

> Berlin: Georg Runge (Johann Kall), 1625.

Kurtzer und verstendtlicher Unterricht, recht und leichtlich Singen zu lernen . . . [*Rism* B/VI/1, p. 245.]

> Berlin: Georg Runge (Johann Kall), 1625.

Synopsis musica, continens rationem constituendi et componendi melos harmonicum, conscripta variisque exemplis illustrata [*Rism* B/VI/1, p. 246.]

> [Berlin]: Johann Kall, 1630. [LCPS: C-109.]
>
> > Enlarged edition, as *Synopsis musica, continens 1. Methodum . . .; 2. Instructionem brevem . . .:*

> Berlin: the author and Christoph Runge, 1654.

Quaestiones musicae practicae, sex capitibus comprehensae, quae perspicuâ, facili, & quâ fieri potuit, succinctâ methodo ad praxin necessaria continent, . . . conscriptae, variisque idoneis exemplis, una cum utilissima XII. modorum doctrina illustratae [Rism B/VI/1, p. 246.]

> Derived from *Kurtzer und verstendtlicher Unterricht* and *Praecepta musicae practicae figuralis*, above.

Berlin: Christoph Runge (Johann Kall), 1650.

Musicae practicae praecepta brevia et exercitia pro tyronibus varia: Der rechte Weg zur Singekunst . . . [Rism B/VI/1, p. 245.]

> Derived from *Quaestiones musicae practicae*, above.

Berlin: the author, 1660.

LITERATURE:

Fischer-Krückeberg, Elisabeth. "Johann Crüger als Musiktheoretiker." *ZfMw* 12/11-12 (1929-30):609-29.

> Extract from "Johann Crüger: Ein Beitrag zur Musikgeschichte Berlins im 17. Jahrhundert" (Ph.D. dissertation, The University of Berlin, 1919).

Brodde, Otto. *Johann Crüger: Sein Weg und sein Werk.* WG, no. 13. Leipzig and Hamburg: Gustav Schloeßmanns Verlagsbuchhandlung (Gustav Fick), 1936.

Blankenburg, Walter. "Crüger, Johannes." In *MGG* (1949-68). Bibliog.

Brodde, Otto. "Johann Crüger zum Gedenken." *Musica* 16/3 (1962):161.

Buszin, Walter E. "Johann Crüger: On the Tercentenary of His Death." *Response* 4/2 (1962):89-97.

● ● ● Buelow, George J. "Crüger, Johannes." In *NGrove* (1980). Bibliog.

See also BELLERMANN: (1858); FÉTIS: (1833-44); HERBST: Allerup (1931); LIPPIUS: Rivera (1974/1980); Howard (1985); SWEELINCK: Seiffert (1891); VIADANA: Haack (1964/1974); WALTHER: (1732); Gehrmann (1891); LITERATURE SUPPLEMENT: **Apfel (1981)**; Becker (1836-39/1964); **Benary (1956/1961)**; Beyschlag (1907/1953); Blankenburg ["Harmonie"] (1959); Bruck (1928); Buelow (1972), (1982); Bukofzer (1947); Burney (1776-89/. . ./1957); Cahn ["Transitus"] (1972-); Chevaillier (1925/1931-32); Dahlhaus ["Termini"] (1955), ["Untersuchungen"] (1966/. . ./1988); Eitner (1900-1904/1959-60); Falck (1965); Feil (1955); Feldmann (1958); Forchert (1986); Forkel (1792/1962); Gerber (1790-92/1977), (1812-14/1966); Ghislanzoni (1949-51); Gissel (1980/1983), (1986); Goldschmidt (1890/1892), (1907); Harrán (1986); Heimann (1970/1973); **Lester** (1974), ● ● ● (1977), **(1989)**; Moser (1936/. . ./1959); Müller-Blattau (1923/. . ./1963); Neumann, Frederick (1978), (1987); Norton (1984); Palisca (1949-68); **Powers** ["Mode"] **(1980)**; Preußner (1924), (1939); Reese (1957/1970); Rivera (1978), (1984); Robbins (1938); Rogers (1955); Ruhnke (1949-68); Schünemann (1928/1931); Unger (1941/1969); Walker (1987).

CARL CZERNY

[1791–1857]

Whereas some of the authors whose theories we study are known to the general musical public through their music, one—Carl Czerny—is recognized primarily for his technical exercises for piano. Though these works more nearly capture the digital demands of Beethoven's music than its structural complexity or emotional depth, they nevertheless reflect the trends of Viennese musical life in the first half of the nineteenth century, an era whose predilections are only palely represented by the concert programming of our day.

Though the practice has long since died out (for better or for worse), improvisation was a feature common to many early nineteenth-century piano performances. In the hands of a Beethoven or a Liszt (the teacher and pupil of Czerny, respectively), such offerings could be both moving and fascinating. Czerny is one of the few guides to this art, in his *Systematische Anleitung zum Fantasieren auf dem Pianoforte* [ca. 1829] and *Die Kunst des Präludirens*. Incorporating numerous music examples, Czerny worked his way from elementary preludes and the expansions that may occur as cadenzas to the art of improvisation on a given theme or themes, the popular potpourri (recommended when the audience is not particularly refined), variations, contrapuntal improvisations, and the capriccio.

As an industrious teacher of pianists, Czerny endeavored to provide comprehensive instruction through numerous publications. He translated REICHA's theoretical works during the 1830s and later created his own multivolume treatise on composition, *Die Schule der praktischen Tonsetzkunst*, which appeared just before the midpoint of the century, though it may have been written somewhat earlier. (Dating Czerny's works is complicated by the rarity of some volumes, the fact that translations may have appeared in print before the original German, and Czerny's habit of "saving" every hundredth opus number for his most important treatises. More work remains to be done in this area.) Typically conservative in character, Czerny's *Schule* offers a panoramic view of the diverse compositional forms then in use, as well as an extensive summary of instrumentation, accompanied by numerous examples in full score. Unlike many earlier discussions, Czerny is much more influenced by a work's thematic content than by its tonal organization in his assessment of its form. Form is, for him, a given which the composer is not free to modify, but through which the full potential of the thematic ideas can be realized.

Briefe über den Unterricht auf dem Pianoforte vom Anfange bis zur Ausbildung als Anhang zu jeder Clavierschule

    Vienna: A. Diabelli, n.d.

    T● Hamilton, James A., trans. *Letters to a Young Lady, on the Art of Playing the Pianoforte . . .* New York: Hewitt & Jaques, [ca. 1837-41]; New York: Firth, Pond & Co., 1851; later editions; reprint edition (MPT), New York: Johnson Reprint Corporation, 1966; reprint edition (DCPMRS), New York: Da Capo Press, 1982; reprint edition, Wolfeboro, N.H.: Longwood Publishing Group.

        Review in *JALS* 12 (1982):96-98 (William S. Newman). See also Horatio Richmond Palmer's *Piano Primer: A Systematic and Clear Explanation of the Fundamental Principles of Piano-Forte Playing* (New York: H. R. Palmer, 1885) and Ferdinand Beyer's *Preliminary School for the Piano-Forte* (Boston: Oliver Ditson, n.d.).

    T● *Pis'ma Karla Cherni, ili Rukovodstvo k izucheniiu igry na fortepiano ot nachal'nykh osnovanii do polnago usovershenstvovaniia s kratkim obiasneniem generalbasa.* St. Petersburg: 1842.

    T● Hamilton, James Alexander, trans. *Letters on Thorough Bass, with an Appendix on the Higher Branches of Musical Execution and Expression, Forming the Second Part of the "Letters on the Teaching of the Pianoforte".* London: Robert Cocks, [1846]; other editions; reprint edition (MPT), New York: Johnson Reprint Corporation, 1966.

    T● Hamilton, James Alexander, trans. *A Treatise on Thorough-Bass; or, Harmony Made Easy, as Contained in a Series of Familiar Letters.* Boston: O. Ditson, n.d.

    T● *New Exercises on Harmony and Thorough Bass, to Be Filled Up by the Student, Forming a Practical Appendix to His Celebrated Letters on Those Subjects.* London: Robert Cocks, [1846]; facsimile edition (MPT), New York: Johnson Reprint Corporation, 1966.

Systematische Anleitung zum Fantasieren auf dem Pianoforte (Op. 200)

    Cassel: C. Loeber, [ca. 1829].

        Review in *AmZ* 31/35-36 (1829):573-82, 589-94 (G. W. Fink).

    Vienna: A. Diabelli, n.d.

    T● *L'art d'improviser, mis à la portée des pianistes.* Paris: Maurice Schlesinger, [ca. 1840]; Paris: A. Leduc, [1847?]; 2nd edition, [1854?].

        This translation is perhaps by Czerny himself.

    T● ●●● Mitchell, Alice Levine, trans. and ed. *A Systematic Introduction to Improvisation on the Pianoforte . . .,* Op. 200. LMS. New York: Longman, 1983.

        Reviews in *AMT* 34/6 (1984-85):51 (Jo Ann La Torra Smith), *Clavier* 22/10 (1983):10-11 (Carol Montparker), *JALS* 14 (1983):124-26 (William S. Newman), and *NCM* 8/2 (1984-85):164-76 (Richard Swift).

Die Kunst des Präludirens in 120 Beispielen, Präludien, Modulationen, Cadenzen und Fantasien von allen Gattungen für das Piano-Forte . . . als 2ter Theil der Fantasie-Schule/L'art de préluder, mis en pratique pour le piano-forte . . . (Op. 300)

    Vienna: A. Diabelli, n.d.

    T● *L'art de préluder, mis en pratique pour le piano par 120 exemples de préludes, modulations, cadeses et fantasies de tous genres.* Paris: M. Schlesinger, [ca. 1840].

Vollständige theoretisch-practische Pianoforte-Schule von dem ersten Anfang bis zur höchsten Ausbildung fortschreitend, und mit allen nöthigen, zu diesem Zwecke eigens componirten zahlreichen Beispielen (Op. 500)

    and

Supplement: *Die Kunst des Vortrags der ältern und neuen Clavier-Compositionen; oder, Die Fortschritte bis zur neuesten Zeit*

    Vienna: Diabelli, n.d. 3 vols.; 1 vol.

    S● *Kleine theoretisch-praktische Pianoforte-Schule für Anfänger* (Op. 584). Vienna: Diabelli, n.d.

    T● Hamilton, James A., trans. *Complete Theoretical and Practical Pianoforte School, from the First Rudiments of Playing, to the Highest and Most Refined State of Cultivation . . .* London: Robert Cocks, [ca. 1842-46]. 3 vols.

    S● Badura-Skoda, Paul, ed. *Carl Czerny: Über den richtigen Vortrag der sämtlichen Beethoven'schen Klavierwerke.* Vienna: Universal Edition, 1963.

        Contains excerpts from Vol. 4 of Op. 500.

Die Schule der praktischen Tonsetzkunst; oder, Vollständiges Handbuch der Composition (Op. 600)

    Bonn: Simrock, [ca. 1849-50?]. 3 vols.

T ● Bishop, John, trans. *School of Practical Composition; or, Complete Treatise on the Composition of All Kinds of Music . . . Together with a Treatise on Instrumentation.* 3 vols. London: Robert Cocks, [ca. 1848] (Bibliog.); facsimile edition (DCPMRS), New York: Da Capo, 1979.

T ● *Traité de l'instrumentation, faisant suite à l'école du piano.* Paris: n.d.

T ● See Rowen (1979).

See also LÖHLEIN: (1765-81):(1825); REICHA: (1814); [1818]; [1824-25]; (1833).

LITERATURE:

Steger, Hellmuth. "Beiträge zu Karl Czernys Leben und Schaffen." Ph.D. dissertation, The University of Munich, 1924 (1925).

> A brief excerpt was published around 1925.

Textor, K. A. "Een vergeten werk: Carl Czerny, systematische Anleitung zum Fantasieren auf dem Pianoforte, Op. 200 . . ." In *ScheurleerFs* (1925):339-45.

Kahl, Willi. "Czerny, Karl." In *MGG* (1949-68). Bibliog.

Newman, William S. "About Carl Czerny's Op. 600 and the 'First' Description of 'Sonata Form'." *JAMS* 20/3 (1967):513-15. [*Rilm* 67-1689.]

> See REICHA: Weiss (1968).

Esteban, Julio. "On the Origin of the Confusion on Bach's Ornamentation." *AMT* 17/3 (1968):18, 33.

Cole, Malcolm Stanley. "Czerny's Illustrated Description of the Rondo or Finale." *MR* 36/1 (1975):5-16. [*Rilm* 75-2702.]

Goebels, Franzpeter. "Plädoyer für Carl Czerny: Eine Revision." *MB* 12/11 (1980):694-97. [*Rilm* 80-4576.]

Mitchell, Alice L. "Czerny, Carl." In *NGrove* (1980). Bibliog.

Wehmeyer, Grete. "Sage mir, wie Du zu Bach stehst . . ." *Musica* 37/3 (1983):221-29.

● ● ● Mitchell, Alice Levine. "A Systematic Introduction to the Pedagogy of Carl Czerny." In *LangFs* (1984):262-69.

Hinson, Maurice. "Carl Czerny Remembered (1791-1857)." *Clavier* 24/8 (1985):15-19.

Cahn, Peter. "Carl Czernys erste Beschreibung der Sonatenform (1832)." *Mth* 1/3 (1986):277-79.

Malloch, William. "Carl Czerny's Metronome Marks for Haydn and Mozart Symphonies." *EM* 16/1 (1988):72-82.

See also FÉTIS: (1833-44); FUX: Federhofer (1988); GALEAZZI: Churgin (1968); LITERATURE SUPPLEMENT: Ahlgrimm (1973); Alekseev (1974); Allen ["Philosophies"] (1939); Badura-Skoda et al. (1980); Balthazar (1983); Becker (1836-39/1964); **Bent**, I. ["Analytical Thinking"] ● ● ● (1980), ["Analysis"] **(1980/1987)**, (1984); Bruck (1928); Cole (1969); David and Mendel (1945/1966); Donington (1963/. . ./1974); Dunsby and Whittall (1988); Ferand [*Improvisation*] (1956/1961); Ganz (1976); Gardavský (1963); Hailparn (1981); Henneberg (1983); Horsley [*Fugue: History*] (1966); Houle (1987); Jackson (1988); Krones (1988); Lawrence (1978); Levenson (1981); Moyer (1969); Newman (1985); Newman (1946), (1963/. . ./1983), (1969/. . ./1983), (1976); Ortmann (1924); Polezhaev (1982); Ratner (1949), (1970); Reimer ["Concerto"] (1972-); **Ritzel (1967/1968)**; Rosen (1971/. . ./1983), (1980/1988); Rosenblum (1988); Rothschild (1953), (1961); Sachs (1972-); Schmalzriedt ["Durchführen"] (1972-), ["Exposition"] (1972-), ["Reprise"] (1972-), (1985); Schoffman (1979); Shamgar (1978), (1981), (1984); Stevens (1974); Subirá (1947/. . ./1958); Tittel (1966); Todd (1983); Troeger (1987); **Wason (1981/1985).**

GHISELIN DANCKERTS

[ca. 1510–after August 1565]

Ghiselin Danckerts, a judge of LUSITANO and VICENTINO in the famous debate on the three genera in 1551, wrote a treatise which promoted his conservative opinion against the *"nuova maniera"* in music. He felt that the uncontrolled use of accidentals by fledgling composers destroyed the integrity of the eight-mode system and corrupted the art of counterpoint. Danckerts's position in his "Trattato sopra una differentia musicale" [three versions, ca. 1551 to 1560] correctly points out errors in VICENTINO's arguments. Its thrust was more powerfully manifested by ZARLINO in *Le istitutioni harmoniche* (1558).

"Trattato . . . sopra una differentia musicale"

> Mss., [ca. 1551-60]. [Rome: Biblioteca Vallicelliana; Rome: Biblioteca Casanatense.]

LITERATURE:

Straeten, Edmund vander. *La musique aux pays-bas avant le XIXᵉ siècle*. Vol. 6. Brussels: G.-A. van Trigt, 1882; reprint edition (with an Introduction by Edward E. Lowinsky), New York: Dover Publications, 1969.

de Bruyn, P. J. "Ghisilinus Danckerts, kapelaan-zanger van de Pauselijke kapel van 1538 tot 1565 — Zijn leven, werken en onuitgegeven tractaat." *TvNm* 16/4 (1946):217-52; 17/2 (1949):128-57.

Borren, Charles van den. "Ghiselin Danckerts." Translated by Hans Albrecht. In *MGG* (1949-68). Bibliog.

Lockwood, Lewis. "A Dispute on Accidentals in Sixteenth-Century Rome." *Anamu* 2 (1965):24-40. Bibliog.

Lockwood, Lewis. "Danckerts, Ghiselin." In *NGrove* (1980). Bibliog.

See also ARTUSI: (1600); LUSITANO: Barbosa (1970/1977); VICENTINO: (1555); Kaufmann (1960/1966); LITERATURE SUPPLEMENT: Ambros (1878/. . ./1909); Bent et al. (1980); **Berger ● ● ● (1975/1980)**, (1980); Eitner (1900-1904/1964); Gerber (1812-14/1966); Haar (1977); Harrán (1986); Hawkins (1776/. . ./1969); Jackson (1988); Kroyer (1901/. . ./1970); La Fage (1864/1964); **Maniates (1979)**; Palisca (1953), (1959), (1974/1977); Reese (1954/1959).

JOHANN FRIEDRICH DAUBE

[ca. 1730–1797]

The theoretical works of Johann Friedrich Daube, whose career was shaped in the musical cultures of Berlin, Stuttgart, Augsburg, and Vienna, confirm his orientation as a performer and composer. His *General-Baß in drey Accorden* (1756) attracted particular attention due to the similarity of its basic tenets and the theories of RAMEAU, although Daube, in a letter to MARPURG [see MARPURG: (1754-78):Vol. 3 (1757-78):69-70], maintained that he had known nothing of RAMEAU's writings at the time. *Der musikalische Dilettant: Eine Abhandlung des Generalbasses*, which was published in fifty-three installments during 1770 and 1771 and then united into a two-part volume, covers essentially the same material but with an orientation towards Vienna's numerous and sophisticated dilettanti. The second of the four volumes projected for the *Dilettant* series appeared in 1773. Subtitled *Eine Abhandlung der Komposition*, it provides straightforward instruction in the free style of the day (with examples of two- through ten-voice composition), in the techniques of variation, and in contrapuntal procedures. The *Anleitung zur Erfindung der Melodie* (1797-98) was probably written during the 1770s as a later volume of the *Dilettant* series. Published around the time of Daube's death, it survives in various editions, some of which substitute the title *Anleitung zum Selbstunterricht in der musikalischen Komposition*

sowohl für die Instrumental- als Vocal-Musik. The word *"Selbstunterricht,"* like *"Dilettant"* before it, does not diminish the value of Daube's pedagogy. Instead, it commends the dedication of the Viennese amateur of the late eighteenth century.

General-Baß in drey Accorden . . . [*Rism* B/VI/1, pp. 252-53.]

> Frankfurt am Main: Johann Benjamin Andrä (Leipzig: J. G. I. Breitkopf), 1756. [LCPS: D-008. SMLMS.]
>
> > Review in MARPURG: (1754-78):Vol. 2/4-6 (1756):325-66, 464-74, 542-47. Response in MARPURG: (1754-78):Vol. 3/1 (1757-58):69-70. Another review in MARPURG: (1754-78):Vol. 3/6 (1757-58):465-86; Vol. 4/3 (1758-59):196-246 (Fried. Wilhelm Sonnenkalb).
>
> T ● Wallace, Barbara K. "J. F. Daube's *General-Bass in drey Accorden* (1756): A Translation and Commentary." Ph.D. dissertation, North Texas State University, 1983. [*Rilm* 83-2634. *DA* 44/05A, p. 1240. UMI 83-20246.]

Der musikalische Dilettant [*Rism* B/VI/1, p. 253.]

> 1) *Eine Abhandlung des Generalbasses . . .*

2) *Eine Abhandlung der Komposition . . .*
Vienna: Joseph Kurtzböck, 1770-71. Vol. 1.
[LCPS: D-009a.]
Vienna: Johann Thomas Edler von Trattner,
1773. Vol. 2. [LCPS: D-009b. SMLMS.]

T● Snook, Susan Pauline. "J. F. Daube's *Der
musikalische Dilettant: Eine Abhandlung der
Komposition* (1773): A Translation and Commentary." 2 vols. Ph.D. dissertation, Stanford
University, 1978. Bibliog. [*Rilm* 78-2820. *DA*
39/06A, p. 3220. UMI: 78-22576.]

Anleitung zur Erfindung der Melodie und ihrer Fortsetzung
[*Rism* B/VI/1, p. 252.]

1) *Erster Theil* [*von Erfindung der Melodie und ihrer
Fortsetzung*]

2) *Zweyter Theil, welcher die Composition enthält*
Vienna: Christian Gottlob Täubel, 1797. Vol. 1.
[LCPS: D-007a. SMLMS.]
Vienna: In Commission der Hochenleitterschen
Buchhandlung, 1798. Vol. 2. [LCPS: D-007a.
SMLMS.]
Vienna: J. Funk, 1798. Both volumes. [LCPS: D-
007b.]

> Further editions, under the title *Anleitung zum
> Selbstunterricht in der musikalischen Komposi-
> tion sowohl für die Instrumental- als Vocal-
> Musik*:

Vienna: Schaumburg in Kommission, 1798. Both
volumes.
Vienna: Binz, 1798. Both volumes.
Linz: Commission der Akademischen Buchhandlung, 1798. Vol. 2.

LITERATURE:

Reichert, Georg. "Daube, Johann Friedrich." In *MGG*
(1949-68). Bibliog.

Karbaum, Michael. "Das theoretische Werk Johann Friedrich Daubes—Der Theoretiker J. F. Daube: Ein
Beitrag zur Kompositionslehre des 18. Jahrhunderts." Ph.D. dissertation, The University of
Vienna, 1968 (1969). [*Rilm* 70-485.]

Buelow, George J. "Daube, Johann Friedrich." In *NGrove*
(1980). Bibliog.

See also FÉTIS: (1833-44); (1840); (1844); HEINICHEN:
(1728):Buelow (1961/. . ./1986); KOCH: Baker
(1976); Sisman (1982); RAMEAU: Pischner
(1961/. . ./1967); RIEMANN: (1898); VOGLER:
Stevens (1983); LITERATURE SUPPLEMENT:
Arnold (1931/. . ./1965); Becker (1836-39/1964); **Benary (1956/1961)**; **Buelow ● ● ●** (1979), ["Rhetoric"] **(1980)**; Chevaillier (1925/1931-32); David
and Mendel (1945/1966); Donington (1963/
. . ./1974); Eitner (1900-1904/1959-60); Fellerer
(1962); Fischer (1957); Forkel (1792/1962); Gerber
(1790-92/1977), (1812-14/1966); Hartmann (1923);
Horsley [*Fugue: History*] (1966); Imig (1969/1970);
Jones (1934); Kauko (1958); Mallard (1978); Nelson (1984); Newman (1963/. . ./1983); Oberdoerffer
(1949-68), (1967); Ratner (1956), (1970), (1980);
Reichenbach (1948); Reimer ["Kenner"] (1972-);
Ritzel (1967/1968); Rohwer (1949-68); Rosenblum
(1988); Sheldon (1982); **Shirlaw (1917/. . ./1970)**;
Sisman (1978); Stein (1983); Telesco (forthcoming);
Thomson (1960/1978); Todd (1983); Troeger
(1987); Ulrich (1931/1932); Vogel (1962); **Wagner
(1974)**; **Wason (1981/1985)**; Wessel (1955); Williams, P. (1970); Wirth (1966).

ALFRED DAY

[1810–1849]

Alfred Day entered theoretical territories which had
been left unexplored by British theorists until his time, yet
his contemporaries remained contemptuous of his results.
One hundred years after RAMEAU's demonstration that
acoustical principles could serve effectively as theoretical
underpinnings, Day based his *Treatise on Harmony* (1845)
upon what he took to be overtones for the tonic, dominant,
and supertonic pitches, though he suggested, curiously, that
either D or D-flat may serve as ninth of C, A or A-flat as
thirteenth of C, etc., thus exposing a less than rigorous adherence to acoustical dictates. The result was awkward from
a variety of standpoints, including the question of temperament and the system's nonconformity with the practices of
composers. On the one hand, the prescriptions by which Day
derived the various chords created contradictions when applied to the tuning of an instrument; while on the other his
derivation of chords led to peculiar chromatic spellings and
illogical explanations of chord progression. For example, he
regarded the submediant as no more than upper partials
(the ninth, eleventh, and thirteenth) of the dominant, thus
calling into question what sort of "progression" a motion
from dominant to submediant might represent.

Day's system encompasses two categories of writing:
diatonic harmony (harmony in the strict style), and chromatic harmony (harmony in the free style). In the strict style,
all dissonances must be prepared. Thus the seventh of the
dominant is regarded as a derivation from the preceding

subdominant chord when prepared (strict style), and as an acoustical outcome of the dominant's root when not prepared (free style). In addition, he formulated an analytical system wherein a letter placed under a bass pitch indicated the inversion of the chord which was to be sounded. "A" was used when the root was on the bottom, "B" when the third was, and so on. In C major, a chord constructed of the pitches A-flat, D, F, B (reading from bottom to top) was labeled "E" since A-flat is the fourth pitch (proceeding by stacked thirds) above the chord's structural root, G. The augmented-sixth chord, which was derived by combining elements of the dominant (particularly its minor ninth) and supertonic (particularly its major third), was also labeled with an "E" owing to the fact that the dominant's ninth resided in the bass. Though the system continued to rankle after Day's untimely demise, it was supported—and modified—by influential teachers and authors, including MACFARREN (who edited the second edition), OUSELEY, and PROUT.

Treatise on Harmony

> London: Cramer, Beale, 1845.
> London: Harrison & Sons, 1885. Edited by G. A. MACFARREN.

S ● See Jacobi (1957-60/1971).

> Contains a facsimile of a large segment of the 1845 edition plus a portion of MACFARREN's 1885 edition.

S ● Facsimile edition. CTME. Kinkenny, Ireland: Boethius Press, forthcoming.

LITERATURE:

"Dr. Alfred Day." [Obituary.] *MW* 24/7 (1849):97.

Stephens, Charles Edward. "On the Fallacies of Dr. Day's Theory of Harmony, with a Brief Outline of the Elements of a New System." *PMA 1874-75* 1 (1875):51-73.

> Includes discussion by Henry Charles Banister, William Chappell, Alexander J. Ellis, John Hullah, and William Pole.

Parry, C. Hubert H. "Day, Alfred." In *DMM* (1879-89).

Pearce, Charles William. "Some Further Modifications of Day's System of Harmony, Suggested from an Educational Point of View." *PMA 1887-88* 14 (1888):173-99.

> Includes discussion by J. F. Bridge, Ebenezer PROUT, and Charles E. Stephens.

PROUT, Ebenezer. "Some Suggested Modifications of Day's Theory of Harmony." *PMA 1887-88* 14 (1888):89-117.

> Includes discussion by J. Frederick Bridge, Ebenezer PROUT, Thomas Lea Southgate, and Charles E. Stephens.

Haydon, Glen. "Alfred Day and the Theory of Harmony." *PAMS 1939* (1944):233-40.

Harman, R. A. "Day, Alfred." Translated by Herta Goos. In *MGG* (1949-68).

Jones, Patricia Collins. "Alfred Day and Nineteenth-Century Theory of Harmony in England." Ph.D. dissertation, Rutgers University, 1977. [*Rilm* 77-1566. *DA* 38/05A, p. 2403. UMI 77-24990.]

● ● ● Jones, Patricia Collins. "Day, Alfred." In *NGrove* (1980).

See also MACFARREN: (1860); (1867); Banister (1891); STAINER: (1871); LITERATURE SUPPLEMENT: Bircher (1970); Bridges (1984); Burke (1963); Cazden (1948); Cobb (1884); Finney (1957); Jacobi (1957-60/1971); Jones (1934); Jorgenson (1957); Kauko (1958); Lecky (1880); Mitchell, J. W. (1963); Prout (1893); Scholes (1947); **Seidel and Cooper (1986)**; Sheldon (1982); **Shirlaw (1917/.../1970)**; Thompson (1980); Whatley (1981).

SIEGFRIED (WILHELM) DEHN

[1799–1858]

Among the nineteenth century's more learned theorists, Siegfried Dehn, who held a professorship at Berlin's Royal Academy of the Arts, was attuned to the music of Lassus and Palestrina and to the fugal writing of Bach and its theoretical interpretation by MARPURG, rather than to the music of his contemporaries and the theoretical constructs they were devising. Among his correspondents was FÉTIS, who benefited from Dehn's generosity in providing materials for the *Biographie universelle*. (Dehn, like FÉTIS, served as a librarian.) Dehn considered the mathematical/acoustical formulations which had pervaded theoretical discourse (in

the works of TARTINI, for example) to be pointless. Theory was, instead, the abstraction of critical thinkers who based their formulations upon the practice of great composers.

A. B. MARX, among others, found fault with Dehn's narrowly focused *Theoretisch-praktische Harmonielehre* (1840). His later works recede further from modern practice and deal instead with his beloved contrapuntists. Mikhail Glinka was perhaps Dehn's most famous student. Their relationship was maintained throughout Glinka's career—he even returned to Dehn late in his life to study modal practices in an attempt to reconcile Western and Orthodox Russian principles of church music. Though no significant compositions resulted from this interaction, one might find a hint of Dehn's teaching method in the numerous exercises which were preserved and published in the complete-works edition of Glinka's compositions.

Theoretisch-praktische Harmonielehre mit angefügten Generalbaßbeispielen

> Berlin: W. Thome, 1840.

>> Response in MARX: (1841). Review in *AmZ* 43/38-39 (1841):761-71, 785-94 (G. W. Fink).

> Berlin: Schlesinger, 1860.

Analysen dreier Fugen aus Johann Sebastian Bach's Wohltemperirtem Clavier und einer Vokal-Doppelfuge A. M. Bononcini's

> Leipzig: C. F. Peters, 1858.

Lehre vom Contrapunkt, dem Canon und der Fuge, nebst Analysen von Duetten, Terzetten etc. von Orlando di Lasso, Marcello, Palestrina u. A. und Angabe mehrerer Muster-Canons und Fugen

> Berlin: F. Schneider, 1859. Edited by Bernhard Scholz.
> Berlin: W. Weber, 1883.

"Kurs muzykal'no-teoreticheskikh lektsii" [A Course of Musical Theoretical Lectures]

> In M. I. Glinka, *Polnoe sobranie sochinenii* [A Complete Collection of Works], Vol. 17, pp. 247-70. Moscow: Izdatel'stvo muzyka, 1969.

>> Contains the original German and the Russian translation of V. V. Uspensky.

See also MARPURG: (1753-54):(1858).

LITERATURE:

Krabbe, Wilhelm. "Dehn, Siegfried Wilhelm." In *MGG* (1949-68). Bibliog.

Brown, David. *Mikhail Glinka: A Biographical and Critical Study*. London: Oxford University Press, 1974. [*Rilm* 74-473.]

> Reviews in *AJME* 16 (1975):65-66 (W. L. Hoffmann), *AMT* 23/6 (1974):44-45 (Gwendoline Harper), *BB* 19/6 (1973-74):82-83 (Frank Granville Barker), *Choice* 11/4 (1974):611, *Dmt* 49/3 (1974-75):70 (Erling Fagerberg), *Éc* 42/4 (1974):437-38 (J. Legrand), *LJ* 99/10 (1974-75):1393 (C. Gerald Parker), *LMl* 14/1 (1974):128-32 (April Fitzlyon), *MB* 8/2 [67] (1976):101-2 (Detlef Gojowy), *MEJ* 62/9 (1975-76):81, *Mf* 31/3 (1978):379-80 (Detlef Gojowy), *MiE* 38/368 (1974):177-78 (Michael Hurd), *Miscm* 8 (1975):159-61 (Andrew D. McCredie), *ML* 55/3 (1974):341-43 (Edward Garden), *MO* 98/1173 (1974-75):513 (Basil Ramsey), *MQ* 61/1 (1975):141-51 (Richard Taruskin), *MR* 35/3-4 (1974):324-26, *MT* 115/1576 (1974):476 (Geoffrey Norris), *MuMus* 22/10 [262] (1973-74):43-44 (Peter Palmer), *Notes* 31/4 (1974-75):775-76 (Laurel Fay), *Nrmi* 8/3 (1974):454-56 (William Weaver), *NS* 87/2248 (1974):553-54 (Bayan Northcott), *NZfM* 135/5 (1974):334-35 (Hans Hollander), *Opera* 25/9 (1974):776-77 (John Warrack), *Smuz* 4 (1976):127-28, and *Strad* 85 [reads 86]/1017 (1974-75):555-57 (A. D.).

Warrack, John. "Dehn, Siegfried (Wilhelm)." In *NGrove* (1980). Bibliog.

See also BELLERMANN: (1858); (1862); CATEL: Asaf'ev (1978); FÉTIS: (1833-44); LITERATURE SUPPLEMENT: Beiche ["Dux"] (1972-); Cahn ["Repercussio"] (1972-); **Dahlhaus** (1967), ["Geschichte"] (1980), (**1984**); **Dahlhaus and Sachs (1980)**; Fellerer (1927/. . ./1972); Jeppesen (1922/. . ./1970), (1930/. . ./1974), (1935); McQuere (1983); Müller-Blattau (1949-68); Schmalzriedt ["Durchführen"] (1972-), ["Episode"] (1972-), ["Exposition"] (1972-); Tittel (1959); **Wagner (1974)**; Wason (1988); Wirth (1966); **Zaminer (1985)**.

JOHANNES CHRISTOPH DEMANTIUS

[1567–1643]

The *Isagoge artis musicae* [1602?] of Johannes Christoph Demantius, like its predecessor, *Forma musices* (1592), offered students a basic introduction to *musica practica*. A number of elementary music examples, as well as suggestions for correct singing, complement the text. Of greater interest are two supplements which Demantius later incorporated. In the 1617 edition a section on mode derived from Nicolaus Roggius [*Musicae practicae* (1566/. . ./1596)] appeared. Beginning with the 1632 edition a glossary of musical terms

was appended. Many of the terms and their definitions were derived from a similar list compiled by Michael PRAETORIUS for his *Syntagma musicum* (1614-20). The work of Demantius served, in turn, as a model for several other glossaries in seventeenth-century theory manuals.

Forma musices: Gründlicher und kurtzer Bericht der Singkunst . . . [*Rism* B/VI/1, p. 257.]

> Bautzen: Michael Wolrab, 1592.

Isagoge artis musicae . . .: Kurtze Anleitung, recht und leicht singen zu lernen [Rism B/VI/1, pp. 257-58.]

[1602?]. [Lost.]

Numerous editions through 1684, including:

Nuremberg: Valentin Fuhrmann, 1607.
Onoldsbach: Paulus Bohemius, 1611. [LCPS: D-018a. SMLMS.]

A single edition titled *Cui additus est Nicolai Roggii gottingensis tractatus de intervallis et modis musicis, etc.*:

Goslar: Johann Vogt, 1617.

Editions from 1632 onward with the supplement *Kurtzer, doch gründlicher Erklärung der griechischen, lateinischen und italiänischen Wörtlein, so bey den Neotericis oder jetzigen newen Musicis hin und wieder üblichen und in Gebrauch seyn*, including:

Freiberg: Georg Beuther, 1632. [IDC.]
Freiberg: Georg Beuther (Jena: Samuel Krebs), 1656. [LCPS: D-018b.]

S ● Eggebrecht, Hans Heinrich. "Ein Musiklexikon von Christoph Demantius." *Mf* 10/1 (1957):48-60.

S ● Facsimile of the 1607 edition. Dm, no. 3. Buren: Fritz Knuf, 1975.

Although this facsimile edition was published in the series "Dictionarium musicum," the 1607 version of the work, which the publisher chose to reproduce, does not contain the glossary supplement.

LITERATURE:

Kade, Reinhard. "Christoph Demant: 1567-1643." *VMw* 6 (1890):469-552. Bibliog.

Adrio, Adam. "Demantius, (Johannes) Christoph." *MGG* (1949-68).

Blankenburg, Walter. "Demantius, (Johannes) Christoph." *NGrove* (1980). Bibliog.

See also FÉTIS: (1833-44); PRAETORIUS: (1614-20); VIADANA: Haack (1964/1974); WALTHER: (1732); LITERATURE SUPPLEMENT: Abraham (1968/1969); Becker (1836-39/1964); Beiche ["Dux"] (1972-); Chybiński (1911-12); Coover (1980); Eitner (1900-1904/1959-60); Falck (1965); Fellerer (1983); Forkel (1792/1962); Frobenius ["Homophonus"] (1972-); Gerber (1812-14/1966); Hüschen (1986); Katz (1926); Lester (1977), (1989); Livingstone (1962); Niemöller (1964/1969); Oberdörffer (1949-68); Pietzsch (1936-42); Preußner (1924); Sannemann (1903/1904); Schäfke (1934/1964); Schünemann (1928/1931); Taddie (1984); Walker (1987).

JEAN DENIS

[ca. 1600–1672]

As a harpsichord builder and organist, Jean Denis proudly asserted that his perspective on matters such as tuning and the French church *tons* would be of more value to readers than the speculations of academics. Though neither elegantly nor precisely worded, his *Traité de l'accord de l'espinette* (1643; expanded edition, 1650) offered a useful perspective on meantone tuning for keyboard instruments and on the interaction of church musicians (singers and organist) at a time when, due to the limitations of the meantone system, a careful assessment of the appropriate transposition of the *ton* was required in order to attain both a comfortable range for the singers and a suitable position on the keyboard. Especially to be avoided was the interval represented by the accidentals G-sharp and E-flat, the one "fifth" in Denis's meantone system that remained intolerable. Vincent Panetta, in commentary to his translation of the treatise, reports that Denis's instructions could have applied only to the one-quarter comma meantone system. Denis was not an advocate of equal temperament, as some modern commentators have suggested.

Traité de l'accord de l'espinette avec la comparison de son clavier avec la musique vocale [Rism B/VI/1, p. 259.]

Paris: the author, 1643.
Paris: Robert Ballard, 1650. Expanded edition. [LCPS: D-019.]

S ● Curtis, Alan, ed. Facsimile of the 1650 edition, with selected pages from the 1643 edition. New York: Da Capo Press, 1969.

Review in *AR* 12/2 (1971):58 (Dale Higbee).

T ● ● ● ● Panetta, Vincent J., Jr., trans. *Treatise on Harpsichord Tuning by Jean Denis*. CMTM. Cambridge: Cambridge University Press, 1987. Bibliog.

Reviews in *Brio* 24/1 (1987):45 (Clifford Bartlett), *Diapason* 79/5 [942] (1988):7 (James B. Hartman), *ML* 69/3 (1988):374-75 (Howard Schott), *MT* 130/1754 (1989):213-15 (Stewart Pollens), *Notes* 44/3 (1987-88):467-69 (Thomas

McGeary), and *Theoria* 4 (1989) (Paul A. Le-prade).

LITERATURE:

Lesure, François. "Denis." Translated by Hans Albrecht. In *MGG* (1949-68). Bibliog.

Dufourcq, Norbert. "Une dynastie française: Les Denis." *Rdm* 38 (1956):151-55.

Lesure, François. "Denis." In *NGrove* (1980). Bibliog.

See also FÉTIS: (1833-44); MERSENNE: (1636-37); (1644); LITERATURE SUPPLEMENT: Alekseev (1974); Asselin (1981); Atcherson (1973); **Barbour** (1949-68), **(1951/. . ./1972)**; Cohen (1966/1978), ["Symposium"] (1972), (1988); **Dahlhaus et al. (1987)**; Eitner (1900-1904/1959-60); Ferran (1979); Gerber (1790-92/1977); Launay (1972); Lindley ["Temperaments"] (1980), (1984); Miller and Cohen (1987); Rogers (1955); Subirá (1947/. . ./1958); Tolkoff (1973).

RENÉ DESCARTES

[1596–1650]

René Descartes, French philosopher, conducted numerous precise scientific experiments relating to music and sound and studied natural phenomena in an attempt to determine their mechanistic characteristics. His *Musicae compendium*, written in 1618, was published posthumously in 1650. The work reveals that Descartes placed the major third after the octave and fifth in order of consonance while denying such status for the fourth. The fourth was, he argued, merely the shadow of the fifth.

Descartes corresponded with MERSENNE about music and scientific analysis. Both men had contact with Rosicrucian thought and attempted to determine whether the scientific experiments of that group had a rational basis. Descartes's mathematical and acoustical approach to music had a strong influence on subsequent theorists, including PRINTZ and SAUVEUR. In addition, his *Les passions de l'âme* (1649) transformed European thought regarding notions such as emotions and the soul—concepts which were carefully considered by music theorists during the next hundred years.

Musicae compendium [*Rism* B/VI/1, pp. 261-63.]

Dated 1618.

Utrecht: typis Gisberti à Zÿll & Theodori ab Ackersdÿck, 1650. [LCPS: D-025a. HoM: 447.]
Amsterdam: J. Jansson junior, 1656. [LCPS: D-025b. HoM: 448.]
Amsterdam: typographia Blaviana, 1683. [LCPS: D-025c.]
Frankfurt am Main: Friedrich Knoch, 1695. [LCPS: D-025d.]

T ● [Brouncker, William Lord, trans.] *Renatus Descartes: Excellent Compendium of Musick . . .* London: Thomas Harper (for Humphrey Moseley), 1653. [*Rism* B/VI/1, p. 262. LCPS: D-025e. HoM: 446. IDC.]

T ● Glazemaker, J. H. *Kort begryp der zangkunst.* Amsterdam: Jan Rieuwertsz (Tymon Hout-

haak), 1661; reprinted in *Proeven der wysbegeerte*, Amsterdam: Jan ten Hoorn, 1692. [*Rism* B/VI/1, pp. 262-63.]

T ● Poisson, Nicolas, trans. and ed. *Traité de la mechanique . . . de plus l'abrégé de musique . . .* Paris: Charles Angot, 1668; Compagnie des libraires, 1724. [*Rism* B/VI/1, pp. 262-63. LCPS: D-025f.]

T ● Robert, Walter, trans. *Compendium of Music.* Introduction and notes by Charles Kent. MSD, no. 8. Rome: American Institute of Musicology, 1961.

S ● Facsimile of the 1650 edition. Strasbourg: Heitz, [1965].

Contains a Preface of six pages.

S ● Facsimile of the 1650 edition. MMMLF, ser. 2, no. 87. New York: Broude Brothers, 1968.

ST ● Brockt, Johannes, trans. and ed. *Musicae compendium/Leitfaden der Musik (1656).* TzF, no. 28. Darmstadt: Wissenschaftliche Verlagsanstalt, 1978.

Review in *Rmuz* 24/20 (1980):7 (mm).

T ● Zanoncelli, Luisa, trans. and ed. *Breviario di musica.* Venice: Corbo & Fiore Editori, 1979.

ST ● Buzon, Frédéric de, ed. and trans. *Abrégé de musique/Compendium musicae.* ÉEp. Paris: Presses universitaires de France, 1987.

T ● See **Katz and Dahlhaus (1987-)**:Vol. 2.

ST ● See Collected Works editions, below.

Correspondence (1619-50)

S ● Roth, Leon, ed. *Correspondance of Descartes and Constantyn Huygens, 1635-1647 . . .* Preface by Charles Adam. Oxford: The Clarendon Press, 1926.

Reviews in *JPh* 24/18 (1927):499-501 (Richard McKeon), *Personalist* 8/2 (1927):132 (R. T. F.), *Phil* 2/5 (1927):100-102 (Edwin A. Burtt), and *PhR* 36/1 (1927):91-92 (H. R. Smart).

S ● *Descartes: Correspondance*. Introduction and notes by Charles Adam and Gérard Milhaud. 8 vols. Paris: Librairie Felix Alcan; Presses universitaires de France, 1936-63; reprint edition, Nendeln, Liechtenstein: Kraus Reprint, 1970.

Reviews in *Isis* 26/2 (1936):464-65 (Jean Pelseneer) and *JPh* 33/16 (1936):443; 36/22 (1939):612-13 (George Boas).

S ● See Stephan (1949-68), below, and Sebba (1959/1964), below, for further bibliographical information.

ST ● See Collected Works editions, below.

Les passions de l'âme

Paris: Henry LeGras, 1649.

Numerous other editions.

T ● [Desmarets, Henri, trans.] *Passiones animae*. Amsterdam: apud Ludovicum Elzevirium, 1650; later printings.

T ● *The Passions of the Soule*. London: J. Martin & J. Ridley, 1650.

T ● Tilesio, Balthasar Heinrich, trans. and ed. *Tractat von den Leidenschafften der Seele*. Frankfurt: E. G. Krugen, 1723.

T ● Kirchmann, J. H. v., trans. *Über die Leidenschaften der Seele*. PBSHPZ, no. 26. Berlin: L. Heimann, 1870.

T ● [Buchenau, Artur, trans.] *Über die Leidenschaften der Seele*. PB, no. 29. Leipzig: F. Meiner, 1911.

S ● *Traité des passions*. L'intelligence, no. 10. With a Study by Émile Chartier [Alain]. Paris: H. Jonquières, 1928.

S ● Mesnard, Pierre, ed. Bph. Paris: Boivin, 1937; reprint edition, Paris: Hatier-Boivin, 1955.

T ● Chmaj, Ludwik, trans. *Namietności duszy*. Bfk, [no. 30]. Warsaw, 1938.

S ● Touchet, J., illustrator. Paris: Kieffer, 1940.

T ● Cairola, Giovanni, trans. *Le passioni dell'anima*. Gss, no. 146. Turin: Unione tipografico-editrice torinese, 1951.

S ● Rodis-Lewis, Geneviève, ed. Btp. Paris: J. Vrin, 1955. Bibliog.

Reviews in *Bdp* 2/4 (1955):no. 752 (Camille de Vregille) and *Nrt* 87/10 [77] (1955):1112 (J. Gilbert).

ST ● See Collected Works editions, below.

COLLECTED WORKS EDITIONS:

Glazemaker, Jan Hendrik, trans. *Werken*. 6 vols. Amsterdam: Jan Rieuwertsz, 1657-61. [*Rism* B/VI/1, p. 262.]

Translations into Dutch.

Principia philosophiae. Amsterdam: apud Danielem Elzevirium, 1664; later editions; French translation by C. Picot, Paris: Theodore Girard, 1668.

Cousin, Victor, ed. *Œuvres de Descartes*. 11 vols. Paris: F. G. Levrault, 1824-26.

Aimé-Martin, L., ed. *Œuvres philosophiques*. Paris: Lefèvre, 1838; 1884.

Simon, Jules, ed. *Œuvres de Descartes*. Paris: Charpentier, 1844.

Adam, Charles, and Tannery, Paul, eds. *Œuvres de Descartes*. 13 vols. Paris: Léopold Cerf, 1897-1913; reprint edition, J. Vrin, 1957-58; reprint edition, Brookhaven Press.

Haldane, Elizabeth S., and Ross, G. R. T., trans. *The Philosophical Works of Descartes*. 2 vols. Cambridge: Cambridge University Press, 1911; 1931; 1967-70; 1973-74; reprint edition, New York: Dover; London: Vision Press, 1955.

Reviews in *IJE* 23 (1912-13):236-37 (Philip E. B. Jourdain), *JPhil* 11/7 (1914):189-92 (Lina Kahn), *Mind* New Series 20/80 (1911):542-52 (A. E. Taylor) and 22/87 (1913):406-8 (A. E. Taylor), and *Thought* 31/120 (1956):120 (James Collins).

Œuvres. Paris: René Hilsum, [1932].

Bridoux, André, ed. *Œuvres et lettres*. Paris: Éditions de la Nouvelle revue française, 1937; enlarged edition (BP, no. 40), Paris: Librairie Gallimard, 1949-53.

Œuvres philosophiques et morales. Bl. Paris: Aubin, 1948.

Smith, Norman Kemp, trans. *Philosophical Writings*. London: Macmillan, 1952; New York: The Modern Library, 1958.

Reviews in *BJPS* 5/18 (1954-55):174 (J. O. Wisdom), *Ethics* 66/3 (1956):228-29 (Alan Gewirth), *HibJ* 52/3 (1953-54):307-8 (L. J. Beck), *Isis* 46/1 [143] (1955):377-80 (Thomas S. Kuhn), *JPhil* 51/5 (1954):192-94 (Albert G. A. Balz), *Phil* 30/112 (1955):77-78 (D. J. McCracken), and *Thought* 29/113 (1954):277-83 (James Collins).

Alquié, Ferdinand, ed. *Œuvres philosophiques de Descartes*. CG. Paris: Éditions Garnier Frères, [1963-73].

Reviews in *Eras* 19/19-20 (1967):580-81 (André Mercier), *FrR* 41/5 (1967-68):729-30 (Gregor Sebba), *FrS* 20/4 (1966):398-99 (Ian W. Alexander), and *JHP* 2/2 (1964):260-61 (Gregor Sebba) and 6/2 (1968):174-75 (Gregor Sebba).

Cottingham, John; Stoothoff, Robert; and Murdoch, Dugald, trans. *The Philosophical Writings*. 2 vols. London: Cambridge University Press, 1985.

> Reviews in *BJHS* 20/2 [65] (1987):232-33 (Alistair Duncan), *StL* 18/1 (1986):94-96 (Desmond M. Clarke), and *TLS* 85/4335 (1986):482 (Margaret D. Wilson).

LITERATURE:

Mercadier, E. "Les théories musicales de Descartes." *Rhcm* 1/4-6 (1901):129-37, 189-95, 237-41.

Gandillot, Maurice. "Le débat sur la gamme: Les conceptions de Pythagore et de Descartes." *Rgspa* 18/17(1907):714-21.

Pirro, André. *Descartes et la musique*. Paris: Fischbacher, 1907; reprint edition, Geneva: Minkoff Reprint, 1973. Bibliog.

Racek, Jan. "Contribution au problème de l'esthétique musicale chez René Descartes." *Rm* 11/109 (1930):288-301.

Locke, Arthur W. "Descartes and Seventeenth-Century Music." *MQ* 21/4 (1935):423-31.

Almeida, D. de. "Una faceta poco explorada: Descartes en su *Compendium musicae*." *Estudios* 57 (1937):441-47.

Orrilard. "Descartes et la musique." *Gch* 4/14 (1937).

Victoria, Marcos. "Descartes y la música." In *Buenos Aires (City) Universidad nacional, Instituto de filosofía: Descartes—Homenaje en el tercer centenario del "Discurso del método"*, edited by Luis Juan Guerrero, vol. 1, pp. 353-67. 3 vols. Buenos Aires: [Imprenta de la Universidad], 1937.

Prenant, Lucie. "Esthétique et sagesse cartésiennes." *Rhphgc* 10/29-30 (1942):3-13, 99-114.

Stephan, Rudolf. "Descartes, René." In *MGG* (1949-68). Bibliog.

Roland-Manuel, M. "Descartes et le problème de l'expression musicale." In *Descartes: Cahiers de Royaumont, Philosophie, no. II.*, pp. 438-42. [Paris]: Les éditions de minuit, [1957].

Massenkeil, Günther. "Bemerkungen zum *Compendium musicae* (1618) des René Descartes." In *Bericht Köln 1958* (1959):188-91.

Sebba, Gregor. *Descartes and His Philosophy: A Bibliographical Guide to the Literature, 1800-1958*. Athens, Ga.: The University of Georgia, College of Business Administration, Bureau of Business Research, 1959; revised edition (as *Bibliographia cartesiana: A Critical Guide to the Descartes Literature, 1800-1960*; Aihi, no. 5), The Hague: Martinus Nijhoff, 1964. Bibliog.

> Reviews in *BSAP* 58/4 (1964):496-98 (Robert L. Perkins), *Eras* 17/3-4 (1965):72-75 (Wilhelm Halbfass), *Isis* 56/4 [186] (1965):459 (J. F Scott), *JHP* 4/3 (1966):257-60 (Jean A. Potter), *Phil* 40/153 (1965):258-59 (A. M. Ritchie), and *RMet* 18/2 [70] (1964-65):386 (Carleton Dallery).

Sadowsky, Rosalie D. Landres. "Jean-Baptiste Abbe Dubos: The Influence of Cartesian and Neo-Aristotelian Ideas on Music Theory and Practice." Ph.D. dissertation, Yale University, 1960. [*DA* 31/05A, p. 2425. UMI 70-20362.]

Augst, Bertrand. "Descartes's Compendium on Music." *JHI* 26/1 (1965):119-32. Bibliog.

Seidel, Wilhelm. "Descartes' Bemerkungen zur musikalischen Zeit." *AfMw* 27/4 (1970):287-303. [*Rilm* 70-3195.]

> Response by Luisa Zanoncelli in *Ridm* 17/2 (1982):350-56. [The title page of this fascicle inadvertently reads Vol. 18.]

Berselli, Raffaella. "Acustica e psicologia nel *Compendium musicae* di Cartesio." Thesis, The University of Parma, 1973-74.

Smith, F. J. "Music Theory and the History of Ideas." In *In Search of Musical Method*, edited by F. J. Smith, pp. 125-49. London: Gordon & Breach, 1976; also published in *MuM* 2/1-2 (1976):125-49. [*Rilm* 76-4957.]

Lohmann, Johannes. "Descartes' *Compendium musicae* und die Entstehung des neuzeitlichen Bewußtseins." *AfMw* 36/2 (1979):81-104. [*Rilm* 79-3966.]

Cohen, Albert. "Descartes, René." In *NGrove* (1980). Bibliog.

Massera, Giuseppe. "Akustyka i psychologia w *Compendium musicae* Kartezjusza." *Pagine* 4 (1980):63-79. [*Rilm* 80-4523.]

Buzon, Frédéric de. "Sympathie et antipathie dans le *Compendium musicae*." *Arphil* 46/4 (1983):647-53. Bibliog.

Salazar, Adolfo. "Descartes teórico de la música." *Het* 19/1 [92] (1986):39-43.

See also FÉTIS: (1833-44); LIPPIUS: Rivera (1974/1980); MERSENNE: (1617-48); Ludwig (1933/. . ./1971); Mace (1970); Walker (1976); MONTEVERDI: Schrade 1950/. . ./1981); RAMEAU: Chailley (1965); Paul (1966); RIEMANN: (1898); SAUVEUR: Scherchen (1946/. . ./1972); LITERATURE SUPPLEMENT: Alekperova (1982); Alette (1951); Allen ["Philosophies"] (1939); Apfel and Dahlhaus (1974); Archibald (1924); Auhagen (1982/1983); Becker (1836-39/1964); Beiche ["Inversio"] (1972-); Bell et al. (1980); Blumröder (1972-); Boomgaarden (1985/1987); **Buelow** (1973-74), ["Rhetoric"] **(1980)**, (1987); Bukofzer (1947); Burke (1963); Burton (1956); Cazden (1948), (1980); Chailley (1967); Chenette (1967); Cohen

(1966/1978), ["Symposium"] (1972), (1977), (1981), (1984); Cohen (1984); Cowart (1987), ["Inventing"] (1989); Crombie (1969); **Dahlhaus et al. (1987)**; Dammann (1958/1967); Deutsch (1980); Dill (1989); Donà (1967); Donington (1963/. . ./1974); Dostrovsky (1969), (1974-75); **Dürr and Gerstenberg (1949-68), (1980)**; Duparcq (1977); Eimert (1926-27); Eitner (1900-1904/1959-60); Federhofer (1985); Fellerer (1927/. . ./1972); ["Zur Kontrapunktlehre"] (1973), (1983); Flindell (1983-84); Forkel (1792/1962); Frobenius ["Dauer"] (1972-), ["Tactus"] (1972-); Fubini (1971/1983); Gerber (1790-92/1977), (1812-14/1966); Godwin (1987); Gouk (1980); Green (1969); Grout (1960/. . ./1980); Gruber (1969); Gut (1976); Haase (1969); Handschin (1948); Harrán (1986); Hartmann (1923); Hawkins (1776/. . ./1969); Heckmann (1953); Hein (1954); Hoffman (1953); Hosler (1978/1981); Houle (1987); Hüschen (1949-68); **Hunt (1978)**; Jacobi (1957-60/1971); Jeppesen ([1951]/1952); Jonckbloet and Land (1882); Jones (1981); Jones (1934); **Kassler (1979)**; Kassler and Oldroyd (1983); Kauko

(1958); Kivy (1980); Koenigsberger (1979); Lang (1941), (1967-68); Lawrence (1978); Levi (1962-63/1964); **Lindley (1982), (1984)**; Lippman (1986); List (1976); Mace (1964/1966); Mallard (1978); Miller (1939-40); Miller and Cohen (1987); Mitchell, J. W. (1963); Mitchell, W. J. (1963); Möller (1971); Norton (1984); Nowak (1975); Ottenberg (1973/1978); **Palisca** (1961), [*Baroque*] (1968/1981), (1974/1977), ["Theory"] **(1980)**; Palisca and Spender (1980); Palm (1965); Ratner (1980); Reckow (1972-); **Ritzel (1967/1968)**; Rowell (1983); Ruff (1970); Schäfke (1934/1964); Schavernoch (1981); **Schneider (1972)**; Seidel (1976); **Seidel and Cooper (1986)**; Sheldon (1975); **Shirlaw (1917/ . . ./1970)**; Smith (1974); Subirá (1947/. . ./1958); Taddie (1984); Taylor (1980); Tenney (1988); Thieme (1982-83); Tolkoff (1973); Truesdell (1960); Tuksar (1978/1980); Vogel (1955/1954); Waite (1970); **Walker** (1976), **(1978)**; Warrack (1945); Weber (1976); Wienpahl (1953); Wightman (1972); Yates (1947), (1964); **Zaminer (1985)**; Zimmermann (1976).

GIROLAMO DIRUTA

[ca. 1554–after 1610]

Girolamo Diruta felt, reasonably, that performers should understand the theoretical underpinnings of the music which they performed. Thus *Il transilvano* (1593 and 1609), a work addressed to organists, includes a substantial body of contrapuntal studies organized according to individual categories or species and thus comprised an early phase of a pedagogical tradition which would come to dominate contrapuntal instruction in the coming centuries. Diruta delineated two contrasting styles: the conservative *contrapunto osservato* and the freer *contrapunto commune*, the latter of which was demonstrated by numerous studies which he composed for the treatise. The work is also helpful regarding the art of diminution, as a variety of ornaments intended for the tasteful adornment of keyboard compositions is presented. The method of fingering advanced (wherein the second and fourth fingers take the consonant notes on strong beats) further reinforces Diruta's conviction that a work must be understood mentally, not just choreographed digitally. As might be expected, Diruta offered numerous tips and strategies for the keyboard performer, thereby preserving the essence of keyboard technique and performance style in Venice at the turn of the seventeenth century.

Il transilvano: Dialogo sopra il vero modo di sonar organi, et istromenti da penna . . . [*Rism* B/VI/1, p. 268.]

and

Seconda parte del transilvano: Dialogo . . . [*Rism* B/VI/1, pp. 268-69.]

    Venice: Giacomo Vincenti, 1593. Vol. 1. [LCPS: D-034.]

    Venice: Giacomo Vincenti, 1597. Vol. 1.

    Venice: Giacomo Vincenti, 1609. Vol. 2.

    Venice: Giacomo Vincenti, 1612. Vol. 1.

    Venice: Alessandro Vincenti, 1622. Vol. 2. [LCPS: D-035.]

    Venice: Alessandro Vincenti, 1625. Vol. 1. [LCPS: D-035. SMLMS.]

        Other editions may exist.

T ● Trost, Johann Caspar, ed. and trans. German translation. Ms. [?], mid seventeenth century. [Lost.]

S ● Cervelli, Luisa, ed. Facsimile of the 1593 and 1622 editions. 2 vols. BmB, ser. 2, no. 33. Bologna: Forni, [1969].

T ● ● ● Soehnlein, Edward John. "Diruta on the Art of Keyboard-Playing: An Annotated Translation and Transcription of *Il Transilvano*, Parts I (1593) and II (1609)." 2 vols. Ph.D. dissertation, The University of Michigan, 1975. Bibliog. [*DA* 36/04A, p. 1897. UMI 75-22083.]

T ● See MacClintock (1979).

S ● Zászkaliczky, Tamás; Pernye, András; and Barlay, Szabolcs Ö., eds. *Il Transilvano*. MtKM, no. 3. Budapest: Edition Musica (Presser), 1981.

> Music examples only. Review in *Notes* 39/4 (1982-83):941-42 (Ross Wood).

S ● Bradshaw, Murray C., and Soehnlen, Edward J., eds. Facsimile of the 1593 and 1609 editions. Bo, no. 44. Buren, The Netherlands: Fritz Knuf, 1983.

> Review in *AmO:AGO* 20/9 (1986):26-28 (Bruce Gustafson).

T ● Soehnlen, Edward J., and Bradshaw, Murray C., trans. *The Transylvanians (Il Transilvano)*. 2 vols. WAMS, no. 28. Henryville, [Pa.]: Institute of Mediaeval Music, 1984. Bibliog.

LITERATURE:

Krebs, Carl. "Girolamo Diruta's *Transilvano*: Ein Beitrag zur Geschichte des Orgel -und Klavierspiels im 16. Jahrhundert." Ph.D. dissertation, The University of Rostock, 1893; published in *VMw* 8 (1892):307-88. Bibliog.

> Contains excerpts from the treatise in German translation.

Haraszti, Emile. "Les rapports italo-transilvains de *Il Transylvano* de Girolamo Diruta." In *LaurencieFs* (1933):73-84; also in *Aeco* 6 (1940):312-24. Bibliog.

Crozier, Catharine Pearl. "The Principles of Keyboard Technique in *Il Transilvano* by Girolamo Diruta." M.M. thesis, The University of Rochester, 1941. Bibliog. [SMLMS.]

Haraszti, Emile. "Diruta, Girolamo." Translated by Hans Albrecht. In *MGG* (1949-68). Bibliog.

Briganti, Francesco. "Il primo libro dei 'Contrappunti' di Girolamo Diruta ignorato dagli storici della musica." *Perugia* 6 (23 September 1950); reprint edition, Perugia: Donnini, 1951.

> Review in *Rmi* 54/2 (1952):180-81.

Falvy, Z. "Diruta: *Il Transilvano*, 1593." *Stm* 11 (1969):123-31. Bibliog.

Barlay, O. Szabolcs. "Girolamo Diruta: *Il Transilvano* — Jelentösége külföldön és Magyarországon." *Magyar* 19/1 (1978):3-24.

Barlay, O. Szabolcs, and Pernye, András. "Girolamo Diruta: *Il Transilvano* — Stíluskritikai analízis és forráskutatási adalékok. Történelmi elözmények." *Magyar* 19/3 (1978):298-313. "Girolamo Diruta: *Il Transil-*

vano — Történeti elözmények, stíluskritikai analízis és forráskutatási adalékok. II.-III.-IV." *Magyar* 19/4 (1978):335-60; 20/1-2 (1979):39-59, 130-46. Bibliog.

Pernye, András. "Girolamo Diruta: *Il Transilvano* — Reflections on a Renaissance Keyboard School." *NHQ* 20/74 (1979):214-19.

● ● ● Palisca, Claude V. "Diruta, Girolamo." In *NGrove* (1980). Bibliog.

Wesołowski, F. ["*Il transilvano* by Girolamo Diruta: The Meaning of the Work for Today's Interpreters."] In *Organy i muzyka organowa, III*, edited by Janusz Krassowski. Psp, no. 20. Gdańsk, Poland: Państwowa Wyższa Szkoła Muzyczna, 1980.

Bradshaw, Murray C. "The Craft of the Renaissance Organist." *AmO:AGO* 15/2 (1981):44-45.

See also BANCHIERI: (1609); (1628); FÉTIS: (1833-44); HERBST: (1643); MATTHESON: Buelow and Marx (1983):Palisca; SWEELINCK: Walker (1986); VIADANA: Haack (1964/1974); WALTHER: (1732); LITERATURE SUPPLEMENT: Abraham (1968/1969); Alekseev (1974); Ambros (1878/. . ./1909); Apel (1936/. . ./1972); **Apfel (1981)**; **Arnold (1931/. . ./1965)**; Babitz (1952); Babitz and Pont (1973); Becker (1836-39/1964); **Bent** ["Analysis"] **(1980/1987):(1987)**; Beyschlag (1907/1953); Brown (1976); Burney (1776-89/. . ./1957); Chomiński (1962/1981); **Dahlhaus and Sachs (1980)**; Dolmetsch (1915/. . ./1969); Donington (1963/. . ./1974); Dupont (1933/. . ./1986); Eitner (1900-1904/1959-60); Fellerer ["Ausdruck"] (1982), (1983); Ferand (1937/1938), [*Improvisation*] (1956/1961); Forkel (1792/1962); Ganz (1972), (1976); Gerber (1790-92/1977), (1812-14/1966); Ghislanzoni (1949-51); Gleason (1981); Goldschmidt (1907); Harich-Schneider ([1939]/. . ./1970); Harrán (1986); Hawkins (1776/. . ./1969); Haydon (1933/1970); Horsley (1963), [*Fugue: History*] (1966), (1972), (1977); Houle (1960), (1987); Hüschen (1986); Jackson (1988); Jeppesen (1930/. . ./1974); Keller (1955/1965); Kinkeldey (1910/1968); Kuhn (1902); Lawrence (1978); **Maniates (1979)**; **Mann (1955/. . ./1987)**; Meier (1974/ 1988); Mendel (1948), (1978); Müller-Blattau (1923/. . ./1963); **Neumann**, Frederick (1978), [*Essays*] **(1982)**; Newman (1985); Palisca (1949-68), ["Artusi-Monteverdi"] (1968/1985), ["Theory"] **(1980)**; Reese (1954/1959), (1957/1970); Robbins (1938); Roberts (1967); Rodgers (1971); Rogers (1955); Sachs (1972-); Schneider (1917/. . ./1971); Soderlund (1980); Taddie (1984); Tagliavini (1975/1983); Tittel (1959), (1966); Troeger (1987); Wagner (1981); Walker (1987).

GIOVANNI BATTISTA DONI

[bapt. 1595–1647]

From the perspective of the seventeenth century, Giovanni Battista Doni studied what was by then a considerable quantity of books and pamphlets relating to Greek music theory. He regarded much of what he read to be ill-founded—particularly the perspectives of GLAREAN and of VICENTINO. Like his illustrious precedessors GALILEI and MEI, Doni sought to inject elements of the ancient tonal system into modern practice, though with little success. Unlike his sixteenth-century counterparts, however, Doni's thought was influenced by a body of music—the fledgling operatic repertoire—which formed an approximation of the Greek theatrical heritage.

In his *Compendio del trattato de' generi e de' modi della musica* (1635) Doni laid the foundation for a resuscitation of the Greek *tonoi* and of the chromatic and enharmonic genera in accordance with his own views on these controversial topics. This scholarship motivated his interest in creating new musical instruments which could accommodate the Greek tonal system. At around the same time, he completed "Lyra Barberina" (named after an instrument of his own invention), which remained unpublished at his death and whose title was used for the much larger collection of his works published by Gori and Passeri in 1763. Unfortunately, much of the illustrative documentation on Greek stringed instruments for that edition was haphazardly assembled and does not represent Doni's intentions.

Doni also completed a "Trattato della musica scenica" (not published until 1763), which offers a useful overview of developments in theatrical music up to his time. The category *stile rappresentativo* is further clarified in his *Annotazioni* (1640), wherein three types of monodic song are defined: the narrative (characterized by many repeated notes and a close interaction with the rhythms of speech); the recitational (wherein melodic formulae and frequent cadences can sometimes lead to monotony); and the expressive (the most daring of the three in terms of dissonance treatment and harmonic content).

At his death Doni left a large number of unpublished works, many of which were included within the *Lyra Barberina* collection in 1763. Today Doni's writings are of value chiefly for his observations concerning the development of opera in Italy and as evidence of the conflicts in aesthetic attitudes which then prevailed. As late as 1647—almost one hundred years after VICENTINO's debate with LUSITANO—Doni, in his *De Praestantia musicae veteris*, championed the ancient practice as a viable alternative to the modern tonal system. For better or for worse, his contemporaries paid little attention.

Correspondence

S● Dati, Carlo Roberto, ed. [*Raccolta di*] *Prose fiorentine* [*raccolte dallo Smarrito . . .*], Vol. 16

[= Part 4, vol. 3]. Florence: Stamperia Granducale per li Tartini, e Franchi, 1743.

    See pp. 277-97.

S● Gori, Antonio Francisco, ed. *Io. Baptistae Donii patricii Florentini: Commercium litterarium.* Florence: in typographio Caesareo, 1754.

S● See MERSENNE: (1617-48).

Compendio del trattato de' generi e de' modi della musica . . . con un discorso sopra la perfettione [*delle melodie o*] *de' concenti . . .* [*Rism* B/VI/1, p. 272.]

    Rome: Andrea Fei, 1635. [LCPS: D-040. HoM: 474.]

S● See Solerti (1903/. . ./1969):222-28.

S● Facsimile edition. MFm, no. 22. Lucca: Libreria musicale italiana editrice, forthcoming.

Annotazioni sopra il compendio de' generi e de' modi della musica . . . [*Rism* B/VI/1, p. 272.]

    Rome: Andrea Fei, 1640.

S● Gallico, Claudio, ed. "Discorso di G. B. Doni sul recitare in scena." *Ridm* 3/2 (1968):286-302. [*Rilm* 71-2200.]

> Includes "Discorso sesto sopra il recitare in scena con l'accompagnamento d'instrumenti musicali" from Doni's *Annotazioni*.

"Deux traictez de musique: 1. Nouvelle introduction de musique . . .; 2. Abrégé de la matière des tons . . ."

    Ms., 1640. [Paris: Bibliothèque nationale; Florence: Biblioteca Marucelliana.]

De praestantia musicae veteris libri tres totidem dialogis comprehensi . . . [*Rism* B/VI/1, p. 273.]

    Florence: Amatore Massa Foroliuien, 1647. [LCPS: D-042. HoM: 475. SMLMS.]

S● See (1763), below.

S● Facsimile edition. BmB, ser. 2, no. 49. Bologna: Forni, [1970].

S● Facsimile edition. Hildesheim: Georg Olms.

Lyra Barberina Αμφιχορδος: *Accedunt eiusdem opera . . .* [*Rism* B/VI/1, p. 273.]

> A compilation of various works left unpublished at Doni's death, including the important "Trattato della musica scenica" (1633-35). Abert (1949-68), below, Palisca (1980), below, and especially Solerti (1903/. . ./1969) provide detailed listings of its contents. The second

volume bears the title "De' trattati di musica di Gio. Batista Doni . . . tomo secondo."

Florence: typis Caesareis, 1763. 2 vols. Edited by Antonius Franciscus Gori and Giovanni Battista Passeri. [LCPS: D-041. HoM: 476.]

S ● See Solerti (1903/. . ./1969):186-221.

Extracts from "Trattato della musica scenica."

ST ● Kretzschmar, Hermann. *Geschichte der Oper.* KHMG, no. 6. Leipzig: Breitkopf & Härtel, 1919.

Contains an extract from "Trattato della musica scenica."

S ● Facsimile edition. BmB, ser. 2, no. 151. Bologna: A. Forni, 1974.

T ● See MacClintock (1979).

S ● Palisca, Claude. *G. B. Doni's "Lyra Barberina"; Commentary and Iconographical Study; Facsimile edition with Critical Notes.* Bologna: A.M.I.S., 1981.

A more comprehensive listing of Doni's unpublished writings is found in Bandini (1755), below.

LITERATURE:

Bandini, Angelo Maria. *Commentariorum de vita et scriptis Ioannis Bapt. Doni . . .* Florence: typis Caesareis, 1755.

Solerti, Angelo. "Lettere inedite sulla musica di Pietro della Valle a G. B. Doni ed una Veglia drammatica-musicale del medesimo." *Rmi* 12/2 (1905):271-338.

Vatielli, Francesco. "L'autografo della *Lyra Barberina* di G. B. Doni." *Nuomu* 10/4/114 (1905):45-47.

Vatielli, Francesco. *La "Lyra Barberina" di Giovanni Battista Doni.* Pesaro: A. Nobili, 1908.

Abert, Anna Amalie. "Doni, Giovanni Battista." In *MGG* (1949-68). Bibliog.

Schaal, Richard. "Ein unbekannter Brief von Giovanni Battista Doni." *Am* 25/1-3 (1953):88-91.

Ledda, Primarosa. "Giovanni Battista Doni: Il *De praestantia musicae veretis*." In *Congresso Monteverdi 1968* (1969):409-20.

Grossman, Margaret Rosso. "G. B. Doni and Theatrical Music." Ph.D. dissertation, The University of Illinois at Urbana-Champaign, 1977. [*Rilm* 77-434. ● ● ●*DA* 38/06A, pp. 3128-29. UMI 77-26671.]

● ● ●Palisca, Claude V. "Doni, Giovanni Battista." In *NGrove* (1980). Bibliog.

● ● ●Palisca, Claude V. "G. B. Doni, Musicological Activist, and His 'Lyra Barberina'." In *Oxford Symposium 1977* (1980):180-205. Bibliog.

Palisca, Claude V. "Stile rappresentativo." In *NGrove* (1980). Bibliog.

Fellerer, Karl Gustav. "Giambattista Donis *Dissertatio de musica sacra*." *KJb* 66 (1982):59-64.

Schleiner, Louise. "Milton, G. B. Doni, and the Dating of Doni's Works." *MilQ* 16/2 (1982):36-42. Bibliog. [*Rilm* 82-2363.]

See also AGAZZARI: Rose (1965); BONTEMPI: (1695); FÉTIS: (1833-44); KIRCHER: (1650); MATTHESON: Buelow and Marx (1983):Palisca; MONTEVERDI: Schrade (1950/. . ./1981); Gianuario (1969); Anfuso and Gianuario [1971]; Fabbri (1985); OUSELEY: (1882); RIEMANN: (1898); WALTHER: (1732); LITERATURE SUPPLEMENT: Abraham (1968/1969); Allen ["Philosophies"] (1939); Barbieri (1983); **Barbour** (1932), **(1951/. . ./1972)**; Baron (1968); Becker (1836-39/1964); Boetticher (1954); Borgir (1971/1987); Bukofzer (1947); Burney (1776-89/. . ./1957); **Coover (1980)**; Cowart ["Inventing"] (1989); Crombie (1969); **Dahlhaus et al. (1987)**; Dammann (1958/1967); Donà (1967); Donington (1963/. . ./1974); Dürr and Gerstenberg (1980); Eitner (1900-1904/1959-60); Fellerer ["Zur Kontrapunktlehre"] (1972), ["Ausdruck"] (1982), ["Wesen"] (1982), (1983), (1984); Ferand (1937/1938); Flindell (1983-84); Forkel (1792/1962); Frobenius ["Homophonus"] (1972-), ["Monodie"] (1972-), ["Polyphon"] (1972-); Gaillard (1971); Gerber (1790-92/1977), (1812-14/1966); Goldschmidt (1901-4/1967); Hanning (1969/1980); Harrán (1986); Hawkins (1776/. . ./1969); Houle (1987); Hüschen (1986); Isgro (1968); Jackson (1988); Jeppesen (1922/. . ./1970); Jonckbloet and Land (1882); **Kassler (1979)**; Katz (1926); Katz (1985); Kinkeldey (1910/1968); Kleinman (1971/1974); Kroyer (1901/. . ./1970); Kuhn (1902); La Fage (1864/1964); Launay (1972); **Lindley** ["Just"] (1980), ["Temperaments"] **(1980)**, (1984); Lippman (1986); **Maniates (1979)**; Martin (1932-33); Meier (1974/1988); Mendel (1978); Neumann (1955/1962); Oberdoerffer (1967); **Palisca** ["Alterati"] (1968), [*Baroque*] (1968/1981), ["Rezitativ"] (1972-), ["Camerata"] (1972), (1979), (1981), **(1985)**, [*Florentine*] (1989); Pirrotta (1953/. . ./1984); Preußner (1939); Reese (1954/1959); Reimer ["Concerto"] (1972-); Schäfke (1934/1964); **Seidel and Cooper (1986)**; Solerti (1903/. . ./1969); **Strunk (1950)**; Subirá (1947/. . ./1958); Tuksar (1978/1980); Walker (1941-42/. . ./1985), (1976); Wessely (1967); Wichmann (1966); Wolff (1972-); **Zaminer (1985)**.

GALLUS DRESSLER

[1533–ca. 1580-89]

As musical structures became more complex in the sixteenth century, theories of mode and of counterpoint were revised and coordinated with ideas borrowed from rhetoric, resulting in a line of thought called *musica poetica*, which, since directed towards composers, complemented the performer's *musica practica* and the more speculative *musica theorica*. Gallus Dreßler, in lectures delivered at Magdeburg beginning in 1559 and in a related manuscript source ("Praecepta musicae poeticae"), aligned traditional contrapuntal study with modal theory, paying particular attention to matters such as imitation and the cadence possibilities for the eight modes. Later, in *Musicae practicae elementa* (1571), he adopted the twelve-mode system of GLAREAN. Dreßler's careful consideration of the parallel between music and oratory is an early example of what later became a major current of theoretical thought. In particular, his discussion of how the imitative opening, the middle, and the cadence in music relate to the *exordium*, *medium*, and *finis* of an oration is an important step in the development of a theory for form.

Practica modorum explicatio . . . [*Rism* B/VI/1, p. 277.]

Jena: Donatus Richzenhain, 1561.

"Praecepta musicae poeticae"

Ms., 1563-64.

S ● Engelke, Bernhard. *GSLM* 49-50 (1914-15):213-50.

Musicae practicae elementa in usum scholae Magdeburgensis [*Rism* B/VI/1, p. 277.]

Magdeburg: Wolfgang Kirchner, 1571. [LCPS: D-051.]

Three other editions through 1601.

LITERATURE:

Engelke, Bernhard. "Einige Bemerkungen zu Dreßlers 'Praecepta musicae poeticae'." *GSLM* 49-50 (1914-15):395-401.

Luther, Wilhelm Martin. "Gallus Dreßler (1533 bis etwa 1589): Ein Beitrag zur Geschichte des protestantischen Schulkantorats im 16. Jahrhundert." Ph.D. dissertation, The University of Göttingen, 1936 (1942); published edition (GmA, no. 1), Kassel: Bärenreiter, [1942].

Review in *Mf* 1/2-3 (1948):209-13 (Hans Albrecht).

Luther, Wilhelm Martin. "Dreßler, Gallus." In *MGG* (1949-68).

Blankenburg, Walter. "Dressler, Gallus." In *NGrove* (1980). Bibliog.

See also FABER: Meier (1958); FÉTIS: (1833-44); LIPPIUS: Rivera (1974/1980); WALTHER: (1732); LITERATURE SUPPLEMENT: ● ● ● **Apfel (1981)**; Atcherson (1960), (1970); Becker (1836-39/1964); Beebe (1976); **Bent** ["Analysis"] **(1980/1987)**; **Buelow** (1972), ["Rhetoric"] **(1980)**; ● ● ● Butler (1977); Cahn ["Repercussio"] (1972-); Dahlhaus ["Untersuchungen"] (1966/. . ./1988), ["Zur Tonartenlehre"] (1976); Dammann (1958/1967); Eitner (1900-1904/1959-60); Feldmann (1958); Fellerer (1969); Ferand (1951); Forkel (1792/1962); Gerber (1812-14/1966); Gissel (1980/1983), (1986); Gurlitt (1942/1966); Harrán (1986); Hüschen (1986); Kirkendale (1979); Krantz (1989); Leuchtmann (1957/1959); Luoma (1976), (1977); Mahlert and Sunter (1972-); Meier (1949-68), (1963), (1969), (1974/1988); Moser (1936/. . ./1959); Niemöller (1964/1969); Palisca (1959); Pietzsch (1936-42); **Powers** ["Language"] (1980), ["Mode"] ● ● ● **(1980)**, (1981); Reimer ["Kenner"] (1972-); Ruhnke (1949-68), (1973), (1974); Sachs (1972-); Sannemann (1903/1904); Schünemann (1928/1931); Seidel (1979); Taddie (1984); Unger (1941/1969); Walker (1987).

THÉODORE DUBOIS

[1837–1924]

The career of Théodore Dubois paralleled that of many other nineteenth-century Parisian teachers but attained somewhat greater heights. Like many others, he taught at the Conservatoire (first in the harmony division, later in the composition, counterpoint, and fugue division) and held important church posts. Like a few, he ascended to the directorship of the Conservatoire. And as many aspired to do, he succeeded in creating texts that were widely used.

Building upon the success of REBER's harmony treatise (for which he supplied a supplementary volume), Dubois devised his own *Traité d'harmonie théorique et pratique* (1891), a typical mix of chordal progressions, expositions concerning various non-harmonic pitches, and explorations of how "foreign" pitches could infiltrate chords as substitutes for their diatonic counterparts. An exceptionally broad coverage of the contrapuntal art is found in his *Traité de contrepoint et de fugue* (1901), which, unfortunately, relies more heavily upon prize-winning fugues by Conservatoire pupils than upon works from the eighteenth-century repertoire. Like GÉDALGE, Dubois promoted the pedagogically straightforward yet comparatively bland *fugue d'école*, making the more varied and ingenious procedures of Bach and Handel seem less normative than they in fact were.

Notes et études d'harmonie pour servir de supplément au traité de H. Reber

> Paris: Henry Heugel, [ca. 1889-90].
> Paris: Henry Heugel, n.d.

87 leçons d'harmonie, basses et chants: Suivies de 34 leçons réalisées par les premiers prix de sa classe d'harmonie aux Concours du Conservatoire (1873-1891)

> Paris: Heugel, [1891].

Traité d'harmonie théorique et pratique

> and

Réalisations des basses et chants du Traité d'harmonie

>> Derived from REBER: (1862), and from *Notes et études d'harmonie*, above.

> Paris: Heugel, 1891.
> Paris: Heugel, [1921].
> Paris: Heugel, [1948].

> T ● Italian translation. Paris: Heugel, n.d.

Traité de contrepoint et de fugue

> Paris: Heugel, 1901.

>> Copyright renewed 1928.

> T ● de' Guarinoni, Eugenio, trans. *Trattato di contrappunto e di fuga*. Milan: G. Ricordi, 1905.

Leçons de solfège à changements de clef

> Paris: Heugel, 1905. 2 vols.

Petit manuel théorique de l'harmonie

> Paris: Heugel, [1918].

"L'enseignement musical"

> In *Encyclopédie de la musique et dictionnaire du Conservatoire. Deuxième partie: Technique, esthétique et pédagogie*, edited by Albert Lavignac and Lionel de la Laurencie, Vol. 6, pp. 3437-71. Paris: C. Delagrave, 1931.

See also REBER: (1862).

LITERATURE:

Raugel, Félix. "Dubois, François-Clément-Théodore." Translated by Hans Albrecht. In *MGG* (1949-68). Bibliog.

Mongrédien, Jean. "Dubois, (François Clément) Théodore." In *NGrove* (1980). Bibliog.

See also MOMIGNY: Chailley (1982); LITERATURE SUPPLEMENT: Chevaillier (1925/1931-32); ● ● ●**Groth (1983)**; Horsley [*Fugue: History*] (1966); Packard (1952); Subirá (1947/. . ./1958).

ANTOINE DU [DE] COUSU

[ca. 1600–1658]

The French musical public that absorbed MERSENNE's *Harmonie universelle* was also the intended audience for Antoine Du Cousu's *La musique universelle*, which apparently was abandoned near the end of the publication process during the 1650s, some twenty years after it had been written. French theory thus was not affected by this monumental, though quite conservative, guide to the foundations of practical composition and complement to MERSENNE's more speculatively oriented works.

ZARLINO was Du Cousu's chief model, and though he created original music examples for his work, the rules of counterpoint and guidance concerning dissonance which he propagated are not much liberated from the Renaissance Italian tradition. In fact, Du Cousu offered a detailed explanation of mensural music at a time when practice was demanding other information from the theorist. Perhaps the remainder of the work (that for which proofs were never made or have not survived) included a summary of more recent procedures.

Système royale

> [Lost.]

"La musique universelle contenant toute la pratique et toute la théorie" [*Rism* B/VI/1, p. 241.]

>> Completed ca. 1635. Plates of three volumes were made ca. 1650-58 by Ballard (Paris). Two copies of printer's proofs survive. [Paris: Bibliothèque Mazarine; Brussels: Bibliothèque royale Albert 1er.]

S ● Facsimile edition. Geneva: Minkoff Reprint, 1972.

LITERATURE:

Jumilhac, Pierre-Benoît de. *La science et la pratique du plain-chant*. Paris: Louis Bilaine, 1673 [LCPS: J-018. SMLMS.]; reprint edition (edited by Théodore Nisard [pseud.] and Alexandre Le Clercq), Paris: Alexandre Le Clercq, 1847.

Roquet, Antoine Ernest [Thoinan, Er.]. *Antoine de Cousu et les singulières destinées de son livre rarissime: "La musique universelle"*. Paris: A. Claudin, 1866.

Pottier, R.-J. "Antoine de Cousu: La musique universelle. Comment a été retrouvé l'exemplaire de la Bibliothèque Mazarine." *Bmus* 1/4 (1872):64-67.

Verchaly, André. "Du Cousu, Antoine." Translated by Hans Albrecht. In *MGG* (1949-68). Bibliog.

Cohen, Albert. "Du Cousu, Antoine." In *NGrove* (1980). Bibliog.

See also FÉTIS: (1833-44); MERSENNE: (1617-48); OUVRARD: (1658):Boulay (1984); WALTHER: (1732); LITERATURE SUPPLEMENT: **Apfel (1981)**; Becker (1836-39/1964); Blumröder (1972-); Cohen (1966/1978); Eitner (1900-1904/1959-60); Forkel (1792/1962); Frobenius ["Isotonos"] (1972-); Gerber (1812-14/1966); Houle (1987); Launay (1972); Ortigue (1853/. . ./1971); Sachs (1972-); **Schneider (1972)**; ● ● ●**Seidel and Cooper (1986)**.

WOLFGANG EBNER

[1612–1665]

By the middle of the seventeenth century, figured bass had become a standard component of musical scores, though the extent to which the appropriate figures were actually written in was quite variable. Wolfgang Ebner created a brief listing of fifteen rules, with examples, to assist performers in this art, while Johann Andreas HERBST ensured a wider circulation for them by translating Ebner's Latin into German and printing the result in his *Arte prattica et poëtica* (1653). Among the suggestions offered are to play below the soloist's pitch and in a relatively narrow range; to increase the number of voices in accordance with the number of parts being accompanied; and to end always with the major triad.

Rules on figured bass

   T ● "Eine Instruction und Unterweisung zum Generalbaß." See HERBST: (1653).

LITERATURE:

Orel, Alfred. "Ebner, Wolfgang." In *MGG* (1949-68). Bibliog.

Arnn, John D. "Ebner, Wolfgang." In *NGrove* (1980). Bibliog.

See also ADLUNG: (1758); FÉTIS: (1833-44); WALTHER: (1732); LITERATURE SUPPLEMENT: **Apfel (1981);** ● ● ●**Arnold (1931/ . . ./1965);** Becker (1836-39/1964); Burney (1776-89/. . ./1957); Eitner (1900-1904/1959-60); Falck (1965); Federhofer (1964); Gerber (1812-14/1966); Morel (1967); Oberdoerffer (1967); Subirá (1947/. . ./1958); Wienpahl (1953); Williams, P. (1970).

PETER EICHMANN

[1561–1623]

Among the authorities cited in Peter Eichmann's *Oratio de divina origine . . . artis musicae* (1600) are the Bible and Boethius. His *Praecepta musicae practicae* (1604) contains information typical of elementary instruction books (keys, intervals, modes, etc.) and includes definitions of terms then in use to divide music and its study into various components. It is particularly rich in examples of motets which both demonstrate modal usage and document the musical proclivities of the time.

Oratio de divina origine atque utilitate multiplici . . . artis musicae [*Rism* B/VI/1, pp. 289-90.]

   Stettin: M. Müller, 1600.

Praecepta musicae practicae . . . [*Rism* B/VI/1, p. 290.]

   Stettin: Mylianis, 1604.

LITERATURE:

Ruhnke, Martin. "Eichmann, Peter." In Supplement (1973-79) to *MGG* (1949-68). Bibliog.

Ruhnke, Martin. "Eichmann, Peter." In *NGrove* (1980).

See also BURMEISTER: Ruhnke (1955); FÉTIS: (1833-44); LITERATURE SUPPLEMENT: Becker (1836-39/1964); Boetticher (1954); Dahlhaus ["Termini"] (1955); Dahlhaus ["Untersuchungen"] (1966/. . ./1988); Eitner (1900-1904/1959-60); Feldmann (1958); Fellerer (1969); Gerber (1790-92/1977); Gissel (1980/1983); Hüschen (1986); **Lester** (1977), **(1989);** Meier (1974/1988); Niemöller (1964/1969); Ruhnke (1974).

LEONHARD EULER

[1707–1783]

When ZARLINO developed his *senario*, he regarded his numbers as representatives of actual physical objects: a string twice as long as another would sound, if all other factors were equal, an octave lower. When Leonhard Euler used the same numbers, he invoked instead the notion of frequencies: if one string sounded an octave lower than another, it was because the higher-pitched string vibrated twice as fast. A mathematician of formidable energy and insight, Euler sought to derive the frequencies of various sounds from variables such as pressure and density (for oscillations of air in a chamber such as an organ pipe) or from tension, length, and weight (for vibrating solids such as strings). Similar issues occupied the attention of d'ALEMBERT, with whom Euler quarreled in arguments unresolvable by the mathematics of their time. Though Euler's formulations were not accurate, they were nevertheless proportionate to the correct readings, and so his comparisons of frequencies produced equivalent ratios for the consideration of consonance.

Euler's interest in acoustics was evident in his youth, before he left his native Switzerland to assume a post at the Academy of Sciences in St. Petersburg. At age nineteen he completed the essay *Dissertatio physica de sono* [1727], which, as a summary of knowledge regarding sound generation and propagation and inventory of topics yet unexplored, remained influential for the remainder of the century. His most rigorous application of mathematical principles to the study of music is found in *Tentamen novae theoriae musicae* (1739), wherein the issue of musical consonance is investigated. Euler proposed that various degrees of consonance, ranked precisely through his *gradus suavitatis*, were inherent in musical sounds and that consonance was an attribute not only of individual intervals, but also of chords, progressions of chords, and even voice leading. The work concludes with a chapter on changing from one mode or system to another. The theory's applicability to the music of the time is doubtful, while its tenets, as Euler pointed out, contradicted RAMEAU's principles of octave equivalence and inversion theory.

In a less technical vein, Euler wrote, when employed at Berlin, a series of letters to Princess d'Anhalt Dessau, the niece of Prussia's King Frederick II, touching upon a broad spectrum of scientific issues. First published beginning in 1768 and later translated into a wide variety of languages, they became their era's most popular introduction to science. Among the issues addressed are several relating to music, including the properties of sound, the concepts of consonance and dissonance, and parallels between sound and color theory.

"Musices theoreticae systema" [fragments]

Ms., [ca. 1726].

Correspondence

S● Unger, Johann Friedrich. *Entwurf einer Maschine, wodurch alles was auf dem Clavier gespielet wird, sich von selber in Noten setzt . . . nebst dem mit dem Herrn Direktor Euler darüber geführten Briefwechsel, und einigen andern diesen Entwurf betreffenden Nachrichten.* Brunswick: im Verlag der Fürstl. Waisenhaus-Buchhandlung, 1774. [LCPS: U-003.]

S● Pelseneer, J. "Une lettre inéd. d'Euler à Rameau." *ArBBs* 5/37 (1951):480-82.

Access to this letter is provided also in *Autographes de Mariemont*, part 1, vol. 2 (1955):475-79; in RAMEAU: Kintzler and Malgoire (1980); and in RAMEAU: Collected Works: (1967-72):Vol. 5 (including a facsimile).

S● Juškevič [Youschkevitch], A. P.; Winter, E.; et al., eds. *Die Berliner und die Petersburger Akademie der Wissenschaften im Briefwechsel Leonhard Eulers*, vol. 2. DAWBQS, no. 3. Berlin: Akademie-Verlag, 1959- .

T● Juškevič [Youschkevitch], A. P., and Winter, E., eds. *Leonhard Euler und Christian Goldbach: Briefwechsel.* Translated by P. Hoffmann. ADAWB, year 1965, no. 1. Berlin: Akademie-Verlag, 1965.

S● Further bibliographical information is found in Youschkevitch (1970-80), below, and Truesdell (1972), below. See also Collected Works: Ser. 4A (1975-), below.

Dissertatio physica de sono . . .

Basel: typis E. & J. R. Thurnisiorum, [1727].

S● See Collected Works: Ser. 3, no. 1 (1926):181-96, below.

Tentamen novae theoriae musicae ex certissimus harmoniae principiis dilucide expositae [Rism B/VI/1, p. 298.]

St. Petersburg: ex typographia Academiae scientiarum, 1739. [LCPS: E-016. HoM: 525. SMLMS.]

Review/translation in MIZLER: (1736-54):Vols. 3/1-3 (1746-47):61-136, 305-46, 539-58; 4/1 (1754):69-103.

T● *Œuvres complètes en français*, vol. 5. Brussels: Établissement géographique (près La Porte de Flandres), 1839; microfilm edition, New York: Datamics.

T● *Musique mathématique.* Paris: Librairie scientifique et philosophique, 1865.

S ● See Collected Works: Ser. 3, no. 1 (1926):197-427, below.

T ● Smith, Charles Samuel. "Leonhard Euler's *Tentamen novae theoriae musicae*: A Translation and Commentary." Ph.D. dissertation, Indiana University, 1960. Bibliog. [*DA* 21/03A, pp. 642-43. UMI 60-02844.]

S ● Facsimile edition. MMMLF, ser. 2, no. 90. New York: Broude Brothers, [1968].

> Review in *Music* 4/4 (1970):24 (Charles Huddelston Heaton).

Lettres à une princesse d'Allemagne sur divers sujets de physique et de philosophie [*Rism* B/VI/1, p. 297.]

> 1760-62.

S ● St. Petersburg: Imprimerie de l'Académie impériale des sciences, 1768-72.

> Numerous editions.

T ● Engel, J. J., trans. *Briefe an eine deutsche Prinzessin über verschiedene Gegenstände aus der Physik und Philosophie*. Leipzig: Johann Friedrich Junius, 1769; later editions, including Leipzig: Reclam, 1983. [*Rism* B/VI/1, pp. 297-98.]

T ● In *WNAMb* 4/3/31-34 (1770):237-44, 245-51, 253-58, 261-65.

> Response in SORGE: (1770).

T ● Hunter, Henry, trans. *Letters . . . to a German Princess, on Different Subjects in Physics and Philosophy*. London: the translator and H. Murray, 1795; numerous later editions, including some edited by David Brewster, Edinburg: J. Brewster, and London: Longman, Hurst, . . ., 1823; New York: J. & J. Harper, 1833; reprint of the 1833 edition, New York: Arno Press, 1975.

> Reviews in *BC* 6 (1795):618-25, *BEMag* 13 (1823):613, and *MonR* 21 (1796):163-69 (Ralph Griffiths).

S ● See Collected Works: Ser. 3, nos. 11-12 (1960).

ST ● This work exists in well over one hundred editions, in a wide variety of languages. See Collected Works: Ser. 3, no. 11 (1960):lxi-lxx, below, for a more comprehensive listing of these sources.

"Conjecture sur la raison de quelques dissonances généralement reçues dans la musique"

> *MArsB* 20 (1764):165-73.

S ● See Collected Works: Ser. 3, no. 1 (1926):508-15, below.

"Du véritable caractère de la musique moderne"

> *MArsB* 20 (1764):174-99.

S ● See Collected Works: Ser. 3, no. 1 (1926):516-39, below.

"De harmoniae veris principiis per speculum musicum repraesentatis"

> In *NcasP* 18 (1773):330-53.

> S ● See Collected Works: Ser. 3, no. 1 (1926):568-86.

See Bell et al. (1980) for more comprehensive coverage of Euler's acoustical writings. See also primary materials in Collected Works: Ser. 3, no. 1 (1926), below.

COLLECTED WORKS EDITION:

Leonhardi Euler Opera omnia sub auspiciis Societatis scientiarum naturalium Helveticae. Ser. 3, no. 1, edited by Eduard Bernoulli, Rudolf Bernoulli, Ferdinand Rudio, and Andreas Speiser (Leipzig and Berlin: B. G. Teubner, 1926); Ser. 3, nos. 11-12, edited by Andreas Speiser [incorporating "Die Musikschriften Leonhard Eulers" by Martin Vogel, pp. xliv-lx] (Zürich: Orell Füssli, 1960); and Ser. 4A, edited by Adolf P. Juškevič, Vladimir I. Smirnov, Walter Habicht, et al. (Zürich: Orell Füssli, 1975-).

LITERATURE:

Fuß, Nicolaus. *Éloge de monsier Leonard Euler, lu à l'Academie impériale des sciences, dans son assemblée du 23 octobre 1783*. St. Petersburg: 1783; German translation by Fuß (as *Lobrede auf Herrn Leonhard Euler . . .*), Basel: Johann Schweighauser, 1786; reprinted in 1797; reprint edition in *Leonhardi Euleri Opera omnia sub auspiciis Societatis scientiarum naturalium Helveticae*, ser. 1, no. 1 (Leipzig and Berlin: B. G. Teubner, 1911), pp. xliii-xcv; English translation published in (1760-62):Hunter (1795/. . ./1975), above.

> Summary (in English) in *NRev* 5 (March 1784):188-204.

Burgess, Henry Thacker. "The Art of Music Making: XX: The Ensemble; XXI: Ensemble and Euler's *Tentamen*; XXII: The Ensemble (Conclusion)." *MO* 30/355, 357-60 (1906-7):501-2, 661-62, 736-37, 813-14, 887-88.

Schulz-Euler, Sophie, ed. *Leonhard Euler: Ein Lebensbild zu seinem 200. Geburtstage nach Quellen und Familienpapeiren*. Frankfurt am Main: C. F. Schulz, 1907.

Knapp, M. "Leonhard Eulers Stellung zur 'modernen' Musik (1766)." *SMz* 51/2-4, 6 (1911):13-14, 27-28, 39-40, 63-64.

Du Pasquier, Louis Gustave. *Leonhard Euler und ses amis*. Paris: J. Hermann, 1927.

Spieß, Otto. *Leonhard Euler: Ein Beitrag zur Geistesgeschichte des XVIII. Jahrhunderts*. SdG, no. 63-64. Frauenfeld and Leipzig: Huber, 1929.

Fokker, Adriaan Daniël. *Rekenkundige bespiegeling der muziek*. Nwr, no. 21. Gorinchem: [J. Noorduijn en zoon n. v.], 1944.

Winckel, Fritz. "Euler, Leonhard." In *MGG* (1949-68).

Fokker, Adriaan Daniël, and Dijk, Jan van. "Expériences musicales avec les genres musicaux de Leonhard Euler contenant la septième harmonique." In *Congress Basle 1949* [1950?]:113-15; also in *TS* 3/10 (1951):133-46.

Winckel, Fritz. *Klangwelt unter der Lupe: Aesthetisch-naturwissenschaftliche Betrachtungen, Hinweise zur Aufführungspraxis in Konzert und Rundfunk*. SzJ, no. 1. Berlin: M. Hesse, [1952].

> Review in *Melos* 21/11 (1954):315-17 (Kreichgauer).

Winter, Eduard, ed. *Die Registres der Berliner Akademie der Wissenschaften, 1746-1766: Dokumente für das Wirken Leonhard Eulers in Berlin, zum 250. Geburtstag*. Berlin: Akademie-Verlag, 1957.

Truesdell, Clifford Ambrose. *Essays in the History of Mechanics*. Berlin: Springer-Verlag, 1968.

> Reviews in *ApA* 31/1 (1970):106 (P. Urban), *BSmB* 22/3 (1970):302-5 (Guy Hirsch), *Isis* 61/1 [206] (1970):115-18 (Stephen G. Brush), *MathR* 39/4 (1970):718-19 (I. N. Veselovskii), *Nature* 223/5212 (1969):1290 (L. Rosenfeld), *NwMPG* 57/7 (1970):362-63 (Willy Hartner), *Science* 168/3929 (1970):354 (J. L. Synge), *Viet* 32 (1970):69-71 (G. K. Michajlov), and *ZfGNTM* 7/2 (1970):139-40 (H. Wussing).

Wicklein, Gerald. "Zu philosophischen Ansichten L. Eulers und deren Beziehung zur deutschen Philosophie (Chr. Wolffs)." Ph.D. dissertation, The University of Berlin, 1968.

Ripin, Edwin M. "A Scottish Encyclopedist and the Piano Forte." *MQ* 55/4 (1969):487-99. [*Rilm* 69-4736.]

Busch, Hermann Richard. "Leonhard Eulers Beitrag zur Musiktheorie." Ph.D. dissertation, The University of Cologne, 1970; published edition (KBzMf, no. 58), Regensburg: Boße, 1970. Bibliog.

> Abstract in *Mf* 24/4 (1971):448-49. Reviews in *Mf* 27/2 (1974):242-43 (Michael Dickreiter) and ●●●*Notes* 29/3 (1972-73):450-51 (Joel Lester).

Youschkevitch, A. P. "Euler, Leonhard." In *DSB* (1970-80). Bibliog.

Truesdell, Clifford Ambrose. "Leonhard Euler, Supreme Geometer (1707-1783)." In *Irrationalism in the Eighteenth Century*, edited by Harold E. Pagliaro, pp. 51-95. SECC, no. 2. Cleveland: The Press of Case Western Reserve University, 1972. Bibliog.

> Review in *AHR* 79/1 (1974):112-14 (John H. Middendorf).

Maedel, Rolf. *Das transzendentale Tonsystem*. Salzburg: Institut für musikalische Grundlagenforschung, 1973; (as SHMS, no. 1) Munich: Musikverlag Emil Katzbichler, 1975. [*Rilm* 73-4311.]

Fellmann, Emil Alfred. "Leonhard Euler." In *Die Grossen der Weltgeschichte*, edited by Kurt Fassmann et al., Vol. 6, pp. 496-531. Zürich: Kindler Verlag, 1975. Bibliog.

"Euler, Leonhard." In *NGrove* (1980).

Fellmann, Emil. A. (with Beatrice Bosshart and Eugen Dombois). "Leonhard Euler—Ein Essay über Leben und Werk." In *Leonhard Euler 1707-1783: Beiträge zu Leben und Werk*, edited by J. J. Burckhardt, E. A. Fellmann, and W. Habicht. Basel: Birkhäuser, 1983. Bibliog.

See also d'ALEMBERT: Hankins (1964/1970); FÉTIS: (1833-44); (1840); HELMHOLTZ: (1862); RAMEAU: ["Extrait"] (1752); Jacobi (1963); Paul (1966); RIEMANN: (1898); SERRE: (1753); SORGE: (1770); LITERATURE SUPPLEMENT: Archibald (1924); Auhagen (1982/1983); Badings (1978); **Barbour (1951/. . ./1972)**; Becker (1836-39/1964); Beer (1969); ●●●Bell et al. (1980); Bukofzer (1947); Cannon and Dostrovsky (1981); Cazden (1948), (1980); Chevaillier (1925/1931-32); Cohen (1981); Cohen (1984); **Dahlhaus et al. (1987)**; Diderot (1748/. . ./1875-77); Eitner (1900-1904/1959-60); Forkel (1792/1962); Frobenius ["Dauer"] (1972-); Gerber (1790-92/1977), (1812-14); Godwin (1987); Gouk (1981-82); Green (1969); Haase (1969); Handschin (1948); Harburger (1928-29); Hartmann (1923); **Hunt (1978)**; **Kassler (1979)**; Kauko (1958); Kelletat [*Temperatur*] (1960); Krehbiel (1964); Lang (1941); Lippman (1986); Lottermoser (1949-68); McQuere (1983); Meer (1980); Mendel (1978); **Palisca (1949-68)**, ["Theory"] **(1980)**; Pole (1879/. . ./1924); Révész (1946/. . ./1954); Rohwer (1949-68); **Shirlaw (1917/. . ./1970)**; Sondheimer (1925); Toncitch (1973); Truesdell (1960); Vogel (1955/1954), (1962), (1975/1984); Warrack (1945); Wellek (1949-68); Winckel (1949-68).

ANTONIO EXIMENO (Y PUJADES)

[1729–1808]

The Spaniard Antonio Eximeno attained notoriety not by creating new theories but by broadcasting his opposition to those of others. He criticized the use of rules and mathematical formulations as aids to the mastery of music. Certainly during his lifetime there was much that he must have found annoying, including works by TARTINI and MARTINI in his adoptive homeland, Italy. When he returned to Spain after an absence of over three decades, he was alarmed to find CERONE still widely read and revered. His novel, "Don Lazarillo Vizcardi," which remained unpublished due to Spain's political turmoil in the early years of the nineteenth century, is a biting attack on the seventeenth-century theorist and on the conservative Spanish music establishment which compared unfavorably with those of Italy and other more progressive musical cultures.

Dell'origine e delle regole della musica, colla storia del suo progresso, decadenza e rinnovazione [*Rism* B/VI/1, p. 299.]

> Rome: Michel' Angelo Barbiellini, 1774. [LCPS: E-17a. SMLMS. IDC.]
>
>> See MARTINI: (1774-[75]).

T ● Gutiérrez, Francisco Antonio, trans. *Del origen y reglas de la música* . . . 3 vols. Madrid: Imprenta real, 1796 [*Rism* B/VI/1, p. 299. LCPS: E-017b. HoM: 526.]; reprint edition (edited by Francisco Otero, Blph, no. 36), Madrid: Editora nacional, 1978.

T ● Kiesewetter, Raphael Georg, trans. "Über den vermeintlichen Zusammenhang der Musik mit der Mathematik." In *Der neuen Aristoxener: Zerstreute Aufsätze über das Irrige der musikalischen Arithmetik und das Eitle ihrer Temperaturrechnung*, pp. 17-24. Leipzig: Breitkopf & Härtel, 1846.

S ● Reprint edition. Hildesheim: Georg Olms, 1983.

Risposta al giudizio delle Efemeridi letterarie di Roma . . . sopra l'opera . . . circa l'origine e le regole della musica [*Rism* B/VI/1, p. 300.]

> [Rome: Bouchard & Gravier], 1774. [LCPS: E-019.]

Dubbio . . . sopra il saggio fondamentale pratico di contrappunto del . . . Martini [*Rism* B/VI/1, p. 299.]

> Rome: Michelangelo Barbiellini, 1775. [LCPS: E-018a. SMLMS.]
>
>> Reply to MARTINI: (1774-[75]). See MARTINI: (1781).

T ● Gutiérrez, Francisco Antonio, trans. *Duda . . . sobre el ensayo fundamental práctico de contrapunto del . . . Martini*. Madrid: Imprenta real por D. Pedro Julián Pereyra, 1797. [*Rism* B/VI/1, p. 299-300. LCPS: E-018b.]

"Don Lazarillo Vizcardi: Sus investigaciones músicas con ocasión del concurso a un magisterio de capilla vacante, recogidas y ordenadas"

> Ms., [1802-6].
>
> S ● Barbieri, Francisco Asenjo, ed. 2 vols. Sdbe. Madrid: M. Rivadeneyra, 1872-73.

LITERATURE:

Otaño, Nemesio. "El P. Antonio Eximeno." *Msh* 7/7 (1914):102-10.

Pedrell, Felipe. *P. Antonio Eximeno: Glosario de la gran remoción de ideas que, para mejoramiento de la técnica y estética del arte músico, ejerció el insigne jesuita valenciano*. BV. Madrid: Unión musical española (antes Casa Dotesio), 1920.

Chavarri, Eduardo L. "Un tratadista teórico español." *Musicalia* 2/9 (1929-30):85-87.

Otaño, Nemesio. *El P. Antonio Eximeno: Estudio de su personalidad a la luz de nuevos documentos*. Madrid: Talleres Ferga, 1943.

Subirá, José. "Eximeno, Antonio." Translated by Christel Blume. In *MGG* (1949-68). Bibliog.

● ● ● Pollin, Alice M. "Toward an Understanding of Antonio Eximeno." *JAMS* 10/2 (1957):86-96. Bibliog.

Ferracin, Gianni. "A. Eximeno, S. Artega, V. Requeno, musicografi spagnoli del secondo '700: Loro scritti in lingua italiana, con particolare riguardo alla musica greca." Thesis, The University of Padua, 1969-70.

Stevenson, Robert. "Eximeno (y Pujades), Antonio." In *NGrove* (1980). Bibliog.

See also CERONE: (1613):(1969):Stevenson (1971); FÉTIS: (1833-44); MARTINI: (1781); Ionta (1969); Stefani (1970); LITERATURE SUPPLEMENT: Becker (1836-39/1964); Cazden (1948); Eitner (1900-1904/1959-60); Forkel (1792/1962); Forrester (1973); Gerber (1790-92/1977), (1812-14/1966); León Tello (1974); **Palisca** ["Theory"] **(1980)**; Subirá (1947/. . ./1958), (1953); Wittwer (1934/1935).

HEINRICH FABER

[before 1500–1552]

For over one hundred years Heinrich Faber's *Compendiolum musicae pro incipientibus* (1548) remained a standard textbook for students in the Lutheran Latin schools of Germany. Both the original work and several translations contain a basic introduction to the practical matters of notes, notation, time, and modes, as well as music for practice in singing. In the various manuscript versions of his "Musica poetica," Faber compared improvised and composed music, focusing particularly upon the latter.

Compendiolum musicae pro incipientibus . . . [Rism
    B/VI/1, pp. 301-4.]

    Brunswick: 1548.

        Forty-six editions through 1617, including:

    Nuremberg: Johann Berg & Ulrich Neuber, 1555.
    ◞ [LCPS: F-003.]

T ● Rid, Christoph. *Musica: Kurtzer Innhalt der Sing-
    kunst . . .* Nuremberg: Dietrich Gerlach, 1572;
    thirteen editions through 1655; see GUM-
    PELZHAIMER: (1591).

ST ● See GUMPELZHAIMER: (1591).

T ● Colhardt, Johann, trans. *Musica: Kurtze und ein-
    feltige Anleitung der Singkunst.* Leipzig: Johann
    Rose, 1605.

ST ● Vulpius, Melchior, trans. and ed. *Musicae com-
    pendium . . .* Jena: Johann Weidner, Heinrich
    Birnstiel, 1608.

        Various printings through 1665. With additions
        borrowed from Michael PRAETORIUS.

T ● See Livingstone (1962).

S ● See Bellingham (1971).

S ● Facsimile of an "ex officina Gerlachiana per
    Paulum Kauffmannum" edition of 1594. BmB,
    ser. 2, no. 20. Bologna: Arnaldo Forni, 1980.

"Musica poetica"

    Mss., [ca. 1548-50]. [Zwickau: Ratsschulbibli-
    othek.]

S ● Stroux, Christoph. "Die 'Musica poetica' des
    Magister Heinrich Faber." Ph.D. dissertation,
The University of Freiburg im Breisgau, 1967.
[*Rilm* 73-3251.]

Ad musicam practicam introductio . . . [Rism B/VI/1, p.
    301.]

    Nuremberg: Johann Berg & Ulrich Neuber, 1550.

        At least four other editions through 1571.

LITERATURE:

Eitner, Robert. "Magister Heinrich Faber." *MMg* 2/2
    (1870):17-30.

Meier, Bernhard. "Eine weitere Quelle der 'Musica poetica'
    von Heinrich Faber." *Mf* 11/1 (1958):76.

    Response in *Mf* 11/3 (1958):340-41 (Ernest T.
    Ferand: "Bemerkungen zu der neuen Quelle von
    Heinrich Fabers 'Musica poetica' ").

Albrecht, Hans. "Faber, Heinrich." In *MGG* (1949-68). Bib-
    liog.

● ● ● Miller, Clement A. "Faber, Heinrich." In *NGrove*
    (1980). Bibliog.

See also BELLERMANN: (1858); FÉTIS: (1833-44);
    LIPPIUS: Rivera (1974/1980); WALTHER:
    (1732); LITERATURE SUPPLEMENT: Albrecht
    (1948); ● ● ● **Apfel (1981)**; Atcherson (1960);
    Becker (1836-39/1964); Beebe (1976); Bellingham
    (1980); Berger (1987); Brennecke (1953); Buelow
    (1972); Collins (1963); Eitner (1900-1904/1959-60);
    Falck (1965); Feldmann (1958); Fellerer (1969),
    ["Zur Kontrapunktlehre"] (1972); Ferand (1951);
    Forkel (1792/1962); Gerber (1812-14/1966); Gurlitt
    (1942/1966), (1954/1966); Harrán (1986); Hender-
    son (1969); Hawkins (1776/. . ./1969); Hüschen
    (1986); Kätzel (1951/1957); **Lester** ● ● ● (1977),
    (1989); Livingstone (1962), (1971); Meier (1974/
    1988); Neumann (1987); Niemöller (1964/1969);
    Palisca (1959); Pietzsch (1936-42/1971); Preußner
    (1939); Ruhnke (1949-68); Sannemann (1903/1904);
    Sachs (1972-); Schünemann (1928/1931); Taddie
    (1984); Walker (1987); Wiora (1962); Witkowski
    (1975).

FRANÇOIS-JOSEPH FÉTIS

[1784–1871]

François-Joseph Fétis, a Belgian by birth, studied the theories of RAMEAU as a student at the Paris Conservatoire during the opening years of the nineteenth century. In 1821 CHERUBINI invited him to return as a professor of composition. His various books written over the next few decades reflect a strong commitment to pedagogy, an uncommon historical awareness, and a unique and influential perspective concerning the stages of musical development from early chant to the enharmonic experimentation of his own day. Fétis also founded and edited a journal (*Revue musicale*) and for many years served as director of the Conservatoire royal de musique in Brussels (1833-71). His most enduring work has proved to be the *Biographie universelle des musiciens et bibliographie générale de la musique*, although he himself regarded his treatises on counterpoint (1824) and harmony (1844) as his most original and significant contributions. The latter did, in fact, go through twenty-one printings, not counting the Italian and Spanish editions.

A historical orientation is clearly apparent in the *Traité du contrepoint et de la fugue*. Fétis promoted a solid grounding in species counterpoint, with examples in two through eight parts. Sections on *contrepoint simple* (including imitation and canon) and *contrepoint double* (invertible counterpoint at the octave, tenth, and twelfth) lead to a consideration of fugue, wherein terminology such as *sujet et répose*, *contresujet*, and *episodes ou imitations transitionelles* is introduced and examples by Bach, Beethoven, and CHERUBINI are presented.

The *Esquisse de l'histoire de l'harmonie* documents Fétis's considerable knowledge of historical treatises, many of which were a part of his splendid personal library, now housed at the Bibliothèque royale in Brussels. One must proceed with caution, however, for the work is permeated with a singular and not necessarily salutary bias. The final paragraph, following a summary of Fétis's own theory of *tonalité*, contains the following typical and troubling remarks: "The [i.e., my] theory of harmony is the last word in this art and science; it is now complete, and there is nothing more to be added. I have given the summary of this theory in my *Méthode élémentaire d'harmonie et d'accompagnement*, and my major *Traité d'harmonie* [as yet unpublished] contains the development of it. Rameau, Sorge, Schroeter, Kirnberger, and Catel have all found the first elements of it, and I have completed it by positing it on a firm foundation. What demonstrates such invincible excellence is that it is at the same time the history of the progress of the art and the best analysis of the art of composition."

The *Traité complet de la théorie et de la pratique de l'harmonie*, particularly the enlarged edition of 1849, contains Fétis's most mature statements regarding *tonalité* (a term he often used when describing the tendencies of individual scale components, such as the force generated by the interaction of the leading tone and fourth scale degree) and the related division of Western music into four categories or *ordres*: *unitonique*, *transitonique*, *pluritonique*, and *omnitonique*. The third and fourth of these categories, involving enharmonic reinterpretation of single and multiple pitches, respectively, offer insights regarding the expanded modulatory range displayed by compositions of the period.

Méthode élémentaire et abrégée d'harmonie et d'accompagnement . . .

> Paris: Petit, [1823 or 1824].
> Paris: Lemoine, [1836]. Revised edition.
> Paris: Aulagnier, [1840 or 1841]. New format.
>
>> Numerous printings.

> T ● Bishop, John, trans. *An Elementary and Abridged Method of Harmony and Accompaniment . . .* London: Robert Cocks, [1835].

> T ● *Metodo elementaire e ristretto di armonia e di accompagnemento del basso*. Naples: Girard, [1836].

> T ● *Metodo elementare e abbreviato di armonia e di accompagnamento*. Turin: Pomba, n.d.

Traité du contrepoint et de la fugue, contenant l'exposé analytique des règles de la composition musicale, depuis deux jusqu'à huit parties réelles

> Paris: Charles Michel Ozu (au magasin de musique du Conservatoire), [1824].
> Paris: Troupenas, [1846]. Enlarged edition.
>
>> Numerous printings.

> S ● Facsimile of the Troupenas edition of 1825. Osnabrück: Zeller, 1972.

Revue musicale [= *Rm*(F)]

> Paris: 1827-35.
>
>> Under Fétis's editorship until merger with *Gazette musicale de Paris* to form *Revue et gazette musicale de Paris* (= *RgmdP*) in 1835.

> S ● Facsimile edition.

"Questions sur la diversité d'opinions et de doctrines des auteurs didactiques en musique . . . par P. Macarry" [A review]

> *Rm*(F) Year 1, Vol. 1, Nos. 10 and 13 (1827):245-56, 324-34.

"Des révolutions de l'orchestre"

> *Rm*(F) Year 1, Vol. 1, No. 11 (1827):269-80.

> S ● See *Curiosités historiques* (1830):272-91, below.

"Introduction à l'étude de l'harmonie, ou exposition d'une nouvelle théorie de cette science, par M. Victor Derode . . ." [A review]

> *Rm*(F) Year 2, Vol. 3 (1828):217-23, 321-27.

Curiosités historiques de la musique; complément nécessaire de la musique mise à la portée de tout le monde

> Paris: Janet et Cotelle; Brussels: Librairie Parisienne, 1830.

"De la nécessité de résumer les nouvelles formes de l'art d'écrire en musique"

> *Rm*(F) [Year 4], Vol. 10 [= Ser. 2, Vol. 4] (1830-31):290-95.

La musique mise à la portée de tout le monde: Exposé succinct de tout ce qui est nécessaire pour juger de cet art, et pour en parler sans l'avoir étudié

> Paris: Alexandre Menier, 1830.
>
> > Several later editions.

T ● Blum, Carl. *Die Musik: Anleitung, sich die nöthigen Kenntnisse zu verschaffen, um über alle Gegenstände der Musik richtige Urtheile fällen zu können.* Berlin: Schlesinger, 1830.

T ● Belaikov, P., trans. *Muzyka, poniatnaia dlia vsekh, ili kratkoe izlozhenie vsego nuzhnogo, chtob sudit' i govorit' ob iskusstve sem, ne uchivshis onomu.* St. Petersburg: 1833.

T ● [Eliot, Samuel Atkins, and Cushing, Luther Stearns, trans.] *Music Explained to the World; or, How to Understand Music and Enjoy Its Performance.* For the Boston Academy of Music. Boston: O. Ditson, n.d.; numerous later printings; facsimile edition, Boethius Press; facsimile edition (edited by Peter Bloom; DCPMRS. Bibliog.), New York: Da Capo Press, 1987; reprint of Bloom's preface in *NCM* 10/1 (1986-87):84-88.

T ● Fargas y Soler, Antonio, trans. *La música puesta al alcance de todas.* Barcelona: Imprenta de Joaquin Verdaguer, 1840.

T ● Predari, Erberto, trans. *La musica accomodata alla intelligenze di tutti.* Turin: Unione tipografico-editrice, 1858.

S ● Facsimile of the 1847 edition. Geneva: Minkoff Reprint, n.d.

"Sur les dictionnaires de musique"

> *Rm*(F) Year 5, Vol. 11, Nos. 38-39, 41 (1831):301-4, 309-12, 325-28.

Traité élémentaire de musique, contenant la théorie de toutes les parties de cet art

> Brussels: A. Jamar (Société pour l'émancipation intellectuelle), [1831-32].

Numerous printings.

"Cours de philosophie musicale et d'histoire de la musique"

> *Rm*(F) Year 6, Vol. 12, Nos. 17-18, 20-25 (1832):131-33, 139-41, 155-58, 161-64, 169-71, 177-79, 185-87, 196-98.

Biographie universelle des musiciens et bibliographie générale de la musique

> Brussels: Leroux; Meline; Paris: H. Fournier; A. Roger, 1833-44. 8 vols.
> Paris: H. Firmin-Didot, 1860-65. 8 vols.
>
> > Later editions, with a two-volume *Supplément et complément* (1870-75), edited by Arthur Pougin.

S ● Facsimile of the 1873-75 edition, with 1878-80 Supplement. 10 vols. Brussels: Culture et civilisation (Joseph Adam), 1963; 1972.

> > Review in *Sh* 10/9 (1966):431 (J. P.).

S ● Microfilm of the second edition. LaCrosse, Wis.: Brookhaven Press.

Résumé philosophique de l'histoire de la musique

> Brussels: Leroux; Paris: Fournier, 1835.
>
> > The work exists in two states: as an independent volume and as Vol. 1, pp. [xxxvii]-ccliv of the *Biographie universelle* (first edition), above.

Manuel des compositeurs, directeurs de musique, chefs d'orchestre et de musique militaire, ou traité méthodique de l'harmonie, des instrumens, des voix et de tout ce qui est relatif à la composition, à la direction et à l'exécution de la musique

> Paris: Maurice Schlesinger, [1837].
>
> > Other editions.

T ● [Navarro, Francisco, trans.] *Manual de compositores . . .* Madrid: 1845.

T ● Guernsey, Wellington, trans. *A Manual for Composers . . .* London: Davison, n.d.

Esquisse de l'histoire de l'harmonie considérée comme art et comme science systématique

> Paris: Bourgogne & Martinet, 1840.
>
> > The printing of this volume was limited to fifty copies. A larger readership for its contents was guaranteed, however, since it was serialized in *RgmdP* 7 (1840): issues 9, 20, 24, 35, 40, 52, 63, 67, 68, 72, 73, 75, 76, and 77. In addition, portions of the work were incorporated within Book 4 of the *Traité complet . . . de l'harmonie*, below.

T ● Arlin, Mary Irene. "*Esquisse de l'historie* [sic] *de l'harmonie considérée comme art et comme science systématique* of François-Joseph Fétis: An Annotated Translation." Ph.D. dissertation,

Indiana University, 1972. [*Rilm* 72-1778. *DA* 33/06A, p. 2966. UMI 72-30396.]

Abstract in *ITR* 2/1 (1978):58.

"Considérations sur l'étude de contre-point dans ses rapports avec la musique actuelle"

RgmdP 11/47 (1844):387-91.

Reaction in *Frm* 48 (1844). Reply in *RgmdP* 11/51 (1844):422-23.

Traité complet de la théorie et de la pratique de l'harmonie contenant la doctrine de la science et de l'art

Paris: Maurice Schlesinger; Brussels: au Conservatoire [royal de musique de Bruxelles], [1844]. Paris: Brandus, 1849. Enlarged edition.

Numerous printings.

T ● Gambale, Emanuele, trans. *Trattato completo della teoria e della pratica dell'armonia*. Milan: Lucca, n.d.

T ● Mazzucato, Alberto, trans. *Trattato completo della teoria e della pratica dell'armonia*. Milan: Ricordi, [1842].

T ● Gil, François d'Assise, trans. *Tratado completo de la teoria y practica de la armonia*. Madrid: M. Salazar, [1850].

T ● Reymann, Rita Marie. "François-Joseph Fétis, 1784-1871, *Traité complet de la théorie et de la pratique de l'harmonie*: An Annotated Translation of Book I and Book III." Master's thesis, Indiana University, 1966.

S ● Vanderdoodt, Jean-Baptiste. *Harmonie-Leer ten gebruike der organisten . . .* Brussels: 1852.

A Flemish summary of the contents of the *Traité*.

T ● Kosar, Anthony Jay. "An Introduction to the Theory of F.-J. Fétis: A Translation with Commentary of the Conclusion from His *Traité complet de la théorie et de la pratique de l'harmonie*." Forthcoming.

"Système général de la musique"

RgmdP 13/8-12, 16-17, 19, 21 (1846):57-62, 65-67, 73-74, 83-84, 89-91, 121-23, 129-30, 145-47, 161-63.

"Première lettre à M. Halévy, concernant la théorie de la musique"

RgmdP 17/49 (1850):403-5.

"Théorie de la musique: Sur les principes fondamentaux de la musique"

RgmdP 17/4, 7, 10, 13 (1850):25-27, 57-59, 77-79, 105-6.

"Du développement futur de la musique dans le domaine du rhythme"   (CMA trans.)

RgmdP 19/35-37, 40, 43-44, 48, 50, 52 (1852):281-84, 289-92, 297-300, 325-27, 353-56, 361-63, 401-4, 457-60, 473-76.

"Effets des circonstances sur la situation actuelle de la musique, au point de vue de la composition; ce qu'il faudrait faire pour améliorer cette situation"

RgmdP 30/32, 35, 38, 41, 44 (1863):251-52, 275-77, 297-99, 321-23, 345-47.

"De la méthode dans l'enseignement de l'harmonie et de la composition"

RgmdP 33/3, 5, 7 (1866):17-19, 33-35, 49-52.

"Note sur un point de l'histoire de l'harmonie et de la tonalité"

RgmdP 35/48 (1868):381.

A reaction to GEVAERT: (1867-68). Response in GEVAERT: (1868).

See also ALBRECHTSBERGER: (1790):CHORON (1830); Seyfried (1833); MARX: (1837-47):(1840); MOMIGNY: Chailley (1982); OUSELEY: (1881-82); REICHA: (1814); WEBER: (1717-21).

The bibliographies and appendices of Nichols (1971), below, and Bloom (1972), below, provide further information on Fétis's publications and their translations, his manuscripts, and his correspondence.

LITERATURE:

Gollmick, Karl. *Herr Fétis, Vorstand der Brüsseler Conservatoriums, als Mensch, Kritiker, Theoretiker und Componist*. Leipzig: Hinze, 1852.

Gil, François d'Assise. *Tratado elemental teorico-practico de armonia*. Madrid: Casimiro Martin, 1856.

Loquin, Anatole. *Essai philosophique sur les principes constitutifs de la tonalité moderne*. Bordeaux: Sauvat & Féret, 1864-69.

Contains "Appendice: Théorie de M. Fétis," pp. 119-34, 171-234.

Herlin, Théodore. *Du rapport synchronique du ré de la gamme*. MSisaaL, Concours de 1865. Lille: Danel, 1866.

A mathematical demonstration of Fétis's theory of tonality, opposing that of Delezenne.

Brussels, Bibliothèque royale de Belgique. *Catalogue de la bibliothèque de F.-J. Fétis, acquise par l'État belge*. Introduction by L. Alvin. Brussels: Muquardt; Paris: Firmin-Didot, 1877; reprint edition (Bmb, ser. 1, no. 7), Bologna: Forni, [1969].

"Portrait Sketches from the Life. IV: François Joseph Fétis." *MMR* 21/245 (1891):100-102.

Niecks, Frederick. "François-Joseph Fétis." *MMR* 48/573-75 (1918):193-95, 217-19, 243-45.

Wangermée, Robert. "Fétis, François-Joseph." In *MGG* (1949-68). Bibliog.

Wangermée, Robert. *François-Joseph Fétis, musicologue et compositeur: Contribution à l'étude du goût musical au XIXe siècle*. ArB, ser. 6, no. 4. Brussels: Palais des académies, 1951. Bibliog.

> Contains as an Appendix "Œuvres completes de F.-J. Fétis concernant la théorie de la musique" from a Ms. [Brussels: Bibliothèque du Conservatoire royal de musique]. Reviews in *ML* 33/1 (1952):81-82 (Richard Capell), *MR* 13/3 (1952):222-24 (H. F. Redlich), *Notes* 9/2 (1951-52):284-85 (Charles Warren Fox), and *Rdm* 29 (1951):132-33 (François Lesure).

Fryklund, Daniel. "Några Fétis-brev à propos ett nyutkommet arbete." *Stfm* 34 (1952):123-39.

Vander Linden, Albert. "Un collaborateur russe de Fétis: Alexis de Lvoff (1798-1870)." *Rbdm* 19/1-4 (1965):64-81.

Vander Linden, Albert. "Contribution à l'histoire de la formation d'une bibliothèque musicale." *Rbdm* 19/1-4 (1965):101-12.

Cantarella, Marie-Paule. "Vallonska tonsättare under 1800-talet." *Musikrevy* 24/3 (1969):135-36.

Nichols, Robert Shelton. "François-Joseph Fétis and the Theory of *tonalité*." Ph.D. dissertation, The University of Michigan, 1971. Bibliog. [*Rilm* 71-757. *DA* 32/11A, p. 6480. UMI 72-14956.]

Arlin, Mary Irene. "Fétis's Contribution to Practical and Historical Music Theory." *Rbdm* 26-27 (1972-73):106-15. [*Rilm* 76-7132.]

Becquart, Paul. "La bibliothèque d'un artiste et d'un savant." *Rbdm* 26-27 (1972-73):146-56. [*Rilm* 76-693.]

Bloom, Peter Anthony. "François-Joseph Fétis and the *Revue musicale* (1827-1835)." Ph.D. dissertation, The University of Pennsylvania, 1972. Bibliog. [*Rilm* 72-1787. *DA* 33/04A, pp. 1760-61. UMI 72-25546.]

Bloom, Peter Anthony. "Critical Reaction to Beethoven in France: François-Joseph Fétis." *Rbdm* 26-27 (1972-73):67-83.

François-Joseph Fétis et la vie musicale de son temps: 1784-1871. Brussels: Bibliothèque royale Albert 1er, 1972. Bibliog.

Nichols, Robert Shelton. "Fétis's Theories of *tonalité* and the Aesthetics of Music." *Rbdm* 26-27 (1972-73):116-29. [*Rilm* 76-1652.]

Lesure, François. "L'affaire Fétis." *Rbdm* 28-30 (1974-76):214-21. [*Rilm* 75-1233.]

Huys, Bernard. "La Section de la musique de la Bibliothèque royale Albert 1er à Bruxelles." *Fam* 23/3 (1976):108-13.

Groth, Renate. "Zur Theorie der Musik bei François-Joseph Fétis." In *SieversFs* (1978):47-57. Bibliog. [*Rilm* 78-6015.]

Huglo, Michel. "Les anciens manuscrits du fonds Fétis." *Rbdm* 32-33 (1978-79):35-39. [*Rilm* 79-2115.]

● ● ● Wangermée, Robert. "Fétis: (1) François-Joseph Fétis." In *NGrove* (1980). Bibliog.

Kosar, Anthony Jay. "François-Joseph Fétis' Theory of Chromaticism and Early Nineteenth-Century Music." Ph.D. dissertation, The Ohio State University, 1984. [*DA* 45/08A, p. 2298. UMI 84-26423.]

Kosar, Anthony Jay. "The Concept of *Modulation* in the Theoretical Writings of François-Joseph Fétis." *JGMSOSU* 9 (1985):1-27.

Brody, Elaine, and LaRue, Jan. "*Trois nouvelles études* (Chopin)." *MQ* 72/1 (1986):1-15.

Bloom, Peter. "A Review of Fétis's *Revue musicale*." In *Music in Paris in the Eighteen-Thirties/La musique à Paris dans les années mil huit cent trente* (MLNCF, no. 4), edited by Peter Bloom, with an Introduction by Jacques Barzun, pp. 55-79. Stuyvesant, N.Y.: Pendragon Press, 1987.

Lewin, David. "Concerning the Inspired Revelation of F.-J. Fétis." *Theoria* 2 (1987):1-12.

See also CHORON: Simms (1971), ● ● ● (1975); GEVAERT: (1868); RIEMANN: (1898); ROUSSEAU, J.-J.: Blum (1985); LITERATURE SUPPLEMENT: Alekseev (1974); Allen ["Philosophies"] (1939); **Barbour (1951/. . ./1972)**; Baron (1968); Beach (1967); Becker (1836-39/1964); **Bent** ["Analysis"] **(1980/1987):(1987)**; Beswick (1950); Bronfin (1974); Burdick (1977); Burke (1963); Carpenter (1988); Cazden (1948), (1980); Chevaillier (1925/1931-32); Cohen (1977); Cohen (1873-74); Čolič (1976); **Coover (1980); Dahlhaus** ["Tonalität"] (1949-68), ["Untersuchungen"] (1966/. . ./1988), ["Harmony"] **(1980)**, ["Tonality"] **(1980)**, **(1984)**; DeFotis (1982-83); de Zeeuw (1983); Dunsby and Whittall (1988); Einstein (1947); Federhofer (1985); Ferand (1937/1938); ● ● ● **Groth (1983)**; Gut (1972-); Handschin (1948); Haydon (1933/1970); Horsley [*Fugue: History*] (1966); Imig (1969/1970); Jacobi (1957-60/1971); Jones (1934); Jorgenson (1957), (1963); **Kassler (1979)**; Kauko (1958); Kroyer (1901/. . ./1970); La Fage (1864/1964); Lang (1941); Lawrence (1978); le Huray (1978-79); le Huray and Day (1981); Levenson (1981), (1983-84); Lewin (1981); Lindley (1982); **Mann (1955/. . ./1987)**; McQuere (1983); Mitchell, J. W. (1963); Müller-Blattau (1923/. . ./1963), (1949-68); Newman (1946), (1963/. . ./1983), (1969/. . ./1983); Norton (1984);

Oldroyd (1948); Ortique (1853/. . ./1971); Packard (1952); **Palisca** ["Theory"] **(1980)**; Peters (1988); Pinsart (1980-81); Pole (1879/. . ./1924); Rea (1978); Reckow (1972-); Reese (1954/1959); Reichenbach (1948); **Ritzel (1967/1968)**; Rohwer (1949-68); Sanders (1919); Schmalzriedt ["Coda"] (1972-), ["Episode"] (1972-), ["Exposition"] (1972-); Schoffman ["Descriptive"] (1983), ["Pedal"] (1983);

Seidel (1972-); **Shirlaw (1917/. . ./1970)**; Stowell (1985); Subirá (1947/. . ./1958); Taddie (1984); Tenney (1988); Thompson (1980); Tirabassi (1925); Tittel (1966); Todd (1983); Tuksar (1978/1980); Vertrees (1974); ● ● ● **Wagner (1974)**; **Wason (1981/1985)**, (1988); Wichmann (1966); Wirth (1966).

HERMANN FINCK

[1527–1558]

After considering standard topics such as solmization, mensural notation, and the modes, Hermann Finck, in his *Practica musica* (1556), set down useful insights on the performance of vocal music. The final chapter is devoted to improvised embellishment, with numerous examples of *coloraturae* supplementing the text. Finck's remarks concerning mode reflect progressive developments in the art of composition, for he discussed works in which not all *fugae* and cadences could be analyzed within a single mode. He attributed such advanced procedures to the fact that composers were striving to express more accurately the meaning of their texts.

Practica musica . . . [*Rism* B/VI/1, p. 317.]

Wittenberg: Georg Rhaus Erben, 1556.

Enlarged edition:

Wittenberg: Georg Rhaus Erben, 1556. [SMLMS.]

T ● Schlecht, Raymund, trans. "Hermann Finck über die Kunst des Singens, 1556." Foreword by Robert Eitner. *MMg* 11/8-9 (1879):129-33, 135-41, 151-66.

T ● Kirby, Frank Eugene. "Hermann Finck's *Practica musica*: A Comparative Study in Sixteenth-Century German Musical Theory." Ph.D. dissertation, Yale University, 1957. [*DA* 25/07, p. 4185. UMI 64-11874.]

S ● Facsimile edition. BmB, ser. 2, no. 21. Bologna: Forni, 1969.

S ● Facsimile edition. Hildesheim: Georg Olms, [1970].

T ● See MacClintock (1979).

LITERATURE:

Eitner, Robert. "Hermann Finck." In *PaptM* 8 (1879):IX-XVI.

Albrecht, Hans. "Finck." In *MGG* (1949-68). Bibliog.

Matzdorf, Paul. "Die *Practica musica* Hermann Fincks." Ph.D. dissertation, The University of Frankfurt, 1957. Bibliog.

> Distributed by Bärenreiter-Antiquariat, Kassel. Review in *Mf* 12/3 (1959):348-50 (Klaus Wolfgang Niemöller).

● ● ● Kirby, Frank Eugene. "Hermann Finck's *Practica musica*." *JAMS* 11/1 (1958):82-83. Bibliog.

Kirby, Frank Eugene. "Hermann Finck on Methods of Performance." *ML* 42/3 (1961):212-20.

Meier, Bernhard. "Hermann Fincks *Practica musica* als Quelle zur musikalischen Dynamik." *Mf* 30/1 (1977):43-46. Bibliog. [*Rilm* 77-3649.]

● ● ● Kirby, F. E. "Finck, Hermann." In *NGrove* (1980). Bibliog.

See also CHORON: (1810-11); FÉTIS: (1833-44); HERBST: Allerup (1931); LIPPIUS: Rivera (1974/1980); MONTEVERDI: Schrade (1950/. . ./1981); WALTHER: (1732); LITERATURE SUPPLEMENT: Abraham (1968/1969); Alette (1951); Babitz (1952); Becker (1836-39/1964); ● ● ● Beebe (1976); Bent, M. (1984); Berger (1987); Beyschlag (1907/1953); Blumröder (1972-); Brown (1976); Chomiński (1962/1981); Chybiński (1911-12); Collins (1963), (1964); Crocker (1966); Dahlhaus ["Termini"] (1955); Donington (1963/. . ./1974); Eitner (1900-1904/1959-60); Fellerer (1969), ["Zur Kontrapunktlehre"] (1972), (1983); Ferand (1937/1938), (1951), [*Improvisation*] (1956), ["Improvised"] (1956); Flindell (1983-84); Geering (1949-68); Gerber (1790-92/1977); Gissel (1980/1983), (1986); Gurlitt (1942/1966); Harrán (1986); Hawkins (1776/. . ./1969); Horsley (1951), (1963), ["Fugue and Mode"] (1966/1978); Houle (1987); Jackson (1988); Kroyer (1901/. . ./1970); Kuhn (1902); Lawrence (1978); Lowinsky (1946/1967), (1948), (1974); Luoma (1976), (1977); **Maniates (1979);** McKinnon (1978); Meier (1963), (1969), (1974/1988); Mitchell, J. W. (1963); Neumann, Frederick (1978); Niemöller (1964/1969); Palisca (1959); Pietzsch (1936-42/1971);

Powers   ["Mode"]   (1980),   (1981);   Reese
(1954/1959), (1957/1970); Sovík (1985); Straková

(1975); Subirá (1947/. . ./1958); Taddie (1984);
Wichmann (1966); Zenck (1942).

ROBERT FLUDD

[baptized 1574–1637]

A powerful clash between early and reformed conceptions of music and procedures of investigation resulted when Robert Fludd unleashed his philosophical system upon the world, causing KEPLER and MERSENNE, among others, to respond with strong and negative comments. Fludd was a thinker bent on propagating the mediaeval teachings of *musica mundana* and *musica humana* as representations of the harmonious relations in the celestial macrocosm and human microcosm, respectively. Though not himself a brother, Fludd was enamored of the Rosicrucian fraternity, which had published several tracts through which ideals for the reform of learning were enunciated. Fludd addressed this mysterious society of alchemists, astrologers, and mystical Christians in his brief *Apologia* (1616) in defense of the brotherhood against the criticisms of Andreas Libavius, and the next year expanded his discussion considerably for his *Tractatus apologeticus*, in which his conception of the heavens is first articulated in detail.

It is the massive *Utriusque cosmi* of 1617-21 that presents the fullest view of Fludd's conceptions, though several later tracts hurled at his critics include further clarifications and revisions. In its first volume, on the history of the macrocosm, a section called "De musica mundana" reveals that, if Fludd is to be believed, a giant monochord stretches between earth and the heavens, and once set in motion by some divine force creates *musica mundana*. In one of numerous interesting illustrations, a hand protruding from a cloud in a region above the smiling sun and stars is seen tightening the string of the monochord. The harmonious numbers which Fludd supplied for his celestial blueprint did not, unfortunately, correspond to established facts, as KEPLER pointed out in an Appendix to his *Harmonices mundi* (1619). Fludd attempted an improvement in his *Monochordum mundi* (1622).

In the second tract of his history of the macrocosm, Fludd addressed a wide range of practical topics, including arithmetic, art, time, geography, astrology, and the military arts. Music is the subject of the second of its eleven sections. Confronting the reader at the outset is a large fold-out engraving of a musical temple whose various components correspond to the diverse aspects of practical musical knowledge. For example, men using hammers of varying weights are shown at work in the lower level, while symbols of music notation adorn the exterior. The text provides commentary on each portion of this structure, so that readers, by examining or bringing to mind the entire image, can remember the details of practical music through simple visual cues. Though this material helps confirm the breadth of Fludd's erudition and fills out the mediaeval plan by addressing *musica instrumentalis*, it reflects an ignorance, or at least an ignoring, of the more advanced musical practices then current in England.

The second volume of the *Utriusque cosmi* is devoted to the microcosm, or the internal workings of man. Fludd was a successful, though undoubtedly singular, doctor in London, and his writings have attracted attention among historians of medicine. In numerological discussions and through analogies with music, Fludd created a microcosm which corresponds to his macrocosm, thus suggesting an intimate relationship between these two universes.

It is no wonder, then, that advocates of scientific observation and reasoned thought were perturbed by such reactionary views coming from one of England's leading philosophical authors. Despite his similar goal of demonstrating a universal harmony, KEPLER could not accept Fludd's unscientific methodology. With perhaps greater urgency MERSENNE and his ally Gassendi attempted to dissuade readers from taking Fludd's theological and musical notions seriously, considering them antithetical to their own progressive stance on these issues.

Apologia compendiaria fraternitatem de Rosea Cruce suspicionis et infamiae maculis aspersam veritas quasi fluctibus abluens et abstergens

    Leiden: [Godfrey Basson], 1616.

Tractatus apologeticus integritatem societatis de Rosea Cruce defendens . . .

        An expansion of the *Apologia* (1616), above.

    Leiden: Godfrey Basson, 1617.

T ● Booz, Ada Mah [Adam Michael Birkholz], trans. *Schutzschrift für die Aechtheit der Rosenkreutzergesellschaft . . .* Leipzig: A. F. Böhme, 1782.

T ● See Godwin (1986).

Utriusque cosmi, maioris scilicet et minoris metaphysica, physica atque technica historia . . . [*Rism* B/VI/1, pp. 319-20.]

    I. *De macrocosmi historia*
    1) *De metaphysico macrocosmi et creaturarum illius ortu; De physico macrocosmi in generatione et corruptione progressu*
    2) *De naturae simia seu technica macrocosmi historia*

II. *De supernaturali, naturali, praeternaturali et contranaturali microcosmi historia*

1) *De integra microcosmi harmonia*
2) *De praeternaturali utriusque mundi historia*

Oppenheim: Johann Theodor de Bry (Hieronymus Galler), 1617. Vol. I:1. [LCPS: F-035a and F-035b (incomplete).]

Oppenheim: Johann Theodor de Bry (Hieronymus Galler), 1618. Vol. I:2.

Oppenheim: Johann Theodor de Bry (Hieronymus Galler), 1619[-20?]. Vol. II:1.

Frankfurt am Main: Johann Theodor de Bry (Erasmus Kempffer), 1621. Vol. II:2.

Frankfurt am Main: Johann Theodor de Bry Erben (Caspar Rötell), 1624. Vol. I:2, 2nd edition. [LCPS: F-035c.]

T ● Robledo, Luis, ed. *Escritos sobre música*. Madrid: Editora nacional, 1979.

> Review in *Pauta* 4/13 (1985):99 (Júan Arturo Brennan).

Veritas proscenium . . . seu demonstratio quaedam analytica, in qua cuilibet comparationis particulae, in appendice quadam a Ioanne Kepplero, nuper in fine harmoniae suae mundanae edita, factae inter harmoniam suam mundanam, et illam Roberti Fludd, ipsissimis veritatis argumentis respondetur [Rism B/VI/1, p. 320.]

> A response to KEPLER: (1619).

Frankfurt am Main: Johann Theodor de Bry (Erasmus Kempffer), 1621. [LCPS: F-036.]

Monochordum mundi symphoniacum, seu replicatio . . . ad apologiam . . . Ioannis Kepleri adversus demonstrationem suam analyticam, nuperrime editam . . . [Rism B/VI/1, p. 319.]

> A response to KEPLER: (1622).

Frankfurt am Main: Johann Theodor de Bry, 1622.

> Another edition, as an Appendix to his *Anatomiae amphitheatrum . . .*:

Frankfurt am Main: Johann Theodor de Bry (Erasmus Kempffer), 1623.

Sophiae cum moria certamen . . .

> A response to MERSENNE: (1623).

[Frankfurt am Main: Erasmus Kempffer], 1629.

Summum bonum quod est verum subjectum verae magiae, cabalae, alchimiae fratrum Rosea Crucis verorum . . .

> A response to MERSENNE: (1623), under the name Joachim Frizius but probably written in part by Fludd.

Frankfurt am Main: Joachim Frizius, 1629.

Clavis philosophiae et alchymiae . . .

> A response to Gassendi (1630), below.

Frankfurt am Main: Guilhelmum Fitzerum, 1633.

LITERATURE:

Gassendi, Pierre. *Epistolica exercitatio, in qua principia philosophiae Roberti Fluddi medici retegunter . . .* Paris: Sebastian Cramoisy, 1630; reprint edition (as *Examen philosophiae Roberti Fulddi medici*, in his *Opera omnia*, vol. 3), Leiden: sumptibus Lavrentii Anisson & Ioan. Bapt. Devenet, 1658; reprint edition (in his *Opera omnia*, vol. 3, edited by Nicolao Averanio), Florence: apud Joannem Cajetanum Tartini & Sanctem Franchi (typis Regiae Celsitudinis), 1727; facsimile of the 1658 edition (with an Introduction by Tullio Gregory, translated into German by Franz Rauhut and Hermann Dommel), Stuttgart-Bad Cannstatt: Friedrich Frommann Verlag (Günther Holzboog), 1964.

Manget, Jean Jacques, ed. *Bibliotheca scriptorum medicorum . . .* Geneva: Perachon & Cramer, 1731. Bibliog.

Craven, James Brown. *Doctor Robert Fludd (Robertus de Fluctibus), the English Rosicrucian: Life and Writings*. Kirkwall: William Peace, 1902; reprint edition, New York: Occult Research Press, n.d. Bibliog.

Blume, Friedrich. "Fludd, Robert." In *MGG* (1949-68). Bibliog.

Machabey, A. "Le temple de la musique." *L'orgue* 83 (1957):101-4.

Cafiero, Luca. "Robert Fludd e la polemica con Gassendi." *Rcsf* 19/4 (1964):367-410; 20/1 (1965):3-15. Bibliog.

Debus, Allen G. *The English Paracelsians*. Oldbourne History of Science Library. London: Oldbourne, 1965; New York: F. Watts, 1966.

> Reviews in *AS* 21/3 (1965):205-6 (William P. D. Wightman), *BHM* 44/2 (1970):182-83 (Robert P. Multhauf), *BJHS* 3 (1966-67):296-97 (C. H. Josten), *PharH* 11/1 (1969):19 (David C. Cowen), *SBF* 2/4 (1967):253, *Science* 154/3750 (1966):758 (Henry M. Leicester), and *SEL* 7/1 (1967):159 (Howard Schultz).

● ● ● Ammann, Peter J. "The Musical Theory and Philosophy of Robert Fludd." *JWCI* 30 (1967):198-227. [*Rilm* 67-1475.]

Ammann, Peter. "Musik und Weltanschauung bei Robert Fludd." Ph.D. dissertation, The University of Zürich, 1968.

Yates, Frances Amelia. *Theatre of the World*. Chicago: The University of Chicago Press, 1969. Bibliog.

> Reviews in *BW* 4 (March 1, 1970):10 (Vincent Cronin), *Cresset* 33/7 (1969-70):18 (Richard Pick), *DQTR* 94 (1969):54 (John Russell Brown), *Dss* (1980):90 (H. Himelfar), *ELN* 8/3 (1970-71):217-21 (Mary Del Villar), *History*

56/187 (1971):263-64 (Robin Briggs), *JEGP* 69/4 (1970):671-75 (Charles H. Shattuck), *Listener* 82/2106 (1969):191-92 (Frank Kermode), *LJ* 95/7 (1970):1372, *MLR* 67/3 (1972):614-16 (Tom Lawrenson), *MPhil* 69/2 (1971-72):159-63 (Stephen Orgel), *NQ* 16/12 (1969):475-78 (A. J. Turner), *NYRB* 14/1-2 (1970):23-26 (Wylie Sypher), *PS* 44/3 (1970-71):278, *RQ* 23/4 (1970):482-85 (D. S. Bland), *SEL* 11/2 (1971):391-93 (Alvin Kernan), *ShakS 1970* 6 (1973):391-96 (Richard Hornby), *Spectator* 223/7364 (1969):209-10 (Roy Strong), and *TLS* 68/3523 (1969):980.

Debus, Allen G. "Fludd, Robert." In *DSB* (1970-80). Bibliog.

Stefani, Gino. "Su *Questo* di Franco Donatoni." *Spetm* (Oct.-Nov. 1970):13-16. [*Rilm* 70-4129.]

Yates, Frances Amelia. *The Rosicrucian Enlightenment*. London & Boston: Routledge & Kegan Paul, 1972.

> Reviews in *AHR* 78/5 (1973):1448 (Otakar Odlozilik), *Ambix* 20/2 (1973):132-33 (C. H. Josten), *AS* 31/1 (1974):85-86 (Colin A. Ronan), *BB* 18/6 (1972-73):42-46 (Colin Wilson), *BBN* (May 1983), *BJHS* 4 (1972-73):442-44 (A. J. Turner), *Choice* 10/3 (1973-74):440, *Daily Telegraph* (Dec. 21, 1972) (Anthony Powell), *EHR* 89/351 (1974):434-35 (Charles Webster), *HJ* 16/4 (1973):865-68 (R. J. W. Evans), *JMH* 47/3 (1975):543-45 (Owen Hannaway), *JMH* 51/2 (1979):287-316 (Brian Vickers: "Frances Yates and the Writing of History"), *Isis* 66 (1975):581-82 (Bettyjo Teeter Dobbs), *Listener* 89/2286 (1973):87-88 (Hugh Trevor-Roper), *LJ* 98/4 (1973):543 (H. G. Hahn), *MLR* 69/1 (1974):149-51 (P. F. Corbin), *NS* 85/2184 (1973):128-29 (J. H. Elliott), *NSc* 56/821 (1972):473 (Asa Briggs), *NYRB* 20 (1973):23-24 (Christopher Hill), *Observer* (Jan. 28, 1973):35 (John Kenyon), *Observer* 9598 (July 13, 1975):21, *PhilQ* 53/4 (1974):561-62 (Constant Noble Stockton), *RQ* 28/3 (1975):366-67 (Charles G. Nauert, Jr.), *Spectator* 230/7543 (1973):78-79 (Frederick Copleston), *STimes* 7801 (Dec. 17, 1972):38 (Hugh Trevor-Roper), *Tablet* (Feb. 24, 1973) (Lisa Jardine), *Times (London)* 58696 (Feb. 1, 1973):12 (Joel Hurstfield), and *TLS* 72/3711 (1973):445-46.

Godwin, Joscelyn. "Instruments in Robert Fludd's *Utriusque cosmi . . . historia.*" *GSJ* 26 (1973):2-14.

Godwin, Joscelyn. "Robert Fludd on the Lute and Pandora." *LSJ* 15 (1973):11-19.

Godwin, Joscelyn. "Robert Fludd's Symbolic Recorder." *AR* 14/1 (1973):17. [*Rilm* 73-2726.]

Debus, Allen G., ed. *Robert Fludd and His Philosophicall Key: Being a Transcription of the Manuscript at Trinity College, Cambridge*. PSSR. New York: Science History Publications, 1979.

> Reviews in *AS* 38/4 (1981):488-90 (Kathleen Ahonen), *BJHS* 14/3 (1981):290-91 (A. T. Grafton), and *Nature* 284/5758 (1980):702 (P. M. Rattansi).

Godwin, Joscelyn. *Robert Fludd: Hermetic Philosopher and Surveyor of Two Worlds*. Boulder: Shambhala (New York: Random House); London: Thames & Hudson, 1979.

> Reviews in *Choice* 16/8 (1979-80):1046, *Parabola* 4/3 (1979):123-24 (Todd Barton), and *SCJ* 12/1 (1981):100 (William Eamon).

Ashbee, Andrew. "Fludd, Robert." In *NGrove* (1980).

Huffman, William H. *Robert Fludd and the End of the Renaissance*. New York and London: Routledge, 1988.

See also FÉTIS: (1833-44); KEPLER: (1596):(1621); (1619); Pauli (1952/1955); Dickreiter (1971/1973); MERSENNE: (1617-48); (1623); (1627); Ludwig (1935); Lenoble (1943); WALTHER: (1732); LITERATURE SUPPLEMENT: Atcherson (1972); **Barbour (1951/. . ./1972)**; Becker (1836-39/1964); Blankenburg ["Harmonie"] (1959); Buelow (1972); Bukofzer (1947); Carpenter (1955); **Coover (1980)**; **Dahlhaus et al. (1987)**; Dammann (1958/1967); Dostrovsky (1969); Eitner (1900-1904/1959-60); Forkel (1792/1962); Gerber (1790-92/1977); Godwin (1987); Haase (1969); Hawkins (1776/. . ./1969); Kassler (1982); Kayser (1950); Lippman (1986); Möller (1971); Niemöller (1970); Pulver (1927/. . ./1973); Rowell (1983); Ruhnke (1949-68); Schäfke (1934); Schavernoch (1981); **Seidel and Cooper (1986)**; Taddie (1984); Walker (1976), (1978); Wightman (1972); Wolf (1939); Yates (1964); Zimmermann (1976).

JOHANN JOSEPH FUX

[1660–1741]

The musical world of 1725 might have seemed an unlikely market for a counterpoint manual founded upon the modes and devoted, for the most part, to a style of music that, though it might have been resurrected during Lent, was regarded as archaic. Yet Johann Joseph Fux's *Gradus ad Parnassum* soon became and remains one of the most beloved documents in the history of music, and it influenced, either directly or indirectly, composers such as Haydn, Mozart, Beethoven, and Schubert. Written in Latin at a level that would be accessible to beginners, the work found its way into German, Italian, French, and English within a few decades, and echoes of its tenets reverberate in most counterpoint treatises written since, including those by ALBRECHTSBERGER, CHERUBINI, BELLERMANN, and SCHENKER.

The species approach to counterpoint, wherein several different categories of exercises lead to the gradual mastery of the art, was not unique to Fux. BANCHIERI and DIRUTA, among others, had used this pedagogical method over a century earlier. Fux's formulation begins with five types of two-part writing. The first species involves the creation of a counterpoint in whole notes either above or below a cantus firmus in whole notes. The second species involves half notes against the whole-note cantus firmus; the third species, quarter notes; the fourth species, suspensions; and finally the fifth species integrates the possibilities of the preceding species. Once these concepts are mastered in two-part writing, various combinations of note values in three- and four-part writing are introduced, culminating in an example wherein a cantus firmus in whole notes appears in conjunction with three other lines each incorporating different note values (half notes, quarter notes, and suspensions).

The *Gradus* continues with a systematic treatment of fugue in two, three, and four parts, as well as of the concept of double counterpoint. Less well known, in part because English translations of the *Gradus* have been incomplete, is the concluding portion of the work, wherein Fux considered the recitative style of his day, text setting, and the affective nature of music.

The endurance of the *Gradus* resulted, in part, from the excellent pedagogical framework, wherein the kindly teacher Aloysius guides the bright and inquisitive student Josephus through the species. Yet perhaps more important is the underlying assumption that composition in the styles of the eighteenth century (and, by extension, of the nineteenth century as well) depends upon the correct understanding of basic voice-leading principles, and that these principles are most accessible to students when isolated from their typically ornate and complicated compositional environments. SCHENKER, in his own two-volume counterpoint treatise [SCHENKER: (1906-35):(1910-22)], expanded upon Fux's doctrines and revealed how the basic principles of voice-leading, as demonstrated by species counterpoint, affect musical perception and creativity.

Correspondence with MATTHESON

Ms., 1717-18.

S ● See MATTHESON: (1722-25):Vol. 2 (1725):185-205.

T ● See MATTHESON: (1722-25):Lester (1977).

Gradus ad Parnassum, sive manuductio ad compositionem musicae regularem, methodo nova, ac certa, nondum ante tam exacto ordine in lucem edita [*Rism* B/VI/1, pp. 340-41.]

Vienna: Johann Peter van Ghelen, 1725. [LCPS: F-075a. HoM: 562. SMLMS. IDC.]

T ● MIZLER, Lorenz Christoph, trans. *Gradus ad Parnassum; oder, Anführung zur regelmässigen musikalischen Composition* . . . [*Rism* B/VI/1, p. 340.] Leipzig: Mizler, 1742 [LCPS: F-075b.]; reprint editions, Leipzig: Johann Samuel Heinsius, 1797 [*Rism* B/VI/1, p. 340.]; Hildesheim: Georg Olms, 1974.

Reviews in MIZLER: (1736-54):Vol. 2/4 (1743):118-22 and *OrganYb* 8 (1977):89 (Peter Williams).

T ● Delfini, Carlo. "Guida armonica . . . ove si trattano delle regole del contrapunto . . ." Ms., [ca. 1753]. [Bologna: Civico museo bibliografico musicale.]

T ● Manfredi, Alessandro, trans. *Salita al Parnasso, o sia guida alla regolare composizione della musica* . . . [*Rism* B/VI/1, pp. 340-41.] Carpi: Carmignani, 1761 [LCPS: F-075c. HoM: 563. SMLMS.]; reprint edition (BmB, ser. 2, no. 46), Bologna: Forni, 1972.

T ● [Heck, John Casper, trans.] *Practical Rules for Learning Composition.* [*Rism* B/VI/1, p. 341.] London: [Peter or Mary] Welcker, [1767?]; reprint editions, including London: John Preston, [ca. 1778-87]. [LCPS: F-075d. SMLMS.]

T ● Denis, Pietro, trans. *Traité de composition musicale* . . . [*Rism* B/VI/1, p. 341.] Paris: adresses ordinaires, [1773-75]. 3 vols. [LCPS: F-075e. SMLMS.]; reprint edition, Paris: Bignon, [c. 1780].

T ● *On peut en l'étudiant avec attention parvenir à bien composer en très peu de temps* . . . [*Rism* B/VI/1, p. 341.] Paris: Boyer, [1788]; reprint editions to ca. 1800.

T ● Haydn, Franz Joseph, trans. [in the hand of F. C. Magnus]. "Elementarbuch der verschiedenen Gattungen des Contrapunkts, aus dem größeren Werke des Kappelmeister Fux, von Joseph Haydn zusammengezogen." Ms., 1789. [Budapest: Országos Széchényi Könyvtára.]

T ● See CHORON: (1836-39):Vol. 4.

A separate, annotated translation by CHORON, called *Traité de contre-point antique*, may have appeared, though no copies survive.

T ● Mann, Alfred, trans. *Die Lehre vom Kontrapunkt: Gradus ad Parnassum, 2. Buch, 1.-3. Übung.* Celle: Moeck, 1938.

Review in *Rmi* 42 (1938):669-70.

T ● Mann, Alfred, trans. *Steps to Parnassus: The Study of Counterpoint.* With John St. Edmunds. New York: W. W. Norton, 1943; London: Dent, 1944; revised edition (as *The Study of Counterpoint from Johann Joseph Fux's "Gradus ad Parnassum"*), 1965.

Reviews in *ABBW* 37/4 (1966):298, *Choice* 2/12 (1965-66):864, *Composer* 21 (1966):11-12 (John Gardner), *ML* 25/4 (1944):249 (Eric Blom), *MT* 107/1476 (1966):124 (Stanley Sadie), *Notes* 23/4 (1966-67):744-45 (Arthur Daniels), *PP* 58/4 (1966):20 (Melva Peterson), and *Tempo* 77 (1966):24-26 (Peter Evans).

T ● Mann, Alfred, trans. "The Study of the Fugue: A Dialogue (in Four Parts)." *MQ* 36/4 (1950):525-39; 37/1-3 (1951):28-44, 203-19, 376-93.

T ● See **Strunk (1950)**:535-63.

T ● See **Mann (1955/.../1987)**:75-138.

S ● Facsimile edition. MMMLF, ser. 2, no. 24. New York: Broude Brothers, 1966.

Reviews in *Consort* 26 (1970):461 (Lillian M. Ruff), *Mf* 21/4 (1968):531-32 (Carl Dahlhaus), *ML* 48/1 (1967):85-86 (Jack A. Westrup), and *MT* 107/1481 (1966):605 (Charles Cudworth).

S ● ● ● ● Federhofer, Hellmut, and Wessely, Othmar, eds. *Johann Joseph Fux: Sämtliche Werke.* Ser. 7, no. 1. Preface by Alfred Mann. Johann-Joseph-Fux-Gesellschaft, Graz. Graz: Akademische Druck- und Verlagsanstalt (Kassel: Bärenreiter), 1967.

S ● Facsimile edition. Hildesheim: Georg Olm, 1974.

T ● See **Lester (1989)**.

"Exempla dissonantiarum ligatarum et non ligatarum"

Ms., [after 1700]. [Vienna: Minoritenkonvent.]

S ● Federhofer, Hellmut. "Drei handschriftliche Quellen zur Musiktheorie in Österreich um

1700." In *VetterFs* (1969):139-51. [*Rilm* 70-1681.]

"Singfundament"

Ms., [early eighteenth century].

LITERATURE:

Köchel, Ludwig Ritter von. *Johann Joseph Fux.* Vienna: Hölder, 1872; reprint edition, Hildesheim: Georg Olms, 1974.

La Fage, Adrien de. "*Gradus ad Parnassum.*" *Bmus* 1/6 (1872):113-14.

Jeppesen, Knud. "Johann Joseph Fux und die moderne Kontrapunkttheorie." In *Bericht Leipzig 1925* (1926):187-88.

Wonderlich, Elvera. "Johann Josef Fux, Contrapuntist." M.M. thesis, The University of Rochester, 1939.

Liess, Andreas. *Johann Joseph Fux, ein Steirischer Meister des Barock.* Vienna: L. Doblinger, 1948.

Review in *NZfM* 113/9 (1952):515-16 (A. Scharnagl).

Liess, Andreas. "Fux, Johann Joseph." In *MGG* (1949-68). Bibliog.

Liess, Andreas. "Bach, Fux und die Wiener Klassik." *Musica* 4/7-8 (1950):261-65.

Liess, Andreas. "Alte Meister: Johann Joseph Fux." *Mleb* 5/9 (1952):254-55.

Arnold, Denis. "Haydn's Counterpoint and Fux's *Gradus*." *MMR* 87/980 (1957):52-58.

Federhofer, Hellmut. "Der *Gradus ad Parnassum* von Johann Joseph Fux und seine Vorläufer in Österreich: Auszug aus einem Vortrag, gehalten vor der Johann-Joseph-Fux-Gesellschaft in Graz am 7. Mai 1957." *Me* 11/1 (1957-58):31-35.

Feil, Arnold. "Zum *Gradus ad Parnassum* von J. J. Fux." *AfMw* 14/3 (1957):184-92. Bibliog.

Liess, Andreas. "Johann Joseph Fux." *NZfM* 118/5 (1957):285-86.

Liess, Andreas. *Fuxiana.* Vienna: Bergland, 1959.

Reviews in *Mf* 13/2 (1960):226 (Hellmut Federhofer) and *ML* 40/2 (1959):191-92 (Denis Arnold).

Federhofer, Hellmut. "Biographische Beiträge zu Georg Muffat und Johann Joseph Fux." *Mf* 13/2 (1960):130-42.

Tittel, Ernst. "J. J. Fux und sein *Gradus ad Parnassum*: Zum 300. Geburtstag des 'österreichischen Palestrina'." *ÖM* 15 (1960):129-30.

Riedel, Friedrich Wilhelm. "Johann Joseph Fux und die römische Palestrina-Tradition." *Mf* 14/1 (1961):14-22.

Federhofer, Hellmut. "Johann Joseph Fux als Musik-theoretiker." In *AlbrechtFs* (1962):109-15. Bibliog.

Wellesz, Egon. *Fux*. OSC, no. 1. London: Oxford University Press, 1965.

> Reviews in *ABBW* 37/5 (1966):410, *Composer* 21 (1966):11-12 (John Gardner), *Listener* 74/1914 (1965):928-29 (Edward Lockspeiser), *ML* 47/2 (1966):170 (Michael Tilmouth), *MO* 89/1067 (1965-66):671 (B. R.), *MT* 107/1476 (1966):124 (Stanley Sadie), *MuMus* 14/6 (1965-66):64 (Stanley Sadie), *ÖM* 22/11 (1967):673 (B.S.), *PP* 59/1 (1966):33 (Melva Peterson), *RS* 21 (1966):31 (A. H.), *Tablet* 219/6550 (1965):1360 (Rosemary Hughes), *Tempo* 75 (1965-66):34-35 (Gerald Abraham), and *TLS* 5/3339 (1966):136.

Wessely, Othmar. "J. J. Fuxens 'Singfundament' als Violinschule." In *SteirischerFs* (1967):24-32.

Kraft, Leo. "In Search of a New Pedagogy." *CMS* 8 (1968):109-16. [*Rilm* 68-4131.]

Mann, Alfred. "Eine Textrevision von der Hand Joseph Haydns." In *VötterleFs* (1968):433-37. [*Rilm* 68-1969.]

Mann, Alfred. "Haydn as Student and Critic of Fux." In *GeiringerFs* (1970):323-32. [*Rilm* 71-586.]

Wessely, Othmar. "Johann Joseph Fux im Urteil der Umwelt und Nachwelt." *ÖM* 25/10 (1970):579-85. [*Rilm* 73-1837.]

Wollenberg, Susan. "The Unknown *Gradus*." *ML* 51/4 (1970):423-34. [*Rilm* 70-3212.]

Mann, Alfred. "Haydn's Elementarbuch: A Document of Classic Counterpoint Instruction." *MuF* 3 (1973): 197-237. [*Rilm* 73-1880.]

Wollenberg, Susan. "Haydn's Baryton Trios and the *Gradus*." *ML* 54/2 (1973):170-78. [*Rilm* 75-1059.]

Wollenberg, Susan. "The 'Jupiter' Theme: New Light on Its Creation." *MT* 116/1591 (1975):781-83. [*Rilm* 75-3654.]

Sovik, Thomas Jon. "*Gradus ad Parnassum*: A Manual of Sixteenth-Century Fundamentals." *JGMSOSU* 7 (1978):17-35.

Federhofer, Hellmut. "Fux, Johann Joseph." In *NGrove* (1980). Bibliog.

Federhofer, Hellmut. "25 Jahre Johann Joseph Fux-Forschung." *Am* 52/2 (1980):155-94; also in *Jahresgabe der Johann Joseph Fux Gesellschaft 1980* (Graz: J.-J. Fux-Gesellschaft, 1981). Bibliog. [*Rilm* 80-2691; 81-218.]

Kraft, Leo. "A New Approach to Species Counterpoint." *CMS* 21/1 (1981):60-66. [*Rilm* 81-3671.]

Federhofer, Hellmut. "Fux's *Gradus ad Parnassum* as Viewed by Heinrich Schenker." Translated by Alfred Mann. *MTS* 4 (1982):66-75. Bibliog. [*Rilm* 82-5762.]

Federhofer, Hellmut. "Johann Joseph Fux: Choral Styles and the *Gradus ad Parnassum*." *ACR* 24/2-3 (1982):14-26. [*Rilm* 82-2318.]

Walter, Horst. "Haydns Schüler." In *Haydn Ausstellung 1982* (1982):311-15. [*Rilm* 82-568.]

Somer, Avo. Review of Richard S. Parks's *Eighteenth-Century Counterpoint and Tonal Structure*. *ITO* 8/7 (1984-85):29-42.

Mazzola, Guerino, and Wieser, Heinz-Gregor. "Musik, Gehirn und Gefühl: Wie sich Konsonanzen und Dissonanzen im Hirnstrombild des Menschen unterschelden." *NZfM* 146/2 (1985):10-14.

Trummer, Johann, and Flotzinger, Rudolf, eds. *Johann Sebastian Bach und Johann Joseph Fux: Bericht über das Symposion anläßlich des 58. Bachfestes der Neuen Bachgesellschaft 24.-29. Mai 1983 in Graz*. Kassel: Bärenreiter, 1985.

> Contains several studies, including "Bach und die Fuxsche Lehre: Theorie und Kompositionspraxis" by Alfred Mann (pp. 82-86) and "Podiumsgespräch: Bach und Fux in Unterricht und Praxis," edited by Rudolf Flotzinger (pp. 87-94).

Federhofer, Hellmut. "Johann Joseph Fux und die gleichschwebene Temperatur." *Mf* 41/1 (1988):9-15.

See also BELLERMANN: (1862); BONONCINI: Holler (1955/. . ./1963); Tittel (1963-64); CHORON: (1810-11); FÉTIS: (1833-44); HELMHOLTZ: Dahlhaus (1970); KIRNBERGER: [*Gedanken*] (1782); Sumner (1975); KUHNAU: Schenk (1965); KURTH: (1917); MARTINI: Wiechens (1968); Mann (1973); MATTHESON: (1722-25); (1739); (1740); Wessely (1965); Schenkman (1978-79), (1981); MOMIGNY: (1791-1818):(1818); RIEMANN: (1898); SCACCHI: (1649):Palisca (1972); SCHENKER: (1906-35):Vol. II (1910-22); Salzer and Schachter (1969); VIADANA: Haack (1964/1974); WALTHER: (1732); WEITZMANN: (1859); LITERATURE SUPPLEMENT: Abraham (1968/1969); Allen ["Philosophies"] (1939); Apfel (1977); **Arnold (1931/. . ./1965)**; Atcherson (1973); Audbourg-Popin (1986); Auhagen (1982/1983); Babbitt (1987); Becker (1836-39/1964); Beiche ["Dux"] (1972-), ["Inversio"] (1972-); **Benary (1956/1961); Bent** ["Analysis"] **(1980/1987)**; Beswick (1950); Bircher (1970); Boomgaarden (1985/1987); Bukofzer (1947); **Bullivant (1980)**; Cahn ["Retardatio"] (1972-); Cazden (1948); Chew (1983); Chomiński (1962/1981); Cohen (1873-74); Crocker (1966); Dahlhaus ["Geschichte"] (1980), ["Über"] (1980), (1984); **Dahlhaus and Sachs (1980)**; Dammann (1958/1967); David and Mendel (1945/1966); Dean (1977); Duckles (1970); Dunsby and Whittall (1988); Eitner (1900-1904/1959-60); Falck (1965); Federhofer (1944/1950), (1958), (1964), (1969), (1970), (1980), (1981), (1985); Feil (1955); Fellerer

(1927/. . ./1972), ["Zur Kontrapunktlehre"] (1973); Forkel (1792/1962); Frobenius ["Cantus"] (1972-), ["Vollstimmig"] (1972-); Geering (1949-68); Gerber (1812-14/1966); Ghislanzoni (1949-51); Grave (1985); **Groth (1983)**; Hansell (1968); Hawkins (1776/. . ./1969); Haydon (1933/1970); Hein (1954); Horsley [*Fugue: History*] (1966); Hucke (1969); Jacobi (1957-60/1971); Jeppesen (1922/. . ./1970), (1930/. . ./1974), (1935); **Kassler** (1971), **(1979)**; Kaufmann (1969); Kelletat [*Temperatur*] (1960); Komma (1972); Kramer (1975), (1987-88); Krenek (1952); Lang (1941); Lawrence (1978); Lester (1978), (1979-81); Lindley (1982); Loach (1957); Mann (1955/. . ./1987), (1970/1971), (1981), (1987); Morel (1967); Müller-Blattau (1923/. . ./1963), (1949-68); Munkachy (1968); Neumann (1969);

Newman (1963/. . ./1983); Norton (1984); O'Donnell (1979); Oldroyd (1948); Pacchioni (1983); **Palisca** (1949-68), (1959), [*Baroque*] (1968/1981), ["Theory"] **(1980)**; Ratner (1980); Reese (1954/1959); Reimer ["Kammermusik"] (1972-); **Ritzel (1967/1968)**; Roberts (1967); Rosenblum (1988); Ruhnke (1973); Sachs (1972-); Sanders (1919); Schenkman (1976); Scholes (1947); **Seidel and Cooper (1986);** Serwer (1974); Shellhous (1988); Straková (1975); Subirá (1947/. . ./1958); Taddie (1984); Tenney (1988); Tittel (1959), (1966); Todd (1983); Walker (1987); **Wason (1981/1985)**, (1983); Wellesz and Sternfeld (1973); Wessely (1967); Whatley (1981); Wichmann (1966); Williams, P. (1970), (1979); Wirth (1966); **Zaminer** (1985); Zenck (1965).

FRANCESCO GALEAZZI

[1758–1819]

An impressive array of materials relating to musical practices in late eighteenth-century Italy is contained within the covers of Francesco Galeazzi's *Elementi teorico-pratici di musica* (1791-96). A prominent violinist, Galeazzi included a substantial section on the art of violin playing, incorporating information on both technique and interpretation (particularly ornamentation and improvisation). Yet his most important contributions are found within the second volume, which, after a brief synopsis of the history of music, consists of a penetrating discourse on composition, including the aspects of harmony, counterpoint, melody, rhythm, and form.

Galeazzi departed from the practice of his contemporaries by defining sonata form principally according to its thematic structure. In a carefully articulated formulation—and with a sixty-four bar sample melody to exemplify his points—he described the components of the form's two sections. His second section begins with what we today call the development. Galeazzi understood and revealed how melodic ideas are reused and transformed over the course of a movement. Similar discussions focus upon other sorts of compositions, such as fugues and concertos. A wide variety of information concerning composition and interpretation further adds to the value his work possesses for the study of Classic music and performance practice.

Elementi teorico-pratici di musica con un saggio sopra l'arte di suonare il violino . . . [*Rism* B/VI/1, p. 344.]

> Rome: Pilucchi Cracas, 1791. Vol. 1. [LCPS: G-006. HoM: 571.]
> Rome: Michele Puccinelli, 1796. Vol. 2. [LCPS: G-006.]
> Ascoli: Francesco Cardi, 1817. 2nd edition of Vol. 1.

T● Frascarelli, Angelo. "*Elementi teorico-pratici di musica* by Francesco Galeazzi: An Annotated English Translation and Study of Volume One." D.M.A. dissertation, The University of Rochester, 1968.

T● Harwood, Gregory W. "Francesco Galeazzi's *Elementi teorico-pratici di musica*, IV/2: An Annotated Translation and Commentary." M.A. thesis, Brigham Young University, 1980. [*Rilm* 80-549.]

LITERATURE:

Barblan, Guglielmo. "Galeazzi, Francesco." Translated by Anna Amalie Abert. In *MGG* (1949-68). Bibliog.

●●● Churgin, Bathia. "Francesco Galeazzi's Description (1796) of Sonata Form." *JAMS* 21/2 (1968):181-99; reprinted in Rosand (1985):Vol. 7, pp. 1-19. Bibliog. [*Rilm* 68-433.]

Sutter, Milton. "Francesco Galeazzi on the Duties of the Leader or Concertmaster." *Consort* 32 (1976):185-92. [*Rilm* 76-1590.]

Churgin, Bathia. "Galeazzi, Francesco." In *NGrove* (1980). Bibliog.

Benedetto, Renato di. "Lineamenti di una teoria della melodia nella trattatistica italiana fra il 1790 e il 1830." In *Colloquium Rom 1978* (1982):421-43. [*Rilm* 82-3557.]

See also CHORON: (1810-11); FÉTIS: (1833-44); VOGLER: Stevens (1983); LITERATURE SUPPLEMENT: Allanbrook (1981); Becker (1836-39/1964); Blake (1988); Bremner (1979); Broyles (1982-83); Eitner (1900-1904/1959-60); Gerber (1812-14/1966); Gwilt (1983-84); Horsley [*Fugue: History*] (1966); Jackson (1988); La Fage (1864/1964); Lange (1899-1900); Lindley (1982); Moyer (1969); Neumann (1986); Ratner (1970), (1980); Rosen (1980/1988); Schmalzriedt ["Coda"] (1972-), ["Reprise"] (1972-), (1985); Schoffman (1979); Shellhous (1988); Smiles (1978); **Steblin (1981/1983)**; Stevens (1974); Stowell (1985), (1988); Telesco (forthcoming); Zaslaw (1979).

VINCENZO GALILEI

[late 1520s?–1591]

The writings of Vincenzo Galilei document the intense conflicts in musical thought towards the end of the sixteenth century. Having studied under ZARLINO, Galilei absorbed MEI's distinctly superior conceptions of ancient music and became a bitter enemy of his former teacher, a lively spokesman for Bardi's Camerata, and a visionary architect of powerful new manners of composition.

Galilei's work with ZARLINO sometime around 1563 gave the Camerata a direct link to what was then regarded as the summit of contemporary musical erudition. *Fronimo* (1568-69) displays none of the invective found in Galilei's later writings, yet, in its straightforward exploration of lute playing and related theoretical and practical issues, it adumbrates the simplicity of style which later emerged as monody.

Soon thereafter, as Galilei was reworking ZARLINO's ideas for his "Compendio nella theorica della musica" (1570-72), the incompatibility of Greek theory and its Renaissance reconstruction became evident, leading to urgent requests for assistance from MEI and, eventually, to a bitter dispute with ZARLINO, beginning with several letters late in the decade and spilling over into print with the *Dialogo* (1581), ZARLINO's *Sopplimenti musicali* (1588-89), and the *Discorso* (1589).

Central to Galilei's complaint was the sense of loss: the Greeks described powerful and varied emotional responses to music, whereas Galilei saw pleasure, not affect, as the goal of the music of his contemporaries. He felt that by eliminating the juxtaposition of several melodies (counterpoint) and by exploiting the natural contrasts in vocal ranges and tempi, music's emotive powers could be regained. Confusion concerning the proper tuning for choral singing further divided the two antagonists. ZARLINO's distinctions between consonance and dissonance were based upon numerical relationships, despite the facts that the system thereby created contained numerous unused intervals and that the precision of intonation required was unattainable. In the *Discorso* and in various unpublished studies Galilei explored the accepted dogma of numerical relationships, in the process exploding it by revealing that the collection of acceptable ratios could not be limited as ZARLINO had insisted. For example, if a string's tension, instead of its length, is considered (as when weights are hung from one end of each string), then the disconcerting ratio 9:4 replaces the universally accepted 3:2 as the generator of the perfect fifth. This freedom from the tyranny of numbers allowed Galilei to support equal temperament.

In the years before his death Galilei prepared a counterpoint treatise which survives in a group of four manuscripts. By disregarding the authority of earlier authors Galilei created a document which vibrantly captures the most progressive elements of contemporary compositional practice, including, in particular, a considerably expanded role for dissonance and a pervasive attentiveness to the emotional character of the text. While Galilei's system fails to accord with what he knew of actual Greek music, it clearly represents the new path upon which he and a number of his contemporaries were journeying.

Fronimo: Dialogo . . . nel quale si contengono le vere, et necessarie regole del intavolare la musica nel liuto . . . [*Rism* A/I/3/p. 140; B/I/1, p. 323; B/VI/1, p. 345.]

> Venice: Girolamo Scotto, 1568-69.
>
> > As *Fronimo: Dialogo . . . sopra l'arte del bene intavolare . . .*:
>
> Venice: appresso l'herede di Girolamo Scotto, 1584. [LCPS: G-010. HoM: 574.]

S ● Rapp, Rolf, ed. Facsimile of the 1584 edition. BmB, ser. 2, no. 22. Bologna: Forni, 1969.

S ● Facsimile of the 1584 edition. Leipzig: Zentralantiquariat der Deutschen Demokratischen Republik; Kassel: Bärenreiter, 1978.

T ● MacClintock, Carol, ed. and trans. Translation of the 1584 edition. MSD, no. 39. Rome: American Institute of Musicology (Neuhausen-Stuttgart: Hänssler-Verlag), 1985.

"Compendio nella tehorica della musica"

> Ms., [ca. 1570-72]. [Florence: Biblioteca nazionale centrale.]

Dialogo . . . della musica antica, et della moderna [*Rism* B/VI/1, p. 344.]

> Florence: Giorgio Marescotti, 1581. [LCPS: G-008a. HoM: 573. SMLMS.]
>
> > As *Dialogo della musica antica e moderna in sua difesa contro Ioseffo Zerlino*:
>
> Florence: Filippo Giunti, 1602. [LCPS: G-008b.]

S ● Fano, Fabio, ed. Facsimile of the 1581 edition. Rome: Reale accademia d'Italia, 1934.
> Review in *ML* 17/1 (1936):73-74 (F. Bonavia).

S ● Fano, Fabio., ed. Abbreviated edition. Estetica, no. 11. Milan: A. Minuziano, 1947.

T ● See **Strunk (1950)**:302-22.

S ● Facsimile of the 1581 edition. MMMLF, ser. 2, no. 20. New York: Broude Brothers, [1968].

T ● Herman, Robert Henry. "*Dialogo della musica antica et della moderna* of Vincenzo Galilei: Translation and Commentary." Ph.D. dissertation, North Texas State University, 1973. [*Rilm* 76/9331. *DA* 34/08A, pp. 5228-29. UMI 74-04032.]

T ● See **Katz and Dahlhaus (1987-)**:Vol. 2.

"Il primo libro della prattica del contrapunto . . . intorno all'uso delle consonanze"

> Mss., 1588-91. [Florence: Biblioteca nazionale centrale.]

S ● See Collected Works (1980), below.

"Discorso . . . intorno all'uso delle dissonanze"

> Mss., 1588-91. [Florence: Biblioteca nazionale centrale.]

S ● See Collected Works (1980), below.

"Critica fatta . . . intorno ai Supplementi musicali di Gioseffo Zarlino"

> Ms., [ca. 1589-91]. [Florence: Biblioteca nazionale centrale.]

"Discorso intorno a diversi pareri che hebbono le tre sette piu famose degl'antichi musici, intorno alla cosa de suoni, et degl acchordi"

>　Ms., [ca. 1589]. [Florence: Biblioteca nazionale centrale.]

>　ST ● See Palisca [*Florentine*] (1989).

Discorso . . . intorno all'opere di messer Gioseffo Zarlino da Chioggia, et altri importanti particolari attenenti alla musica [*Rism* B/VI/1, pp. 344-45.]

>　Florence: Giorgio Marescotti, 1589. [LCPS: G-009. SMLMS. IDC.]

>　S ● See 1602 edition of *Dialogo* (1581), above.

>　S ● Facsimile edition. Ctma. Milan: Bollettino bibliografico musicale, 1933.

>　T ● See **Katz and Dahlhaus (1987-)**:Vol. 2.

>　S ● Facsimile edition. MMMLF, ser. 2, no. 62. New York: Broude Brothers, forthcoming.

"Discorso particolare intorno alla diversita delle forme del diapason"

>　Ms., [ca. 1589-90]. [Florence: Biblioteca nazionale centrale.]

>　ST ● See Palisca [*Florentine*] (1989).

"Discorso . . . intorno all'uso dell'enharmonio et di chi fusse autore del cromatico"

>　Ms., 1590-91. [Florence: Biblioteca nazionale centrale.]

>　S ● See Collected Works (1980), below.

"Discorso particolare intorno all'unisono"

>　Ms., [ca. 1590]. [Florence: Biblioteca nazionale centrale.]

>　ST ● See Palisca [*Florentine*] (1989).

"Dubbi intorno a quanto io ho detto dell'uso dell'enharmonio, con la solutione di essi"

>　Ms., 1591. [Florence: Biblioteca nazionale centrale.]

>　S ● See Collected Works (1980), below.

"Traduzione d'un discorso latino fatto da Carlo Valgulio Bresciano, sopra la Musica di Plutarco"

>　Ms. [Florence: Biblioteca nazionale centrale.]

"Trattato di musica di Plutarco"

>　Ms. [Florence: Biblioteca nazionale centrale.]

COLLECTED WORKS EDITION:

Rempp, Frieder. "Die musiktheoretischen Traktate des Vincenzo Galilei." Ph.D. dissertation, The University of Tübingen, 1975; published edition (as *Die Kontrapunkttraktate Vincenzo Galileis*, VSIMPK, no. 9), Cologne: Arno Volk Verlag (Hans Gerig), 1980. Bibliog.

LITERATURE:

[*Edizione nazionale delle*] *opera di Galileo Galilei*, vols. 10 and 19. Florence: G. Barbèra, 1900, 1907; reprint edition, 1934, 1938.

Chilesotti, Oscar. "Di Nicola Vicentino e dei generi greci secondo Vicentio Galilei." *Rmi* 19/3 (1912):546-65.

Fleissner, Otto. "Vincentio Galilei und sein *Dialogo della musica antica e moderna*." Ph.D. dissertation, The University of Munich, 1923.

Fano, Fabio, ed. *La Camerata fiorentina: Vincenzo Galilei, 1520?-1591; La sua opera d'artista e di teorico come expressione di nuove idealità musicali.* Imami, no. 4. Milan: Ricordi, 1934. Bibliog.

>　Review in *ML* 15/3 (1934):265-67 (F. Bonavia).

Fano, Fabio. "Alcuni chiarimenti su Vincenzo Galilei." *Rasm* 10/3 (1937):85-90.

Bignami, Giovanni. "Uno scritto di Galileo sulle onde sonore." *Rmi* 45/1 (1941):16-19.

Palisca, Claude V. "Galilei, Vincenzo." Translated by Friedrich Baake. In *MGG* (1949-68). Bibliog.

Palisca, Claude V. "Vincenzo Galilei's Counterpoint Treatise: A Code for the *seconda pratica*." *JAMS* 9/2 (1956):81-96.

"Um texto de Vincenzo Galilei." *Amus* 28/9 (1960):260-62.

Palisca, Claude V. "Vincenzo Galilei and Some Links Between 'Pseudo-Monody' and Monody." *MQ* 46/3 (1960):344-60.

Drake, Stillman. *Galileo Studies: Personality, Tradition, and Revolution.* Ann Arbor, Mich.: University of Michigan Press, 1970.

>　See Chapter Two: "Vincenzio Galilei and Galileo," pp. 43-62. Reviews in *AHR* 77/5 (1972):1436-37 (Harry Woolf), *BJHS* 6/1 [21] (1972-73):93-94 (J. R. Ravetz), *Booklist* 67/20 (1971):845, *Choice* 8/9 (1971-72):1198, *Isis* 62/4 [214] (1971):546-47 (E. J. Aiton), *LJ* 96/7 (1971):1280 (George Basalla), *Lychnos 1971/72* (1973):507-8 (Lennart Bromander), *RQ* 25/3 (1972):319-21 (Vern L. Bullough), *SBF* 7/2 (1971):109-10, *Science* 172/3984 (1971):710-11 (E. W. Strong), *SS* 36/1 (1972):111-13 (Irving Adler), *STel* 42/1 (1971):37-40 (Edward Rosen), and *ZfMG* 241 (1973):4-5 (H.-J. Treder).

● ● ● Walker, David Pickering. "Some Aspects of the Musical Theory of Vincenzo Galilei and Galileo Galilei." *PMA 1973-74* 100 (1974):33-47. [*Rilm* 74-3888.]

> Reprinted in Walker (1978).

Rempp, Frieder. "Der Musiktheoretiker Vincenzo Galilei und das Ende des 'klassischen' Kontrapunkts." *JSIM 1978* (1979):19-34. Bibliog. [*Rilm* 79-335.]

● ● ● Palisca, Claude V. "Galilei, Vincenzo." In *NGrove* (1980). Bibliog.

Szweykowski, Zygmunt M. "Krytyka kontrapunktu w *Dialogo della musica antica, et della moderna* Vincenza Galilei." *Muzyka* 30/3-4 [118-19] (1985):3-16.

Troccoli, Gaetano. "Vincenzo Galilei: Le due stesure del 'Fronimo' e le 'Intavolature del lauto, madrigali e ricercate, libro primo'." Thesis, The University of Pavia (Cremona), 1985-86.

Harrán, Don. "Sulla genesi della famosa disputa fra Gioseffo Zarlino e Vincenzo Galilei, un nuovo profilo." *Nrmi* 21/3 (1987):467-75.

See also ARTUSI: (1588); (1590); BONINI: [ca. 1649-50]; DIRUTA: Soehnlein (1975); FÉTIS: (1833-44); KEPLER: Dickreiter (1971/1973); MEI: (1572-81); Palisca (1954); Palisca (1960/1977); MERSENNE: (1617-48); MOMIGNY (1791-1818):(1818); MONTEVERDI: Schrade (1950/. . ./1981); Gianuario (1969); Anfuso and Gianuario [1971]; Monterosso (1976); WALTHER: (1732); ZARLINO (1588); LITERATURE SUPPLEMENT: Allen ["Philosophies"] (1939); Ambros (1878/. . ./1909); **Apfel (1981)**; Arnold (1957); **Barbour** (1932), (1938), (1949-68), **(1951/. . ./1972)**; Becker (1836-39/1964); Bell et al. (1980); ● ● ● **Berger (1975/1980)**; Boetticher (1954); Brown (1973); Buelow (1972); Burney (1776-89/. . ./1957); Cazden (1980); Chilesotti (1912); Chomiński (1962/1981); Cohen (1984); Cowart ["Inventing"] (1989); Crombie (1969); Dahlhaus ["Untersuchungen"] (1966/. . ./1988); **Dahlhaus and Sachs (1980); Dahlhaus et al. (1987)**; Dammann (1958/1967); Deutsch (1980);

Donà (1967); Dostrovsky (1969), (1974-75); Drake (1970); **Dürr and Gerstenberg** (1949-68), (1980); Duparcq (1977); Dyson (1967); Eitner (1900-1904/1959-60); Fellerer ["Wesen"] (1982), (1983), (1984); Ferand (1937/1938); Forchert (1986); Forkel (1792/1962); Fubini (1971/1983), (1987); Gable (1979); Gerber (1790-92/1977), (1812-14/1966); Giacotti (1968); Grout (1960/. . ./1980); Haar (1983), (1986); Haase (1969); Hanning (1969/1980); Harrán (1986); Hawkins (1776/. . ./1969); Hein (1954); Hill (1983); Horsley (1963), [*Fugue: History*] (1966); Hosler (1978/1981); Hüschen (1986); Hutchinson and Knopoff (1979-81); Isgro (1968), (1979); Jacobi (1957-60/1971); Jeppesen (1922/. . ./1970); **Kassler (1979)**; Katz (1985); Kelletat ["Tonordnung"] (1960); Kinkeldey (1910/1968); Kirkendale (1979); Kivy (1984); Koenigsberger (1979); Kretzschmar (1911-12); Kunze (1979-83); La Fage (1864/1964); Le Coat (1978); Leuchtmann (1957/1959); **Lindley** ["Temperaments"] **(1980), (1984)**; Mace (1964/1966); **Maniates (1979); Mann (1955/. . ./1987)**; Martin (1932-33); McKinnon (1978); Meier (1974/1988); Müller (1976); Müller-Blattau (1923/. . ./1963); Neumann, Frederick (1978); Norton (1984); **Palisca** (1949-68), (1953), (1961), ["Alterati"] (1968), ["Artusi-Monteverdi"] (1968/1985), [*Baroque*] (1968/1981), ["Rezitativ"] (1972-), ["Camerata"] (1972), (1974/1977), (1979), ["Camerata"] (1980), ["Theory"] (1980), (1981), ● ● ● (1985), [*Florentine*] (1989); Palisca and Spender (1980); Pirrotta (1953/. . ./1984); Pöhlmann (1969); Reese (1954/1959), (1957/1970); Reimer ["Concerto"] (1972-); Sachs (1972-); Schavernoch (1981); Scher (1975); Seidel and Cooper (1986); Subirá (1947/. . ./1958); Tenney (1988); Tirabassi (1925); Tuksar (1978/1980); Vogel (1976); **Walker** (1941-42/. . ./1985), (1950/1985), (1976), **(1978)**; Walker (1987); Warren (1980); Wienpahl (1953); Wightman (1972); Wolff (1972-); Yates (1947); Yeston (1974/1976); **Zaminer (1985)**.

FRANCESCO GASPARINI

[1661 – 1727]

The sophistication which continuo accompaniments had attained at the beginning of the eighteenth century is documented in Francesco Gasparini's *L'armonico pratico al cimbalo* (1708). While aiding inexperienced students in understanding unfigured basses and their realization, Gasparini also divulged the essence of stylistic continuo playing, including the art of diminution, the relationship between the keyboard's melodic line and the solo melody, the judicious use of dissonant embellishment, and voice leading in the context of full-voiced chords. HEINICHEN, though not always in agreement with Gasparini's suggestions, regarded him highly and incorporated portions of *L'armonico pratico* in his own figured-bass manual.

L'armonico pratico al cimbalo; Regole, osservazioni, ed avvertimenti per ben suonare il basso, e accompagnare sopra il cimbalo, spinetta, ed organo [*Rism* B/VI/1, pp. 349-50.]

> Venice: Antonio Bortoli, 1708. [LCPS: G-023a.]

>> Several editions through 1802, including:

> Venice: Antonio Bortoli, 1729. [LCPS: G-023b. HoM: 584.]

> Venice: Antonio Bortoli, 1745. [LCPS: G-023c. SMLMS. IDC.]

> Venice: Antonio Bortoli, 1764. [LCPS: G-023d.]

T ● "Mss.: Lessons for the Harpsichord." Ms., [mid-eighteenth century]. [Durham, England: Durham Cathedral Library.]

> A translation from Chapters 8 and 9. See "An Unknown Bach Source," *MT* 113/1558 (1972):1167-69 (Barry Cooper).

S ● Facsimile of the 1708 edition. MMMLF, ser. 2, no. 14. New York: Broude Brothers, [1967].

> Reviews in *Consort* 26 (1970):460 (Lillian M. Ruff), *ML* 50/4 (1969):509-10 (John A. Caldwell), and *MT* 110/1512 (1969):159 (Charles Cudworth).

T ● ● ● ● Stillings, Frank S., trans. *The Practical Harmonist at the Harpsichord.* Edited by David L. Burrows. MTTS, no. 1. New Haven, Ct.: Yale School of Music, 1963; reprint edition, Yale University Press, 1968; reprint edition, New York: Da Capo Press, 1980.

> Reviews in *AR* 14/2 (1973):72 (Sabina Teller Ratner), *ARG* 31/9 (1964-65):907-10 (Igor Kipnis), *Clavier* 2/5 (1963):6, *JAMS* 18/2 (1965):255-56 (Glen Haydon), *JMT* 8/1 (1964):120-22 (William J. Mitchell), *Mf* 24/4 (1971):485-86 (Peter Cahn), *MiE* 34/341 (1970):37-38, *ML* 45/3 (1964):283-84 (J. A. Westrup), *MO* 93/1115 (1970):595 (B. R.), *RBBR* 26/2 (1981):9 (Donald McRoe), and *TLS* 68/3532 (1969):1276.

"Guida ossia dizionario armonico, in cui si trova il modo di ben modulare"

> Ms. [Bologna: Civico museo bibliografico musicale.]

"Li principii della composizione"

> Ms. [Berlin: Deutsches Staatsbibliothek; Hamburg: Staats- und Universitätsbibliothek.]

LITERATURE:

Ruhnke, Martin. "Gasparini, Francesco." In *MGG* (1949-68). Bibliog.

Rose, Gloria. "A Fresh Clue from Gasparini on Embellished Figured-Bass Accompaniment." *MT* 107/1475 (1966):28-29.

Libby, Dennis, and Jackman, James L. "Gasparini, Francesco." In *NGrove* (1980). Bibliog.

Tagliavini, Luigi Ferdinando. "*L'armonico pratico al cimbalo*: Lettura critica." In *Gasparini convegno 1978* (1981):133-55. [*Rilm* 81-4712.]

See also FÉTIS: (1833-44); HEINICHEN: (1728); (1728):Buelow (1961/. . ./1986); MATTHESON: (1740); MOMIGNY: (1791-1818):(1818); RIEMANN: (1898); SAINT-LAMBERT: (1707):Burchill (1979); WALTHER: (1732); LITERATURE SUPPLEMENT: Ahlgrimm (1973); **Arnold (1931/. . ./1965)**; Badura-Skoda et al. (1980); Beach (1983); Becker (1836-39/1964); Beyschlag (1907/1953); ● ● ● Borgir (1971/1987); Brown and McKinnon (1980); Bukofzer (1947); Chevaillier (1925/1931-32); Chew (1983); Dahlhaus ["Konsonanz"] (1949-68); Dean (1977); Donington (1963/. . ./1974); Dreyfus (1987); Eitner (1900-1904/1959-60); Fellerer (1927/. . ./1972); Ferand [*Improvisation*] (1956/1961); Forkel (1792/1962); Geering (1949-68); Gerber (1790-92/1977), (1812-14/1966); Hansell (1968); Harich-Schneider ([1939]/. . ./1970); Hawkins (1776/. . ./1969); Helm (1960); Henderson (1969); Ibberson (1984); Jackson (1988); **Kassler (1979)**; Kauko (1958); Kroyer (1901/. . ./1970); Lawrence (1978); Lewis (1975); Mahlert and Sunter (1972-); Morche (1974); Nelson (1984); Neumann, Frederick (1978); North (1987); Oberdoerffer (1967); **Palisca ["Theory"] (1980)**; Ratner (1980); Rogers (1955); Rothgeb (1968); Ruhnke (1973); **Seidel and Cooper (1986)**; **Shirlaw (1917/. . ./1970)**; Sisman (1978); Subirá (1947/. . ./1958); Tenney (1988); Tirabassi (1925); Troeger (1987); Williams, P. ["Harpsichord"] (1968), (1970).

ANDRÉ GÉDALGE

[1856 — 1926]

Though he intended to publish three volumes on counterpoint and fugue, the *Traité de la fugue* by André Gédalge remains incomplete. Only *De la fugue d'école* [1904] appeared, despite the fact that Gédalge lived for two more decades and attained greater prominence owing to his appointment in 1905 as a professor of counterpoint and fugue at the Paris Conservatoire. A culmination of nineteenth-century contrapuntal pedagogy, with borrowings from or expansions upon REICHA, CHERUBINI, and FÉTIS, Gédalge's masterful synthesis has served as a valued tool for generations of students, including those who read only German, Italian, or English. Avoiding the abstract and sometimes unmusical dictates which mar other treatises, Gédalge emphasized in his examples the music of master composers, in particular J. S. Bach, even though the admittedly contrived school fugue, which was intended to demonstrate a specific set of attributes not characteristically assembled in the practice of any particular composer, offered students an exposure to but a part of the fugal art's essence. One must lament the fact that Gédalge did not complete his monumental undertaking, for the first volume demonstrates both a keen understanding of the subject and an apt manner of presentation. Nevertheless, one finds therein a cogent summary of basic principles (including the concepts of subject, answer, countersubject, episode, stretto, and pedal) as well as revealing comments on the compositional process as practiced in the context of this sophisticated framework.

Traité de la fugue

1) *De la fugue d'école*

Paris: Enoch, [1904]

Later printings.

T ● Stier, Ernst, trans. and ed. *Lehrbuch der Fuge. Erster Teil: Die Schulfuge.* Brunswick: Henry Litolff (Boston: Arthur P. Schmidt), [1906].

T ● Parodi, Renato, trans. *Trattato della fuga.* Milan: Curci (Toni), 1953.

T ● Levin, A., trans. *Treatise on Fugue. Part I: The School Fugue.* Edited and with an Introduction by S. B. Potter. Mattapan, Mass.: Gamut Music, 1964.

Review in *MEJ* 51/6 (1964-65):86 (Theodore F. Normann).

T ● Davis, Ferdinand, trans. and ed. *Treatise on the Fugue.* Foreword by Darius Milhaud. Norman, Okla.: The University of Oklahoma Press, 1965.

Reviews in *ABBW* 37/5 (1966):408, *AmO* 49/4 (1966):6 (Harry W. Gay), *ARG* 32/8 (1965-66):735 (Walter S. Kimmel), *Choice* 3/5-6 (1966-67):416, *Clavier* 5/5 (1966):10, *Instrumentalist*

20/11 (1966):14, *MJ* 24/3 (1966):134 (William Mayer), *MusT* 45 (1966):245 (J. R. T.), and *Strad* 77/924 (1966-67):481-82 (Samuel and Sada Applebaum).

"Les rapports de l'harmonie et du contrepoint: Définitions et considérations générales"

Rhcm 4 (1904):326-29.

L'enseignement de la musique par l'éducation méthodique de l'oreille . . .

1) *Partie théorique*

2) *Exercises*

Paris: Librairie Gedalge, 1921-22. 2 vols.

Later printings. Review in *Rmi* 29/2 (1922):361-62 (G. M.).

T ● Mealand, Anna Mary, trans. *The Teaching of Music by the Methodical Education of the Ear.* Paris: Librairie Gedalge, n.d.

A brief pamphlet describing the system.

LITERATURE:

Elliott, Gilbert. "A French Master of Musical Theory." *MAm* 12/3 (1916):23.

Koechlin, Charles. "André Gedalge." *Rm* 7/5 (1925-26):242-54.

Reprinted in *André Gedalge* (1926), below.

André Gedalge: 1856-1926. Corbeil: Crété, 1926.

Pelliot, Alice. "Gedalge, André." Translated by Renate Albrecht. In *MGG* (1949-68). Bibliog.

Louvier, Alain. "Gédalge, André." In *NGrove* (1980). Bibliog.

See also LITERATURE SUPPLEMENT: **Bullivant (1980)**; **Dahlhaus (1984)**; ● ● ● **Groth (1983)**; Horsley [*Fugue: History*] (1966); Kleinman (1971/1974); Lindley (1982); **Mann (1955/. . ./1987)**; Müller-Blattau (1923/. . ./1963); Subirá (1947/. . ./1958); Walker (1987).

FRANCESCO GEMINIANI

[bapt. 1687–1762]

Having distinguished himself as one of Corelli's finest Italian pupils, Francesco Geminiani settled in London in 1714 and cultivated his musical career on British soil. In his later years he created an impressive set of practical texts to document his teaching and his aesthetic perspective, and perhaps also to supply sufficient income to maintain a

household. The facts of publication for these works are tangled in a web of inaccuracy and conjecture. The dates suggested by scholars for several of his works have diverged widely; numerous violin tutors which have nothing to do with Geminiani's *Art of Playing on the Violin* (1751) bear his name or have been attributed to him; the English translation of

Antoniotto's *L'arte armonica* (1760) perhaps ought to be attributed to him; and we suspect that he undertook a major theoretical treatise which was stolen from him and destroyed under unusual circumstances.

As one of the leading violinists of his day (in a country which lavished attention upon foreign virtuosi), Geminiani scored a clear success with his violin treatise of 1751 – five years before Leopold MOZART's more comprehensive work, which was not available in English translation during the eighteenth century. Addressed to skilled performers rather than beginners, *The Art of Playing on the Violin* asserts that music's emotional impact is of the greatest importance and reveals how various techniques of ornamentation, improvisation, vibrato, and bowing can assist in realizing the composer's intent. Its aesthetic perspective echoes Geminiani's earlier *Rules for Playing in a True Taste on the Violin* [ca. 1739] and *A Treatise of Good Taste in the Art of Musick* (1749), the first of which includes scores replete with a wide variety of unique markings which were intended to foster various nuances of musical expression in performance.

Geminiani irritated his professional colleagues in publishing *Guida harmonica, o dizionario armonico* [ca. 1742]. Rather than actually teaching composition, it supplies a repository of ready-made segments of compositions which amateurs could assemble with little effort or understanding. Geminiani's impressive list of practical works also includes *The Art of Accompaniament* [ca. 1754-57] and *The Art of Playing the Guitar or Cittra* (1760). His perspective received a wider circulation through a number of French, German, and Dutch translations.

Rules for Playing in a True Taste on the Violin, German Flute, Violoncello, and Harpsichord, Particularly the Thorough-Bass, Exemplify'd in a Variety of Compositions on the Subjects of English, Scotch and Irish Tunes [*Rism* A/I/3, pp. 213-14; B/VI/1, p. 356.]

> [London]: Royal License [Philips], [ca. 1739.] [SMLMS. IDC.]
>
> > Reprinted ca. 1745.

Guida armonica, o dizionario armonico: Being a Sure Guide to Harmony and Modulation . . . [*Rism* B/VI/1, p. 356.]:

> London: the author (John Johnson), [ca. 1742 (or ca. 1754?)]. Two versions. [LCPS: G-032a. SMLMS.]
>
> > See SERRE: (1763).
> >
> > In addition, *A Supplement to the Guida armonica, with Examples Shewing It's Use in Composition*:
>
> London: the author (John Johnson), [ca. 1742 (or ca. 1754?)]
>
> > Reprinted ca. 1745. [?]

T ● *Dictionaire harmonique ou guide sûr pour la vraie modulaison/Dictionarium harmonicum of Zeekere wegwyzer tot de waare modulatie . . .* Amsterdam: the author (J. Vermaazen), 1756. [*Rism* B/VI/1, p. 356. LCPS: G-032b. SMLMS. IDC.]

A Treatise of Good Taste in the Art of Musick [*Rism* A/I/3, p. 214; B/VI/1, p. 356.]

> [London]: 1749. [LCPS: G-031. SMLMS.]

S ● Donington, Robert, ed. Facsimile edition. DCPMRS. New York: Da Capo Press, 1969.

> Review in *AR* 11/3 (1970):100 (Dale Higbee).

The Art of Playing on the Violin, Containing All the Rules Necessary to Attain to a Perfection on That Instrument . . . [*Rism* A/I/3, p. 214; B/VI/1, pp. 354-56.]

> London: [Philips], 1751. [LCPS: G-030b. IDC.]
> London: the author (John Johnson), 1751.
> London: Robert Bremner, [after 1777].
> London: Preston & Son, [after 1789].
>
> > Several other editions, as well as tutors with other titles printed under Geminiani's name, bear little resemblance to this work. [LCPS: G-030c through G-030f. SMLMS.]

T ● *L'art de jouer le violin . . .*; Paris: 1752 [LCPS: G-030g.]; later editions, including Paris: de la Chevardière; Lyon: les frères Le Goux, [1763?] [LCPS: G-030h. SMLMS.].

S ● *An Abstract of Geminiani's Art of Playing on the Violin.* Boston: John Boyles, 1769.

T ● *Gründliche Anleitung oder Violin Schule; ou fundament pour le violin.* Vienna: Christoph Torricella, [1782]; Artaria, [ca. 1785-1805].

> German and French translations.

T ● *L'art du violon, ou méthode raisonnée pour aprendre à bien jouer de cet instrument.* Paris: Louis [Sieber?] fils, [ca. 1800-1803] [LCPS: G-030i.]; later editions.

S ● Boyden, David D., ed. Facsimile edition. London: Oxford University Press, [1952]. Bibliog.

> Reviews in *AR* 11/3 (1970):103 (Dale Higbee), *JAMS* 6/2 (1953):184-85 (Hans T. David), *MC* 146/9 [3261] (1952):30 (Kemp Stillings), *MQ* 39/2 (1953):302-4 (Ross Lee Finney), *MT* 93/1318 (1952):548-49 (André Mangeot), *Notes* 10/2 (1952-53):276 (Paul Gelrud), *Rmi* 55/4 (1953):449 (A.), and *VV* 14/4 [124] (1953):186.

S ● See MacClintock (1980).

The Art of Accompaniament; or, A New and Well Digested Method to Learn to Perform the Thorough Bass on the Harpsichord, with Propriety and Elegance [*Rism* A/I/3, pp. 214-15; B/VI/1, p. 354.]

London: the author (John Johnson), [ca. 1754-57]. 2 vols. Two versions. [LCPS: G-029. SMLMS. IDC.]

Later printings (London: Preston and Son).

T ● *L'art de bien accompagner du clavecin.* Paris: adresses ordinaires, 1754. [*Rism* B/VI/1, p. 353.]

T ● *Arte d'accompagnare col'cimbalo o sia nuovo metodo per accompagnare propriamente il basso continuo.* Paris: Madame Boivin, Le Clerc, n.d. [*Rism* B/VI/1, p. 354.]

The Art of Playing the Guitar or Cittra . . . [*Rism* A/I/3, p. 215.]

Edinburgh: the author (Robert Bremner), 1760. [LCPS: G-034.]

L'arte armonica; or, A Treatise on the Composition of Musick . . . [*Rism* B/VI/1, p. 91.]

London: John Johnson, 1760. 2 vols. [LCPS: A-041. HoM: 61. SMLMS.]

The work of Giorgio Antoniotto appearing in an English translation attributed by some to Geminiani. Review in *MonR* 24 (1761):293-99.

LITERATURE:

Betti, Adolfo. *La vita e l'arte di Francesco Geminiani.* Lucca: G. Giusti, 1933.

Gutheil, Crystal H. "F. Geminiani's Violin Methods." M. M. thesis, The University of Rochester, 1943. Bibliog.

Giegling, Franz. "Geminiani, Francesco Saverio." In *MGG* (1949-68). Bibliog.

Boyden, David D. "Prelleur, Geminiani, and Just Intonation." *JAMS* 4/3 (1951):202-19.

McArtor, Marion E. "Francesco Geminiani, Composer and Theorist." Ph.D. dissertation, The University of Michigan, 1951. Bibliog. [*DA* 11/02, p. 374. UMI 00-02363.]

McArtor, Marion E., and Reilly, Edward. "A Study of Free Ornamentation Based on Works by Geminiani and Quantz [Abstract]." *JAMS* 5/2 (1952):142-43.

Boyden, David D. "Geminiani and the First Violin Tutor." *Am* 31/3-4 (1959):161-70; 32/1 (1960):40-47.

Betti, Adolfo. "Francesco Geminiani, His Life and His Art." Translated by Helen L. Kaufmann. *Strad* 73/870-71 (1962):215-21.

Boyden, David D. "Francesco Geminiani: A Reappraisal." *Lucca: Rassegna del Comune* 4/4 (1962):3ff.

Dart, Thurston. "Francesco Geminiani and the Rule of Taste: A Bi-centenary Appreciation." *Consort* 19 (1962):122-27.

Wood, Godfrey. "Lot with Hidden Assets." *Strad* 78/930 (1967-68):233-37.

Oshibuchi, Takako. "Francesco Geminiani no *The Art of Playing on the Violin* ni tsuite." *Djdgkn* 19 (1968):215-29.

Donington, Robert. "Geminiani and the Gremlins." *ML* 51/2 (1970):150-55. [*Rilm* 70-365.]

Friedmann, Martin George. "Francesco Geminiani's *The Art of Playing on the Violin* in Perspective." D.M.A. dissertation, The University of Washington, 1971. [*DA* 32/05A, p. 2728. UMI 71-28405.]

Tonazzi, Bruno. "*L'arte di suonare la chitarra o cetra* di Francesco Geminiani." *Fronimo* 1/1 (1972-73):13-20. [*Rilm* 74-3719.]

Boyden, David D., and Ladewig, James. "Geminiani, Francesco (Xaverio)." In *NGrove* (1980). Bibliog.

Hickman, Roger. "The Censored Publications of *The Art of Playing on the Violin*, or Geminiani Unshaken." *EM* 11/1 (1983):73-76.

Kirakowska, Susan. "Geminiani the Editor." *MR* 44/1 (1983):13-24.

Walls, Peter. " 'Ill-Compliments and Arbitrary Taste'? Geminiani's Directions for Performers." *EM* 14/2 (1986):221-35.

Beechey, Gwilym. "Francesco Geminiani (1687-1762) and the Art of String Playing." *Consort* 43 (1987):24-34.

See also FÉTIS: (1833-44); SERRE: (1763); WALTHER: (1732); LITERATURE SUPPLEMENT: Almond (1979); **Arnold (1931/. . ./1965)**; Babitz (1952), (1967/1969); Babitz and Pont (1973); Barbour (1952); Becker (1836-39/1964); Bent et al. (1980); Beyschlag (1907/1953); Bremner (1979); Brown and McKinnon (1980); Burke (1963); Burney (1776-89/. . ./1957); Castellani (1976); Chevaillier (1925/1931-32); Derr (1985); Dolmetsch (1915/. . ./1969); Donington (1963/. . ./1974), (1977), (1980); Eitner (1900-1904/1959-60); Fischer (1957); Forkel (1792/1962), (1799-1800); Gerber (1790-92/1977), (1812-14/1966); Gillingham (1981); Goldsmith (1978-79); Hansell (1968); Harich-Schneider ([1939]/. . ./1970); Hawkins (1776/. . ./1969); Houle (1960), (1987); Jackson (1988); Jacobi (1957-60/1971); Jasinsky (1974); ● ● ● **Kassler (1979)**; Krehbiel (1964); Lawrence (1978); **Lindley** ["Just"] **(1980)**; Lippman (1986); Nelson (1984); Neumann, Frederick (1978); Newman (1985); Oberdörffer (1949-68); Pincherle (1958); Ratner (1980); Robison (1982); **Seidel and Cooper (1986)**; Sheppard (1978-79); Sisman (1978); Stowell (1985); Subirá (1947/. . ./1958); Troeger (1987); Wessel (1955); Williams, P. ["Harpsichord"] (1968), (1970); Zaslaw (1979).

FRANÇOIS-AUGUSTE GEVAERT

[1828–1908]

Few nineteenth-century authors on music possessed quite the breadth of interests and accomplishments that François-Auguste Gevaert commanded. After a successful career as an opera composer in Paris, Gevaert spent nearly half of his life as director of the Brussels Conservatory, a post he undertook with vigor and success. His writings range from scholarly studies of ancient Greek and early church music through instrumentation and orchestration to a catholic perspective on harmony.

Gevaert's name was spread to many nations through his *Traité général d'instrumentation* (1863) and its two-part revision, *Nouveau traité d'instrumentation* (1885) and *Cours méthodique d'orchestration* (1890). The music examples depend heavily upon the opera composers who had inspired Gevaert's own development. Wagner is prominently represented, for example. In the 1885-90 version, all instruments are categorized as string, wind, or percussion. A devoted student of early musical practices, Gevaert promoted the view that the Greeks had known polyphony, questioned the role of Pope Gregory I in the formulation of Gregorian chant, and countered FÉTIS's assertion that MONTEVERDI had been the first to utilize the dominant-seventh chord. His *Traité d'harmonie théorique et pratique* (1905-7) mirrors his eclectic tastes. One finds therein an extraordinary range of examples, including folk tunes in unusual modes, chorales and other Baroque music, French opera, and, of course, Wagner.

Leerboek der harmonij en begeleiding

[Ghent: Gevaert?]

T ● *Méthode d'harmonie et d'accompagnement, contenant tout ce qui est nécessaire pour acquérir en peu de temps et sans le secours d'un maître, une connaissance théorique et pratique de l'harmonie et de la basse chiffrée.* 2 vols. Brussels: Cranz; Ghent: V. & C. Gevaert et fils, [1857].

Under the pseudonym Albert Kennig.

Leerboek van den Gregoriaenschen zang, voornamelyk toegepast op de orgelbegeleiding, gevolgd van talryke voorbeelden

Ghent: Gevaert, 1856.

T ● *Méthode pour l'enseignement du plain-chant et de la manière de l'accompagner . . .* Brussels: Cranz; Ghent: Gevaert, 1856.

Traité général d'instrumentation: Exposé méthodique des principes de cet art dans leur application à l'orchestre, à la musique d'harmonie et de fanfares etc.

Ghent and Liége: V. & C. Gevaert et fils, 1863.
Ghent and Paris: Katto, 1863.

Revised and expanded version of the technical part, as *Nouveau traité d'instrumentation*:

Paris and Brussels: Henry Lemoine et fils, 1885.

Revised and expanded version of the practical part, as *Cours méthodique d'orchestration*:

Paris and Brussels: Henry Lemoine, [1890].

T ● CHAIKOVSKY, Petr Il'ich. *Rukovodstvo k instrumentovke*. Moscow: 1866; 1901.

Russian translation of the 1863 edition.

T ● RIEMANN, Hugo, trans. *Neue Instrumenten-Lehre*. Leipzig: Otto Junne (Breitkopf & Härtel); Paris and Brussels: Henry Lemoine, 1887; Paris; Leipzig: Otto Junne, 1897.

A German translation of the *Nouveau traité*.

S ● *Abrégé du nouveau traité d'instrumentation*. Paris and Brussels: Henry Lemoine, 1892.

T ● Rebikov, Vladimir Ivanovich, trans. Moscow: 1899.

A Russian translation of the *Cours méthodique*.

T ● Suddard, E. F. E., trans. *A New Treatise on Instrumentation*. Paris and Brussels: Henry Lemoine; London: Gérard, [ca. 1906-9].

T ● Neuparth, Júlio Cândido, trans. Lisbon: n.d.

A Portuguese translation of the *Nouveau traité*.

"Les origines de la tonalité moderne"

Mén 35/50-52 [1154-56] (1867-68):393-95, 401-2, 414-15.

See FÉTIS: (1868), to which Gevaert responded in (1868), below.

Réponse à M. Fétis sur l'origine de la tonalité moderne

Paris: Kugelmann, 1868.

T ● See FÉTIS: (1840):Arlin (1972):219-26.

Vade-mecum de l'organiste

Ghent: Gevaert; Brussels: Schott, 1871.

Histoire et théorie de la musique de l'antiquité

Ghent: C. Annoot-Braeckman, 1875-81. 2 vols.

S ● Facsimile edition. Hildesheim: Georg Olms, 1965. 2 vols.

Académie royale des sciences, des lettres et des beaux-arts de Belgique: Discours prononcé dans le séance publique de la classe des Beaux-Arts en présence de LL. MM. le roi et la reine, le 24 septembre 1876

Ghent: C. Annoot-Braeckman, 1876.

See [Rouxel] (1876), below.

S ● *Annuaire du Conservatoire royal de musique de Bruxelles* 1 (1877).

25 leçons de solfège à changement de clefs

Paris and Brussels: Henry Lemoine, 1887.

Les origines du chant liturgique de l'église latine: Étude d'histoire musicale

Ghent: A. Hoste, 1890.

See Morin (1890), below.

T ● RIEMANN, Hugo, trans. *Der Ursprung des römischen Kirchengesanges: Musikgeschichtliche Studie.* Leipzig: Breitkopf & Härtel, 1891.

S ● Facsimile edition. Hildesheim: Georg Olms, 1971.

La mélopée antique dans le chant de l'église latine: Suite et complément de l'Histoire et théorie de la musique de l'antiquité

Ghent: A. Hoste, 1895-96. 2 vols.

S ● Facsimile edition. Osnabrück: Otto Zeller, 1967.

Les problèmes musicaux d'Aristote: Texte grec avec traduction française, notes philologiques, commentaire musical et appendice

Ghent: A. Hoste, 1899-1903. 3 vols. With J. C. Vollgraff.

Review by James Green, as *Aristotle's "Musical Problems"...: A Paper Read before the American Antiquarian Society...*, Worcester, Mass.: Charles Hamilton, 1903.

S ● Facsimile edition. Osnabrück: Biblio-Verlag, 1977.

Traité d'harmonie théorique et pratique

Paris and Brussels: Henry Lemoine, 1905[-7]. 2 vols.

Review in *Gm* 51/30-31, 32-33 (1905):521-24, 539-41; 54/23-24, 27-28 (1908):447-550, 471-75 (Ernest Closson).

See also CACCINI: (1601):GEVAERT:(1873-74).

LITERATURE:

[Rouxel, Mathurin.] *Histoire politique des écoles de musique: Réponse au discours prononcé par M. Gevaert, a l'Académie des beaux-arts à Bruxelles le 24 septembre 1876, par un trouvere.* Paris: Baur, 1876.

Wichmann, Hermann. *Über Gevaerts Histoire et théorie de la musique de l'antiquité.* Berlin: Mitscher & Röstell, 1876.

Morin, Germain. *Les véritables origines du chant grégorien, à propos du livre de M. Gevaert...* Saint-Gérard, Namur, Belgium: Abbaye de Maredsous, Bureau de la *Revue bénédictine*, 1890; as *Der Ursprung des gregorianischen Gesanges...* (translated by Thomas Elsässer), Paderborn: F. Schöningh., 1892.

Extract from *Rbén* 7/2, 7, 8 (1890):62-70, 289-323, 337-69.

Meerens, Charles. *À propos de la Mélopée antique dans le chant de l'église latine par Fr. Aug. Gevaert.* Brussels: J.-B. Katto, 1896.

Catoire, Georgii Lvovich. *Teoreticheskii kurs garmonii.* [The Theoretical Course of Harmony.] 2 vols. Moscow: 1924-26.

Based on Gevaert.

Van der Linden, Albert. "Gevaert, François-Auguste." Translated by Renate Albrecht. In *MGG* (1949-68). Bibliog.

Sutter, Albert de. "Den flamländska 1800-talsmusiken." *Musikrevy* 24/3 (1969):134-35.

Potiron, Henri. "Les modes liturgiques d'après Gevaert: *La mélopée antique dans le chant de l'église latine* (Gand, 1895)." *Ég* 11 (1970):181-85. [*Rilm* 70-1343.]

Hucke, Helmut. "Toward a New Historical View of Gregorian Chant." *JAMS* 33/3 (1980):437-67. Bibliog. [*Rilm* 80-4429.]

Riessauw, Anne-Marie. "Gevaert, François-Auguste." In *NGrove* (1980). Bibliog.

Zaminer, Frieder. "Hypate, Mese und Nete im frühgriechischen Denken: Ein altes musikterminologisches Problem in neuem Licht." *AfMw* 41/1 (1984):1-26.

See also FÉTIS: (1833-44); RIEMANN: (1898); WESTPHAL: Sokolowsky (1887); LITERATURE SUPPLEMENT: Auda (1930/1979); Auhagen (1982/1983); Carpenter (1988); Carse (1925/1964); Cazden (1948); Chevaillier (1925/1931-32); Ferand (1937/1938); ● ● ● **Groth (1983)**; Imig (1969/1970); Jorgenson (1957); Norton (1984); Peters (1988); Pole (1879/.../1924); Seidel (1972-); Subirá (1947/.../1958); Tuksar (1978/1980); Wichmann (1966); **Zaminer (1985)**.

OTTO GIBELIUS

[1612–1682]

German youths learned singing in seventeenth-century church schools through a pedagogical method in which basic precepts were established and later drilled. Otto Gibelius, in his popular manuals of instruction, sought to reorient the process by using practice as the basis for the gradual emergence of concepts. His successful method continued beyond mere *Syllabication* (using *ut* through *la*): clear procedures for the incorporation of rhythm and of text were included. In this way students in the Latin schools attained skills which would be useful in the context of the worship service.

Gibelius's potential as a significant author of more technical theoretical works was stifled by pecuniary difficulties, which prevented the full realization of his conception. The *Introductio musicae theoreticae didacticae* (1660) forms the foundation for what might have emerged, while the *Propositiones mathematico-musicae* (1666) treats issues of temperament and includes a discussion of a fourteen-note octave in which D-sharp, E-flat, G-sharp, and A-flat would each be available on the keyboard.

Seminarium modulatoriae vocalis; Das ist, Ein Pflantzgarten der Singkunst . . . [Rism B/VI/1, pp. 363-64.]

    Celle: Elias Holwein, 1645.
    Bremen: Jacob Köhler, 1657.

      With *Compendium modulatoriae*, below:

    Rinteln: Lucius Witwe, 1658.

Compendium modulatoriae . . .

    Jena: 1651. [Lost.]

      With *Seminarium modulatoriae vocalis*, above:

    Rinteln: Lucius Witwe, 1658.

Kurtzer, jedoch gründlicher Bericht von den vocibus musicalibus, darin gehandelt wird von der musicalischen Syllabication . . . [Rism B/VI/1, p. 363.]

    Bremen: Jacob Köhler, 1659.

      Review in MIZLER: (1736-54):Vol. 1/3 (1737):16-33.

Introductio musicae theoreticae didacticae . . . [Rism B/VI/1, p. 363.]

    Bremen: Jacob Köhler, 1660. [LCPS: G-045. IDC.]

Propositiones mathematico-musicae; Das ist, Etliche fürnehme und gar nützliche musicalische Auffgaben, auß der Mathesi demonstriret . . . [Rism B/VI/1, p. 363.]

    Minden an der Weser: Johann Ernst Heydorn (Hiddewigs Witwe), 1666. [LCPS: G-046. IDC.]

LITERATURE:

Ganse, Albrecht. "Der Cantor Otto Gibelius (1612-1682): Sein Leben und seine Werke, unter besonderer Berücksichtigung seiner Schriften zur Schulgesangsmethodik." Ph.D. dissertation, The University of Kiel, 1931 (1934); published edition, Leipzig: Frommhold & Wendler, 1934. Bibliog.

Ruhnke, Martin. "Gibel, Otto." In *MGG* (1949-68). Bibliog.

Buelow, George J. "Gibelius, Otto." In *NGrove* (1980).

See also FÉTIS: (1833-44); HERBST: Allerup (1931); LIPPIUS: Rivera (1974/1980); MATTHESON: (1717); (1740); WALTHER: (1732); LITERATURE SUPPLEMENT: Becker (1836-39/1964); Buelow (1972); **Dahlhaus et al. (1987)**; Eitner (1900-1904/1959-60); Forkel (1792/1962); Gerber (1790-92/1977), (1812-14/1966); Lange (1899-1900); ● ● ● Preußner (1924); Schünemann (1928/1931); Vogel (1955/1954).

HEINRICH GLAREAN

[1488–1563]

Despite our inclination to regard the creator of the twelve-mode system as progressive, Heinrich Glarean worked under a conservative humanist influence in sixteenth-century Switzerland. A disciple of Erasmus, Glarean carefully studied older theoretical treatises. One fruit of this labor was an edition of Boethius's *De musica*, published in 1546. The influences of Boethius and of Gaffurio are strongly in evidence in *Dodecachordon* (1547), wherein Glarean argued that his additional modes represented a restoration of ancient thought rather than a modern innovation. The new modes were, in fact, a case of theory adapting to practice, for the Dorian and Lydian with B-flat were in use, but not yet labelled Aeolian and Ionian. The corresponding plagals—Hypoaeolian and Hypoionian—led to the number twelve of Glarean's title. Two additional modes—an authentic on B and a plagal on F—were considered but rejected due to the B-F and F-B divisions that would result.

The maturation of Glarean's views concerning the modes was not spread over thirty years, as the publication dates of the conservative pedagogical manual *Isagoge in musicen* (1516) and of *Dodecachordon* would seem to indicate. Glarean's correspondence reveals that the latter work was much delayed due to publishers' apprehensions about its production cost. The numerous examples of monophonic and polyphonic music, now regarded as a valuable Renaissance anthology, must have contributed to this problem. Access to Glarean's theory was later made available in a much less sumptuous format, in a compendium of *Dodecachordon* published in Latin and in German. Acknowledged or unacknowledged (as was the case with ZARLINO), Glarean's innovations affected much of what was written about the modes by later generations, while the added modes provided a necessary foundation for the major-minor system which eventually replaced modal theory as a central issue in theoretical discourse.

Isagoge in musicen . . . [*Rism* B/VI/1, p. 366.]

> Basel: Johannes Frobenius, 1516. [LCPS: G-051. SMLMS. IDC.]

T ● Turrell, Frances Berry, trans. "The *Isagoge in musicen* of Henry Glarean." *JMT* 3/1 (1959):97-139. Bibliog.

"Boethii de musica" [*Rism* B/VI/1, p. 157.]

> Edited by Glarean.

> In *Anitii Manlii Severini Boethi, . . . Opera, quae extant, omnia . . .: Inter quos in omni literarum genere summus uir Henrichus Loritus Glareanus arithmeticam & musicam demonstrationibus & figuris auctiorem redditam suo pristino nitori restituit . . .* Basel: Heinrich Petri, 1546; 2nd edition, 1570.

Δωδεκαχορδον [*Dodecachordon*] [*Rism* B/VI/1, p. 366.]

> Basel: Heinrich Petri, 1547. [LCPS: G-049. HoM: 619. SMLMS. IDC.]

S ● See (1557), below.

S ● *De modis musicis* [*Rism* B/VI/1, p. 365.] Hamburg: Jakob Rebenlein, 1635.

T ● Bohn, Peter, trans. *Glareani Dodecachordon.* 3 vols. PaptM, no. 16. Leipzig: Breitkopf & Härtel, 1888-90; reprint edition (in 1 vol.), New York: Broude Brothers, 1966.

> Review in *VMw* 5 (1889):591-600 (Philipp Spitta).

T ● ● ● ● Miller, Clement Albin. "The *Dodecachordon* of Heinrich Glarean." 2 vols. Ph.D. dissertation, The University of Michigan, 1950; published edition (MSD, no. 6), n.p.: American

Institute of Musicology, 1965. Bibliog. [*DA* 11/02, p. 375.]

> Review in *JAMS* 20/2 (1967):292-95 (Edward F. Houghton).

T ● See **Strunk (1950)**:219-27.

S ● Facsimile edition. MMMLF, ser. 2, no. 65. New York: Broude Brothers, 1967.

> Reviews in *Consort* 25 (1968-69):405-6 (Lillian M. Ruff), *ML* 49/4 (1968):398 (Jack A. Westrup), and *MT* 110/1512 (1969):159 (Charles Cudworth).

S ● Facsimile edition. Hildesheim: Georg Olms, 1969.

T ● See Rowen (1979).

Musicae epitome sive compendium ex Glareani Dodecachordo [*Rism* B/VI/1, p. 366.]

> Edited by Johannes Litavicus Wonnegger.

> Basel: Heinrich Petri, 1557. [SMLMS.]
> Basel: officina Hieronymi Curionis (Heinrich Petri), [1559]. [LCPS: G-050.]

T ● *Auß Glareani Musick ein Ußzug* . . . [*Rism* B/VI/1, p. 366.], Basel: Heinrich Petri, 1557; reprint edition, Basel: Heinrich Petri (H. P. Mertz), 1559 [SMLMS.]; facsimile of the 1559 edition, Kassel: Bärenreiter, 1975.

LITERATURE:

Dörffel, A. "Isagoge in musicen Henrici Glareani, 1516." *MMg* 1/4 (1869):67-68.

Fritzsche, Otto Fridolin. *Glarean: Sein Leben und seine Schriften*. Frauenfeld: J. Huber, 1890. Bibliog.

> Review in *VMw* 7 (1891):123-26 (Philipp Spitta).

Willfort, E. St. "Glarean's Erwiderung." *ZIMG* 10/11-12 (1908-9):337-41.

Schering, Arnold. "Die Notenbeispiele in Glarean's *Dodekachordon* (1547)." *SIMg* 13 (1911-12):569-96.

> Comment in *SIMg* 14 (1912-13):183-84 (Bernhard Ulrich).

Birtner, Herbert. "Studien zur niederländisch-humanistischen Musikanschauung." Habilitationsschrift, The University of Marburg, 1928 (1930); published edition (incomplete), Heidelberg: Carl Winters Universitätsbuchhandlung, 1930.

Kirsch, Ernst. "Studie zum Problem des Heinrich Loriti (Glarean)." In *ScheringFs* (1937):125-36.

Levitan, Joseph S. "Ockeghem's Clefless Compositions." *MQ* 23/4 (1937):440-64.

Crevel, Marcus van. *Adrianus Petit Coclico: Leben und Beziehungen eines nach Deutschland emigrierten Josquinschüler*. The Hague: Martinus Nijhoff, 1940.

Albrecht, Hans. "Glarean(us), Heinrich." In *MGG* (1949-68). Bibliog.

Miller, Clement A. "Heinrich Glarean, Humanist and Teacher [Abstract]." *JAMS* 5/2 (1952):143-44.

Meier, Bernhard. "Glareans *Isagoge in musicen* (1516)." In *Kongress Wien 1956* (1958): 397-401.

Meier, Bernhard. "Heinrich Loriti Glareanus als Musiktheoretiker." In *BFWU* 22 (1960): 65-112.

> Review in *Mf* 22/2 (1969):252-53 (Wolf Frobenius).

Voisé, Waldemar. "*Le Dodecachordon* d'Henri Glaréan d'aprés sa correspondance avec Jean Laski." *RdS* 81 (1960):107-10.

Miller, Clement A. "The *Dodecachordon*: Its Origins and Influence on Renaissance Musical Thought." *Md* 15 (1961):155-66.

Mompellio, Federico. "Il Glareano e il suo *Dodekachordon*." In *Celebrazioni 1963* (1963):3-8.

Frei, Walter. "Einheit in der Musik." *MGot* 18/3 (1964):69-73.

Heckenbach, Willibrord. "Glareanus." In *Rheinische Musiker, 4. Folge*, edited by Karl Gustav Fellerer, pp. 19-22. BrM, no. 64. Cologne: Arno Volk Verlag, 1966. Bibliog.

Fuchss, W. "Musik und Erziehung als Mittler zwischen Ungarn und der Schweiz: Ein Ausschnitt aus der Geschichte der schweizerisch-ungarischen Beziehung." *Stm* 10/1-2 (1968):55-68.

Loach, Donald Glenn. "Aegidius Tschudi's Songbook (St. Gall Ms. 463): A Humanistic Document from the Circle of Heinrich Glarean." 2 vols. Ph.D. dissertation, The University of California at Berkeley, 1969. [*DA* 31/04A, p. 1833. UMI 70-17607.]

Lichtenhahn, Ernst. " 'Ars Perfecta': Zu Glareans Auffassung der Musikgeschichte." In *GeeringFs* (1972): 129-38. Bibliog.

● ● ● Miller, Clement A. "Glarean, Heinrich." In *NGrove* (1980). Bibliog.

Bossuyt, Ignace. "Die *Psalmi Poenitentiales* (1570) des Alexander Utendal: Ein Künstlerisches Gegenstück der Bußpsalmen von O. Lassus und eine praktische Anwendung von Glareans Theorie der zwölf Modi." *AfMw* 38/4 (1981):279-95. [*Rilm* 81-4517.]

Aschmann, Rudolf. "Glarean als Musiktheoretiker." In *Der Humanist Heinrich Loriti, genannt Glarean, 1488-1563: Beiträge zu seinem Leben und Werk*. Glarus: Buchhandlung Baeschlin, 1983.

Westendorf, Craig J. "Glareanus's *Dodecachordon* in German Theory and Practice: An Expression of Confessionalism." *CM* 37-38 (1984):33-48.

Schubert, Peter N. "The Modal System of Illuminato Aiguino." Ph.D. dissertation, Columbia University, 1987.

See also BELLERMANN: (1858); (1862); BONTEMPI: (1695); CALVISIUS: Dahlhaus (1956); CHORON: (1810-11); COCLICO: Meier (1956); DONI: (1647); FÉTIS: (1833-44); KEPLER: Dickreiter (1971/1973); LIPPIUS: Rivera (1974/1980); MEI: (Mss., 1567-73); MERSENNE: (1617-48); MONTEVERDI: Schrade (1950/. . ./1981); MORLEY: Stevenson (1952); RIEMANN: (1898); SALINAS: (1577); VIADANA: Haack (1964/1974); WALTHER: (1732); ZARLINO: (1558):Cohen (1977/1983); LITERATURE SUPPLEMENT: Abraham (1968/1969); Alekperova (1982); Ambros (1878/. . ./1909); Apel (1936/. . ./1972), (1942/. . ./1961); **Apfel (1981)**; Atcherson (1960), (1970), (1973); Auda (1930/1979); Auhagen (1982/1983); Beck (1973); Becker (1836-39/1964); Beebe (1976); Beiche ["Dux"] (1972-); Bellingham (1971); **Bent**, I. ["Analysis"] **(1980/1987)**; Bent, M. (1984); Bent et al. (1980); Berger (1987); Beyer (1958); Bircher (1970); Blumröder (1972-); Buelow (1972); Burney (1776-89/. . ./1957); Chomiński (1962/1981); Chybiński, (1911-12); Cohen (1984); Čolić (1976); Collins (1963), (1964); Coover (1980); **Dahlhaus** ["Termini"] (1955), (1960), ["Untersuchung"] (1966/. . ./1988), ["Zur Tonartenlehre"] (1976), ["Tonality"] **(1980), (1984); Dahlhaus et al. (1987)**; Dammann (1958/1967); Dunsby and Whittall (1988); Dupont (1933/. . ./1986); Eitner (1900-1904/1959-60); Federhofer (1944/1950); Feldmann (1958); Fellerer (1927/. . ./1972), (1969), ["Zur Kontrapunktlehre"] (1972), ["Ausdruck"] (1982), (1983); Ferand (1937/1938), (1956); Forkel (1792/1962); Frobenius ["Tactus"] (1972-); Gerber (1812-14/1966); Ghislanzoni (1949-51); Gissel (1980/1983), (1986); Green (1969); Gurlitt (1944/1966), (1954/1966); Gut (1972-), (1976); Haar (1983); Haase (1972); Handschin (1948); Harrán (1973), (1986); Hawkins (1776/. . ./1969); Hein (1954); Horsley ["Fugue and Mode"] (1966/1978), [*Fugue: History*] (1966), (1972); Houle (1987); Hüschen (1949-68), (1986); Isgro (1968), (1979); Jackson (1988); Jeppesen (1930/. . ./1974); Kahl (1953); **Kassler (1979)**; Katz (1985); Kauko (1958); Kinkeldey (1910/1968); Koenigsberger (1979); Kramer (1978); Krantz (1989); Kroyer (1901/. . ./1970); La Fage (1864/1964); Lang (1941); Lange (1899-1900); Launay (1972); **Lester** ● ● ● (1977), **(1989)**; Levitan (1938); Livingstone (1971); Lowinsky (1946/1967), (1961/1989); Luoma (1976), (1977); Luper (1938); **Maniates (1979)**;

Mann (1955/. . ./1987); McKinnon (1978); Meier (1963), (1966), (1974/1988); Mendel (1948), (1978); Mitchell, J. (1963); Müller-Blattau (1923/. . ./1963); Neumann (1987); Niemöller (1964/1969); Norton (1984); **Palisca** (1959), ["Artusi-Monteverdi"] (1968/1985), ["*Ut oratoria musica*"] (1972), ["Theory"] **(1980)**, (1981), **(1985)**; Pesce (1987); Pietzsch (1936-42/1971); Powers (1974), ["Mode"] ● ● ● (1980), (1981); Ratner (1970); Reckow (1972-); Reese (1954/1959), ● ● ● (1957/1970);

Reichenbach (1948); Rogers (1955); Rohwer (1949-68); Schäfke (1934); Schering (1926); Schmalzriedt ["Subiectum"] (1972-); Schulenberg (1985-86); Seidel (1976); **Seidel and Cooper (1986)**; **Shirlaw (1917/. . ./1970)**; Stevenson (1976); Subirá (1947/. . ./1958); Taddie (1984); Tenney (1988); Tolkoff (1973); Tuksar (1978/1980); Turrell (1956), (1958); Walker (1941-42/. . ./1985), (1950/1985); Wessely (1967); Wienpahl (1953); Wiora (1962); Yates (1947); **Zaminer (1985)**; Zenck (1942).

HEINRICH GRIMM

[1593 – 1637]

We remember Heinrich Grimm more in his relationship with other theorists than for his own writings. His work on solmization (1624) is apparently not extant, though echoes of his conception must certainly reverberate in his pupil Otto GIBELIUS's *Kurtzer, jedoch gründlicher Bericht von den vocibus musicalibus* (1659). Grimm also wrote painstakingly on the monochord and its use in "Instrumentum instrumentorum . . .," which remains in manuscript (unless Forkel's reference to a *De monochordo* refers instead to a printed work lost to posterity). His dependence upon earlier authors, particularly LIPPIUS and PRAETORIUS (his former teacher), is clearly apparent.

Another pupil, Conrad MATTHAEI, claimed in his *Kurtzer, doch ausführlicher Bericht von den Modis Musicis* (1652) that Grimm was the work's actual author. Its dependence upon earlier writers (PRAETORIUS again and GLAREAN, in particular) seems in keeping with Grimm's method. Works by BARYPHONUS and CALVISIUS were published under Grimm's supervision in 1630.

Unterricht, wie ein Knabe nach der alten guidonischen Art zu solmisieren leicht angeführt werden kann [*könne*]

Magdeburg: 1624. [Lost?]

"Instrumentum instrumentorum, hoc est monochordum vel potius dodecachordum ad utramque scalam diatonam scilicet veterem et syntonam novam accurate declinatum additâque brevi declaratione . . ."

Ms., 1629. [Wolfenbüttel: Neidersächsisches Staatsarchiv.]

See also BARYPHONUS: (1615):(1630); CALVISIUS: (1592):(1630).

LITERATURE:

Reimer, Otto. "Heinrich Grimm, ein mitteldeutscher Musiker." In *ScheringFs* (1937):180-93. Bibliog.

Lorenzen, Hermann. "Der Cantor Heinrich Grimm (1593-1637): Sein Leben und seine Werke mit Beiträgen zur Musikgeschichte Magdeburgs und Braunschweigs." Ph.D. dissertation, The University of Hamburg, 1940.

Lorenzen, Hermann. "Grimm, Heinrich." In *MGG* (1949-68). Bibliog.

Wilkinson, Christopher. "Grimm, Heinrich." In *NGrove* (1980). Bibliog.

See also BURMEISTER: Ruhnke (1954/1955); FÉTIS: (1833-44); GIBELIUS: (1659); Ganse (1931/1934); MATTHAEI: (1652); MATTHESON: (1717); WALTHER: (1732); LITERATURE SUPPLEMENT: **Apfel (1981)**; Becker (1836-39/1964); Eggebrecht (1955); Eitner (1900-1904/1959-60); Forkel (1792/1962); Gerber (1790-92/1977), (1812-14/1966); ● ● ● Lester (1977); Preußner (1939).

ADAM GUMPELZHAIMER

[1559 – 1625]

Adam Gumpelzhaimer borrowed extensively from Heinrich FABER's *Compendiolum musicae* of 1548 to create an elementary pedagogical work, called *Compendium musicae* (1591), under his own name. An abundance of music examples, many in two parts, are incorporated, thereby continuing the *bicinium* tradition of the Lutheran Latin schools. Since Christoph Rid had already published a German translation of FABER's work in 1572, the task of assembling parallel texts in Latin and German for all but the last chapter of Gumpelzhaimer's work was simplified.

Compendium musicae . . . [*Rism* B/VI/1, pp. 387-88.]

Augsburg: Valentin Schönig, 1591.

> Fifteen editions through 1681, including:

Augsburg: Johann Udalrich Schönig, 1616. [LCPS: G-081a. SMLMS. IDC.]

Augsburg: Johann Udalrich Schönig, 1632. [LCPS: G-081b. SMLMS.]

Ingolstadt: Wilhelm Eder (Johann Weh), 1646. [SMLMS.]

Augsburg: Jacob Enderlin, 1681. [HoM: 647.]

S ● Cuyler, Louise, ed. Facsimile of an unidentified seventeenth-century edition. Ann Arbor, Mich.: University Microfilms, 1965.

LITERATURE:

Mayr, Otto. "Adam Gumpelzhaimer: Ein Beitrag zur Musikgeschichte der Stadt Augsburg im 16. und 17. Jahrhundert." Ph.D. dissertation, The University of Munich, 1908 (1907); published edition, Augsburg: T. Lampart, 1908.

> See also the Introduction to *DTB* 19 [10/2] (1909):ix-lxxxii; reprint edition, Wiesbaden: Breitkopf & Härtel, 1962.

Dekker, Wil. "Ein Karfreitagsrätselkanon aus Adam Gumpelzhaimers *Compendium musicae* (1632)." *Mf* 27/3 (1974):323-32. Bibliog. [*Rilm* 74/1611.]

Adrio, Adam. "Gumpelzhaimer, Adam." In *MGG* (1949-68). Bibliog.

Wessely, Othmar. "Jodoc Entzenmüller – Der Lehrer Adam Gumpelzhaimers." *Mf* 7/1 (1954):65-66.

Hettrick, William E. "Gumpelzhaimer, Adam." In *NGrove* (1980). Bibliog.

See also BELLERMANN: (1858); FABER: (1548); FÉTIS: (1833-44); LIPPIUS: Rivera (1974/1980); WALTHER: (1732); LITERATURE SUPPLEMENT: Atcherson (1960); Becker (1836-39/1964); Bellingham (1971), (1980); Buelow (1972); Collins (1963); Eitner (1900-1904/1959-60); Falck (1965); Federhofer (1964); Fellerer (1927/. . ./1972), ["Musikwissenschaft"] (1972); Forkel (1792/1962); Gerber (1790-92/1977), (1812-14/1966); Gissel (1980/1983), (1986); Hannas (1934); Hüschen (1986); **Lester** (1977), **(1989)**; Livingstone (1971); Niemöller (1964/1969); Rogers (1955); Sannemann (1903/1904); Schäfke (1934); Schünemann (1928/1931); Taddie (1984); Walker (1987).

AUGUST OTTO HALM

[1869 — 1929]

The rich and varied writings of August Halm offer a unique perspective on the musical art, coming from the portentous period at the beginning of the current century, when the monumental works of Wagner and BRUCKNER were occupying the attention of many musicians and the philosophical outlook of Schopenhauer was influencing their dispositions. Halm's youthful *Harmonielehre* (1900) offers a dynamic interpretation of what he regarded as the universal side of the musical will (as opposed to the individual character of each composer's melodic invention). Harmonic progression is a result of the forces and attractions that derive ultimately from the cadence, from the essential motion of a descending fifth. The common I-IV-V-I succession was viewed, in this perspective, as the synthesis of two fifth-descending progressions, with an "abyss" between them in the juxtaposition of IV and V.

Von zwei Kulturen der Musik (1913) advances the notion that two basic musical natures had developed during the preceding centuries, epitomized by the melodic-polyphonic tendencies of the fugue and the harmonic-formal tendencies of the sonata. Halm assayed how the two stood in opposition to one another and suggested that their synthesis was to be found in BRUCKNER's symphonies, which he addressed in a separate work published the following year. During the next decade he completed two additional books, notably a study on works of Beethoven's middle period (1927). His contributions to journals (numbering over two hundred articles and reviews) are equally impressive and include two early appreciations of SCHENKER. Two sets of selections from his writings have been published: *Von Grenzen und Ländern der Musik* (1916) and *August Halm: Von Form und Sinn der Musik* (1978).

Harmonielehre (SGös, no. 120)

> Leipzig: G. J. Göschen'sche Verlagshandlung, 1900.
>
>> Numerous editions. That of 1939 reviewed in *Rmi* 44/1 (1940):131-32 (Galladol).

T ● Jeanson, Gunnar, trans. *Harmonilära*. Uppsala: Almquist & Wiksells Förlag, 1925.

Von zwei Kulturen der Musik

> Munich: Georg Müller, 1913.
>
>> Reprinted in 1916[?]. Reviews in *Kunstwart* 27/3 (1913-14):79-82 (Wolfgang Schumann) and *Rhein* 13 (1913):477 (Wilhelm Schäfer).

> Stuttgart: Ernst Klett, 1947. Introduction by Gustav Wyneken.

Die Symphonie Anton Bruckners

> Munich: Georg Müller, [1914].
> Munich: Georg Müller, 1923.

S ● Facsimile edition. Hildesheim: Georg Olms, 1975.

Von Grenzen und Ländern der Musik: Gesammelte Aufsätze

> Incorporates twenty-four articles, including "Über Richard Wagners Musikdrama" (pp. 1-78).

> Munich: Georg Müller, 1915.
>
>> Reprinted in 1916. Reviews in *FS* 6 (1915-16):53 (Otto Hausdorff), *MnN* 69/187 (April 12, 1916):3 (Alfred Einstein), and *PR* 41/15 (Supplement, April 11, 1917) (Fritz Jöde).

"Heinrich Schenker"

> *FS* 8 (1917-18):11-15.

S ● See (1978):271-74, below.

"Über J. S. Bachs Konzertform"

> In *BachJb 1919* 16 (1920):1-44.

S ● See (1978):119-51, below.

"Heinrich Schenkers *Neue musikalische Theorien und Phantasien*"

> *Merker* 11/17, 21 (1920):414-17, 505-7.

"H. Riemanns Analysen von Beethovens Klavier-Sonaten 1-11"

> *FS* 11 (1920-21):36.

"Chromatik und Tonalität"

> *NMZ* 45/11 (1924):270-78; 46/2 (1925):44-46.

S ● See (1978):182-99, below.

Einführung in die Musik

> Berlin: Deutsche Buch-Gemeinschaft, 1926.

S ● Facsimile edition. Darmstadt: Wissenschaftliche Buchgesellschaft, 1966.

Beethoven (HiH, no. 85)

> Berlin: Max Hesse, 1926.
>
>> Review in *MFKKH* 4 (1927):177-80 (Karl Schmid).

S ● Facsimile edition. Darmstadt: Wissenschaftliche Buchgesellschaft, 1971; 1979.

>> Review in *Orch* 20/5 (1972):288 (Erich F. W. Altwein).

"Über den Wert musikalischen Analysen"

> *Musik* 21/7-8 (1928-29):481-84, 591-95.

S ● See (1978):83-90, below.

August Halm: Von Form und Sinn der Musik (Gesammelte Aufsätze)

Wiesbaden: Breitkopf & Härtel, 1978. Edited, with an Introduction [see below], by Siegfried Schmalzriedt. Bibliog.

Reviews in *Musica* 33/4 (1979):381 (Peter Nitsche) and *WF* 64 (1980):315 (Rudolf Chmelar).

See (1978), above, or Stephan (1949-68), below, for a more complete listing of Halm's varied output.

LITERATURE:

Schmid, Karl. "Tonsetzer der Gegenwart: August Halm." *NMZ* 31/23 (1910):469-74.

Mohr, Wilhelm. "August Halm." *Musik* 21/7 (1928-29):507-11.

Schmid, Theodor Karl. "Zum Tode August Halms." *Sg* 5 (1928-29):98-104.

Schilling, Rudolf. "Die Musikanschauung August Halms." Ph.D. dissertation, The University of Strasbourg, 1944.

Stephan, Rudolf. "Halm, August Otto." In *MGG* (1949-68). Bibliog.

Schaedlich, Hans-Werner. "August Halm zum Gedächtnis." *NMzs* 4/2-3 (1950):51-52.

Kinzel, Hugo Jos. "In memoriam: August Halm." *Musica* 8/2 (1954):69-70.

Dahlhaus, Carl. "*Von zwei Kulturen der Musik*. Die Schlußfuge aus Beethovens Cellosonate Opus 102/2." *Mf* 31/4 (1978):397-405. [*Rilm* 78-6035.]

● ● ● Schmalzriedt, Siegfried. "August Halms musikalische Ästhetik: Versuch einer Darstellung." In (1978):3-56, above. Bibliog. [*Rilm* 78-6447.]

Goodman, Alfred Grant. "Halm, August Otto." In *NGrove* (1980). Bibliog.

Busch, Regina. "August Halm über die Konzertform." In *Notizbuch 5/6: Musik*, edited by Reinhard Kapp, pp. 107-53. Berlin and Vienna: Medusa, 1982. [*Rilm* 82-3574.]

See also KURTH: Nishihara (1979); Rothfarb (1985/1988); SCHENKER: Federhofer (1985); LITERATURE SUPPLEMENT: Beiche ["Inversio"] (1972-); **Bent** ["Analysis"] **(1980/1987):(1987)**; Busch (1980); Cahn (1982); **Dahlhaus** ["Untersuchungen"] (1966/. . ./1988), (1967), ["Tonalität"] (1983), **(1984)**; Federhofer (1944/1950), (1985); Frobenius ["Vollstimmig"] (1972); Ghislanzoni (1949-51); Gut (1972-); Jorgenson (1957); La Motte-Haber (1976); Mahlert and Sunter (1972-); Möllers (1978); Moos (1902/1922); Moyer (1969); Müller-Blattau (1923/. . ./1963), (1949-68); Neumann (1969); Newcomb (1981-82); Oberdörffer (1949-68); Rohwer (1949-68); Scher (1975); Schering (1930/1974); Schmalzriedt ["Durchführen"] (1972-), ["Episode"] (1972-), ["Reprise"] (1972-); Schuhmacher ["Notwendige Ergänzung"] (1974); Thaler (1984); **Wason** ● ● ● **(1981/1985)**, (1983); Wolff (1978); **Zaminer (1985)**.

MORITZ HAUPTMANN

[1792 – 1868]

The quest for a foundation upon which to build a music theory had led through the domains of mathematics and acoustics when, in the middle of the nineteenth century, the German composer and teacher Moritz Hauptmann developed a powerful and influential, though abstract, perspective based upon philosophical reasoning. The Hegelian dialectic served as the impetus for his view, which perhaps was formulated more directly from principles enunciated by Goethe. Both the harmonic system and meter were generated through the principle of a unity (thesis) being subjected to an opposition (antithesis), the coordination of the two resulting in a new, mediated unity (synthesis). This principle, existing in the broader range of philosophical thought, purportedly guided music into conformity with general truth, rather than with the more specific inferences derived from acoustics, or, for that matter, with the conceptions of composers or perceptions of listeners.

The octave (or its equivalent, the unison) represents a thesis, to which the antithesis of a perfect fifth leads to the synthesis of the major third, thus generating, *in toto*, the major triad. The thesis of a subdominant (e.g., F-major) and antithesis of a dominant (G-major) produce the synthesis of a tonic (C-major), creating an interlocking network consisting of F-A-C, C-E-G, and G-B-D and resulting in the pitch collection of the C-major scale. A two-beat, strong/weak rhythmic pattern (thesis) and a three-beat pattern (antithesis) find their synthesis in a four-beat pattern. Though these and similar conceptual formulations flourished in the minds of Hauptmann's disciples (many of whom were his students at the Leipzig Conservatory), the inherent problem of making himself understood to musical laymen was never adequately addressed. Instead, a second generation of thought, in which OETTINGEN, HELMHOLTZ, and particularly RIEMANN were, each in a unique way, the chief representatives, found easier acceptance within the German musical mind.

In that an undertone series was seriously contemplated by some of these thinkers, Hauptmann's conception of the minor triad requires careful consideration. He dealt with philosophical issues, not with acoustical phenomena. It was less problematical for him than it had been for RAMEAU, for example, to formulate the minor triad by following the same steps which produce the major triad but changing their direction. If C serves as thesis and, this time, F (below) counters as antithesis, then the synthesis of these pitches would be A-flat, and F minor would be generated. (Note that the top pitch, C, is the thesis. Hauptmann commented that whereas the thesis in the positive direction "has" a fifth, that in the negative direction "is" a fifth.) Remarkably similar to one of RAMEAU's derivations, Hauptmann also offered the suggestion that the fifth of the minor triad could be dually generated, as when C serves as the antithesis of F (forgetting the synthesis A-natural) and synthesis of A-flat (forgetting the antithesis E-flat). Hauptmann thus joins the list of theorists who could not quite make up their minds how this most difficult chord was to be generated. He was, however, more definitive regarding the dominant seventh and other more complicated chords: they result from the merger of elements from two separate triads. For example, both G-B-D-F and B-D-F-A combine elements of dominant and subdominant in the key of C.

Though his work has been overshadowed by other types of theory oriented towards other goals, Hauptmann influenced both the methodology and direction of theoretical inquiry in Germany during the latter half of the nineteenth century. His exploration of the relationships among metrical levels was particularly useful to RIEMANN and others, while the logical rigor to which he aspired put the discipline of music theory on a higher plane.

Correspondence

S ● Schöne, Alfred, ed. *Briefe von Moritz Hauptmann . . . an Franz Hauser*. 2 vols. Leipzig: Breitkopf & Härtel, 1871.

S ● Hiller, Ferdinand. *Briefe von Moritz Hauptmann . . . an Ludwig Spohr und andere*. Leipzig: Breitkopf & Härtel, 1876.

T ● Coleridge, A. D., trans. and ed. *The Letters of a Leipzig Cantor*. 2 vols. London: Novello, Ewer, 1892; facsimile edition, New York: Vienna House, 1972.

Derived from the Schöne and Hiller volumes, above.

Erläuterungen zu Joh. Sebastian Bachs Kunst der Fuge

Leipzig and Berlin: C. F. Peters, 1841.

Reprinted in 1861, 1881, and ca. 1929.

T ● Boyd, George R., trans. "Hauptmann's Commentary on the *Art of Fugue*: A Translation." *ITR* 8/2 (1987):45-66.

Die Natur der Harmonik und der Metrik: Zur Theorie der Musik

Leipzig: Breitkopf & Härtel, 1853.

Review in *NZfM* 43/16-21 (1855):165-66, 177-78, 189-90, 197-98, 209-10, 221-23 (Louis Köhler).

Leipzig: Breitkopf & Härtel, 1873.

T ● Heathcote, William Edward, trans. and ed. *The Nature of Harmony and Metre*. London: Swan Sonnenschein; New York: Novello, Ewer, 1888; reprint edition, 1893; reprint edition, New York: Da Capo Press, 1989.

"Brief über Helmholtz' Lehre von den Tonempfindungen"

AmZ (Neue Folge) 1/40 (1863):669-73.

"Klang"

JfmW 1 (1863):17-27.

S ● See (1874), below.

"Temperatur"

JfmW 1 (1863):28-54.

S ● See (1874), below.

Die Lehre von der Harmonik, mit beigefügten Notenbeispielen

Leipzig: Breitkopf & Härtel, 1868. Edited by Oscar Paul.

Reprinted in 1873.

Opuscula: Vermischte Aufsätze

Leipzig: F. E. C. Leuckart (Constantin Sander), 1874. Bibliog.

A compilation of articles, some previously published in German periodicals, introduced by Hauptmann's son Ernst. Included are "Klang," "Temperatur," "Der Dreiklang und seine Intervalle," "Dreiklang mit der pythagoräischen Terz," "Zum Quintenverbot," "Zur Auflösung des Dominantseptimenaccordes durch Erweiterung der Septime zur Octav," "Einige Regeln zur richtigen Beantwortung des Fugenthemas," "Das Hexachord," "Authentisch und Plagalisch," "Contrapunkt," "Metrum," "Zur Metrik," "Über die Recitative in J. S. Bach's Matthäus-Passion," "Kunstvollendung," "Form in der Kunst," "Ironie der Kunst," "Männlich und Weiblich," "Egoismus," "Mechanik," and "Die Sinne."

Aufgaben für den einfachen und doppelten Kontrapunkt, zum Gebrauch beim Unterricht aus Studienhefte seiner Schüler

> Leipzig: Bartholf Senff, n.d. Edited by Ernst Friedrich Karl Rudorff.

LITERATURE:

Naumann, Carl Ernst. "Über die verschiedenen Bestimmungen der Tonverhältnisse und die Bedeutung des pythagoreischen oder reinen Quinten-Systemes für unsere heutige Musik." Ph.D. dissertation, The University of Leipzig, 1858; published edition, Leipzig: Breitkopf & Härtel, 1858.

Paul, Oscar. *Moritz Hauptmann: Eine Denkschrift zur Feier seines siebenzigjährigen Geburtstages am 13. October 1862.* Leipzig: A. Dörffel, 1862.

Hiller, Ferdinand. *Aus dem Tonleben unserer Zeit.* Vol. 3. Leipzig: F. E. C. Leuckart (Constantin Sander), 1871.

Köhler, Louis. "Über die Verwerthung der Hauptmann'schen Theorie im Unterricht." *NZfM* 69/37 (1873):373-75.

Phillips, R. C. "Hauptmann's Doctrines." *MO* 31/361 (1907-8):26-27.

KREHL, Stephan. "Moritz Hauptmann: Ein Dank- und Gedenkwort." In *LeipzigFs* (1918).

Hetsch, Gustav. "Moritz Hauptmann som lærer, belyst af Ham Selv." *MTft* 6/6 (1922):75-78; 7/2 (1923):18-21.

Ruhnke, Martin. "Hauptmann, Moritz." In *MGG* (1949-68). Bibliog.

Rummenhöller, Peter. "Moritz Hauptmann als Theoretiker: Eine Studie zum erkenntniskritischen Theoriebegriff in der Musik." Ph.D. dissertation, The University of Saarbrücken, 1963; published edition, Wiesbaden: Breitkopf & Härtel, 1963. Bibliog.

> Reviews in *NZfM* 125/11 (1964):512-13 (Carl Dahlhaus) and *Stfm* 46 (1964):198-201 (Ingmar Bengtsson).

Rummenhöller, Peter. "Moritz Hauptmann, der Begründer einer transzendental-dialektischen Musiktheorie." See Vogel (1966):11-38. Bibliog.

Rummenhöller, Peter. "Der dialektische Theoriebegriff: Zur Verwirklichung Hegelschen Denkens in Moritz Hauptmanns Musiktheorie." In *Kongress Leipzig 1966* (1970):387-91. [*Rilm* 72-1203.]

Seidel, Wilhelm. "Moritz Hauptmanns organische Lehre: Tradition, Inhalt und Geltung ihrer Prämisse." *IRASM* 2/2 (1971):243-66. [*Rilm* 71-4558.]

Hoffmann, Mark. "Hauptmann, Moritz." In *NGrove* (1980). Bibliog.

Lewin, David. "On Harmony and Meter in Brahms's Op. 76, No. 8." *NCM* 4/3 (1980-81):261-65. [*Rilm* 81-1661.]

Caplin, William. "Moritz Hauptmann and the Theory of Suspensions." *JMT* 28/2 (1984):251-69.

> Abstract in *MA* 5/2-3 (1986):303-4.

● ● ● Jorgenson, Dale A. *Moritz Hauptmann of Leipzig.* SHIM, no. 2. Lewiston, N.Y.: Edwin Mellen Press, 1986. Bibliog.

> Reviews in *JMT* 32/2 (1988):381-93 (Mark P. McCune) and *ML* 69/2 (1988):390-92 (William J. Gatens).

McCune, Mark. "Moritz Hauptmann: Ein *Haupt Mann* in Nineteenth Century Music Theory." *ITR* 7/2 (1986):1-28. Bibliog.

See also FÉTIS: (1833-44); HELMHOLTZ: (1863); d'INDY: (1903-50); ÖTTINGEN: (1866); RIEMANN: (1898); Wuensch (1977); SCHOENBERG: Rexroth (1969/1971); WEITZMANN: (1859); (1861); LITERATURE SUPPLEMENT: Abbado (1964); Abel (1980/1982); Abraham (1966); Alette (1951); Auhagen (1982/1983); Babbitt (1961/1972); Beach (1967); Beiche ["Inversio"] (1972-); **Bent** ["Analysis"] **(1980/1987)**; Bridges (1984); Burke (1963); Caplin (1978), (1981), (1983); Cazden (1980); Chevaillier (1925/1931-32); Chew (1980); Chomiński (1962/1981); **Dahlhaus** ["Konsonanz"] (1949-68), ["Tonsystem"] (1949-68), ["Über"] (1966), ["Untersuchungen"] (1966/.../1988), ["Relationes"] (1975), (1975/1977), ["Harmony"] ● ● ● (1980), ["Über"] (1980), **(1984)**, ["Zum Taktbegriff"] (1988); Devore (1987); de Zeeuw (1983); **Dürr and Gerstenberg** (1949-68), **(1980)**; Dunsby and Whittall (1988); Federhofer (1944/1950), (1985); Fillmore (1887); Ghislanzoni (1949-51); Handschin (1948); Henneberg (1972/1974), (1983); Heinlein (1927/1928); Hoffman (1953); Imig (1969/1970); Jacobi (1957-60/1971); Jeppesen ([1951]/1952); Jones (1934); Jorgenson (1957), (1963); Kauko (1958); Kelletat [*Temperatur*] (1960); La Motte-Haber (1969), (1971); Levenson (1981), (1983-84); Lewin (1981), (1982); Mitchell, J. W. (1963); Morgan (1978); Moyer (1969); Müller-Blattau (1923/.../1963); Newman (1969/.../1983); Oberdörffer (1949-68); **Palisca** ["Theory"] **(1980)**; Parncutt (1988-89); Phillips (1979); Rea (1978); Révész (1946/.../1954); Rohwer (1949-68); Rothärmel (1963/1968); Ruhnke (1974); Rummenhöller (1967), (1971); Sachs (1972-); Seidel (1972-), (1975), (1976); **Shirlaw (1917/.../1970)**, (1931), (1957), (1960); Skyllstad (1968); Smither (1960); Snyder (1980-81); Stein (1983); Taddie (1984); Thompson (1980); Thürlings (1877); Todd (1983); Vogel (1962); **Wason (1981/1985)**, (1988); Wirth (1966); Yeston (1974/1976); **Zaminer (1985)**.

JOHANN DAVID HEINICHEN

[1683 – 1729]

Learning to play continuo was, in the early eighteenth century, an essential step in mastering the art of composition. No one provided more thorough or better information on the topic than Johann David Heinichen, whose early *Neu erfundene und gründliche Anweisung* (1711) blossomed, after its author had spent several years in Venice and had interacted with GASPARINI and others, into the monumental *General-Bass in der Composition* (1728).

Heinichen's perspective encompassed the full range of twenty-four major and minor keys, displayed in a circle to reveal their interrelations. Motion in either direction on the circle was permitted. One could move to an adjacent position on the circle (which would be a key of the opposite mode), or skip one or two positions. A representative succession of adjacent keys on the circle reads as follows (clockwise): C major, A minor, G major, E minor, D major, B minor, etc. Heinichen viewed the typical modulations from a major key as the first three steps clockwise, while more extraordinary would be the first two steps counterclockwise. From a minor key, the first step counterclockwise and the first two steps clockwise were the typical modulations, while the second and third steps counterclockwise were more extraordinary. Keys a tritone apart were, it turns out, furthest from each other on the circle. His endorsement of temperament (though not of equal temperament) both allowed the use of all keys and created subtle differences among them.

The scope of Heinichen's discussion was unprecedented, and its stylistic norms deserve much closer examination by performers of Baroque music. In response to the increased size of the orchestral ensemble for Italian operas, Heinichen developed a full-voiced style of accompaniment for use on the harpsichord, such that both right and left hands would strike numerous keys. Yet even in more moderate accompanimental writing, he was surprisingly liberal in allowing voice-leading with parallel perfect intervals, except between outer voices.

Heinichen enumerated a wide variety of ways in which dissonant pitches could be specially treated in the theatrical style. Later theorists, including MARPURG, benefited from Heinichen's precedent when establishing their own perspectives. The concept of *anticipatio transitus*, or the anticipation of a passing note, is typical of Heinichen's reasoning. It explains how, for example, a chord might contain a seventh from the outset, rather than as a passing note in an 8-7 configuration. Other topics within Heinichen's purview include the treatment of unfigured basses (for which specific guidelines are listed), the interpretation of basses which are themselves embellished, and the additional considerations required whenever text is involved.

Neu erfundene und gründliche Anweisung, wie ein Musik-Liebender auff gewisse vortheilhafftige Arth könne zu

vollkommener Erlernung des General-Basses . . . [*Rism* B/VI/1, p. 403.]

Hamburg: Benjamin Schiller, 1711. [LCPS: H-023a. SMLMS. IDC.]

Der General-Bass in der Composition . . . [*Rism* B/VI/1, p. 403.]

Dresden: the author (Freiberg: Christoph Matthaeus), 1728. [LCPS: H-023b. HoM: 740. SMLMS.]

Derived from the work of 1711, above.

T ● ● ● ● Buelow, George J. "Johann David Heinichen's *Der General-Bass in der Composition*: A Critical Study with Annotated Translation of Selected Chapters." Ph.D. dissertation, New York University, 1961; published edition (as *Thorough-Bass Accompaniment According to Johann David Heinichen*), Berkeley and Los Angeles: University of California Press, 1966; revised edition (SiM, no. 84), Ann Arbor, Mich.: UMI Research Press, 1986. Bibliog. [*DA* 23/03, p. 1034-35.]

Reviews in *AmO* 50/4 (1967):6 (Harry W. Gay), *JAMS* 21/3 (1968):393-96 (Bathia Churgin), *JMT* 11/2 (1967):281-85 (Albert Cohen), *MEJ* 56/8 (1969-70):85-86 (Donald M. McCorkle), *Mf* 21/3 (1968):381-82 (Walter Reckziegel), *MiE* 33/337 (1969):143, *ML* 50/2 (1969):314-15 (Bernard W. G. Rose), *MO* 92/1100 (1969):417 (B. R.), *MT* 110/1518 (1969):837 (Robert Donington), *MusT* 48/4 (1969):27 (Kenneth Simpson), *Notes* 23/4 (1966-67):730-32 (Robert Donington), and *Rdm* 53/1 (1967):74-76 (Denise Launay).

S ● Facsimile edition. Hildesheim: Georg Olms, 1969.

LITERATURE:

Hiller, Johann Adam. "Lebenslauf des Herrn Johann David Heinichen . . ." *WNAMb* 1/28-29 (1766-67):213-17, 221-25.

Haußwald, Günter. "Heinichen, Johann David." In *MGG* (1949-68). Bibliog.

Buelow, George J. "Heinichen's Treatment of Dissonance." *JMT* 6/2 (1962):216-74.

Reprinted in (1728):Buelow (1961):(1986), above.

Buelow, George J. "The Full-voiced Style of Thorough-Bass Realization." *AM* 35/4 (1963):159-71.

Buelow, George J. "The *Loci Topici* and Affect in Late Baroque Music: Heinichen's Practical Demonstration." *MR* 27/3 (1966):161-76. Bibliog.

Buelow, George J. "Heinichen, Johann David." In *NGrove* (1980). Bibliog.

Review in *MQ* 68/2 (1982):161-81 (Allen Forte).

See also FÉTIS: (1833-44); (1840); LÖHLEIN: (1765-81):Wilson (1979); MATTHESON: (1717); (1719); (1722-25); (1731); Schenkman (1978-79); Schenkman ["Theory"] (1981); Werts (1985); RAMEAU: Pischner (1961/. . ./1967); RIEMANN: (1898); SAINT-LAMBERT: (1707):Burchill (1979); SCHEIBE: (1738-40); VIADANA: Haack (1964/1974); WALTHER: (1732); LITERATURE SUPPLEMENT: Ahlgrimm (1969-70), (1973); **Arnold (1931/. . ./1965)**; Auhagen (1982/1983); Babitz (1952), (1967/1969); Badura-Skoda et al. (1980); Beach (1967); Becker (1836-39/1964); **Benary (1956/1961)**; **Bent** ["Analysis"] **(1980/1987)**; Beyschlag (1907/1953); Bircher (1970); Boomgaarden (1985/1987); Braun (1970), (1986); Brown and McKinnon (1980); Buelow (1973-74), ["Rhetoric"] (1980); Bukofzer (1947); Burdick (1977); Burney (1776-89/. . ./1957); Cahn ["Retardatio"] (1972-), ["Transitus"] (1972-); Chafe (1981), (1982); Chevaillier (1925/1931-32); Crocker (1966); **Dahlhaus** ["Konsonanz"] (1949-68), ["Untersuchungen"] (1966/. . ./1988), **(1984)**; **Dahlhaus et al. (1987)**; **Dahlhaus and Sachs (1980)**; Dammann (1958/1967); David (1956); David and Mendel (1945/1966); Dean (1977); Derr (1985); Donington (1963/. . ./1974), (1980); Dreyfus (1987); Duckles (1970); Eitner (1900-1904/1959-60); Emig (1977); Federhofer (1969); Feil (1955); Ferand [*Improvisation*] (1956/1961); Forkel (1792/1962); Frobenius ["Isotonos"] (1972-), ["Vollstimmig"] (1972-); Gerber (1812-14/1966); Hammel (1977-78); Hansell (1968); Harich-Schneider ([1939]/. . ./1970); Harrán (1986); Heimann (1970/1973); Helm (1960); Hiller (1784); Houle (1960), (1987); Ibberson (1984); Jackson (1988); Kauko (1958); Keller (1931/. . ./1966); Kretzschmar (1911-12); Lang (1941); **Lester** (1977), (1978), **(1989)**; **Lindley** ["Just"] **(1980)**, ["Temperaments"] **(1980)**, (1982); Lippman (1986); Maier (1984); McQuere (1983); Mitchell, J. W. (1963); Mitchell, W. J. (1963); Morche (1974); Nelson (1984); **Neumann**, Frederick (1978), [*Essays*] **(1982)**; North (1987); Norton (1984); Oberdoerffer (1949-68), (1967); **Palisca (1949-68)**, ["Theory"] **(1980)**; **Powers** ["Mode"] **(1980)**; Ratner (1970), (1980); Reckow (1972-); Reese (1957/1970); Reilly (1984-85); Reimer ["Kenner"] (1972-); Rogers (1955); Rohwer (1949-68); Rothgeb (1968); Rothschild (1953); Sachs (1972-); Schäfke (1934); Schering (1926); Schmalzriedt ["Durchführen"] (1972-); Schmitz (1950); Schneider (1917/ . . ./1971); Schulenberg (1984); **Seidel and Cooper (1986)**; Sheldon (1975), (1981), (1982); **Shirlaw (1917/. . ./1970)**; Sisman (1978); Speak (1973); Tenney (1988); Tittel (1966); Todd (1988-89); Uemura (1969); Ulrich (1931/1932); Unger (1941/1969); Werts (1983); Wessely (1971-72); Williams, P. ["Harpsichord"] (1968), (1970); Wirth (1966); Yeston (1974/1976); **Zaminer (1985)**; Zenck (1942).

HERMANN VON HELMHOLTZ

[1821 – 1894]

The research of Hermann von Helmholtz concerning the characteristics of tone and our capacity for its perception added many new insights to what was then still a rather mysterious part of musical study. To be sure, RAMEAU had made use of SAUVEUR's formulations concerning overtones, and ZARLINO's *senario* had grown out of ancient Greek speculation on the nature of consonance, yet the precision and comprehensiveness of Helmholtz's views and the sophistication of his methodology transformed the discipline of acoustics and established a groundwork for modern research on musical perception.

Helmholtz published extensively and on an extraordinarily wide range of topics. For the musician, however, one work—*Die Lehre von den Tonempfindungen als physiologische Grundlage für die Theorie der Musik* (1863)—was so overpowering in its breadth and specificity that it became, almost immediately, the essential volume on musical acoustics. Within a dozen years, French, English, and Russian translations were available. Though some of its physiological hypotheses have since been supplanted, the work remains a remarkable and fascinating document, filled with penetrating observations and provocative charts, diagrams, and formulae.

Unlike many of his contemporaries, whose perspectives were dominated by acquired aesthetic expectations relating to compositional processes, Helmholtz took raw sound into the laboratory for minute observation. With the device called a siren, which emitted puffs of air with such control and at sufficient frequency that specific desired pitches could be created and compared, Helmholtz had at his disposal an untiring and flexible generator of fundamental sounds. The 3:2 ratio of the perfect fifth could be empirically tested by mechanically producing the same relationship in the number of air puffs emitted per unit of time. One of the two sound-generating chambers was subject to an adjustment that would either reduce or increase the time between adjacent puffs entering that chamber and thus would affect the relationships between the two generated sounds. Helmholtz scrutinized the beats that resulted, both revealing how the interaction of waves caused them and assessing the appropriateness of the terms "consonant" and "dissonant" that might be applied to characterize the generating interval. Another sound source for Helmholtz was a harmonium of twenty-four pitches per octave, through which he obtained a large number of justly-tuned intervals for study. His laboratory also contained "Helmholtz resonators"—glass globes with one hole to let in an external sound source and another to funnel a specific frequency into the ear of the researcher. In this way, Helmholtz could isolate individual components of a complex sound.

Many of the explanations which modern students of acoustics take for granted were formulated first by Helmholtz. For example, the role of partial tones in the determination of timbre was elucidated through his research. Those curious difference tones noted a century earlier by TARTINI, and summation tones—a similar phenomenon involving pitches higher than the generating tones—were defined with mathematical precision, while a theory for their generation explained how the ear might produce a response reflex in certain contexts even when the external sound that normally would be required to induce it was absent. Helmholtz undertook a careful exploration of the ear's functioning and postulated various ways in which the anatomical structure of that organ might analyze and separate the complex sounds that confronted it. Though this aspect of his work has undergone revision in the light of more recent and sophisticated research, it nevertheless brought to public attention the great complexity of the listening process and offered several hypotheses concerning how individual rods or, later, the basilar membrane of the cochlea, absorbed external sounds and sent the appropriate signals to the brain.

"Über die physiologischen Ursachen der musikalischen Harmonien"

    Lecture, 1857.

S ● *Vorträge und Reden von Hermann von Helmholtz.* Brunswick: Fr. Vieweg, 1865.

    Numerous later editions.

T ● Ellis, Alexander J., trans. "On the Physiological Causes of Harmony in Music." In *Popular Lectures on Scientific Subjects by H. Helmholtz,* translated by Edmund Atkinson, with an Introduction by Professor Tyndall, pp. 61-106. New York: D. Appleton, 1873; reprint edition, New York: Dover Publications, 1962.

    Review in *FR* 19/77 (1873):664-65 (Edith Simcox).

T ● *O fizicheskikh prichinakh muzykal'noi garmonii.* St. Petersburg: 1896.

T ● Warren, Richard M., and Warren, Roslyn P., eds. *Helmholtz on Perception: Its Physiology and Development.* New York: John Wiley, [1968].

    Reviews in *Apsy* 70/1 (1970):295-96 (A. Lévy-Schoen), *Choice* 6/1 (1969-70):80, and *Science* 161/3842 (1968):679 (Conrad G. Mueller).

T ● Kahl, Russell, ed. *Selected Writings of Hermann von Helmholtz.* Middletown, Ct.: Wesleyan University Press, [1971].

    Reviews in *AS* 30/2 (1973):243-44 (Colin A. Ronan), *BJHS* 7/1 (1974):95 (P. M. Heimann), *JHBS* 10/2 (1974):270-71 (J. A. Cardno), *LJ* 96/13 (1971):2331 (Frank N. Jones), *SBF* 8/1 (1972-73):19-20, and *ScAm* 226/4 (1972):114-15 (Philip Morrison).

S ● Krafft, Fritz, ed. Munich: Kindler, 1971.

    Contains "Nachwort: Von der mathematischen zur physikalischen Harmonie," pp. 56-63.

Die Lehre von den Tonempfindungen als physiologische Grundlage für die Theorie der Musik

    Brunswick: Fr. Vieweg & Sohn, 1863.

    Later editions in 1865, 1870, 1877, and 1896. Review in *AmZ* (Neue Folge) 1/27-29 (1863):467-71, 483-89, 495-501 (E. Krüger).

    Brunswick: Fr. Vieweg & Sohn, 1913. Edited by R. Wachsmuth.

T ● Guéroult, M. Georges, trans. *Théorie physiologique de la musique, fondée sur l'études des sensations auditives.* Paris: Victor Masson, 1868; 2nd edition, 1874.

T ● Ellis, Alexander J., trans. *On the Sensations of Tone as a Physiological Basis for the Theory of Music.* London: Longman, Green, & Co., 1875; 2nd edition, 1885; later printings in 1895, 1912, 1930, and (New York: P. Smith) 1948; reprint of the 2nd edition (with an Introduction by Henry Margenau and extensive bibliography of Helmholtz's writings), New York: Dover Publications, 1954. Bibliog.

    Reviews in *MR* 10/1 (1949):65 and *Spectator* 49/2485 (1876):211-13.

T ● Petukhov, Mikhail, trans. *Uchenie o slukhovykh oshchushcheniiakh kak fizicheskaia osnova dlia teorii muzyki.* St. Petersburg: 1875.

S ● Facsimile of the 1913 edition. Hildesheim: Georg Olms, 1968.

S ● Facsimile of the 1863 edition. Frankfurt am Main: Minerva, 1981.

T ● See **Katz and Dahlhaus (1987-)**:Vol. 3.

T ● See Bujić (1988).

Collected articles pertaining to musical acoustics

S ● *Wissenschaftliche Abhandlungen von Hermann Helmholtz*. Vol. 1. Leipzig: Johann Ambrosius Barth, 1882.

> Contains, among others, the following articles: "Bericht über die theoretische Akustik betreffenden Arbeiten vom Jahre 1848 und 1849," "Über Combinationstöne" (two versions), "Über die Klangfarbe der Vokale," "Über Klangfarben," "Über die Bewegung der Violinsaiten," "Über musikalische Temperatur," and "Über die persisch-arabische Tonleiter."

A listing of articles by Helmholtz is found in (1863):Ellis (1875):(1954), above, and in Lottermoser (1949-68), below.

LITERATURE:

Mach, Ernst. *Einleitung in die Helmholtz'sche Musiktheorie*. Graz: Leuschner & Lubensky: 1866; Russian translation (as *Vvedenie k izucheniiu o zvukovykh oshchushcheniiakh Gel'mgol'tsa*), St. Petersburg, 1879.

Laugel, [Antoine] Auguste. *La voix, l'oreille et la musique*. Paris: Germer Baillière; New York: Baillière Brothers, 1867.

Mach, Ernst. *Beiträge zur Analyse der Empfindungen*. Jena: Gustav Fischer, 1886.

> Excerpt in *VMw* 3 (1887):151-56.

STUMPF, Carl. "Hermann von Helmholtz und die neuere Psychologie." *AfGPh* 8/3 (1895):303-14.

Lotze, Hermann. *Geschichte der Ästhetik in Deutschland*. GWDNZ, no. 7. Munich: J. G. Cotta, 1868; reprint edition (HPON, no.1, edited by the Historische Commission bei der K. Academie der Wissenschaften), Leipzig: F. Meiner, 1913.

Taylor, Sedley. *Sound and Music: A Non-Mathematical Treatise on the Physical Constitution of Musical Sounds and Harmony, Including the Chief Acoustical Discoveries of Professor Helmholtz*. London: Macmillan, 1873; 2nd edition (as *Sound and Music: An Elementary Treatise . . .*), London: Macmillan, 1883; reprint edition, New York: Johnson Reprint Corporation, 1967.

> Review in *Choice* 5/8 (1968-69):970.

Blaserna, Pietro. *La teoria del suono nei suoi rapporti colla musica*. Bibsi, no. 1. Milan: Fratelli Dumolard, 1875; English edition (as *The Theory of Sound and Its Relation to Music*, ISS, no. 22), London: H. S. King; New York: D. Appleton, 1876; German edition (as *Die Theorie des Schalls in Beziehung zur Musik*, IwB, no. 24), Leipzig: Brockhaus, 1876;

French edition (as *Le son et la musique . . . suivis des causes physiologiques de l'harmonie musicale*, Bsi, no. 24), Paris: G. Baillière, 1877; numerous later editions.

Taylor, Sedley. *The Science of Music; or, The Physical Basis of Musical Harmony*. New York: D. Appleton, 1875; later editions.

> Review in *Nation* 21/523 (1875):28-29.

Koenigsberger, Leo. *Hermann von Helmholtz*. 3 vols. Brunswick: Fr. Vieweg & Sohn, 1902-3; English translation (abridged; translated by Frances A. Welby, with a Preface by Lord Kelvin), Oxford: Clarendon Press, 1906; reprint edition, New York: Dover, 1965; abridged German edition, Brunswick: Fr. Vieweg & Sohn, 1911.

> Reviews in *JPhil* 4/26 (1907):715-17 (J. McKeen Cattell), *Nation* 84/2183 (1907):416, *ScAm* 214/6 (1966):143, and *STel* 32/4 (1966):224.

Manz, Gustav. "Hermann von Helmholtz und die Musik." *Musik* 3/7 (1903-4):17-25.

Conrat, Friedrich. *Hermann von Helmholtz' psychologische Anschauung*. AzPG, no. 18. Halle: Max Niemeyer, 1904.

Sabine, W. C. "Melody and the Origin of the Musical Scale." *Science* 27/700 (1908):841-47.

Wesendonk, K. von. "Über Helmholtz' Lehre von der Dissonanz und Konsonanz." *NR* 25/20-21 (1910):249-51, 261-64.

Watt, Henry J. "Hermann von Helmholtz, 1821-1894." *ML* 2/3 (1921):235-43.

Zurmühl, Georg. "Abhängigkeit der Tonhöhenempfindung von der Lautstärke und ihre Beziehung zur Helmholtz'schen Resonanztheorie des Hörens." Ph.D. dissertation, The University of Marburg, 1930; published in *ZfS* 61 (1930):40-86.

Gerlach, Walther. "Hermann von Helmholtz: 1821-1894." In *Die großen Deutschen: Neue deutsche Biographie*, vol. 3, pp. 456-65. Berlin: Propyläen-Verlag, 1935-36; 2nd edition, 1956.

Lloyd, Llewelyn Southworth. "Helmholtz and the Musical Ear." *MQ* 25/2 (1939):167-75.

Boring, Edwin Garrigues. *Sensation and Perception in the History of Experimental Psychology*. CPS. New York: D. Appleton-Century, 1942.

Ebert, Hermann *Hermann von Helmholtz*. GN, no. 5. Stuttgart: Wissenschaftliche Verlagsgesellschaft M. B. H., 1949.

Lottermoser, Werner. "Helmholtz, Hermann von." In *MGG* (1949-68). Bibliog.

Husmann, Heinrich. *Vom Wesen der Konsonanz*. MGf, no. 3. Heidelberg: Müller-Thiergarten-Verlag, 1953.

Reviews in *Mf* 8/3 (1955):369-71 (Wilhelm Stauder) and *Musica* 8/11 (1954):522 (Karl G. Fellerer).

Wever, Ernest Glen, and Lawrence, Merle. *Physiological Acoustics*. Princeton, N.J.: Princeton University Press, 1954.

Pringsheim, Klaus. "Zwischen Helmholtz und Schönberg." *SMz* 96/10 (1956):385-90.

Pringsheim, Klaus. "Helmholtz und das arabische Tonsystem." *SMz* 98/10 (1958):370-74.

Besseler, Heinrich. *Das musikalische Hören der Neuzeit*. Berlin: Akademie-Verlag, 1959.

Reviews in *Mf* 13/4 (1960):478-80 (Carl Dahlhaus), *Rasm* 29/4 (1959):353-55 (Alfredo Bonaccorsi), and *Sh* 4 (1960):333-34.

London, S. J. "The Origins of Psychoacoustics." *HFMA* 13/4 (1963):44-47, 117.

Bartley, S. Howard. *Principles of Perception*. New York: Harper, 1958; 2nd edition, New York: Harper & Row, 1969. [*Rilm* 69-2970.]

Review in *AJO* 69/1 (1970):161 (Joel Pokorny).

Dahlhaus, Carl. "Hermann von Helmholtz und der Wissenschaftscharakter der Musiktheorie." In *Referate Berlin 1970* (1970):49-58. Bibliog. [*Rilm* 72-1064.]

Sunderman, F. William. "Medicine, Music, and Academia." *AST* 20/2 (1970):42-47.

● ● ● Turner, R. Steven. "Helmholtz, Hermann von." In *DSB* (1970-80). Bibliog.

Weyer, Rolf-Dieter. "Modelle zur Analyse stationärer und insbesondere nichtstationärer Schallvorgänge." In *FellererFs* (1973):673-85. [*Rilm* 74-4191.]

Cogan, Robert. "Reconceiving Theory: The Analysis of Tone Color." *CMS* 15 (1975):52-69. [*Rilm* 75-2673.]

Zenkl, Luděk. "Helmholtzovo pojetí konsonance a česká hudební teorie." *Hv* 12/3 (1975):328-50. [*Rilm* 76-1656.]

Terhardt, E. "Ein psychoakustisch begründetes Konzept der musikalischen Konsonanz." *Acustica* 36/3 (1976-77):121-37. Bibliog. [*Rilm* 76-7664.]

Moorer, James A.; Grey, John; and Strawn, John. "Lexicon of Analyzed Tones." *CMJ* 1/3 (1977):12-29. Bibliog. [*Rilm* 77-4034.]

Turner, R. Steven. "The Ohm-Seebeck Dispute, Hermann von Helmholtz, and the Origins of Physiological Acoustics." *BJHS* 10/1/34 (1977):1-24.

Terhardt, Ernst. "Conceptual Aspects of Musical Tones." *HAR* 30/1-2 (1979):46-57.

Bell, James F. "Helmholtz, Hermann (Ludwig Ferdinand) von." In *NGrove* (1980).

Review in *MQ* 68/2 (1982):182-88 (Robert Cogan).

Rasch, Rudolf A. "Theory of Helmholtz-Beat Frequencies." *MP* 1/3 (1983-84):308-22.

Terhardt, Ernst. "The Concept of Musical Consonance: A Link between Music and Psychoacoustics." *MP* 1/3 (1983-84):276-95. Bibliog.

● ● ● Warren, Richard M. "Helmholtz and His Continuing Influence." *MP* 1/3 (1983-84):253-75. Bibliog.

Roberts, Linda, and Shaw, Marilyn L. "Perceived Structure of Triads." *MP* 2/1 (1984-85):95-124.

Bailhache, Patrice. "Valeur actuelle de l'acoustique musicale de Helmholtz." *Stp* 11 (1986/87):152-74.

See also HAUPTMANN: ["Brief"] (1863); HOLDER: Stanley (1983); d'INDY: (1903-50); OETTINGEN: (1866); RIEMANN: (1877); (1898); (1914-15); Gurlitt (1950); Wuensch (1977); SAUVEUR: (1704):Maxham (1976); SCHOENBERG: Rexroth (1969/1971); Dahlhaus (1971); STUMPF: (1883-90); (1898-1924); TARTINI: Meyer (1957); LITERATURE SUPPLEMENT: Abbado (1964); Abel (1980/1982); Archibald (1924); Auhagen (1982/1983); **Barbour** (1938), (1949-68), **(1951/. . ./1972)**; Beach (1967); Bell et al. (1980); Beswick (1950); Burke (1963); Caplin (1978); Cavallini (1949); Cazden (1948), (1961-62), (1980); Chailley (1967); Chevaillier (1925/1931-32); Cobb (1884); ● ● ● Cohen (1984); Crombie (1969); **Dahlhaus** ["Tonalität"] (1949-68), ["Über"] (1966), ["Untersuchungen"] (1966/. . ./1988), ["Neue Musik"] (1976), ["Harmony"] **(1980)**, ["Über"] (1980), **(1984)**; **Dahlhaus et al. (1987)**; Deutsch (1980); de Zeeuw (1983); Dostrovsky (1969); Dubovsky et al. (1934-35); Duchez (1979); Federhofer (1985); Frobenius ["Homophonus"] (1972-), ["Polyphon"] (1972-), ["Vollstimmig"] (1972-); Geering (1949-68); Godley (1952); Gouk (1980); Green (1969); Gut (1976); Haase (1969); Handschin (1948); Hartmann (1923); Heinlein (1927/1928); Hoffman (1953); Hunt (1978); Hutchinson and Knopoff (1979-81); Imig (1969/1970); Jacobi (1957-60/1971); Jeppesen ([1951]/1952); Jones (1934); Jorgenson (1957), (1963); Kauko (1958); Kayser (1950); Keislar (1987); Kelletat [*Temperatur*] (1960); Kleinman (1971/1974); Krumhansl (1983-84); Kümmel (1973); La Motte-Haber (1969), (1971); Lang (1941); Lawrence (1978); Lecky (1880); **Lindley** ["Just"] **(1980)**, (1982); Lloyd (1940-41), (1955); Lottermoser (1949-68); Mach (1892); Marvin (1987); McCredie (1968); McQuere (1983); Mendel (1948); Miller (1939-40); Mitchell, J. W. (1963); Moos (1902/1922); Norton (1984); **Palisca** ["Theory"] **(1980)**; Palisca and Spender (1980); Parncutt (1988-89); Perinello (1936); Pikler (1966); Pole (1879/. . ./1924); Reinecke (1970); Révész (1946/. . ./1954); Rohwer (1949-68); Rowen (1979); Rummenhöller (1967), (1971); Schmidt (1979); Sheppard (1975); **Shirlaw**

(1917/. . ./1970), (1931); Smith (1967); Spender and Shuter-Dyson (1980); Subirá (1947/. . ./1958); Taddie (1984); Taylor (1980); Tenney (1988); Thürlings (1877); Toncitch (1973); Truesdell (1960); Vauclain (1978); Vogel (1955/1954), (1962),

(1975/1984), (1976); Warrack (1945); **Wason (1981/1985)**; Wellek (1949-68); Winckel (1949-68); Wunderlich (1940-41); **Zaminer (1985)**; Zimmermann (1976).

JOHANN ANDREAS HERBST

[bapt. 1588 – 1666]

Johann Andreas Herbst's several instruction manuals reflect the state of German music theory near the middle of the seventeenth century. Because he borrowed materials from a variety of sources, not all of his pronouncements are consistent with one another. He also supplied German translations of what he considered to be useful Latin works: treatises on counterpoint by Chiodino and on figured bass by EBNER comprise most of his *Arte prattica et poëtica* (1653).

As were many other Germans, Herbst was enamored of Italian compositional practices. He even devoted his first book, *Musica practica* (1642), to an elaboration of Italian vocal principles. Revised twice before his death, it served as a model for later works on vocal ornamentation, just as PRAETORIUS's discussion on the topic had established a foundation for Herbst. While consisting almost exclusively of music examples, *Musica practica* also includes a list of thirty-seven musical terms and their definitions.

Herbst's most important work is certainly his *Musica poëtica* (1643), in which a debt to BANCHIERI, DIRUTA, ZACCONI, Bernardi, Chiodino, CALVISIUS, Harnisch, BARYPHONUS, Bulichius, and ALSTED is acknowledged. Like other composition manuals of the era (though here in the vernacular German), an account of consonance and dissonance is followed by discussion on chord construction, modes, cadences, imitation, text-setting, musical rhetoric, and affect.

Musica practica sive instructio pro symphoniacis; Das ist, Eine kurtze Anleitung, wie die Knaben . . . auff jetzige Italienische Manier . . . können informiret und unterrichtet werden . . . [Rism B/VI/1, pp. 406-7.]

    Nuremberg: Jeremias Dümler, 1642. [LCPS: H-029a. SMLMS.]

        Expanded editions, as *Musica moderna prattica, overo maniera del buon canto . . .*:

    Frankfurt am Main: Anton Humm (Georg Müller), 1653.
    Frankfurt am Main: Fievettische Druckerey (Georg Müller), [1658]. [LCPS: H-029b. IDC.]

S ● Facsimile of the 1642 edition. MMMLF, ser. 2, no. 104. New York: Broude Brothers, forthcoming.

Musica poëtica, sive compendium melopoëticum; Das ist, Eine kurtze Anleitung und gründliche Unterweisung, wie

man eine schöne Harmoniam, oder lieblichen Gesang, nach gewiesen Praeceptis und Regulis componiren, und machen soll . . . [Rism B/VI/1, p. 406.]

    Nuremberg: Jerimias Dümler, 1643. [LCPS: H-028. SMLMS. IDC.]

S ● Facsimile edition. MMMLF, ser. 2, no. 103. New York: Broude Brothers, forthcoming.

Compendium musices; Das ist, Kurtzer doch gründlicher Unterricht . . . den Tyronibus und Incipienten

    Frankfurt am Main: 1652. [Lost.]

Arte prattica et poëtica; Das ist, Ein kurtzer Unterricht, wie man einen Contrapunkt machen und Componiren sol lernen . . . [Rism B/VI/1, p. 406.]

    Frankfurt am Main: Anton Humm (Thomas Matthias Götze), 1653. [LCPS: H-027. SMLMS.]

LITERATURE:

Allerup, Albert. "Die *Musica practica* des Johann Andreas Herbst und ihre entwicklungsgeschichtliche Bedeutung: Ein Beitrag zur Geschichte der deutschen Schulmusik." Ph.D. dissertation, The University of Münster, 1931; published edition (MBzMw, no. 1), Kassel: Bärenreiter (Emsdetten, Westphalia: Heinr. & J. Lechte), 1931. Bibliog.

Stauder, Wilhelm. "Herbst, Johann Andreas." In *MGG* (1949-68). Bibliog.

Eggebrecht, Hans Heinrich. "Zum Wort-Ton-Verhältnis in der *Musica poetica* von J. A. Herbst." In *Bericht Hamburg 1956* (1957):77-80.

● ● ● Samuel, Harold E. "Herbst, Johann Andreas." In *NGrove* (1980). Bibliog.

See also FÉTIS: (1833-44); LIPPIUS: Rivera (1974/1980); RIEMANN: (1898); WALTHER: (1732); LITERATURE SUPPLEMENT: Abraham (1968/1969); **Apfel (1981)**; **Arnold (1931/. . ./1965)**; Audbourg-Popin (1984); Badura-Skoda et al. (1980); Becker (1836-39/1964); Beiche ["Dux"] (1972-); Benary (1956/1961); Buelow (1972), (1982); Bukofzer (1947); Cahn ["Repercussio"] (1972-); ["Transitus"] (1972-); **Coover (1980)**;

Dahlhaus ["Untersuchungen"] (1966/. . ./1988); Dammann (1958/1967); Donington (1963/. . ./1974); Eggebrecht (1955), (1957), (1959); Eitner (1900-1904/1959-60); Falck (1965); Feldmann (1958); Fellerer ["Musikwissenschaft"] (1972), (1983); Ferand (1937/1938), (1951), ["Improvised"] (1956), [*Improvisation*] (1956/1961); Flindell (1983-84); Forchert (1986); Forkel (1792/1962); Geering (1949-68); Gerber (1790-92/1977), (1812-14/1966); Gissel (1980/1983), (1986); Goldschmidt (1890/

1892), (1907); Gurlitt (1942/1966), (1954/1966); Harrán (1986); Hawkins (1776/. . ./1969); Heimann (1970/1973); Horsley (1963); Houle (1987); Jackson (1988); Kirkendale (1979); Krones (1988); Kuhn (1902); **Lester** ● ● ● (1977), **(1989)**; Leuchtmann (1957/1959); Meier (1974/1988); Neumann, Frederick (1978); Palisca (1949-68); Rivera (1984); Robbins (1938); Rogers (1955); Ruhnke (1949-68); Sachs (1972-); Subirá (1947/. . ./1958); Tittel (1966); Unger (1941/1969); Walker (1987); Zenck (1942).

EUCHARIUS HOFFMANN

[d. 1588]

Eucharius Hoffmann's *Musicae practicae praecepta* (1572) retained the traditional eight-mode system, but his more important *Doctrina de tonis seu modis musicis* (1582) reveals the strong influence of GLAREAN. In addition to considering modal theory (including how the concept of *repercussio* might be applied to polyphonic music), Hoffmann dealt with the chromaticism of his day, including the elusive practice of *musica reservata*. His writings and the examples selected display a great respect for composers of earlier generations, especially Josquin.

Musicae practicae praecepta [*Rism* B/VI/1, pp. 418-19.]

Wittenberg: Johann Schwertel, 1572.

Other editions in 1578 and 1588.

Doctrina de tonis seu modis musicis [*Rism* B/VI/1, p. 418.]

Greifswald: Augustin Ferber, 1582.

Another edition in 1588.

Brevis synopsis de modis seu tonis musicis [*Rism* B/VI/1, p. 418.]

Derived from (1582/1588), above.

Rostock: Myliander, 1605.

LITERATURE:

Ruhnke, Martin. "Hoffmann, Eucharius." In *MGG* (1949-68). Bibliog.

Meier, Bernhard. "Eine weitere Quelle der Musica Reservata." *Mf* 8/1 (1955):83-85.

Ruhnke, Martin. "Hoffmann, Eucharius." In *NGrove* (1980). Bibliog.

See also BURMEISTER: Ruhnke (1955); FÉTIS: (1833-44); GLAREAN: Miller (1961); WALTHER: (1732); LITERATURE SUPPLEMENT: Atcherson (1960); Becker (1836-39/1964); Burney (1776-89/. . ./1957); Dahlhaus ["Zur Entstehung"] (1961); **Dahlhaus et al. (1987)**; Dunning (1980); Eitner (1900-1904/1959-60); Feldmann (1958); Fellerer (1983); Forkel (1792/1962); Gerber (1812-14/1966); Gissel (1980/1983), (1986); Hüschen (1986); Luoma (1976); Meier (1969); Meier (1949-68), ● ● ● (1974/1988); Mitchell, J. W. (1963); Niemöller (1964/1969); Palisca (1959); Preußner (1924); Ruhnke (1974); Sannemann (1903/1904).

JOHN HOLDEN

[died ca. 1771]

Though overlooked by most modern scholars, John Holden's *Essay towards a Rational System of Music* (1770) was favorably received in its day, particularly in Scotland. The work is divided into two parts: "The Rudiments of Practical Music" and "The Theory of Music." In the former, one finds the expected exposition of scales, consonance and dissonance, rhythm, and so on. The more interesting second part delves into the science of music (sound generation, per-

ception, tuning) as well as recent developments in harmonic theory.

A Collection of Church-Music . . . [*Rism* A/I/4, p. 372.]

Glasgow: the author, 1766.

Under the pseudonym Philarmonikos. The Preface contains a description of the projected *Essay* of 1770.

An Essay towards a Rational System of Music [*Rism* B/VI/1, p. 419.]

> Glasgow: the author (Robert Urie), 1770.
> Glasgow: the author; London: R. Baldwin, 1770. [LCPS: H-056a.]
>
>> Reviews in *CrR* 33 (1771):323-25 and *MonR* 44 (1771):121-24 [John Langhorne].
>
> Calcutta: the editor (Ferris & Greenway), [1799]. Edited by A. U. [LCPS: H-056b.]
> In J. Sibbald's *Vocal Magazine* [ca. 1802-3]. [Partial printing.]
> Edinburgh: William Blackwood (C. Stewart at the University Press), 1807.

S ● Gunn, Anne. *An Introduction to Music* . . . Edinburgh: Muir, Wood, & Co., 1803; later editions.

> Based on HOLDEN's *Essay*. Review in *BC* 25 (1805):64-72, 163-71 (J. W. Callcott).

LITERATURE:

Farmer, Henry George. "Holden, John." Translated by Theodora Holm. In *MGG* (1949-68). Bibliog.

Kassler, Jamie Croy. "Holden, John." In *NGrove* (1980). Bibliog.

See also FÉTIS: (1833-44); KOLLMANN: (1799); LITERATURE SUPPLEMENT: Allanbrook (1981); Becker (1836-39/1964); Burke (1963); Cazden (1948); Chenette (1967); Eitner (1900-1904/1959-60); Farmer (1947/1970); Forkel (1792/1962); Gerber (1812-14/1966); Houle (1987); **Kassler** (1971), ● ● ● **(1979)**; **Seidel and Cooper (1986)**.

WILLIAM HOLDER

[1616 – 1696]

The growing appreciation of scientific rigor among the English is manifested in William Holder's *Treatise of the Natural Grounds, and Principles of Harmony* (1694), which treats the physical basis for musical sound. Holder's earlier *Elements of Speech* (1669) had already displayed a concern for precise observation, there analyzing the sounds fundamental to the English language. With the investigations of authorities such as Robert Hooke, Francis NORTH, and MERSENNE as a foundation, Holder carefully explored the nature of musical sound, the concepts of consonance and dissonance, the role of proportions in music, and issues of tuning and temperament. His work was highly regarded by later generations. It was paired with KELLER's short manual on figured bass for a revised edition in 1731.

Elements of Speech: An Essay of Inquiry into the Natural Production of Letters, with an Appendix concerning Persons Deaf and Dumb

> London: J. Martyn (T. N.), 1669.

S ● Facsimile edition. ELin, no. 49. Menston, England: Scolar Press, 1967.

S ● Facsimile edition. New York: AMS Press, 1975.

Correspondence with John Baynard

> Mss., 1692-93. [London: British Library.]

A Treatise of the Natural Grounds, and Principles of Harmony [*Rism* B/VI/1, p. 420.]

> London: John Carr (John Heptinstall), 1694. [LCPS: H-057a.]

>> Abstract in *PTRS* 18 (1694):67-76 [Robert Hooke].

> London: Philip Monckton (John Heptinstall), 1701. [LCPS: H-057b.]

>> Revised by Gottfried KELLER and published with KELLER's *Rules for Playing a Thorow-Bass*:

> London: J. Wilcox and T. Osborne (W. Pearson), 1731. Two versions. [LCPS: H-057c. HoM: 755. IDC.]

S ● Facsimile of the 1694 edition. MMMLF, ser. 2, no. 32. New York: Broude Brothers, 1967.

LITERATURE:

Cudworth, Charles L. "Holder, William." Translated by Wilhelm Pfannkuch. In *MGG* (1949-68). Bibliog.

Poole, H. Edmund. "The Printing of William Holder's *Principles of Harmony*." *PMA 1974-75* 101 (1975):31-43. Bibliog. [*Rilm* 76-7814.]

Tilmouth, Michael. "Holder, William." In *NGrove* (1980). Bibliog.

Stanley, Jerome Merlin. "William Holder: His Position in Seventeenth Century Philosophy and Music Theory." Ph.D. dissertation, The University of Cincinnati, 1983. [*DA* 45/03A, p. 861. UMI 84-13709.]

See also FÉTIS: (1833-44); JONES: (1781); NORTH, R.: Wilson (1959); RIEMANN: (1898); LITERA-

TURE SUPPLEMENT: Atcherson (1972); Barbieri (1983); **Barbour (1951/. . ./1972)**; Becker
(1836-39/1964); Boomgaarden (1985/1987); Burney
(1776-89/. . ./1957); Cazden (1948), (1961-62);
● ● ●Chenette (1967); **Dahlhaus et al. (1987)**;
Eitner (1900-1904/1959-60); Forkel (1792/1962);
Frobenius ["Isotonos"] (1972-); Gerber (1790-
92/1977), (1812-14/1966); Gouk (1980), (1982);
Green (1969); Hawkins (1776/. . ./1969); Hutchin-
son and Knopoff (1979-81); Jacobi (1957-60/1971);
Kassler (1978), ● ● ● **(1979)**; Kassler and Oldroyd
(1983); Miller (1960); Miller and Cohen (1987);
Pulver (1927/. . ./1973); Ruf (1972-); Ruff (1970);
Seidel and Cooper (1986); **Shirlaw (1917/. . ./1970)**.

CHRISTIAAN HUYGENS

[1629 – 1695]

The physical and mathematical aspects of musical
sound occupied the prominent Dutch scientist Christiaan
Huygens at various times during his life, though he never
published a major work devoted to his findings. He did,
however, address a letter—now known as "Novus cyclus
harmonicus"—to the editor of the *Histoire des ouvrages des
sçavans* (1691), wherein he added his view on keyboard
tuning to the controversy then raging. At about the same
time WERCKMEISTER was proposing a well-tempered
system, which Huygens dismissed as purely empirical. A
strong supporter of mean-tone temperament, Huygens
devised a means of permitting transposition to any key (but
not modulation to any key during a performance) through
the use of a movable keyboard which would select the appropriate strings or pipes from a selection of thirty-one prepared choices per octave. Through his study he had noted
that if the octave were divided into thirty-one equal parts,
then all the pitches necessary for mean-tone temperament
would be approximated. (The means of dividing the 2:1 ratio
into such segments had only recently been made possible, as
a result of logarithms.) For example, between C and D there
would be four intervening pitches, the second of which
would function as C-sharp and the third as D-flat. Since the
pattern persisted throughout the octave, sliding the keyboard up and down this grid of possibilities would create
uniformly successful results. Yet at the same time the difference between the chromatic and diatonic half steps, a significant asset of the mean-tone system, would be retained.

Huygens had studied the ancient and Renaissance
authors on music and was particularly devoted to
MERSENNE, whose correspondent Huygens's father Constantijn had been (and with whom the young Huygens had
also interacted in that medium). In manuscript jottings we
observe Huygens attempting to rationalize a new hierarchy
of consonance wherein the major third surpassed the fourth
in its perfection. Huygens also studied vibrating strings, and
he pondered what happened to sound in a vacuum. In his
celebrated "Κοσμοθεωρος" (first published posthumously in
1698), he advanced the idea that music would certainly be a
part of the culture developed by inhabitants of other planets.

"Novus cyclus harmonicus"

Ms., 1661.

S ● As "Lettre touchant le cycle harmonique" (a letter to the editor, Basnage de Beuval). *Hos* (October 1691):78-88; reprinted in Collected
Works: (1888-1950/1967-):Vol. 10, pp. 169-74,
below.

S ● See Collected Works: 'sGravesande (1724):Vol.
4, pp. 745-54; reprinted in (1661):(1986), below.

T ● *Christiani Hugenii . . . Opera mechanica,
geometrica, astronomica et miscellanea*. Leiden:
G. Potvliet, 1751.

S ● See Collected Works: (1888-1950/1967-):Vol. 20,
pp. 139-73, below.

ST ● Rasch, Rudolf, ed. and trans. *Le cycle harmonique (Rotterdam 1691); Novus cyclus
harmonicus (Leiden 1724)*. TTL, no. 6. Utrecht:
The Diapason Press, 1986.

Contains English and Dutch translations, as well
as the French and Latin versions indicated. Reviews in *JMT* 32/2 (1988):379-81 (Thomas
Christensen) and *ML* 69/1 (1988):68-70 (Albert
Cohen).

"Κοσμοθεωρος [Kosmotheoros], sive de terris coelesti-
bus, earumque ornatu, conjecturae"

Ms., [ca. 1683-89].

S ● Edition in Latin and French. The Hague: apud
Adrianum Moetjens, 1698; 2nd edition, 1699;
Frankfurt and Leipzig: 1704.

T ● Childe, Timothy, trans. *The Celestial Worlds Dis-
cover'd; or, Conjectures Concerning the Inhabitants, Plants & Productions of the Worlds in the
Planets*. London: T. Childe, 1698; 2nd edition
(revised and enlarged), London: James Knap-
ton, 1722; facsimile of the 1698 edition (CLSC,
no. 10), London: Cass, 1968; as *Cosmotheros;
or, Conjectures Concerning the Planetary Worlds
and their Inhabitants*, Glasgow: Rob. & And.
Foulis, 1757; Glasgow: Robert Urie, [1762?].

S ● See Collected Works: 'sGravesande (1724):Vol.
3, pp. 641-722, below.

T ● Dufour, I., trans. *Nouveau traité de la pluralité des mondes, où l'on prouve par des raisons philosophiques, que toutes les planètes sont habitées & cultivées comme notre terre.* Paris: J. Moreau, 1702; Amsterdam: aux dépens d'E. Roger, 1718.

T ● *De la pluralité des mondes.* The Hague: J. Neaulme, 1724.

T ● *New Conjectures Concerning the Planetary Worlds, their Inhabitants and Productions.* n.p., [17 – ?].

S ● See Collected Works: (1888-1950/1967-):Vol. 21, pp. 677-821, below.

> The discussion of music is on pp. 750-55.

See Collected Works: (1888-1950/1967-):Vol. 20, below, for other manuscript works on music. Vol. 19 contains further useful material.

COLLECTED WORKS EDITIONS:

'sGravesande, G. J., ed. *Christiani Hugenii Zulichemor . . . Opera varia.* Leiden: apud Janssonios Vander Aa, 1724 [*Rism* B/VI/1, p. 427.].

Œuvres complètes de Christiaan Huygens. The Hague: M. Nijhoff, 1888-1950; reprint edition, Amsterdam: Swets & Zeitlinger, 1967- .

LITERATURE:

Land, J. P. N. "Het toonstelsel van Christiaan Huygens." *TvNm* 3/4 (1891):197-203.

Kalff, S. "Huygens en de muziek." *CHmu* 85/1, 4, 6 (1927-28):3-5, 52-56, 82-83.

Bell, Arthur E. *Christian Huygens and the Development of Science in the Seventeenth Century.* London: E. Arnold; New York: Longmans Green, 1947.

> Reviews in *AS* 6/1 (1948-50):103-4 (A. Armitage) and *Isis* 40/1 [119] (1949):272-73 (Mark Graubard).

Fokker, Adriaan D. "Huygens . . . Christiaan." In *MGG* (1949-68).

Farrar, Lloyd P. "Christiaan Huygens: His Musical Contributions to Seventeenth-Century Science." Ph.D. dissertation, The University of Texas, 1962.

Bos, H. J. M. "Huygens, Christiaan." *DSB* (1970-80). Bibliog.

Bister, Heribert, and Schneider-Klement, Albrecht. "Die Huygens-Fokker-Orgel im Museum Teyler zu Haarlem und die Möglichkeiten der 31-Ton-Temperierung." *Ao* 6 (1972):123-31. Bibliog. [*Rilm* 74-3587.]

● ● ● Hayes, Deborah. "Christian Huygens and the Science of Music." *Musicology at the University of Colorado*, edited by William Kearns, pp. 17-31. [Boulder?]: The Regents of the University of Colorado, 1977. Bibliog. [*Rilm* 77-4533.]

Cohen, H. F. "Christiaan Huygens on Consonance and the Division of the Octave." In *Huygens Symposium 1979* (1980):271-301. Bibliog.

Tollefsen, Randall H. "Huygens, Christiaan." In *NGrove* (1980).

See also FÉTIS: (1833-44); MERSENNE: (1617-48); RIEMANN: (1898); SERRE: (1763); LITERATURE SUPPLEMENT: Archibald (1924); Badings (1978); Barbieri (1983); **Barbour (1951/. . ./1972)**; Beer (1969); Bell et al. (1980); Cannon and Dostrovsky (1981); Cazden (1980); Chailley (1967):Cazden (1968) [Review]; Cohen (1981); ● ● ● Cohen (1984); **Dahlhaus et al. (1987)**; Dostrovsky (1969), (1974-75); Dupont (1933/. . ./1986); Eitner (1900-1904/1959-60); Fokker (1955), (1966); Gerber (1812-14/1966); Gouk (1980), (1981-82), (1982); Green (1969); **Hunt (1978)**; **Kassler (1979)**; Kassler and Oldroyd (1983); Koenigsberger (1979); Lottermoser (1949-68); Miller and Cohen (1987); Révész (1946/. . ./1954); Pikler (1966); **Shirlaw (1917/. . ./1970)**; Toncitch (1973); Truesdell (1960); Vogel (1955/1954), (1962), (1975/1984), (1976); **Walker (1976), (1978)**.

VINCENT D'INDY

[1851–1931]

When the Paris Conservatoire asked for Vincent d'Indy's help in formulating a new curriculum in theory and composition, they inspired a concept so revolutionary that it had to be rejected. D'Indy, whose artistic life was inspired by his study with César Franck and interactions with Wagner and Liszt, realized his plan instead at a new school, the Schola Cantorum, which from its inception in 1896 (and in particular after he became director in 1900) he shaped into a solid and distinctive institution. It nevertheless faltered soon after his death, and many faculty and students banded together to form the École César Franck to keep its principles alive.

As its name suggests, the Schola Cantorum was conceived to bring new vitality to Catholic church music, including Gregorian chant and the Renaissance repertoire. D'Indy added the composition course which he had proposed for the Paris Conservatoire. It was intended to follow after a rigorous program of harmony instruction. His efforts might have remained but a footnote in the history of theory pedagogy had he not undertaken to see his perspective into print. Happily, we possess the remarkable *Cours de composition musicale* (1903-50), one of the most comprehensive works of its kind ever created.

In sharp contrast to the operatic orientation and virtuosic expectations of the Conservatoire, d'Indy's course, which took from seven to ten years to complete, was broadly focused. The four published volumes grew out of actual classroom instruction. The students Auguste Sérieyx and, later, Guy de Lioncourt were responsible for assembling the texts and made independent contributions of their own. Book 1 is devoted to early music (what d'Indy classified as the rhythmic-monodic and the polyphonic periods) and includes brief chapters on harmony, tonality, and expression, as well as a synopsis of harmonic theories. Book 2, which was published in two volumes, inaugurates the investigation of the third of d'Indy's periods — the metrical period. Fugue, sonata, variations, concerto, symphony, string quartet, and symphonic poem are among the genres investigated. Book 3 completes the series with a study of dramatic music, oratorio, cantata, and song. Though this final volume was published posthumously in 1950, it retains d'Indy's perspective in its neglect of the modern repertoire. D'Indy was critical of Debussy's music and, as a resident of Paris, was forced to witness firsthand the gradual deflation of the stylistic and aesthetic principles he had spent his lifetime championing. The series offered a refreshing alternative to the excessively "academic" textbooks which flooded the market. Merging historical and technical information, particularly that which pertained to form, the *Cours* supplied what at least one of France's leading composers felt was essential for personal — and national — development in the art of composition.

Projet d'organisation des études du Conservatoire de musique de Paris

> Paris: Imprimerie nationale, 1892.

Une école de musique répondant aux besoins modernes: Discours d'inauguration de l'école de chant liturgique ... fondée par la Schola Cantorum en 1896

> Paris: Schola Cantorum, 1900.

Cours de composition musicale

> Paris: A. Durand & fils, 1903. Book 1. With Auguste Sérieyx.
>
> > Later printings.
>
> Paris: A. Durand & fils, 1909. Book 2, Part 1. With Auguste Sérieyx.
>
> > Review in *Rhcm* 10/7 (1910):182-89 (Henri Quittard).
>
> Paris: Durand, 1933. Book 2, Part 2. With Auguste Sérieyx.
>
> > Published posthumously. Review in *ML* 15/2 (1934):180-82 (F. Bonavia).
>
> Paris: Durand, 1950. Book 3. Edited by Guy de Lioncourt.
>
> > Published posthumously. Several later printings. Review in *Fm* 4/3 (1951) (Pierre Meylan).

T● Montgomery, Merle. "A Comparative Analysis [and Translation] of Vincent d'Indy's *Cours de composition musicale*." 7 vols. Ph.D. dissertation, The University of Rochester, 1946.

Cent thèmes d'harmonie et réalisations (Op. 71)

> Paris: Roudanez, 1907-18.

Correspondence

S● Sérieyx, Marie Louise, ed. *Lettres à Auguste Sérieyx*, by d'Indy, Henri Duparc, and Albert Roussel. Cdc, no. 5. Lausanne: Éditions du Cervin; Paris: Librairie E. Ploix, [1961].

See Ferchault (1949-68), below, for an extensive listing of d'Indy's articles in periodicals and newspapers.

LITERATURE:

Laloy, Louis. "Un nouvelle école de musique: La cours de M. Vincent d'Indy." *Rhcm* 1/10 (1901):393-98.

Castéra, René de. "Le cours de composition de V. d'Indy." *Occ* 2 (1902):355-58.

Saint-Saëns, Camille. *Les idées de M. Vincent d'Indy*. Paris: Éditions P. Lafille, [1919].

Honegger, A. "La classe de d'Indy au Conservatoire." *Rm* 13/122 (1932):40-41.

Fraguier, Marguerite-Marie de. *Vincent d'Indy: Souvenirs d'une élève, accompagnés de lettres inédites du maître*. Preface by Louis de Serres. Paris: Jean Naert, 1934 [colophon 1933].

> Review in *ML* 15/3 (1934):271 (M. R. Bonavia).

Gabeau, A. *Auprès du maître Vincent d'Indy: Souvenirs des cours de composition*. Paris: 1938.

Guenther, Ralph Russell. "Vincent d'Indy." Ph.D. dissertation, The University of Rochester, 1948.

Ferchault, Guy. "d'Indy, Paul Marie Théodore Vincent." Translated by Dorothea Schmidt-Preuß. In *MGG* (149-68). Bibliog.

● ● ● Demuth, Norman. *Vincent d'Indy 1851-1931: Champion of Classicism*. London: Rockliff, 1951; Westport, Ct.: Greenwood Press, 1974. Bibliog.

> Reviews in *Ches* 26/169 (1952):61-63 (Herbert Antcliffe), *MMR* 81/931 (1951):244-45 (G. A.), *MO* 75/891 (1951-52):157 (H. H.), *MR* 13/1 (1952):63 (E. H. W. Meyerstein), *MT* 93/1308 (1952):74 (W. R. A.), *MusT* 30/12 (1951):571 (W. R. A.), and *Tempo* 23 (1952):33 (Harold Truscott).

Le centenaire de Vincent d'Indy: 1851-1951. Paris: Jean Naert, 1952. Bibliog.

> Includes an extensive listing of publications which celebrate d'Indy's centenary.

Eckhart-Bäcker, Ursula. "Die Pariser Schola Cantorum in den Jahren um 1900: Eine Skizze unter besonderer Berücksichtigung historischer und pädagogischer Aspekte." In *HüschenFs* (1980):91-99. [*Rilm* 80-3907.]

Orledge, Robert. "Indy, (Paul Marie Théodore) Vincent d'." In *NGrove* (1980). Bibliog.

Nattiez, Jean-Jacques. "The Concepts of Plot and Seriation Process in Music Analysis." Translated by Catherine Dale. *MA* 4/1-2 (1985):107-18.

See also KOCH: Dahlhaus (1978); LITERATURE SUPPLEMENT: Alette (1951); Auda (1930/1979); Beswick (1950); Carse (1925/1964); Chailley (1967); Chevaillier (1925/1931-32); Cole (1969); Cooper (1974); Godley (1952); ● ● ● **Groth (1983)**; Jorgenson (1957), (1963); Lang (1941); Lawrence (1978); Lindley (1982); Longyear and Covington (1985); Müller-Blattau (1923/. . ./1963); Newman (1959/. . ./1983), (1963/. . ./1983), (1969/. . ./1983); Reese (1957/1970); Schmalzriedt ["Coda"] (1972-), ["Exposition"] (1972-); Seidel (1972-); Subirá (1947/. . ./1958); Vauclain (1978); Vogel (1962).

SALOMON JADASSOHN

[1831 – 1902]

Holders of major teaching posts have tended to write textbooks. Salomon Jadassohn, a prominent member of the Leipzig Conservatory's faculty late in the nineteenth century, wrote many. Unfortunately his career depended more upon industry than upon inspiration, and his texts, though influential both in Europe and America, led students towards a dull, mechanical familiarity with what is now generally regarded as inadequate analytical and compositional techniques. His harmonic perspective fostered a jumble of key changes that segmented chordal progressions into small compartments, often with no apparent relationship among them. The opening phrase of the *Tristan* Prelude, for example, is analyzed in his *Melodik und Harmonik bei Richard Wagner* (1899) as "fis: VII°7 a: II°7 H: VII°7 a: V7." His pronouncements in the contrapuntal arts included a questioning of the integrity of many masterworks, since they were not in conformity with his perspective.

The quantity of material published under Jadassohn's name—in at least six languages—tells us something important about the era and its pedagogical climate. Though the question of truth in art is never fully resolved, at a time when Wagner's and others' intensely chromatic music was in vogue Jadassohn's perspective was served to thousands of young practitioners as the best possible introduction to music's structure. Today, as we continue to ponder this repertoire, the dusty books by Jadassohn are not among those often consulted.

"Der streng-polyphonische Stil in der Gegenwart"

Under the pseudonym L. Lübenau.

MuWb 12/17-18 (1881):201-2, 213-15.

Musikalische Kompositionslehre

I. *Die Lehre vom reinen Satz*

1) *Lehrbuch der Harmonie*

2) *Lehrbuch des einfachen, doppelten, drei- und vierfachen Contrapunkts*

3) *Die Lehre vom Canon und von der Fuge*

II. *Die Lehre von der freien Komposition*

4) *Die Formen in den Werken der Tonkunst: Analysirt und in stufenweise geordnetem Lehrgange für die praktischen Studien der Schüler und zum Selbstunterricht dargestellt*

5) *Lehrbuch der Instrumentation*

Leipzig: Breitkopf & Härtel, 1883. Vol. I:1.

Later editions through 1923.

Leipzig: Breitkopf & Härtel, 1884. Vol. I:2.

Later editions through 1926.

Leipzig: Breitkopf & Härtel, 1884. Vol. I:3.

Later editions through 1928. An Appendix, "Erläuterungen der in Joh. Seb. Bach's Kunst der Fuge enthaltenen Fugen und Canons," appeared beginning with the 1898 edition and was published separately in 1899. Review in *Rmi* 5/3 (1898):598-99 (L. Torchi).

Leipzig: Fr. Kistner [Breitkopf & Härtel], 1885. Vol. II:4.

Later editions through 1923. Review in *Rmi* 3/1 (1896):195 (L. Torchi).

Leipzig: Breitkopf & Härtel, 1889. Vol. II:5.

Later editions through 1924.

T● Torek, Paul, and Pasmore, H. B., trans. *Manual of Harmony* [= Vol. I:1]. Leipzig: Breitkopf & Härtel, 1884; numerous later editions.

T● Wolff, Gustav (Tyson-), trans. *Treatise on [Manual of] Simple, Double, Triple and Quadruple Counterpoint* [= Vol. I:2]. Leipzig: Breitkopf & Härtel; New York: G. Schirmer, 1887; several later editions, revised by E. M. Barber.

T● Wolff, Gustav (Tyson-), trans. *A Course of Instruction on Canon and Fugue* [= Vol. I:3]. Leipzig: Breitkopf & Härtel; New York: G. Schirmer, 1887; later editions, which include an Appendix, "An Analysis of the Fugues and Canons Contained in Joh. Seb. Bach's 'Art of Fugue'," translated by Ernest Brentnall [published independently in French in 1895 (see below) and separately printed in English translation in 1899].

T● Wilkins, Harry P., trans. *A Course of Instruction in Instrumentation* [= Vol. II:5]. Leipzig: Breitkopf & Härtel, 1891; reprinted in 1899.

T● Barber, E. M., trans. *Manual of Musical Form* [= Vol. II:4]. Leipzig: Breitkopf & Härtel, 1892.

T● Baker, Theodore, trans. *A Manual of Harmony* [= Vol. I:1]. New York: G. Schirmer, [1893]; numerous later editions.

T● Brahy, Edouard, trans. *Traité d'harmonie* [= Vol. I:1]. Leipzig: Breitkopf & Härtel, 1893; later editions.

T● Jodin, Mathieu, trans. *Traité de contrepoint simple, double, triple et quadruple* [= Vol. I:2]. Paris: Fischbacher; Leipzig: Breitkopf & Härtel, 1896.

Review in *Rmi* 5/1 (1898):172-73 (L. Torchi).

T● Gherzfeld, Gherzoff, trans. *Trattato d'armonia* [= Vol. I:1]. Leipzig: Breitkopf & Härtel, 1898; reprinted in 1911.

> Review in *Rmi* 6/1 (1899):212-13 (L. Torchi).

T● Hartog, J., trans. *Leerboek der harmonie* [= Vol. I:1]. Leipzig: Breitkopf & Härtel, 1898; reprinted in 1912.

> Review in *Rmi* 6/2 (1899):429 (L. Torchi).

T● Perinello, Carlo, trans. *Trattato di contrappunto semplice, doppio, triplo e quadruplo* [= Vol. I:2]. Leipzig: Breitkopf & Härtel, 1898; reprinted 1925.

> Review in *Rmi* 6/1 (1899):212-13 (L. Torchi).

T● Montillet, William, trans. *Les formes musicales dans le chef-d'œuvres de l'art . . .* [= Vol. II:4]. Leipzig: Breitkopf & Härtel, 1900; reprinted in 1926.

T● Berg, Alfred, trans. *Lärobok i enkla, dubbla, tre- och fyrdubbla kontrapunkten* [= Vol. I:2]. Lund: Gleerup, 1901.

T● Baker, Theodore, trans. *A Manual of Single, Double, Triple and Quadruple Counterpoint.* New York: G. Schirmer: [1902]; later editions.

T● Hartog, Jacques, trans. *Leerboek van het eenvoudige, dubbele drie- en viervoudige contrapunt* [= Vol. I:2]. Leipzig: Breitkopf & Härtel, 1905.

T● Schinelli, Achille, trans. *Le forme nelle opera musicali . . .* [= Vol. II:4]. Leipzig: Breitkopf & Härtel, 1906; reprinted in 1925.

Aufgaben und Beispiele für die Studien in der Harmonielehre, mit Bezugnahme auf des Verfassers Lehrbuch der Harmonie/Exercises and Examples for the Study in Harmony Appertaining to the Manual of Harmony

Leipzig: Breitkopf & Härtel, 1886.

> Later editions through 1934. Review in *Rmi* 11/3 (1904):638 (L. Torchi).

T● *Thèmes et examples pour l'étude de l'harmonie/Oefeningen en voorbeelden voor de leer der harmonie.* Leipzig: Breitkopf & Härtel, 1901; several later editions.

Erläuternde Anmerkungen und Hinweise für die Bearbeitung der Aufgaben des Lehrbuchs der Harmonie, mit besonderer Berücksichtigung des Selbstunterricht

Leipzig: Breitkopf & Härtel, 1886.

T● *Explanatory Remarks and Suggestions for the Working of the Exercises in the Manual of Harmony, with Special Consideration for Self-Instruction.* Leipzig: Breitkopf & Härtel, 1886.

Erläuternde Anmerkungen und Hinweise für die Bearbeitung der Aufgaben im Lehrbuche des Contrapunkts, mit besonderer Berücksichtigung des Selbstunterrichts

Leipzig: Breitkopf & Härtel, 1887.

Erläuterungen zu ausgewählten Fugen aus Johann Sebastian Bach's wohltemperirtem Clavier: Supplement zu des Verfassers Lehrbuch des Canons und der Fuge

Leipzig: F. E. C. Leuckart, [ca. 1887]; Breitkopf & Härtel, 1899.

Die Kunst zu moduliren und zu präludiren: Ein praktischer Beitrag zur Harmonielehre, in stufenweise geordnetem Lehrgange dargestellt (BHmH, no. 9)

Leipzig: Breitkopf & Härtel, 1890.

> Later editions in 1902 and 1914.

Gesangschule/Singing Tutor

Leipzig: Breitkopf & Härtel, 1891.

Allgemeine Musiklehre

Leipzig: Breitkopf & Härtel, 1892.

Aufgaben und Beispiele für die Studien im Kontrapunkt, mit Bezugnahme auf des Verfassers Lehrbuch des Kontrapunkts/Exercises and Examples for the Studies in Counterpoint Appertaining to the Treatise on Counterpoint

Leipzig: Breitkopf & Härtel, 1892.

> Reprinted in 1910.

T● Sandré, Gustave, and Hartog, Jacques, trans. *Exercises et exemples pour l'étude du contrepoint appendice au traité de contrepoint/Oefeningen en voorbeelden voor de studie van het contrapunt in verband met zijn leerboek voor contrapunt.* Leipzig: Breitkopf & Härtel, 1905.

Anhang zu den hinweisen für die Bearbeitung der Aufgaben des Lehrbuches; Speziell für den Selbstunterricht

Leipzig: Breitkopf & Härtel, 1894.

T● *Appendix to the Remarks for the Working of the Exercises in the Manual of Harmony, with Special Consideration for Self-Instruction.* Leipzig: Breitkopf & Härtel, 1894.

Elementar-Harmonielehre für den Schul- und Selbstunterricht

Leipzig: Breitkopf & Härtel, 1894.

> Review in *Rmi* 2/4 (1895):742-43 (L. Torchi).

T● *Elementary Principles of Harmony, for School and Self-Instruction.* Leipzig: Breitkopf & Härtel, 1895.

"Erläuterungen der in Joh. Seb. Bach's Kunst der Fuge enthaltenen Fugen und Canons"

T ● " 'L'art de la fugue' de Jean Séb. Bach." *Rmi* 2/1 (1895):57-84.

T ● Brentnall, Ernest, trans. *An Analysis of the Fugues and Canons Contained in Joh. Seb. Bach's "Art of Fugue"*. Leipzig: Breitkopf & Härtel, 1899.

S ● Leipzig: Breitkopf & Härtel, 1899.

   Review in *Rmi* 6/4 (1899):877-78 (L. Torchi).

S ● See (1883-89):Vol. I:3 (1884), later editions, above.

T ● See (1883-89):Wolff (1887):later editions, above.

Schlüssel zu den Aufgaben der Elementar-Harmonielehre/Key to the Examples in the Elementary Principles of Harmony.

   Leipzig: Breitkopf & Härtel, 1895.

   Review in *Rmi* 4/1 (1897):166 (L. Torchi).

Methodik des musiktheoretischen Unterrichtes

   Leipzig: Breitkopf & Härtel, 1898.

   Review in *Rmi* 6/2 (1899):430 (L. Torchi).

Melodik und Harmonik bei Richard Wagner

   Leipzig: Breitkopf & Härtel, [1899].
   Berlin: Verlagsgesellschaft für Literatur und Kunst ['Harmonie'], n.d.

Ratschläge und Hinweise für die Instrumentationsstudien der Anfänger

   Leipzig: Breitkopf & Härtel, 1899.

   Reviews in *Rmi* 6/3-4 (1899):655-56, 877-78 (L. Torchi).

Das Tonbewußtsein: Die Lehre vom musikalischen Hören

   Leipzig: Breitkopf & Härtel, 1899.

   Review in *Rmi* 6/4 (1899):877-78 (L. Torchi).

T ● Campbell, Le Roy B., trans. *A Practical Course in Ear Training; or, A Guide for Acquiring Relative and Absolute Pitch* . . . Leipzig: Breitkopf & Härtel, 1899; reprinted in 1905.

   Review in *Rmi* 13/1 (1906):181-82 (L. Torchi).

Das Wesen der Melodie in der Tonkunst

   Leipzig: Breitkopf & Härtel, 1899.

   Review in *Rmi* 6/3 (1899):654 (L. Torchi).

Zur Einführung in J. S. Bach's Passions-Musik nach dem Evangelisten Matthaeus. Berlin: Harmonie, [ca. 1899].

   Review in *Rmi* 6/4 (1899):874 (A. Engelfred).

Der Generalbaß: Eine Anleitung für die Ausführung der Continuo-Stimmen in den Werken der alten Meister/ Thoroughbass: Instruction Leading to the Performance of the Continuo-Parts in the Works of the Old Masters/La basse continue: Une instruction pour l'exécution des parties chiffrées dans les chef-d'œuvres des anciens maîtres

   Leipzig: Breitkopf & Härtel, 1901.

   Review in *Rmi* 8/2 (1901):484-85 (L. Torchi).

LITERATURE:

Wihtol, Austris A., ed. *A Manual of Elementary Harmony, Quoted from the Works of Solomon Jadassohn*. Glendale, Calif.: Hama Conservatory, n.d.

Levi, Josef. "Zum 100. Geburtstag von Solomon Jadassohn." *CVZ* 10/33 (1931):408-9.

Feder, Georg. "Jadassohn, Salomon." In *MGG* (1949-68). Bibliog.

Grove, George. "Jadassohn, Salomon." Revised. In *NGrove* (1980).

See also FÉTIS: (1833-44); LITERATURE SUPPLEMENT: Babbitt (1987); **Bent** ["Analysis"] **(1980/1987)**; Burke (1963); Carse (1925/1964); Chevaillier (1925/1931-32); Devore (1987); Dziebowska (1976); Horsley [*Fugue: History*] (1966); Jacobi (1957-60/1971); Jeppesen (1930/. . ./1974), (1935); Lang (1941); **Mann (1955/. . ./1987)**; Moyer (1969); Nielsen (1971); Phillips (1979); Schmalzriedt ["Coda"] (1972-); Schoffman ["Descriptive"] (1983); Skinner (1891); Subirá (1947/. . ./1958); Thaler (1984); Thompson (1980); Tittel (1959), (1966); Vogel (1962); ● ● ●**Wason (1981/1985)**; Weigl (1914-15).

TOMÁŠ BALTAZAR JANOVKA

[1660? – 1715?]

The Czech organist Tomáš Baltazar Janovka produced an impressive though not widely circulated volume called *Clavis ad thesaurum magnae artis musicae* (1701), which presents a large body of theoretical information in dictionary format. The titles of some of the longer articles give an indication of its scope: *Tactus, Tonus, Scala, Transpositio*. Janovka was particularly sensitive to the wide variety of styles then practiced in Europe, and he dutifully supplied terms for the various categories he discerned. Somewhat vague in his understanding of past modal usage, he asserted, quite daringly, that all twenty-four keys were available to composers, going so far as to list them all with appropriate key signatures.

Clavis ad thesaurum magnae artis musicae seu elucidarium omnium ferè rerum ac verborum, in musica figurali tam vocali, quàm instrumentali obvenientium . . .
[*Rism* B/VI/1, p. 432.]

  Prague: Georg Labaun, 1701. [LCPS: J-005.]

  As Clavis ad musicam in elucidatione potissimum dictionum, seu terminorum musicorum consistens:

  Prague: Georg Labaun, 1715.

S ● Facsimile of the 1701 edition. Dm, no. 2. Amsterdam: Fritz Knuf, 1973.

T ● See **Lester (1989)**.

LITERATURE:

Burda, Antonín. "*Clavis ad thesaurum magnae artis musicae* Tomáše Balthasara Janovky z r. 1701." Ph.D. dissertation, The University of Prague, 1946.

Ruhnke, Martin. "Janowka, Thomas Balthasar." In *MGG* (1949-68). Bibliog.

Burda, Antonín. "M. Vogt a T. B. Janovka: Vogtovo Conclave slíbeným pokračováním Janovkova Clavisu?" *Hv* 2/4 (1965):672-82. Bibliog.

Cígler, Radovan. "Notes on the History of Musical Lexicography in Czechoslovakia." English translation by John Tyrrell. *SpFfBU* 3 (1968):87-97.

Sehnal, Jiří. "Janovkas Clavis und die Musik in Prag um das Jahr 1700." In *SpFfBU* 6 (1971):25-42.

Volek, Tomislav. "Tomáš Baltazar Janovka, představitel české barokní hudební a vzdělanecké tradice." *Hv* 9/4 (1972):344-55. [*Rilm* 76-9878.]

Burda, Antonín. "Thomas Balthasar Janovka, der Fürst der Musiktheoretiker Böhmens des 17. Jahrhunderts." In *Musica antiqua V* (1978).

Clapham, John, and Volek, Tomislav. "Janovka, Tomáš Baltazar." In *NGrove* (1980). Bibliog.

See also DEMANTIUS: Eggebrecht (1957); FÉTIS: (1831); (1833-44); WALTHER: (1732); LITERATURE SUPPLEMENT: Ahlgrimm (1969-70); Bartel (1982/1985); Becker (1836-39/1964); Beiche ["Dux"] (1972-), ["Inversio"] (1972-); Beyschlag (1907/1953); Chafe (1981), (1982); ● ● ● Coover (**1980**); Dammann (1958/1967); Eitner (1900-1904/1959-60); Feldmann (1958); Frobenius ["Isotonos"] (1972-), ["Monodie"] (1972-), ["Vollstimmig"] (1972-); Gerber (1812-14/1966); Goldschmidt (1907); Harich-Schneider ([1939]/ . . ./1970); Katz (1926); Kirkendale (1984); Lester (1977), ● ● ● (1978); Mendel (1955), (1978); Müller-Blattau (1923/. . ./1963); Neumann, Frederick (1978); Newman (1959/. . ./1983); Ritzel (**1967/1968**); Sachs (1972-); Schmalzriedt ["Reprise"] (1972-); Schwartz (1908); Seidel (1972-); Straková (1975); Subirá (1947/. . ./1958); Taddie (1984); Unger (1941/1969); Walker (1987).

WILLIAM JONES

[bapt. 1726 – 1800]

William Jones, an English clergyman, lamented the increasingly secular explanations which were offered for music and considered the compositional practices of his day to be "depraved." His reactionary musical theory is based upon the Old Testament and upon seventeenth-century mechanistic theory. For him, God played an important role in the creative process. Jones's lifelong fascination with science fostered his awareness of basic acoustical principles, which inform his chapter "On Sound and Music" from the *Physiological Disquisitions* of 1781 and even a sermon, *The Nature and Excellence of Music* (1787), delivered at the dedication of a new organ. God's handiwork was apparent in the coordination of pulses observable in consonant sounds, though man's intervention was required in the form of temperament in order for the modern tonal system to function. Music, whose foundational harmonies were based upon a Trinity of three notes, could move men's upright passions and instill noble and worthwhile thoughts. On the practical side, his *Treatise on the Art of Music* (1784) attempts to establish a perspective in which harmony serves as foundation for melody (defined by rhythm as well), all under the control of expression. His view promoted a monotonous mapping of subjects over the span of a composition. Notably, it fails to account for the subtle developmental characteristics of music then being written. Handel's works—not Haydn's—are the models from which Jones created his ill-received theory.

Letters from a Tutor to His Pupils

> London: for G. Robinson, [ca. 1780 or earlier].
>> Numerous later editions.

S ● See Collected Works (1801):Vol. 11, below.

Physiological Disquisitions: or, Discourses on the Natural Philosophy of the Elements . . . VI. On Sound and Music . . .

> London: J. Rivington & Sons, G. Robinson, D. Prince, etc., 1781.

S ● See Collected Works (1801):Vols. 9-10, below.

A Treatise on the Art of Music, in Which the Elements of Harmony and Air Are Practically Considered . . . Preparatory to the Practice of Thorough-Bass and Musical Composition [*Rism* B/VI/1, p. 435.]

> Published anonymously.

> Colchester: the author (W. Keymer), 1784. [LCPS: J-011.]
>> Reviews in *CrR* 59 (1785):449-53, *EurM* 6 (1784):131-34 [Samuel Arnold], and *MonR* 75 (1786):105-12, 174-81 [Charles Burney].

> Sudbury: G. W. Fletcher; London: Longman & Co. and E. Whitaker, 1827.
>> Reviews in *GMag* 98/1 (1828):145-46 and *Harmon* 6/1 (1828):81-83.

The Nature and Excellence of Music: A Sermon . . . [*Rism* B/VI/1, p. 435.]

> London: G. G. J. and J. Robinson, etc., 1787.

S ● See Collected Works (1801):Vol. 6, below.

COLLECTED WORKS EDITION:

Stevens, William, ed. *The Theological, Philosophical and Miscellaneous Works of the Rev. William Jones . . . to Which is Prefixed a Short Account of His Life and Writings*. 12 vols. London: F. and C. Rivington, J. Robson, and J. Hatchard, 1801; later editions.

LITERATURE:

Cudworth, Charles L. "Jones, William." Translated by Wilhelm Pfannkuch. In *MGG* (1949-68). Bibliog.

Lonsdale, Roger. "Dr. Burney and the *Monthly Review*, Part 1." *RES* 14/56 (1963):346-58.

Schofield, Robert E. *Mechanism and Materialism: British Natural Philosophy in an Age of Reason*. Princeton, N.J.: Princeton University Press, 1970. Bibliog.

> Reviews in *AHR* 76/2 (1971):479-80 (Brooke Hindle), *AS* 27/3 (1971):300-301 (Richard Hunter), *BHM* 47/2 (1973):211-12 (Theodore M. Brown), *BJHS* 5/4 [20] (1970-71):418-19 (J. E. McGuire), *BSM* 2/3 (1972):71, *Choice* 7/5-6 (1970-71):699, *JHM* 27/2 (1972):230-33 (Arthur Donovan), *PhQ* 22/87 (1972):178-79 (P. M. Heimann), *Science* 169/3950 (1970):1068 (Robert H. Kargon), *SRis* 65/11-12 [106] (1971):1117-18 (G. Montalenti), and *TLS* 69/3576 (1970):1000.

Kassler, Jamie Croy. "The Systematic Writings on Music of William Jones (1726-1800)." *JAMS* 26/1 (1973):92-107. Bibliog. [*Rilm* 73-1214.]

Kassler, Jamie Croy. "Jones, William (i)." In *NGrove* (1980). Bibliog.

See also FÉTIS: (1833-44); LITERATURE SUPPLEMENT: Becker (1836-39/1964); Burke (1963); Burney (1776-89/. . ./1957); **Dahlhaus et al. (1987)**; Eitner (1900-1904/1959-60); Gerber (1790-92/1977), (1812-14/1966); Houle (1987); Jacobi (1957-60/1971); **Kassler** (1971), (1976), ● ● ● **(1979)**; Kirkendale (1979); **Ritzel (1967/1968)**; **Seidel and Cooper (1986)**.

GOTTFRIED KELLER

[died 1704]

Despite a somewhat haphazard format and error-laden text, Gottfried Keller's posthumous *Rules for Playing a Thorough Bass* (1705) was popular in England during the early decades of the eighteenth century. Two sections deserve special mention: "Short Lessons by Way of Fugeing," in which nine examples invite students to apply a fugal subject at specified spots within the chordal fabric; and "Rules for Tuning an Harpsichord," which perhaps undeservedly circulated in treatises by Prelleur and TANS'UR. Though Keller was German, his work lacks the sophistication of the best Continental treatises of the era, such as those by SAINT-LAMBERT and HEINICHEN.

Rules for Playing a Thorough Bass

> London: J. Walsh and J. Hare, 1705.

>> As *A Compleat Method, for Attaining to Play [a] Thorough Bass upon either Organ, Harpsichord or Theorbo-Lute* . . . [*Rism* B/VI/1, pp. 442-43.]:

> London: J. Cullen, John Young, 1707.
> London: J. Walsh, J. Hare, P. Randall, [1707].
> London: Richard Meares, [ca. 1715-21]. [LCPS: K-006.]

>> Further editions, under the title *Rules, or a Compleat Method* . . . [*Rism* B/VI/1, p. 443.]:

> London: J. Walsh & J. Hare, [ca. 1708-13].
> London: J. Walsh & J. Hare, [1717].
> London: J. Walsh & J. Hare, [ca. 1730].

S ● See HOLDER: (1694):(1731).

S ● Keller's tuning rules found their way into Peter Prelleur's *The Modern Musick-Master* [*Rism* B/VI/2, pp. 667-68.], Part 6: "The Harpsichord Illustrated and Improv'd . . . with Rules for Tuning the Harpsichord or Spinnet" (London: Printing Office of Bow Church Yard, 1730; later editions; facsimile edition, Kassel: Bärenreiter, 1965) and into TANS'UR: (1746).

LITERATURE:

Nef, Albert. "Gottfried Keller und die Musik." *SMz* 51/36 (1911):475-77; 52/1-3 (1912):2-3, 12-13, 21-23.

> See also *SMz* 52/5 (1912):44 (A. Niggli).

Tilmouth, Michael. "Keller, Gottfried." Translated by Wilhelm Pfannkuch. In *MGG* (1949-68). Bibliog.

Tilmouth, Michael. "Keller, Gottfried." In *NGrove* (1980). Bibliog.

Evans, Jeffrey. "The Keyboard Tuning Rules of *The Modern Musick-Master*." *EM* 11/3 (1983):360-63.

See also FÉTIS: (1833-44); RIEMANN: (1898); SAINT-LAMBERT: (1707):Burchill (1979); LITERATURE SUPPLEMENT: Ahlgrimm (1973); **Arnold (1931/. . ./1965)**; **Barbour** (1949-68), **(1951/. . ./1972)**; Becker (1836-39/1964); Boomgaarden (1985/1987); Chenette (1967); Chevaillier (1925/1931-32); **Dahlhaus et al. (1987)**; Eitner (1900-1904/1959-60); Forkel (1792/1962); Gerber (1812-14/1966); Green (1969); Hawkins (1776/. . ./1969); ● ● ●**Kassler (1979)**; Kauko (1958); Mitchell, W. J. (1963); Oberdörffer (1949-68); Riedel (1956/1959); Rogers (1955); Rohwer (1949-68); **Seidel and Cooper (1986)**; **Shirlaw (1917/. . ./1970)**; Williams ["Equal"] (1968).

DAVID KELLNER

[ca. 1670 – 1748]

A brief, popular, and largely derivative manual on figured bass came into being when David Kellner published, in 1732, *Treulicher Unterricht im General-Baß*. Swedish, Dutch, and, eventually, Russian translations followed, making Kellner's work especially appealing to various segments of the European populace. Unlike HEINICHEN's massive *General-Bass in der Composition*, published just four years earlier, Kellner's book, at about a tenth the size (and lower cost), gave musicians an appealing introduction to the basic principles of figured-bass realization. Since Kellner had access to HEINICHEN's work, the *Treulicher Unterricht* incorporated recent innovations such as full-voiced accompaniment and a musical circle that revealed which keys were most closely related to any given tonic.

Treulicher Unterricht im General-Baß . . . [*Rism* B/VI/1, pp. 444-45.]

> Hamburg: Kissner, 1732. [HoM: 799. SMLMS.]

>> Review in MIZLER: (1736-54):Vol. 1/1 (1736): 25-27. Numerous later printings, including the following:

> Hamburg: Christian Herold, 1737. Foreword by Georg Philipp TELEMANN. [LCPS: K-007a.]

Hamburg: Christian Herold, 1743. Foreword by Daniel Solander. [LCPS: K-007b.]

Hamburg: Christian Herold seel. Wittwe, 1773. [LCPS: K-007d.]

Hamburg: J. G. Herold, 1796. [LCPS: K-007e.]

T ● L[ondée], J[onas]. trans. *Trogen underrättelse uti general-basen . . .* Stockholm: Benj. Gottl. Schneider Enckia, 1739 [*Rism* B/VI/1, p. 445.]; reprinted (by Miklin) in 1782.

T ● Havingha, Gerhardus, trans. *Korte en getrouwe onderregtinge van de generaal bass, of bassus continuus . . .* [*Rism* B/VI/1, p. 445.] Amsterdam: G. F. Witvogel, 1741 [SMLMS.]; Amsterdam: J. Covens junior, 1751 [LCPS: K-007f.].

T ● Zubrilov, I., trans. *Vernoe nastavlenie v sochinenii general'basa . . .* [*Rism* B/VI/2, p. 996.] Moscow: v Universitetskoi tipografii u V. Okorokova, 1791.

S ● Facsimile of the 1737 edition. Hildesheim: Georg Olms, 1979.

S ● Facsimile of the 1743 edition. DfMMF, no. 9. Laaber: Laaber-Verlag, 1980.

S ● Hobohm, Wolf, ed. Facsimile of the 1737 edition. Michaelstein: Kultur- und Forschungsstätte Michaelstein, [1985].

LITERATURE:

Haase, Hans. "Kellner, David." In *MGG* (1949-68). Bibliog.

● ● ● Buelow, George J. "Kellner, David." In *NGrove* (1980).

See also ADLUNG: (1758); FÉTIS: (1833-44); HEINICHEN: (1728):Buelow (1961/. . ./1986); RAMEAU: Pischner (1961/. . ./1967); RIEMANN: (1898); SCHRÖTER: (1772); LITERATURE SUPPLEMENT: **Arnold (1931/. . ./1965)**; Auhagen (1982/1983); Babitz (1967/1969); Becker (1836-39/1964); Bircher (1970); Carpenter (1988); Donington (1963/. . ./1974); Dreyfus (1987); Duckles (1970); Eitner (1900-1904/1959-60); Forkel (1792/1962); Frobenius ["Isotonos"] (1972-), ["Vollstimmig"] (1972-); Gerber (1790-92/1977), (1812-14/1966); Gurlitt (1954/1966); Hammel (1977-78); **Lester (1989)**; McQuere (1983); Nelson (1984); Oberdoerffer (1949-68), (1967); Reilly (1984-85); **Ritzel (1967/1968)**; Rothgeb (1968); Sheldon (1982); Subirá (1947/. . ./1958); Ulrich (1931/1932); Vogel (1955/1954); Werts (1983); Williams, P. (1970); Wirth (1966).

JOHANNES KEPLER

[1571 – 1630]

The early seventeenth century was a time of diverse scientific speculations relating to music. FLUDD's macrocosmic and microcosmic universes provide a whimsical contrast to the rigors of mathematics found in works by MERSENNE, among others. Johannes Kepler mixed the ancient notion of a harmony of the spheres with empirical data and mathematical precision to create a view of planetary behavior which powerfully affected science but had little impact upon musical thought. Kepler set out, in his *Prodromus dissertationum cosmographicarum, continens mysterium cosmographicum* (1596), to prove that the music of the spheres actually existed but was inaudible due to lack of air in the heavens. To generate evidence he studied the characteristics of the planetary orbits around the sun. Through his decades of observation and calculation, he developed the modern science of astronomy almost as a byproduct of his doomed astrological quest.

Though his preoccupation with cosmic harmony emerges in much of his writing, it is the *Harmonices mundi libri V* (1619) which best reveals his mature conception. The first four books of this work contain materials—both scientific and musical—which are useful as a prelude to the description of cosmic harmony in the fifth book (from which scientists extracted his famous Third Law of Planetary Motion while avoiding as much as possible its astrological context). Kepler measured the speed of the six known planets at the points on their elliptical orbits closest to the sun (the maximum speed) and farthest from the sun (the minimum speed). These values were compared against one other, creating numerous possibilities for proportions among the planets. Fortunately for Kepler, these numbers produced a variety of consonant intervals. For example, Saturn's lowest note forms a minor third against Jupiter's lowest note. In general, the closer the planet is to the sun, the higher are its pitches; the more variable its speed, the greater the range of pitches possible between its lowest and highest notes. Earth, one of the more stable planets, fluctuates by only half a step during the year. Obviously, rarely would the planets be so aligned that the combination of all six pitches would create a consonant harmony. Kepler speculated that the moment of the Creation may have been the only time when this potential for harmonic beauty had been realized.

In a separate line of inquiry Kepler explored the question of what distinguishes musical consonance from dissonance. Unsatisfied with ZARLINO's numerology, he made a somewhat forced derivation of consonances by positioning geometrical figures (only those that could be created by compass and ruler) on the circumferences of circles. Such a triangle would divide the circle into three equal arcs, giving the ratios 1:2, 1:3, and 2:3. Unfortunately he required the octagon's 5:8 ratio to generate the minor sixth, thereby inviting what would seem equally logical, the unacceptable ratios 1:7 and 7:8.

Kepler is closer in spirit to the views of FLUDD — whose works, on account of their dubious scientific precision, he publicly opposed both in an Appendix to the *Harmonices mundi libri V* and in his later *Apologia* (1621) — than to those of MERSENNE, who established a new front in the conquest of musical understanding with his revelations on the physics of sound. The scientific precision and dependence upon empirical data inherent in Kepler's works eventually emerged as such overpowering forces that scientists summarily dismissed his accompanying poetical, sometimes nonsensical notions, despite their central position within his *œuvre*. One senses that the considerable attention his musical thought has received is proportionate to his standing as a major figure in the history of science rather than to his importance in the history of music theory.

Correspondence

Mss., 1590-1630.

T ● Caspar, Max, and von Dyck, Walther, trans. and ed. *Johannes Kepler in seinen Briefen.* 2 vols. Munich and Berlin: R. Oldenbourg, 1930.

S ● See Collected Works: von Dyck et al. (1937-):Vols. 13-18, below.

T ● Baumgardt, Carola, trans. *Johannes Kepler: Life and Letters.* Introduction by Albert Einstein. New York: Philosophical Library, 1951.

> Reviews in *BJPS* 3/2 (1952-53):272-73 (G. J. Whitrow), *Phil* 27/100 (1952):92-93 (Stephen Toulmin), and *PPR* 12/3 (1951-52):455-56 (Louis O. Kattsoff).

Prodromus dissertationum cosmographicarum, continens mysterium cosmographicum . . .

Tübingen: Georgius Gruppenbachius, 1596.

> Published in conjunction with his *Apologia* (1622), below:

Frankfurt: Godefredus Tampachius (Erasmus Kempfer), 1621.

S ● See Collected Works: Frisch (1858-71/1971-): Vol. 1, below.

T ● Bryk, Otto J., trans. and ed. *Die Zusammenklänge der Welten . . .* KNwT. Jena: Eugen Diederichs, 1918.

T ● Caspar, Max, trans. and ed. *Mysterium cosmographicum: Das Weltgeheimnis.* Augsburg: Benno Filser, 1923; reprint edition (as *Das Weltgeheimnis: Mysterium cosmographicum*), Munich and Berlin: R. Oldenbourg, 1936.

S ● See Collected Works: von Dyck et al. (1937):Vols. 1 and 8, below.

T ● Skrzypczak, Mirosława, and Zakrzewska-Gebka, Elżbieta, trans. *Tajemnica kosmosu.* Zródła do dziejów nauki i techniki, no. 15. Gdańsk: Zakład Narodowy im. Ossolińskich [Oddz. w Gdańsk] 1972.

ST ● Duncan, Alistair M., trans. *Mysterium cosmographicum: The Secret of the Universe.* Facsimile of the 1621 edition and English translation. Introduction and commentary by Eric J. Aiton. Preface by I. Bernard Cohen. BECPS, ser. 3. New York: Abaris Books, 1981. Bibliog.

> Reviews in *AS* 39/3 (1982):323-25 (Aug. Ziggelaar), *BJHS* 17/55 (1984):108-9 (N. Jardine), *Centaurus* 26/2-3 (1982):221-22 (K. P. Moesgaard), *Choice* 19/3 (1981-82):394, and *STel* 65/1 (1983):39 (Owen Gingerich).

Harmonices mundi libri V . . . [Rism B/VI/1, p. 446.]

Linz: Godofredus Tampachius (Joannes Plancus), 1619. [LCPS: K-009.]

S ● See Collected Works: Frisch (1858-71/1971-): Vol. 5, below.

T ● See (1596):Bryk (1918), above.

T ● Harburger, Walter, trans. and ed. *Johannes Keplers kosmische Harmonie.* DBdM. Leipzig: Insel-Verlag, 1925.

T ● Trede, Hilmar, trans. and ed. *Harmonice mundi Buch III.* SBHF, no. 1. Ostermundigen: 1936.

S ● See Collected Works: von Dyck et al. (1937-): Vol. 6, below.

T ● Caspar, Max, trans. and ed. *Harmonice mundi: Weltharmonik.* Munich and Berlin: R. Oldenbourg, 1939; reprint edition, Munich and Darmstadt: R. Oldenbourg (Wissenschaftliche Buchgesellschaft), 1967.

T ● Wallis, Charles Glenn, trans. *The Harmonies of the World.* GBWW, no. 16. Chicago, London, & Toronto: Encyclopaedia Britannica, 1952.

> A translation of Book 5 of Kepler's work.

S ● Facsimile edition. Brussels: Culture et civilisation, 1968.

S ● Facsimile edition. BmB, ser. 2, no. 58. Bologna: Forni, [1969].

T ● See Godwin (1986).

T ● See **Katz and Dahlhaus (1987-)**:Vol. 1.

Pro suo opere harmonices mundi apologia adversus demonstrationem analyticam . . . Roberti de Fluctibus . . . [*Rism* B/VI/1, p. 446.]

A response to FLUDD: [*Veritas*] (1621).

Frankfurt: Godefredus Tempachius, 1622.

> Published in conjunction with the 1621 edition of his *Prodromus* (1596):Vol. 5, above.

S ● See Collected Works: Frisch (1858-71/1971-): Vol. 5, below.

S ● See Collected Works: von Dyck et al. (1937-): Vol. 6, below.

More comprehensive listings of Kepler's works are found in Caspar (1936/1968), below, and in Haase (1949-68), below.

COLLECTED WORKS EDITIONS:

Frisch, Christian, ed. *Joannis Kepleri Astronomi: Opera omnia.* Frankfurt and Erlangen: Heyder & Zimmer, 1858-71; reprint edition, Hildesheim: Gerstenberg, 1971- .

von Dyck, Walther; Caspar, Max; Hammer, Franz; and List, Martha, eds. *Johannes Kepler: Gesammelte Werke.* Munich: C. H. Beck, 1937- .

LITERATURE:

Pfaff, [J. W.]. "Über Keplers Weltharmonie." *JCP* 10 (1814):36-43.

Apelt, Ernst Friedrich. *Johann Kepler's astronomische Weltansicht.* Leipzig: T. O. Weigel, 1849.

Thimus, Albert, Freiherr von. *Die harmonicale Symbolik des Alterthums.* 2 vols. Cologne: M. Du Mont-Schauberg, 1868-76; reprint edition [with Hasenclever (1870), below], Hildesheim: Georg Olms, 1972.

Hasenclever, Richard. *Die Grundzüge der esoterischen Harmonik des Alterthums.* Cologne: M. Du Mont-Schauberg, 1870; reprint edition, see Thimus (1868-76), above.

Förster, Wilhelm. "Johann Kepler und die Harmonie der Sphären." Berlin: F. Dümmler, 1862; reprint edition

(in his *Sammlung wissenschaftlicher Vorträge*, pp. 30-60), Berlin: Ferd. Dümmler, 1876.

Schick, Joseph. "Keplers Mysterium Cosmographicum." In *Sammler* 94/13-15 (1925).

Wehrli, Werner. "Das musiktheoretische System Johannes Keplers (1571–1630) im Lichte der Weltanschauung des Forschers." *SMz* 69/7 (1929):213-21.

Speiser, Andreas. "Kepler und die Lehre von der Weltharmonie." In his *Die mathematische Denkweise*, pp. 110-35. Zürich: Rascher, 1932; 2nd edition (Wk, no. 1), Basel: Birkhäuser, 1945; 3rd edition, 1952.

Caspar, Max. *Johannes Keplers wissenschaftliche und philosophische Stellung.* SC, no. 13. Munich, Berlin, and Zürich: R. Oldenbourg, 1935.

Caspar, Max, ed. *Bibliographia Kepleriana: Ein Führer durch das gedruckte Schrifttum von Johannes Kepler.* Munich: C. H. Beck, 1936; 2nd edition (edited by Martha List), Munich, 1968. Bibliog.

> An update appears in Beer and Beer (1975), below. Reviews in *Isis* 60/4 (1969):567-68 (Owen Gingerich) and *Lychnos 1969/70* (1971):349 (K.-G. Hagstroem).

Trunz, Erich. "Kepler und die Prager Musik." *BMäh* 3 (1942):220-21.

Warrain, Francis. *Essai sur l'Harmonices mundi: Ou musique du monde de Johann Kepler.* 2 vols. Asi, nos. 912-13. Paris: Hermann, 1942.

Knöfel, E. "Johann Keplers philosophische Mathematik als Grundlage seines Weltbildes." Ph.D. dissertation, The University of Hamburg, 1945.

Kayser, Hans. *Akróasis: Die Lehre von der Harmonik der Welt.* Basil: Benno Schwabe, 1946; Stuttgart: G. Hatje, 1947; Basel and Stuttgart: Schwabe, 1964. Bibliog.

Kayser, Hans. "Johannes Kepler und die Sphärenharmonie." *SR* 46/7-8 (1946-47):545-53.

Caspar, Max. *Johannes Kepler.* Stuttgart: W. Kohlhammer, [1948]; 2nd edition, [1950]; English translation (translated and edited by C. Doris Hellman, LSL, no. 36), London and New York: Abelard-Schuman, [1959].

> Reviews in *AHR* 66/1 (1960-61):150 (Edward Rosen), *CCen* 77/41 (1960):1187, *GLL* 3/3 (1949-50):239, *Isis* 41/2 [124] (1950):216-19 (C. Doris Hellman), *Listener* 63/1609 (1960):185-86 (Harold Spencer Jones), *LJ* 85/8 (1960):1571 (George Basalla), *RN* 13/4 (1960):330-32 (S. K. Heninger, Jr.), *ScAm* 203/2 (1960):173-76 (Gerald Holton), *Science* 131/3408 (1960):1203 (William D. Stahlman), and *TLS* 59/3026 (1960):132.

Haase, Rudolf. "Kepler, Johannes." In *MGG* (1949-68). Bibliog.

Koch, Walter Albert. *Aspektenlehre nach Johannes Kepler: Die Formsymbolik von Ton, Zahl und Aspekt*. ASh. Hamburg: [Kosmobiosophische Gesellschaft], 1950.

Pauli, Wolfgang. "Der Einflusz archetypischer Vorstellungen auf die Bildung naturwissenschaftlicher Theorien bei Kepler." In *Naturerklärung und Psyche*, by Carl Gustav Jung and Wolfgang Pauli, pp. 109-94. SJIZ, no. 4. Zürich: 1952; English version (as "The Influence of Archetypal Ideas on the Scientific Theories of Kepler," in *The Interpretation of Nature and the Psyche*, translated by Priscilla Manton Kramer Silz, pp. 147-240; BS, no. 51 [48]), New York: Pantheon; London: Routledge & Kegan Paul, 1955.

Wörner, Karl H. "Hindemith, Kepler und die Zahl." *Melos* 22/11 (1955):319-21.

Holton, Gerald. "Johannes Kepler's Universe: Its Physics and Metaphysics." *AJPh* 24/5 (1956):340-51.

Bayerische Akademie der Schönen Künste, ed. *Die Harmonie der Welt: Kepler, Hindemith. Zur Uraufführung der Oper am 11. August 1957 in München.* Munich: Bayerische Akademie der Schönen Künste (Kastner & Callwey), 1957.

Haase, Rudolf. *Die harmonikale Bedeutung der Zahl Fünf.* VIHF, no. 3. Cologne: Eckhardt, 1958.

Koestler, Arthur. *Sleepwalkers: A History of Man's Changing Vision of the Universe.* Introduction by Herbert Butterfield. London: Hutchinson, 1959; reprint edition, New York: Macmillan, 1968.

> Reviews in *BW* 360 (1969):6 (H. E. F. Donohue), *Isis* 50 (1959):255-60 (Giorgio de Santillana and Stillman Drake), *JPhil* 59/18 (1962):500-503 (Stephen Toulmin), *LM* 6/4 (1959):73-75 (Colin Wilson), *Mind* NS69/274 (1960):281 (R. Harré), *Spectator* 202/6813 (1959):125 (Geoffrey Barraclough), and *TC* 165/985 (1959):296-98 (J. G. Weightman).

Koyré, Alexandre. *La révolution astronomique* . . . Hp, no. 3. Paris: Hermann, 1961; English translation (as *The Astronomical Revolution* . . ., translated by R. E. W. Maddison), Paris: Hermann; London: Methuen; Ithaca, N.Y.: Cornell University Press, [1973]. Bibliog.

> Reviews in *AS* 16/4 (1960):271 (A. Armitage), *BJHS* 7/3 [27] (1974):293-94 (Eric G. Forbes), *Choice* 11/2 (1974-75):278, *Edeavour* 33/118 (1974):52 (J. W. Herivel), *Isis* 53/4 [174] (1962):517-19 (Edward Rosen), *JHA* 5/3 [14] (1974):201-3 (Edward Rosen), *JRASC* 70/1 [538] (1976):45-47 (J. F. Heard), *Nature* 249/5460 (1974):865-66 (Eric G. Forbes), *SBF* 10/2 (1974-75):115, *STel* 47/3 (1974):182-83 (Edward Rosen), and *TLS* 72/3730 (1973):994.

Haase, Rudolf. "Keplers Weltharmonik und das naturwissenschaftliche Denken." In *Antaios* 5/3 (1963-64):225-36; reprinted in *ZfGf* 12 (1968). Bibliog.

Bindel, Ernst. *Harmonien im Reiche der Geometrie in Anlehnung an Keplers "Weltharmonik".* Stuttgart: Verlag Freies Geistesleben, 1964.

Gerlach, Walther, and List, Martha. *Johannes Kepler: Leben und Werk.* Munich: Piper, 1966; Ehrenwirth, 1971.

> Reviews in *Isis* 63/216 (1972):101-3 (C. Doris Hellman), *MathR* 41/4 (1971):945 (J. A. Lohne), *MpS* 20/1 (1973):137-40 (Fritz Krafft), *TG* 37/4 (1970):360-61 (Menso Folkerts), and *ZfMG* 215/1 (1971):41 (J. E. Hofmann).

Nádor, Georg. "Die heuristische Rolle des Harmoniebegriffs bei Kepler." *Sgen* 19/9 (1966):555-58.

● ● ● Werner, Eric. "The Last Pythagorean Musician: Johannes Kepler." In *ReeseFs* (1966/1978):867-82. Bibliog.

Haase, Rudolf. "Gehörte Normen: Eine erkenntnistheoretische Studie." *Me* 21/5 (1967-68):213-18. [*Rilm* 68-4218.]

Haase, Rudolf. *Kaysers Harmonik in der Literatur der Jahre 1950 bis 1964.* OSGM. Düsseldorf: Verlag der Gesellschaft zur Förderung der systematischen Musikwissenschaft, 1967.

> Reviews in *Me* 21/5 (1967-68):253-54 (Eugen Banauch), *Mf* 22/3 (1969):403-4 (Carl Dahlhaus), *Musica* 24/1 (1970):66-67, *Melos/NZfM* 131/2 (1970):95-96 (Erich F. W. Altwein), and *ÖM* 22/11 (1967):686 (Walter Szmolyan).

Walker, David Pickering. "Kepler's Celestial Music." *JWCI* 30 (1967):228-50; reprinted in Walker (1978). Bibliog. [*Rilm* 67-1530.]

Haase, Rudolf. *Hans Kayser: Ein Leben für die Harmonik der Welt.* Basel and Stuttgart: Schwabe, 1968.

> Reviews in *Me* 25/1 (1971-72):46-47 (Eugen Banauch), *Musica* 23:4 (1969):395 (Gerhard Schuhmacher), and *ÖM* 24/3 (1969):193-94 (Walter Szmolyan).

Haase, Rudolf. "Harmonikale Grundlagenforschung: Eine neue Wissenschaft." *Me* 22/3-4 (1968-69):120-23, 164-68; reprinted in Haase [*Aufsätze*] (1974), below. [*Rilm* 69-2930.]

Kayser, Hans. "Johannes Kepler und seine Weltharmonik." In *Die Harmonie der Welt*, edited by Rudolf Haase, pp. 20-25. BhG, no. 1. Vienna: Elisabeth Lafite, 1968. [*Rilm* 69-2939.]

> Reviews in *Me* 25/1 (1971-72):46-47 (Eugen Banauch), *Musica* 24/1 (1970):66-67 (Anton Würze), and *ÖM* 24/2 (1969):111 (Walter Szmolyan).

Haase, Rudolf. "350 Jahre Weltharmonik: Dem Gedächtnis Johannes Kepler." *Musica* 23/1 (1969):44. [*Rilm* 69-4968.]

Haase, Rudolf. "Keplers harmonikale Denkweise." *Me* 23/2 (1969-70):53-56. [*Rilm* 69-4967.]

Atteln, Horst. "Das Verhältnis Musik-Mathematik bei Johannes Kepler: Ein Beitrag zur Musiktheorie des frühen 17. Jahrhunderts." Ph.D. dissertation, The University of Erlangen-Nürnberg, 1970 (1971). [*Rilm* 70-3104.]

Gingerich, Owen. "Kepler, Johannes." In *DSB* (1970-80). Bibliog.

Dickreiter, Michael. "Dur und Moll in Keplers Musiktheorie: Ein Beitrag zur Theorie der Dur-Moll-Tonalität." In Maar (1971):41-50, below. Bibliog. [*Rilm* 73-2583.]

Dickreiter, Michael. "Der Musiktheoretiker Johannes Kepler." Ph.D. dissertation, The University of Heidelberg, 1971; published edition (NHSzMw, no. 5), Bern and Munich: Francke, 1973. Bibliog. [*Rilm* 75-2610.]

> Reviews in *Isis* 67/236 (1976):126-27 (Rudolf Haase), *Janus* 61 (1974):222-23 (H. A. M. Snelders), *Melos/NZfM* 1/6 (1975):509-10 (Carl Dahlhaus), *Mf* 30/4 (1977):533-34 (Albrecht Riethmüller), *Muh* 25/8 (1974):406 (F. W. D.), *ÖM* 29/3 (1974):163-64 (Rudolf Haase), *Rdm* 60/1-2 (1974):227-28 (Denise Launay), and *Ridm* 8/2 (1973):349-54 (Giovanni Morelli).

Gerlach, Walther, and List, Martha, eds. *Johannes Kepler . . .: Dokumente zu Lebenszeit und Lebenswerk.* Munich: Ehrenwirth, 1971.

> Reviews in *AVZ* 78/12 (1971):492-93 (H. Draheim), *Isis* 63 (1972):101-3 (C. Doris Hellman), *JHA* 5/2 [13] (1974):133-34 (Zdeněk Horský), *MathR* 41/4 (1971):945 (J. A. Lohne), *MpS* 20/1 (1973):137-40 (Fritz Krafft), *SHZ* 22/4 (1971):250-51 (Friedrich Seck), and *ZfMG* 215/1 (1971):41 (J. E. Hofmann).

Haase, Rudolf. "Fortsetzungen der Keplerschen Weltharmonik." In Maar (1971):61-72, below; reprinted in Haase [*Aufsätze*] (1974), below. Bibliog. [*Rilm* 73-2728.]

Haase, Rudolf. "Johannes Keplers wahre Bedeutung." *Kunstjahrbuch der Stadt Linz 1970* (1971):9-21. [*Rilm* 71-4610.]

Haase, Rudolf. "Keplers Planetenharmonien." In *Anton Bruckner: Zum 75. Todestag*, pp. 33-38. Linz: Brucknerbund für Oberösterreich, 1971. [*Rilm* 76-7715.]

Haase, Rudolf. "Marginalien zur 3. Keplerschen Gesetz." In *Kepler Festschrift 1971: Zur Erinnerung an seinen Geburtstag vor 400 Jahren*, edited by Ekkehard Preuß, pp. 159-65. AAR, no. 32. Regensburg: Naturwissenschaftlicher Verein Regensburg e. V. (Mittelbayerische Druckerei- und Verlags-Gesellschaft), 1971; reprinted in Haase [*Aufsätze*] (1974), below. [*Rilm* 74-4112.]

Klein, Ulrich. "Johannes Keplers Bemühungen um die Harmonieschriften des Ptolemaios und Porphyrios." In Maar (1971):51-60, below. Bibliog.

Maar, Gerold, ed. *Johannes Kepler, Werk und Leistung: Ausstellung im Steinernen Saal des Linzer Landhauses, 19. Juni bis 29. August 1971.* KOöL, no. 74; KSL, no. 9. Linz: Gutenberg, 1971. [*Rilm* 73-2728.]

Haase, Rudolf. "Kepler und der Gedanke der Weltharmonie." *JoM* 117 (1972):213-22. [*Rilm* 73-2730.]

Haase, Rudolf. "Zur 400. Wiederkehr des Geburtstages von Johannes Kepler." *ÖM* 27/2 (1972):88-90. [*Rilm* 73-2731.]

Hannas, Ruth. "Johannes Kepler's Excursion into Political Proportions." *Diapason* 63/5 [= 749] (1972):8-9, 12, 19. [*Rilm* 72-1185.]

Maasih, Camelia. "Barresihaje Elmije dar Boreje Harmoniehoje Gahoni." *Magnus* 136 (1972):76-78. [*Rilm* 73-2735.]

Haase, Rudolf. "Keplers Weltharmonik in Vergangenheit, Gegenwart und Zukunft." *SA* 57/1 (1973):41-70. [*Rilm* 73-4307].

Haase, Rudolf. *Aufsätze zur harmonikalen Naturphilosophie.* Graz: Akademische Druck- und Verlagsanstalt, 1974. [*Rilm* 74-1694.]

> Reviews in *Me* 28/3 (1974-75):143, *ÖM* 31/4-5 (1976):256 (Walter Szmolyan), and *SK* 23/1 (1975-76):43 (Hans Haselböck).

Haase, Rudolf. "Keplers drittes Plantengesetz und seine Weltharmonik." *ZfGf* 18/2 (1974):88-92. [*Rilm* 76-16907.]

Beer, Arthur, and Beer, Peter, eds. *Kepler, Four Hundred Years: Proceedings of Conferences Held in Honour of Johannes Kepler.* [*Vistas in Astronomy* 18 (1975).] Oxford: Pergamon Press, 1975. Bibliog.

> Section Nine (pp. 471-539) is devoted to "Celestial Harmonie" and incorporates contributions by Michael W. Ovenden, D. G. King-Hele, Rudolf Haase, and Giorgio Abetti. There is also a "Bibliographia Kepleriana: 1967-1975" by Martha List, pp. 955-1012. Reviews in *Choice* 13/4 (1976-77):542, *JHA* 7/1 [18] (1976):57-61 (D. T. Whiteside), *JRASC* 70/1 [538] (1976):44-45 (Helen Sawyer Hogg), *NR* 29/4 (1976):136-37 (Schmedler), *Observatory* 96/1014 (1976):209-11 (David W. Dewhirst), *STel* 52/2 (1976):125-27 (I. Bernard Cohen), and *SW* 15/9 (1976):296 (H. Elsässer).

Schedl, Claus. "Die logotechnische Struktur des Psalmes VIII und Keplers Weltharmonik." In *Johannes Kepler: 1571-1971: Gedenkschrift der Universität Graz*, edited by Paul Urban and Berthold Sutter, pp. 105-23. Graz: Leykam-Verlag, 1975.

Haase, Rudolf. "Johannes Keplers Weltharmonik." *WW* 29/3-4 (1976):157-67. [*Rilm* 77-3922.]

Aiton, Eric. "Johannes Kepler and the *Mysterium cosmographicum*." *SA* 61/2 (1977):173-94.

Haase, Rudolf. "Keplers zweifache Weltharmonik." *GW* 26/2 (1977):89-105. [*Rilm* 77-3923.]

Rogers, John, and Ruff, Willie. "Kepler's Harmony of the World: A Realization for the Ear." *AmSc* 67/3 (1979):286-92.

Jeans, Susi. "Kepler, Johannes." In *NGrove* (1980). Bibliog.

Haase, Rudolf. "Von Keplers 'Weltharmonik' zu Hindemiths 'Harmonie der Welt'." *ÖM* 35/7-8 (1980):380-85.

Wahsner, Renate. "Weltharmonie und Naturgesetz: Zur wissenschaftstheoretischen und wissenschaftshistorischen Bedeutung der Keplerschen Harmonielehre." *DZP* 29/5 (1981):531-45. Bibliog.

Dickreiter, Michael. "Der Musiktheoretiker Johannes Kepler." In *Kepler-Symposion 1980* (1982):19-28. [*Rilm* 82-1789.]

Haase, Rudolf. "Die Bedeutung von Analogie und Finalität für Kepler und für die Gegenwart." In *Kepler-Symposion 1980* (1982):37-44. [*Rilm* 82-1792.]

Hamel, Peter Michael. "Harmonikales Denken." *HindJb* 10 (1982):32-42. [*Rilm* 82-6137.]

Rubeli, Alfred. "Johannes Keplers Harmonik in Paul Hindemiths Oper *Die Harmonie der Welt*." In *Kepler-Symposion 1980* (1982):107-16. [*Rilm* 82-892.]

Haase, Rudolf, and Haase, Ursula. *Literatur zur harmonikalen Grundlagenforschung, V.* Vienna: Braumüller, 1983. [*Rilm* 83-131.]

Field, J. V. *Kepler's Geometrical Cosmology*. Chicago: The University of Chicago Press, 1988.

See also CALVISIUS: Pietzsch (1930-31); Dahlhaus (1956); DESCARTES: (1619-50):Adam and Gérard (1936-63); FÉTIS: (1833-44); FLUDD: [*Veritas*] (1621); (1622); Craven (1902/n.d.); Debus (1965/66); Ammann (1967), (1968); KIRCHER: (1650); LEIBNIZ: Haase (1963); MERSENNE: (1617-48); (1627); (1636-37); Lenoble (1943); Walker (1976); Beaulieu (1982); VOGLER: [*Tonwissenschaft*] (1776):*AmZ* (1818); WALTHER: (1732); LITERATURE SUPPLEMENT: Allen ["Baroque"] (1939), ["Philosophies"] (1939); Archibald (1924); **Barbour (1951/. ./1972)**; Barford (1975); Becker (1836-39/1964); Bell et al. (1980); Blankenburg ["Harmonie"] (1959); Boomgaarden (1985/1987); Buelow (1972); Bukofzer (1947); Burney (1776-89/. ./1957); Cazden (1948), (1980); Cohen (1981), ● ● ● Cohen (1984); Crombie (1969); **Dahlhaus et al. (1987)**; Dammann (1958/1967); Deutsch (1980); Dostrovsky (1969); Drake (1970); Dupont (1933/. . ./1986); Eitner (1900-1904/1959-60); Gerber (1790-92/1977); Godwin (1987); Green (1969); Haase (1963), (1969), (1972), (1976), (1986); Handschin (1948); Harburger (1928-29); Hartmann (1980); Hawkins (1776/. . ./1969); Heckmann (1953); Hüschen (1949-68); **Hunt (1978)**; Jacobi (1957-60/1971); **Kassler (1979)**, (1982); Kassler and Oldroyd (1983); Katz (1985); Kayser (1950); Kelletat [*Temperatur*] (1960), (1966); Koenigsberger (1979); Lange (1899-1900); **Lindley (1982)**, **(1984)**; Lippman (1986); Lowinsky (1946/1967); Meer (1988); Miller and Cohen (1987); Müller (1976); Pole (1879/. . ./1924); Rohwer (1949-68); Schäfke (1934); Schavernoch (1981); **Seidel and Cooper (1986)**; Subirá (1947/. . ./1958); Taddie (1984); Truesdell (1960); Tuksar (1978/1980); Vauclain (1978); Vogel (1955/1954); **Walker (1976)**, **(1978)**; Weber (1976); Wienpahl (1953); Wightman (1972); Winckel (1949-68); Yates (1964); **Zaminer (1985)**; Zenck (1942); Zimmermann (1976).

ATHANASIUS KIRCHER

[1601—1680]

Among seventeenth-century writers on music, none possessed quite the breadth of erudition demonstrated by Athanasius Kircher, a German priest who spent most of his life teaching and writing in Rome. Twentieth-century minds may easily find Kircher's numerous works disturbing: separating scientific observation from fairy tale, established fact from conjecture, informed discussion from mystical speculation is not always as straightforward as we might wish. The plethora of full-page and fold-out illustrations displaying everything from mythological creatures and the compartments of Noah's ark to birdsongs in staff notation and a depiction of why the Tower of Babel could not have reached the moon further confound our expectations, despite their considerable fascination. Nevertheless, Kircher was among the most respected linguists and Egyptologists of his time, and his massive books were widely circulated and were highly regarded long after his death.

None of his treatises has stood the test of time better than *Musurgia universalis* (1650), an enormous volume replete with multifarious information. A familiarity with ZARLINO's writings is apparent in Kircher's treatment of counterpoint. The affections are discussed, as is the relationship between music and rhetoric. Plates showing keyboards outfitted with an abundance of added keys bring the numerical ponderings he offered regarding tuning and temperament into the sphere of practical musicmaking. The propagation of sound is given a prominent position: numerous illustrations involving room acoustics, echoes, and the construction of a megaphone reveal the workings of a fertile imagination, if not a perfect understanding of the subject. These acoustical materials were augmented and reissued as *Phonurgia nova* in 1673 to prove that he had invented the megaphone, instead of a Sir Samuel Morland, who also laid claim to that distinction. Despite his sometimes muddled, sometimes fanciful pronouncements, his works served as comprehensive and, to be sure, entertaining sourcebooks in an era which had yet to see this sort of musical knowledge assembled in dictionary format.

Correspondence

S ● See Langenmantel (1684/1901), below.

S ● See Scharlau (1969), below.

Magnes sive de arte magnetica . . . [*Rism* B/VI/1, p. 448.]

> Rome: Ludovico Grignani (Hermann Scheus), 1641. [SMLMS.]
> Cologne: Iodocus Kalcoven, 1643. Revised version. [LCPS: K-010.]
> Rome: Vitale Mascardi (Blasius Deversin and Zanobio Masotti), 1654.

Ars magna lucis et umbrae . . .

> Rome: Hermann Scheus (Ludovico Grignani), 1646.
> Amsterdam: apud Joannem Janssonium à Waesberge, 1671.

Musurgia universalis sive ars magna consoni et dissoni . . . [*Rism* B/VI/1, p. 449.]

> Rome: eredi di Francesco Corbelletti, 1650. Vol. 1. [LCPS: K-011a. HoM: 807. SMLMS. IDC.]
> Rome: Ludovico Grignani, 1650. Vol. 2. [LCPS: K-011a. HoM: 807. SMLMS. IDC.]
>
>> Occasional references to editions of 1654, 1662, and 1690 appear in the literature, probably in error.

T ● Hirsch, Andreas, trans. *Germaniae redonatus, sive artis magnae de consono et dissona ars minor: Das ist, Philosophischer Extract und Auszug aus . . . Musurgia universali . . .* Schwäbisch Hall: Hans Reinhard Laidigen & Johann Christoph Gräter, 1662. [*Rism* B/VI/1, pp. 449-50. LCPS: K-011b.]

T ● Crane, Frederick Baron. "Athanasius Kircher, *Musurgia universalis* (Rome, 1650): The Section on Musical Instruments." M.A. thesis, The University of Iowa, 1956. [SMLMS.]

S ● Sharlau, Ulf, ed. Facsimile edition. Hildesheim: Georg Olms, 1970.

T ● See Godwin (1986).

T ● See **Katz and Dahlhaus (1987-)**:Vol. 3.

S ● Goldhan, Wolfgang, ed. Facsimile edition. Leipzig: Zentralantiquariat der DDR, 1988.

Oedipus aegyptiacus . . .

> Rome: Vitale Mascardi, 1652-54. 3 vols.

Itinerarium exstaticum quo mundi . . . siderumque . . . natura, vires, proprietates, singulorumque compositio et structura explorata

> Rome: 1656.
>
>> As *Iter exstaticum coeleste . . .*, edited by Gaspar Schott:
>
> Würzburg: sumptibus Joh. Andr. & Wolffg. Jun. Endterorum haeredibus, 1660.
> Würzburg: sumptibus Johannis Andreae Endteri & Wolfgangi junioris haeredum, 1671.

Organum mathematicum . . . quo per paucas ac facillimè parabiles tabellas . . . plerasque mathematicae disciplinae, modo novo ac facili traduntur

> Würzburg: sumptibus Johannis Andreae Endteri & Wolfgang jun. haeredum (J. Hertz), 1668. With Gaspar Schott.
>
>> A second edition appeared in 1670.

Ars magna sciendi, . . . qua . . . per artificosum combinationum contextum de omni re . . . disputari, omniumque summaria quaedam cognitione comparari potest

> Amsterdam: apud J. Janssonium à Waesberge, 1669.

"Vita admodum reverendi P. Athanasii Kircher SJ viri toto orbe celebratissimi"

> Ms., [ca. 1669].

S ● See Langenmantel (1681/1901), below.

Phonurgia nova siva conjugium mechanico-physicum artis et naturae paranympha phonosophia concinnatum . . . [*Rism* B/VI/1, pp. 450-51.]

> Kempten: Rudolph Dreherr, 1673. [LCPS: K-012a. HoM: 808.]

T ● Nislen, Tobias [Carione, Agatho], trans. *Neue Hall- und Thon-Kunst . . .* Nördlingen: Friedrich Schultes (Ellwangen: Arnold Heyl), 1684; facsimile edition (edited by Ulf Scharlau), Hanover: Th. Schäfer, 1983. [LCPS: K-012b.]

>> Reviews in *BrB* 48 (1984):93-94 (Edward H. Tarr), *Mi* 33/1 (1984):220, *Orch* 32/9 (1984):786 (Kurt Janetzky), and *Tibia* 8/3 (1983):454 (Reinhold Quandt).

S ● Facsimile edition. MMMLF, ser. 2, no. 44. New York: Broude Brothers, 1966.

> Reviews in *Consort* 27 (1971):64 (Lillian M. Ruff), *ML* 48/4 (1967):371-73 (Jack A. Westrup), and *MT* 108/1498 (1967):1112 (Charles Cudworth).

Tariffa Kircheriana sive Mensa Pythagorica expansa . . .

> Rome: typis & sumptibus Nicolai Angeli Tinassij, 1679.

Physiologia Kircheriana experimentalis, qua summa argumentorum multitudine et varietate, naturalium rerum scientia per experimenta . . . musica . . . comprobatur atque stabilitur . . .

> Amsterdam: ex officinâ Janssonio-Waesbergiana, 1680. [LCPS: K-012c.]

See Sommervogel (1893), below, for a more comprehensive listing of Kircher's works, particularly those which do not relate to music.

LITERATURE:

Langenmantel, Hieronymus Ambrosius. *Fasciculus epistolarum adm. R. P. Athanasii Kircheri Soc. Jesu, viri in mathematicis et variorum idiomatum scientiis celebratissimi* . . . Augsburg: Vindelicorum, 1684; German translation in Seng, Nikolaus, *Selbstbiographie des P. Athanasius Kircher aus der Gesellschaft Jesu*, Fulda: Fuldaer Actiendruckerei, 1901.

Sommervogel, Carlos. "Kircher, Athanase." In *Bibliothèque de la Compagnie de Jésus*, edited by Carlos Sommervogel, vol. 4, cols. 1046-77. Brussels: Oscar Schepens; Paris: Alphonse Picard, 1893. Bibliog.

Scarlatti, Americo. "La Musurgia!" *MM* 59/2 (1904):67-72.

Kaul, Oskar. "Athanasius Kircher als Musikvelehrter." In *WürzburgFs* (1932):363-70.

Gutmann, Joseph. "Athanasius Kircher (1602-1680) und das Schöpfung- und Entwicklungsproblem." Ph.D. dissertation, The University of Würzburg, 1938; published edition, Fulda: Parzeller, 1938.

Stauder, Wilhelm. "Kircher, Athanasius." In *MGG* (1949-68). Bibliog.

Tutenberg, Fritz. "*Musurgia universalis*: Zum 350. Geburtstage des Athanasius Kircher." *ZfM* 113/5 (1952): 278-79.

Reilly, P. Conor. "Father Athanasius Kircher S. J.: Master of a Hundred Arts." *Studies* 44 (1955):457-68.

Scharlau, Ulf. "Athanasius Kircher (1601-1680) als Musikschriftsteller: Ein Beitrag zur Musikanschauung des Barock." Ph.D. dissertation, The University of Frankfurt am Main, 1969; published edition (ShMg,

no. 2), Marburg: Görich & Weiershäuser, 1969. Bibliog. [*Rilm* 69-949.]

> Review in *Nrmi* 4/5 (1970):945-50 (Gino Stefani).

Kangro, Hans. "Kircher, Athanasius." In *DSB* (1970-80). Bibliog.

Reilly, P. Conor. *Athanasius Kircher S. J.: Master of a Hundred Arts, 1602−1680*. SKir, no. 1. Wiesbaden and Rome: Edizioni del Mondo, 1974. Bibliog.

Scharlau, Ulf. "Athanasius Kircher (1601-1680), or Some Aspects of Acoustical Developments in the 17th Century." *Fam* 25/1 (1978):86-89.

● ● ● Godwin, Joscelyn. *Athanasius Kircher: A Renaissance Man and the Quest for Lost Knowledge*. London: Thames & Hudson; Boulder, Colo.: Shambhala (New York: Random House), 1979. Bibliog.

> Reviews in *BMag* 126/974 (1984):298 (Fred Brauen) and *BSel* 40/4 (1980-81):122 (Gerald J. Bobango).

Wessely, Othmar. "Athanasius Kircher: Zur 300. Wiederkehr seines Todestages." *Me* 33 (1979-80):147-52. [*Rilm* 80-512.]

● ● ● Buelow, George J. "Kircher, Athanasius." In *NGrove* (1980). Bibliog.

Brashovanova, L. "Novi danni za Yoan Kukuzel." *Bulmuz* 32/1 (1981):23-26.

Fletcher, John. "Athanasius Kircher and His *Musurgia universalis* (1650)." *Mus* 7 (1982):73-83. [*Rilm* 82-4525.]

Nichihara, Minoru. "A. Kircher ni okeru ongaku no renkinjutsu−ongaku no seisakugaku to Affekt, yoshiki no riron." *BTNU* 8 (1982):1-43.

Alexitch, Antonietta. "Musica, teologia e scienza nella *Musurgia universalis* di A. Kircher." *Nrmi* 18/2 (1984):182-90. Bibliog.

Tornifore, Tonino. "L'origine delle sinestesie: Mersenne, Kircher e le corrispondenze fra suoni e colori." *IRsi* 7 (1987):21-51.

See also BONTEMPI: (1695); FÉTIS: (1833-44); KEPLER: Dickreiter (1971/1973); LIPPIUS: Rivera (1974/1980); MATTHESON: Buelow and Marx (1983): Palisca; MERSENNE: (1617-48); Ludwig (1933/ . . ./1971); MOMIGNY: (1791-1818):(1791); PRAETORIUS: (1614-20):Fleming (1979); RIEMANN: (1898); SOLER: (1765); WALTHER: (1732); Gehrmann (1891); LITERATURE SUPPLEMENT: Abraham (1968/1969); Ahlgrimm (1969-70); Allen ["Baroque"] (1939); Allen ["Philosophies"] (1939); **Apfel (1981)**; Auda (1930/1979); Audbourg-Popin (1984); Auhagen (1982/1983); **Barbour (1932), (1951/. . ./1972)**, (1952); Barbieri (1983); Baron (1968); Bartel (1982/1985); Becker (1836-39/1964); Beiche ["Dux"] (1972-); **Benary (1956/1961)**; Blankenburg ["Harmonie"] (1959); Boetticher (1954); Boomgaarden (1985/1987); Borgir (1971/1987); Brandes (1935); Braun (1970); **Buelow** (1972), ["Affections"] (1980), ["Rhetoric"] **(1980)**; Bukofzer (1947); Burney (1776-89/. . ./1957); Butler (1977); Cohen (1981); **Coover (1980)**; **Dahlhaus** ["Termini"] (1955), (1981), **(1984)**, (1986); **Dahlhaus et al. (1987)**; Dammann (1958/1967); David and Mendel (1945/1966); Donà (1967); Donington (1963/. . ./1974); Dostrovsky (1969); Duckles (1970); Dupont (1933/. . ./1986); Eitner (1900-1904/1959-60); Federhofer (1964); Feldmann (1958); Fellerer ["Musikwissenschaft"] (1972); ["Zum Bild"] (1973), ["Zur Kontrapunktlehre"] (1973), ["Wesen"] (1982), (1983); Ferand (1951), [*Improvisation*] (1956/1961); Flindell (1977), (1983-84); Forchert (1986); Forkel (1792/1962); Frobenius ["Monodie"] (1972-), ["Polyphon"] (1972-); Gerber (1790-92/1977), (1812-14/1966); Godwin (1987); Gouk (1980), (1981-82); Gurlitt (1942/1966); Haase (1969); Hannas (1934); Harich-Schneider ([1939]/. . ./1970); Harrán (1986); Hawkins (1776/. . ./1969); Heckmann (1953); Hein (1954); Hiller (1768-69); Houle (1960), (1987); **Hunt (1978)**; **Kassler (1979)**; Katz (1926); Kauko (1958); Kayser (1950); Kirken-

dale (1979), (1984); Kleinman (1971/1974); Kroyer (1901/. . ./1970); Krützfeldt (1961); Krummacher (1979); La Fage (1864/1964); Lang (1941), (1967-68); Lester (1978); Leuchtmann (1957/1959); **Lindley** (1982), **(1984)**; Lippman (1986); Lottermoser (1949-68); Mann (1955/. . ./1987); McKinnon (1978); Meier (1974/1988); Mendel (1978); Miller and Cohen (1987); Möller (1971); Moser (1936/. . ./1959); Müller-Blattau (1923/. . ./1963); Nelson (1984); Neumann, Frederick (1978); Newman (1959/. . ./1983); Palisca [*Baroque*] (1968/1981); Ratner (1970); Rauhe (1959-60); **Ritzel (1967/1968)**; Rowen (1979); Ruhnke (1949-68); Sachs (1972-); Schäfke (1934); Schering (1926); Schmitz (1950); Schulenberg (1984); Seidel (1972-), (1976); **Seidel and Cooper (1986)**; Sheppard (1975); **Shirlaw (1917/. . ./1970)**; Sirch (1981); Sponheuer (1986); Stoll (1978/1981); Straková (1975); Subirá (1947/. . ./1958); Taddie (1984); Thieme (1982-83); Todd (1983); Unger (1941/1969); Walker (1987); Wienpahl (1953); Winternitz (1970); Wittwer (1934/1935); Wolf (1939); Yates (1964); Zenck (1942); Zimmermann (1976).

JOHANN PHILIPP KIRNBERGER

[1721 – 1783]

Countering the prevailing preoccupation with mathematical and acoustical speculations, Johann Philipp Kirnberger based his theoretical perspective upon contextual associations of chords. To a much greater extent than did RAMEAU, whose theory he disdained while nevertheless absorbing its notions of inversion and fundamental bass (albeit in adapted form), Kirnberger was inclined to consider dissonances within their compositional environments and therefore to note the diverse ways in which they could occur. Some, such as the seventh of the 7/5/3 chord, he regarded as "essential": they resolve only when the bass moves. Others, such as suspensions, were "nonessential" or "incidental": they resolve within the existing harmony rather than by change of harmony.

Kirnberger's view of the 6/4 chord is startlingly modern: it is sometimes consonant (a true inversion), sometimes dissonant (as in the double suspension leading to the dominant harmony). Only by examining the context could one decide which principle was operational, and only by deciding could one know which pitches might be doubled and where they should lead. Such sophisticated thinking made the process of creating an analytical fundamental bass more complex than RAMEAU's perspective required, yet the result, though still lacking the powerful hierarchical organization of later perspectives, established the process of

distinguishing between harmonic and linear factors, leading the way for nineteenth-century theorists such as SECHTER and culminating in SCHENKER's theory. On occasion Kirnberger interpolated an extra bass note within his analysis of a progression, a practice which was particularly upsetting to his adversary MARPURG, a fellow resident of Berlin and indefatigable defender of his own befuddled version of RAMEAU's theory. He also incorporated progressive conceptions of melody, phrase structure, and texture.

Kirnberger's perspective is thoroughly articulated in *Die Kunst des reinen Satzes in der Musik* (1771-79). Intending the work as a replication of the educational process advocated by J. S. Bach (with whom he had studied during his youth), Kirnberger first fostered an understanding of temperament, then chords and their contexts, cadences, modulation, simple counterpoint, and eventually double counterpoint. One may speculate that an additional volume devoted to fugue might have succeeded the two existing volumes had Kirnberger lived longer. He did produce, however, *Grundsätze des Generalbasses als erste Linien zur Composition* [ca. 1781] to serve as preparation for his more advanced *Kunst*.

Kirnberger's student J. A. P. SCHULZ was responsible for *Die wahren Grundsätze zum Gebrauch der Harmonie* (1773), a brief summary of his teacher's harmonic theory. The two had earlier collaborated with J. G. SULZER on the music articles for SULZER's *Allgemeine Theorie der schönen Künste* (1771-74). This interaction helped stimulate Kirnberger's interest in writing treatises. He was reportedly neither well organized nor articulate and therefore required prodding and probably assistance in putting his theory into words. Also interesting, though curious, are publications which aid amateurs in creating musical compositions, either by throwing dice to select prefabricated portions of pieces (in *Der allezeit fertige Polonoissen- und Menuettencomponist* of 1757) or by modifying existing works (in *Methode, Sonaten aus'm Ermel zu schüddeln* of 1783).

Der allezeit fertige Polonoisen- und Menuettencomponist [*Rism* B/VI/1, pp. 451-52.]

Berlin: Georg Ludewig Winter, 1757. [LCPS: K-015a.]

T ● *L'art de composer des minuets et des polonoises sur la champ* [*Rism* B/VI/1, p. 452.] Berlin: Georg Ludewig Winter, 1757. [LCPS: K-015b.]

Allegro für das Clavier alleine, wie auch für die Violin mit dem Violoncell zu accompagniren [*Rism* B/VI/1, p. 451.]

Berlin: Georg Ludewig Winter, 1759. [LCPS: K-014.]

See MARPURG: (1759-63):Vol. 1 (1759-60):Letters 6, 23-28, 30.

Construction der gleichschwebenden Temperatur [*Rism* B/VI/1, p. 452.]

Berlin: Friedrich Wilhelm Birnstiel, [ca. 1760]. [LCPS: K-017.]

S ● Facsimile edition. Hildesheim: Georg Olms, 1970.

Includes also (1773), below.

Die Kunst des reinen Satzes in der Musik, aus sicheren Grundsätzen hergeleitet und mit deutlichen Beyspielen erläutert [*Rism* B/VI/1, pp. 453-54.]

Berlin: Christian Friedrich Voß in Commission, 1771. Vol. 1. [LCPS: K-020a. HoM: 811. SMLMS.]
Berlin and Königsberg: G. J. Decker & G. L. Hartung, 1774. Vol. 1. [HoM: 812. IDC.]
Berlin: Heinrich August Rottmann, [ca. 1776]. Vol. 1.
Berlin and Königsberg: G. J. Decker & G. L. Hartung, 1776, 1777, 1779. Vol. 2 (in three parts). [LCPS: K-020b. HoM: 812. SMLMS. IDC.]

Review in VOGLER: (1778-81):Vol. 3/2/7-9 (1780-81):2ff.

Vienna: Musikalisch-typographische Gesellschaft, 1793. Both volumes.

S ● Facsimile of the [1776] and 1776-1779 editions. Hildesheim: Georg Olms, 1968.

T ● Winzenburger, Walter, trans. "Translation from *Die Kunst des reinen Satzes in der Musik* (Johann Philip Kirnberger, 1779)." *Bach* 2/1-2 (1971):42-46, 31-34. [*Rilm* 71-2333.]

T ● See Rowen (1979).

T ● ● ● ● Beach, David, and Thym, Jürgen, trans. *The Art of Strict Musical Composition by Johann Philip Kirnberger*. Introduction and Explanatory Notes by David Beach. MTTS, no. 4. New Haven, Ct.: Yale University Press, 1982. [*Rilm* 82-4551.]

Reviews in *Choice* 19/11-12 (1981-82):1568, *JMT* 28/1 (1984):124-28 (William Caplin), *ML* 65/1 (1984):64-65 (Philip Whitmore), *MR* 44/1 (1983):55-56 (C. Malcolm Boyd), and *MTS* 6 (1984):100-103 (Raymond Haggh).

Die wahren Grundsätze zum Gebrauch der Harmonie, darinn deutlich gezeiget wird, wie alle möglichen Accorde aus dem Dreyklang und dem wesentlichen Septimenaccord, und deren dissonirenden Vorhälten, herzuleiten und zu erklären sind, als ein Zusatz zu der Kunst des reinen Satzes in der Musik [*Rism* B/VI/1, p. 454.]

Johann Abraham Peter SCHULZ's rendering of Kirnberger's ideas.

Berlin and Königsberg: G. J. Decker & G. L. Hartung, 1773. [LCPS: K-022. HoM: 813. SMLMS. IDC.]
Vienna: Verlag der K. K. priv. chemischen Druckerey am Graben, [1793].

S ● Facsimile of the 1773 edition. See [ca. 1760]:(1970), above.

T ● Winzenburger, Walter, trans. "Translation from *Die wahren Grundsätze zum Gebrauch der Harmonie*, Johann Philip Kirnberger, 1773." *Bach* 1/4 (1970):41-46. [*Rilm* 70-3270.]

T ● Beach, David W., and Thym, Jürgen. "*The True Principles for the Practice of Harmony* by Johann Philip Kirnberger: A Translation." *JMT* 23/2 (1979):163-225.

Recueil d'airs de danse caractéristiques, pour servir de modèle aux jeunes compositeurs ... [*Rism* A/I/5, p. 50.]

Berlin: Johann Julius Hummel; Amsterdam: au grand magazin de musique, [ca. 1777].

T ● Powell, Newman Wilson. "Kirnberger on Dance, Rhythm, Fugues, and Characterization." In *Hoelty-NickelFs* (1967):65-76. Bibliog. [*Rilm* 69-2686.]

Correspondence with Forkel [and others]

143

Mss., 1779-83.

S● BELLERMANN, H., ed. "Briefe von Kirnberger an Forkel." *AmZ*(L) 6/34-36, 39-43 (1871):529-34, 550-54, 565-72, 614-18, 628-30, 645-48, 661-64, 677-78; 7/28-29 (1872):441-42, 457-60.

Grundsätze des Generalbasses als erste Linien zur Composition [*Rism* B/VI/1, pp. 452-53.]

Berlin: J. J. Hummel, [ca. 1781]. Two volumes. [LCPS: K-019. SMLMS. IDC.]

Several later editions.

T● Fling, Robert Michael. "Kirnberger, Johann Philipp: *Grundsätze des Generalbasses als erste Linien zur Composition* (1781)." M.A. thesis, The University of Iowa, 1964.

S● Facsimile of the 1781 edition. Hildesheim: Georg Olms, 1974.

Includes also [*Gedanken*] (1782), below.

Anleitung zur Singekomposition mit Oden in verschiedenen Sylbenmaassen begleitet [*Rism* B/VI/1, p. 452.]

Berlin: Georg Jacob Decker, 1782. [LCPS: K-016. SMLMS.]

Gedanken über die verschiedenen Lehrarten in der Komposition, als Vorbereitung zur Fugenkenntniss [*Rism* B/VI/1, p. 452.]

Berlin: Georg Jacob Decker, 1782. [LCPS: K-018. IDC.]

Vienna: Verlag der K. K. priv. chemischen Druckerey am Graben (Musikalisch-typographische Gesellschaft), 1793. [HoM: 810. SMLMS.]

S● Facsimile of the 1782 edition. See [ca. 1781]:(1974), above.

T● Nelson, Richard B., and Boomgaarden, Donald R., trans. "Kirnberger's *Thoughts on the Different Methods of Teaching Composition as Preparation for Understanding Fugue*." *JMT* 30/1 (1986):71-94.

Methode, Sonaten aus'm Ermel zu schüddeln [*Rism* B/VI/1, p. 454.]

Berlin: Friedrich Wilhelm Birnstiel, 1783. [LCPS: K-021.]

S● Fischer, Hans, ed. *Die Sonate*. MFhR, no. 18. Berlin: C. F. Vieweg, [1936].

ST● Newman, William S. "Kirnberger's Method for Tossing Off Sonatas." *MQ* 47/4 (1961):517-25.

See also SULZER: (1771-74).

LITERATURE:

Tempelhof, Georg Friedrich. *Gedanken über die Temperatur des Herrn Kirnberger...* [*Rism* B/VI/2, p. 823.] Berlin and Leipzig: Georg Jacob Decker, 1775. [LCPS: T-019.]

Seiffert, Max. "Aus dem Stammbuche Johann Philipp Kirnbergers." *VMw* 5 (1889):365-71.

Borris(-Zuckermann), Siegfried. "Kirnbergers Leben und Werk und seine Bedeutung im Berliner Musikkreis um 1750." Ph.D. dissertation, The University of Berlin, 1933; published edition, Kassel: Bärenreiter; Ohlau: Eschenhagen, 1933.

Review in *ML* 15/4 (1934):360-61 (Eric Blom).

Kraus, Hedwig. "Musikalisches Würfelspiel: Seltsames aus der Werkstatt eines deutschen Musiktheoretikers." *AMuZ* 66/48 (1939):628-29.

Dadelsen, Georg von. "Kirnberger, Johann Philipp." In *MGG* (1949-68). Bibliog.

Kloppenburg, W. C. M. "Een 18e eeuwse methode om sonates uit de mouw te schudden." *Mens* 5/11 (1950):357-58.

Bose, Fritz. "Anna Amalie von Preußen und Johann Philipp Kirnberger: Bemerkungen zu drei Briefen der Prinzessin aus der Autographinsammlung des Instituts für Musikforschung Berlin." *Mf* 10/1 (1957):129-35.

Schwinger, Wolfram. "In memoriam: Johann Philipp Kirnberger zum 175. Todestag am 27. Juli." *Musica* 12/7-8 (1958):487-88.

Mekeel, Joyce. "The Harmonic Theories of Kirnberger and Marpurg." *JMT* 4/2 (1960):169-93.

Hławiczka, Karol. "Ze studiów nad historia poloneza." *Muzyka* 10/2 [37] (1965):33-46.

Vogel, Martin. "Die Kirnberger-Stimmung vor und nach Kirnberger." In *Schmidt-GörgFsII* (1967):441-49. [*Rilm* 67-1248.]

Aldrich, Putnam. " 'Rhythmic Harmony' as Taught by Johann Philipp Kirnberger." In *GeiringerFs* (1970):37-52.

Arakawa, Tsuneko. "J. P. Kirnberger no ongakuriron—*Die Kunst des reinen Satzes in der Musik* o chushin ni." *Og* 19/1 (1973):1-12. [*Rilm* 73-409.]

Beach, David Williams. "The Harmonic Theories of Johann Philipp Kirnberger: Their Origins and Influences." Ph.D. dissertation, Yale University, 1974. [*Rilm* 74-3869. *DA* 35/07A, p. 4582. UMI 75-01338.]

Engelhardt, Ruth. "Untersuchungen über Einflüsse Johann Sebastian Bachs auf das theoretische und praktische Wirken seines Schülers Johann Philipp Kirnberger." Ph.D. dissertation, The University of

Erlangen, 1974; published edition, Erlangen: J. Hogl, [1974?]. [*Rilm* 75-3482.]

Rensch, Richard. "The Kirnberger Temperament and Its Effects on Organ Sound/Die Kirnberger-Temperierung und ihre Auswirkung auf den Orgelklang." Translated by H. D. Blanchard. *ISOI* 12 (1974):831-40.

Sumner, Floyd G. "Haydn and Kirnberger: A Documentary Report." *JAMS* 28/3 (1975):530-39. Bibliog. [*Rilm* 75-3646.]

Grant, Cecil Powell. "Kirnberger versus Rameau: Toward a New Approach to Comparative Theory." Ph.D. dissertation, The University of Cincinnati, 1976. [*Rilm* 76-1622. *DA* 37/09A, pp. 5429-30. UMI 77-06194.]

Grant, Cecil Powell. "The Real Relationship between Kirnberger's and Rameau's Concept of Fundamental Bass." *JMT* 21/2 (1977):324-38.

Jung, Karl. "Zwei mitteltönige Temperaturen." *Mi* 28/3 (1979):531-32. [*Rilm* 79-1649.]

● ● ● Serwer, Howard. "Kirnberger, Johann Philipp." In *NGrove* (1980). Bibliog.

Greenfield, Jack. "Later 18th-Century Music and Tuning in Germany." *PTJ* 27 (1984):30-32.

Roth, Lynette. "Kirnberger's Concept of Reductive Analysis." *ITO* 9/8 (1986-87):21-29.

Abstract in *MA* 7/3 (1988):365-66 (Wai-Ling Cheong).

Spanyi, M. "A Kirnberger-temperalas tifkai." *Muzsika* 30/8 (1987):24-27.

See also BACH: (1754-78):Helm (1966); BELLERMANN: (1862); CATEL: George (1982); CHORON: Simms (1975); FÉTIS: (1833-44); (1840); FUX: Federhofer (1988); HAUPTMANN: Caplin (1984); HEINICHEN: (1728):Buelow (1961/. . ./1986); KOCH: Baker (1976); Sisman (1982); KOLL-MANN: (1806); MARPURG: (1759-63); (1776); Frederick (1951); Serwer (1969); (1970); RAMEAU: Pischner (1961/. . ./1967); RIEMANN: (1898); SCHENKER: Slatin (1967); SCHULZ: Reichardt (1800-1801); TÜRK: (1806); VOGLER: (1800); Grave (1979-80); LITERATURE SUPPLEMENT: Alette (1951); Allanbrook (1981); Apfel and Dahlhaus (1974); Apfel (1977); Arakawa (1973); **Arnold (1931/. . ./1965)**; Atcherson (1960); Auhagen (1982/1983); Babbitt (1987); **Barbour** (1932), (1947), **(1951/. . ./1972)**; Beach (1967), (1974); Becker (1836-39/1964); **Benary (1956/1961)**; Benjamin (1981); **Bent** ["Analytical Thinking"] (1980), ["Analysis"] **(1980/1987)**; Bircher (1970); Blake (1988); Blumröder (1972-); Boomgaarden (1985/1987); Burdick (1977); Burke (1963); Burney (1776-89/. . ./1957); Cahn ["Retardatio"] (1972-), ["Transitus"] (1972-); Caplin (1978), (1981); Car-

penter (1988); Carr (1974); Chevaillier (1925/1931-32); Chew (1980); Collins (1963), (1966); **Coover (1980)**; **Dahlhaus** (1967), ["Harmony"] **(1980)**, (1981), **(1984)**, (1985); **Dahlhaus et al. (1987)**; **Dahlhaus and Sachs (1980)**; David and Mendel (1945/1966); Dekker (1979); de Zeeuw (1983); Donington (1963/. . ./1974); Dreyfus (1987); **Dürr and Gerstenberg** (1949-68), **(1980)**; Dunsby and Whittall (1988); Dupont (1933/. . ./1986); Eitner (1900-1904/1959-60); Federhofer (1944/1950), (1981); Feil (1955); Fellerer ["Zum Bild"] (1973); Forkel (1792/1962), (1799-1800); Frobenius ["Cantus"] (1972-), ["Vollstimmig"] (1972-); Gerber (1790-92/1977), (1812-14/1966); Gernhardt (1977); Gjerdingen (1988); Grave (1980), (1985); Gruber (1982); Gut (1972-); Hartmann (1923); Heckmann (1953); Hedges (1978); Heimann (1970/1973); Helm (1960); Henneberg (1972/1974); Hiller (1768-69); Hoffman (1953); Horsley [*Fugue: History*] (1966); Hosler (1978/1981); Houle (1960), (1987); Jackson (1988); Jacobi (1957-60/1971); Jenne (1973-74); Jeppesen (1930/. . ./1974), (1935); Jones (1934); **Kassler (1979)**, (1983-85); Kaufmann (1969); Kauko (1958); Kelletat [*Temperatur*] (1960), ["Tonordnung"] (1960), (1966); Konecne (1984); Kramer (1975), (1987-88); Kubota (1986); Lawrence (1978); **Lester** (1978), **(1989)**; Levenson (1981); **Lindley** ["Temperaments"] **(1980)**, (1982), (1988); Mainka (1965/1969); **Mann (1955/. . ./1987)**, (1987); Maier (1984); McQuere (1983); Meer (1980); Mitchell, J. W. (1963); Mitchell, W. J. (1963); Möllers (1978); Morgan (1978); Moyer (1969); Müller-Blattau (1923/. . ./1963); Munkachy (1968); Nelson (1984); **Neumann**, Frederick (1978), [*Essays*] **(1982)**; Newman (1946), (1963/. . ./1983), (1969/. . ./1983); Newman (1985); Oldroyd (1948); Ottenberg (1973/1978); **Palisca** (1949-68), [*Baroque*] (1968/1981), ["Theory"] **(1980)**; Rasch (1981); Ratner (1949), (1956), (1970), (1980); Reichert (1978); Reilly (1984-85); Ritzel (1967/1968); Rivera (1984); Rohwer (1949-68); Rosenblum (1988); Rothschild (1961); Sachs (1972-); Schoffman ["Descriptive"] (1983); Schulenberg (1982), (1984); Seaton (1981); Seidel (1971), (1972-), (1975); **Seidel and Cooper (1986)**; Sheldon (1975), (1981), (1982); Shellhous (1988); **Shirlaw (1917/. . ./1970)**; **Steblin (1981/1983)**; Stein (1983); Stevens (1974); Telesco (forthcoming); Tenney (1988); Thomson (1960/1978); Tittel (1959), (1966); Todd (1983), (1988-89); Troeger (1987); Unger (1941/1969); Vogel (1955/1954), (1975/1984), (1976); **Wagner (1974)**; **Wason (1981/1985)**, (1983); Wellesz and Sternfeld (1973); Wessel (1955); Wichmann (1966); Williams, P. ["Equal"] (1968), (1970); Wintle (1982); Wirth (1966); Yeston (1974/1976).

CHARLES HERBERT KITSON

[1874–1944]

The British penchant for formal examinations led to a pedagogy geared more towards a successful showing on exam days than towards a thorough grounding in the infinitely more varied possibilities of the actual repertoire. Bach's fugues were somewhat inconvenient: it was much more "beneficial" for the student to master the procedures of the examination fugue, since it would contain *all* of the principal features of fugal composition, rather than just some of them, as did many of Bach's fugues. And, of course, such a fugue should be written within three hours.

Charles Herbert Kitson was a master at preparing students for their examinations. His teaching in Dublin and London coincided with the musical establishment's expectations regarding appropriate musical training. His influence spread further through his administrative duties within the British system and through his numerous texts, each of which addresses a specific aspect of harmonic or contrapuntal technique. In all, fourteen works were published over the span of thirty years. Unlike his prolific German counterpart, RIEMANN, Kitson did not venture into more speculative realms.

The Art of Counterpoint and Its Application As a Decorative Principle

> Oxford: Clarendon Press, 1907.
>
>> Reviews in *MT* 48/775 (1907):607 and *Nation* 85/2200 (1907):193.
>
> Oxford: Clarendon Press; London: Oxford University Press (Humphrey Milford), 1924.
>
>> Later printings.

S ● Facsimile of the 1924 edition. DCPMRS. New York: Da Capo, 1975.

Studies in Fugue

> Oxford: Clarendon Press, 1909.
>
>> Later printings.

The Evolution of Harmony: A Treatise on the Material of Musical Composition, Its Gradual Growth and Elementary Use

> Oxford: Clarendon Press, 1914.
> Oxford: Clarendon Press, 1924.
>
>> Later printings.

Applied Strict Counterpoint

> Oxford: Clarendon Press, 1916.
>
>> Later printings.

S ● Facsimile edition. New York: AMS Press.

Elementary Harmony

> Oxford: Clarendon Press, 1920. 3 vols.
>
>> Later printings. Reviews in *MEJ* 14/3 (1927-28):79-81 (Will Earhart) and *Rmi* 28/1 (1921):165 (A. G.).

"Modern Harmony from the Standpoint of the Teacher"

>> Includes discussion by Evelyn Broadwood, Wm. J. Phillips, J. Swinburne, T. H. Yorke Trotter, and Charles Wood.

> In *PMA 1924-25* 51 (1925):57-72.

Additional Exercises to Elementary Harmony

> London: Oxford University Press (Humphrey Milford), 1926.
>
>> Review in *MEJn* 14/1 (1927-28):82 (Will Earhart).

Counterpoint for Beginners

> London: Oxford University Press (Humphrey Milford), [1927].
>
>> Later printings. Review in *MEJ* 14/1 (1927-28):82 (Will Earhart).

Invertible Counterpoint and Canon

> London: Oxford University Press (Humphrey Milford), 1927.

Rudiments of Music

> London: Oxford University Press (Humphrey Milford), 1927.
>
>> Later printings. Review in *MEJ* 14/1 (1927-28):81 (Will Earhart).

The Elements of Fugal Construction

> London: Oxford University Press (Humphrey Milford), 1929.
>
>> Review in *ML* 11/2 (1930):199-200 (S. Goddard).

S ● Facsimile edition. Westport, Ct.: Greenwood Press, 1981.

Six Lectures on Accompanied Vocal Writing

> London: Oxford University Press (Humphrey Milford), 1930.

Contrapuntal Harmony for Beginners

> London: Oxford University Press (Humphrey Milford), 1931.
>
>> Review in *ML* 13/2 (1932):243 (S. Goddard).

S ● Facsimile edition. Westport, Ct.: Greenwood Press, 1978.

Rudiments of Music for Junior Classes

London: Oxford University Press (Humphrey Milford), 1931.

The Elements of Musical Composition

London: Oxford University Press (Humphrey Milford), 1936.

LITERATURE:

Webber, W. S. Lloyd. "A Master Craftsman." *MiE* 9/98-99 (1945-46):43-44.

Williamson, Winifred F. "Kitson, Charles Herbert." Translated by Wilhelm Pfannkuch. In *MGG* (1949-68). Bibliog.

Shaw, Watkins. "Kitson, Charles Herbert." In *NGrove* (1980).

See also RIEMANN: (1898):Mickelsen (1970/1977); LITERATURE SUPPLEMENT: **Bullivant (1980)**; Burke (1963); Cazden (1948); Jeppesen (1922/. . ./1970), (1930/. . ./1974), (1935); Mann (1955/. . ./1987), (1987); Roberts (1967); Sanders (1919); Scholes (1947).

HEINRICH CHRISTOPH KOCH

[1749 – 1816]

One of the eighteenth century's most vivid and penetrating explorations of the compositional art was undertaken by Heinrich Christoph Koch. Writing in relative obscurity and drawing upon the work of RIEPEL and SULZER, Koch established, in his *Versuch einer Anleitung zur Composition* (1782-93), a precise and convincing mechanism for describing the various interactions among phrase segments, phrases, periods, and the extended periods which shape the largest musical forms. His perspective sharply contrasted the mathematical, contrapuntal, and figured-bass conventions of less innovative eighteenth-century treatises and influenced nineteenth-century writers on form, including CHORON, who translated a portion of the *Versuch* into French.

Koch readily acknowledged the extraordinary power of genius in creating and coordinating materials for a composition. Both inspiration and craftsmanship were required for success. Following SULZER's lead (in a formulation similar to that proposed by MATTHESON), Koch demonstrated how the compositional process could be divided into three separate phases: that of developing a plan or central body of musical materials (the *Anlage*), articulating this plan within the larger shape of an actual composition (the *Ausführung*), and then working out elaborations to embellish or refine the basic design (the *Ausarbeitung*). In coordination with this premise, he offered numerous suggestions for how a basic model might be expanded or altered. Repetition of a phrase or melodic segment was possible; an expansion of the end of a phrase could be carried out, using repetition or the addition of an appendix; or a melodic section could be internally expanded, using devices such as repetition and interpolation. Koch's numerous music examples are peppered (somewhat haphazardly) with triangles and squares (derived

from RIEPEL) which demark the phrase segments and complete phrases, respectively.

Koch's innovative and extensive discussion of phrase structure complements his equally provocative conception of form. He viewed the symphony first movement as the most significant of the larger forms and related his treatments of sonata and concerto first movements to the symphony model. Two parts, each of which might be repeated, unite to shape the symphony movement. The first consists of a single principal period which typically leads to the dominant; the second consists of two principal periods, the first in a related key, the second reinforcing the tonic key. Whereas sonata first movements are similarly structured, the concerto incorporates ritornello sections surrounding the three constituent periods borrowed from the symphony structure. Koch also explored a variety of smaller forms and supplied numerous possibilities for their harmonic plans.

Koch's preoccupation with the periodicity of phrases and with the means by which normal two- and four-measure units can be expanded, combined, and interpolated led to useful insights regarding phrase rhythm. Phrase lengths of five, six, and seven measures result from procedures which he documented in detail. For example, a compound phrase of seven measures may result when the fourth measure of one four-measure phrase doubles as the first measure of another. Such a phrase is perceived as if it occupied eight measures.

The industry and acumen with which Koch undertook his musical studies are further reflected in his short-lived *Journal der Tonkunst* (1795) and in his extensive *Musikalisches Lexicon* (1802), wherein many of the ideas from the *Versuch* are reiterated or brought up to date. (Koch had become acquainted with Mozart's music in the years between the *Versuch* and the *Lexicon*.) Koch also contributed, often anonymously, to the *Speyerschen musikalische Zeitung*, *Allgemeine musikalische Zeitung*, and *Jenaischen allgemeine Literaturzeitung*.

Versuch einer Anleitung zur Composition [*Rism* B/VI/1, p. 458.]

> Leipzig: Adam Friedrich Böhme (Rudolstadt: gedruckt mit Schriften der Löwischen Erben, und Schirach), 1782. Vol. 1. [LCPS: K-031. SMLMS. IDC.]
>
>> Review in *MagM* 1/2 (1783):1304-8 [reprinted in Johann Nicolaus Forkel's *Musikalischer Almanach für Deutschland auf das Jahr 1784*, pp. 1-4 (Leipzig: im Schwickertschen Verlag, [1783]; reprint edition, Hildesheim: Georg Olms, 1974)].
>
> Leipzig: Adam Friedrich Böhme, 1787. Vol. 2. [LCPS: K-031. SMLMS. IDC.]
> Leipzig: Adam Friedrich Böhme, 1793. Vol. 3. [LCPS: K-031. SMLMS. IDC.]

T ● See CHORON: (1836-38).

S ● Facsimile edition. Hildesheim: Georg Olms, 1969.

T ● See Rowen (1979).

T ● Baker, Nancy Kovaleff, trans. *Introductory Essay on Composition: The Mechanical Rules of Melody, Sections 3 and 4*. MTTS. New Haven, Ct.: Yale University Press, 1983. Bibliog.

> Reviews in *Choice* 21/10 (1983-84):1475, *JMT* 29/2 (1985):341-47 (Elaine R. Sisman), *MA* 6/1-2 (1987):196-202 (Esther Cavett-Dunsby), *ML* 66/2 (1985):149-50 (Philip Whitmore), *MTS* 8 (1986):143-48 (Nola Reed Knouse), and *Notes* 41/1 (1984-85):64-65 (Roger L. Lustig).

Journal der Tonkunst [*Rism* B/VI/1, p. 458.]

> Erfurt: Georg Adam Keyser, 1795. Vol. 1. [SMLMS.]
> Erfurt: Georg Adam Keyser (Brunswick: In dem Musikalisches Magazin auf der Höhe), 1795. Vol. 2. [SMLMS.]

Musikalisches Lexikon, welches die theoretische und praktische Tonkunst, encyclopädisch bearbeitet, alle alten und neuen Kunstwörter erklärt, und die alten und neuen Instrumente beschrieben, enthält

> Frankfurt am Main: Hermann, 1802. 2 vols.
>
>> Review in *AmZ* 6/3 (1803-4):33-45.
>
> Offenbach am Main, J. André, n.d.
> Heidelberg: [Mohr?], 1817.

S ● *Kurzgefaßtes Handwörterbuch der Musik für praktische Tonkünstler und für Dilettanten*. Leipzig: Joh. Friedr. Hartknoch, 1807; an excerpt, Ulm:

1828; facsimile of the 1807 edition, Hildesheim: Georg Olms, 1981.

> An abridged version of the 1802 work. Review in *AmZ* 9/48 (1806-7):757-70.

T ● Lassen, H. C. F., trans. *Musikalsk haand-lexicon . . . Udtog af H. C. Kochs musikalske Encyclopaedie*. Copenhagen: 1826.

S ● Dommer, Arrey von, ed. Revised edition. Heidelberg: J. C. B. Mohr, 1864.

> Review in *AmZ* (Neue Folge) 2/37 (1864):626-30.

S ● Facsimile of the 1802 edition. Hildesheim: Georg Olms, 1964.

"Über den technischen Ausdruck: Tempo rubato"

> *AmZ* 10/33 (1807-8):513-19.

Handbuch bey dem Studium der Harmonie

> Leipzig: Joh. Friedr. Hartknoch; Hofmeister, 1811.
>
>> Related to Book 1 of the *Versuch* (1782), above. Review in *AmZ* 13/46 (1811):765-75.

S ● "Bruchstücke aus Heinrich Christoph Kochs Handbuch beym Studium der Harmonie." *AmZ* 12/63, 65 (1809-10):1001-6, 1045-52.

Versuch, aus der harten und weichen Tonart jeder Stufe der diatonisch-chromatischen Tonleiter vermittelst des enharmonischen Tonwechsels in die Dur- und Molltonart der übrigen Stufen auszuweichen

> Rudolstadt: Hof- Buch- und Kunsthandlung, 1812.
>
>> Review in *AmZ* 14/42 (1812):679-84. Response by Koch and replies by the reviewer and editor in *AmZ: Intelligenz-Blatt* [15]/1 (1813):1-9.

"Über die physischen und mathematischen Gegenstände der Musik, oder über die Frage: Was muß in der Musik unabänderlich bleiben, wenn auch Melodie und Harmonie eine ganz neue Gestalt annehmen?"

> Ms. [Lost.]

"Vergleichung der verschiedenen Systeme der harmonie, veranlaßt durch das von Momigny im Jahre 1808 [*sic*] zu Paris ersch. Werk: Cours complet d'harmonie et de composition d'après une theorie neuve et générale et de la musique . . ."

> Ms. [Lost.]

LITERATURE:

Eggebrecht, Hans Heinrich. "Koch, Heinrich Christoph." In *MGG* (1949-68). Bibliog.

Burde, Wolfgang. "Versuch über einen Satz Theodor W. Adornos." *NZfM* 132/11 (1971):578-83. [*Rilm* 74-1283.]

Pečman, Rudolf. "Die Musik in der Auffassung Heinrich Christoph Kochs (Ein Kapitel aus der Geschichte der Musiktheorie und -lexikographie)." *SpFfBU* 6 (1971):51-62. [*Rilm* 71-3266.]

Seidel, Wilhelm. "Heinrich Christoph Kochs Begriff des musikalischen Metrums." In *Bericht Bonn 1970* (1971), pp. 570-73. [*Rilm* 73-4322.]

Stevens, Jane R. "An Eighteenth-Century Description of Concerto First-Movement Form." *JAMS* 24/1 (1971):85-95. [*Rilm* 71/628.]

Jones, Gregory Paul. "Heinrich Christoph Koch's Description of the Symphony and a Comparison with Selected Symphonies of C. P. E. Bach and Haydn." M.A. thesis, The University of California at Los Angeles, 1973. [*Rilm* 73-1873.]

Baker, Nancy Kovaleff. "From *Teil* to *Tonstück*: The Significance of the *Versuch einer Anleitung zur Composition* by Heinrich Christoph Koch." Ph.D. dissertation, Yale University, 1975. [*Rilm* 75-2606. *DA* 36/12A, p. 7719. UMI 76-13694.]

Baker, Nancy Kovaleff. "Heinrich Koch and the Theory of Melody." *JMT* 20/1 (1976):1-48. [*Rilm* 76-1641.]

Baker, Nancy Kovaleff. "The Aesthetic Theories of Heinrich Christoph Koch." *IRASM* 8/2 (1977):183-209. Bibliog. [*Rilm* 77-5941.]

Dahlhaus, Carl. "Der rhetorische Formbegriff H. Chr. Kochs und die Theorie der Sonatenform." *AfMw* 35/3 (1978):155-77. [*Rilm* 78-4947.]

Henneberg, Gudrun. "Heinrich Christoph Kochs Analysen von Instrumentalwerken Joseph Haydns." *HS* 4 (1978):105-12. [*Rilm* 78-4969.]

● ● ● Ratner, Leonard G. "Koch, Heinrich Christoph." In *NGrove* (1980). Bibliog.

Baker, Nancy Kovaleff. "Heinrich Koch's Description of the Symphony." *Sm* 9/2 (1980):303-16. [*Rilm* 80-5631.]

Sisman, Elaine Rochelle. "Small and Expanded Forms: Koch's Model and Haydn's Music." *MQ* 68/4 (1982):444-75. [*Rilm* 82-4691.]

Davis, Shelley. "H. C. Koch, the Classic Concerto, and the Sonata-Form Retransition." *JM* 2/1 (1983):45-61. [*Rilm* 83-1643.]

Forschner, Hermann. *Instrumentalmusik Joseph Haydns aus der Sicht Heinrich Christoph Kochs.* Munich: Emil Katzbichler, 1984.

Wagner, Günther. "Anmerkungen zur Formtheorie Heinrich Christoph Kochs." *AfMw* 41/2 (1984):86-112.

Baker, Nancy K. " 'Der Urstoff der Musik': Implications for Harmony and Melody in the Theory of Heinrich Koch." *MA* 7/1 (1988):3-30.

See also FÉTIS: (1833-44):Vol. 5:365-66; MARX: Eicke (1966); RAMEAU: Pischner (1961/. . ./1967); RIEMANN: (1895-1901):(1900); (1898); RIEPEL: Schwarzmaier (1936/1948); SULZER: (1771-

74):Churgin (1980); VOGLER: Stevens (1983); LITERATURE SUPPLEMENT: Allanbrook (1981); Apfel and Dahlhaus (1974); Arakawa (1973); Auhagen (1982/1983); Becker (1836-39/1964); Beiche ["Dux"] (1972-), ["Inversio"] (1972-); **Benary (1956/1961)**, (1963); **Bent**, I. ["Analytical Thinking"] (1980), ["Analysis"] **(1980/1987)**, ● ● ● (1984); Blake (1988); Blumröder (1972-); Broyles (1983); Bruck (1928); Budday (1982/1983), (1987); Buelow (1979); Burde (1976); Cahn ["Retardatio"] (1972-); Carse (1925/1964); Chew (1980); Cole (1969); **Coover (1980)**; **Dahlhaus** (1967), (1970/1983), (1978), **(1984)**, ["Zum Taktbegriff"] (1988); **Dahlhaus et al. (1987)**; **Dürr and Gerstenberg** (1949-68), **(1980)**; Dunsby and Whittall (1988); Eggebrecht (1955); Eitner (1900-1904/1959-60); Federhofer (1944/1950); Feil (1955); Fischer (1957); Forkel (1792/1962); Frobenius ["Cantus"] (1972-), ["Homophonus"] (1972-), ["Isotonos"] (1972-), ["Polyphon"] (1972-), ["Vollstimmig"] (1972-); Gerber (1790-92/1977), (1812-14/1966); Grave (1980), (1985); Gwilt (1983-84); Hamilton (1854); Hartmann (1923); Henneberg (1972/1974), (1983); Hosler (1978/1981); Houle (1960), (1987); Jones (1934); Karube (1969); **Kassler (1979)**; Kauko (1958); Kelletat [*Temperatur*] (1960); Kob (1965); Krones (1988); Kubota (1986); Larsen (1963/1988); Laudon (1978); **Lester** (1978), **(1989)**; Levenson (1981); Lindley (1982); Mann (1987); Meer (1980); Möllers (1978); Moyer (1969); Müller-Blattau (1923/. . ./1963); Munkachy (1968); Nelson (1984); **Neumann** (1981/**1982**), ["Appoggiatura"] (1982), [*Essays*] **(1982)**, (1986); Newman (1946), (1963/. . ./1983), (1969/. . ./1983); Oberdoerffer (1967); Orr (1983); **Palisca** ["Theory"] **(1980)**; **Powers** ["Language"] (1980), ["Mode"] **(1980)**; Ratner (1949), (1956), (1970), (1980); Reichenbach (1948); Reimer ["Concerto"] (1972-), ["Kammermusik"] (1972-), ["Kenner"] (1972-), (1973); **Ritzel (1967/1968)**; Rohwer (1949-68); Rosen (1971/. . ./1983), (1980/1988); Rosenblum (1988); Rothärmel (1963/1968); Rothgeb (1968); Rothschild (1961); Sachs (1972-); Schmalzriedt ["Coda"] (1972-), ["Durchführen"] (1972-), ["Episode"] (1972-), ["Reprise"] (1972-); Schoffman (1979); Seidel (1975), (1976), (1979), (1980), (1986); Serwer (1974); Shamgar (1978), (1981), (1984); Sheldon (1975), (1981), (1982); Shellhous (1988); **Shirlaw (1917/. . ./1970)**; Sisman (1978); Spitzer and Zaslaw (1986); Steinbeck (1981); Stevens (1974); Stowell (1985), (1988); Telesco (forthcoming); Thaler (1984); Thieme (1982-83); Todd (1983); Tsuchida (1979), (1981); Vogel (1976); **Wagner (1974)**; Wessel (1955); Whittall (1980); Wirth (1966); Wolff (1972-); **Zaminer (1985)**.

AUGUSTUS FREDERIC CHRISTOPHER KOLLMANN

[1756 – 1829]

The writings of Augustus Frederic Christopher Kollmann supplied British musicians with a wide scope and high quality of instruction, comparable to what was produced in the principal Continental musical capitals. Influenced by KIRNBERGER (with whom he shared what was then an uncommon devotion to the works of J. S. Bach), Kollmann developed a systematic and straightforward theory guided by strong pedagogical inclinations. Practical considerations dominate, especially in his thoroughbass manuals and sets of compositions for which analytical commentary was supplied. His longer treatises were intended to enhance his readers' understanding of the various facets of music's grammar and rhetoric. Among the most important outcomes of his quest were clear descriptions of various musical forms, including sonata, concerto, and rondo. Kollmann also edited a journal, the *Quarterly Musical Register* (1812), and entered into the polemic regarding LOGIER's system of keyboard instruction (1821).

The *Essay on Musical Harmony* (1796) and its successor, *A New Theory of Musical Harmony* (1806), are devoted to the grammatical aspects of music, such as scales, intervals, chords and their connection, cadences, rhythm, the elements of counterpoint, and the like. The rhetorical aspects of music, including form, instrumentation, and tonal structure, are scrutinized in *An Essay on Practical Musical Composition* (1799). Kollmann's hierarchical perspective draws heavily upon the harmonic plan of a movement, as opposed to its thematic content. The sonata movement, for example, is divided into two parts (at the double bar which separates what we now call exposition and development). Each of these two parts is itself typically divided into two sections, in accordance with the arrival of the dominant (or, in minor, the mediant) in the first section and the return of tonic in the second section. For Britons who had grown accustomed to importing composers and performers, it should not have been surprising that Kollmann, a native German, was producing some of their best theoretical formulations. Fortunately for them, his treatises were published in English.

An Introduction to the Art of Preluding and Extemporizing ... (Op. 3) [*Rism* A/I/5, p. 83; B/VI/1, p. 460.]

London: R. Wornum, [1792]. [LCPS: K-035.]

The First Beginning on the Piano Forte, According to an Improved Method of Teaching Beginners; Containing an Explanatory Introduction ... (Op. 5) [*Rism* B/VI/1, p. 460.]

London and Edinburgh: the author (Corri, Dussek & Co.), [ca. 1795-96].

Review in *MMag* 7/3 (1799):226 [Thomas Busby].

An Essay on Musical Harmony, According to the Nature of That Science and the Principles of the Greatest Musical Authors [*Rism* B/VI/1, p. 460.]

London: J. Dale, 1796. [LCPS: K-034a.]

Superseded by (1806), below. Reviews in *BC* 8 (1796):322-23, *BC* 16 (1800):169-72, 393-97 [J. W. Callcott], *CrR* 18 (September 1796):88-91, *MMag* 7/45-46 (1799):389-90, 477, and *MonR* 21 (1796):27-30 [Charles Burney].

Utica, N.Y.: Seward & Williams, 1817. 1st American edition.

Proposals for Publishing by Subscription, A New Theoretical Musical Work, Entitled "An Essay on Practical Musical Composition"

London: 1798.

A Symphony for the Piano-Forte, A Violin, and a Violoncello; With Analytical Explanations of the Subjects and Imitations, the Modulations, the Counterpoint Inversions, and the Rhythmical Order It Contains ... (Op. 7) [*Rism* A/I/5, p. 83.]

London: the author (Longman and Broderip), [1798].

An Essay on Practical Musical Composition, According to the Nature of That Science and the Principles of the Greatest Musical Authors [*Rism* B/VI/1, p. 460.]

London: the author, 1799. [LCPS: K-034b.]

Reviews in *BC* 17 (1801):399-406 [J. W. Callcott], *CrR* 28 (1800):219-20, *MMag* 8/48-49 (1799):561, 644 (Thomas Busby), and *MonR* 31 (1800):127-31 [Charles Burney].

London: the author, 1812. Revised edition.

Compatible with *New Theory* (1806), below.

S ● Horsley, Imogene, ed. Facsimile of the 1799 edition. DCPMRS. New York: Da Capo Press, 1973.

Review in ●●●*Notes* 31/2 (1974-75):296-97 (Michael Kassler).

A Practical Guide to Thorough-Bass [*Rism* A/I/5, p. 83.]

London: the author, 1801.

Reviews in *MonR* 36 (1801):303-7 [Charles Burney], *MMag* 11/70 (1801):159-60 [Thomas Busby], and *BC* 18 (1801):389-99 [J. W. Callcott]. Discussed by Matthew Peter King (whom Kollmann had criticized in *A Practical Guide*) in *A General Treatise on Music* ..., 2nd edition (London: the author, 1801), to which Kollmann responded with *A. C. F. Kollmann's Vindication of a Passage in His "Practical Guide to Thorough-Bass," against an Advertisement of Mr. M. P. King* (London: the author, 1801), reviewed in *BC* 20 (1802):487-93 [J. W. Callcott], *MMag* 13/84 (1802):154 [Thomas Busby], and *MonR* 38 (1802):216-17 [Charles Burney].

T ● *Praktische Anleitung zum Generalbass*. Offenbach am Main: Johann André, 1808.

> Review in *AmZ* 11/25 (1808-9):390-95.

A New Theory of Musical Harmony, According to a Complete and Natural System of That Science

> Derived from (1796), above.

London: W. Bulmer, 1806.

> Review in *GMag* 84/2 (1814):155-56.

London: the author (W. Nicol), 1823. Revised edition.

"An Essay on Earl Stanhope's 'Principles of the Science of Tuning Instruments with Fixed Tones' "

> *Ba* 2-3 (1807):321-23; 99-101.

A Second Practical Guide to Thorough-Bass

London: the author, 1807.

> Compatible with *New Theory* (1806), above. Review in *MMag* 23/156 (1807):379 (Thomas Busby).

ST ● *A Practical Guide to Thorough Bass . . ./Practische Anleitung zum Generalbass* [*Rism* A/I/5, p. 83]. Offenbach am Main: Johann André, [1808].

The Melody of the Hundredth Psalm, with Examples and Directions for an Hundred Different Harmonies (Op. 9)

London: the author, 1809.

[A Series of] Twelve Analyzed Fugues for Two Performers with Double Counterpoint at All Intervals, and Introductory Explanations (Op. 10) [*Rism* A/I/5, p. 83]

London: the author, [ca. 1810].
London: the author, 1822.

The Quarterly Musical Register

1812. Two issues only.

> Includes items such as "A Retrospect of the State of Music in Great Britain since the Year 1789" (pp. 6-28), "An Account of the Theoretical Works of A. F. C. Kollmann . . ." (pp. 40-59, 105-15), and a review of John Wall Callcott's *A Musical Grammar* (pp. 59-74, 115-31). Review in *GMag* 83/1 (1813):354-56.

An Introduction to Extemporary Modulation . . . (Op. 11)

London: the author, [ca. 1820].

Reviews in *AcR* 11/61 (1821):57-58 (G. L. Engelbach) and *MMag* 50/5 [347] (1820):464-66.

See also LOGIER: KOLLMANN:(1821).

LITERATURE:

Mathews, William Smythe Babcock. "A Remarkable Token of American Progress in 1818." *MuMM* 21 (1901-2):419-20.

"Notes on an Old Music Journal: *The Quarterly Musical Register*." *MT* 48/776 (1907):645-48.

Redlich, Hans Ferdinand. "Kollmann, August Friedrich Christoph." In *MGG* (1949-68). Bibliog.

Jacobi, Erwin R. "Augustus Frederic Christopher Kollmann als Theoretiker." *AfMw* 13/3-4 (1956):263-70.

Cole, Malcolm Stanley. "Rondos, Proper and Improper." *ML* 51/4 (1970):388-99. [*Rilm* 70-3239.]

● ● ● Kassler, Michael. "Kollmann: (1) Augustus Frederic Christopher Kollmann." In *NGrove* (1980). Bibliog.

Kassler, Michael. "Transferring a Tonality Theory to a Computer." In *Report Berkeley 1977* (1981):339-47. [*Rilm* 81-6105.]

> Remarks by Stephen W. Smoliar and discussion on pp. 347-51.

Lambert, J. Philip. "Eighteenth-Century Harmonic Theory in Concept and Practice: Kollmann's Analysis of J. S. Bach's Chromatic Fantasy." *ITO* 8/3 (1984-85):11-29.

See also FÉTIS: (1833-44); KIRNBERGER: Beach (1974); LOGIER: (1824); LITERATURE SUPPLEMENT: Balthazar (1983); Beach (1974); Becker (1836-39/1964); Bent ["Analytical Thinking"] (1980); Broyles (1982-83), (1983); Chevaillier (1925/1931-32); **Dahlhaus et al. (1987)**; David and Mendel (1945/1966); Dreyfus (1987); Eitner (1900-1904/1959-60); Forkel (1799-1800); Gerber (1812-14/1966); ● ● ● Gwilt (1983-84); Horsley [*Fugue: History*] (1966); Houle (1960), (1987); Irving (1986); Jacobi (1957-60/1971); Jones (1934); **Kassler** (1971), ● ● ● **(1979)**; Konecne (1984); Lindley (1982); Miller and Cohen (1987); Nelson (1984); Newman (1963/. . ./1983); Ratner (1949), (1980); Reimer ["Kammermusik"] (1972-); **Ritzel (1967/1968)**; Schmalzriedt ["Exposition"] (1972-), ["Reprise"] (1972-); **Seidel and Cooper (1986)**; Sheldon (1982); Sisman (1978); Stevens (1974); Telesco (forthcoming); Todd (1983); Williams, P. ["Equal"] (1968), (1970).

STEPHAN KREHL

[1864–1924]

In over two decades of service at the Leipzig Conservatory, including several years as director, Stephan Krehl influenced a generation of German musicians. His numerous textbooks, on the standard topics of harmony, counterpoint, and form, were popular throughout Germany though they were not, as were many of RIEMANN's, translated into numerous languages. Following in the pedagogical tradition of JADASSOHN and RIEMANN, Krehl attempted, in his *Kontrapunkt* (1908), to bring about a synthesis of harmony and counterpoint, wherein the two-voice textures of the species exercises were formulated in accordance with actual harmonic progressions. Though outwardly similar to the various categories of species writing, the inner logic upon which these efforts were founded represented a negation of the sort of contrapuntal craftsmanship which FUX had in mind.

Musikalische Formenlehre (Kompositionslehre) (SGös, nos. 149-50)

> Leipzig: G. J. Göschen, 1902-3. 2 vols.
> Berlin and Leipzig: Walter de Gruyter, 1917-20. Enlarged edition.
>
>> Numerous printings. Review in *Rmi* 28/3 (1921):522-23 (A. G.).

Allgemeine Musiklehre (SGös, no. 220)

> Leipzig: G. J. Göschen, 1904.
> Berlin and Leipzig: Walter de Gruyter, 1933. Edited by Robert Hernried.
>
>> Several other printings. Review in *Rmi* 28/3 (1921):519-21 (G. C.).

Fuge: Erläuterung und Anleitung zur Komposition derselben (SGös, no. 418)

> Leipzig: G. J. Göschen, 1908.
>
>> Later printings.

> T ● Ribera y Maneja, Antonio, trans. *Fuga*. CL, ser. 5, no. 230. Barcelona: Editorial Labor, 1930; 2nd edition, 1953.

Kontrapunkt: Die Lehre von der selbständigen Stimmführung (SGös, no. 390)

> Leipzig: G. J. Göschen, 1908.
>
>> Several later printings.

> T ● Ribera y Maneja, Antonio, trans. *Contrapunto*. CL, ser. 5, no. 229. Barcelona: Editorial Labor, 1930; 2nd edition, 1953.

Beispiele und Aufgaben zum Kontrapunkt

> Berlin and Leipzig: Vereinigung wissenschaftlicher Verleger (Walter de Gruyter), 1908.
>
>> Later printings.

Kompositionsunterricht und moderne Musik (MusMag, no. 25)

> Langensalza: H. Beyer & Söhne, 1909.

"Die Dissonanz als musikalisches Ausdrucksmittel"

> *ZfMw* 1/11 (1918-19):645-54.

Theorie der Tonkunst und Kompositionslehre

> Berlin and Leipzig: Vereinigung wissenschaftlicher Verleger (Walter de Gruyter), 1920-22. 2 vols.

Harmonielehre [Tonalitätslehre] (SGös, nos. 809-11)

> Berlin and Leipzig: Vereinigung wissenschaftlicher Verleger (Walter de Gruyter), 1921. 3 vols.
>
>> Reprint of vol. 1 in 1928.

See also HAUPTMANN: KREHL (1918).

LITERATURE:

Reuter, Fritz. *Stephan Krehl*. LKC, no. 3. Leipzig: P. Beutel, 1921.

Moser, Hans Joachim. *Allgemeine Musiklehre: Unter gelegentlicher Benutzung des gleichnamigen Werkes von Stephan Krehl*. SGös, no. 220. Berlin: W. de Gruyter, 1940; 1955.

Schaal, Richard. "Krehl, Stephan." In *MGG* (1949-68). Bibliog.

Goodman, Alfred Grant. "Krehl, Stephan." In *NGrove* (1980).

See also KOCH: Dahlhaus (1978); LITERATURE SUPPLEMENT: Dahlhaus (1978); Frobenius ["Isotonos"] (1972-); ● ● ● Jeppesen (1930/ . . ./1974); La Motte-Haber (1969); Müller (1976); Sachs (1972-); Schmalzriedt ["Reprise"] (1972-); Thaler (1984); Tittel (1966).

JOHANN KUHNAU

[1660 – 1722]

Though noted primarily as a composer and distinguished predecessor of Bach in Leipzig, Johann Kuhnau also wrote on music. His *Musicalische Quack-Salber* (1700) is a novel devoted to the exploits of the quack musician Caraffa, who exhibits many characteristics which must have irritated Kuhnau when he saw them among his living contemporaries. Along more traditional lines, Kuhnau created at least three treatises, only one of which, the "Fundamenta compositionis" (1703), still exists in manuscript. Commentators have noted its close identification with manuscript treatises by BERNHARD and by WALTHER, though it seems likely that both WALTHER and Kuhnau shared an as yet undetermined source rather than borrowed from one another. In a letter published in MATTHESON's *Critica musica* (1725), Kuhnau expressed the conservative view that the modes—at least the Phrygian, characterized by its half step between first and second scale degrees—should not be displaced by the twenty-four major and minor keys.

Der musicalische Quack-Salber, nicht alleine denen verständigen Liebhabern der Music, sondern auch allen andern, welche in dieser Kunst keine sonderbahre Wissenschaft haben, in einer kurtzweiligen und angenehmen Historie zur Lust und Ergetzlichkeit beschreiben . . . [Rism B/VI/1, p. 465.]

Dresden: Johann Christoph Mieth and Johann Christoph Zimmermann, 1700.

S● Benndorf, Kurt, ed. DLd, nos. 83-88. Berlin: B. Behr (E. Bock), 1900; facsimile edition, New York: Kraus Reprint, 1966.

Musicalische Vorstellung einer biblischer Historien in 6. Sonaten auff dem Clavier zu spielen [Rism A/I/5, pp. 179-80.]

Leipzig: the author (Immanuel Tietz), 1700.

S● Stone, Kurt, trans. and ed. *Six Biblical Sonatas for Keyboard (1700) with the Original Preface and Introductions in German (Facsimile) and English.* New York: Broude Brothers, 1953.

"Fundamenta compositionis"

Anonymous. Attributed to Kuhnau.

Ms., 1703. [Berlin: Deutsche Staatsbibliothek.]

[Ausspruch über dem Orchester-Streit]

Letter dated 1717.

S● See MATTHESON: (1722-25):Vol. 2/7 (1725): 229-39.

"De triade harmonica"

Ms. [Lost.]

"Tractatus de tetrachordo seu musica antiqua ac hodierna"

Ms. [Lost.]

LITERATURE:

Münnich, Richard. "Johann Kuhnau." Ph.D. dissertation, The University of Berlin, 1902.

Extract (as "Kuhnaus Leben") in *SIMg* 3 (1901-2):473-509.

Riedel, Friedrich Wilhelm. "Kuhnau, Johann." In *MGG* (1949-68). Bibliog.

Hahn, Kurt. "Johann Kuhnaus 'Fundamenta compositionis'." In *Bericht Hamburg 1956* (1957):103-5. Bibliog.

Stockhammer, Robert. "Johann Kuhnau: Zur Wiederkehr seines 300. Geburtstages." *Me* 13/3 (1959-60):131-33.

Moser, Hans Joachim. "In memoriam: Johann Kuhnau zur 300. Wiederkehr seines Geburtstages." *Musica* 14/4 (1960):246.

Schenk, E. "Kuhnau und Fux." *AÖAW* 102/23 (1965):359-66.

Ingen, F. J. van. "Een muziekroman uit het einde van de 17de eeuw: Johann Kuhnau's *Musikalischer Quack-Salber*." *Mens* 17/7 (1962):202-6.

Buelow, George J. "Kuhnau, Johann." In *NGrove* (1980). Bibliog.

Merkley, Lora L. "Johann Kuhnau (1660-1722): Life, Music, and Writings." Ph.D. dissertation, Brandeis University, forthcoming.

See also ADLUNG: (1758); BERNHARD: [ca. 1649]: Müller-Blattau (1922/. . ./1963); FÉTIS: (1833-44); MATTHESON: (1740); PRINTZ: Stöpfgeshoff (1960); SCHEIBE: (1737-40):(1745); VOSSIUS, I.: Serauky (1955); WALTHER: (1732); LITERATURE SUPPLEMENT: Allen ["Philosophies"] (1939); Audbourg-Popin (1986); Becker (1836-39/1964); **Benary (1956/1961)**; Beyschlag (1907/1953); Buelow (1972); Bukofzer (1947); Chafe (1981); Dammann (1958/1967); David (1956); David and Mendel (1945/1966); Dreyfus (1987); Eggebrecht (1959); Eitner (1900-1904/1959-60); Fellerer (1927/. . ./1970); Forkel (1792/1962); Frobenius ["Vollstimmig"] (1972-); Gerber (1790-92/1977), (1812-14/1966); Gurlitt (1944/1966); Hartmann (1980); Hoffman (1970); **Lester (1978)**, **(1989)**; Menck (1931); Mendel (1955), (1978); Moser (1936/. . ./1959); Neumann, Frederick

also Jura circa Musicos ecclesiasticos Leipzig 1688 (Dammann)

(1978); Newman (1985); Newman (1959/. . ./1983); Ottenberg (1973/1978); Reimer ["Kenner"] (1972-); Riedel (1956/1959); Schäfke (1934); Scher-

ing and Wustmann (1941); Schmitz (1950); Sheldon (1975); Subirá (1947/. . ./1958); Walker (1987); Wessely (1971-72); Ziebler (1933); Zenck (1942).

ERNST KURTH

[1886—1946]

Assessing the tonal repertoire during the early decades of the current century, Ernst Kurth developed potent and novel ideas focused upon Bach's counterpoint, Wagner's harmony, and BRUCKNER's form, all from a psychological perspective. He drew upon the writings of Schopenhauer, Bergson, and Freud, as well as upon the premises of Gestalt psychology, while at the same time rejecting traditional pedagogical and speculative orientations. A pupil of Adler in Vienna, he assumed teaching duties in Bern and influenced a generation of Continental scholars. Reactions to Kurth have been sharply divided, ranging from accusations of incompetence and irrelevance to displays of fierce loyalty. In any event, his works are challenging and, in their own way, insightful.

Psychic tension is the ultimate creative force in Kurth's system. As much as was possible, he avoided the acoustical derivations of pitches, instead regarding the emergence of sound as the result of an internal creative process. The kinetic energy of melodic motion and potential energy of chordal formations control the pitch successions of compositions. The tendency of the leading tone and of similarly situated pitches (as in the half-step relationship between third and fourth scale degrees in major and the chromatic pitches of altered chords) is the primary instance of potential energy—even in major and minor triads, whose thirds tend to move up or down, respectively, by half step, and so to cause chord progressions by fifth.

Linear melodic considerations pervade Kurth's exploration of Bach's practice in *Grundlagen des linearen Kontrapunkts* (1917). More than almost any other author, Kurth curtailed consideration of the harmonic component of Bach's music in favor of the contrapuntal, or "linear," aspects. Yet his technical assurance in analysis was at times insufficient for the task of delineating the linear parameters of Bach's complex scores in a convincing manner. In *Romantische Harmonik* (1920) Kurth turned his attention to Wagner, in particular to *Tristan und Isolde*. He acknowledged that as the nineteenth century progressed, coloristic effects gradually replaced traditional syntactic principles as the basis for harmonic progression. The individual chords of Wagner's operas were strongly charged with tendencies due to the half-step resolutions which they held in check momentarily. Whereas the pure triad was self-preserving and a tonally constructive force in harmony, the chromatic and dissonant components that were increasingly incorporated during the nineteenth century were energetic and tonally de-

structive. Kurth continued his prolific output with *Bruckner* (1925), a large, detailed study of the composer's symphonies with emphasis upon their formal characteristics, defined in terms of "waves" (intensification/deintensification), signs of the composer's control of psychic energy through time. His final published work, *Musikpsychologie* (1931), is a synthesis and summary of his perspective, one which seeks the impulses for music as a manifestation of the human will, rather than in the external environment of the physical universe.

"Der Stil der Oper seria von Christoph Willibald Gluck bis zum *Orfeo*"

>Ph.D. dissertation, The University of Vienna, 1908.

>As "Die Jugendopern Glucks bis *Orfeo*":

>*SMw* 1 (1913):193-277.

"Die Voraussetzungen der theoretischen Harmonik und der tonalen Darstellungssysteme"

>Habilitationsschrift, The University of Bern, 1913. Bern: Akademische Buchhandlung von Max Drechsel (E. Bollmann), 1913.

>S ● Dahlhaus, Carl, ed. Facsimile edition. SzM, no. 14. Munich: Emil Katzbichler, 1973.

>>Reviews in *Mf* 29/2 (1976):226 (Emil Platen) and *NZfM* 135/8 (1974):528 (Christian Möllers).

>T ● Rothfarb, Lee Allen. "Ernst Kurth's *The Requirements for a Theory of Harmony*: An Annotated Translation with an Introductory Essay." M.M. thesis, The University of Hartford, 1979.

Grundlagen des linearen Kontrapunkts: Einführung in Stil und Technik von Bach's melodischer Polyphonie

>Bern: M. Drechsel, 1917.

>>Several later printings, with the subtitle *Bachs melodische Polyphonie*. Reviews in *BachJb 1917* 14 (1918):173-75 (Hermann Wetzel), *FZ* 62 (March 27, 1918):1 (Paul Bekker), *NMZ* 42/21 (1921):340-42 (Hugo Holle), and *NZfM* 86/9-10 (1919):60. See RIEMANN: (1918-19), to which Kurth replied with "Zur Stilistik und Theorie des Kontrapunkts: Eine Erwiderung" in *ZfMw* 1/3 (1918-19):176-82.

>T ● Eval'd, Z., trans. *Osnovy linearnogo kontrapunkta*. Foreword by Boris Vladimirovich ASAFIEV. Moscow: 1931.

S ● Facsimile of the 1956 edition. Hildesheim: Georg Olms, 1977.

T ● See Rothfarb (forthcoming), below.

"Zur Motivbildung Bachs: Ein Beitrag zur Stilpsychologie"

BachJb 1917 14 (1918):80-136.

Romantische Harmonik und ihre Krise in Wagners "Tristan"

Bern and Leipzig: P. Haupt, 1920.

Later editions in 1922 and 1923. Reviews in *Musik* 16/4 (1923-24):255-62 (Alfred LORENZ) and *Rmi* 28/2 (1921):331-33 (A. C.).

S ● Facsimile of the 1923 edition. Hildesheim: Georg Olms, 1968.

Reviews in *Mf* 25/2 (1972):225 (Carl Dahlhaus) and *SMz* 109/5 (1969):306.

T ● Etinger, M., trans. and ed. *Romanticheskaia garmoniia i ee krizis v "Tristan" Vagnera.* Moscow: Muzyka, 1975.

Review in *Smuz* /8 (1977):118-25 (I. Barsova).

T ● See Rothfarb (forthcoming), below.

Bruckner

Berlin: Max Hesse, 1925. 2 vols.

Reviews in *Musik* 18/3 (1925-26):200-208 (Frank Wohlfahrt) and *NZfM* 93/12 (1926):682-83 (Georg Göhler).

S ● *Musik* 16/12 (1923-24):861-69.

S ● "Bruckners Fernstand." *MAn* 6/9 (1924):351-57.

S ● "Der musikalische Formbegriff." *Melos* 4/7-8 (1924-25):364-70.

S ● Facsimile edition. Hildesheim: Georg Olms, 1971.

T ● See Rothfarb (forthcoming), below.

Musikpsychologie

Berlin: Max Hesse, 1931.

Reviews in *Am* 3/2 (1931):64-68 (Kurt Herbst) and *Musik* 23/3 (1930-31):182-87 (Alfred LORENZ).

Bern: Krompholz, 1947.

S ● Facsimile of the 1931 edition. Hildesheim: Georg Olms, 1969.

T ● Manion, Mark Martin. "The Origin and Essence of Music: Ernst Kurth's *Musikpsychologie* — A Translation and Commentary." Ph.D. dissertation, Stanford University, forthcoming.

See Rothfarb (1985/1988), below, for a more comprehensive listing of articles by Kurth.

LITERATURE:

Bücken, Ernst. "Ernst Kurth als Musiktheoretiker." *Melos* 4/7-8 (1924-25):358-64.

Akimov, P. V. *Vvedenie v polifoniiu na osnove energeticheskikh uchenii (Ernst Kurth).* [An Introduction to Polyphony on the Basis of the Study of Energy (Ernst Kurth).] Leningrad: 1928.

Schole, Heinrich. *Tonpsychologie und Musik-Ästhetik: Art und Grenzen ihrer wissenschaftlichen Begriffsbildung.* Gottingen: Vandenhoeck & Ruprecht, 1930.

Mazel, Lev Abramovich. "O muzykal'no-teoreticheskoi kontseptsii Kurta." [About the Musical-Theoretical Conceptions of Kurth.] In *Muzykal'nyi al'manakh* [A Musical Almanac], edited by N. I. Cheliapov, pp. 31-60 (Moscow: 1932).

Fischer, Kurt von. "In memoriam Ernst Kurth." In *Der Musik-Almanach,* edited by Viktor Schwarz, pp. 228-52. Munich: Kurt Desch, 1948.

Fischer, Kurt von. "Kurth, Ernst." In *MGG* (1949-68). Bibliog.

Kreidler, Walter. "Ernst Kurth." *Mf* 2/1 (1949):9-13.

Hsu, Dolores Menstell. "Ernst Kurth and His Concept of Music as Motion." *JMT* 10/1 (1966):2-17.

Lieberman, Ira. "Some Representative Works from Beethoven's Early Period Analyzed in Light of the Theories of Ernst Kurth and Kurt von Fischer." D.M.A. dissertation, Columbia University, 1968. [*Rilm* 76-15562. *DA* 30/04A, pp. 1588-89. UMI 69-15692.]

Yasuda, Hiroshi. "Ernst Kurt no ongaku-bigaku no kiso-gainen no kaimei." M.A. dissertation, Kunitachi Music College, 1973. [*Rilm* 75-3028.]

Nishihara, Minoru. "Kurth kenkyû josetsu: Kurth ni okeru shinteki keiki to ongaku tetsugaku no shomondai o megutte." M.A. thesis, Tokyo University of Fine Arts and Music, 1978. [*Rilm* 78-2046.]

Bose, Madelon. "The Sound and the Theory: A Novel Look at Word and Music." *IRASM* 10/1 (1979):57-71. [*Rilm* 79-4729.]

Nishihara, Minoru. "E. Kurth no shokishisô no tenkai — kyôju shikakuronbun ni okeru waseiron no igi." *Og* 25/2 (1979):116-26. [*Rilm* 79-1627.]

Nishihara, Minoru. "Kurth no ongakuriron ni okeru bigakuteki mondai." *Bigaku* 118 (1979):49-61. [*Rilm* 79-5872.]

Edler, Arnfried. "Hinweise auf die Wirkung Bachs im Werk Franz Schuberts." *Mf* 33/3 (1980):279-91. [*Rilm* 80-4693.]

Fischer, Kurt von, and Schnapper, Edith B. "Kurth, Ernst." In *NGrove* (1980). Bibliog.

● ● ● McCreless, Patrick. "Ernst Kurth and the Analysis of the Chromatic Music of the Late Nineteenth Century." *MTS* 5 (1983):56-75.

>Abstract in *MA* 3/3 (1984):295-96 (Celia Duffy).

● ● ● Rothfarb, Lee Allen. "Ernst Kurth as Theorist and Analyst." Ph.D. dissertation, Yale University, 1985; published edition (SCTM), Philadelphia: University of Pennsylvania Press, 1988. Bibliog. [*DA* 46/12A, p. 3531.]

Stoffer, Thomas H. "Parallelen zwischen Ernst Kurths Konzeption der Musikpsychologie und der gegenwärtigen Entwicklung einer kognitiven Musikpsychologie." *MPsy* 2 (1985):87-99. Bibliog.

La Motte-Haber, Helga de. "In memoriam." *MPsy* 3 (1986):7-8.

● ● ● Parkany, Stephen. "Kurth's *Bruckner* and the Adagio of the Seventh Symphony." *NCM* 11/3 (1987-88):262-81.

Rothfarb, Lee. "Ernst Kurth's *Die Voraussetzungen der theoretischen Harmonik* and the Beginnings of Music Psychology." *Theoria* 4 (1989).

Rothfarb, Lee. "Ernst Kurth in Historical Perspective: His Intellectual Inheritance and Music-Theoretical Legacy." *SJMw* 6-7 (1989).

Rothfarb, Lee. *Ernst Kurth: Selected Readings*. Cambridge: Cambridge University Press, forthcoming.

See also ASAFIEV: Mazel (1957); Rozin (1983); BONONCINI: Holler (1955/1963); LORENZ: (1924-33); RIEMANN: (1898):Mickelsen (1970/1977); Mazel (1934-39):(1939); SCHENKER: (1925-30):Vol. 1 (1925); SCHOENBERG: Falck (1982); VIADANA: Haack (1964/1974); YAVORSKY: Tiulin (1937); LITERATURE SUPPLEMENT: Abraham and Dahlhaus (1972); Albersheim (1980); Alette (1951); Apfel ["Wandlungen"] (1964), (1977); Auhagen (1982/1983); Babbitt (1987); Barford (1975); **Benary (1956/1961)**; **Bent** ["Analysis"] **(1980/1987)**; Billeter (1970/1971); Braun (1986); Cahn (1982); Cazden (1948), (1980); ● ● ● Chew (1983); Cook (1987); Dadelsen (1972); **Dahlhaus** ["Tonsystem"] (1949-68), ["Untersuchungen"] (1966/. . ./1988), (1972), (1975/1977), ["Harmony"] **(1980)**, ["Tonality"] **(1980)**, **(1984)**; **Dahlhaus and Sachs (1980)**; Dunsby and Whittall (1988); Eimert (1926-27); Erpf (1959/1974); Federhofer (1944/1950), (1981), (1985), (1989); Fellerer (1927/. . ./1972); Ferand (1937/1938); Fischer (1976); Flechsig (1977); Frobenius ["Polyphon"] (1972-), ["Vollstimmig"] (1972-); Ghislanzoni (1949-51); Handschin (1948); Hartmann (1923); Henneberg (1972/1974); Imig (1969/1970); Jeppesen (1922/. . ./1970), (1930/. . ./1974), (1935); Jiránek (1967); Jorgenson (1957); Kauko (1958); Keller (1955/1965); Kinderman (1983); Konecne (1984); Krenek (1952); La Motte-Haber (1976); Larsen (1963/1988); Mahlert and Sunter (1972-); **Mann (1955/. . ./1987)**; ● ● ● Marvin (1987); Mazel (1937); McQuere (1983); Moyer (1969); Müller-Blattau (1923/. . ./1963), (1949-68); Murray (1978); Natale (1971); Neumann (1939); Neumann (1969); Newcomb (1981-82); Nielsen (1971); **Palisca** ["Theory"] **(1980)**; Palm (1965); Parncutt (1988-89); Révész (1946/. . ./1954); Rohwer (1949-68); Sachs (1972-); Scher (1975); Schmalzriedt ["Coda"] (1972-), ["Durchführen"] (1972-), ["Reprise"] (1972-); Schuhmacher ["Notwendige Ergänzung"] (1974); Seidel (1972-), (1975), (1976), (1979), (1986); Skyllstad (1968); Tittel (1959); Vogel (1955/1954), (1962); **Wason (1981/1985)**; **Zaminer (1985)**.

HONORÉ FRANÇOIS MARIE LANGLÉ

[1741–1807]

The founding of Paris's Conservatoire de musique in 1795 brought about a demand for systematic texts of music instruction. Honoré François Marie Langlé, who served as professor of harmony and librarian of the new school, helped fill this void by writing or contributing to a variety of manuals on harmony, solfège, counterpoint, and fugue.

Langlé's harmonic theory, expounded in his *Traité d'harmonie et de modulation* [1797], is founded upon the interval of the third, the four triadic configurations of which bear major, minor, augmented, and diminished qualities. His *"accord de l'harmonie complette"* consists of five adjacent thirds (an 11/9/7 chord), though its application in actual music (wherein elevenths and ninths typically resolved to tenths and octaves, respectively) was rare. His *Traité de la fugue* [1805] includes a discussion of eight basic fugal types: *fugue réelle, fugue d'imitation, fugue du ton, fugue irrégulière, fugue à la seconde, fugue à la septieme, fugue inverse,* and *fugue mixte.* History has been unkind to Langlé. FÉTIS, for example, at one point exclaimed *"Quelle absurdité!"* in his *Biographie universelle* overview of Langlé, while the modern commentary in Groth (1983) points out critical flaws.

Traité d'harmonie et de modulation [*Rism* B/VI/1, p. 480.]

Paris: Boyer (Marie), [1797]. [LCPS: L-033a.]
Paris: Cochet [Vᵛᵉ Nàderman], [ca. 1797]. [LCPS: L-033b. SMLMS.]

Traité de la basse sous le chant, précédé de toutes les règles de la composition [*Rism* B/VI/1, p. 480.]

Paris: Naderman (Marie), [ca. 1798]. [LCPS: L-032. SMLMS.]

Principes élémentaires de musique

Paris: à l'imprimerie du Conservatoire de musique (Mᵐᵉ Le Roy), *An* VIII [1799-1800].

Joint author, along with CATEL, CHERUBINI, and others.

Nouvelle méthode pour chiffrer les accords

Paris: chez tous les marchands de musique (Goujon fils), *An* IX [1800-1801].

Solfèges pour servir à l'étude dans le Conservatoire de musique

Paris: à l'imprimerie du Conservatoire de musique (Mᵐᵉ Le Roy), *An* X [1801-2].

Joint author, along with CATEL, CHERUBINI, and others.

Edition of *Méthode de chant du Conservatoire de musique . . .,* left incomplete by Bernardo Mengozzi upon his death.

Paris: Janet & Cotelle (Mᵐᵉ Le Roy), *An* XII [1803-4].

Reprinted ca. 1815.

T ● Leipzig: Breitkopf & Härtel, n.d.

Traité de la fugue

Paris: the author (Mᵐᵉ Le Roy), [1805].

LITERATURE:

Favre, Georges. "Langlé, Honoré François Marie." Translated by Wilfried Brennecke. In *MGG* (1949-68).

Favre, Georges. "Un compositeur monégasque: Honoré Langlé (1741-1807)." *Anmon* 1 (1977):55-66. [*Rilm* 77-529.]

Druilhe, Paule. "Langlé, Honoré (François Marie)." In *NGrove* (1980). Bibliog.

See also FÉTIS: (1833-44); LITERATURE SUPPLEMENT: Becker (1836-39/1964); Chevaillier (1925/1931-32); Chew (1980); Cohen (1873-74); Eitner (1900-1904/1959-60); Geering (1949-68); ● ● ●**Groth** (1983); Horsley [*Fugue: History*] (1966); Nelson (1984); Ratner (1970), (1980); **Shirlaw (1917/. . ./1970); Wagner (1974).**

DE LA VOYE-MIGNOT

[d. 1684]

French theorist and geometrician La Voye-Mignot is best known for his study of cadences, which he demonstrated using a two-voiced framework. Perfect, interrupted, and suspensive cadences are described in his *Traité de musique* (1656). The perfect category includes the typical descending-fifth bass, as well as the leading-tone and Phrygian cadences, while the interrupted category includes what we would today label V to VI and V to I⁶. Suspensive cadences are, to use the modern term, half cadences. Different durational values are assigned to each cadence type: perfect end with a longa, interrupted with a brevis, and suspensive with a semibrevis. In a section on the modes, he dismissed the traditional plagal forms, since a polyphonic setting renders them meaningless. This practical handbook, addressed to singers and composers, also includes instruction in the reading of musical notation, techniques for writing simple counterpoint, and rules governing embellished counterpoint, resolution of dissonances, and fugue.

Traité de musique pour bien et facilement apprendre à chanter & composer tant pour les voix que pour instruments . . . [Rism B/VI/1, p. 487.]

>> Paris: Robert Ballard, 1656. [LCPS: L-045. SMLMS.]
>> Paris: Robert Ballard, 1666. 2nd edition, enlarged.

> T ● *Trattato di musica*. Paris: Robert Ballard, 1659. [*Rism* B/VI/1, p. 487.]

> T ● ● ● Gruber, Albion, trans. *Treatise on Music (Traité de la musique)*. MTT, no. 11. Brooklyn: Institute of Mediaeval Music, 1972.

>> The 1656 edition was the source for this translation.

S ● Facsimile of the 1666 edition. Geneva: Minkoff Reprint, 1972.

> Review in *Rdm* 58/2 (1972):271-72 (André Verchaly).

LITERATURE:

Siohan, Robert. "La Voye-Mignot, de." Translated by Dorothea Schmidt-Preuß. In *MGG* (1949-68). Bibliog.

Cohen, Albert. "La Voye-Mignot, de." In *NGrove* (1980). Bibliog.

See also FÉTIS: (1833-44); OUVRARD: (1658):Boulay (1984); LITERATURE SUPPLEMENT: **Apfel (1981)**; Atcherson (1973); Butler (1977); Cohen (1966/1978), ["Symposium"] (1972), (1981); Eitner (1900-1904/1959-60); Gerber (1790-92/1977); Gruber (1969); Horsley [*Fugue: History*] (1966); Houle (1960), (1987); Schmalzriedt ["Reprise"] (1972-); **Schneider (1972)**; **Seidel and Cooper (1986)**; Taddie (1984).

GOTTFRIED WILHELM LEIBNIZ

[1646 – 1716]

Though more influential in the realms of mathematics and philosophy, Gottfried Wilhelm Leibniz maintained a sincere interest in the theory of music, revealed principally in his correspondence with Christoph Goldbach and Conrad Henfling. Not surprisingly, the issue of consonance was of particular concern to the father of differential calculus. Leibniz maintained that the aesthetic appreciation fostered by consonance resulted from the unconscious calculation of interval ratios. In this manner, the process of actual human assessment replaced the prescriptive ratios offered by authorities such as ZARLINO as the determinant of consonance. Proof that such measurements were indeed occurring as a component of perception did not appear, however.

"Principes de la nature et de la grâce, fondés en raison"

> Mss., ca. 1712-14. [Hanover: Niedersächsische Landesbibliothek (3 versions); Vienna: Nationalbibliothek; Paris: Bibliothèque nationale.]

S ● Robinet, André, ed. Bpc. Paris: Presses universitaires de France, 1954.

Correspondence

> Mss. [The correspondence with Conrad Henfling is at Hanover: Niedersächsische Landesbibliothek.]

S ● Kortholt, Christian, ed. *Epistolae ad diversos*. Leipzig: Bern. Christoph Brettkopf, 1734-42.

S ● Bodemann, Eduard, ed. *Der Briefwechsel des Gottfried Wilhelm Leibniz in der königlichen öffentlichen Bibliothek zu Hannover*. Hanover: Hahnsch Buchhandlung, 1889.

S ● Haase, Rudolf, ed. *Der Briefwechsel zwischen Leibniz und Conrad Henfling: Ein Beitrag zur Musiktheorie des 17. Jahrhunderts*. VLA, no. 9. Frankfurt am Main: Vittorio Klostermann, 1982. [*Rilm* 82-2329.]

S ● "Briefwechsel zwischen Conrad Henfling und Gottfried Wilhelm Leibniz." *Mth* 2/2 (1987): 169-81.

LITERATURE:

Henfling, Conrad. "Epistola de novo suo systemate musico." *MBis* 1 (1710):265-94; German translation by Werner Schulze in *Mth* 2/2 (1987):169-81 and 3/2 (1988):171-81.

> Published through Leibniz's influence.

Żymalkowski, Ulrich. "Die Bedeutung der prästabilierten Harmonie im Leibnizischen Systeme." Ph.D. dissertation, The University of Erlangen, 1905; published edition, Berlin: Die Post, 1905.

Mahnke, Dietrich. *Leibniz und Goethe: Die Harmonie ihrer Weltansichten*. WTFpS, no. 4. Erfurt: Kurt Stenger, 1924.

Haase, Rudolf. "Leibniz, Gottfried Wilhelm." In *MGG* (1949-68). Bibliog.

Bugg, Eugene G. "A Criticism of Leibniz's Theory of Consonance." *JAAC* 20/3 (1961-62):295-99 [defective]; 21/4 (1962-63):467-72 [corrected].

Haase, Rudolf. "Leibniz und die pythagoreisch-harmonikale Tradition." *Antaios* 4/4 (1962-63):368-76. Bibliog.

Haase, Rudolf. *Leibniz und die Musik: Ein Beitrag zur Geschichte der harmonikalen Symbolik*. Hommerich: Paul Eckhardt Verlag, 1963. Bibliog.

Müller, Kurt, ed. *Leibniz-Bibliographie: Die Literatur über Leibniz*. VLA, no. 1. Frankfurt am Main: Klostermann, 1967. Bibliog.

> Review in *ZfMG* 183/1 (1970):4-5 (J. E. Hofmann).

Vonessen, Franz. "Reim und Zahl bei Leibniz." *Antaios* 8/2 (1966-67):99-120. Bibliog.

Serres, Michel. *Le système de Leibniz et ses modèles mathématiques*. 2 vols. Paris: Presses universitaires de France, 1968. Bibliog.

> Reviews in *JHP* 8/1 (1970):105-7 (G. H. R. Parkinson), *PRund* 17/1-2 (1970):144-45 (J. E. Hofmann), and *Rcsf* 27/3 (1972):351-53 (Paolo Parrini).

Müller, Kurt, and Kröner, Gisela. *Leben und Werk von Gottfried Wilhelm Leibniz: Eine Cronik*. VLA, no. 2. Frankfurt am Main: Klostermann, 1969.

> Reviews in *NJL* 43 (1971):310-11 (Georg Schnath) and *TG* 36/4 (1969):338-39 (Ludolf v. Mackensen).

Haase, Rudolf. "Leibniz und die harmonikale Tradition." *Me* 26/2 (1972-73):78.

Haase, Rudolf. "Leibniz und die Musiktheorie." *ÖM* 27/10 (1972):547-48. [*Rilm* 72-3125.]

Haase, Rudolf. "Leibniz und die harmonikale Tradition." *Leibniz-Kongress 1972* (1973-75):Vol. 1:123-34. [*Rilm* 76-16497.]

Galeffi, Romano. "À propos de l'actualité de Leibniz en esthétique." *Resth* 27/2 (1974):161-70.

Baas, Bernard. "L' 'animal musicien': Philosophie et musique chez Leibniz." *Mujeu* 25 (1976):49-72. [*Rilm* 76-5293.]

Haase, Rudolf, ed. "Korrespondenten von G. W. Leibniz: 3. Conrad Henfling." *StL* 9/1 (1977):111-19. Bibliog. [*Rilm* 77-4531.]

● ● ● Haase, Rudolf. "Leibniz, Gottfried Wilhelm." In *NGrove* (1980). Bibliog.

Luppi, Andrea. " 'Imitation de l'harmonie universelle': G. W. Leibniz e la musica." Thesis, The Catholic University of the Sacred Heart in Milan, 1985-86.

Schulze, Werner. "Henflings Brief über sein neues Musik-System." *Mth* 2/2 (1987):183-86.

Schulze, Werner. "Anmerkungen zu Henflings 'Epistola'." *Mth* 3/2 (1988):183-85.

See also FÉTIS: (1833-44); KEPLER: Thimus (1868-76/ 1972); MERSENNE: (1617-48); LITERATURE SUPPLEMENT: Allen ["Philosophies"] (1939); Auhagen (1982/1983); Babbitt (1987); Becker (1836-39/1964); **Bent** ["Analysis"] **(1980/1987)**; Birke (1966); Blankenburg ["Harmonie"] (1959); Boomgaarden (1985/1987); **Buelow** ["Rhetoric"] **(1980)**; Bukofzer (1947); Cazden (1948); Cohen (1981); Cohen (1984); Crombie (1969); **Dahlhaus (1984)**; **Dahlhaus et al. (1987)**; Dammann (1958/1967); Eggebrecht (1955); Eitner (1900-1904/1959-60); Fellerer (1927/. . ./1972); Flindell (1983-84); Forkel (1792/1962); Fubini (1971/1983); Gerber (1790-92/1977), (1812-14/1966); Godwin (1987); Göttert (1985-86); Gouk (1980); Gurlitt (1944/1966); Haase (1963), (1969), (1976), (1986); Handschin (1948); Harich-Schneider ([1939]/. . ./ 1970); Hosler (1978/1981); Hüschen (1949-68); Jorgenson (1963); **Katz and Dahlhaus (1987-)**; Kauko (1958); Kayser (1950); Kirkendale (1984); Kivy (1984); Koenigsberger (1979); Lippman (1986); Lottermoser (1949-68); Moos (1902/1922); Nowak (1975); Palisca and Spender (1980); Révész (1946/. . ./1954); Rohwer (1949-68); Schäfke (1934); Schavernoch (1981); Schering and Wustmann (1941); Seidel (1976); Sheldon (1986); **Shirlaw (1917/. . ./1970)**; Spender and Shuter-Dyson (1980); Subirá (1947/. . ./1958); Truesdell (1960); Vogel (1955/1954); Walker (1976); Wellek (1949-68); Wightman (1972); **Zaminer (1985)**; Zenck (1942); Zimmermann (1976).

JOHANNES LIPPIUS

[1585 – 1612]

The gradual development of triadic thinking coalesced in the writings of Johannes Lippius, whose notion of *trias harmonica* is introduced as the logical continuation of his discussion of monads and dyads. A theologian and philosopher, Lippius infused his theoretical discussions with references to the Trinity, comparing the root of his triad with the Father, the fifth with the Son, and the third with the Holy Spirit. The concept of inversion, both of intervals and of triads, is systematically articulated, though its implications were not then fully developed either in theory or in practice.

The substance of Lippius's theoretical conceptions is found in the three disputations published in Wittenberg (1609-10), though the *Synopsis musicae novae* (1612), as a summary of these ideas, found wider circulation and was mimicked by various later authors, including CRÜGER, BARYPHONUS, and ALSTED. Lippius's writings reveal a strong (and, at that time in Germany, uncommon) interest in speculative thinking, complementing his discussions of practical matters. Though his formulation is less detailed than that of BURMEISTER, Lippius based his conception of form upon rhetoric. The meaning of the text specified for the composer the appropriate choices for chordal construction and the degree of ornamentation. Modal theory is modified in keeping with the new triadic emphasis, and the six modal pairs, while maintaining specific individual characters, are categorized according to the quality of triad—major or minor—formed above the final.

Lippius advocated a shift away from the solmization of hexachords to the system of bocedisation, wherein the syllables *bo, ce, di, ga, lo, ma*, and *ni* provide the means for traversing an entire octave. Like his proposal that the standard letter names (C, D, E, etc.) be replaced by the first letters of these syllables, the system was not universally adopted.

Disputatio musica prima . . . [*Rism* B/VI/1, p. 206.]

     Wittenberg: Johann Gormann, 1609. [LCPS: C-019. SMLMS.]

Disputatio musica secunda . . . [*Rism* B/VI/1, p. 206.]

     Wittenberg: Johann Gormann, 1609. [LCPS: C-020. SMLMS.]

Disputatio musica tertia . . . [*Rism* B/VI/1, p. 206.]

     Wittenberg: Johann Gormann, 1610. [LCPS: C-021. SMLMS.]

Thematia [sic] *musica ut multis forte paradoxa* . . . [*Rism* B/VI/1, p. 206.]

     Jena: Johann Weidner, 1610.

Breviculum errorum musicorum . . . [*Rism* B/VI/1, p. 206.]

     Jena: Johann Weidner, 1611.

Themata fontem omnium errantium musicorum aperientia . . . [*Rism* B/VI/1, p. 206.]

     Jena: Johann Weidner, 1611.

Synopsis musicae novae omnino verae atque methodicae universae . . . [*Rism* B/VI/1, p. 505.]

     Derived from *Disputatio musica secunda* and *tertia*, above.

     Strasbourg: Paul Ledertz (Carl Kieffer), 1612. [LCPS: L-083. IDC.]

     Reprinted in *Philosophiae verae* (1614), vol. 1, below.

T ● Rivera, Benito V., trans. *Synopsis of New Music.* CCMPT, no. 8. Colorado Springs, Colo.: Colorado College Music Press, 1977.

     Reviews in *Choice* 15/5-6 (1978-79):700-701, *JMT* 23/2 (1979):310-15 (Joel Lester), and *ML* 60/3 (1979):357-61 (Ronald Woodley).

Philosophiae verae ac sincerae synopticae [*Rism* B/VI/1, p. 505.]

     1) *Praeparatio per musicam diam*
     2) *Perfectio interior: Realis per metaphysicam, rationalis per logicam; Exterior: Realis per ethicam, rationalis per rhetoricam*
     Erfurt: Johann Bischoff, [1614].
     Erfurt: Johann Bischoff, [1615]. [LCPS: L-082. HoM: 896.]

See Rivera (1974/1980), below, for a listing of all known works by Lippius, including those on theological and philosophical topics.

LITERATURE:

Ruhnke, Martin. "Lippius, Johannes." In *MGG* (1949-68). Bibliog.

Rivera, Benito V. "Johannes Lippius and His Musical Treatises: A Study of German Musical Thought in the Early Seventeenth Century." Ph.D. dissertation, Rutgers University, 1974; published edition (as *German Music Theory in the Early Seventeenth Century: The Treatises of Johannes Lippius*, SiM, no. 17), Ann Arbor, Mich.: UMI Research Press, 1980. Bibliog. [*Rilm* 76-9802. *DA* 35/10A, p. 6755.]

Reviews in *JMT* 25/2 (1981):326-34 (Lyle Hanna), *MA* 1/2 (1982):209-13 (Geoffrey Chew), *Notes* 37/3 (1980-81):586-87 (Joel Lester), and *Rh* 265/4 [540] (1981):535 (Édith Weber).

● ● ● Buelow, George J. "Lippius, Johannes." In *NGrove* (1980).

Howard, John Brooks. "Form and Method in Johannes Lippius's *Synopsis musicae novae*." *JAMS* 38/3 (1985):524-50. Bibliog.

See also BELLERMANN: (1858); BURMEISTER: Ruhnke (1954/1955); CALVISIUS: Bendorf (1894); FÉTIS: (1833-44); KEPLER: Dickreiter (1971/1973); RIEMANN: (1898); WALTHER: (1732); Gehrmann (1891); WERCKMEISTER: Dammann (1954); ZARLINO: Dahlhaus (1957); LITERATURE SUPPLEMENT: **Apfel (1981)**; Atcherson (1973); Audbourg-Popin (1984); Becker (1836-39/1964); Beiche ["Inversio"] (1972-); **Benary (1956/1961)**; **Bent** ["Analysis"] **(1980/1987)**; Blankenburg ["Harmonie"] (1959); Braun (1986); **Buelow** (1972), ["Rhetoric"] **(1980)**; Bukofzer (1947); Chominski (1962/1981); **Dahlhaus** ["Kon-

sonanz"] (1949-68), ["Dreiklang"] (1955), ["Termini"] (1955), ["Untersuchungen"] (1966/. . ./ 1988), ["Harmony"] **(1980)**; Dammann (1958/1967); Eitner (1900-1904/1959-60); Federhofer (1944/1950); Fellerer ["Zur Kontrapunktlehre"] (1972), ["Zur Kontrapunktlehre"] (1973), (1983); Ferand (1951); Flindell (1983-84); Forchert (1986); Forkel (1792/1962); Gerber (1790-92/1977), (1812-14/1966); Gissel (1980/1983); Gut (1976); Hannas (1934); Harrán (1986); Heckmann (1953); Hein (1954); Horsley ["Fugue and Mode"] (1966/1978); Hüschen (1986); Kauko (1958); Lange (1899-1900); **Lester** (1974), ● ● ●(1977), (1978), **(1989)**; Leuchtmann (1957/1959); Lippman (1986); Meier (1974/1988); Müller-Blattau (1923/. . ./1963); Niemöller (1970); Palisca (1949-68); **Powers** ["Mode"] **(1980)**; Preußner (1924); Rauhe (1959-60); Reckow (1972-); **Ritzel (1967/1968)**; Rivera (1978), (1984); Robbins (1938); Rogers (1955); Ruhnke (1949-68); Sachs (1972-); **Shirlaw (1917/ . . ./1970)**; Taddie (1984); Tenney (1988); Unger (1941/1969); Vogel (1955/1954); Walker (1987); Wienpahl (1953).

NIKOLAUS LISTENIUS

[born ca. 1510]

The modest instruction manual which Nikolaus Listenius (Listen, Lysten) devised during the 1530s became, along with FABER's *Compendiolum musicae*, one of the most popular music tutors used in the Lutheran schools of the German lands. Listenius was the first to introduce the term *musica poetica*, referring to the art of composition, as a coequal of the traditional classifications *musical theoretica* (the science of music) and *musica practica* (the concerns of performance). This influential categorization motivated numerous later books about compositional technique (by FABER, DRESSLER, BURMEISTER, and HERBST, among others) and fostered an improved status for the composer and the works which were created.

Though the standard topics of music fundamentals which Listenius covered differ little from earlier manuals, such as those of Georg Rhau, his commentaries sometimes provide new insights, such as his discussion of *musica ficta* and other matters related to late-Renaissance chromatic practice. Through his efforts, sophisticated Lutheran musical amateurs filled the German parishes, creating an environment ripe for the flowering of musical creativity in the developing Protestant musical tradition.

Rudimenta musicae in gratiam studiosae juventutis diligenter comportata . . . [*Rism* B/VI/1, pp. 509-10.]

Wittenberg: Georg Rhau, 1533.

Several later editions, including:

Augsburg: Heinrich Steyner, 1540. [LCPS: L-086.]

Revised, as *Musica . . . ab authore denuo recognita, multisque novis regulis et exemplis adaucta* [*Rism* B/VI/2, pp. 506-9.]:

Wittenberg: Georg Rhau, 1537. [LCPS: L-085a.]

Numerous later editions through 1583, including:

Wittenberg: Georg Rhau, 1544. [LCPS: L-085b.]
Leipzig: Michael Blum, 1547. [HoM: 897.]
Wittenberg: Georg Rhau, 1548. [SMLMS.]
Nuremberg: Johann Petreius, 1549. [LCPS: L-085c.]
Nuremberg: Johann Petreius, 1550. [LCPS: L-085d.]
Nuremberg: Gabriel Heyn, 1557. [LCPS: L-085e.]

S ● Schünemann, Georg, ed. Facsimile of the 1549 Nuremberg edition. VMbPH, no. 8. Berlin: Martin Breslauer, 1927. Bibliog.

T ● Seay, Albert, trans. *Music (Musica)*. CCMPT, no. 6. Colorado Springs, Colo.: Colorado College Music Press, 1975.

Reviews in *ML* 57/2 (1976):199-200 (John Caldwell), *Notes* 33/1 (1976-77):77-78 (Dale Jay Bonge), and *Rdm* 62/2 (1976):300-302 (Michel Huglo).

LITERATURE:

Niemöller, Klaus Wolfgang. "Listen(ius), Nikolaus." In *MGG* (1949-68). Bibliog.

Niemöller, Klaus Wolfgang. "Listenius, Nikolaus." In *NGrove* (1980).

See also BURMEISTER: Ruhnke (1954/1955); DRESSLER: Luther (1936/1942); FÉTIS: (1833-44); FINCK: Matzdorf (1957); LIPPIUS: Rivera (1974/1980); WALTHER: (1732); LITERATURE SUPPLEMENT: Apfel (1981); Becker (1836-39/1964); Bellingham (1971), (1980); **Benary (1956/1961)**; **Bent** ["Analysis"] **(1980/1987):(1987)**; Bent, M. (1984); Berger (1987); Brennecke (1953); **Buelow** (1972), ["Rhetoric"] **(1980)**; **Dahlhaus (1984)**; Eitner (1900-1904/1959-60); Falck (1965); Federhofer (1985); Feldmann (1958); Fellerer (1969), ["Zur Kontrapunktlehre"] (1972); Frobenius ["Tactus"] (1972-); Gerber (1812-14/1966); Gurlitt (1942/1966), (1954/1966); Houle (1987); Hüschen (1986); Jackson (1988); Kätzel (1951/1957); Livingstone (1971); Lowinsky (1946/1967), (1948):(1949); ● ● ● **Maniates (1979)**; Niemöller (1964/1969); Pietzsch (1936-42/1971); Sannemann (1903/1904); Schünemann (1928/1931); **Seidel and Cooper (1986)**; Sovík (1985); Straková (1975); Zenck (1942).

JOHANN CHRISTIAN LOBE

[1797 – 1881]

The published work of Johann Christian Lobe typifies the career of the nineteenth-century theorist: there is the popular, often-translated *Katechismus der Musik* (1851) for the amateur; the ambitious, multi-volume *Lehrbuch der musikalischen Komposition* (1850-67) for the professional; and compilations of his letters and essays, *Musikalische Briefe* (1852) and *Consonanzen und Dissonanzen* (1869). Also typical is his stint as editor of a journal: he spent two years with Leipzig's *Allgemeine musikalische Zeitung* in the late 1840s.

Lobe's interest in the works of earlier composers served as an inspiration for his provocative *Lehrbuch*. By studying the few published samples of Beethoven's sketches, he developed a conception of how such compositions evolved. He was particularly interested in motives and their elaboration. The music of Bach served as model for the volume on counterpoint and fugue. Not contented with the abstractions which other theorists were utilizing in their fugal analyses, Lobe stripped away much of the terminology and the sectional orientation, asserting instead that such works were continuous fabrics of compositional development and formulating a new vocabulary to define his perspective. His harmonic theory incorporates the ninth above all diatonic roots as a potential chord component. By altering or omitting some of these pitches (root, third, fifth, seventh, and ninth), he derived a large variety of choices for chordal structures.

"Andeutungen über meine Lehrmethode der musikalischen Komposition"

AmZ 44/28-30 (1842):553-56, 569-72, 585-89.

Compositions-Lehre; oder, Umfassende Theorie von der thematischen Arbeit und den modernen Instrumentalformen . . .

Weimar: Bernhard Friedrich Voigt, 1844.

Lehrbuch der musikalischen Komposition

1) *Von den ersten Elementen der Harmonielehre an bis zur vollständigen Komposition des Streichquartetts und aller Arten von Klavierwerken*

2) *Die Lehre von der Instrumentation*

3) *Lehre von der Fuge, dem Kanon und dem doppelten Kontrapunkte, in neuer und einfacher Darstellung mit besonderer Rücksicht auf Selbstunterricht*

4) *Die Oper*

Leipzig: Breitkopf & Härtel, 1850, 1855, 1860, 1867. 4 vols.

Other editions through the end of the century, including:

Leipzig: Breitkopf & Härtel, 1884-87. Edited by Hermann Kretzschmar.

T ● Sandré, Gustave, trans. *Traité pratique de composition musicale depuis les premiers éléments de l'harmonie jusqu'à la composition raisonnée du quatuor et des principales formes de la musique pour piano.* Leipzig and Brussels: Breitkopf & Härtel, 1889; 2nd edition, 1897.

T ● Kashkin, Nicholai Dmitrievich, trans. *Rukovodstvo k sochinenii muzyki: Opera*. Moscow: 1898.

> A translation of Vol. 4.

Katechismus der Musik (WiKat, no. 4)

> Leipzig: J. J. Weber, 1851.
>
>> Numerous later editions, including some edited by Franz Eschweiler [ca. 1910], by Hugo Leichtentritt (1913), by Richard Hofmann (1918), and by Werner Neumann (1949). Reviews of Neumann's 1965 edition appear in *MG* 18/7 (1968):495 (Ingrid Hauk) and *MSch* 19/4 (1968):174-75 (Hans Pollack).

T ● *Katechismus der muzijk*. The Hague: 1857.

T ● Ritter, Fanny Raymond. *Catechism of Music*. New York: J. Schuberth, [1867]; Philadelphia: F. A. North, [1876?]; Boston: O. Ditson, New York: C. H. Ditson, [1880]; revised edition (edited by Th. Baker), New York: G. Schirmer, [1881]; revised edition (edited by J. H. Cornell), New York: G. Schirmer, 1896.

T ● CHAIKOVSKY, Petr I'lich, trans. *Muzykal'nyi katekhizis, sochinenïe I. K. Lobe*. Moscow: Petr Jurgenson, 1870; 2nd edition, 1882.

T ● Bache, Constance, trans. *Catechism of Music*. London: Augener, [ca. 1885].

> Review in *MMR* 15/179-80 (1885):241-43, 265-68 (Frederick Niecks).

T ● Sandré, Gustave, trans. [*Le bréviaire du musicien:*] *Manuel général de musique par demandes et par réponses à l'usage des professeurs, des élèves et des amateurs*. Leipzig: Brietkopf & Härtel, 1886; other editions.

T ● Coon, Oscar, ed. and trans. *A New Catechism of Music on the Plan of J. C. Lobe*. New York: C. Fischer, [ca. 1905].

Musikalische Briefe: Wahrheit über Tonkunst und Tonkünstler

> Published anonymously.

> Leipzig: Baumgärtner, 1852. 2 vols.

> Leipzig: Baumgärtner, 1860. 2 vols.

Vereinfachte Harmonielehre

> Leipzig: C. F. W. Siegel, 1861.

Katechismus der Compositionslehre (WiKat, no. 50)

> Leipzig: J. J. Weber, [ca. 1862].
>
>> Later editions, including those edited by Richard Hofmann (1902) and by Otto Klauwell (1914).

T ● Ritter, Fanny Raymond. *Catechism of Composition*. New York: J. Schuberth, [1868].; revised edition (edited by Theod. Baker), New York: G. Schirmer, 1891.

Consonanzen und Dissonanzen: Gesammelte Schriften aus älterer und neuerer Zeit

> Leipzig: Baumgärtner, 1869.

S ● Reich, Willi, ed. *Gespräche mit Komponisten: Von Gluck bis zur Elektronik*. MBWl. Zürich: Manesse Verlag, 1965.

LITERATURE:

Sietz, Reinhold. "Lobe, Johann Christian." In *MGG* (1949-68). Bibliog.

Rakijaš, Branko. "Razvoj muzičke terminologije u hrvatskoj poslije kuhača, u razdoblju 1918-1941." *Armus* 6 (1975):71-83. [*Rilm* 75-4089.]

Warrack, John. "Lobe, Johann Christian." In *NGrove* (1980).

See also FÉTIS: (1833-44); LITERATURE SUPPLEMENT: Beiche ["Dux"] (1972-); **Bent, I.** ["Analysis"] **(1980/1987)**, ● ● ● (1984); Blumröder (1972-); Bullivant (1980); Carpenter (1988); Carse (1925/1964); Dunsby and Whittall (1988); Dziebowska (1976); Frisius (1969/1970); Frobenius ["Polyphon"] (1972-); Henneberg (1983); Krones (1988); **Mann (1955/. . ./1987)**; McQuere (1983); Moyer (1969); Müller-Blattau (1923/. . ./1963), (1949-68); Nielsen (1971); Oberdörffer (1949-68); Ratner (1949), (1980); **Ritzel (1967/1968)**; Rothärmel (1963/1968); Rummenhöller (1967); Seidel (1972-), (1976); Sheldon (1982); Steinbeck (1981); Tittel (1966); **Wason (1981/1985)**, (1988); Wirth (1966).

MATTHEW LOCKE

[1621-22 — 1677]

In the preface to his *Melothesia*, Matthew Locke set down what may be the first instructions for realizing a figured bass in English. The rules are sound and thorough, with clear comments on figures which indicate the altered thirds, chords of the sixth, and suspensions. Locke also supplied comments about modulating basses—that is, the placing of chords of the sixth on certain notes of the key plus on sharp notes outside of the key. In addition, basses with alternately descending thirds and rising steps or half steps are harmonized. Suggestions are given for establishing a chordal foundation in passages involving a rapid succession of notes. Various ornaments are listed, but there is no table of execution is shown.

Locke championed English music with a sharp pen, which was used for hateful attacks on Thomas SALMON, whose *Essay* proposed a novel alternative for the multiplicity of clefs in use at that time. Locke was a well-established composer; SALMON was a young amateur musician. Locke saw SALMON's proposals to abolish the Guidonian gamut as an attack on professional musicians. He successfully showed that the octave division of G to G proposed by SALMON was not convenient for most voices, and that his system would require inordinate use of ledger lines and shifting from clef to clef.

Observations upon a Late Book, Entitled, "An Essay to the Advancement of Musick," etc., Written by Thomas Salmon . . . [Rism B/VI/1, p. 511.]

> A response to SALMON: [*Essay*] (1672). Countered in SALMON: [*Vindication*] (1672), to which Locke replied in *The Present Practice* (1673), below.

London: John Playford (W. G[odbid]), 1672. [LCPS: L-089.]

Melothesia; or, Certain General Rules for Playing upon a Continued-Bass . . . [Rism B/VI/1, p. 511.]

London: J. Carr, 1673. [LCPS: L-088.]

S ● See ● ● **Arnold (1931/. . ./1965)**.

S ● Kooiker, Anthony. "Locke's *Melothesia*: Its Place in the History of Keyboard Music in Restoration England." 2 vols. Ph.D. dissertation, The University of Rochester, 1962. [*DA* 26/04, p. 2255. UMI 63-02381.]

S ● Facsimile edition. MMMLF, ser. 2, no. 30. New York: Broude Brothers, 1975.

S ● Hogwood, Christopher, ed. Facsimile edition. Oxford: Oxford University Press, 1987.

Reviews in *ML* 68/4 (1987):401 (Howard Ferguson) and *OrR* 74/1 (1988):72.

The Present Practice of Musick Vindicated against the Exceptions and New Way of Attaining Musick Lately Publish'd by Thomas Salmon . . . To Which is Added "Duellum musicum" by John Philipps . . . Together with a Letter from John Playford to Mr. T. Salmon by Way of Confutation of His Essay [Rism B/VI/1, p. 512.]

> A response to SALMON: [*Vindication*] (1672).

London: N. Brooke & J. Playford, 1673. [LCPS: L-090.]

S ● Facsimile edition. MMMLF, ser. 2, no. 16. New York: Broude Brothers, 1974.

LITERATURE:

le Huray, Peter. "Locke, Matthew." Translated by Wilhelm Pfannkuch. In *MGG* (1949-68). Bibliog.

Lefkowitz, Murray. "Matthew Locke at Exeter." *Consort* 22 (1965):5-16.

Tilmouth, Michael. "Matthew Locke, 1622-77: A Tercentenary Note." *MT* 118/1610 (1977):295-98. [*Rilm* 77-496.]

Lefkowitz, Murray. "Locke, Matthew." In *NGrove* (1980). Bibliog.

See also FÉTIS: (1833-44); HEINICHEN: Buelow (1961/. . ./1986); MACE: (1676); NORTH, R.: Wilson (1959); RIEMANN: (1898); SALMON: Ruff (1964); Baldwin and Wilson (1970); LITERATURE SUPPLEMENT: Babbitt (1987); Burney (1776-89/. . ./1957); Chenette (1967); Chew (1980); Dahlhaus ["Untersuchungen"] (1966/. . ./1988); Dolmetsch (1915/. . ./1969); Donington (1980); Eitner (1900-1904/1959-60); Forkel (1792/1962); Gerber (1790-92/1977), (1812-14/1966); Hancock (1977); Hawkins (1776/. . ./1969); Jackson (1988); **Kassler** (1971), **(1979)**; Kivy (1984); Lawrence (1978); Lewis (1981); Miller (1960); Mitchell, J. W. (1963); **Palisca** [*Baroque*] (1968/1981), ["Theory"] **(1980)**; Pulver (1927/. . ./1973); Rogers (1955); Ruf (1972-); Ruff (1962), (1970); **Seidel and Cooper (1986)**; Shute (1972); Subirá (1947/. . ./1958); Traficante (1970); Wienpahl (1953), (1955); Williams, P. (1970).

GEORG SIMON LÖHLEIN

[1725 – 1781]

The German music teacher Georg Simon Löhlein assembled useful manuals for the musical instruction of amateurs: a two-volume *Clavier-Schule* (1765-81) and a violin method called *Anweisung zum Violinspielen* (1774). He depended upon the writings of C. P. E. BACH, SORGE, and HEINICHEN for his keyboard primer, while Leopold MOZART was his model for the *Anweisung*.

Keyboard students were introduced to the basic symbols and concepts necessary for attaining basic proficiency in their art in the first volume of the *Clavier-Schule*. In the second volume, which came some sixteen years later, Löhlein addressed the more theoretical topics of consonance and dissonance, chord construction and voice leading in figured-bass accompaniment, and the realization of an unfigured bass. The various editions differ markedly in their content. That of 1779-81 contains an early description of sonata form, focusing upon the interaction between set dance forms and the inventive freedom of improvisation. By the 1804 Müller edition, the work had deteriorated into routine technical studies. Löhlein's works offer the modern scholar a contemporary perspective on the stylistic elements which define *galant* practice, including both theoretical issues such as daring dissonance usage and modulations, particularly in recitatives, and practical matters such as improvised ornamentation.

Clavier-Schule; oder, Kurze und gründliche Anweisung zur Melodie und Harmonie, durchgehends mit practischen Beyspielen erkläret [Rism B/VI/1, p. 513.]

and

Clavier-Schule, zweyter Band, worinnen eine vollständige Anweisung zur Begleitung der unbezifferten Bäße, und andern im ersten Band fehlenden Harmonien gegeben wird durch sechs Sonaten, mit Begleitung einer Violine erkläret; Nebst einem Zusatze vom Recitativ [Rism B/VI/1, p. 513.]

> Leipzig and Züllichau: Waisenhaus- und Frommannische Buchhandlung, 1765. Vol. 1. [LCPS: L-093a.]
> Leipzig and Züllichau: Waisenhaus- und Frommannische Buchhandlung, 1773. Vol. 1.
> Leipzig and Züllichau: Waisenhaus- und Frommannische Buchhandlung, 1779. Vol. 1.
> Leipzig and Züllichau: Waisenhaus- und Frommannische Buchhandlung, 1781. Vol. 2. [LCPS: L-093d.]
> Leipzig: Waisenhaus- und Frommannische Buchhandlung, 1782. [LCPS: L-093c.] Vol. 1.
> Züllichau and Freystadt: Nathanael Sigismund Frommanns Erben, 1788. Vol. 2.

> As *Georg Simon Löhleins Clavier-Schule; oder, Kurze Anweisung zum Clavierspielen und dem Generalbaße, mit practischen Beyspielen*:

Leipzig and Züllichau: Nathanael Sigismund Frommanns Erben, 1791. Two vols. Edited by Johann Georg Witthauer.

> As *Klavierschule; oder, Anweisung zum Klavier- und Fortepiano-Spiel nebst vielen practischen Beyspielen und einem Anhange vom Generalbaße*:

Jena: Friedrich Frommann, 1804. In one volume. Edited by August Eberhard Müller.

> Review in *AmZ* 8/13-14 (1805-6):203-7, 209-19.

> As *Fortepiano-Schule*:

Leipzig: Peters, 1819.

> As *Große Fortepiano-Schule*:

Leipzig: Peters, 1825. Edited by Carl CZERNY. 1848. Edited by F. Knorr.

T ● Gablitst, Fedor, trans. *Klavikordnaia shkola, ili kratkoe i osnavatel'noe pokazanie k soglasiu i melodii prakticheskimi primerami iziasnennoe.* Moscow: Christian-Ludwig Weber, 1773. [Rism B/VI/1, p. 514.]

> Russian translation of the first volume.

T ● "Clavier onderwys." Ms., [ca. 1778?]. [Amsterdam: Universiteitsbibliotheek.]

T ● Wilson, Dora Jean. "Georg Simon Lohlein's *Klavierschule*: Translation and Commentary." Ph.D. dissertation, The University of Southern California, 1979. [Rilm 79-2713. *DA* 39/12A, p. 7049.]

Anweisung zum Violinspielen, mit pracktischen Beyspielen und zur Übung mit vier und zwanzig kleinen Duetten erläutert [Rism B/VI/2, p. 512.]

> Leipzig and Züllichau: Waisenhaus- und Frommannische Buchhandlung, 1774. [LCPS: L-092a.]
> Leipzig and Züllichau: Waisenhaus- und Frommannische Buchhandlung, 1781.
> Leipzig and Züllichau: Friedrich Frommann, 1797. Edited by Johann Friederich Reichardt.

LITERATURE:

Glasenapp, Franzgeorg von. "Georg Simon Löhlein (1725-1781): Sein Leben und seine Werke, insbesondere seine volkstümlichen Musiklehrbücher." Ph.D. dissertation, The University of Halle, 1937; published edition, Halle: Akademischer Verlag, 1937. Bibliog.

Hoffmann-Erbrecht, Lothar. "Löhlein, Georg Simon." In *MGG* (1949-68).

Hoffmann-Erbrecht, Lothar. "Löhlein, Georg Simon." In *NGrove* (1980).

● ● ● Wilson, Dora. "Löhlein's *Klavierschule*: Toward an Understanding of the *Galant* Style." *IRASM* 12/2 (1981):103-15. Bibliog. [*Rilm* 81-4854.]

See also FÉTIS: (1833-44); FUX: Federhofer (1988); VOGLER: Knecht (1785); LITERATURE SUPPLE-MENT: Alekseev (1974); Babitz (1952); Becker (1836-39/1964); **Benary (1956/1961)**; Carpenter (1988); Chybiński (1911-12); Collins (1963), (1966); **Coover (1980)**; David and Mendel (1945/1966); Duckles (1970); Eitner (1900-1904/1959-60); Forkel (1792/1962); Gerber (1812-14/1966); Goldsmith (1978-79); Hiller (1768-69); Jackson (1988); McQuere (1983); Nelson (1984); **Neumann**, Frederick (1977/**1982**), (1978), (1979/**1982**), [*Essays*] (**1982**), (1986), (1987); Newman (1963/. . ./1983); Palisca ["Rezitativ"] (1972-); Pfeiffer (1978); Ratner (1980); Rauschning (1931); Rosenblum (1988); Rothgeb (1968); Schering and Wustmann (1941); Stowell (1985), (1988); Vanhulst (1971); Wagner (1981); Williams, P. (1970).

JOHANN BERNHARD LOGIER

[1777 – 1846]

Among the early nineteenth century's most controversial music educators was Johann Bernhard Logier, who set out to conquer British piano instruction and later extended his influence to Germany and France as well. His method was centered upon an apparatus for the piano called a chiroplast, into which the student entrusted his or her hands, allowing it, with its wrist rests and finger holes, to ensure that a proper position was maintained. Logier also fabricated a gamut-board, which, when placed just beyond the keys, served as a guide to how each pitch appeared in staff notation. These devices and the necessary accompanying literature comprised a more economical way to begin one's piano study than did the hours of private instruction otherwise available. Of course, the money spent on Logier's equipment and texts was siphoned from other teachers' incomes!

Logier emphasized group instruction, wherein several students simultaneously performed the same work. Chiroplast Clubs were organized. Examinations of student progress were held at Dublin's Chiroplast Hall and other locations. Instructors were certified by Logier to teach his method. The system generated a huge outpouring of critical response, mostly from others who were engaged in piano instruction themselves and who may have felt threatened by "chiromania."

Logier's interest in piano performance and pedagogy was complemented by a sincere if somewhat regimented commitment to music theory and analysis. In the public examinations presented by his students, their capacities in coping with chordal constructions and modulations were demonstrated. To ensure an adequate preparation, he published a series of texts, including *Theoretical and Practical Studies for the Pianoforte* (1816), *Thorough Bass* (1818), and *A System of the Science of Music and Practical Composition* (1827). His "analyzations" included a fundamental bass line with abundant figures, and his perspective embraced matters such as periodic structure and the use of non-harmonic tones.

The chiroplast's construction could not accommodate the passing of the thumb under the second finger. The group performances led to uninteresting interpretations. Yet for a large segment of the amateur musical public Logier's system held a special allure. The considerable negative press could not erase its influence.

A Treatise on Practical Composition and Harmony, Founded on the Diatonic and Chromatic Scales in All the Major and Minor Modes with Their Fundamental Harmony and Inversions

Dublin: [ca. 1813].

An Explanation and Description of the Royal Patent Chiroplast, or Hand-Director . . .

London: Clementi (T. Davison), [1814?].
Dublin: J. Carrick, 1816. 2nd edition.

An American edition was published ca. 1817. Review in *GMag* 85/1 (1815):347.

A [The First] Companion to the Royal Patent Chiroplast, or Hand-Director

London: the author (Clementi), [ca. 1815].

Numerous printings, translations into French and German, and several related volumes (*A Second Companion . . ., Sequel the the First Companion . . ., and Sequel to the Second*

Companion . . .) appeared in several countries for several decades. Reviews in *AcR* 13 (February 1815):105-7 (G. L. Engelbach) and *EurM* 67 (1815):235-37 [Samuel Wesley].

A Syllabus of the Second Examination of Mr. Logier's Pupils, on His New System of Musical Education, to Which is Prefixed a Prospectus of Its Course of Instruction . . .

    Dublin: J. Carrick, 1816.

Theoretical and Practical Studies for the Pianoforte, Comprising a Series of Compositions Selected from the Most Classical Works Ancient and Modern

    London: Clementi, 1816. 12 vols.
    London: J. Green, [ca. 1832].

    T ● *Theoretisch-praktisch Studien für das Pianoforte . . .Berlin: Heinrich Adolph Wilhelm Logier, 1826-32. 14 vols.*

Prospectus of the Musical Academy of Messrs. Logier, Webbe, and Kalkbrenner, Established on Mr. Logier's New System of Musical Education . . .

    London: J. M'Creery, [ca. 1817]

An Authentic Account of the Examination of Pupils, Instructed in the New System of Musical Education; Before Certain Members of the Philharmonic Society, and Others

    London: R. Hunter, 1818.

A Refutation of the Fallacies and Misrepresentations Contained in a Pamphlet, Entitled "An Exposition of the New System of Musical Education," Published by a Committee of Professors in London

    London: R. Hunter (J. M'Creery), 1818.

    A second printing appeared in 1818. Reviews in *GMag* 89/1 (1819):240 and *MMag* 46 (1818):57 [Thomas Busby?].

Thorough Bass, Being a Second Series of Theoretical and Practical Study for the Piano Forte Comprising Selections from the Most Classical Modern Compositions, Fingered Throughout, Arranged with Inverted and Fundamental Basses, Also a Separate Part Figured and Arranged Expressly as a Theoretical and Practical Study of Thoro' Bass . . .

    London: J. Green, 1818.

    T ● *Anweisung zum Unterricht im Clavierspiel und der musikalischen Composition.* Berlin: Heinrich Adolph Wilhelm Logier, [1819?]; 1827-29.

    Review in *BamZ* 7/52 (1830):413-14 (A. B. MARX).

A Short Account of the Progress of J. B. Logier's System of Musical Education in Berlin . . .

    London: R. Hunter (J. M'Creery), 1824.

A System of the Science of Music and Practical Composition: Incidentally Comprising What is Usually Understood by the Term Thorough Bass

    London: J. Green (W. Clowes), 1827.

    Many editions (with variant titles) throughout the remainder of the century.

    T ● *Nouveau système d'enseignement musical, ou traité de composition.* Paris: Maurice Schlesinger, 1827.

    Review in *Rm*(F) [2]/3 (1828):61-66 (François-Joseph FÉTIS).

    T ● [MARX, A. B., trans.] *System der Musik-Wissenschaft und der praktischen Composition mit Inbegriff dessen was gewöhnlich unter dem Ausdrucke General-Bass verstanden wird.* Berlin: Heinrich Adolph Wilhelm Logier, 1827.

    Reviews in *AmZ* 30/51-52 (1828):8477-56, 862-72 (G. W. Fink) and *BamZ* 7/52 (1830):413-14 (A. B. MARX). Extract as *Lehrbuch der musikalischen Composition* (Berlin: Heinrich Adolph Wilhelm Logier, 1827).

    S ● Stein, Carl, ed. *Logier's Comprehensive Course in Music, Harmony, and Practical Composition . . . with an Abridged Treatise from Hector Berlioz's Standard Work on Instrumentation, with Hints on Conducting.* Boston: Jean White; New York: Carl Fischer, 1888; facsimile of the Fischer 1888 edition (DCPMRS), New York: Da Capo Press, 1976.

    Reviews in *MT* 118/1615 (1977):732 (William Drabkin) and *RBBR* 22/3 (1977):26 and 22/4 (1977):17.

    S ● Facsimile of the 1827 London edition. DCPMRS. New York: Da Capo Press, 1976.

    Reviews in *MT* 118/1615 (1977):732 (William Drabkin) and *RBBR* 24/3 (1979):14 (Josef Alexander).

A Manual, Chiefly for the Use of Preceptors, Parents, Governesses, etc. Exhibiting the Peculiar Method of Teaching the Art and Science of Music . . .

    London: J. Green (L. Harrison), 1828.

Themes . . . for Those Who Are Desirous of Additional Subjects for Exercise in Harmony, during the Study of the Science of Music and Composition . . .

    London: J. Green, [1829?].

    T ● *Nachträgliche Sammlung von Aufgaben und Beispielen zu J. B. Logier's System der Musik-Wissenschaft und der praktischen Komposition.* Berlin: Heinrich Adolph Wilhelm Logier, 1827 [or 1829?].

Programme of a Public Examination of Mr. Logier's Pupils in the Theory and Practice of Music

    Dublin: W. Holden, 1834.

LITERATURE:

[Graham, George Farquhar.] *General Observations upon Music, and Remarks on Mr. Logier's System of Musical Education; With an Appendix, Containing a Reprint of the Letters Relative to Mr. Logier's System, Which Were Published in the Edinburgh Newspapers, and Also Some Additional Letters.* Edinburgh: Robert Purdie (Duncan Stevenson), 1817.

> Contains reprints of numerous newspaper reviews. Two editions and an appendix appeared, perhaps all within the year 1817.

de Monti, Henry. *Strictures on Mr. Logier's System of Musical Education.* Glasgow: William Turnbull et al. (J. Hedderwick), 1817; Dublin: 1817.

Anonymous. *Joel Collier Redivivus: An Entirely New Edition, of That Celebrated Author's "Musical Travels," Containing, among a Variety of Interesting Particulars, a Faithful Account of His Many Ingenious Experiments, Valuable Discoveries, and Inestimable Inventions, for the Improvement of Students, and the Advancement of Science in This Country.* London: J. Asperne; Budd & Calkin; L. Lavenu (E. Justins), 1818.

[Ayrton, William.] *The Logierian System of Teaching Music Carefully Surveyed, Analyzed, and Exploded, by a Master, Member of the Royal Society of Musicians.* London: Phillips (D. Jaques), 1818.

[Bacon, R. M. (?).] "Mr. Logier's New System of Musical Instruction." *QMMR* 1/1 (1818-19):111-39.

A Committee of Professors in London [Attwood, Crotch, Smart, et al.]. *An Exposition of the Musical System of Mr. Logier; With Strictures on His Chiroplast.* London: Budd & Calkin (B. M'Millan), 1818.

> Logier responded in ["Refutation"] (1818), above.

[Graham, George Farquhar.] *The Musical Tour of Dr. Minim, A.B.C. und D.E.F.G., with a Description of a New Invented Instrument, a New Mode of Teaching Music by Machinery, and an Account of the Gullabaic System in General.* London: W. Glindon, 1818.

M[ichaelis], C[hristian] F[riedrich]. "Einige Nachricht über den Chiroplasten und die neue musikalische Unterweisung des Herrn Logier in England." *AmZ* 20/52 (1818):893-98.

Cummins, Charles. *Logierian Sensibility; or, Marsayas in the Chiroplast: Exemplified in Letters . . . Originally Written for the Bristol Mercury.* Bath: 1819.

Eager, J. *A Brief Account, with Accompanying Examples, of What was Actually Done, at the Second Examination of Mr. Eager's Pupils in Music, Educated upon Mr. Logier's "System" . . . to Which are Added, Observations on the Chiroplast . . .* London: R. Hunter et al. (J. M'Creery), 1819; 2nd edition, 1819.

Spohr, Louis. "Musikalische Notizen." *AmZ* 22/31 (1820):521-30; reprinted in his *Selbstbiographie* (Kassel and Göttingen: G. H. Wigand, 1860-61; English and revised editions).

> A derivative article, "Logier's System of Musical Education," is found in *Eut* 1/5 (1830):33-34.

KOLLMANN, Augustus Frederic Christopher. "Bemerkungen über Hrn. J. B. Logier's sogenanntes neues System des Musikunterrichts (New System of Musical Education)." *AmZ* 23/46-48 (1821):769-74, 785-94, 801-14.

> Continued with "Nachtrag zu den Bemerkungen . . ." in *AmZ* 24 (1822):Intelligenz-Blatt 3, cols. 9-13. An English translation by KOLLMANN was published as *Remarks on What Mr. J. B. Logier Calls His New System of Musical Education; with a Sequel* [London: for the author (W. Nicol), 1824; enlarged edition, 1824]. The *Remarks* were reviewed in *PJLR* 2 (1825):433-50. A related document appeared as *Über Logier's Musikunterrichts-System* (Munich: Falter & Sohn, [ca. 1822-24]), by KOLLMANN and C. F. Müller. See also *AmZ* 31/39 (1829):651-52 (KOLLMANN).

"The Logierian System." *EMI* 2/3 (1821-22):19.

Blewitt, Jonathan. *Epitome of the Logierian System of Harmony.* Dublin: [ca. 1823].

> See also Richard Andrews, *General Observations on Music as a Science . . . and Explanatory Remarks upon Blewitt's "Epitome . . ."* (Manchester: J. Heywood, [ca. 1865]).

Hentschel, E. "Die Logier'sche Methode beim musikalischen Unterricht." In *Der Volksschullehrer*, I, 1, edited by W. Harnisch. Halle: Anton, 1824.

Loewe, K. "Über Logiers Musik-System." *BamZ* 2/4-6, 8 (1825):25, 33-35, 41-42, 57-58.

Girschner, Christian Friedrich Johann. *Über J. B. Logier's neues Systeme des musicalischen Unterrichts; oder, Wodurch unterscheidet sich das Logier'sche System von dem alten? . . .* Berlin: Trautwein, 1826.

Ilgner, C. F. *Kurze Darstellung des Logierschen Systems.* Danzig: 1827.

Stöpel, Franz David Christoph. *Freimüthige Worte: Ein Beitrag zur Beurtheilung der Schrift, "System der Musik-*

Wissenschaft und der praktischen Composition" von *J. B. Logier.* Munich: Sidler, 1827.

Michaelis, Christian Friedrich. *Katechismus über J. B. Logier's System der Musikwissenschaft und der musikalischen Composition.* Leipzig: 1828.

Examiner 21/1062 (1828):384 and 21/1086 (1828):767.

Advertisements only.

Erdmann [pseud. for Élie Häseler]. *Die höhe Wichtigkeit des von J. B. Logier erfundenen Musikunterricht-Systems: Eine patriotische Phantasie.* Hamburg: Bitter, 1830.

Herschel, J. F. W. "Sound." In *Encyclopaedia metropolitana; or, Universal Dictionary of Knowledge, on an Original Plan . . .,* vol. 4, pp. 747-820. London: B. Fellowes et al., 1845.

Maitland, J. A. Fuller. "Gymnastics." In *Grove's Dictionary of Music and Musicians,* 2nd edition. London and New York: Macmillan, 1904-10.

Pügner, Georg. "Logier, Johann Bernhard." In *MGG* (1949-68). Bibliog.

Becker, Heinz. "Das System Logier: Ein Wegbereiter moderner Musikpädagogik." *Musica* 11/11 (1957):616-20.

Pügner, Georg. "Johann Bernhard Logier, Leben und Werke: Ein Beitrag zur Entwicklung des musikalischen Gruppenunterrichts." Ph.D. dissertation, The University of Leipzig, 1959 (1960).

Abstract in *WZKMU* 10/1 (1961):119-22.

Pügner, Georg. "Johann Bernhard Logier: Wegbereiter des Gruppenunterrichts." *MSch* 10/1 (1959):38-43.

Bouws, Jan. "Groeps-piano-orderwijs in de vorige eeuw." *Mens* 30/10 (1975):313-15 (Jan Bouws).

Charlton, David. "Logier, Johann Bernhard." In *NGrove* (1980). Bibliog.

See also FÉTIS: (1833-44); MARX: Eicke (1966); LITERATURE SUPPLEMENT: Allen ["Philosophies"] (1939); Beach (1974); Becker (1836-39/1964); ● ● ● **Bent** ["Analysis"] **(1980/1987)**; Eitner (1900-1904/1959-60); Jacobi (1957-60/1971); **Kassler** (1971), (1976), ● ● ● **(1979)**; Konecne (1984); **Ritzel (1967/1968)**; Scholes (1947); **Shirlaw (1917)/ . . ./1970)**; **Wagner (1974)**; Whatley (1981); Wirth (1966).

ANDRÉS LORENTE

[bapt. 1624 – 1703]

Spanish theory mirrored a national musical life of unchanging liturgical orthodoxy bent on preserving sixteenth-century practice intact. Treatises, such as Andrés Lorente's *El porqué de la música* (1672), were not intended as transmitters of the latest foreign innovations; instead, they reinforced and solidified existing Spanish practices. Lorente, like others before him, found it expedient to borrow extensive passages from earlier authors, most notably CERONE. The resulting compendium was certainly a useful guide for musicians active in Spain, as it provided extensive instruction in matters of importance to church music—modes, mensural notation, counterpoint, styles, etc.—as well as abundant music examples. At the same time, topics which were regarded as indispensable by more progressive European authors were neglected.

El porqué de la música en que se contiene los quatro artes de ella: Canto llano, canto de órgano, contrapunto, y composición . . . [*Rism* B/VI/1, p. 516.]

Alcalá de Henares: Nicolás de Xamares, 1672. [LCPS: L-096. HoM: 902.]
Alcalá de Henares: Nicolás de Xamares, 1690. [?]
Alcalá de Henares: Juan Fernández, 1699.

LITERATURE:

Querol, Miguel. "Lorente, Andrés." Translated by Friedrich Suck. In *MGG* (1949-68). Bibliog.

● ● ● Howell, Almonte. "Lorente, Andrés." In *NGrove* (1980). Bibliog.

See also FÉTIS: (1833-44); OUSELEY: (1882); LITERATURE SUPPLEMENT: Anglés and Subirá (1946-51); **Apfel (1981)**; Becker (1836-39/1964); Collins (1963), (1966); Eitner (1900-1904/1959-60); Forrester (1973); Gerber (1790-92/1977), (1812-14/1966); Hannas (1934); Hawkins (1776/. . ./1969); Howell (1972); León Tello (1974); Pedrell (1888); Subirá (1947/. . ./1958), (1953).

ALFRED (OTTOKAR) LORENZ

[1868 – 1939]

Wagner's music dramas present analysts with formidable challenges, no less so today than in the early 1920s, when Alfred Lorenz completed his intensive study of the *Ring*. In all, four volumes were published under the title *Das Geheimnis der Form bei Richard Wagner* (1924-33). Treating in turn *Der Ring des Nibelungen*, *Tristan und Isolde*, *Die Meistersinger von Nürnberg*, and *Parsifal*, each includes an extraordinary assemblage of data and interpretation, including summaries in innovative tabular and grid formats. The work impressed the scholarly community at the time—and revealed the "secret" that indeed Wagner's craft did incorporate elements of form, in particular the *Bogen* form (A-B-A) and the *Bar* form (A-A-B). The latter even served as an element of plot in *Die Meistersinger*.

Lorenz formulated hierarchical arrangements of these simple forms. The three acts of *Tristan* complete a gigantic A-B-A form, for example. His method involved a segmentation of the score into discrete units each of which was analyzed in terms of a specific tonal center. Perhaps owing to the close identification of Wagner's music with the Nazi cause during the 1930s and 40s, critical assessment of Lorenz's perspective was slow to develop. More recent critics, led by Dahlhaus, have succeeded in demonstrating that arbitrary and superficial interpretations permeate this once admired and always daunting study.

"Die formale Gestaltung des Vorspiels zu *Tristan und Isolde*"

>*ZfMw* 5/9-10 (1922-23):546-57.

>S ● See Schuhmacher [*Zur musikalischen Analyse*] (1974).

"Gedanken und Studien zur musikalischen Formgebung in Richard Wagners *Ring des Nibelungen*"

>Ph.D. dissertation, The University of Frankfurt am Main, 1922.

>S ● See (1924-33), Vol. 1, below.

"Betrachtungen über Beethovens Eroica-Skizzen (Ein Beitrag zur Psychologie des Schaffens)"

>*ZfMw* 7/7 (1924-25):409-22.

Das Geheimnis der Form bei Richard Wagner

>1) *Der musikalische Aufbau des Bühnenfestspieles "Der Ring des Nibelungen"*

>2) *Der musikalische Aufbau von Richard Wagners "Tristan und Isolde"*

>3) *Der musikalische Aufbau von Richard Wagners "Die Meistersinger von Nürnberg"*

>4) *Der musikalische Aufbau von Richard Wagners "Parsifal"*

>Berlin: Max Hesse, 1924, 1926, 1931, 1933. 4 vols.

>>Review in *Musik* 20/2 (1927-28):93-103 (Hans Lafred Grunsky).

>S ● Facsimile edition. Tutzing: Hans Schneider, 1966. 4 vols.

>>Review in *Muh* 19/5 (1968):246 (Paul Mies).

"Der formale Schwung in Richard Strauss' *Till Eulenspiegel*"

>*Musik* 17/9 (1924-25):658-69.

"Das Finale in Mozarts Meisteropern"

>*Musik* 19/9 (1926-27):621-32.

"Der Begriff der 'Tonalitäts-Auflösung' "

>*RMTZ* 28/43-44 (1927):477-78.

Abendländische Musikgeschichte im Rhythmus der Generationen: Eine Anregung

>Berlin: Max Hesse, 1928.

"Homophone Großrhythmik in Bachs Polyphonie"

>*Musik* 22/4 (1929-30):245-53.

"Das Relativitätsprinzip in den musikalischen Formen"

>In *AdlerFs* (1930/1971):179-86.

"Klangmischung in Anton Bruckners Orchester"

>*AMuZ* 63/47 (1936):717-20.

"Neue Formerkenntnisse, angewandt auf Richard Straußens *Don Juan*"

>*AfMf* 1/4 (1936):452-66.

"Neue Gedanken zur Klangspaltung und Klangverschmelzung"

>In *ScheringFs* (1937):137-50.

See also KURTH: (1920):Review; (1931):Review.

See Schaal (1949-68), below, for a more comprehensive listing of Lorenz's articles and other publications.

LITERATURE:

Herzfeld, Friedrich. "Alfred Lorenz, der Wagner-Forscher." *AMuZ* 63/30-31 (1936):481-82.

Schaal, Richard. "Lorenz, Alfred Ottokar." In *MGG* (1949-68). Bibliog.

Stein, Herbert von. *Dichtung und Musik im Werk Richard Wagners*. Berlin: Walter de Gruyter, 1962.

> Reviews in *Me* 18/2 (1964-65):94 (Hanns Zimmerl), *ML* 46/3 (1965):258-59 (Gerald Abraham), *Musica* 17/3 (1963):139 (Fritz Bose), and *NZfM* 125/3 (1964):126 (G. A. Trumpff).

Zuckerman, Elliott. *The First Hundred Years of Wagner's "Tristan"*. New York: Columbia University Press, 1964.

> Reviews in *ARG* 32/4 (1965):384 (C. J. Luten), *LJ* 89/14 (1964):3011 (Catharine K. Miller), *MJ* 25/2 (1967):72 (James Browning), *ML* 46/1 (1965):63-64 (J. A. Westrup), *MR* 26/2 (1965):152-53, *MT* 106/1469 (1965):520-21 (H. A. Hammelmann), and *PP* 57/4 (1965):18 (Melva Peterson).

Grasberger, Franz. "Zur Geschichte der Musikforschung: Alfred Ottokar Lorenz." *ÖM* 23/10 (1968):555-56. [*Rilm* 69-341.]

Dahlhaus, Carl. "Formprinzipien in Wagners *Ring des Nibelungen*." In *Beiträge zur Geschichte der Oper*, edited by Heinz Becker, pp. 95-129. SMg, no. 15. Regensburg: Gustav Boße, 1969. Bibliog. [*Rilm* 69-3893.]

Stephan, Rudolf. "Gibt es ein Geheimnis der Form bei Richard Wagner?" In *Das Drama Richard Wagners als musikalisches Kunstwerk*, edited by Carl Dahlhaus, pp. 9-16. SMg, no. 23. Regensburg: Gustav Boße, 1970.

Jackson, Roland. "*Leitmotive* and Form in the *Tristan* Prelude." *MR* 36/1 (1975):42-53. [*Rilm* 75-1204.]

Voss, Egon. "Noch einmal: Das Geheimnis der Form bei Richard Wagner." In *Theaterarbeit an Wagners "Ring"*, edited by Dietrich Mack, pp. 251-67. Munich: R. Piper, 1979.

Breig, Werner. "Der 'Rheintöchtergesang' in Wagners *Rheingold*." *AfMw* 37/4 (1980):241-63. Bibliog.

"Lorenz, Alfred (Ottokar)." In *NGrove* (1980). Bibliog.

McCreless, Patrick. "Wagner's *Siegfried*: Its Drama, Its History, and Its Music." Ph.D. dissertation, The University of Rochester, 1981; published edition (as *Wagner's "Siegfried": Its Drama, History, and Music*; SiM, no. 59), Ann Arbor, Mich.: UMI Research Press, 1982. [*Rilm* 81-2777. *DA* 42/04A, p. 1366.]

> Reviews in *Choice* 20/7 (1983):999, *Mf* 40/3 (1987):279-84 (Werner Breig), *NYRB* 30/20 (1983):23-37 (Joseph Kerman), *OQ* 1/3 (1983-84):240-41 (M. Mitchell), and *TLS* 83/4236 (1984):646 (Derrick Puffett).

Seelig, Wolfgang. "Ambivalenz und Erlösung: Wagners *Parsifal*: Zweifel und Glauben." *ÖM* 37/6 (1982):307-17.

Stein, Herbert von. "Richard Wagners Begriff der dichterisch-musikalischen Periode." *Mf* 35/2 (1982):162-65. [*Rilm* 82-3895.]

Lek, Robbert van der. "Zum Begriff Übergang und zu seiner Anwendung durch Alfred Lorenz auf die Musik von Wagners *Ring*." *Mf* 35/2 (1982):129-47. [*Rilm* 82-3575.]

Wildgruber, Jens. "Das Geheimnis der 'Barform' in R. Wagners *Die Meistersinger von Nürnberg*: Plädoyer für einer neue Art der Formbetrachtung." In *BeckerFs* (1982):205-13. [*Rilm* 82-1531.]

Gloede, Wilhelm. "Dichterisch-musikalische Periode und Form in Brünnhildes Schlussgesang." *ÖM* 38/2 (1983):84-92.

See also KURTH: McCreless (1983); LITERATURE SUPPLEMENT: Babbitt (1987); ● ● ● **Bent** ["Analysis"] **(1980/1987)**; **Dahlhaus** (1975/1977), ["Tonalität"] (1983), **(1984)**; Dunsby and Whittall (1988); Federhofer (1944/1950); Fellerer (1927/. . ./1972); Ferand (1937/1938); Kerman (1980-81), (1985); Kinderman (1980-81), (1983); Lewin (1983-84); Morgan (1969); Moyer (1969); Murray (1978); Newcomb (1981-82); Nielsen (1971); **Palisca** ["Theory"] (1980); Powers ["Language"] (1980); Seidel (1972-); Vogel (1955/1954), (1962); **Wason (1981/1985)**; Wintle (1982).

RUDOLF LOUIS

[1870–1914]

and

LUDWIG THUILLE

[1861–1907]

Rudolf Louis and Ludwig Thuille were two of Munich's most influential musical thinkers at the turn into the current century. Louis, a critic and author of numerous books on composers—including Wagner, Liszt, Berlioz, and Bruckner—possessed the greater proclivity towards abstraction, though Thuille, a composer and professor at the Königliche Musikschule, was by no means uninvolved in the theoretical portions of their *Harmonielehre* [1907]. It was left to Louis, who survived Thuille by seven years, to draft a response to RIEMANN's charges that their work was derivative of his own writings, to make revisions and supplements for later editions, and to create several pedagogical offshoots—*Grundriß des Harmonielehre* [1908], *Aufgaben für den Unterricht in der Harmonielehre* (1911), and *Schlüssel zum Harmonielehre* [1912]. Though virtually unknown in the United States until recently, their work was among the more popular texts in German-speaking countries during the first half of the century. In addition to numerous perceptive analyses of excerpts, the book offers a large number of challenging figured-bass and melody-harmonization assignments.

As did RIEMANN, Louis and Thuille recognized three essential chord functions: tonic, dominant, and subdominant. Their detailed and multi-layered Roman-numeral analyses reveal—through the use of parentheses—that VI relates to I and that II relates to IV; or, in another context, that VI relates to IV; or, that III relates to V; etc. However, their perspective is markedly different from RIEMANN's and much closer to the Viennese tradition and SCHENKER's early formulations in their effective integration of a linear perspective regarding passing, neighboring, and suspended notes into the context of their analytical scheme. The so-called "interpretation-dissonance" (*Auffassungsdissonanz*) concept effectively overrode the tendency to label a pitch formation in accordance with the inversion-theory interpretation of its root. In effect, the context of a composition could convert what in an abstract state might seem perfectly acceptable as a harmonic formation into what would be interpreted more appropriately as the confluence of various linear forces lingering in stasis for a moment. In a

text made vivid by numerous fascinating and well-chosen music examples the authors succeeded in drawing a convincing picture of the harmonic workings of music.

Having completed their exposition on diatonic harmony, Louis and Thuille ventured into the less well charted regions of chromatic and enharmonic practice, which typified the music they held in highest esteem. Many altered chords are catalogued. They are assayed both through abstract progressions of a few chords each and through excerpts from the literature (Bruckner, Wagner, and Strauss being among the more frequently consulted composers). The augmented triad, diminished-seventh chord, and the various augmented-sixth chords are carefully considered and their modulatory potentials demonstrated. Among all the books written while the chromatic tonal art was still flourishing, their *Harmonielehre* is among the most lucid and significant.

"Der Widerspruch in der Musik: Bausteine zu einer Ästhetik der Tonkunst auf realdialektischer Grundlage"

The work of Louis alone.

Ph.D. dissertation, The University of Vienna, 1893.
Leipzig: Breitkopf & Härtel, 1893.

Review in *Rmi* 1/3 (1894):557-58 (A. U.).

S ● Facsimile edition. Walluf bei Wiesbaden: Martin Sändig, 1972.

"Unsere Harmonielehre"

SdM 3/2 (1906):430-37.

Written by Louis.

"Eine Neue Harmonielehre"

NMZ 28 (1907):225-27.

Harmonielehre

Stuttgart: Carl Grüninger (Klett & Hartmann), [1907].

Reviews in *AMuZ* 34/16 (1907):291 (Otto Lessman), *BHKM* 11/7 (1907):112 (Ernst Rabich), *KL* 30/16 (Aug. 20, 1907):249-50 (Arno Kleffel), *Kunstwart* 21/16 (1908):231-34 (Ernst Decsey), *LZD* 62/3 (1910):103-4 (J. M.), *Msac* 25 (1933):461, *Musik* 6/18 (1906-7):365-69, *MuWb* 38/22 (1907):488-89 (Edgar Istel), *NMZ* 29 (1908):40, *SdM* 4/1 (1907):500-504 (Hugo RIEMANN) [to which Louis responded in 4/1 (1907):614-20 and RIEMANN replied in 4/2 (1907):138], and *ZIMG* 8/10-11 (1907):437-39 (Herman Wetzel). Numerous later editions, including:

Stuttgart: Ernst Klett Verlag, [1933]. 10th edition, revised by Walter Courvoisier, Richard G'schrey, Gustav Geierhaas, and Karl Blessinger.

S ● *Grundriß des Harmonielehre*. Stuttgart: Carl Grüninger, [1908]; later editions.

Published by Louis alone after Thuille's death. Review in *Kunstwart* 22/4 (1909):271-74.

T ● Schwartz, Richard Isadore. "An Annotated English Translation of *Harmonielehre* of Rudolf Louis and Ludwig Thuille." Ph.D. dissertation, Washington University, 1982. [*Rilm* 82-3573. *DA* 43/09A, p. 2921. UMI 83-02360.]

Aufgaben für den Unterricht in der Harmonielehre

Published by Louis alone after Thuille's death.

Stuttgart: Carl Grüninger, 1911.

Numerous later editions. Review in *Musik* 10/17 (1910-11):309 (Max Steinitzer).

Schlüssel zum Harmonielehre: Lösungen der in dem Louis-Thuilleschen Harmonielehrbuche und in dem dazu gehörigen Louisschen Aufgabenbuche enthaltenen übungsaufgaben

Published by Louis alone after Thuille's death.

Stuttgart: Carl Grüninger (Klett & Hartmann), [1912].

Later editions. Reviews in *KZ* 32 (August 6, 1933) and *Musik* 12/21 (1912-13):172-73 (Edgar Istel).

LITERATURE:

Munter, Friedrich. *Ludwig Thuille: Ein erster Versuch*. Munich: Drei Masken Verlag, 1923.

Review in *Rmi* 31/2 (1924):446 (A. E.).

Kaul, Oskar. "Louis, Rudolf." In *MGG* (1949-68). Bibliog.

Kaul, Oskar. "Thuille, Ludwig." In *MGG* (1949-68). Bibliog.

Zentner, Wilhelm. "In memoriam: Ludwig Thuille zur 100. Wiederkehr seines Geburtstages." *Musica* 15/11 (1961):619-20.

Goodman, Alfred Grant. "Louis, Rudolf." In *NGrove* (1980). Bibliog.

Kravitt, Edward F. "Thuille, Ludwig." In *NGrove* (1980). Bibliog.

See also SCHOENBERG: Rexroth (1969/1971); Falck (1982); LITERATURE SUPPLEMENT: Blumröder (1972-); Breig (1972-); Cazden (1980); Dahlhaus ["Konsonanz"] (1949-68); Federhofer (1944/1950), (1981); Forster (1966); Frischknecht (1979); Haydon (1930/1970); Imig (1969/1970); La Motte-Haber (1971); Levenson (1981), (1983-84); McCredie (1968); Moos (1902/1922); Neumann (1939); Rohwer (1949-68); Vogel (1962); **Wason** ● ● ● **(1981/1985)**, (1983); Weigl (1914-15).

ÉTIENNE LOULIÉ

[ca. 1655 – ca. 1707]

Étienne Loulié, a student of OUVRARD, was a practical theorist whose goals included making the acquisition of musical knowledge easy for his readers. He incorporated a variety of examples, as well as exercises for the student. His *Éléments ou principes de musique* (1696) is an excellent source of information on French melodic ornamentation in the late seventeenth century. Active as an inventor as well, he devised a *chronomètre* – a pendulum for setting tempi – and a *sonomètre* – a device for tuning keyboard instruments in equal temperament.

Loulié's treatises address such issues as the dotting of a note, how to execute trills, musical symbols, custos marks, fermatas, repeat signs, and ornaments. The treatment of scales and of transposition is clear and orderly. Pains were taken to explain terms which might be obscure to his readers or have several meanings. He was among those who documented the practice of playing notes with unequal duration even when the score showed notes of the same rhythmic value.

Éléments ou principes de musique, mis dans un nouvel ordre très-clair, très-facile, et très-court, . . . [Rism B/VI/1, pp. 518-19.]

> Paris: Christophe Ballard and the author, 1696. [LCPS: L-100a.]
>
> Amsterdam: Estienne Roger, 1698. [LCPS: L-100b.]
>
> > The 1698 edition contains numerous errors.

S ● *Abrégé des principes de musique . . .* Paris: Christophe Ballard, 1696. [*Rism* B/VI/1, p. 518.]

T ● ● ● ● Cohen, Albert, trans. and ed. *Elements or Principles of Music.* MTT, no. 6. New York: Institute of Mediaeval Music (Assen: Koninklijke van Gorcum), 1965; reprint edition, Henryville, Pa., 1971. Bibliog.

> > Review in *JMT* 10/2 (1966):372-75 (Almonte C. Howell, Jr.).

S ● Facsimile of the 1696 edition. Geneva: Minkoff Reprint, 1971.

> > Review in *Rdm* 58/2 (1972):271-72 (André Verchaly).

Nouveau système de musique, ou nouvelle division du monocorde . . . avec la description et l'usage du sonomètre . . . [Rism B/VI/1, p. 519.]

> Paris: Christophe Ballard, 1698.

Élémens ou principes de musique avec la manière du chant

> Amsterdam: Estienne Roger, n.d. [Lost.]

"Supplément des principes ou éléments de musique"

> Ms. [Paris: Bibliothèque nationale.]

Manuscript collection

> [Paris: Bibliothèque nationale.]
>
> > The manuscripts collected under the number "fonds fr. n. a. 6355" treat a variety of topics, including counterpoint, transposition, improvisation, and performance. See Cohen (1965), below, and Semmens (1980), below, for further information.

T ● Semmens, Richard, trans. and ed. "A Translation of Etienne Loulié's Method for Learning How to Play the Recorder." *AR* 24/4 (1983):135-45.

LITERATURE:

Elvers, Rudolf. "Loulié, Étienne." In *MGG* (1949-68). Bibliog.

Cohen, Albert. "Étienne Loulié as a Music Theorist." *JAMS* 18/1 (1965):70-72.

Cohen, Albert. "Loulié, Étienne." In *NGrove* (1980). Bibliog.

Semmens, Richard Templar. "Étienne Loulié as Music Theorist: An Analysis of Items in Ms. Paris, Bibliothèque nationale, Fonds Français, N. A. 6355." Ph.D. dissertation, Stanford University, 1980. [*DA* 41/02A, p. 456. UMI 80-16862.]

Fuller, David. "An Unknown French Ornament Table from 1699." *EM* 9/1 (1981):55-61. [*Rilm* 81-1604.]

Semmens, Richard. "The Early Eighteenth-Century Discussion of Musical Acoustics by Étienne Loulié." *CUMR* 2 (1981):177-206. Bibliog. [*Rilm* 83-6666.]

Semmens, Richard. "Étienne Loulié's *Method for Learning How to Play the Recorder.*" *SMUWO* 6 (1981):7-23. [*Rilm* 81-1583.]

Semmens, Richard. "Étienne Loulié and the New Harmonic Counterpoint." *JMT* 28/1 (1984):73-88.

See also FÉTIS: (1833-44); RAMEAU: Verba (1978); SAUVEUR: (1704):Maxham (1976); WALTHER: (1732); LITERATURE SUPPLEMENT: Atcherson (1973); Auhagen (1987); Babitz (1952), (1967/1969); Becker (1836-39/1964); Beyschlag (1907/1953); Borrel (1928); Bukofzer (1947); Byrt (1967); Cohen (1971), ["Symposium"] (1972), (1988); Cohen and Miller (1979); Collins (1967), (1973); **Dahlhaus et al. (1987)**; Dolmetsch (1915/ . . ./1969); Donington (1963/. . ./1974); (1980); Dürr and Gerstenberg (1949-68), (1980); Eitner (1900-1904/1959-60); Fellerer (1927/. . ./1972); Forkel (1792/1962); Gerber (1812-14/1966); Goldschmidt (1907); Gruber (1969); Harding (1938); Harich-Schneider ([1939]/. . ./1970); Houle (1960), (1987); Jackson (1988); **Kassler (1979)**; Kleinman (1971/1974); Kooiman (1980), (1981); Lange (1899-1900); Launay (1982); **Lindley** ["Temperaments"] **(1980)**; **Neumann**, Frederick (1964/**1982**), (1977/**1982**), (1978), (1981/**1982**), [*Essays*] **(1982)**; Newman (1985); O'Donnell (1979); Schmalzriedt ["Reprise"] (1972-); Schwartz (1908); **Seidel and Cooper (1986)**; Taddie (1984); Tolkoff (1973); Troeger (1987); Turner (1974).

VICENTE LUSITANO

(Sixteenth Century)

The dispute between the Portuguese Vicente Lusitano and the Italian Nicola VICENTINO concerning the application of Greek genera to more recent music led to a public dispute settled in Rome during June, 1551. Lusitano advocated the conservative position that music was diatonic unless two consecutive semitones (chromatic genus) or enharmonic dieses (enharmonic genus) were present. VICENTINO sought—unsuccessfully as far as the two judges were concerned—to accommodate all three genera by emphasizing the presence of thirds, which in the diatonic genus would necessarily be derived as combinations of two seconds but which occur naturally in the remaining two genera. Ghiselin DANCKERTS, one of the judges, ultimately responded better to VICENTINO's challenge than did Lusitano, for his manuscript "Trattato sopra una differentia musicale" directly addresses the issues involved while Lusitano's *Introdutione facilissima et novissima de canto fermo* (1553), in addition to providing a necessary foundation on clefs, notation, cadences, and the like, is more useful today for its discussion of improvised counterpoint than for any unique interpretation of chromatic practice. A more ambitious work, which exists only in manuscript, survives. Its erudition more closely parallels the writings of SALINAS than the more practical treatises of BERMUDO or SANTA MARÍA.

Introdutione facilissima, et novissima, di canto fermo, figurato, contraponto simplice, et inconcerto, con regole generali per far fughe differenti sopra'il canto fermo, à 2. 3. et 4. voci, et compositioni, proportioni, generi. s. diatonico, cromatico, enharmonico [*Rism* B/VI/1, p. 521.]

    Rome: Antonio Blado, 1553.
    Venice: Francesco Marcolini, 1558. [HoM: 907.]
    Venice: Francesco Rampazetto, 1561.

    T ● An unpublished Portuguese translation. Ms., 1603.

    S ● Gialdroni, Giuliana, ed. Facsimile of the 1553 edition. MFm, no. 7. Lucca: Libreria musicale italiana editrice, 1988.

A manuscript treatise in Spanish.

    Ms. [Paris: Bibliothèque nationale.]

    S ● Collet, Henri, ed. *Un tratado de canto de órgano (siglo XVI), manuscrito en la Biblioteca nacional de París: Edición y comentarios*. Madrid: Librería Gutenberg (Ruiz hermanos), 1913.

LITERATURE:

Sampayo Ribeiro, Mário de. "Lusitano, Vicente." Translated by Henning Ferdinand. In *MGG* (1949-68). Bibliog.

Dahlhaus, Carl. "Die Formen improvisierter Mehrstimmigkeit im 16. Jahrhundert." *Musica* 13 (1959):163-67.

Stevenson, Robert. "Vicente Lusitano: New Light on His Career." *JAMS* 15/1 (1962):72-77. Bibliog.

Barbosa, Maria Augusta. "Vincentinus Lusitanus, ein portugiesischer Komponist und Musiktheoretiker des 16. Jahrhunderts." Ph.D. dissertation, The University of Cologne, 1970; published edition, Lisbon: Secretaria de Estado da Cultura/Portugal, 1977. [*Rilm* 77-339.]

Kaufmann, Henry W. "Lusitano, Vicente." In *NGrove* (1980). Bibliog.

Stevenson, Robert. "The First Black Published Composer." *IAMR* 5/1 (1982-83):79-103. [*Rilm* 82-4468.]

See also ARTUSI: (1600); BERMUDO: Stevenson (1960); BOTTRIGARI: (1602); DANCKERTS: (manuscript treatise); FÉTIS: (1833-44); VICENTINO: (1555):Lowinsky (1959); Kaufmann (1960/1966); LITERATURE SUPPLEMENT: ● ● ● **Apfel (1981)**; Badura-Skoda et al. (1980); Becker (1836-39/1964); ● ● ● **Berger (1975/1980)**; Collins (1963); Dahlhaus (1960); Dürr (1980); Dupont (1933/. . ./1986); Eitner (1900-1904/1959-60); Fellerer ["Ausdruck"] (1982); Ferand (1937/1938), ["Improvised"] (1956); Gerber (1790-92/1977), (1812-14/1966); Hawkins (1776/. . ./1969); Hüschen (1986); Jackson (1988); La Fage (1864/1964); Lange (1899-1900); Lowinsky (1967); Luper (1938); Mahlert and Sunter (1972-); **Maniates (1979)**; Meier (1974/1988); Palisca (1959), ["Artusi-Monteverdi"] (1968/1985); Reese (1954/1959); Reimer ["Concerto"] (1972-); Stevenson (1976); Subirá (1947/. . ./1958).

MATHIS LUSSY

[1828 – 1910]

As one of Paris's leading piano pedagogues during the second half of the nineteenth century, the Swiss author Mathis Lussy commanded the attention of a large public with his *Traité de l'expression musicale* (1874) and several related publications. Whereas the pitch content of a work was more or less set by the composer, the performer's role was much more influential in parameters such as accentuation, dynamics, and tempo. Lussy sought ways to improve the expressive performance of music through a systematic review of these techniques. In the process he revitalized and expanded upon the phrase-structure perspectives of his predecessors KOCH, REICHA, and MOMIGNY while offering fertile ideas for his contemporaries, including RIEMANN.

Lussy divided considerations of accentuation into three categories. The most general is that involving metrical accent, wherein the first beat of a measure is typically emphasized. Second is Lussy's careful overview of rhythmic accent, wherein contraction, expansion, repetition, sequence, and echo affect the melodic structure. Since composers were often quite imprecise in their use of slurs to indicate phrase structure, it is important for performers to develop a sensitivity concerning how pitches should be grouped, as well as ways in which these groupings should be performed. (For example, a pianist should use a single wrist motion for all pitches under a single slur, in Lussy's view.) The third category is expressive (or pathetic) accent, resulting from exceptional, unexpected pitches which have the greatest potential to create an emotional response if properly executed. Even though such pitches tend to contradict the prevailing elements of key, mode, meter, or rhythm, their presence within the musical fabric is a vital factor in a composition's expressive capacity.

Lussy's unique perspective, drawn from his study of the editorial practices of distinguished musicians from the past (e.g., Moscheles) as well as from observation of contemporary performers, represents factors too often lacking in written musical discourse. Though some modern interpreters might disagree with various of his notions, such as his encouragement to use subtle shifts in tempo for expressive purposes and his prescriptions for the application of crescendo and decrescendo, his treatises offer insights that were not written down by others who were living at the time—a time that antedates the first sound recordings. Though the movement towards an authentic performance practice for music of the nineteenth century is still in its infancy, as it develops we will likely find in Lussy a potent voice whose importance may parallel those of QUANTZ, C. P. E. BACH, and Leopold MOZART for music of the eighteenth century.

Traité de l'expression musicale: Accents, nuances et mouvements dans la musique vocale et instrumentale

> Paris: Berger-Levrault and Heugel, 1874.
>
>> Numerous editions, some revised on the basis of his later publications. Reviews in *Bmus* 4/24 (1875):407-15 (Ernest David) and *Chmus* 2/5/25 (1874):35-38 (H. Marcello).

T ● Glehn, M. E. von, trans. *Musical Expression, Accents, Nuances, and Tempo, in Vocal and Instrumental Music*. NMPES, no. 25. London: Novello, Ewer & Co., [1885]; later editions.

T ● Vogt, Felix, trans. *Die Kunst des musikalischen Vortrags* . . . Leipzig: F. E. C. Leuckart, 1886.

T ● Chechott, V. A., trans. *Teoriia muzykal'nogo vyrazheniia*. St. Petersburg: Bösselt, 1888.

S ● *Concordance entre la mesure et la rythme*. Paris: Fischbacher, 1893.

Histoire de la notation musicale depuis ses origines
> With Ernest David.
>
> Paris: Imprimerie nationale (Heugel et fils), 1882.

Le rythme musical: Son origine, sa fonction et son accentuation
> Paris: Heugel et fils, 1883.
> Paris: Librairie Fischbacher, 1884.
>
>> Four editions through 1911. Review in *MMR* 13/156 (1883):274-77 (Frederick Niecks). See also Fuchs (1885).

T ● Fowles, Ernest, trans. *A Short Treatise on Musical Rhythm* . . . Abridged by E. Dutoit. London: Vincent Music Co., [1908]; Boston: T. J. Donlan, 1909.

"Die Correlation zwischen Takt und Rhythmus"
> *VMw* 1 (1885):141-57. Translated by Heinrich Rietsch.

"Zur neueren Literatur über die Reform der musikalischen Vortragszeichen"
> *VMw* 1 (1885):546-59. Translated by Heinrich Rietsch.

L'anacrouse dans la musique moderne
> Paris: Heugel, 1903.
>
>> Later editions. Review in *Mén* 70 (1904):323-24 (Raymond Bouyer).

La sonata pathétique de L. van Beethoven, op. 13: Édition rhythmée et annotée

> Paris: Costallat, 1912. Edited by A. Dechevrens.

LITERATURE:

Witting, C. "Ein Beitrag zum Rhythmus." *KL* 29/16 (1906):262-65.

Combe, Edouard. "Mathis Lussy." *SI* 16/764 (1908):397-400.

"Mathis Lussy [Obituary]." *SMz* 50/7 (1910):63-65.

Monod, Edmond. *Mathis Lussy et le rhythme musicale*. Éns. Neuchâtel: Attinger frères, 1912.

Reviews in *Rmi* 19/4 (1912):1048-51 (Oscar Chilesotti) and *SMz* 52/17 (1912):237-38.

Schanzlin, Hans Peter. "Lussy, Mathis." In *MGG* (1949-68).

Hoffman, Mark. "Lussy, Mathis." In *NGrove* (1980).

Woźna, Małgorzata. "O *prawach ekspresji muzycznej* Mathiasa Lussy'ego." *Pagine* 4 (1980):79-92. Bibliog. [*Rilm* 80-5891.]

See also KOCH: ● ● ● Baker (1976); RIEMANN: Vianna de Motta (1905); LITERATURE SUPPLEMENT: Alette (1951); **Bent** ["Analysis"] **(1980/1987)**; Chew (1979), (1980); **Dahlhaus (1984)**; Dürr and Gerstenberg (1949-68), (1980); Rosenblum (1988); Seidel (1972-), (1975); ● ● ● Smither (1960); Steblin (1987); Winick (1974).

THOMAS MACE

[1612-13 – 1706?]

Thomas Mace, impassioned English eccentric, pleaded for continued use of lutes and viols at a time when the guitar and the violin were becoming increasingly popular. *Musick's Monument*, much of which is written in verse (epistle, dedication, thanks, apology, and even his censure of ignoramuses), includes valuable information on problems of the tuning, fretting, stringing, and handling of the lute as well as instructions for the performance of ornaments. The art of continuo playing is considered, as is the use of organ and harpsichord in consort music. Commentary on Mace ranges from those who see him as a minor composer concerned mostly with his own music to those who savor his wit and sparkle. In his comments about the French lute, he revealed important information on musicmaking in England around the middle of the seventeenth century.

Musick's Monument; or, A Remembrancer of the Best Practical Musick, both Divine, and Civil, That Has Ever Been Known, to Have Been in the World . . . [*Rism* B/VI/2, pp. 523-24.]

London: the author and John Carr (T. Ratcliffe & N. Thompson), 1676. [LCPS: M-002. HoM: 911. SMLMS. IDC.]

S • Jacquot, Jean, and Souris, André, eds. Facsimile edition. 2 vols. Ccm. Paris: Éditions du Centre national de la recherche scientifique, 1958 (Vol. 1 only); 1966 (both volumes).

Reviews in *GSJ* 23 (1970):129-32 (Michael W. Prynne), *JAMS* 21/1 (1968):110-12 (Philip Brett), *Mf* 21/1 (1968):130-32 (Kurt Dorfmüller), *ML* 48/2 (1967):160-62 (J. A. Westrup), *MT* 108/1498 (1967):1112 (Charles Cudworth), *Notes* 24/4 (1967-68):706-7 (Robert Donington), and *Rdm* 53/1 (1967):71-72 (André Verchaly).

S • Facsimile edition. MMMLF, ser. 2, no. 17. New York: Broude Brothers, 1966.

Review in *ML* 48/4 (1967):371-73 (J. A. Westrup) and *MT* 108/1498 (1967):1112 (Charles Cudworth).

S • See SIMPSON: (1659):Eggers (1983).

LITERATURE:

Watson, Henry. "Thomas Mace: The Man, the Book, and the Instruments." *PMA 1908-9* 35 (1909):87-107.

Kinkeldey, Otto. "Thomas Mace and His *Musick's Monument*." *BAMS* 2 (1937):21.

Pulver, Jeffrey. "The English Theorists: XV – Thomas Mace." *MT* 78/1133 (1937):601-4.

Jacquot, Jean. "Mace, Thomas." Translated by Wilhelm Pfannkuch. In *MGG* (1949-68). Bibliog.

Jacquot, Jean. *"Musick's Monument* de Thomas Mace (1676) et l'évolution du goût musical en Angleterre." *Rdm* 34/101-2 (1952):21-37.

Mackerness, E. D. "Thomas Mace: Additions to a Biography." *MMR* 83/944 (1953):43-46.

Mackerness, E. D. "Thomas Mace and the Fact of Reasonableness." *MMR* 85/970-71 (1955):211-13, 235-39.

Jones, Edward Huws. "The Theorbo and Continuo Practice in the Early English Baroque." *GSJ* 25 (1972):67-72.

Jacquot, Jean. "Thomas Mace et la vie musicale de son temps." In *MeyerFs* (1973):215-22. [*Rilm* 76-508.]

• • • Tilmouth, Michael. "Mace, Thomas." In *NGrove* (1980). Bibliog.

See also FÉTIS: (1833-44); LITERATURE SUPPLEMENT: Abraham (1968/1969); Becker (1836-39/1964); Burney (1776-89/. . ./1957); Burton (1956); Butler (1977), (1984); Chenette (1967); Dolmetsch (1915/. . ./1969); Donington (1963/. . ./1974), (1980); Eitner (1900-1904/1959-60); Fischer (1957); Forkel (1792/1962); Gable (1979); Gerber (1790-92/1977), (1812-14/1966); Gouk (1981-82); Green (1969); Hancock (1977); Hannas (1934); Hawkins (1776/. . ./1969); Hoshino (1979); Houle (1987); Jackson (1988); Jacobi (1957-60/1971); Kivy (1980); Lawrence (1978); Lewis (1981); Miller (1960); Miller and Cohen (1987); Neumann, Frederick (1978); North (1987); Pulver (1927/. . ./1973); Rothschild (1953); Rowen (1979); Ruf (1972-); **Seidel and Cooper (1986)**; Sheppard (1978-79); Shute (1972); Subirá (1947/. . ./1958); Traficante (1970); Troeger (1987); Williams, P. (1970); Wolf (1939).

Sir GEORGE ALEXANDER MACFARREN

[1813 – 1887]

Few theorists of reputation have been as totally submerged in the ideas of another as was George Alexander Macfarren. It was to Alfred DAY, who survived the publication of his *Treatise on Harmony* (1845) by only a few years, that Macfarren owed his conception of music's theory, as is reflected in his several pedagogical works published in the 1860s and 1870s and his edition of DAY's treatise in 1885. Macfarren did, however, accept more of the traditional theory than had DAY, as, for example, in his acknowledgment that the supertonic, subdominant, and submediant possessed unique roots. His works featured topics typical of British theory at the time—namely, harmony and counterpoint. His text on the latter topic is devoted mainly to species-type exercises.

Given that Macfarren was, during his lifetime, very highly regarded—even knighted—, it is not surprising that two publications are devoted to his lectures. In fact, his renown as a composer helped mollify the initially hostile reception which DAY's treatise had received and therefore influenced the course of British theory in the later nineteenth and early twentieth centuries. Though we might now regard this sort of theory as rigid and misguided, the paucity of alternatives available to English-speaking musicians at that time should be noted.

Analytical Essay on Beethoven's Fidelio

London: Cramer, Beale & Co., [1852].

Published with the score of *Fidelio*.

London: *Musical World* Office, 1853.

The Rudiments of Harmony, with Progressive Exercises

London: Cramer, Beale & Chappell, 1860.

The 20th edition appeared in 1889.

Six Lectures on Harmony, Delivered at the Royal Institution of Great Britain

London: Longmans, Green, Reader, & Dyer, 1867.

The 4th edition appeared in 1892.

On the Structure of a Sonata

London: Rudall, Carte & Co., 1871.

Review in *MT* 15/345 (1871-73):282.

Eighty Musical Sentences, to Illustrate Chromatic Chords

London: J. B. Cramer, [1875].

Counterpoint: A Practical Course of Study

Cambridge: University Press, 1879.

The 6th edition appeared in 1886; a revised edition appeared in 1887.

Addresses and Lectures

London: Longmans, Green & Co., 1888.

See also DAY (1845):(1885).

LITERATURE:

Vickess, S. E. *Questions on Macfarren's Harmony and Counterpoint*. Liverpool: J. B. Cramer & Co., [1887].

Banister, Henry Charles. "The Life and Work of Sir G. A. Macfarren." *PMA 1887-88* 14 (1888):67-88.

Banister, Henry Charles. *George Alexander Macfarren: His Life, Works, and Influence*. London: G. Bell & Sons, 1891.

Harman, Richard Alexander. "Macfarren, George Alexander." Translated by Wilhelm Pfannkuch. In *MGG* (1949-68). Bibliog.

Temperley, Nicholas. "Macfarren, Sir George (Alexander)." In *NGrove* (1980). Bibliog.

See also DAY: Haydon (1944); Jones (1977); FÉTIS: (1833-44); LITERATURE SUPPLEMENT: Bircher (1970); Bridges (1984); Burke (1963); Cobb (1884); Finney (1957); ● ● ●Jacobi (1957-60/1971); Jones (1934); Jorgenson (1957); Lecky (1880); Newman (1969/. . ./1983); Pole (1879/. . ./1924); Prout (1893); Sanders (1919); ● ● ●**Shirlaw (1917/. . ./1970)**; Sholes (1947); Subirá (1947/. . ./1958); Thompson (1980); Whatley (1981).

PIERRE MAILLART

[1550 – 1622]

The Flemish theorist Pierre Maillart offered a thorough and influential account of seventeenth-century modal and rhythmic practices in *Les tons ou discours sur les modes de musique et les tons de l'église* (1610). Distinguishing carefully between modes, which comprise a full octave, and the tones of church music, which are scalar patterns used for chanting and which are dependent upon their dominant pitch, Maillart's work was regarded as authoritative by later scholars such as DONI and MERSENNE.

*Les tons ou discours sur les modes de musique et les
   tons de l'église, et la distinction entre iceux . . . [Rism
   B/VI/2, p. 528.]*

> Tournai: Charles Martin, 1610.

> S ● Facsimile edition. Geneva: Minkoff Reprint, 1972.

>> Review in *Rdm* 58/2 (1972):271-72 (André Verchaly).

LITERATURE:

Meier, Bernhard. "Maillart, Pierre." In *MGG* (1949-68):Supplement (1973-79).

● ● ● Cohen, Albert. "Maillart, Pierre." In *NGrove* (1980). Bibliog.

See also FÉTIS: (1833-44); GLAREAN: Meier (1960); MERSENNE: (1617-48); OUVRARD: (1658):Boulay (1984); WALTHER: (1732); LITERATURE SUPPLEMENT: Atcherson (1973); Auda (1930/1979); Becker (1836-39/1964); Brennecke (1953); Cohen (1966/1978), ["Symposium"] (1972); Eitner (1900-1904/1959-60); Ferand (1937/1938); Forkel (1792/ 1962); Gerber (1812-14/1966); Hüschen (1986); Kleinman (1971/1974); Lester (1977); Meier (1974/1988); **Schneider (1972); Seidel and Cooper (1986)**.

ALEXANDER MALCOLM

[1685 – 1763]

When Alexander Malcolm offered *A Treatise of Musick: Speculative, Practical, and Historical* (1721) to the musical public, he acknowledged that it should be regarded as a convenient and well-organized compilation of existing theory rather than as an original contribution to that theory. What the reader found was over six hundred pages documenting the basic premises of the art, with special emphasis upon the physics of music. Malcolm, who later settled in America, was apparently not gifted as a composer and was aided by a ghost writer—PEPUSCH has been suggested—in creating his terse remarks upon the compositional art. Though the book is insightful in some matters of tonal practice, such as modulation and the use of figuration, its greater merit resides in its clear pedagogical framework, rather than in its artistic outlook.

A Treatise of Musick: Speculative, Practical, and Historical [Rism B/VI/2, pp. 530-31.]

> Edinburgh: for the author, 1721. Printed twice during this year. [LCPS: M-014a. HoM: 918. SMLMS.]
> London: J. Osborn & T. Longman; F. Fayram & E. Symon, 1730.

> London: J. Osborn & T. Longman; J. Maceun, 1731. [LCPS: M-014b.]
> London: Strahan, 1751. [Lost?]

>> Much abbreviated editions:

> London: J. French, 1776. [LCPS: M-014c. HoM: 919.]
> Issued in *NMUM* 2 [ca. 1774-76].
> London: J. French; Fielding & Walker, 1778.
> London: J. Murray; Dublin: Luke White, 1779.

> S ● Facsimile of the 1721 edition. DCPMRS. New York: Da Capo, 1970.

>> Reviews in *Consort* 28 (1972):122 (Lillian M. Ruff), *ML* 52/2 (1971):207-8 (J. A. Westrup), *MT* 112/1537 (1971):241 (Michael Tilmouth), and ● ● ●*Notes* 28/2 (1971-72):237 (James R. Heintze).

> S ● Facsimile of the 1721 edition. Geneva: Minkoff Reprint.

A New System of Arithmetick, Theoretical and Practical . . .

> London: J. Osborn & T. Longman; F. Fayram & E. Symon, 1730.

LITERATURE:

Burney, Charles. "Alexander Malcolm." In *Cyc* (1802-20).

Maurer, Maurer. "Alexander Malcolm in America." *ML* 33/3 (1952):226-31.

Stone, Reppard. "An Evaluative Study of Alexander Malcolm's *Treatise of Music: Speculative, Practical and Historical*." Ph.D. dissertation, The Catholic University of America, 1974. [*Rilm* 75-2624. *DA* 35/01A, pp. 504-5. UMI 74-14948.]

Heintze, James R. "Alexander Malcolm: Musician, Clergyman, and Schoolmaster." *MHM* 73/3 (1978):226-35. [*Rilm* 78-4862.]

Heintze, James R. "Malcolm, Alexander." In *NGrove* (1980). Bibliog.

Rishton, Timothy J. "Plagiarism, Fiddles and Tarantulas." *MT* 125/1696 (1984):325-27.

See also FÉTIS: (1833-44); WALTHER: (1732); LITERATURE SUPPLEMENT: Alette (1951); Allen ["Philosophies"] (1939); **Barbour** (1948), (1949-68), **(1951/. . ./1972)**; Becker (1836-39/1964); Blumröder (1972-); Boomgaarden (1985/1987); Burke (1963); Burney (1776-89/. . ./1957); Burton (1956); Cazden (1948); Chenette (1967); Cohen (1971); Donington (1963/. . ./1974); Eitner (1900-1904/1959-60); Farmer (1947/1970); Fischer (1978); Forkel (1792/1962); Frobenius ["Dauer"] (1972-); Gerber (1812-14/1966); Green (1969); Hannas (1934); Harding (1938); Hawkins (1776/. . ./1969); Houle (1960), (1987); Jacobi (1957-60/1971); **Kassler** (1971), ● ● ● **(1979)**; Kelletat [*Temperatur*] (1960), (1966); **Lester** (1978), **(1989)**; Lonsdale (1979); **Ritzel (1967/1968)**; Ruf (1972-); **Seidel and Cooper (1986)**; Speak (1973).

VINCENZO MANFREDINI

[1737 – 1799]

Vincenzo Manfredini's *Regole armoniche* (1775) addresses the basic topics of time values, note names, and ornaments, as well as chordal construction (including diminished and half-diminished sevenths) and the distinction between the performed basso continuo and the abstraction of fundamental bass. Various styles of figured-bass realization are displayed, along with a set of fingering patterns for keyboardists. The second edition of the work was expanded to include commentary on singing and counterpoint. (Manfredini had entered into a dispute with Giambattista Mancini regarding the teaching of singing.) In an extended polemic with Esteban Arteaga, whose *La rivoluzioni del teatro musicale italiano* (1783) he had reviewed, Manfredini defended modern operatic practices against reactionary criticism.

Regole armoniche, o sieno precetti ragionati per apprendere i principj della musica, il portamento della mano, e l'accompagnamento del basso sopra gli strumenti da tasto, come l'organo, il cembalo ec. [*Rism* B/VI/2, p. 533.]

> Venice: Guglielmo Zerletti, 1775. [LCPS: M-019a. HoM: 922. IDC.]
> Venice: Adolfo Cesare, 1797. An enlarged edition. [LCPS: M-019b.]

> T ● Degtiarev, Stepan, trans. *Pravila garmonicheskie i melodicheskie dlia obucheniia vsei muzyki*. St. Petersburg: 1805.

> S ● Facsimile of the 1775 edition. MMMLF, ser. 2, no. 10. New York: Broude Brothers, [1966].

Review of Esteban Arteaga's *Le rivoluzioni del teatro musicale italiano, dalla sua origine fino al presente*, vol. 2 (1785)

> In *Giornale enciclopedico di Bologna* 13 (April 1786).

> S ● Arteaga, Esteban. *Le rivoluzioni del teatro musicale italiano, dalla sua origine fino al presente*. 3 vols. Bologna: Carlo Trenti, 1783-88; 2nd edition, Venice: Carlo Palese, 1785 [*sic*]; facsimile of the 1783-88 edition (BmB, ser. 3, no. 6), Bologna: Forni, 1969. [*Rism* B/VI/1, p. 98. LCPS: A-054a and 054b. HoM: 109. SMLMS.]

>> Contains the text of Manfredini's review of vol. 2 with extensive commentary, as "Osservazioni intorno ad un estratto del tomo secondo della presente opera inserito nel Giornale Enciclopedico di questa città [Bologna] N. XIII. del Mese d' Aprile, anno 1786., colle 'Repliche' fatte a queste 'Osservazioni' dallo stesso autor dell' estratto, e intitolate 'Difesa della musica moderna'." Manfredini replied in (1788), below.

Difesa della musica moderna e de' suoi celebri esecutori [*Rism* B/VI/2, p. 533.]

> Bologna: Carlo Trenti, 1788. [LCPS: M-018. IDC.]

> S ● Facsimile edition. BmB, ser. 2, no. 73. Bologna: Forni, [1972].

> S ● Facsimile edition. Geneva: Minkoff Reprint.

LITERATURE:

Mancini, Giambattista. *Lettera . . . diretta all'illustrissimo signor conte N. N.* [Vicenzo Manfredini]. Vienna: Mathias Andreas Schmidt, 1796. [*Rism* B/VI/2, p. 532.]

Monici, A. " 'Delle regole più essenziali per imparare a cantare' secondo un vecchio autore [Vincenzo Manfredini]." *Rmi* 18/1 (1911):85-94.

Monici, A. "Di un nuovo metodo per apprendere l'accompagnamento del basso secondo un vecchio autore [Vincenzo Manfredini]." *Rmi* 23/3-4 (1916):453-90.

Giegling, Franz. "Manfredini . . . Vincenzo." In *MGG* (1949-68). Bibliog.

Varda, Maria Paola de. "Il musicista Vincenzo Manfredini (1737–1799) e la sua posizione teorica nel quadro dell'Illuminismo." In *Tesi di laurea in storia della musica, Milano Universita, Facolta di lettere e filosofia, Anno accademico, 1966-67*.

Libby, Dennis. "Manfredini, Vincenzo." In *NGrove* (1980). Bibliog.

Baird, Julianne. "An 18th-Century Controversy about the Trill: Mancini v. Manfredini." *EM* 15/1 (1987):36-45.

See also FÉTIS: (1833-44); LITERATURE SUPPLEMENT: Alekseev (1974); Badura-Skoda et al. (1980); Becker (1836-39/1964); Carpenter (1988); Eitner (1900-1904/1959-60); Fellerer (1927/. . ./ 1972); Forkel (1792/1962); Fubini (1971/1983); Gerber (1790-92/1977), (1812-14/1966); Houle (1987); Jackson (1988); Lange (1899-1900); McQuere (1983); **Neumann** ["Appoggiatura"] (1982), [*Essays*] **(1982)**, (1986); **Ritzel (1967/1968)**; Rosenblum (1988); Smiles (1978); Williams, P. (1970).

FRIEDRICH WILHELM MARPURG

[1718–1795]

RAMEAU's principal champion in the German lands was Friedrich Wilhelm Marpurg, whose vigorous activities as author of numerous treatises, editor of three journals, and translator of d'ALEMBERT's *Élémens de musique, théorique et pratique, suivant les principes de M. Rameau* make him a central figure of eighteenth-century theoretical thought. His legacy, which served as inspiration for KOCH, SECHTER, and BRUCKNER, among others, combines a reworking of Rameau's theories and a penetrating yet somewhat arbitrary synthesis of Bach's fugal techniques.

Marpurg was in Paris during the 1740s and, inevitably, absorbed aesthetic and theoretical perspectives from which German musicians benefited upon his return. Though we should not blame him for losing track of RAMEAU's many revisions and expansions through numerous treatises and articles, we must concede that RAMEAU was ill served by Marpurg's unyielding and skewed perspective. Whereas RAMEAU derived melody from harmony, Marpurg erected an octave scale of twenty-one pitches for building chords; and whereas RAMEAU eventually acknowledged that his undertone hypothesis was fallacious, Marpurg never did. It was Marpurg more than RAMEAU himself who was responsible for the overwhelming attention that was paid, for the next two hundred years, to vertical chordal constructions at the expense of even the most elementary of linear melodic events.

Marpurg's harmonic theory, first articulated in a short-lived popular journal which he called *Der critische Musicus an der Spree* (1749-50) and treated in greater detail in his *Handbuch bey dem Generalbasse und der Composition* (1755-60), develops RAMEAU's concept of *supposition*. Not only are the ninth, eleventh, and thirteenth chords generated by adding a third, fifth, or seventh below the root of a seventh chord, but these constructs are, at least in his initial formulation, subject to inversion, thereby creating a wide variety of unusual sonorities.

A bitter dispute ensued with SORGE, whose *Compendium harmonicum* (1760), based on the more solid footing of overtones, poked at Marpurg's weak spots. As a result Marpurg further clarified his theory: in an edition of SORGE's work with commentary added by Marpurg, published during the same year; in an important article, "Untersuchung der sorgischen Lehre von der Entstehung der dißonirenden Sätze" (1761), published in Marpurg's journal *Historisch-kritische Beyträge zur Aufnahme der Musik*; and in a new edition of the first volume of the *Handbuch* (1762). What resulted was a so-called "combined Rameau-Marpurg system," an expansion upon RAMEAU's more speculative orientation through the manufacture and evaluation of a large number of two-, three-, and four-note pitch combinations. Some are listed as "classic" (*claßische*) chords, while others which incorporate elements of two keys are labelled "fantastic" (*fantastische*).

KIRNBERGER also suffered from Marpurg's pontification in the name of RAMEAU when he began experimenting with means for acknowledging non-essential dissonances, that is, those pitches which, though they may sound along with chord members, do not actually contribute to the formation of a harmony. He was so bold as to interpolate additional pitches into his fundamental bass, thereby acknowledging the role of context in its determination. Marpurg, intolerant of this departure from dogma (as he defined it), attacked KIRNBERGER in his *Versuch über die musikalische Temperatur, nebst einem Anhang über den Rameau- und Kirnbergerschen Grundbaß* (1776). By then, the two had been antagonistic towards one another for several decades, for they had sparred earlier on the concept of fugue in another of Marpurg's journals, *Kritische Briefe über die Tonkunst*, issued between 1759 and 1763.

　　Marpurg's reputation as an articulate spokesman for the *galant* musical aesthetic makes his equally important role in codifying Baroque fugal practice a bit surprising. His *Abhandlung von der Fuge* (1753-54) was at the time unprecedented in its depth of penetration into that complicated art. Marpurg had enjoyed direct consultation with J. S. Bach before the master's death. Thus with seemingly unquestionable authority Marpurg established normative procedures regarding subjects, answers, the injection of episodic passages, and the like. RAMEAU's and MATTHESON's earlier formulations were taken into account, as was a large body of repertoire. Yet in its very decisiveness the work promoted the sort of dry, rule-laden exercise that choked the study of fugue during the nineteenth century. Thus in contrapuntal as well as harmonic theory Marpurg potently influenced later thought, but in ways that many today find antithetical to the true purposes of the discipline.

Der critische Musicus an der Spree [*Rism* B/VI/2, p. 542.]

　　March 4, 1749-February 17, 1750. Issued weekly. Berlin: A. Haude & J. C. Spener, 1750. Vol. 1. [LCPS: M-040. HoM: 934. SMLMS. UME.]

S ● Facsimile edition. Hildesheim: Georg Olms, 1970.

Die Kunst das Clavier zu spielen . . . [*Rism* B/VI/2, pp. 544-45.]

　　Berlin: Henning, 1750.
　　Berlin: Haude & Spener, 1751. [LCPS: M-045a. HoM: 938.]
　　Berlin: A. Haude & J. C. Spener (G. L. Winter), 1760. [SMLMS.]
　　Augsburg: J. J. Lotters Erben, 1761.
　　Berlin: A. Haude & J. C. Spener, 1762. [LCPS: M-045b.]

　　　　A second part, "worinnen die Lehre vom Accompagnement abgehandelt wird":

　　Berlin: A. Haude & J. C. Spener, 1761. [LCPS: M-045c.]

T ● Lustig, Jaques Guillaume, trans. *L'art de joüer le clavessin . . .* [*Rism* B/VI/2, p. 545.] Amsterdam: J. J. Hummel, [ca. 1763-65].

　　A translation of the second part.

T ● Roeser, Valentin, trans. *L'art de toucher le clavecin . . .* [*Rism* B/VI/2, p. 545.] Paris: Le Menu, [1764]; Paris: Naderman, [ca. 1795]; Paris: Boyer (Nadermann), [ca. 1794-96]; facsimile edition, Geneva: Minkoff Reprint, 1973.

　　A translation of the first part.

S ● Facsimile of the 1762 (Part 1) and 1761 (Part 2) editions. Hildesheim: Georg Olms, 1969.

"Vorbericht" to J. S. Bach's *Die Kunst der Fuge*, second edition [*Rism* A/I/1, pp. 187-88.]

　　[Leipzig: 1752.]

T ● See David and Mendel (1945/1966).

*Abhandlung von der Fuge, nach dem Grundsätzen und Exempeln der besten deutschen und ausländischen Meiste*r [*Rism* B/VI/2, p. 540.]

　　Berlin: A. Haude & J. C. Spener, 1753-54. 2 vols. [LCPS: M-033. SMLMS. IDC. UME.] Leipzig: Kühnel, 1806.

　　　　Review in *BmZ* 2/32 (1806):125-27.

T ● *Traité de la fugue et du contrepoint* [*Rism* B/VI/2, p. 540.]. 2 vols. Berlin: A. Haude & J. C. Spener, 1756-61; Paris: Imbault, 1801.

　　　　Marpurg's own translation. Contains a "Histoire abrégée du contrepoint et de la fugue," which was translated into German for DEHN's edition of 1858, below.

T ● "A Treatise of Fugue and Counterpoint." Ms. [London: Royal College of Music.]

T ● See CHORON: [1809].

S ● *Exempel in LXII and LX Kupfertafeln zur Abhandlung von der Fuge*. Leipzig: Peters, [181-].

T ● See CHORON: (1836-38).

S ● SECHTER, Simon, ed. Vienna: Ant. Diabelli, [1843].

　　　　Review in *AmZ* 45/35 (1843):627-28 (N.).

S ● DEHN, S. W., ed. 2 vols. Leipzig: Peters, 1858.

T ● See **Mann (1955/. . ./1987)**.

S ● Facsimile of the 1753-54 edition. Hildesheim: Georg Olms, 1970.

Historisch-kritische Beyträge zur Aufnahme der Musik [*Rism* B/VI/2, p. 543.]

　　　　Includes "Untersuchung der sorgischen Lehre von der Entstehung der dißonirenden Sätze," 5/203 (1760-78):131-220.

Berlin: J. J. Schützens Witwe, G. A. Lange, 1754-62, 1778. 5 vols. [LCPS: M-042. HoM: 935. SMLMS. IDC. UME.]

> Review in *BsW* 2/2 (1757-58):421-22.

S ● Eggebrecht, Hans Heinrich, ed. "Rehabilitierung des Plagiates: Brief vom musikalischen Ausschreiben, worinnen zugleich eine neue Erfindung in der Musik bekanntgemacht wird." *Mleb* 6/2 (1953):55-56.

S ● Facsimile edition. Hildesheim: Georg Olms, 1970.

Anleitung zum Clavierspielen, der schönern Ausübung der heutigen Zeit gemäß [*Rism* B/VI/2, p. 541.]

> Berlin: A. Haude & J. C. Spener, 1755. [LCPS: M-036a. HoM: 932.]
> Berlin: A. Haude & J. C. Spener, 1765. [LCPS: M-036b. IDC. UME.]

T ● *Principes du clavecin* [*Rism* B/VI/2, p. 541.], Berlin: A. Haude & J. C. Spener (G. L. Winter), 1756 [LCPS: M-036c.]; facsimile editions (BmB, ser. 2, no. 44), Bologna: Forni, 1971; Geneva: Minkoff Reprint, 1974.

> Marpurg's own translation.

T ● Lustig, Jacob Wilhelm, trans. *Aanleiding tot het clavier-speelen . . .* [*Rism* B/VI/2, p. 545.] Amsterdam: J. J. Hummel, 1760 [LCPS: M-045d.]; reprint edition, [Amsterdam: A. J. Heuwekemeijer, 1970].

S ● Facsimile of the 1765 edition. MMMLF, ser. 2, no. 110. New York: Broude Brothers, 1969.

S ● Facsimile of the 1765 edition. Hildesheim: Georg Olms, 1970.

T ● Hayes, Elizabeth Loretta. "F. W. Marpurg's *Anleitung zum Clavierspielen* (Berlin, 1755); and *Principes du Clavecin* (Berlin, 1756): Translation and Commentary." 2 vols. Ph.D. dissertation, Stanford University, 1977. [*DA* 37/12A, pp. 7392-93. UMI 77-12641.]

Handbuch bey dem Generalbasse und der Composition mit zwey- drey- vier- fünf- sechs- sieben- acht und mehreren Stimmen; nebst einem vorläuffigen kurzen Begriff der Lehre vom Generalbasse für Anfänger [*Rism* B/VI/2, pp. 541, 542-43.]

> Berlin: Johann Jacob Schützens Witwe, Gottlieb August Lange, 1755-58. 3 vols. [LCPS: M-041a and M-041b. SMLMS. IDC. UME.]

> See SORGE: (1760) for a reaction to the *Handbuch*, as well as Marpurg's edition of SORGE's work for his rebuttal.

Berlin: Gottlieb August Lange, 1762. Vol. 1 only. [LCPS: M-041c. UME.]

> A Supplement, entitled *Anhang zum Handbuche . . .; worinnen, zur Übung der gewöhnlichern harmonischen Dreyklänge und Septimenaccorde, Probeexempel vorgeleget werden, und hiernächst dasjenige, was ein jeder Componist von dem doppelten Contrapunct und der Verfertigung einer Fuge wissen muß, gezeiget wird:*

Berlin: Gottlieb August Lange, 1760. [LCPS: M-035. SMLMS.]

T ● [Miklin, J., trans.] *Kort begrepp om general-basen* [*Rism* B/VI/2, p. 543.]. Stockholm: Carl Stolpe, 1782.

T ● See CHORON: [1809]; (1836-38).

S ● Facsimile of the 1755-60 volumes. Hildesheim: Georg Olms, 1974.

T ● Sheldon, David A., trans. *Marpurg's "Thoroughbass and Composition Handbook": A Narrative Translation and Critical Study.* HSMT, no. 2. Stuyvesant, N.Y.: Pendragon Press, 1989.

Anfangsgründe der theoretischen Musik [*Rism* B/VI/2, pp. 540-41.]

> Leipzig: Johann Gottlob Immanuel Breitkopf, 1757. [LCPS: M-034. HoM: 931. SMLMS.]

S ● Facsimile edition. MMMLF, ser. 2, no. 33. New York: Broude Brothers, 1966.

Anleitung zur Singcomposition [*Rism* B/VI/2, p. 542.]

> Berlin: Gottlieb August Lange, 1758. [LCPS: M-038. SMLMS.]

Kritische Briefe über die Tonkunst, mit kleinen Clavierstücken und Singoden, begleitet von einer musikalischen Gesellschaft in Berlin [*Rism* B/VI/2, pp. 543-44.]

> 1759-1763. Issued weekly.
> Berlin: Friedrich Wilhelm Birnstiel, 1760-64. Three collected volumes. [LCPS: M-043. HoM: 936. SMLMS. IDC. UME.]

S ● Facsimile edition. 2 vols. Hildesheim: Georg Olms, 1974.

Clavierstücke mit einem practischen Unterricht für Anfänger und Geübtere [*Rism* A/I/5, p. 430; B/II, p. 131; and B/VI/2, p. 542.]

> Berlin: Haude & Spener, 1762-63. 3 vols. [LCPS: M-039.]

The third volume contains "Discurs des Herrn Quanz über das Clavieraccompagnement."

Anleitung zur Musik überhaupt, und zur Singkunst besonders [*Rism* B/VI/2, pp. 541-42.]

> Berlin: Arnold Wever, 1763. [LCPS: M-037. SMLMS. IDC.]

> S ● Facsimile edition. Leipzig: Zentralantiquariat der DDR, 1975.

Versuch über die musikalische Temperatur, nebst einem Anhang über den Rameau- und Kirnbergerschen Grundbaß . . . [*Rism* B/VI/2, p. 546.]

> Breslau: Johann Friedrich Korn, 1776. [LCPS: M-048. HoM: 940. SMLMS. IDC.]

Neue Methode, allerley Arten von Temperaturen dem Claviere aufs bequemste mitzutheilen . . . [*Rism* B/VI/2, p. 546.]

> Berlin: Gottlieb August Lange, 1790. [LCPS: M-047. SMLMS. UME.]

> S ● Facsimile edition. Hildesheim: Georg Olms, 1970.

See also d'ALEMBERT: (1752); SORGE: (1760).

LITERATURE:

Lessing, Gotthold Ephraim. "An den Herrn Marpurg über die Regeln der Wissenschaften zum Vergnügen; besonders der Poesie und Tonkunst." 1753.

> A poem of about five pages found in collected works editions of Lessing's writings.

Pulver, Jeffrey. "Friedrich Wilhelm Marpurg." *MT* 53/832 (1912):375-77.

Bieder, Eugen. "Über Friedrich Wilhelm Marpurgs System der Harmonie, des Kontrapunkts und der Temperatur." Ph.D. dissertation, The University of Berlin, 1923.

Fox, Charles Warren. "Friedrich Wilhelm Marpurg, His *Historisch-kritisch Beyträge zur Aufnahme der Musik*, and Musical Life in Berlin." *BAMS* 2 (1937):13-14.

Hoke, Hans Gunter. "Marpurg, Friedrich Wilhelm." In *MGG* (1949-68). Bibliog.

Frederick, Kurt. "Friedrich Wilhelm Marpurg's *Abhandlung von der Fuge*." M.M. thesis, The University of Rochester, 1951. [SMLMS.]

Frerichs, Elli. "Lebendige Regeln eines alten Lehrbuches: *Die Kunst, das Klavier zu spielen*." *MiU* 43/3 (1952):74-76.

Link, John W., Jr. *Theory and Tuning: Aron's Meantone Temperament and Marpurg's Temperament "1"*. Boston: Tuners Supply Co., 1963; reprint edition, 1972.

Serwer, Howard Jay. "Friedrich Wilhelm Marpurg (1718-1795): Music Critic in a *Galant* Age." Ph.D. disserta-tion, Yale University, 1969. [*Rilm* 69-1163. *DA* 30/09A, pp. 3977-78. UMI 70-02801.]

Serwer, Howard. "Marpurg versus Kirnberger: Theories of Fugal Composition." *JMT* 14/2 (1970):209-36.

● ● ● Serwer, Howard. "Marpurg, Friedrich Wilhelm." In *NGrove* (1980). Bibliog.

See also BELLERMANN: (1862); DAUBE: Karbaum (1968/1969); FÉTIS: (1833-44); FUX: Federhofer (1988); HEINICHEN: (1728): Buelow (1961/. . ./ 1986); HERBST: Allerup (1931); KEPLER: Dickreiter (1971/1973); KIRNBERGER: Borris-Zuckermann (1933); Mekeel (1960); Beach (1974); Grant (1977); KOCH: Baker (1988); LÖHLEIN: (1765-81):Wilson (1979); MATTHESON: Buelow and Marx (1983): Sheldon; RAMEAU: Pischner (1961/. . ./1967); RIEMANN: (1898); SCHENKER: Slatin (1967); SCHRÖTER: ["Bedenken"] (1763); SCHULZ: (1799-1800):Spazier (1799-1800); SERRE: (1763); SORGE: (1760): Martin (1981); Frisch [dissertation] (1954); LITERATURE SUPPLEMENT: Ahlgrimm (1973); Allen ["Philosophies"] (1939); Apfel and Dahlhaus (1974); Arlt (1974); **Arnold (1931/. . ./ 1965)**; Asselin (1981); Atcherson (1960); Auhagen (1982/1983); Babitz (1952); Babitz and Pont (1973); Balthazar (1983); **Barbour** (1947), (1948), (1949-68), **(1951/. . ./1972)**; Beach (1967); Becker (1836-39/1964); Beiche ["Dux"] (1972-), ["Inversio"] (1972-); **Benary (1956/1961**; Bent, I. (1984); Beyschlag (1907/1953); Bircher (1970); Blake (1988); Blume (1984); Blumröder (1972-); Boomgaarden (1985/1987); Braun (1970); Bruck (1928); Buelow ["Affections"] (1980); **Bullivant (1980)**; Burney (1776-89/. . ./1957); Butler (1977); Cahn ["Repercussio"] (1972-); Carse (1925/ 1964); Chevaillier (1925/1931-32); Chybiński (1911-12); Cohen (1873-74); Collins (1963) (1966), (1967), (1973); **Dahlhaus (1984); Dahlhaus et al. (1987)**; David and Mendel (1945/1966); Dean (1977); de Zeeuw (1983); Dolmetsch (1915/. . ./1969); Donington (1963/. . ./1974) (1980); Duckles (1970); **Dürr and Gerstenberg (1949-68)**, **(1980)**; Dunsby and Whittall (1988); Dupont (1933/. . ./1986); Eitner (1880), (1900-1904/1959-60); Feil (1955); Fellerer (1927/. . ./1972); ["Zum Bild"] (1973); Ferand (1937/1938); Fischer (1957); Flaherty (1989); Forkel (1792/1962); Frisius (1969/1970); Frobenius ["Cantus"] (1972-), ["Homo-phonus"] (1972-), ["Isotonos"] (1972-), ["Polyphon"] (1972-); Ganz (1972), (1976); Gerber (1790-92/1977), (1812-14/1966); Ghislanzoni (1949-51); Goldmann (1987); Goldschmidt (1890/1892); Grave (1985); Gruber (1982); Gut (1972-); Harich-Schneider ([1939]/. . ./1970); Hawkins (1776/. . ./1969); Hedges (1978); Helm (1960); Hiller (1768-69); Hoffman (1953); Horsley (1963), [*Fugue: History*] (1966); Hosler (1978/1981); Houle (1960),

(1987); Jackson (1988); Jacobi (1957-60/1971); Jenne (1973-74); Jones (1934); Jorgensen (1971), (1978); Jorgenson (1957); **Kassler (1979)**; Katz (1926); Kaufmann (1969); Kauko (1958); Keller (1955/1965); Kelletat [*Temperatur*] (1960), ["Tonordnung"] (1960), (1966); Kivy (1980), (1984); Krehbiel (1964); Kretzschmar (1911-12); Krome (1896); Kümmerling (1977); Lang (1967-68); Lange (1899-1900); Lawrence (1978); **Lester (1989)**; Levenson (1981); Lewis (1975/1978); **Lindley** ["Temperaments"] **(1980), (1982), (1984)**; Maier **(1984)**; Mainka (1965/1969); Mallard (1978); **Mann (1955/. . ./1987),** (1987); Mendel (1978); Mitchell, J. W. (1963); Mitchell, W. J. (1963); Möller (1971); Müller-Blattau (1923/. . ./1963), (1949-68); Munkachy (1968); **Neumann,** Frederick (1977/1982), (1978), ["Appoggiatura"] (1982), [*Essays*] **(1982)**, (1986); Neumann, F.-H. (1955/1962); Newman (1985); Newman (1946), (1959/. . ./1983), (1963/. . ./ 1983), (1976); Oberdoerffer (1949-68), (1967); Oldroyd (1948); Ottenberg (1973/1978); **Palisca** ["Rezitativ"] (1972-), ["Theory"] **(1980)**, [" 'Baroque' "] (1989); Pikler (1966); Rasch (1981), (1983); Ratner (1956), (1980); Reichenbach (1948); Reilly (1984-85); Reimer ["Kammermusik"] (1972-); Ritzel (1967/1968); Rohwer (1949-68); Rosenblum (1988); Rothschild (1953), (1961); Rummenhöller (1967); Sachs (1972-); Schäfke (1934); Schering and Wustmann (1941); Schmalzriedt ["Durchführen"] (1972-), ["Episode"] (1972-); Schünemann (1928/1931); Schulenberg (1982); Schwartz (1908); Seaton (1981); Seidel (1972-); Serauky (1929); Sheldon (1975), (1981), ● ● ●(1982), (1986); **Shirlaw (1917/ . . ./1970)**; Sisman (1978); Smiles (1978); Sondheimer (1925); Spitzer and Zaslaw (1986); **Steblin (1981/1983)**; Stege (1927-28); Stein (1983); Stowell (1985); Tenney (1988); Thieme (1982-83); Tittel (1959), (1966); Todd (1983); Troeger (1987); Ulrich (1931/1932); Vanhulst (1971); Vogel (1955/1954); (1975/1984); Wagner (1981); Waite (1970); Walker (1987); **Wason (1981/1985),** (1983); Wessel (1955); Wichmann (1966); Williams, P. (1968), (1970); Wirth (1966); **Zaminer (1985)**; Zimmermann (1976).

GIOVANNI BATTISTA MARTINI

[1706 – 1784]

The beloved Bolognese ecclesiastic and scholar Giovanni Battista Martini held an extraordinary position in European musical life. His devotion to the contrapuntal tradition of Palestrina found a fruitful outlet through his teaching. An international assemblage of students, including J. C. Bach and the young Mozart, lingered in Bologna to work with him, while famous and powerful men from all of Europe were recipients of his letters.

Despite the difficulties and expenses involved, Martini assembled an amazing library of theoretical treatises and scores, numbering some seventeen thousand volumes, now housed in the Civico museo bibliografico musicale in Bologna. Various of his correspondents were also voracious buyers for him at the booksellers of their native cities. Sometimes works of great rarity were copied out longhand so that Martini could have access to them. No one was better qualified in music scholarship than Martini, and as a result he was frequently consulted for his opinions. His writings, not surprisingly, emphasize history. For example, the *Storia della musica* (1757-81) is the beginning of a large-scale history of music which, after three volumes, had progressed only through Greek antiquity.

RAMEAU submitted his "Nouvelles réflexions sur le principe sonore" (published with his *Code de musique pra-* *tique* in 1760) to Bologna's Accademia delle scienze, into which Martini had been initiated in 1758. The academy chose Martini as the principal evaluator of this document. Rather than examining this work out of context, Martini saw to it that the major works of RAMEAU were shipped from Paris and promptly had them translated into Italian. He also interacted with RAMEAU by mail (through special arrangements, since Geneva's chief postal officer was uncooperative with the French post). The resulting document, the text for Martini's presentation before the academy [ca. 1761], reveals a careful and fair assessment of RAMEAU's ideas, with, as would be expected for someone as conservative as Martini, certain reservations concerning the acoustical principles upon which RAMEAU had based his harmonic theory.

Of particular interest for modern scholars (who might find his history of Hebrew and Greek music rather dull, as did Martini's contemporaries) is the *Exemplare o sia saggio fondamentale pratico di contrappunto sopra il canto fermo* (1774-75), a fascinating and challenging compendium of musical scores and perceptive commentary. Continuing on the path of FUX's *Gradus ad Parnassum* (1725), Martini assembled materials appropriate for the more advanced students he was accustomed to encountering. The work is particularly useful for its clear articulation of terminology for contrapuntal analysis. Though its central focus is the reper-toire of Palestrina's generation, its perspective was regarded as vital even for composers whose works might venture beyond that tradition.

Correspondence

> Mss., 1730-84. [Bologna: Civico museo biblio-grafico musicale; and various other libraries.]

> S ● Parisini, Federico, ed. *Carteggio inedito del P. Giambattista Martini coi più celebri musicisti del suo tempo.* Vol. 1. Bologna: N. Zanichelli, 1888; reprint edition (BmB, ser. 5, no. 22), Bologna: Forni, 1969.

> S ● See Schnoebelen (1979), below, and Brofsky (1980), below, for information on further sources. See also RAMEAU: Collected Works (1967-72):Vol. 6; Jacobi (1964); SOLER: (1765-72).

Regola agli organisti per accompagnare il canto fermo [*Rism* B/VI/2, p. 552.]

> Bologna: Dalla Volpe, [ca. 1756].

> S ● Facsimile edition. BmB, ser. 4, no. 201. Bologna: Forni, 1969.

Storia della musica [*Rism* B/VI/2, pp. 552-53.]

> Bologna: Lelio dalla Volpe, 1757 [appeared in 1760 or 1761], 1770, 1781. 3 vols. [HoM: 943. SMLMS. IDC.]
> Ms., [ca. 1780-84]. [Bologna: Civico museo bibli-ografico musicale.] A fourth volume.

> S ● Wessely, Othmar, ed. Facsimile edition. GDMgBA, no. 3. Graz: Akademische Druck- und Verlagsanstalt, 1967.

>> Reviews in *Mf* 22/2 (1969):238-39 (Werner Friedrich Kümmel), *ML* 49/1 (1968):55-57 (J. A. Westrup), and *Musica* 22/5 (1968):369-70 (Ludwig Finscher).

> S ● Vecchi, Giuseppe. " 'Alcune memorie intorno alla musica figurata' di Padre Giambattista Martini (dalla *Storia della Musica*, volume 4)." In *HaberlFs* (1977):303-10. [*Rilm* 77-289.]

[Report on Rameau's Theoretical Writings (especially the "Nouvelles réflexions sur le principe sonore") for the Accademia delle scienze dell'Istituto di Bologna]

> Ms., [ca. 1761]. [Bologna: Civico museo biblio-grafico musicale.]

> S ● See RAMEAU: Collected Works (1967-72):Vol. 6, pp. 387-407.

"Onomasticum, seu synopsis musicarum graecarum atque obscuriorum vocum, cum earum interpreta-tione ex operibus Io. Baptistae Doni Patrici Floren-tini"

> In DONI: (1763):Vol. 2:268-76.

"Dissertatio de usu progressionis geometricae in musica"

> In *Commentari dell'Istituto delle scienze di Bologna* 5/2 (1767):372-94.
> [Ca. 1767]. [*Rism* B/VI/2, p. 551. LCPS: M-056.]
>> Reprinted in 1775.

> S ● Facsimile of the [ca. 1767] edition. BmB, ser. 2, no. 72. Bologna: Arnaldo Forni, 1980.

Compendio della teoria de' numeri per uso del musico [*Rism* B/VI/2, p. 551.]

> [Bologna: Lelio dalla Volpe], 1769.

> S ● Facsimile edition. BmB, ser. 2, no. 63. Bologna: Forni.

Esemplare o sia saggio fondamentale pratico di contrap-punto sopra il canto fermo [*Rism* B/VI/2, pp. 551-52.]

> Bologna: Lelio dalla Volpe, 1774[-75]. 2 vols. [LCPS: M-057. HoM: 942.]

> T ● See ● ● ● **Mann (1955/.../1987)**.

> S ● Facsimile edition. Ridgewood, N.J.: Gregg Press, 1965.

Lettere di un accademico filarmonico sull'Eximeno [*Rism* B/VI/2, p. 552.]

> Pisaro: Savelli, 1781.

"Intorno alle quinte successive nel contrappunto"

> In *Lettere del Sig. Francesco Maria Zanotti*. Milan: Pirola, 1782.

"Nomenclatura musicale . . . a guisa di dizionario"

> Ms. [Bologna: Civico museo bibliografico musi-cale.]

See also RAMEAU (passim) for translations of RAMEAU's works undertaken by or for Martini.

LITERATURE:

Zanotti, Francesco Maria. *Lettere . . . nelle quale si propongono, e risolvano alcuni dubbj appartementi al trattato: Della divisione del tempo nella musica, nel ballo, e nella poesia*. Milan: Malatesta, 1770. [*Rism* B/VI/2, p. 905. LCPS: Z-002.]

Parisini, Federico. *Della vita e delle opere del Padre Gio. Battista Martini*. Bologna: Nicola Zanichelli, 1887.

Gaspari, Gaetano, ed. *Catalogo della Biblioteca musicale G. B. Martini di Bologna*. Vol. 1: *Opere teoriche*. Bologna: Libreria Romagnoli dall' Acqua, 1890; reprint edition (edited by Napoleone Fanti, Oscar Mischiati, and Luigi Ferdinando Tagliavini; Stmus, no. 1), Bologna: Arnaldo Forni, 1961.

Busi, Leonida. *Il padre G. B. Martini, musicista-letterato del secolo XVIII*. Bologna: N. Zanichelli, 1891; facsimile edition (BmB, ser. 3, no. 2), Bologna: Forni, [1969].

Reich, Wilhelm. "Padre Martini als Theoretiker und Lehrer." Ph.D. dissertation, The University of Vienna, 1934.

Tebaldini, Giovanni. "La scolastica del P. Martini." *Rmi* 43/3-4, 5 (1939):305-14, 517-30; 44/1 (1940):1-17.

Bolis, Luciano. "G. B. Martini, compositore, teorico e storico della musica." Thesis, The University of Pavia, 1941-42.

Pauchard, P. Anselm. "Ein italienischer Musiktheoretiker: Pater Giambattista Martini, Franziskaner-Konventual (1706-1784): Eine literarische Quellenuntersuchung zur *Storia della musica*." Ph.D. dissertation, The University of Freiburg (Switzerland), 1941 (1942); published edition, Lugano: Cesare Mazzucconi, 1941.

Tagliavini, Luigi Ferdinando. "Martini, Giovanni Battista." In *MGG* (1949-68). Bibliog.

Tagliavini, Luigi Ferdinando. "Glorioso passato e problemi presenti della Biblioteca musicale 'G. B. Martini' di Bologna." *Fam* 2/1 (1955):62-68.

Reich, Willi. "In memoriam: Padre Martini." *Musica* 10/4 (1956):283-84.

Brofsky, Howard. "Students of Padre Martini: A Preliminary List." *Fam* 13/2-3 (1966):159-60.

Wiechens, Bernward. "Die Kompositionstheorie und das kirchenmusikalische Schaffen Padre Martinis." Ph.D. dissertation, The University of Cologne, 1968; published edition (KBzMf, no. 48), Regensburg: Boße, 1968. Bibliog. [*Rilm* 69-3856.]

> Abstract in *Mf* 22/4 (1969):501-2. Review in *Musica* 23/4 (1969):394 (Lothar Hoffmann-Erbrecht: "Padre Martinis Kirchenmusik").

Ionta, Sylvester John. "The Eximeno-Martini Polemic." Ph.D. dissertation, Syracuse University, 1969. [*DA* 30/08A, pp. 3491-92. UMI 70-01957.]

Zaccaria, Vittore. *Padre Giambattista Martini compositore musicologo e maestro, con il catalogo di tutte le opere*. Padua: Messaggero, 1969.

> Reviews in *Nrmi* 4/2 (1970):361 (Agostino Ziino) and *SK* 17/4 (1969-70):186 (Dr. Kundi).

Stefani, Gino. "Padre Martini e l'Eximeno: Bilancio di una celebre polemica sulla musica di chiesa." *Nrmi* 4/3 (1970):463-81. Bibliog. [*Rilm* 70-1901.]

Duckles, Vincent. "The Revival of Early Music in 18th-Century Italy: Observations on the Correspondence between Girolamo Chiti and Padre Giambattista Martini." *Rbdm* 26-27 (1972-73):14-24. [*Rilm* 76-594.]

Di Toma, Gabriele. "Aspetti della figura e dell'opera di Padre Giambattista Martini." Thesis, The University of Padua, 1973-74.

Mann, Alfred. "Padre Martini and Fux." In *MeyerFs* (1973):253-55. [*Rilm* 76-638.]

Schnoebelen, Anne. "Padre Martini's Collection of Letters: An Overview." *CM* 19 (1975):81-88. Bibliog.

Kirk, Elise K. "Padre Giambattista Martini: Some Little-Known Aspects." *AMT* 26/6 (1976-77):16-18. Bibliog. [*Rilm* 77-2620.]

Schnoebelen, Anne. "The Growth of Padre Martini's Library as Revealed in His Correspondence." *ML* 57/4 (1976):379-97. [*Rilm* 76-5626.]

Brofsky, Howard. "Doctor Burney and Padre Martini: Writing a General History of Music." *MQ* 65/3 (1979):313-45. [*Rilm* 79-2618.]

Schnoebelen, Anne. *Padre Martini's Collection of Letters in the Civico museo bibliografico musicale in Bologna: An Annotated Index*. ARTM, no. 2. New York: Pendragon Press, 1979. Bibliog.

> Reviews in *EM* 8/4 (1980):533-35 (Michael Talbot), *Fam* 27/3-4 (1980):225-27 (Pierluigi Petrobelli), *Mf* 35/2 (1982):186 (Eva Renate Wutta), *ML* 61/3-4 (1980):376-78 (Vincent Duckles), *Notes* 36/4 (1979-80):893-94 (John Walter Hill), and *Rh* 264/535 (1980):219 (Edith Weber).

Brofsky, Howard. "Martini, Padre Giovanni Battista." In *NGrove* (1980). Bibliog.

Haberl, Ferdinand. "Martin Gerbert von St. Blasien und seine Beziehungen zu Padre Giambattista Martini von Bologna." *SK* 32/3 (1985):101-4.

See also BELLERMANN: (1858); EXIMENO: (1775); FÉTIS: (1833-44); MOMIGNY: (1791-1818):(1791); RAMEAU: Collected Works (1967-72); Pischner (1961/. . ./1967); Jacobi (1964); RIEMANN: (1898); SABBATINI, L. A.: ["Studi"] (n.d.); TARTINI: Cavallini (1979-80); VALLOTTI: Cattin (1981); VIADANA: Haack (1964/1974); LITERATURE SUPPLEMENT: Allen ["Philosophies"] (1939); Austin (1980); Baron (1968); Becker

(1836-39/1964); Beiche ["Dux"] (1972-); Bircher (1970); Boetticher (1954); Borgir (1971/1987); **Bullivant (1980)**; Burney (1776-89/. . ./1957); Cahn ["Transitus"] (1972-); Chesnut (1976); Cohen (1873-74); **Coover (1980); Dahlhaus and Sachs (1980)**; David and Mendel (1945/1966); Eitner (1900-1904/1959-60); Federhofer (1985); Fellerer (1927/. . ./1972); ["Zum Bild"] (1973); Ferand (1937/ 1938), ["Improvised"] (1956), [*Improvisation*] (1956/ 1961); Fischer (1957); Forkel (1792/1962); Frobenius ["Cantus"] (1972-), ["Vollstimmig"] (1972-); Gerber (1790-92/1977), (1812-14/1966); Ghislanzoni (1949-51); Grave (1985); Gut (1972-); Hawkins (1776/. . ./1969); Horsley [*Fugue: History*] (1966); Isgro (1968); Jeppesen (1930/. . ./1974); **Kassler (1979)**; Kroyer (1901/. . ./1970); La Fage (1864/1964); Lang (1941); Lindley (1982); Mahlert and Sunter (1972-); Mann (1970/1971), (1987); McKinnon (1978); McQuere (1983); Mendel (1948); Müller-Blattau (1923/. . ./1963); Neumann, Frederick (1978), (1986); Newman (1963/. . ./1983); Ortigue (1853/. . ./1971); Ratner (1980); Roberts (1967); Schmalzriedt ["Coda"] (1972-), ["Episode"] (1972-), ["Exposition"] (1972-), ["Subiectum"] (1972-); Seidel (1972-); Sondheimer (1925); Subirá (1947/. . ./1958); Tittel (1959); Todd (1983); Tuksar (1978/1980); Wessely (1967); Williams, P. (1970); Wirth (1966); Wolff (1972-); **Zaminer (1985)**.

ADOLF BERNHARD MARX

[ca. 1795 – 1866]

The Berlin professor Adolf Bernhard Marx undertook a huge project on behalf of his students: the four-volume *Lehre von der musikalischen Komposition, praktisch-theoretisch* (1837-47). He was not contented to circumscribe his efforts within the domains of harmony and counterpoint, as some of his contemporaries were doing, much to his consternation. [His views on the pedagogy of Siegfried DEHN were vented in *Alte Musiklehre im Streit mit unserer Zeit* (1841).] Instead, he embraced the study of rhythm, melody, and, especially, form.

Countering the historical association of form with harmonic plan, Marx paid greater attention to the role of melody in determining the form of a movement. As a Hegelian, he was inclined to emphasize the thematic contrasts that may exist in a given work and to reveal how the composer achieved, ultimately, a synthesis of opposing ideas. Rather than postulating a set of rigid formulae for the various musical forms, Marx acknowledged the wide range of individual possibilities for a work's form when controlled by a master composer. He suggested that the sonata form (*Sonatenform*, a term he coined) consisted of three—not two—parts and was subject to an infinite variety of modifications based upon composers' creative inspirations. The concerto form was regarded as a type of sonata movement, rather than as a separate category of form. Marx also formulated several basic types of rondo form, as well as a hybrid which merged sonata and rondo characteristics. In addition, his treatise embraces contrapuntal procedures (including an influential ternary interpretation of fugue), other standard forms (scherzo, variations, etc.), and procedures of composition for various instruments and ensemble groupings.

Marx did not confine himself to materials intended for his university students. Early in his career, he served as editor for the *Berliner allgemeine musikalische Zeitung* and pro-moted the keyboard pedagogy of LOGIER. While still writing his *Lehre von der musikalischen Komposition*, he produced a more elementary *Allgemeine Musiklehre* (1839), which went through numerous editions and appeared in two different English translations. As an offshoot of his study on Beethoven, he published *Anleitung zum Vortrag Beethovenscher Klavierwerke* (1863). Unlike his contemporaries HAUPTMANN and SECHTER, Marx retained a practical orientation and was thoroughly committed to what was then emerging as the standard repertory—from Bach through mid-Beethoven.

Berliner allgemeine musikalische Zeitung [BamZ]

> Berlin: A. M. Schlesinger, 1824-30. Edited by Marx.

Die Kunst des Gesanges, theoretisch-praktisch

> Berlin: A. M. Schlesinger, 1826.

Die Lehre von der musikalischen Komposition, praktisch-theoretisch, zum Selbstunterricht, oder als Leitfaden bei Privatunterweisung und öffentlichen Vörtragen

> Leipzig: Breitkopf & Härtel, 1837, 1838, 1845, 1847. 4 vols.

> > Numerous editions of the various volumes, including those of vols. 1, 2, and 4 by RIEMANN in 1887-90. Reviews in *AmZ* 40/7-8 (1838):101-8, 117-26 (G. W. Fink), *AmZ* 44/43-44 (1842):850-55, 865-75, *AmZ* 47/29-30 (1845):481-87, 497-501 (Dr. Keferstein), *AmZ* 50/11-12 (1848): 179-82, 201-5 (Dr. Keferstein), and *RgmdP* 7 (1840):13-15 (François-Joseph FÉTIS).

T ● Saroni, Hermann S., trans. and ed. *Theory and Practice of Musical Composition*. New York: F. J.

Huntington and Mason & Law, [ca. 1851]; later editions (edited by Emilius Girac).

T ● Wehrhan, August Heinrich, trans. *The School of Musical Composition, Practical and Theoretical*. Vol. 1. London: R. Cocks, 1852.

Allgemeine Musiklehre: Ein Hülfsbuch für Lehrer und Lernende in jedem Zweige musikalischer Unterweisung

Leipzig: Breitkopf & Härtel, 1839.

Numerous editions. Review in *AmZ* 43/26 (1841):510-12.

T ● Lemokh, Vikenti Osipovich, trans. *Obshchee rukovodstvo k izucheniiu muzyki*. Moscow: 1848.

T ● Wehrhan, August Heinrich, trans. *The Universal School of Music: A Manual for Teachers and Students in Every Branch of Musical Art*. London: R. Cocks, 1853; Louisville: American Printing House for the Blind, 1877; other editions.

T ● Macirone, George, trans. *General Musical Instruction (Allgemeine Musiklehre): An Aid to Teachers and Learners in Every Branch of Musical Knowledge*. Boston: O. Ditson, n.d.; revised edition (edited by Josiah Pittman; NLDMK), London: Novello, 1854.

T ● Famintsyn, A. S., trans. *Vseobshchii uchebnik muzyki: Rukovodstvo dlia uchitelei i uchashchikhsia po vsem otrabliam muzykal'nogo obrazovanniia*. St. Petersburg: 1872.

Die alte Musiklehre im Streit mit unserer Zeit

Leipzig: Breitkopf & Härtel, 1841.

An attack on DEHN: (1840). Response by G. W. Fink, as *Der neumusikalische Lehrjammer; oder, Beleuchtung der Schrift: Die alte Musiklehre im Streit mit unserer Zeit* (Leipzig: Mayer & Wigand, 1842).

Die Musik des neunzehnten Jahrhunderts und ihre Pflege: Methode der Musik

Liepzig: Breitkopf & Härtel, 1855.
Liepzig: Breitkopf & Härtel, 1873.

T ● Wehrhan, August Heinrich; Clarke, James; and MacFarren, C. Natalia, trans. *The Music of the Nineteenth Century, and Its Culture: System of Musical Instruction*. London: R. Cocks, 1855.

"Die Form in der Musik"

WnJ 2/2 (1857):21-48.

Anleitung zum Vortrag Beethovenscher Klavierwerke

Derived from Marx's *Ludwig van Beethoven: Leben und Schaffen* (2 vols.; Berlin: Otto Janke, 1859).

Berlin: Otto Janke, 1863.

Later editions, including:

Berlin: Otto Janke, 1875. Edited by Gustav Behncke.

Later editions. Review in *Rmi* 5/4 (1898):849 (A. E.).

Leipzig: Reinecke, [1903]. Edited by R. Hövker. Regensburg: G. Boße, [1912]. Edited by Eugen Schmitz.

T ● Gwinner, Fannie Louise, trans. *Introduction to the Interpretation of the Beethoven Piano Works*. Chicago: Clayton F. Summy, 1895.

Review in *Rmi* 3/4 (1896):782-85 (Luigi Torchi).

See also LOGIER: (1818) [*Thorough*]:[1819?]:Review (1830); (1827):MARX (1827); (1827):MARX (1827):Review (1830).

See Hahn (1949-68), below, for a more comprehensive worklist.

LITERATURE:

Decker, C. v. *Bildliche Darstellung des Systems der Tonarten; oder, Gedächtnißtafel zur Versinnlichung der Tonarten, ihrer Harmonien, Modulationen und Verwandtschaften; Basirt auf die musikalische Kompositionslehre des Herrn Professor Dr. Marx*. Berlin: Mittler, 1838.

"Uber das Studium der komposition mit besonderer Beziehung auf die Kompositionslehre von A. B. Marx vom Verfasser." *AmZ* 41/46 Extrablatt (1839):909-16.

Hentschel, Ernst Julius. *Streitfragen über Musik und Methode der Musik und des musikalischen Unterrichts: Fink und Marx*. Essen: Bädeker, 1843.

Girac, Emilius. *Appendix and Notes to Marx's Theory of Musical Composition*. New York: Mason, 1854.

Selle, Gustav F. "Zur Charakteristik von Marx' Unterricht." In *Aus Adolf Bernhard Marx' litterarischem Nachlaß: Ein Gedenkblatt zum hundertjährigen Geburtstage des . . . Dr. A. B. Marx*, edited by Gustav F. Selle, pp. 53-60. Berlin: Janke, 1898.

Mendelssohn, J. *A Complete Method of Musical Composition According to the System of A. B. Marx*. New York and Boston: C. Fischer, 1910.

Hahn, Kurt. "Marx, Adolf Bernhard." In *MGG* (1949-68). Bibliog.

Fellerer, Karl Gustav. "Adolf Bernhard Marx und Gottfried Wilhelm Fink." In *OrelFs* (1960):59-65. Bibliog.

Edler, Arnfried. "Zur Musikanschauung von Adolf Bernhard Marx." In Salmen (1965):103-12. Bibliog.

Kirchmeyer, Helmut. "Ein Kapitel Adolf Bernhard Marx: Über Sendungsbewußtsein und Bildungsstand der Berliner Musikkritik zwischen 1824 und 1830." In Salmen (1965):73-101. Bibliog.

Eicke, Kurt-Erich. "Der Streit zwischen Adolph Bernhard Marx und Gottfried Wilhelm Fink um die Kompositionslehre." Ph.D. dissertation, The University of Cologne, 1966; published edition (KBzMf, no. 42), Regensburg: Boße, 1966. Bibliog.

Abstract in *Mf* 20/3 (1967):312-13.

Eicke, Kurt-Erich. "Das Problem des Historismus im Streit zwischen Marx und Fink." In *Die Ausbreitung des Historismus über die Musik*, edited by Walter Wiora, pp. 221-32. SzMg, no. 14. Regensburg: Gustav Boße, 1969. Bibliog. [*Rilm* 70-2924.]

Ottlová, Marta. "Tektonické problémy ve Smetanových studijních skladbách." *Hv* 11/2 (1974):150-61. [*Rilm* 76-10601.]

Slavický, Milan. "Polyfonie ve Smetanově počátečním období." *Hv* 11/2 (1974):136-47. [*Rilm* 76-10711.]

Slavická-Hachová, Eva. "Ke Smetanovým studiím u Josefa Prokše." *Hv* 11/2 (1974):147-49. [*Rilm* 76-10710.]

Dahlhaus, Carl. "Formenlehre und Gattungstheorie bei A. B. Marx." In *SieversFs* (1978):29-35. [*Rilm* 78-6059.]

Forchert, Arno. "Adolf Bernhard Marx und seine *Berliner Allgemeine musikalische Zeitung*. In Dahlhaus ["Geschichte"] (1980):381-404. Bibliog. [*Rilm* 80-5856.]

Moyer, Birgitte. "Marx, Adolf Bernhard." In *NGrove* (1980). Bibliog.

Roske, Michael. "Der private Klavierlehrer im 19. Jahrhundert." *Musica* 35/2 (1981):137-41. Bibliog. [*Rilm* 81-4038.]

Dahlhaus, Carl. "Ästhetische Prämissen der 'Sonatenform' bei Adolf Bernhard Marx." *AfMw* 41/2 (1984):73-85.

Burnham, Scott Gordon. "Aesthetics, Theory and History in the Works of Adolph Bernhard Marx." Ph.D. dissertation, Brandeis University, 1988. [*DA* 49/07A, p. 1614. UMI 88-19744.]

Schmidt, Lothar. "Die Kompositionslehre von Adolf Bernhard Marx." Ph.D. dissertation, The University of Marburg, forthcoming.

See also FÉTIS: (1833-44); HELMHOLTZ: Dahlhaus (1970); KOCH: Baker (1976); Dahlhaus (1978);

LOGIER: Pügner (1959); RIEMANN: Denecke (1937); SCHOENBERG: Rexroth (1969/1971); VOGLER: Stevens (1983); LITERATURE SUPPLEMENT: Allanbrook (1981); Allen ["Philosophies"] (1939); Apfel and Dahlhaus (1974); Auhagen (1982/1983), (1987); Beiche ["Dux"] (1972-), ["Inversio"] (1972-); **Bent**, I. ["Analytical Thinking"] (1980), ["Analysis"] ● ● ● **(1980/1987)**, (1984); Budday (1982/1983); **Bullivant (1980)**; Burde (1976); Busch (1980); Cahn ["Repercussio"] (1972-), ["Retardatio"] (1972-), (1982); Carpenter (1988); Cavett-Dunsby (1988); Černý (1976); Cole (1969): Cook (1987); Dadelsen (1972); **Dahlhaus** (1967), (1970/1983), (1975/1977), (1978), ["Harmony"] **(1980)**, [*Studien*] (1980), ["Über"] (1980), **(1984)**; Dunsby and Whittall (1988); Dziebowska (1976); Federhofer (1944/1950), (1985); Fischer (1957); Frisius (1969/1970); Frobenius ["Cantus"] (1972-), ["Dauer"] (1972-), ["Polyphon"] (1972-), ["Vollstimmig"] (1972-); Gut (1972-); Gwilt (1983-84); Hahn (1960); Henneberg (1972/1974), (1983); Horsley [*Fugue: History*] (1966); Imig (1969/1970); Jacobi (1957-60/1971); Jeppesen (1930/. . ./1974); Kähler (1958); Kivy (1984); Kümmel (1967), (1973); Kunze (1968); Larsen (1963/1988); Levenson (1981), (1983-84); Lindley (1982); Longyear and Covington (1985); Mann (1987); McQuere (1983); Meier (1966), (1969), (1974); Moyer (1969); Müller-Blattau (1923/. . ./1963), (1949-68); Nelson (1984); Newman (1946), (1959/. . ./1983), (1963/. . ./1983), (1969/. . ./1983); Nielsen (1971); Palisca ["Rezitativ"] (1972-); Polezhaev (1982); Ratner (1949), (1980); Rea (1978); Reimer ["Concerto"] (1972-), ["Kammermusik"] (1972-), (1973); **Ritzel (1967/1968)**; Rohwer (1949-68); Rosen (1980/1988); Rothärmel (1963/1968); Rummenhöller (1967), (1971); Ryzhkin (1933), (1934-39); Sachs (1972-); Schmalzriedt ["Coda"] (1972-), ["Durchführen"] (1972-); ["Episode"] (1972-), ["Reprise"] (1972-), (1985); Schmidt (1979); Schoffman (1979); Seaton (1981); Seidel (1972-), (1975), (1979), (1986); Serauky (1929); Serwer (1974); Shamgar (1978), (1981); Sheldon (1982); Smither (1960); Steinbeck (1981); Stevens (1974); Thaler (1987); Thompson (1980); Tittel (1959); Todd (1983), (1988-89); Tsuchida (1979); Vogel (1955/1954), (1962); **Wagner (1974); Wason (1981/1985)**; Weigl (1914-15); Whittall (1980); Wirth (1966); **Zaminer (1985)**.

CHARLES MASSON

[fl. 1680 – 1700]

Charles Masson's *Nouveau traité des règles de la composition de la musique* (1697) is one of the most important French treatises on practical music theory from the period before RAMEAU, whose references to it attest to its usefulness, as does its long publication history. Masson accepted only two modes — major and minor, derived from Ionian and Dorian, respectively. Their essential notes (namely, the final, mediant, and dominant) were to be emphasized in composition. Two-, three-, and four-part examples are discussed, with special emphasis given to the use of the various dissonant intervals. Four categories of fugue (that is, imitative writing) are mentioned: exact repetition at the unison or octave; imitation at the fourth or fifth (with variant interval sizes permitted to accommodate the tonal context); imitation through inversion; and "double fugue," wherein two different motives are utilized in imitative writing.

Nouveau traité des règles de la composition de la musique par lequel on apprend à faire facilement un chant sur des paroles . . . [*Rism* B/VI/2, pp. 554-55.]

> Paris: the author and Jacques Collombat, 1697 [*not* 1694].
>
> > As *Nouveau traité des règles pour la composition de la musique . . .*:
>
> Paris: Christophe Ballard, 1699.
>
> > This edition was reprinted in 1700 and 1701.
>
> Paris: Christophe Ballard, 1705. [LCPS: M-060a.]
> Amsterdam: Estienne Roger, [ca. 1708]. [LCPS: M-060b.]
> Paris: J. B. C. Ballard, 1738. [LCPS: M-060c.]
> Paris: Ch. Ballard, 1755.

S ● ● ● ● Horsley, Imogene, ed. Facsimile of the 1699 edition. DCPMRS. New York: Da Capo Press, 1967.

> Reviews in *ABBW* 41/4 (1968):281, *ARG* 35/2 (1968-69):164-65 (James Ringo), *Choice* 4/11 (1967-68):1252, *Consort* 25 (1968-69):406-7 (Lillian M. Ruff), and *Notes* 25/1 (1968-69):46 (Robert Donington).

S ● Facsimile of the 1705 edition. Geneva: Minkoff Reprint, 1971.

T ● Hoiseth, Gary Thomas. "Charles Masson's *Nouveau traité des règles pour la composition de la musique* and *Divers traitez sur la composition de la musique*: A Translation and Commentary." M.A. thesis, The University of Iowa, 1972.

T ● Schaffer, John William, trans. Forthcoming.

Divers traitez sur la composition de la musique. Premier traité: Secret de l'harmonie, pour apprendre d'une manière très-sûre et très-facile à faire une basse à un dessus [*Rism* B/VI/2, p. 554.]

> Paris: J. Colombat, 1705.

T ● See (1697):Hoiseth (1972), above.

LITERATURE:

● ● ● Schneider, Herbert. "Charles Masson und sein *Nouveau traité*." *AfMw* 30/4 (1973):245-74. Bibliog. [*Rilm* 74-344.]

Horsley, Imogene. "Masson, Charles." In *NGrove* (1980).

See also FÉTIS: (1833-44); LOULIÉ: Semmens (1984); RAMEAU: Verba (1978); RIEMANN: (1898); WALTHER: (1732); LITERATURE SUPPLEMENT: **Apfel (1981)**; Audbourg-Popin (1986); Auhagen (1982/1983); Becker (1836-39/1964); Burney (1776-89/. . ./1957); Cohen ["Symposium"] (1972); **Dahlhaus et al. (1987)**; **Dahlhaus and Sachs (1980)**; Donington (1963/. . ./1974); Eitner (1900-1904/1959-60); Forkel (1792/1962); Gerber (1812-14/1966); Gruber (1969); Horsley [*Fugue: History*] (1966); Houle (1960), (1987); Kauko (1958); O'Donnell (1979); **Palisca (1949-68)**, ["Theory"] **(1980)**; **Ritzel (1967/1968)**; Rogers (1955); Schmalzriedt ["Reprise"] (1972-); **Seidel and Cooper (1986)**; **Shirlaw (1917/. . ./1970)**; **Steblin (1981/1983)**; Tolkoff (1973); Wienpahl (1953).

CONRAD MATTHAEI

[1619 – 1667?]

Published at a time when modal composition was on the wane, Conrad Matthaei's *Kurtzer, doch ausführlicher Bericht von den Modis Musicis* (1652) offered German Baroque musicians an exceptionally comprehensive and, because the German language was utilized instead of Latin, easily accessible overview of that subject, derived from a wide assortment of authorities, including GLAREAN, PRAETORIUS, and LIPPIUS. It is possible that Matthaei was not the work's author. If his prefatory remarks are to be taken at face value, he merely made available a manuscript treatise by his teacher Heinrich GRIMM. The list of authors consulted includes, however, several theorists whose works had not yet appeared in print at the time of GRIMM's death in 1637.

The *Bericht* documents a lamentable deterioration in contemporary musicians' understanding of the modes, and notes various ill effects of this state of affairs upon the arts of composition and improvisation. The solution, of course, would be to absorb and utilize the materials that are provided so abundantly within the book. The basic concepts of ambitus, final, and arithmetic and harmonic divisions of the octave serve as a prelude to more complicated issues, such as progressive assertions on modal transposition to other scale degrees and a forced explanation of why the Ionian mode should be regarded as the first. Missing from the discussion are comments on the purported affective quality of each mode and a rigorous treatment of modal usage in polyphonic composition. Though LIPPIUS was among the authors consulted, his categorization of the modes according to the type of third above the final was not adopted.

Kurtzer, doch ausführlicher Bericht von den Modis Musicis, welchem aus den besten, aeltesten, berühmtesten und bewerthesten Autoribus der Music zusammen getragen . . . [Rism B/VI/2, p. 557.]

[Kaliningrad]: the author (Johann Reusner), 1652. [LCPS: M-064.]
Kaliningrad: Johann Reusner, 1658. [IDC.]

LITERATURE:

Forchert, Arno. "Matthaei, Conrad." In *MGG* (1949-68). Bibliog.

Forchert, Arno. "Ein Traktat über die Modi musici vom Jahre 1652." In *StäbleinFs* (1967):57-63. Bibliog. [*Rilm* 67-1561]

Wilkinson, Christopher. "Matthaei, Conrad." In *NGrove* (1980). Bibliog.

See also FÉTIS: (1833-44); LIPPIUS: Rivera (1974/1980); RIEMANN: (1898); WALTHER: (1732); LITERATURE SUPPLEMENT: Auhagen (1982/ 1983); Becker (1836-39/1964); Eitner (1900-1904/1959-60); Forkel (1792/1962); Gerber (1790-92/1977); Gissel (1980/1983); **Lester** (1974), ● ● ● (1977), (1978), (**1989**); Rivera (1978); Taddie (1984).

JOHANN MATTHESON

[1681 – 1764]

The practical and artistic aspects of musicmaking were a lifelong fascination for Johann Mattheson, whose attainments as an opera singer and composer in Hamburg preceded an even more distinguished career as an author on musical subjects. In sharp contrast to the quasi-scientific theories of RAMEAU and others, Mattheson wrote perceptively and profusely on matters relating to figured bass and improvisation, melody, the affective nature of music, and aesthetics, meanwhile involving himself in polemical arguments on matters such as keys versus modes, the consonant status of the perfect fourth, and the outdated practice of solmization. He inaugurated one of the first German music periodicals, *Critica musica* (1722-25), as a forum for his initiatives and later assembled a useful collection of biographies and autobiographies of German musicians, published as *Grundlage einer Ehren-Pforte* (1740).

The three *Orchestre* volumes, published between 1713 and 1721, established Mattheson as a champion of modernism and foe of the sort of speculative, mathematically oriented theory that would assert the consonance of the perfect fourth purely from its numerical characteristics, rather than from its compositional usage. Following HEINICHEN, Mattheson established a list of all twenty-four keys and wrote disparagingly of Guidonian solmization, which still held a footing in Germany. Johann Heinrich BUTTSTETT published two volumes countering the views that Mattheson presented in 1713 and 1717, and though Mattheson may be regarded as the victor in the argument, the challenge helped him to clarify his views and solidify his synthesis of the many ideas he absorbed from others, most notably from KIRCHER and DESCARTES.

Mattheson dedicated his *Beschützte Orchestre* to thirteen prominent musicians, asking them to respond to his views (and to help him silence BUTTSTETT). These testimonials appeared in the second volume of his *Critica musica* (1725). That of FUX is particularly informative, as it counters Mattheson's notions.

In keeping with his penchant for the practical, Mattheson compiled several works intended for keyboardists. His *Exemplarische Organisten-Probe* (1719) and its expanded version, *Grosse General-Bass-Schule* (1731), are devoted to improvisation. Two sets of twenty-four test pieces (the second more difficult than the first, and each containing a representative from every key) are presented, along with critical commentary and suggestions for attaining artistic results. The more basic aspects of figured-bass realization in the context of accompaniment are examined in his later *Kleine General-Bass-Schule* (1735), which also includes Mattheson's version of a musical circle for shifting keys. Reading clockwise (the only direction one should traverse the circle), a typical succession of keys reads: D minor, A minor, C major, G major, E minor, B minor, D major, A major. His formulation was dependent upon equal temperament, which he advocated.

The appearance of *Der vollkommene Capellmeister* in 1739, like that of RAMEAU's *Traité* and FUX's *Gradus* in the preceding decade, offered a powerful and distinctive perspective on how music might be conceived. Mattheson advocated a strong melodic character for compositions and insisted that emotional impact be an ever-present consideration. Basing his notions on DESCARTES's *Les passions de l'âme* (1649), Mattheson formulated means by which various emotional states could be replicated through music, including rhetorical devices (earlier described by BERNHARD and PRINTZ, among others), the choice of genre for a given work, and the selection of key and mode (in a formulation that Mattheson suggested might pertain to his own music but should not be regarded as universally valid). Discussing form when the topic was still rarely mentioned in treatises, Mattheson delineated six sections which might occur in a work, borrowing the terms Exordium, Narratio, Propositio, Confirmatio, Confutatio, and Peroratio from rhetorical theory. Expanding upon HEINICHEN's views, he clarified some of the more daring ways in which dissonances were being treated at the time, thereby contributing to an emerging analytical perspective for music. It is a work that today, as then, rewards careful study.

Das neu-eröffnete Orchestre; oder, Universelle und gründliche Anleitung, wie ein Galant Homme einen vollkommen Begriff von der Hoheit und Würde der edlen Music erlangen, seinen Gout darnach formiren, die Terminos technicos verstehen und geschicklich von dieser vortrefflichen Wissenschafft raisonniren möge [Rism B/VI/2, pp. 562-63.]

Hamburg: the author & Benjamin Schillers Wittwe, 1713. [LCPS: M-079a. HoM: 961.]
Hamburg: Benjamin Schillers Wittwe, 1713. [LCPS: M-079b.]

Das beschützte Orchestre; oder, desselben zweyte Eröffnung, worinn nicht nur einem würcklichen galant-homme, der eben kein Profeßions-Verwandter, sondern auch manchem Musico selbst die alleraufrichtigste und deutlichste Vorstellung musicalischer Wissenschafften, wie sich dieselbe vom Schulstaub tüchtig gesäubert, eigentlich und wahrhafftig verhalten, ertheilet . . . [Rism B/VI/2, p. 558.]

A response to BUTTSTETT: [ca. 1715].

Hamburg: im Schillerischen Buchladen, 1717. [LCPS: M-066. HoM: 948. SMLMS.]

S ● Facsimile edition. Zentralantiquariat der DDR.

Exemplarische Organisten-Probe im Artikel vom General-Bass . . . [Rism B/VI/2, p. 559.]

Hamburg: Schiller- und Kissnerischer Buch-Laden, 1719. [LCPS: M-069. HoM: 952. SMLMS.]

See also (1731), below.

T ● Schenkman, Walter. "Johann Mattheson's *Organisten-Probe: Erlaeuterungen*: A Translation, Part 1." *Bach* 12/4 (1981):10-16.

Das forschende Orchestre; oder, desselben dritte Eröffnung, darinn Sensus vindiciae et quartae blanditiae, D. i. der beschirmte Sinnen-Rang und der schmeichelnde Quarten-Klang, allen unpartheyischen Syntechnitis zum Nutzen und Nachdenken; Keinem Menschen aber zum Nachtheil, sana ratione et autoritate untersuchet, und vermuhtlich in ihr rechtes Licht gestellet werden [Rism B/VI/2, pp. 559-60.]

Hamburg: Benjamin Schillers Wittwe & Johann Christoph Kißner, 1721. [LCPS: M-070. HoM: 953. SMLMS.]

S ● Facsimile edition. Hildesheim: Georg Olms, 1976.

Critica musica . . . [Rism B/VI/2, p. 558.]

Hamburg: the author, 1722-23. Vol. 1. [LCPS: M-067a. HoM: 950. SMLMS. IDC.]
Hamburg: Thomas von Wierings Erben, 1725. Vol. 2. [LCPS: M-067b. HoM: 950. SMLMS. IDC.]

S ● Facsimile edition. Amsterdam: Frits A. M. Knuf, 1964.

Review in *Sos* 42/31-32 (1970):31-32 (Frans Brüggen).

T ● Lester, Joel. "The Fux-Mattheson Correspondence: An Annotated Translation." *CM* 24 (1977):37-62. [Rilm 77-430.]

Grosse General-Bass-Schule; oder, Der exemplarischen Organisten-Probe zweite, verbesserte und vermehrte Auflage . . . [Rism B/VI/2, p. 560.]

Hamburg: Johann Christoph Kißner, 1731. [LCPS: M-073. HoM: 954, 955. SMLMS.]

Derived from the work of 1719, above.

S ● Fortner, Wolfgang, ed. Mainz: Schott, 1956.

An abridged version. Review in *Mf* 11/1 (1958):110 (Lothar Hoffmann-Erbrecht).

T ● Reddick, Harvey Phillips. "Johann Mattheson's Forty-Eight Thorough-Bass Test-Pieces: Translation and Commentary." 2 vols. Ph.D. dissertation, The University of Michigan, 1956. [*DA* 17/01, p. 152. UMI 00-19715.]

S ● Facsimile edition. Hildesheim: Georg Olms, 1968.

Kleine General-Bass-Schule . . . [*Rism* B/VI/2, pp. 560-61.]

> Hamburg: Johann Christoph Kißner, 1735. [LCPS: M-074a. HoM: 958. SMLMS.]
>
>> Review in MIZLER: (1736-54):Vol. 1/4 (1738):45-54.

S ● [Heck, John Casper, ed.] *A Complete Treatise of Thorough Bass, Containing the True Rules with a Table of All the Figures and Their Proper Accompanyments, to Which is Added Several Examples of Each Figure.* [*Rism* B/VI/2, p. 561.] London: P. Hodgson, [ca. 1776]. [LCPS: M-074b.]

> Contains some thirty pages of music examples derived from Mattheson.

T ● Inada, Hiroko. "Tsuso-teion no rekishi-teki kenkyu: Mattheson no sho-tsuso-teion renshu-sho ni tsuite." M.A. thesis, Tokyo University of Arts, 1968. [*Rilm* 68-348.]

S ● Facsimile edition. Laaber: Laaber-Verlag, 1980.

Kern melodischer Wissenschaft, bestehend in den auser-lesensten Haupt- und Grund-Lehren der musicalischen Setz-Kunst oder Composition, als ein Vorläuffer des Vollkommenen Capellmeisters [*Rism* B/VI/2, p. 561.]

> Hamburg: Christian Herold, 1737. [LCPS: M-075. HoM: 957. SMLMS IDC.]
>
>> Absorbed within (1739), below. Review in MIZLER: (1736-54):Vol. 1/6 (1738):16-44.

S ● Facsimile edition. Hildesheim: Georg Olms, 1976.

Gültige Zeugnisse über die jüngste Matthesonische-musicalische Kern-Schrifft . . . [*Rism* B/VI/2, p. 560.]

> Hamburg: the author, 1738. [LCPS: M-072. HoM: 956.]

Der vollkommene Capellmeister; Das ist, Gründliche Anzeige aller derjenigen Sachen, die einer wissen, können, und vollkommen inne haben muß, der einer Capelle mit Ehren und Nutzen vorstehen will [*Rism* B/VI/2, p. 564.]

> Hamburg: Christian Herold, 1739. [LCPS: M-084. HoM: 967. SMLMS. IDC.]
>
>> Review in MIZLER: (1736-54):Vols. 1/6 (1738):76-85; 2/1 (1740):38-71; 2/2 (1740):204-

47; 2/3 (1742):72-119; 2/4 (1743):96-118; 3/1 (1746):46-61; 3/2 (1746):276-304; 3/3 (1747):477-539.

S ● Reimann, Margarete, ed. Facsimile edition. IGMDm, ser. 1, no. 5. Kassel: Bärenreiter, 1954; reprint editions, 1969; 1980.

> Reviews in *JAMS* 9/1 (1956):40-46 (A. Tillman Merritt), *Musica* 8/10 (1954):460-61 (Otto Riemer), and *OrganYb 1983* 14 (1983):124-25 (Peter Williams).

T ● Lenneberg, Hans. "Johann Mattheson on Affect and Rhetoric in Music." *JMT* 2/1-2 (1958):47-84, 193-236; reprinted in *PT* 6/5 (1963-64):10-16.

T ● ● ● Harriss, Ernest Charles. "Johann Mattheson's *Der vollkommene Capellmeister*: A Translation and Commentary." D.M.A. dissertation, George Peabody College for Teachers, 1969; published edition (SiM, no. 21), Ann Arbor, Mich.: UMI Research Press, 1981. Bibliog. [*Rilm* 76-9657. *DA* 30/11A, p. 5016.]

> Review in *AmO:AGO* 19/1 (1985):20.

T ● Winzenburger, Walter, trans. "Translation from *Der vollkommene Capellmeister* [by] Johann Mattheson, 1739." *Bach* 2/3-4 (1971):33-36; 38-41. [*Rilm* 71-3696.]

T ● See Rowen (1979).

S ● "Von der Leichtigkeit einer Melodie." *Musica* 36/6 (1982):499.

T ● See Lippman (1986).

T ● See **Katz and Dahlhaus (1987-)**: Vol. 3.

Grundlage einer Ehren-Pforte, woran der tüchtigsten Capellmeister, Componisten, Musikgelehrten, Tonkünstler &c. Leben, Wercke, Verdienste &c. erscheinen sollen [*Rism* B/VI/2, p. 560.]

> Hamburg: the author, 1740. [LCPS: M-071. SMLMS.]

S ● Schneider, Max, ed. Berlin: Kommissionsverlag von L. Liepmannssohn, 1910; facsimile edition, Kassel: Bärenreiter; Graz: Akademische Druck- und Verlagsanstalt, 1969.

> Reviews in *ArsOr* 22/44 (1974):1978 (Alfred Reichling), *GK* /5 (1970):175-76 (Hans Schmidt), *Mf* 24/4 (1971):356 (Werner Braun), *Muh* 21/4 (1970):192, *Musica* 24/3 (1970):287 (Fritz Bose), *Rmi* 5/4 (1971):713-15 (Gino Stefani), and *Zvuk* 106-7 (1970):312-13 (Josip Andreis).

Phthongologia systematica: Versuch einer systemtischen Klang-Lehre wider die irrigen Begriffe von diesem geistigen Wesen, von dessen Geschlechten, Ton-Arten, Dreyklängen, und auch vom mathematischen Musikanten, nebst einer Vor-Erinnerung wegen der behaupteten himlischen Musik [Rism B/VI/2, p. 557.]

Under the pseudonymn Aristoxeni iunior.

Hamburg: Johann Adolph Martini, 1748. [HoM: 964.]

Plus ultra, ein Stückwerk von neuer und mancherley Art [Rism B/VI/2, p. 564.]

Hamburg: Johann Adolph Martini, 1754-56. 4 vols. [HoM: 966. SMLMS.]

Review in MARPURG: (1754-78):Vol. 1/2 (1754):142-45.

See also NIEDT: (1700-1717):(1717) and (1721); WALTHER: (1702-47).

See Cannon (1939/. . ./1968), below, for a complete listing of Mattheson's publications on music.

LITERATURE:

Meinardus, Ludwig. "Johann Mattheson und seine Verdienste um die deutsche Tonkunst." In *SmV* 1 (1879):213-72.

Schmidt, Heinrich. *Johann Mattheson, ein Förderer der deutschen Tonkunst, im Lichte seiner Werke.* Leipzig: Breitkopf & Härtel, 1897; reprint edition, Walluf bei Wiesbaden: Martin Sändig, 1973.

Stege, Fritz. "Johann Mattheson und die Musikkritik des 18. Jahrhunderts." *ZfM* 106/4 (1939):407-11.

● ● ● Cannon, Beekman Cox. "Johann Mattheson, Spectator in Music." Ph.D. dissertation, Yale University, 1939; published edition (YSHM, no. 1), New Haven, Ct.: Yale University Press, 1947; reprint edition, [Hamden, Ct.]: Archon Books, 1968. Bibliog.

Reviews in *Md* 1 (1946):295-96 (J. M. Coopersmith), *Mf* 1 (1948):69-72 (F. Blume), *ML* 29/4 (1948):407-8 (J. A. Westrup), *MQ* 33/2 (1947):274-78 (Paul Henry Lang), *MR* 9/1 (1948):57-58, *Notes* 4/3 (1946-47):336-37 (Charles Warren Fox), *Rmi* 50/2 (1948):183-84 (Andrea della Corte), and *ThA* 31/11 (1947):81.

Turnow, Hans. "Mattheson, Johann." In *MGG* (1949-68). Bibliog.

Braun, Werner. "Johann Mattheson und die Aufklärung." Ph.D. dissertation, The University of Halle, 1951 (1952).

Becker, Heinz. "Johann Matthesons handschriftliche Einzeichnungen im *Musicalischen Lexicon* Johann Gottfried Walthers." *Mf* 5/4 (1952):346-50.

Heckmann, Harald. "*Critica musica*: Aus der Geschichte der Musikzeitschriften." *Musica* 10/1 (1956):41-47. Bibliog.

Feldmann, Fritz. "Mattheson und die Rhetorik." In *Bericht Hamburg 1956* (1957):99-103. Bibliog.

Wessely, Othmar. *Johann Joseph Fux und Johann Mattheson: Vortrag gehalten vor der Jahreshauptversammlung der Johann-Joseph-Fux-Gesellschaft am 10. Oktober 1963.* Graz: [Johann-Joseph-Fux-Gesellschaft], 1965.

Ariga, Noyuri. "Mattheson no chosei-byosha, Bach no Clavier-sakuhin tono kanren." *Djdgkn* 20 (1969):19-42. [Rilm 76-5290.]

Buelow, George J. "An Evaluation of Johann Mattheson's Opera, *Cleopatra* (Hamburg, 1704)." In *GeiringerFs* (1970):92-107. [Rilm 71-402.]

Kivy, Peter. "What Mattheson Said." *MR* 34/2 (1973):132-40; reprinted in Kivy (1980):Ch. 5. [Rilm 73/4475.]

Isoyama, Tadashi. ["Music and Erudition, with Particular Reference to the Works of J. Mattheson."] *Og* 20/3 (1974):129-43. [Rilm 76-9677.]

In Japanese.

Isoyama, Tadashi. "Mattheson ni okeru Gelehrsamkeit no shomondai." 2 vols. M.A. thesis, Tokyo University, 1974.

Apfel, Ernst. "Ein Menuett bei Johann Mattheson." *Mf* 29/3 (1976):295-99. [Rilm 76-5287.]

Siegmund-Schultze, Walther. "Zu Fragen der Aufführungspraxis der Musik des frühen 18. Jahrhunderts." In *Konferenzbericht Blankenburg/Harz 1976* (1977):Vol. 1, pp. 10-16. [Rilm 77-1502.]

Schenkman, Walter. "Portrait of Mattheson, the Editor, Together with His Correspondents." *Bach* 9/4 (1978):2-10; 10/1-2 (1979):3-12, 2-8.

Isoyama, Tadashi. "Johann Mattheson no ongaku jonenron." *SHA* 5 (1979):105-38. [Rilm 79-519.]

● ● ● Buelow, George J. "Mattheson, Johann." In *NGrove* (1980). Bibliog.

Bergmann, Walter. "Double Tercentenary." *RecMus* 7/1 (1981-83):2-3.

Gudel, Joachim. "Telemanninterpretation damals und heute." In *Zur Aufführungspraxis und Interpretation der Instrumentalmusik von Georg Philipp Telemann*, edited by Eitelfriedrich Thom, pp. 16-21. BSAII, no. 17. Blankenburg: 1981. [Rilm 82-5700.]

Schenkman, Walter. "Johann Mattheson." *Keyboard* 7/9 (1981):26-32, 66. [Rilm 81-4692.]

Schenkman, Walter. "Mattheson's 'Forty-Eight' and Their Commentaries." *MR* 42/1 (1981):9-21. [Rilm 81-2528.]

Schenkman, Walter. "Theory and Practice: Mattheson's Differing Key Arrangements." *Bach* 12/3-4 (1981):2-10, 3-9.

Walker, Geoffrey. "Mattheson the Practicus." *Consort* 37 (1981):389-93. [*Rilm* 81-2551.]

Comploi, Franz. "Musik und Rhetorik insbesondere bei Johann Sebastian Bach." M.A. thesis, Hochschule für Musik "Mozarteum," Salzburg, 1982. [*Rilm* 82-2304.]

Forchert, Arno. "Französische Autoren in den Schriften Johann Matthesons." In *BeckerFs* (1982):382-91. Bibliog. [*Rilm* 82-377.]

Forchert, Arno. "Mattheson und die Kirchenmusik." In *Kieler Tagung 1980* (1982):114-22. [*Rilm* 82-2323.]

Krummacher, C. "Articulation und rhetorische Deutlichkeit: Überlegungen zur Interpretation alter Orgelmusik anhand der Lehrschriften von Mattheson und Walther." *Km* 33/2 (1982):37-51.

Mann, Alfred. "Internationales Johann Mattheson Symposium in Wolfenbüttel (26. bis 28. September 1981)." *Mf* 35/3 (1982):283-84.

Marx, Hans Joachim. *Johann Mattheson (1681-1764): Lebensbeschreibung des Hamburger Musikers, Schriftstellers und Diplomaten, nach der "Grundlage einer Ehrenpforte" und den handschriftlichen Nachträgen des Verfassers*. Hamburg: Karl Dieter Wagner, 1982. Bibliog. [*Rilm* 82-398.]

> Reviews in *Mf* 38/2 (1985):141-42 (Franz Giegling), *ML* 65/2 (1984):197 (George J. Buelow), *Musica* 37/2 (1983):178 (Werner Braun), and *NZfM* 144/3 (1983):38 (Matthias Henke).

Zejfas, Natalija. "Iogann Mattezon." *Smuz* /2 (1982):91-98. [*Rilm* 82-436.]

● ● ● Buelow, George J., and Marx, Hans Joachim, ed. *New Mattheson Studies*. Cambridge and New York: Cambridge University Press, 1983. Bibliog.

> Contains twenty-three studies, including: "The Legacy of Johann Mattheson: A Retrospective Evaluation" (Beekman C. Cannon); "*Der vollkommene Capellmeister* as a Stimulus to J. S. Bach's Late Fugal Writing" (Gregory G. Butler); "Zur Handhabung der 'inventio' in der deutschen Musiklehre des frühen achtzehnten Jahrhunderts" (Wulf Arlt); "Johann Mattheson and the Invention of the *Affektenlehre*" (George J. Buelow); "The Genesis of Mattheson's Style Classification" (Claude V. Palisca); "*Verwechselung, Vorausnehmung,* and *Verzögerung*: Important Mattheson Contributions to Eighteenth-Century Music Theory" (David A. Sheldon); and "Johann Mattheson's Historical Significance: Conflicting Viewpoints" (Ernest Harriss). Reviews in *BJECS* 8/1 (1985):120-21 (Basil Smallman), *EM* 12/4 (1984):539-41 (Hans Lenneberg), *ML* 67/1 (1986):74-76 (Susan Wollenberg), *MQ* 71/1 (1985):98-101 (Georgia Cowart), *MT* 125/ 1700 (1984):576 (Geoffrey Webber), *Muh* 37/1 (1986):40 (F. W. D.), *Notes* 41/3 (1984-85):506-8 (Roger Lustig), *NZfM* 145/6 (1984):44-45 (Peter Cahn), and *Opera* 35/10 (1984):1092-93 (John Warrack).

Marx, Hans Joachim. "Johann Matthesons Nachlaß: Zum Schicksal der Musiksammlung der alten Stadtbibliothek Hamburg." *Am* 55/1 (1983):108-24.

Braun, Werner. "Mattheson und Händel: Bedingungen einer Konfrontation." *Concerto* 2/5 (1984-85):24-29. Bibliog.

Kivy, Peter. "Mattheson as Philosopher of Art." *MQ* 70/2 (1984):248-65.

Werts, Daniel. "The Musical Circle of Johannes Mattheson." *Theoria* 1 (1985):97-131.

Radice, Mark A. "Johann Mattheson and the *Stylus narrativus*." *Bach* 18/3 (1987):3-9.

Walker, Geoffrey J. "St. Evremond, François Raguenet and Johann Mattheson: A Critical Assessment of Their Views on Opera." Ph.D. dissertation, Cambridge University (King's), forthcoming.

N.B.: A most useful annotated bibliography of the Mattheson literature was compiled by Ernest Harriss and published in Buelow and Marx (1983), above.

See also BONONCINI: Holler (1955/1963); BUTTSTETT: [ca. 1717]; [1718]; FÉTIS: (1833-44); (1840); HEINICHEN: (1728):Buelow (1961/. . ./1986); HERBST: Allerup (1931); KEPLER: Dickreiter (1971/1973); KOCH: Dahlhaus (1978); LIPPIUS: Rivera (1974/1980); MARPURG: (1759-63); Serwer (1969); MIZLER: Richter (1967); Pinegar (1984); NIEDT: Espinosa (1981); RAMEAU: Pischner (1961/ . . ./1967); RIEMANN: (1898); SAINT-LAMBERT: (1707):Burchill (1979); SCACCHI: (1649): Palisca (1972); SCHEIBE: (1737-40):(1745); Willheim (1963); SORGE: (1767); VIADANA: Haack (1964/1974); VOSSIUS, I.: Serauky (1955); WALTHER: (1732); LITERATURE SUPPLEMENT: Abraham and Dahlhaus (1972); Ahlgrimm (1968), (1969-70), (1973); Albrecht (1981); Alette (1951); Allen ["Philosophies"] (1939); Apfel and Dahlhaus (1974); Arakawa (1973); Arlt (1974); **Arnold (1931/. . ./1965)**; Auhagen (1982/1983); Babbitt (1961/1972), (1987); Babitz (1952), (1967/1969); Babitz and Pont (1973); **Barbour (1947), (1951/. . ./ 1972)**, (1952); Baron (1968); Bartel (1982/1985); Beach (1967); Beck (1973), (1974); Becker (1836-39/1964); Beiche ["Dux"] (1972-), ["Inversio"] (1972-); **Benary (1956/1961)**, (1963); **Bent**, I. ["Analytical Thinking"] (1980), ["Analysis"] **(1980/ 1987)**, (1984); Beyer (1958); Beyschlag (1907/1953); Blankenburg ["Harmonie"] (1959); Blumröder (1972-); Boomgaarden (1985/1987); Braun (1970), (1986); Brown and McKinnon (1980); Broyles (1983); Bruck (1928); **Buelow (1973-74)**, (1979), ["Affections"] (1980), ["Rhetoric"] **(1980)**, (1987); Bukofzer (1947); Burney (1776-89/. . ./1957); Butler (1977), (1984); Cahn ["Repercussio"] (1972-), ["Retardatio"] (1972-), ["Transitus"] (1972-); Carse (1925/1964); Chafe (1982); Chevaillier (1925/1931-

32); Chybiński (1911-12); Cohen (1873-74); Cole (1969); Collins (1963), (1966); Constantini (1975); **Coover (1980)**; Cowart (1987); **Dahlhaus** ["Untersuchungen"] (1966/. . ./1988), (1967), (1981), **(1984)**, (1985), ["Zum Taktbegriff"] (1988); **Dahlhaus et al. (1987); Dahlhaus and Sachs (1980)**; Dammann (1958/1967); David and Mendel (1945/1966); Dean (1977); Dolmetsch (1915/. . ./1969); Donington (1963/. . ./1974), (1980); Dreyfus (1987); Duckles (1970); **Dürr and Gerstenberg (1980)**; Dunsby and Whittall (1988); Dupont (1933/. . ./1986); Eggebrecht (1955); Eitner (1900-1904/1959-60); Emig (1977); Federhofer (1964), (1969), (1970), (1985); Feil (1955); Feldmann (1958); Fellerer (1927/. . ./1972), ["Zum Bild"] (1973), (1983); Ferand (1937/1938); Fischer (1957); Flaherty (1989); Flindell (1983-84); Forchert (1986); Forkel (1792/1962); Frobenius ["Cantus"] (1972-), ["Isotonos"] (1972-), ["Monodie"] (1972-), ["Vollstimmig"] (1972-); Fuller (1977); Geering (1949-68); Gerber (1790-92/1977), (1812-14/1966); Ghislanzoni (1949-51); Gissel (1986); Godwin (1987); Göttert (1985-86); Grave (1985); Grusnick (1964-66); Gurlitt (1944/1966); Haase (1969); Handschin (1948); Harich-Schneider ([1939]/. . ./1970); Harrán (1986); Hartmann (1980); Hawkins (1776/. . ./1969); Heimann (1970/1973); Hein (1954); Helm (1960); Henderson (1969); Hiller (1768-69); Horsley (1963), [*Fugue: History*] (1966); Hosler (1978/1981); Houle (1960), (1987); Ibberson (1984); Jackson (1988); Jenne (1973-74); Jung (1969); **Kassler** (1971), **(1979)**; Kaufmann (1969); Katz (1926); Katz (1985); Kauko (1958); Keller (1931/. . ./1966), (1955/1965); Kelletat [*Temperatur*] (1960); Kirkendale (1979), (1984); Kivy (1980), (1984); Kleinman (1971/1974); Kob (1965); Komma (1972); Kramer (1975); Kretzschmar (1911-12); Krome (1896); Krones (1988); Kroyer (1901/. . ./1970); Krummacher (1979), (1986); Kümmerling (1977); Kunze (1979-83); Lang (1941), (1967-68); Lange (1899-1900); Lawrence (1978); Lester (1974), (1978), (1979-81); Leuchtmann (1957/1959); Lewis (1975/1978); **Lindley** ["Temperaments"] **(1980)**, (1982), (1985); Mahlert and Sunter (1972-); Maier (1984); Mallard (1978); **Mann**

(1955/. . ./1987), (1970/1971), (1987); McQuere (1983); Meier (1966), (1974/1988); Mendel (1948), (1955), (1978); Mitchell, W. J. (1963); Möller (1971); Moser (1936/. . ./1959); Moyer (1969); Müller-Blattau (1923/. . ./1963), (1949-68); Nelson (1984); **Neumann**, Frederick (1977/**1982**), (1978), (1979/**1982**), [*Essays*] **(1982)**, (1986), (1988); Neumann, Friedrich (1978); Neumann, F.-H. (1955/1962); Newman (1985); Newman (1946), (1959/. . ./1983), (1963/. . ./1983); Norton (1984); Oberdoerffer (1949-68), (1967); Ottenberg (1973/1978); **Palisca** (1949-68), [*Baroque*] (1968/1981), ["Rezitativ"] (1972-), ["Theory"] **(1980)**; Pfeiffer (1978); Pole (1879/. . ./1924); Powers ["Language"] (1980), ["Mode"] (1980); Preußner (1924), (1939); Ramírez (1967); Rasch (1981); Ratner (1956), (1970), (1980); Reckow (1972-); Reese (1957/1970); Reimer ["Concerto"] (1972-), ["Kammermusik"] (1972-), ["Kenner"] (1972-); **Ritzel (1967/1968)**; Rogers (1955); Rohwer (1949-68); Rosenblum (1988); Rothgeb (1968); Sachs (1972-); Schäfke (1934); Schenkman (1976); Scher (1975); Schering (1926); Schering and Wustmann (1941); Schmalzriedt ["Coda"] (1972-), ["Durchführen"] (1972-), ["Episode"] (1972-), ["Subiectum"] (1972-); Schmidt (1979/1981); Schmitz (1950); Schoffman ["Descriptive"] (1983); Schünemann (1928/1931); Schulenberg (1982), (1984); Schwartz (1908); Seaton (1981); Seidel (1972-), (1975), (1976), (1979); **Seidel and Cooper (1986)**; Serauky (1929); Serwer (1974); Sheldon (1975), (1981), (1982); Shellhous (1988); **Shirlaw (1917/. . ./1970)**; Sisman (1978); Sondheimer (1925); Spender and Shuter-Dyson (1980); Sponheuer (1986); Steblin (1981/1983), (1987); Stege (1927-28); Struthers (1902); Subirá (1947/. . ./1958); Sydow-Saak (1972-); Thieme (1982-83); Tittel (1966); Todd (1983); Troeger (1987); Uemura (1969); Ulrich (1931/1932); Unger (1941/1969); Vogel (1955/1954); Waite (1970); Walker (1987); **Wason (1981/1985)**; Werts (1983); Wessely (1967), (1971-72); Wessel (1955); Wichmann (1966); Williams, P. (1970), (1979); Wirth (1966); Wolff (1972-); **Zaminer (1985)**; Zenck (1942); Ziebler (1933); Zimmermann (1976).

GIROLAMO MEI

[1519 – 1594]

The first scholar to evaluate and interpret the extant writings of the Greeks on music in a systematic way was Girolamo Mei. A skilled philologist with access to and interest in sources unavailable to GLAREAN or ZARLINO, Mei came to conclusions which diverged from the cloudy conception which prevailed in his day. In particular, he determined that the Greek *tonoi* and the ecclesiastical modes bore little similarity in conception or result, and he established that monody—and not polyphony—typified Greek music. Both the characteristics of the *tonoi* and the intimate relationship between text and music were constituents of what gave Greek music its affective potential, he felt, while

198

their absence from sixteenth-century music produced a poverty of emotional impact.

Not inclined towards an aggressive promulgation of his findings, Mei allowed his major work, "De modis musicis antiquorum" (1567-73), to remain unpublished. It contains the first careful comparison of the views of Aristoxenus, Ptolemy, and others, while the errors of Boethius and GLAREAN are exposed. The *tonoi* are represented as transpositions of the Greek tonal system—a presentation which, though not entirely in accordance with the modern interpretation, nevertheless countered the confusion which existed concerning the relationship between Greek theory and Renaissance modal practice. Finally, the ethical aspects of Greek music are discussed, and the important role of music in Greek theater is clarified. Though the work remained in manuscript, part of it was circulated among friends, and Mei's ideas were later assimilated by DONI and incorporated in his published work.

Though Mei spent much of his adult life in Rome, connections with friends in his native Florence led to a correspondence with Vincenzo GALILEI (a pupil of ZARLINO and a principal figure in Bardi's Camerata), who in the early 1570s knew enough to realize that there were problems in his teacher's treatment of Greek theory but not enough to resolve them, especially considering the corrupt, poorly translated, and incomplete state of his textual sources. The interaction between these men amounted to over thirty letters (plus at least two visits), through which Mei led GALILEI away from ZARLINO's defective conception of Greek theory. GALILEI's *Dialogo della musica antica, et della moderna* (1581) both attacks ZARLINO and serves as a vessel for Mei's views in a dispute which was not put to rest even with the death of its protagonists during the early 1590s. ZARLINO's advocacy of Ptolemy's diatonic *syntonon* tuning, which coordinated so well with his *senario* numerology, was denigrated in favor of the Pythagorean diatonic *ditoniaion*, while the practice of polyphony was sharply condemned as being antagonistic to the relationship between music and poetry.

A manuscript treatise which begins "Come potesse tanto la musica" includes a summary of Greek theory and of compositional and performance practices and provides information concerning rhythmics. "Do nomi delle cordi del monochordo" espouses a new system of solmization and considers notation up to the time of Guido in the context of Mei's views regarding ancient and modern music. The *Discorso sopra la musica antica e moderna*, published posthumously in 1602, derives from a letter to GALILEI (not from "De modis musicis antiquorum," as several sources indicate) and treats the differences in emotional effect between Greek and modern music and the reasons for this discrepancy.

Through Mei the ancient pronouncements in works such as Aristotle's *Poetics* and Ptolemy's *Harmonics* are linked to the progressive thinkers of the late sixteenth century, leading ultimately to revolutionary conceptions for the art of song and to the birth of opera.

Letters to Vincenzo Borghini and Piero Vettori

    Mss.

    S • [*Raccolta di*] *Prose fiorentine* [*raccolte dallo Smarrito . . .*], Vol. 15 [= Part 4, vol. 2]. Florence: Stamperia Granducale per li Tartini, e Franchi, 1734; another edition, Venice: dalla Stamperia Remondini, 1751-54.

"De modis musicis antiquorum libri IV"

    Mss., 1567-73. [Rome: Biblioteca Apostolica Vaticana; Paris: Bibliothèque nationale; Bologna: Civico museo bibliografico musicale; Florence: Biblioteca Riccardiana e Moreniana.]

Letters to Vincenzo Galilei and Giovanni Bardi

    Mss., 1572-81. [Rome: Biblioteca Apostolica Vaticana.]

        Copies of six letters, out of at least thirty which were written, are extant.

    S • • • • Palisca, Claude V. *Girolamo Mei (1519-1594): Letters on Ancient and Modern Music to Vincenzo Galilei and Giovanni Bardi: A Study with Annotated Texts.* MSD, no. 3. Rome: American Institute of Musicology, 1960; reprint edition (with corrections), 1977. Bibliog.

    T • See Lippman (1986).

    T • See Palisca [*Florentine*] (1989).

"De nomi delle corde del monochordo"

    Ms. [Milan: Biblioteca Ambrosiana; Rochester, N.Y.: Sibley Music Library.]

"Trattato di musica: Come potesse tanto la musica appresso gli antichi . . ."

    Incomplete.

    Ms., [ca. 1570s-early 80s]. [Paris: Bibliothèque nationale; Rome: Biblioteca Apostolica Vaticana.]

Discorso sopra la musica antica e moderna [*Rism B/VI/2, p. 568.*]

        Derived from a portion of Mei's letter to Vincenzo GALILEI dated May 8, 1572.

    Venice: Gio. Battista Ciotti, 1602. Edited by Piero del Nero. [LCPS: M-093.]

S • Facsimile edition. Ctma. Milan: Bollettino bibliografico musicale, 1933.

S • Massera, G., ed. Facsimile edition. BmB, ser. 2, no. 35. Bologna: Forni, 1968.

LITERATURE:

Palisca, Claude V. "Mei, Girolamo." Translated by Ellen Hickmann. In *MGG* (1949-68). Bibliog.

Palisca, Claude V. "Girolamo Mei: Mentor to the Florentine Camerata." *MQ* 40/1 (1954):1-20. Bibliog.

Giorgi, Cecilia. "La figura di Gerolamo Mei nella Camerata fiorentina." Thesis, The University of Milan, 1972-73.

• • • Palisca, Claude V. "Mei, Girolamo." In *NGrove* (1980). Bibliog.

See also DONI: (1763); FÉTIS: (1833-44); GALILEI: (1581); MARTINI: (1757-81); MERSENNE: (1617-48); WALTHER: (1732); LITERATURE SUPPLEMENT: Becker (1836-39/1964); **Berger (1975/1980)**; Burney (1776-89/. . ./1957); Cazden (1980); Cohen (1984); Cowart ["Inventing"] (1989); **Dahlhaus et al. (1987)**; Dostrovsky (1969); Eitner (1900-1904/1959-60); Fellerer ["Wesen"] (1982), (1983); Forkel (1792/1962); Gerber (1812-14/1966); Hanning (1969/1980); Harrán (1986); Hüschen (1986); Jones (1981); Katz (1985); Koenigsberger (1979); La Fage (1864/1964); Le Coat (1978); **Maniates (1979)**; Martin (1932-33); Meier (1963); **Palisca** (1953), ["Alterati"] (1968), [*Baroque*] (1968/1981), ["Camerata"] (1972), (1979), ["Camerata"] (1980), ["Theory"] **(1980)**, **(1985)**, [*Florentine*] (1989); Pöhlmann (1969); Tuksar (1978/1980); **Walker** (1941-42/. . ./1985), **(1978)**.

MARIN MERSENNE

[1588 – 1648]

Marin Mersenne, a French Jesuit who displayed a remarkable range of learning and devotion to scholarship, absorbed and wrote on many aspects of contemporary musical knowledge. He favored scientific pursuits but also contemplated topics such as the differences between the French and Italian music of his day. His experiments on the vibrations of strings of variable length, diameter, mass, and tension established fundamental acoustical laws, while he also explored partials and tuning systems. His mention of a harmonic series antedates SAUVEUR's more definitive statements. The major second, augmented fourth, and major seventh were named as the three principal dissonances, while the octave, fifth, and major third held the status as most consonant. The priority of the bass and soprano lines, one of Mersenne's assertions, is a notion in keeping with his preference for the newer monophonic style.

A prolific writer, Mersenne neither composed nor performed music. Much of his data was attained through a massive correspondence with some of the most prominent musicians, philosophers, and scientists of his time. His descriptions of instruments have proved useful to modern scholars. The observation of natural phenomena, from which general principles were derived, was stressed. It was expected that the student of music must be immersed in all other sciences and the liberal arts, an expectation fulfilled by Mersenne's career.

Mersenne's most comprehensive examination of musical issues is found in his celebrated *Harmonie universelle, contenant la théorie et la pratique de la musique* (1636-37),

which covers topics of acoustics, singing, fundamentals of theory (consonance and dissonance, the three genera, the modes, and various aspects of composition, including counterpoint and rhythm), and musical instruments. The work is carefully organized and displays Mersenne's wide-ranging curiosity. It remained the most respected of French musical treatises for generations.

An advocate of standards for pitch and tempo, Mersenne suggested that each note of the scale be tuned slightly at odds with the true mathematical proportion. He conducted experiments with open and closed pipes, and was a founder of the French Academy of Science. Many of his most advanced ideas exist in his correspondence rather than in his treatises. He recommended study of cadence formulas expressed by ZARLINO and CERONE. Although he has been criticized for trying to be an expert on too many subjects, he is remembered as a conscientious and erudite thinker whose influence spanned several generations.

Correspondence

Mss., 1617-48.

S • de Waard, Cornélis, with Armand Beaulieu, René Pintard, or Bernard Rochot, eds. *Correspondance du P. Marin Mersenne, religieux minime*. Paris: Beauchesne, Éditions du Centre national de la recherche scientifique, 1932 [i.e., 1933]- .

The editors and publishers of this complete edition have varied over the years. Volume 16, published in 1985, completes the correspondence. An index for the first ten volumes was published in 1972. Another index (as well as a list of errata) is due as Vol. 17. Reviews in *Isis* 27/2 (1937):334-36 (Jean Pelseneer), *Isis* 39/3 (1948):179-81 (George Sarton), *Isis* 78/292 (1987):303-4 (William R. Shea), *Rdm* 24/1 (1945):33 (J.-G. P.), and *Rhsa* 39 (1986):92-93.

S ● See DONI: Correspondence.

Quaestiones celeberrimae in Genesim . . . [*Rism* B/VI/2, pp. 573-74.]

Paris: Sébastien Cramoisy, 1623. [LCPS: M-107. HoM: 991.]

La vérité des sciences . . . [*Rism* B/VI/2, p. 575.]

Paris: Toussaint Du Bray, 1625.

S ● Facsimile edition. Stuttgart/Bad Cannstatt: Frommann (Holzboog), 1969.

"Livre de la nature des sons"

Ms. [Paris: Bibliothèque de l'Arsenal.]

Traité de l'harmonie universelle, où est contenu la musique théorique et pratique des anciens et modernes, avec les causes de ses effets . . . [*Rism* B/VI/2, p. 574.]

Paris: Guillaume Baudry, 1627. [LCPS: M-108.]

T ● Egan, John Bernard. "Marin Mersenne: *Traité de l'harmonie universelle*: Critical Translation of the Second Book." Ph.D. dissertation, Indiana University, 1962. [*DA* 23/06, pp. 2164-65. UMI 62-05029.]

Les préludes de l'harmonie universelle, ou questions curieuses . . . [*Rism* B/VI/2, p. 573.]

Paris: Henry Guenon, 1634. [LCPS: M-106. HoM: 990. SMLMS.]

Les questions théologiques, physiques, morales, et mathématiques . . . [*Rism* B/VI/2, p. 574.]

Paris: Henry Guenon, 1634.

Questions harmoniques, dans lesquelles sont contenuës plusieurs choses remarquables pour la physique, pour la morale, et pour les autres sciences [*Rism* B/VI/2, p. 574.]

Paris: Jaques Villery, 1634. [HoM: 992.]

S ● Facsimile edition. Stuttgart/Bad Cannstatt: Friedrich Frommann Verlag (Günther Holzboog), 1972.

Questions inouyes ou récréation des savans . . . [*Rism* B/VI/2, p. 574.]

Paris: Jaques Villery, 1634.

S ● Facsimile edition. Cœplf. Paris: Fayard, 1985.

Harmonicorum libri in quibus agitur de sonorum natura, causis, et effectibus . . . [*Rism* B/VI/2, p. 572.]

Paris: Guillaume Baudry, , 1635-36. [LCPS: M-104a.]

Together with the *Harmonicorum instrumentorum libri IV* (1636), below, as *Harmonicorum libri XII* [*Rism* B/VI/2, pp. 572-73.]:

Paris: Guillaume Baudry, 1648. [LCPS: M-104b. HoM: 988.]
Paris: Thomas Jolly, 1652.

S ● Facsimile of the 1648 edition. Geneva: Minkoff Reprint, 1973.

Review in *ISOI* 10 (1973):755 (Martin A. Vente).

ST ● Cook, Frederick, trans. "The 'Batteries' on the Spanish Baroque Guitar According to Marin Mersenne." *GLM* 19 (1981):35-37.

Harmonicorum instrumentorum libri IV

Paris: Guillaume Baudry, 1636.

S ● See *Harmonicorum libri* (1635-36):(1973), above.

Harmonie universelle, contenant la théorie et la pratique de la musique . . . [*Rism* B/VI/2, p. 573.]

Paris: Sébastien Cramoisy, 1636-37. [LCPS: M-105. HoM: 989. SMLMS. IDC.]

T ● Chapman, Roger E. "The Books on Instruments in the *Harmonie universelle* of Marin Mersenne." Ph.D. dissertation, The University of California at Los Angeles, 1954; published edition (as *Harmonie universelle: The Book on Instruments*), The Hague: Martinus Nijhoff, 1957.

Reviews in *Mf* 13/1 (1960):97-100 (Margarete Reimann) and *MQ* 44/4 (1958):534-40 (Emanuel Winternitz).

S ● Lesure, François, ed. Facsimile edition. 3 vols. Paris: Centre national de la recherche scientifique, 1963; 1986.

The copy chosen for this facsimile contains autograph annotations by Mersenne. Reviews in *ML* 45/3 (1964):282-83 (J. A. Westrup), *Notes* 21/1-2 (1963-64):126-27 (Hans Lenneberg), *Rdm* 50/128 (1964):131 (André Verchaly), and *Stfm* 47 (1965):118-20 (Ingmar Bengtsson).

T ● Williams, Robert Fortson. "Marin Mersenne: An Edited Translation of the Fourth Treatise of the *Harmonie universelle*." 3 vols. Ph.D. dissertation, The University of Rochester, 1972. [*Rilm* 76-9882. *DA* 33/07A, pp. 3705-6. UMI 73-00983.]

T ● Leroy, Edmund Walter. "Book One of the 'Traitez de la voix, et des chants' from Marin Mersenne's *Harmonie universelle*: A Translation." D.M.A. dissertation, The Julliard School, 1978.

T ● See MacClintock (1979).

ST ● See (1635-36):(1648):Cook (1981), above.

T ● Köhler, Wolfgang. "Marin Mersenne, *Livre cinquiesme des instruments à vents*: Kritische Edition und Kommentar." Ph.D. dissertation, The University of Bochum, 1983.

T ● See Lippman (1986).

T ● See **Katz and Dahlhaus (1987-)**:Vol. 2.

T ● Russell, William F., trans. "Translation of Livre premier: *De la voix* and Livre second: *Des chants*." Available from the American Musicological Society/Music Library Association Translations Center, Brooklyn College Music Department.

Cogita physico-mathematica . . . [*Rism* B/VI/2, p. 572.]

Paris: Antoine Bertier, 1644. [LCPS: M-103.]

Novarum observationum physico-mathematicarum [*Rism* B/VI/2, p. 573.]

Paris: Antoine Berthier, 1647.

LITERATURE:

FÉTIS, François-Joseph. "Du P. Mersenne, de ses écrits sur la musique, et particulièrement de l'*Harmonie universelle*." *Rm*(F) 7/13/11-13 (1833):81-83, 89-91, 98-100.

Eitner, Robert. "Die Druckwerke P. Marin Mersenne über Musik." *MMg* 23/4 (1891):60-68. Bibliog.

Ludwig, Hellmut. "Marin Mersenne und seine Musiklehre." Ph.D. dissertation, The University of Halle, 1933 (1934); published edition (BzMf, no. 4), Halle (Saale) and Berlin: Buchdruckerei des Waisenhauses G.m.b.H., 1934; 1935; reprint edition, Hildesheim: Georg Olms, 1971. Bibliog.

Lenoble, Robert. *Mersenne, ou la naissance de mécanisme*. Bhp. Paris: J. Vrin, 1943. Bibliog.

> Contains an extraordinary "Notice bibliographique," pp. XI-LVII.

Dräger, Hans-Heinz. "Mersenne, Marin." In *MGG* (1949-68). Bibliog.

Hyde, Frederick Bill. "The Position of Marin Mersenne in the History of Music." Ph.D. dissertation, Yale University, 1954. [*DA* 28/12A, p. 5093. UMI 68-07557.]

Cohen, Albert. "Jean Le Maire and 'La musique almerique'." *Am* 35/4 (1963):175-81.

Vaught, Raymond. "Mersenne's Unknown English Viol Player." *GSJ* 17 (1964):17-23.

Anthony, James M. "The Organ As Described by Marin Mersenne." M.A. thesis, The University of Michigan, 1967.

Whitmore, P. J. S. *The Order of Minims in Seventeenth-Century France*. IAHI, no. 20. The Hague: Martinus Nijhoff, 1967. Bibliog.

> Reviews in *CathHR* 56/3 (1970-71):564 (Louis J. Lekai), *ChH* 38/4 (1969):536-37 (Robert K. Kingdon), *EHR* 84/330 (1969):186 (W. R. Fryer), *Eras* 21/5-6 (1969):184-86 (Alfred Cohausz), and *Historian* 30/4 (1967-68):653-54 (Edward J. Kealey).

Gruber, Albion. "Mersenne and Evolving Tonal Theory." *JMT* 14/1 (1970):36-67. [*Rilm* 70-3145.]

Mace, Dean T. "Marin Mersenne on Language and Music." *JMT* 14/1 (1970):2-34. [*Rilm* 70-3165.]

Hilton, Wendy. "A Dance for Kings: The 17th-Century French *Courante*—Its Character, Step-Patterns, Metric and Proportional Foundations." *EM* 5/2 (1977):160-72.

● ● ● Cohen, Albert. "Mersenne, Marin." In *NGrove* (1980). Bibliog.

Lindley, Mark. "Mersenne on Keyboard Tuning." *JMT* 24/2 (1980):167-203. [*Rilm* 80-5495.]

Duncan, David Allen. "The Tyranny of Opinions Undermined: Science, Pseudo-Science and the Scepticism in the Musical Thought of Marin Mersenne." Ph.D. dissertation, Vanderbilt University, 1981. Bibliog. [*DA* 42/04A, p. 1746. UMI 81-20196.]

Feingold, Mordechai, and Gouk, Penelope. "An Early Critique of Bacon's *Sylva sylvarum*: Edmund Chilmead's Treatise on Sound." *AS* 40/2 (1983):139-57. [*Rilm* 83-469.]

Dear, Peter Robert. "Mersenne and the Learning of the Schools: Continuity and Transformation in the Scientific Revolution." Ph.D. dissertation, Princeton University, 1984; Ithaca, N.Y.: Cornell University Press, 1988. [*DA* 45/05A, p. 1504.]

Greenfield, Jack. "Meantone Temperament Variations: Marin Mersenne." *PTJ* 27/2 (1984):20-22.

Shiloah, Amnon, and Berthier, Annie. "A propos d'un 'Petit livre arabe de musique' (Oxford, Bodleian Library, Manuscrits Turcs XLII: Paris, Bibliothèque nationale, Arabe 2480)." *Rdm* 71/1-2 (1985):164-77.

De Luccia, Paolo. "I riferimenti alla modalità nell' *Harmonie universelle* di Marin Mersenne." Thesis, The University of Pavia (Cremona), 1986-87.

Koehler, W. "Die Blasinstrumente aus der *Harmonie universelle* des Marin Mersenne und ihre Bedeutung für die Aufführungspraxis heute." *Tibia* 13/1 (1988):1-14.

Duncan, David Allen. "Persuading the Affections: Rhetorical Theory and Mersenne's Advice to Harmonic Orators." In Cowart [*French*] (1989):149-75. Bibliog.

Duncan, David Allen. *The Science of Harmony: Music and Cultural Reunion in the Career of Marin Mersenne.* Forthcoming.

See also BAN: Walker (1976/1978); DENIS: (1643):Panetta (1987); DESCARTES: (1619-50):Roth (1926); (1619-50):Adam and Gérard (1936-63); Pirro (1907/1973); FÉTIS: (1833-44); FLUDD: Craven (1902/n.d.); Debus (1965/1966); Ammann (1967); Yates (1972); HOLDER: (1694); KEPLER: Dickreiter (1971/1973); KIRCHER: (1650); Tornifore (1987); MOMIGNY: (1791-1818):(1818); ÖTTINGEN: (1866); OUSELEY: (1882); OUVRARD: (1658):Boulay (1984); PRAETORIUS: (1614-20):Fleming (1979); Hayes (1927); RIEMANN: (1891); (1898); SAUVEUR: (1704):Maxham (1976); Scherchen (1946/. . ./1972); WALTHER: (1732); LITERATURE SUPPLEMENT: Abbado (1964); Abraham (1968/1969); Ahlgrimm (1969-70); Alette (1951); Allen ["Baroque"] (1939), ["Philosophies"] (1939); Archibald (1924); Atcherson (1973); Auhagen (1982/1983); Babbitt (1961/1972); Barbieri (1983); **Barbour** (1932), (1938), (1947), (1948), (1949-68), **(1951/. . ./1972)**; (1952); Becker (1836-39/1964); Beiche ["Dux"] (1972-), ["Inversio"] (1972-); Bell et al. (1980); Bent, M. (1984); Beyschlag (1907/1953); Boomgaarden (1985/1987); Borrel (1928); Brown (1976); **Buelow** (1972), ["Affections"] (1980), ["Rhetoric"] **(1980)**; Bukofzer (1947); Burney (1776-89/. . ./1957); Butler (1977); Cahn ["Transitus"] (1972-); Cazden (1948), (1980); Chevaillier (1925/1931-32); Cohen (1966/1978), (1971), ["Symposium"] (1972), (1977), (1981); Cohen (1984); Collins (1973); **Coover (1980)**; Crombie (1969); Dahlhaus ["Zur Entstehung"] (1961); **Dahlhaus et al. (1987)**; David and Mendel (1945/1966); Diderot (1748/. . ./1875-77); Dill (1989); Dolmetsch (1915/. . ./1969); Donà (1967); Donington (1963/. . ./1974), (1977), (1980); Dostrovsky (1969), (1974-75); Drake (1970); Duchez (1979); **Dürr and Gerstenberg** (1949-68), **(1980)**; Dupont (1933/. . ./1986); Eggebrecht (1955); Eitner (1900-1904/1959-60); Federhofer (1985); Fellerer

["Zur Kontrapunktlehre"] (1972), ["Zur Kontrapunktlehre"] (1973), (1983); Ferand (1937/1938), [*Improvisation*] (1956/1961); Flindell (1983-84); Forkel (1792/1962); Frobenius ["Isotonos"] (1972-); Fubini (1971/1983); Gable (1979); Gerber (1790-92/1977), (1812-14/1966); Godwin (1987); Goldschmidt (1907); Gouk (1980), (1981-82), (1982); Green (1969); Gremion (1974); Gruber (1969); Hall (1975); Hannas (1934); Harding (1938); Harich-Schneider ([1939]/. . ./1970); Harrán (1986); Hawkins (1776/. . ./1969); Heckmann (1953); Hein (1954); Horsley [*Fugue: History*] (1966); Hoshino (1979); Houle (1960), (1987); **Hunt (1978)**; Hutchinson and Knopoff (1979-81); Jackson (1988); Jander (1980); Jonckbloet and Land (1882); Jones (1934); **Kassler (1979)**, (1982); Kayser (1950); Keislar (1987); Keller (1955/1965); Kirkendale (1979); Koenigsberger (1979); Kramer (1978); Kuhn (1902); La Borde (1780/1978); La Fage (1864/1964); Lang (1967-68); Lange (1899-1900); Launay (1972), (1982); Le Coat (1978); Levi (1962-63/1964); Lewis (1980); Lewis (1975/1978); **Lindley** ["Just"] **(1980)**, ["Temperaments"] **(1980)**, (1982), **(1984)**; Lloyd (1940-41); Lottermoser (1949-68); Mace (1964/1966); Mach (1892); **Mann (1955/. . ./1987)**; Meer (1980); Mendel (1955), (1978); Miller and Cohen (1987); Neumann, Frederick (1978); Newman (1959/. . ./1983); Norton (1984); **Palisca** (1961), [*Baroque*] (1968/1981), ["Rezitativ"] (1972-), ["Theory"] **(1980)**, **(1985)**; Palisca and Spender (1980); Pikler (1966); Pole (1879/. . ./1924); Ratner (1970), (1980); Reckow (1972-); Reese (1957/1970); Ritzel (1967/1968); Rogers (1955); Rowen (1979); Schäfke (1934); Schavernoch (1981); **Schneider (1972)**; Schwartz (1908); Seidel (1972-); **Seidel and Cooper (1986)**; Sheppard (1978-79); **Shirlaw (1917/. . ./1970)**; Sirch (1981); Smith (1974); Stoll (1978/1981); Subirá (1947/. . ./1958); Taddie (1984); Taylor (1980); Truesdell (1960); Tuksar (1978/1980); Unger (1941/1969); Vogel (1955/1954), (1975/1984); **Walker** (1941-42/. . ./1985), (1950/1985), (1976), **(1978)**; Warrack (1945); Weber (1976); Wichmann (1966); Wienpahl (1953); Wightman (1972); Winternitz (1970); Wolff (1972-); Yates (1947); **Zaminer (1985)**; Zimmermann (1976).

LORENZ CHRISTOPH MIZLER VON KOLOF

[1711–1778]

Drawing from the legacy of Pythagoras and the mediaeval quadrivium, as well as from the work of LEIBNIZ and EULER, Lorenz Christoph Mizler von Kolof developed a mathematical perspective on music and found effective means for its promulgation. Beginning with his master's thesis, *Dissertatio, quod musica ars sit pars eruditionis philosophicae* (1734), Mizler promoted the notion that music should be classified as a mathematical component of philosophy. Through his periodical *Neue eröffnete musikalische Bibliothek*, which was issued between 1736 and 1754, he persistently projected his scientific viewpoint through extensive summaries and commentaries on a wide range of music books, including treatises by MATTHESON, PRINTZ, and SCHEIBE, among others. Contributions for the *Bibliothek* were generated in part through Mizler's founding and directorship of what was called the Korrespondierenden Sozietät der Musicalischen Wissenschaften, which was devoted to the mathematical perspective. In addition to motivating numerous papers on musical topics, it provoked one of its select members, J. S. Bach, to compose his Canonic Variations (and, in accordance with the rules of the Society, induced him to sit for what is now probably his most famous portrait).

Among Mizler's more traditional undertakings is a treatise on thoroughbass, *Anfangs-Gründe des General-Baßes* (1739), which was sold with an elaborate, color-coded machine made of brass to aid the learning process, and a translation of FUX's *Gradus ad Parnassum* (1742).

Dissertatio, quod musica ars sit pars eruditionis philosophicae [*Rism* B/VI/2, p. 628.]

> Leipzig: Joh. G. Schniebes, [1734].

> > As *Dissertatio quod musica scientia sit et pars eruditionis philosophicae*:

> Liepzig and Wittenberg: Officina Hakiana, 1736. [LCPS: O-008.]

> S • In *Gründliche Auszüge aus denen neuesten theologisch-philosophisch- und philologischen Disputationibus* . . . Leipzig: Friedrich Matthias Friese, 1738.

Lusus ingenii de praesenti bello . . . [*Rism* B/VI/2, p. 589.]

> Wittenberg: Literis Schlomachianis, 1735. [HoM: 997.]

> T • As "Einfall auf den gegenwärtigen Krieg . . ." In (1736-54):Vol. 1/3 (1737):65-70, below.

Neu eröffnete musikalische Bibliothek; oder, Gründliche Nachricht nebst unpartheyischem Urtheil von

musikalischen Schriften und Büchern [*Rism* B/VI/2, p. 589.]

> Leipzig: im Verlag des Verfassers and bey Brauns Erben in Commission, 1736-54. [LCPS: M-141. SMLMS. IDC.]

> > Review in *HBgS* 42 (June 14, 1737) (Johann Adolph SCHEIBE).

> S • Facsimile edition. 3 vols. Hilversum: Frits Knuf, 1966.

Anfangs-Gründe des General-Baßes, nach mathematischer Lehr-Art abgehandelt, und vermittelst einer hierzu erfundenen Maschine auf das deutlichste vortragen [*Rism* B/VI/2, pp. 588-59.]

> Leipzig: the author, [1739]. [LCPS: M-139. SMLMS.]

> > Review in (1736-54): 2/1 (1740):97-131, above.

> S • Facsimile edition. Hildesheim: Georg Olms, 1972.

Musikalischer Staarstecher, in welchem rechtschaffener Musikverständigen Fehler bescheiden angemerket, eingebildeter und selbst gewachsener so genannten Componisten Thorheiten aber lächerlich gemachet werden . . . [*Rism* B/VI/2, p. 589.]

> Leipzig: the author (Graff), 1739-40. [LCPS: M-140. SMLMS.]

Preface to *Gespräch von der Musik, zwischen einem Organisten und Adjuvanten* . . . [*Rism* B/VI/2, pp. 870-71.], by Johann Carl Voigt.

> Erfurt: Johann David Jungnicol, 1742. [LCPS: V-036. SMLMS.]

See also FUX: (1725):MIZLER (1742); WALTHER: (1702-47).

LITERATURE:

Wöhlke, Franz. "Lorenz Christoph Mizler: Ein Beitrag zur musikalischen Gelehrtengeschichte des 18. Jahrhunderts." Ph.D. dissertation, The University of Würzburg, 1940; published edition (MuG, no. 3), Würzburg-Aumühle: Konrad Triltsch, 1940. Bibliog.

> Review in *AfMf* 7/4 (1942):240-42 (Friedrich Blume).

Hoke, Hans Gunter. "Mizler von Kolof, Lorenz Christoph." In *MGG* (1949-68). Bibliog.

Richter, Lukas. " 'Des Psellus vollständiger kurzer Inbegriff der Musik' in Mizlers *Bibliothek*: Ein Beitrag zur Rezeption der byzantinischen Musiktheorie im 18. Jahrhundert." *BzMw* 9 (1967):45-54; as " 'Psellus' Treatise on Music' in Mizler's *Bibliothek*" in *Studies in Eastern Chant II*, edited by Miloš Velimirovič, pp. 112-28. London: Oxford University Press, 1971. Bibliog. [*Rilm* 67-2434 and 68-1990.]

Falenciak, Joanna. "Lorenz Christoph Mizler a polska kultura muzyczna w drugiej połowie XVIII wieku." *Muzyka* 20/4 [79] (1975):95-103. Bibliog.

Hoke, Hans Gunter. "Neue Studien zur *Kunst der Fuge* BWV 1080." *BzMw* 17/2-3 (1975):95-115.

● ● ● Buelow, George J. "Mizler von Kolof, Lorenz Christoph." In *NGrove* (1980). Bibliog.

Pinegar, Sandra. "Perspective on the Musical Essays of Lorenz Christoph Mizler (1711-1778)." M.A. thesis, North Texas State University, 1984. [*MAb* 23/01, p. 11. UMI 13-23637.]

See also ADLUNG: (1758); FÉTIS: (1833-44); MATTHESON: (1740); RIEMANN: (1898); SCHEIBE: (1737-40):(1745); SCHRÖTER: (1772); LITERATURE SUPPLEMENT: **Arnold (1931/. . ./1965)**; Auhagen (1982/1983); Babbitt (1987); Badura-Skoda et al. (1980); Becker (1836-39/1964); Beiche ["Dux"] (1972-); **Benary (1956/1961)**; Birke (1966); Boomgaarden (1985/1987); Burney (1776-89/. . ./1957); Chybiński (1911-12); **Dahlhaus et al. (1987)**; Dammann (1958/1967); David and Mendel (1945/1966); Donington (1963/. . ./1974); Dreyfus (1987); Duckles (1970); Eitner (1900-1904/1959-60); Federhofer (1970); Feil (1955); Fellerer ["Musikwissenschaft"] (1972); Ferand [*Improvisation*] (1956/1961); Forkel (1792/1962); Frobenius ["Isotonos"] (1972-), ["Vollstimmig"] (1972-); Goldmann (1987); Gurlitt (1944/1966); Hein (1954); Hiller (1768-69); Hosler (1978/1981); Jackson (1988); Jeppesen (1922/. . ./1970); Jung (1969); Krome (1896); Kümmel (1967); Kümmerling (1977); Lang (1967-68); Lawrence (1978); **Lester (1978)**, **(1989)**; Lindley (1982), (1988); List (1976); Mallard (1978); Mann (1955/. . ./1987), (1987); Möller (1971); Müller-Blattau (1923/. . ./1963); Neumann, Frederick (1978); Newman (1985); Newman (1963/. . ./1983); Palisca [*Baroque*] (1968/1981); Rasch (1987); Ratner (1980); Reimer ["Concerto"] (1972-); **Ritzel (1967/1968)**; Rohwer (1949-68); Schering (1926); Schering and Wustmann (1941); Sheldon (1982); Sondheimer (1925); Stege (1927-28); Struthers (1902); Todd (1983); Ulrich (1931/1932); Vogel (1955/1954); Werts (1983); Wessely (1971-72); Williams, P. (1970).

JÉRÔME-JOSEPH DE MOMIGNY

[1762 – 1842]

The Belgian theorist and music publisher Jérôme-Joseph de Momigny made Paris his home, and though he never won the acceptance of the Conservatoire, for which his *Cours complet d'harmonie et de composition* (1803-6) might have served as a useful text, his works were both progressive and distinctive. He challenged the standard arrangement of the scale and questioned the duplication of a pitch at both top and bottom. For Momigny, the tonic pitch C, for example, should be symmetrically surrounded by two tetrachords: one descending to G, the other ascending to F. All seven diatonic pitches are thereby generated, while none are doubly generated. He also was adept in supplying a complete story line for a movement, as in Haydn's Symphony 103, wherein the opening drum roll represents the thunder of threatening weather and the development section represents the cackling of individuals in dispute over whether the fear of a storm (and resulting prayer during the Introduction) were warranted. He even concocted a vocal work (complete with appropriate text) based upon a Mozart quartet and published it below its model as a stimulus for developing the feelings which the version for strings should evoke. To be sure, readers of the early nineteenth century harbored different expectations of their commentators, yet even in that more poetic time, Momigny's contributions were exceptional.

Momigny's commitment to the analytical exploration of music surpassed that of his contemporaries. As were KOCH and REICHA, he was concerned with the interactions among strata of phrases and phrase groups and developed a vocabulary to explain it. His discussion of figuration is enhanced by the use of open and closed noteheads to render the structural and embellishing pitches, respectively. In some of his analytical plates, certain pitches are printed smaller than others. His analysis of a fugue by Bach contains a variety of descriptive annotations, including *Sujet en montant* (Subject), *Réponse* (Answer), *Sujet en descendant* (Inversion of the Subject), and *Sujet coupé* (Fragment of the Subject).

Momigny viewed the rhythmic character of music in what was then a novel way. His ideas were to influence the later development of rhythmic theory in the works of LUSSY and RIEMANN. He perceived a contrast between the written notation, wherein the first beat of a metrical unit appears at the beginning of a measure, and the observed sound, wherein the segmentation would appear more naturally before an upbeat. He suggested, in *La seule vraie théorie de la musique* [1821], that the beats of a 2/4 measure be counted as 1 / 2 1 / 2 1 / 2 etc., while those of a 3/4 measure would be counted as 1 2 / 3 1 2 / 3 etc. or as 1 / 2 3 1 / 2 3 etc.

A dictionary of nearly forty pages was appended to the *Cours complet d'harmonie*. Momigny's skill in such endeavors was further demonstrated in the *Encyclopédie méthodique* (1791-1818), a huge undertaking whose two volumes on music were entrusted to the editorship of Nicolas-Étienne Framery and Pierre-Louis Ginguené, and later to Momigny (the others having died before the second volume was in print). Though the work depends to a large extent on J.-J. ROUSSEAU's existing definitions, Momigny's unique perspective is clearly apparent. As compared with the earlier portion of the dictionary, Momigny's contributions (beginning in the letter G) display a keener interest in theorists of earlier generations, including ZARLINO, VICENTINO, MERSENNE, RAMEAU, and many others.

Encyclopédie méthodique, ou par ordre des matières
. . .: Musique [*Rism* B/VI/1, p. 326.]

>　Edited by Nicolas-Étienne Framery, Pierre-Louis Ginguené, and (particularly in vol. 2) Momigny.

>　Paris: Panckoucke, 1791. Vol. 1. [LCPS: F-050. SMLMS.]
>　Paris: veuve Agasse, 1818. Vol. 2. [LCPS: F-050. SMLMS.]

>　S ● Facsimile edition. DCPMRS. New York: Da Capo Press, 1971.

>>　Reviews in *ML* 54/2 (1973):237-39 (Jack A. Westrup) and *MT* 113/1555 (1972):868 (Julian Rushton).

Méthode de piano à l'aide de laquelle les progrès des élèves sont rendus plus faciles et plus rapides

>　Paris: the author, 1802.

La première année de leçons de piano-forté . . .

>　Issued as a periodical, in 24 installments.

>　Paris: the author, 1802-3.

Cours complet d'harmonie et de composition, d'après une théorie neuve et générale de la musique . . .

>　Paris: the author and Bailleul, *An* XI [1802-3]-1806. 3 vols.

>>　Sold by subscription beginning in 1803. The complete work was offered by Momigny in 1806.

>　Paris: the author; Strasbourg: Amand Koenig, 1808. 2 vols.

>　See KOCH ["Vergleichung"] (lost). Reviews in *AmZ* 11/1, 2, 4, 5 (1808-9):3-10, 19-27, 49-54, 65-73 and *JdP* /355 (*An* XI [1802-3]):2266-67 [Nicolas-Étienne Framery].

>　T ● [Bacon, R. M. (?)], trans. "M. Momigny's Theory." *QMMR* 5/17-19 (1823):57-64, 182-90, 330-38.

>>　Selections from Momigny's work in English.

Le nouveau solfège avec accompagnement de piano, dans lequel le phrasé est réduit en principes . . .

>　Paris: the author, 1808.

Exposé succinct du seul système musical qui soit vraiment fondé et complet, ou seul système qui soit partout d'accord avec la nature, avec la raison et avec la pratique

>　Paris: the author, [ca. 1809].

La seule vraie théorie de la musique, utile à ceux qui excellent dans cet art comme à ceux qui en sont aux premiers élémens, ou moyen le plus court pour devinir mélodiste, harmoniste, contrepointiste et compositeur

>　Paris: the author, [1821].

>>　Review in *ZTM* 1 (1 December 1821):191 (August Kuhn). Review by Alexander-Jean Morel as *Observations sur la seule vraie théorie de la musique de M. de Momigny* (Paris: Bachelier, 1822), which provoked Momigny's *Réponse aux observations de M. Morel . . .* (Paris: Hocquet, [1822]).

>　T ● Santerre, E. M. E., trans. *La sola e vera teoria della musica*. Bologna: Cipriani, 1823; reprint edition (BmB, ser. 2, no. 66), Bologna: Forni, 1969.

>　S ● Facsimile edition. Geneva: Minkoff Reprint, 1980.

À l'Académie des Beaux-Arts, et particulièrement à la Section de musique en réponse aux sept questions adressées par celle-ci à M. de Momigny le 25 avril de cette année 1831

>　Paris: Decourchant, 1831.

Cours général de musique, de piano, d'harmonie et de composition depuis A jusqu' à Z, pour les élèves, quelle que soit leur infériorité, et pour tous les musiciens du monde, quelle qui soit leur supériorité réelle; divisé en douze parties théoriques et pratiques . . .

>　Paris: the author (Everat), 1834. Incomplete (24 pages).

See Palm (1957/1969), below, for information on early press announcements concerning and responses to Momigny's works.

LITERATURE:

[Mocquereau, André.] "Jérôme de Momigny et la rythme musical." *Pm* [ser. 1], no. 7 (1901):[356]-66.

RIEMANN, Hugo. "Ein Kapitel vom Rhythmus." *Musik* 3/15 (1903-4):155-62.

Palm, Albert. "Momigny, Jérôme-Joseph de." In *MGG* (1949-68).

Palm, Albert. "Jérôme-Joseph de Momigny (1762-1842), Leben und Werk: Ein Beitrag zur Geschichte der Musiktheorie im 19. Jahrhundert." Ph.D. dissertation, The University of Tübigen, 1957; published edition, Cologne: Arno Volk Verlag, 1969. Bibliog. [*Rilm* 70-631.]

> Reviews in *Mf* 25/3 (1972):393-94 (Carl Dahlhaus), *ML* 51/4 (1970):459-61 (Mosco Carner), *Musica* 24/2 (1970):178-79 (Fritz Bose), and *SMz* 110/4 (1970):262-63 (Willi Schuh).

Gerstenberg, Walter. "Ein Dictionnaire Momignys und seine Lehre vom musikalischen Vortrag." In *FellererFsI* (1962):182-86.

Palm, Albert. "Mozart und Haydn in der Interpretation Momignys." In *Bericht Kassel 1962* (1963):187-90. Bibliog.

Palm, Albert. "Ein Beitrag zum solfège aus den Anfängen der Schulmusik in Frankreich." In *GerstenbergFs* (1964):107-21.

Palm, Albert. "Mozarts Streichquartett D-moll, KV 421, in der Interpretation Momignys." *Mozart-Jb 1962/63* (1964):256-79.

Chailley, Jacques. "Un grand théoricien belge méconnu de la musique, J.-J. de Momigny (1762-1842)." *ArBB* 48/2-3 (1966):80-98.

Palm, Albert. "Eine unbekannte Klavierschule aus der Zeit des Übergangs vom Cembalo zum Hammerklavier." *Mf* 19/1 (1966):9-19.

Palm, Albert. "Contribution à la connaissance de J.-J. de Momigny." *Rmfc* 7 (1967):127-53. [*Rilm* 68-1980.]

Palm, Albert. "Händels Nachwirkung in Frankreich: Ein Beitrag zu Momignys Händelverständnis." *HJb* 13-14 (1967-68):61-82. Bibliog. [*Rilm* 68-3388.]

Palm, Albert. "Mozart im Spiegel der *Encyclopédie méthodique*." *Mozart-Jb 1967* (1968):314-25. [*Rilm* 68-496.]

Palm, Albert. "Unbekannte Haydn-Analysen." *HaydnJb* 4 (1968):169-94. [*Rilm* 68-3389.]

Palm, Albert. "Zum Erwachen des Bachverständnisses in Frankreich." *MK* 38/4 (1968):169-76. [*Rilm* 68-3390.]

Cole, Malcolm S. "Momigny's Analysis of Haydn's Symphony No. 103." *MR* 30/4 (1969):261-84. [*Rilm* 69-3756.]

Heughebaert, H. "Muziekopvatting en muziekanalyse v. J.-J. de Momigny." *Vm* 22 (1970).

Mongrédien, Jean. "Momigny, Jérôme-Joseph de." In *NGrove* (1980). Bibliog.

Chailley, Jacques. "Momigny, Maleden et l'École Niedermeyer: Un épisode de la lutte entre ramistes et antiramistes." In *PalmFs* (1982):8-18. Bibliog. [*Rilm* 82-2531.]

Görner, Rüdiger. "Die Sprache in der Musiktheorie Jérôme-Joseph de Momignys." In *PalmFs* (1982):100-119. [*Rilm* 82-4029.]

See also FÉTIS: (1831); (1833-44); LITERATURE SUPPLEMENT: Apfel and Dahlhaus (1974); Beck (1973), (1974); Becker (1836-39/1964); Beiche ["Dux"] (1972-); ● ● ●Bent ["Analysis"] **(1980/1987)**; Blumröder (1972-); Cazden (1948); Chevaillier (1925/1931-32); **Coover (1980)**; **Dahlhaus (1984)**; **Dahlhaus and Sachs (1980)**; **Dürr and Gerstenberg** (1949-68), **(1980)**; Dunsby and Whittall (1988); Eitner (1900-1904/1959-60); Fischer (1957); Frobenius ["Isotonos"] (1972-); **Groth (1983)**; Hartmann (1923); Henneberg (1972/1974); Houle (1960), (1987); Jones (1934); **Kassler** (1971), **(1979)**; Kauko (1958); Konecne (1984); Kunze (1968); Laudon (1978); Mongrédien (1974); Moyer (1969); Newman (1963/. . ./1983), (1969/. . ./1983); **Palisca** ["Theory"] **(1980)**; Palm (1965); Ratner (1949), (1980); Ritzel (1967/1968); Schmalzriedt ["Coda"] (1972-), ["Durchführen"] (1972-), ["Episode"] (1972-), ["Exposition"] (1972-), ["Reprise"] (1972-); Seidel (1972-), (1975), (1976), (1979); Shamgar (1978), (1981), (1984); **Shirlaw (1917/. . ./1970)**; Stevens (1974); Taddie (1984); **Wagner (1974)**; **Wason (1981/1985)**; Wirth (1966); **Zaminer (1985)**.

FRANCISCO DE MONTANOS

[c. 1528 – after 1592]

The *Arte de canto llano* of Franciso de Montanos was popular in Spain from the late sixteenth century well into the eighteenth. In that Spain remained relatively isolated from modern innovations in the art of composition, both Montanos and CERONE (who took materials from Montanos) retained their appeal despite their Renaissance perspective. Montanos's work is devoted to sacred vocal polyphony, including that of Palestrina, and contains numerous music examples. The text is practical rather than speculative and treats plainsong, mensural notation, counterpoint, composition, and proportions.

Arte de música theórica y prática [*Rism* B/VI/2, p. 593.]

Valladolid: Diego Fernández de Córdova y Obiedo, 1592. [LCPS: M-145.]

T ● Urquhart, Dan Murdock. "Francisco de Montaños's *Arte de música theórica y prática*: A Translation and Commentary." 2 vols. Ph.D. dissertation, The University of Rochester, 1969. Bibliog. [*DA* 30/10A, pp. 4484-85. UMI 69-19780.]

Arte de canto llano . . . [*Rism* B/VI/2, pp. 592-93.]

Derived from *Arte de música theórica y prática*, above.

Valladolid: Andrés de Merchán, 1594.

Numerous editions through 1756, including:

Salamanca: Andrés López (Francisco de Cea Tesa), 1610.
Salamanca: Antonio Vázquez, 1625. [LCPS: M-144a.]

Edited by Sebastián López de Velasco:

Madrid: Imprenta Real, 1635.
Saragossa: Iván de Ibar, 1670. [LCPS: M-144b.]
Saragossa: Francisco Moreno, 1756. [LCPS: M-144d.]

With *El arte práctico de canto de órgano* by Joseph de Torres:

Madrid: Imprenta de música (Diego Lucas Ximénez), 1705.
Madrid: Imprenta de música (Miguel de Rézola), 1728. [LCPS: M-144c.]

LITERATURE:

Gallardo, Bartolomé José. *Ensayo de una biblioteca española de libros raros y curiosos*. Edited by M. R. Zarco del Valle, J. Sancho Rayón, and Marcelino Menéndez y Pelayo. Madrid: Manuel Rivadeneyra, 1863-66; M. Tello, 1888-89; facsimile of the 1888-89 edition (Brh, no. 9), Madrid: Editorial Gredos, 1968.

Palau y Dulcet, Antonio. *Manual del librero hispanoamericano*. Vol. 10. Barcelona: Librería anticuaría, 1923-27; 2nd edition, Librería Palau, 1957.

Review in *Hisp* 33/2 (1950):190-91 (John Kenneth Leslie).

Querol, Miguel. "Montanos, Francisco de." Translated by Gerda Dürr. In *MGG* (1949-68).

Stevenson, Robert. "Montanos, Francisco de." In *NGrove* (1980).

See also FÉTIS: (1833-44); WALTHER: (1732); LITERATURE SUPPLEMENT: Abraham (1968/1969); Anglés and Subirá (1946-51); ● ● ● **Apfel (1981)**; Becker (1836-39/1964); Collet (1912); Eitner (1900-1904/1959-60); Forrester (1973); Gerber (1790-92/1977), (1812-14/1966); Howell (1972); León Tello (1962); Luper (1938); Reese (1954/1959); Sachs (1972-); Subirá (1947/. . ./1958), (1953).

CLAUDIO MONTEVERDI

[1567–1643]

and

GIULIO CESARE MONTEVERDI

[bapt. 1573 – ca. 1630-31]

Though Claudio Monteverdi preferred to demonstrate the power of his new compositional practice through actual music rather than through words, the abusive treatment several excerpts from his works had received under ARTUSI's scrutiny [in *L'Artusi* (1600 and 1603), where several examples from Monteverdi's unpublished madrigals were printed without text or attribution] led him to write a brief preface for his Fifth Book of Madrigals (1605), wherein he established the notion that two separate practices—one that of ZARLINO (*prima prattica*), the other his own (*seconda prattica*)—coexisted. He also promised to publish his own treatise, to be called "Seconda Pratica, ovvero perfezioni della moderna musica," which, unfortunately, did not materialize.

ARTUSI continued the interaction with *Discorso musicale di Antonio Braccino da Todi* [Lost], which induced Claudio's brother Giulio Cesare Monteverdi to draft a commentary on the preface, published as a "Dichiaratione" appended to Claudio's *Scherzi musicali* (1607). This document provides a more detailed picture of the attitudes which formed the progressive stance and draws upon the authority of Plato in explaining that the text should be the mistress of the harmony, not its servant, as ARTUSI would have it. ARTUSI, never shy to pick up the pen, responded with a second *Discorso* in 1608.

Preface ("Studiosi lettori") to *Il quinto libro de' madrigali a cinque voci* . . . [*Rism* A/I/6, pp. 11-12.]

and

"Dichiaratione della lettera stampata nel Quinto libro de suoi madregali" in *Scherzi musicali a tre voci* [*Rism* A/I/6, p. 12.]

Venice: Ricciardo Amadino, 1605. (*Madrigali.*)

Numerous later printings.

Venice: Ricciardo Amadino, 1607. (*Scherzi.*)

Numerous later printings.

T ● Pereyra, Marie Louise. *Explication de la lettre qui est imprinmée dans le cinquième livre de madrigaux de Claudio Monteverde*. Paris: Bureau d'édition de la "Schola cantorum", 1911.

Contains a French translation of the "Dichiaratione."

S ● Facsimile of the 1606 (*Madrigali*) and 1632 (*Scherzi*) editions. In *Claudio Monteverdi: Tutte le opera*, edited by G. Francesco Malipiero, vols. 5, p. [iii], and 10, pp. 69-72. Asolo: nel Vittoriale degli italiani, 1927 and 1929; reprint editions.

S ● Malipiero, Gian Francesco. *Claudio Monteverdi*. IGmis. Milan: Fratelli Treves, 1929.

T ● See ● ● ● **Strunk (1950)**:405-12.

T ● See Gerboth et al. (1964).

S ● Paoli, Domenico de', ed. *Lettere, dediche e prefazioni: Edizione critica*. Cdm, no. 4. Rome: Edizioni de Santis, 1973. [*Rilm* 76-9753.]

Reviews in *ML* 55/2 (1974):235-37 (Denis Arnold), *MQ* 61/2 (1975):314-19 (Barbara R. Hanning), *NZfM* 135/4 (1974):267 (Dietrich Kämper), and *TLS* 74/3818 (1975):507 (Denis Stevens).

T ● See Rowen (1979).

S ● Caraci, Maria, ed. Facsimile of the 1605 (*Madrigali*) edition. *Opera omnia*, ser. 1, no. 5:6: *Madrigali a 5 voci, Libro quinto*, p. 75. SpfmuP. Cremona: Fondazione Claudio Monteverdi, 1984.

T ● "Iz pisem Klaudi Monteverdi." *Smuz* /1 (1986):104-11.

LITERATURE:

Vogel, Emil. "Claudio Monteverdi: Leben, Wirken im Lichte der zeitgenössischen Kritik und Verzeichniss seiner im Druck erschienenem Werke." *VMw* 3 (1887):315-450. Bibliog.

Tessier, André. "Monteverdi e la filosofia dell'arte." *Rasm* 2/10 (1929):459-68.

Redlich, Hans Ferdinand. *Claudio Monteverdi: Leben und Werk*. Olten, Switzerland: Otto Walter, 1949; English translation by Kathleen Dale (as *Claudio Monteverdi: Life and Work*), London: Oxford University Press (Geoffrey Cumberlege), 1952.

Reviews in *Dmt* 25/1 (1950):18 (Bengt Johnsson), *JAMS* 5/3 (1952):247-52 (Alexander L. Ringer), *MAm* 73/2 (1953):25 (Robert Sabin), *MC* 146/5 (1952):30, *Mf* 4/1 (1951):64-68 (Anna Amalie Abert), *ML* 33/2 (1952):175-78 (R. Thurston Dart), *MMR* 82/939 (1952):186 (A. H.), *MO* 75/896 (1951-52):473 (H. H.), *MQ* 39/1 (1953):120-26 (Joseph Kerman), *MR* 11/3 (1950):246-47 (Adam Carse), *MR* 13/4 (1952):318-20 (J. A. Westrup), *MSur* 2/3 (1950):192 (Denis W. Stevens), *MT* 93/1310 (1952):163-64 (Denis Stevens), *Musica* 6/9 (1952):389-90 (Hellmuth Christian Wolff), *Notes* 9/4 (1951-52):601-3 (Edward E. Lowinsky), *Punch* 222/5813 (1952):382 (J. Durrant), and *Tempo* 23 (1952):28 (Denis Stevens).

Redlich, Hans Ferdinand. "Monteverdi, Claudio Zuan Antonio." In *MGG* (1949-68). Bibliog.

Schrade, Leo. *Monteverdi, Creator of Modern Music*. NLS, no. 490. New York: W. W. Norton, 1950; reprint edition, 1969; (DCPMRS), New York: Da Capo Press, 1979; French translation (as *Monteverdi*, translated by Jacques Drillon; Mmus), Paris: Lattès, 1981.

Reviews in *AmO* 34/5 (1951):146, *CCh* 36/4 (1950):184-85 (J. Vincent Higginson), *Choice* 6/9 (1969-70):1232, *Éc* 51/2 (1983):162 (Yves Lenoir), *Etude* 69/3 (1951):8-9 (Thomas Faulkner), *JAAC* 9/4 (1950-51):341 (Frederick Dorian), *JAMS* 4/2 (1951):153-59 (Alexander L. Ringer), *MAm* 71/13 (1951):34 (Robert Sabin), *MC* 142/10 (1950):26, *MCM* 30/3 (1950-51):18 (Hazel G. Weaver), *Mf* 4/4 (1951):318-32 (Hans F. Redlich), *ML* 33/1 (1952):64-65 (Thurston Dart), *MN* 43 (1951):22, *MQ* 37/2 (1951):272-78 (Charles Warren Fox), *MR* 13/4 (1952):316-18 (Hans F. Redlich), *MT* 93/1310 (1952):163-64 (Denis Stevens), *MT* 106/1469 (1965):522 (Jeremy Noble), *Notes* 8/2 (1950-51):336-38 (Hans Tischler), *PP* 43/4 (1950-51):257 (Gladys Wilson), *Punch* 221/5785 (1951):309 (J. Durrant), *RBBR* 25/1 (1980):13 (James B. Boskey), *Rmi* 56/1 (1954):72-81 (Luigi Ronga), *SatR* 34/4 (January 27, 1951):50 (Kathleen O'Donnell Hoover), *Strad* 80/953 (1969-70):235, *TES* 3328 (1980):26 (Michael Trend), *TLS* 64/3280 (1965):4, and *YR* 42/1 (1952-53):120-21 (Louise Talma).

Bonino, Mary Ann Teresa. "Monteverdi's Use of Musical and Dramatic Expression in His First Four Books of Madrigals." M.A. thesis, The University of Southern California, 1963.

Claro, Samuel. "Claudio Monteverdi—Giovanni Maria Artusi: Una controversia musica." *RmC* 19/93 (1965):86-94.

Gallico, Claudio. "Monteverdi e i dazi di Viadana." *Ridm* 1/2 (1966):242-45.

Fano, Fabio. "Il Monteverdi sacro, la *prima prattica* e la scuola veneziana." *Ridm* 2/1 (1967):264-69. [*Rilm* 73/318.]

Fortune, Nigel. "Monteverdi and the *Seconda prattica*." In Arnold and Fortune (1968/1985).

Roche, Jerome. "Monteverdi and the *Prima prattica*." In Arnold and Fortune (1968/1985).

Gianuario, Annibale. "Proemío all'*Oratione* di Monteverdi." *Ridm* 4 (1969):32-47.

Anfuso, Nella, and Gianuario, Annibale. *Preparazione alla interpretazione della* Ποιησις' *Monteverdiana.* CsrmF. Florence: OTOS, [1971]. [*Rilm* 74-4086.]

> Reviews in *KJb* 55 (1971):87 and *ML* 54/1 (1973):96-97 (Denis Arnold).

Moses, Gavriel Josef. "Literary Genre in Monteverdi." Ph.D. dissertation, Brown University, 1974. [*DA* 35/11A, p. 7262. UMI 75-09211.]

Monterosso, Raffaello. "Claudio Monteverdi: la nouvelle musique." Translated by Marie-Hélène Poli. In *Avs* 5 (1976):15-19. [*Rilm* 76-7574.]

Arnold, Denis, and Arnold, Elsie M. "Monteverdi, Claudio (Giovanni Antonio)." In *NGrove* (1980). Bibliog.

Arnold, Denis. "Monteverdi, Giulio Cesare." In *NGrove* (1980).

Beaudoin, Russell Martin. "The Seconda Pratica of Claudio Monteverdi as Used in His *Quinto libro de madrigali a cinque voci* (1605)." M.M. thesis, Michigan State University, 1984. [*MAb* 23/01, p. 8. UMI 13-23679.]

Fabbri, Paolo. *Monteverdi*. Bcm. Turin: EDT/Musica, 1985.

> Review in *EM* 13/4 (1985):575-76 (Jerome Roche).

See also ARTUSI: (1600); (1603); (1608); Massera (1966); BANCHIERI: (1609); (1628); BOTTRIGARI: (1600); (1603); [ca. 1606]; (1608); DONI: (1763); FÉTIS: (1833-44); GALILEI: Fabo (1934); LIPPIUS: Howard (1985); MARTINI: (1774-75); PRAETORIUS: (1614-20):Vol. 3 (1618); RIEMANN: (1898); WALTHER: (1732); LITERATURE SUPPLEMENT: Abraham (1968/ 1969); Arnold (1957); **Berger (1975/1980)**; Beyschlag (1907/1953); Buelow (1972); Bukofzer (1947); Chomiński (1962/1981); Cohen (1984); Crocker (1966); **Dahlhaus** ["Untersuchungen"] (1966/ . . ./1988), (1984); **Dahlhaus and Sachs (1980); Dahlhaus et al. (1987)**; Dammann (1958/1967); Donà (1967); Eggebrecht (1957); Eitner (1900-1904/1959-60); Federhofer (1969), (1985); Fellerer (1983); Ferand (1937/1938); Frobenius ["Monodie"] (1972-), ["Vollstimmig"] (1972-); Fubini (1971/1983); Gerber (1790-92/1977), (1812-14/1966); Gianuario (1979); Goldschmidt (1901-4/1967); Grout (1960/. . ./1980); Grusnick (1964-66); Haar (1986); Harrán (1986); Houle (1987); Hucke (1969); Isgro (1968); Katz (1985); Koenigsberger (1979); Kuhn (1902); Lang (1941); Lang (1967-68); **Lindley** (1982), (1984); Luoma (1977); **Maniates (1979)**; Mann (1987); Massera (1969); Meier (1974/1988); Neumann, Frederick (1978); Oberdörffer (1949-68); **Palisca** ["Artusi-Monteverdi"] ● ● ● (1968/1985), [*Ba-roque*] (1968/1981), ["Theory"] **(1980), (1985)**; Pöhlmann (1969); Reese (1954/1959); Reimer ["Concerto"] (1972-), ["Kammermusik"] (1972-); Sirch (1981); Subirá (1947/. . ./1958); Tenney (1988); Vecchi (1969); Vogel (1955/1954); Wichmann (1966); Williams, P. (1970); Yamaguchi (1977); **Zaminer (1985)**.

THOMAS MORLEY

[ca. 1557 – 1602]

Thomas Morley wrote at a time of musical experimentation, though he remained, as both composer and theorist, conservative. His *Plaine and Easie Introduction to Practicall Musicke* (1597) deals with hexachords, mensural notation, counterpoint, canon, and cadences. The work is divided into three sections, each of which is accompanied by explanatory notes. Part I deals with notation, Part II with two-part counterpoint, and Part III with composition (multi-voiced counterpoint and forms).

The book's dialogue format is enriched by the colorfully portrayed personalities of the tutor and two youths. Master Gnorimus, the tutor, is stern taskmaster, hypochondriac, and wise mentor. The student and his brother tease the tutor playfully and fall for every trap he has set with his contrapuntal examples. Morley speaks of the aesthetic side of music frequently, particularly in his discussion on setting of songs, in the third book.

Morley leaned heavily on ZARLINO and TIGRINI but surpassed them pedagogically. Although his book addresses the music of the immediate past, there is some indication of increasing tonal feeling and importance of the bass voice. The modes are interpreted, essentially, as major or minor.

A Plaine and Easie Introduction to Practicall Musicke, Set Downe in Forme of a Dialogue . . . [*Rism* B/VI/2, p. 598.]

> London: Peter Short, 1597. [LCPS: M-156a. HoM: 1032. SMLMS.]
> London: Humfrey Lownes, 1608. [LCPS: M-156b. HoM: 1033. SMLMS.]
> London: William Randall (George Bigg), 1771. Revisions by Arthur Burton and Samuel Howard. [LCPS: M-156c. HoM: 1034.]

S ● Southgate, T. L., ed. "An Unpublished Chapter from an Early Manuscript of Morley's *Plaine and Easy Introduction to Practicall Musicke.*" *ChaM* 4 (1913):33-36.

S ● Fellowes, Edmund H., ed. Facsimile of the 1597 edition. SAF, no. 14. London: Humphrey Milford, Oxford University Press, 1937.

> Reviews in *LonM* 36/214 (1937):382 (B. H. New-digate), *ML* 18/4 (1937):403-4 (A. H. Fox Strang-ways), and *MLR* 34/2 (1939):294 (Bruce Pattison).

S ● See **Strunk (1950)**:274-78.

S ● Harman, R. Alec, ed. Edition in modern typeface. Foreword by Thurston Dart. London: J. M. Dent, 1952; New York: W. W. Norton, 1953; 2nd edition (NLS, no. 682), 1963; reprint edition, 1973.

> Reviews in *JAMS* 6/1 (1953):74-77 (Robert Stevenson), *MQ* 39/3 (1953):442-55 (Otto Kinkeldey), *Musart* 26/1 (1973-74):41, *Notes* 10/1 (1952-53):98-99 (David D. Boyden), and *PP* 66/4 (1973-74):24 (Melva Peterson).

S ● Facsimile of the 1597 edition. EE, no. 207. Amsterdam: Theatrum Orbis Terrarum; New York: Da Capo Press, 1969.

S ● Facsimile of the 1597 edition. Farnborough, England: Gregg International, 1971.

S ● See MacClintock (1979).

S ● See Rowen (1979).

LITERATURE:

STAINER, Sir John. "Morley's *Plaine and Easie Introduction to Practicall Musicke.*" *MT* 43/713 (1902):457-60.

Pulver, Jeffrey. "The English Theorists: XIII — Thomas Morley." *MT* 76/1107 (1935):411-14.

Deutsch, Otto Erich. "The Editions of Morley's *Introduction.*" *Libr* 23/2-3 (1942-43):127-29.

Harman, Richard Alexander. "Morley, Thomas." Translated by Helene Wessely. In *MGG* (1949-68). Bibliog.

Stevenson, Robert. "Thomas Morley's 'Plaine and Easie' Introduction to the Modes." *Md* 6/4 (1952):177-84.

Nutting, Geoffrey. "Cadence in Late-Renaissance Music." *Miscm* 8 (1975):32-55. [*Rilm* 76-9414.]

Brett, Philip. "Morley, Thomas." In *NGrove* (1980). Bibliog.

See also DIRUTA: Soehnlein (1975); FÉTIS: (1833-44); GLAREAN: Miller (1961); NORTH, R.: [ca. 1726]; RIEMANN (1898); VIADANA: Haack (1964/1974); WALTHER: (1732); LITERATURE SUPPLEMENT: Abraham (1968/1969); Apel (1942/. . ./1961); **Apfel (1981)**; **Barbour (1951/. . ./1972)**; Becker (1836-39/1964); Beiche ["Dux"] (1972-), ["Inversio"] (1972-); Blanken-burg ["Kanonimprovisationen"] (1959); Bukofzer (1947); **Bullivant (1980)**; Burney (1776-89/. . ./1957); Burton (1956); Bush (1939), (1946); Butler (1977), (1980); Cahn ["Transitus"] (1972-); Carpenter (1955); Cazden (1948); Chew (1980); Chomiński (1962/1981); Colles (1928-29); Dahlhaus ["Untersuchungen"] (1966/. . ./1988); **Dahlhaus et al. (1987)**; Dolmetsch (1915/. . ./1969); Donington (1963/. . ./1974); Eggebrecht (1955); Eitner (1900-1904/1959-60); Fellerer ["Zur Kontrapunktlehre"] (1972); Ferand (1937/1938), ["Improvised"] (1956), [*Improvisation*] (1956/1961); Forkel (1792/ 1962); Frobenius ["Vollstimmig"] (1972-); Gerber (1812-14/1966); Hancock (1977); Harding (1938); Harrán (1973), (1986); Hawkins (1776/. . ./1969); Haydon (1933/1970); Hein (1954); Henderson (1969); Hoffman (1970); Horsley [*Fugue: History*] (1966); Houle (1960), (1987); Hüschen (1986); Isgro (1968); Jackson (1988); Jacobi (1957-60/1971); Jeppesen (1922/. . ./1970); **Kassler (1976), ● ● ● (1979)**; Kassler and Oldroyd (1983); Kauko (1958); Kleinman (1971/1974); Lawrence (1978); Lewis (1981); **Lindley (1982)**, **(1984)**; Lloyd (1940-41); Luper (1938); **Maniates (1979)**; **Mann (1955/. . ./1987)**, (1987); Meier (1974/1988); Mendel (1948), (1978); Moyer (1969); Müller-Blattau (1923/. . ./1963); O'Donnell (1979); **Palisca (1949-68)**, ["*Ut oratoria musica*"] (1972), ["Theory"] **(1980)**; Powers (1974); Pulver (1927/ . . ./1973); Reese (1954/1959); Roberts (1967); Rogers (1955); Rothschild (1953); Ruf (1972-); Ruff (1970); Sachs (1972-); Schenkman (1976); **Seidel and Cooper (1986)**; Shute (1972); Subirá (1947/. . ./1958); Taddie (1984); Tenney (1988); Walker (1987); Wienpahl (1953), (1955); Williams (1979); Wolf (1939).

LEOPOLD MOZART

[1719 – 1787]

First QUANTZ, then C. P. E. BACH, and finally Leopold Mozart issued a major work devoted to a specific instrument during the 1750s. As are the flute and keyboard manuals, so also is Mozart's *Versuch einer gründlichen Violinschule* (1756) an informative guide for all who aspire towards stylistic performances of music from the eighteenth century. In fact, a comparison of the three works reveals numerous differences of opinion concering performance practices, thus warning modern practitioners of earlier music to avoid dogmatic adherence to any specific set of rules.

Of the three treatises, Mozart's is the least informative theoretically. One finds basic information (time signatures, clefs, rhythmic notation, and so on), definitions of technical terms borrowed from the Italian, a summary of the mechanics of performance, and explanations for a wide variety of ornaments. Yet extensive discussions of musical taste and explanations of compositional procedures are lacking. Perhaps his concern that the book not become too expensive for performers of modest means influenced his decision not to write more. In any event, the *Versuch* was enormously popular and served as a model and source for violin method books well into the nineteenth century.

Correspondence

S ● "Brief an Meinrad Spieß." *AMoz* 34/4 (1987):77-82.

Versuch einer gründlichen Violinschule, entworfen und mit 4. Kupfertafeln sammt einer Tabelle versehen [*Rism* B/VI/2, pp. 600-602.]

Augsburg: the author (Johann Jacob Lotter), 1756. [LCPS: M-160a. HoM: 1038. SMLMS. IDC.]

Reviews in *BsW* 10/1-2 (1763-64):50-53 and MARPURG: (1754-78):Vol. 3/2 (1757-58):160-63.

As *Gründliche Violinschule*:

Augsburg: the author (Johann Jacob Lotter), 1769 and 1770. [LCPS: M-160b. HoM: 1039.]
Augsburg: Johann Jacob Lotter & Sohn, 1787. [LCPS: M-160c.]
Frankfurt and Leipzig: 1791. [LCPS: M-160d.]
Augsburg: Johann Jacob Lotter & Sohn, 1800. [LCPS: M-160e.]

T ● *Grondig onderwÿs in het behandelen der viool.* Haarlem: Joannes Enschede, 1766 [*Rism* B/VI/2, p. 601. LCPS: M-160f. IDC.]; reprint edition (edited by Adolphe Poth), Utrecht: A. Oosthoek, 1965.

T ● Roeser, Valentin, trans. *Méthode raisonnée pour apprendre à jouer du violon*. Paris: Le Menu, [1770]; Boyer & Le Menu, [ca. 1783]; Boyer, [ca. 1788]; Naderman, [ca. 1800]. [*Rism* B/VI/2, pp. 601-2.]

S ● Frankfurt and Leipzig: 1791. [*Rism* B/VI/2, p. 601. LCPS: M-160d.]

An unauthorized edition.

S ● Perlinger, Joseph, ed. *Neue vollständige theoretische und praktische Violin-Schule für Lehrer und Lernende*. 2 vols. Vienna: Musikalisch-typographische Verlagsgesellschaft (Christian Gottlob Täubel), 1799-1800; reprint edition(s). [*Rism* B/VI/2, p. 602.]

S ● Woldemar, Michel, ed. *Méthode de violin par L. Mozart*. Paris: Cochet, 1801.

T ● *Osnovatel'noe skripichnoe uchilishche*. [St. Petersburg:] 1804.

S ● *Violinschule; oder, Anweisung die Violin zu spielen*. Leipzig: Hoffmeister & Kühnel, [1804]; C. F. Peters, [1817]; abridged edition (edited by Joh. Bapt. Schiedermayr), Mainz: Schott, [1818]; other editions [?].

S ● Paumgartner, Bernhard, ed. Facsimile of the 1756 edition. Vienna: Carl Stephenson, [1922].

T ● Knocker, Editha, trans. *A Treatise on the Fundamental Principles of Violin Playing*. Preface by Alfred Einstein. London: Oxford University Press, 1948; revised edition, 1951; reprint edition (EMS, no. 6), 1985.

Reviews in *AST* 37/1 (1987):84 (Barbara Jackson), *JAMS* 2/3 (1949):187-88 (Alfred Mann), *MQ* 35/1 (1949):147-51 (David D. Boyden), and *Notes* 6/1 (1948-49):165 (Paul G. Gelrud).

T ● See **Strunk (1950)**:599-608.

S ● Moser, Hans Joachim, ed. Facsimile of the 1787 edition. Leipzig: Breitkopf & Härtel, 1956.

S ● Jung, Hans Rudolf, ed. Facsimile of the 1787 edition. Introduction by David Oistrach. Leipzig: VEB Deutscher Verlag für Musik, 1968; 1978.

Reviews in *BzMw* 12/2 (1970):140-41 (Cornelia Schröder-Auerbach), *Dmt* 44/2 (1969):53-54

(Sigurd Berg), *Greg* 94/3 (1970):149 (Piet Visser), *Me* 22/5 (1969):237-38, *MG* 19/8 (1969):560-61 (Frank Schneider), *Muzsika* 12/11 (1969):30, *Nrmi* 4/1 (1970):149-52 (Remo Giazotto), and *Zvuk* 94 (1969):191-92 (Josip Andreis).

T ● Tsukahara, Tetsuo, trans. *Violin soho*. Tokyo: Zenon-gakufu-shuppan, 1974.

T ● See MacClintock (1979).

"Nachricht von dem gegenwärtigen Zustande der Musik Sr. Hochfürstlichen Gnaden des Erzbischoffs zu Salzburg im Jahre 1757"

Published anonymously. Attributed to Mozart.

In MARPURG: (1754-78):Vol. 3/3 (1757-58):183-98.

LITERATURE:

Gerhartz, Karl. "Die Violinschule von Leopold Mozart (1756)." *MozJ* 3 (1929):243-302.

Bittner, Carl. "Was bedeutet Phil. Em. Bachs *Versuch* für die Gegenwart?" *DTZ* 33/6 (1936-37):154-55.

Hahn, Grete. "Leopold Mozarts Violinschule (1756)." *DTZ* 33/6 (1936-37):155-57.

Steinhardt, Milton. "Leopold Mozart's Violin Method." M.M. thesis, The University of Rochester, 1937.

Fischer, Kurt von. "Eine Neubearbeitung von L. Mozarts Violinschule aus dem Jahre 1804: Ein Stilvergleich." *Mf* 2 (1949):187-92.

Schmidt, Ernst Fritz. "Mozart, Johann Georg Leopold." In *MGG* (1949-68). Bibliog.

Egk, W. "Anmerkungen zur Violinschule von Leopold Mozart." *GG* 4 (1957):28-35.

Lidke, Wolfgang. "Übereinstimmung und Gegensatz der Violinschulen von Leopold Mozart und Louis Spohr." *SpohrFs* (1959):67-77.

Ruddick, James D. "Leopold Mozart and His Violinschule." *Strad* 73/872 (1962):293-95.

Valentin, E. "Was der Schüler beobachten muß . . . Zu Leopold Mozarts Lehrtätigkeit." In *Neues Augsburger Mozartbuch: Zeitschrift des historischem Vereins für Schwaben*, nos. 62/63. Augsburg: M. Seitz, 1962.

Apps, Howard Llewellyn. "Leopold Mozart and His *Violinschule*." *Strad* 80/959 (1969-70):511-15.

Layer, Adolf. "Johann Jakob Lotter d. J., Leopold Mozarts Augsburger Verleger." In *Leopold Mozart, 1719-1787: Bild einer Persönlichkeit*, edited by Ludwig Wegele, pp. 117-28. Augsburg: Die Brigg, 1969. [*Rilm* 70-1859.]

Cherubini, Ralph. "Leopold Mozart's *Violinschule* as a Guide to the Performance of W. A. Mozart's Sonatas for Violin and Keyboard." Ph.D. dissertation, Case Western Reserve University, 1976.

Chesnut, John Hind. "Mozart's Teaching of Intonation." *JAMS* 30/2 (1977):254-71. [*Rilm* 77-4597.]

Plath, Wolfgang. "Mozart. (1) (Johann Georg) Leopold Mozart." In *NGrove* (1980). Bibliog.

Szegö, Júlia. *A két Mozart hétköznapjai*. Budapest: Zenemükiadó Vállalat; Bucharest: Ion Creangá Könyvkiadó, [1980].

Hofmiller, Josef. "Der alte Mozart und seine Violinschule." *AMoz* 34/1 (1987):1-7.

Kerr, David Wallis. "A Performance Edition of W. A. Mozart's *Eine kleine Nachtmusik*, K. 525, Based upon Performance Principles Propounded in Leopold Mozart's *Versuch einer gründlichen Violinschule*." D.A. dissertation, The University of Northern Colorado, 1986. [*DA* 48/04A, pp. 774-75. UMI 87-13007.]

See also FÉTIS: (1833-44); MARPURG: (1759-63):Vol. 1 (1759-60); LITERATURE SUPPLEMENT: Almond (1979); Aulabaugh (1958); Babitz (1952), (1967/1969); Babitz and Pont (1973); Badura-Skoda et al. (1980); Badura-Skoda (1983); Barbour (1952); Becker (1836-39/1964); Beyschlag (1907/1953); Blake (1988); Boomgaarden (1985/1987); Bremner (1979); Brown and McKinnon (1980); Bruck (1928); Budday (1982/1983); Buelow ["Rhetoric"] (1980); Burde (1976); Cahn ["Retardatio"] (1972-); Chesnut (1976); Chiba (1976); Cole (1988); Collins (1963), (1966), (1967); Coover (1980); Dahlhaus (1984); Dahlhaus et al. (1987); Donington (1963/. . ./1974), (1977), (1980); Duckles (1970); Eggebrecht (1955); Eitner (1900-1904/1959-60); Federhofer (1964), (1985); Ferand (1937/1938), [*Improvisation*] (1956/1961); Fischer (1957); Flaherty (1989); Forkel (1792/1962); Ganz (1972), (1976); Gerber (1790-92/1977), (1812-14/1966); Goldmann (1987); Goldschmidt (1907); Hartig (1982); Hiller (1768-69); Hoffmann (1974); Hosler (1978/1981); Houle (1960), (1987); Jackson (1988); Jasinsky (1974); Kamieński (1918-19); Kretzschmar (1911-12); Lawrence (1978); Lester (1989); Lindley (1982); Mann (1987); Neumann, Frederick (1967/1982), (1977/1982), (1978), [*Essays*] (1982), (1986); Newman (1985); Newman (1963/. . ./1983), (1976); Petrobelli (1968); Pincherle (1958); Reichert (1978); Reimer ["Kenner"] (1972-); Robison (1982); Rosenblum (1988); Rothschild (1953), (1961); Schwartz (1908); Sheppard (1978-79); Smiles (1978); Sondheimer (1925); Spitzer and Zaslaw (1986); Steblin (1981/1983), (1987); Stowell (1985), (1988); Subirá (1947/. . ./1958); Tittel (1966); Troeger (1987); Vogel (1976); Wessel (1955); Yeston (1975); Zaslaw (1979).

GEORG MUFFAT

[bapt. 1653 – 1704]

The informative and practical writings of Georg Muffat confirm his position as one of seventeenth-century Austria's leading organists and most progressive composers. Having interacted with both Lully and Corelli, Muffat brought both French and Italian influences into play in his compositions and remarked upon them (in four languages) in prefaces to his various collections. Orchestration, ornamentation, tempo, bowing, and dynamics are among the topics considered.

Of greater interest for the study of theory is Muffat's manuscript treatise on figured bass, which influenced a small circle of his contemporaries but remained relatively unknown until its publication in 1961. The uses of the various intervals are listed and demonstrated in uncommonly artistic examples which utilize alternatively three, four, or more voices. Devoted less to the basic mechanics of figured bass than were most contemporary treatises, its primary value is in its keen discrimination among potential realizations and in the care with which the numerous outstanding examples are annotated.

Preface to *Apparatus musico-organisticus* . . . [*Rism* A/I/6, p. 280.]

> Salzburg: the author and Johann Baptist Mayr, 1690.
> Passau: Georg Adam Höller, n.d.
> Vienna: Gottfried Muffat, [ca. 1704 – 1709].
> Vienna: Johann Peter von Ghelen, n.d.

S ● Walter, Rudolf, ed. Altötting: Alfred Coppenrath (H. Pawelek), [1957]; reprint edition (SdOB, no. 3), 1968; reprint edition, 1987.

> Review in *ArsOr* 35/1 (1987):67 (Hermann J. Busch).

S ● Kolneder, Walter. *Georg Muffat zur Auffühungs-praxis*. SmA, no. 50. Strasbourg and Baden-Baden: Heitz, 1970. [*Rilm* 71-1488.]

S ● Radulescu, Michael, ed. Vienna: Dilmu, nos. 825-28. Doblinger/Universal, 1982.

> Reviews in *ML* 66/3 (1985):294-95 (Susan Wollenberg) and *MT* 125/1694 (1984):233 (Ann Bond).

Preface to *Suavioris harmoniae instrumentalis hyporchematicae florilegium primum* . . . [*Rism* A/I/6, p. 280.]

> Augsburg: Wilhelm Panneker (Jacob Koppmayr), 1695.

S ● Rietsch, Heinrich, ed. *DTÖ* 2 (I:2). Vienna: Artaria, 1894; reprint edition, Graz: Akademische Druck- und Verlagsanstalt.

T ● See **Strunk (1950)**:442-45.

S ● See (1690):Kolneder (1970), above.

Preface to *Suavioris harmoniae instrumentalis hyporchematicae florilegium secundum* [*Rism* A/I/6, p. 280.]

> Passau: the author (Georg Adam Höller), 1698.

S ● [Stollbrock, Ludwig, ed.] "Georg Muffat's musiktheoretische Abhandlung 1698." *MMg* 23/3-4 (1891):37-48; 53-60.

S ● Rietsch, Heinrich, ed. *DTÖ* 4 (II:2). Vienna: Artaria, 1895; reprint edition, Graz: Akademische Druck- und Verlagsanstalt.

T ● See **Strunk (1950)**:445-48.

T ● Cooper, Kenneth, and Zsako, Julius, trans. and ed. "Georg Muffat's Observations on the Lully Style of Performance." *MQ* 53/2 (1967):220-45; reprinted in Rosand (1985):Vol. 6, pp. 70-95. [*Rilm* 67-676.]

T ● Waite, Russell T. "A Translation of Georg Muffat's *Première Observations*." D.M.A. dissertation, The University of Washington, 1967. [*DA* 28/07A, p. 2724. UMI 67-14230.]

S ● See (1690):Kolneder (1970), above.

T ● See MacClintock (1979).

"Regulae concentuum partiturae"

> Ms., [copy dated 1699]. [Vienna: Minoritenkonvent.]

S ● ● ● ● Federhofer, Helmut, ed. *An Essay on Thoroughbass*. MSD, no. 4. Rome: American Institute of Musicology, 1961. Bibliog.

> Muffat's text is in German, while Federhofer's extensive Introduction is in English. Review in *Muzyka* 8/1-2 [28-29] (1963):213-14 (Adam Sutkowski).

Preface to *Außerlesener mit Ernst- und Lust-gemengter Instrumental-Music, Erste Versamblung* . . . /*Exquisitioris harmoniae instrumentalis gravi-jucundae selectus primus* . . . [*Rism* A/I/6, p. 280.]

> Passau: Maria Margaretha Höller, 1701.

S ● Luntz, Erwin, ed. *DTÖ* 23 (XI:2). Vienna: Artaria, 1904; reprint edition, Graz: Akademische Druck- und Verlagsanstalt, 1959.

> Review in *ZIMG* 5 (1903-4):365-68 (A. Schering).

T ● See **Strunk (1950)**:449-52.

S ● See (1690):Kolneder (1970), above.

"Nothwendige Anmerkungen bey der Musik"

> Ms. [Lost.]

LITERATURE:

Stollbrock, Ludwig. "Georg Muffat und sein *Florilegium* I." *MMg* 22/6 (1890):87-94.

Federhofer, Hellmut. "Muffat, Georg." In *MGG* (1949-68). Bibliog.

Walter, Rudolf. "Georg Muffat und sein *Apparatus musico-organisticus*." *MuA* 11/3 (1958-59):116-25.

Damp, Georg Edward. "The *Apparatus musico-organisticus* of Georg Muffat (1653-1704): A Study of Stylistic Synthesis and Aspects of Performance Practice." D.M.A. dissertation, The University of Rochester, 1973. [*Rilm* 74-2080. *DA* 34/05A, p. 2677. UMI 73-28176.]

Radulescu, Michael. "Die 12 Toccaten von Georg Muffat." In *Orgelsymposium Innsbruck 1979* (1980):169-84. Bibliog. [*Rilm* 80-2731.]

Wagner, Karl Friedrich. "Die Originalnotation des *Apparatus musico-organisticus* von Georg Muffat und ihr aufführungspraktischer Informationswert." In *Or-gelsymposium Innsbruck 1979* (1980):185-200. [*Rilm* 80-3732.]

Wollenberg, Susan. "Muffat, Georg." In *NGrove* (1980). Bibliog.

Stampfl, Inka. *Georg Muffat: Orchesterkompositionen. Ein musikhistorischer Vergleich der Orchestermusik 1670-1710.* Passau: Verlag Passavia, 1984.

> Reviews in *ÖM* 42/12 (1987):634 and *Orch* 33/6 (1985):614-15 (Rudolf Walter).

See also FÉTIS: (1833-44); FUX: Federhofer (1960); HEINICHEN: (1728):Buelow (1961/. . ./1986); RIEMANN: (1898); SAINT-LAMBERT: (1707): Burchill (1979); WALTHER: (1732); LITERATURE SUPPLEMENT: Atcherson (1973); Audbourg-Popin (1986); Babitz (1952), (1967/ 1969); Babitz and Pont (1973); Becker (1836-39/1964); Beyschlag (1907/1953); Burney (1776-89/. . ./1957); Byrt (1967); Chafe (1981); Chew (1980); Collins (1967); Dolmetsch (1915/. . ./1969); Donington (1980); Dotzauer (1976); Dreyfus (1987); Eitner (1900-1904/1959-60); Federhofer (1964); Fellerer (1927/. . ./1972); Flotzinger (1981); Gerber (1812-14/1966); Goldschmidt (1907); Harich-Schneider ([1939]/. . ./1970); Heimann (1970/1973); Hosler (1978/1981); Houle (1987); Jackson (1988); Kohlschütter (1979); Kooiman (1981); Mendel (1978); **Neumann**, Frederick (1965/. . ./**1982**), (1977/ **1982**), (1978), (1981/**1982**), [*Essays*] ● ● ● **(1982)**, (1988); Newman (1985); Norton (1984); Oberdoerffer (1967); O'Donnell (1979); Pacchioni (1983); Palisca [*Baroque*] (1968/1981); Reimer ["Concerto"] (1972-), ["Kenner"] (1972-); Rothgeb (1968); Rothschild (1953); Sirch (1981); Spitzer and Zaslaw (1986); Williams, P. (1970).

PABLO NASSARRE

[ca. 1654—1730]

Musical traditions did not evolve at the same pace throughout all of Europe. Spain, for example, retained Renaissance ideals of composition long after the chordal emphasis of figured bass had swept through much of the continent. It is thus difficult to evaluate Pablo Nassarre's comprehensive *Escuela música según la práctica moderna* (1723-24), a work which we might more comfortably regard as a product of the seventeenth century, or even, in some respects, the sixteenth. Nassarre himself claimed that his monumental, two-volume treatise was fifty years in the making. Certainly there was no need to discuss topics such as figured bass in a Spanish treatise if Spain remained isolated from those practices. Instead we find a wide array of materials ranging from plainsong and mathematical proportions to species counterpoint and tuning systems. This conservative perspective earned Nassarre the disdain of EXIMENO, whose scathing "Don Lazarillo Vizcardi" heaped abuses upon both Nassarre and CERONE.

Nassarre cited numerous authorities from both ancient and modern times, including Aristotle and SALINAS. His discussions of contemporary instruments, especially those with keyboard, and of the responsibilities of church musicians are particularly illuminating for modern readers. His smaller *Fragmentos músicos* (1683/1700), a popular composition manual, offers practical information without the large dose of speculation found in the later *Escuela*.

Fragmentos músicos: Reglas generales, y muy necessarias para canto llano, canto de órgano, contrapunto, y composición [*Rism* B/VI/2, p. 610.]

> Saragossa: Tomas Gaspar Martinez, 1683. [LCPS: N-005a.]

>> Expanded edition, as *Fragmentos músicos, repartidos en quatro tratados, en que se hallan reglas generales, y muy necessarias para canto llano . . .*:

> Madrid: Imprenta de música, 1700. Preface by Joseph de Torres. [LCPS: N-005b. HoM: 1058. SMLMS.]

T ● Forrester, Donald Williams. "Pablo Nasarre's *Fragmentos músicos*: Translation and Commentary." Ed.D. dissertation, The University of Geor-

gia, 1969. [*Rilm* 69-3632. *DA* 30/12A, p. 5468. UMI 70-10186.]

Escuela música según la práctica moderna . . . [*Rism* B/VI/2, p. 610.]

> Saragossa: herederos de Manuel Román, Impressor de la Universidad, 1723. Vol. 2. [LCPS: N-004. SMLMS.]
> Saragossa: herederos de Diego de Larumbe, 1724. Vol. 1. [LCPS: N-004. SMLMS.]

S ● Facsimile of both volumes. Saragossa: Portico librerias, 1980.

LITERATURE:

Querol, Miguel. "Nassarre, Pablo." Translated by Dorothea Schmidt-Preuß. In *MGG* (1949-68). Bibliog.

● ● ● Howell, Almonte C., Jr. "Pablo Nasarre's *Escuela música*: A Reappraisal." In *HaydonFs* (1969):80-108. Bibliog. [*Rilm* 69-1087.]

Forrester, Donald W. "Conducting Practice in the Spanish Polyphonic Choral Tradition: Implications for Modern Performers." *CJ* 15/2 (1974-75):7-8. [*Rilm* 75-2559.]

Howell, Almonte. "Nassarre, Pablo." In *NGrove* (1980). Bibliog.

Forrester, Donald W. "Pablo Nasarre's Contrapuntal Method." *Bach* 15/4 (1984):23-31.

See also EXIMENO: [1802-6]; Pedrell (1920); FÉTIS: (1833-44); OUSELEY: (1882); SOLER: (1765); LITERATURE SUPPLEMENT: Alette (1951); Anglés and Subirá (1946-51); **Apfel (1981)**; **Barbour (1951/. . ./1972)**; Becker (1836-39/1964); Cohen (1971); Eitner (1900-1904/1959-60); Forkel (1792/1962); Forrester (1973); Gerber (1790-92/1977); Howell (1972); Jackson (1988); León Tello (1974); **Lindley (1982)**, **(1984)**; Meer (1988); Parkins (1983); Pedrell (1888); Subirá (1947/. . ./1958), (1953).

JOHANN GEORG NEIDHARDT

[ca. 1685—1739]

When organists of the seventeenth century modulated on their instruments, they changed not only the tonal center, but also the subtle relationships among the various scale degrees. Depending upon how the instrument was tuned, certain keys would possess a noble purity in the sound of its basic triads, while others might be intolerable. This diversity of key characteristics was a powerful tool for expressing the affections, and the change of tonal center within the course of a composition had a more pronounced effect, especially to ears that were not, as ours are, conditioned to the modulatory freedom of more recent music. As composers became more daring, they inevitably confronted two basic facts: ascending four consecutive pure (3:2) fifths exceeds the result of ascending a compound pure (5:1) major third; and, ascending the full circle of twelve pure fifths exceeds an octave equivalent of the starting pitch. These differences, the syntonic comma and Pythagorean comma, respectively, were devastating to the success of the circle of fifths if an entire comma was positioned in one spot. Therefore attempts were made to alter, or temper, the tuning of a large number of intervals, each of which would accept a tolerable portion of the inconvenient but inevitable remainder. Equal temperament emerged as the ultimate solution to the dilemma, but during the early eighteenth century several authors, of whom WERCKMEISTER and Johann Georg Neidhardt were the most distinguished, devised reasonable alternatives to the colorless uniformity of our modern system.

Neidhardt's goal was to create methods for tempering the pitches in such a way that the full circle of fifths would be practicable, while at the same time permitting different keys to retain some individual character. Through the course of his numerous handbooks (1706-1734), he offered a wide variety of strategies, each of which spreads the departures from pure fifths in a different way. Typically the greatest divergences were positioned in those keys which require the most sharps or flats. Such temperaments are appropriate—even better suited than equal temperament, in the view of many—for compositions of the Baroque, including Bach's *Well-Tempered Clavier*.

Neidhardt faced a number of difficult mathematical and practical challenges. The precise way by which a comma should be divided was open to question. There were both arithmetic and geometric divisions to consider. Then, having created these theoretical models, the actual tuning of an organ required further skill, especially since tuning an organ pipe to a sound created on a monochord was more difficult than tuning one pipe to another. The equal division of the octave—for Neidhardt regarded equal temperament as a valid possibility—presented its own mathematical challenges, though one wonders if the six-digit tables which Neidhardt assembled after studying MERSENNE's and others' works on the subject could be put into practice with equivalent precision.

The study of Neidhardt's treatises reminds us that many temperaments were in use during the early eighteenth century, and that equal temperament was not necessarily the most popular of them. His own recommendations, in his *Sectio canonis harmonici* (1724), reveal that organs in village and town churches might typically tolerate greater degrees of inequality among keys than those in cities and at court. Among the many temperaments which he devised, he favored those which, while sharing the burden of hiding the comma among the various fifths, also produced the purest thirds in the most frequently used keys.

Beste und leichteste Temperatur des Monochordi, vermittelst welcher das heutiges Tages bräuchliche Genus diatonico-chromaticum also eingerichtet wird, dass alle Intervalla, nach gehöriger Proportion, einerley Schwebung überkommen, und sich daher die Modi regulares in alle und iede Claves, in einer angenehmen Gleichheit transponiren lassen . . . [Rism B/VI/2, pp. 611-12.]

    Jena: Johann Bielcke, 1706. [LCPS: N-009.]

Sectio canonis harmonici, zur völligen Richtigkeit der generum modulandi [Rism B/VI/2, p. 612.]

    Kaliningrad: Christoph Gottfried Eckart, 1724. [LCPS: N-011.]

Gäntzlich erschöpfte, mathematische Abtheilungen des diatonisch-chromatischen, temperirten Canonis Monochordi, alwo in unwiedersprechlichen Regeln und handgreiflichen Exempeln, gezeigt wird, wie alle Temperaturen zu erfinden, in Linien und Zahlen darzustellen, und aufzutragen seyn . . . [Rism B/VI/2, p. 612.]

    Kaliningrad: Christoph Gottfried Eckart, 1732. [LCPS: N-010.]
    Kaliningrad and Leipzig: Christoph Gottfried Eckart, 1734.

T ● *Canon monochordus, temperamenta generis diatonico-chromatici omnia arithmetice et geometrice edocens* . . . [Rism B/VI/2, p. 612.] Kaliningrad: Stelter, [1734 or 1735].

Systema generis diatonico-chromatici, ex numeris serie naturali procedentibus evolutum, atque temperamenti aequalis, quod terminis geometricae proportionis paret, calculo et usu comitatum [Rism B/VI/2, p. 612.]

    Kaliningrad: F. Reusner, 1734.

T ● *Beschaffenheit der diatonisch-chromatischen Oktave, aus der Ordnung der natürlichen Zahlen herbeigeführt.* [Rism B/VI/2, p. 611.] Kaliningrad: F. Reusner, 1734.

Compositio harmonica problematice tradita

    [Lost.]

T ● *Tractat von der Kompos. nach mathematischer Lehrart.* [Lost.]

LITERATURE:

Forchert, Arno. "Neidhardt, Johann Georg." In *MGG* (1949-68). Bibliog.

Adkins, Cecil. "Neidhardt, Johann Georg." In *NGrove* (1980). Bibliog.

Greenfield, Jack. "The Well-Tempered Keyboards of Bach and Neidhardt." *PTJ* 27 (1984):24-26.

See also ADLUNG: (1758); (1768); FÉTIS: (1833-44); MATTHESON: (1722-25):(1725); (1739); (1740); MERSENNE: Lindley (1980); SORGE: [1748]; WALTHER: (1732); LITERATURE SUPPLE-MENT: Ahlgrimm (1973); **Barbour** (1932), (1948), (1949-68), ● ● ● **(1951/. . ./1972)**; Becker (1836-39/1964); Blood (1979); **Buelow** ["Rhetoric"] **(1980)**; Bukofzer (1947); Dekker (1979); **Dahlhaus et al. (1987)**; Dupont (1933/. . ./1986); Eitner (1900-1904/1959-60); Forkel (1792/1962); Gerber (1790-92/1977), (1812-14/1966); Gernhardt (1977); Jackson (1988); Jorgensen (1978); Kelletat [*Temperatur*] (1960), ["Tonordnung"] (1960); **Lindley** ["Temperaments"] **(1980)**, (1985), (1988); Meer (1988); Nelson (1984); Rasch (1981), (1983).

FRIEDRICH ERHARD NIEDT

[bapt. 1674 – 1708]

The slower pace at which new ideas were propagated in former times led to a more varied musical scene in Europe. While Italian keyboardists had absorbed and become proficient in figured-bass practice, many of their German counterparts, particularly organists in the smaller villages, were mired in the complexities of tablature, from which improvisational genius was less likely to flow. Friedrich Erhard Niedt sought to remedy the situation by sharing of his knowledge through his three-volume *Musicalische Handleitung* (1700-1717), wherein the priority of attaining a solid grounding in figured-bass realization is firmly established. J. S. Bach was among Niedt's readers, it appears, for the notes of one of Bach's pupils, Carl August Thieme, bear a direct relationship to Part 1 of the *Handleitung*.

Following the examples of KUHNAU and PRINTZ, Niedt used prose narrative as a vehicle for influencing the pedagogical direction the reader might take. The story of a group of musicians performing, drinking, and discussing music in a woodland setting occupies a large portion of Part 1 of the *Handleiting*. After many hours of convivial interaction, the party agrees that organ tablature takes years to master and does not foster the same level of musical proficiency as the easier, but at that time still novel, thoroughbass practice. Niedt proceeded by exploring the basic skills of that tradition in Part 1, developing the notion further in Part 2 with a discussion of improvisation over a figured bass. The third part of the work, devoted to counterpoint and traditional types of Baroque composition (including motet, chorale, and recitative style), owes its dissemination to MATTHESON, who edited it for publication after Niedt's death. MATTHESON also undertook an extensive revision of Part 2 for an edition published in 1721.

Musicalische Handleitung; oder, gründlicher Unterricht . . . [*Rism* B/VI/2, pp. 616-17.]

1) *Handelt vom General-Baß, denselben schlechtweg [schlichtweg] zu spielen*

2) *Handleitung zur Variation, wie man den General-Baß, und darüber gesetzte Zahlen variiren, artige Inventiones machen, und aus einen schlechten [schlichten] General-Baß Praeludia, Ciaconen, Allemanden, Couranten, Sarabanden, Menueten, Giguen und dergleichen leichtlich verfertigen könne samt andern nötigen Instructionen*

3) *Handlend vom Contra-Punct, Canon, Motetten, Choral, Recitativ-Stylo und Cavaten . . .*

Hamburg: Nicolaus Spieringk, 1700. Vol. 1.
Hamburg: Benjamin Schiller, 1706. Vol. 2. [LCPS: N-025a. SMLMS.]
Hamburg: Benjamin Schiller, 1710. Vol. 1. [LCPS: N-024. SMLMS.]
Hamburg: Benjamin Schillers Erben, 1717. Vol. 3. Edited by MATTHESON. [LCPS: N-025c. SMLMS.]

　As *Von der Variation des General-Baßes . . .*, revised by MATTHESON:

Hamburg: Benjamin Schillers Wittwe & Johann Christoph Kißner, 1721. Vol. 2. [LCPS: N-025b.]

S ● Thieme, Carl August. [Formerly attributed to Johann Peter Kellner.] "Vorschriften und Grundsätze zum vierstimmigen Spielen des General-Baß oder Accompagnement . . ." Ms., 1738. [Brussels: Conservatoire royal de musique, Bibliothèque.] Published in Philipp Spitta's *Johann Sebastian Bach* (2 vols., Leipzig: Breitkopf & Härtel, 1873-80; later editions; English edition (translated by Clara Bell and J. A. Fuller-Mait-land), London: Novello Ewer, & Co., 1884-85; later editions, including New York: Dover Publications, 1951).

T ● See **Strunk (1950)**:453-70.

S ● Facsimile of the 1710, 1717, and 1721 editions. Bo, no. 32. Buren, The Netherlands: Frits Knuf, 1976.

> Review in *ISOI* 18 (1978):79 (Maarten A. Vente).

T ● ● ● Poulin, Pamela L., trans. and ed.; and Taylor, Irmgard C., trans. *The Musical Guide: Parts I (1700/1710), II (1721), and III (1717)*. Oxford: Clarendon Press; New York: Oxford University Press, 1988. Bibliog.

Musicalisches A B C zum Nutzen der Lehr- und Lernenden [*Rism* B/VI/2, p. 617.]

> Hamburg: Benjamin Schiller, 1708. [LCPS: N-026.]

LITERATURE:

Chrysander, Friedrich. "Ein alter deutscher Tonlehrer, Friedrich Erhard Niedt." *AmZ* 12/35-36 (1877):551-56; 566-73.

Spitta, Philipp. "Der Tractat über den Generalbaß und F. Niedts *Musikalische Handleitung*." In his *Musikgeschichtliche Aufsätze*, pp. 121-28. Berlin: Paetel, 1894; reprint edition, Hildesheim: Georg Olms, 1976.

Oberdörffer, Fritz. "Niedt, Friedrich Erhard." In *MGG* (1949-68). Bibliog.

Sietz, Reinhold. "Friedrich Erhardt Niedt: Gegen den gesaltzenen, gespickten und gebratenen Contra-Punct." *Mleb* 5/1 (1952):15-16.

Gerstenberg, Walter. "Generalbaßlehre und Kompositionstechnik in Niedts *Musikalischer Handleitung*." In Osthoff (1954):152-55.

● ● ● Buelow, George J. "Niedt, Friedrich Erhard." In *NGrove* (1980).

> Review in *MQ* 68/2 (1982):161-81 (Allen Forte).

Sachs, Klaus-Jürgen. "Die 'Anleitung . . ., auff allerhand Arth einen Choral durchzuführen', als Paradigma der Lehre und der Satzkunst Johann Sebastian Bachs." *AfMw* 37/2 (1980):135-54. Bibliog. [*Rilm* 80-485.]

Espinosa, Alma. "More on the Figured-Bass Accompaniment in Bach's Time: Friedrich Erhard Niedt and *The Musical Guide*." *Bach* 12/1 (1981):13-20.

See also FÉTIS: (1833-44); (1840); HERBST: Allerup (1931); KIRNBERGER: Borris (1933); MATTHESON: Werts (1985); RIEMANN: (1898); WALTHER: (1732); LITERATURE SUPPLEMENT: ● ● ● Arnold (1931/. . ./1965); Becker (1836-39/1964); **Benary (1956/1961)**, (1963); Braun (1970); Buelow (1972); Bukofzer (1947); **Coover (1980)**; Dammann (1958/1967); David and Mendel (1945/1966); Donington (1963/. . ./1974); Dreyfus (1987); Eggebrecht (1955); Eitner (1900-1904/1959-60); Feil (1955); Fischer (1957); Forkel (1792/1962); Frobenius ["Vollstimmig"] (1972-); Gerber (1812-14/1966); Gurlitt (1954/1966); Heimann (1970/1973); Jackisch (1966); Jackson (1988); Jenne (1973-74); Kauko (1958); Keller (1931/. . ./1966); Krummacher (1979); **Lester (1978)**, **(1989)**; Maier (1984); Mallard (1978); McIntyre (1965); Mendel (1955), (1978); Nelson (1984); Newman (1959/. . ./1983); North (1987); Oberdoerffer (1949-68), (1967); **Ritzel (1967/1968)**; Rogers (1955); Rohwer (1949-68); Sachs (1972-); Schulenberg ● ● ● (1982), (1984); Sheldon (1982); **Shirlaw (1917/. . ./1970)**; Sisman (1978); Tenney (1988); Todd (1983); Ulrich (1931/1932); Walker (1987); Werts (1983); Wienpahl (1953); Williams, P. (1970); Wirth (1966); Zenck (1942); Zinar (1983).

GUILLAUME GABRIEL NIVERS

[ca. 1632 – 1714]

Guillaume Gabriel Nivers, Master of Music to the Queen, wrote not for the beginner but for the serious student of composition. He classified intervals as true (major, minor, and perfect) or false (diminished and augmented) and cadences as perfect (as when the bass descends by perfect fifth or a major sixth expands out to the octave), imperfect (with bass descending by perfect fourth), or deceptive (in which one or both parts avoid their natural conclusion). His treatises covered topics such as Gregorian chant, intervals, modes, cadences, fugue, continuo playing, realizing figured basses, part-writing, and contrapuntal rules (of which he offered sixteen). He supplied many tonal answers for fugue subjects. As a composer, he was an important figure in the French organ school of the period.

"Observations sur le toucher et jeu de l'orgue"

> In *Livre d'orgue contenant cent pieces de tous les tons de l'eglise* [*Rism* A/I/6, p. 334; B/VI/2,

p. 619.]. Paris: the author and Robert Ballard (Luders), 1665.

> Reprinted in 1667.

S ● Dufourcq, Norbert, ed. Reprint edition with transcriptions. Paris: Bornemann, 1963.

Méthode facile pour apprendre à chanter la musique [*Rism* B/VI/2, p. 620.]

> Attributed also to Charles Le Maire.

> Paris: Robert Ballard, 1666.

> > Reprinted in 1670 and 1696.

Traité de la composition de musique [*Rism* B/VI/2, p. 620.]

> Paris: the author and Robert Ballard, 1667. [LCPS: N-031. HoM: 1075. IDC.]
> Paris: Christophe Ballard, 1712.

ST ● Roger, Estienne, trans. *Traitté de la composition de musique/Tractaat van de saamenstellinge der sangkunst*. Amsterdam: J. L. de Lorme & E. Roger, 1697. [*Rism* B/VI/2, p. 620. HoM: 1076. IDC.]

> Text in French and Flemish.

T ● ● ● ● Cohen, Albert, trans. and ed. *Treatise on the Composition of Music*. MTT, no. 3. Brooklyn: Institute of Mediaeval Music, 1961; reprint edition, Henryville, Pa.: n.d.

Dissertation sur le chant grégorien [*Rism* B/VI/2, p. 619.]

> Paris: the author and Christophe Ballard, 1683. [LCPS: N-030a. HoM: 1073.]

"L'art d'accompagner sur la basse continue pour l'orgue et le clavecin"

> In his *Motets à voix seule* . . . [*Rism* A/I/6, p. 334.]. Paris: the author (Ballard), 1689.

> > Further editions through 1741.

Méthode certaine pour apprendre le pleinchant de l'église [*Rism* B/VI/2, p. 619.]

> Paris: Christophe Ballard, 1698 or 99.

> > Other printings through 1749, including:

> Paris: Christophe Ballard, 1711. [HoM: 1074.]

Paris: Jean-Baptiste-Christophe Ballard, 1745. [LCPS: N-030b.]

LITERATURE:

Garros, Madeleine. "Nivers, Guillaume-Gabriel." Translated by Dorothea Schmidt-Preuß. In *MGG* (1949-68). Bibliog.

Garros, Madeleine. "L'art d'accompagner sur la basse-continue d'après Guillaume-Gabriel Nivers." In *MassonFs* (1955):II:43-51.

Howell, Almonte C., Jr. "French Baroque Organ Music and the Eight Church Tones." *JAMS* 11/2-3 (1958):106-18.

Beechey, Gwilym. "Guillaume Gabriel Nivers (1632-1714): His Organ Music and His *Traité de la composition*." *Consort* 25 (1968-69):373-83. [*Rilm* 69-3585.]

Pruitt, William. "Bibliographies des œuvres de Guillaume Gabriel Nivers." *Rmfc* 13 (1973):133-56. Bibliog. [*Rilm* 73-2899.]

Howell, Almonte. "Nivers, Guillaume Gabriel." In *NGrove* (1980). Bibliog.

Gorenstein, N. "G.-G. Nivers: Un repère historique fausse par l'histoire." *Trorg* 37/4 (1985):1-10.

Pruitt, William. "A Seventeenth-Century French Manuscript on Organ Performance." *EM* 14/2 (1986):237-51.

See also FÉTIS: (1833-44); LOULIÉ: Semmens (1984); RIEMANN: (1898); SAINT-LAMBERT: (1707):Burchill (1979); WALTHER: (1732); LITERATURE SUPPLEMENT: **Apfel (1981)**; Atcherson (1973); Becker (1836-39/1964); Beiche ["Inversio"] (1972-); Cohen (1966/1978), (1971), ["Symposium"] (1972); Eitner (1900-1904/1959-60); Forkel (1792/1962); Gerber (1790-92/1977), (1812-14/1966); Hall (1975); Harich-Schneider ([1939]/. . ./1970); Hawkins (1776/. . ./1969); Horsley [*Fugue: History*] (1966); Kleinman (1971/1974); Kooiman (1980), (1981); Lange (1899-1900); **Lester (1989)**; Lewis (1975/1978); **Lindley (1984)**; **Mann (1955/. . ./1987)**; Mendel (1978); **Neumann**, Frederick (1978), [*Essays*] **(1982)**, (1988); Sachs (1972-), (1984); **Seidel and Cooper (1986)**; Soderlund (1980); Subirá (1947/. . ./1958); Taddie (1984); Tolkoff (1973); Troeger (1987).

FRANCIS NORTH

[bapt. 1637 – 1685]

Not all attempts at elucidating music's foundations came from professional musicians, as Francis North's *Philosophical Essay* (1677) attests. North (whose brother and biographer Roger NORTH was also drawn to musical speculations) practiced law, served in Parliament, and eventually attained the title Lord Keeper of the Great Seal. He composed, played the bass viol, and, despite limited vocal endowment, enjoyed singing.

His lordship's brief *Essay* advances a geometric perspective for the notion of consonance. It was noted by several prominent English scientists, including Newton and WALLIS, and was to influence the musical writings of HOLDER. North created a grid of parallel lines to show the relationship among vibrations of various pitches. These lines represented pulses, too swiftly passing to be individually perceived. Consonant intervals display a degree of coordination among their pulses. For example, every second pulse of a pitch an octave above a bass would coincide with the bass's pulse. Experimentation upon a monochord confirmed for North that his formulation was correct. The exactitude of his presentation stimulated further attempts at codifying the nature of consonance and dissonance, which, as his brother remarked, "every one is sensible of . . . but scarce any know why or by what means they are produced."

A Philosophical Essay of Musick Directed to a Friend [*Rism* B/VI/2, p. 621.]

Published anonymously.

London: John Martyn, 1677. [LCPS: N-034.]

See NORTH, R.: ["Some Notes"] [before ca. 1703].

LITERATURE:

NORTH, Roger. *The Life of . . . Francis North, Baron of Guilford . . .* BSL. London: John Whiston, 1742; various later editions (including that edited by Augustus Jessopp, London: George Bell & Sons, 1890).

See also NORTH, R.: Selected Writings (1959).

Dale, Sir Henry H., ed. "A Hitherto Unpublished Letter of Isaac Newton." *HMYB* 2-3 (1945-46):400-403.

Wilson, John. "North, Francis." Translated by Hans Haase. In *MGG* (1949-68). Bibliog.

Wilson, John. "North, Francis." In *NGrove* (1980). Bibliog.

See also FÉTIS: (1833-44); HOLDER: Stanley (1983); NORTH, R.: [ca. 1698-ca. 1703]:Chan and Kassler (1986); Wilson (1959); LITERATURE SUPPLEMENT: Becker (1836-39/1964); Burney (1776-89/. . ./1957); Chenette (1967); Eitner (1900-1904/ 1959-60); Forkel (1792/1962); Gerber (1812-14/1966); Gouk (1980), (1981-82), (1982); Hawkins (1776/. . ./ 1969); **Kassler (1979)**; Kassler and Oldroyd (1983); Lewis (1981); Miller (1960); Miller and Cohen (1987); Randall (1981); Ruff (1970); **Seidel and Cooper (1986)**.

ROGER NORTH

[ca. 1651 – 1734]

Unlike most other authors on music, Roger North held no professional position as a musician. He was embarked upon a distinguished career in government when political circumstances in Britain forced him to retire from public life in 1688. His remaining years were devoted to writing for his own pleasure and for his family's education. Music was one of his favorite topics: some two thousand pages of manuscript survive. Though much of the musical material has been published in excerpts, only now is a critical edition of North's writings being undertaken, and that only tentatively.

Like his elder brother Francis NORTH, Roger was fascinated by the science of music. The generation of sound through motion of an elastic body and its transmission through air were topics upon which he devoted considerable attention throughout his writings. His study led him both in the direction of aesthetics, where the physical characteristics of sounds influenced their "goodness," and compositional practice, where his study of pitch led him to an inversion theory antedating that of RAMEAU.

North fervently supported the lifestyle of the country gentleman, whose family obligations afforded ample opportunities for amateur music performance. He disparaged the concerts and opera productions of the city, dismissing them as fit only for "idle people." Through his ambitious program of self-development, he attained a remarkably sophisticated perspective on the art of music. Yet he neglected to establish a mechanism whereby his observations could be transmitted to other serious students of the art.

Various untitled manuscripts

Mss., [ca. 1690-1726]. [London: British Library, Reference Division.]

S ● See Selected Writings (1959), below.

"Some M[emoran]dums, concerning Musick"

Ms., [completed ca. 1695-1701]. [London: British Library, Reference Division.]

A source for parts of North's "Cursory Notes of Musicke," below.

"Cursory Notes of Musicke . . ."

> Ms., [ca. 1698-ca. 1703]. [Rougham Hall, King's Lynn, Norfolk, Great Britain: Library of the late Robert North (d. 1985).]

> S ● ● ● ● Chan, Mary, and Kassler, Jamie C., eds. *Roger North's "Cursory Notes of Musicke" (c. 1698-c. 1703): A Physical, Psychological and Critical Theory*. Kensington, N.S.W., Australia: Unisearch, 1986. Bibliog.

>> Reviews in *EM* 15/3 (1987):401-3 (Barry Cooper), *Isis* 79/297 (1988):347-48 (Thomas Christensen), *ML* 68/3 (1987):271-72 (Penelope Gouk), and *The Organ* 67/264 (1988):94.

"Notes of Me"

> Ms., [before 1703]. [London: British Library, Reference Division.]

> S ● Jessopp, Augustus, ed. *Autobiography of the Hon. Roger North*. London: David Nutt; Norwich: A. H. Goose & Co., 1887; reprint edition, see NORTH, F.: NORTH, R.: (1742):(1890).

>> Review in *EHR* 3/9 (1888):174-78 (Osmund Airy).

> S ● See Selected Writings (1959), below.

"Some Notes upon an Essay of Musick Printed, 1677, by Way of Comment and Ammendment"

> Ms., [before ca. 1703]. [London: British Library, Reference Division.]

>> Pertains to NORTH, F.: (1677).

Annotations to Capt. Prencourt's "Short, Easy, and Plaine Rules to Learne in a Few Days the Principles of Musick" and "The Treatis of the Continued or Thro-Base"

> Mss., [ca. 1710]. [London: British Library, Reference Division.]

> S ● See Selected Writings (1959), below.

> S ● Chan, Mary, and Kassler, Jamie C., eds. Forthcoming.

"An Essay of Musicall Ayre, Tending Cheifly to Shew the Foundations of Melody Joyned with Harmony . . ."

> Ms., [ca. 1715-20]. [London: British Library, Reference Division.]

> S ● See Selected Writings (1959), below.

> S ● Stinson, John. "Roger North's 'Essay of Musicall Ayre': An Edition . . . with Introduction and Com-

mentary." Master's essay, Australian National University, [in progress as of 1979].

> S ● Chan, Mary, and Kassler, Jamie C., eds. Forthcoming.

"The Theory of Sounds Taking Rise from the First Principles of Action That Affect the Sense of Hearing, and Giving Phisicall Solutions of Tone, Harmony, and Discord . . ."

> Mss., [ca. 1715-26]; revised 1726; revised (as "Theory of Sounds Shewing the Genesis, Propagation, Augmentation, and Application of Them . . ."), 1728. [London: British Library, Reference Division.]

> S ● See Selected Writings (1959), below.

> S ● Chan, Mary, and Kassler, Jamie C., eds. *Roger North's "The Musical Grammarian" and "Theory of Sounds."* Kensington, N.S.W., Australia: New South Wales University Press, 1988.

>> Review in *MT* 130/1756 (1989):348 (Penelope Gouk).

"The Musicall Gramarian; or, A Practick Essay upon Harmony, Plain and Artificiall, with Notes of Comparison between the Elder and Later Musick, and Somewhat Historicall of Both"

> Ms., [ca. 1726]. [London: British Library, Reference Division.]

>> As "The Musicall Grammarian, Being a Scientifick Essay upon the Practise of Musick":

> Ms., 1728. [Hereford: Cathedral Library.]

> S ● Andrews, Hilda, ed. *Roger North's Musicall Gramarian*. Foreword by Sir Richard Terry. London: Oxford University Press (Humphrey Milford), [pref. 1925].

> S ● See Selected Writings (1959), below.

> S ● See MacClintock (1979).

> S ● See [ca. 1715-26]:Chan and Kassler (1988), above.

"Memoires of Musick, being Some Historico-Critticall Collections of That Subject"

> Ms., 1728. [Hereford: Cathedral Library.]

> S ● Rimbault, Edward Francis, ed. *Memoirs of Musick, by the Hon. Roger North . . . Now First Printed from the Original Ms. and Edited, with Copious Notes*. London: George Bell, 1846; facsimile edition, New York: AMS Press.

S ● See Selected Writings (1959), below.

S ● See MacClintock (1979).

See also NORTH, F.: NORTH, R.: (1742).

More detailed accounts of North's numerous writings are found in [ca. 1698-ca. 1703]:Chan and Kassler (1986), above, and in Kassler (1979).

SELECTED WRITINGS:

● ● ● Wilson, John, ed. *Roger North on Music, Being a Selection from His Essays Written during the Years c. 1695-1728*. London: Novello, 1959. Bibliog.

> Reviews in *CanMJ* 6/2 (1961-62):73-76 (George Falle), *GSJ* 14 (1961):80-81 (James A. MacGillivray), *MEv* 15 (1960):29, *Mf* 16/2 (1963):191-92 (Carl Dahlhaus), *ML* 41/2 (1960):176-77 (J. A. Westrup), *MO* 83/988 (1960):257-59 (H. H.), *MR* 22/1 (1961):64-65 (G. Abraham), *MT* 100/1402 (1959):662-63 (Franklin B. Zimmerman), and *Notes* 17/2 (1959-60):227-28 (Henry Leland Clarke).

LITERATURE:

Bridge, Frederick. "A Seventeenth-Century View of Musical Education." *PMA 1900-1901* 27 (1901):121-30.

> Responses by A. H. D. Prendergast, Thomas Lea Southgate, Jas. S. Shedlock, Charles Maclean, and Frederick Bridge.

Venn, Lyn. "Roger North and the 'Memoires of Musick'." *MO* 42/503 (1918-19):687-88.

Pulver, Jeffrey. "North's 'Memoires of Musick'." *MT* 66/989 (1925):594-96.

Pulver, Jeffrey. "Unpaid Debts: V. Roger North." *MN* 72/1814 (1927):8-9.

Wilson, John. "North, Francis . . .; Roger." Translated by Hans Haase. In *MGG* (1949-68). Bibliog.

Mackerness, E. D. "A Speculative Dilettante." *ML* 34/3 (1953):236-42.

Sommerset, H. V. F. "Roger North on Music in Education." *MMR* 83/951 (1953):231-35.

Burton, Martin C. "Mr. Prencourt and Roger North on Teaching Music." *MQ* 44/1 (1958):32-39.

Wilson, John. "North, Roger." In *NGrove* (1980). Bibliog.

Korsten, F. J. M. "Roger North (1651–1734), Virtuoso and Essayist: A Study of His Life and Ideas, Followed by an Annotated Edition of a Selection of His Unpublished Essays." Thesis, The University of Nijmegen, 1981; published edition, Amsterdam: APA–Holland University Press, 1981. Bibliog.

> Review in *NQ* 30/1 [228] (1983):80-81 (Peter Millard).

Hine, Janet, ed., with Mary Chan and Jamie C. Kassler. *Roger North's Writings on Music to c. 1703: A Set of Analytical Indexes, with Digests of Manuscripts*. Kensington, N.S.W., Australia: School of English, University of New South Wales, 1986.

> Reviews in *Isis* 79/297 (1988):347-48 (Thomas Christensen), *ML* 70/1 (1989):96 (Penelope Gouk), *Mus* 10 (1987):81-83, and *The Organ* 67/264 (1988):94.

See also FÉTIS: (1833-44); LITERATURE SUPPLEMENT: Allen ["Philosophies"] (1939); Babitz (1967/1969); Babitz and Pont (1973); Becker (1836-39/1964); Boomgaarden (1985/1987); Burney (1776-89/. . ./1957); Butler (1977); Chenette (1967); **Dahlhaus** ["Untersuchungen"] (1966/. . ./1988), ["Harmony"] **(1980)**; **Dahlhaus et al. (1987)**; Dean (1977); Donington (1963/. . ./1974); Eitner (1900-1904/1959-60); Forkel (1792/1962); Fuller (1977); Gerber (1812-14/1966); Gouk (1982); Green (1969); Hancock (1977); Hawkins (1776/. . ./1969); Jackson (1988); **Kassler** ● ● ● **(1979)**; Kassler and Oldroyd (1983); Kivy (1980); Larsson (1980); Lawrence (1978); Lewis (1975/1978); **Neumann, Frederick (1978), (1981/1982), [*Essays*] (1982)**; Newman (1985); Oberdoerffer (1967); O'Donnell (1979); Pulver (1927/. . ./1973); Randall (1981); Robison (1982); Ruf (1972-); Ruff (1970); **Seidel and Cooper (1986)**; Spitzer and Zaslaw (1986); Stowell (1985); Troeger (1987); Williams, P. ["Harpsichord"] (1968), (1970).

JOHANNES NUCIUS

[ca. 1556-63 – 1620]

The facets of compositional practice which an author chooses to emphasize give a hint of the trends in musical style and in pedagogy at a given time. In 1613, when Johannes Nucius's *Musices poeticae* was published, the study of counterpoint retained, for many, a close alliance with sixteenth-century practice, while the works of many composers of earlier generations were venerated. Countering the recent innovation of allowing the bass to control the structure of a composition, Nucius advocated the time-honored practice of starting with the tenor and soprano. The requisite considerations of consonance and dissonance, cadential formulae, and the modes and their affective characters are all to be found, yet they are enlivened with the notion of an alliance between text and music via rhetorical devices. Though not as detailed as BURMEISTER's earlier formulations, Nucius created seven specific types of rhetorical usage, such as melodic imitation, repetition, and unexpected silence. His work was of singular importance to THURINGUS, whose *Opusculum bipartitum* (1624) drew abundantly from Nucius as well as from other sources.

Musices poeticae sive de compositione cantûs: Praeceptiones absolutissimae nunc primùm [*Rism* B/VI/2, p. 623.]

Nisa, Poland: Crispinus Scharffenberg, 1613.

S ● Facsimile edition. Leipzig: Zentralantiquariat der Deutschen Demokratischen Republik, 1976.

> Review in *JLH* 23 (1979):183-86 (Konrad Ameln).

LITERATURE:

Starke, Reinhold. "Johannes Nux (Nucis oder Nucius)." *MMg* 36/12 (1904):195-209. Bibliog.

Widmann, Bernhard. "Johann Nucius, Abt von Himmelwitz: Ein Altmeister der klassischen Polyphonie." *CistC* 32/371, 374-75, 378-81 (1920):1-4, 49-51, 70-74, 113-22, 132-36, 150-55, 161-63.

Rubsamen, Walter H. "Nucius, Johannes." Translated by Helene Wessely. In *MGG* (1949-68). Bibliog.

Feldmann, Fritz. "Musiktheoretiker in eigenen Kompositionen: Untersuchungen am Werk des Tinctoris, Adam von Fulda und Nucius." *DJbMw* 1 (1956):39-65. Bibliog.

● ● ● Buelow, George J. "Nucius, Johannes." In *NGrove* (1980). Bibliog.

Nishihara, Minoru. "Ongaku to shujigaku—Nucius to 17 seiki no musica poetica." *Og* 27/1 (1982):35-47. [*Rilm* 82-406.]

See also FÉTIS: (1833-44); KIRCHER: (1650); LIPPIUS: Rivera (1974/1980); MATTHESON: (1722-25):Vol. 1 (1722-23); PRAETORIUS: (1614-20); THURINGUS: (1624); WALTHER: (1732); LITERATURE SUPPLEMENT: **Apfel (1981)**; Audbourg-Popin (1984); Bartel (1982/1985); Becker (1836-39/1964); Brandes (1935); Braun (1986); **Buelow** (1972), ["Rhetoric"] **(1980)**; Bukofzer (1947); **Bullivant (1980)**; Butler (1980); Cahn ["Repercussio"] (1972-), ["Transitus"] (1972-); Dahlhaus ["Untersuchungen"] (1966/. . ./ 1988); Dammann (1958/1967); Eggebrecht (1955); Eitner (1900-1904/1959-60); Feldmann (1958); Fellerer (1983); Ferand (1951); Flindell (1983-84); Forkel (1792/1962); Frobenius ["Isotonos"] (1972-); Gerber (1812-14/1966); Gissel (1980/1983), (1986); Gurlitt (1942/1966); Harrán (1986); Hawkins (1776/. . ./1969); Hein (1954); Hüschen (1986); Kirkendale (1979), (1984); Krützfeldt (1961); Leuchtmann (1957/1959); Lindley (1982); **Mann (1955/. . ./1987)**; Meier (1974/ 1988); Müller-Blattau (1923/. . ./1963); Rauhe (1959-60); Rivera (1984); Robbins (1938); Ruhnke (1949-68); Sachs (1972-); Schering (1908); Unger (1941/1969); Walker (1987); Ziebler (1933).

ARTHUR JOACHIM VON OETTINGEN

[1836–1920]

The unrelentingly empirical perspective of HELM-HOLTZ fostered the belief that the minor mode was an altered form of major—that only the latter was inherent in the overtone series and that it therefore served as the foundation for both modal possibilities. Within three years of HELM-HOLTZ's *Lehre von den Tonempfindung*, Arthur Joachim von Oettingen published his first monograph espousing a dualistic view of major and minor, his *Harmoniesystem in dualer Entwickelung* (1866). To be sure, the notion of minor as some sort of mirror inversion of major had been advanced by RAMEAU and had recently resurfaced in the writings of HAUPTMANN. Oettingen, a scientist, developed a methodology for such a perspective and offered it in several publications from the *Harmoniesystem* of 1866 through the rigorously systematic "Grundlage der Musikwissenschaft und das duale Reininstrument" of 1916. His most passionate convert was Hugo RIEMANN, whose unabashed advocacy of an undertone series extended the theory further than Oettingen was willing to take it himself.

Oettingen based his system upon two incontrovertible facts: the pitches C, E, and G are overtones of a common pitch C two octaves lower; and, the pitches C, E-flat, and G are common fundamentals for an overtone G two octaves higher. From this symmetrical relationship, Oettingen established a system segmented into tonality (for major) and phonality (for minor). Note that despite the symmetry, the two components are not equivalent: whereas the tonic E and G are *derived from* C, it cannot be claimed that the phonic E-flat and C are likewise derived from G. The *Tonika* C has a third and fifth, while the *Phonika* G *is* a third (of E-flat) and fifth (of C).

In keeping with the opposition in direction between tonality and phonality, what we generally call "C minor" was classified as a chord dependent upon G and notated as g°, in contrast to the notation of C major as c⁺. Whereas a *Tonika* (e.g., c⁺) possessed *Dominante* (g⁺) and *Unterdominante* (f⁺) chords, the *Phonika* (e.g., g°) was supported by a *Regnante* (c°) and *Oberregnante* (d°). Oettingen could not, however, counter the fact that in both major and minor, composers tended to proceed from I through IV to V, rather than, in minor, I-V-IV. He displayed little interest in what composers elected to do.

Oettingen's system, like that of HAUPTMANN, is dependent upon just intonation, and his musical notation accommodated many subtle differentiations. At the back of *Das duale Harmoniesystem* one finds a diagram showing fifty-three pitches per octave, arranged on fifty-seven keys. Indeed, his writings incorporate a number of charts showing pitch relationships in fascinating arrays. One suspects that they are derived from pure speculation, rather than from an observation of compositional practice. This was, however, the era of composer/theorists such as Reger and SCHOENBERG. Oettingen's perspective maps a plethora of chordal interrelationships at the very time when the more restrictive patterns of chordal succession were crumbling.

Harmoniesystem in dualer Entwickelung: Studien zur Theorie der Musik

Dorpat and Leipzig: W. Gläser, 1866.

Neue rationelle Gesangschule, by O. Sefferi.

Translated by Oettingen.

Leipzig: J. H. Zimmermann, 1894.

Reprinted in 1897.

"Das duale System der Harmonie"

AdN 1 (1902):62-75; 2 (1903):375-403; 3 (1904):241-69; 4 (1905):116-36, 301-38; 5 (1906):449-503.

Das duale Harmoniesystem

Leipzig: C. F. W. Siegel's Musikalienhandlung (R. Linnemann), 1913.

"Die Grundlage der Musikwissenschaft und das duale Reininstrument"

AKSGW 34/2 (1916):155-361 (Leipzig: B. G. Teubner, 1917).

LITERATURE:

Dahlhaus, Carl. "Oettingen, Arthur Joachim von." In *MGG* (1949-68).

Vogel, Martin. "Arthur v. Oettingen und der harmonische Dualismus." In Vogel (1966):103-32. Bibliog.

Tokawa, Seicchi. ["Oettingen's System of Harmony."] In *NomuraFs* (1969):276-95. [*Rilm* 70-1150.]

Schubert, Giselher. "Zur Kritik der Musiktheorie." *ZfMt* 2/1 (1971):35-37. [*Rilm* 71-1515.]

Keller, Wilhelm. "Die Modulationen in Mozarts Fantasie KV 475." In *ValentinFs* (1976):79-88. [*Rilm* 76-15549.]

● ● ● Hoffman, Mark. "Oettingen, Arthur Joachim von." In *NGrove* (1980).

See also d'INDY: (1903-50); RIEMANN: (1898); (1905); Wuensch (1977); LITERATURE SUPPLEMENT: Abbado (1964); Albersheim (1980); Billeter (1970/1971); Blumröder (1972-); Cavallini (1949); Cazden (1948); Chailley (1967); Chevaillier (1925/1931-32); Chew (1980); **Dahlhaus** ["Konsonanz"] (1949-68), ["Tonsystem"] (1949-68), ["Über"] (1966), ["Untersuchungen"] (1966/. . ./

1988), ["Relationes"] (1975), **(1984)**; ● ● ● Devore (1987); Fillmore (1887); Fox Strangways (1923); Gut (1972-); Hartmann (1923); Hoffman (1953); Imig (1969/1970); Jacobi (1957-60/1971); Jeppesen ([1951]/1952); Jones (1934); Jorgenson (1957), (1963); Kauko (1958); Kayser (1950); Lang (1941); Lewin (1982); McCredie (1968); Münnich

(1909/1965); Perinello (1936); Révész (1946/. . ./ 1954); Rohwer (1949-68); Rummenhöller (1967); **Shirlaw (1917/. . ./1970)**, (1931); Snyder (1980-81); Taddie (1984); Thürlings (1877); Vogel (1955/1954), (1962), (1975/1984), (1976); **Wason (1981/1985)**; Wellek (1949-68).

ANDREAS ORNITHOPARCHUS

[born ca. 1490]

One sign of a book's significance is the degree to which it resonates even generations after its first appearance. Like the volumes by GLAREAN and ZARLINO, Ornithoparchus's *Musicae activae micrologus* (1517) served as an authoritative guide for later authors, including BERMUDO and SEBASTIANI, just as Ornithoparchus himself had relied on existing sources, particularly Boethius, Tinctoris, and Gaffurio. In addition to offering an effective, concise summary of contrapuntal rules, Ornithoparchus touched upon a range of other topics, including mensural theory, the chanting of scripture, and singing. Yet unlike dozens of other worthwhile Renaissance treatises, that by Ornithoparchus was given new life through an English translation by John Dowland. Appearing in 1609, nearly one hundred years after the first Latin edition and at a time when MORLEY's more progressive *Introduction* (1597) was finding favor in England, the work must have seemed curiously at odds with prevailing practices, though its basic definitions and introduction to contrapuntal procedures might be regarded as timeless. One may speculate on how Dowland attained his copy of the treatise (apparently one of the Cologne editions) and what motivated him to translate it, but the evidence leads one to conclude that he sincerely regarded the material as of great importance and utility for lute players of his own day, and thus worthy of his attention and the trouble of publication.

Musicae activae micrologus . . . libris quatuor digestus . . . [*Rism* B/VI/2, pp. 627-28.]

Leipzig: Valentin Schumann, January 1517.
Leipzig: Valentin Schumann, November 1517. [LCPS: O-007a.]
Leipzig: Valentin Schumann, 1519. [SMLMS.]

As *De arte cantandi micrologus . . .*:

Cologne: Hero Alopecius, 1524. [HoM: 1085.]

Later editions by I. Gymnicus in 1833, 1935, and 1840.

Within the collection *Libelli titulum inscriptionemque iocus*:

Leipzig: Valentin Schumann, 1555.

T ● Dowland, John, trans. *Andreas Ornithoparcus: His Micrologus, or Introduction, Containing the Art of Singing . . .* [*Rism* B/VI/2, p. 628. LCPS:

O-007b. IDC.]; facsimile edition (EE, no. 160), Amsterdam: Theatrum Orbis Terrarum; New York: Da Capo Press, 1969; excerpt in *CJ* 15/2 (1974-75):17-18.

See also (1517):(1973), below.

S ● Facsimile of the 1519 edition. Hildesheim: Georg Olms, 1970; 1977.

S ● ● ● Reese, Gustave, and Ledbetter, Steven, eds. *A Compendium of Musical Practice. . .* Facsimile of the November 1517 edition and 1609 Dowland translation. AMS/MLARS. New York: Dover Publications, 1973. Bibliog. [*Rilm* 73-3223.]

Reviews in *Clavier* 13/8 (1974):6 and *Notes* 31/1 (1974-75):50-51 (Richard Wingell).

S ● Facsimile of the November 1517 edition. Hildesheim: Georg Olms, 1977.

LITERATURE:

Starowolski, Szymon. *Musices practicae erotemata . . .* Cracow: officina Franc. Caesarij, 1650. [*Rism* B/VI/2, p. 804.]

Lyra, Justin Wilhelm. *Andreas Ornithoparchus aus Meiningen, der zeitgenosse Luthers, und dessen Lehre von den Kirchenaccenten . . .* Gütersloh: C. Bertelsmann, 1877.

Review in *MMg* 10/8 (1878):105-11 (Julius Richter).

Niemöller, Klaus Wolfgang. "Ornithoparchus, Andreas." In *MGG* (1949-68). Bibliog.

Michels, L. C. "Een music-dialectologische tekst." In *Neo* 40/4 (1956):310-14.

Poulton, Diana. *John Dowland*. Berkeley and Los Angeles: University of California Press; London: Faber & Faber, 1972; revised edition, 1982. Bibliog.

Reviews in *AR* 26/3 (1985):125-26 (Carolyn Bryant), *BBN* (1982):697 (Richard Luckett), *Choice* 9/10 (1972):1298-1300, *Consort* 28 (1972):119 (Richard D. C. Noble), *Eng* 22/114 (1973):113-

14 (Michael Hattaway), *GR* 37 (1972):23-24 (Suzanne Bloch), *GR* 53 (1983):21-23 (Eliot Fisk), *GuW* 106/20 (May 13, 1972):20 (Wilfred Mellers), *HTo* 22/6 (1972):445 (A. L. Rowse), *Listener* 87/2255 (1972):796-97 (Denis Arnold), *MakM* 81 (1973):21 (Ian Graham-Jones), *MEJ* 60/1 (1973):86, *Mf* 30/1 (1977):127-29 (Winfried Kirsch), *ML* 55/1 (1974):99-100 (David Greer), *ML* 64/1-2 (1983):96 (Christopher Wilson), *MT* 113/1557 (1972):1085-86 (Jeremy Noble), *MT* 124/1681 (1983):171 (John Steele), *MuMus* 21/1 [241] (1972-73):52-53 (Nicholas Sandon), *Notes* 30/2 (1973-74):275-77 (Richard Wang), *Nrmi* 17/2 (1983):282-84 (Dinko Fabris), *RQ* 26/3 (1973):331 (John H. Long), *SCN* 31/3-4 (1973):98-99 (Mortimer H. Frank), *Spec* 228/7511 (June 10, 1972): 895-96 (Richard Luckett), *TES* 3456 (1982):31 (Peter Holman), and *TLS* 71/3686 (1972):1293.

Pamuła, Maria. "Pojecie tonów i śpiewu kościelnego w Musices practicae erotemata Starowolskiego." *Muzyka* 19/1 (1974):54-68. [*Rilm* 74-2169.]

Rivera, Benito V. "Harmonic Theory in Musical Treatises of the Late Fifteenth and Early Sixteenth Centuries." *MTS* 1 (1979):80-95. [*Rilm* 79-2477.]

Niemöller, Klaus Wolfgang. "Ornithoparchus, Andreas." In *NGrove* (1980). Bibliog.

See also BERMUDO: Stevenson (1960); FÉTIS: (1833-44); LIPPIUS: Rivera (1974/1980); MORLEY: Stevenson (1952); WALTHER: (1732); LITERATURE SUPPLEMENT: Allen ["Philosophies"] (1939); **Apfel (1981)**; **Barbour (1951/. . ./1972)**; Becker (1836-39/1964); Bellingham (1971); Bent, M. (1984); Berger (1987); Burney (1776-79/. . ./1957); Bush (1939), (1946); Cahn ["Repercussio"] (1972-); Collins (1963), (1964); **Dahlhaus et al. (1987)**; Eitner (1900-1904/1959-60); Fellerer ["Ausdruck"] (1982); Ferand (1937/1938), (1951); Forkel (1792/1962); Frobenius ["Tactus"] (1972-); Gerber (1812-14/1966); Gurlitt (1944/1966), (1954/1966); Hannas (1934); Harrán (1986); Hawkins (1776/. . ./1969); Houle (1960), (1987); Hüschen (1986); Jackson (1988); Koenigsberger (1979); Krantz (1989); Leuchtmann (1957/1959); Levitan (1938); Lowinsky (1948), (1948):(1949); Luoma (1976), (1977); Mahlert and Sunter (1972-); Meier (1974/1988); Niemöller (1964/1969); Pesce (1987); Pietzsch (1936-42/1971); Reese (1954/1959); Rogers (1955); Sachs (1972-); Schünemann (1928/1931); **Seidel and Cooper (1986)**; Straková (1975); Taddie (1984).

DIEGO ORTIZ

[ca. 1510 – ca. 1570]

A sixteenth-century manner of improvised performance, foreshadowing the Baroque convention of figured bass, was described by Diego Ortiz, whose rare *Trattado de glosas* (1553), though primarily a compendium of cadential diminution formulae, offers terse instructions for creative interaction between a viol player and keyboardist. With only a bass as a guide (and no figures), the keyboard player was advised to devise a chordal accompaniment to a more ornate and spontaneously developed viol melody, sometimes resorting to imitative counterpoints and producing a delightful interplay between the performers. Less challenging, but equally effective, would be to have the keyboardist play the parts of a vocal composition while the viol player freely embellished one or another of these lines, or even added a new line. Through his abundant examples, Ortiz has supplied unique and valuable documentation of sixteenth-century ornamentation and diminution practices.

Trattado de glosas sobre clausulas y otros generos de puntos en la musica de violones . . . [*Rism* A/I/6, p. 350.]

Rome: Valerio Dorico, y Luis su hermano, 1553.

T ● [Ortiz, Diego, trans.?] *Tratta delle glose sopra le cadenze et altre sorte de punti in la musica del violone . . .* Rome: Valerio Dorico, 1553.

ST ● Schneider, Max, ed. and trans. VOBIMg, no. 1. Berlin: Kommissionsverlag L. Liepmannssohn, 1913; Kassel: Bärenreiter, 1936; 1961; 1967.

Review in *Rdm* 18 (1937):62 (Yvonne Rokseth), *Rmi* 21/1 (1914):154-55 (G. C.), and *Rmi* 40/3 (1936):563-64 (Benvenuto Disertori).

T ● Farrell, Peter, trans. "Diego Ortiz' *Tratado de glosas.*" *JVGSA* 4 (1967):5-9.

LITERATURE:

Horsley, Imogene. "Ortiz, Diego." Translated by Hans Haase. In *MGG* 1949-68). Bibliog.

Gerson-Kiwi, Edith. "Drone and 'Dyaphonia basilica'." *YIFMC* 4 (1972):9-22. [*Rilm* 73-3090.]

Griffin, Julia Ann. "Diego Ortiz's Principles of Ornamentation for the Viol: *Tratado de glosas.*" *JVGSA* 10 (1973):88-95.

Stevenson, Robert. "Ortiz, Diego." In *NGrove* (1980). Bibliog.

See also FÉTIS: (1833-44); RIEMANN: (1898):Mickelsen (1970/1977); VIADANA: Haack (1964/1974); WALTHER: (1732); LITERATURE SUPPLE-

MENT: **Arnold (1931/. . ./1965)**; Babitz (1952); Badura-Skoda et al. (1980); Becker (1836-39/1964); Borgir (1971/1987); Brown (1973), ● ● ● (1976); Brown and McKinnon (1980); Chomiński (1962/1981); Crocker (1966); Dolmetsch (1915/. . ./1969); Donington (1963/. . ./1974), (1980); Eggebrecht (1955); Eitner (1900-1904/1959-60); Fellerer (1983), (1984); Ferand (1937/1938), [*Improvisation*] (1956/1961); Forkel (1792/1962); Gerber (1790-92/1977), (1812-14/1966); Goldschmidt (1890/ 1892); Haar (1986); Hammel (1977-78); Harrán (1986); Horsley (1951); Houle (1987); Jackson (1988); Johnson (1973); Kinkeldey (1910/1968); Kuhn (1902); Mahlert and Sunter (1972-); Neumann, Frederick (1978); Newman (1959/. . ./1983); **Palisca** ["Theory"] **(1980)**; Reimer ["Concerto"] (1972-); Rosenblum (1988); Rowen (1979); Schneider (1917/. . ./1971); Schulenberg (1984); Stevenson (1960); Subirá (1947/. . ./1958); Troeger (1987); Wienpahl (1953); Wolff (1972-).

Sir FREDERICK ARTHUR GORE OUSELEY

[1825 – 1889]

Basing his perspective primarily upon the theories of Alfred DAY and Johann Bernhard LOGIER, Sir Frederick Arthur Gore Ouseley created a series of texts encompassing harmony (1868), counterpoint (1869), and form (1875). As an Oxford professor and founding father of the Musical Association, Ouseley held a position of great influence in the Victorian musical world. He also devoted considerable energy and much of his wealth to the establishment of the College of St. Michael and All Saints at Tenbury, intending that it serve as a leading force in the restoration and development of Anglican church music.

Though each of his texts went through at least two editions, they were not enormously popular, as were some of the later efforts of STAINER and PROUT. His reliance upon overtones in the basic formulations for his *Treatise on Harmony* is sometimes willful, sometimes capricious. He regarded the Neapolitan chord as a melding of elements from dominant and tonic (e.g., in C minor, F and A-flat from the dominant ninth and D-flat from the tonic ninth), while he suspended the control of overtones in order to improve the tuning of the dominant root's seventh partial, causing one commentator to refer caustically to "the dominant chord of Nature, corrected by Ouseley" [Shirlaw (1917):432]. Though his *Treatise on Counterpoint* contains more examples from the literature than does his harmony book, his rules seem sometimes more dependent upon his own whims than upon the practices of the composers (including Purcell, Handel, and Bach) he called into service. The *Treatise on Musical Form* includes an exposition on sonata form, influenced by the writings of REICHA.

A Treatise on Harmony (ClPS)

> Includes as an Appendix the following materials by William Pole: "Explanation of the Diagrams of the Musical Scale and Its Component Intervals," "Diagram of the Musical Scale," "Diagram of Various Small Intervals," and other tables.

Oxford: Clarendon Press, 1868.
Oxford: Clarendon Press, 1875.
Oxford: Clarendon Press: 1883.

A Treatise on Counterpoint, Canon and Fugue, Based Upon That of Cherubini (ClPS)

> Oxford: Clarendon Press (London: Macmillan), 1869.

> > Review in *MT* 14/317 (1869-71):149.

> Oxford: Clarendon Press, 1880.

A Treatise on Musical Form and General Composition (ClPS)

> Oxford: Clarendon Press, 1875.
> Oxford: Clarendon Press, 1886.

"On the Early Italian and Spanish Treatises of Counterpoint and Harmony"

> *PMA 1878-79* 5 (1879):76-99.

> > Includes discussion by J. Frederick Bridge, William Chappell, Arthur Duke Coleridge, W. H. Cummings, Thomas Helmore, George Alexander Osborne, William Pole, and John STAINER.

"On Some Italian and Spanish Treatises of Music of the Seventeenth Century"

> *PMA 1881-82* 8 (1882):83-98.

> > Includes discussion by J. Frederick Bridge, William Chappell, W. H. Cummings, Thomas Helmore, G. A. MACFARREN, George Alexander Osborne, William Pole, John STAINER, and Charles Edward Stephens.

LITERATURE:

STAINER, Sir John. "The Character and Influence of the Late Sir Frederick Ouseley." *PMA 1889-90* 16 (1890):25-39.

> Includes discussion by W. H. Cummings.

Joyce, Frederick Wayland. *The Life of Rev. Sir F. A. G. Ouseley*. With G. R. Sinclair. London: Methuen, 1896.

Contains an analysis (by [Thomas Lea] South-gate) of four papers presented by Ouseley before the Musical Association, pp. 166-73.

Harman, Richard Alexander. "Ouseley, Sir Frederick Arthur Gore." Translated by Irmgard Vilmar. In *MGG* (1949-68). Bibliog.

Temperley, Nicholas. "Ouseley, Sir Frederick Arthur Gore." In *NGrove* (1980). Bibliog.

Harrison, W. H. John. "Sir Frederick Gore-Ouseley and His Orbit." Ph.D. dissertation, The University of Wales (Aberystwyth), 1982.

Gedge, David. "Ouseley's Dream." *MO* 109/1308 (1986):395-401; 110/1309-11 (1987):15-18, 46-49, 79-85.

See also DAY: Jones (1977); FÉTIS: (1833-44); LITERATURE SUPPLEMENT: Bircher (1970); Burke (1963); Cazden (1948); Cobb (1884); Finney (1957); Jacobi (1957-60/1971); Jones (1934); Jorgenson (1957); Kassler (1983-85); Kauko (1958); Mendel (1978); Mitchell, J. W. (1963); Pole (1879/. . ./1924); **Ritzel (1967/1968)**; Sanders (1919); Schmalzriedt ["Exposition"] (1972-); Scholes (1947); **Shirlaw (1917/. . ./1970)**; Steblin (1987); ● ● ●Thompson (1980); Whatley (1981).

RENÉ OUVRARD

[1624–1694]

René Ouvrard, continuing a strong tradition of objective scientific thinking, considered many aspects of music's theory and history. His perspective evolved from a careful evaluation of works by ZARLINO, CERONE, KIRCHER, and MERSENNE. Adumbrating RAMEAU, he posited that harmony's perfection was contained in the triad in root position.

Ouvrard's acoustical studies touched upon principles of vibrating bodies, the derivation of partials, sympathetic vibrations, echo, and sound transmission. Intervallic proportions were related to those found in architecture.

Ouvrard's classification of music history is based on style characteristics. Ten ages were proposed, his own being that dominated by the use of figured bass. His interests included music lexicography and the etymology of musical terms. His theological writings suggest that faith was being replaced by reason, subjectivity by objectivity, and theological proof by scientific inquiry.

Secret pour composer en musique par un art nouveau, si facile, que ceux mesdames qui ne sçavent pas chanter, pourront en moins d'un jour composer à quatre parties sur toute sorte de basses . . . [*Rism* B/VI/2, p. 630.]

Published anonymously.

Paris: Jacques de Senlecque, veuve Gervais Alliot et Antoine Clément, 1658.

Reprinted in 1660, under the pseudonym Du Reneau.

T ● Boulay, Jean-Michel. "Rene Ouvrard's *Secret pour composer en musique* (1658): Translation and Commentary." M.A. thesis, The University of Rochester, 1984. Bibliog.

Correspondence with Abbé Nicaise

Mss, 1663-93. [Paris: Bibliothèque nationale.]

L'art et la science des nombres

Paris: L. Roulland & C. Ballard, 1677.

Architecture harmonique ou application de la doctrine des proportions de la musique à l'architecture [*Rism* B/VI/2, p. 630.]

Paris: R. J. B. de La Caille, 1679.

Commentary by François Blondel in his *Cours d'architecture* (3 vols. Paris: P. Auboin & F. Clouzier (vol. 1); the author and Nicolas Langlois (vols. 2 and 3), 1675-83; 2nd edition, Paris: the author; Amsterdam: Pierre Mortier, 1698.), Book 5, Chapters 11-12.

"La musique rétablie depuis son origine, et l'histoire des divers progrez qui s'y sont faits jusqu'à notre tems"

Ms. 2 vols. [Tours: Bibliothèque municipale.]

LITERATURE:

Launay, Denise. "Ouvrard, René." Translated by Anna Frese. In *MGG* (1949-68). Bibliog.

● ● ●Cohen, Albert. "René Ouvrard (1624-1694) and the Beginnings of French Baroque Theory." In *Congress Copenhagen 1972* (1974):336-42. Bibliog. [*Rilm* 76-466.]

Cohen, Albert. "The Ouvrard-Nicaise Correspondence (1663-93)." *ML* 56/3-4 (1975):356-63. Bibliog.

Cohen, Albert. "Ouvrard, René." In *NGrove* (1980). Bibliog.

See also FÉTIS: (1833-44); WALTHER: (1732); LITERATURE SUPPLEMENT: Becker (1836-39/1964); Cohen (1966/1978), (1971), ["Symposium"] (1972); Eitner (1900-1904/1959-60); Forkel (1792/1962); Gerber (1812-14/1966); Launay (1982); **Schneider (1972)**; **Seidel and Cooper (1986)**; Subira (1947/. . ./1958); **Zaminer (1985)**.

GIUSEPPE PAOLUCCI

[1726 – 1776]

MARTINI's student and friend Giuseppe Paolucci anticipated the format of his mentor's *Esemplare o sia saggio fondamentale prattico di contrappunto fugato* (1774-75) in his *Arte pratica di contrappunto* (1765-72), which includes a large collection of music examples representative of contrapuntal techniques from the sixteenth through eighteenth centuries. These scores are marked with numbers which cue the reader to consult specific points in Paolucci's commentary. Some of the selections are a cappella, while others include a figured-bass line. In several instances, scores for sixteen voices plus continuo are printed on larger paper which has been folded into the book. Also of interest is Paolucci's extensive correspondence with MARTINI, though access is hindered since the MARTINI collection in Bologna remains, for the most part, in manuscript.

Correspondence with MARTINI

> Mss., 1757-76. [Bologna: Civico museo bibliografico musicale.]

S ● See MARTINI: (1730-84).

Arte pratica di contrappunto dimostrata con esempj di varj autori e con osservazioni [*Rism* B/VI/2, p. 635.]

> Venice: Antonio de Castro, 1765, 1766, 1772. 3 vols. [HoM: 1101. SMLMS.]

LITERATURE:

Mischiati, Oscar. "Paolucci, Giuseppe." Translated by Gerda Dürr. In *MGG* (1949-68). Bibliog.

● ● ● Brofsky, Howard. "Paolucci, Giuseppe." In *NGrove* (1980). Bibliog.

See also FÉTIS: (1833-44); MOMIGNY: (1791-1818): (1818); LITERATURE SUPPLEMENT: Abraham (1968/1969); Becker (1836-39/1964); Boetticher (1954); Burney (1776-89/. . ./1957); Eitner (1900-1904/1959-60); Fellerer (1927/. . ./1972), ["Zum Bild"] (1973); Forkel (1792/1962); Gerber (1790-92/1977), (1812-14/1966); Ghislanzoni (1949-51); Mendel (1948), (1978); Müller-Blattau (1923/. . ./1963); Niecks (1891).

ANTOINE PARRAN

[1587 – 1650]

Antoine Parran, who was a correspondent of MERSENNE, was, like MERSENNE, Jesuit-trained. He worked as a professor and composer. His *Traité de la musique théorique et pratique* (1639) is a thorough manual of counterpoint in the Renaissance tradition, with examples from Du Caurroy and Le Jeune. In his view, Gaffurio, KEPLER, and de CAUS were important transmitters of musical information. Initially Parran omitted the sixths from his list of consonances, but he later accepted them. He also noted that the fourth blends well with imperfect consonances and identified cadences as final, dominant, or mediant, the latter including cadences ending on the third and sixth scale degrees.

Traité de la musique théorique et pratique contenant les préceptes de la composition [*Rism* B/VI/2, p. 637.]

> Paris: Pierre Ballard, 1639.
> Paris: Robert Ballard, 1646. [LCPS: P-013. HoM: 1108. SMLMS.]

S ● Facsimile of the 1639 edition. Geneva: Minkoff Reprint, 1972.

Review in *Rdm* 58/2 (1972):271-72 (André Verchaly).

LITERATURE:

Verchaly, André. "Parran, Antoine." Translated by Dorothea Schmidt-Preuß. In *MGG* (1949-68).

Cohen, Albert. "Parran, Antoine." In *NGrove* (1980). Bibliog.

See also FÉTIS: (1833-44); MERSENNE: (1617-1648); OUVRARD: (1658):Boulay (1984); LITERATURE SUPPLEMENT: **Apfel (1981)**; Atcherson (1973); Becker (1836-39/1964); Cohen (1966/1978); Eitner (1900-1904/1959-60); Fellerer ["Zur Kontrapunktlehre"] (1973); Ferand (1951); Forkel (1792/1962); Gerber (1790-92/1977), (1812-14/1966); Gruber (1969); Jonckbloet and Land (1882); Kleinman (1971/1974); Launay (1972); Ortigue (1853/. . ./1971); **Schneider (1972)**; **Seidel and Cooper (1986)**; Taddie (1984).

NICCOLO PASQUALI

[ca. 1718–1757]

The Italian musician Niccolo Pasquali spent his brief adult life in Great Britain, where he wrote what was to become one of the most popular English figured-bass manuals of the latter third of the eighteenth century. *Thorough-Bass Made Easy* (1757), as he named it, contains a wide assortment of exercises upon which students might hone their skills, as well as various model examples and a brief text. It is perhaps more useful today for its hints on stylistic performance than for any keen insight into chord construction or voice-leading. In some of the examples, the various numbers for the figured bass compete with the numbers 0 through 4 used to indicate fingering.

Pasquali specified what he called "first" and "second" chords for each of the seven diatonic triads. They were distinguished according to which of their pitches was placed at the top of the texture. His rules fostered a choice between these two positionings such that parallel perfect intervals would be prevented or the melody would be more linear. Yet his plan was somewhat complicated, as the following explanation of an example attests: "According to the third Rule, the G *, because near C, ought to have its second Chord, but, upon Consideration, that the following C must have its second Chord also, as being near D, agreeable to the first Rule, and that its Chord happens to be its highest one, the playing G, with its second, which is its lowest, would make a troublesome Skip, and therefore, as an Exception to the third Rule, it must have its first Chord, as at **, which is the Step from one to the other."

Upon Pasquali's death in 1757 a manuscript entitled "The Art of Fingering the Harpsichord" was found in a state suitable for publication. The work addresses elementary issues of keyboard playing, as well as the topics of ornamentation and articulation. A legato style is recommended. A project on harmony, which has been referred to simply as "Theory," was left in a less complete state. Its current whereabouts are unknown.

Thorough-Bass Made Easy; or, Practical Rules for Finding and Applying Its Various Chords with Little Trouble, Together with Variety of Examples in Notes, Shewing the Manner of Accompanying Concertos, Solos, Songs, and Recitatives [Rism B/VI/2, pp. 638-39.]

> Edinburgh: Robert Bremner, 1757. [LCPS: P-016a. HoM: 1111. SMLMS.]
> London: Robert Bremner, [ca. 1760-65]. [LCPS: P-016b.]
>
>> Later editions. That of 1810 (edited by A. Hamilton with alterations by John Jousse) was reviewed in *GMag* 85/1 (1815):159-60.

T ● Lustig, Jaques Guillaume, trans. and ed. *La basse continuë renduë aisée; ou, explication succinte des accords que le clavessin renferme . . .* Amsterdam: J. J. Hummel, [ca. 1763]. [Rism B/VI/2, p. 639. IDC.]

> Text in French and Dutch.

S ● Churchill, John, ed. Facsimile of the ca. 1760-65 edition. London: Oxford University Press, [ca. 1974.]

> Reviews in *EM* 3/3 (1975):271-73 (Robert Donington), *MakM* 89 (1975):14 (W. R. Pasfield), *ML* 56/3-4 (1975):407 (J. A. Westrup), *MT* 116/1593 (1975):974 (Peter Williams), and *MusT* 54 (1975):27 (John Morehen).

The Art of Fingering the Harpsichord, Illustrated with Examples in Notes; To Which Is Added, an Approved Method of Tuning That Instrument [Rism B/VI/2, p. 638.]

> Published posthumously.

> Edinburgh: Robert Bremner, [ca. 1757-58]. [LCPS: P-015a. HoM: 1110. SMLMS.]
> London: Robert Bremner, [ca. 1760-65]. [LCPS: P-015b.]
>
>> Later editions.

S ● See HOLDEN: (1770):[1799].

"Theory"

> Ms. [Lost.]

LITERATURE:

Cudworth, Charles, and Redlich, Hans F. "Pasquali, Niccolo." Translated by Hans Haase. In *MGG* (1949-68). Bibliog.

Cooper, Barry. "Alberti and Jozzi: Another View." *MR* 39/3-4 (1978):160-66. [Rilm 78-4941.]

Johnson, David. "Pasquali, Niccolo." In *NGrove* (1980). Bibliog.

See also FÉTIS: (1833-44); LITERATURE SUPPLEMENT: Badura-Skoda et al. (1980); Becker (1836-39/1964); Borgir (1971/1987); Burney (1776-89/. . ./1957); Chenette (1967); Dean (1977); Eitner (1900-1904/1959-60); Farmer (1947/1970); Forkel (1792/1962); Gerber (1790-92/1977), (1812-14/1966); Houle (1987); Johnstone (1966); **Kassler** (1971), ● ● ● **(1979)**; North (1987); Rosenblum (1988); **Seidel and Cooper (1986)**; Troeger (1987); Williams, P. (1970).

LORENZO PENNA

[1613 – 1693]

A popular and well organized guide to the musical art, Lorenzo Penna's *Li primi albori musicali* (1672) spans the spectrum of practical theory from its basic foundations through counterpoint and figured bass. In the first of its three volumes, conservative and progressive elements of pedagogy and practice are intermingled. Guido's hand, accompanied by solmization instructions using the syllables *do* through *la*, is given a place alongside a discussion of contemporary time signatures, including examples of signatures for five and seven beats per measure. The second volume is devoted to counterpoint. A pedagogical method akin to that of FUX leads the reader step by step from consonance through the various dissonance usages and more florid rhythmic patterns. Canon and cadential formulas are also explored. The final volume is an excellent manual on both figured and unfigured bass. It reveals considerable refinement over formulations made earlier in the century. His discussion focuses upon accompaniments using the organ, and his advice on supporting vocal lines in their various ranges and his detailed explanations of how to construct, connect, and embellish chords should be useful to modern keyboardists, as they must have been in the late seventeenth century.

Li primi albori musicali per li principianti della musica figurata . . . [*Rism* B/VI/2, pp. 642-43.]

1) *Primo libro, da cui spuntano li principii del canto figurato*

2) *Secondo libro, da doue si spiccano le regole del contrapunto*

3) *Terzo libro, di onde appariscono li fondamenti per suonare l'organo sopra la parte*

Bologna: Giacomo Monti, 1672. 3 vols. [LCPS: P-022a.]
Bologna: M. Silvani, 1674. Vol. 1 (incomplete).
Venice: Gioseppe Sala, 1678. Vol. 2. (as *Albori musicali per li studiosi della musica figurata* . . .) [LCPS: P-022b.]
Bologna: Giacomo Monti, 1679. 3 vols. [SMLMS.]
Bologna: Giacomo Monti, 1684.
Antwerp: Henrico Aertssens, 1690.
Bologna: Pier-maria Monti, 1696. 3 vols. [LCPS: P-022c. HoM: 1115.]

S • Facsimile of the 1684 edition. BmB, ser. 2, no. 38. Bologna: Forni, 1969.

Direttorio del canto fermo . . . [*Rism* B/VI/2, p. 642.]

Modena: eredi Cassiani, 1689. [LCPS: P-021.]

LITERATURE:

Oberdörffer, Fritz. "Penna, Lorenzo." In *MGG* (1949-68). Bibliog.

Lederer, Josef-Horst. "Lorenzo Penna und seine Kontrapunkttheorie." Ph.D. dissertation, The University of Graz, 1970 (1971). [*Rilm* 73-344.]

Caputo, Maria Carmela. "*Li primi albori musicali* di Lorenzo Penna." Thesis, The University of Messina, 1972-73.

Lederer, Josef-Horst. "Zur Kontrapunkttheorie Lorenzo Pennas." *SzMw* 28 (1977):105-13. Bibliog.

Lederer, Josef-Horst. "Penna, Lorenzo." In *NGrove* (1980). Bibliog.

See also BONONCINI: Holler (1955/1963); FÉTIS: (1833-44); HEINICHEN: (1728):Buelow (1961/. . ./ 1986); MOMIGNY: (1791-1818):(1818); SAINT-LAMBERT: (1707):Burchill (1979); WALTHER: (1732); LITERATURE SUPPLEMENT: **Apfel (1981)**; ● ● ● **Arnold (1931/. . ./1965)**; Becker (1836-39/1964); Borgir (1971/1987); Burney (1776-89/. . ./1957); Collins (1966); Dahlhaus ["Untersuchungen"] (1966/. . ./1988); **Dahlhaus et al. (1987)**; David (1956); Donington (1963/. . ./ 1974); Eitner (1900-1904/1959-60); Fellerer ["Zur Kontrapunktlehre"] (1973), (1984); Forkel (1792/1962); Gerber (1790-92/1977); Hammel (1977-78); Hannas (1934); Harich-Schneider ([1939]/. . ./1970); Hein (1954); Horsley [*Fugue: History*] (1966), (1972); Houle (1960), (1987); Jackson (1988); La Fage (1864/1964); Mitchell, J. W. (1963); Nelson (1984); **Neumann**, Frederick (1978), [*Essays*] **(1982)**; North (1987); Oberdörffer (1949-68); Pacchioni (1983); **Palisca** (1949-68); ["Theory"] **(1980)**; Rogers (1955); Rothgeb (1968); Schulenberg (1984); Schwartz (1908); Speak (1973); Tagliavini (1975/1983); Troeger (1987); Walker (1987); Wienpahl (1953); Williams, P. ["Harpsichord"] (1968), (1970).

JOHANN CHRISTOPH PEPUSCH

[1667 – 1752]

Though he had begun a career in Berlin, Johann Christoph Pepusch sought an improved political climate in England and spent some fifty years there. Though it appears he never quite mastered the language (his students and friends aided him in this regard), he contributed several interesting and popular treatises and was in great demand as a teacher. His success as a composer for the stage, with the *Beggar's Opera* (1728) in particular, created enemies within the Handel camp, yet among the more conservative members of London's musical establishment, such as those who applauded his efforts in founding the Academy of Ancient Music, he was highly revered.

Though published anonymously, scholars generally accept *Rules, or a Short and Compleat Method for Attaining to Play a Thorough Bass* [ca. 1730] and *A Short Treatise on Harmony* (1730) as works by Pepusch, or at least as works transcribed from his teaching. The latter includes, in its 1731 edition, chapters on plain counterpoint; the keys of C and A (as representatives of sharp [major] and flat [minor] modes); descant or figurate counterpoint (including a discussion of discords); further discussion of discords (including "by Supposition" — wherein the "Discord so brought in is *Suppos'd* to be a Note higher, or a Note lower than it is"); cadences; modulation; solmization (wherein the hexachord system is endorsed); the techniques of fugue, canon, and imitation; and transposition.

Upon initiation into the Royal Society, Pepusch prepared a lecture, "Of the Various Genera and Species of Music among the Ancients," which was published in 1747. In it he endorsed HUYGENS's division of the octave into thirty-one parts. Numerous other papers and teaching materials are preserved in a variety of British and American libraries.

A Short Explication of Such Foreign Words, as Are Made Use of in Musick Books [*Rism* B/VI/2, p. 919.]

> Attributed to Pepusch.

> London: J. Brotherton, 1724. [LCPS: Anon-013.]
> London: [ca. 1730].

> S ● See [ca. 1730], below.

Rules, or a Short and Compleat Method for Attaining to Play a Thorough Bass upon the Harpsichord or Organ; . . . Also an Explanation of Figur'd Time, with the Several Moods and Characters Made Use Of in Musick, to Which Is Added, a Dictionary, or Explication of . . . Italian Words, or Terms . . . [*Rism* B/VI/2, p. 982.]

> Published anonymously.

> London: J. Walsh, [ca. 1730]. [LCPS: Anon-092.]

A Short Treatise on Harmony, Containing the Chief Rules for Composing in Two, Three, and Four Parts . . . [*Rism* B/VI/2, p. 643.]

> Published anonymously.

> London: J. Watts, 1730. [LCPS: P-023a.]

> As *A Treatise on Harmony . . .*:

> London: W. Pearson, 1731. Enlarged [by James Hamilton?]. [LCPS: P-023b. SMLMS. IDC.]

> > Reviewed in the Ms. "Classified Papers" of the Royal Society of London and in John Frederick Lampe's *The Art of Musick* (London: C. Corbett, 1740), pp. 36-46.

> S ● Facsimile of the 1731 edition. MMMLF, ser. 2, no. 28. New York: Broude Brothers, [1966].

> S ● Facsimile of the 1731 edition. Hildesheim: Georg Olms, 1970; 1976.

["A Short Account of the Thoro Bass as It Is Taught by Mr. Pepusch"]

> Ms., [ca. 1740]. [Rochester, N.Y.: Sibley Music Library.]

"Of the Various Genera and Species of Music among the Ancients, with Some Observations concerning Their Scale"

> *PTRS 1746* 44/1/481 (1747):266-74.

> > Appears also in abridgments of *PTRS*.

"A Short Account of the Twelve Modes of Composition and Their Progression in Every Octave"

> Ms., 1751. [Rochester, N.Y.: Sibley Music Library.]

"Rules for to Play a Thorough Bass"

> Ms. [Glasgow: University Library, The University of Glasgow.]

["Various Papers . . . Relating to Harmony and the Scales and Modes of the Ancients"]

> Ms. [London: British Library.]

[Writings on scales, clefs, thoroughbass, etc.]

> Ms. [Evanston, Ill.: Music Library, Northwestern University.]

Pepusch has been suggested as a contributor to MALCOLM: (1721).

LITERATURE:

Burney, Charles. "Counterpoint." In *Cyc* (1802-20).

Hughes, Charles W. "John Christopher Pepusch." *MQ* 31/1 (1945):54-70.

Cudwort[h], Charles. "Pepusch, Johann Christoph." Translated by Dorothea Schmidt-Preuß. In *MGG* (1949-68). Bibliog.

Williams, J. G. "The Life, Work and Influence of J. C. Pepusch." D.Phil. dissertation, The University of York, 1976.

Boyd, Malcolm. "Pepusch, Johann Christoph." In *NGrove* (1980). Bibliog.

Cook, D. F. "J. C. Pepusch: An 18th-Century Musical Bibliophile." *Soun* 9 (1982):11-28.

See also FÉTIS: (1833-44); NORTH, R.: Wilson (1959); LITERATURE SUPPLEMENT: Becker (1836-39/1964); Beiche ["Dux"] (1972-); Blumröder (1972-); Boomgaarden (1985/1987); Burney (1776-89/. . ./1957); Cazden (1948); Chenette (1967); Chevaillier (1925/1931-32); Eitner (1900-1904/1959-60); Forkel (1792/1962); Gerber (1790-92/1977), (1812-14/1966); Hawkins (1776/. . ./1969); Jacobi (1957-60/1971); **Kassler** (1971), ● ● ● **(1979)**; Miller and Cohen (1987); **Seidel and Cooper (1986)**.

AGOSTINO PISA

[active early seventeenth century]

The practice of beating time suffered from too great a diversity of methods and interpretations in early seventeenth-century Rome. Agostino Pisa, in several publications dating from 1611, attempted to create a more uniform and understandable system by scrutinizing the technique of raising and lowering the hand. In addition to the moments of action (downward and upward), there were moments of repose. Pisa maintained that the beat resided in the motions, rather than in the stops. Furthermore, the music should conform to the established beat, rather than the beat bending to the music. Pisa's documentation influenced later treatments of the topic and put the primitive art of conducting on a more secure foundation.

Breve dichiarazione della battuta musicale . . . Opera non solo utile mà necessaria à quelli che desiderano fare profitto nella musica [*Rism* B/VI/2, p. 656.]

> Rome: Bartolomeo Zannetti, 1611.
>
>> Revised edition, as *Battuta della musica . . .:*
>
> Rome: Bartolomeo Zannetti, 1611.
>
>> Extract, as *Brevissima dichiaratione della battuta della musica*:
>
> Rome: 1611.

S ● Facsimile of the revised 1611 edition. BmB, ser. 2, no. 32. Bologna: Forni Editore, 1969.

LITERATURE:

Valentini, Pier Francesco. "Trattato della battuta musicale." Ms., 1643. [Rome: Biblioteca Apostolica Vaticana.]

Schünemann, Georg. *Geschichte des Dirigirens*. Leipzig: Breitkopf & Härtel, 1913; reprint edition (KHMG, no. 10), Wiesbaden: Breitkopf 7 Härtel; Hildesheim: Georg Olms, 1965.

Mischiati, Oscar. "Pisa, Agostino." Translated by Dorothea Schmidt-Preuß. In *MGG* (1949-68). Bibliog.

Ziino, Agostino. "Pisa, Agostino." In *NGrove* (1980). Bibliog.

See also BANCHIERI: (1601):Cranna (1981); FÉTIS: (1833-44); WALTHER: (1732); LITERATURE SUPPLEMENT: Collins (1964); Dürr (1964); Eitner (1900-1904/1959-60); Fellerer (1984); Gerber (1790-92/1977); Houle (1987); Hüschen (1986); **Palisca** ["Theory"] **(1980)**; Schwartz (1908).

JOHN PLAYFORD

[1623 – 1686]

John Playford, a prominent London music publisher, compiled *A Breefe Introduction to the Skill of Musick* (1654), borrowing freely from writings by many of England's best-known theorists. His sources were acknowledged whenever possible, and one treatise, Thomas CAMPION's *A New Way* *of Making Fowre Parts in Counter-point* [ca. 1612-14], was incorporated in toto (with annotations and minor changes by SIMPSON) as "The Art of Setting or Composing Musick in Parts" (editions from 1655 to 1662) and "The Art of Descant or Composing Musick in Parts" (editions from 1664 to 1679).

Playford's work appeared in at least twenty editions. PUR-CELL's hand was involved in the edition of 1694. In addition to coverage of the usual musical rudiments, there is a section devoted to the bass viola or viol da gamba.

Playford's book includes one segment of his own creation. It demonstrates how discords may be taken elegantly. Numerous examples of 9ths, 7ths, and augmented 4ths are provided. Playford, as LOCKE's publisher, also became involved in the SALMON-LOCKE controversy.

A Musicall Banquet . . . to Which is Added Some Few Rules and Directions for Such as Learne to Sing, or to Play on the Viol [*Rism* I, p. 529.]

London: J. Benson and J. Playford (T. H.), 1651.

A Breefe Introduction to the Skill of Musick for Song and Violl [*Rism* B/VI/2, pp. 657-59.]

London: John Playford, 1654.

> Numerous editions through 1730, with the title *An Introduction to the Skill of Musick . . .* The contents vary from edition to edition. [LCPS: P-042a through P-042m (various editions from 1666 through 1730). HoM: 1168-89 (various editions from 1654 through 1730). SMLMS (edition of 1683). IDC (edition of 1730).]

S ● Facsimile of the seventh edition (1674). Ridgewood, N.J.: Gregg Press, 1966.

S ● Zimmerman, Franklin B., ed. Facsimile of the twelfth edition (1694), with portions of the thirteenth and fourteenth editions and facsimiles of title pages from many other editions. DCPMRS. New York: Da Capo Press, 1972.

> Review in *Choice* 10/3 (1973-74):470, *ML* 54/3 (1973):368 (Jack A. Westrup), and *MT* 114/1565 (1973):704-5 (David Scott).

See also LOCKE: [*Present Practice*] (1673).

LITERATURE:

Kidson, Frank. "John Playford, and Seventeenth-Century Music Publishing." *MQ* 4/4 (1918):516-34.

Pulver, Jeffrey. "Playford's *Introduction to the Skill of Musick*." *MMR* 52/619 (1922):154-55.

Playford's "Brief Introduction to the Skill of Musick": An Account, with Bibliographical Notes, of an Unique Collection Comprising All the Editions from 1654 to 1730 in the Possession of Messrs. Ellis. London: 1926.

Pulver, Jeffrey. "Unpaid Debts: VI—John Playford." *MN* 72/1816 (1927):209-10.

Dean-Smith, Margaret. "Playford." Translated by Hans-Joachim Beier. In *MGG* (1949-68). Bibliog.

Carapetyan, Leon. "A Few Remarks on John Playford and His *Introduction to the Skill of Musick* [Abstract]." *JAMS* 9/1 (1956):65-66.

Spink, Ian. "Playford's 'Directions for Singing after the Italian Manner'." *MMR* 89/994 (1959):130-35.

● ● ● Meyer, Ramon E. "John Playford's *An Introduction to the Skill of Musick*." Ph.D. dissertation, The Florida State University, 1961. [*DA* 22/08, pp. 2819-20. UMI 61-05650.]

● ● ● Ruff, Lillian M. "A Survey of John Playford's *Introduction to the Skill of Musick*." *Consort* 22 (1965):36-48.

Dean-Smith, Margaret. "Playford. (1) John Playford (i)." In *NGrove* (1980). Bibliog.

Munstedt, Peter Alan. "John Playford, Music Publisher: A Bibliographical Catalogue." Ph.D. dissertation, The University of Kentucky, 1983. [*Rilm* 83-78. *DA* 44/06A, pp. 1621-22. UMI 83-22712.]

See also COPRARIO: Ruff (1963); FÉTIS: (1833-44); PURCELL: (1654):(1694):Squire (1904-5); SALMON: Baldwin and Wilson (1970); LITERATURE SUPPLEMENT: Abraham (1968/1969); Apfel (1976); Atcherson (1972); Becker (1836-39/1964); Brown (1976); Burke (1963); Burney (1776-89/. . ./1957); Burton (1956); Chenette (1967); Colles (1928-29); Collins (1963), (1966); Dolmetsch (1915/. . ./1969); Donington (1963/ . . ./1974), (1980); Eitner (1900-1904/1959-60); Ferand [*Improvisation*] (1956/1961); Gerber (1790-92/1977), (1812-14/1966); Gouk (1980); Grashel (1981); Hancock (1977); Hawkins (1776/. . ./ 1969); Horsley [*Fugue: History*] (1966); Houle (1960), (1987); Jackson (1988); Jacobi (1957-60/1971); **Kassler (1979)**; Kleinman (1971/1974); Lange (1899-1900); Lawrence (1978); Lewis (1981); **Mann (1955/. . ./1987)**; Miller (1960); Neumann, Frederick (1978); Pulver (1927/. . ./1973); Robison (1982); Rogers (1955); Rothschild (1953); Ruf (1972-); Ruff (1962), (1970); Sachs (1972-); Schmalzriedt ["Reprise"] (1972-); **Seidel and Cooper (1986)**; Shute (1972); Subirá (1947/. . ./ 1958); Taddie (1984); Traficante (1970); Wienpahl (1953); Wolf (1939).

PIETRO PONTIO

[1532–1595]

If, as the brothers MONTEVERDI were to suggest, two separate compositional practices coexisted at the end of the sixteenth century, then certainly books which sustain and clarify the *prima prattica* were an essential component of the theoretical literature. Unlike ZARLINO's extensive *Istitutione harmoniche* (1558), wherein practical theory coexists with learned speculative pondering, the two treatises by Pietro Pontio (Ponzio) emphasize basic components of contrapuntal writing in two parts. *Ragionamento di musica* (1588) contains an introduction to each interval, a discussion of the eight original ecclesiastical modes, and informative commentary on rhythm and meter. Pontio also made important distinctions in the procedures for writing various types of compositions, such as motets and magnificats. The *Dialogo ove si tratta della theorica è prattica di musica* (1595) presents an abundance of interval ratios and designations (e.g., "supertripartiente quarta divisa" for 14:8) and continues the development of contrapuntal theory with topics such as cadences outside the mode of the piece, types of imitation, and means for evoking a mood appropriate to a work's liturgical function or text.

Ragionamento di musica . . . ove si tratta de' passaggi delle consonantie, et dissonantie, buoni, et non buoni; et del modo di far motetti, messe, salmi et altre compositioni . . . [*Rism* B/VI/2, p. 663.]

Parma: Erasmo Viotto, 1588. [LCPS: P-050.]

S ● Clercx, Suzanne, ed. Facsimile edition. IGMDm, ser. 1, no. 16. Kassel: Bärenreiter, 1959.

Reviews in *Mf* 13/1 (1960):96-97 (Walther Dürr) and *ML* 41/1 (1960):82-83 (Jack A. Westrup).

Dialogo . . . ove si tratta della theorica è prattica di musica, et anco si mostra la diversità de' contraponti, et canoni [*Rism* B/VI/2, p. 663.]

Parma: Erasmo Viotto, 1595. [LCPS: P-049. HoM: 1218.]

LITERATURE:

Sartori, Claudio. "Ponzio, Pietro." Translated by Albert Müry. In *MGG* (1949-68). Bibliog.

● ● ● Jackson, Roland. "Pontio, Pietro." In *NGrove* (1980). Bibliog.

Murray, Russell Eugene, Jr. "Pietro Pontio (1532-1595): Musician of Parma." Ph.D. dissertation, The University of North Texas, forthcoming.

See also ARTUSI: (1600); FÉTIS: (1833-44); MATTHESON: Buelow and Marx (1983):Palisca; RIEMANN: (1898); WALTHER: (1732); LITERATURE SUPPLEMENT: **Apfel (1981)**; Armstrong (1978); Becker (1836-39/1964); Beiche ["Inversio"] (1972-); **Bent** ["Analysis"] **(1980/1987)**; Blumröder (1972-); **Bullivant (1980)**; Cahn ["Transitus"] (1972-); Dahlhaus ["Zur Tonartenlehre"] (1976); **Dahlhaus and Sachs (1980)**; Eitner (1900-1904/1959-60); Fellerer ["Zur Kontrapunktlehre"] (1973); Ferand [*Improvisation*] (1956/1961); Gerber (1790-92/1977), (1812-14/1966); Harrán (1986); Hein (1954); Horsley ["Fugue and Mode"] (1966/1978); Hüschen (1986); Katz (1926); Krantz (1989); Lockwood (1966/1978); Mahlert and Sunter (1972-); Meier (1963); Reckow (1972-); Robbins (1938); Ruhnke (1949-68); Schmalzriedt ["Subiectum"] (1972-); Sydow-Saak (1972-); Tilmouth (1980); Walker (1987); Wolff (1972-).

JOHANN GOTTLIEB PORTMANN

[1739–1798]

Though little remembered today, Johann Gottlieb Portmann published several informative treatises near the end of the eighteenth century. Among them, his *Leichtes Lehrbuch der Harmonie, Composition und des Generalbaßes* (1789) stands out for its account of contemporary perceptions concerning musical form. Portmann relied upon harmonic, rather than thematic, guideposts in determining how a movement was organized. In fact, his grids showing the arrangement of harmonic regions amount to a "middleground" perspective.

Portmann understood that a given harmony could be expanded through what we now call antecedent and consequent phrases, which he described in terms of their questioning and answering characters, respectively. He also displayed convincing examples of how phrases might be modified or segmented through various techniques to produce melodic material for use later within a movement, thereby enhancing its continuity.

Musikalischer Unterricht. Zum Gebrauch für Anfänger und Liebhaber der Musik überhaupt, so viel sie von den ersten Gründen der Musik, Melodie, Harmonie, Metrum, Rhythmus u. s. w. verstehen müssen, um größere Fortschritte darinnen zu machen; und alsdann insbesondere für Schulmeister und Schulkandidaten, so viel sie von dem Choralspielen, der Erfindung der Präludien und Zwischenspiele, ingleichen vom Singen, zum Lehren und Lernen zu wissen nöthig haben [Rism B/VI/2, pp. 664-65.]

> Darmstadt and Speyer: Krämer & Boßler, 1785. [LCPS: P-053.]
> 1802. Edited by J. K. Wagner.

Leichtes Lehrbuch der Harmonie, Composition und des Generalbaßes, zum Gebrauch für Liebhaber der Musik, angehende und fortschreitende Musici und Componisten [Rism B/VI/2, p. 664.]

> Darmstadt: Fürstl. Hof- und Kanzleibuchdruckerei (J. J. Will), 1789. [LCPS: P-052a.]
>
>> Reviews in *AdB* 117/1 (1794):71-77 (Os.) and *MRz 1790* /21 (1790):161-62 (Heinrich Philipp Karl Boßler).
>
> Darmstadt: Georg Friedrich Heyer, 1799. [LCPS: P-052b.]

Die neuesten und wichtigsten Entdeckungen in der Harmonie, Melodie und dem doppelten Contrapuncte: Eine Beilage zu jeder musicalischen Theorie [Rism B/VI/2, p. 665.]

> Darmstadt: [Georg Friedrich Heyer], 1798. [LCPS: P-054.]
>
>> Review in *AmZ* 1/29-32 (1798-99):454-60, 471-78, 487-94, 507-11.

See also Portmann's reviews of ALBRECHTS-BERGER: (1790) and TÜRK: (1791), as well as other reviews in *AdB* 104/1 (1791):159-66 and 112/1 (1792):96-105.

LITERATURE:

Noack, Elisabeth. "Portmann, Johann Gottlieb." In *MGG* (1949-68). Bibliog.

See also FÉTIS: (1833-44); LITERATURE SUPPLEMENT: Bauman (1977); Becker (1836-39/1964); Eitner (1900-1904/1959-60); Forkel (1792/1962); Gerber (1790-92/1977), (1812-14/1966); Moyer (1969); Nelson (1984); Newman (1963/. . ./1983); Ratner (1949), (1956), (1970), (1980); **Ritzel (1967/1968)**; Shamgar (1978), (1981), (1984); ● ● ● Sheldon (1982); Wirth (1966).

MICHAEL PRAETORIUS

[ca. 1569-73 — 1621]

The state of music in Germany soon after the turn of the seventeenth century is well documented in the mammoth yet incomplete *Syntagma musicum* (1614-20) of Michael Praetorius. BARYPHONUS was to have supplied material for a fourth volume on composition, but Praetorius's death intervened. What survives are three rich volumes which treat, respectively, the music of the ancients and of the church; the musical instruments of the day, particularly the organ; and the genres of composition and the technical background necessary for professional musicians.

As a Lutheran church musician and prolific composer of music for worship, Praetorius was particularly enamored of the organ, its construction, and its tuning. His meantone temperament divides the syntonic comma equally among four fifths to produce a pure major third (5:4 rather than 81:64). He also favored Italian developments in composition and performance practice, from which his discussion of figured bass is derived. His detailed description and written-out realization of figured bass give a clear picture of the state of that art during its infancy. There were few authorities for Praetorius to cite, but in quoting VIADANA, AGAZZARI,

and others, he brought recent Italian ideas to German-speaking readers. (Beginning with the second volume of *Syntagma musicum*, Praetorius wrote in German.)

Praetorius's main contribution is his documentation of existing musical practices rather than the development of new ideas. He tells us about the state of modal, metrical, and fugal theory, about the prevailing combinations of instruments and of voices in ensembles, about the standard pitch in chamber and church music. Occasionally he suggests new alternatives, such as a revision in the standard pitch or refinements in the conventions of figured bass. With the diversity of his subject matter and the penetration of his writing Praetorius has emerged as a trusted guide through an often neglected segment of our musical past.

Syntagma musicum ex veterum et recentiorum ecclesiasticorum autorum lectione, polyhistorûm consignatione, variarum linguarum notatione, hodierni seculi usurpatione, ipsius denique musicae artis observatione . . . [Rism B/VI/2, p. 666.]

1) *Musicae artis analecta*

2) *De organographia*

  Appendix: *Sciagraphia*

3) *Termini musicali*

  Wolfenbüttel; Elias Holwein, 1614. Vol. 1. [HoM: 1220.]
  Wittenberg: Johannis Richter, 1615. Vol. 1. [LCPS: P-056. SMLMS. IDC.]
  Wolfenbüttel: Elias Holwein, 1618. Vols. 2 and 3.
  Wolfenbüttel: Elias Holwein, 1619. Vols. 2 and 3. [LCPS: P-056. HoM: 1220. SMLMS. IDC.]
  Wolfenbüttel: Elias Holwein, 1620. Appendix to Vol. 2. [LCPS: P-056. HoM: 1220. SMLMS. IDC.]

S ● Trost, Johann Caspar. "Organographia rediviva Michaelis Praetorii." [Ms.?, mid seventeenth century.] [Lost.]

S ● [Eitner, Robert, ed.] "Einiges aus Michael Praetorius *Syntagma musicum*, 3. Tomus, Wolfenbüttel 1619." *MMg* 10/3-4 (1878):33-44, 49-54.

S ● Eitner, Robert, ed. *Von den Instrumenten*. PaptM, no. 13. Berlin: Trautwein, 1884; reprint edition, Leipzig: Breitkopf & Härtel, 1894.

  Volume 2 (*De organographia*).

S ● Bernoulli, Eduard, ed. Modern edition of Volume 3. Leipzig: C. F. Kahnt, 1916. ⸱ ⸱⸱

S ● Gurlitt, Wilibald, ed. Facsimile edition of Vol. 2. Kassel: Bärenreiter, 1929.

T ● Blumenfeld, Harold, trans. *The "Syntagma musicum" of Michael Praetorius, Volume Two: "De Organographia," First and Second Parts*. New Haven, Ct.: Yale University (Chinese Printing Office), 1949; reprint edition (expanded), New York: Bärenreiter, 1962; reprint edition (further expanded; DCPMRS), New York: Da Capo Press, 1980.

  Review in *Notes* 7/3 (1949-50):481-82 (Karl Geiringer).

T ● Lampl, Hans. "A Translation of *Syntagma musicum*, Volume III, by Michael Praetorius." D.M.A. dissertation, The University of Southern California, 1957.

S ● Gurlitt, Wilibald, ed. Facsimile edition. 3 vols. IGMDm, ser. 1, nos. 14, 15, 21. Kassel: Bärenreiter, 1958-59. Bibliog.

  Reviews in *GK* 5 (1971):183 (Hans Schmidt), *Mf* 14/1 (1961):103-4 (Harald Heckmann), *ML* 40/2 (1959):190-91 (D. W. Stevens), and *ML* 41/4 (1960):384 (J. A. Westrup).

T ● Lampl, Hans, trans. and ed. "Michael Praetorius on the Use of Trumpets." *BQ* 2/1 (1958-59):3-7.

T ● Fleming, Michael David. "Michael Praetorius, Music Historian: An Annotated Translation of *Syntagma musicum* I, Part 1." Ph.D. dissertation, Washington University, 1979. [*Rilm* 79-2523. *DA* 40/02A, pp. 525-26. UMI 79-18595.]

T ● See Rowen (1979).

T ● See MacClintock (1980).

T ● ● ● Crookes, David Z., trans. and ed. *Syntagma musicum II: De organographia, Parts I and II* [and Facsimile of the *Sciagraphia* (1620)]. EMSer, no. 7. Oxford: Clarendon Press, 1986. Bibliog.

  Reviews in *EM* 15/2 (1987):253-55 (Ian Harwood), *RecMus* 9/6 (1988):155-56, *RQ* 40/2 (1987):342-43 (Laurence Libin), *SCN* 45/1-2 (1987):18-19 (David Fallon), and *TLS* 85/4336 (1986):496 (David Fallows).

"Kurzer Bericht waß bey uberliefferung einer klein und grosverfertigten orgell zu observiren" ["Orgeln Verdingnis"]

  With the collaboration of Esaias Compenius.

  Ms. [Wolfenbüttel: Herzog August Bibliothek.]

S ● Blume, Friedrich, ed. *Michael Praetorius und Esaias Compenius: Orgeln Verdingnis*. KieBzMw, no. 4. Wolfenbüttel and Berlin: G. Kallmeyer, 1936.

See Blume (1960/1963), below, for a listing of lost works.

LITERATURE:

Gurlitt, Wilibald. "Michael Praetorius (Creuzbergensis): Sein Leben und seine Werke." Ph.D. dissertation, The University of Leipzig, 1915; published edition (partial), Leipzig: Breitkopf & Härtel, 1915; reprint edition, Hildesheim: Georg Olms, 1968. Bibliog.

Hayes, Gerald R. "Praetorius and Mersenne." *MT* 68/1016 (1927):889-91.

Blume, Friedrich. "Das Werk des Michael Praetorius." *ZfMw* 17/8, 12 (1935):321-31, 482-502.

Forchert, Arno. "Praetorius, Michael." In *MGG* (1949-68). Bibliog.

Watanabe, Ruth. "Michael Praetorius and His *Syntagma musicum*." *URLB* 10/3 (1954-55):46-52.

Dadelsen, Georg von. "Zu den Vorreden des Michael Praetorius." In *Kongress Wien 1956* (1958):107-11.

Vellekoop, Gerrit. "Michaël Praetorius en zijn *Syntagma musicum*." *Mens* 14/8 (1959):256-58.

Blume, Friedrich. "Schlußbericht des Herausgebers." In *Gesamtausgabe der musikalischen Werken von Michael Praetorius*, edited by Friedrich Blume, pp. XLV-LII. Wolfenbüttel: Möseler, 1960; reprinted in his *Syntagma musicologicum: Gesammelte Reden und Schriften* (edited by Martin Ruhnke; Kassel: Bärenreiter, 1963), pp. 265-74.

Abraham, Lars Ulrich. *Der Generalbaß im Schaffen des Michael Praetorius und seine harmonischen Voraussetzungen*. BSzMw, no. 3. Berlin: Merseburger, 1961.

> Reviews in *Mf* 18/1 (1965):104-5 (Carl Dahlhaus), *MK* 37/2 (1967):75-76 (Gerhard Schuhmacher), *NZfM* 123/10 (1962):482 (Bernhard Hansen), *OrganYb 1976* 7 (1976):166-67 (Peter Williams), and *QdRm* 3 (1965):265 (Alfredo Bonaccorsi).

Krützfeldt, Werner. "Satztechnische Untersuchungen am Vokalwerk des Michael Praetorius auf der Basis der Musiktheorie seiner Zeit und unter besonderer Berücksichtigung des Wort-Ton-Verhältnisses in den motettischen Sätzen." Ph.D. dissertation, The University of Hamburg, 1961.

Hiekel, Hans Otto. "Der Madrigal- und Motettentypus in der Mensurallehre des Michael Praetorius." *AfMw* 19-20/1 (1962-63):40-55.

Brainard, Paul. "Zur Deutung der Diminution in der Tactuslehre des Michael Praetorius." *Mf* 17/2 (1964):169-74.

Dahlhaus, Carl. "Zur Taktlehre des Michael Praetorius." *Mf* 17/2 (1964):162-9.

Grüß, Hans. "Über die objektive Verlangsamung musikalischer Verläufe als Erscheinungsweise der historischen Entwicklung musikalischer Formen." In *Kongress Leipzig 1966* (1970):242-45. [*Rilm* 72-333.]

Hübsch-Pfleger, Lini. "Michael Praetorius: Komponist und Theoretiker an der Schwelle des Barock." *Muh* 22/1 (1971):8-9.

Ruhnke, Martin. "Michael Praetorius." *MK* 41/5 (1971):229-42.

Forchert, Arno. "Michael Praetorius: Werk und Wirkung." *Sagittarius* 4 (1973):98-110. [*Rilm* 76-2559.]

Dahlhaus, Carl. "Über den Motettenbegriff des Michael Praetorius." In *GudewillFs* (1978):7-14. [*Rilm* 78-4847.]

Crane, Frederick. "Tobias Schönfeld's *Compendium instrumentorum musicalium* (Liegnitz, 1625)." *JAMIS* 5-6 (1979-80):37-41. [*Rilm* 80-1528.]

Blankenburg, Walter. "Praetorius, Michael." In *NGrove* (1980). Bibliog.

Ferrari, Giorgio. "Liuto, arciliuto, chitarrone, strumenti dell'età barocca in Italia." *Fronimo* 39 (1982):11-18. [*Rilm* 82-1390.]

Smith, Anne. "Belege zur Frage der Stimmtonhöhe bei Michael Praetorius." In *Alte Musik: Praxis und Reflexion*, edited by Peter Reidemeister and Veronika Gutmann, pp. 340-45. BJhM:Sonderband. Winterthur: Amadeus Verlag, 1983. [*Rilm* 83-4734.]

Myers, Herbert W. "Praetorius's Pitch." *EM* 12/3 (1984):369-71.

> See Segerman (1985), below.

Segerman, Ephriam. "Praetorius's Pitch?" *EM* 13/2 (1985):261-63.

Hickmann, Ellen. " 'Aussländische, barbarische, bäwrische' Klangwerkzeuge als frühe klassifikatorische Kategorie bei Michael Praetorius (1619)." *OmSM* 9A (1986-87):177-91. Bibliog.

Vogelsanger, Siegfried. *Michael Praetorius beim Wort genommen: Zur Entstehungsgeschichte seiner Werke*. Ormus, no. 2. Aachen: Edition Herodot, Rader Verlag, 1987. Bibliog.

Möller, Dietlind. "Studien zu M. Praetorius' *Syntagma musicum*." Ph.D. dissertation, The University of Cologne, forthcoming.

See also BELLERMANN: (1858); DEMANTIUS: (1602):Eggebrecht (1957); FABER: (1548):Vulpius (1608); FÉTIS: (1833-44); HEINICHEN: (1728): Buelow (1961/. . ./1986); HERBST: Allerup (1931); KEPLER: Dickreiter (1971/1973); LIPPIUS: Rivera (1974/1980); MERSENNE: (1617-48); RIEMANN: (1898); SAINT-LAMBERT: (1707): Burchill (1979); SORGE: [1748]; VIADANA: Haack (1964/1974); WALTHER: (1732); LITERATURE SUPPLEMENT: Abraham (1968/1969); Allen ["Baroque"] (1939), ["Philosophies"] (1939); Ambros (1878/. . ./1909); ● ● ● **Arnold (1931/ . . ./1965)**; Auhagen (1982/1983); Babitz (1967/1969); Badura-Skoda et al. (1980); Barbieri (1983); **Barbour (1932), (1951/. . ./1972)**; Becker (1836-39/1964); **Bent** ["Analysis"] **(1980/1987)**; Beyschlag (1907/1953); Boetticher (1954); Borgir (1971/1987); Braun (1986); Brennecke (1953); Brown (1973); Brown and McKinnon (1980); **Buelow (1972)**, ["Rhetoric"] **(1980)**, (1982); Bukofzer (1947); **Bullivant (1980)**; Burney (1776-89/. . ./ 1957); Cahn ["Retardatio"] (1972-); Carse (1925/1964); Chafe (1982); Chew (1980); Chomiński (1962/1981); Collins (1963); **Coover (1980)**; Dahlhaus ["Zur Entstehung"] (1961); ["Untersuchungen"] (1966/. . ./1988), (1981); **Dahlhaus et al. (1987)**; Dammann (1958/1967); Dolmetsch (1915/. . ./1969); Donington (1963/. . ./ 1974),

1974), (1980); Dreyfus (1987); **Dürr and Gerstenberg** (1949-68), **(1980)**; Dupont (1933/. . ./1986); Eggebrecht (1955), (1957); Eitner (1880), (1900-1904/1959-60); Federhofer (1967); Feldmann (1958); Fellerer (1983), (1984); Ferand (1937/1938), (1951), [*Improvisation*] (1956/1961); Fischer (1978); Forkel (1792/1962); Frobenius ["Tactus"] (1972-), ["Vollstimmig"] (1972-); Gable (1979); Gernhardt (1977); Ghislanzoni (1949-51); Gissel (1980/1983), (1986); Goldschmidt (1890/1892), (1907); Green (1969); Guion (1980); Gurlitt (1942/1966); Haase (1969); Hammel (1977-78); Harich-Schneider ([1939]/. . ./1970); Harrán (1986); Hawkins (1776/. . ./1969); Haydon (1933/1970); Heckmann (1953); Heimann (1970/1973); Hiller (1768-69); Horsley (1963); Hoshino (1979); Houle (1960), (1987); Hucke (1969); Hüschen (1986); Jackisch (1966); Jackson (1988); Jacobi (1957-60/1971); Jeppesen (1922/. . ./1970); Kätzel (1951/1957); Kahl (1953); Kassler (1984); Katz (1926); Katz (1985); Kauko (1958); Keller (1931/. . ./1966), (1955/1965); Kelletat [*Temperatur*] (1960), ["Tonordnung"] (1960); Kinkeldey (1910/1968); Kirkendale (1979); Kroyer (1901/. . ./1970); Krützfeldt (1961); Krummacher (1979); Kuhn (1902); Launay (1972); Lawrence (1978); **Lester** (1977), **(1989)**; Lewis (1980); **Lindley** ["Temperaments"] **(1980)**, (1982), (1988); Livingstone (1971); Lowinsky (1946/1967); Mahlert and Sunter (1972-); **Maniates (1979)**; **Mann (1955/. . ./1987)**; Meer (1980); Meier (1974/1988); Mendel (1948), (1955), (1978); Mitchell, J. W. (1963); Moser (1936/. . ./1959); Moyer (1969); Müller-Blattau (1923/. . ./1963); **Neumann**, Frederick (1978), [*Essays*] **(1982)**; Newman (1985); Newman (1959/. . ./1983); Niemöller (1964/1969); North (1987); Oberdoerffer (1949-68), (1967); **Palisca** [*Baroque*] (1968/1981), ["Theory"] **(1980)**; Preußner (1924), (1939); Ratner (1980); Rauhe (1959-60); Reckow (1972-); Reese (1954/1959); ● ● ● (1957/1970); Reichenbach (1948); Reimer ["Concerto"] (1972-); **Ritzel (1967/1968)**; Robison (1982); Rogers (1955); Rothgeb (1968); Ruf (1972-); Ruhnke (1949-68), (1974); Schäfke (1934/1964); Schmitt (1974-75); Schulenberg (1984); Seidel (1976); Sirch (1981); Sponheuer (1986); Stowell (1985); Subirá (1947/. . ./1958); Sydow-Saak (1972-); Taddie (1984); Tagliavini (1975/1983); Tittel (1966); Troeger (1987); Tyler (1975); Ulrich (1931/1932); Walker (1987); Wessely (1971-72); Wichmann (1966); Wienpahl (1953); Williams, P. (1970); Winternitz (1970); Wolff (1972-); **Zaminer (1985)**; Zenck (1942).

WOLFGANG CASPAR PRINTZ

[1641 – 1717]

Every theorist transmits some part of what is already known—modifying and augmenting, to be sure, but nevertheless participating in a continuing exchange among thinkers. Young devotees continually emerge to take the place of the old, whose death does not necessarily diminish their impact, but only prevents them from responding to any further developments of their notions. Wolfgang Caspar Printz, active in Germany during the last third of the seventeenth century, was particularly affected by the works of DESCARTES and KIRCHER, and to a lesser extent by those of ZARLINO, LIPPIUS, and PRAETORIUS, among others. He brought to German-speaking musicians a variety of materials which they might not have encountered otherwise, and his commentary and synthesis put these perspectives into an organized framework for comparison. His original observations concerning rhythm and meter and his clarification of cadential procedures had lasting influence, and his summary of the history of music from ancient times through the seventeenth century, in his *Historische Beschreibung* (1690), was an important step in establishing an awareness of music's past.

Though Printz listed an output of over twenty books on music, only a handful survive. He also indulged in musical fiction, made available recently in facsimile. *Phrynis; oder,* *Satyrischer Componist* (1676-96) is his most comprehensive treatment of theoretical issues, ranging from intervals and cadences to variation techniques, figured bass, tuning and temperament, rhythm, and counterpoint. He made perceptive comments on the nuances of rhythmic performance (wherein the stress of individual beats does not conform to exact mathematical standards and thus must be considered when setting a text) and clarified through numerous examples the possibilities for cadences in each of the modes (emphasizing the first, fifth, and third scale degrees except when that degree would serve as the foundation for a diminished triad).

Printz displayed impressive rigor in his organizational skill, evident not only in the documentation of cadence types and diminution formulae, but also in his categorization of music's components. The 1668 *Compendium musicae* presents a system organized according to harmonic, melodic, rhythmic, dynamic, and formal criteria.

Further evidence of his systematic methodology appears in his *Exercitatione musicae* (1687-89), wherein he treated each consonant interval in turn, first exploring theoretical issues such as the degree to which the interval is consonant (he suggested, for example, that the 5:1 major third and its 5:4 offshoot were perfect while the 4:3 fourth was imperfect) and the necessity of tempering each fifth so that four ascending fifths (3/2 to the fourth power, or 81:16) might coincide with the major third (5:1, or 80:16). Then, with extraordinary and to some readers probably daunting rigor, he discussed voice-leading from each of the consonant intervals using every conceivable type of motion. For example, in the chapter on the perfect fifth, he explained motion from a fifth to a fifth or to another interval. If to a fifth, then the composer would choose motion either to the same pitches or to different pitches, either by step (whole or half) or by leap. (Not surprisingly, most of these possibilities were condemned.) If to another interval, then the composer would choose motion either to a suspension or to another consonance, accomplished using similar motion (ascending or descending), oblique motion, or contrary motion (either inward or outward). Throughout these discussions of voice-leading one finds suggestions for how certain motions that might otherwise be frowned upon (such as one involving a cross relation) would be acceptable if brought to the service of a specific affect.

Though not among the century's more creative theorists, Printz's writings offer a particularly thorough overview of theoretical speculation and practice in an era which was becoming comfortable with triadic thinking and sophisticated voice-leading.

Anweisung zur Singe-Kunst; oder, Kurtzer Bericht, wie man einen Knaben auff das Leichteste nach jetziger Manier könne singen lehren [*Rism* B/VI/2, p. 669.]

> Zittau: 1666. [Lost.]
> Guben: Christoph Gruber, 1671.
> 1685. [Lost.]

Compendium musicae in quo breviter ac succinte explicantur et traduntur omnia ea quae ad Oden artificiose componendam requiruntur

> Guben: 1668.

Phrynis [*Mytilenaeus*]; *oder, Satyrischer Componist, welcher vermittelst einer satyrischen Geschicht alle und jede Fehler der ungelehrten, selbstgewachsenen, ungeschickten und unverständigen Componisten höfflich darstellet und darneben lehret, wie ein musikalisches Stück rein, ohne Fehler und nach dem rechten Grunde zu componiren und zu setzen sey* [*Rism* B/VI/2, p. 670.]

> 1) *Synopsin musices poeticae; oder, Eine kurtze Einleitung zur Kunst noch dem rechten Grunde zu componiren . . .*
>
> 2) [*So in sich hält mancherley musicalische Discurse als von denen Proportionibus, den Requisitis eines guten Componisten de Variationibus, vom General-Baß und dergleichen . . .*]

3)[*So in sich hält unterschiedliche musicalische Discurse sonderlich aber von denen Generibus Modulandi, und darbey von unterschiedenen Temperaturen, Musicâ Rhythmicâ, mancherley Contrapuncten, Prolation des Texts, einer Arth des musicalischen Labyrinths samt andem so wohl lustigen als ernsthafften Sachen ans Licht gegeben*]

> Quedlinburg: Christian Okel, 1676. Vol. 1. [LCPS: P-065a.]
> Sagan: Christian Okel, 1677. Vol. 2. [LCPS: P-065a.]
> Dresden and Leipzig: Johann Christoph Mieth & Johann Christoph Zimmermann (Johann Riedel/C. S. Hoff-Buchdrucker), 1696. Vols. 1-3. [LCPS: P-065b. SMLMS. IDC.]
>
> > The third volume was ready for publication in 1679 but remained in manuscript until the 1696 edition. Two additional volumes were in preparation when Printz's library was destroyed by fire. See *AmZ* 31/34 (1829):569-70.
>
> Dresden: Joh. Nic. Gerlach, 1744.

Musica modulatoria vocalis; oder, Manierliche und zierliche Sing-Kunst . . . [Rism B/VI/2, p. 671.]

> Schweidnitz: Christian Okel, 1678. [LCPS: P-068.]

Refutation des Satyrischen Componistens, oder so genannten Phrynis . . . [Rism B/VI/2, p. 672.]

> Gedruckt in der Welt, 1678.
>
> > Published under the names Matz Tapinsmus and Charis Läusimpeltz. Perhaps written by Printz himself as a pretext for his *Declaration* (1679), below. Reprinted in (1676-77):(1696), above.

Declaration oder weitere Erklärung der Refutation des Satyrischen Componistens

> Cosmopolis: 1679.
>
> > A response to the *Refutation* of 1678. Reprinted in (1676-77):(1696), above.

Exercitationes musicae theoretico-practicae curiosae de concordantiis singulis; Das ist, Musicalische Wissenschaft und Kunst-Übungen von jedweden Concordantien . . . [Rism B/VI/2, p. 670.]

> Dresden [Frankfurt and Leipzig]: Johann Christoph Mieth, 1687-89. [LCPS: P-066. SMLMS.]
>
> > Review in MIZLER: (1736-54):Vols. 1/1 (1736):10-18; 1/2 (1737):35-48; 1/3 (1737):33-52; 1/4 (1738):4-27; 1/5 (1738):32-67; 1/6 (1738):44-61; 2/1 (1740):132-44; 2/2 (1740):247-55; 2/3 (1742):50-62.

Compendium musicae signatoriae et modulatoriae vocalis; Das ist, Kurtzer Begriff aller derjenigen Sachen, so einem, der die Vocal-Music lernen will, zu wissen von nöthen seyn [*Rism* B/VI/2, pp. 669-70.]

Dresden: Johann Christoph Mieth (Johann Riedel), 1689.

Dresden and Leipzig: Johann Christoph Mieth, 1714. [LCPS: P-064. SMLMS.]

S • Facsimile of the 1689 edition. Hildesheim: Georg Olms, 1974.

Historische Beschreibung der edelen Sing- und Kling-Kunst . . . [*Rism* B/VI/2, p. 671.]

Dresden: Johann Christoph Mieth (Johann Georgen), 1690. [LCPS: P-067. SMLMS. IDC.]

Review in MARPURG: (1754-78):Vol. 1/2 (1754):172-79.

S • Wessely, Othmar, ed. Facsimile edition. GDMgBA, no. 1. Graz: Akademische Druck- und Verlagsanstalt, 1964.

Review in *Me* 24/4 (1971):191.

See MATTHESON: (1740) for Printz's own listing of his works, some of which are not extant, others of which do not pertain to music theory.

LITERATURE:

Schmitz, Eugen. "Studien über W. C. Printz als Musikschriftsteller." *MMg* 36/6-7 (1904):100-21. Bibliog.

Heckmann, Harald. "Printz, Wolfgang Caspar." In *MGG* (1949-68). Bibliog.

Heckmann, Harald. "Wolfgang Caspar Printz (1641-1717) und seine Rhythmuslehre." Ph.D. dissertation, The University of Freiburg im Breisgau, 1952.

Stöpfgeshoff, Susanne. "Die Musikerromane von Wolfgang Caspar Printz und Johann Kuhnau zwischen Barock und Aufklärung." Ph.D. dissertation, The University of Freiburg im Breisgau, 1960. Bibliog.

Eberhard, Otto. "Wolfgang Caspar Printz, ein oberpfälzischer Musiker." *Die Oberpfalz* 10 (1967):218-21. [*Rilm* 69-3682.]

• • • Buelow, George J. "Printz, Wolfgang Caspar." In *NGrove* (1980). Bibliog.

See also AHLE: Sevier (1976); FÉTIS: (1833-44); HERBST: Allerup (1931); LIPPIUS: Rivera (1974/1980); MATTHESON: (1740); RAMEAU: Pischner (1961/. . ./1967); SORGE: [1748]; VIADANA:

Haack (1964/1974); WALTHER: (1732); LITERATURE SUPPLEMENT: Allen ["Baroque"] (1939), ["Philosophies"] (1939), **Apfel (1981)**; Apfel and Dahlhaus (1974); Arlt (1974); **Arnold (1931/. . . / 1965)**; Auhagen (1982/1983); Badura-Skoda et al. (1980); **Barbour (1951/. . ./1972)**; Baron (1968); Bartel (1982/1985); Becker (1836-39/1964); **Benary (1956/1961)**; Blumröder (1972-); Boomgaarden (1985/1987); Braun (1970), (1986); Buelow (1972), ["Affections"] (1980), (1982); Bukofzer (1947); Burney (1776-89/. . ./1957); Cahn ["Repercussio"] (1972-); Chybiński (1911-12); Collins (1963), (1966); **Coover (1980)**; Dahlhaus ["Zur Entstehung"] (1961), ["Untersuchungen"] (1966/ . . . /1988); **Dahlhaus et al. (1987)**; Dammann (1958/1967); Duckles (1970); **Dürr and Gerstenberg (1949-68), (1980)**; Dupont (1933/. . ./1986); Eitner (1900-1904/1959-60); Fellerer (1962), ["Musikwissenschaft"] (1972), ["Zum Bild"] (1973); Fischer (1978); Flindell (1983-84); Forchert (1986); Forkel (1792/1962); Frobenius ["Homophonus"] (1972-), ["Isotonos"] (1972-), ["Monodie"] (1972-), ["Polyphon"] (1972-), ["Vollstimmig"] (1972-); Gerber (1790-92/1977), (1812-14/1966); Goldschmidt (1907); Green (1969); Gurlitt (1954/1966); Harrán (1986); Hartmann (1980); Hawkins (1776/. . ./ 1969); Heckmann (1953); Hiller (1768-69); Horsley (1963), [*Fugue: History*] (1966); Houle (1960), (1987); Kähler (1958); **Kassler (1979)**; Kirkendale (1984); Krützfeldt (1961); Lange (1899-1900); **Lester (1974), (1977), (1978), (1989)**; Leuchtmann (1957/1959); **Lindley ["Temperaments"] (1980)**; Maier (1984); Mainke (1969); McKinnon (1978); Meier (1974/1988); Menck (1931); Moser (1936/. . ./ 1959); Müller-Blattau (1923/. . ./1963); Nelson (1984); **Neumann**, Frederick (1978), [*Essays*] **(1982)**; Newman (1985); Preußner (1924); Ratner (1970); Reckow (1972-); Reese (1957/1970); Reichenbach (1948); Riedel (1956/1959); Rivera (1978); Rivera (1984); Ruhnke (1949-68); Schäfke (1934/1964); Schünemann (1928/1931); Schulenberg (1982), (1984); Seidel (1972-), (1975), (1976); Sheldon (1975); Spitzer and Zaslaw (1986); Troeger (1987); Vogel (1955/1954); Walker (1987); Wessely (1971-72); Williams, P. (1970), (1979); **Zaminer (1985)**.

EBENEZER PROUT

[1835–1909]

The most comprehensive set of music theory texts to emerge in England during Victoria's reign was written by Ebenezer Prout, who taught in London and Dublin, helped George Grove with a number of articles for his *Dictionary*, and edited for a time the *Monthly Musical Record*. His works cover many aspects of harmony, counterpoint, form, and orchestration. A number of them were published concurrently in America, while several volumes appeared in translation—German, Italian, or Russian.

As was typical of British harmony manuals of the time, Prout's synthesis, in his *Harmony: Its Theory and Practice* (1889), is muddled by his monumental efforts to derive his system from the harmonic series (following the precedent of DAY), while in later editions he abandoned these speculations but offered no better alternative. The works which address counterpoint and fugue (1890-92) and form (1893-95) are of greater interest. The former represents a refreshing about-face from the unstylistic exercises then in vogue. Prout had carefully examined the fugal works of Bach, Handel, Beethoven, and others, and achieved a considerable degree of success in creating an analytical framework for understanding their characteristic procedures. His *Musical Form* and *Applied Forms* develop out of RIEMANN's conceptions of phrase structure and offer a potent perspective on the larger forms, including rondo form, sonata form, sonata-rondo form, and the symphonic poem.

Instrumentation (NMPES, no. 15)

London: Novello, [1877].

> Numerous later editions, some edited by Sir John STAINER and Sir C. Hubert H. Parry. Reviews in *NAR* 190/645 (1909):266 and *Nation* 88/2273 (1909):72-73.

T ● Bachur, Bernhard, trans. *Elementar-Lehrbuch der Instrumentation*. BHmH, no. 5. Leipzig: Breitkopf & Härtel, 1880; later editions.

> Review in *Rmi* 11/3 (1904):641 (Luigi Torchi).

T ● Ricci, Vittorio, trans. *Strumentazione*. MH. Milan: Ulrico Hoepli, 1901.

S ● Facsimile of the 1877 edition. SMus. New York: Haskell House, 1969.

S ● Facsimile of the 1877 edition. St. Clair Shores, Mich.: Scholarly Press, 1970.

Articles in Grove's *Dictionary of Music and Musicians* [*DMM*]

London: Macmillan, 1879-89.

A Third Book on the Theory of Music

> By Louisa Gibson.

London: Weekes, [1887]. 2nd edition, with the assistance of Prout.

Harmony: Its Theory and Practice

London: Augener, [1889].

> Numerous editions, including a reworking in 1903 (sixteenth edition). Reviews in *MMR* 19/226-28 (1889):225-26, 242-46, 265-69

(Frederick Niecks) [response by Prout in *MMR* 19/228 (1889):269-72 and 20/229 (1890):2-5; reply by Niecks in *MMR* 20/230 (1890):27-32], *MMR* 33/393 (1903):163-66, *Nation* 78/2035 (1904):517-18, and *Rmi* 11/2 (1904):381 (Luigi Torchi).

S ● Facsimile of the 1903 edition. St. Clair Shores, Mich.: Scholarly Press, 1970.

S ● Facsimile of the 1903 edition. New York: AMS Press, [1971].

Additional Exercises to "Harmony: Its Theory and Practice"

London: Augener, [1890].

> Numerous editions. Review in *MMR* 21/242 (1891):30-31 (Charles W. Pearce).

Counterpoint: Strict and Free

London: Augener, [1890].

> Numerous editions. Review in *MMR* 20/233 (1890):97-103 (Charles W. Pearce).

S ● Facsimile of the 14th impression. St. Clair Shores, Mich.: Scholarly Press, 1970.

S ● Facsimile edition. New York: AMS Press, [1971].

Additional Exercises, Melodies, and Unfigured Basses for Harmonizing to "Counterpoint: Strict and Free"

London: Augener, [1890].

> Numerous editions. Review in *MMR* 21/246 (1891):128-30 (Charles W. Pearce).

Double Counterpoint and Canon

London: Augener, [1891].

> Numerous editions. Review in *MMR* 21/250-51 (1891):219-23, 242-45 (Charles W. Pearce).

S ● Facsimile of the 1893 edition. Westport, Ct.: Greenwood Press, [1969].

S ● Facsimile of the 1893 edition. SMus, no. 42. New York: Haskell House, 1969.

Fugue

London: Augener, [1891].

> Numerous editions. Review in *MMR* 22/256-57 (1892):74-77, 97-101 (Charles W. Pearce).

T ● Timitseva-Gering, A., trans. *Fuga*. Moscow: 1900.

S ● Facsimile of the 1891 edition. Westport, Ct.: Greenwood Press, [1969].

S ● Facsimile of the 1891 edition. SMus, no. 42. New York: Haskell House, 1969.

S ● Facsimile of the 1891 edition. St. Clair Shores, Mich.: Scholarly Press, 1970.

Key to the Exercises in "Harmony: Its Theory and Practice"

London: Augener, [1891].

Numerous editions. Review in *MMR* 21/243 (1891):52-53 (Charles W. Pearce).

Key to the Additional Exercises to "Harmony: Its Theory and Practice"

London: Augener, [1891].

Numerous editions. Review in *MMR* 21/244 (1891):80-81 (Charles W. Pearce).

Fugal Analysis: A Companion to "Fugue," Being a Collection of Fugues of Various Styles, Put into Score and Analyzed

London: Augener, [1892].

Numerous editions. Review in *MMR* 22/260 (1892):170-74 (Charles W. Pearce).

T ● Beliaev, Viktor Mikhailovich, trans. *Analiz fug.* Moscow: 1915.

Musical Form

London: Augener, [1893].

Numerous editions.

T ● Tolstoi, S. L., trans. *Muzykal'naia forma.* Moscow: 1896.

S ● Facsimile of the 1893 edition. St. Clair Shores, Mich.: Scholarly Press, 1970.

S ● Facsimile of the 1893 edition. New York: AMS Press, [1971].

"Musical Form: A Paper Read before the Incorporated Society of Musicians, at the Conference at Scarborough, January 4th, 1894"

In *MMR* 24/278-79 (1894):27-31, 50-52.

Applied Forms: A Sequel to "Musical Form"

London: Augener, [1895].

Numerous editions. Reviews in *MMR* 25/294 (1895):121-25 (Charles W. Pearce), *MMR* 25/299 (1895):250, and *Rmi* 3/1 (1896):195-98 (E. N.).

T ● Slavinsky, Y. *Prikladnye formy.* Moscow: 1910.

S ● Facsimile of the 1895 edition. St. Clair Shores, Mich.: Scholarly Press, 1970.

S ● Facsimile of the 1895 edition. New York: AMS Press, [1971].

"The Relation of Musical Theory to Practice"

MMR 25/292 (1895):73-77.

The Orchestra

1) *Technique of the Instruments*

2) *Orchestral Combination*

London: Augener, [1898-99]. 2 vols.

Reviews in *Nation* 71/1827 (1900):19, *Rmi* 5/3 (1898):602-3 (Luigi Torchi), and *Rmi* 7/1 (1900):196-98 (Luigi Torchi).

T ● Nikitis, O., trans. *Das Orchester.* 2 vols. 1905-6.

S ● Facsimile edition. Melville, N.Y.: Belwin Mills (Kalmus Publication), [1960?].

S ● Facsimile edition. St. Clair Shores, Mich.: Scholarly Press, 1972.

Analytical Key to the Exercises in [the Sixteenth and Subsequent Editions of] Harmony: Its Theory and Practice

London: Augener, [1903].

"Chromatic Harmony"

MMR 33/386-87 (1903):21-24, 41-44.

A Course of Lectures on Orchestration

London: C. Jaques, 1905.

Analysis of J. S. Bach's Forty-Eight Fugues (Das wohltemperirte Clavier)

London: Edwin Ashdown, [ca. 1910]. Edited by Louis B. Prout.

See also DAY: Pearce (1888); DAY: PROUT (1888).

LITERATURE:

Knowles, C. H. G. . . . *Rhymes on the Rules of Harmony, Founded on Dr. Prout's "Harmony".* London: Augener, [1899].

Westrup, J. A. "Ebenezer Prout (1835-1909)." *MMR* 65/765 (1935):53-54.

Harman, Richard Alexander. "Prout, Ebenezer." Translated by Hans-Joachim Beier. In *MGG* (1949-68). Bibliog.

Musicus [pseud.]. Letter to the Editor. *MT* 91/1284 (1950):66.

Frank, Jonathan. "Ebenezer Prout—A Revaluation." *MO* 83/988 (1959-60):247-49.

Shaw, Watkins. "Prout, Ebenezer." In *NGrove* (1980). Bibliog.

See also DAY: Jones (1977); KOCH: Dahlhaus (1978); LITERATURE SUPPLEMENT: **Bent** ["Analysis"] **(1980/1987)**; Bircher (1970); Bridges (1984); **Bullivant (1980)**; Burdick (1977-78); Burke (1963); Carpenter (1988); Carse (1925/1964); Cavett-

Dunsby (1988); Cazden (1948); Chew (1980); Cobb (1884); Cole (1969); Dunsby and Whittall (1988); Finney (1957); Horsley [*Fugue: History*] (1966); Jacobi (1957-60/1971); Jeppesen (1922/. . ./ 1970), (1935); Jones (1934); Jorgenson (1957); Kauko (1958); Lang (1941); Laudon (1978); Lindley (1982); **Mann (1955/. . ./1987)**;

McQuere (1983); Mitchell, J. W. (1963); Müller-Blattau (1923/. . ./1963); **Neumann** [*Essays*] **(1982)**; Niecks (1891); Oldroyd (1948); Prout (1893); Sanders (1919); Scholes (1947); ● ● ● **Shirlaw (1917/. . ./1970)**; Stevens (1974); Thompson (1980); Whatley (1981).

HENRY PURCELL

[1659 – 1695]

Henry Purcell edited the twelfth edition (1694) of PLAYFORD's *Introduction to the Skill of Music* and inserted his own rules of descant for those of Thomas CAMPION. Purcell rejected CAMPION's method of composing from the bass and advised readers to compose from the treble. He also introduced and illustrated the procedures of imitation, double counterpoint, inversion, augmentation, diminution, retrograde, and canon. Various harmonic sonorities are presented, including what we now label as the dominant seventh chord with the leading tone in the bass, the diminished-seventh chord on the raised fourth degree in the minor mode, the 6/5 (added-sixth) chord, the Neapolitan-sixth chord, the dominant pedal, and the technique of composing upon a ground (variations over a repeated bass).

"A Brief Introduction to the Art of Descant; or, Composing Musick in Parts."

In PLAYFORD: (1654):(1694).

S ● Squire, W. Barclay, ed. "Purcell as Theorist." *SIMg* 6 (1904-5):521-67.

S ● "Examples of Counterpoint and Canon." In *The Works of Henry Purcell*, vol. 31. PSE. London: Novello, 1959.

LITERATURE:

Westrup, Jack Allan. "Purcell . . . Henry (II)." Translated by Christiane Blume. In *MGG* (1949-68). Bibliog.

Westrup, Jack. "Purcell (3) Henry Purcell (ii)." In *NGrove* (1980). Bibliog.

See also FÉTIS: (1833-44); LITERATURE SUPPLEMENT: Apfel (1981); **Arnold (1931/. . ./1965)**; Colles (1928-29); **Dahlhaus et al. (1987)**; Dolmetsch (1915/. . ./1969); Donington (1963/. . ./ 1974), (1980); Eitner (1900-1904/1959-60); Gerber (1790-92/1977), (1812-14/1966); Hancock (1977); Harding (1938); Hawkins (1776/. . ./1969); Houle (1987); **Lester (1989)**; Miller (1960); Rothschild (1953); Ruff (1970); Sachs (1972-); **Seidel and Cooper (1986)**; Shamgar (1981), (1984); Sheldon (1982); Williams, P. (1970); Wolf (1939).

JOHANN JOACHIM QUANTZ

[1697 – 1773]

Among the many pedagogical works intended for performers of specific instruments, a few stand out for their unique and penetrating perspectives on the musical practices and conditions of their era. Johann Joachim Quantz's *Versuch einer Anweisung, die Flöte traversiere zu spielen* (1752) treats the attainment of proficiency on the transverse flute not only in its technical sense, but also in terms of developing full artistry and taste. His work therefore deserves the attention of anyone interested in eighteenth-century performance practices and conventions of composition. Quantz emphasized the flautist's interactions with the larger musical establishment: how an ensemble should be organized, what its leader must accomplish, standards for accompaniment. His discussions of articulation, rhythmic delivery, tempo, dynamics, and improvised ornamentation have stimulated many modern scholars and performers. Never dry or abstract, his treatment emphasizes both style and the arousal of the appropriate passions as essential goals of performance.

Quantz developed his skill as a flautist in Dresden, his principal residence from 1716 through 1741. Frederick the Great, who had studied with Quantz intermittently since 1728, offered him an esteemed position in his Berlin musical establishment soon after his ascent to the throne in 1740. Through the flourishing musical life in which he participated in these two cities, Quantz gained the broad perspective from which his book is derived. Another figure at the Berlin court, C. P. E. BACH, followed Quantz's lead by producing a manual for keyboardists, while Leopold MOZART performed the same service for violinists.

Solfeggi

Ms. [Copenhagen: Det Kongelige Bibliotek.]

T ● Michel, Winfried, and Teske, Hermien, eds. *Solfeggi pour la flute traversière avec l'enseignement, par Monsieur Quantz*. Winterthur: Amadeus Verlag, 1978.

Reviews in *AR* 21/3 (1980):134 (Dale Higbee) and *Notes* 36/1 (1979-80):104-5 (Jane P. Ambrose).

Versuch einer Anweisung, die Flöte traversiere zu spielen; mit verschiedenen, zur Beförderung des guten Geschmackes in der praktischen Musik dienlichen Anmerkungen begleitet, und mit Exempeln erläutert, nebst XXIV Kupfertafeln [*Rism* B/VI/2, pp. 676-78.]

Berlin: Johann Friedrich Voß, 1752. [LCPS: Q-002a. HoM: 1251. SMLMS.]

Review in *BsW* 10/1-2 (1763-64):50-53.

Breslau: Johann Friedrich Korn der Ältere, 1780.
Breslau: Johann Friedrich Korn der Ältere, 1789.
[LCPS: Q-002b. HoM: 1252.]

T ● *Essai d'une méthode pour apprendre à jouer de la flûte traversière . . .* [*Rism* B/VI/2, p. 677.] Berlin: Cretien Frederic Voß, 1752; facsimile edition (Introduction by Antoine Geoffrey-Dechaume; Essay by Pierre Sechet), Paris: Éditions A. Zurfluh, 1975. [*Rilm* 76-7024.]

T ● Lustig, Jacob Wilhelm, trans. *Grondig onderwys van den aardt en de regte behandeling der dwarsfluit . . .* [*Rism* B/VI/2, p. 677.] Amsterdam: A. Olofsen, 1754; partial reprint, [ca. 1765]; facsimile edition (edited by Frans Brüggen), Utrecht: A. Oosthoek, 1965.

Review in *Mens* 20/8 (1965):250-52 (Charles Havelaar).

T ● "Trattato di un metodo per imparare a suonare il flauto traversiere . . ." Ms. [Bologna: Civico museo bibliografico musicale.]

S ● See MARPURG: (1762-63).

S ● See (1770), below.

T ● [?Heck, Johann Caspar, trans.] *Easy and Fundamental Instructions . . . How to Introduce Extempore Embellishments or Variations; as Also Ornamental Cadences, with Propriety, Taste, and Regularity*. [*Rism* B/VI/2, pp. 677-78.] London: Welcker, [ca. 1770-80] [LCPS: Q-002c.]; London: Longman & Broderip, [ca. 1780-98]; as *Extemporary Cadences*, Dublin: Edmund Lee, [ca. 1795].

Translation of Chapters 13 and 15.

S ● Schering, Arnold, ed. Abridged edition. Leipzig: Kahnt, 1906; reprint edition, 1926.

Reviews in *MMR* 37/440-42 (1907):169-72, 194-96, 218-22 (Ebenezer Prout) and *Rmi* 41/4-5 (1937):499-501 (Benvenuto Disertori).

T ● Christman, Arthur H. "Johann Joachim Quantz on the Musical Practices of His Time." S.M.D. dissertation, Union Theological Seminary (New York), 1950.

T ● See **Strunk (1950)**:577-98.

S ● Schmitz, Hans-Peter, ed. Facsimile of the 1789 edition. Afterword by Horst Ausbach. IGMDm, ser. 1, no. 2. Kassel: Bärenreiter; Beverly Hills, Calif.: Gottlieb, 1953; reprint edition, Kassel: Bärenreiter, 1964; 1968; 1983; VEB Deutscher Verlag für Musik, 1986.

> Review in *JAMS* 9/1 (1956):40-46 (A. Tillman Merritt).

T ● ● ● Reilly, Edward Randolph. "Quantz's *Versuch einer Anweisung, die Flöte traversiere zu spielen*: A Translation and Study." 2 vols. Ph.D. dissertation, The University of Michigan, 1958; published edition (as *On Playing the Flute*), New York: Free Press; London: Faber & Faber, 1966; reprint edition, 1976; 2nd edition, New York: Schirmer, 1985. Bibliog. [*DA* 21/01A, p. 207.]

> See Babitz and Pont (1973). Reviews in *AJME* 21 (1977):63 (Owen Fisenden), *AMT* 27/1 (1977):42 (Fredda L. Stang), *AR* 8/1 (1967):25 (Erich Katz), *AR* 27/4 (1986):163 (Jane P. Ambrose), *Choice* 4/5-6 (1967-68):539, *Diapason* 66/12 [792] (1975):11-12 (Robert Schuneman), *HFMA* 26/3 (1976):MA38 (Patrick J. Smith), *Instrumentalist* 21/2 (1966):36, *JAAC* 26/3 (1967-68):402 (Charles W. Hughes), *JAMS* 20/2 (1967):300-302 (Howard Mayer Brown), *MakM* 62 (1966):20 (John Milne), *MEJ* 53/5 (1966-67):66-67 (Curtis Coffee), *Mf* 22/1 (1969):129-30 (Peter-Hans Schmitz), *MO* 90/1075 (1967):393 (B. R.), *MT* 107/1485 (1966):962 (Stanley Sadie), *Notes* 25/1 (1968-69):37-38 (Judith L. Schwartz), *NS* 73/1879 (1967):376 (Rosalyn Tureck), *Spectator* 238/7757 (1977):23 (Anthony Burgess), and *Tempo* 79 (1966-67):29-30 (Robert Donington).

T ● Reilly, Edward R. "Quantz on National Styles of Music." *MQ* 49/2 (1963):163-87.

T ● Arakawa, Tsuneko. "J. J. Quantz no *Versuch einer Anweisung die Flöte traversiere zu spielen* ni tsuite — honyaku to shiron." M.A. thesis, Tokyo University of Arts, 1966. [*Rilm* 67-172.]

T ● Arakawa, Tsuneko. *Flute soho*. Tokyo: Zen On Gakufu, 1976.

T ● Imoto, Shoji, and Ishihala, Toshinori, trans. *Flute soho shiron — Baroque ongaku enso no genri*. Tokyo: Sinfonia, 1976.

T ● See MacClintock (1980).

Letter to G. P. TELEMANN

> Ms., 1753. [Tartu: Universitetskaya biblioteka.]

T ● See Reilly (1971), below.

"Hrn. Johann Joachim Quanzens Antwort auf des Herrn von Moldenit gedrucktes so genanntes Schreiben an Hrn. Quanz, nebst einigen Anmerkungen über dessen Versuch einer Anweisung die Flöte traversiere zu spielen"

> S ● In MARPURG: (1754-78):Vol. 4/3 (1758-59):153-91.

> > The rare work to which Quantz refers was apparently published in May, 1758. Moldenit's name appears with some regularity in MARPURG: (1754-78), while the affair was noted in *BsW* 4/2 (1758-59):821-22.

Articles under the pseudonym "Neologos" in MARPURG: (1759-63):Vol. 1 (1759-60) are perhaps by Quantz.

"Anweisung, wie ein Musikus und eine Musik zu beurteilen sey"

> In *UKK* 9/6 (1770):445-82; 10/1 (1770):3-38.

> > An excerpt from the *Versuch*.

See (1752):Reilly (1958/. . ./1985), above, and Reilly (1971), below, for further information on the dissemination of Quantz's treatise through published excerpts and plagiarisms and on the initial critical reaction.

LITERATURE:

Lorenzoni, Antonio. *Saggio per ben sonare il flaute traverso . . .* [*Rism* B/VI/1, p. 516.] Vicenza: Francesco Modena, 1779. [LCPS: L-097. SMLMS.]

Schlegel, Franz Anton. *Gründliche Anleitung, die Flöte zu spielen, nach Quanzens Anweisung.* [*Rism* B/VI/2, p. 764.] Graz: J. G. Weingand & Franz Ferstl, 1788. [LCPS: S-041.]

> Derived from Part 1 of (1752), above. Review in *AdB* 110 (1792):118-19.

Castilon, F. D. "Flute traversiere." In *Supplément à l'encyclopédie ou dictionnaire raisonné des sciences, des arts et des métiers . . .* Vol. 3. Amsterdam: M. M. Rey, 1777.

> Translation in Halfpenny (1956), below, and in Reilly (1971):98-101, below.

[Eitner, Robert.] "Quantz and Emanuel Bach." *MMg* 34/3-4 (1902):39-46, 55-63.

Schäfke, Rudolf. "Quantz als Aesthetiker: Eine Einführung in die Musikästhetik des galanten Stils." *AfMw* 6/2 (1924):213-42.

Scheck, Gustav. "Johann Joachim Quantz' Flötenschule (1752)." *DTZ* 33/6 (1936-37):152-54.

Bose, Fritz. "Quantz, Johann Joachim." In *MGG* (1949-68). Bibliog.

Halfpenny, Eric. "A French Commentary on Quantz." *ML* 37/1 (1956):61-66.

Kolneder, Walter. "Ausdrucksdynamik im Lehrwerk von Quantz." *Haus* 23/3 (1959):73-77.

Reilly, Edward R. "Further Musical Examples for Quantz's *Versuch*." *JAMS* 17/2 (1964):157-69.

Neumann, Frederick. "The French *Inégales*, Quantz, and Bach." *JAMS* 18/3 (1965):313-58; reprinted in Neumann [*Essays*] (1982):17-54.

> Replies in *JAMS* 19/1 (1966):112-14 (Robert Donington) [Response by Neumann in *JAMS* 19/3 (1966):435-37], *JAMS* 19/3 (1966):437-37 (Graham Pont), *JAMS* 20/3 (1967):473-76 (Sol Babitz), *JAMS* 20/3 (1967):476-80 (John Byrt), and *JAMS* 20/3 (1967):481-85 (Michael B. Collins).

Rasmussen, Mary. "Some Notes on the Articulations in the Melodic Variation Tables of Johann Joachim Quantz's *Versuch einer Anweisung die Flöte traversiere zu spielen* (Berlin 1752, Wroclaw 1789)." *BWQ* 1-2 (1966-67):3-26.

Allihn, Ingeborg. *Georg Philipp Telemann und Johann Joachim Quantz: Der Einfluß einiger Kammermusikwerke G. Ph. Telemanns auf das Lehrwerk des J. J. Quantz "Versuch einer Anweisung, die Flöte traversiere zu spielen"*. MTS, no. 3. Magdeburg: Deutscher Kulturbund, 1971. [*Rilm* 71-387.]

Reilly, Edward R. *Quantz and His 'Versuch': Three Studies*. AMSSD, no. 5. New York: Galaxy, 1971. Bibliog. [*Rilm* 71-3711.]

> Reviews in *AR* 12/4 (1971):142 (Dale Higbee) and *MT* 113/1552 (1972):565 (Pippa Drummond).

Reilly, Edward R. "A Realization by J. C. Heck: An *Affettuoso di molto* by Johann Joachim Quantz (1697-1773)." In *CuylerFs* (1974):154-62. [*Rilm* 76-15227.]

Dahlhaus, Carl. "Quantz und der 'vermanierierte Mannheimer goût'." *Melos/NZfM* 2/3 (1976):184-86.

Michel, Winfried. "*Solfeggi pour la flute traversiere avec l'enseignement, par Monsr. Quantz*: Einige Bemerkungen über ein ungewöhnliches, lange vermißtes Dokument zur Aufführungspraxis des 18. Jahrhunderts." *Tibia* 2/1 (1977):201-6. [*Rilm* 77-1493.]

Lasocki, David. "Quantz and the Passions: Theory and Practice." *EM* 6/4 (1978):556-67. Bibliog.

Meredith, Henry. "Baroque Trumpet Ornamentation: Another View." *ITGN* 7/3 (1980-81):22-23.

Reilly, Edward R. "Quantz, Johann Joachim." In *NGrove* (1980). Bibliog.

Allihn, Ingeborg. "Johann Joachim Quantz: Überlegungen zur Rolle der Kleinmeister im Spannungsfeld zwischen Beharrungsvermögen und Veränderungszwang." In *Konferenzbericht Blankenburg/Harz 1980* (n.d.):69-73. Bibliog.

Brixel, Eugen. "Unterweisung auf der Flöte zur Zeit Mozarts und Goethes." *ÖB* 29/3 (1981):1-2. [*Rilm* 81-1563.]

Erig, Richard. "Zum 'Pulsschlag' bei Johann Joachim Quantz." *Tibia* 7/3 (1982):168-75. [*Rilm* 82-5698.]

Gersmann, Friedrich. "Klassisches Tempo für klassische Musik." *GitL* 8/3 (1986):14-18.

Prior, Susan. "Baroque Etudes." *AR* 27/3 (1986):107-12.

Crockett, Charlotte Gwen. "The Berlin Flute Sonatas of Johann Joachim Quantz: A Study of the Repertory and Its Performance Options." Ph.D. dissertation, The University of Texas at Austin, 1987. [*DA* 48/05A, p. 1049. UMI 87-17590.]

Hefling, Stephen E. " 'Of the Manner of Playing the Adagio': Structural Levels and Performance Practice in Quantz's *Versuch*." *JMT* 31/2 (1987):205-23.

Schmitz, Hans-Peter. *Quantz heute: Der "Versuch einer Anweisung, die Flöte traversiere zu spielen" als Lehrbuch für unser Musizieren*. Kassel: Bärenreiter, 1987.

> Reviews in *NZfM* 149/10 (1988):54 (Dorothea Redepenning) and *ÖM* 43 (1988):143.

Ljungar-Chapelon, A. "Tre hundra års flötspel." *Musikrevy* 43/4 (1988):116-17.

See also ADLUNG: (1758); BACH: (1753-62); FÉTIS: (1833-44); GEMINIANI: McArtor and Reilly (1952); HEINICHEN: (1728): Buelow (1961/. . ./ 1986); KOCH: Stevens (1971); MARPURG: (1754-78):Vol. 1/1 (1754):v; (1759-63):Vol. 1 (1759-60):429-59; (1762-63); SAINT-LAMBERT: (1707):Burchill (1979); SORGE in MARPURG: (1754-78):Vol. 4 (1758-59):1-17; SCHRÖTER: (1772); TELEMANN, G. M.: (1773); TOSI: (1723):AGRICOLA:(1757); TÜRK: (1789); WALTHER: (1732); LITERATURE SUPPLEMENT: Ahlgrimm (1968), (1969-70); Almond (1979); **Arnold (1931/. . ./1965)**; Audbourg-Popin (1986); Auhagen (1982-83), (1987); Aulabaugh (1958); Babitz (1952), (1967/1969); Badura-Skoda et al. (1980); Balthazar (1983); Barbour (1952); Becker (1836-39/1964); **Benary (1956/1961)**, (1963); Beyschlag (1907/1953); Blake (1988); Boomgaarden (1985/1987); Borgir (1971/1987); Bremner (1979); Brown (1976); Brown and McKinnon (1980); Bruck (1928); **Buelow** ["Affections"] (1980), ["Rhetoric"] **(1980)**; Burde (1976); Burney (1776-89/. . ./1957); Butler (1984); Byrt (1967); Cahn ["Retardatio"] (1972-); Carse (1925/1964); Castellani (1976); Chesnut (1976); Chew (1980); Chiba (1976); Cole (1988); Collins (1963), (1966), (1967), (1969); **Dahlhaus (1984)**; **Dahlhaus et al. (1987)**; David and Mendel (1945/1956); Dolmetsch (1915/. . ./1969); Donington (1963/. . ./1974), (1980); Dreyfus

(1987); Duckles (1970); Dupont (1933/. . ./1986); Eggebrecht (1955); Eitner (1900-1904/1959-60); Ferand [*Improvisation*] (1956/1961); Fischer (1957); Forkel (1792/1962); Frobenius ["Vollstimmig"] (1972-); Fubini (1971/1983); Fürstenau (1861-62); Fuller (1977); Ganz (1972); Gerber (1790-92/1977), (1812-14/1966); Gerboth et al. (1964); Goldschmidt (1907); Grout (1960/. . ./1980); Gurlitt (1944/1966); Hailparn (1981); Harding (1938); Harich-Schneider ([1939]/. . ./1970); Hartig (1982); Helm 1960); Hiller (1768-69). (1784); Hoffmann (1974); Hosler (1978/1981); Houle (1960), (1987); Jackson (1988); Johnstone (1966); Jung (1969); **Kassler (1979)**; Keller (1931/. . ./1966), (1955/1965); Kinkeldey (1910/1968); Kooiman (1981); Kretzschmar (1911-12); Kubota (1986); Kümmerling (1977); Kuhn (1902); Lawrence (1978); **Lester (1989)**; Lindley (1982); Lippman (1986); List (1976); Mahlert and Sunter (1972-); McIntyre (1965); Mendel (1955), (1978); Moyer (1969); Nelson (1984); **Neumann**, Frederick (1965/. . ./ **1982**), (1967/**1982**), (1977/**1982**), (1978), (1979/**1982**), (1981/**1982**), [*Essays*] **(1982)**, (1986), (1988); Newman (1985); Newman (1946), (1959/. . ./1983), (1963/. . ./1983); North (1987); O'Donnell (1979); Orr (1983); Ottenberg (1973/1978); Petrobelli (1968); Pfeiffer (1978); Pincherle (1958); Ratner (1980), (1980); Reese (1957/1970); Reichert (1978); Reimer ["Concerto"] (1972-), ["Kammermusik"] (1972-), ["Kenner"] (1972-), (1973); **Ritzel (1967/1968)**; Robison (1982); Rosen (1980/1988); Rosenblum (1988); Rothschild (1953), (1961); Sachs (1972-); Schäfke (1934/1964); Scher (1975); Schulenberg (1982); Serauky (1929); Sheldon (1975), (1981); Sisman (1978); Smiles (1978); Sondheimer (1925); Spitzer and Zaslaw (1986); **Steblin (1981/1983)**; Stevens (1974); Stowell (1985), (1988); Subirá (1947/. . ./1958); Swain (1988); Thieme (1982-83); Todd (1983); Troeger (1987); Ulrich (1931/1932); Unger (1941/1969); Vanhulst (1971); Vogel (1976); Wessel (1955); Whitmore (1988); Wichmann (1966); Williams, P. (1970); Wirth (1966); Zaslaw (1979).

GEORG QUITSCHREIBER

[1569 – 1638]

Georg Quitschreiber's *Musicbüchlein für die Jugend* (1605), part of a flourishing pedagogical tradition, is one of the more interesting and multifaceted works in its genre. In addition to the typical fare of such works, Quitschreiber introduced transposition and even touched upon tuning for the voice. A more expanded account of singing is found in his *De canendi elegantia* (1598). Of greater importance for composers of his day was his *De Παροδια* (1611), wherein we find an early theoretical account of the common technique of parody, or fusion of old and new elements by borrowing substantial material from one's own or another's work in molding a new composition.

De canendi elegantia, octodecim praecepta, musicae studiosis necessaria [*Rism* B/VI/2, p. 679.]

Jena: Donatus Richtzenhan, 1598.

Another edition in 1606.

Musicbüchlein für die Jugend . . . [*Rism* B/VI/2, p. 680.]

Leipzig: 1605.
Jena: Johan Weidner (Leipzig: Johan Börner), 1607. [IDC.]

De Παροδια [*parodia*], *tractatus musicalis musicae studiosis propositus* [*Rism* B/VI/2, p. 680.]

Jena: Johann Weidner, [1611].

Quarta exercitatio musicalis: De confusionibus publicis in choro musico, . . . [*Rism* B/Vi/2, p. 680.]

Jena: the author (Johann-Christoph Weidner), 1637.

LITERATURE

Ruhnke, Martin. "Quitschreiber, Georg." In *MGG* (1949-68). Bibliog.

Braun, Werner. "Zur Parodie im 17. Jahrhundert." In *Bericht Kassel 1962* (1963):154-55.

Dart, Thurston. "How They Sang in Jena in 1598." *MT* 108/1490 (1967):316-17; reprinted in *CJ* 15/9 (1975):20.

● ● ● Ruhnke, Martin. "Quitschreiber, Georg." In *NGrove* (1980). Bibliog.

See also BURMEISTER: Ruhnke (1955); FÉTIS: (1833-44); LIPPIUS: Rivera (1974/1980); PRAETORIUS: (1614-20); WALTHER: (1732); LITERATURE SUPPLEMENT: Becker (1836-39/1964); Collins (1963), (1966); Dahlhaus ["Zur Entstehung"] (1961); Eitner (1900-1904/1959-60); Forkel (1792/1962); Gerber (1790-92/1977), (1812-14/1966); Harrán (1986); Houle (1987); Hüschen (1986); Jackson (1988); Livingstone (1962); Moser (1936/. . ./1959); Neumann (1987); Sannemann (1903/1904); Taddie (1984); Tilmouth (1980); Walker (1987).

JEAN-PHILIPPE RAMEAU

[1683 – 1764]

Through their scope, originality, and influence, the writings of Jean-Philippe Rameau have attained a prominence nearly unparalleled in the history of music theory. Many of the ideas which shape modern analytical practice were established initially by Rameau. No scholar of tonal theory may remain ignorant of concepts such as the sonorous body (*corps sonore*) and fundamental bass (*basse fondamentale*), regardless of his or her own theoretical orientation or reaction to these formulations.

Rameau's habit of perpetually revising his theories complicates the process of study, and it must have irked his contemporary detractors, some of whom, such as d'ALEMBERT, perhaps better understood the limits of science's ability to explain art than did Rameau. Yet it is within the realm of science that Rameau's formulations must be understood. His qualifications as a composer would have made him successful had he chosen merely to manufacture composition manuals for dilettanti, but Rameau chose the more treacherous route of courting Europe's leading savants. Though his writings were certainly impressive, he succeeded in irritating or offending several of them in the process.

Rameau desired not only that his theory be deemed correct, but also that it be perceived as inevitable, as the one — and only — result of the careful observation of natural phenomena. To Rameau, and to the rationalists of the era, a musical theory was as logical a candidate for submission to a scientific academy for verification as was a theory involving the physical sciences. Indeed, Rameau's "Mémoire où l'on expose les fondemens du système de musique théorique et pratique," which was submitted to the Académie royale des sciences (Paris) in 1749, was titled *Démonstration du principe de l'harmonie* (1750) in the published version, which contained the Académie's report on the memoir as if it were the confirmation of a demonstration.

Ironically, the foundation upon which Rameau based his theory in his landmark *Traité de la harmonie* (1722) was supplanted in his later writings. The numbers 1 through 6 had served ZARLINO as determinants for intervallic relationships; with Rameau they also established the character of the tonic triad, wherein the ratio 3:1 generated the fifth and 5:1 generated the third. The monochord, upon which a string and its divisions into 1/3 and 1/5 produced the appropriate sounds, provided the only empirical test for these assertions. Louis Bertrand Castel, who reviewed the *Traité* in the *Journal de Trevoux*, injected the notion of overtones into the discussion, and as a result Rameau thereafter incorporated SAUVEUR's researches, so that the foundation of the tonal system was inherent within the sound generated by a single sonorous body (*corps sonore*). Following DESCARTES's methodology, Rameau further proposed that other parameters of music, such as melody and the succession of chords, derived from the basis created by this initial construct, the tonic triad, which was itself generated from the root pitch.

Vibration theory was not well understood at this time, though Daniel Bernoulli, EULER, and d'ALEMBERT were actively pursuing the topic. This state of ignorance allowed Rameau to posit, in his *Génération harmonique* (1737), a fanciful derivation of the minor triad as emanating downward from a fundamental pitch: just as G and E appear prominently among the upper partials of C, so also might F and A-flat as lower partials. This theory conformed to the fact that strings tuned a twelfth and seventeenth below a vibrating string would also begin to resound. Yet as he later realized, only the upper partials of such strings' fundamental pitches were set into motion. Abandoning his undertone theory in *Démonstration du principe de l'harmonie* (1750), Rameau proposed, among other ideas, that two tones a minor third apart, such as A and C (both of which generate E), together establish the minor triad. His lack of success regarding this issue remained one of his theory's critical flaws and plagued his successors as well.

Rameau's doctrines regarding the inversion and succession of chords remained a focal point of theoretical inquiry for over two hundred years. Whereas the consonant status of the perfect fourth was, for many of Rameau's predecessors, an issue of considerable controversy, Rameau's formulation depended upon octave equivalence, wherein the pitches C, E, and G, for example, would represent the same chord (with root C) regardless of which of the notes was placed at the bottom. The determination of the chordal root was critical in decisions regarding chord succession, for the fundamental bass (*basse fondamentale*), or succession of such roots, was controlled by criteria dependent upon the intervals between successive roots. These roots were a theoretical construct, not entities intended to be performed, and as such served as an early version of an analytical observation which was later rendered through Roman numerals.

To accommodate the variety of normative chordal successions, Rameau developed several novel ideas regarding chord construction. For example, a succession of chords for the bass progression C-F-G-C would, in its C-F phase, perfectly follow Nature's model, for the fifth (or its inversion, the fourth) was the most prominent interval generated by the *corps sonore*. Yet F-G was not so endowed. Rameau's solution was to declare that the chord on F possessed both a 6th and a 5th, whether these pitches actually sounded or not. Thus in the succession C-F, F was to be regarded as the chordal root of a chord with "added sixth." But in moving F-G, the chord was to be regarded as an inversion of a seventh chord rooted upon D, and thus the succession of roots was D-G. This process was called double employment (*double-emploi*). Similarly, he sought an explanation for the linear resolution of suspensions in harmonic terms. If, for example, the stable pitches G and D were combined with another voice which moved from C to B (4-3 above G in figured bass), then the G-B-D chord would be preceded, in Rameau's view (at least in the *Traité*), with a D^7 chord (the D and C) with an added lower fifth (G). This process was called *supposition*. The succession of this example would be analyzed with fundamental bass D-G rather than simply G.

Rameau was prone to fierce verbal combat with his detractors. D'ALEMBERT, who had favorably reviewed Rameau's 1749 "Mémoire" and had created a summary of Rameau's ideas in his *Élémens de musique, théorique et pratique, suivant les principes de M. Rameau* (1752), was eventually compelled to oppose Rameau, for Rameau's criticisms of d'ALEMBERT and Diderot's *Encyclopédie* demanded a firm response. (The project was on a somewhat delicate political footing, and certainly the opposition of France's greatest composer and theorist was not welcome. The editors had, in fact, requested that Rameau himself write music articles for the *Encyclopédie*. When J.-J. ROUSSEAU and d'ALEMBERT took up the task after Rameau's refusal, they had in Rameau a critic who was not easily pleased.) Other battles and his bold requests for attention from various scientists and scientific academies confirm Rameau's reputation as being a difficult and rather isolated individual.

Controversy regarding Rameau continues. Just as MATTHESON and d'ALEMBERT expressed disfavor with Rameau during his lifetime, some members of later generations likewise responded to the theory in a negative way. SCHENKER gave one of his more mature articles [in *Meisterwerk* (1930)] the bold title "Rameau or Beethoven? Torpidity or Spiritual Vitality in Music?" Yet many sensitive musicians utilize analytical techniques and harbor assumptions derived from Rameau. Thus, whether for strengthening one's understanding of important developments in the history of tonal theory or for enriching one's own conception of tonal practice, the varied and extensive output of Rameau offers many rewards.

Traité de l'harmonie réduite à ses principes naturels . . . [*Rism* B/VI/2, pp. 685-86.]

> Paris: Jean-Baptiste-Christophe Ballard, 1722. [LCPS: R-012a. HoM: 1264. SMLMS.]
>
> > Review in *JTr* (October-November 1722):1713-43, 1876-1910 [Louis Bertrand Castel], reprinted

in Collected Works: (1967-72):Vol. 1, below; excerpts of Castel's review in translation in *NZGS* /84, 90 (1723):818-21, 878-80, reprinted in Collected Works: (1967-72):Vol. 6, below.

T ● *A Treatise of Musick, Containing the Principles of Composition* . . . [*Rism* B/VI/2, pp. 685-86.] London: John Walsh (Robert Brown), 1752 [LCPS: R-012c. SMLMS.]; 2nd edition, London: J. Murray, 1779; Dublin: White, 1779 [HoM: 1265]; a pirated edition published by J. French of London, spuriously dated 1737 [LCPS: R-012b].

> An English translation of Part 3 of the *Traité*.

T ● [MARTINI, Giovanni Battista, trans. (?)] "Trattato dell'armonia ridotta a'suoi principj naturali." Ms., [ca. 1759]. [Bologna: Civico museo bibliografico musicale.]

T ● Jones, Griffith, trans. *A Treatise on Harmony, in Which the Principles of Accompaniment are Fully Explained and Illustrated by a Variety of Examples* [*Rism* B/VI/2, p. 686.] London: Longman & Broderip, [ca. 1795]; a later edition, ca. 1805.

> An English translation of Part 4 of the *Traité*.

T ● See **Strunk (1950)**:564-74.

T ● See Gerboth et al. (1964).

S ● Facsimile edition. MMMLF, ser. 2, no. 3. New York: Broude Brothers, 1965.

> Reviews in *Mf* 22/4 (1969):532-34 (Helmut Haack), *ML* 48/1 (1967):85 (Jack A. Westrup), *Notes* 25/2 (1968-69):241-42 (J. Murray Barbour), and *Notes* 28/3 (1971-72):440-43 (Neal Zaslaw).

S ● See Collected Works: (1967-72):Vol. 1, below.

T ● Gossett, Philip, trans. and ed. *Treatise on Harmony*. New York: Dover, 1971. [*Rilm* 71-2250, 76-15434.]

> Reviews in *JAMS* 27/1 (1974):148-54 (Charles B. Paul), *JMT* 17/1 (1973):164-67 (Erwin R. Jacobi), and *Notes* 28/3 (1971-72):440-43 (Neal Zaslaw).

S ● See Kintzler and Malgoire (1980), below.

S ● Cook, Martha, ed. Facsimile edition. MFa, ser. A/MFa, no. 34. Madrid: Arte Tripharia, 1984.

S ● Kremer, Joseph-François, ed. Facsimile edition. Cmus. Paris: Foundation Singer-Polignac and Librairie Méridiens (Klincksieck), 1986.

Includes Kremer's "Rameau, l'harmonie et les méprises de la tradition," pp. VIII-LXXV. Review in *DH* 324 (1987):29 (Philippe-A. Autexier).

T ● See **Katz and Dahlhaus (1987-)**: Vol. 3.

Nouveau système de musique théorique, où l'on découvre le principe de toutes les règles nécessaires à la pratique, pour servir d'introduction au traité de l'harmonie [*Rism* B/VI/2, pp. 683-84.]

Paris: Jean-Baptiste-Christophe Ballard, 1726. [*LCPS*: R-009. *HoM*: 1258. *SMLMS*.]

Review in *JTr* (March 1728):472-81 [Louis Bertrand Castel], reprinted in Collected Works: (1967-72):Vol. 2, below; excerpts of Castel's review in translation in *NZGS* /1 (1731):4-5, reprinted in Collected Works: (1967-72):Vol. 6, below.

T ● [MARTINI, Giovanni Battista, trans. (?)] "Nuovo sistema di musica teorica, nel qual si scuopre il principio di tutte le regole necessarie alla pratica . . ." Ms., [ca. 1759]. [Bologna: Civico museo bibliografico musicale.]

S ● Facsimile edition. MMMLF, ser. 2, no. 7. New York: Broude Brothers, 1965.

Reviews in *Mf* 22/4 (1969):532-34 (Helmut Haack), *ML* 48/1 (1967):85 (Jack A. Westrup), *Notes* 25/2 (1968-69):241-42 (J. Murray Barbour), and *Notes* 28/3 (1971-72):440-43 (Neal Zaslaw).

S ● See Collected Works: (1967-72):Vol. 2, below.

T ● Chandler, B. Glenn. "Rameau's *Nouveau système de musique théorique*: An Annotated Translation with Commentary." Ph.D. dissertation, Indiana University, 1975. [*Rilm* 75-2608. *DA* 36/05A, p. 2475. UMI 75-23465.]

T ● See Rowen (1979).

Polemic with Michel Pignolet de Montéclair in *MdFr*, including the following articles:

"Conférence sur la musique" (June 1729):1281-89 (Pignolet).
"Examen de la conférence sur la musique" (October 1729):2369-77 (Rameau).
"Observations sur la méthode d'accompagnement pour le clavecin qui est en usage, et qu'on appelle échelle ou règle de l'octave" (February 1730):253-63 (Rameau).
"Plan abrégé d'une méthode nouvelle d'accompagnement pour le clavecin" (March 1730):489-501 (Rameau).

"Réponse du second musicien au premier musicien, auteur de l'Examen" (May 1730):880-92 (Pignolet).
"Réponse du second musicien au premier musicien, sur les deux écrits qui concernent l'accompagnement du clavecin" (June 1730):1079-85 (Pignolet).
"Réplique du premier musicien à la réponse du second" (June 1730):1337-44 (Rameau).
"Lettre de M. à M. sur la musique" (September 1731):2126-45 (Rameau).

S ● See Collected Works: (1967-72):Vol. 6, below.

Dissertation sur les différentes métodes [*sic*] *d'accompagnement pour le clavecin, ou pour l'orgue . . .* [*Rism* B/VI/2, pp. 683-84.]

Paris: Boivin, Le Clair, 1732. [*LCPS*: R-005a.]

Review in *JTr* (March 1732):445-79, reprinted in Collected Works: (1967-72):Vol. 5, below.

Paris: Antoine Bailleux, [ca. 1772]. [*LCPS*: R-005b. *SMLMS*.]

Review in *JTr* (August 1772):197-208, reprinted in Collected Works: (1967-72):Vol. 5, below.

S ● See Collected Works: (1967-72):Vol. 5, below.

T ● Hayes, Deborah, trans. "Dissertation on the Different Methods of Accompaniment." Ann Arbor, Mich.: Xerox University Microfilms, 1974. [*Rilm* 76-9797. *MonAb* 00033.]

"Lettre au R. P. Castel, au sujet de quelques nouvelles réflexions sur la musique"

JTr (July 1736):1691-1709.

A reply to three articles by Castel appearing in *JTr* (August-September 1735):1444-82, 1619-66, 1807-39 [and continued later in *JTr* (October-December 1735):2018-53, 2335-72, 2642-68]. Castel responded in *JTr* (September 1736):1999-2026, to which Rameau replied in *Pc* 14/196-97 (1738):74-96, 141-43 [cited also under *Génération harmonique*, below].

S ● See Collected Works: (1967-72):Vol. 6, below, for Rameau's letter and reply and a portion of Castel's material.

Génération harmonique, ou traité de musique théorique et pratique [*Rism* B/VI/2, p. 683.]

Paris: Prault fils (Charles Osmont), 1737. [*LCPS*: R-008. *HoM*: 1257. *SMLMS*.]

Remarks on this work in *MdFr* (February, June 1737):326-29, 1137-46. Reviews in *Jds* (January-February 1738):3-10, 80-89 [see also *Jds* 8 (1758):309 for an abstract]; *JTr* (December 1737):2142-67 [Louis Bertrand Castel]; *Oém* 10/*Lettres* 138, 139, 150 (August, October

1737):68-72, 73-86, 349-60; and *Pc* 13/179 (1737):34-48 [Thérèse Deshayes]. Response to Castel by Rameau in *Pc* 14/196-97 (1738):74-96, 141-43. Of further interest is "Réflexions sur l'origine des arts," *Pc* 13/179 (1737):25-34 (Abbé Prévost). All of these materials, plus other items, appear in Collected Works: (1967-72):Vol. 6, below.

T ● [MARTINI, Giovanni Battista, trans. (?)] "Generazione armonica, o sia trattato di musica teorico e pratico." Ms., [ca. 1759]. [Bologna: Civico museo bibliografico musicale.]

S ● Facsimile edition. MMMLF, ser. 2, no. 6. New York: Broude Brothers, 1966.

S ● See Collected Works: (1967-72):Vol. 3, below.

T ● Hayes, Deborah. "Rameau's Theory of Harmonic Generation: An Annotated Translation and Commentary of *Génération harmonique* by Jean-Philippe Rameau." Ph.D. dissertation, Stanford University, 1968; revised edition (as "Harmonic Generation, or Treatise on Theoretical and Practical Music"), Ann Arbor, Mich.: Xerox University Microfilms, 1974. Bibliog. [*Rilm* 68-1182, 76-15415. *DA* 29/05A, p. 1557. UMI 68-15055.]

> Review in *ML* 56/3-4 (1975):387-88 (J. A. Westrup).

"L'art de la basse fondamentale"

> Ms., [ca. 1739-44]. [Paris: Bibliothèque de l'Institut de France.]

> > See Christensen ["Rameau's 'L'art'"] (1987), below, for Table of Contents.

S ● Paris: Bibliothèque nationale (Music Division), Film 551.

"Mémoire où l'on expose les fondemens du système de musique théorique et pratique"

> Ms., 1749. [Paris: Archives de l'Académie des sciences.]

> > See d'ALEMBERT: (1749).

S ● See *Démonstration* (1750), below.

Démonstration du principe de l'harmonie servant de base à tout l'art musical théorique et pratique [*Rism* B/VI/2, p. 682.]

> Paris: Durand, Pissot, 1750. [LCPS: R-004. HoM: 1255. SMLMS.]

> > Reviews in d'ALEMBERT: (1749) [reprinted in the *Démonstration*], *HArs, An 1750* (1754):160-65 (under "Acoustique"); d'ALEMBERT: (1751-65):"Discourse préliminaire"; *JTr* (June

1751):1368-84 [Louis Bertrand Castel (?)]; *Lét* 3 (November 1750):200-210 (Elie-Catherine Fréron); and *MdFr* (May 1750):144-46. All of these materials, plus other items, appear in Collected Works: (1967-72):Vol. 6, below.

T ● [MARTINI, Giovanni Battista, trans. (?)] "Dimostrazione del principio dell'armonia che serve di base a tutta l'arte musicale teorica e pratica . . ." Ms., [ca. 1759]. [Bologna: Civico museo bibliografico musicale.]

T ● Lesser, Elisabeth, trans. and ed. *Darstellung des Prinzips der Harmonie als Grundlage aller theoretischen und praktischen Musik*. QMt, no. 1. Wolfenbüttel and Berlin: G. Kallmeyer, 1930.

S ● Facsimile edition. MMMLF, ser. 2, no. 4. New York: Broude Brothers, 1965.

> Reviews in *Mf* 22/4 (1969):532-34 (Helmut Haack), *ML* 48/1 (1967):85 (Jack A. Westrup), *Notes* 25/2 (1968-69):241-42 (J. Murray Barbour), and *Notes* 28/3 (1971-72):440-43 (Neal Zaslaw).

S ● See Collected Works: (1967-72):Vol. 3, below.

T ● Papakhian, Arsen Ralph. "Jean-Philippe Rameau's *Démonstration du principe de l'harmonie* (1750) and Pierre Esteve's *Nouvelle découverte de principe de l'harmonie* (1752): A Translation." M.M. thesis, Western Michigan University, 1973. [*Rilm* 76-2752.]

T ● Briscoe, Roger Lee. "Rameau's *Démonstration du principe de l'harmonie* and *Nouvelles réflexions de M. Rameau sur sa démonstration du principe de l'harmonie*: An Annotated Translation of Two Treatises by Jean-Philippe Rameau." Ph.D. dissertation, Indiana University, 1975. [*Rilm* 76-9549. *DA* 36/08A, pp. 4835-36. UMI 76-02791.]

S ● See Kintzler and Malgoire (1980), below.

Nouvelles réflexions de M. Rameau sur sa démonstration du principe de l'harmonie, servant de base à tout l'art musical théorique et pratique [*Rism* B/VI/2, p. 684.]

> Paris: Durand, Pissot (J. Chardon), 1752. [LCPS: R-010. SMLMS.]

> > Reviews in *JTr* (August-September 1752):1856-70, 1961-77 [Louis Bertrand Castel (?)] and *MdFr* (June 1752):115-17, both reprinted in Collected Works: (1967-72):Vol. 5, below.

T ● [MARTINI, Giovanni Battista, trans. (?)] "Nuove riflessioni di Mr. Rameau sopra la sua dimostrazione del principio dell'armonia." Ms., [ca. 1759]. [Bologna: Civico museo bibliografico musicale.]

S ● Facsimile edition. MMMLF, ser. 2, no. 138. New York: Broude Brothers, 1969.

S ● See Collected Works: (1967-72):Vol. 5, below.

T ● See Briscoe (1975), above.

"Réflexions sur la manière de former la voix et d'apprendre la musique, et sur nos facultés en général pour tous les arts d'exercice"

> In *MdFr* (October 1752):87-100.

S ● Moreau, Marie-Germaine. "Jean-Philippe Rameau et la pédagogie." *Rm* 260 (1965):47-64.

S ● See Collected Works: (1967-72):Vol. 6, below.

"Extrait d'une réponse de M. Rameau à M. Euler, sur l'identité des octaves . . ." [*Rism* B/VI/2, p. 683.]

> In *MdFr* (December 1752):6-31.
> Paris: Durand, 1753. [LCPS: R-007. SMLMS.]
>
> > Review in *JTr* (June 1753):1327-31, reprinted in Collected Works: (1967-72):Vol. 5, below.

T ● [MARTINI, Giovanni Battista, trans. (?)] "Risposta di Mons. Rameau a M. Eulero sopra l'identita delle ottave." Ms., [ca. 1759]. [Bologna: Civico museo bibliografico musicale.]

S ● See Collected Works: (1967-72):Vol. 5, below.

Observations sur notre instinct pour la musique, et sur son principe . . . [*Rism* B/VI/2, p. 684.]

> Paris: Prault fils, Lambert, Duchesne, 1754. [LCPS: R-011. SMLMS.]
>
> > Reviews in *Aaad* (June 12, 1754):94, *Alit* 3/*Lettre* 15 (June 28, 1754):340-48 [Elie-Catherine Fréron], *Corlit* (June 15, 1754) [Baron von Grimm], *JTr* (August 1754):1997-2008 [partial translation and commentary in MATTHESON: (1754-56): 3 (1755):471-74], and *Nlit* (June 28, 1754) [Abbé Raynal]. All of these materials appear in Collected Works: (1967-72):Vol. 6, below.

S ● Facsimile edition. MMMLF, ser. 2, no. 54. New York: Broude Brothers, 1967.

> Reviews in *Consort* 27 (1971):64 (Lillian M. Ruff), *ML* 50/2 (1969):311-12 (Frederick W. Sternfeld), and *Notes* 26/3 (1969-70):528-29 (Philip Gossett).

S ● See Collected Works: (1967-72):Vol. 3, below.

S ● Facsimile edition. Geneva: Slatkine, 1971.

S ● See Kintzler and Malgoire (1980), below.

T ● See Lippman (1986).

T ● Middleton, Alain Henri. "Jean-Philippe Rameau: *Observations sur notre instinct pour la musique*, Paris, 1754. Annotated Translation and Commentary." Ph.D. dissertation, Columbia University, forthcoming.

Erreurs sur la musique dans l'Encyclopédie [*Rism* B/VI/2, p. 683.]

> Published anonymously.

> Paris: Sébastien Jorry, 1755. [LCPS: R-006. HoM: 1256. IDC.]
>
> > Notices and reviews in *Aaad* (January 21, 1756):10; *Corlit* 3 (November 1755) [Baron von Grimm]; *JTr* (February 1756):493-513; *MdFr* (March 1756):101-3; and *Shdom* 2 (1756):109-18 (Antoine-Jacques Labbet de Morambert) [response in ROUSSIER: (1756-57)]. Responses in d'ALEMBERT: (1751-65):Vol. 6 (1756) and ROUSSEAU, J.-J.: (1755). All of these materials appear in Collected Works: (1967-72):Vol. 5, below.

S ● Facsimile edition. MMMLF, ser. 2, no. 137. New York: Broude Brothers, 1969.

> Review in *Notes* 28/3 (1971-72):440-43 (Neal Zaslaw).

S ● See Collected Works: (1967-72):Vol. 5, below.

S ● Facsimile edition. Geneva: Slatkine, 1971.

> Contains all three works related to the *Encyclopédie*. [See related entries of 1756 and 1757, below.]

Suite des erreurs sur la musique dans l'Encyclopédie [*Rism* B/VI/2, p. 683.]

> Published anonymously.

> Paris: Sébastien Jorry, 1756. [HoM: 1263.]

S ● See Collected Works: (1967-72):Vol. 5, below.

S ● See (1755):(1971), above.

Prospectus, où l'on propose au public, par voye de souscription, un code de musique-pratique, composé de sept méthodes [*Rism* B/VI/2, p. 684.]

> [Paris: 1757.]
>
> > Notices and reviews in *AAAd* (December 14, 1757):199 and (November 2, 1758):187; *Corlit* (1757); *Jenc* (December 1, 1757):134-39; *JTr* (January 1758):176-90; and *MdFr* (December 1757):157-58. All of these materials appear in Collected Works: (1967-72):Vol. 6, below.

S ● See Collected Works: (1967-72):Vol. 4, below.

*Réponse de M. Rameau à MM. les éditeurs de l'Ency-
clopédie sur leur dernier avertissement* [*Rism*
B/VI/2, p. 685.]

> London and Paris: Sébastien Jorry, 1757. [HoM:
> 1262. SMLMS.]

S ● See Collected Works: (1967-72):Vol. 5, below.

S ● See (1755):(1971), above.

*Code de musique pratique, ou méthodes pour ap-
prendre la musique . . . avec de nouvelles réflexions sur le principe sonore* [*Rism* B/VI/2, p. 682.]

> Paris: Imprimerie royale, 1760 [appeared early
> 1761]. [LCPS: R-003. HoM: 1254. SMLMS.]

>> Reviews in *Corlit* (April 1, 1761), *JTr* (April
>> 1761), and *MdFr* (March-April 1761):92-101, 85-
>> 96. These materials, as well as documentation
>> concerning Rameau's interactions with MAR-
>> TINI and J. P. Beccari pertaining to the "Nou-
>> velles réflexions," appear in Collected Works:
>> (1967-72):Vol. 6, below.

S ● Facsimile edition. MMMLF, ser. 2, no. 5. New
York: Broude Brothers, 1965.

>> Reviews in *ML* 48/1 (1967):85 (Jack A. West-
>> rup), *Notes* 25/2 (1968-69):241-42 (J. Murray
>> Barbour), and *Notes* 28/3 (1971-72):440-43
>> (Neal Zaslaw).

S ● See Collected Works: (1967-72):Vol. 4, below.

S ● See Kintzler and Malgoire (1980), below.

T ● See le Huray and Day (1981).

> A brief excerpt.

*Lettre à M. d'Alembert, sur ses opinions en musique, in-
sérées dans les articles "Fondamental" et "Gamme"
de l'Encyclopédie* [*Rism* B/VI/2, p. 683.]

> [Paris: 1760.]

>> D'ALEMBERT responded in *MdFr* (April
>> 1761):124-26 and (March 1762):132-52, as well
>> as the 1762 edition of d'ALEMBERT: (1752).
>> Rameau replied in *MdFr* (April, July 1761):127-
>> 29, 150-58 and in his *Origine* [1762]:17-28,
>> below. The three letters of 1761, as well as two ar-
>> ticles by Rameau—"Source où, vraisemblable-
>> ment, on a dû puiser la première idée des
>> proportions" *MdFr* (April 1761):129-33 and
>> "Origine des modes et du tempérament" *MdFr*
>> (June 1761):152-70—were collected and pub-
>> lished as a set in 1761, were translated by MAR-
>> TINI (?) [Ms., Vienna: Österreichische
>> Nationalbibliothek], and were reprinted in Col-
>> lected Works: (1967-72):Vol. 5, below. The
>> other materials were reprinted in Collected
>> Works: (1967-72):Vol. 6, below.

S ● See Collected Works: (1967-72):Vol. 4, below.

S ● See Kintzler and Malgoire (1980), below.

"Lettre aux Philosophes, concernant le corps sonore
et la sympathie des tons"

> *JTr* (August 1762):2035-53.

> T ● [MARTINI, Giovanni Battista, trans. (?)]
> "Lettera di Mr. Rameau a lei filosofi." Ms.
> [Vienna: Österreichische Nationalbibliothek.]

S ● See Collected Works: (1967-72):Vol. 6, below.

*Origine des sciences, suivie d'une controverse sur le
même sujet* [*Rism* B/VI/2, p. 684.]

> Published anonymously.

> [Paris: Sébastien Jorry, 1762.]

>> Notice and letters in *MdFr* (March-April
>> 1762):152-54, 103-19, 125-43, reprinted in Col-
>> lected Works: (1967-72):Vol. 6, below.

S ● See Collected Works: (1967-72):Vol. 4, below.

"Observations de M. Rameau, sur son ouvrage inti-
tulé origine des sciences"

> *MdFr* (June 1762):139-43.

"Vérités également ignorées et interressantes tirées
du sein de la nature"

> Ms., 1764. [Stockholm: Stiftelsen Musikkulturens
> Främjande; Paris: Bibliothèque nationale.]

S ● Chantavoine, Jean. "Fragments d'un ouvrage in-
édit de J.-Ph. Rameau." *RB* 12 (1924):667-89.

S ● Jacobi, Erwin R. " 'Vérités intéressantes': Le dernier manuscrit de Jean-Philippe Rameau." *Rdm*
50 (1964):76-109.

S ● Schneider, Herbert, ed. *Jean-Philippe Rameaus
letzter Musiktraktat, "Vérités également ignorées et
interressantes tirées du sein de la nature" (1764):
Kritische Ausgabe mit Kommentar*. BAfMw, no.
25. Stuttgart: Franz Steiner Verlag, 1986. Bibliog.

>> Reviews in *ML* 68/3 (1987):272-73 (Albert
>> Cohen) and *Mth* 3/1 (1988):81-85 (Thomas
>> Christensen; translated by Renate Groth).

See also d'ALEMBERT: (1752):Review (1752):Re-
sponse.

More comprehensive coverage of Rameau's writings,
particularly his correspondence, and of reviews
and notices of his works is available in Jacobi's editorial commentary for the Collected Works Edition, below. This edition contains facsimile
reproductions of most of these materials.

COLLECTED WORKS EDITION:

● ● ● Jacobi, Erwin R., ed. *The Complete Theoretical Writings of Jean-Philippe Rameau*. 6 vols. PAIM:M, ser. 3. American Institute of Musicology, 1967-72. Bibliog. [*Rilm* 68-1881, 68-1882, 69-927, 69-929, 69-930, 72-376.]

> Reviews in *Consort* 24 (1967):326-27 (Lillian M. Ruff), *JAMS* 27/1 (1974):148-54 (Charles B. Paul), *Jmf* 193-94 (1970):49 (Norbert Dufourcq), *Mf* 22/4 (1969):532-34 and 27/4 (1974):493-96 (Helmut Haack), *ML* 49/2 (1968):170-71, 53/1 (1972):81-82, and 55/1 (1974):116 (Jack A. Westrup), *MQ* 57/4 (1971):677-84 (Paul Henry Lang), *Notes* 25/2 (1968-69):241-42 (J. Murray Barbour), *Notes* 28/3 (1971-72):440-43 (Neal Zaslaw), *Rdm* 62/2 (1976):316-21 (Jacques Chailley), and *Ridm* 7/2 (1972):299-303 (Alberto Basso).

LITERATURE:

Castel, Louis Bertrand. *Des nouvelles expériences d'optique et d'acoustique*. 1735.

Voltaire, François Marie Arouet de. *Lettre à Rameau*. June, 1738; reprinted in Collected Works: (1967-72):Vol. 6, above.

Estève, Pierre. *Nouvelle découverte du principe de l'harmonie, avec un examen de ce que M. Rameau a publié sous le titre de Démonstration de ce principe.* [*Rism* B/VI/1, p. 296.] Paris: Huart et Moreau fils, Durand, 1751; Paris: Sébastien Jorry, 1752 [LCPS: E-013. SMLMS.]; English translation: See (1750):Papakhian (1973), above.

> Review in *JTr* (June 1751):1368-84 [Louis Bertrand Castel (?)] and in *HArs, An 1750* (1754):165-67.

Bernoulli, Daniel. "Réflexions et éclaircissemens sur les nouvelles vibrations des chordes exposées dans les mémoires de 1747 & 1748." *AWBH* 9 (1753):147-72.

La Porte, Claude-Nicolas de. *Traité théorique et pratique de l'accompagnement du clavecin.* [*Rism* B/VI/1, p. 481.] Paris: the author, Mme. Boivin, Le Clerc, [1753].

> Review in *JTr* (November-December 1753):2543-53, 3034-37.

Arnaud, Abbé François. "Lettre sur la musique à Monsieur le Comte de Caylus . . ." [*Rism* B/VI/1, p. 96.] N.p.: 1754 [LCPS: A-047. HoM: 64.]; reprinted in La Borde (1780/1978):Vol. 3:551-67.

> Reviews in *Alit* 2 (1754):270-80 (Elie-Catherine Fréron) and *JTr* (April 1754):829-43.

Gallimard, Jean-Edme. *La théorie des sons applicables à la musique* . . . [*Rism* B/VI/1, p. 346.] Paris: Ballard, Bauche, Saugrin, 1754. [LCPS: G-014.]

Review in *JTr* (October 1754):2398-2403.

Ducharger. *Réflexions sur divers ouvrages de M. Rameau.* [*Rism* B/VI/1, p. 281.] Rennes: J. Ch. Vatar, 1761.

"Éloge de M. Rameau, par M. de Chabanon . . ." *Jdm* [1/3] (March 1770):12-21.

"Réflexions . . . sur une question concernant la basse fundamentale." *Jdm An 1777/4* (1777):5-8.

Berlioz, Hector. "De Rameau et de quelques uns de ses ouvrages." *RgmdP* 9/32-33 (1842):321-24, 329-32.

Henry, Charles. *La théorie de Rameau sur la musique.* Paris: Hermann, 1887.

Brenet, Michel. "La jeunesse de Rameau." *Rmi* 9/3-4 (1902):658-93, 860-87; 10/1-2 (1903):62-85, 185-206.

Laloy, Louis. "Les idées de Jean-Philippe Rameau sur la musique." *RmSIM* 3/11 (1907):1144-59.

Brenet, Michel. "Bibliographie de M. J.-P. Rameau." *Cmu* 11/10 (1908):323-27.

Debussy, Claude. [Article on Rameau. Ms., 1912.] Facsimile edition in Collected Works: (1967-72):Vol. 6, above; transcription in *Claude Debussy: Lettres inédites à André Caplet (1908-1914)*, edited by Edward Lockspeiser, pp. 62-64 (Monaco-Ville: Éditions du Rocher, 1957).

Schnürmann, Leo. "Das System Rameaus und sein Einfluß auf die Theorie der Folgezeit." Ph.D. dissertation, The University of Vienna, 1913.

Lasserre, Pierre. *L'esprit de la musique française (de Rameau à l'invasion wagnérienne).* Paris: Payot, 1917; English translation (as *The Spirit of French Music*) by Denis Turner, London: Kegan Paul, Trench, Trubner; New York: Dutton, 1921.

> Reviews in *ML* 2/3 (1921):289-90 (D. Calvocoressi) and *YR* 12/3 (1922-23):661-64 (Bruce Simonds).

Tiersot, Julien. "Rameau: Théoricien et praticien de la musique." *Mén* 93/36-42 (1931):379-81, 387-89, 396-98, 403-5, 412-14, 421-23, 433-35.

Ryzhkin, Iosif. "Nashi spory i Zh. F. Ramo." [Our Arguments and J.-P. Rameau.] *Smuz* /5 (1933):101-11.

Ryzhkin, Iosif. "Klassicheskaia teoriia (Zh. F. Ramo)." [Classical Theory (J.-P. Rameau).] In Ryzhkin and Mazel (1934-39):vol. 1 (1934):3-78.

Masson, Paul-Marie. "Une polémique musicale de Claude Rameau en faveur de son frère (1752)." *Rdm* 18 (1937):39-47.

Miller, Poland. "Fundamental Bass: The Parallelism of Rameau and Bach." *JMus* 2/4 (1940-41):181-86.

Gil-Marchex, Henri. "Las ideas de Rameau sobre el papel primordial de la armonía en la creación musical." *Rmen* (1944):62-75.

Girdlestone, Cuthbert (trans. Christiana Blume); Jacobi, Erwin R.; and Pfannkuch, Wilhelm. "Rameau, Jean-Philippe." In *MGG* (1949-68). Bibliog.

Ahnell, Emil Gustave. "The Concept of Tonality in the Operas of Jean-Philippe Rameau." Ph.D. dissertation, The University of Illinois at Urbana-Champaign, 1957. Bibliog. [*DA* 18/02, p. 605. UMI 00-25188.]

> Contains a chapter, "The Theories of Rameau."

Berthier, Paul. *Réflexions sur l'art et la vie de Jean-Philippe Rameau (1683-1764)*. Paris: J. Picard, 1957.

> Reviews in *Mf* 12/1 (1959):112-13 (Margarete Reimann) and *Rdm* 40 (1957):225 (Eugène Borrel).

Girdlestone, Cuthbert Morton. *Jean-Philippe Rameau: His Life and Work*. London: Cassell, 1957; revised edition, New York: Dover, 1969; a French translation (as *Jean-Philippe Rameau: Sa vie, son œuvre*), n.p.: Desclée de Brouwer, 1962; reprint edition, 1983.

> Reviews in *Composer* 38 (1970-71):34-35 (Bernard Barrell), *Fm* 15/8 (1962):162 (Pierre Meylan), *Mf* 13/1 (1960):90-92 (Erwin R. Jacobi), *ML* 39/1 (1958):73-76 (Wilfrid Mellers), *MR* 19/2 (1958):152-54, *MT* 99/1379 (1958):22-23 (Watkins Shaw), *MT* 111/1532 (1970):1003-4 (Stanley Sadie), *MuMus* 19/9 [225] (1970-71):44 (Bayan Northcott), *MusDisq* 110 (1963):59, *MusT* 50/3 (1971):31 (John Standen), *Rasm* 29/1 (1959):77-79 (Alfredo Bonaccorsi), *Rbdm* 21/1-4 (1967):128-29 (André Souris), *RCMM* 54/1 (1958):21, and *Rdm* 41 (1958):128-29 (Elisabeth Lebeau).

Pischner, Hans. "Zur Vorgeschichte einiger im theoretischen Werk Jean Philippe Rameaus behandelter Probleme der Harmonik." In *MünnichFs* (1957):9-39.

Doolittle, James. "A Would-be *Philosophe*: Jean Philippe Rameau." *PMLAA* 74/3 (1959):233-48. Bibliog.

● ● ● Ferris, Joan. "The Evolution of Rameau's Harmonic Theories." *JMT* 3/2 (1959):231-56.

Suaudeau, René. "Le premier système harmonique (dit clermontois) de Jean-Philippe-Rameau." Clermont-Ferrand, 1958; published edition (expanded and revised, as *Introduction à l'harmonie de Rameau*), Clermont-Ferrand: École nationale de musique de Clermont-Ferrand, 1960.

Farmer, Henry George. "Diderot and Rameau." *MR* 22/3 (1961):181-88.

Keane, Sister Michaela Marie. *The Theoretical Writings of Jean-Philippe Rameau*. CUASM, no. 9. Washington, D.C.: The Catholic University of America Press, 1961.

> Reviews in *Mf* 16/4 (1963):404-5 (Richard Schaal) and *Notes* 19/3 (1961-62):441 (Roy T. Will).

Pischner, Hans. "Die Harmonielehre Jean-Philippe Rameaus: Ihre historischen Voraussetzungen und ihre Auswirkungen im französischen, italienischen und deutschen musiktheoretischen Schrifttum des 18. Jahrhunderts. Ein Beitrag zur Geschichte des musikalischen Denkens." Ph.D. dissertation, The University of Berlin (Humboldt-Universität), 1961; published edition, Leipzig: Breitkopf & Härtel, 1963; 1967; excerpts in *MG* 14/10 (1964):593-97.

> Review in *Mens* 19/3 (1964):93-94 (Gerrit Vellekoop).

Jacobi, Erwin R. "Nouvelles lettres inédites de Jean-Philippe Rameau." *Rmfc* 3 (1963):145-58.

Jacobi, Erwin R. "Rameau and Padre Martini: New Letters and Documents." Translated by Piero Weiss. *MQ* 50/4 (1964):452-75.

Moberg, Carl-Allan. "Jean-Philippe Rameau som musikteoretiker." *Musikrevy* 19/5 (1964):185-87.

Chailley, Jacques. "Rameau et la théorie musicale." *Rm* 260 (1965):65-95.

Duparcq, Jean-Jacques. "De la conception du principe de l'harmonie selon Jean-Philippe Rameau et Jean-Sébastien Bach." *Rm* 260 (1965):123-43.

Leipp, E. "Critique des fondements de la théorie de Jean-Philippe Rameau." *Rm* 260 (1965):97-111.

Machabey, Armand. "Jean-Philippe Rameau et la tempérament égal (*Nouveau système de musique théorique . . . 1726*)." *Rm* 260 (1965):113-22.

Paul, Charles Bennett. "Rameau's Musical Theories and the Age of Reason." Ph.D. dissertation, The University of California at Berkeley, 1966. [*DA* 27/11A, p. 3799. UMI 67-05139.]

Cavallotti, Enrico. "Rameau e la rivoluzione intellettuale de '700." Thesis, The University of Palermo, 1969-70.

Paul, Charles Bennett. "Jean-Philippe Rameau (1683-1764): The Musician as *Philosophe*." *PAPS* 114 (1970):140-54. [*Rilm* 70-3176.]

McKay, James R. "Rameau and the Subdominant." Master's thesis, The University of Chicago, 1971.

Paul, Charles Bennett. "Music and Ideology: Rameau, Rousseau and 1789." *JHI* 32/3 (1971):395-410.

Potashnikova, M. [Rameau as the Founder of Scientific Theoretical Musicology.] In *Metodologicheskie voprosy teoreticheskogo muzykoznaniia*, edited by Susanna Matveeva. [*Rilm* 76-4942.]

Billeter, Bernhard. "Der Naturbegriff bei Jean-Philippe Rameau: Aus Anlass des soeben erschienenen Gesamtausgabe der theoretischen Schriften." *NZZ* 194/92 (1973):51-52. [*Rilm* 74-4089.]

Jacobi, Erwin R. "Jean-Philippe Rameau und die Schweiz." *NZZB* 310 (July 1973):51-52. [*Rilm* 73-3221.]

Verba, E. Cynthia. "The Development of Rameau's Thoughts on Modulation and Chromatics." *JAMS* 26/1 (1973):69-91; reprinted in Rosand (1985):Vol. 6, pp. 279-301. [*Rilm* 73-1209.]

Hayes, Deborah. "Rameau's 'Nouvelle méthode'." *JAMS* 27/1 (1974):61-74. [*Rilm* 74-2115.]

Lewin, David. "Two Interesting Passages in Rameau's *Traité de l'harmonie*." *ITO* 4/3 (1978-79):3-11. [*Rilm* 78-3953.]

Verba, E. Cynthia. "Rameau's Views on Modulation and Their Background in French Theory." *JAMS* 31/3 (1978):467-79. Bibliog. [*Rilm* 78-4922.]

Lindsey, David Ray. "A Study of Root Motion in Passages Leading to Final Cadences in Selected Masses of the Late Sixteenth Century." Ph.D. dissertation, North Texas State University, 1979. [*Rilm* 79-3669. *DA* 40/07A, p. 3618. UMI 80-00792.]

Verba, E. Cynthia. "A Hierarchic Interpretation of the Theories and Music of Jean-Philippe Rameau." Ph.D. dissertation, The University of Chicago, 1979. [*Rilm* 79-2599. *DA* 40/11A, p. 5645.]

Bernard, Jonathan W. "The Principle and the Elements: Rameau's Controversy with d'Alembert." *JMT* 24/1 (1980):37-62. [*Rilm* 80-423.]

> Response in *JMT* 25/1 (1981):174 (B. Glenn Chandler) [Reply in *JMT* 25/1 (1981):175 (Jonathan Bernard)].

● ● ● Cohen, Albert; Cyr, Mary; and Girdlestone, Cuthbert. "Rameau, Jean-Philippe." In *NGrove* (1980); reprint edition (as *The New Grove French Baroque Masters . . .*, CBioS), New York: W. W. Norton, 1986. Bibliog.

Kintzler, Catherine, and Malgoire, Jean-Claude, eds. *Jean-Philippe Rameau: Musique raisonnée*. Paris: Stock, 1980.

Zimmermann, Michael. "Jean-Philippe Rameau (1683-1764)." *Musica* 34/5 (1980):445-51. [*Rilm* 80-5614.]

Anderson, Gene Henry. "Musical Terminology in J.-P. Rameau's *Traité de l'harmonie*: A Study and Glossary Based on an Index." Ph.D. dissertation, The University of Iowa, 1981. [*Rilm* 81-376. *DA* 42/05A, p. 1842. UMI 81-23296.]

Keiler, Allan R. "Music as Metalanguage: Rameau's Fundamental Bass." In Browne (1981):83-100. [*Rilm* 81-1640.]

Kintzler, Catherine. "Rameau et Voltaire: Les enjeux théoriques d'une collaboration orageuse." *Rm* 67/2 (1981):139-68. [*Rilm* 81-4643.]

Yoshida, Kazuko. "Jean Philippe Rameau no *Waseiron* to clavecin sakuhin no kenkyu." *Bulletin of Showa Junior Music College* 1 (1981):27-58. [*Rilm* 81-496.]

Beaussant, Philippe, ed. *Rameau de A à Z*. Paris: Fayard/IMDA, [ca. 1983]. Bibliog. [*Rilm* 83-2129.]

> Review in *Rmuz* 28/3 (1984):7-8 (Izabella Bauer).

Billeter, Bernhard. "Jean-Philippe Rameau: Zum dreihundertsten Geburtstag des Komponisten." *NZZ* 223 (1983):67-68. [*Rilm* 83-4754.]

Kintzler, Catherine. *Jean-Philippe Rameau: Splendeur et naufrage de l'esthétique du plaisir à l'âge classique.* Paris: Le sycomore, 1983.

> Reviews in *Alash* 26/3-4 (1984):459-60 (Dezsö Baróti), *Ép* (1986):568-70 (Patrice Henriot), *FrR* 60/4 (1987):575-76 (Buford Norman), *JAMS* 38/1 (1985):169-78 (Cynthia Verba), *Nrmi* 20/2 (1986):272-75 (Paolo Russo), and *Rdm* 70/1 (1984):138-40 (Serge Martin).

Malignon, Jean. *Petit dictionnaire Rameau*. Paris: Aubier, 1983. [*Rilm* 83-44.]

Massip, Catherine, and Noiray, Michel. "Le colloque Rameau (Dijon, 21-24 septembre 1983)." *Rdm* 69/2 (1983):217-21.

Miller, Leta E. "Rameau and the Royal Society of London: New Letters and Documents." *ML* 66/1 (1985):19-33.

Robrieux, Jean-Jacques. "Jean-Philippe Rameau et l'opinion philosophique en France au dix-huitième siècle." *SVEC* 238 (1985):269-395. Bibliog.

Skowron, Zbigniew. "Debaty estetyczne w kregu encyklopedystów." *Rmuz* 29/12 (1985):14-16.

Dahlhaus, Carl. "Ist Rameaus *Traité de l'harmonie* eine Harmonielehre?" *Mth* 1/2 (1986):123-27.

> Response entitled "Analogie- und Kausalprinzip bei Rameau" in *Mth* 1/2 (1986):185-86 (Michael Zimmermann).

Duchez, Marie-Élisabeth. "Valeur épistémologique de la théorie de la basse fondamentale de Jean-Philippe Rameau: Connaissance scientifique et représentation de la musique." *SVEC* 245 (1986):91-130. Bibliog.

Schneider, Herbert. "Rameaus musiktheoretisches Vermächtnis." *Mth* 1/2 (1986):153-61.

● ● ● Christensen, Thomas. "Eighteenth-Century Science and the *corps sonore*: The Scientific Background to Rameau's Principle of Harmony." *JMT* 31/1 (1987):23-50. Bibliog.

Christensen, Thomas. "Rameau's 'L'art de la basse fondamentale'." *MTS* 9 (1987):18-41.

Gorce, Jérôme de la, ed. *Jean-Philippe Rameau: Colloque international organisé par la Société Rameau, Dijon— 21-24 septembre 1983. Actes publiés avec le concours du C.N.R.S. et du Ministère de la culture.* Paris: Champion; Geneva: Slatkine, 1987.

> Includes a wide assortment of articles, including "Pour une lecture critique du premier chapitre de la *Génération harmonique*" (Jacques Chailley), "Connaissance scientifique et représentation de la

musique, valeur épistémologique de la théorie de la basse fondamentale" (Marie-Élisabeth Duchez), *"Conclusions sur l'origine des sciences*, un texte méconnu de Jean-Philippe Rameau" (Philippe Lescat), "Présupposés, contours et prolongements de la polémique autour des écrits théoriques de Jean-Philippe Rameau (Anne-Marie Chouillet), "Le concept de nature dans l'esthétique de Rameau" (Michel Baridon), and "Rameau: Le sujet de la science et le sujet de l'art à l'âge classique" (Catherine Kintzler).

Sjöqvist, Gunnar. "Jean-Philippe Rameau: Musiker, teoretiker, kompositör." *Musikrevy* 42/6 (1987):252-54.

Cohen, Albert. "Rameau, Equal Temperament, and the Academy of Lyon: A Controversy Revisited." In Cowart [*French*] (1989):121-27. Bibliog.

Christensen, Thomas. *The Music Theory of Jean-Philippe Rameau.* Forthcoming.

See also ADLUNG: (1758); d'ALEMBERT: (1751-65); (1752); (1752):Elsberry (1984); (1759); Escal (1983), (1984); Christensen (1985); Christensen (1989); Isherwood (1989); BÉTHIZY: (1754); Earhart (1985); CATEL: George (1982); CHORON: (1810-11); Simms (1975); DAUBE: Karbaum (1968/1969); EULER: (1739); Correspondence: Pelseneer (1951); FÉTIS: (1831); (1833-44); (1840); FUX: Federhofer (1988); GASPARINI: (1708):Tagliavini (1981); HAUPTMANN: Caplin (1984); HEINICHEN: (1728):Buelow (1961/. . ./ 1986); d'INDY: (1903-50); JONES: (1784); KIRNBERGER: (1771-79):Beach and Thym (1982); Beach (1974); Grant (1976), (1977); KOCH: Baker (1988); KOLLMANN: (1801); LIPPIUS: Rivera (1974/1980); LOULIÉ: Semmens (1984); MARPURG: (1754-78); (1759-63); (1776); Serwer (1969); MARTINI: (1757-81); MATTHESON: (1722-25); (1731); (1735); (1739); Zejfas (1982); MOMIGNY: (1791-1818); Chailley (1982); RIEMANN: (1895-1901); (1898); ROUSSEAU, J.-J.: (1768); Kisch (1947); Gossman (1964); Wokler (1974); Strauss (1978); Kintzler (1979); Blum (1985); Marshall (1986); ROUSSIER: (1764); (1783); SAINT-LAMBERT: (1707):Burchill (1979); SAUVEUR: (1704):Maxham (1976); SCHEIBE: (1773); SCHENKER: (1925-30):(1930); Slatin (1967); Morgan (1978); SCHOENBERG: Rexroth (1969/1971); SERRE: (1753); (1763); SORGE: (1760); VIADANA: Haack (1964/1974); VOGLER: (1800); WALTHER: (1732); WEITZMANN: (1859); LITERATURE SUPPLEMENT: Abbado (1964); Alekseev (1974); Alette (1951); Allen ["Philosophies"] (1939); Apfel (1967); Archibald (1924); **Arnold (1931/. . ./1965)**; Asselin (1981), (1983/1985); Atcherson (1973); Auhagen (1982/1983); Babbitt (1961/1972), (1987); **Barbour** (1932), (1947), (1948), (1949-68), **(1951/. . ./1972)**, (1952); Beach (1967), (1974); Becker (1836-

39/1964); Beer (1969); Beiche ["Dux"] (1972-), ["Inversio"] (1972-); Bell et al. (1980); **Benary (1956/1961)**; Benjamin (1981); **Bent, I.** ["Analytical Thinking"] (1980), ["Analysis"] **(1980/1987)**, (1984); Beswick (1950); Beyschlag (1907/1953); Bircher (1970); Blumröder (1972-); Boomgaarden (1985/1987); Buelow (1979); Bukofzer (1947); Burdick (1977); Burke (1963); Burney (1776-89/. . ./ 1957); Burton (1956); Cahn ["Repercussio"] (1972-); Caplin (1981), (1983); Cavallini (1949); Cazden (1948); Chailley (1967); Chesnut (1976); Chevaillier (1925/1931-32); Chew (1980); Cohen (1971), (1981), (1987), (1988); Cohen and Miller (1979); Cohen (1984); Čolič (1976); Collins (1963); **Coover (1980)**; Cotte (1951); Crocker (1962), (1966); **Dahlhaus** ["Untersuchungen"] (1966/. . ./1988), (1972), ["Relationes"] (1975), ["Harmony"] **(1980)**, ["Tonality"] **(1980)**, ["Über"] (1980), **(1984)**; **Dahlhaus et al. (1987)**; **Dahlhaus and Sachs (1980)**; Dekker (1979); Devore (1987); de Zeeuw (1983); Diderot (1748/. . ./1875-77); Dolmetsch (1915/ 1969); Donington (1963/. . ./1974), (1980); Dreyfus (1987); Duchez (1979); Dunsby and Whittall (1988); Dupont (1933/. . ./1986); Eitner (1900-1904/1959-60); Federhofer (1944/1950), (1989); Fellerer (1962); Ferran (1979); Forkel (1792/1962); Fox Strangways (1923); Frobenius ["Dauer"] (1972-); Fubini (1969), (1971/1983); Ganz (1972), (1976); Gerber (1790-92/1977), (1812-14/1966); Ghislanzoni (1949-51); Godwin (1987); Green (1969); Greenfield (1984); Gremion (1974); **Groth (1981/1983)**; Grout (1960/. . ./1980); Gruber (1982); Gut (1972-), (1976); Haase (1969); Handschin (1948); Harich-Schneider ([1939]/. . ./ 1970); Hartmann (1923); Hawkins (1776/. . ./1969); Haydon (1933/1970); Hedges (1978); Heimann (1970/1973); Hein (1954); Heinlein (1927/1928); Helm (1960); Hiller (1768-69); Hoffman (1953); Hoffmann (1974); Horsley (1963), [*Fugue: History*] (1966); Hosler (1978/1981); Houle (1960), (1987); Hüschen (1949-68); Hutchinson and Knopoff (1979-81); Imig (1969/1970); Isgro (1968), (1979); Jackson (1988); Jacobi (1957-60/1971); Jeppesen (1930/. . ./ 1974), ([1951]/1952); Jones (1934); Jorgenson (1957), (1963); Jullien (1873); **Kassler** (1971), **(1979)**, (1983-85); Kaufmann (1969); Kauko (1958); Kelletat [*Temperatur*] (1960); Kleinman (1971/1974); Komma (1972); Krehbiel (1964); La Borde (1780/1978); La Fage (1864/1964); La Motte-Haber (1971); Lang (1941), (1967-68); Lawrence (1978); Lecky (1880); le Huray (1978-79); le Huray and Day (1981); Lester (1974), (1979-81); Levarie (1986); Levenson (1981), (1983-84); Lewin (1982); Lewis (1975/1978); **Lindley** ["Temperaments"] **(1980)**, (1982), **(1984)**, (1988); Lippman (1986); Lloyd (1940-41), (1955); Lottermoser (1949-68); Mahlert and Sunter (1972-);

Mainka (1965/1969); **Mann (1955/. . ./1987)**, (1981), (1987); McQuere (1983); Meer (1980); Meier (1966), (1969); Miller and Cohen (1987); Miller (1939-40); Mitchell, J. W. (1963); Mitchell, W. J. (1963); Morche (1974); Munkachy (1968); Nelson (1984); **Neumann,** Frederick (1964/**1982)**, (1978), [*Essays*] **(1982)**, (1986); Newman (1985); Newman (1959/. . ./1983), (1963/. . ./1983); Norton (1984); Oberdoerffer (1949-68), (1967); Oliver (1949/1947); **Palisca** (1949-68), (1961), [*Baroque*] (1968/1981), ["Rezitativ"] (1972-), ["Theory"] **(1980)**, [" 'Baroque' "] (1989); Parncutt (1988-89); Perinello (1936); Pikler (1966); Pincherle (1958); Pole (1879/. . ./1924); Ramírez (1967); Ratner (1980); Reckow (1972-); Reese (1954/ 1959), (1957/1970); Révész (1946/. . ./1954); **Ritzel (1967/1968)**; Rivera (1984); Rohwer (1949-68); Rosenblum (1988); Rowell (1983); Ruf (1972-); Ryzhkin (1933), (1934-39); Scher (1975);

Schmalzriedt ["Reprise"] (1972-); Schoffman ["Descriptive"] (1983), ["Pedal"] (1983); Schulenberg (1984); **Seidel and Cooper (1986)**; Serwer (1974); Sheldon (1975), (1982); **Shirlaw (1917/. . ./ 1970)**, (1931), (1957), (1960); Smith (1974); Smith (1967); Snyder (1980-81); Speak (1973); Spender and Shuter-Dyson (1980); **Steblin (1981/1983)**; Stein (1983); Stowell (1985); Subirá (1947/. . ./1958); Taddie (1984); Telesco (forthcoming); Tenney (1987); Thompson (1980); Thürlings (1877); Tittel (1966); Todd (1983), (1988-89); Tolkoff (1973); Troeger (1987); Truesdell (1960); Vauclain (1978); Vogel (1955/1954); (1962), (1975/1984); **Wagner (1974)**, (1981); **Walker (1978)**; Walker (1987); Warrack (1944); **Wason (1981/1985)**, (1983); Wessel (1955); Whatley (1981); Wichmann (1966); Williams, P. (1970); Wintle (1982), Wirth (1966); Wittwer (1934/1935); Yates (1947); **Zaminer (1985)**; Zimmermann (1976).

THOMAS RAVENSCROFT

[ca. 1582? – ca. 1635]

Though Thomas Ravenscroft consulted recognized authorities, such as GLAREAN and MORLEY, his treatment of mensural theory, the topic of his *Briefe Discourse*, falls short. While attempting innovations and clarifications, he achieved a set of prescriptions which would have put severe restrictions on England's early seventeenth-century composers, had they heeded him. Fortunately he included an appendix of madrigals (including some he composed himself) which made the treatise a more worthwhile purchase in its day.

A Briefe Discourse of the True (but Neglected) Use of Charact'ring the Degrees by Their Perfection, Imperfection, and Diminution in Measurable Musicke, against the Common Practise and Custome of These Times . . . [*Rism* B/VI/2, p. 689.]

     London: Thomas Adams (Edwin Allde), 1614. [LCPS: R-020.]

S ● Mateer, David G. "A Critical Study and Transcription of *A Brief Discourse* by Thomas Ravenscroft." Dissertation, The University of London, 1970.

S ● Facsimile edition. EE, no. 409. Amsterdam: Theatrum Orbis Terrarum; New York: Da Capo Press, 1971.

S ● Facsimile edition. MMMLF, ser. 2, no. 22. New York: Broude Brothers, n.d.

S ● Payne, Ian, ed. Facsimile edition. MSo, no. 22. Kilkenny, Ireland: Boethius Press, 1984.

"A Treatise of Musick."

     Ms. [London: British Library, Reference Division.]

LITERATURE:

Pulver, Jeffrey. "The English Theorists: XII – Thomas Ravenscroft." *MT* 76/1104 (1935):124-26.

Gleason, Harold. "*A Briefe Discourse*." *BAMS* 8 (1944):7-8.

Tilmouth, Michael. "Ravenscroft, Thomas." Translated by Rainer Huck. In *MGG* (1949-68). Bibliog.

Mateer, David. "Ravenscroft, Thomas." In *NGrove* (1980). Bibliog.

See also FÉTIS: (1833-44); LITERATURE SUPPLEMENT: Atcherson (1972); Becker (1836-39/1964); Bukofzer (1947); Burney (1776-89/. . ./1957); Burton (1956); Collins (1963); Eitner (1900-1904/1959-60); Forkel (1792/1962); Gerber (1790-92/1977),(1812-14/1966); Hawkins (1776/. . ./ 1969); Houle (1960), (1987); Hüschen (1986); **Kassler (1979)**; Lawrence (1978); Pulver (1927/. . ./1973); **Seidel and Cooper (1986)**.

HANS MIKKELSEN RAVN

[ca. 1610–1663]

The mainstream of early Baroque music theory was channeled to Denmark by Hans Mikkelsen Ravn (alias Johann Michael Corvinus), whose *Heptachordum danicum seu nova solsisatio* (1646), though written in Latin, provides not only a distinctly Danish perspective on folksongs, hymns, and the behavior of choirboys, but also draws upon the teachings of a diverse group of theorists ranging from ZARLINO and GLAREAN to PRAETORIUS, LIPPIUS, and CALVISIUS.

The word *solsisatio* (instead of *solmisatio*) draws attention to Ravn's addition of *si* as a seventh syllable in solmization. Besides an exposition of techniques for composition, Ravn included a dictionary of terms and musical instruments and a section on overtones and ratios. Among the book's more progressive elements is its adoption of LIPPIUS's *trias harmonica* as the basis for musical composition.

Brevia et facilia praecepta componendi . . .

Copenhagen: 1644.

Heptachordum danicum seu nova solsisatio in qua musicae practicae usus, tàm qui ad canendum, quàm qui ad componendum cantum, sive choralem seu planum, sive mensuralem seu contrapunctum pertinet, dilucidè, planè, et apertè, ostenditur; Cui accessit logistica harmonica musicae theoricae vera et firma praestruens fundamenta . . . [*Rism* B/VI/1, p. 239.]

Copenhagen: Melchior Martzan, 1646. [LCPS: C-093. IDC.]

S ● Facsimile edition. BmB, ser. 2, no. 61. Bologna: Forni.

ST ● ● ● Johnsson, Bengt, trans. and ed. Partial facsimile edition and Danish translation, with commentary. 2 vols. Horsens: G. E. C. Gads Forlag (A. Backhausens Bogtrykkeri ved Holger J. Sørensen), 1977. Bibliog.

The section on acoustics has been omitted. Reviews in *Dafmf 1979* 10 (1980):186-88 (Bent Stellfeld) and *Mf* 33/3 (1980):395-96 (Werner Braun).

LITERATURE:

Johnsson, Bengt. "Ravn, Hans Mikkelsen." Translated by Gerhard Hahne. In *MGG* (1949-68). Bibliog.

Johnsson, Bengt. "Hans Mikkelsen Ravn's Heptachordum Danicum 1646." *Dafmf 1962* (1962):59-92. Bibliog.

Bergsagel, John. "Ravn, Hans Mikkelsen." In *NGrove* (1980). Bibliog.

See also FÉTIS: (1833-44); HERBST: Allerup (1931); WALTHER: (1732); LITERATURE SUPPLEMENT: **Apfel (1981)**; Becker (1836-39/1964); Eitner (1900-1904/1959-60); Ferand [*Improvisation*] (1956/1961); Flindell (1983-84); Gerber (1812-14/1966); Jeppesen (1922/. . ./1976); Lange (1899-1900); Mahlert and Sunter (1972-); Rivera (1978); Taddie (1984); Unger (1941/1969).

HENRI REBER

[1807–1880]

As had CATEL over half a century earlier, Henri Reber (like CATEL a professor at the Paris Conservatoire) created a single book—but one that attained a very enduring circulation. Whereas CATEL's *Traité d'harmonie* reached German, English, Spanish, and Italian audiences in their native tongues, Reber's *Traité d'harmonie* (1862) retained its French wording but persisted in its appeal well into the twentieth century. In fact, as late as 1950 a companion volume, written by Paule Maurice and Pierre Lantier, was published to accommodate more recent developments in harmonic practice. Earlier, Théodore DUBOIS had made revisions and had supplied a supplemental volume.

In keeping with the precedent of many nineteenth-century harmony treatises, Reber's work addresses issues such as the progression of harmonies, harmonizing a given bass or melody, figured bass, and even elementary principles of counterpoint. He shed light on harmonic practices involving pitches foreign to the tonality and rigorously categorized the various types of non-harmonic tones. His perspective affected generations of students who passed through the Paris Conservatoire and other music institutions in France.

Traité d'harmonie

Paris: Colombier, 1862.

With additions by Théodore DUBOIS:

Paris: Colombier, 1889.

Numerous printings.

LITERATURE:

Rapport du Comité des études musicales du Conservatoire sur le Traité d'harmonie de M. Reber. Paris: 1862.

Saint-Saëns, Camille. *Notice sur Henri Reber.* Paris: Firmin-Didot, 1881.

Werner, L.-G. "Henri Reber (1807–1881)." *BMhM* 48 (1928):123-65. Bibliog.

Ferchault, Guy. "Reber, Napoléon-Henri." Translated by Anna Frese. In *MGG* (1949-68).

Maurice, Paule, and Lantier, Pierre. *Complément du Traité d'harmonie de Reber: Commentaires et nombreux*

textes destinés à faciliter l'assimilation de l'écriture moderne . . . Preface by Jean and Noël Gallon. Paris: Gallet et fils, [1950].

Robert, Frédéric. "Reber, (Napoléon-)Henri." In *NGrove* (1980). Bibliog.

See also DUBOIS: [ca. 1889-90]; (1891); LITERATURE SUPPLEMENT: Chevaillier (1925/1931-32); ● ● ● Groth (1983); Gut (1972-); Kauko (1958); Mitchell, J. W. (1963); Packard (1952); Peters (1988).

ANTOINE-JOSEPH REICHA

[1770–1836]

Antoine-Joseph Reicha offered an original and fascinating perspective on music during the early decades of the nineteenth century. Of Czech descent, Reicha (or Rejcha) was educated in Vienna, where he studied under ALBRECHTSBERGER and Salieri, interacted with Haydn, and befriended Beethoven. He later settled in Paris, where he was appointed professor of counterpoint and fugue at the Conservatoire in 1818, having distinguished himself as a lucid author of pedagogically oriented theory books. Liszt, Berlioz, and Franck came under his direct influence, while many readers knew his popular works either through the numerous French editions or through CZERNY's voluminous French/German versions.

Though apparently not acquainted with KOCH's formulation, Reicha created, in his *Traité de mélodie* (1814), a similarly detailed perspective on the organization of musical materials into phrases, periods, and larger forms. The smallest unit is called a *dessin*, and through various stages—each punctuated by a cadence of a specific strength—the components of a composition are erected. Depending upon the extent of this hierarchical organization and whether two or three sections are involved, one of the following four forms is created: *petite coupe binaire, petite coupe ternaire, grande coupe binaire,* or *grande coupe ternaire.* Though he preferred a symmetrical organization, he indicated how expansions or contractions of phrases could be accomplished. Furthermore his methodology was attractive as a means for analyzing existing repertoire, rather than only as a prescription for the creation of new compositions. His analytical symbols (such as brackets) appear in the context of musical scores and are complemented, in a separate volume, by written commentary.

Reicha's perspective on form was expanded considerably in his *Traité de haute composition musicale* [ca. 1824-26], wherein an entire sonata-form movement (Reicha's *grande coupe binaire*) is displayed in a clear, innovative diagram. The first part, or exposition of ideas, consists of four com-

ponents: the first basic idea (*idée mère*), a bridge passage, a second basic idea, and subordinate ideas leading to the conclusion of the first part. The second part consists of two segments, separately diagrammed. The first contains the principal development, characterized by continuous modulating, followed by a stopping on the dominant. The second repeats the first three components of the first part (with a tonal adjustment so that the second basic idea appears now in the tonic key) and continues with a coda. Reicha's treatment of what we call the sonata-rondo form is equally detailed.

In his *Cours de composition musicale* [ca. 1816], which replaced CATEL's treatise at the Conservatoire, Reicha insisted upon a practical, rather than a speculative, approach to the study of harmony. He formulated thirteen basic chords, as follows: G B D, G B-flat D, G B-flat D-flat, G B D-sharp, G B D F, G B-flat D F, G B-flat D-flat F, G B D F-sharp, G B D F A, G B D F A-flat, D-flat F A-flat B-natural, D-flat F G B-natural, and G F-natural B D-sharp. His perspective included the topics of voice leading and spacing, dissonance treatment, non-harmonic tones, and modulations (for which the diminished-seventh and augmented-sixth chords were called into action when a remote key was targeted). For analysis, he recommended sorting out the essential tones from embellishments and then writing out a structural bass line on a separate staff so that root movements and modulations could be noted more easily.

Early in his career Reicha published a set of thirty-six fugues of astonishing modernity. They were supplemented, in the Vienna edition of around 1803-5, by an essay, "Über das neue Fugensystem." Later, in his *Traité de haute composition musicale* [ca. 1824-26], Reicha addressed the topics of counterpoint, canon, and fugue at greater length and somewhat more conservatively. Not only did he experiment with answers on unusual scale degrees, but he also reformulated notions of what an appropriate fugal subject might sound like. In fact, he borrowed themes from chamber and symphonic works by Haydn and Mozart as subjects for fugal elaboration! His *fugue phrasée* melded traditional fugal procedures and the periodic phrase structures of his day.

Though he enjoyed better success as a composer of chamber pieces than with opera, Reicha addressed music for the stage in his *Art du compositeur dramatique* (1833), which offers an abundance of advice to would-be opera composers and includes a volume of examples from his own works.

Études ou exercises pour le piano-forte, dirigées d'une manière nouvelle (Op. 30)

>Paris: Imbault, [ca. 1800-1801].

"Praktische Beispiele: Ein Beitrag zur Geisteskultur des Tonsetzers . . . mit philosophisch-praktische Anmerkungen zu den praktischen Beispielen"

>Ms., 1803. [Paris: Bibliothèque nationale.]

>>Incorporates materials from [ca. 1800-1801], above.

Trente-six fugues pour le pianoforte, composée d'après un nouveau system (Op. 36)

>Contains "Über das neue Fugensystem."

>Vienna: Au magazin de l'imprimerie chymique, [ca. 1803-5].

>>Other editions. Reviews in *AmZ* 10/23 (1807-8):353-61 and 35/5 (1833):73.

S ● Sýkora, Václav Jan, ed. *36 Fugen für Klavier*. 3 vols. Kassel: Bärenreiter; Prague: Supraphon (Artia), 1973.

>>Lacks Reicha's comments on his new fugal system.

L'art de varier ou 57 Variations pour le piano-forte (Op. 57)

>Leipzig: Breitkopf & Härtel, [ca. 1803-4].

>Other editions.

S ● Racek, Jan, and Šetková, Dana, eds. MaBo, no. 50. Prague: Státní hudební vydavatelství (Artia), 1961. Bibliog.

S ● Zahn, Dana, and Weinmann, Alexander, eds. *Ausgewählte Klavierwerke*. Munich/Duisburg: G. Henle (Roundelay), 1971.

>>Reviews in *Mf* 26/2 (1973):287-88 (Paul Mies), *MT* 113/1553 (1972):666-67 (Adrienne Simpson), and *Notes* 29/3 (1972-73):536-37 (Nathan Schwartz).

"Sur la musique comme art purement sentimental, avec des remarques philosophiques et critiques sur les opérations morales de notre être"

Mss., [before 1814(?)]. Two versions. [Paris: Bibliothèque nationale.]

Petit traité d'harmonie pratique à deux parties, suivi d'exemples en contrepoint double et de douze duos pour violon et violoncelle, pouvant être joués aussi sur le piano (Op. 84)

>Contains a preface on two-part writing.

>Paris: Gambaro, [ca. 1814].

T ● See [ca. 1816]:Merrick [1854], below.

Traité de mélodie, abstraction faite de ses rapports avec l'harmonie; suivi d'un supplément sur l'art d'accompagner la mélodie par l'harmonie, lorsque la première doit être prédominante appuyé sur les meilleus modéles mélodiques

>Paris: the author (J. L. Scherff), 1814. 2 vols.

>>Later editions. Reviews in *AmZ* 22/5 (1820):69-76 and *Rm*(F) 6/12/39 (1832):305-7 (François-Joseph FÉTIS).

ST ● CZERNY, Carl, ed. and trans. *Reicha's Compositions-Lehre: Cours de composition musicale ou traité complet d'harmonie pratique, de melodie, de l'emploi des voix et des instrumens, de haut composition et du contrepoint double, de la fugue et du canon etc./Vollständiges Lehrbuch der musikalischen Composition; oder, Ausführliche und erschöpfende Abhandlung über die Harmonie (den Generalbass) die Melodie, die Form und Ausarbeitung der verschiedenen Arten von Tonstücken, den Gebrauch der Gesangstimmen, die gesammte Instrumentirung, den höhern Tonsatz im doppelten Contrapunct, die Fuge und den Canon, und über den strengen Satz im Kirchenstyl.* 4 vols. Vienna: A. Diabelli, [ca. 1832-34]; reprint edition, Amsterdam: Heuwekemeijer, [1974?]; a segment, "Über die Formen und den Bau jedes Tonstückes," in *Mth* 1/3 (1986):261-76.

>This work combines the contents of several of Reicha's treatises. See below. The title *Vollständiges Lehrbuch der Harmonielehre, des Generalbaßes, der Melodie . . .* occasionally seen in bibliographies is apparently an abbreviation of the above. The four volumes are arranged as follows: Vol. 1: *Die Abhandlung von der praktischen Harmonie*; Vol. 2: *Die Abhandlung von der Melodie*; Vol. 3: *Die Abhandlung von der höheren musikalischen Compositionoder vom Contrapunkt, den Imitationen und den Canons*; Vol. 4: *Die Abhandlung von der Fuge, und von der Kunst, seine Ideen zu benützen, oder dieselben zu entwickeln.* Among CZERNY's comments is, on

pp. 316-32 of Volume 3, "Über die Formen und den Bau jedes Tonstückes."

T ● *Trattato della melodia considerata fuori de' suoi rapporti coll' armonia . . . 2 vols. Milan: Giovanni Ricordi, n.d.

T ● Metcalf, Edwin Styles, trans. *Treatise on Melody, Considered Apart from its Relations to Harmony; Followed by Observations upon the Art of Accompanying the Melody with Harmony.* Chicago: E. S. Metcalf, 1893.

A translation from the Italian edition.

Études pour le piano-forte dans le genre fugué précédées de quelques remarques instructives sur différentes propositions musicales à l'usage des jeunes compositeurs (Op. 97)

Paris: Erard, [1815-17]. 2 vols.

As *La fugue et le contrepoint mis en pratique et appliqués au clavier du piano en trente quatre études avec les notes à l'usage de jeunes compositeurs:*

Paris: Schonenberger, [ca. 1840].

Cours de composition musicale, ou traité complet et raisonné d'harmonie pratique

Paris: Gambaro, [ca. 1816]. 1 vol.

Review in *AmZ* 22/10 (1820):157-68.

As *Traité d'harmonie pratique:*

Paris: H. Lemoine, Janet & Cotelle, [ca. 1818]. 2 vols.

Numerous later printings.

T ● Kurpinski, Karol, trans. Polish translation. [1820.]

ST ● See (1814):CZERNY: [1832], above.

T ● Merrick, Arnold, trans. *Course of Musical Composition; or, Complete and Methodical Treatise of Practical Harmony.* Edited by John Bishop. London: Robert Cocks, [1854].

Includes translation of remarks by CZERNY in his edition.

T ● Rossi, Luigi Felice, trans. and ed. *Corso di composizione musicale, ossia trattato completo e ragionato d'armonia pratica.* Milan: F. Lucca, [18—].

Traité de haute composition musicale, faisant suite au cours d'harmonie pratique et au traité de mélodie

Paris: Zetter, [ca. 1824-26]. 2 vols.

Later editions.

T ● Hamilton, James Alexander, trans. *A New Theory of the Resolution of Discords, According to the Modern System.* London: Robert Cocks, [ca. 1830].

Translation of Chapter 6, Book 1.

T ● Hamilton, James Alexander, trans. *One Hundred Twenty-Nine Formulas of Interrupted Cadences.* London: Robert Cocks, [ca. 1830].

T ● Hamilton, James Alexander, trans. *Table of Harmonic Phrases, Formed of Suspensions Invented by A. Reicha.* London: Robert Cocks, [ca. 1830].

Excerpts from Chapter 8, Book 1.

ST ● See (1814):CZERNY: [1832], above.

T ● Rudolphus, C., trans. *Practical Harmony and Composition.* London: n.d.

T ● Tonassi, Pietro, trans. *Trattato d'armonia . . .* 2 vols. Milan: Giovanni Ricordi, [ca. 1842].

Review in *AmZ* 44/38 (1842):740.

Art du compositeur dramatique ou cours complet de composition vocale

Paris: A. Farrenc and the author, 1833. 2 vols.

ST ● CZERNY, Carl, ed. and trans. *Die Kunst der dramatischen Composition; oder, Vollständiges Lehrbuch der vocal Tonsetzkunst . . ./Art du compositeur dramatique . . .* Vienna: A. Diabelli, [ca. 1835-40].

"Contrepoint"

Encyclopédie des gens du monde 6/2 (Paris: Treuttel & Würtz, 1836):716-17.

La fugue et la contrepoint

Paris: Schonenberger, [1840].

"Cours de mélodie"

Ms. [Paris: Bibliothèque nationale.]

"Fragments harmoniques"

Ms. [Paris: Bibliothèque nationale.]

"Die Grundsätze der practischen Harmonie"

Ms. [Paris: Bibliothèque nationale.]

"Haute composition musicale"

Ms. [Paris: Bibliothèque nationale.]

"Kunst der praktischen Harmonie"

Ms. [Paris: Bibliothèque nationale.]

"Notes et exemples musicaux sur la permutation"

Ms. [Paris: Bibliothèque nationale.]

Other manuscripts are found at the Bibliothèque nationale and the Bibliothèque et Musée de l'Opére, Paris. See Vysloužil (1970), below, for more complete coverage.

LITERATURE:

Dun, Finlay. "On the Elements of Musical Harmony and Composition." *Harmon* 7 (1829):211-14.

Delaire, Jacques Auguste. *Notice sur Reicha, musicien compositeur et théoriste*. Paris: Lacombe, 1837; Czech version (translated by J. Fiala) in *Chud* 36 (1933):263-74.

Amory, A. H. "Iets uit Ant. Reicha's *Traité de haute composition musicale* (1826)." *CMvm* 68/6 (1911):224-28.

Bücken, Ernst. "Anton Reicha: Sein Leben und seine Kompositionen." Ph.D. dissertation, The University of Munich, 1912; published edition, Munich: Kgl. Hof- und Üniversitätsbuchdruckerei, 1912.

Bücken, Ernst. "Beethoven und Anton Reicha." *Musik* 12/12 (1912-13):341-45.

Bücken, Ernst. "Anton Reicha als Theoretiker." *ZfMw* 2/3 (1919-20):156-69.

Medvedeva, Marie. "Anton Reikha—opyt izucheniia ego teoreticheskikh rabot." [Anton Reicha—An Experimental Study of His Theoretical Works.] *Biulleteny GAKhN* 10 (1927-28):42.

Medvedeva, Marie. "Novaia sistema fugi A. Reikha." [A New System of Fugue of A. Reicha.] *Biulleteny GAKhN* 11 (1928):49.

Emmanuel, Maurice. "Notes sur Anton Reicha, pédagogue." *Mmu* 41/11 (1930):373-75.

Emmanuel, Maurice. *Antonin Reicha*. Mucél. Paris: Librairie Renouard (Henri Laurens), 1937. Bibliog.

Gilson, Paul. "Antonin Reicha." *Rim* 1/2 (1938-39):313-15.

Demuth, Norman. "Antonín Reicha." *ML* 29/2 (1948):165-72.

Bužga, Jaroslav. "Reicha . . . Antonín." In *MGG* (1949-68). Bibliog.

Laing, Millard Myron. "Anton Reicha's Quintets for Flute, Oboe, Clarinet, Horn, and Bassoon." Ed.D. dissertation, The University of Michigan, 1952. [*DA* 12/4, pp. 432-33. UMI 00-03697.]

Contains as an Appendix an English translation (by Gordon Hallman) of Reicha's manuscript autobiography.

Nedbal, Miroslav. "Antonín Rejcha jako pedagog a teoretik." Ph.D. dissertation, The University of Prague, 1952.

Blum, Klaus. "Bemerkungen Anton Reichas zur Aufführungspraxis der Oper." *Mf* 7/4 (1954):429-40.

Gardavský, Č. "Liszt und seine tschechischen Lehrer." *Stm* 5/1 (1963):69-76.

Kunze, Stefan. "Anton Reichas 'Entwurf einer phrasirten Fuge': Zum Kompositionsbegriff im frühen 19. Jahrhundert." *AfMw* 25/4 (1968):289-307. [*Rilm* 68-3483.]

Weiss, Piero. "Communication." *JAMS* 21/2 (1968):233-34.

Procházka, Jaroslav. "Ohlas Rejchova díla v Polsku a otázka jeho vlivu na Frederyka Chopina." *Hv* 7/4 (1970):470-77.

Šotolová, Olga. "Antonín Rejcha–pedagog a skladatel." *Hv* 7/4 (1970):459-67.

Vysloužil, Jiří, ed. *Zápisky o Antonínu Rejchovi/Notes sur Antoine Reicha*. Translated by Jaroslav Fryčer. Brno: Opus musicum, 1970. Bibliog.

Contains French and Czech versions of Reicha's manuscript autobiography. Reviews in *BzMw* 14/4 (1972):342-48 (Peter Gülke) and *Öm* 27/4 (1972):229 (Günter Brosche).

Zenkl, Luděk. "L'art de varier, op. 57, Antonín Rejchy." *Hv* 7/4 (1970):467-70.

P., P. "Antonin Rejcha." *RasmC* 29/3 (1976):43-45.

Magee, Noel Howard. "Anton Reicha as Theorist." Ph.D. dissertation, The University of Iowa, 1977. Bibliog. [*Rilm* 77-4639. *DA* 39/01A, p. 15. UMI 78-10364.]

Šotolová, Olga. *Antonín Rejcha*. Prague: Supraphon, 1977. Bibliog. [*Rilm* 77-601.]

Review in *Opmus* 10/8 (1978):V (rp).

Smith, Martin Dennis. "Antoine Joseph Reicha's Theories on the Composition of Dramatic Music." Ph.D. dissertation, Rutgers University, 1979. [*Rilm* 79-539. *DA* 40/10A, p. 5244. UMI 80-08922.]

Morris, Mellasenah Young. "A Style Analysis of the Thirty-Six Fugues for Piano, Opus 36, by Anton Reicha." D.M.A. dissertation, The Peabody Institute of the Johns Hopkins University, 1980. [*Rilm* 80-764. *DA* 41/04A, p. 1274. UMI 80-21959.]

● ● ● Stone, Peter Eliot. "Reicha, Antoine." In *NGrove* (1980). Bibliog.

Caswell, Austin. "Anton Reicha on Vocal Embellishment." In *KaufmannFs* (1981):283-307. [*Rilm* 81-2571.]

Simpson, Adrienne. "An Introduction to Antoine Reicha." *Consort* 40 (1984):13-19.

Bulley, Michael. "Reicha's 13th Fugue." *MR* 46/3 (1985):163-69.

Elsberry, Thomas Norman. "Anto Reicha's *Thirty-Six Fugues for Piano*, Op. 36: A Comparative Study with Representative Fugues of His Contemporaries." Ph.D. dissertation, Florida State University, forthcoming.

McCachren, Renee. "The Origins and Influences of Antoine Reicha's Theories of Form." Ph.D. dissertation, The University of North Texas, forthcoming.

See also CZERNY: Newman (1967); Cahn (1986); FÉTIS: (1833-44); KOCH: Baker (1976); Dahlhaus (1978); Sisman (1982); LORENZ: Vanderlek (1982); MOMIGNY: Chailley (1982); VOGLER: Stevens (1983); LITERATURE SUPPLEMENT: Apfel and Dahlhaus (1974); Babbitt (1961/1972), (1987); Becker (1836-39/1964); Beiche ["Dux"] (1972-), ["Inversio"] (1972-); **Bent**, I. ["Analytical Thinking"] (1980), ["Analysis"] ● ● ● **(1980/1987)**, (1984); Blumröder (1972-); Bronfin (1974); Broyles (1982-83); Burke (1963); Carpenter (1988); Chevaillier (1925/1931-32); Cohen (1873-74); Cole (1969); **Dahlhaus (1984)**; Eitner (1900-1904/1959-60); Frisius (1969/1970); Gardavský (1963); Gerber (1812-14/1966); Grave (1985); ● ● ●**Groth (1983)**; Hamilton (1854); Henneberg (1972/1974); Horsley [*Fugue: History*] (1966); Jacobi (1957-60/1971); Jones (1934); **Kassler** (1971), **(1979)**; Kauko (1958); Lang (1941); Lawrence (1978); Levenson (1981), (1983-84); Lindley (1982); **Mann (1955/. . ./ 1987)**; McQuere (1983); Mitchell, J. W. (1963); Moyer (1969); Müller-Blattau (1923/. . ./1963), (1949-68); Newman (1963/. . ./1983), (1969/. . ./ 1983); Packard (1952); Powers ["Language"] (1980); Ratner (1980); Rea (1978); Reimer ["Concerto"] (1972-); **Ritzel (1967/1968)**; Rosen (1980/1988); Rosenblum (1988); Ryzhkin (1933), (1934-39); Sachs (1972-); Schmalzriedt ["Coda"] (1972-), ["Durchführen"] (1972-), ["Episode"] (1972-), ["Exposition"] (1972-), ["Reprise"] (1972-), ["Subiectum"] (1972-), (1985); Seidel (1972-); Serwer (1974); Shamgar (1978), (1981), (1984); Sisman (1978); **Steblin (1981/1983)**; Stevens (1974); Straková (1975); Subirá (1947/. . ./1958); Thomson (1960/1978); Tittel (1959); Todd (1983); Vertrees (1974); **Wagner (1974)**; **Wason (1981/1985)**; Wirth (1966).

ERNST FRIEDRICH RICHTER

[1808 – 1879]

The Leipzig Conservatory played an important role in European musical life and even influenced pedagogy in the United States, since it attracted a number of foreign students as well as native Germans. Among its faculty were Moritz HAUPTMANN, whose theory of music was among the most abstract of the nineteenth century, and Ernst Friedrich Richter, who focused upon practical issues. Richter created a series of texts incorporating the study of harmony (1853), fugue (1859), and counterpoint (1872), eventually assembled under the general title *Die praktischen Studien zur Theorie der Musik*. He had earlier completed a monograph on form, *Die Grundzüge der musikalischen Formen und ihre Analyse* (1851). The popularity of these works is attested by the number of editions and translations that were published. Students from Russia, France, England, Italy, Denmark, Spain, Holland, Sweden, Poland, and the United States studied Richter's method in their own tongue. Richter's success was due, in part, to a straightforward, compact, uncontroversial style that was deemed appropriate for young conservatory students, whether they trained in Leipzig, Cambridge (Massachusetts), or Oberlin (Ohio). His influence on theory instruction was considerable and, in the view of some modern teachers who still confront vestiges of his system, unfortunate.

Expanding upon WEBER's already extensive use of Roman numerals, Richter acknowledged the augmented triad as a fundamental chord. Thus, in addition to the discrimination made between major and minor triads (using capital and small Roman numerals), the further distinction involving diminished and augmented triads was notated by the circle (e.g., vii°) and the apostrophe (e.g., III') or, in the United States, the plus sign (III+). (WEBER had introduced the circle, but had suggested that the leading-tone seventh chord, which Richter accepted as a fundamental chord, represented an incomplete dominant ninth.) An indication of the chord's inversion was typically affixed to the Roman numeral through the use of Arabic numerals whenever the chord was not in root position.

Perhaps because of its pervasive influence, SCHENKER singled Richter's method out for particular criticism in his *Harmonielehre* (1906). His principal complaint was that Richter confused the roles of harmony and counterpoint by attempting to teach principles of voice-leading rather than the artistic progression of scale-steps, using sterile, one-dimensional examples of his own concoction. SCHENKER claimed that Richter did not draw upon excerpts from the masterworks because the principles he was embracing were not representative of compositional practice. His condemnation of Richter reflected his universal concern regarding almost all received theory: "How can [the student] ever see the light of truth?" (Borgese translation, p. 177).

Die Grundzüge der musikalischen Formen und ihre Analyse. . .

Leipzig: Breitkopf & Härtel, 1851.
Leipzig: Georg Wigand, 1852.

Die Elementarkenntnisse zur Harmonielehre und zur Musik überhaupt

> Leipzig: Georg Wigand, 1852.

> T ● Famintsyn, A., trans. *Elementarnaia teoria muzyki*. St. Petersburg: 1878.

Lehrbuch der Harmonie: Praktische Anleitung zu den Studien in derselben

> Leipzig: Breitkopf & Härtel, 1853.

>> At least thirty-six editions through 1953, some edited by Alfred Richter.

> T ● Taylor, Franklin, trans. *Treatise on Harmony*. London: Cramer & Co., [1864]; at least fourteen editions through 1898.

> T ● Morgan, John P., trans. *Manual of Harmony: A Practical Guide to Its Study*. New York: G. Schirmer, [1867]; numerous editions.

> T ● Famintsyn, A., trans. *Uchebnik garmonii: Prakticheskoe rukovodstvo k ee izucheniiu*. St. Petersburg: 1868.

> T ● Parker, J. C. D., trans. *Manual of Harmony: A Practical Guide to Its Study*. Boston: Oliver Ditson; New York: C. H. Ditson, [1873].

> T ● Gebauer, Joh. Chr., trans. *Harmonilære*. Edited by J. D. Bondesen. Copenhagen: T. Petersen, 1883.

> T ● Sandré, Gustave., trans. and ed. *Traité d'harmonie théorique et pratique*. Leipzig: Breitkopf & Härtel, 1884; at least eleven editions through 1911.

> T ● Pedrell, Filipe, trans. *Tratado de armonía, teórico y práctico*. Leipzig: Breitkopf & Härtel, 1892; at least nine editions through 1928.

> T ● Coon, Oscar, ed. [and trans.?]. *Manual of Harmony: A Practical Guide to Its Study*. New York: Carl Fischer, [1896]; later editions.

> T ● Hartog, Jacques, trans. *Leerboek der harmonie* . . . 1896.

> T ● Baker, Theodore, trans. *Manual of Harmony: A Practical Guide to Its Study*. New York: G. Schirmer, 1912.

> T ● Zingerle, Francesco G., trans. *Trattato d'armonia*. Milan: G. Ricordi, 1935.

Lehrbuch der Fuge: Einleitung zur Komposition derselben und zu den sie vorbereitenden Studien in den Nachahmungen und in dem Canon . . .

> Leipzig: Breitkopf & Härtel, 1859.

>> At least nine editions through 1921, some edited by Alfred Richter.

> T ● Famintsyn, A., trans. *Uchebnik fugi*. St. Petersburg: 1873.

> T ● Taylor, Franklin, trans. *Treatise on Canon and Fugue*. London: J. B. Cramer, 1878.

> T ● Foote, Arthur W., trans. *A Treatise on Fugue, including the Study of Imitation and Canon*. Boston: Oliver Ditson; New York: C. H. Ditson, 1878; as *A Treatise on Canon and Fugue* . . ., 1888.

> T ● Sandré, Gustave. *Traité de fugue, précédé de l'étude des imitations et du canon*. Benm. Leipzig: Breitkopf & Härtel, 1902; later editions.

Lehrbuch des einfachen und doppelten Kontrapunkts: Praktische Anleitung zu dem Studium desselben

> Leipzig: Breitkopf & Härtel, 1872.

>> At least fifteen editions through 1920, some edited by Alfred Richter. Review in *Rmi* 11/3 (1904):637-38 (Luigi Torchi).

> T ● Famintsyn, A., trans. *Uchebnik prostogo i dvoinogo kontrapunkta*. St. Petersburg: 1874; at least three editions through 1903.

> T ● Taylor, Franklin, trans. *Treatise on Counterpoint*. London: J. B. Cramer; New York: G. Schirmer, [1874]; 2nd edition (with an Appendix by James Cutler Dunn Parker), Boston: Ditson, [1878].

> T ● Morgan, J. P., trans. *Manual of Simple and Double Counterpoint*. New York: G. Schirmer, [1884]; later editions.

> T ● Rollinson, T. H., ed. *Treatise on Harmony, Counterpoint, Instrumentation and Orchestration* . . . Philadelphia: J. W. Pepper & Son, 1886.

>> The segment on counterpoint is Richter's.

> T ● Sandré, Gustave, trans. *Traité complet de contrepoint*. Leipzig: Breitkopf & Härtel, 1892; at least three editions through 1924.

>> Review in *Rmi* 1/1 (1894):156-58 (G. Branzoli).

Die praktischen Studien zur Theorie der Musik

>> The general title later affixed to the above works on harmony (1853), fugue (1859), and counterpoint (1872). Review in *Rmi* 20/4 (1913):924-25 (P. C.).

LITERATURE:

Richter, Alfred. *Aufgabenbuch zu E. Friedr. Richter's Harmonielehre.* BHmH, no. 4. Leipzig: Breitkopf & Härtel, 1879; at least sixty-four editions through 1952; translated by John P. Morgan (as *Additional Exercises to Manual of Harmony by E. F. Richter*), New York: G. Schirmer, [1882]; as *Exercises pour servir à l'étude de l'harmonie pratique . . .* (translated by Gustave Sandré), Leipzig: Breitkopf & Härtel, 1883; at least seven editions through ca. 1910.

Richter, Alfred. *Schlüssel zu dem Aufgabenbuch, . . . zum Selbstunterricht.* BHmH, no. 11. Leipzig: Breitkopf & Härtel, 1880; numerous editions.

> Review in *Rmi* 16/1 (1909):211 (Luigi Torchi).

Richter, Alfred. *Nachtrag [Aufgabenbuch] zu E. Fried. Richter's Lehrbuch des einfachen und doppelten Contrapunkts.* BHmH, no. 7. Leipzig: Breitkopf & Härtel, 1884; as *Book of Exercises to Accompany E. Friedrich Richter's Manual of Simple and Double Counterpoint* (translated by J. H. Cornell), New York: G. Schirmer, 1888; as *Supplement to E. F. Richter's Manual . . .,* New York: G. Schirmer; Leipzig: Breitkopf & Härtel, 1888.

Stockmann, Bernhard. "Richter, Ernst Friedrich Eduard." In *MGG* (1949-68). Bibliog.

Gehring, Franz, and Charlton, David. "Richter, Ernst Friedrich (Eduard)." In *NGrove* (1980). Bibliog.

See also RIEMANN: (1898); SCHENKER: (1906-35):(1906); SCHOENBERG: Rexroth (1969/1971); LITERATURE SUPPLEMENT: Abraham (1966); Beach (1983); **Bent** ["Analysis"] **(1980/1987)**; Blumröder (1972-); **Bullivant (1980)**; Burdick (1977), (1977-78); Burke (1963); Chew (1980); Čolič (1976); **Dahlhaus (1984)**; Devore (1987); Federhofer (1944/1950); Harris (1969); Hoffmann (1974); Horsley [*Fugue: History*] (1966); Imig (1969/1970); Jacobi (1957-60/1971); Jeppesen (1930/. . ./1974), (1935); Konecne (1984); **Mann (1955/. . ./1987)**; McQuere (1983); Moyer (1969); Nielsen (1971); Palisca (1949-68); Phillips (1979); Pole (1879/. . ./1924); Prout (1893); **Ritzel (1967/1968)**; **Rummenhöller (1967)**; Schmalzriedt ["Durchführen"] (1972-), ["Reprise"] (1972-); Skinner (1891); Skyllstad (1968); Thaler (1984); Thompson (1980); Tittel (1959); **Wason (1981/1985)**; Weigl (1914-15); Wirth (1966).

(KARL WILHELM JULIUS) HUGO RIEMANN

[1849–1919]

Building upon the theoretical and philosophical foundations of HAUPTMANN and OETTINGEN, and drawing upon the acoustical perspective of HELMHOLTZ, Hugo Riemann created a remarkably comprehensive system which explicates music from a variety of angles and includes particularly influential notions regarding harmony and meter and early investigations on the nature of musical perception. Though his prolific output in these areas alone surpasses the life work of most other music theorists, Riemann also compiled an important music dictionary (1882), authored a landmark work on the history of music theory (1898), and made significant contributions in the field of musicology.

The Riemann holdings in major research libraries attest the importance which earlier generations ascribed to his work; yet recent scholarship in music theory has neglected to some extent the speculative side of his contribution. To be sure, there are aspects to his work that are simply untenable. Riemann spent a good part of his life believing in and championing the notion of an undertone series which would complement the overtone series of acoustical physics. As a result, his harmonic system instructs that major triads are founded upon their bottom pitch, while minor triads are founded upon what in traditional theory is regarded as the chordal fifth.

Riemann's functional theory of harmony, articulated in his *Vereinfachte Harmonielehre; oder, Die Lehre von den tonalen Funktionen der Akkorde* (1893) and in later writings, is based upon the duality of the overtone and undertone series. The fifths above and below the tonic root generate the only non-tonic functions—dominant and subdominant. No other chords attain a status independent of this triumvirate. The system incorporates a number of symbols, such as T (Tonic), D (Dominant), S (Subdominant), p (for parallel, as in A minor being Tp of a C-major Tonic), + (for major), ° (for minor), intersecting letters (such as two Ds joined to indicate the Dominant's Dominant), and small crescendo and decrescendo marks (to indicate raised or lowered pitches or chordal roots). The system dutifully supplies a symbol for any conceivable chord, yet the theory is unable to assist in determining which possible successions might be more appropriate than others. Riemann's work on harmony pervaded the musical culture of his time and persists in some music pedagogy today, particularly in northern Europe.

Riemann devoted considerable attention to matters such as meter, rhythm, and phrasing. His *Musikalische Dynamik und Agogik* (1884) and *System der musikalischen Rhythmik und Metrik* (1903), as well as numerous practical editions and performance guides, extend KOCH's treatment of phrase structure into a complete hierarchical system. For Riemann the *Motiv*, a small unit which passes from an upbeat through the following downbeat (and thus displays the characteristics of growth, peak, and decay), was the essential component of all musical structures. Their combination into two-, four-, and eight-bar segments created the normative constructions of music, though numerous situations involving elision, repetition, dovetailing, and so on, were carefully enumerated and displayed using special slur symbols in the music examples. His remarks are particularly pertinent for performers, as the variables of accentuation, dynamics, and tempo are closely allied with metrical organization.

Riemann's numerous books testify to an indefatigable energy and intense curiosity. (Note that the worklist below is selective and excludes his contributions in the field of musicology.) Riemann's numerous "Catechisms" touch upon counterpoint, aesthetics, orchestration, ear-training, figured-bass, acoustics, and composition, as well as the harmonic and metric concerns of his more speculative books. His *Geschichte der Musiktheorie im IX.-XIX. Jahrhunderts* (1898), a work which is only now being replaced by a *fifteen-volume* survey [see Zaminer (1985) for contents], has served generations of students as their primary introduction to the field—despite its numerous flaws and bias in favor of Riemann's perspective (for example, the "dualistic" treatment of ZARLINO concerning the distinction between major and minor). Though few will continue to study Riemann with the vigor that he once elicited, an acquaintance with the nature of his questions, the direction of his responses, and the scope of his undertaking will benefit those for whom nineteenth-century repertoire and musical theories are matters of importance.

"Musikalische Logik: Ein Beitrag zur Theorie der Musik"

> *NZfM* 68/28-29, 36-38 (1872):279-82, 287-88, 353-55, 363-64, 373-74.
>
>> Under the pseudonym Hugibert Ries.

S ● See (1895-1901):Vol. 3 (1901), below.

"Über Tonalität"

> *NZfM* 68/45-46 (1872):443-44, 453-54.
>
>> Under the pseudonym Hugibert Ries.

S ● See (1895-1901):Vol. 3 (1901), below.

ST ● McCune, Mark P. "Hugo Riemann's 'Über Tonalitat': A Translation." *Theoria* 1 (1985):132-50.

"Über das musikalische Hören"

> Ph.D. dissertation, The University of Göttingen, 1873.
>
>> Incorporates materials from the two articles of 1872, above.

> Göttingen: Vandenhoeck & Ruprecht, 1874.
> Leipzig: F. Andrä, 1874.
>
>> As *Musikalische Logik: Hauptzüge der physiologischen und psychologischen Begründung underes Musiksystems*:

> Leipzig: C. F. Kahnt, [1874].

"Musikalische Grammatik"

> Ms., 1874. [Destroyed.]

"Neue Schule der Harmonik"

> Ms., 1874. [Destroyed.]

"Die Hilfsmittel der Modulation: Studie"

> *AdM* 2/30-33, 35, 37, 39-40, 43, 45 (1875):245-46, 253-54, 261-62, 269-70, 285-87, 303-5, 318-19, 326-27, 350-51, 365-66.
> Kassel (Berlin: F. Luckhardt): 1875.

Die objektive Existenz der Untertöne in der Schallwelle: Skizze

> Kassel (Berlin: F. Luckhardt): 1875.

Musikalische Syntaxis: Grundriß einer harmonischen Satzbildungslehre

> Leipzig: Breitkopf & Härtel, 1877.
>
> S ● Facsimile edition. Niederwalluf bei Wiesbaden: Martin Sändig, 1971.

Studien zur Geschichte der Notenschrift

>> Contains, as Chapter 3, a discussion of major and minor as they relate to early music.

> Leipzig: Breitkopf & Härtel, 1878.
>
> S ● Facsimile edition. Hildesheim: Georg Olms.

Skizze einer neuen Methode der Harmonielehre

> Leipzig: Breitkopf & Härtel, 1880.
>
>> Enlarged, as *Handbuch der Harmonielehre*:

> Leipzig: Breitkopf & Härtel, 1887.
> Leipzig: Breitkopf & Härtel, 1898. 3rd edition, revised.
>
>> Review in *Rmi* 5/3 (1898):599. Numerous other printings.

> T ● Calvocoressi, Michel D., trans. *Manuel de l'harmonie*. Leipzig: Breitkopf & Härtel, 1902.
>
>> Review in *Rmi* 9/3 (1902):743 (Luigi Torchi).

T ● Setaccioli, Giacomo, trans. *Manuale di armonia.* Leipzig: Breitkopf & Härtel, 1906.

> Review in *Rmi* 13/3 (1906):558 (Luigi Torchi).

T ● Spanish translation. Leipzig: 1906.

"Zarlino als harmonischer Dualist"

MMg 12/10 (1880):155-57, 174.

Musik-Lexikon: Theorie und Geschichte der Musik, die Tonkünstler alter und neuer Zeit mit Angabe ihrer Werke, nebst einer vollständigen Instrumentenkunde (MFl)

> Leipzig: Bibliographisches Institut, 1882.

>> Numerous later editions, with considerable revision. Reviews in *Nation* 91/2358 (1910):225-26, *Rmi* 1/2 (1894):362-63 (A. Untersteiner), *Rmi* 17/1 (1909):268 (Fausto Torrefranca), and *Rmi* 36/3 (1929):646-47 (B.).

T ● Schytte, Henrik Vissing, trans. *Nordisk Musik-Lexikon.* Copenhagen: W. Hansen, 1888-92; Supplement, [ca. 1906].

T ● Shedlock, John South, trans. [*Encyclopaedic*] *Dictionary of Music.* London: Augener, 1893; New York: Schirmer, [1893]; Philadelphia: Presser, [ca. 1899]; later editions; reprints of the 1908 edition: (DCPMRS) New York: Da Capo Press, 1970; St. Clair Shores, Mich.: Scholarly Press, 1972.

>> Reviews in *Diapason* 64/6 [762] (1973):10-11, *MMR* 23/272 (1893):171-72, *MMR* 27/314 (1897):28-31 (Charles W. Pearce), and *MT* 112/1536 (1971):140 (Stanley Sadie).

T ● Humbert, Georges, trans. *Dictionnaire de musique de Hugo Riemann.* Paris: Perrin, 1895-1902; later editions, revised.

>> A French translation of the 4th German edition. Review in *Rmi* 3/1 (1896):201-2 (G. Branzoli).

T ● Engel, Yuly Dmitrievich, trans. *Muzykal'nyi slovar.* 19 vols. Moscow: Petr Jurgenson, 1901-4.

"Die Natur der Harmonik"

SmV 4/40 (1882):157-90.

T ● Fillmore, John Comfort, trans. "The Nature of Harmony." In his *New Lessons in Harmony.* Philadelphia: Presser, [1886 or 1887].

Elementar-Musiklehre

> Hamburg: K. Grädener [J. F. Richter], 1883.

Neue Schule der Melodik: Entwurf einer Lehre des Contrapunkts nach einer gänzlich neuen Methode

> Hamburg: K. Grädener [J. F. Richter], 1883.

Phrasierungsausgabe

> 1) *Sonaten für Klavier* by W. A. Mozart.

> 2) *Sonaten für Klavier* by Ludwig van Beethoven. Berlin: N. Simrock, 1883. Vol. 1 Berlin: N. Simrock, 1885. Vol. 2.

"Der Ausdruck in der Musik"

SmV 5/50 (1884):41-64.

Musikalische Dynamik und Agogik: Lehrbuch der musikalischen Phrasierung auf Grund einer Revision der Lehre von der musikalischen Metrik und Rhythmik

> Hamburg: D. Rahter, 1884.

>> Review in *MMR* 15/170 (1885):25-28 (Frederick Niecks).

Systematische Modulationslehre als Grundlage der musikalischen Formenlehre

> Hamburg: J. F. Richter, 1887.

T ● Engel, Yuly Dmitrievich, trans. *Sistematicheskoe uchenie o moduliatsii, kak osnova ucheniia o muzykal'nykh formakh.* Moscow: 1898.

Katechismus der Musik (Allgemeine Musiklehre) (MHiK, no. 5)

> Leipzig: Max Hesse, 1888.

>> Later editions, as *Handbuch der Musik.*

T ● English translation. London: Augener.

T ● Ribera y Maneja, Antonio, trans. *Teoría general de la música.* CL, ser. 5, no. 172. Barcelona: Editorial Labor; 2nd edition, 1932; 3rd edition (with José Subirá), 1945.

Katechismus der Musikinstrumente ([Kleine] Instrumentationslehre) (MHiK, no. 1)

> Leipzig: Max Hesse, 1888.

>> Later editions, as *Handbuch der Musikinstrumente.* Review in *Rmi* 11/3 (1904):641 (Luigi Torchi).

T ● *Catechism of Musical Instruments (Guide to Instrumentation).* London: Augener, n.d.

Lehrbuch des einfachen, doppelten und imitierenden Kontrapunkts

> Leipzig: Breitkopf & Härtel, 1888.

>> Later editions. Review in *Rmi* 16/1 (1909):211 (Luigi Torchi).

T ● Lovewell, S. Harrison, trans. *Text-Book of Simple and Double Counterpoint Including Imita-*

tion and Canon. Leipzig: Breitkopf & Härtel, 1904.

> Reviews in *Nation* 80/2084 (1905):463-64 and *Rmi* 11/3 (1904):637-38 (Luigi Torchi).

Wie hören wir Musik? Drei Vorträge

> Leipzig: Max Hesse, 1888.

> > As *Grundlinien der Musik-Ästhetik (Wie hören wir Musik?)* (MHiK, no. 17):

> Leipzig: Max Hesse, 1890.

> > Later editions, under the title *Katechismus der Musik-Ästhetik.* Reviews in *Rmi* 11/1 (1904):151-52 (Luigi Torchi) and *Rmi* 19/2 (1912):470 (Fausto Torrefranca).

T ● Bewerunge, Henry, trans. *Catechism of Musical Aesthetics.* London: Augener, [ca. 1895].

T ● See Bujić (1988).

Katechismus des Generalbaß-Spiels (Harmonie-Übungen am Klavier) (MHiK, no. 10)

> Leipzig: Max Hesse, 1889.

> > Later editions, under the title *Anleitung zum Generalbaß-Spielen* or *Handbuch des General-baß-Spiels.*

Katechismus der Kompositionslehre (Musikalische Formenlehre) (MHiK, nos. 8-9)

> Leipzig: Max Hesse, 1889. 2 vols.

> > Later editions, under the title *Grundriß der Kompositionslehre.*

T ● English translation. London: Augener, n.d.

T ● Ribera y Maneja, Antonio, trans. *Composición musical (Teoría de las formas musicales).* CL, ser. 5, nos. 211-12. Barcelona: Editorial Labor, [1929]; 2nd edition (with Roberto Gerhard), [1950].

Katechismus des Musik-Diktats (Systematische Gehörs-bildung) (MHiK, no. 11)

> Leipzig: Max Hesse, 1889.

> > Later editions, as *Handbuch des Musikdiktats.*

T ● Ladukhin, A., trans. *Katekhizis muzykal'nogo dik-tanta.* St. Petersburg and Moscow: 1894.

Katechismus der Fugen-Komposition (Analyse von J. S. Bachs "Wohltemperiertem Klavier" und "Kunst der Fuge") (MHiK, nos. 18, 19, 29)

> Leipzig: Max Hesse, 1890-94. 3 vols.

> > Later edition, under the title *Handbuch der Fugen-Komposition.* Reviews in *MMR* 23/269 (1893):98-101 (Ebenezer PROUT) and *Rmi* 14/2 (1907):452-53 (Luigi Torchi).

T ● Shedlock, John South, trans. *Analysis of J. S. Bach's Wohltemperirtes Clavier (48 Preludes and Fugues).* 2 vols. London: Augener, n.d.

S ● See Schuhmacher [*Zur Analyse*] (1974):3-9.

> An excerpt dealing with the Prelude and Fugue in D Minor from Volume 1 of Bach's *Well-Tempered Clavier.*

Katechismus der Harmonie- [und Modulations]lehre (Praktische Anleitung zum mehrstimmigen Tonsatz) (MHiK, no. 15)

> Leipzig: Max Hesse, 1890.

> > Later editions, some under the title *Handbuch der Harmonie- und Modulationslehre.* Review in *Rmi* 8/2 (1901):485 (Luigi Torchi) and *Rmi* 17/1 (1910):276 (Luigi Torchi).

Katechismus der Phrasierung (Praktische Anleitung zum Phrasieren . . .) (MHiK, no. 16)

> Leipzig: Max Hesse, 1890. With Carl Fuchs.

S ● Fuchs, Carl Dorius Johann. *Die Zukunft des musikalischen Vortrages und sein Ursprung: Studien im Sinne der Riemannischen Reform und zur Aufklärung des Unterscheides zwischen antiker und musikalischer Rhythmik, nebst einem Vortrage von Dr. H. Riemann "Über musikalische Phra-sirung . . ."* [Danzig: A. W. Kafemann, 1884.]

T ● *Practical Guide to the Art of Phrasing . . .* New York: G. Schirmer, 1890.

T ● Ribera y Maneja, Antonio, trans. *Fraseo musi-cal.* CL, ser. 5, no. 162. Barcelona: Editorial Labor, [1928]; 2nd edition (with Otto Mayer), [1936].

Katechismus der Akustik (Musikwissenschaft) (MHiK, no. 21)

> Leipzig: Max Hesse, 1891.

> > Reprinted as *Handbuch der Akustik.*

T ● *Akustika s tochki zreniia muzykal'noi nauki.* Mos-cow: 1898.

Katechismus der Gesangkomposition (MHiK, no. 20)

> Leipzig: Max Hesse, 1891.

> > Later editions, as *Handbuch der Gesangkomposi-tion.*

"Kurzgefaßte Harmonielehre"

> In *Musik-Taschenbuch,* 5th and later editions. Leipzig: Steingräben, [1892].

Vereinfachte Harmonielehre; oder, Die Lehre von den tonalen Funktionen der Akkorde

> London: Augener; New York: Schirmer, 1893.

> > Reprinted in 1903.

> T ● Bewerunge, Henry, trans. *Harmony Simplified; or, The Theory of the Tonal Functions of Chords*. London: Augener, [1895]; reprint edition, Ann Arbor, Mich.: Xerox University Microfilms.

> T ● Engel, Yuly Dmitrievich, trans. *Uproshchennaia garmoniia ili uchenie o tonal'nykh funktsiiakh akkordov*. Moscow and Leipzig: P. Yurgenson, 1896; 1901.

> > Review in *Rmg* /41-42 (1902):986-90, 1020-22 (Yury Vladimirovich Kurdiumov).

> T ● Humbert, Georges, trans. *L'harmonie simplifiée ou théorie des fonctions tonales des accords*. London: Augener, [1899].

Präludien und Studien: Gesammelte Aufsätze zur Ästhetik, Theorie und Geschichte der Musik

> > Contains numerous individual essays (some previously published), including "Zur Theorie der Konsonanz und Dissonanz," "Die musikalische Phrasierung," and "Über Agogik."

> Frankfurt am Main: Bechhold, 1895. Vol. 1.

> > Review in *Rmi* 3/2 (1896):371-72 (Luigi Torchi).

> Leipzig: Hermann Seemann, 1900. Vol. 2.
> Leipzig: Hermann Seemann, 1901. Vol. 3.

> S ● Facsimile edition. Hildesheim: Georg Olms, 1967. 3 vols. in 1.

> S ● Facsimile edition. MSt, nos. 1, 2, 7. 3 vols. in 2. Nendeln/Leichtenstein: Kraus Reprint, 1976.

Geschichte der Musiktheorie im IX.-XIX. Jahrhundert

> 1) *Organum; Dé chant; Fauxbourdon*

> 2) *Die Mensuraltheorie und der geregelte Kontrapunkt*

> 3) *Die Harmonielehre*

> Leipzig: Max Hesse, 1898. 3 books in 1.

> > Reprinted in 1921 (edited by Gustav Becking). Reviews in *AMuZ* 27/1-7 (1900):4-7, 23-24, 39-40, 55-56, 71-72, 87-88, 103-4 (Bernhard ZIEHN) [reprinted in ZIEHN: Goebel (1926-27)] and *Rmi* 6/1 (1899):189-96 (Luigi Torchi).

> T ● Spratt, John Fenton, trans. "The Relation of Theory to Practice in Selected Musical Examples, 1300-1500." M.A. thesis, Florida State University,

> > 1954; excerpts published as "Contrapuntal Theory of the Fourteenth and Fifteenth Centuries, from the *Geschichte der Musiktheorie*." *FSUS* 18 (1955):41-128.

> S ● Facsimile of the 1921 edition. Hildesheim: Georg Olms, 1961.

> T ● Haggh, Raymond Herbert. "Hugo Riemann's *Geschichte der Musiktheorie im IX.-XIX. Jahrhundert*, Books I and II: A Translation with Commentary and Annotated Bibliography." Ph.D. dissertation, Indiana University, 1961; published edition (as *History of Music Theory, Books 1 and 2: Polyphonic Theory to the Sixteenth Century*), Lincoln, Nebr.: University of Nebraska Press, 1962; reprint edition (DCPMRS), New York: Da Capo Press, 1974. Bibliog. [*DA* 22/04A, p. 1203-4.]

> > Reviews in *JAMS* 17/3 (1964):395-400 (Lawrence A. Gushee), *JMT* 7/1 (1963):127-30 (Lewis Rowell), *JRME* 11/2 (1963):145-46 (Johannes Riedel), *MEJ* 49/4 (1963):153, *MJ* 21/1 (1963):104 (Ruth de Cesare), *ML* 44/4 (1963):394-96 (Frank Harrison), *MR* 26/1 (1965):68-69, and *RN* 16/3 (1963):229-31 (Carl Parrish).

> T ● Mickelsen, William Cooper. "Hugo Riemann's History of Harmonic Theory with a Translation of *Harmonielehre*." Ph.D. dissertation, Indiana University, 1970; published edition (as *Hugo Riemann's Theory of Harmony, with a Translation of Riemann's "History of Music Theory," Book 3*. Lincoln, Nebr.: University of Nebraska Press, 1977. Bibliog. [*Rilm* 71-1529. *DA* 32/02A, p. 1002.]

> > Reviews in *JMT* 22/2 (1978):316-19 (Lewis Rowell), *MEJ* 65/2 (1978):90, *MR* 41/3 (1980):246-47 (Peter J. Pirie), ●●●*NCM* 2/2 (1978-79):178-85 (Ruth A. Solie), and *Notes* 35/3 (1978-79):626-28 (Hedi Siegel).

Die Elemente der musikalischen Ästhetik

> Berlin and Stuttgart: W. Spemann, 1900.

> T ● Humbert, Georges, trans. *Les élémens de l'esthétique musicale*. Bpc. Paris: F. Alcan, 1906.

> > Review in *Rmi* 13/2 (1906):366 (R. G.).

> T ● Spanish translation. Madrid: 1914.

Vademecum der Phrasierung (MHiK, no. 16)

> > Replaced *Katechismus der Phrasierung* (1890), above, as vol. 16 of MHiK.

> Leipzig: Max Hesse, 1900.

Later editions, under the title *Handbuch der Phrasierung*. Review in *Rmi* 8/2 (1901):485-86 (Luigi Torchi).

Große Kompositionslehre

1) *Der homophone Satz (Melodielehre und Harmonielehre)*

2) *Der polyphone Satz (Kontrapunkt, Fuge und Kanon)*

3) *Der Orchestersatz und der dramatische Gesangstil*
Berlin and Stuttgart: W. Spemann, 1902-3. Vols. 1 and 2.

Reviews in *Rmi* 9/1 (1902):199-200; 10/1 (1903):147-48 (Luigi Torchi).

Berlin and Stuttgart: W. Spemann, 1912-13. All three volumes.

Katechismus der Orchestrierung (Anleitung zum Instrumentieren) (MHiK, no. 31)

Leipzig: Max Hesse, 1902.

Later editions, as *Handbuch der Orchestrierung*. Review in *Rmi* 10/2 (1903):403-5 (Luigi Torchi).

T ● *Catechism of Orchestration (Introduction to Instrumentation)*. London: Augener, n.d.

Beethoven's Streichquartette (SMb; Mfüh, no. 12)

Berlin: Schlesinger (Robert Lienau); Vienna: Haslinger, 1903; [1910].

Riemann editions of the late quartets of Beethoven were first published ca. 1899-1903. Review in *Rmi* 17/4 (1910):974-75 (Fausto Torrefranca).

S ● See Schuhmacher [*Zur Analyse*] (1974):115-21.

A brief excerpt.

System der musikalischen Rhythmik und Metrik

Leipzig: Breitkopf & Härtel, 1903.

S ● Facsimile edition. Niederwalluf bei Wiesbaden: Martin Sändig, 1971.

"Das Problem des harmonischen Dualismus[: Ein Beitrag zur Ästhetik der Musik]"

NZfM 72/1-4 (1905):3-5, 23-26, 43-46, 67-70. Leipzig: C. F. Kahnt, 1905.

Review in *Rmi* 13 (1906):182.

S ● Reprint edition. Scarsdale, N.Y.: Schnase, 1969.

T ● Lovewell, S. Harrison, trans. "Consonance and Dissonance: A Discussion of the Principles of

Harmonic Dualism." Ms., 1925. [Boston: Boston Public Library.]

Elementar-Schulbuch der Harmonielehre

Leipzig: Max Hesse, 1906.

Later editions. Review in *Rmi* 13/4 (1906):748-49 (Luigi Torchi).

T ● Lovewell, S. Harrison, trans. "An Elementary Textbook of Harmony Designed for Use in Schools." Arlington, Mass.: 1925. [Ms.?]

Copies are found in the Boston and New York Public Libraries.

Kleines Handbuch der Musikgeschichte mit Periodisierung nach Stilprinzipien und Formen (HMl, no. 2)

Leipzig: Breitkopf & Härtel, 1908.

Later editions.

"Ideen zu einer 'Lehre von der Tonvorstellungen' "

JMbP 1914/15 21-22 (1916):1-26.

S ● In *Musikhören*, edited by Bernhard Dopheide, pp. 14-47. WdF, no. 429. Darmstadt: Wissenschaftliche Buchgesellschaft, 1975.

T ● Marvin, Elizabeth West, and Wason, Robert, trans. "Hugo Riemann's 'Ideas for a *Theory of Tonal Perception*'." Forthcoming.

"Neue Beiträge zu einer 'Lehre von den Tonvorstellungen' "

JMbP 1916 23 (1917):1-21.

L. van Beethovens sämtliche Klavier-Solosonaten: Ästhetische und formal-technische Analyse mit historischen Notizen (MHiK, nos. 51-53)

Berlin: Max Hesse, 1917-19. 3 vols.

Later editions. See HALM: (1920-21). Reviews in *Rmi* 28/1 (1921):164 (A. E.) and *ZfMw* 1/10 (1918-19):629-30 (Hermann Wetzel).

"Die Phrasierung im Lichte einer Lehre von den Tonvorstellungen"

ZfMw 1/1 (1918-19):26-39.

A response to KURTH: (1917).

See also GEVAERT: (1863):(1887); (1890):(1891); LOUIS AND THUILLE: [1907]:Review (1907); MARX: (1837-47):(1887-90); MOMIGNY: RIEMANN (1903-4). See ["Verzeichnis"] (1909/1965), below, for a more thorough listing of Riemann's publications.

LITERATURE:

Charnova, Anna Ivanovna. "Gugo Riman, novator v oblasti teorii i garmonii." [Hugo Riemann, An Innovator in the Sphere of Theory and Harmony.] *Teatr* [Theater] /284, 287 (1897).

Charnova, Anna Ivanovna. "Gugo Riman i ego novyi metod prepodavaniia teorii garmonii." [Hugo Riemann and His New Method of Teaching the Theory of Harmony.] *Muzp* /3 (1898).

Boutroux, Léon. "Réflexions sur le système d'harmonie de M. Hugo Riemann." *Rhcm* 3/16-17 (1903):628-30, 663-65.

Calvocoressi, Michel D. "Le système d'harmonie de M. Hugo Riemann." *Rhcm* 3/13-14 (1903):542-46, 565-68.

> Responses in *Rhcm* 3/16-17 (1903):628-30, 663-65 (Léon Boutroux) and *Rhcm* 4/5, 7 (1904):139-43, 186-88 (Paul Landormy); followed by "Les fonctions variables des accords d'après M. Hugo Riemann" in *Rhcm* 4/21 (1904):525-28 (Paul Landormy).

Engel, Yuly Dmitrievich. "Osnovy sistemy garmonii Rimana." [The Principles of the System of Harmony of Riemann.] *Rmg* /25-26 (1904):611-12.

Landormy, Paul. "La nouvelle théorie de l'harmonie de M. Hugo Riemann." *Rhcm* 4/5, 7 (1904):139-43, 186-88.

Capellen, Georg. *Die Zukunft der Musiktheorie (Dualismus oder "Monismus"?) und ihre Einwirkung auf die Praxis.* Leipzig: Kahnt, 1905.

Marnold, Jean. "Les sons inférieurs et la théorie de M. Hugo Riemann." *RmSIM* 1/1, 3, 5, 11, 13 (1905):25-38, 119-28, 214-27, 293-98, 435-39, 530-37; 2/1, 7, 9, 11 (1906):11-20, 289-98, 399-408, 494-504.

Vianna da Motta, J. "Mathis Lussy und Hugo Riemann." *KL* 28/20 (1905):309-11.

"Verzeichnis der Werke Hugo Riemanns." In *RiemannFs* (1909/1965):xxv-xl. Bibliog.

Altmann, Wilhelm. "Nachträge zu Hugo Riemanns Verzeichnis der Druckausgaben und thematischem Katalog der Mannheimer Kammermusik des XVIII Jahrhunderts." *ZfMw* 1/10 (1918-19):620-28.

Becking, Gustav Wilhelm. " 'Hören' und 'Analysieren': Zu Hugo Riemanns Analyse von Beethovens Klaviersonaten." *ZfMw* 1/10 (1918-19):587-603.

Einstein, Alfred. "Hugo Riemann zum 70. Geburtstag" *ZfMw* 1/10 (1918-19):569-70.

Gurlitt, Wilibald. "Hugo Riemann und die Musikgeschichte." *ZfMw* 1/10 (1918-19):571-87.

Kühn, Walter. "Die Lehre von den Tonvorstellungen und ihre Anwendung im Elementarmusikunterricht." *ZfMw* 1/7 (1918-19):414-22.

Steglich, Rudolf. "Hugo Riemann als Wiedererwecker älterer Musik." *ZfMw* 1/10 (1918-19):603-20.

Niecks, Frederick. "The Late Hugo Riemann." *MMR* 49/587 (1919):242-44.

Grabner, Hermann. *Die Funktionstheorie Hugo Riemanns und ihre Bedeutung für die praktische Analyse.* Munich: Halbreiter, 1923.

Frey, Martin. "Wiehmayer contra Riemann." *NMZ* 46/19 (1925):450-52.

Wiehmayer, Theodor. "Die Auswirkung der Theorie Hugo Riemanns." *NMZ* 46/15 (1925):345-50.

> Comment in *NMZ* 46/19 (1925):448-50 (Paul Wermbter).

Maecklenburg, Albert. "Riemanns Tonsystem — Ein Markstein in der Geschichte der Musiktheorie." *NZfM* 96/7 (1929):376-80.

Nadel, Siegfried. "Hugo Riemann und Karl Stumpf." *NZfM* 96/7 (1929):381-84.

Mazel, Lev Abramovich. "Funktsional'naia shkola (G. Riman)." In Ryzhkin and Mazel (1934-39):Vol. 1 (1934):122-80.

Mazel, Lev Abramovich. "Funktsional'naia shkola v oblasti teoreticheskogo muzykoznaniia." [The Functional School in the Sphere of Theoretical Musicology.] *Smuz* /4 (1934):76-90.

Mazel, Lev Abramovich. "Obshchii obzor teoreticheskogo muzykoznaniia posle Rimana." [A General Survey of Theoretical Musicology after Riemann.] In Ryzhkin and Mazel (1934-39):Vol. 2 (1939).

Denecke, Heinz Ludwig. "Die Kompositionslehre Hugo Riemanns, historisch und systematisch dargestellt." Ph.D. dissertation, The University of Kiel, 1937; published edition, Kiel: Kleinert, 1937.

Hurlbut, Ira D. *Practical Chord Signs: A Scientific Terminology Consistent with the Harmonic Theory of Dr. Hugo Riemann, with Universal Modulating Harmony Chart and Illustrations of Harmonic Analyses.* Prairie du Chien, Wisc.: Hurlbut, [1945].

Bonaccorsi, Alfredo. *Elementi di forme musicali, appunti dal Riemann.* Milan: Edizioni Curci, [1946].

Wolff, Hellmuth Christian. "Riemann, Karl Wilhelm Julius Hugo." In *MGG* (1949-68). Bibliog.

Sievers, Gerd. "Die Grundlagen Hugo Riemanns bei Max Reger." Ph.D. dissertation, The University of Hamburg, 1949 (1950); published edition, Wiesbaden: Breitkopf & Härtel, 1967.

> Review in *Mf* 23/4 (1970):485-86 (Bernhard Hansen).

Gurlitt, Wilibald. "Hugo Riemann (1849–1919)." *AMAWL* 25 (1950):1865-1905; Wiesbaden: Franz Steiner, [1951].

> Reviews in *Mf* 6/2 (1953):167-68 (Walther Vetter), *Notes* 9/2 (1951-52):292-93 (Ernest C.

Krohn), *Rbdm* 6/1 (1952):57 (A. Van der Linden), and *Rmi* 54/2 (1952):186.

Sievers, Gerd. "Max Regers Kompositionen in ihrem Verhältnis zu der Theorie Hugo Riemanns." *Mf* 3/3-4 (1950):212-23.

Thoor, Alf. "Hugo Riemann, mannheimskolan och 'Denkmälerstriden'." *Stfm* 34 (1952):5-27.

Wienke, Gerhard. "Voraussetzungen der *Musikalischen Logik* bei Hugo Riemann: Studien zur Musikästhetik in der zweiten Hälfte des 19. Jahrhunderts." Ph.D. dissertation, The University of Freiburg im Breisgau, 1952 (1953).

Blom, Eric. "Phrase-Lengths." *MT* 95/1333 (1954):124-27.

Wolff, Hellmuth Christian. "Hugo Riemann, der Begründer der systematischen Musikbetrachtung." In *SchneiderFs* (1955):265-70.

Federhofer, Hellmut. "Die Funktionstheorie Hugo Riemanns und die Schichtenlehre Heinrich Schenkers." In *Kongress Wien 1956* (1958):183-90.

Seidel, Elmar. "Die Harmonielehre Hugo Riemanns." In Vogel (1966):39-92.

Dahlhaus, Carl. "Eduard Hanslick und der musikalische Formbegriff." *Mf* 20/2 (1967):145-53. [*Rilm* 68-1291.]

Hayashi, Mikinori. "Ongaku-Bigakusha to shiteno Hugo Riemann." *Og* 8/4 (1967):234-40. [*Rilm* 68-1297.]

Bessler, Heinrich. "M. Ugolini de Maltero Thuringi 'De cantu fractibili': Ein scherzhafter Traktat von Hugo Riemann." *Am* 41/1-2 (1969):107-8.

Siegmund-Schultze, Walther. "Hugo Riemann zum 50. Todestag (16.7.1849 – 10.7.1919)." *MG* 19/7 (1969):466-69.

Volek, T. "Eggebrechtuv Riemann." *Hroz* 22/15 (1969):459-61.

Byrt, John Clare. "Form and Style in the Works of J. S. and C. P. E. Bach." Ph.D. dissertation, Oxford University, 1970. [*Rilm* 75-2679.]

Haack, Helmut. "Das Phrasierungsproblem." In *Bericht Bonn 1970* (1971):415-16. [*Rilm* 73-4288.]

Dahlhaus, Carl. "Terminologisches zum Begriff der harmonischen Funktion." *Mf* 28/2 (1975):197-202. [*Rilm* 76-7136.]

● ● ● Wuensch, Gerhard. "Hugo Riemann's Musical Theory." *SMUWO* 2 (1977):108-24. [*Rilm* 77-5724.]

● ● ● Hoffman, Mark. "Riemann, (Karl Wilhelm Julius) Hugo." In *NGrove* (1980). Bibliog.

Christensen, Tom. "The *Schichtenlehre* of Hugo Riemann." *ITO* 6/4 (1981-83):37-44. [*Rilm* 82-3569.]

Whiteman, Michael. "Reflections on the Teaching of Harmony and Composition." *SAMT* 98 (1981):19-23.

Dadelsen, Georg von. "Urtext und Spielpraxis: Einige Gedanken anhand des Allegro aus Bachs Violin-Solo-Sonata a-Moll BWV 1003." In *PalmFs* (1982):19-23. [*Rilm* 82-2307.]

Caplin, William E. "Hugo Riemann's Theory of 'Dynamic Shadings': A Theory of Musical Meter?" *Theoria* 1 (1985):1-24.

Tveit, S. "Harmoniske moenstre hos J. S. Bach." *Smn* 13 (1987):43-44.

See also BONONCINI: Holler (1955/1963); GLAREAN: Willfort (1908-9); HALM: (1920-21); HELMHOLTZ: Dahlhaus (1970); d'INDY: (1903-50); KOCH: Baker (1976), Dahlhaus (1978); KURTH: (1913); (1931); Nishihara (1978), (1979); LIPPIUS: Rivera (1974/1980); LORENZ: (1924-33); Lewin (1984); MOMIGNY: Chailley (1982); SCHENKER: Morgan (1978); Yokota (1982); Wintle (1985); SCHOENBERG: Rexroth (1969/1971); VIADANA: Haack (1964/1974); ZARLINO: Dahlhaus (1957), (1975); Wienpahl (1959); LITERATURE SUPPLEMENT: Abbado (1964); Abraham (1968/1969); Albersheim (1980); Alette (1951); Allen ["Philosophies"] (1939); Apel (1936/. . ./ 1972), (1942/. . ./1961); Apfel (1967), (1976), (1977); Apfel and Dahlhaus (1974); Auhagen (1982/1983); Babbitt (1987); **Barbour (1951/. . ./ 1972)**; Baron (1968); Beach (1967); Beck (1973), (1974); Beiche ["Dux"] (1972-); **Benary (1956/ 1961)**; ● ● ● **Bent** ["Analysis"] **(1980/1987)**; Berry (1985); Beswick (1950); Beyer (1958); Billeter (1970/1971); Blume (1984); Blumröder (1972-); Böckl (1972); Boomgaarden (1985/1987); Braun (1970); Breig (1972-); Bridges (1984); Budday (1982/1983); **Bullivant (1980)**; Burke (1963); Cahn ["Repercussio"] (1972-); Caplin (1978), (1981), (1983); Carpenter (1988); Carse (1925/1964); Cavallini (1949); Cavett-Dunsby (1988); Cazden (1948), (1980); Chailley (1967); Chevaillier (1925/1931-32); Chew (1979), (1980); Čolič(1976); Conley (1977); Cook (1987); **Coover (1980)**; Covington (1985); Crocker (1966); **Dahlhaus** ["Konsonanz"] (1949-68), ["Tonalität"] (1949-68), ["Tonsystem"] (1949-68), ["Über"] (1966), ["Untersuchungen"] (1966/. . ./ 1988), (1967), (1972), ["Relationes"] (1975), (1975/ 1977), ["Neue Musik"] (1976), (1978), ● ● ● ["Harmony"] **(1980)**, ["Tonality"] **(1980)**, ["Über] (1980), (1981), ["Hindemiths"] (1983), ["Tonalität"] (1983), **(1984)**, (1985), ["Zum Taktbegriff"] (1988); **Dahlhaus et al. (1987)**; Devore (1987); de Zeeuw (1983); Dubovsky et al. (1934-35); Duchez (1979); Dürr and Gerstenberg (1949-68), (1980); Dunsby and Whittall (1988); Dziebowska (1976); Eggebrecht (1955), (1957), (1975); Eimert (1926-27); Erpf (1959/1974); Federhofer (1944/1950), (1981), (1985), (1989); Feil (1955); Fellerer (1927/. . ./1972); Ferand (1937/1938); Fillmore (1887); Fischer (1976); Flechsig (1977); Forster (1966); Frischknecht (1979); Frisius (1969/1970); Frobenius ["Cantus"] (1972),

["Homophonus"] (1972-), ["Vollstimmig"] (1972-); Fubini (1971/1983); Fuchs (1885); Green (1969); Gurlitt (1944/1966); Gut (1972-), (1976); Haase (1969), (1972); Hahn (1960); Handschin (1948); Harrán (1986); Hartmann (1923); Haydon (1933/1970); Heckmann (1953); Hein (1954); Henneberg (1972/1974); Hoffman (1953), (1974); Horsley [*Fugue: History*] (1966); Imig (1969/1970); Jackson (1988); Jacobi (1957-60/1971); Jeppesen (1922/. . ./1970), (1930/. . ./1974), (1935), ([1951]/1952); Jiránek (1967); Jones (1934); Jorgenson (1957), Jorgenson (1963); Kauko (1958); Kayser (1950); Keller (1955/1965); Kelletat (1966); Kerman (1985); Kinkeldey (1910/1968); Komma (1972); Kroyer (1901/. . ./1970); La Motte-Haber (1971), (1976); Lang (1941); Lange (1899-1900); Lerdahl (1988); Lester (1977); Levarie (1986); Levenson (1981); Levitan (1938); Lewin (1981), (1982), (1983-84); Lindley (1982); List (1976); Loach (1957); Longyear and Covington (1985); Luoma (1977); Mahlert and Sunter (1972-); Mainka (1965/1969); **Mann (1955/. . ./1987)**, (1987); Marvin (1987); Mazel (1937); McQuere (1983); Meier (1966), (1974/1988); Mendel (1948), (1978); Mitchell, J. W. (1963); Mitchell, W. J. (1963); Möllers (1978); Moos (1902/1922); Morgan (1978); Moyer (1969); Müller (1976); Müller-Blattau (1923/. . ./1963), (1949-68); Münnich (1909/1965); Natale (1971); Neumann, Frederick (1986); Neumann, Friedrich (1978); Newman (1959/. . ./1983), (1969/. . ./1983); Nielsen (1971); Norton (1984); Ortmann (1924); **Palisca** ["Theory"] **(1980)**; Parncutt (1988-89); Perinello (1936); Powers ["Language"] (1980); Ratner (1980); Reese (1954/1959); Reichert (1978); Révész (1946/. . ./1954); Riechenbach (1948); **Ritzel (1967/1968)**; Rohwer (1949-68); Rosen (1971/. . ./1983); Rosenblum (1988); Rothärmel (1963/1968); Rothschild (1953); **Rummenhöller (1967)**, (1971); Sachs (1972-); Schmalzriedt ["Coda"] (1972-), ["Durchführen] (1972-), ["Episode"] (1972-), ["Exposition"] (1972-), ["Reprise"] (1972-); Schoffman ['Descriptive"] (1983); Scholz (1981/1983); Schuhmacher ["Notwendige Ergänzung"] (1974); Schulenberg (1984); Seidel (1972-), (1975), (1976), (1979), (1980), (1986); **Seidel and Cooper (1986)**; **Shirlaw (1917/. . ./1970)**, (1931), (1957); Silberman (1949); Smith (1974); Smith (1967); Smither (1960); Snyder (1980-81); Sondheimer (1925); Stein (1983); Steinbeck (1981); Subirá (1947/. . ./1958); Taddie (1984); Tenney (1988); Thaler (1984); Tittel (1959); Vauclain (1978); Vertrees (1974); Vogel (1955/1954), (1962), (1970), (1975/1984); **Wagner (1981)**; Wagner (1974); **Wason (1981/1985)**, (1983), (1987); Whittall (1980); Wichmann (1966); Yeston (1974/1976); **Zaminer (1985)**.

JOSEPH RIEPEL

[1709 – 1782]

In Joseph Riepel we find a true trailblazer of the mid-eighteenth century. The startling changes in music's fabric—the organization by phrases, the techniques for expansion, the patternings of key areas—were a focus of his explorations, from which resulted embryonic formulations for concepts such as antecedent and consequent phrases, periodic structure, and motivic development.

As might be expected, such novel ideas were not easily conceived: chapters from *Anfangsgründe zur musicalischen Setzkunst* were published separately in 1752, 1755, 1757, 1765, and 1768. Another chapter remained in manuscript, while four others were projected but never completed. That Riepel's ideas were evolving is evident through comparison of the various chapters. Though his theory is imperfectly articulated, it was nevertheless of great importance to KOCH, who later offered a more elegant and further refined formulation.

Riepel was the first theorist to examine systematically the role of phrases in the development of larger musical entities. He dealt with phrase units of from two to nine measures, though his preference was (as it was also for composers of the era) the four-measure phrase. Sometimes these phrases were divided into smaller components, called *incises*, while irregular phrases might be assembled additively (e.g., seven measures consisting of three measures plus four measures). Phrases were categorized according to their harmonic and melodic roles. (Did the phrase modulate, or did it confirm its opening harmony? Was its concluding melodic pitch an octave doubling of the bass pitch, or another pitch?)

Riepel offered the progressive view that larger works were, essentially, expansions of the structures from which the most basic of compositions were derived. He showed, for example, three stages in the developmental process, wherein a simple model served as the underpinning for a symphony Allegro, which itself provided the foundation for a more elaborate symphonic work. Several types of expansion are described, including the repetition of material and the interpolation of one body of material within another.

Drawing upon his era's fascination with games of chance and with novel ways of examining phenomena, Riepel made serious use of permutation theory (*ars combinatoria*) as a compositional tool. Through his procedures a large variety of candidate melodies and harmonic plans were generated, and from these the best were selected through ar-

tistic discrimination. Melodies were subjected to permutation by pitch, by measure, and by phrase, while rhythms also
were subjected to this process on occasion. Though many
possible harmonic successions were generated, Riepel
issued a clear statement on which keys he felt were most
closely related to a major tonic—namely, the dominant, submediant, and mediant.

Anfangsgründe zur musicalischen Setzkunst: Nicht zwar
nach alt-mathematischer Einbildungs-Art der Zirkel-
Harmonisten, sondern durchgehends mit sichtbaren
Exempeln abgefasset [Rism B/VI/2, pp. 704-5.]

1) *De Rhythmopoeïa, oder von der Tactordnung* . . .

2) *Grundregeln zur Tonordnung insgemein* . . .

3) *Gründliche Erklärung der Tonordnung insbe-*
   sondere, zugleich aber für die mehresten Organisten
   insgemein . . .

4) *Erläuterung der betrüglichen Tonordnung* . . .

5) *Unentbehrliche Anmerkungen zum Contrapunct,*
   über die durchgehend- verwechselt- und
   ausschweifenden Noten . . .

Regensburg and Vienna: Emerich Felix Bader
   (Augsburg: Johann Jacob Lotter), 1752. Vol. 1.
   [HoM: 1296.]
Frankfurt, Leipzig, etc.: (Augsburg: Johann Jacob
   Lotter), 1752. Vol. 1. [LCPS: R-049a.]
Regensburg: Johann Leopold Montag, 1754. Vol.
   1., 2nd edition.
Frankfurt, Leipzig, etc.: [Regensburg: Johann
   Leopold Montag]; (Ulm: Christian Ulrich
   Wagner), 1755. Vol. 2. [LCPS: R-049b.]

   Review in MARPURG: (1754-78):Vol. 2/6
   (1756):514-21.

Frankfurt, Leipzig, etc.: [Regensburg: Johann
   Leopold Montag], 1757. Vol. 3. [LCPS: R-
   049c.]
Augsburg: Johann Jakob Lotter, 1765. Vol. 4.
   [LCPS: R-049d.]

   Review in *WNAMb* 1/2-3 (1766-67):14-15, 17-19.

Regensburg: Jacob Christian Krippner; Augsburg: Johann Jacob Lotter (Ulm: Christian Ulrich Wagner), 1768. Vol. 5. [LCPS: R-049e.]
Augsburg: Johann Jacob Lotter, 1768. Vol. 5.

   A sixth volume, "Vom Contrapunct," remained
   unpublished. [Berlin: Deutsche Staatsbibliothek.]

Harmonisches Syllbenmaß, Dichtern melodischer
Werke gewiedmet, und angehenden Singcomponisten
zur Einsicht mit platten Beyspielen gesprächweise
abgefaßt [Rism B/VI/2, p. 706.]

1) *Von dem Rezitativ*

2) *Von Arien*

Regensburg: J. L. Perile, 1776. 2 vols. [LCPS: R-
   051.]

   A third volume remained unpublished. [Berlin:
   Deutsche Staatsbibliothek.]

Baßschlüssel; Das ist, Anleitung für Anfänger und Lieb-
haber der Setzkunst, die schöne Gedanken haben
und zu Papier bringen, aber nur klagen, daß sie kei-
nen Baß recht dazu zu setzen wissen [Rism B/VI/2,
pp. 705-6.]

Regensburg: Johann Leopold Montags Erben,
   1786. Edited by Johann Kaspar Schubarth.
   [LCPS: R-050.]

"Eine Abhandlung vom Kanon"

Ms. [Lost?]

"Der Fugen-Betrachtung"

Ms. 2 parts. [Berlin: Deutsche Staatsbibliothek.]

"Silva rerum, ein Notiz-Exzerptenbuch"

Ms. [Regensburg.]

LITERATURE:

Twittenhoff, Wilhelm. "Die musiktheoretischen Schriften
   Joseph Riepels (1709-1782) als Beispiel einer an-
   schaulichen Musiklehre." Ph.D. dissertation, The
   University of Halle, 1933 (1934); published edition
   (BzMf, no. 2), Halle (Saale) and Berlin: Buchhandlung des Waisenhauses G.m.b.H., 1935; reprint edition, Hildesheim: Georg Olms, 1971. Bibliog.

Schwarzmaier, Ernst. "Die Takt- und Tonordnung Joseph
   Riepels: Ein Beitrag zur Geschichte der For-
   menlehre im 18. Jahrhundert." Ph.D. dissertation,
   The University of Munich, 1934; published edition,
   Wolfenbüttel: Verlag für musikalische Kultur und
   Wissenschaft, 1936; reprint edition (with a new Af-
   terword by Hermann Beck; RBzMw, no. 4), Re-
   gensburg: Boße, 1978. Bibliog.

Hoke, Hans Gunter. "Riepel, Joseph." In *MGG* (1949-68).
   Bibliog.

● ● ● Ratner, Leonard G. "Riepel, Joseph." In *NGrove*
   (1980). Bibliog.

Reed, Nola Jane. "The Theories of Joseph Riepel as Expressed in His *Anfangsgründe zur musicalischen*
   Setzkunst (1752-68)." Ph.D. dissertation, The University of Rochester, 1983. [Rilm 83-4984. *DA*
   44/08A, p. 2288. UMI 83-25697.]

Emmerig, Thomas. *Joseph Riepel (1709-82), Hofkapellmeis-*
   ter des Fürsten von Thurn und Taxis: Biographie,
   Thematisches Werkverzeichnis, Schriftenverzeichnis.
   TTS, no. 14. Kallmünz: Michael Lassleben, 1984.
   Bibliog.

Reviews in *CM* 37-38 (1984):221-23 (Nola Reed Knouse), *MiB* 30 (1985):96-99 (Thomas Röder), *Orch* 33/6 (1985):614 (Rudolf Stöckl), *VhVOR* 124 (1984):481 (A. Scharnagl), and *ZfbL* 48/3 (1985):795-96 (Alois Schmid).

Emmerig, Thomas. "Joseph Riepel (1709-1782) und seine musiktheoretischen Schriften." *Mf* 38/1 (1985):16-21. Bibliog.

Knouse, Nola Reed. "Joseph Riepel and the Emerging Theory of Form in the Eighteenth Century." *CM* 41 (1986):46-62. Bibliog.

See also FÉTIS: (1833-44); KOCH: (1782-93); (1782-93):Baker (1983); Baker (1975), ● ● ● (1976); Dahlhaus (1978); ● ● ● Sisman (1982); VIADANA: Haack (1964/1974); VOGLER: Stevens (1983); LITERATURE SUPPLEMENT: Apfel and Dahlhaus (1974); Arakawa (1973); Balthazar (1983); Becker (1836-39/1964); **Benary (1956/1961)**, (1963); **Bent** ["Analytical Thinking"] (1980), ["Analysis"] **(1980/1987)**; Budday (1982/1983), (1987); Buelow (1979); Cahn ["Retardatio"] (1972-); Chybiński (1911-12); Dahlhaus ["Zum Taktbegriff"] (1988); Duckles (1970); Eitner (1900-1904/1959-60); Feil (1955); Fellerer (1927/. . ./ 1972); ["Musikwissenschaft"] (1972); Forkel (1792/1962); Gerber (1790-92/1977), (1812-14/1966); Grave (1985); Henneberg (1972/1974); Hiller (1768-69); Houle (1960), (1987); Karube (1969); **Kassler (1979)**; Kelletat [*Temperatur*] (1960); Kob (1965); Krones (1988); Lester (1979-81); Maier (1984); **Mann (1955/. . ./1987)**; Moyer (1969); Munkachy (1968); Nelson (1984); Newman (1963/. . ./1983); **Palisca** ["Theory"] **(1980)**; Ratner (1956), (1970), (1980); Reichenbach (1948); Reimer ["Concerto"] (1972-), (1973); **Ritzel (1967/1968)**; Sachs (1972-); Seidel (1979); **Seidel and Cooper (1986)**; Sheldon (1981); **Wason (1981/1985)**; Wirth (1966); Yeston (1974/1976); **Zaminer (1985)**.

NIKOLAI ANDREEVICH RIMSKY-KORSAKOV

[1844 – 1908]

Whereas CHAIKOVSKY established a norm for the teaching of harmony in Moscow, Nikolai Andreevich Rimsky-Korsakov ruled in St. Petersburg [Leningrad], where he served on the faculty at the Conservatory and at the school of the Imperial Court Capella. A strict regimen was followed at the Conservatory. Though every composition student began with the study of harmony, only a few survived the courses on counterpoint and fugue and were permitted to enter the culminating three-year program of composition study and the orchestration course.

Motivated by his teaching duties, Rimsky-Korsakov developed texts in both harmony and orchestration. His *Prakticheskii uchebnik garmonii* (1886) offers an innovative synthesis of basic harmonic principles, one which was to persist in the work of many later Russian authors. Unlike CHAIKOVSKY's pedagogy, Rimsky-Korsakov's establishes the functional relationships among the tonic, subdominant, and dominant chords before any others are incorporated. Furthermore, by introducing a "harmonic" variant of the major scale—as in C D E F G A-flat B C, for example—he generated chords such as the minor subdominant and diminished-seventh on the leading tone in the major mode.

Harmonization of melodies and effective modulation from one tonal center to another are of central importance in Rimsky-Korsakov's method. The former was taught with a pedagogy that initially limited chord choices; the latter was clarified through a careful assessment of the relatedness of any of the twenty-three potential goal triads for a modulation from a given tonal center. Whereas keys whose tonics were deemed closely related could be approached through common-chord modulation, Rimsky-Korsakov also devised means whereby seemingly unrelated keys might be linked using modulatory techniques dependent upon intermediate tonalities. He also explored ways in which modal and enharmonic shifts might contribute to modulatory practice.

Though of less interest from a purely theoretical point of view, Rimsky-Korsakov's orchestration manual, *Osnovy orkestrovki* (published posthumously in 1913), has attained the stature of a classic both inside Russia and in many other countries, owing to its numerous translations. Examples from his own works in full score occupy a large portion of the treatise.

Uchebnik garmonii [*Kurs Pridvornoi kapelly. Vypusk pervyi: Garmonizatsiia akkordami v predelakh lada*] [Textbook of Harmony, A Course of the Court Capella. First Volume: Harmonization with Chords in the Limits of the Mode]

St. Petersburg: 1884. Vol. 1 only.
St. Petersburg: 1885. Two vols.

A preliminary version of (1886), below, appearing only in a lithograph edition.

Prakticheskii uchebnik garmonii [Practical Textbook of Harmony]

St. Petersburg: Büttner, 1886.

Numerous printings. Those after 1912 were revised by Joseph Withol and Maximilian Steinberg.

T ● Schmidt, Hans, trans. *Praktisches Lehrbuch der Harmonie*. Leipzig: M. P. Belaieff, 1895; later editions.

> Review in *Rmi* 2/4 (1895):741-42 (Luigi Torchi).

T ● Dorfmann, Félix, trans. *Traité d'harmonie théorique et pratique*. Paris: Alphonse Leduc, 1910.

T ● Bucchi, G. F., and Zamorski, A., trans. *Trattato pratico d'armonia*. Milan: Sonzogno, 1913; 1932.

T ● Achron, Joseph, trans. *Practical Manual of Harmony*. New York: Carl Fischer, [1930].

S ● See Collected Works (1955-70):Vol. IV, below.

"Razbor *Snegurochki*" [An Analysis of *Snowmaiden*]

Ms.

S ● See Collected Works (1955-70):Vol. IV, pp. 393-426, below.

Osnovy orkestrovki [Principles of Orchestration]

St. Petersburg, Berlin, and Moscow: Rossiiskoe muzykal'noe izdatel'stvo, 1913. 2 vols. Edited by Maximilian Steinberg.
Moscow: Gosudarstvennoe muzykal'noe izdatel'stvo, 1946. 2 vols.

T ● Calvocoressi, Michel-D., trans. *Principes d'orchestration*. Berlin: Edition russe de musique; Paris: Max Eschig, 1914; Paris: Musique russe, 1921.

T ● Agate, Edward, trans. *Principles of Orchestration*. 2 vols. Berlin and New York: Édition russe de musique, [1922-23]; reprint edition, Scarsdale, N.Y.: E. F. Kalmus, [ca. 1948]; reprint edition, New York: Boosey & Hawkes, [1950]; reprint edition, New York: Dover, [1964]; reprint edition, Gloucester, Mass.: 1966; Magnolia, Mass.: Peter Smith.

> Reviews in *AmO* 50/1 (1967):5-6 (Harry W. Gay), *MiE* 29/313 (1965):140-41, *MO* 88/1055 (1964-65):673 (B. R.), *MuMus* 13/9 (1964-65):52 (Stephen Dodgson), *MusT* 44/5 (1965):223 (W. R. A.), *Notes* 8/1 (1950-51):173-74 (Walter E. Nallin), and *NZfM* 128/4 (1967):167 (G. A. Trumpff).

T ● Elukhen, Alexander, trans. *Grundlagen der Orchestration*. 2 vols. Berlin and New York: Russischer Musikverlag, [ca. 1922].

T ● Riesemann, O. von, trans. *Grundlagen der Instrumentation*. [Berlin]: Russischer Musikverlag, 1922 or 1928.

T ● Agate, Edward, trans. *Principles of Orchestration: Digest*. New York: Édition russe de musique, [1922?]; [New York: Boosey & Hawkes, 1950].

T ● Ficher, Jacobo, and Jurafsky, A. *Principios de orquestación*. Bmm. Buenos Aires: Ricordi americana, [1946].

S ● See Collected Works (1955-70):Vol. III, below.

T ● Bucharest: 1960.

Articles and miscellaneous writings

S ● Rimsky-Korsakov, Nadezhda Nikolaevna, ed. *Muzykal'nye stat'i i zametki (1869-1907)*. [Articles and Notes on Music (1869-1907).] Introduction by M. F. Gnesin. St. Petersburg: 1911.

S ● Shelkov, N. V., ed. "Materialy, sviazannye s deiatel'nostiu pridvornoi pevcheskoi kapelly." [Materials Connected with Activity at the Court Choir Capella.] In Collected Works (1955-70):Vol. II, pp. 129-68, below.

S ● Shelkov, N. V., ed. "Materialy, sviazannye s deiatel'nostiu v peterburgskoi konservatorii." [Materials Connected with Activity in the Petersburg Conservatory.] In Collected Works (1955-70):Vol. II, pp. 169-222, below.

S ● Shelkov, N. V., ed. "Materialy, sviazannye s deiatel'nostiu v russkom muzykal'nom obshchestve i v kachestve uchreditelia vysshikh muzykal'nykh kursov." [Materials Connected with Activity in the Russian Musical Society and in the Capacity of Founder of Higher Musical Courses.] In Collected Works (1955-70):Vol. II, pp. 223-32, below.

COLLECTED WORKS EDITION:

Shelkov, N. V. (Vol. II); Dmitriyev, A. N. (Vol. III); and Protopopov, Vladimir Vasil'evich (Vol. IV), eds. *N. A. Rimskii-Korsakov: Polnoe sobranie sochinenii: Literaturnye proizvedeniia i perepiska*. [N. A. Rimsky-Korsakov: Complete Collected Works: Literary Works and Correspondence.] Moscow: Gosudarstvennoe muzykal'noe izdatel'stvo, 1955-70.

LITERATURE:

CHAIKOVSKY, Petr I'lich. "Zamechaniia na poliakh *Uchebnika garmonii* N. Rimskogo-Korsakova." [Notes in the Margins of *The Textbook of Harmony* by N. Rimsky-Korsakov.] Ms., 1885; published in CHAIKOVSKY: Collected Works (1957):Vol. 3-A, pp. 226-49.

Gnesin, Mikhail Fabianovich. "Muzykal'no-nauchnye trudy N. A. Rimskogo-Korsakova." [The Musical Scientific Works of N. A. Rimsky-Korsakov.] *Muzïka* 133 (1913):403-15.

Kotov, Petr Aleksandrovich. *Prakticheskii kurs garmonii v zadachakh, primenitel'no k uchebniku N. A. Rimskogo-Korsakova. Chast' 1.: Formuly i tsifrovannyi bas.* [The Practical Course of Harmony in Problems, Applicable to the Textbook of N. A. Rimsky-Korsakov. Part 1: Formulas and Figured Bass.] Moscow: 1915.

Levenson, Boris. *How Rimsky-Korsakoff Taught: An Intimate Personal Picture Showing the Enormously Painstaking Teaching Methods Employed in Russian Conservatories.* New York: Edw. B. Marks Music Co, [ca. 1928].

> Reprinted from *Etude* 46/3 (1928):197-98.

Mutli, Andrei Fedorovich. *O moduliatsii: K voprosu o razvitii ucheniia N. A. Rimskogo-Korsakova o srodstve tonal'nostei.* [About Modulation: On the Question of the Development of the Doctrine of N. A. Rimsky-Korsakov on the Relatedness of Tonalities.] Moscow and Leningrad: Gosudarstvennoe muzykal'noe izdatel'stvo, 1948.

Abraham, Gerald. "Rimski-Korssakow, Nikolai Andréjewitsch." Translated by Christiane Blume. In *MGG* (1949-68). Bibliog.

Ryzhkin, Iosif Yakovlevich. "Novoe izdanie uchebnika garmonii." [A New Edition of a Textbook of Harmony.] *Smuz* /2 (1950):108-10.

Berkov, Viktor Osipovich. *Uchebnik garmonii Rimskogo-Korsakova.* [The Textbook of Harmony of Rimsky-Korsakov.] Moscow: Gosudarstvennoe muzykal'noe izdatel'stvo, 1953.

Rimsky-Korsakov, Vladimir Nikolaevich. "Muzykal'no-esteticheskie printsipy *Osnov orkestrovki* N. Rimskogo-Korsakova (Neopublikovannye materialy)." [The Musical Aesthetic Principles of *Principles of Orchestration* of N. Rimsky-Korsakov (Unpublished Material).] *Smuz* /9 (1955):56-70.

Protopopov, Vladimir Vasil'evich. "Ob uchebnike garmonii Rimskogo-Korsakova." [About the Textbook of Harmony of Rimsky-Korsakov.] *Smuz* /6 (1958):56-57.

Ginzburg, Semyon L'vovich, ed. *N. A. Rimskii-Korsakov i muzykal'noe obrazovanie* [N. A. Rimsky-Korsakov and Musical Education.] Leningrad: Gosudarstvennoe muzykal'noe izdatel'stvo, 1959.

> Includes "N. A. Rimsky-Korsakov i A. K. Liadov" [N. A. Rimsky-Korsakov and A. K. Liadov], by M. K. Mikhailov (pp. 158-70), "Mysli N. A. Rimskogo-Korsakova ob analize muzykal'nykh proizvedenii" [Thoughts of N. A. Rimsky-Korsakov on the Analysis of Musical Works], by Elena Mikhailovna Orlova (pp. 107-18), "Ob istoricheskom znachenii uchebnika garmonii N. A. Rimskogo-Korsakova" [On the Historical Significance of the Textbook of Harmony of N. A. Rimsky-Korsakov], by Yury Nikolaevich Tiulin (pp. 81-93), and "Voprosy muzykal'noi pedagogiki v perepiske N. A. Rimskogo-Korsakova s S. N. Kruglikovym" [Questions of Music Pedagogy in Correspondence of N. A. Rimsky-Korsakov with S. N. Kruglikov], by A. P. Zorina (pp. 71-80).

Stepanov, Aleksei Alekseevich. "O razlichnykh sistemakh rodstva tonal'nostei (iz istorii russkoi i sovetskoi muzykal'no-teoreticheskoi pedagogiki)." [About the Different Systems of the Relatedness of Tonalities (from the History of Russian and Soviet Music Theory Pedagogy).] In Rags (1972):Vol. 1, pp. 129-51.

Rukavishnikov, V. "Nekotorye dopolneniia i utochneniia sistemy tonal'nogo rodstva N. A. Rimskogo-Korsakova i vozmozhnye puti ee razvitiia." [Some Additions and Clarifications of the System of Tonal Relatedness of N. A. Rimsky-Korsakov and Possible Paths of Its Development.] In *Voprosy teorii muzyki* [Questions of the Theory of Music], edited by Teodor Miuller, Vol. 3, pp. 70-103. Moscow: Muzyka, 1975. [*Rilm* 76-1682.]

Abraham, Gerald. "Rimsky-Korsakov, Nikolay Andreyevich." In *NGrove* (1980). Bibliog.

See also CHAIKOVSKY: Miasoedov (1972); LITERATURE SUPPLEMENT: Burke (1963); Carpenter (1988); Carse (1925/1964); Chevaillier (1925/1931-32); Lawrence (1978); Lindley (1982); ● ● ● McQuere (1983); Ryzhkin (1933), (1934-39); Subirá (1947/. . ./1958).

ANTONIO VENTURA ROEL DEL RÍO

[active mid eighteenth century]

As was typical of Spanish theorists at the time, Antonio Ventura Roel del Río drew heavily upon past authors, particularly CERONE and KIRCHER, in the development of his own treatise on music, *Institución harmónica: O doctrina musical, theórica, y práctica* (1748). He utilized his position as an authority to poor advantage in his later *Re-*

paros músicos (1764), for SOLER, the target of its criticism, responded brilliantly in his *Satisfacción a los reparos precisos* (1765).

Institución harmónica: O doctrina musical, theórica, y práctica, que trata del canto llano, y de órgano; Exactamente, y según el moderno estilo explicada, de suerte que escusa casi de maestro . . . [*Rism* B/VI/2, p. 711.]

>		Madrid: herederos de la viuda de Juan García Infanzón, 1748. [LCPS: R-062. SMLMS.]

>			A manuscript treatise of the same title [a revised version?], from 1766, is housed at the Biblioteca nacional in Madrid. See Martin Moreno (1975), below.

Razón natural, y científica de la música en muchas de sus más importantes materias: Carta a D. Antonio Rodríguez de Hita . . .

>		Santiago: Ignacio Aguayo i Aldemunde, 1760.

>			An attack on Rodríguez de Hita's *Diapasón instructivo* (1757).

Reparos músicos precisos a la llave de la modulación del . . . Soler . . . [*Rism* B/VI/2, p. 711.]

>		Madrid: Antonio Muñóz del Valle, 1764.

An attack on SOLER: (1762). Reply in SOLER: (1765).

LITERATURE:

Anonymous. *Anti-crysis a la crysis de don Antonio Ventura Roel del Rio: Oro fino de la verdad contra la alchimia musical de Ventura; Mycroscopio a la carta escrita por Roel; Y confirmación de la doctrina música del maestro don Gregorio Santiso Bermúdez. Obra útil, y provechosa para los facultativos, y aficionados a la indagación fundamental de sus reglas.* [*Rism* B/VI/2, p. 916.] Stockholm: en la Oficina de Mufti Beij, 1737.

Querol, Miguel. "Roel del Rio, Antonio Ventura." Translated by Reinhard Schmidt-Preuß. In *MGG* (1949-68). Bibliog.

Martín Moreno, Antonio. "Un tratado de composición manuscrito (1766) de Antonio V. Roel del Río (siglo XVIII). *Anmu* 30 (1975):109-22.

Howell, Almonte. "Roel del Río, Antonio Ventura." In *NGrove* (1980). Bibliog.

See also LITERATURE SUPPLEMENT: Anglés and Subirá (1946-51); Eitner (1900-1904/1959-60); León Tello (1974); Subirá (1947/. . ./1958), (1953).

JEAN ROUSSEAU

[1644 – ca. 1700?]

Jean Rousseau moved a step towards the modern perspective by noting that only two basic modal types existed: that exemplified by Ionian, with a major third above its final, and that exemplified by Dorian, with a minor third above its final. His *Méthode claire, certaine et facile pour apprendre à chanter* (1678) incorporates this notion, making frequent use of transpositions of these basic modes to accommodate various vocal ranges. His *Traité de la viole*, a compendium of useful information on the viol, was published in 1687. In addition to matters such as bowing and transposition, the work includes instructions concerning ornamentation, accompanying, and tuning the instrument. In response to remarks by Demachy (in his *Pièces de violle* of 1685), Rousseau defended — both in the *Traité* and a later *Réponse* (1688) — the use of unharmonized melodies as an alternative to harmonic music.

Méthode claire, certaine et facile pour apprendre à chanter la musique, sur les tons transposez comme sur les naturels . . . [*Rism* B/VI/2, p. 719.]

>		Paris: Ballard, 1678.
>		Paris: the author, 1683. [LCPS: R-077a.]
>		Amsterdam: P. & J. Blaeu, 1691. Edited by A. Le Chevalier.

>		Paris: the author and Christophe Ballard, 1691. 4th edition.
>		Amsterdam: Estienne Roger, [1700]. 4th edition. [SMLMS.]
>		Amsterdam: Pierre, [ca. 1707-10]. 5th edition. [LCPS: R-077b.]

>	S ● Facsimile of the ca. 1707-10 edition. Geneva: Minkoff Reprint, 1976.

>	T ● Green, Robert Anthony. "Annotated Translation and Commentary of the Works of Jean Rousseau: A Study of Late Seventeenth-Century Musical Thought and Performance Practice." Ph.D. dissertation, Indiana University, 1979. [*Rilm* 79-1583. *DA* 40/10A, p. 5241. UMI 80-07961.]

Traité de la viol, qui contient une dissertation curieuse sur son origine. Une démonstration generale de son manche en quatre figures, avec leurs explications. L'explication de ses jeux differents, et particulierement des pieces par accords, et de l'accompagnement à fond. Des regles certaines, pour connoître tous les agrémens qui se peuvent pratiquer sur cét instrument dans toutes sortes de pieces de musique. La veritable maniere de gouverner l'archet, et des moyens faciles pour transposer sur toutes sortes de tons [*Rism* B/VI/2, p. 720.]

> Paris: Christophe Ballard, 1687. [LCPS: R-078. HoM: 1308. SMLMS. IDC.]

S ● Facsimile edition. Amsterdam: Antiqua, 1965.

S ● Lesure, François, ed. Facsimile edition. Geneva: Minkoff Reprint, 1975.

T ● ● ● ● Dolmetsch, Nathalie, trans. "Jean Rousseau's *Traité de la viole* 1687." *Consort* 33 (1977): 225-36; 34 (1978):302-11; 36 (1980):365-70; 37 (1981):402-11; 38 (1982):463-66. [*Rilm* 82-2359.]

T ● See (1678):Green (1979), above.

ST ● Erhard, Albert, trans. and ed. *Jean Rousseau's "Traité de la viole": Faksimile der Ausgabe Paris 1687 mit Einführung, Übersetzung und Kommentar.* MwS, no. 6. Munich: Emil Katzbichler, 1980. Bibliog.

> Review in *Mf* 35/3 (1982):322-23 (Veronika Gutmann).

Réponse . . . à la lettre d'un de ses amis qui l'avertit d'un libelle diffamatoire que l'on a écrit contre luy [*Rism* B/VI/2, p. 720.]

> An attack on Demachy, who had already induced remarks in Rousseau's *Traité* (above) in response to the Preface of his *Pièces de violle . . .* (Paris: the author and H. Bonneuil, 1685). [*Rism* A/I/5, p. 386.]

> Paris: 1688.

S ● Lesure, François, ed. "Une querelle sur le jeu de la viole en 1688: Jean Rousseau contre Demachy." *Rdm* 46/122 (1960):181-99.

> Contains the text of Rousseau's *Réponse* (1688).

LITERATURE:

Pauls, Karlheinz. "Rousseau, Jean." In *MGG* (1949-68).

Green, Robert A. "Jean Rousseau and Ornamentation in French Viol Music." *JVGSA* 14 (1977):4-41. [*Rilm* 77-1411.]

Kinney, Gordon J. "A 'Tempest in a Glass of Water'; or, A Conflict of Esthetic Attitudes." *JVGSA* 14 (1977):42-52. [*Rilm* 77-1418.]

Hancock, Wendy. "The Frequency and Positioning of Ornaments in French Viol Music (1685-89)." *Chelys* 8 (1978-79):38-50. [*Rilm* 79-4598.]

Pond, Celia. "Ornamental Style and the Virtuoso—Solo Bass Viol in France c. 1680-1740." *EM* 6/4 (1978):512-18. [*Rilm* 78-5976.]

Thompson, Clyde H. "Rousseau, Jean." In *NGrove* (1980). Bibliog.

Rose, Adrian P. "Some Eighteenth Century French Sources of Treble Viol Technique." *Consort* 38 (1982):431-39. Bibliog. [*Rilm* 82-3519.]

See also FÉTIS: (1833-44); WALTHER: (1732); LITERATURE SUPPLEMENT: Atcherson (1973); Auhagen (1982/1983); Babitz and Pont (1973); Badura-Skoda et al. (1980); **Barbour (1951/. . ./ 1972)**; Becker (1836-39/1964); Beyschlag (1907/1953); Bruck (1928); Burney (1776-89/. . ./ 1957); Carse (1925/1964); Cohen ["Symposium"] (1972), (1988); Collins (1963), (1973); **Dahlhaus et al. (1987)**; Dolmetsch (1915/. . ./1969); Donington (1963/. . ./1974), (1977), (1980); Eitner (1900-1904/1959-60); Ferand (1937/1938), [*Improvisation*] (1956/1961); Gable (1979); Gerber (1790-92/1977), (1812-14/1966); Goldschmidt (1907); Harich-Schneider ([1939]/. . ./1970); Houle (1960), (1987); Jackson (1988); Kooiman (1980), (1981); La Borde (1780/1978); **Lindley (1984)**; Mahlert and Sunter (1972-); **Neumann**, Frederick (1964/**1982**), (1978), [*Essays*] **(1982)**; **Palisca** ["Theory"] **(1980)**; Pincherle (1958); Rothschild (1953); Schwartz (1908); **Seidel and Cooper (1986)**; **Steblin (1981/1983)**; Tolkoff (1973).

JEAN-JACQUES ROUSSEAU

[1712 – 1778]

The multi-faceted career of Jean-Jacques Rousseau was enlivened through the completion of several music essays and two large lexicographical projects, which in turn add interest to our study of eighteenth-century theory and aesthetics. Reared on the harmonic formulations of RAMEAU, Rousseau entered the French capital hoping to dazzle the Académie with his notational system (which amounted to rows of Arabic numerals embellished by occasional dots). Unfortunately his judges were not impressed; nor was RAMEAU. Nevertheless he published his formulation, as *Dissertation sur la musique moderne* (1743), and retained an interest in it throughout his life.

An invitation of great importance came Rousseau's way after RAMEAU refused to aid Diderot and d'ALEMBERT in writing the music articles for their *Encyclopédie* (1751-65). The task fell upon Rousseau, who perhaps too speedily fabricated hundreds of contributions. RAMEAU's irritation at the result was caused less by the errors of fact than by the general philosophical outlook represented by Rousseau, who, though he depended upon RAMEAU's theory, was philosophically opposed to the mathematical and, in his view, emotionless perspective which RAMEAU was promulgating.

In the heated "Lettre sur la musique françoise" (1753) and dispassionate "Essai sur l'origine des langues" [ca. 1760], Rousseau's extraordinary sensitivity to the subtle, emotional effects of melody is exposed. Elaborate accompaniments and refined imitative devices did not, in his view, promote the communicative capabilities of music. In counterpoint, one line was apt to neutralize the effect of another. Only through a reaffirmation of pure melody would music regain the direct and intense character of its origins, wherein sounds served as indicators of human feelings.

Rousseau reformulated much of the material he had contributed to the *Encyclopédie* for his *Dictionnaire de musique* (1768), a work notable both for its elaborations of Rousseau's philosophy and as an advance in the development of musical lexicography. Unlike the neutral entries of more recent dictionaries, Rousseau peppered his articles with his distinctive personality, offering strong and interesting opinions in lively and appealing prose. It remains a useful source for information on the forms, performance practices, and aesthetic views which dominated French culture at the time.

N.B.: Numerous editions of Rousseau's collected writings have appeared. They have not been catalogued below. See Dufour (1925), below, and *Rism* B/VI/2, pp. 720-37 for more comprehensive information. Readers of German should note Peter Gülke's recent edition of Rousseau's writings, *Musik und Sprache: Ausgewählte Schriften*, with translations into German by Dorothea Gülke. (TzMw, no. 99; Wilhelmshaven: Heinrichshofen's Verlag, 1984), which has been reviewed in *Mf* 40/1 (1987):74-75 (Walter Wiora), *Mth* 3/2 (1988):188-89 (Herbert Schneider), and *NZfM* 146/5 (1985):57 (Hans Christoph Worbs).

"Projet concernant de nouveaux signes pour la musique . . . à l'Académie des sciences, le 22 août 1742" [*Rism* B/VI/2, pp. 736-37.]

> *Registre des procès-verbaux de l'Académie des sciences, An 1742.*

S ● Revised as (1743), below.

S ● In *Traités sur la musique*. Geneva: 1781; facsimile edition (MMMLF, ser. 2, no. 31) New York: Broude Brothers. [LCPS: R-080b, R-081a, R-082a, R-084a, R-085a, R-087a, R-088a, R-088. HoM: 1349. SMLMS. IDC.]

> This early compilation of Rousseau's writings on music, sometimes referred to as *Projet*. . . since a separate title page appears for that contribution, includes also the works of 1743, 1754, 1755, ca. 1760, and ca. 1777, below. It appears also in collected works editions. [HoM: 1350.]

ST ● Rainbow, Bernarr, trans., with Introduction. *Projet concernant de nouveau signes pour la musique, 1742/Project Concerning New Symbols for Music, 1742*. CTME, no. 1. Kilkenny, Ireland: Boethius Press (Leslie Hewitt), 1982. [*Rilm* 82-414.]

> Reviews in *Brio* 19/2 (1982):53-54 (Clifford Bartlett) and *ML* 65/3 (1984):302-3 (Watkins Shaw).

S ● See various collected works editions. [HoM: 1346-47.]

Dissertation sur la musique moderne [*Rism* B/VI/2, pp. 723-25.]

> Derived from (1742), above.

Paris: G. F. Quillau, père, 1743. [LCPS: R-080a. HoM: 1320. SMLMS.]

T ● George, Jonathan C., trans. Available from the American Musicological Society/Music Library Association Translations Center at the Brooklyn College Music Department.

S ● See various collected works editions. [HoM: 1321.]

Articles on music in the *Encyclopédie, ou dictionnaire raisonné des sciences, arte et métiers* (1751-65) of Diderot and d'ALEMBERT.

> The articles by Rousseau are signed S.

See d'ALEMBERT: (1751-65).

> Reactions in RAMEAU: (1755); (1756); (1757).

S ● See (1768), below.

Lettre sur la musique françoise [*sic*] [*Rism* B/VI/2, pp. 734-36.]

[Paris]: 1753. [LCPS: R-086a. HoM: 1339.]
[Paris]: 1753. [LCPS: R-086b. HoM: 1340. IDC.]

T ● See **Strunk (1950)**:636-54.

S ● See various collected works editions. [HoM: 1341-45.]

"Lettre à Monsieur l'Abbé Raynal au sujet d'un nouveau mode de musique, inventé par M. Blainville" [*Rism* B/VI/2, pp. 730-31.]

> Written in 1754.

> S ● First published in *Œuvres . . . Nouvelle édition*, vol. 5. Neuchâtel: 1764.

> S ● See various collected works editions. [HoM: 1333-34.]

"Examen de deux principes avancés par M. Rameau, dans sa brochure intitulée: 'Erreurs sur la musique dans l'Encyclopédie' " [*Rism* B/VI/2, pp. 726-27.]

> Written in 1755.

> S ● First published in (1742):(1781), above.

> S ● Duchez, Marie-Élisabeth. " 'Principe de la mélodie' et 'Origine des langues': Un brouillon inédit de Jean-Jacques Rousseau sur l'origine de la mélodie." *Rdm* 60/1-2 (1974):33-86. [*Rilm* 74-4107.]

>> Presents texts of two manuscripts which served as stages in the development of the "Essai sur l'origine des langues" and "Examen des deux principes avancés par M. Rameau." See also Wokler (1974), below, for further discussion of and an excerpt from the "Principe."

> S ● See various collected works editions. [HoM: 1326-28.]

"Essai sur l'origine des langues, où il est parlé de la mélodie et de l'imitation musicale . . ." [*Rism* B/VI/2, pp. 725-26.]

> Written ca. 1760, as a supplement to *Discours sur l'origine et les fondemens de l'inégalité parmi les hommes* (1755).

> S ● First published in (1742):(1781), above.

> T ● Moran, John H., and Gode, Alexander, trans. and ed. *On the Origin of Language: Jean-Jacques Rousseau, "Essay on the Origin of Languages . . ."* MoT. New York:F. Ungar, 1966; Chicago: The University of Chicago Press, 1986.

> S ● Facsimile of the 1817 (A. Belin) edition. BdG. Paris: Bibliothèque du Graphe, [1970].

> S ● Porset, Charles, ed. Bordeaux: G. Ducros, 1968; 1970.

>> Reviews in *ASJJR* (1975):395-98 (Jean Starobinski) and *TLS* 71/3688 (1972):1367-68.

T ● See Fubini (1969).

S ● See (1755):Duchez (1974), above.

S ● Kremer-Marietti, Angele, ed. *La philosophie en poche*. Paris: Aubier Montaigne, [1974].

> Contains "Jean-Jacques Rousseau; ou, La double origine et son rapport au systeme Langue-Musique-Politique."

S ● See Lippman (1986).

S ● See various collected works editions. [HoM: 1323-25.]

Dictionnaire de musique [*Rism* B/VI/2, pp. 720-23.]

> Paris: veuve Duchesne, 1768. [LCPS: R-079a. HoM: 1314. SMLMS. IDC.]

>> Published in November or December 1767. Reviews in *Jdm* [2/1, 3, 4] (1771):3-23, 171-86, 251-68 and *MonR* 38 (1802):215-16.

> Amsterdam: Marc Michel Rey, 1768. [LCPS: R-079b.]

T ● See BROSSARD: Grassineau (1740):(1769).

T ● Waring, William, trans. *Dictionary of Music*. London: for J. French, [ca. 1775-78] [*Rism* B/VI/2, p. 723. HoM: 1312.]; 2nd edition (as *The Complete Dictionary of Music . . .*), London: for J. Murray, Fielding and Walker, [ca. 1779] [LCPS: R-079d.]; London: for J. Murray; Dublin: Luke White, 1779 [LCPS: R-079e.]; facsimile of the London ca. 1779 edition, New York: AMS Press, 1975.

> Reviews in *MonR* 60 (1779):422-26 and *GMag* 49 (1779):414.

S ● See Supplement (1776-77) to d'ALEMBERT: (1751-65).

S ● See MOMIGNY: (1791-1818).

T ● Blacklock, Thomas. Articles on music in the *Encyclopaedia Britannica*, 2nd and 3rd editions.

T ● Burney, Charles. Music articles in *Cyc* (1802-20).

S ● Castil-Blaze [Blaze, François Henri Joseph]. *Dictionnaire de musique moderne*. Paris: au magazin de musique de la Lyre moderne, 1821; later editions.

S ● Facsimile of the 1768 edition. Hildesheim: Georg Olms; (MPT) New York: Johnson Reprint, 1969.

> Review in *BSAP* 64/4 (1970):483.

T ● See Rowen (1969).

S ● Facsimile of the 1832 edition (Paris: A. Aubrée), with historical notes and critiques by contemporary commentators. 2 vols. Paris: Art et culture, 1977.

T ● Lynn, Michael, trans. "Early Music Dictionary: J. J. Rousseau on Various Subjects." *Courant* 1/3 (1983):31-32.

S ● See various collected works editions. [HoM: 1315-19.]

"Lettre à M. Burney sur la musique, avec fragmens d'observations sur l'Alceste italien de M. le chevalier Gluck" [*Rism* B/VI/2, pp. 731-34.]

Written ca. 1777.

S ● First published in (1742):(1781), above.

S ● See various reprint and collected works editions. [HoM: 1331-32.]

"Leçons de musique"

Ms. 2 vols. [Geneva: Bibliotheque publique et universitaire.]

Both Kling (1905), below, and Tiersot ["Les leçons"] (1912), below, include excerpts from this work.

Additional items are listed in Cotte (1949-68), below; Sélenier (1949/1950), below; and Heartz (1980), below.

LITERATURE:

See Conlon (1981), below, for an extensive listing of eighteenth-century materials relating to Rousseau's work.

Villoteau, Guillaume André. *Recherches sur l'analogie de la musique avec les arts qui ont pour objets l'imitation du langage, pour server d'introduction à l'étude des principes naturels de cet art . . .* Paris: de l'imprimerie impériale, 1807.

Jansen, Albert. *Jean-Jacques Rousseau als Musiker*. Berlin: Georg Reimer, 1884; facsimile edition, Geneva: Slatkine, 1971.

Pougin, Arthur. *Jean-Jacques Rousseau, musicien*. Paris: Fischbacher, 1901.

Kling, H. "Jean-Jacques Rousseau et ses études sur l'harmonie et la contrepoint." *Rmi* 12/1 (1905):40-62.

Brunold, P., ed. "Réponse à la lettre sur la musique française." *L'echo musicale* (1912).

Findeisen, Wilhelm. "Über Rousseaus Beziehung zur Musik." *NZfM* 79/27 (1912):384-85.

Istel, Edgar. "Jean-Jacques Rousseau's Position in the History of Music." *MMR* 42/499 (1912):170-72.

Masson, Paul-Marie. "Les idées de Rousseau sur la musique." *RmSIM* 8/6, 7-8 (1912):1-17, 23-32.

Tiersot, Julien. *J.-J. Rousseau*. Mamu. Paris: Félix Alcan, 1912; 1920; reprint of the 1920 edition (MTFSEC), New York: AMS Press, 1978. Bibliog.

Reviews in *Harmonie* 136 (1978):93 (P. B.) and *Rmi* 19/3 (1912):772-78 (Oscar Chilesotti).

Tiersot, Julien. "Les leçons de musique de Jean-Jacques Rousseau." *SIMg* 14 (1912-13):253-77.

Erckmann, Fritz. "Rousseau und die Musik." *NMZ* 42/19, 21 (1921):296-98, 337-40.

Dufour, Théophile. *Recherches bibliographiques sur les œuvres imprimées de J.-J. Rousseau . . .* Introduction by Pierre-Paul Plan. 2 vols. Paris: L. Giraud-Badin, 1925. Bibliog.

Gysi, Fritz. "Jean-Jacques Rousseau als Musiker." *NSR* 22 (1929):778-86, 871-80.

Somerset, H. V. F. "Jean Jacques Rousseau as a Musician." *ML* 17/1, 3 (1936):37-46, 218-24.

Hansen, Peter. "The *Dictionnaire de musique* of Jean-Jacques Rousseau." *BAMS* 2 (1937):28.

Pochon, Alfred. *J.-J. Rousseau, musicien, et la critique: Essai de mise au point*. Éms. [Montreux: Imprimerie nouvelle, C. Corbaz], 1940. Bibliog.

From *Mois suisse* (1940):23-47, 96-116.

Kisch, Eve. "Rameau and Rousseau." *ML* 22/2 (1941):97-114.

Cotte, Roger. "Rousseau, Jean-Jacques." Translated by Dorothea Schmidt-Preuß. In *MGG* (1949-68). Bibliog.

Sénelier, Jean. *Bibliographie générale des œuvres de J.-J. Rousseau*. Paris: Encyclopédie française, [1949]; Presses universitaires de France, 1950. Bibliog.

Review in *MPhil* 50/1 (1952-53):67-68 (Marecel Françon).

Taylor, Eric. "Rousseau's Conception of Music." *ML* 30/3 (1949):231-42.

Noll, Günther. "Untersuchungen über die musikerzieherische Bedeutung J.-J. Rousseaus und seiner Ideen: Allgemeiner Überblick und spezielle Darstellung seiner Ziffernschrift als Anfang einer modernen Musikmethodik; Ein Beitrag zu ihrer Geschichte." Pedagogy dissertation, The University of Berlin, 1960.

Cotte, Roger, "Bemerkungen über das Verhältnis Jean-Jacques Rousseaus zur Musik." Translated by Waltraud and Johannes Klare. *BzMw* 5 (1963):81-96.

Heintze, H. "Bemerkungen zu Rousseaus Brief an d'Alembert." *WZMLU* 12/12 (1963):1015-20.

Noll, Günther. "Jean-Jacques Rousseau als Musikerzieher." In *Bericht Kassel 1962* (1963):282-84. Bibliog.

Gossman, Lionel. "Time and History in Rousseau." *SVEC* 30 (1964):311-49.

Osmont, Robert. "Les théories de Rousseau sur l'harmonie musicale et leurs relations avec son art d'écrivain." In *Jean-Jacques Rousseau et son œuvre: Problèmes et recherches. Commémoration et colloque de Paris 16-20 octobre 1962 organisés par le Comité national pour la commémoration de J.-J. Rousseau*, pp. 329-48. Acol, no. 2. Paris: C. Klincksieck, 1964.

Hunt, Thomas Webb. "The *Dictionnaire de musique* of Jean-Jacques Rousseau." Ph.D. dissertation, North Texas State University, 1967. Bibliog. [● ● ●*DA* 28/09A, p. 3701. UMI 68-02776.]

Simpson, Kenneth. "Some Great Music Educators: 2. Jean-Jacques Rousseau." *MusT* 46/10-11 (1967):16, 12.

Westrup, J. A. "Editorial." *ML* 48/1 (1967):1-3. [*Rilm* 67-483.]

> Response in *ML* 48/3 (1967):308-10 (Edward E. Lowinsky).

Ebisawa, Bin. "[Rousseau and Burney.]" In *NomuraFs* (1969). [*Rilm* 70-470.]

> In Japanese.

Lazzari, Maria Grazia. "La musica nell'opera e nella vita di Jean-Jacques Rousseau." Thesis, The University of Padova, 1970-71.

Winzenburger, Janet, and Barber, Elinore. "Riemenschneider Bach Library Vault Holdings (*Dictionnaire de musique*, 1768-1775)." *Bach* 3/1 (1972):32-33. [*Rilm* 72-7.]

Zijlstra, Miep. "Rousseau in de branding." *Mens* 27/4 (1972):119-22.

Kleinman, Sidney. *La solmisation mobile de Jean-Jacques Rousseau à John Curwen*. Paris: Heugel, 1974.

> Review in *MT* 116/1588 (1975):542 (Bernarr Rainbow).

Siegele, Ulrich. " 'La cadence est une qualité de la bonne musique'." In *MendelFs* (1974):124-35. [*Rilm* 74-2376.]

● ● ● Wokler, Robert. "Rameau, Rousseau and the *Essai sur l'origine des langues*." *SVEC* 117 (1974):179-238.

Ettelson, Trudy Gottlieb. "Jean-Jacques Rousseau's Writings on Music: A Quest for Melody." Ph.D. dissertation, Yale University, 1974. [*DA* 36/01A, pp. 309-10. UMI 75-14567.]

Cotte, Roger. *Jean-Jacques Rousseau, le philosophe musicien*. Braine-le-Comte: Éditions du Baucens, 1976.

Porset, Charles. "L' 'inquiétance étrangeté' de l'*Essai sur l'origine des langues*: Rousseau et ses exégètes." *SVEC* 154 (1976):1729-58.

Attali, Jacques. *Bruits: Essai sur l'économie politique de la musique*. Paris: 1977; English edition (as *Noise: The Political Economy of Music*, translated by Brian Massumi; THL, no. 16), Minneapolis: The University of Minnesota Press, 1985.

Bonham, Gillian. "Australian Music Education: Traditions of the Enlightenmnent." *AJME* 20 (1977):17-21.

Paquette, Daniel. "Ile Saint-Pierre/Bienne: Jean-Jacques Rousseau." *SMz* 118/4 (1978):237-39.

Strauss, John F. "Jean Jacques Rousseau: Musician." *MQ* 64/4 (1978):474-82. Bibliog.

Hagmann, Peter. "Jean-Jacques Rousseau musicien: 59. Hauptversammlung der Schweizerischen Musikforschenden Gesellschaft Biel, 20./21. Mai 1978." *Mf* 32/1 (1979):68.

Kintzler, Catherine. Preface ("Rameau et Rousseau: Le choc de deux esthétiques") to *Rousseau: Écrits sur la musique, avec des notes, éclaircissements historiques, etc.* (Reprint of Paris: Éditions Pourrat, 1838 edition.) Paris: Stock, 1979. [*Rilm* 79-1978.]

Fulcher, Jane. "Melody and Morality: Rousseau's Influence on French Music Criticism." *IRASM* 11/1 (1980):45-57. Bibliog. [*Rilm* 80-3996.]

Heartz, Daniel. "Rousseau, Jean-Jacques." In *NGrove* (1980). Bibliog.

Robinson, P. E. J. "Jean-Jacques Rousseau's Doctrine of the Arts." Ph.D. dissertation, The University of Wales (Swansea), 1980.

Conlon, Pierre M. *Ouvrages français relatifs à Jean-Jacques Rousseau, 1751-1799: Bibliographie chronologique*. Hicl, no. 196. Geneva: Librairie Droz, 1981. Bibliog.

> Reviews in *BbF* 27/2 (1982):117-18 (Louis Desgraves), *BJECS* 5/2 (1982):266-68 (Philip Robinson), *FrS* 37/1 (1983):83-84 (J. S. Spink), *MLR* 78/1 (1983):190 (Malcolm Carroll), *RoF* 95/1-2 (1983):196 (Kurt Kloocke), and *SZG* 32/3 (1982):457-61 (Jean-Daniel Candaux).

Duchez, Marie-Élisabeth. "Modernité du discours de Jean-Jacques Rousseau sur la musique." In *Rousseau Colloquium* (1982):263-83. Bibliog.

Haspeslagh, Jan. "Jean-Jacques Rousseau: Eerste moderne muziekpedagoog." *Adem* 18/5 (1982):247-49. [*Rilm* 82-5843.]

Madou, Jean-Pol. "Langue, mythe, musique." *Lmus* 28 (1982):75-110. [*Rilm* 82-1822.]

Gülke, Peter. *Rousseau und die Musik; oder, Von der Zuständigkeit des Dilettanten*. TzMw, no. 98. Wilhelmshaven: Heinrichshofen's Verlag, 1984. Bibliog.

> Review in *Mf* 40/1 (1987):75-76 (Walter Wiora) and *NZfM* 146/5 (1985):57 (Hans Christoph Worbs).

Blum, Stephen. "Rousseau's Concept of *Sistême musical* and the Comparative Study of Tonalities in Nineteenth-Century France." *JAMS* 38/2 (1985):349-61.

Marshall, W. A. "Rousseau and His Dictionary." *Consort* 42 (1986):35-39.

Verba, Cynthia. "Jean-Jacques Rousseau: Traditional and Radical Views in His *Dictionnaire de musique*." *JM* 7 (1989).

See also d'ALEMBERT: Isherwood (1989); BELLER-MANN: (1858); FÉTIS: (1831); (1833-44); MOMIGNY: (1791-1818); Görner (1982); RAMEAU: Pischner (1961/. . ./1967); Paul (1971); Verba (1973); Verba (1978); Kintzler (1981); Beaussant (1983); Kintzler (1983); Robrieux (1985); Skowron (1985); RIEMANN: (1898); SERRE: (1763); LITERATURE SUPPLEMENT: Alekperova (1982); Allen ["Philosophies"] (1939); Apfel and Dahlhaus (1974); Arlt (1974), (1976); Asselin (1981), (1983/1985); Auhagen (1982/1983); Austin (1980); Babitz (1952), (1967/1969); **Barbour (1951 / . . ./1972)**; Bauman (1981); Becker (1836-39/1964); Beiche ["Inversio"] (1972-); Beyschlag (1907/1953); Bircher (1970); Blumröder (1972-); Bremner (1979); Bruck (1928); Burdick (1977); Burney (1776-89/. . ./1957); Byrt (1967); Carse (1925/1964); Cazden (1948), (1961-62); Chernin (1986); Cohen (1987); Cohen and Miller (1979); Cole (1969); **Coover (1980)**; Cotte (1951); **Dahlhaus (1967), (1984), (1985); Dahlhaus et al. (1987)**; David (1956); David and Mendel (1945/1966); Dolmetsch (1915/. . ./1969); Donington (1963/. . ./1974); Dreyfus (1987); Duchez (1979); Duckles (1970); Eggebrecht (1955); Eitner (1900-1904/1959-60); Fellerer (1927/. . ./1972), (1962), (1983); Ferand (1937/1938); Fischer (1957); Flaherty (1989); Forkel (1792/1962); Frobenius ["Dauer"] (1972-), ["Isotonos"] (1972-); Fubini (1969), (1971/1983); Gerber (1790-92/1977), (1812-14/1966); Ghislanzoni (1949-51); Godwin (1987); Goldschmidt (1907); Greenfield (1984); Gremion (1974); Haase (1969); Hailparn (1981); Hall (1975); Handschin (1948); Harding (1938); Harich-Schneider ([1939]/. . ./1970); Hiller (1768-69); Hosler (1978/1981); Houle (1960), (1987); Jackson (1988); Jorgenson (1963); Jullien (1873); **Kassler** (1971), (1976), **(1979)**; Keller (1955/1965); Kirkendale (1979), (1984); Kivy (1980), (1984); Krehbiel (1964); Kretzschmar (1911-12); Krones (1988); La Borde (1780/1978); La Fage (1864/1964); Lange (1899-1900); Laudon (1978); Lawrence (1978); le Huray (1978-79); ● ● ● le Huray and Day (1981); Lewis (1975/1978); **Lindley** ["Temperaments"] **(1980)**, (1982), **(1984)**, (1988); Lippman (1986); Lonsdale (1979); Mahlert and Sunter (1972-); Mann (1987); Mendel (1978); Mongrédien (1974); Müller-Blattau (1923/. . ./1963); Nelson (1984); **Neumann**, Frederick (1977/**1982**), (1978), (1979/**1982**), [*Essays*] **(1982)**; Neumann, F.-H. (1955/1962); Newman (1946), (1959/. . ./1983), (1963/. . ./1983); Oberdoerffer (1949-68), (1967); Oliver (1949/1947); Orr (1983); Ottenberg (1973/1978); Palisca [*Baroque*] (1968/1981), ["Rezitativ"] (1972-), [" 'Baroque' "] (1989); ; Rainbow (1964/1967); Ratner (1980); Reimer ["Concerto"] (1972-), ["Kammermusik"] (1972-), ["Kenner"] (1972-); Révész (1946/. . ./1954); Rex (1981); **Ritzel (1967/1968)**; Rosenblum (1988); Rothgeb (1968); Rothschild (1953), (1961); Schäfke (1934/1964); Scher (1975); Schmalzriedt ["Reprise"] (1972-), ["Subiectum"] (1972-); Schneider (1985); Schünemann (1928/1931); **Seidel and Cooper (1986)**; Serauky (1929); Shellhous (1988); **Shirlaw (1917/. . ./1970)**; Sondheimer (1925); Spitzer and Zaslaw (1986); **Steblin (1981/1983)**, (1987); Stowell (1985); Subirá (1947/. . ./1958); Taddie (1984); Telesco (forthcoming); Tittel (1966); Truesdell (1960); Vogel (1955/1954); Waite (1970); Wellesz and Sternfeld (1973); Wichmann (1966); Wienpahl (1953); Williams, P. (1970); Wittwer (1934/1935); Yates (1947); **Zaminer (1985)**; Zaslaw (1979); Zimmermann (1976); Zinar (1983).

PIERRE-JOSEPH ROUSSIER

[1716 or 17 – 1792]

With RAMEAU, French harmonic theory was much changed, to say the least. In his wake came Pierre-Joseph Roussier, a staunch defender whose *Traité des accordes, et de leur succession* (1764) attempted a simplification of RAMEAU's theory, essentially by deleting the more speculative elements and concentrating upon practical considerations. One finds therein a careful exposition on chord construction and succession, followed by a description of some new chord types. Most of the music examples which amplify the text did not appear until around 1775, as

L'harmonie pratique, ou exemples pour le traité des accords. This supplement includes a system for analyzing chords using letters (A through G), numbers (2 through 9), accidentals, and other symbols.

Roussier's other writings include a collaboration with another RAMEAU-inspired French scholar, Jean-Benjamin de La Borde. In addition, several titles betray an interest in non-Western musical cultures. His discussions of temperament in these works coexist with an endorsement of Pythagorean tuning.

Replies to Labbet's review of RAMEAU: (1755)

> *MdFr* (October 1756-September 1757):passim.

*Traité des accords, et de leur succession, selon le sys-
téme de la basse-fondamentale; pour servir de principes d'harmonie à ceux qui étudient la composition
ou l'accompagnement du clavecin, avec une
méthode d'accompagnement* [*Rism* B/VI/2, p. 739.]

> See [1775], below.

> Paris: Duchesne, Dessain junior; Lyon: Jean-
> Marie Bruyset (Ballard), 1764. [HoM: 1355.
> SMLMS.]
> Paris: M. Bailleux (Ballard), 1764. [LCPS: R-095.
> HoM: 1354.]

>> Review in *WNAMb* 1/32 (1766-67):245-47 (Jo-
>> hann Adam Hiller).

> S ● Facsimile of the 1764 (Bruyset) edition. Geneva:
> Minkoff Reprint, 1972.

>> Lacks the music examples, found in [1775],
>> below.

Observations sur différens points d'harmonie [*Rism*
B/VI/2, pp. 738-39.]

> Geneva and Paris: d'Houry, 1765. [LCPS: R-
> 094b.]

>> Review in *WNAMb* 1/32 (1766-67):245-47 (Jo-
>> hann Adam Hiller).

> Geneva and Paris: Bailleux, [ca. 1775 (title page
> states 1755)]. [LCPS: R-094a. HoM: 1353.
> SMLMS.]

*Mémoire sur la musique des anciens, où l'on expose le
principe des proportions authentiques, dites de Pythagore, et de divers systêmes de musique chez les
grecs, les chinois et les égyptiens, avec un parallèle
entre le systême des egyptiens et celui des modernes*
[*Rism* B/VI/2, p. 738.]

> Paris: Lacombe, 1770. [LCPS: R-091. HoM: 1352.
> SMLMS.]

>> Review in *Jdm* [1/8] (August 1770):54-62.

>> As *Mèmoire historique et pratique sur la musique
>> des anciens . . .*:

> Paris: Lacombe, 1774.

> S ● Facsimile of the 1770 edition. MMMLF, ser. 2,
> no. 41. New York: Broude Brothers, 1966.

"Lettre . . . touchant la division du zodiaque et l'institution de la semaine planétaire, relativement à
une progression géométrique, d'où dépendent les
proportions musicales" [*Rism* B/VI/2, p. 738.]

> In *Jbas* (November-December 1770; August
> 1771).
> [Paris: 1771.]

A reissue of the 1770 segment from the journal.
Review in *Jdm* [2/1] (January 1771):85-87.

*L'harmonie pratique, ou exemples pour le traité des ac-
cords* [*Rism* B/VI/2, p. 737.]

> Paris: l'éditeur; Lyon: Castaud; Toulouse: Brunet;
> etc., [1775]. [LCPS: R-090. HoM: 1351.
> SMLMS.]

*Mémoire sur la musique des chinois, tant anciens que
modernes* [*Rism* B/VI/1, p. 85.]

> By Joseph-Marie Amiot, edited by Roussier.

> Paris: Nyon l'aîné, 1779. [LCPS: A-031. HoM: 54.]
> Paris: Nyon l'aîné, 1780.

> S ● Facsimile of the 1779 edition. Geneva: Minkoff
> Reprint, 1973.

"Remarques . . . sur les observations de M.
Vandermonde"

> In *Mémoires sur les proportions musicales, le genre
> énarmonique des grecs et celui des modernes:
> Supplément à l'essai sur la musique*, by Jean-
> Benjamin de La Borde, pp. 42-68. Paris: Phi-
> lippe Denys Pierres, 1781. [*Rism* B/VI/1, p.
> 467. LCPS: L-007.]

*Mémoire sur le nouveau clavecin chromatique de M. de
Laborde . . . Suite du supplément à l'essai sur la
musique* [*Rism* B/VI/2, p. 738.]

> Paris: Philippe-Denys Pierres, 1782.

> S ● Facsimile edition, in *Textes sur les instruments de
> musique au XVIIIe siècle*. Geneva: Minkoff Re-
> print, 1982.

*Mémoire sur la nouvelle harpe de M. Cousineau, luthier
de la riene* [*Rism* B/VI/2, p. 738.]

> Paris: Lamy, 1782. [LCPS: R-092.].

> S ● See (1782):(1982), above.

"Lettre . . . sur l'acception des mots *Basse fondamentale*, dans le sens des Italiens et dans le sens
de Rameau"

> *Jenc* [56]/6/2 (September 1783):330-36.

N.B.: A work called *Méthode de musique sur un nouveau plan* (1769) is often erroneously attributed to
Roussier.

LITERATURE:

Birkner, Günter. "Roussier, Pierre-Joseph." In *MGG* (1949-
68). Bibliog.

Osborne, Richard Dale. "The Theoretical Writings of Abbé
Pierre-Joseph Roussier." Ph.D. dissertation, The

Ohio State University, 1966. Bibliog. [*DA* 27/09A, p. 3074. UMI 67-02508.]

Cohen, Albert. "Roussier, Pierre-Joseph." In *NGrove* (1980). Bibliog.

See also CHORON: (1810-11); FÉTIS: (1833-44); (1840); MOMIGNY: (1791-1818):(1791); RAMEAU: Collected Works (1967-72):Vols. 5 and 6; SAINT-LAMBERT: (1707):Burchill (1979); LITERATURE SUPPLEMENT: Becker (1836-39/1964); Blumröder (1972-); Burney (1776-89/. . ./1957); Chevaillier (1925/1931-32); Cohen and Miller (1979); Eitner (1900-1904/1959-60); Fellerer (1962); Forkel (1792/1962); Gerber (1790-92/1977), (1812-14/1966); Godwin (1987); ● ● ●Groth (1983); Jacobi (1957-60/1971); Jones (1934); Krehbiel (1964); La Borde (1780/1978); Mitchell, J. W. (1963); **Ritzel (1967/1968); Shirlaw (1917/. . ./ 1970).**

GALEAZZO SABBATINI

[1597 – 1662]

When Galeazzo Sabbatini's *Regola facile e breve per sonare sopra il basso continuo* appeared in Venice in 1628, the art of accompanying from a bass was still in its infancy. His work thus fulfilled a useful function in educating would-be continuo players. However, the very novelty of the procedure and relative lack of interaction among expert practitioners from different cities resulted in individual variants upon the practice.

The left hand is given a prominent role in Sabbatini's method. He divided the bass register into five regions, so that the number and type of intervals which might concurrently be struck by the left hand could be prescribed exactly. For example, the lowest of the potential bass notes should not be struck with an upper third, while the higher notes should not be struck with the larger intervals, such as the octave. The right hand fills in where necessary to complete the construction of the chords. It does not perform a melodic role.

Sabbatini's rules pertain to the use of five-three and six-three chords only. More advanced procedures were to have been introduced in a planned but apparently never realized second segment of the work. One was to assume five-three position unless confronted with the bass B (in the context of the key of C), E (in the context of the key of F), or a chromatically raised pitch. Thus his work comprises an early formulation of rules regarding unfigured basses.

KIRCHER noted Sabbatini's study of just intonation. The keyboard instrument which Sabbatini devised for his experiments with microtonal pitches contained thirty-four keys per octave. His formulation demonstrates that interest in such complicated instruments did not cease after VICENTINO's celebrated championing of his *arcicembalo*.

Regola facile e breve per sonare sopra il basso continuo nell'organo, manacordo ò altro simile stromento [*Rism* B/VI/2, p. 742.]

At its publication, the work was announced as the first part of a larger treatise. There is no evidence that a second part was ever completed or published.

Venice: Salvatori, 1628.
Venice: Alessandro Vincenti, 1644.
Rome: Paolo Moneta, 1669.

T ● Trost, Johann Caspar, ed. and trans. German translation. Ms. [?], [mid seventeenth century]. [Lost.]

LITERATURE:

Oberdörffer, Fritz. "Sabbatini, Galeazzo." In *MGG* (1949-68). Bibliog.

Roche, Jerome. "Sabbatini, Galeazzo." In *NGrove* (1980). Bibliog.

See also FÉTIS: (1833-44); HEINICHEN: (1728):Buelow (1961/. . ./1986); KIRCHER: (1650); MERSENNE: (1617-48); SAINT-LAMBERT: (1707):Burchill (1979); VIADANA: Haack (1964/1974); WALTHER: (1732); LITERATURE SUPPLEMENT: ● ● ● Arnold (1931/. . ./1965); Barbour (1949-68), (1951/ . . ./1972), (1952); Burney (1776-89/. . ./1957); Dahlhaus ["Untersuchungen"] (1966/. . ./1988); Donington (1963/. . ./1974); Eitner (1900-1904/1959-60); Forkel (1792/1962); Gerber (1790-92/1977), (1812-14/1966); Kroyer (1901/. . ./1970); Lindley ["Just"] (1980); Meer (1980); Rothgeb (1968); Subirá (1947/. . ./1958); Tenney (1988); Tirabassi (1925)

LUIGI ANTONIO SABBATINI

[1732? – 1809]

The works of Luigi Antonio Sabbatini reflect the strong influence of MARTINI, VALLOTTI, and TARTINI. In *La vera idea delle musicali numeriche segnature* (1799) he developed the notion that all chords are derived from the triad (which might be augmented or diminished) through processes such as inversion and adding a third above the chordal fifth. Since the dissonant pitch of the dominant seventh corresponded approximately to the seventh partial, he granted it the special privilege of entering without pre-

paration. His treatment of ninths, elevenths, and thirteenths is extraordinary: the ninth and octave, the eleventh and tenth, or the thirteenth and twelfth are juxtaposed in his models, creating harsh clashes. Developing MARTINI's perspective on counterpoint and incorporating VALLOTTI's study of fugal models, Sabbatini's *Trattato sopra le fughe musicali* (1802) is an important contribution to that discipline. He attempted to codify the various types of fugue, thereby establishing norms for the future development of the art.

Elementi teorici della musica colla pratica de' medesimi, in duetti, e terzetti a canone accompagnati dal basso, ed eseguibili sì a solo, che a più voci [*Rism* B/VI/2, p. 743.]

> Rome: Pilucchi Cracas & Giuseppe Rotilj, 1789-90. 3 vols. [LCPS: S-001.]
> Rome: Pilucchi Cracas & Giuseppe Rotilj, 1795. First two parts only. [LCPS: S-001.]

> S ● *Solfèges ou leçons élémentaires de musique*
> Paris: 1810. Edited by A.-É. CHORON.
>
>> Reprinted in 1834.

La vera idea delle musicali numeriche segnature diretta al giovane studioso dell'armonìa [*Rism* B/VI/2, p. 743.]

> Venice: Sebastian Valle, 1799. [LCPS: S-002. HoM: 1356.]

> S ● Facsimile edition. BmB, ser. 2, no. 65a. Bologna: Forni (Presso Sebastian Valle), 1969.

Trattato sopra le fughe musicali di . . . Sabbatini . . . corredato da copiosi saggj del suo antecessore . . . Vallotti

> Venice: Sebastiano Valle, 1802. 2 vols. [IDC.]

> S ● Facsimile edition. BmB, ser. 2, no. 65b. Bologna: Forni, 1969.

"Canoni sui principi elementare"

> Two mss. [Milan: Conservatorio di musica Giuseppe Verdi.]

"Esame d'uno scolaro del Padre L. A. Sabbatini"

> Ms. [Bologna: Civico museo bibliografico musicale.]

"Studi di contrappunto fatti alla scuola del Padre Martini"

> Ms. [Bologna: Civico museo bibliografico musicale.]

"Trattato di contrappunto"

> Incomplete mss. [Piacenza: Collegio Alberoni; Venice: Biblioteca nazionale Marciana.]

See also VALLOTTI: SABBATINI, L. A. (1780).

LITERATURE:

Balbi, Melchiorre, ed. *Trattato del sistema armonico di Antonio Calegari*. Padua: Valentino Crescini, 1829.

Prota-Giurleo, Ulisse. "Sabbatini, Luigi Antonio." Translated by Ruth Blume. In *MGG* (1949-68). Bibliog.

Hansell, Sven. "Sabbatini, Luigi Antonio." In *NGrove* (1980). Bibliog.

See also CHORON: [1804]; (1810-11); FÉTIS: (1833-44); (1840); LITERATURE SUPPLEMENT: Becker (1836-39/1964); Butler (1977); Cazden (1948); Chevaillier (1925/1931-32); Eitner (1900-1904/1959-60); Gerber (1812-14/1966); Horsley [*Fugue: History*] (1966); Jacobi (1957-60/1971); Kauko (1958); La Fage (1864/1964); **Mann (1955/. . ./1987)**; Neumann (1986); Ratner (1980); Schmalzriedt ["Coda"] (1972-); **Shirlaw (1917/. . ./1970)**; Wessely (1967); Wirth (1966).

DE SAINT-LAMBERT

[active ca. 1700-1710]

The obscure French keyboardist named de Saint-Lambert (who is easily confused with his countryman Michel Lambert and therefore sometimes erroneously provided with the first name "Michel") wrote two popular volumes during the first decade of the eighteenth century. The first, *Les principes du clavecin* (1702), is aimed at youngsters just beginning their study of harpsichord playing. In addition to the technical details of fingering and ornamentation, it includes a basic course in the fundamentals of music theory. Of more interest to grownups is his discussion of how the various time signatures relate to one another and to a vaguely described walking pace of perhaps about 125 pulses per minute. A further confirmation of Saint-Lambert's practical stance is his suggestion that keyboard music be written using clefs which retain the same positioning of the pitches, but in three different octaves.

More important from the standpoint of music theory is his *Nouveau traité de l'accompagnement du clavecin, de l'orgue et des autres instruments* (1707), which, according to a comment in the *Traité* itself, was published after the *Principes* but which numerous scholars have assigned, with no direct evidence, to the year 1680. HEINICHEN knew and benefited from Saint-Lambert's formulation, as did RAMEAU, who, without acknowledgment, borrowed Saint-Lambert's commentary on accompaniment for his *Traité de l'harmonie* (1722). A thorough and exemplary treatment of figured-bass practice is offered, though with some ambiguity. Saint-Lambert's recommendation that the signatures for minor keys involving flats include a flat for the sixth scale degree corresponds to what in fact became the standard procedure as the eighteenth century progressed.

Les principes du clavecin, contenant une explication exacte de tout ce qui concerne la tablature et le clavier . . . [*Rism* B/VI/2, pp. 747-48.]

>
> Paris: Christophe Ballard, 1702. [LCPS: S-010.] Amsterdam: Estienne Roger, [ca. 1710].

T ● Gallet, Anne. "*Les principes du clavecin*, by Monsieur de Saint Lambert. Paris, 1702. Partial Translation and Commentary." M.A. thesis, Washington University, 1970.

S ● Facsimile of the 1702 edition. Geneva: Minkoff Reprint, 1974.

> Also contains a facsimile of the *Nouveau traité* (1707), below. Review in *OrganYb 1974* 5 (1974):137-38 (Peter Williams).

T ● See MacClintock (1979).

T ● ● ● Harris-Warrick, Rebecca, trans. and ed. *"Principles of the Harpsichord" by Monsieur de Saint Lambert*. CMTM. Cambridge: Cambridge University Press, 1984. Bibliog.

> Reviews in *AmO:AGO* 22/4 (1988):36, *AR* 27/1 (1986):25 (George H. Lucktenberg), *EM* 12/4 (1984):541-43 (David Ledbetter), *ML* 67/2 (1986):164-65 (Howard Schott), *MT* 125/1699 (1984):504-5 (Howard Ferguson), *NAMIS* 13/3 (1984):11 (Darcy Kuronen), and *TLS* 83/4241 (1984):773 (Robert Donington).

S ● Bordonaro, Adriana Viola, trans. *I principi del clavicembalo (Parigi 1702); Nuovo trattato dell'accompagnamento (Parigi 1707)*. Bologna and Rome: Associazione clavicembalistica bolognese, 1986.

> Review in *Nrmi* 21/4 (1987):707-8 (Giorgio Cerasoli).

Nouveau traité de l'accompagnement du clavecin, de l'orgue et des autres instruments [*Rism* B/VI/2, p. 747.]

> Paris: Christophe Ballard, 1707 [*not* 1680]. [LCPS: S-009a.]

> Review in *JTr* (July 1708):1257-61.

> Amsterdam: Estienne Roger, [ca. 1710]. [LCPS: S-009b.]

S ● See (1702):(1974), above.

T ● Wills, Harold Edward. "*Nouveau traité de l'accompagnement du clavecin, de l'orgue et des autres instruments* (1707) by Michel de Saint Lambert: A Translation from the French with Commentary." M.A. thesis, American University, 1978. [*MAb* 16/03, p. 174. UMI 13-11382.]

T ● ● ● Burchill, James Frederick. "Saint-Lambert's *Nouveau traité de l'accompagnement*: A Translation with Commentary." 2 vols. Ph.D. dissertation, The University of Rochester, 1979. Bibliog. [*DA* 40/09A, p. 4791. UMI 80-05138.]

T ● See (1702):(1986), above.

LITERATURE:

Oberdörffer, Fritz. "Saint-Lambert, de." In *MGG* (1949-68). Bibliog.

Tessier, André, and Fuller, David. "Saint-Lambert, ?Michel de." In *NGrove* (1980).

See also FÉTIS: (1833-44); HEINICHEN: (1728):Buelow (1961/. . ./1986); RAMEAU: (1722):Gossett (1971); Pischner (1961/. . ./1967); Verba (1978); LITERATURE SUPPLEMENT: Ahlgrimm (1973); Alekseev (1974); **Arnold (1931/. . ./1965)**; Atcherson (1973); Auhagen (1987); Babitz (1952); Beyschlag (1907/ 1953); Chevaillier (1925/1931-32); Cohen, A. ["Symposium"] (1972); (1988); Dahlhaus ["Untersuchungen"] (1966/. . ./1988); Donington (1963/. . ./1974), (1980); Gut (1972-); Eitner (1900-1904/1959-60); Hammel (1977-78); Harich-Schneider ([1939]/. . ./ 1970); Houle (1960), (1987); Ibberson (1984); Jackson (1988); **Lester** (1978), **(1989)**; Mitchell, J. W. (1963); Morche (1974); Nelson (1984); **Neumann**, Frederick (1967/**1982**), (1978), [*Essays*] **(1982)**, (1986); Newman (1985); North (1987); Oberdoerffer (1949-68), (1967); **Palisca** ["Theory"] **(1980)**; Pincherle (1958); Rogers (1955); Rothgeb (1968); Schulenberg (1984); **Seidel and Cooper (1986)**; Tagliavini (1975/1983); Tenney (1988); Tolkoff (1973); Troeger (1987); Wagner (1981); Williams, P. ["Harpsichord"] (1968), (1970).

FRANCISCO DE SALINAS

[1513 – 1590]

Francisco de Salinas was for scholarship in Spain what Girolamo MEI was for scholarship in Italy: a thorough and devoted student of the ancient authors on music. Having spent over twenty years of his adulthood in Rome and Naples, Salinas had ample opportunities for exposure to rare source materials, though his blindness must have complicated the research process. The result was *De musica libri septem* (1577), a work of great importance in the realm of *musica theorica*, especially in its careful reconstruction of Greek tunings and its consideration of temperaments, including equal temperament and one-third comma meantone temperament. Salinas did not restrict himself to twelve pitches per octave, though he felt that VICENTINO's suggestion of thirty-one pitches per octave was excessive. He responded to the ideas of a variety of theorists, including ZARLINO, and was indebted to a number of the older authorities. The latter portion of the work is devoted to metrics. Of particular interest are the various folk songs which were included as illustrations.

"Musices liber tertius . . ."

Ms., 1566. [Madrid: Biblioteca nacional.]

"De musica quatuor priores libri"

Ms. [Madrid: Biblioteca nacional.]

De musica libri septem . . . [*Rism* B/VI/2, pp. 748-49.]

Salamanca: Mathias Gastius, 1577. [LCPS: S-013a. HoM: 1370. SMLMS.]
Salamanca: haeredes Cornelii Bonardi (Claudius Curlet), 1592. [LCPS: S-013b.]

S ● Kastner, Macario Santiago, ed. Facsimile of the 1577 edition. IGMDm, ser. 1, no. 13. Kassel and Basel: Bärenreiter, 1958.

Reviews in *ML* 39/4 (1958):392-94 (Thurston Dart), *Mog* 3/9 (1960):437-38 (Luigi Rognoni), and *MR* 19/4 (1958):345-46 (J. A. Westrup).

T ● La Cuesta, Ismael Fernández de, trans. Madrid: Editorial Alpuerto.

T ● See Rowen (1979).

LITERATURE:

Trend, J. B. "Salinas: A Sixteenth Century Collector of Folk Songs." *ML* 8/1 (1927):13-24.

Palisca, Claude V. "Salinas, Francisco de." Translated by Klaus Hortschansky. In *MGG* (1949-68). Bibliog.

Lowinsky, Edward E. "A Treatise on Text Underlay by a German Disciple of Francisco de Salinas." In *BesselerFs* (1961):231-51. Bibliog.

See also *JAMS* 16/2 (1963):241-43.

Daniels, Arthur Michael. "The *De musica libri VII* of Francisco de Salinas." Ph.D. dissertation, The University of Southern California, 1962. Bibliog. [*DA* 23/06, pp. 2163-64. UMI 62-06046.]

Review in ●●●*CM* 1 (1965):97-100 (Peter Bergquist).

García Matos, M. "Pervivencia en la tradición actual de canciones populares recogidas en el siglo XVI por Salinas en su tradado *De musica libri septem*." *Anmu* 18 (1963):67-84. Bibliog.

●●● Daniels, Arthur. "Microtonality and Mean-Tone Temperament in the Harmonic System of Francisco Salinas." *JMT* 9/1-2 (1965):2-51, 234-80. Bibliog.

●●● La Cuesta, Ismael Fernández de. "General Introduction to the *De musica libri septem* of Francisco Salinas, and to Its First Translation." Translated by Rodrigo de Zayas. *Consort* 31 (1975):101-8. Bibliog. [*Rilm* 75-585.]

Stevenson, Robert. "Salinas, Francisco de." In *NGrove* (1980). Bibliog.

See also FÉTIS: (1833-44); LIPPIUS: Rivera (1974/1980); MERSENNE: (1617-48); MOMIGNY: (1791-1818): (1791); MORLEY: Stevenson (1952); OUSELEY: (1879); (1882); RIEMANN: (1898); WALTHER: (1732); LITERATURE SUPPLEMENT: Abraham (1968/1969); Alette (1951); Anglés and Subirá (1946-51); Barbieri (1983); **Barbour** (1932), (1938), (1947), **(1951/. . ./1972)**; Becker (1836-39/1964); Beiche ["Dux"] (1972-), ["Inversio"] (1972-); Berger (1975/ 1980); Brown (1976); Burney (1776-89/. . ./1957); Chomiński (1962/1981); Cohen (1981); Cohen (1984); Collet (1912); Dahlhaus ["Konsonanz"] (1949-68), ["Tonsystem"] (1949-68), ["Untersuchungen"] (1966/ . . ./1988); **Dahlhaus et al. (1987); Dürr and Gerstenberg (1980)**; Dupont (1933/. . ./1986); Eitner (1900-1904/1959-60); Fellerer ["Zur Kontrapunktlehre"] (1972); Fokker (1955); Forkel (1792/1962); Frobenius ["Dauer"] (1972-); Gerber (1790-92/1977), (1812-14/1966); Green (1969); Gut (1976); Haase (1969); Handschin (1948); Harrán (1973), (1986); Hartmann (1923); Hawkins (1776/. . ./1969); Houle (1987); Jackson (1988); Jacobi (1957-60/1971); Jonckbloet and Land (1882); Katz (1985); Keislar (1987); Kelletat (1966); Kinkeldey (1910/1968); Kramer (1978); Kroyer (1901/. . ./1970); Launay (1972); León Tello (1962); Levitan (1938); **Lindley** ["Temperaments"] **(1980)**,

(1984); Luper (1938); **Maniates (1979)**; **Mann (1955/. . ./1987)**; **Palisca** (1953), ["Theory"] **(1980)**, **(1985)**; Pikler (1966); Rasch (1983); Reese (1954/1959), (1957/1970); Révész (1946/. . ./1954); Ruhnke (1949-68); (1974); Schmalzriedt ["Subiectum"] (1972-); Seidel (1972-), (1976); **Seidel and**

Cooper (1986); Stevenson (1960), (1976); Subirá (1947/. . ./1958); Taddie (1984); Tuksar (1978/1980); Vellekoop (1959); Vogel (1955/1954); **Walker** (1941-42/. . ./1985), (1950/1985), **(1978)**; Wienpahl (1953), (1955); **Zaminer (1985)**.

THOMAS SALMON

[1648 – 1706]

Clergyman Thomas Salmon was a musical amateur who saw no strong need for the continuation of the Guidonian hexachord nomenclature. In its place he proposed, in *An Essay to the Advancement of Musick* (1672), a system in which all clefs except the F clef would be abolished. A letter indicating bass, mean, or treble would be placed at the beginning of the staff. He also urged that lute music be written on the staff rather than in tablature. Salmon could not claim to have induced the decline of the hexachordal system, however, as its demise was imminent even before his *Essay*.

Matthew LOCKE responded swiftly and vehemently with a pamphlet, entitled *Observations upon a Late Book*, which promoted the existing notational system and demonstrated why Salmon's alternative would not work. Salmon responded with *A Vindication of an Essay to the Advancement of Musick from Mr. Matthew Lock's Observations* (1672). LOCKE countered with *The Present Practice of Music Vindicated* (1673). This heated controversy contained verbal abuse of all sorts from both parties, particularly from LOCKE.

Salmon also advanced a tuning system which resulted in a natural major third, fourth, and fifth in relation to the reference pitch, but considerable variance from pure intonation elsewhere. Since modulation was impossible, frets were to be affixed by performers to overcome this limitation. Not surprisingly, the system had little more following than did his appeal for clef reform.

An Essay to the Advancement of Musick by Casting Away the Perplexity of Different Cliffs and Writing All Sorts of Musick . . . in One Universal Character [*Rism* B/VI/2, p. 749.]

> London: John Carr (J. Macock), 1672. [LCPS: S-014. HoM: 1371.]

> > Review in LOCKE: (1672).

> S ● Facsimile edition. MMMLF, ser. 2, no. 11. New York: Broude Brothers, 1966.

> > Reviews in *ML* 48/4 (1967):371-73 (Jack A. Westrup), *MT* 108/1498 (1967):1112 (Charles Cudworth), and *Notes* 24/3 (1967-68):496 (Peter Bergquist).

A Vindication of "An Essay to the Advancement of Musick" from Mr. Matthew Lock's "Observations" by Enquiring into the Real Nature and Most Convenient Practise of That Science [*Rism* B/VI/2, p. 749.]

> London: John Carr (A. Maxwell), 1672. [LCPS: S-016.]

> > A response to LOCKE: (1672). Countered in LOCKE: [*Present Practice*] (1673).

A Proposal to Perform Musick in Perfect and Mathematical Proportions . . . with Large Remarks upon This Whole Treatise by . . . John Wallis [*Rism* B/VI/2, p. 749.]

> London: J. Lawrence, 1688. [LCPS: S-015.]

"The Theory of Musick Reduced to Arithmetical and Geometrical Proportions"

> *PTRS* 24/302 (1705):2072-77 (erratic pagination).

> S ● Motte, Benj., ed. *The Philosophical Transactions [of the Royal Society, London] from the Year MDCC . . . to the Year MDCCXX, Abridged and Disposed under General Heads.* 2 vols. London: R. Wilkin, etc., 1721. Vol. 1, pp. 429-32 plus gatefold.

> S ● Baddam, ed. *Memoirs of the Royal Society; or, A New Abridgement of the Philosophical Transactions . . .* London: T. Cooper, etc. (G. Smith), 1739-41; 2nd edition, London: John Nourse, 1745. Vol. 4, pp. 454-58 plus Plate XIII.

LITERATURE:

La Fond, Jean François de. *A New System of Music . . .* London: the author, 1725. [*Rism* B/VI/1, pp. 472-73.]

Hayes, Gerald R. "A Forgotten Prophet." *MT* 65/974 (1924):327-28.

Harman, Richard Alexander. "Salmon, Thomas." Translated by Peter Schleuning. In *MGG* (1949-68). Bibliog.

Harley, John. "Thomas Salmon's *Perfect and Mathematical Proportions*." *MT* 97/1358 (1956):191-92.

Ruff, Lillian M. "Thomas Salmon's *Essay to the Advancement of Musick*." *Consort* 21 (1964):266-75.

Baldwin, Olive, and Wilson, Thelma. "Musick Advanced and Vindicated." *MT* 111/1524 (1970):148-50. [*Rilm* 70-322.]

Tilmouth, Michael. "Salmon, Thomas." In *NGrove* (1980). Bibliog.

See also FÉTIS: (1833-44); MALCOLM: (1721); NORTH, R.: Wilson (1959); WALTHER: (1732); LITERATURE SUPPLEMENT: Atcherson (1972), (1973);

Becker (1836-39/1964); Boomgaarden (1985/1987); Chenette (1967); Chew (1980); **Dahlhaus et al. (1987)**; Eitner (1900-1904/1959-60); Gerber (1790-92/1977), (1812-14/1966); Gouk (1980), (1982); Hannas (1934); Hawkins (1776/. . ./1969); Kassler (1976); Kassler and Oldroyd (1983); Lawrence (1978); **Lindley (1984)**; Miller (1960); Miller and Cohen (1987); Pulver (1927/. . ./1973); Ruf (1972-); Ruff (1970); **Seidel and Cooper (1986)**; Shute (1972); Traficante (1970); **Walker (1978)**; Williams ["Equal"] (1968); Wolf (1939).

JOHANN BAPTIST SAMBER

[bapt. 1654 — buried 1717]

The Salzburg organist and teacher Johann Baptist Samber developed, over the first decade of the eighteenth century, a series of three manuals to enhance the effectiveness of Austrian musical education, particularly that of organists and composers. His first volume, *Manuductio ad organum* (1704), is devoted to the foundations of music and includes a large section on solmization. The second, *Continuatio ad manuductionem organicam* (1707), begins with a lengthy chapter on figured bass and continues with expositions on the organ and its specifications, compositional procedures (including cadences and diminution), and fugal writing. His brief summary of musical figures, akin to that of BERNHARD, includes commentary on and examples of *accentus, subsumptio, variatio, multiplicatio, eclypsis, retardatio, mutilatio, quasi diminutio oder transitus,* and *abruptio*. The final volume, *Elucidatio musicae choralis* (1710), is devoted to the musical practices of the Catholic church.

Manuductio ad organum; Das ist, Gründlich- und sichere Handleitung durch die höchst-nothwendige Solmisation, zu der edlen Schlag-Kunst . . . [*Rism* B/VI/2, p. 751.]

Salzburg: Johann Baptist Mayrs seel. Witwe und Erben, 1704. [LCPS: S-020. SMLMS.]

T ● Holden, Stephen S., trans. Ms., 1964. [Berkeley: The University of California.]

T ● Boomgaarden, Donald R., and Nelson, Richard B. "Johann Baptist Samber's (1654-1717) *Manuductio ad organum*: The First Discussion of Fugue in German." *JMR* (forthcoming).

S ● Facsimile edition. Bo, no. 54. Buren, The Netherlands: Fritz Knuf, forthcoming.

Continuatio ad manuductionem organicam; Das ist, Fortsetzung zu der Manuduction oder Hand-Leitung zum Orgl-Schlagen . . . [*Rism* B/VI/2, p. 751.]

Salzburg: Johann Baptist Mayrs Witwe und Sohn, 1707. [LCPS: S-021.]

S ● Facsimile edition. Bo, no. 54. Buren, The Netherlands: Fritz Knuf, forthcoming.

Elucidatio musicae choralis; Das ist, Gründlich und wahre Erläuterung oder Unterweisung, wie die edle und uralte Choral-Music fundamentaliter nach denen wolgegründten Reglen mit leichter Mühe möge erlehrnet werden . . . [*Rism* B/VI/2, p. 750.]

Salzburg: Johann Joseph Mayr, 1710. [LCPS: S-019. SMLMS.]

LITERATURE:

Federhofer, Hellmut. "Samber, Johann Baptist." In *MGG* (1949-68). Bibliog.

● ● ● Buelow, George J. "Samber, Johann Baptist." In *NGrove* (1980).

See also FÉTIS: (1833-44); MUFFAT: [ca. 1699]:Federhofer (1961); Damp (1973); WALTHER: (1732); LITERATURE SUPPLEMENT: Becker (1836-39/1964); Collins (1966); Eitner (1900-1904/1959-60); Federhofer ● ● ● (1964), (1969), (1985); Fellerer ["Musikwissenschaft"] (1972); Forkel (1792/1962); Frobenius ["Cantus"] (1972-); Gerber (1812-14/1966); Heimann (1970/1973); Horsley (1963), [*Fugue: History*] (1966); Jackson (1988); Kohlschütter (1979); Mendel (1948); Neumann, Frederick (1978); Oberdoerffer (1967); Troeger (1987); Walker (1987); Williams, P. (1970).

TOMÁS DE SANTA MARÍA

[d. 1570]

Published in 1565, Tomás de Santa María's *Libro llamado arte de tañer fantasía* reflects the musical ideals of Antonio de Cabezón. Since theory in Spain remained quite conservative into the seventeenth century and beyond, CERONE and LORENTE were able to borrow materials from this work for their own treatises. Santa María's remarks on keyboard performance are of great utility for modern practitioners of this repertoire. In addition, one finds a detailed description of the musical structures and compositional techniques used by Cabezón.

Libro llamado arte de tañer fantasía . . . [*Rism* B/VI/2, pp. 752-53.]

Valladolid: Francisco Fernández de Córdova, 1565. [LCPS: S-025. HoM: 1501. SMLMS.]

T ● See Kinkeldey (1910/1968).

T ● Harich-Schneider, Eta, and Boadella, Ricard, trans. *Anmut und Kunst beim Clavichordspiel: Wie mit aller Vollkommenheit und Meisterschaft das Klavichord zu spielen, 1565*. Leipzig: Kistner & Siegel, 1937; reprint edition, 1962.

See also *AfMf* 2/2 (1937):243-45. Review in *Rmi* 42/2 (1938):227-28 (Benvenuto Disertori).

S ● Stevens, Denis, ed. Facsimile edition. Farnborough, England: Gregg International, 1972.

S ● Facsimile edition. Geneva: Minkoff Reprint, 1973.

Review in *OrganYb 1975* 6 [1975]:162-63 (Peter Williams).

T ● Aranguren, Julia, and Ochse, Orpha, trans. "How to Play with Complete Perfection and Excellence." *AmO:AGO* 13/6 (1979):30-38.

S ● Facsimile edition. MMMLF, ser. 2, no. 124. New York: Broude Brothers, [?].

LITERATURE:

Kastner, Santiago. "Santa María, Tomás de." In *MGG* (1949-68). Bibliog.

Ward, John M. "The *Vihuela de mano* and Its Music." Ph.D. dissertation, New York University, 1953. [*DA* 32/05A, p. 2735. UMI 71-28669.]

Murphy, Richard Miller. "Fantasia and Ricercare in the Sixteenth Century." Ph.D. dissertation, Yale University, 1954. [*DA* 30/04A, p. 1589. UMI 69-13918.]

Jacobs, Charles. *La interpretación de la mùsica española del Siglo XVI para instrumentos de Teclado*. Madrid: Dirección general de relaciones culturales, 1959.

Hultberg, Warren Earl. "Sancta María's *Libro llamado arte de tañer fantasía*: A Critical Evaluation." 2 vols. Ph.D. dissertation, The University of Southern California, 1964. [*DA* 26/04A, p. 2254. UMI 65-01277.]

Lange, Helmut. "A Tutor by Santa Maria." *DFB* 14 (1968):5-6.

Poulton, Diana. *"How to Play with Good Style* by Thomas de Sancta Maria." *LSJ* 12 (1970):23-30. [*Rilm* 76-3956.]

● ● ● Howell, Almonte. "Santa María, Tomás de." In *NGrove* (1980). Bibliog.

Frolkin, Viktor. "Nekorotye voprosy ispolnitel'skoi praktiki ispanskogo klavirizma epokhi Renessansa, po traktatu Tomasa de Sankta Mariia *Iskusstvo igry fantazii* (1565)." [Some Aspects of Spanish Keyboard Performance Practice in the Renaissance, According to Tomás de Santa María's Treatise *Libro llamado arte de tañer fantasia* (1565).] In *Muzykal'noe ispolnitel'stvo: Sbornik statei, II* [Performance Practice: A Collection of Articles, II], edited by Vladimir Grigor'ev and Vladimir Natanson. Moscow: Muzyka, 1983. [*Rilm* 83-1567.]

Roig-Francolí, Miguel A. "Compositional Theory and Practice in Mid-Sixteenth Century Castilian Instrumental Music: The *Arte de tañer fantasía* by Tomás de Santa María and the Music of Antonio de Cabezón." Ph.D. dissertation, Indiana University, forthcoming.

Roig-Francolí, Miguel A. "Bass Emancipation in Sixteenth-Century Spanish Instrumental Music: The *Libro llamado arte de tañer fantasía* by Tomás de Santa María." Forthcoming.

See also DIRUTA: (1593-1609):Soehlein (1975); FÉTIS: (1833-44); LIPPIUS: Rivera (1974/1980); VIADANA: Haack (1964/1974); WALTHER: (1732); LITERATURE SUPPLEMENT: Abraham (1968/1969); Ahlgrimm (1969-70); **Apfel** (1962), (1964), ● ● ● **(1981)**; Babitz (1952), (1967/1969); Badura-Skoda et al. (1980); **Barbour** (1932), **(1951/. . ./1972)**; Becker (1836-39/1964); Brown (1976); **Bullivant (1980)**; Chew (1980); Chomiński (1962/1981); Collet (1912); Crocker (1966); Dahlhaus ["Untersuchungen"] (1966/. . ./1988); **Dahlhaus et al. (1987)**; Donington (1963/. . ./1974); Eggebrecht (1955); Eitner (1900-1904/1959-60); Ferand (1937/1938), [*Improvisation*] (1956/1961); Ganz (1972); Gerber (1812-14/1966); Harich-Schneider ([[1939]/. . ./1970); Hawkins (1776/. . ./1969); Hoag (1976); Horsley (1963), [*Fugue: History*] (1966); Houle (1987); Howell (1972); Jackson (1988); Jacobi (1957-60/1971); Jacobs (1968); Jeppesen (1922/. . ./1970); Johnson

(1973), (1978); Kastner (1973-74/1987); Kooiman (1981); Léon Tello (1974); **Lindley (1984)**; Luper (1938); **Mann (1955/. . ./1987)**; Müller-Blattau (1923/. . ./1963); **Neumann** [*Essays*] **(1982)**, (1988); Newman (1985); Oberdoerffer (1967); **Palisca** ["Theory"] **(1980)**; Parkins (1983); Pedrell (1888);

Pfeiffer (1978); Reese (1954/1959), (1957/1970); Reimer ["Concerto"] (1972-); Rodgers (1971); Rosenblum (1988); Schneider (1917/. . ./1971); Soderlund (1980); Stevenson (1960); Subirá (1947/. . ./1958); Troeger (1987); Wagner (1981).

JOSEPH SAUVEUR

[1653 – 1716]

To Joseph Sauveur music was a component of a broader science pertaining to sound. He dubbed it "acoustique." Whereas music was limited to agreeable aural stimulations, acoustics covered the entire realm of sonic possibilities. Sauveur's perspective was already developed in his manuscript "Traité de la théorie de la musique" (1697), while his central points were worked out in detail during the following two decades and presented with great success before the Académie royale des sciences, whose *Mémoires* preserve Sauveur's lucid reports.

The phenomenon of beats had long been recognized, yet Sauveur put it to a new use. Studying a 25:24 semitone created by low-pitched organ pipes, he measured the frequency of the resulting beats and used this information to unlock the mysteries of absolute pitch. Finally, within a narrow range of error, scientists could determine the frequency of vibration for any pitch. Continuing his quest for precise measurement tools, he developed a system for specifying where pitches fell within an octave. The octave contained forty-three equal segments, or *mérides* (determined logarithmically), and each of these was divided into seven units (*heptamérides*) which were in turn segmented into ten parts (*décamérides*). Though a bit cumbersome when compared with the modern division of the octave into 1200 cents, the system performed the same role when comparing various temperaments. Sauveur attempted, unsuccessfully, to persuade musicians to adapt solmization to the formulations of his system. Another practical suggestion involving the elimination of staff notation was likewise rejected.

The theory that a sound was characterized by the covibration of a fundamental and various *sons harmoniques* (overtones) was developed by Sauveur, though other scientists had come to the same conclusion independently at about the same time. Upon examining the art of organ building, Sauveur was delighted to learn that skilled craftsmen had discovered through empirical experimentation the same conclusions he had derived from his exploration of beats and nodes. From the resulting perspective Sauveur was able to extract generalizations concerning the nature of consonance and dissonance.

"Traité de la théorie de la musique"

Ms., 1697. [Paris: Bibliothèque nationale.]

ST ● Semmens, Richard. "Joseph Sauveur's *Treatise on the Theory of Music*: A Study, Diplomatic Transcription and Annotated Translation." *SMUWO* 11 (1986):entire issue. Bibliog.

"Système général des intervalles des sons, et son application à tous les systêmes et à tous les instrumens de musique"

In *MArs, An 1701.*

S ● *Principes d'acoustique et de musique, ou système général des intervalles des sons, et de son application à tous les systêmes et à tous les instrumens de musique.* Paris: 1701 [*Rism* B/VI/2, p. 755. HoM: 1380.]; reprint edition, Geneva: Minkoff Reprint, 1973.

T ● See Collected Works: Maxham (1976), below.

T ● Whelden, Roy M., III. "*Système général des intervalles des sons, et son application à tous les systèmes et à tous les instrumens de musique* by Joseph Sauveur: A Translation and Commentary." M.M. thesis, Indiana University, 1976.

S ● See Collected Works: Rasch (1984), below.

"Application des sons harmoniques à la composition des jeux d'orgues"

In *MArs, An 1702.*

S ● Paris: 1702. [*Rism* B/VI/2, p. 755. HoM: 1379.]

T ● See Collected Works: Maxham (1976), below.

S ● Souberbielle, Léon. *Le plein-jeu de l'orgue français à l'époque classique (1660-1740)* ... Montoire-sur-le-Loir: Léon Souberbielle (Jean-François Proux), 1977. [*Rilm* 77-1366.]

Reviews in *ArsOr* 27/58 (1979):503 (Ch.-W. L.) and *Ég* 18 (1979):262-66 (Jacques Froger).

S ● See Collected Works: Rasch (1984), below.

"Méthode générale pour former les systèmes temperés de musique, et du choix de celui qu'on doit suivre"

In *MArs, An 1707*.

T ● See Collected Works: Maxham (1976), below.

S ● See Collected Works: Rasch (1984), below.

"Table générale des sistèmes temperés de musique"

In *MArs, An 1711*.

Response to LEIBNIZ: Henfling (1710).

T ● See Collected Works: Maxham (1976), below.

S ● See Collected Works: Rasch (1984), below.

"Rapport des sons des cordes d'instruments de musique, aux flèches des cordes; et nouvelle détermination des sons fixes"

In *MArs, An 1713*.

S ● Amsterdam: Pierre Mortier, 1736.

T ● See Collected Works: Maxham (1976), below.

S ● See Collected Works: Rasch (1984), below.

See Cohen (1981):115-16 for a listing of references to Sauveur in the ms. "Registres des procès-verbaux" of the Académie des sciences.

COLLECTED WORKS EDITIONS:

Maxham, Robert Eugene. "The Contribution of Joseph Sauveur (1653-1716) to Acoustics." 2 vols. Ph.D. dissertation, The University of Rochester, 1976. [*Rilm* 76-4426. *DA* 37/04A, p. 1866. UMI 76-21658.]

Rasch, Rudolf, ed. *Collected Writings on Musical Acoustics (Paris, 1700-1713)*. Facsimile editions. TTL, no. 2. Utrecht: Diapason Press, 1984.

Reviews in *Mf* 40/1 (1987):81 (Klaus-Ernst Behne) and *ML* 69/1 (1988):68-70 (Albert Cohen).

LITERATURE:

Fontenelle, Bernard le Bouvier de. Entries in *HArs*.

The following reports relate specifically to Sauveur: *An 1700*: "Sur la détermination d'un son fixe"; *An 1701*: "Sur un nouveau système de musique"; *An 1702*: "Sur l'application des sons harmoniques aux jeux d'orgues"; *An 1707*: "Sur les sistèmes temperés de musique"; *An 1711*: "Sur les systèmes temperés de musique"; *An 1713*: "Sur les cordes sonores, et sur une nouvelle détermination du son fixe."

Fontenelle, Bernard le Bouvier de. *Éloges des académiciens*. 2 vols. The Hague: Isaac vander Kloot; Florence: Pierre Bouchard, 1740; reprint edition, Brussels: Culture et civilisation, 1969.

That of Sauveur also found in *HArs, An 1716*.

Scherchen, Hermann. *Vom Wesen der Musik*. MMMw, no. 1. Zürich: Mondial, 1946; reprint edition, Regensburg: Boße, 1955; English edition (as *The Nature of Music*, translated by William Mann), Chicago: Regnery; London: Dennis Dobson, 1950; reprint edition, St. Clair Shores, Mich.: Scholarly Press, 1972.

Reviews in *Etude* 69/11 (1951):7-8 (Thomas Faulkner), *MAm* 71/13 (1951):34 (C. S.), *MC* 144/6 (1951):28, *ML* 32/3 (1951):273-75 (Wilfrid Mellers), *MMR* 81/928 (1951):159-61 (Hans Ferdinand Redlich), *MO* 74/888 (1950-51):647 (H. H.), *MSur* 4/1 (1951):356 (Hans Keller), *MT* 92/1299 (1951):213, *MusT* 30/7 (1951):321 (W. R. A.), *Notes* 9/1 (1951-52):132 (Scott Goldthwaite), *SatR* 34/50 (1951):29 (Rudolph Reti), and *Tempo* 20 (1951):37 (Elizabeth Godley).

Auger, Léon. "Les apports de J. Sauveur (1653-1716) à la création de l'acoustique." *Rhsa* 1/4 (1947-48):323-36.

Winckel, Fritz. "Sauveur, Joseph." In *MGG* (1949-68). Bibliog.

Auger, Léon. "Un fondateur de l'acoustique: Joseph Sauveur, membre de l'Académie des sciences." Thesis (Lettres), The University of Paris, 1956.

● ● ● Dostrovsky, Sigalia. "Sauveur, Joseph." In *DSB* (1970-80). Bibliog.

Sirker, Udo. "Joseph Sauveurs musikakustische Untersuchungen: Ein Beitrag zu experimentellen Forschungen um 1700." In *HüschenFs* (1980):412-15. Bibliog. [*Rilm* 80-3756.]

Truesdell, C. "Sauveur, Joseph." In *NGrove* (1980).

Li[e]bermann, Marc L. "A Scientist's Account of the French Organ in 1704." *Diapason* 73/2 [867] (1982):16-17. Bibliog. [*Rilm* 82-1346.]

See also FÉTIS: (1833-44); MERSENNE: (1619-48); MOMIGNY: (1791-1818):(1818); RIEMANN: (1898); WALTHER: (1732); LITERATURE SUPPLEMENT: Abbado (1964); Asselin (1981), (1983/1985); Auhagen (1982-83); (1987); Barbieri (1983); **Barbour** (1932), **(1951/. . ./1972)**; Becker (1836-39/1964); Bell et al. (1980); Borrel (1928); Bukofzer (1947); Cannon and Dostrovsky (1981); Cazden (1961-62), (1980); Chew (1980); Cohen ["Symposium"] (1972), (1977), ● ● ● (1981); Cohen and Miller (1979); Cohen (1984); **Dahlhaus (1984)**; **Dahlhaus et al. (1987)**; Diderot (1748/ . . ./1875-77); Dostrovsky (1969), (1974-75); Eitner (1900-1904/1959-60); Federhofer (1985); Forkel (1792/1962); Gerber (1790-92/1977); Gouk (1980), (1981-82); Green (1969); Gut (1972-); Handschin

(1948); Harding (1938); Hartmann (1923); Hosler (1978/1981); Hutchinson and Knopoff (1979-81); Jackson (1988); Jones (1934); **Kassler (1979)**; Kauko (1958); La Borde (1780/1978); Lang (1941); Lange (1899-1900); **Lindley (1984)**, (1988); Lloyd (1940-41); Mach (1892); Mendel (1948), (1955),

(1978); Norton (1984); **Palisca** ["Theory"] **(1980)**; Perinello (1936); Pikler (1966); Rasch (1983); Rohwer (1949-68); Schavernoch (1981); **Seidel and Cooper (1986)**; **Shirlaw (1917/. . ./1970)**; Truesdell (1960); Vogel (1955/ 1954), (1962), (1975/1984); **Walker (1978)**; Zimmermann (1976).

MARCO SCACCHI

[ca. 1600 — between 1681 and 1687]

The Italian Marco Scacchi spent several decades as Kapellmeister at the Warsaw court and brought a progressive southern disposition to the northern musical climate. Though the ideals of the second practice had had an impact there by the 1640s, not all composers were willing converts. Particularly at odds with the new manner was Paul Siefert, a SWEELINCK pupil who defended the practice of Palestrina. Scacchi came to the defense of Kasper Förster, Siefert's adversary, with *Cribrum musicum ad triticum Syferticum* (1643), which posits that Siefert neither understood the new style nor followed the old style with particular acumen. The return volley was Siefert's *Anticribratio musica ad avenam Scacchianam* (1645), which motivated Scacchi to clarify his position regarding the stylistic norms of his day. In a letter to Christoph Werner around 1648 Scacchi delineated three stylistic classifications: the *stylus ecclesiasticus* or church style, continuing the *prima prattica* tradition; the *stylus cubicularis* or chamber style, which incorporates some *seconda prattica* elements; and the *stylus scenicus seu theatralis*, the stage or theatre style, in which the most daring elements of the *seconda prattica* are incorporated. A similar classification, perhaps derived from Scacchi, made its way into various other theory books, including those of BERNHARD, BERARDI, FUX, and MATTHESON.

To defend his position, Scacchi collected commentary from various contemporaries, published as *Judicium cribri musici* [ca. 1649]. Schütz's contribution suggests that Scacchi was preparing a thorough treatise on counterpoint, though only the *Breve discorso sopra la musica moderna* (1649), which promises more to come, is extant. That work summarizes Scacchi's advocacy of recent advances in composition and compares the seeming lunacy of daring composers to the once fantastic notions which motivated Columbus in his explorations.

Cribrum musicum ad triticum Syferticum, seu examinatio succinta psalmorum . . . [Rism B/VI/2, p. 756.]

Venice: Alessandro Vincenti, 1643.

Lettera per maggiore informazione a chi leggerà il mio Cribrum

Venice: 1644. [Lost.]

S ● Ms. (transcription found in two copies of *Cribrum musicum*). [Berlin: Staatsbibliothek Preussischer Kulturbesitz; Bologna: Civico museo bibliografico musicale.]

An Attack on Romano Micheli's *Canoni musicali*

[Ca. 1645-47.] [Lost.]

"Epistola ad Excellentissimum Dn. CS. Wernerum"

Ms., [ca. 1648]. [Hamburg: Staatsbibliothek.]

S ● See Katz (1926).

Breve discorso sopra la musica moderna [Rism B/VI/2, p. 755.]

Warsaw: Pietro Elert, 1649.

T ● ● ● ● Palisca, Claude V. "Marco Scacchi's Defense of Modern Music (1649)." In *MerrittFs* (1972):189-235. [*Rilm* 73-3363.]

Judicium cribri musici

Warsaw: Pietro Elert, [ca. 1649]. [Lost.]

S ● Ms. (transcription). [Bologna: Civico museo bibliografico musicale.]

LITERATURE:

Siefert [Syfert], Paul. *Anticribratio musica ad avenam Scacchianam, hoc est, ocularis demonstratio crassissimorum [sic] errorum, quos Marchus Schachius . . . quem Cribrum musicum ad triticum Syferticum baptizavit, passim in eo commisit . . .* Gdańsk: Georgius Rhetius, 1645. [*Rism B/VI/2, p. 782.*]

Seiffert, Max. "Paul Siefert." *VMw* 7 (1891):397-428.

Palisca, Claude V. "Scacchi, Marco." Translated by Klaus Hortschansky. In *MGG* (1949-68). Bibliog.

Kmicic-Mieleszyński, Wacław. "Geneza *Cribrum musicum*." *Muzyka* 2/3 (1957):3-17. Bibliog.

Dahlhaus, Carl. "*Cribrum musicum*: Der Streit zwischen Scacchi und Siefert." In *Kieler Tagung 1963* (1965):108-12. Bibliog.

Kmicic-Mieleszyński, Wacław. "Poglady Marca Scacchiego na znajamość kontrapunktu Pawła Sieferta." *Zeszyty naukowe. Państwowej Wyszej Szkoły Muzycznej w Gdańsku* 6 (1969):1-57; 10 (1971):1-25. [*Rilm* 69-3662; 72-1649.]

Szweykowski, Zygmunt M. "Poglady Scacchiego na muzyke jako sztuke." *Pag* 1 (1972):17-29. Bibliog.

Szweykowski, Zygmunt M. "*Stile imbastardito* i *stile rappresentativo* w systemie teoretycznym Marka Scacchiego." *Muzkya* 19/1 (1974):11-34. Bibliog. [*Rilm* 74-2212.]

Szweykowski, Zygmunt M. "*Audites mortales* jako problem wykonawczy." *Rmuz* 21/14 (July 1977):3-5. [*Rilm* 77-3659.]

Szweykowski, Zygmunt Marian. *Musica moderna w ujeciu Marka Scacchiego: Z dziejów teorii muzyki w XVII wieku.* Kraków: Polskie Wydawnictwo Muzyczne, 1977. Bibliog. [*Rilm* 78-4916.]

> Contains a summary translated into English by Jerzy Zawadzki, pp. 276-95.

Gudel, Joachim. ["Scacchi's Letter to Krzysztof Werner, described by Mattheson as a Singer in Gdańsk."] In *Zeszyty naukowe XVIII*, edited by Janusz Krassowski. Gdańsk: Państwowa Wyższa Szkoła Muzyczna, 1979.

> In Polish.

Palisca, Claude V. "Scacchi, Marco." In *NGrove* (1980). Bibliog.

Gudel, Joachim. "Ponadczasowe znaczenie listu Marco Scacchiego do kantora gdańskiego Krzysztofa Wernera." *Rocg* 42/1 (1982):249-57. [*Rilm* 82-4533.]

See also BERARDI: (1687); BERNHARD: [ca. 1649]:Hilse (1973); Dahlhaus (1964); Federhofer (1964); FÉTIS: (1833-44); MATTHESON: (1722-25); (1739); Gudel (1981); Buelow and Marx (1983):Palisca; SWEELINCK: Walker (1986); WALTHER: (1732); LITERATURE SUPPLEMENT: Abraham (1968/ 1969); Becker (1836-39/1964); Bukofzer (1947); **Dahlhaus (1984)**; Eitner (1900-1904/1959-60); Federhofer (1969); Fellerer (1983); Forkel (1792/1962); Frobenius ["Vollstimmig"] (1972-); Gerber (Grusnick (1964-66); Hawkins (1776/. . ./1969); Hucke (1969); Mainke (1969); Moser (1936/. . ./1959); **Palisca** (1949-68), ["Artusi-Monteverdi"] (1968/1985), [*Baroque*] (1968/ 1981), ["Theory"] **(1980)**; Rauschning (1931); Reimer ["Concerto"] (1972-); Walker (1987).

JOHANN ADOLPH SCHEIBE

[1708–1776]

A few unkind words concerning J. S. Bach's compositions hurled Johann Adolph Scheibe into battle with prominent Bach supporters Johann Abraham Birnbaum, Lorenz Christoph MIZLER, and Christoph Gottlieb SCHRÖTER. The offensive passage was published in the sixth issue of *Der critische Musikus* (May 14, 1737), of which Scheibe, influenced by Georg Philipp TELEMANN, served as founder, editor, and author. Underlying the controversy was the issue of aesthetic values: Was music to be an intricate and elaborate meshing of pitches, or instead a simpler, more poetic undertaking? Scheibe's values looked forward to the ideals of the Classic era, while by the 1730s Bach's music seemed, despite its mastery, somewhat antiquated.

Beyond the unfortunate stigma resulting from the Bach controversy, one finds in Scheibe a compelling musical personality informed by a broad acquaintance with the stylistic diversity of his time. His concern for various genres and their affective potential parallels the similar development of his fellow Hamburg resident MATTHESON, who was influenced by the same rhetorical theories and published his synthesis at about the same time. Scheibe's classification of music into high, middle, and low styles appeared first (in Issue 13 of *Der critische Musikus*). An earlier discussion of style appears in Scheibe's youthful "Compendium musices theoretico-practicum" [ca. 1730], which remained in manuscript during his lifetime. After a brief résumé of elementary principles, the treatise offers a perspective on the principal musical figures, counterpoint, and church, theatrical, and chamber styles.

"Compendium musices theoretico-practicum; Das ist, Kurzer Begriff derer nötigsten Compositions-Regeln"

> Ms., [ca. 1730]. [Leipzig: Musikbibliothek der Stadt.]

S ● See Benary (1956/61).

Der critische Musicus [*Rism* B/VI/2, p. 760.]

> Hamburg: Thomas von Wierings Erben, 1737-38. Vol. 1. [SMLMS.]
> Hamburg: Rudolph Beneke, 1739-40. Vol. 2. [SMLMS.]
>
> > Response to Issue 6 by Johann Abraham Birnbaum as *Unpartheyische Anmerckungen über eine bedenckliche Stelle in dem sechsten Stücke des critischen Musicus* [Leipzig: 1738] [*Rism* B/VI/1, p. 151.]; reprinted in MIZLER: (1736-54):Vol.

1/4 (1738):62-73 and in (1737-40):(1745):833-58, below. Scheibe responded in an Appendix to Vol. 1, which was published as *Beantwortung der unpartheyschen Anmerkungen über eine bedenkliche Stelle in dem sechsten Stück des critischen Musicus* [*Rism* B/VI/2, p. 760.] (Hamburg: 1738) and which also appeared in (1737-40):(1745):859-98, below. Birnbaum replied with *Vertheidigung seiner unpartheyischen Anmerkungen, über eine bedenckliche Stelle in dem sechsten Stück des critischen Musicus, wider Johann Adolph Scheibens Beantwortung derselben* [*Rism* B/VI/1, p. 151.] ([Leipzig]: 1739), which was reprinted in (1737-40):(1745):899-1031, below. Review of Vol. 1 in MIZLER: (1736-54):Vol. 1/4-6 (1738): 54-62, 71-73, 62-76. General review in MIZLER: (1736-54):Vol. 3/2-3 (1746-47):201-76, 409-63 (as "Die Nothwendigkeit der Mathematik bey gründlicher Erlernung der musikalischen Composition, dem hier mit nachdrücklicher Bescheidenheit beurtheilten critischen Musice erwiesen . . .," by Christoph Gottlieb SCHRÖTER).

Leipzig: Bernhard Christoph Breitkopf, 1745. 2nd edition, expanded. [LCPS: S-032. HoM: 1384. SMLMS. IDC.]

> Review in MIZLER: (1736-54):Vol. 3/4 (1752): 726-54 (Christoph Gottlieb SCHRÖTER). See also *AmZ* 5/30 (1802-3):499-508 (Franz Horn).

ST ● Items pertaining to Issue 6 of *Der critische Musikus* appear in English translation in David and Mendel (1945/1966) and in the original German in *Fremdschriftliche und gedruckte Dokumente zur Lebensgeschichte J. S. Bachs* (edited by Werner Neumann and Hans-Joachim Schulze; BD, no. 2; Kassel: Bärenreiter, 1969). [See numbers 400, 409, 413, 417, 441, 442, 533, and 552.]

S ● Facsimile edition. Amsterdam: Antiqua, 1966.

S ● Facsimile of the 1745 edition. Hildesheim: Georg Olms; Wiesbaden: Breitkopf & Härtel, 1970.

T ● See **Katz and Dahlhaus (1987-)**:Vol. 2.

"Sendschreiben . . . über den Kern melodischer Wissenschaft, von dem Verfasser des sogenannten critischen Musici abgelassen"

In MATTHESON: (1738):6-15.

Eine Abhandlung von den musicalischen Intervallen und Geschlechten [*Rism* B/VI/2, pp. 760-61.]

Hamburg: the author, 1739. [LCPS: S-033. SMLMS.]

Abhandlung vom Ursprunge und Alter der Musik, insonderheit der Vokalmusik . . . mit einer historischen und critischen Vorrede versehen, worinn vom Inhalte dieser Abhandlung, und von einigen andern musikalischen Sachen gehandelt wird [*Rism* B/VI/2, p. 760.]

Altona and Flensburg: in der Kortischen Buchhandlung, 1754. [LCPS: S-031. IDC.]

"Abhandlung über das Rezitativ"

In *BsW* 11/2 (1764):209-68; 12 (1765):217ff.

Über die musikalische Composition. Erster Theil: Die Theorie der Melodie und Harmonie [*Rism* B/VI/2, p. 761.]

Leipzig: Schwickert, 1773. [LCPS: S-035. SMLMS.]

See also MIZLER: (1736-54):Review (1737).

LITERATURE:

Reichel, Eugen. "Gottsched und Scheibe." *SIMg* 2 (1900-1901):654-68.

Rabich, Ernst. "Scheibe gegen Bach." *BHKM* 9/2 (1904-5):35-37.

Rosenkaimer, Eugen. "Johann Adolf Scheibe als Verfasser des *Critischen Musicus*." Ph.D. dissertation, The University of Bonn, 1923 (1929).

Storch, Karl Arno. "Johann Adolph Scheibes Anschauung von der musikalischen Historie, Wissenschaft und Kunst." Ph.D. dissertation, The University of Leipzig, 1923.

> Abstract in *Jahrbuch der Phlosophischen Fakultät zu Leipzig für das Jahr 1923* (Weida i. Thüringen: Thomas & Hubert, [1923]), vol. 1, pp. 81-82.

Cahn-Speyer, Rudolf. "J. S. Bach und J. A. Scheibe." *AMuZ* 55/19 (1928):553-54.

Gleason, Harold. "The Scheibe-Bach Controversy." *BAMS* 4 (1940):24-25.

Bergner, Caroline, and Hoke, Hans Gunter. "Scheibe . . . Johann Adolph." In *MGG* (1949-68). Bibliog.

Eggebrecht, Hans Heinrich. "Scheibe gegen Bach: Im Notenbeispiel." *Mleb* 5/4 (1952):106-8.

Benary, Peter. "Johann Adolf Scheibes 'Compendium musices'." *Mf* 10/4 (1957):508-15.

Bowman, Elsa McPhee. "The Theoretical Writings of Johann Adolph Scheibe." M.A. thesis, Yale University, 1957. Bibliog.

Schwinger, Wolfram. "In memoriam: Johann Adolf Scheibe zum 250. Geburtstag am 3. Mai." *Musica* 12/5 (1958):298.

Skapski, George J. "The Recitative in Johann Adolph Scheibe's Literary and Musical Work." Ph.D. dissertation, The University of Texas at Austin, 1963. [*DA* 24/10, pp. 4225-26. UMI 64-03814.]

Willheim, Imanuel. "Johann Adolph Scheibe: German Musical Thought in Transition." Ph.D. dissertation, The University of Illinois at Urbana-Champaign, 1963. [*DA* 24/01, pp. 324-25. UMI 63-05159.]

Review in *CM* [1] (1965):211-17 (Konrad Wolff).

Keller, Hermann. "Johann Adolph Scheibe und Johann Sebastian Bach: Eine Beitrag zur Ornamentik im 'Wohltemperierten Klavier'." In *VötterleFs* (1968): 383-86. [*Rilm* 68-1842.]

Barber, Elinore L. "J. S. Bach and the Critics." *Bach* 2/3 (1971):4-6. [*Rilm* 71-3237.]

Winzenburger, Janet. "Riemenschneider Bach Library Vault Holdings (*Critischer Musikus*). *Bach* 2/1 (1971):35-37. [*Rilm* 71-1819.]

● ● ● Buelow, George J. "In Defence of J. A. Scheibe against J. S. Bach." *PMA 1974-75* 101 (1975):85-100. [*Rilm* 76-5320.]

Mainka, Jürgen. "Zum Naturbegriff bei Bach: Aspekte des Scheibe-Birnbaum-Disputs." In *Bach-Fest 1975* (1977):155-63. [*Rilm* 77-464.]

Buelow, George J. "Scheibe, Johann Adolph." In *NGrove* (1980). Bibliog.

Becker, Peter. "Bach, Scheibe und wir: Didaktische Materialien." *MB* 14/2 (1982):76-84. Bibliog. [*Rilm* 82-351.]

Wagner, Günther. "J. A. Scheibe – J. S. Bach: Versuch einer Bewertung." *BachJb 1982* 68 (1983):33-50. [*Rilm* 82-4590.]

Zenck, Martin. "Stadien der Bach-Deutung in der Musikkritik, Musikästhetik und Musikgeschichtsschreibung zwischen 1750 und 1800." *BachJb 1982* 68 (1983):7-32. [*Rilm* 82-4601.]

Kolneder, Walter. "Forum." Reply by Karl-Heinz Göttert. *Concerto* /1 (1987):4.

Steil, Anneli. "Johann Adolph Scheibe und Johann Christoph Gottsched." Ph.D. dissertation, The University of Bonn, forthcoming.

See also ADLUNG: (1758); FÉTIS: (1833-44); KOCH: Sisman (1982); LIPPIUS: Rivera (1974/1980); MATTHESON: (1740); Buelow and Marx (1983):Palisca; MIZLER: (1739-54); Pinegar (1984); RAMEAU: Pischner (1961/. . ./1967); VIADANA: Haack (1964/1974); LITERATURE SUPPLEMENT: Ahlgrimm (1968); Allanbrook (1981); Allen ["Philosophies"] (1939); Bartel (1982/1985); Becker (1836-39/1964); Beiche

["Dux"] (1972-), ["Inversio"] (1972-); **Benary (1956/1961)**, (1963); **Bent** ["Analysis"] **(1980/1987)**; Birke (1966); Boomgaarden (1985/1987); Buelow ["Affections"] (1980); Bukofzer (1947); Burke (1963); Butler (1977); Cahn ["Repercussio"] (1972-), ["Retardatio"] (1972-), ["Transitus"] (1972-); Cazden (1980); Chafe (1981); Chybiński (1911-12); Dahlhaus (1985), (1986); Dammann (1958/1967); David and Mendel (1945/1966); Donington (1963/. . ./1974), (1980); Dreyfus (1987); Duckles (1970); Eitner (1900-1904/1959-60); Federhofer (1969); Fellerer (1927/ . . ./1972); Fischer (1957); Forchert (1986); Forkel (1792/1962); Fubini (1971/1983); Gerber (1790-92/ 1977); Ghislanzoni (1949-51); Göttert (1985-86); Goldmann (1987); Grave (1985); Gurlitt (1944/1966); Harich-Schneider ([1939]/. . ./1970); Heimann (1970/ 1973); Hiller (1768-69); Horsley (1963), [*Fugue: History*] (1966); Hosler (1978/1981); Houle (1960), (1987); Jackson (1988); Jones (1934); Jung (1969); Katz (1926); Kaufmann (1969); Krome (1896); Krützfeldt (1961); Kümmerling (1977); Lawrence (1978); **Lester (1989)**; Lindley (1982); Mahlert and Sunter (1972-); Maier (1984); Mallard (1978); **Mann (1955/. . ./1987)**; Mitchell, W. J. (1963); Müller-Blattau (1923/. . ./1963), (1949-68); Nelson (1984); **Neumann**, Frederick (1978), (1981/**1982**), [*Essays*] **(1982)**; Neumann (1955/1962); Newman (1985); Newman (1946), (1959/. . ./1983), (1963/. . ./1983); O'Donnell (1979); **Palisca** [*Baroque*] (1968/1981), ["Rezitativ"] (1972-), ["Theory"] **(1980)**; Ratner (1980); Reese (1957/1970); Reichenbach (1948); Reimer ["Concerto"] (1972-), ["Kammermusik"] (1972-), (1973); **Ritzel (1967/1968)**; Sachs (1972-); Schering (1908); Schering and Wustmann (1941); Schmalzriedt ["Durchführen"] (1972-); Schmitz (1950); Schwartz (1908); Seidel (1972-), (1975); Serauky (1929); Sheldon (1975), (1986); Sisman (1978); Sondheimer (1925); Spitzer and Zaslaw (1986); Stege (1927-28); Stevens (1974); Stowell (1985); Struthers (1902); Todd (1983); Troeger (1987); Unger (1941/1969); Viertel (1976); Waite (1970); Wellesz and Sternfeld (1973); Wessel (1955); Wichmann (1966); Wirth (1966); Ziebler (1933); Zimmermann (1976).

HEINRICH SCHENKER

[1868 – 1935]

Not since RAMEAU has a theorist so commanded the attention of the professional musical community or generated such a proliferation of output from other authors as has Heinrich Schenker. Even thirty years ago the followers of RIEMANN or of SCHOENBERG might have wished to make such a claim. Yet the recent and spectacular alteration of the analytical and pedagogical landscapes, particularly in the United States (where several of Schenker's most prominent pupils spent the years of World War Two and remained later) and in England (where American scholarship has been assimilated most readily) confirm Schenkerian theory as the preeminent methodology of our day.

Schenker categorically rejected the scientific perspective attempted by RAMEAU, who, since he had not known the music of J. S. Bach, let alone Mozart, Beethoven, or Brahms, could not have formulated a theory adequate to the task of elucidating the full-blossomed intricacies of tonality. And whereas SCHOENBERG continued the path of nineteenth-century writers, Schenker bypassed the century almost entirely in his theoretical formulations. He had little use (except as objects of derision) for notions such as the undertone series or the sterile harmonic progressions and contrapuntal instructions of textbook theory. Instead, he brought new life to the perspectives of FUX and C. P. E. BACH and developed, over a period of about thirty years, a tonal theory of extraordinary vitality and complexity, in the process devising a system of graphic analysis which elucidated a work's structure using score notation and special symbols rather than poetical or technical language.

Schenker regarded himself as an artist—he even signed his *Harmonielehre* with the words "von einem Künstler" in place of his own name—and maintained careers as a pianist (particularly in the lieder and chamber repertoire) and piano teacher, though his lessons were, to be sure, unlike those offered in any other Viennese studio. His intensive study of the masterworks led to the gradual development of his analytical perspective. In the process of gaining better access to the actual intentions of the composers, he transformed the notion of what a published score should and should not contain and demonstrated the value of manuscript study.

Schenker's work was not accepted by a large following during his lifetime. Yet the very notion of mass appeal was antithetical to his philosophy. To Schenker, music was an art of such refinement and complexity that few would be able to penetrate its meaning. Even fewer—the true geniuses of music—could create masterworks possessing deeper levels of structural coherence and organic development. That most

of these "genius" composers were German is perhaps no more remarkable than the fact that most great Impressionist painters were French, yet Schenker's strong nationalistic sentiments, amplified by the difficult political climate between the two World Wars, figured prominently in his musical writings. In fact, several works were abridged after his death to minimize the impact of these powerful political meanderings. Schenker felt that only an aristocratic environment could adequately support the development of genius—that the materialistic and democratic principles of so much of the West, and also the leveling influence resulting from socialist thought, were spawning a non-culture devoid of either the yearning or capacity for serious artistic creation. He deplored "modern" composers and their works, lamented the demise of music as it had been practiced by the masters, and wrote feverishly concerning his discoveries so that a future generation (certainly not his decadent contemporaries) might rediscover the true essence of music as revealed in the masterworks of the eighteenth and nineteenth centuries.

Schenker's numerous publications, many of which were sponsored by generous patrons, offer a fascinating view of the development of his theory, which attained its definitive stage only with the works of the 1930s, *Fünf Urlinie-Tafeln* and *Der freie Satz*. The first part of his *Neue musikalische Theorien und Phantasien* (of which *Der freie Satz* was the culmination) is *Harmonielehre* (1906). The young Schenker turned away from the conventions of harmony instruction which prevailed in his day, embracing instead "a purely spiritual universe, a system of ideally moving forces, born of Nature or of art" (Borgese translation). The notion that adjacent chords deserve separate Roman-numeral classifications was alien to his thinking. The concept of structural levels thus was already being invoked to counteract the monotonous foreground successions of his contemporary pedagogues. Even at this point, Schenker utilized a narrow range of repertoire (mainly J. S. and C. P. E. Bach, Beethoven, Brahms, Chopin, Haydn, Mozart, Schubert, and Schumann, though there are a few examples by Berlioz, Liszt, and Wagner (but none by Debussy, Reger, or Strauss).

The progress of *Neue musikalische Theorien und Phantasien* continued apace with the publication of the first part of *Kontrapunkt*, which deals with two-part species writing, in 1910. However, the continuation of this project was interrupted both by the First World War and several other publications of great interest, including careful studies of Beethoven's Ninth Symphony and late piano sonatas. It was in the process of preparing these latter works that he began utilizing diagrams in staff notation to demonstrate a variety of motivic, melodic, harmonic, and contrapuntal relationships.

The completion of *Kontrapunkt* in 1922 was, in fact, not a culmination of his original intentions. A segment on "Der freie Satz" (to contrast the "strenge Satz" of the species exercises) was postponed and would eventually fill two volumes as the third part of the *Neue musikalische Theorien und Phantasien*. Nevertheless, the second *Kontrapunkt* volume reveals an unprecedented awareness of the importance of linear forces in music. Schenker had discerned that the contrapuntal exercises which so many of the great composers had completed as part of their musical educations played a critical role in the organization of tonal works at a level beyond the immediate surface. For this reason, he regarded the development of a masterful technique in the art of counterpoint as a necessary step in attaining a comprehensive understanding of tonal compositions. In particular, such study was useful in training the musical ear to perceive the subtle interactions between consonance and dissonance in the context of passing and neighboring motions and suspensions.

During the early 1920s Schenker launched a periodical, *Der Tonwille*, of which he was the sole author. Numerous essays and analyses (particularly an extended study of Beethoven's Fifth Symphony, which was later published separately) were offered. In the latter half of the same decade, Schenker changed the format to that of a yearbook, titled *Das Meisterwerk in der Musik*. Three volumes (1925, 1926, and 1930) were issued. Their contents include perceptive analyses and several probing essays. The third volume is devoted primarily to a study of Beethoven's Third Symphony.

A few months after Schenker's death in January 1935, and not long before the Nazis took control of Vienna and banned this product of a Jewish mind, *Der freie Satz* was published. Here we find the full formulation of Schenker's mature thought, with chapters devoted to the background, the fundamental structure, the forms of the fundamental structure, the middleground in general, specific characteristics of the middleground, the concepts of strict counterpoint, the later structural levels, specific foreground events, meter and rhythm, and form. Accompanying the text is a volume filled with Schenker's characteristic graphic analyses, which even today inspire wonder among the uninitiated. Though the work is both difficult and terse, the extraordinary editorial efforts that have been devoted to the English translation (Forte, Jonas, Oster, and Rothgeb were each involved) give the English-speaking student guidance in ways the original German does not. The availability of secondary materials concerning Schenker and his work, and the increasing number of English translations of his earlier works (including the entire *Neue musikalische Theorien und Phantasien*), give

Schenker's ideas an accessibility matched by few important authors on music theory.

The concept of structural levels is central to Schenker's mature thought. The persistent use of three terms—foreground, middleground, and background—does not, however, imply that only three levels exist. As one progresses from foreground to background in reading Schenker's graphs one perceives deeper structural layers, which serve as the controlling forces in the tonal design of a work. Ultimately, every composition which Schenker cared to analyze possesses a fundamental structure, whose upper voice is characterized by a descending, tonic-defining linear progression from either the third, fifth, or (rarely) eighth scale degree to the tonic pitch. Coordinating with this melody in the fundamental structure is a bass arpeggiation traversing the path from first to fifth scale degree and back. Though this ultimate stage of reduction is an important discovery of Schenker's, its realization in every analysis is not, ultimately, the goal of the undertaking. Much more important is the perception of how the elements of the fundamental structure are prolonged (or "composed-out") in the various intermediate layers which lead to the actual composition.

Der freie Satz displays a remarkable independence from the Roman-numeral saturation that has typified most analytical methodologies both before and after Schenker. Schenker used Roman numerals to indicate scale degrees upon which the bass was grounded in the path between tonic (I) and dominant (V) in the fundamental structure's bass arpeggiation. Since such patterns are replicative at levels closer to the foreground, various layers of Roman numerals—each at a different structural level—are possible. This concept both allows for a large number of chords to be subsumed by one Roman numeral (which represents a level deeper than that of the succession of chords) and radically alters the traditional notion of modulatory technique. No motion from scale degree to scale degree is independent of the overriding tonic prolongation which is represented by the fundamental structure, and therefore every so-called "modulation" is, instead, a tonicization of a point within the control of the tonal center of the work or movement.

The dedicated work of Schenker's students and other practitioners during the decades after Schenker's death has contributed profoundly to the development of music theory in the United States and Britain. Among the earlier generation Oswald Jonas, Ernst Oster, and Felix Salzer, in particular, established through painstaking effort the environment in which the propagation of Schenkerian theory became possible and fostered the transmission of their knowledge to younger musicians whose teaching and publications (amply though not exhaustively represented on the following pages) continue the tradition. Various expansions and criticisms of

Schenker's thought have been offered as well. (See especially the work of Salzer and of Schachter for the the former, and of Narmour for the latter.) Yet one wonders if the cantankerous Schenker would be any more contented with the current musical scene than with his own: though a greater number of students are exposed to his ideas, few—especially few performers, for whom his perspective is particularly helpful—become competent in analysis; and despite the continuing vitality of compositional practices bearing some relationship with tonality, he probably would not wish to alter his view that Brahms was the last of the great composers.

Essays and Reviews

> See Rast (1988), below, for a comprehensive listing.

T ● Dunsby, Jonathan, and Loeschmann, Horst B., trans. "Three Essays from *Neue Revue* (1894-97)." *MA* 7/2 (1988):133-41.

"Der Geist der musikalischen Technik"

> *MuWb* 26/19-26 (1895):245-46, 257-59, 273-74, 285-86, 297-98, 309-10, 325-26.

> > The contents of this article are listed (and a brief passage translated) in Pastille (1984-85), below.

S ● *Mth* 3/3 (1988):237-42.

T ● Pastille, William, trans. "The Spirit of Musical Technique." *Theoria* 3 (1988):86-104.

Ein Beitrag zur Ornamentik, als Einführung zu Ph. Em. Bachs Klavierwerken, mitumfassend auch die Ornamentik Haydns, Mozarts, Beethovens etc.

> Founded upon BACH: (1753-62).

> Vienna: Universal Edition; London: E. Ascherberg, [1904].
> Vienna: Universal Edition, 1908. Revised edition.

S ● Facsimile of the 1908 edition. Vienna: Universal Edition, [1954].

T ● Siegel, Hedi, trans. "A Contribution to the Study of Ornamentation." *MuF* 4 (1976):1-139.

T ● Noro, Aiko, and Tamemoto, Akiko, trans. *Koten piano soshokuon soho*. Japan: Ongaku no tomo, 1979.

Neue musikalische Theorien und Phantasien

  I. *Harmonielehre*

> Published anonymously "von einem Künstler."

  II. *Kontrapunkt*
    1: *Cantus Firmus und zweistimmiger Satz*

    2: *Drei- und mehrstimmiger Satz; Übergänge zum freien Satz*

  III. *Der freie Satz*

> Stuttgart and Berlin: J. G. Cotta; Vienna: Universal Edition, 1906. Vol. I.
> Stuttgart and Berlin: J. G. Cotta; Vienna: Universal Edition, 1910. Vol. II:1.

> > Review in *Rmi* 18/2 (1911):457 (Luigi Torchi).

> Vienna: Universal Edition, 1922. Vol. II:2.
> Vienna: Universal Edition, 1935. Vol. III (in two parts).

> > Published posthumously. Review in *ModM* 15/3 (1939):192-97 (Roger Sessions).

T ● Borgese, Elisabeth Mann, trans. *Harmony*. Edited and annotated by Oswald Jonas. Chicago: The University of Chicago Press, 1954; reprint edition, 1980; paperback edition, Cambridge, Mass.: The MIT Press, 1973.

> Reviews in *ChR* 9/1 (1955-56):132-35 (Robert Bloch), *MEJ* 61/9 (1974-75):92, *ML* 37/2 (1956):180-82 (H. K. Andrews), *MQ* 41/2 (1955):256-60 (William J. Mitchell), *MR* 18/3 (1957):249-51, *Notes* 13/1 (1955-56):53-56 (Charles Seeger), and *SchM* 47/9 (1976):24.

S ● Jonas, Oswald, ed. Revised edition (Vol. III). Vienna: Universal Edition, [1956].

> Some controversial materials were omitted from this edition. Reviews in *Mf* 12/4 (1959):523-25 (Carl Dahlhaus) and *SmpB* 47 (1959) (Franz Eibner).

T ● Krueger, Theodore Howard, trans. "*Der freie Satz* by Heinrich Schenker: A Complete Translation and Re-editing. Volume 1: The Complete Text. Volume 2: Supplement of Musical Examples." Ph.D. dissertation, The State University of Iowa, 1960. [*DA* 20/12, pp. 4678-79. UMI 60-01558.]

T ● Dunn, John Petrie. English translation of *Kontrapunkt*, Part 1. University of Edinburgh.

T ● See Komar (1971), below.

S ● Frisius, Rudolf, ed. Facsimile of the 1906 edition (Vol. I). Vienna: Universal Edition, 1978.

> Reviews in *HFS* 19/6 (1980):713 (Ulrich Dibelius), *Me* 33 (1979-80):239-40 (Franz Eibner), *Mf* 33/3 (1980):374-75 (Diether de la Motte), *ML* 60/3 (1979):332-33 (Derrick Puffett), *MT* 120/1636 (1979):485-86 (William Drabkin), *NZfM* 141/1 (1980):65-66 (Erhard

Karkoschka), and *Öm* 34/11 (1979):578-80 (Heinz Kratochwil).

T ● Oster, Ernst, trans. and ed. *Free Composition (Der freie Satz): Volume III of New Musical Theories and Fantasies*. 2 vols. Introduction by Allen Forte. LMS. New York and London: Longman, 1979. [*Rilm* 79-1708.]

Reviews in *Choice* 17/3 (1980):398, *JMT* 25/1 (1981):115-42 (Carl E. Schachter), *JMT* 25/1 (1981):143-53 (David Epstein), *JMT* 25/1 (1981):155-73 (William E. Benjamin), *MA* 1/1 (1982):101-7 (Michael Musgrave), *MQ* 67/1 (1981):113-18 (Roger Kamien), *MT* 121/1651 (1980):560-62 (Arnold Whittall), *MTS* 3 (1981):158-84 (Edward Laufer), *Mus* 8 (1985):51-55 (Craig Ayrey), *Notes* 36/4 (1979-80):879-81 (Gregory Proctor), *RCMM* 78/2 (1982):199-201 (R. B. Swanston), *RMARC* 16 (1980):140-48 (Jonathan Dunsby), *Tempo* 136 (1981):37-38 (Richard Evans), and *TLS* 79/4042 (1980):1046 (Christopher Wintle).

T ● Stewart, James, trans. "Heinrich Schenker's *Kontrapunkt* I and II: A Translation and Commentary." Ph.D. dissertation, The Ohio State University, 1983. [*DA* 44/11A, p. 3203. UMI 84-03579.]

T ● See **Katz and Dahlhaus (1987-)**:Vol. 3.

T ● Rothgeb, John, ed. and trans., and Thym, Jürgen, trans. *Counterpoint: A Translation of "Kontrapunkt" by Heinrich Schenker: Volume II of "New Musical Theories and Fantasies"*. 2 vols. New York: Schirmer Books, 1987.

Reviews in *Brio* 25/1 (1988):36-37 (Clifford Bartlett), *Choice* 25/5 (1987-88):778 (R. Stahura), *MT* 129/1748 (1988):524-29 (Carl Schachter), and *Theoria* 3 (1988):161-69 (William Pastille).

T ● See **Bujić (1988)**.

S ● Kosar, Anthony Jay, and Phillips, Joel. *A Companion to Schenker's "Free Composition": The Musical Scores*. Forthcoming.

Instrumentations-Tabelle

Under the pseudonym Artur Niloff.

Vienna: Universal Edition, 1908.

Later editions.

S ● Joppig, G., ed. Facsimile of the 1908 edition. Vienna: Universal, 1986.

Review in *BrB* 61 (1988):124 (Clemens Gottfried).

J. S. Bach, Chromatische Phantasie und Fuge: Kritische Ausgabe.

Vienna: Universal Edition, 1910.

S ● Jonas, Oswald, ed. Revised edition. Vienna: Universal Edition, 1969.

T ● Siegel, Hedi, trans. and ed. *J. S. Bach's Chromatic Fantasy and Fugue*. New York: Longman, 1984. Bibliog.

Reviews in *Choice* 22/2 (1984-85):280 (J. E. Johnson), *MA* 7/2 (1988):225-33 (John Rink), and *MTS* 7 (1985):203-7 (William Rothstein).

Beethovens neunte Sinfonie: Eine Darstellung des musikalischen Inhaltes, unter fortlaufender Berücksichtigung auch des Vortrages und der Literatur

Vienna: Universal Edition, 1912.

Reprinted in 1925.

S ● Facsimile edition. WUA. Vienna: Universal Edition, 1969.

T ● Rothgeb, John, trans. Forthcoming.

Die letzten fünf Sonaten Beethovens: Kritische Ausgabe mit Einführung und Erläuterung

Vienna: Universal Edition, 1913, 1914, 1915, 1920. 4 vols.

The projected edition of Op. 106 was not realized. Review in *Rmi* 32/4 (1925):658-60 (A. E.).

S ● Jonas, Oswald, ed. Revised edition. 4 vols. Vienna: Universal Edition, 1971-72. [*Rilm* 76-2766.]

Reviews in *Mf* 27/3 (1974):383 (Hellmut Federhofer), *NZfM* 134/7 (1973):465 (Rudolf Stephan), *ÖM* 26/5-6 (1971):334 (Rudolf Klein), and *PNM* 12/1-2 (1973-74):319-30 (William Drabkin) [*Rilm* 74-3873].

L. van Beethoven: Sonate, Op. 27, Nr. 2 (MSel, no. 1)

A facsimile of the manuscript, plus three of Beethoven's sketches.

Vienna: Universal Edition, 1921.

Der Tonwille: Flugblätter zum Zeugnis unwandelbarer Gesetze der Tonkunst, einer neuen Jugend dargebracht

Vienna: Tonwilleverlag Albert J. Gutmann; Leipzig: F. Hofmeister, 1921-24. Ten [nine] issues.

S ● See (1925), below.

S ● Facsimile edition. Vienna: Universal Edition, [1969]. 3 vols.

T ● Pastille, William, trans. "Franz Schubert: 'Ihr Bild'." *Sonus* 6/2 (1985-86):31-37.

T ● Larson, Steve, trans. "C. P. E. Bach: *Kurze und leichte Klavierstücke mit veränderten Reprisen* (1766), No. 1, Allegro." *ITO* 10/4 (1987-88):5-10.

T ● Petty, Wayne, trans. "Haydn: Sonata in E-flat Major." *Theoria* 3 (1988):105-60.

Beethoven V. Sinfonie: Darstellung des musikalischen Inhaltes nach der Handschrift unter fortlaufender Berücksichtigung des Vortrages und der Literatur

Vienna: Tonwille-Verlag (A. Gutmann), 1925.

> Derived from *Tonwille* (1921-24), nos. 1, 5, and 6, above.

S ● Vienna: Universal Edition, n.d.; reprint edition, 1969.

T ● Forbes, Elliott, and Adams, F. John, Jr., trans. "Beethoven: Fifth Symphony, First Movement." In Forbes (1971):164-82.

Das Meisterwerk in der Musik: Ein Jahrbuch

Munich: Drei Masken Verlag, 1925, 1926, 1930. 3 vols.

> Reviews in *ML* 12/3 (1931):306-7 (E. W.) and *ZfMw* 15/2 (1932-33):92-94 (Oswald Jonas). A portion of "Das Organische der Fuge" from *Meisterwerk* 2 (1926) appeared as "Joh. Seb. Bach: Wohltemperiertes Klavier, Band I, Präludium C-Moll" in *Musik* 15/9 (1922-23):641-51.

T ● Grossman, Orin, trans. "Organic Structure in Sonata Form." *JMT* 12/2 (1968):164-83; reprinted in Yeston (1977):38-53, below, and in Rosand (1985):Vol. 7, pp. 112-31.

T ● Siegel, Hedi, trans. "The Sarabande of J. S. Bach's Suite No. 3 for Unaccompanied Violoncello [BWV 1009]." *MuF* 2 (1970):274-82.

T ● Kalib, Sylvan Sol. "Thirteen Essays from the Three Yearbooks *Das Meisterwerk in der Musik* by Heinrich Schenker: An Annotated Translation." 3 vols. Ph.D. dissertation, Northwestern University, 1973. [*Rilm* 76-15546. *DA* 34/06A, p. 3452. UMI 73-30626.]

> The essays included are "The Art of Improvisation," "Let's Do Away With the Phrasing Slur," "J. S. Bach: Six Sonatas for Unaccompanied Violin: Sonata III, Largo," "Chopin: Etude in G-flat Major, Op. 10, No. 5," "Resumption of Urlinie Considerations," and "Clarifications" from the first yearbook; "Resumption of Urlinie Considerations," "The Organic Aspect of Sonata Form," "The Organic Aspect of the Fugue,"

"Mozart: Symphony in G Minor," "Haydn: The Creation: The Representation of the Chaos," and "A Negative Example: Max Reger, Op. 81" from the second yearbook; and "Rameau or Beethoven? Paralytic Standstill or Ingenious Life in Music?" from the third yearbook.

S ● Facsimile edition. 3 vols. in 1. Hildesheim: Georg Olms, 1974.

S ● "Haydn: *Die Schöpfung*: 'Die Vorstellung des Chaos'." In Schuhmacher [*Zur musikalischen Analyse*] (1974):59-71. [*Rilm* 74-2369.]

T ● Rothgeb, John, trans. "The Largo of J. S. Bach's Sonata No. 3 for Unaccompanied Violin [BWV 1005]." *MuF* 4 (1976):141-59; reprinted in Rosand (1985):Vol. 14, pp. 259-77.

T ● Bent, Ian, trans. "Essays from *Das Meisterwerk in der Musik*, Vol. 1 (1925)." *MA* 5/2-3 (1986):151-91.

T ● See **Katz and Dahlhaus: (1987-)**:Vol. 3.

T ● Cambridge: Cambridge University Press, forthcoming.

Fünf Urlinie-Tafeln

Vienna: Universal Edition, 1932.

S ● Weisse, Hans, ed. *Fünf Urlinie-Tafeln/Five Analyses in Sketchform*. New York: David Mannes Music School, [1933]; reprint edition (as *Five Graphic Music Analyses/Fünf Urlinie-Tafeln*, edited by Felix Salzer), New York: Dover Publications, 1969. [*Rilm* 69-2762.]

> Reviews in *MT* 112/1536 (1971):140 (Eric Sams) and *NYRB* 16/11 (1971):32-34 (Charles Rosen).

Johannes Brahms, "Oktaven und Quinten" u[nd] A[nderes]

Vienna: Universal Edition, 1933.

T ● Mast, Paul, trans. "*Oktaven und Quinten, u. A.*: A Critical Edition of Brahms' Notebook with Schenker's Commentary Translated and Compared." M.A. thesis, The University of Rochester, 1971; revised edition (as "Brahms's Study, *Octaven u. Quinten u. A.*, with Schenker's Commentary Translated") in *MuF* 5 (1980):1-196. [*Rilm* 80-1847.]

> A complete facsimile of Brahms's manuscript (from which Schenker's edition was made) is included with the *MuF* translation.

"Kommentar zu Ph. E. Bach's Versuch . . ."

Ms. [New York: New York Public Library, Music Division, Special Collections.] Incomplete.

"Die Kunst des Vortrags"

>   This working title is applied to several Schenker
>   manuscripts, including "Vom Vortrag" [ca. 1910]
>   and "Entwurf einer 'Lehre vom Vortrag'."

>   Ms. [Riverside, Cal.: Oswald Jonas Collection,
>   The University of California at Riverside.]

>   S ● Esser, Heribert, ed. Vienna: Universal Edition,
>   forthcoming.

>   T ● Scott, Irene Schreier, trans. Forthcoming.

"Von dem Stimmführung des Generalbasses"

>   Ms. [New York: New York Public Library, Music
>   Division, Special Collections.]

>   T ● Siegel, Hedi, trans. *MuF* 6/2 (forthcoming).

Correspondence

>   S ● Jonas, Oswald, ed. "Ein Brief Bernhard Paum-
>   gartners an Heinrich Schenker." *ÖM* 31/7-8
>   (1976):371-72.

>   ST ● See SCHOENBERG: (1903-7):Erwin and
>   Simms (1981).

>   T ● Rothgeb, John, and Siegel, Hedi, trans. "The
>   Opening of Beethoven's Sonata, Op. 111: A Let-
>   ter." *T&P* 8/1 (1983):3-13.

>   S ● See Federhofer (1985), below.

Posthumously published articles

>   S ● See Jonas and Salzer (1937-38), below.

>   The editors Oswald Jonas and Felix Salzer pub-
>   lished several items from among Schenker's
>   papers, as well as excerpts from his published
>   work, in the short-lived periodical, *Der Dreiklang,*
>   just before the Second World War. Included are
>   Schenker's "Vom Hintergrund in der Musik,"
>   "Von der Stimmführung im Generalbaß," "Von
>   der Diminution," "Urlinietafel zu Haydns
>   'Chorale St. Antoni'," "Über Anton Bruckner,"
>   and "Ein Kommentar zu Schindler, Beethovens
>   Spiel betreffend" [reprinted in *Me* 18/4 (1964-
>   65):152-57].

Additional information on Schenker's works (particularly his numerous early articles and reviews), on
his editions of music, and on recent work of
analysts influenced by Schenker's writings is provided in Beach (1969/1977), below, Beach (1979),
below, and Beach (1985), below. See also Federhofer (1985), below, and Rast (1988), below. Many
interesting documents, ranging from Schenker's
diary to sketches on random scraps of paper, are
housed in the Oswald Jonas Memorial Collection
at the University of California, Riverside, and at
the Music Division of the New York Public Library
at Lincoln Center. Both of these collections are
being microfilmed and will eventually be available
for purchase by libraries and scholars in that medium.

LITERATURE:

Moormann, Ludwig. "Das Werk Heinrich Schenkers: Eine
Übersicht." *Mgil* 1/7 (1922-23):80-84.

Vrieslander, Otto. "Heinrich Schenker und sein Werk."
MAn 5/2-3 (1923):41-44, 72-79.

Carrière, Paul. "Schenkers Urlinie." *AMuZ* 52/7-8
(1925):139-40, 163-65.

Roth, Hermann. *Elemente der Stimmführung (Der strenge
Satz)*. Stuttgart: Carl Grüniger Verlag (Ernst Klett),
1926.

Vrieslander, Otto. "Heinrich Schenker." *Musik* 19/1 (1926-
27):33-38.

Riezler, Walter. "Die Urlinie." *Musik* 22/7 (1929-30):502-10.

Vrieslander, Otto. "Heinrich Schenker." *Kunstwart* 43/9
(1929-30):181-89.

Albersheim, Gerhard. "Heinrich Schenker: Grundlagen und
Bedeutung seines Werkes." *RMTZ* 31/15-16 (1930):
259-61, 270-74.

Citkowitz, Israel. "The Role of Heinrich Schenker." *ModM*
11/1 (1933-34):18-23; reprinted in *T&P* 10/1-2
(1985): 17-22.

Jonas, Oswald. "Heinrich Schenker." *AMuZ* 60/36-37
(1933):425-27, 437-38.

Jonas, Oswald. "The Photogram-Archives in Vienna." *ML*
15/4 (1934):344-47; as "Das Wiener Photogramm-
Archiv" in *Anbruch* 18/1 (1936):6-7.

Jonas, Oswald. *Das Wesen des musikalischen Kunstwerks:
Eine Einführung in die Lehre Heinrich Schenkers*.
Vienna: Saturn-Verlag, 1934; revised edition (as
Eine Einführung . . .), Vienna: Universal Edition,
1972; as *Introduction to the Theory of Heinrich
Schenker (Einführung in die Lehre Heinrich
Schenkers): The Nature of the Musical Work of Art*,
translated and edited by John Rothgeb (LMS),
New York and London: Longman, 1982. [*Rilm* 76-
4064.]

>   Reviews in *Choice* 19/11-12 (1981-82):1568, *Cnv*
>   65, p. 19 (John Swackhamer), *JMT* 27/2
>   (1983):273-81 (William Rothstein), *Me* 26/2
>   (1972-73):93, *Mf* 27/2 (1974):251 (Hellmut
>   Federhofer), *ML* 16/4 (1935):341 (E. Lock-
>   speiser), *MTS* 5 (1983):127-31 (Bruce B. Camp-
>   bell), *NCM* 8/2 (1984-85):164-76 (Richard
>   Swift), *NZfM* 134/2 (1973):123-24 (Carl
>   Dahlhaus), and *TLS* 82/4187 (1983):697 (Chris-
>   topher Wintle).

Reich, Willi. "Kant, Schenker und die Nachläufer." *DzWMz*
15-16 (1934):29-32.

Sessions, Roger. "Heinrich Schenker's Contribution." *ModM* 12/4 (1934-35):170-78; reprinted in *CI* 2/1 (1975-76):113-19.

"The Late Heinrich Schenker." *NYT* (February 3, 1935); reprinted in *T&P* 10/1-2 (1985):7.

Katz, Adele T. "Heinrich Schenker's Method of Analysis." *MQ* 21/3 (1935):311-29; reprinted in *T&P* 10/1-2 (1985):77-95.

Salzer, Felix. *Sinn und Wesen der abendländische Mehrstimmigkeit.* Vienna: Saturn-Verlag, 1935.

> Review in *ML* 16/3 (1935):249-50 (E. Lockspeiser).

Waldeck, Arthur, and Broder, Nathan. "Musical Synthesis as Expounded by Heinrich Schenker." *MMer* 11/4 (1935):56-64; reprinted in *T&P* 10/1-2 (1985):65-73.

Zuckerkandl, Victor. "Bekenntnis zu einem Lehrer." *Anbruch* 17/5 (1935):121-25.

Bamberger, Carl. "Das Schenker-Institut am neuen Wiener Konservatorium." *Anbruch* 18/1 (1936):7-8.

Weisse, Hans. "The Music Teacher's Dilemma." *VPMTNA 1935* 30 (1936):122-37; reprinted in *T&P* 10/1-2 (1985):29-48.

Plettner, Arthur. "Heinrich Schenker's Contribution to Theory: Viennese Scholar Sought Broader Base for Analysis of Composition." *MAm* 56/3 (1936):14, 136; reprinted in *T&P* 10/1-2 (1985):11-14.

Jonas, Oswald, and Salzer, Felix, eds. *Der Dreiklang: Monatsschrift für Musik.* Vienna: Krystall-Verlag, 1937-38.

> A journal (nine [seven] issues only) devoted to Schenker's work, including numerous articles by Schenker's pupils. Of particular interest are "Die historische Sendung Heinrich Schenkers" 1 (1937): 2-12 (Felix Salzer), "Ein Bach-Präludium: Ein Weg zum organischen Hören" 1 (1937):13-17 (Oswald Jonas) [reprinted in *Me* 20/5 (1966-67): 205-9], "Der Nachlass Heinrich Schenkers" 1 (1937):17-22 ([Oswald Jonas]), "Mozarts ewige Melodie" 3 (1937):84-92 (Os-wald Jonas) [reprinted in *Me* 30/3-4 (1976-77): 118-21, 158-60], "Zur Betrachtung von Skizzen Beethovens" 6 (1937):150-54 (Oswald Jonas) [reprinted in *Me* 23/5 (1969-70):203-6], "Beethoven in der Interpretation" 6 (1937):154-57 (Oswald Jonas) [reprinted in *Me* 23/4 (1969-70):151-54], "Schenkers Persönlichkeit im Unterricht" 7 (1937):176-84 (Hans Wolf), and "Nachtrag zu Schenkers Aufsatz über Schindler" 8-9 (1937-38):200-207 (Oswald Jonas) [reprinted in *Me* 18/5 (1964-65):205-9].

Sessions, Roger. "Escape by Theory." *ModM* 15/3 (1937-38):192-97.

Sessions, Roger. "The Function of Theory." *ModM* 15/4 (1937-38):257-62.

Dale, Frank Knight. "Heinrich Schenker and Musical Form." *BAMS* 7 (1943):12-13; reprinted in *T&P* 10/1-2 (1985):23.

Katz, Adele T. *Challenge to Musical Tradition: A New Concept of Tonality.* London: Putnam; New York: A. A. Knopf, 1945; reprint edition, New York: Da Capo Press, 1975.

> Reviews in *JAAC* 4/3 (1945-46):196-97 (Hugo Leichtentritt), *ML* 28/4 (1947):390-91 (Percy M. Young), *MQ* 32/2 (1946):296-302 (Paul Henry Lang), *MR* 8/4 (1947):308-10 (Egon J. Wellesz), *Notes* 3/1 (1945-46):41-42 (Herman Reichenbach), *PMM* 8 (1949):58-61 (Edward Clark), and *Scrutiny* 15/2 (1947-48):134-35 (W. H. Mellers).

Mitchell, William J. "Heinrich Schenker's Approach to Detail." *Musicology* 1/2 (1946):117-28; reprinted in *T&P* 10/1-2 (1985):51-62.

Federhofer, Hellmut. "Die Musiktheorie Heinrich Schenkers." *SMz* 87/10 (1947):365-68.

Daniskas, John. *Grondslagen voor de analytische vormleer der musiek.* Rotterdam: W. L. & J. Brusse, 1948.

> Review in *JAMS* 4/1 (1951):51-55 (Alexander Ringer).

Jonas, Oswald. "Schenker, Heinrich." In *MGG* (1949-68). Bibliog.

Mann, Michael. "Schenker's Contribution to Music Theory." *MR* 10/1 (1949):3-26.

Wingert, Hans. "Über die 'Urlinie' und ihren Schöpfer." *ZfM* 111/5 (1950):244-46.

Hartmann, Heinrich. "Heinrich Schenker und Karl Marx." *ÖM* 7/2 (1952):46-52.

Salzer, Felix. *Structural Hearing: Tonal Coherence in Music.* 2 vols. Foreword by Leopold Mannes. New York: Boni, 1952; reprint edition, New York: Dover, 1962; as *Strukturelles Hören: Der tonale Zusammenhang in der Musik* (with a Foreword by Saul Novak; TzMw, nos. 10-11), Wilhelmshaven: Heinrichshofen, 1957; 1977; 2nd German edition (edited by Richard Schaal), 1983.

> Excerpts printed in Komar (1971), below. Reviews in *Dmt* 38/7 (1963):284-85 (Morten Levy), *IMus* 51/5 (1952-53):28 (J. R.), *JAMS* 5/3 (1952): 260-65 (Milton Babbitt), *MC* 145/10 (1952): 30, *Mf* 33/4 (1980):513-14 (Helmut Rösing), *ML* 34/4 (1953): 329-32 (W. Mellers), *MMR* 83/946 (1953):85-87, *MQ* 39/1 (1953):126-29 (Nathan Broder), *MT* 94/1324 (1953):261 (Mosco Carner), *Musica* 32/6 (1978):581-82 (Clemens Kühn), *Notes* 10/3 (1952-53):438 (Norman Lloyd), *Notes* 10/3 (1952-53):439 (Oswald Jonas), and *Tibia* 3/3 (1978):189-91 (Albrecht Riethmüller).

Furtwängler, Wilhelm. "Heinrich Schenker, ein zeitgemäßes Problem." In his *Ton und Wort: Aufsätze und Vorträge* (Wiesbaden: F. A. Brokhaus, 1954; later editions), pp. 198-204; as "Heinrich Schenker: A Contemporary Problem" (translated by Jan Emerson), *Sonus* 6/1 (1985):1-5.

Forte, Allen. *Contemporary Tone-Structures*. TCSE. New York: Bureau of Publications, Teachers College, Columbia University, 1955.

> Reviews in *Etude* 74/6 (1956):8 (William Mitchell), *JMT* 1/1 (1957):112-18 (Howard Boatwright) [Rebuttal in *JMT* 1/2 (1957):201-5 (Allen Forte). Response in *JMT* 2/1 (1958):85-92 (Howard Boatwright).], *JRME* 4/1 (1956):69-70 (John Verrall), *ML* 37/2 (1956):187-89 (Hans Keller), and *Notes* 13/3 (1955-56):431-32 (Herbert Livingston).

Jonas, Oswald. "On the Study of Chopin's Manuscripts." *ChJb 1956* (1956):142-55.

Meyer, Leonard B. *Emotion and Meaning in Music*. Chicago: The University of Chicago Press, 1956.

> Reviews *CanMJ* 1/4 (1956-57):71-76 (Geoffrey B. Payzant), *ChR* 11/2 (1957-58):97-100 (Marcus G. Raskin), *HFMA* 7/4 (1957):29-30 (R. D. Darrell), *JAAC* 16/2 (1957-58):285-86 (Julius Portnoy), *JMT* 1/1 (1957):110-12 (David Kraehenbuehl), *ML* 38/3 (1957):278-79 (F. Howes), *MMR* 88/988 (1958):149-50 (P. T. B.), *MQ* 43/4 (1957):553-57 (Edward Arthur Lippman), *MR* 19/1 (1958):64-67 (Guy A. Marco), *MT* 99/1380 (1958):82 (Henry Raynor), *Notes* 14/1 (1956-57):253-54 (Richard S. Hill), *NY* 32/46 (1957):63-65 (Winthrop Sargeant), *PP* 50/1 (1957):41 (Esther Goetz Gilliland), and *YR* 46/4 (1956-57):627-29 (Kenneth Connelly).

Das Archiv für Photogramme musikalischer Meisterhandschriften in der Musiksammlung der Österreichischen Nationalbibliothek in Wien. BibS, no. 18. Vienna: Österreichische Nationalbibliothek, 1958.

Kessler, Hubert. "On the Value of Schenker's Ideas for Analysis of Contemporary Music." *PTCI* 1 (1958):1-11.

Kolneder, Walter. "Sind Schenkers Analysen Beiträge zur Bacherkenntnis?" *DJbMw* 3 (1958):59-73.

Schmid, Edmund. "Autographe und Originalausgaben Beethovens: Auswertung eines Vergleichs." *NZfM* 119/12 (1958):746-47.

● ● ● Forte, Allen. "Schenker's Conception of Musical Structure." *JMT* 3/1 (1959):1-30; excerpts reprinted in Komar (1971), below; reprinted in Yeston (1977):3-37, below.

Hirschkorn, Kurt. "Die Stimmführung als Leitstern des Geigers: Die Bedeutung Heinrich Schenkers." *Me* 12 (1958-59):233-34.

Travis, Roy. "Towards a New Concept of Tonality?" *JMT* 3/2 (1959):257-84.

> Responses in *JMT* 4/1 (1960):85-98 (Ernst Oster), *JMT* 4/2 (1960):274-75 (Hans Neumann), and *JMT* 5/1 (1961):152-56 (Arthur Komar).

Cooper, Grosvenor, and Meyer, Leonard B. *The Rhythmic Structure of Music*. Chicago: The University of Chicago Press, 1960.

> Reviews in *Instrumentalist* 15/7 (1961):14, *JAMS* 16/2 (1963):270-72 (Hans Tischler), *JMT* 5/1 (1961):129-34 (Ellis B. Kohs), *JRME* 9/1 (1961):77-78 (Charles L. Gary), *MC* 163/8 (1961):46 (Frederick Werlé), *ML* 43/1 (1962):72-74 (A. Hutchings), *Notes* 20/1 (1962-63):60-61 (Wallace Berry), and *Tempo* 59 (1961):32 (Peter Evans).

Oster, Ernst. "Register and the Large-Scale Connection." *JMT* 5/1 (1961):54-71; reprinted in Yeston (1977):54-71, below.

Federhofer, Hellmut. "Heinrich Schenker." In *HobokenFs* (1962):63-72.

Jonas, Oswald. "Die Kunst des Vortrags nach Heinrich Schenker." *Me* 15/3 (1961-62):127-29.

Kerman, Joseph. "A Romantic Detail in Schubert's *Schwanengesang*." *MQ* 48/1 (1962):36-49.

Eibner, Franz. "Die Stimmführung Chopins in der Darstellung Heinrich Schenkers." In *Congress Chopin 1960* (1963):145-67.

Jonas, Oswald. "Ein textkritisches Problem in der Ballade Op. 38 von Frederic Chopin." *Am* 35/2-3 (1963):155-58.

Jonas, Oswald. "Heinrich Schenker und grosse Interpreten." *ÖM* 19/12 (1964):584-89.

Silberman, Israel. "Teaching Composition via Schenker's Theory." *JRME* 12/4 (1964):295-303.

Kaufmann, Harald. "Fortschritt und Reaktion in der Lehre Heinrich Schenkers: Vor 30 Jahren, am 13. Januar 1935, starb der bedeutende Wiener Musiktheoretiker." *NZfM* 126/1 (1965):5-9; reprinted in *Orch* 13 (1965):44-49; reprinted in Kaufmann's *Spurlinien: Analytische Aufsätze über Sprache und Musik* (Vienna: Elisabeth Lafite, 1969), pp. 37-46.

Treitler, Leo. "Musical Syntax in the Middle Ages: Background to an Aesthetic Problem." *PNM* 4/1 (1965-66):75-85.

Federhofer, Hellmut. "Zur neuesten Literatur über Heinrich Schenker." In *Müller-BlattauFs* (1966):69-79.

Keller, Wilhelm. "Heinrich Schenkers Harmonielehre." In Vogel (1966):203-32.

Kassler, Michael. "A Trinity of Essays: Toward a Theory That Is the Twelve-Note Class System; Toward Development of a Constructive Tonality Theory Based on Writings by Heinrich Schenker; Toward a Simple Programming Language for Musical Information Retrieval." Ph.D. dissertation, Princeton University, 1967. [*Rilm* 75-2617. *DA* 28/09A, p. 3702. UMI 68-02490.]

[Mitchell, William J., and Salzer, Felix, eds.] "A Glossary of the Elements of Graphic Analysis." *MuF* 1 (1967):260-68.

Regener, Eric. "Layered Music-Theoretic Systems." *PNM* 6/1 (1967-68):52-62. [*Rilm* 67-2315.]

Slatin, Sonia. "The Theories of Heinrich Schenker in Perspective." Ph.D. dissertation, Columbia University, 1967. [*Rilm* 67-2341. *DA* 28/06A, pp. 2283-84. UMI 67-15521.]

> Review in *CRMEB* 16 (1969):40-43 (Peter Bergquist). See also *ITO* 3/2 (1977-78):4-8 (Henry Martin).

Harris, S. "The Schenkerian Principle." *Composer* 29 (1968):30-32.

Hest, Jeffrey. "A Union Bibliography of the Works of Heinrich Schenker and Works Pertaining to the Schenkerian System of Analysis." Ms., 1968. [New York: Queens College of the City University of New York.] Bibliog.

Komar, Arthur J. "Theory of Suspensions: A Study of Metrical and Pitch Relationships in Tonal Music." Ph.D. dissertation, Princeton University, 1968; published edition (PSM, no. 5), Princeton, N.J.: Princeton University Press, 1971; Austin, Texas: Peer Publications, 1979. [*Rilm* 68-4049. *DA* 29/10A, p. 3633.]

> Reviews in *AJME* 9 (1971):55 (Andrew D. McCredie), *Choice* 8/9 (1971-72):1186, *JMT* 16/1-2 (1972):210-19 (John Rothgeb), *MQ* 59/2 (1973):320-22 (Christopher Hatch), and *Notes* 29/1 (1972-73):52-54 (Graham George).

Beach, David. "A Schenker Bibliography." *JMT* 13/1 (1969):2-37; reprinted in Yeston (1977):273-311, below. Bibliog. [*Rilm* 69-161.]

> See also Beach (1979), below, and Beach (1985), below.

Salzer, Felix, and Schachter, Carl. *Counterpoint in Composition: The Study of Voice Leading.* New York: McGraw-Hill, 1969. [*Rilm* 69-2739.]

> Reviews in *BzMw* 13/3 (1971):226-27 (Jürgen Wilbrandt), *Dmt* 45/4 (1970):112-13 (Morten Levy), *JMT* 13/2 (1969):307-16 (John Rothgeb), *MiE* 34/341 (1970):36 (Leslie Orrey), *MuMus* 20/11 [239] (1971-72):46-47 (Watkins Shaw), and *PNM* 8/1 (1969-70):151-54 (Stanley Persky).

Kudlawiec, Dennis Paul. "The Adaptation of Schenkerian Concepts of Musical Structure to the Analysis Segment of Basic Theory Courses at the College Level." Ed.D. dissertation, The University of Illinois, 1970. [*DA* 31/12A, pp. 6649-50. UMI 71-14836.]

Beeson, Roger A. "Background and Model—A Concept in Musical Analysis." *MR* 32/4 (1971):349-59.

Komar, Arthur, ed. *Schumann: Dichterliebe.* NCS. New York: W. W. Norton, 1971.

Includes excerpts from (1906-35):(1935), above, from Forte (1959/1977), above, and from Salzer (1952/.../1983), above.

Rothgeb, John. "Design as a Key to Structure in Tonal Music." *JMT* 15/1-2 (1971):230-53; reprinted in Yeston (1977):72-93, below. [*Rilm* 72-1092.]

Walker, Alan. "Schenker: A Musician's Musician." *Composer* 43 (1972):9-10.

Gould, Murray J. "Species Counterpoint and Tonal Structure." Ph.D. dissertation, New York University, 1973. [*DA* 34/08A, pp. 5227-28. UMI 74-01984.]

Zuckerkandl, Victor. *Sound and Symbol. Vol. 2: Man the Musician.* Translated by Norbert Guterman. BS, no. 44:2. Princeton, N.J.: Princeton University Press, 1973.

> Reviews in *AMT* 24/6 (1975):57-58 (David Zakeri Kushner), *BJA* 15/3 (1975):278-81 (K. Mitchells), *JAAC* 33/3 (1974-75):354-56 (Bruce N. Morton), *ML* 55/3 (1974):347-48 (Richard Middleton), *MQ* 62/2 (1976):285-89 (Edward A. Lippman), *MR* 36/4 (1975):307-9 (Henry B. Raynor), *MT* 115/1576 (1974):477-48 (Eric Sams), and *Notes* 30/4 (1973-74):790-92 (Daniel Brown).

Austin, John Charles. "A Survey of the Influence of Heinrich Schenker on American Music Theory and Its Pedagogy since 1940." M.M. thesis, North Texas State University, 1974. [*MAb* 13/2, p. 87. UMI 13-06953.]

Bent, Ian D. "Current Methods in Stylistic Analysis." *Congress Copenhagen 1972* (1974):43-45. [*Rilm* 76-1668.]

Hallnäs, Lars. "Heinrich Schenker, Arnold Schering och frågan 'Vad är musik?'." Ph.D. dissertation, The University of Uppsala, 1974.

> Review in *Stfm* 58/1 (1976):44-45.

Levy, Edward. "Structural Analysis in Interdisciplinary Arts Courses." *CMS* 14 (1974):102-21. [*Rilm* 74-3943.]

Narmour, Eugene. "The Melodic Structure of Tonal Music: A Theoretical Study." 2 vols. Ph.D. dissertation, The University of Chicago, 1974. [*Rilm* 77-1557.]

Browne, Richmond. "Initial Readings in Schenker." *ITO* 1/1 (1975):4-5. Bibliog. [*Rilm* 76-4059.]

Gould, Murray. "Schenker's Theory in the World of Teacher and Student." *CMS* 15 (1975):133-49.

> Responses by Richmond Browne, Charles Burkhart, and Oswald Jonas.

Kassler, Michael. *Proving Musical Theorems I: The Middleground of Heinrich Schenker's Theory of Tonality.* TechR, no. 103. Sydney: The University of Sydney, Basser Department of Computer Science, 1975. [*Rilm* 76-15548.]

Levy, Morten. "The Naive Structuralism of Heinrich Schenker." *MForsk* 1 (1975):20-32. [*Rilm* 75-2690.]

"Notes for *Notes*." *Notes* 32/4 (1975-76):744.

311

An announcement concerning the Jonas collection at the University of California, Riverside.

Rothgeb, John. "Strict Counterpoint and Tonal Theory." *JMT* 19/2 (1975):260-84. [*Rilm* 75-4469.]

Frankel, Robert E.; Rosenschein, Stanley J.; and Smoliar, Stephen W. "A LISP-Based System for the Study of Schenkerian Analysis (Report of First Attempts at Modeling Musical Perception on a Digital Computer Using Methodology of Schenker's *Auskomponierung* Theory of Music." *CH* 10/1 (1976):21-32.

Gould, Murray J. "A Commentary on Schenker's Analytic Sketches." In *Brahms: Variations on a Theme of Haydn for Orchestra, Op. 56a and for Two Pianos, Op. 56b* . . ., edited by Donald M. McCorkle, pp. 165-68. NCS. New York: W. W. Norton, 1976. [*Rilm* 76-10326.]

Morgan, Robert P. "Dissonant Prolongation: Theoretical and Compositional Precedents." *JMT* 20/1 (1976):49-91. [*Rilm* 76-1626.]

Schachter, Carl. "Rhythm and Linear Analysis: A Preliminary Study." *MuF* 4 (1976):281-334. [*Rilm* 76-7122.]

Adrian, John Stanley. "Heinrich Schenker's Early Theory of Scale-Step." D.M. dissertation, The University of Alberta, 1977. [*Rilm* 77-1589.]

Hatten, Robert S. "A Critical Re-examination of Schenker's Thought." *ITR* 1/3 (1977-78):22-30.

Kassler, Michael. "Explication of the Middleground of Schenker's Theory of Tonality." *Miscm* 9 (1977):72-81.

Keiler, Allan R. "The Syntax of Prolongation." *ITO* 3/5 (1977-78):3-27.

Narmour, Eugene. *Beyond Schenkerism: The Need for Alternatives in Music Analysis*. Chicago: The University of Chicago Press, 1977. [*Rilm* 77-5699.]

Reviews in *AmO:AGO* 15/1 (1981):12 (Charles Huddleston Heaton), *Choice* 15/3 (1978):410, *HAR* 30/1-2 (1979):114-18 (Annabel Cohen), *Interface* 7/2-3 (1978):169-71 (Frits Weiland), *ITR* 3/1 (1979-80):7-15 (Robert Hatten), *JAAC* 36/4 (1977-78):505-7 (Kay Dreyfus), *JAMS* 32/3 (1979):586-91 (Jan LaRue), *JMT* 23/2 (1979):287-304 (Steven Haflich), *JRME* 26/4 (1978):481-86 (John Rothgeb), *Mf* 33/3 (1980):372-74 (Hellmut Federhofer), *ML* 60/1 (1979):86-90 (Arnold Whittall), *MR* 41/2 (1980):154-55 (Donald Chittum), *MT* 119/1622 (1978):331 (William Drabkin), *NCM* 2/3 (1978-79):267-69 (James McCalla), *Notes* 34/4 (1977-78):857-59 (Ruth A. Solie), *PNM* 17/1 (1978-79):161-96 (Allan Keiler), *PNM* 17/1 (1978-79):196-210 (Henry Martin), *T&P* 3/2 (1978):28-42 (John Rothgeb), and *ZfMt* 9/2 (1978):52-54 (William Earl Caplin).

Schachter, Carl E. "Diversity and the Decline of Literacy in Music Theory." *CMS* 17/1 (1977):150-53. [*Rilm* 77-5702.]

Yeston, Maury, ed. *Readings in Schenker Analysis and Other Approaches*. New Haven, Ct.: Yale University Press, 1977.

Reviews in *Choice* 14/11 (1977-78):1510, *Mf* 33/3 (1980):371-72 (Hellmut Federhofer), *MT* 119/1622 (1978):331 (William Drabkin), *MuMus* 27/6 [318] (1978-79):40-41 (Malcolm Barry), *NCM* 2/3 (1978-79):267-69 (James McCalla), and *ÖM* 33/9 (1978):468.

"Archival Material at the Library of the University of California, Riverside." *Notes* 35/4 (1978-79):863-64.

Burkhart, Charles. "Schenker's 'Motivic Parallelisms'." *JMT* 22/2 (1978):145-75. [*Rilm* 78-6083.]

Frankel, Robert E.; Rosenschein, Stanley J.; and Smoliar, Stephen William. "Schenker's Theory of Tonal Music—Its Explication through Computational Processes." *IJMMS* 10/2 (1978):121-38. Bibliog. [*Rilm* 78-1824.]

Gries, Peter. "Continuity as a Basic Perspective for Piano Teaching: A Discussion of Analytical Techniques and Playing Coordinations for Achieving Aesthetic Continuity in Piano Performance." D.M.A. dissertation, The University of Oregon, 1978. [*Rilm* 79-1475. *DA* 39/10A, pp. 5790-91. UMI 79-07464.]

Johnson, Douglas. "Beethoven Scholars and Beethoven's Sketches." *NCM* 2/1 (1978-79):3-17. [*Rilm* 79-522.]

See also "Viewpoint," *NCM* 2/3 (1978-79):270-79 (Seighard Brandenburg; William Drabkin; Douglas Johnson). [*Rilm* 79-4644.]

Kunselman, Joan D. "The Oswald Jonas Memorial Collection." *WLB* 53/9 (1978-79):624-28.

See also *ITO* 4/4 (1978-79):2 (Judith D. King).

Laskowski, Larry. *Heinrich Schenker: An Annotated Index to His Analyses of Musical Works*. New York: Pendragon Press, 1978.

Reviews in *JMT* 23/2 (1979):304-7 (Harald Krebs) and *Notes* 36/1 (1979-80):98-99 (John Rothgeb).

Morgan, Robert P. "Schenker and the Theoretical Tradition: The Concept of Musical Reduction." *CMS* 18/1 (1978):72-96. [*Rilm* 78-1857.]

Plum, Karl-Otto. "Untersuchung zu Heinrich Schenkers Stimmführungsanalyse." Ph.D. dissertation, The University of Cologne, 1978; published edition (KBzMf, no. 102), Regensburg: Boße, 1979. [*Rilm* 79-1706.]

Reviews in *MA* 2/1 (1983):102-5 (William Drabkin), *Mf* 34/4 (1981):509-11 (Elmar Seidel), and *ML* 62/2 (1981):212-15 (Jonathan Dunsby).

Smith, Charles J. "Beethoven via Schenker: A Review." *ITO* 4/1 (1978-79):37-47. [*Rilm* 78-1748.]

Beach, David W. "A Schenker Bibliography: 1969-1979." *JMT* 23/2 (1979):275-86. Bibliog.

>See also Beach (1969/1977), above, and Beach (1985), below.

Epstein, David. *Beyond Orpheus: Studies in Musical Structure*. Cambridge, Mass.: MIT Press, 1979; Oxford: Oxford University Press, 1987.

>Reviews in *Brio* 24/2 (1987):71-72 (John Wagstaff), *JAAC* 38/4 (1980):480-82 (William Webster), *JASI* 3/2 (1979):194-202 (Jonathan M. Dunsby), *JMT* 25/2 (1981):319-26 (Arnold Whittall) [with rebuttal in *JMT* 26/1 (1982):208-10 (David Epstein) and reply in *JMT* 26/1 (1982):211-12 (Arnold Whittall)], *MA* 2/2 (1983):225-27 (Jonathan Harvey), *ML* 69/3 (1988):407-9 (V. Kofi Agawu), *MuMus* 28/5 (1979-80):38-40 (Malcolm Barry), and *Notes* 36/2 (1979-80):357-58 (Larry Stempel).

Kholopov, Yury Nikolaevich. "Muzykal'no-esteticheskie vzgliady Kh. Shenkera." [H. Schenker's Views on Music Aesthetics.] In *Esteticheskie ocherki* [Essays on Aesthetics], vol. 5, pp. 234-53. Moscow: 1979.

Kunselman, Joan. "Communications." *Am* 51/2 (1979):283-85.

Kunselman, Joan. "Communications." *JMT* 23/1 (1979):151-52.

Kunselman, Joan D. "University of California, Riverside: The Oswald Jonas Memorial Collection." *CM* 28 (1979):7-8.

Lamb, James Boyd. "A Graphic Analysis of Brahms, Opus 118, with an Introduction to Schenkerian Theory and the Reduction Process." Ph.D. dissertation, Texas Tech University, 1979. [*DA* 41/02A, p. 454. UMI 80-13258.]

Lester, Joel. "Articulation of Tonal Structures as a Criterion for Analytical Choices." *MTS* 1 (1979):67-79.

Rahn, John. "Logic, Set Theory, Music Theory." *CMS* 19/1 (1979):114-27. [*Rilm* 79-3653.]

Reynolds, William H. "Comment and Chronicle." *NCM* 3/3 (1979-80):281-82.

Treitler, Leo. "History, Criticism, and Beethoven's *Ninth Symphony*." *NCM* 3/3 (1979-80):193-210. [*Rilm* 80-2147].

Drabkin, William. "Arpeggiation." "Ausfaltung." "Auskomponierung." "Höherlegung." "Koppelung." "Layer." "Oblige Lage." "Prolongation." "Teiler." "Tieferlegung." "Übergreifen." "Unterbrechung." "Untergreifen." "Urlinie." "Ursatz." "Zug (i)." In *NGrove* (1980).

>Review in *MQ* 68/2 (1982):161-81 (Allen Forte).

● ● ●Forte, Allen, with Drabkin, William. "Schenker, Heinrich." In *NGrove* (1980). Bibliog.

Parish, George D. "Tonality: A Multi-leveled System." *MR* 41/1 (1980):52-59. [*Rilm* 80-1892.]

Rahn, John. "On Some Computational Models of Music Theory." *CMJ* 4/2 (1980):66-72.

Schachter, Carl. "Rhythm and Linear Analysis: Durational Reduction." *MuF* 5 (1980):197-232; reprinted in Rosand (1985):Vol. 14, pp. 223-58. [*Rilm* 80-1836.]

Smoliar, Stephen. "A Computer Aid for Schenkerian Analysis." *CMJ* 4/2 (1980):41-59.

Solie, Ruth A. "The Living Work: Organicism and Musical Analysis." *NCM* 4/2 (1980-81):147-56. [*Rilm* 80-5611.]

Whittall, Arnold. "Schenker and the Prospects for Analysis." *MT* 121/1651 (1980):560-62.

Dunsby, Jonathan, and Stopford, John. "The Case for a Schenkerian Semiotic." *MTS* 3 (1981):49-53. [*Rilm* 81-1634.]

Riggins, Herbert Lee. "Heinrich Schenker's Graphic Notation and Contemporary Variants." Ph.D. dissertation, The University of Texas at Austin, 1981. [*Rilm* 81-6212. *DA* 42/11A, p. 4642. UMI 82-08242.]

Riggins, Herbert L. "Change of Register in Schenker's Late Theoretical Works." *ITR* 6/1-2 (1981-83):63-75.

Riggins, Herbert L. "Neighbor Motion and Its Graphic Notation in Schenker's *Free Composition*." *ITO* 6/7 (1981-83):3-11. [*Rilm* 82-5747.]

Rothgeb, John. "Schenkerian Theory: Its Implications for the Undergraduate Curriculum." *MTS* 3 (1981):142-49. [*Rilm* 81-1809.]

>Abstract in *MA* 2/3 (1983):307.

Rothstein, William Nathan. "Rhythm and the Theory of Structural Levels." Ph.D. dissertation, Yale University, 1981. [*Rilm* 81-3732. *DA* 42/06A, p. 2357. UMI 81-25672.]

Wagner, Aleksandra. "Heinrich Schenker ili kakva je zapravo 'Biologija tonova'." *Zvuk* /2 (1981):68-73.

Adorno, Theodor W. "On the Problem of Musical Analysis." Translated and edited by Max Paddison. *MA* 1/2 (1982):169-87. [*Rilm* 82-3835.]

Arias, Enrique Alberto. "The Application of General System Theory to Musical Analysis." *MR* 43/3-4 (1982):236-48. [*Rilm* 82-5733.]

Benjamin, William E. "Models of Underlying Tonal Structure: How Can They Be Abstract, and How Should They Be Abstract?" *MTS* 4 (1982):28-50. [*Rilm* 82-5734.]

Clark, William. "Heinrich Schenker on the Nature of the Seventh Chord." *JMT* 26/2 (1982):221-59. [*Rilm* 82-5760.]

Federhofer, Hellmut. "Heinrich Schenkers Bruckner-Verständnis." *AfMw* 39/3 (1982):198-217. [*Rilm* 82-5140.]

> Abstract in *MA* 2/3 (1983):303.]

Forte, Allen, and Gilbert, Steven E. *Introduction to Schenkerian Analysis.* New York: W. W. Norton, 1982. [*Rilm* 82-5738.]

> Reviews in *ITO* 7/4 (1983-84):45-51 (Peter Bergquist), *JMT* 28/1 (1984):113-23 (Roger Kamien), *MA* 2/3 (1983):281-90 (James Marra), *MQ* 70/2 (1984):269-78 (Joseph Dubiel), *MTS* 6 (1984):110-20 (Larry Laskowski), *Muzyka* 31/4 [123] (1986):91-94 (Andrzej Tuchowski), *NCM* 8/2 (1984-85):164-76 (Richard Swift), *Notes* 41/2 (1984-85):268-70 (Channan Willner), and *Stfm* 69 (1987):160-62.

Hantz, Edwin Charlton. "Towards a Psychology of Tonal Music." Ph.D. dissertation, The University of Michigan, 1982. [*Rilm* 82-1763. *DA* 43/02A, p. 300. UMI 82-15005.]

Lewin, David. "*Auf dem Flüsse*: Image and Background in a Schubert Song." *NCM* 6/1 (1982-83):47-59. [*Rilm* 82-3608.]

Neumeyer, David, and Marcozzi, Rudy T. "An Index to Schenkerian Analyses of Beethoven Piano Sonatas and Symphonies." *ITR* 6/1-2 (1982-83):101-17.

Stern, David. "A Quotation from Josquin in Schenker's *Free Composition*." *T&P* 7/2 (1982):33-40. [*Rilm* 82-5809.]

Tepping, Susan. "An Interview with Felix-Eberhard von Cube." Translated by John Bullard and Susan Tepping. *ITR* 6/1-2 (1982-83):77-100. [*Rilm* 83-1623.]

Yokota, Erisa. "Heinrich Schenker no ongakukan kosatsu—*Harmonielehre* (1906) o chushin to shite." M.A. thesis, Ochanomizu Women's University, Tokyo, 1982. [*Rilm* 82-1503.]

Beach, David, ed. *Aspects of Schenkerian Theory.* New Haven, Ct.: Yale University Press, 1983.

> A collection of articles: "Schenker's Theories: A Pedagogical View" (David Beach); "Thematic Content: A Schenkerian View" (John Rothgeb); "Motive and Text in Four Schubert Songs" (Carl Schachter); "Aspects of Motivic Elaboration in the Opening Movement of Haydn's Piano Sonata in C-Sharp Minor" (Roger Kamien); "Schenker's Theory of Levels and Musical Performance" (Charles Burkhart); "The Analysis of Pre-Baroque Music" (Saul Novack); "Heinrich Schenker and Historical Research: Monteverdi's Madrigal *Oimè, se tanto amate*" (Felix Salzer); "Schenkerian Analysis and Post-Tonal Music" (James Baker); "The *Fantasie-Impromptu*: A Tribute to Beethoven" (Ernst Oster); and "The Dramatic Character of the *Egmont Overture*" (Ernst Oster). Reviews in *Brio* 21/1 (1984):27 (Christopher Marshall), *Choice* 20/8 (1982-83):1147, *ITO* 7/7-8 (1983-84):51-57 (David Allen Damschroder), *JMT* 29/1 (1985):169-77

(Patrick McCreless), *MA* 3/3 (1984):277-83 (Allan R. Keiler), *Mf* 41/1 (1988):88-89 (Hellmut Federhofer), *ML* 65/1 (1984):83-87 (Craig Ayrey), *MusT* 63/7 (1984):20 (John Fenton), *NCM* 8/2 (1984-85):164-75 (Richard Swift), *ÖM* 38/7-8 (1983):452, *T&P* 9/1-2 (1984):119-24 (Christopher Hatch and David Bernstein), and *TLS* 82/4187 (1983):697 (Christopher Wintle).

Dahlhaus, Carl. "Im Namen Schenkers." *Mf* 36/2 (1983):82-87.

> Reply in *Mf* 37/1 (1984):21-24 (Hellmut Federhofer) and in *Mf* 37/1 (1984):24-26 (Karl-Otto Plum). Abstract of the article and replies in *MA* 3/3 (1984):289-92.

Gebuhr, Ann Karen. "Structuralism in Music: A Review of Recent Ideas." Ph.D. dissertation, Indiana University, 1983. [*DA* 44/05A, p. 1235. UMI 83-21374.]

Kassler, Jamie Croy. "Heinrich Schenker's Epistemology and Philosophy of Music: An Essay on the Relations between Evolutionary Theory and Music Theory." In *The Wider Domain of Evolutionary Thought*, edited by David Oldroyd and Ian Langham, pp. 221-260. ASHPS, no. 2. Dordrecht (Holland) and Boston: D. Reidel, 1983. Bibliog. [*Rilm* 83-1614.]

Keiler, Allan. "On Some Properties of Schenker's Pitch Derivations." *MP* 1/2 (1983-84):200-228.

> Abstract in *MA* 3/3 (1984):293-94 (Celia Duffy).

Lerdahl, Fred, and Jackendoff, Ray. *A Generative Theory of Tonal Music.* MITCT. Cambridge, Mass.: MIT Press, 1983. [*Rilm* 83-2083.]

> Reviews in *CJL* 29/2 (1984):157-75 (J. K. Chambers), *CMJ* 8/4 (1984):56-64 (Peter Child), *CPsy* 33/3 (1988):226-28 (Oscar S. M. Marin and John A. Walker), *CUMR* 4 (1983):141-83 (Célestin Deliège), *IJSLP* 29 (1984):189-92 (Emily Klenin), *ITO* 8/6 (1984-85):27-52 (Richard Cohn), *JAAC* 46/1 (1987):94-98 (Robert B. Cantrick), *JAMS* 37/1 (1984):196-205 (Joseph P. Swain), *JMT* 28/2 (1984):271-94 (John Peel and Wayne Slawson), *LiS* 13/1 (1984):133-35 (Steven Feld), *MA* 4/3 (1985):292-303 (David Harvey), *MP* 2/2 (1984-85):275-90 (Burton R. Rosner), *MT* 125/1695 (1984):273 (William Drabkin), *Mth* 2/2 (1987):192-94 (Carl Dahlhaus), *MTS* 7 (1985):190-202 (Edwin Hantz), *Mus* 9 (1986):72-73, *Muzyka* 31/4 [123] (1986):100-106 (Zofia Helman), *Nature* 304/5921 (1983):93 (Christopher Longuet-Higgins), *NCM* 8/2 (1984-85):168-69 (Richard Swift), *Notes* 41/3 (1984-85):502-5 (Frank Retzel), *Psychomusicol* 3/1-2 (1983):60-67 (Henry L. Cady), and *QJEP* 36A/3 (1984):561-62 (John Sloboda).

Lerdahl, Fred, and Jackendoff, Ray. "An Overview of Hierarchical Structures in Music." *MP* 1/2 (1983-84):229-52.

Narmour, Eugene. "Some Major Theoretical Problems Concerning the Concept of Hierarchy in the Analysis of Tonal Music." *MP* 1/2 (1983-84):129-99.

Swain, Joseph Peter. "Limits of Musical Structure." Ph.D. dissertation, Harvard University, 1983. [*Rilm* 83-3891. *DA* 44/06A, p. 1623. UMI 83-22452.]

Barsky, V. "K teorii Kh. Shenkera i *Muzyke nastoyashchego*." *Smuz* /1 (1984):121-22.

Cadwallader, Allen. "Schenker's Unpublished Graphic Analysis of Brahms's Intermezzo Op. 117, No. 2: Tonal Structure and Concealed Motivic Repetition." *MTS* 6 (1984):1-13.

Damschroder, David Allen. "Pedagogically Speaking: Structural Levels and the College Freshman." *ITO* 8/6 (1984-85):17-25.

Deliège, Célestin. *Les fondaments de la musique tonale: Une perspective analytique post-schenkerienne*. Paris: Éditions Jean-Claude Lattès, 1984.

> Reviews in *JMT* 30/1 (1986):122-30 (Joseph P. Swain), *Muzyka* 31/4 [123] (1986):106-10 (Zofia Helman), *Rdm* 73/1 (1987):139-43, and *RmSr* 38/1 (1985):41-42 (Gérard Le Coat).

Drabkin, William. "Felix-Eberhard von Cube and the North-German Tradition of Schenkerism." *PMA 1984-85* 111 (1986):180-207.

> Abstract in *MA* 5/2-3 (1986):305-6.

Holcomb, Margaret Ann. "Rhythmic Theories in Schenkerian Literature: An Alternative View." Ph.D. dissertation, The University of Texas at Austin, 1984. [*DA* 46/02A, p. 296. UMI 85-08280.]

Pastille, William A. "Heinrich Schenker, Anti-Organicist." *NCM* 8/1 (1984-85):29-36.

Rothgeb, John. "Translating Texts on Music Theory: Heinrich Schenker's *Kontrapunkt*." In *Translation Perspectives: Selected Papers, 1982-83*, edited by Marilyn Gaddis Rose, pp. 113-18. Binghamton, N.Y.: National Resource Center for Translation and Interpretation—SUNY/Binghamton, 1984; reprinted in *T&P* 9/1-2 (1984):71-75.

Rothstein, William. "Heinrich Schenker as an Interpreter of Beethoven's Piano Sonatas." *NCM* 8/1 (1984-85):3-28.

> Abstract in *MA* 5/2-3 (1986):310-11.

Wagner, Aleksandra. "Na puta ka novoj teoriji muzike—Heinrich Schenker." *Zvuk* /3 (1984):17-29. Bibliog.

Beach, David. "The Current State of Schenkerian Research." *Am* 57/2 (1985):275-307. Bibliog.

> See also Beach (1969/1977), above, and Beach (1979), above. Abstract in *MA* 6/3 (1987):380-81 (Robert Samuels).

Drabkin, William. "A Lesson in Analysis from Heinrich Schenker: The C Major Prelude from Bach's Well-Tempered Clavier, Book I." *MA* 4/3 (1985):241-58.

Dunsby, Jonathan. "Conference Report: Schenker Symposium." *MA* 4/3 (1985):333-35.

Federhofer, Hellmut. *Heinrich Schenker: Nach Tagebüchern und Briefen in der Oswald Jonas Memorial Collection, University of California, Riverside*. SMw, no. 3. Hildesheim: Georg Olms, 1985. Bibliog.

> Reviews in ●●●*JAMS* 39/3 (1986):667-77 (William Pastille), *MA* 7/2 (1988):233-38 (William Rothstein), *ML* 68/3 (1987):279-81 (William Drabkin), *NZfM* 147/12 (1986):78-79 (Peter Cahn), and *ÖM* 41/6 (1986):337-38 (Rudolf Stephan).

Hoyt, Reed J. "In Defense of Music Analysis." *MQ* 71/1 (1985):38-51.

Johns, Donald. "Aimez-vous Brahms?: A Brief Exchange between Hindemith and Schenker." *HindJb* 14 (1985).

Pancharoen, Natchar. "Distinguishing Musical Styles within the Romantic Era through Schenkerian Analysis." Ph.D. dissertation, Kent State University, 1985. [*DA* 46/05A, pp. 1124-25. UMI 85-14178.]

Pastille, William Alfred. "*Ursatz*: The Musical Philosophy of Heinrich Schenker." Ph.D. dissertation, Cornell University, 1985. [*DA* 46/09A, p. 2481. UMI 85-25718.]

Sloboda, John A. *The Musical Mind: The Cognitive Psychology of Music*. OPS, no. 5. Oxford: Clarendon Press, 1985.

> Reviews in *AJP* 100/1 (1987):132-35 (Stewart H. Hulse), *Apsy* 86 (1986):619 (C. Gérard), *BJME* 3/2 (1986):240-42 (George Pratt), *BJP* 76/4 (1985):551-52 (John Davies), *CPsy* 31/11 (1986): 874-75 (Gerald J. Balzano), *CRMEB* 94 (1987): 77-82 (James W. Sherbon; Kacper Miklaszewski), *JMTP* 2/1 (1988):163-72 (Elizabeth West Marvin), *Leonardo* 20/2 (1987):193 (Allan Shields), *MA* 6/1-2 (1987): 179-92 (Eric Graebner), *Mf* 41/2 (1988):191-92 (Hedga de la Motte-Haber), *ML* 67/3 (1986):320-21 (Christopher Longuet-Higgins), *MP* 3/4 (1986): 427-29 (David Butler), *MPsy* 3 (1986):210-12, *MT* 128/1729 (1987):142-43 (Francis Sparshott), *Nature* 315/6021 (1985):696 (Eric Clarke), *PMS* 61/2 (1985):679, *PsyR* 36/3 (1986):423-24 (Robert W. Lundin), *QJEP* 39A/2 (1987):367-72 (Henry Shaffer), and *Science* 231/4735 (1986):279 (W. Jay Dowling).

Willner, Channan. "Foreword [to issue entitled 'Schenkerian Theory in America: The Early Introductory Articles']." *T&P* 10/1-2 (1985):3-5.

Wintle, Christopher. "Kontra-Schenker: *Largo e mesto* from Beethoven's Op. 10 No. 3." *MA* 4/1-2 (1985):145-82.

Bent, Ian. "Heinrich Schenker, Chopin and Domenico Scarlatti." *MA* 5/2-3 (1986):131-49.

Brown, Matthew. "The Diatonic and the Chromatic in Schenker's Theory of Harmonic Relations." *JMT* 30/1 (1986):1-34.

> Abstract in *MA* 6/3 (1987):383 (Robert Samuels).

Cavett-Dunsby, Esther. "Schenker's Analysis of the *Eroica* Finale." *T&P* 11 (1986):43-51.

Federhofer, Hellmut. "Heinrich Schenker." *Muzyka* 31/4 [123] (1986):5-24.

Gołab, Maciej. "Analiza i dzieło: Na marginesie polemik wokół teorii Heinricha Schenkera." *Muzyka* 31/4 [123] (1986):25-41.

Gołab, Maciej. "Główne nurty badań Schenkerowskich: Bibliografie z lat 1904-1984." *Muzyka* 31/4 [123] (1986):67-84. Bibliog.

Gołab, Maciej. "Leksykon terminologii Schenkerowskiej." *Muzyka* 31/4 [123] (1986):59-66.

Helman, Zofia. "Od metody analitycznej Heinricha Schenkera do generatywnej teorii muzyki tonalnej." *Muzyka* 31/4 [123] (1986):43-58.

Lamblin, André. "L'analyse tonale selon Schenker." *IRASM* 17/2 (1986):187-202.

> Response in *IRASM* 19/1 (1988):117-19 (Jonathan Dunsby). Reply in *IRASM* 19/1 (1988):119 (André Lamblin).

Marston, Nicholas. "Schenker and Forte Reconsidered: Beethoven's Sketches for the Piano Sonata in E, Op. 109." *NCM* 10/1 (1986-87):24-42.

Miller, Malcolm. "Schenkerian Analysis: A Practical Introduction, at Notthingham University 21-2 September 1985." *MA* 5/1 (1986):119-21.

Miller, Patrick. "Report: Symposium on the Life and Music of Heinrich Schenker." *T&P* 11 (1986):5.

Neumeyer, David. "The Urlinie from $\hat{8}$ as a Middleground Phenomenon." *ITO* 9/5-6 (1986-87):3-25.

Riggins, Herbert Lee. "Linear Progressions and Their Graphic Notation in Schenker's Late Theoretical Works." *ThS* 3 (1986):32-46.

Rothstein, William. "The Americanization of Heinrich Schenker." *ITO* 9/1 (1986-87):5-17.

Smith, Charles J. "The Functional Extravagance of Chromatic Chords." *MTS* 8 (1986):94-139.

> Response in *MTS* 9 (1987):173-85 (David Beach). Reply in *MTS* 9 (1987):186-94 (Charles J. Smith).

Cook, Nicholas. "Musical Form and the Listener." *JAAC* 46/1 (1987):23-29.

Don, Gary W. "Goethe and Schenker." *ITO* 10/8 (1987-88):1-14.

Komar, Arthur J. "Pedagogically Speaking: The Pedagogy of Tonal Hierarchy." *ITO* 10/5 (1987-88):23-28.

> Response in *ITO* 10/7 (1987-88):31-35 (Kevin Mooney).

Martin, Henry. "Syntax in Music and Drama." *ITO* 10/1-2 (1987-88):65-78.

Neumeyer, David. "The Ascending *Urlinie*." *JMT* 31/2 (1987):275-303.

Neumeyer, David. "The Three-Part *Ursatz*." *ITO* 10/1-2 (1987-88):3-29.

> Response in *ITO* 10/4 (1987-88):11-31 (Steve Larson). Reply in *ITO* 10/4 (1987-88):33-37 (David Neumeyer).

Schachter, Carl. "Analysis by Key: Another Look at Modulation." *MA* 6/3 (1987):289-318.

Schachter, Carl. "Rhythm and Linear Analysis: Aspects of Meter." *MuF* 6/1 (1987):1-59.

Beach, David. "The Fundamental Line from Scale Degree 8: Criteria for Evaluation." *JMT* 32/2 (1988):271-94.

Cadwallader, Allen. "Prolegomena to a General Description of Motivic Relationships in Tonal Music." *Intégral* 2 (1988):1-35.

Ebcioglu, Kemal. "An Expert System for Harmonizing Four-Part Chorales." *CMJ* 12/3 (1988):43-51.

Forte, Allen. "New Approaches to the Linear Analysis of Music." *JAMS* 41/2 (1988):315-48.

Gołab, Maciej. "Analyse und Werk—zu den Polemiken über Heinrich Schenkers Theorie." *IRASM* 19/2 (1988):197-215.

Graybill, Roger. "Harmonic Circularity in Brahms's F Major Cello Sonata: An Alternative to Schenker's Reading in *Free Composition*." *MTS* 10 (1988):43-55.

Helman, Zofia. "Von Heinrich Schenkers analytischer Methode bis zur generativen Theorie der tonalen Musik." *IRASM* 19/2 (1988):181-95.

Korsyn, Kevin. "Schenker and Kantian Epistemology." *Theoria* 3 (1988):1-58.

Krebs, Harald. "Schenker's Changing View of Rameau: A Comparison of Remarks in *Harmony*, *Counterpoint*, and 'Rameau or Beethoven?'." *Theoria* 3 (1988):59-72.

Lerdahl, Fred. "Tonal Pitch Space." *MP* 5/3 (1988):315-49. Bibliog.

Plum, Karl-Otto. "Towards a Methodology for Schenkerian Analysis." Translated and edited by William Drabkin. *MA* 7/2 (1988):143-64.

Proctor, Gregory, and Riggins, Herbert Lee. "Levels and the Reordering of Chapters in Schenker's *Free Composition*." *MTS* 10 (1988):102-26.

Rast, Nicholas. "A Checklist of Essays and Reviews by Heinrich Schenker." *MA* 7/2 (1988):121-32.

Renwick, William. "Brackets and Beams in Schenker's Graphic Notation." *Theoria* 3 (1988):73-85.

Taruskin, Richard. "The Dark Side of Modern Music [*Music in Fascist Italy* by Harvey Sachs]." *NRep* 3842 (1988):28-34.

McCreless, Patrick. "Schenker and the Norns." In *Analysing Opera: Verdi and Wagner*, edited by Carolyn Abbate and Roger Parker. CSNCM, no. 6. Berkeley, Calif.: The University of California Press, 1989.

Rothstein, William. *Phrase Rhythm in Tonal Music*. New York: Schirmer Books, 1989.

Cadwallader, Allen. *Trends in Schenkerian Research*. New York: Schirmer Books, forthcoming.

> A collection of articles, including "Form and Tonal Process: The Design of Different Structural Levels" (Allen Cadwallader), "The Development of the *Ursatz* in Schenker's Published Works" (William Pastille), "Rhythmic Displacement and Rhythmic Normalization" (William Rothstein), and "Illusory Cadences and Apparent Tonics: The Effect of Motivic Enlargement upon Phrase Structure" (Eric Wen).

Cherlin, Michael. "Hauptmann and Schenker: Two Adaptations of Hegelian Dialectics." *T&P* (forthcoming).

Galand, Joel. "Heinrich Schenker's Theory of Form and Its Application to Historical Criticism." Ph.D. dissertation, Yale University, forthcoming.

Keiler, Allan. *Schenker and Tonal Theory*. Cambridge, Mass.: Harvard University Press, forthcoming.

Kunselman, Joan, and Lang, Robert. *The Oswald Jonas Memorial Collection, Incorporating the Heinrich Schenker Archive at the University of California, Riverside: A Checklist*. In preparation.

McCreless, Patrick. "Schenker and Chromatic Tonicization: A Reappraisal." In *Schenker Studies*, edited by Hedi Siegel. Cambridge: Cambridge University Press, forthcoming.

See also FUX: Federhofer (1982); HALM: (1917-18); (1920); RAMEAU: Lewin (1978-79); RIEMANN: (1898):Mickelsen (1970/1977) and Review (Solie); Federhofer (1958); Christensen (1981-83); SCHOENBERG: (1950):Stein (1975/. . ./1984); Rexroth (1969/ 1971); Dahlhaus (1973-74); Dunsby (1977-78); Simms (1977-78); Dunsby (1980); Federhofer (1981/1982); Phipps (1983); Phipps (1986); Lewis (1987); SIMPSON: Breslauer (1988); VOGLER: Grave (1980); LITERATURE SUPPLEMENT: Albersheim (1980); Apfel (1967); Austin (1966); Babbitt (1961/1972), (1987); Badura-Skoda (1983); Barford (1975); Beach (1967), (1974), (1983); Beiche ["Inversio"] (1972-); Benjamin (1981); ● ● ● **Bent** ["Analysis"] **(1980/1987)**; Berger (1980); Berry (1985); Billeter (1970/1971); Blumröder (1972-); Böckl (1972); Brewer (1967); Bridges (1984); Broyles (1982-83), (1983); Burdick (1977), (1977-78); Burke (1963); Carpenter (1988); Cavett-Dunsby (1988); Chew (1980), (1983); Cole (1988); Cook (1987); Dadelsen (1972); **Dahlhaus** ["Untersuchungen"] (1966/ . . ./1988), (1970/1983), (1972), (1975/1977), ["Harmony"] **(1980)**, ["Hindemiths"] (1983), ["Tonalität"] (1983), **(1984)**; de Zeeuw (1983); Drabkin (1985); Dunsby and Whittall (1988); Federhofer (1944/1950), (1980), (1981), (1985), (1989); Flechsig (1977); Gjerdingen (1988); Godwin (1987); Goldschmidt and Brenneis (1976); Greenberg (1975-76); Gut (1972-); Harris (1969); Henneberg (1972/1974); Jeppesen (1922/. . ./1970), (1930/. . ./1974), (1935); Jorgenson (1957); Kaufmann (1969); Kauko (1958); Kerman (1980-81), (1985); Konecne (1984); Kramer (1987-88); Krantz (1989); Krumhansl (1983-84); Lerdahl (1988); Lester (1979-81); Levenson (1981); Lewin (1977), (1981); Lindley (1982); Mann (1987); McQuere (1983); Mitchell, J. W. (1963); Morgan (1969), (1978); **Neumann** [*Essays*] **(1982)**, (1986); Newman (1963/. . ./1983); Norton (1984); **Palisca** ["Theory"] **(1980)**; Parncutt (1988-89); Phipps (1984); **Powers** ["Mode"] **(1980)**; Ratner (1949); Reese (1957/1970); Rohwer (1949-68); Rosen (1971/. . ./1983); Rosenblum (1988); Rothschild (1961); Sachs (1972-); Schäfke (1934/1964); Scher (1975); Schering (1930/1974); Schoffman ["Descriptive"] (1983), ["Pedal"] (1983); Scholz (1981/1983); Schuhmacher ["Notwendige Ergänzung"] (1974); Schulenberg (1982), (1984), (1985-86); Seidel (1972-); **Seidel and Cooper (1986)**; Serwer (1974); Shellhous (1988); Silberman (1949); Solie (1977); Stein (1983); Swain (1983); Tenney (1988); Thaler (1984); Thompson (1980); Thomson (1952), (1983-84); Tittel (1959); Treibitz (1983); Vertrees (1974); Walsh (1984-85); **Wason (1981/1985)**, (1983); Wintle (1982); Yeston (1974/1976), (1975); **Zaminer (1985)**; Zychowicz (1984).

CYRIACUS SCHNEEGASS

[1546 – 1597]

With his *Nova et exquisita monochordi dimensio* (1590) Cyriacus Schneegass joined the ranks of musicians who sought to improve the methods by which tuning was accomplished. He advocated a tempered fifth with the ratio of 160:107 (i.e., 696.6 cents), and though his suggested procedures do not in fact corroborate this ratio [see Barbour (1951/. . ./1972)], the resultant temperament was serviceable. Two major currents of later theory are anticipated in *Isagoges musicae libri duo* (1591), a manual written in the tradition of FABER's and DRESSLER's works on *musica poetica*. In the preface Schneegass drew a parallel between the three consonant pitches of a triad and the Trinity of Christian theology. (Thus LIPPIUS cannot be regarded as the first theorist to make such an association.) Furthermore, his consideration of the five-three, six-three, and six-four chord types might be viewed as an early precursor of inversion theory.

Nova et exquisita monochordi dimensio . . . [*Rism* B/VI/2, p. 768.]

     Erfurt: Georgius Baumann, 1590.

Isagoges musicae, non ita pridem in lucem editae, methodus

     Erfurt: 1591.

Isagoges musicae libri duo . . . [*Rism* B/VI/2, pp. 767-68.]

     Erfurt: Georgius Baumann, 1591. [SMLMS.]
     Erfurt: Georgius Baumann, 1596.

Deutsche Musica für die Kinder und andere so nicht sonderlich Latein verstehen . . . [*Rism* B/VI/2, p. 767.]

     Erfurt: Georgius Baumann, 1592.

         At least two other editions through 1625.

LITERATURE:

Dahlhaus, Carl. "Schneegaß, Cyriacus." In *MGG* (1949-68).

Flindell, E. Fred. "Schneegass, Cyriacus." In *NGrove* (1980). Bibliog.

See also CALVISIUS: Dahlhaus (1956); FÉTIS: (1833-44); LIPPIUS: Rivera (1974/1980); WALTHER: (1732); LITERATURE SUPPLEMENT: ● ● ● **Apfel (1981)**; Atcherson (1960); Barbieri (1983); **Barbour (1951/. . ./1972)**; Becker (1836-39/1964); Dahlhaus ["Dreiklang"] (1955), ["Termini"] (1955), ["Untersuchungen"] (1966/. . ./1988); **Dahlhaus et al. (1987)**; Eitner (1900-1904/1959-60); Fellerer ["Zur Kontrapunktlehre"] (1972); Forkel (1792/1962); Gerber (1812-14/1966); Gissel (1980/1983), (1986); Haase (1969); Harrán (1986); Hüschen (1986); Luoma (1976); Meier (1963), (1969), (1974/1988); Rivera (1978); Ruhnke (1974); Taddie (1984); Walker (1987).

ARNOLD SCHOENBERG

[1874 – 1951]

The early twentieth century's most radical compositional innovator, Arnold Schoenberg, was also one of its most dedicated and influential teachers of tonal practice. He sought to develop an understanding of tonal procedures — including elements such as harmony, counterpoint, and form, as well as procedures fostering variation and coherence — in part as a basis for new modes of expression. Even at a time when his own style had far surpassed the boundaries of late-Romantic chromatic tonality, he dutifully instilled in his pupils the same rapport with the tonal tradition that had served as the foundation for his own development.

With the exception of *Harmonielehre* (1911), which was created in part to prove his worthiness for appointment to a professorship in Vienna, Schoenberg's legacy amounts to a large assemblage of essays and teaching materials, some of which were pieced together after his death by his senior pupils from the war years and after in California. Schoenberg, a Jew, had moved to the United States in 1933 upon the termination of his tenure at the Prussian Academy of Arts in Berlin. He found his students at the University of Southern California and, later, at the University of California at Los Angeles, to be considerably less well prepared than those he had taught in Vienna and Berlin. Yet another Webern or Berg would have been difficult to lure anywhere, let alone in the California of the 1930s. As a result of a course load that included even the most rudimentary of topics

(taught in part by his assistants), Schoenberg and his pupils/editors assembled an influential series of texts: *Models for Beginners in Composition* (1942), *Structural Functions of Harmony* (1954), *Preliminary Exercises in Counterpoint* (1963), and a manual on form, *Fundamentals of Musical Composition* (1967). Another manuscript (intended as a book) in which Schoenberg pondered compositional problems of a higher order — "Der musikalische Gedanke und die Logik, Technik und Kunst seiner Darstellung" (1934-36) — is the focus of the most recent editorial project. Even posthumously, Schoenberg's ideas continue to proliferate.

Though he failed to acknowlege his debt to past pedagogical traditions, Schoenberg drew upon the Viennese perspective developed by SECHTER and taught by BRUCKNER. Even SCHENKER claimed that Schoenberg had assimilated ideas from his own *Harmonielehre* (1906). (Schoenberg continued to follow SCHENKER's work through the early 1920s.) Yet Schoenberg's notions are decidedly non-Schenkerian. As a composer of music in which dissonances were freed of their former obligation to resolve in a specific manner — the so-called "emancipation of the dissonance" — it is not surprising that Schoenberg had little interest in the hierarchical differentiations that separate harmonic from non-harmonic tones. To Schoenberg, Bach's historical role in so rigorously controlling the contexts for dissonant pitches was to facilitate the gradual acceptance of such sounds by the ear, so that in a later period—that which Schoenberg himself inaugurated—any pitch might serve as an element of the harmony. Schoenberg conceived of harmony as a succession of root functions. His students were expected to create their own root progressions illustrating given techniques. In the process, he declared void the very procedures—figured bass realization and the harmonization of melodies—through which musical craftsmanship traditionally had been attained.

Schoenberg's harmonic perspective is particularly useful for the study of works of the late nineteenth century. His posthumous *Structural Functions of Harmony* contains numerous examples from the repertoire, including many samples by composers who were rejected by SCHENKER. Schoenberg supplied innovative strategies and concepts for revealing how the various chords of a composition interact with one another. Perhaps most provocative is his conception of a "monotonality" which embraces all of the various subsidiary tonal regions that constitute a work. He developed ingenious charts which show the various tonal centers that might potentially occur in major and in minor, such as the flat mediant's major dominant (B-flat major in the context of C major), the flat submediant minor's submediant major (F-flat major in the context of C major), and the sharp submediant major (F-sharp major in the context of A minor). The incorporation of concepts such as substitutes (chromatically altered pitches), transformations (a variety of altered chords), and vagrant and roving harmonies (whose resolutions are subject to considerable variability) creates an elaborate set of possibilities for analyzing challenging progressions. His analyses show chords which he interpreted simultaneously in as many as three different keys (such as a B-major chord as V in the tonic key E major, as I in the dominant key, and as IV in the supertonic [major] key—in his Example 136i, from his own *Pelleas und Melisande*). Many of the Roman numerals are marked with a horizontal line through their centers to indicate some alteration from the pure diatonic state, while occasionally Schoenberg analyzed a passage as "ROVING - - - - -".

The more abstract aspects of Schoenberg's thought have also received considerable attention. A collection of Schoenberg's writings was assembled shortly before his death and published as *Style and Idea* (1950). The volume includes his essay "Composition with Twelve Tones," a revision of a lecture that he presented in 1934 at Princeton. A more comprehensive edition of his writings appeared under the same title in 1975. Spanish, Italian, Japanese, German, and French collections have been published as well. Recent scholarship has emphasized his notions of "musikalische Gedanke" (musical idea) and "Developing Variation" (local motivic variations of the features of rhythm and interval). Thanks to his numerous and devoted students and advo-

cates, Schoenberg's provocative and inspired perspective lives on as a vital force in modern musical thought.

Correspondence with Heinrich SCHENKER

> Mss., 1903-7. [Missing. Photocopies at Riverside, Cal.: The University of California at Riverside, Oswald Jonas Memorial Collection.]

> ST ● Erwin, Charlotte E., and Simms, Bryan R. "Schoenberg's Correspondence with Heinrich Schenker." *JASI* 5/1 (1981):22-43. Bibliog. [*Rilm* 81-2905.]

Harmonielehre

> Leipzig and Vienna: Universal Edition, 1911.
> Leipzig and Vienna: Universal Edition, 1922. 3rd edition, revised.

>> Other editions through 1966 (with editorial contributions by Joseph Rufer). Review in *ML* 37/4 (1956):394 (Mosco Carner).

> T ● Adams, Robert D. W., trans. *Theory of Harmony*. New York: Philosophical Library, 1948; reprint edition, Ann Arbor, Mich.: University Microfilms, 1970.

>> An abridgment. Reviews in *Metronome* 66/1 (1950):31-32 (Barry Ulanov), *MT* 90/1271 (1949):14 (Mosco Carner), and *Notes* 5/4 (1947-48):574-75 (Luther Noss).

> T ● Manzoni, Giacomo, trans. *Manuale di armonia*. 2 vols. Edited by Luigi Rognoni. Csal, no. 28. Milan: Saggiatore, 1963.

> T ● Carter, Roy Everett, trans. "Arnold Schoenberg's *Harmonielehre*: A Complete English Translation." 2 vols. Ph.D. dissertation, The Florida State University, 1971; published edition (as *Theory of Harmony*), Berkeley and Los Angeles: The University of California Press, 1978; (CLRS, no. 121), 1983; London: Faber & Faber, 1978. [*Rilm* 76-15397. *DA* 35/06A, p. 3790.]

>> Reviews in *Composer* 79 (1983):29 (Charles Edwards), *JASI* 3 (1979):179-86 (Claudio Spies), ● ● *JMT* 25/2 (1981):307-16 (Robert W. Wason), *ML* 60/2 (1979):220-22 (Derrick Puffett), *MR* 40/1 (1979):57-58 (Arnold Whittall), *MTS* 4 (1982):155-62 (Bryan R. Simms), *Musikrevy* 33/5 (1978):245 (Holger Larsen), *MusT* 62/10 (1983):29 (David Biermann), *Notes* 36/1 (1979-80):86-88 (Mark DeVoto), *SAMT* 94 (1979):19f, and *Tempo* 127 (1978):35-37 (Peter Paul Nash).

> S ● Klemm, Eberhardt, ed. Facsimile of the 1922 edition. Leipzig: Peters, 1977.

Review in *MG* 33/6 (1983):440 (Frank Schneider).

T ● Gubisch, Gérard, trans. *Traité d'harmonie*. CMm. Paris: J. C. Lattès, 1983.

Review in *RmSr* 36/4 (1983):171-73.

S ● A number of excerpts from *Harmonielehre* have been printed. See Bailey (1980), below, for a listing.

"Das Komponieren mit selbständigen Stimmen: Kritik der alten Kontrapunkt-Lehrmethode und Aufstellung einer neuen"

Ms., 1911. [Vienna: Universal Edition.]

S ● Stephan, Rudolf, ed. "Schönbergs Entwurf über 'Das Komponieren mit selbständigen Stimmen'." *AfMw* 29/4 (1972):239-56. [*Rilm* 73-1208.]

Comments on Busoni's *Entwurf einer neuen Ästhetik der Tonkunst* (1907)

Ms., [ca. 1917].

S ● Stuckenschmidt, H. H., ed. Facsimile of the 1916 edition, with Schoenberg's comments published as an appendix. BSu, no. 397. Frankfurt am Main: Insel Verlag; Suhrkamp Verlag, 1974.

Reviews in *Melos/NZfM* 1/2 (1975):148-49 (Wolfgang Dömling) and *Mf* 30/3 (1977):384-85 (Wolfgang Dömling).

"Instrumentationslehre"

Mss., 1917-49.

"Die Lehre von Kontrapunkt"

Ms., 1926.

Stems from (1911), above, and from "Zusammenhang, Kontrapunkt, Instrumentation, Formenlehre," an unpublished manuscript of 1917. Two later untitled revisions are dated 1936 and 1942. These manuscripts led ultimately to the publication of *Preliminary Exercises in Counterpoint* (1963), below.

"Probleme der Harmonie"

Lecture presented in Berlin, 1927.

T ● Weiss, Adolph, trans. "Problems of Harmony." *ModM* 11/4 (1934):167-87; reprinted in Armitage (1937), below; reprinted in *PNM* 11/2 (1972-73):3-23.

Schoenberg's response to questions from Joseph Yasser regarding this article is published in *JAMS* 6/1 (1953):53-62.

T ● See (1950):Stein (1975/. . ./1984), below.

S ● See (1950):Vojtěch (1976), below.

"Der musikalische Gedanke und die Logik, Technik und Kunst seiner Darstellung"

Ms., 1934-36. [Los Angeles: Arnold Schoenberg Institute, University of Southern California.]

Other related manuscripts and revisions exist (1917-40).

ST ● Carpenter, Patricia, and Neff, Severine, eds. *Schoenberg's Gedanke Manuscripts: A Reconstruction, Edition, and Translation*. New York: Columbia University Press, forthcoming.

Models for Beginners in Composition: Music Examples, Syllabus, and Glossary

Los Angeles: The University of California at Los Angeles, 1942.
New York: G. Schirmer, 1943. Enlarged edition.

Review in *ModM* 21/2 (1943-44):124-25 (Israel Citkowitz) [reprinted in *PNM* 2/2 (1963-64):29-31].

S ● Stein, Leonard, ed. Revised edition. Los Angeles: Belmont Music Publishers; New York: G. Schirmer, 1972.

T ● Stephan, Rudolf, ed. and trans. *Modelle für Anfänger im Kompositionsunterricht*. Vienna: Universal Edition, 1972.

Reviews in *Me* 26/5 (1973):238-39, *Musica* 27/3 (1973):293 (Clemens Kühn), *NMZ* 24/4 (1975-76):16 (Hartmut Lück), *ÖM* 29/6 (1974):316-17 (Walter Pass), and *Rmuz* 23/19 (1979):6.

Style and Idea

New York: Philosophical Library, 1950. Edited and translated (where necessary) by Dika Newlin.
London: Williams & Norgate, 1951.

Reviews in *Critique* 7 (1951):1035-43, *IMus* 49/1 (1950):32 (Hope Stoddard), *LME* 6 (1951):31, *MAm* 70/11 (1950):22 (Cecil Smith), *MC* 143/5 (1951):27, *ML* 31/4 (1950):295-304 (Winton Dean), *MMR* 80/920 (1950):197-200, *MMR* 81/928 (1951):161 (J. H.), *MR* 12/2 (1951):170-71 (E. H. W. Meyerstein), *MT* 91/1292 (1950):382 (Mosco Carner), *MusN* 42 (1950):17, *MusT* 30 (1951):281, *Nmu* 7/25 (1952):65-71 (Michael Greet Field), *Notes* 8/1 (1950-51):167-68 (Richard S. Hill), *NYT* 100/34070 (1951):Sect. 2, p. 7 (Olin Downes), *Strad* 61/724-25 (1950-51):142, 164, *Tempo* 19 (1951):29-30 (Humphrey Searle), and *VV* 11/5 (1950):226.

T ● Esteve, Juan J., trans. *El estilo y la idea*. Introduction by Ramon Barce. Syt, no. 33. Madrid: Taurus, 1951; 2nd edition, 1963.

T ● Moretti, Maria Giovanna, and Pestalozza, Luigi, trans. *Stile e idea*. Edited by Luigi Pestalozza, with a Preface by Luigi Rognoni. Milan: Rusconi & Paolazzi, 1960.

Review in *Rasm* 31/2 (1961):152-54 (g. gr.).

T ● Ueda, Akira, trans. *Ongaku no yoshiki to shiso*. Tokyo: San ichi shobo, 1973.

ST ● Spies, Claudio. "Vortrag / 12 T K / Princeton." *PNM* 13/1 (1974-75):58-136.

This article documents an early version of "Composition with Twelve Tones."

S ● Stein, Leonard, ed. *Style and Idea: Selected Writings of Arnold Schoenberg*. Translated (where necessary) by Leo Black. New York: St. Martin's Press; London: Faber & Faber, 1975; 1982; reprint edition, Berkeley, Calif.: University of California Press, 1984.

Much enlarged from the original edition. Reviews in *AMT* 27/1 (1977-78):41 (E. Eugene Helm), *BJME* 2/2 (1985):214-16 (George Pratt), *Composer* 56 (1975-76):7-9 (Max Harrison), *Mf* 31/1 (1978):97-98 (Reinhold Brinkmann), *MQ* 62/3 (1976):435-41 (George Perle), *MR* 37/2 (1976):153-56 (Ena Steiner), *Notes* 32/3 (1975-76):524-26 (Boris Schwarz), and *PNM* 14/1 (1975-76):174-81 (Seymour Shifrin).

T ● Vojtěch, Ivan, ed. *Arnold Schoenberg: Gesammelte Schriften*. Vol. 1: *Stil und Gedanke; Aufsätze zur Musik*. Translated (where necessary) by Gudrun Budde. Frankfurt: S. Fischer, 1976.

Reviews in *HFS* 16/10 (1977):1926 (Ulrich Schreiber), *JV* 23 (1978):191-92 (Peter Andraschke), *Magyar* 21/2 (1980):210-11 (János Breuer), *Melos/NZfM* 4/6 (1978):548-49 (Rudolf Stephan), *Musica* 31/3 (1977):260 (Wulf Konold), *ÖM* 34/4-5 (1979):231-32 (Walter Szmolyan), *OpW* 18/11 (1977):52 (Peter Dannenberg), and *ZfMp* 3/5 (1978):87-88 (Konrad Vogelsang).

T ● Lisle, Christiane de., trans. *Le style et l'idée*. Paris: Buchet et Chastel, 1977.

Reviews in *Harmonie* 126 (1977):98-99, *Mujeu* 29 (1977):14-17 (Dominique Jameux), and *RmSr* 30/2-3 (1977):79.

T ● See Rosand (1985):Vol. 9, pp. 132-75.

T ● See **Katz and Dahlhaus (1987-)**:Vol. 3.

Structural Functions of Harmony

Posthumously published. Based on Schoenberg manuscripts of the 1940s and collaborations with Leonard Stein.

New York: W. W. Norton; London: Williams & Norgate, 1954. Edited by Humphrey Searle.

Reviews in *Critique* 4/1 (1948):422-28 (René Leibowitz), *Etude* 73/1 (1955):7 (Dale Anderson), *MC* 150/3 [3294] (1954):40 (Harold Schonberg), *MCM* 34/2 (1954-55):13 (Gertrude Friedberg), *ML* 36/1 (1955):80-83 (Colin Mason), *MMR* 85/965 (1955):75-76 (P. T. B.), *MO* 78/927 (1954-55):163-65 (H. H.), *MQ* 41/1 (1955):109-15 (William J. Mitchell), *MT* 96/1343 (1955):23-24 (Mosco Carner), *MusT* 33 (1954):429, *Notes* 11/4 (1953-54):558-59 (Walter Piston), and *Tempo* 36 (1955):29-30 (Erwin Stein).

New York: W. W. Norton; London: Benn, 1969. Revised edition, edited by Leonard Stein.

Reviews in *Composer* 36 (1970):33-34 (W. R. Pasfield), *MiE* 34/341 (1970):36 (Leslie Orrey), *MuMus* 18/4 (1969-70):67 (Bayan Northcott), and *PQ* 18/71 (1970):38.

S ● Reprint of the 1969 edition. London: Faber & Faber, 1983.

Reviews in *MR* 45/3-4 (1984):304-10 (A. F. Leighton Thomas) and *MusT* 64/7 (1985):20 (John Fenton).

T ● Stein, Erwin, trans. *Die formbildenden Tendenzen der Harmonie*. Mainz: B. Schotts Söhne, 1957; 1969.

Reviews in *Melos* 25/12 (1958):400-401 (Willi Reich), *Mens* 13/12 (1958):380-81 (Hennie Schouten), *NZfM* 119/11 (1958):662-63 (Hermann Erpff), and *ÖM* 13/11 (1958):495-96 (Egon Kornauth).

T ● Manzoni, Giacomo, trans. *Funzioni strutturali dell'armonia*. Introduction by Luigi Rognoni. Csal, no. 10. Milan: Saggiatore, 1967.

Review in *Nrmi* 1/3 (1967):609-12 (Roman Vlad).

T ● Ueda, Akira, trans. *Wasei-ho*. Tokyo: Ongaku no tomo, 1968.

T ● See **Katz and Dahlhaus (1987-)**:Vol. 3.

Preliminary Exercises in Counterpoint

Posthumously published. Based upon mss., 1911-50 (see above), in collaboration with Gerald Strang.

London: Faber & Faber, 1963; New York: St. Martin's Press, 1964. Edited by Leonard Stein.

Reviews in *Brio* 25/2 (1988):66 (John Wagstaff), *Dmt* 40/6 (1965):188-91 (Jan Maegaard), *JMT* 9/1 (1965):181-84 (John Verrall), *MEJ* 51/3 (1965):99-100 (John Verrall), *Melos* 32/2 (1965):48-49 (Andres Briner), *Mf* 18/2 (1965):226-28 (Friedrich Neumann), *MJ* 23/2 (1965):80 (Paul

H. Turok), *ML* 45/1 (1964):78-79 (H. K. Andrews), *MT* 104/1449 (1963):795-96 (Alexander Goehr), *MusT* 42/10 (1963):411 (Lionel Salter), *Notes* 22/4 (1965-66):1225-26 (Wendell Margrave), and *Tempo* 66-67 (1963):59 (Edmund Rubbra).

S ● Reprint edition. London: Faber & Faber, 1982.

T ● Saathen, Friedrich, trans. *Vorschule des Kontrapunkts*. Vienna: Universal Edition, 1977.

> Reviews in *Me* 31 (1977):141, *Musica* 31/5 (1977):451-52 (Diether de la Motte), *NMZ* 27/3 (1978-79):18 (Norbert Linke), and *Rmuz* 22/11 (1978):14 (mm).

T ● Yamagata, Shigetaro, trans. *Taiiho nyumon*. Tokyo: Ongaku no tomo, 1977.

Fundamentals of Musical Composition

> Posthumously published. Based on Schoenberg manuscript materials from ca. 1937-48.

New York: St. Martin's Press; London: Faber & Faber, 1967; paperback edition, 1970. Edited by Gerald Strang, with an Introduction by and the collaboration of Leonard Stein. [*Rilm* 68-4090.]

> Reviews in *Composer* 37 (1970):34-35 (Max Harrison), *JRME* 18/1 (1970):95-96 (Richard Swift), *MakM* 74 (1970):21, *MEJ* 55/1 (1968-69):92-93 (Dika Newlin), *Mf* 26/1 (1973):133-34 (Reinhold Brinkmann), *MiE* 32/330 (1968):90, *ML* 49/2 (1968):159-61 (Eric Taylor), *MR* 30/1 (1969):66-67 (Arnold Whittall), *MR* 31/4 (1970):341-43, *MT* 109/1499 (1968):35-36 (Alexander Goehr), *MusT* 49/12 (1970):19 (Lionel Salter), *Notes* 25/2 (1968-69):233-34 (Wendell Margrave), *RCMM* 67/1 (1971-72):28 (Timothy Bond), and *Tempo* 84 (1968):35 (George William Hopkins).

T ● Manzoni, Giacomo, trans. Italian translation. Milan: 1969.

T ● Tallián, Tibor, trans. *A zeneszerzés alapjai*. Budapest: Zenemükiadó, 1971.

> Review in *Magyar* 13/1 (1972):81 (János Breuer).

T ● Yamagata, Shigetaro, and Shigehara, Shinichi, trans. *Sakkyoku no kiso giho*. Tokyo: Ongaku no tomo, 1971. [*Rilm* 73-2603.]

T ● Kolisch, Rudolf, trans. *Die Grundlagen der musikalischen Komposition*. Edited by Rudolf Stephan. Vienna: Universal Edition, 1979.

> Reviews in *HFS* 19 (1980):811, *MB* 11/12 (1979):775 (Christian Möllers), *Me* 33 (1979-80):95 *Mf* 33/4 (1980):543-44 (Hans Oesch), *MG* 31/6 (1980):373-74 (Mathias Hansen), *ÖM* 34/9 (1979):450 (Gottfried Scholz), and *Rmuz* 23/20 (1979):6.

S ● Reprint edition. London: Faber & Faber, 1982.

T ● See **Katz and Dahlhaus (1987-)**:Vol. 3.

See (1950):Stein (1975/. . ./1984), above; Rufer (1959/. . ./1969), below; Bailey (1980), below; McBride (1980), below; and Christensen (1988), below, for more complete accounts of Schoenberg's articles, lectures, manuscripts, and pedagogical materials.

LITERATURE:

Jalowetz, Heinrich. "Die Harmonielehre." In *Arnold Schönberg*, by Alban Berg et al., pp. 49-58. Munich: R. Piper, 1912.

Wellesz, Egon G. *Arnold Schönberg*. Vienna: E. P. Tal (Universal Edition), 1921; reprint edition (edited by Richard Schaal and Carl Dahlhaus; TzMw, no. 101), Wilhelmshaven: Heinrichshofen, 1985; in English (translated by W. H. Kerridge; DILBM), London: J. M. Dent; New York: E. P. Dutton, [1925]; as *Arnold Schoenberg: The Formative Years*, New York: Da Capo Press, 1969.

> Reviews in *AJME* 10 (1972):59-60 (David Symons), *ARG* 35/9 (1968-69):846-47 (Dika Newlin), *ML* 6/3 (1925):276-77, *ML* 50/4 (1969):524-26 (R. T. Beck), *MT* 113/1551 (1972):461-62 (Anthony Payne), *MuMus* 20/6 (1971-72):48-49 (Alexander Goehr), *NQ* 18/12 [216] (1971):480 (R. T. Beck), *NZfM* 147/10 (1986):73 (Albrecht Dumling), *ÖM* 41/11 (1986):608 (Rudolf Stephan), and *TLS* 71/3653 (1972):253.

Stein, Erwin. *Praktischer Leitfaden zu Schönbergs 'Harmonielehre': Ein Hilfsbuch für Lehrer und Schüler*. Vienna: Universal Edition, [1923]; Italian translation (as "Guida pratica . . .") in (1911):Manzoni (1963), above.

> Review in *Rmi* 31/2 (1924):610 (A. E.).

Cort van den Linden, R. "Arnold Schoenberg." *ML* 7/4 (1926):322-31; 8/1 (1927):38-45.

Sewall, Maud G. "Hucbald, Schoenberg, and Others of Parallel Octaves and Fifths." *MQ* 12/2 (1926):248-65.

Weiss, Adolph. "The Lyceum of Schönberg." *ModM* 9/3 (1931-32):99-107.

Armitage, Merle, ed. *Schoenberg*. Foreword by Leopold Stokowski. New York: G. Schirmer, 1937.

Stuckenschmidt, Hans Heinz. "Schönberg, Arnold." In *MGG* (1949-68). Bibliog.

Rufer, Josef. *Das Werk Arnold Schönbergs*. Kassel: Bärenreiter, 1959; 2nd edition, 1975; English edition (as *The Works of Arnold Schoenberg: A Catalogue of His Compositions, Writings, and Paintings*, translated by Dika Newlin), London: Faber & Faber, 1962; New York: Free Press of Glencoe, 1963. Bibliog.

> Reviews in *IME* 2 (1960):86 (Winfried Zillig), *Listener* 69/1762 (1963):39 (Humphrey Searle), *LJ* 88/9 (1963):1886-87 (Catharine K. Miller), *MakM* 51 (1963):19-20, *MAm* 83/6 (1963):36 (Everett Helm), *Melos* 27/7-8 (1960):216-17 (Winfried Zillig), *Mf* 15/4 (1962):403-4 (Carl Dahlhaus), *ML* 44/2 (1963):164-66 (Egon J. Wellesz), *MO* 86/1028 (1962-63):475 (B. R.), *MuL* 95/8 (1963):22 (E. E. P.), *MuMus* 11/9 (1962-63):17 (William Mann), *Musica* 13/12 (1959):815-16 (Willi Reich), *MusT* 42/3 (1963): 129 (J. T.), *Notes* 18/3 (1960-61):409-11 (Dika Newlin), *NS* 64/1659 (1962):933 (David Drew), *NZfM* 121/4 (1960):141 (Ernst Thomas), *Rasm* 30/2 (1960):172-74 (G. M.), *Stfm* 45 (1963):219 (Bengt Hambraeus), *Tempo* 64 (1963):38-40 (Gerald Abraham), and *TLS* 62/3187 (1963):212.

Langlie, Warren M. "Arnold Schoenberg as a Teacher." Ph.D. dissertation, The University of California at Los Angeles, 1960.

Lück, Rudolf. "Die Generalbass-Aussetzungen Arnold Schönbergs." *DJbMw* 8 (1963):26-35.

Oliveri, Giuseppe. "L'opera teorica di Arnold Schoenberg." Thesis, The University of Palermo, 1964-65.

Griesbach, Karl-Rudi. "Der Musiktheoretiker Schönberg: Ein Vorläufer Hindemiths?" *MG* 16/11 (1966):726-29.

Lewin, David. "Inversional Balance as an Organizing Force in Schoenberg's Music and Thought." *PNM* 6/2 (1967-68):1-21.

Pisk, Paul A. "Arnold Schoenberg as Teacher." *ASUCP* 2 (1967):51-53.

Epstein, David Mayer. "Schoenberg's *Grundgestalt* and Total Serialism: Their Relevance to Homophonic Analysis." Ph.D. dissertation, Princeton University, 1968. [*Rilm* 69-2716. *DA* 29/09A, pp. 3168-69. UMI 69-02738.]

Parmentola, Carl. "La *Harmonielehre* di Schoenberg nella crisi del pensiero moderno." *Nmi* 2/1 (1968):81-95. [*Rilm* 75-1589.]

Richter, Lukas. "Schönbergs *Harmonielehre* und die freie Atonalität." *DJbMw* 13 (1968):43-71; related version in *Colloquium Janáček* (1970):339-54. [*Rilm* 70-2552; 71-4427.]

Rexroth, Dieter. "Arnold Schönberg als Theoretiker der tonalen Harmonik." Ph.D. dissertation, The University of Bonn, 1969; published edition, Bonn: Rheinische Friedrich-Wilhelms-Universität, 1971. Bibliog.

Cagianelli, Floriana. *Tra fenomenologia e strutturalismo: L'opera teorica di Schönberg*. Perugia: Salvi, 1971. Bibliog. [*Rilm* 74-2696.]

Dahlhaus, Carl. "Schönbergs Orchesterstück Op. 16, 3 und der Begriff der 'Klangfarbenmelodie'." In *Bericht Bonn 1970* (1971):372-73. [*Rilm* 73-4326.]

Rexroth, Dieter. "Zum Theoretiker Schönberg: Anmerkungen zur *Harmonielehre* von 1911." In *Bericht Bonn 1970* (1971):288-93. [*Rilm* 74-4331.]

Rufer, Josef. "Von der Musik zur Theorie: Der Weg Arnold Schönbergs." *ZfMt* 2/1 (1971):1-3. [*Rilm* 71-1011.]

Spratt, John F. "The Speculative Content of Schoenberg's *Harmonielehre*." *CM* 11 (1971):83-88. [*Rilm* 71-3269.]

Beiche, Michael. "Grundgestalt." "Reihe, Zwölftonreihe." In *HwmT* (1972-). Bibliog.

Dabrowski, Florian. "Arnold Schönberg." *Rf* 6 (1972):65-70. [*Rilm* 72-1916.]

Dahlhaus, Carl. "Schoenberg and Schenker." *PMA 1973-74* 100 (1974):209-15. [*Rilm* 74-3908.]

Federhofer, Hellmut. "Arnold Schönbergs theoretisches Verständnis der Wiener Klassik." *FellererFsII* (1973): 102-9. [*Rilm* 74-3936.]

Goehr, Alexander. "The Theoretical Writings of Arnold Schoenberg." *PMA 1973-74* 100 (1974):85-96; expanded version in *PNM* 13/2 (1974-75):3-16. [*Rilm* 74-2772; 76-10936.]

Kraus, Egon. "Bibliographie: Arnold Schönberg." *MB* 5/2 (1973):79-85. Bibliog.

Breig, Werner. "Schönbergs Begriff des vagierenden Akkordes." In *Bericht Walcker-Stiftung 1972* (1974):83-115. [*Rilm* 76-4031.]

Cone, Edward T. "Sound and Syntax: An Introduction to Schoenberg's Harmony." *PNM* 13/1 (1974-75):21-40. [*Rilm* 74-2714.]

Gerhard, Roberto. "Schoenberg Reminiscences." *PNM* 13/2 (1974-75):57-65.

Gillio, Pier Giuseppe. "Fenomenologia ed espressionismo nell'opera teorica e musicale di A. Schoenberg." Thesis, The University of Turin, 1974-75.

Grandi, Walter, and Grandi, Cesare A. *La verità su Schoenberg teorico*. Padua: G. Zanibon, [1974]. [*Rilm* 76-15340.]

Halbreich, Harry. "Arnold Schoenberg: Discographie critique et éléments de bibliographie." *Harmonie* 99 (1974):29-44. [*Rilm* 75-3313.]

Hilmar, Ernst, ed. *Arnold Schönberg: Gedenkausstellung 1974*. Vienna: Universal Edition, 1974.

> A collection of articles, including "Arnold Schoenberg as an Educator," pp. 92-99 (Warren Langlie) and "Schönbergs *Style and Idea*," pp. 112-18 (Hans Keller).

Meggett, Joan, and Moritz, Ralph. "The Schoenberg Legacy." *Notes* 31/1 (1974-75):30-36.

Stuckenschmidt, H. H. *Schönberg—Leben, Umwelt, Werk*. Zürich: Atlantis, 1974; as *Schoenberg: His Life, World and Work* (translated by Humphrey Searle), London: John Calder, 1977.

Reviews in *Bühne* 193 (1974):26, *HFS* 14/10 (1975):1092-94 (Ulrich Schreiber), *MB* 6/10 (1974):574-75 (Siegfried Borris), *Melos/NZfM* 1/3 (1975):240-41 (Christian Martin Schmidt), *MG* 26/3 (1976):176-78 (Ernst Krause), *MiE* 42/389 (1978):37 (Paul Griffiths), *ML* 56/2 (1975):212-14 (Mosco Carner), *MO* 101/1210 (1978):470-71 (Adrian Thorne), *MQ* 61/3 (1975):476-81 (Alexander L. Ringer), *MR* 39/2 (1978):135-38 (Ena Steiner), *MT* 119 (1978):597 (Jonathan Harvey), *MuMus* 27/3 (1978-79):49 (Adrian Jack), *Musica* 28/3 (1974):269-70 (Wolfram Schwinger), *MusT* 57/7 (1978):26 (John Fenton), *NMZ* 24/4 (1975-76):16 (Hartmut Lück), *ÖM* 30/3 (1975):144 (Walter Szmolyan), *OpW* /10 (1974):40 (Erich Limmert), *Orch* 23/4 (1975):278 (Wolfgang Schreiber), *SMz* 114/6 (1974):373, *Tatzlil* 16 [vol. 9] (1976):61-62, *Tempo* 111 (1974):44-49 (Michael Graubart), and *WM* 16/4 (1974):51-57 (Brigitte Schiffer).

Pisk, Paul A. "Arnold Schoenberg, the Teacher." *AMT* 24/3 (1975):12-13.

Harris, Donald. "Some Thoughts on the Teacher-Student Relationship between Arnold Schoenberg and Alban Berg." *PNM* 15/2 (1976-77):133-44. [*Rilm* 77-3035.]

Pilotto, Ornella. "L'evoluzione del pensiero teorico di Arnold Schönberg." Thesis, The University of Milan, 1976-77.

Dunsby, Jonathan M. "Schoenberg and the Writings of Schenker." *JASI* 2/1 (1977-78):26-33. [*Rilm* 77-4899.]

Goehr, Alexander. "Schoenberg's *Gedanke* Manuscript." With a translation by Olga Termini. *JASI* 2/1 (1977-78):4-25. [77-4912.]

Newlin, Dika. "Notes for a Schoenberg Biography: From My Los Angeles Diary, 1939." *JASI* 1/3 (1976-77):126-36. [*Rilm* 77-3083.]

Newlin, Dika. "Arnold Schoenberg in the Classroom, 1939." *MuN* 7/4 (1977):13-19.

Simms, Bryan R. "New Documents in the Schoenberg-Schenker Polemic." *PNM* 16/1 (1977-78):110-24. [*Rilm* 77-3728.]

Lederer, Josef-Horst. "Pfitzner—Schoenberg: Theorie der Gegensätze." *AfMw* 35/4 (1978):297-309. [*Rilm* 78-6425.]

Satoh, Tetsuo, et al. *A Bibliographical Catalog with Discography and a Comprehensive Bibliography of Arnold Schönberg.* KMCLBS, no. 1. Tokyo: Kunitachi Music College, 1978. Bibliog.

Reviews in *Brio* 16/2 (1979):48-49 (Helen Faulkner), *Fam* 27/3-4 (1980):224-25 (Alexander L. Ringer), *MEJ* 67/5 (1981):24, *ML* 61/2 (1980):193-95 (Jonathan Dunsby), and *ÖM* 34/11 (1979):581.

Stephan, Rudolf. "Zum Thema 'Schönberg und Bach'." *BachJb 1978* 64 (1978):232-44. [*Rilm* 78-3098.]

Swarowsky, Hans. "Schönberg als Lehrer." In *Bericht Wien 1974* (1978):239-40.

Smith, Joan Allen. "Schoenberg's Way." *PNM* 18/1-2 (1979-80):258-85.

Stein, Leonard. "Foreword: Schoenberg and His Pupils (I)." *JASI* 3/2 (1979):125.

Steiner, Ena. "Correspondence." *JASI* 3/1 (1979):114-16.

Steuermann, Clara. "From the Archives: Schoenberg's Library Catalogue." *JASI* 3/2 (1979):203-18.

Zam, Maurice. "How Schoenberg Came to UCLA." *JASI* 3/2 (1979):223-27.

Bailey, Walter B. "Schoenberg's Published Articles: A List of Titles, Sources, and Translations." *JASI* 4/2 (1980):155-91. Bibliog. [*Rilm* 80-4842.]

Breuer, János. "Arnold Schoenberg: Pedagógiai koncepciója." *Parlando* 22 (May-June, 1980):8-12, 1-6.

Cross, Charlotte M. "Three Levels of 'Idea' in Schoenberg's Thought and Writings." *CM* 30 (1980):24-36. [*Rilm* 80-3990.]

Dunsby, Jonathan. "Schoenberg on Cadence." *JASI* 4/1 (1980):41-49. [*Rilm* 80-3780.]

McBride, Jerry. "Teaching Materials in the Arnold Schoenberg Institute Archives." *JASI* 4/1 (1980):103-8. [*Rilm* 80-3087.]

● ● ● Musgrave, Michael. "Schoenberg and Theory." *JASI* 4/1 (1980):34-40. [*Rilm* 80-3753.]

Neighbour, O. W. "Schoenberg, Arnold (Franz Walter)." In *NGrove* (1980); reprinted in *The New Grove Second Viennese School* (CBioS; London: Macmillan; New York: W. W. Norton, 1983). Bibliog.

Reviews in *ML* 65/4 (1984):385-87 (Jonathan Dunsby) and *MT* 125/1696 (1984):331 (Marc Rochester).

Newlin, Dika. *Schoenberg Remembered: Diaries and Recollections (1938-76).* New York: Pendragon Press, 1980.

Reviews in *AmM* 1/2 (1983):97-99 (R. John Specht), *JASI* 4/2 (1980):192-95 (Pauline Alderman), *MEJ* 67/4 (1980):75, *Mf* 36/1 (1983):48-49 (Otto Brusatti), *ML* 62/3-4 (1981):402-3 (Jonathan Dunsby), *MR* 43/3-4 (1982):273-76 (Ena Steiner), *Notes* 37/4 (1980-81):861-62 (Steven Stucky), *PQ* 29/112 (1980-81):44-45 (Conrad Wolff), and *Tempo* 137 (1981):44-45 (Peter Paul Nash).

Reiche, Jens Peter. "Zur Frage der Rezeption aussereuropäischer Musik bei Schönberg und Debussy: Anmerkungen zu einer Fussnote in Arnold Schönbergs *Harmonielehre*." In *Bericht Berlin 1974* (1980):516-18. [*Rilm* 80-987.]

Wintle, Christopher W. "Schoenberg's Harmony: Theory and Practice." *JASI* 4/1 (1980):50-67. [*Rilm* 80-3779.]

Alderman, Pauline. "Arnold Schoenberg at USC." *JASI* 5/2 (1981):203-10. [*Rilm* 81-5289.]

Chapman, Roger E. "Modulation in Haydn's Late Piano Trios in the Light of Schoenberg's Theories." In *Proceedings Haydn 1975* (1981):471-75. [*Rilm* 81-6125.]

Federhofer, Hellmut. *Heinrich Schenkers Verhältnis zu Arnold Schönberg.* Anzeiger/Akademie der Wissenschaften in Wien: Philosophische-historische Klasse, no. 118; Jahrg. (1981): Sonderabdruck; no. 23, Vienna: Verlag der o. A. d W, 1981; reprint edition, Mitteilungen der Kommission für Musikforschung, no. 33. Vienna: Verlag der Österreichischen Akademie der Musikwissenschaft, 1982. [*Rilm* 82-1492.]

Frisch, Walter. "Brahms, Developing Variation, and the Schoenberg Critical Tradition." *NCM* 5/3 (1981-82):215-32. [*Rilm* 82-1567.]

Frisch, Walter Miller. "Brahms's Sonata Structures and the Principle of Developing Variation." Ph.D. dissertation, The University of California at Berkeley, 1981; published edition (as *Brahms and the Principle of Developing Variation*), Berkeley, Calif.: University of California Press, 1984. [*Rilm* 81-6152. *DA* 42/07A, p. 2922-23.]

> Reviews in *AMT* 34/5 (1984-85):49 (David Z. Kushner), *CM* 41 (1986):76-80 (Rebecca R. Pechefsky), *JAMS* 38/3 (1985):628-336 (Michael Musgrave), *JASI* 8/1 (1984):78-82 (Ethan Haimo), *JMT* 30/2 (1986):284-85 (William Rothstein), *MA* 7/1 (1988):99-105 (V. Kofi Agawu), *ML* 67/1 (1986):88-90 (Jonathan Dunsby), *MR* 46/3 (1985):221-26 (Michael T. Roeder), *MTS* 9 (1987):204-15 (John Rothgeb), and *Ridm* 22 (1987):333-42.

Stein, Leonard. "Foreword: Tonal or Atonal?" *JASI* 5/2 (1981):121-23. [*Rilm* 81-5257.]

Wells, Alan. "[Schoenberg's Class at USC.]" *JASI* 5/2 (1981):211-12. [*Rilm* 81-5462.]

Blumröder, Christoph von. "Schoenberg and the Concept of 'New Music'." *JASI* 6/1 (1982):96-105. [*Rilm* 82-2736.]

Delaere, Mark. "Een kerngedachte uit Arnold Schönbergs muziekesthetiek: De noodzakelijke historische evolutie van het muzikale materiaal en de muzikale geest." *Rbdm* 36-38 (1982-84):185-206.

Falck, Robert. "Emancipation of the Dissonance." *JASI* 6/1 (1982):106-11. [*Rilm* 82-2759.]

Stephan, Rudolf. "Der musikalische Gedanke bei Schönberg." *ÖM* 37/10 (1982):530-40. [*Rilm* 82-5062.]

Szmolyan, Walter, ed. "Schönberg aus der Sicht seiner Schüler." Translated by Regina Busch. *ÖM* 37/10 (1982):540-44. [*Rilm* 82-5272.]

Carpenter, Patricia. "*Grundgestalt* as Tonal Function." *MTS* 5 (1983):15-38.

Carter, Roy E. "On Translating Schoenberg's *Harmonielehre*." *CMS* 23/2 (1983):164-76.

Federhofer, Hellmut. "Johannes Brahms — Arnold Schoenberg und der Fortschritt." *SzMw* 34 (1983):111-30. [*Rilm* 83-694.]

Gaudibert, Eric. "Une lecture du *Traité d'harmonie* de Schönberg." *RmSr* 36/4 (1983):171-73.

Phipps, Graham H. "A Response to Schenker's Analysis of Chopin's Etude, Op. 10, No. 12, Using Schoenberg's '*Grundgestalt*' Concept." *MQ* 69/4 (1983): 543-69.

Reif, Jo-Ann. "Adrian Leverkühn, Arnold Schoenberg, Theodor Adorno: Theorists Real and Fictitious in Thomas Mann's *Doctor Faustus*." *JASI* 7/1 (1983):102-12.

Carpenter, Patricia. "Musical Form and Musical Idea: Reflections on a Theme of Schoenberg, Hanslick, and Kant." In *LangFs* (1984):394-427.

Christensen, Jean. "The Spiritual and the Material in Schoenberg's Thinking." *ML* 65/4 (1984):337-44.

Dahlhaus, Carl. "Schönberg als Lehrer." *ÖM* 39/6 (1984):282-85.

Hoffmann, Richard, and Stein, Leonard, eds. "A Schoenberg Centennial Symposium at Oberlin College." *JASI* 8/1 (1984):59-77.

Kandinsky, Wassily. "Commentaires sur l'*Harmonielehre* de Schoenberg." Translated by Vincent Barras and Antoine Courvoisier. In *Schoenberg, Kandinsky: Correspondance, écrits. Contrechamps* 2 (1984):93-95.

McBride, Jerry. "*Dem Lehre Arnold Schönberg*." *JASI* 8/1 (1984):30-38.

Neff, Severine. "Aspects of *Grundgestalt* in Schoenberg's First String Quartet, Op. 7." *T&P* 9 (1984):7-56.

Busch, Regina. "On the Horizontal and Vertical Presentation of Musical Ideas and on Musical Space." Translated by Michael Graubart. *Tempo* 154 (1985):2-10; 156-57 (1986):7-15, 21-26.

> See also "The Translator Speaks . . . !" in *Tempo* 157 (1986):26-29 (Michael Graubart).

Franklin, Peter. *The Idea of Music: Schoenberg and Others.* London: Macmillan, 1985.

> Review in *MT* 127/1720 (1986):387-88 (Paul Griffiths).

Phipps, Graham H. "The Logic of Tonality in Strauss's *Don Quixote*: A Schoenbergian Evaluation." *NCM* 9/3 (1985-86):189-205.

McGeary, Thomas. "The Publishing History of *Style and Idea*." *JASI* 9/2 (1986):181-209. Bibliog.

Ballan, Harry Reuben. "Schoenberg's Expansion of Tonality, 1899-1908." Ph.D. dissertation, Yale University, 1986. [*DA* 47/08A, pp. 2786-87. UMI 86-27258.]

Bauer, Glen Alan. "A Contextual Approach to Schoenberg's Atonal Works: Self-Expression, Religion, and

Music Theory." Ph.D. dissertation, Washington University, 1986. [*DA* 47/12A, p. 4224. UMI 87-08365.]

Dineen, P. Murray. "Schoenberg's Concept of Neutralization." *Theoria* 2 (1987):13-38.

Hoffmann, Richard. "Arnold Schönberg (1874-1951)." Translated by Walter Szmolyan. *ÖM* 42/12 (1987):576-77.

Lewis, Christopher. "Mirrors and Metaphors: Reflections on Schoenberg and Nineteenth-Century Tonality." *NCM* 11/1 (1987-88):26-42.

> Abstract in *MA* 7/3 (1988):364 (Celia Duffy).

Christensen, Jean and Jesper. *From Arnold Schoenberg's Literary Legacy: A Catalog of Neglected Items*. DSMB, no. 59. Warren, Mich.: Harmonie Park Press, 1988.

> Review in *MT* 129/1748 (1988):532-33 (Oliver Neighbour).

Dahlhaus, Carl. "Liszt, Schoenberg und die grosse Form: Das Prinzip den Mehrsätzigkeit in der Einsätzigkeit." *Mf* 41/3 (1988):202-13.

Lesemann, Heidi. "The Arnold Schoenberg Institute of the University of Southern California." *AMT* 37/6 (1988):18-21.

Krämer, Ulrich. "Alban Bergs Unterricht bei Schönberg." Ph.D. dissertation, Freie University of Berlin, forthcoming.

See also HELMHOLTZ: Pringsheim (1956); RAMEAU: Lewin (1978-79); RIEMANN (1898): Mickelsen (1970/1977); SCHENKER: Slatin (1967); Epstein (1979); Federhofer (1985); Wintle (1985); LITERATURE SUPPLEMENT: Abel (1980/1982); Albersheim (1980); Allen ["Philosophies"] (1939); Austin (1966); Barford (1975); Beiche ["Dux"] (1972-), ["Inversio"] (1972-); **Bent** ["Analysis"] **(1980/1987)**; Beswick (1950); Billeter (1970/1971); Breig (1972-); Brewer (1967); Burke (1963); **Cahn** (1982); Cavett-Dunsby (1988); Cazden (1948), (1980); Chailley (1967); Chew (1980), (1983); Čolič (1976); Cooper (1974); Dadelsen (1972); **Dahlhaus** ["Untersuchungen"] (1966/. . ./1988), ["Relationes"] (1975), ["Neue Musik"] (1976), ["Harmony"] **(1980)**, ["Tonality"] **(1980)**, ["Hindemiths"] (1983), ["Tonalität"] (1983), **(1984)**; Dunsby and Whittall (1988); Eggebrecht (1975); Federhofer (1944/1950), (1981), (1985); Fischer (1976); Forster (1966); Frischknecht (1979); Frobenius ["Polyphon"] (1972-), ["Vollstimmig"] (1972-); Fubini (1971/1983); Ghislanzoni (1949-51); Godwin (1987); Goldschmidt and Brenneis (1976); Greenberg (1975-76); Gut (1972-); Handschin (1948); Harris (1969); Henneberg (1972/1974); Imig (1969/1970); Jacobi (1957-60/1971); Kerman (1980-81), (1985); Komma (1972); Krumhansl (1983-84); La Motte-Haber (1969); Lawrence (1978); Lerdahl (1988); Lester (1979-81); Lindley (1982); Longyear and Covington (1985); Mahlert and Sunter (1972-); Mann (1987); Mitchell, J. W. (1963); Neumann (1969); Norton (1984); **Palisca** ["Theory"] **(1980)**; Palisca and Spender (1980); Phipps (1984); Reese (1957/1970); Rohwer (1949-68); Rosen (1971/. . ./1983); Sachs (1972-); Schmalzriedt ["Coda"] (1972-), ["Durchführen"] (1972-), ["Exposition"] (1972-), ["Reprise"] (1972-); Schoffman ["Descriptive"] (1983), ["Pedal"] (1983); Schuhmacher ["Notwendige Ergänzung"] (1974); **Seidel and Cooper (1986)**; Shirlaw (1957); Smith (1974); Stein (1983); Subirá (1947/. . ./1958); Taddie (1984); Tenney (1988); Thomson (1952); Tittel (1966); **Todd** (1988-89); Toncitch (1973); Treibitz (1983); Vogel (1955/1954), (1962); **Wason (1981/1985)**, (1988); Weigl (1914-15); Whittall (1980); Wintle (1982); Wolff (1978); **Zaminer (1985)**; Zimmermann (1976); Zychowicz (1984).

WOLFGANG SCHONSLEDER

[1570 – 1651]

By 1631, when Wolfgang Schonsleder's *Architectonice musices universalis* appeared, the concept of chordal succession had attained a position within the theoretical literature. Not surprisingly, theorists immediately began to explore the ramifications of triadic thinking. Schonsleder dealt with the manner in which four-voiced textures could be created from the foundation of an unfigured bass, noting how various pitch successions required specific solutions in terms of appropriate chord choices. The very emphasis upon four-voiced, rather than two- or three-voiced composition (which he regarded as harder and therefore postponed until later) is evidence of the radical change which had occurred.

Schonsleder supplied numerous musical examples by prominent composers, including MONTEVERDI and Frescobaldi, making his categorization of textual elements which could be specially treated (e.g., evocative or descriptive words such as "weep," "ascend," "fast," and "childhood") more vivid than the similar discussion by NUCIUS (1613). He also specified three means of notation: on a ten-line staff, on a grouping of five-line staves, and using tablature.

Architectonice musices universalis, ex qua melopoeam per universa et solida fundamenta musicorum, proprio marte condiscere possi [*Rism* B/VI/2, p. 769.]

Published under the name Volupius Decorus, Musagetes.

Ingolstadt: Wilhelm Eder (Caspar Sutor), 1631. [LCPS: S-048.]
Ingolstadt: Maenrad Zeller, 1684.

LITERATURE:

Stiefel, Eberhard. "Schonsleder, Wolfgang." In *MGG* (1949-68). Bibliog.

Wolff, Hellmuth Christian. *Die Musik der alten Niederländer (15. und 16. Jahrhundert)*. Leipzig: Breitkopf & Härtel, 1956.

> The index for Schonsleder should read pp. 257f. rather than p. 256. Reviews in *JAMS* 14/3 (1961):402-4 (E. H. Sparks), *MMR* 87/980 (1957):69-70 (G. A.), *MR* 18/3 (1957):251-52 (Everett Helm), and *Rdm* 41 (1958):124 (F. Lesure).

● ● ● Buelow, George J. "Schonsleder, Wolfgang." In *NGrove* (1980).

See also FÉTIS: (1833-44); LIPPIUS: Rivera (1974/1980); WALTHER: (1732); LITERATURE SUPPLEMENT: ● ● ● **Apfel (1981)**; Becker (1836-39/1964); Buelow (1972); Bukofzer (1947); Dahlhaus ["Untersuchungen"] (1966/. . ./1988); Dammann (1958/1967); Eitner (1900-1904/1959-60); Feldmann (1958); Ferand (1951); Gerber (1812-14/1966); Mendel (1978); Pietzsch (1936-42/1971); Reese (1954/1959); Rivera (1984); Ruhnke (1949-68); Sachs (1972-); Unger (1941/1969); Walker (1987); Wittwer (1934/1935).

CHRISTOPH GOTTLIEB SCHRÖTER

[1699–1782]

The career of Christoph Gottlieb Schröter typifies the close alliance between keyboardists and theoreticians during the eighteenth century. Figured bass and temperament are among the topics which Schröter addressed, and, not surprisingly, MIZLER's Society and its organ, the *Neue eröffnete musikalische Bibliothek*, aided the dissemination of his views. He assisted in defending J. S. Bach against the criticism of SCHEIBE and, as did MARPURG, found fault with the pronouncements of SORGE.

We possess only a part of what Schröter created on the topic of thoroughbass: his *Deutliche Anweisung zum General-Baß*, published in 1772 but completed as early as 1754, was to have been complemented by a second volume, "Vom vollstimmigen und unbezifferten General-Baß," which was destroyed during hostilities in 1761. The *Anweisung*, even on its own, is a rich repository of the ideas which informed the mature Baroque. Schröter's derivation of dissonance by adding a sixth to rather than stacking a third above a five-three chord reveals some independence from the strong influence of RAMEAU. The preoccupation with chords and their permutations is certainly symptomatic of his era. He also explored the dissonances that were created through the application of an anticipation or suspension in an individual voice.

Sendschreiben an . . . Mizler . . . , in welchem I. der bevorstehenden Reformation der Musik; II. einer Aufgabe wegen der Temperatur; III. einiger nützlicher Erfindungen gedacht; und etliche nöthige Erinnerungen für die Tonkünstler so bescheiden als freymüthig eingeschaltet worden [*Rism* B/VI/2, p. 772.]

Nordhausen: 1738. [LCPS: S-055.]

S ● See MIZLER: (1736-54):Vol. 3/3 (1747):464-77.

"Der musikalischen Intervallen Anzahl und Sitz"

In MIZLER: (1736-54):Vol. 3/4 (1752):685-713.

"Bedenken über Herrn Sorges schmähend angefangenen Streit wider Herrn Marpurgs im Handbuche bescheidenen Vortrag wegen Herleitung der mancherley harmonischen Sätze"

In MARPURG: (1759-63):Vol. 2/4 (1763):448-50.

"Sendschreiben an die Verfasser der kritischen Briefe"

In MARPURG: (1759-63):Vol. 2/4 (1763):417-26.

Deutliche Anweisung zum General-Baß, in beständiger Veränderung des uns angebohrnen harmonischen Dreyklanges, mit zulänglichen Exempeln; wobey ein umständlicher Vorbericht der vornehmsten vom General-Baße handelnden Schriften dieses Jahrhunderts [*Rism* B/VI/2, p. 772.]

Halberstadt: Johann Heinrich Gross, 1772. [LCPS: S-053.]

Letzte Beschäftigung mit musicalischen Dingen; nebst sechs Temperatur-Plänen und einer Noten-Tafel [*Rism* B/VI/2, p. 772.]

Nordhausen: 1782. [LCPS: S-054.]

"Euclides von der Harmonie aus dem Griechischen übersetzen und mit Beispielen erläutert"

Ms. [Lost.]

"Historie der Harmonie und Melodie"

Ms. [Lost.]

"Vom vollstimmigen und unbezifferten General-Baß"

Ms. [Lost.]

A continuation of (1772), above.

See also SCHEIBE: (1737-40):Review (1746-52); TELEMANN, G. P.: (1736-54):(1752):(1752).

LITERATURE:

Oberdörffer, Fritz. "Schröter, Christoph Gottlieb." In *MGG* (1949-68). Bibliog.

Buelow, George J.; Meisel, Maribel; and Belt, Philip R. "Schröter, Christoph Gottlieb." In *NGrove* (1980). Bibliog.

See also ADLUNG: (1758); FÉTIS: (1833-44); (1840); MARPURG: (1759-63); MIZLER: (1736-54):Vol. 3/3 (1747):577-80; RAMEAU: Pischner (1961/. . ./1967); SORGE: (1754); LITERATURE SUPPLEMENT: ● ● ●**Arnold (1931/. . ./1965)**; **Barbour** (1949-68), **(1951/. . ./1972)**; Becker (1836-39/1964); **Benary (1956/ 1961)**; Chevaillier (1925/1931-32) **Dahlhaus et al. (1987)**; David and Mendel (1945/1966); Dreyfus (1987); Eitner (1900-1904/1959-60); Forkel (1792/ 1962); Gerber (1790-92/1977); Hiller (1784); Kauko (1958); Meer (1980); Mendel (1955); Oberdörffer (1949-68); **Ritzel (1967/1968)**; Schering and Wustmann (1941); Sheldon (1981), (1982); **Shirlaw (1917/. . ./1970)**; Sondheimer (1925); Ulrich (1931/1932); Williams, P. (1970).

JOHANN ABRAHAM PETER SCHULZ

[bapt. 1747 – 1800]

Johann Abraham Peter Schulz, a student of KIRNBERGER, became involved in several of his teacher's projects and made lasting contributions of his own. His summary of basic principles from KIRNBERGER's *Kunst des reinen Satzes in der Musik* was published under KIRNBERGER's name as *Die wahren Grundsätze zum Gebrauch der Harmonie* in 1773. Particularly valuable are its two model analyses of works by J. S. Bach. The responsibility for completing music articles for SULZER's *Allgemeine Theorie der schönen Künste* (1771-74) was shared first between SULZER and KIRNBERGER (from the beginning through the article "Modulation," as well as the article "System"), but later SCHULZ replaced SULZER as KIRNBERGER's collaborator, and from the letter S onward he composed the remaining music articles independently. The articles on Sonata and Symphony are among those for which Schulz supplied influential commentary, with emphasis upon a bold and expressive style and a progressive toleration of unpredictability and seeming disorder. KOCH, in particular, drew from Schulz's perspective for both his treatise on composition and his music dictionary.

Entwurf einer neuen und leichtverständlichen Musiktablatur, deren man sich, in Ermangelung der Notentypen, in kritischen und theoretischen Schriften bedienen kann, und derer Zeichen in allen Buchdruckereyen vorräthig sind, nebst einem Probe Exempel [*Rism* B/VI/2, pp. 773-74.]

Berlin: Rellstab, [1786]. [LCPS: S-060.]

S ● In his *Maria und Johannes* [*Rism* A/I/8, p. 17.]. Copenhagen: S. Sønnichsen, 1789.

Gedanken über den Einfluß der Musik auf die Bildung eines Volks, und über deren Einführung in den Schulen der Königl. Dänischen Staaten [*Rism* B/VI/2, p. 774.]

Copenhagen: Christian Gottlob Prost, 1790.

T ● *Oversaettelse af Hr Kapelmester Schulz's Tanker over Musikens Indflydelse paa et Folks Dannelse og sammes Indførelse i Skolerne i de Kongelige Danske Stater.* Copenhagen: N. E. Lycke, 1790. [*Rism* B/VI/2, p. 774.]

"Über die in Sulzers Theorie der schönen Künste unter dem Artikel Verrückung angeführten zwey Beispiele von Pergolesi und Graun, zum Beantwortung einer Aeusserung des Hrn. v. Dittersdorf in Nr. 13 d. 1. Jahrg. der A. M. Z. S. 204 und 205." *AmZ* 2/15-16 (1799-1800):257-65, 273-80.

Response, as "Einige Worte zur Rechtfertigung Marpurgs, und zur Erinnerung an seine Verdienste," in *AmZ* 2/32-34 (1799-1800):553-60, 569-78, 593-600 (Karl Spazier).

See also KIRNBERGER: (1773); SULZER: (1771-74).

LITERATURE:

Reichardt, J. F. "J. A. P. Schulz." *AmZ* 3/10, 11, 36, 37, 38 (1800-1801):153-57, 169-76, 597-606, 613-20, 629-35; reprint edition (edited by Richard Schaal), Kassel: Bärenreiter, [1948].

Rieß, Otto. "Johann Abraham Peter Schulz' Leben." *SIMg* 15 (1913-14):169-270.

Gottwaldt, Heinz, and Hahne, Gerhard. "Schulz, Johann Abraham Peter." In *MGG* (1949-68). Bibliog.

Hahne, Gerhard. "Johann Abraham Peter Schulz' *Gedanken über den Einfluß der Musik auf die Bildung eines Volkes*." In *Musikerziehung in Schleswig-Holstein: Dokumente der Vergangenheit, Aspekte der Gegenwart*, edited by Carl Dahlhaus and Walter Wiora, pp. 54-67. KieSzMw, no. 17. Kassel: Bärenreiter, 1965.

Mainka, Jurgen. "Johann Abraham Peter Schulz und die musikalische Entwicklung im Zeitalter von Sturm und Drang." Habilitationsschrift, The University of Berlin, 1969 (1970).

Barr, Raymond A. "Schulz, Johann Abraham Peter." In *NGrove* (1980). Bibliog.

See also FÉTIS: (1833-44); KIRNBERGER: Zuckermann (1933), Beach (1974); KOCH: Sisman (1982); RIEMANN: (1898), (1903); SULZER: Leo (1907); LITERATURE SUPPLEMENT: Bauman (1977); Beach (1974); Becker (1836-39/1964); Beiche ["Inversio"] (1972-); Blake (1988); **Bent** ["Analysis"] **(1980/ 1987):(1987)**; Broyles (1983); Bruck (1928); Caplin (1978); Cole (1969); **Coover (1980)**; **Dahlhaus (1984)**; Eitner (1900-1904/1959-60); Fischer (1957); Gerber (1790-92/1977); Keller (1955/1965); Kelletat [*Temperatur*] (1960); Laudon (1978); Maier (1984); Mainka (1965/1969); Mann (1987); Mitchell, W. J. (1963); **Neumann** (1979/**1982**), (1981/**1982**), ["Appoggiatura"] (1982); Newman (1963/. . ./1983), (1976); O'Donnell (1979); Orr (1983); Reimer ["Kenner"] (1972-); **Ritzel (1967/1968)**; Rowen (1979); Schering and Wustmann (1941); Schmidt (1979), (1981); Seidel (1972-), (1975); Sheldon (1982); Shellhous (1988); Sisman (1978); Stowell (1985); Todd (1983); Vogel (1955/1954); **Wason (1981/1985)**, (1983); Williams, P. (1970); Wintle (1982); Wirth (1966).

CLAUDIUS SEBASTIANI

[active mid sixteenth century]

The church musician of the mid sixteenth century viewed the musical repertory as divided into two contrasting categories: the traditional chant melodies, and the more recent developments in polyphony. Their seeming incompatibility provided Claudius Sebastiani with a clever framework for his assessment of contemporary musical practices in his *Bellum musicale* (1563), wherein the two opposing camps and their positions are described in the terminology of war, and their strengths and weaknesses assessed in terms of readiness for battle. This conceit had appeared earlier, though less fully developed, with ORNITHOPARCHUS, whose *Musicae activae micrologus* (1517) was an important source for Sebastiani's pronouncements on traditional theory.

Though neither of the two competing "kings" triumphs decisively, the overview of their attributes permits Sebastiani to remind his readers of the various rules and doctrines upon which music had been grounded, but which he feared were being neglected by more recent practitioners of the art. Strict counterpoint is promoted, as is the development of skill in improvisation. His work documents the state of theory in central Europe just before the influx of ZARLINO's formulations and, later in the century, of the more radical notion of monody.

Bellum musicale inter plani et mensuralis cantus reges de principatu in musicae provincia obtinendo contendentes [*Rism* B/VI/2, pp. 776-77.]

> Strasbourg: Paulus Machaeropoeus, 1563. [LCPS: S-065. SMLMS.]

> Perhaps reissued in 1568.

T ● Schlecht, Raymund, trans. *COKK* 14-16 (1875-77); reprint edition, Trier: 1876.

LITERATURE:

Fellerer, Karl Gustav. "Bella musicale (Musikalische Krieg)." *Musik* 30/10 (1938-39):676-79.

Ruhnke, Martin. "Sebastiani, Claudius." In *MGG* (1949-68). Bibliog.

Ruhnke, Martin. "Sebastiani, Claudius." In *NGrove* (1980).

See also FÉTIS: (1833-44); WALTHER: (1732); LITERATURE SUPPLEMENT: **Apfel (1981)**; Becker (1836-39/1964); Eitner (1900-1904/1959-60); Ferand (1951), [*Improvisation*] (1956/1961); Gerber (1790-92/1977), (1812-14/1966); Grusnick (1964-66); Hannas (1934); Harrán (1986); Hawkins (1776/. . ./1969); Sachs (1972-); Taddie (1984).

SIMON SECHTER

[1788–1867]

Viennese music theory and pedagogy around the middle of the nineteenth century were dominated by Simon Sechter, who both interacted briefly with Schubert (on the young yet dying composer's questions concerning fugue) and strongly influenced Anton BRUCKNER, who later succeeded Sechter as a professor at the Vienna Conservatory. Sechter's rise to prominence was gradual: he served for many years as a music instructor at a school for the blind. Eventually private teaching and, when he was past sixty, the professorship, brought him a more favorable position within the Viennese musical scene.

Sechter's was a conservative view of harmony, dependent upon the fundamental-bass theory that had been proposed by RAMEAU and, with some modifications, championed by KIRNBERGER. Sechter used numerals—sometimes even two sets of numerals for analysis in two keys simultaneously—underneath the staff of music notation, along with the letter names of the chords' fundamentals. The seven numerals were tags which could reveal which of the seven scale degrees (*Stufen*) within a particular tonal context was the foundation for a given sonority. Sechter proposed that adjacent harmonies should relate in specific ways, of which descending fifths and thirds were the most favored. The ascent of the scale degree by a second (as in C-D or F-G in C major) was reconciled with the system by positing that such a motion was an abbreviation of a descending third followed by a descending fifth (as in C-A-D or F-D-G). The Viennese emphasis upon scale degrees, adopted by BRUCKNER and influential in SCHENKER's creative development, contrasted RIEMANN's later partitioning of the available harmonies into three basic functional categories. However, Sechter did regard the chords on the first, fourth, and fifth scale degrees as of greater importance than the remaining diatonic steps.

While Sechter resisted the most progressive elements of nineteenth-century practice (his views on chromatic and modulatory techniques, for example, reflect his reluctance to embrace equal temperament), his harmonic perspective nevertheless avoids a rigid harmonic interpretation of every vertical sonority. He displayed how a single scale step could be prolonged through the succession of several chords, advocating a hierarchical interpretation.

Sechter was also a skilled contrapuntist and even made it his habit to compose a fugue every day. His magnum opus, *Die Grundsätze der musikalischen Komposition* (1853-54), proceeds to matters of counterpoint once the "correct succession of fundamental harmonies" and basic aspects of meter and melody harmonization have been addressed. Further material on canon, intended for a later volume of the *Grundsätze*, survives in manuscript. Sechter had earlier edited MARPURG's *Abhandlung von der Fuge* for an edi-

tion published in 1843, further reflecting his commitment to the traditions of eighteenth-century musical thought.

Zergliederung des Finale aus Mozarts 4ter [i.e., 41st] Sinfonie in C, als Muster einer freien Instrumentalfuge

> Vienna: Anton Diabelli, [ca. 1820].

> S ● See MARPURG: (1753-54):[1843]:Vol. 2, pp. 161-93.

> S ● Eckstein, Friedrich, ed. *Das Finale der Jupiter-Symphonie (C Dur) von W. A. Mozart: Analyse von Simon Sechter (1788– 1867)*. Vienna: Wiener Philharmonischer Verlag A. G., 1923.

Zwölf Variationen im strengen Style für das Piano-Forte (Op. 7)

> Vienna: [1824].

Zwölf Versetten und eine Fuge über das Thema des VIIten Werkes (folgt das Thema in Noten wie vorne angegeben) für die Orgel oder das Pianoforte (Op. 12)

> Vienna: [1826].

Zwölf neue Variationen im strengen Style mit einer Schlussfuge, über das Thema des 7ten und 12ten Werkes . . . (Op. 45)

> Vienna: Joseph Czerny-Witzendorf, [ca. 1826-28].

Practische Generalbaß-Schule, bestehend in 120 progressiven und mehrfach ausgeführten Übungen im Generalbasse, mit besonderer Rücksicht auf jene, welche sich im Orgelspiele vervollkommnen wollen (Op. 49)

> Vienna: Joseph Czerny-Witzendorf, [1830].

Practische und im Zusammenhange anschauliche Darstellung, wie aus den einfachen Grundharmonien die verschiedenen Bezifferungen im Generalbasse entstehen . . . (Op. 59)

> Vienna: Artaria, [1834].

Musikalischer Rathgeber; oder, Sichere Mittel, zwey in einer bestimmten Lage gesetzten Accorde, die gleich nacheinander eine fehlerhafte Folge (als verbotene Quinten und Octaven, unharmonische Querstände und unvorbereitetes Eintreten der Dissonanzen) abgeben würden, durch Zwischentöne oder Zwischenaccorde auf verschiedene Arten zu verbinden . . . (Op. 57)

> Vienna: A. Diabelli, [1835].

Die Grundsätze der musikalischen Komposition

1) *Die richtige Folge der Grundharmonien, oder vom Fundamentalbass und dessen Umkehrungen und Stellvertretern*

2) *Von den Gesetzen des Taktes in der Musik; Vom einstimmigen Satze; Die Kunst zu einer gegebenen Melodie die Harmonie zu finden*

3) *Vom drei- und zweistimmigen Satze; Rhythmische Entwürfe; Vom strengen Satze, mit kurzen Andeutungen des freien Satzes; Vom doppelten Contrapunkte*

Leipzig: Breitkopf und Härtel, 1853-54. 3 vols.

T ● Müller, Carl Christian, trans. and ed. *The Correct Order of Fundamental Harmonies: A Treatise on Fundamental Basses, and Their Inversions and Substitutes*. New York: Wm. A. Pond, 1871; numerous editions through 1912.

Translation of Volume 1.

T ● Chenevert, James. "Simon Sechter's *The Principles of Musical Composition*: A Translation of and Commentary on Selected Chapters." Ph.D. dissertation, The University of Wisconsin at Madison, 1989.

"Abhandlung über die musikalisch-akustischen Tonverhältnisse"

Ms. [Vienna: Gesellschaft der Musikfreunde.]

Intended for Part 4 of *Die Grundsätze*.

"Vom Canon"

Ms. [Vienna: Gesellschaft der Musikfreunde.]

Intended for Part 4 of *Die Grundsätze*.

Miscellanea

Mss. [Vienna: Gesellschaft der Musikfreunde.]

See also MARPURG: (1753-54):(1843).

See Zeleny (1938/1979), below, for an overview of Sechter's publications in newspapers.

LITERATURE:

Bagge, Selmar. "Über S. Sechter's Harmonie-System." *AmZ* Neue Folge 2/45-46 (1864):753-58, 769-74.

Müller, Carl Christian. *Additions to S. Sechter's Fundamental Harmonies*. [New York, 1885.]

Müller, Carl Christian. *Tables for the Writing of Exercises in the Study of Harmony, Arranged in Conformity with S. Sechter's "Fundamental Harmonies"* . . . New York: Schirmer, n.d.

Capellen, Georg. *Ist das System Simon Sechters ein geeigneter Ausgangspunkt für die theoretische Wagnerforschung?* SmA, no. 2. Leipzig: Kahnt, 1902.

Waltz, Hermann. "Simon Sechter: Ein verkannter Musiktheoretiker (1788-1867)." *AMuZ* 63/5 (1936):68-69.

Zeleny, Walter. "Die historischen Grundlagen des Theoriesystems von Simon Sechter." Ph.D. dissertation, The University of Vienna, 1938; published edition (WVzMw, no. 10), Tutzing: Schneider, 1979. Bibliog. [*Rilm* 79-748.]

Reviews in *Mf* 34/3 (1981):359-60 (Carl Dahlhaus) and *ÖM* 35/11 (1980):618.

Spivak, Samuel, ed. *Modern Harmony*. 3 vols. New York: Clef Music, 1943.

Related to the translation by Müller, above.

Tittel, Ernst. "Sechter, Simon." In *MGG* (1949-68). Bibliog.

Tittel, Ernst. "Simon Sechter: Zum 100. Todestag am 10. September 1967." *ÖM* 22/9 (1967):550-51. [*Rilm* 68-2127.]

Kier, Herfrid. "Simon Sechter (1788-1867): Zum 100. Todestag des österreichischen Kirchenmusikers und Theoretikers." *Ms:CVO* 88/1 (1968):16-18. [*Rilm* 68-3471.]

Landon, Christa. "Neue Schubert-Funde: Unbekannte Manuskripte im Archiv des Wiener Männergesang-Vereines." *ÖM* 24/5-6 (1969):299-323. [*Rilm* 74-545.]

Landon, Christa. "New Schubert Finds." *MR* 31/3 (1970):215-31.

Nowak, Leopold. "Ein Doppelautograph Sechter-Bruckner." In *FederhoferFs* (1971):252-59; reprinted in BRUCKNER: Nowak (1985). [*Rilm* 73-638.]

Reich, Willi. "Simon Sechter im eigenen Wort." *NZfM* 132/10 (1971):539-41. [*Rilm* 73-1969.]

Arnold, Donna. "Concerning Schubert and Sechter." In *NewlinFs* (1973):24-30. [*Rilm* 73-543.]

Shurtz, H. Paul. "The Small Sacred Choral Works of Anton Bruckner." M.A. dissertation, Brigham Young University, 1976. [*Rilm* 76-5889.]

Mann, Alfred. "Zu Schuberts Studien im strengen Satz." In *Schubert-Kongreß 1978* (1979):127-39. [*Rilm* 79-2809.]

Mann, Alfred. "Zur Kontrapunktlehre Haydns und Mozarts." In *Bericht Mozart* (1979):195-99. [*Rilm* 79-2810.]

Brown, Maurice J. E. "Sechter, Simon." In *NGrove* (1980). Bibliog.

Review in *NCM* 5/2 (1981-82):167-68 (Graham H. Phipps).

● ● ● Caplin, William Earl. "Harmony and Meter in the Theories of Simon Sechter." *MTS* 2 (1980):74-89. [*Rilm* 80-1829.]

Mann, Alfred. "Schubert's Lesson with Sechter." *NCM* 6/2 (1982-83):159-65. [*Rilm* 82-4834.]

See also BRUCKNER: [Teaching Materials]:Schwanzara (1950); Decsey (1906-7); Klose (1927); FÉTIS: (1833-44); KURTH: (1913); RIEMANN: (1898); SCHENKER: Slatin (1967); Morgan (1978); SCHOENBERG: Rexroth (1969/1971); LITERATURE SUPPLEMENT: Abraham (1966); Auhagen (1982/1983); Babbitt (1987); Becker (1836-39/1964); Benjamin (1981); ● ● ● **Bent** ["Analysis"] **(1980/1987)**; Breig (1972-); Burdick (1977-78); Caplin (1981), (1983); Chew (1980); **Dahlhaus** ["Untersuchungen"] (1966/. . ./1988),

["Harmony"] **(1980)**, **(1984)**; **Dahlhaus and Sachs (1980)**; Devore (1987); Dunsby and Whittall (1988); Hoffmann (1974); Horsley [*Fugue: History*] (1966); Imig (1969/1970); Kauko (1958); Kerman (1980-81); Konecne (1984); Levenson (1981); **Mann (1955/. . ./1987)**, (1981), (1987); Müller-Blattau (1923/. . ./1963), (1949-68); Parncutt (1988-89); Phipps (1984); Rohwer (1949-68); Rowen (1979); **Rummenhöller (1967)**; Schmalzriedt ["Episode"] (1972-); Seidel (1975); Smith (1974); Thomson (1960/1978); Tittel (1959), (1966); Todd (1983); Vogel (1962); **Wagner (1974)**; **Wason** ● ● ● **(1981/1985)**, (1983), (1988); Wirth (1966).

JEAN-ADAM SERRE

[1704 – 1788]

When the Swiss scientist Jean-Adam Serre arrived in Paris in 1751, he confronted a major musical controversy arising from Charles-Henri de Blainville's "Essay sur un troisième mode," which had been delivered to the Académie for a response (favorable, as it happens). Blainville was proposing that a third mode be established, beginning on *mi*. Serre opposed this idea and wrote two critical pieces for the *Mercure de France* (1751 and 1752). Nearly fifty years old, Serre thus inaugurated a series of critical essays devoted to specific theorists and their ideas. The Blainville materials, as well as commentary on RAMEAU and EULER, were assembled as *Essais sur les principes de l'harmonie* (1753), while major pieces on d'ALEMBERT and TARTINI, plus a briefer essay on GEMINIANI, constitute his *Observations sur les principes de l'harmonie* (1763), published after his return to Switzerland.

Serre relied little on music examples in his essays. His perspective was philosophical. In reasoned and dispassionate prose he evaluated what he had read and set a course for future developments. RAMEAU's *basse fondamentale* was compared with his own *basse essentiellement fondamentale*. The premises of harmony and its relationship with natural principles were explored, as was the basis for the minor triad. Though his work had some impact during the eighteenth century, it has been relatively neglected since. This is odd, considering the considerable attention RAMEAU's theories and squabbles with d'ALEMBERT have received.

"Lettre . . . sur la nature d'un mode en e-si-mi naturel, et sur son rapport, tant avec le mode majeur, qu'avec le mode mineur"

> Under the pseudonym Philaetius.

> *MdFr* (September 1751):166-70.

S ● See (1753), below.

"Réflexions sur la supposition d'un troisième mode en musique"

> *MdFr* (January 1752):160-73.

S ● See (1753), below.

Essais sur les principes de l'harmonie, où l'on traite de la théorie de l'harmonie en général, des droits respectifs de l'harmonie et de la mélodie, de la basse fondamentale, et de l'origine du mode mineur [*Rism* B/VI/2, p. 780.]

> Paris: Prault fils, 1753. [LCPS: S-073. HoM: 1413. SMLMS.]

>> Reviews in *JTr* (January-February 1753):307-34, 526-47 and *Jds* (May 1753):294-98.

S ● Facsimile edition. MMMLF, ser. 2, no. 52. New York: Broude Brothers, 1967.

S ● Facsimile edition. Hildesheim: Georg Olms, 1970; 1986.

Observations sur les principes de l'harmonie, occasionnées par quelques écrits modernes sur ce sujet, et particuliérement par l'article Fondamental de M. d'Alembert dans l'Encyclopédie, le Traité de théorie musicale de M. Tartini, et le Guide harmonique de M. Geminiani [*Rism* B/VI/2, p. 780.]

> Geneva: Henri-Albert Gosse & Jean Gosse, 1763. [LCPS: S-074. IDC.]

T ● Hiller, Johann Adam, trans. and ed. *WNAMb* 2/7-11 (1767):49-53, 57-60, 65-69, 73-77, 81-84.

>> Translation of excerpts, with commentary.

S ● Facsimile edition. MMMLF, ser. 2, no. 53. New York: Broude Brothers, 1967.

LITERATURE:

Jacobi, Erwin R. "Serre, Jean-Adam." In *MGG* (1949-68).

● ● ● Jacobi, Erwin R. "Jean-Adam Serre, ein vergessener Schweizer Musiktheoretiker." *SMz* 98/4 (1958):145-48. Bibliog.

Cohen, Albert. "Serre, Jean-Adam." In *NGrove*.

See also FÉTIS: (1833-44); MOMIGNY: (1791-1818): (1791); RAMEAU: Collected Works (1967-72):Vols. 3-6; Pischner (1961/. . ./1967); RIE-MANN: (1898); TARTINI: [*Risposta*] (1767); LITERATURE SUPPLEMENT: Becker (1836-39/1964); Bircher (1970); Burke (1963); Burney (1776-89/. . ./1957); Cazden (1948); Chevaillier (1925/1931-32); Cohen (1981); **Dahlhaus et al. (1987)**; Eitner (1900-1904/1959-60); Forkel (1792/1962); Gerber (1790-92/1977); Gut (1972-); **Kassler (1979)**; Kauko (1958); Krehbiel (1964); La Borde (1780/1978); Vogel (1955/1954), (1962), (1975/1984); **Walker (1978)**.

CHRISTOPHER SIMPSON

[ca. 1605 – 1669]

The writings of Christopher Simpson display clarity, conciseness, and practicality. Simpson was addressing performing musicians, not waging campaigns against other treatise authors. His success in this enterprise is confirmed by the existence of numerous printings of his works, as well as by words of praise from his contemporaries and from modern commentators. *The Division-Violist* (1659) treats the mechanics of playing the viol, basic aspects of theory, and techniques of division, such as breaking the ground ("dividing its Notes into more diminute Notes"), descant division ("that which makes a Different-concording-part unto the Ground"), and "a Mixture of Those, one with the other." Later editions include parallel texts in Latin and English. *A Compendium of Practical Musick* (1667), a more extended volume, includes five sections: "The Rudiments of Song," "The Principles of Composition," "The Use of Discords," "The Form of Figurate Descant," and "The Contrivance of Canon." Derived in part from materials in *The Division-Violist*, it appeared in various forms well into the eighteenth century, sometimes with the modified title *A Compendium: or, Introduction to Practical Music*. The brief *Principles of Practical Musick* (1665) was incorporated, in revised form, within the *Compendium*.

The Division-Violist; or, An Introduction to the Playing upon a Ground . . . [*Rism* B/VI/2, pp. 785-86.]

London: William Godbid (J. Playford), 1659. [LCPS: S-084. HoM: 1429. SMLMS.]

> Later editions, under the title *Chelys, minuritionum artificio exornata . . ./The Division-Viol: or, The Art of Playing Ex tempore upon a Ground*, with parallel Latin translation by William Marsh:

London: Henry Brome (William Godbid), 1665 or 1667. [LCPS: S-085. HoM: 1424. SMLMS.]

> This edition appeared in 1667 after a delay of two years. In many copies the date has been corrected with a hand stamp ("II" added to "M.DC.LXV.").

London: Richard Meares & Alexander Livingstone (William Pearson), 1712.

S ● Dolmetsch, Nathalie, ed. Facsimile of the 1665 [1667] edition. London: Curwen; New York: Schirmer, 1955; reprint edition, 1965.

ST ● Eggers, Wolfgang, ed. and tr. Facsimile of the 1665 [1667] edition, with German translation. MwS, no. 20. Munich: Emil Katzbichler, 1983.

> Review in *Mf* 39/1 (1986):93-95 (Bernhard R. Appel).

T ● Appel, Bernhard R., and Geck, Karl, trans. and ed. Wilhelmshaven: Heinrichshofen, forthcoming.

> Translation into German and commentary.

The Principles of Practical Music Delivered in a Compendious, Easie, and New Method . . . [*Rism* B/VI/2, p. 786.]

London: Henry Brome (William Godbid), 1665. [LCPS: S-086.]

A Compendium of Practical Musick . . . [*Rism* B/VI/2, pp. 784-85.]

London: Henry Brome (William Godbid), 1667. [LCPS: S-083a. HoM: 1425. SMLMS.]
London: Henry Brome (William Godbid), 1667. [LCPS: S-083b.]
London: Henry Brome (M[ary] C[lark]), 1678. [LCPS: S-083c. HoM: 1426. SMLMS.]
London: J. Cullen (William Pearson), 1706. [LCPS: S-083d.]
London: John Young (William Pearson), 1714. [LCPS: S-083e.]
London: John Young (William Pearson), 1714/1722. [LCPS: S-083f.]
London: John Young (William Pearson), 1722. [LCPS: S-083g.]

London: T. Astley, 1727.

London: Arthur Bettesworth & Charles Hitch (William Pearson), 1732. [LCPS: S-083h. HoM: 1427. SMLMS.]

London: Longman, Lukey & Co., [1775?]. [LCPS: S-083i. HoM: 1428. SMLMS.]

S ● Lord, Phillip J., ed. Modern printing of the second 1667 text. Oxford: B. Blackwell, 1970.

> Reviews in *ML* 52/2 (1971):207-8 (Jack A. Westrup), *MR* 33/2 (1972):148-49, and *MT* 112/1540 (1971):557-58 (Michael Tilmouth) .

See also CAMPION, T.: [ca. 1613-14]; PLAYFORD: (1654).

LITERATURE:

Pulver, Jeffrey. "Christopher Simpson." *MN* 50/1299-1302 (1916):82-83, 102-3, 131, 154-55.

Coxon, Carolyn. "Simpson, Christopher." Translated by Ruth Blume. In *MGG* (1949-68). Bibliog.

Vellekoop, Gerrit. "Christopher Simpson's *The Division-Viol.*" *Mens* 13/4 (1958):103-5.

Hullfish, William R. "*The Division Flute*: An Introduction to Playing upon a Ground." *NACWPIJ* 27/2 (1978-79):4-23. [*Rilm* 78-5916.]

● ● ● Field, Christopher D. S. "Simpson, Christopher." In *NGrove* (1980). Bibliog.

● ● ● Appel, Bernhard R. "Christopher Simpsons Systematiker der Divisionsverfahren (1667)." *Mf* 35/3 (1982):223-34. [*Rilm* 82-5694.]

Breslauer, Peter. "Diminutional Rhythm and Melodic Structure." *JMT* 32/1 (1988):1-21.

See also FÉTIS: (1833-44); LOCKE: (1672); NORTH, R.: Wilson (1959); RAMEAU: Verba (1978); WALTHER: (1732); LITERATURE SUPPLEMENT: Abraham (1968/1969); **Apfel (1981)**; Atcherson (1972), (1973); Badura-Skoda et al. (1980); Becker (1836-39/1964); Beiche ["Inversio"] (1972-); Bent et al. (1980); Boomgaarden (1985/1987); Brown (1976); Burke (1963); Burney (1776-89/. . ./1957); Burton (1956); Butler (1977); Cazden (1948); Chenette (1967); Colles (1928-29); Dolmetsch (1915/. . ./1969); Donington (1980); Eggebrecht (1955); Eitner (1900-1904/1959-60); Ferand (1937/1938); Forkel (1792/ 1962); Gerber (1790-92/1977), (1812-14/1966); Gouk (1980); Grashel (1981); Hancock (1977); Harding (1938); Hawkins (1776/. . ./1969); Horsley [*Fugue: History*] (1966); Houle (1960), (1987); Jackson (1988); Jacobi (1957-60/1971); ● ● ●**Kassler (1979)**; Kassler and Oldroyd (1983); Lawrence (1978); **Lester (1989)**; Lewis (1981); Miller (1960); Neumann, Frederick (1978); Newman (1959/ . . ./1983); **Palisca** ["Theory"] **(1980)**; Pulver (1927/. . ./1973); Reese (1954/1959); Robison (1982); Rogers (1955); Rothschild (1953); Ruf (1972-); Ruff (1970); Sachs (1972-); Schulenberg (1982); **Seidel and Cooper (1986)**; Shute (1972); Sisman (1978); Subirá (1947/. . ./1958); Taddie (1984); Wienpahl (1953), (1955); Williams, P. (1970); Wolf (1939).

ANTONIO SOLER

[bapt. 1729 – 1783]

In an environment dominated by conservative ecclesiastical influences and by the musical authority of CERONE's outmoded *El melopeo y maestro* (1613), Antonio Soler's *Llave de la modulacion* (1762) must have seemed remarkably modern. In fact, several authors published criticisms of the work, and that by ROEL DEL RÍO (1764) generated a forceful response from Soler in his *Satisfacción a los reparos* (1765).

In addition to his extensive coverage of matters pertaining to intervals, notation, cadences, and other such foundational elements of music, Soler offered a provocative guide to modulation from any key to any other, in either mode. His examples display a freedom of tonal movement that simultaneously irritated the advocates of traditional musical values and challenged the most progressive of contemporary composers.

Llave de la modulación, y antigüedades de la música, en que se trata del fundamento necessario para saber modular: Theórica, y práctica para el más claro conocimiento de qualquier especie de figuras, desde el tiempo de Juan de Muris, hasta hoy, con algunos canones enigmáticos, y sus resoluciones [*Rism* B/VI/2, p. 791.]

Madrid: Joachin Ibarra, 1762. [LCPS: S-098.]

> Review in ROEL DEL RÍO: (1764). See also Díaz (1765), below, and Bruguera y Morreras (1766), below.

T ● See Carroll (1960), below.

S ● Facsimile edition. MMMLF, ser. 2, no. 42. New York: Broude Brothers, 1967.

T ● Crouch, Margaret Long. "*Llave de la modulación y antiguedades de la música* . . . by Padre Fray Antonio Soler: Translation and Commentary." Ph.D. dissertation, The University of California at Santa Barbara, 1978. [*Rilm* 78-2727. *DA* 39/06A, p. 3207. UMI 78-24176.]

T ● Shipley, Linda Patricia. "An English Translation of Antonio Soler's *Llave de la modulación*." Ph.D. dissertation, The Florida State University, 1978. [*Rilm* 78-4904. *DA* 40/02A, p. 534. UMI 79-17082.]

Satisfacción a los reparos precisos hechos por D. Antonio Roel del Río, a la llave de la modulación [*Rism* B/VI/2, p. 791.]

>A response to ROEL DEL RÍO: (1764).

>Madrid: Antonio Marín, 1765.

Correspondence with MARTINI

>Mss., 1765-72.

S ● Kastner, Santiago. "Algunas cartas del P. Antonio Soler dirigidas al P. Giambattista Martini." *Anmu* 12 (1957):235-41.

S ● See Carroll (1960), below.

Carta escrita a un amigo . . . en que le da parte de un diálogo últimamente publicado contra su llave de la modulación

>Madrid: Antonio Marín, 1766.

>>Soler's response to Díaz (1765), below.

S ● Rubio, Samuel. "Antonio Soler: Carta escrita a un amigo." *Revdm* 2/1 (1979):145-63.

"Theórica, y práctica del temple para los órganos, y claves"

>Ms., [after 1766].

S ● Rubio, Samuel, ed. Facsimile edition. Madrid: Sociedad española de musicología, 1983.

LITERATURE:

Díaz, Gregorio. *Diálogo crítico reflexivo entre Amphión y Orpheo, sobre el estado en que se halla la profesión de la música en España, y principalmente sobre algunos méthodos que han querido introducir en ella ciertos profesores que por acreditar sus hipótesis han venido a caer en el abismo de la confusión . . .* [*Rism* B/VI/1, p. 265.] Madrid: Antonio Mayorál, 1765.

>A criticism of *Llave* (1762), above.

Bruguera y Morreras, Juan Bautista. *Carta apologética que en defensa del labyrinto de labyrintos, compuesto por un autor cuyo nombre saldrá presto al público, escribió . . . contra la llave de la modulación . . .* Barcelona: Francisco Suriá, 1766. [*Rism* B/VI/1, p. 183.]

>A criticism of *Llave* (1762), above.

Vila, José. *Respuesta y dictamen . . . a petición del autor de la Carta apologética, escrita en defensa del Laberinto de Laberintos, contra la Llave de la modulación . . .* Cervera: 1766.

>A defense of Soler against Bruguera y Morreras (1766), above.

Kastner, Santiago. "Soler, Antonio." In *MGG* (1949-68). Bibliog.

Carroll, Frank Morris. "An Introduction to Antonio Soler." 2 vols. Ph.D. dissertation, The University of Rochester, 1960. Bibliog.

Puig, Jose Subirá. "Un insigne musico escurialense: Fray Antonio Soler." In *El Escorial: 1563-1963 (IV centenario de la fundación del Monasterio de San Lorenzo el Real)*, vol. 2, pp. 645-62. Madrid: Ediciones patrimonio nacional, [1963].

Winter, Marion O. "Antonio Soler: A Survey of His Life and Works." *RS* 55-56 (1974):336-52; 59 (1975):463-64.

Sadowsky, Reah. "Antonio Soler: Creator of Spain's Fifth Century of Musical Genius." *AMT* 28/1 (1978):10-15.

● ● ● Stevenson, Robert. "Antonio Soler: A 250th-Anniversary Review Article." *IAMR* 2/1 (1979-80):45-57. Bibliog.

Rubio, Samuel. "Antonio Soler: Catálogo crítico." Madrid: Instituto de música religiosa de la Diputación provincial de Cuenca, 1980. Bibliog.

Stevenson, Robert. "Soler (Ramos), Antonio (Francisco Javier José)." In *NGrove* (1980). Bibliog.

See also FÉTIS: (1833-44); LITERATURE SUPPLEMENT: Anglés and Subirá (1946-51); Blumröder (1972-); Eitner (1900-1904/1959-60); Kastner (1973-74/1987); León Tello (1974); Subirá (1947/. . ./1958), (1953); Troeger (1987).

GEORG ANDREAS SORGE

[1703 – 1778]

Regardless of their strengths or weaknesses, RAMEAU's innovative theories, which were spreading throughout Germany during the middle of the eighteenth century, profoundly influenced the nature and tenor of publications seen thereafter. Without RAMEAU and his German champion MARPURG, Georg Andreas Sorge might have remained a narrowly focused author, treating principally figured bass (using a perspective derived from HEINICHEN), organ construction (taking full advantage of the recent development of logarithms), and temperament (particularly equal temperament). Already predisposed towards mathematics in his study of organs, he endorsed the scientific aura which was then enveloping theoretical discourse, surpassed MARPURG as a disciplined advocate of mathematical precision in musical matters, and was rewarded with membership in MIZLER's Sozietät der Musikalischen Wissenschaften, which had as its goal the establishment of a rigorous mathematical basis for music.

By the middle of the eighteenth century, triadic theory was congested with a wide variety of chord types resulting from added dissonance and inversion. The RAMEAU/MARPURG camp was advocating a theory of supposition, whereby ninths, elevenths, and thirteenths were formed by adding a third, fifth, or seventh below a chord's fundamental pitch. Sorge, whose impressive understanding of acoustics was put to use in his theoretical formulations, could not accept this theory and proposed, in his *Compendium harmonicum* (1760), that the first thirty-two partials should generate all structural chords, which included seventh and ninth chords as well as triads. Earlier, in his *Vorgemach der musicalischen Composition* (1757-59), he had shown how dissonance could result from the suspension of a pitch or pitches from one chord into the domain of the next. In this way a hierarchy was developed: not every vertical entity need be explained independently of its context; some chords accommodate elements of the preceding or following harmonies.

Rejecting any dogmatic formulae for chord succession, yet not restricting himself to the traditional domain of figured-bass realization, Sorge established criteria for the shifting of tonal center to a closely related key. Those keys which he allied most strongly with C major, for example, are G major, then A minor, E minor, F major, and finally D minor. Those so related to A minor are, in order, C major, E minor, G major, D minor, and F major. This conception was important both in the art of composition, where modulation beyond this range was classified as extraordinary, and in improvisation, which Sorge addressed in his *Anleitung zur Fantasie* (1767).

Genealogia allegorica intervallorum octavae diatono-chromaticae; Das ist, Geschlecht-Register der Intervallen der diatonisch-chromatischen Octav in einem verblümten Verstande, nach Anleitung der Klänge, so das grosse Waldhorn gibt . . . [*Rism* B/VI/2, p. 793.]

Hof: Johann Ernst Schultz, [1741]. [LCPS: S-105.]

Anweisung zur Stimmung und Temperatur sowohl der Orgelwerke, als auch anderer Instrumente, sonderlich aber des Claviers; in einem Gespräche zwischen einem Musico theoretico und seinem Scholaren . . . [*Rism* B/VI/2, p. 792.]

Hamburg: gedruckt mit Piscators Schriften, 1744. [LCPS: S-101.]

S ● Facsimile edition. Bo, no. 36. Buren, The Netherlands: Frits Knuf, forthcoming.

Vorgemach der musicalischen Composition; oder, Ausführliche, ordentliche und vor heutige Praxin hinlängliche Anweisung zum General-Bass . . . [*Rism* B/VI/2, p. 794.]

Lobenstein: the author, 1745[-47]. 3 vols. [LCPS: S-108. SMLMS.]

T ● ● ● ● Reilly, Allyn Dixon. "Georg Andreas Sorge's *Vorgemach der musicalischen Composition*: A Translation and Commentary." 2 vols. Ph.D. dissertation, Northwestern University, 1980. Bibliog. [*DA* 41/06a, p. 2348. UMI 80-26907.]

Gespräch zwischen einem Musico theoretico und einem Studioso musices von der Prätorianischen, Printzischen, Werckmeisterischen, Neidhardtischen und Silbermannischen Temperatur, wie auch von dem neuen Systemate Herrn Capellmeister Telemanns, zu Beförderung reiner Harmonie. [*Rism* B/VI/2, p. 793.]

Lobenstein: the author, [1748]. [LCPS: S-106. SMLMS. IDC.]

Ausführliche und deutliche Anweisung zur Rational-Rechnung und der damit verknüpfften Ausmessung und Abtheilung des Monochords . . . [*Rism* B/VI/2, p. 792.]

Lobenstein: the author, 1749. [LCPS: S-102.]

Ausweichungs-Tabellen, in welchen auf vierfache Art gezeiget wird, wie eine jede Tonart in ihre Neben-Tonarten ausweichen könne [*Rism* B/VI/2, pp. 792-93.]

Nuremberg: Johann Ulrich Haffner, [ca. 1753]. [LCPS: S-103.]

Gründliche Untersuchung, ob die . . . Schröterische Clavier-Temperaturen für gleichschwebend passiren können, oder nicht . . . [Rism B/VI/2, p. 793.]

    N.p., 1754.

Zuverlässige Anweisung, Claviere und Orgeln behörig zu temperiren und zu stimmen, nebst einem Kupfer, welches die Ausmessung und Ausrechnung der Temperatur, wie auch das Telemannische Intervallen-System . . . darstellet . . . [Rism B/VI/2, pp. 794-95.]

    Leipzig and Lobenstein: the author & G. F. Authenrieth, [1758]. [LCPS: S-109.]

Compendium harmonicum; oder, Kurzer Begriff der Lehre von der Harmonie, vor diejenigen, welche den Generalbass und die Composition studiren, in der Ordnung, welche die Natur des Klangs an die Hand giebt [Rism B/VI/2, p. 793.]

    Lobenstein: the author & in Kommission in Hof bei Ludwig, 1760. [LCPS: S-104. SMLMS.]

    S ● MARPURG, Friedrich Wilhelm, ed. *Herrn Georg Andreas Sorgens Anleitung zum Generalbass und zur Composition. [Rism B/VI/2, p. 792.]* Berlin: Gottlieb August Lange, 1760. [LCPS: S-100. HoM: 933. SMLMS.]

        Review in MARPURG: (1754-78):Vol. 5/2, 4 (1761-62):100-120, 263-85 (Johann Lorenz Albrecht).

    T ● Martin, James M., II. "The *Compendium harmonicum* (1760) of Georg Andreas Sorge (1703-1778): A Translation and Critical Commentary." Ph.D. dissertation, The Catholic University of America, 1981. [*Rilm* 81-2612. *DA* 42/06A, p. 2354. UMI: 81-23258.]

Kurze Erklärung des Canonis harmonici [Rism B/VI/2, p. 794.]

    [Lobenstein]: the author, [1763].

"Die geheim gehaltene Kunst der Mensuration der Orgel-Pfeiffen"

    Mss., [ca. 1760]. [Winston-Salem, N.C.: Moravian Music Foundation; Bethlehem, Pa.: Archives of the Moravian Church.]

    ST ● ● ● ● Bleyle, Carl O., trans. and ed. Facsimile edition and English translation. *The Secretly Kept Art of the Scaling of Organ Pipes.* Bo, no. 33. Buren, The Netherlands: Frits Knuf, 1978. Bibliog. [*Rilm* 78-1550.]

        Reviews in *ArsOr* 28/3 (1980):180 (Matthias Reichling), *ISOI* 20 (1980):51 (Maarten A. Vente), *Mf* 34/1 (1981):97 (Raimund W. Sterl), *MK* 49/2 (1979):77-78 (Walter Kwasnik), and *Notes* 36/2 (1979-80):360-62 (George Stauffer).

Anleitung zur Fantasie oder zu der schönen Kunst, das Clavier, wie auch andere Instrumente, aus dem Kopfe zu spielen; nach theoretischen und practischen Grundsätzen, wie solche die Natur des Klangs lehrt [Rism B/VI/2, p. 792.]

    Lobenstein: the author, [1767]. [LCPS: S-099.]

"Mathematische Beschreibung der musikalischen Intervallen"

    Ms., 1769. [Rochester, N.Y.: Sibley Music Library.]

"Anmerkung über Professor Eulers Intervallensystem"

    WNAMb 4/3/35 (1770):269-76.

Der in der Rechen- und Meßkunst wohlerfahrne Orgelbaumeister . . . [Rism B/VI/2, p. 794.]

    [Lobenstein]: the author, [1773]. [LCPS: S-107. IDC.]

    S ● Modern edition. Smets, Paul, ed. Mainz: Paul Smets, 1932.

    S ● Facsimile edition. Bo, no. 23. Buren, The Netherlands: Frits Knuf, 1977.

"Die Melodie aus der Harmonie . . . hergeleitet"

    Ms. [Vienna: Gesellschaft der Musikfreunde.]

See (1745-47), above, and (1760), above, for more detailed listings of manuscripts by Sorge.

LITERATURE:

Oberdörffer, Fritz. "Sorge, Georg Andreas." In *MGG* (1949-68). Bibliog.

Frisch, Manfred. "Georg Andreas Sorge: Ein großer Lobensteiner des 18. Jahrhunderts." In *AlbertFs* (1954): 45-57. Bibliog.

Frisch, Manfred. "Georg Andreas Sorge und seine Lehre von der musikalischen Harmonie: Ein Beitrag zur Geschichte der Musiktheorie im 18. Jahrhundert." Ph.D. dissertation, The University of Leipzig, 1954.

Bleyle, Carl O. "Georg Andreas Sorge's Influence on David Tannenberg and Organ Building in America During the Eighteenth Century." 2 vols. Ph.D. dissertation, The University of Minnesota, 1969. Bibliog.

Lange, Helmut K. H. "Gottfried Silbermann's Organ Tuning: A Contribution to the Manner of Performing Ancient Music/Die Orgelstimmung Gottfried Silbermanns: Ein Beitrag zur Aufführungspraxis alter Musik." Translated by H. D. Blanchard. *ISOI* 8 (1972):543-56; *ISOI* 9 (1973):647-58.

Bleyle, Carl O. "Georg Andreas Sorge: An 18th-Century Proponent of Logarithmic Scaling for Organ-Pipes." *OrganYb 1975* 6 (1975):53-63.

● ● ● Buelow, George J. "Sorge, Georg Andreas." In *NGrove* (1980). Bibliog.

Ebersbach, Günther W. "Georg Andreas Sorge, Gräflich Reuss.-Plauischer Hof- und Stadtorganist sowie Lehrer und Musikgelehrter." *AfSf* 48/86 (1982):389-405. [*Rilm* 82-4520.]

Rasch, Rudolf. "Sorge's Monochord." *Mens* 37/5 (1982):232-43. [*Rilm* 82-5636.]

See also FÉTIS: (1833-44); (1840); HEINICHEN: (1728): Buelow (1961/. . ./1986); MARPURG: (1754-78): Vol. 5 (1761):131-220; (1759-63); Serwer (1969); MATTHESON: (1740); RAMEAU: Pischner (1961/. . ./1967); RIEMANN: (1898); SCHRÖTER ["Bedenken"] (1763); LITERATURE SUPPLEMENT: Abraham (1966); **Arnold (1931/. . ./1965)**; **Barbour** (1947), (1949-68), **(1951/. . ./1972)**; Beach (1967); Becker (1836-39/1964); Bell et al. (1980); Benary (1956/1961); Bukofzer (1947); Burke (1963); Cavallini (1949); Cazden (1980); Chevaillier (1925/ 1931-32); Dahlhaus ["Konsonanz"] (1949-68); **Dahlhaus et al. (1987)**; Dammann (1958/1967); David and Mendel (1945/1966); Duckles (1970); Dupont (1933/. . ./1986); Eitner (1900-1904/1959-60); Feil (1955); Ferand (1937/1938), [*Improvisation*] (1956/1961); Forkel (1792/1962); Frisius (1969/1970); Gerber (1790-92/1977), (1812-14/1966); Haase (1969); Hartmann (1923); Hiller (1768-69); Hoffman (1953); Imig (1969/1970); Jackson (1988); Jacobi (1957-60/1971); Jones (1934); Jorgenson (1957); Jung (1969); Kauko (1958); Kelletat [*Temperatur*] (1960), (1966); Krehbiel (1964); **Lester (1989)**; **Lindley** ["Temperaments"] **(1980)**, (1982), (1985), (1988); Lottermoser (1949-68); Mallard (1978); Meer (1980); Mitchell, J. W. (1963); Mitchell, W. J. (1963); Nelson (1984); Newman (1963/. . ./1983); Palisca ["Theory"] (1980); Rasch (1981), (1983); Reilly (1984-85); Révész (1946/ . . ./1954); Rohwer (1949-68); Rothgeb (1968); Schoffman ["Descriptive"] (1983); Sheldon (1981), (1982); Shellhous (1988); **Shirlaw (1917/. . ./1970)**; Stein (1983); Stowell (1985); Telesco (forthcoming); Tittel (1966); Todd (1983), (1988-89); Ulrich (1931/1932); Vanhulst (1971); Werts (1983); Williams, P. (1970); Wirth (1966).

DANIEL SPEER

[1636-1707]

The study of music theory was not limited, of course, to scholars who made it their primary vocation. Few academics would have been interested in Daniel Speer's *Grundrichtiger . . . Unterricht der musicalischen Kunst*, which appeared in 1687 and was expanded considerably for a second edition ten years later. The audience for this volume consisted mainly of performers, who needed information of a practical sort, not too burdened with speculation. Speer offered a pleasing array of materials touching upon singing and both keyboard and instrumental performance. Readers could find information on notation, solmization, meters, figured bass, and instrumental fingerings alongside suggestions on what a singer should eat and drink. The expansion of key possibilities is documented through Speer's advocacy of not only the diatonic keys on A, C, D, E, F, and G, but also major triads on A, B, D, E, B-flat, and E-flat, and minor triads on F, G, and C. His own categorization, however, differentiated according to the use of sharps versus flats rather than according to major and minor, while the key signatures utilized in his keyboard examples later in the book do not conform to our modern standards. The fourth and final section of the work is devoted to the art of composition. Due to its brevity and dependence upon the much earlier writings of HERBST, it is of little importance.

Grund-richtiger, kurtz, leicht und nöthiger Unterricht der musicalischen Kunst, wie man füglich und in kurtzer Zeit Choral und Figural singen, den General-Bass tractiren und componieren lernen soll: Denen Lehr-und Lernenden zu beliebigem Gebrauch [*Rism* B/VI/2, p. 800.]

Ulm: Georg Wilhelm Kühn, 1687. [LCPS: S-114a. SMLMS.]

Revised edition, as *Grund-richtiger, kurtz-, leicht- und nöthiger, jetzt wol-vermehrter Unterricht der musicalischen Kunst, oder vierfaches musicalisches Kleeblatt . . .*:

Ulm: Georg Wilhelm Kühn (Christian Balthasar Kühn), 1697. [LCPS: S-114b. SMLMS. IDC.]

T ● Howey, Henry Eugene. "A Comprehensive Performance Project in Trombone Literature with an Essay consisting of a Translation of Daniel Speer's *Vierfaches musikalisches Kleeblatt* (Ulm, 1697)." D.M.A. dissertation, The University of Iowa, 1971. [*Rilm* 71-446. *DA* 32-09A, p. 5267. UMI 72-08346.]

S ● Ahlgrimm, Isolde, and Burckhardt, Felix, ed. Facsimile of the 1697 edition, with excerpts from the 1687 edition. Leipzig: VEB Edition Peters, 1974.

Reviews in *MG* 30/5 (1980):307-8 (Kurt Petermann), *MK* 46/2 (1976):81-82 (Gerhard Schuhmacher), *ML* 58/1 (1977):81-82 (Susan Wollenberg), *MT* 117/1604 (1976):828 (Rosemary

Roberts), *Rdm* 62/1 (1976):160-61 (D. Launay), and *Tibia* 1 (1977):235 (D.).

LITERATURE:

Moser, Hans Joachim. "Daniel Speer." *Am* 9/3-4 (1937):99-122; reprinted (as "Daniel Speer als Dichter und Musiker") in Moser's *Musik in Zeit und Raum: Ausgewählte Abhandlungen* (Berlin: Merseburger, 1960), pp. 119-44.

> Reviews in *Mf* 14/4 (1961):439-40 (Joseph Müller-Blattau), *MGot* 16/6 (1962):181 (E. N.), *MK* 31/3 (1961):133 (Walter Blankenburg), and *Musica* 15/10 (1961):583 (Hans Georg Bonte)

Eppelsheim, Jürgen. "Speer, Daniel." In *MGG* (1949-68). Bibliog.

Hansen, Bernhard. "Daniel Speer (1687) über den Klavierunterricht." *SMz* 103/6 (1963):336-41.

Cosma, Viorel. "Documente si lucrări muzicale din pragul veacului al XVIII-lea." *Muzica* 14 (1964):67-71.

Burckhardt, Felix. "Daniel Speer: Schulmeister, Musiker und Dichter, 1636-1707." *LSF* 11 (1969):48-68.

Fetter, David. "Daniel Speer." *JITA* 6 (1978):5-6.

Roberts, Rosemary. "Speer, Daniel." In *NGrove* (1980). Bibliog.

See also FÉTIS: (1833-44); WALTHER: (1732); LITERATURE SUPPLEMENT: Becker (1836-39/1964); Braun (1970); Dahlhaus ["Zur Entstehung"] (1961); Dammann (1958/1967); Dreyfus (1987); Eitner (1900-1904/1959-60); Flindell (1983-84); Forkel (1792/1962); Gerber (1790-92/1977), (1812-14/1966); Green (1969); Guion (1980); Harrán (1986); Heimann (1970/1973); Houle (1960), (1987); Jackson (1988); **Lester** (1978), **(1989)**; Leuchtmann (1957/1959); Mendel (1978); Moser (1936/. . ./1959); Newman (1959/. . ./1983); Preußner (1924); Riedel (1956/1959); **Ritzel (1967/1968)**; Sachs (1984); Schünemann (1928/1931); Schulenberg (1984); Sheldon (1975); Sydow-Saak (1972-); Troeger (1987); Unger (1941/1969); Vogel (1955/1954); Walker (1987).

MEINRAD SPIESS

[1683 – 1761]

Coexisting with the progressive theories propounded by HEINICHEN, MATTHESON, and others, a conservative church tradition flourished in eighteenth-century Germany. Sincere and learned men such as Meinrad Spieß, whose *Tractatus musicus compositorio-practicus* was published in 1745, offered composers of ecclesiastical music useful guidance for attaining mastery of their art. As did FUX twenty years earlier, Spieß supported the retention of the church modes, as opposed to the more innovative yet, in his view, less varied or interesting assortment of twenty-four major and minor keys. Though his efforts led in a direction which countered the more secular perspective then prevalent in Germany, Spieß advocated a style influenced by the affective preoccupations of his contemporaries. He also possessed a keen interest in the mathematical aspects of music. As a result, he was admitted as the seventh member of MIZLER's Sozietät der Musicalischen Wissenschaften in 1743.

Tractatus musicus compositorio-practicus; Das ist, Musicalischer Tractat, in welchem alle gute und sichere Fundamenta zur musicalischen Composition aus denen alt- und neuesten besten Autoribus herausgezogen, zusammen getragen, gegen einander gehalten, erkläret, und mit untersetzten Exemplen dermassen klar und deutlich erläutert werden . . . (Op. 8) [*Rism* B/VI/2, pp. 801-2.]

> Augsburg: Johann Jacob Lotters seel. Erben 1745. [SMLMS. IDC.]

Augsburg: Johann Jacob Lotters seel. Erben, 1746.

> Review in MIZLER: (1736-54): 3/4 (1752):754-64.

LITERATURE:

"Ein Kapitel aus P. Meinrad Spieß." *KJb* 18 (1903):67-81.

Goldmann, Alfred. "Spieß, Meinrad." In *MGG* (1949-68). Bibliog.

Federl, Ekkehard. "Der *Tractatus musicus* des Pater Meinrad Spieß (1683-1761)." In *StäbleinFs* (1967):39-46. Bibliog. [*Rilm* 67-2308.]

Irmen, Hans-Josef. "Meinrad Spiess und sein Begriff der Musica und Musica sacra." *Ms:CVO* 90/6 (1970):234-42. [*Rilm* 71-448.]

Buelow, George J. "Spiess, Meinrad." In *NGrove* (1980). Bibliog.

See also ADLUNG: (1758); FÉTIS: (1833-44); MOZART: Correspondence; LITERATURE SUPPLEMENT: Ahlgrimm (1969-70); Bartel (1982/1985); Becker (1836-39/1964); Beiche ["Dux"] (1972-); **Benary (1956/1961)**, (1963); Beyschlag (1907/1953); Blumröder (1972-); Boetticher (1954); Butler (1977); Cahn ["Retardatio"] (1972-); **Coover**

(1980); **Dahlhaus et al. (1987)**; Dammann (1958/1967); Dotzauer (1976); Duckles (1970); Eitner (1900-1904/1959-60); Fellerer (1927/. . ./1972), ["Musikwissenschaft"] (1972); Flindell (1983-84); Frobenius ["Homophonus"] (1972-), ["Vollstimmig"] (1972-); Gerber (1790-92/ 1977); Goldmann (1987); Haase (1969); Hiller (1768-69); Katz (1926); **Lester** (1978), **(1989)**; Neumann, Frederick (1978); Ratner (1980); Reckow (1972-); Reimer ["Kammermusik"] (1972-); **Ritzel (1967/ 1968)**; Sachs (1972-); Schmalzriedt ["Coda"] (1972-), ["Episode"] (1972-); Sheldon (1982); Unger (1941/ 1969); Wirth (1966).

Sir JOHN STAINER

[1840 – 1901]

The organist and Oxford professor Sir John Stainer was strongly influenced by OUSELEY, though he attempted, in his *Theory of Harmony* (1871), to dispense with much of the acoustical speculation that had befogged British theory during the mid-nineteenth century. His advocacy of a tempered scale was an attempt at redirecting speculation along more practical lines, yet his fascination with thirds (and their capacity for stacking into agglomerations incorporating all seven diatonic pitches) produced a strained, counterintuitive theory, especially with regard to chords outside the direct tonic/dominant axis. The pitches F, A, C, and D in the context of C major, for example, are derived not from F or from D, as RAMEAU would have maintained, but from G. As did Alfred DAY, Stainer posited that augmented-sixth chords melded components from two different arrays of stacked thirds. It is astonishing to learn that Stainer's derivative *Harmony* (1878), a part of Novello's Music Primers and Educational Series (of which he served as editor), was a best seller—186,000 copies were in print before Stainer died. His *Dictionary of Musical Terms* (1876), which was coauthored by William Alexander Barrett, was also very popular.

A Theory of Harmony [Founded on the Tempered Scale], with Questions and Exercises for the Use of Students

> London: Rivingtons, 1871.

>> Numerous editions, some with the title *A Treatise on Harmony and the Classification of Chords, with Questions and Exercises for the Use of Students*. Review in *MT* 15/347 (1871-73):341-42.

> S ● *Harmony, with an Appendix Containing One Hundred Graduated Exercises*. NMPES, no. 8. London: Novello, 1878.

>> A simplified version of the above. Numerous editions. Review in *MT* 19/420 (1878):93.

A Dictionary of Musical Terms

> London: Novello, Ewer & Co., 1876. With William Alexander Barrett.

>> Numerous editions. An abridged edition appeared in 1880 (NMPES, no. 21).

> S ● Facsimile of the 1898 edition. Hildesheim: Georg Olms, 1970.

> S ● Facsimile of the 1889 edition. St. Clair Shores, Mich: Scholarly Press, 1974.

Composition

> London: Novello, 1877.

>> Also printed as *Guide to Beginners in Composition*.

Music in Its Relation to the Intellect and Emotions

> London: Novello & Ewer, 1892.

>> One later edition, in 1911 (NMPES, no. 82).

> T ● Pennequin, Louis, trans. *La musique dans ses rapports avec l'intelligence et les émotions, essai d'esthétique musicale*. Paris: Henri Falque, 1911.

See also MORLEY: STAINER (1902); OUSELEY: (1879):Discussion; (1882):Discussion; OUSELEY: STAINER (1890).

A complete listing of Stainer's publications appears in Charlton (1977/1984), below.

LITERATURE:

Harman, Richard Alexander. "Stainer, John." Translated by Käthe Henke. In *MGG* (1949-68). Bibliog.

● ● ● Charlton, Peter. "The Life and Influence of Sir John Stainer." Ph.D. dissertation, The University of East

Anglia, 1977; published edition (as *John Stainer and the Musical Life of Victorian Britain*), Newton Abbot, London, and North Pomfret, Vt.: David & Charles, 1984. Bibliog. [*Rilm* 77-639.]

> Reviews in *AmO:AGO* 20/8 (1986):16-17, *Choice* 21/10 (1984):1474, *Diapason* 76/5 [906] (1985):7 (John Silantien), *Gram* 62/733 (1984): 79 (M. E. O.), *ML* 66/2 (1985):153-55 (William J. Gatens), *MT* 125/1699 (1984):501 (Walter Hillsman), *Organ* 63/250 (1984):187-90 (Richard D. Fenwick), *Organists Review* 68/276 (1984):62-63, *Spec* 253/8140 (1984):28 (Michael Trend), and *TLS* 83/4232 (1984):517 (Nicholas Temperley).

Temperley, Nicholas. "Stainer, Sir John." In *NGrove* (1980). Bibliog.

See also LITERATURE SUPPLEMENT: Bircher (1970); Bridges (1984); Burke (1963); Cobb (1884); Ferand (1937/1938); Finney (1957); Jacobi (1957-60/1971); Jones (1934); Jorgenson (1957); Kauko (1958); Lecky (1880); Mitchell, J. W. (1963); Schmalzriedt ["Exposition"] (1972-); Schoffman ["Descriptive"] (1983); Scholes (1947); ● ● ● **Shirlaw (1917/ . . ./1970)**; Thompson (1980); Whatley (1981).

CARL STUMPF

[1848 – 1936]

Carl Stumpf's contributions to our understanding of sound develop out of, though in critical ways depart from, the scientific and aesthetic achievements of nineteenth-century Germany. Whereas HELMHOLTZ concerned himself with the role of beats in effecting consonance or dissonance and with the ears' capacity to receive and transmit perceptions, Stumpf adopted a psychological perspective: even if each ear is exposed to a different pitch, the mind can determine whether the two sounds are in a consonant or dissonant relationship with one another, despite the absence of beats in the received sounds. Stumpf also challenged RIEMANN's notion that consonance and dissonance are dependent upon the norms of compositional practice: a composer might disregard the status of a particular combination of pitches, but that status cannot be altered.

To Stumpf, concordance and discordance (the terms he preferred when more than two sounds were present) correlate with human reactions to amalgamations of tones. He rejected the view that the character of a multiple-pitched chord depended upon the acoustical charateristics of its dyadic components. He exempted the judgments of trained musicians: the subjects of his experiments held no overt prejudices regarding the objects of his inquiry. Their responses helped him in determining to what extent the fused sounds of various combinations of pitches were perceived as single, indivisible tones. Instead of a stark categorization as concordant or discordant, he formulated a number of grades between these two poles.

Tonpsychologie

Leipzig: S. Hirzel, 1883-90. 2 vols.

> Review in *VMw* 1 (1885):127-38 and 7 (1891):429-40 (Alexius Meinong).

S ● Facsimile edition. Hilversum: Frits A. M. Knuf; Amsterdam: E. J. Bonset, 1965.

T ● See Bujić (1988).

"Musikpsychologie in England: Betrachtungen über Herleitung der Musik aus der Sprache und aus dem thierischen Entwickelungsproceß, über Empirismus und Nativismus in der Musiktheorie"

> *VMw* 1 (1885):261-349.
> Leipzig: Breitkopf & Härtel, 1885.

"Die pseudo-aristotelischen Probleme über Musik"

> *APAWPhK* 3 (1896):1-85.
> Berlin: Königl. Akademie der Wissenschaften (Georg Reimer), 1897.

"Geschichte des Konsonanzbegriffes, I."

> *ABAWPpK* 21/1 (1897):1-78.
> Munich: G. Franz' Verlag, 1901.

Beiträge zur Akustik und Musikwissenschaft

> Leipzig: Johann Ambrosius Barth, 1898-1924. 9 vols. Edited by Stumpf.

>> Contains numerous contributions by Stumpf, including "Konsonanz und Dissonanz" 1 (1898), "Neueres über Tonverschmelzung" 2 (1898), "Differenztöne und Konsonanz" 4 (1909) and 6 (1911), "Über das Erkennen von Intervallen und Accorden bei sehr kurzer Dauer" 4 (1909), "Beobachtungen über Kombinationstöne" 5 (1910), "Konsonanz und Konkordanz" 6 (1911), "Über neuere Untersuchungen zur Tonlehre" 8 (1915), "Singen und Sprechen" 9 (1924), and many others. Also includes Stumpf and Erich Mortiz von Hornbostel's "Über die Bedeutung ethnologischer Untersuchungen für die Psychologie und Ästhetik der Tonkunst" 6 (1911). Reviews in

Rmi 5/3 (1898):604 (Luigi Torchi) and *Rmi* 8/4 (1901):1055-56 (Luigi Torchi).

"Die Anfänge der Musik"

> *IntW* 3/51 (1909):1593-1615.
> Leipzig: Johann Ambrosius Barth, 1911.
>
> > Review in *Rmi* 19/2 (1912):478-9 (G. C.).

> S ● Facsimile of the 1911 edition. Hildesheim: Georg Olms, 1979.

> T ● See Bujić (1988).

Sammelbände für vergleichende Musikwissenschaft

> Munich: Drei Masken Verlag, 1922-23. Vols. 1, 3, and 4. Edited by Stumpf and Erich Moritz von Hornbostel.

> S ● Hildesheim: Georg Olms, 1975. 3 vols. in 1.

Die Sprachlaute: Experimentell-phonetische Untersuchungen nebst einem Anhang über Instrumentalklänge

> Berlin: Julius Springer, 1926.

See also HELMHOLTZ: STUMPF (1895).

See Wellek and Freudenberger (1980), below, for a more comprehensive worklist.

LITERATURE:

Schumann, Erich. "Die Förderung der Musikwissenschaft durch die akustisch-psychologische Forschung Carl Stumpf's." *AfMw* 5 (1923):172-76.

Hornbostel, Erich M. von. "Carl Stumpf und die vergleichende Musikwissenschaft." *ZfvMw* 1/2 (1933):25-28.

Schünemann, Georg. "Carl Stumpf: 25. Dezember 1936." *AfMf* 2/1 (1937):1-7.

Welleck, Albert, and Freudenberger, Berthold. "Stumpf, Friedrich Carl." In *MGG* (1949-68). Bibliog.

Besseler, Heinrich "Das musikalische Hören der Neuzeit." *BVSAWL* 104/6 (1958); Berlin: Akademie-Verlag, 1959.

Wellek, Albert. *Musikpsychologie und Musikästhetik: Grundriss der systematischen Musikwissenschaft.* Frankfurt am Main: Akademische Verlagsgesellschaft, 1963; Bonn: Bouvier Verlag Herbert Grundmann, 1975; 1982. Bibliog.

Sargenti, Simonetta. "Aspetti fenomenologici nella 'Psicologia del suono' di Carl Stumpf." Thesis, The University of Milan, 1975-76.

Wellek, Albert, and Freudenberger, Berthold. "Stumpf, (Friedrich) Carl." In *NGrove* (1980). Bibliog.

La Motte-Haber, Helga de. "In memoriam." *MPsy* 3 (1986):9-10.

See also RIEMANN: (1898); Nadel (1929); SCHOENBERG: Rexroth (1969/1971); Reiche (1980); LITERATURE SUPPLEMENT: Allen ["Philosophies"] (1939); Apfel (1967); Barbour (1938); Bell et al. (1980); Cavallini (1949); Cazden (1948), (1961-62), (1980); Chailley (1967); Chevaillier (1925/1931-32); **Dahlhaus** ["Konsonanz"] (1949-68), ["Untersuchungen"] (1966/. . ./1988), **(1984)**; Duchez (1979); Federhofer (1944/1950), (1985); Ferand (1937/1938); Frobenius ["Homophonus"] (1972-), ["Polyphon"] (1972-); Fubini (1971/1983); Gut (1976); Haase (1969); Handschin (1948); Hartmann (1923); Heinlein (1927/1928); Kauko (1958); Kümmel (1973); La Motte-Haber (1969), (1971), (1976); Lang (1941); Marvin (1987); McCredie (1968); Münnich (1909/1965); Norton (1984); ● ● ●Palisca and Spender (1980); Palm (1965); Parncutt (1988-89); Perinello (1936); Pikler (1966); Reinecke (1970); Révész (1946/. . ./1954); Rohwer (1949-68); Rothärmel (1963/1968); Smith (1974); Spender and Shuter-Dyson (1980); Steblin (1987); Subirá (1947/. . ./1958); Tenney (1988); Vogel (1955/1954), (1962); (1975/1984), (1976); Wellek (1949-68); **Zaminer (1985)**.

JOHANN GEORG SULZER

[1720 – 1779]

Whereas Diderot and d'ALEMBERT had culled an enormous quantity of information concerning the arts for the French *Encyclopédie*, German readers found in the Swiss aesthetician Johann Georg Sulzer's *Allgemeine Theorie der schönen Künste* (1771-74) an impressive assemblage of data and formulations, including a substantial number of articles on music and particularly on aesthetic issues. Whereas Jean-Jacques ROUSSEAU aided the Encyclopedists, so also was Sulzer helped in the creation of the music articles, by KIRN-

BERGER and his student J. A. P. SCHULZ. Though criticized for its moralizing tone and somewhat antiquated perspective, the work enjoyed a wide circulation. It was particularly influential in KOCH's artistic development.

Sulzer established a useful model for the creative process: first an *Anlage*, or general layout, was devised; then came the *Ausführung*, or execution of this plan; finally there was the *Ausarbeitung*, or elaboration of details. This perspective influenced the manner in which articles on the various musical forms were formulated in the work, in that the general plan was described before more specific elements were added to the perspective.

Allgemeine Theorie der schönen Künste in einzeln, nach alphabetischer Ordnung der Kunstwörter auf einander folgenden, Artikeln abgehandelt [*Rism* B/VI/2, pp. 812-13.]

> Leipzig: M. G. Weidmanns Erben und Reich (Berlin: George Ludewig Winter), 1771-1774. 2 vols.
>
>> Reviews in *FgA* (Feb. 11 and Dec. 18, 1772) (J. H. Merck and J. W. von Goethe) [reprinted in *Goethes Werke* I:37:193-97 and 206-14 (Weimar: Hermann Böhlaus Nachfolger, 1896)] and *AdB* 22/1 (1774):5-35 (Tz. [Johann Gottfried Herder]) [reprinted in *Herders Sämmtliche Werke*, edited by Bernhard Suphan, vol. 5, pp. 377-400 (Berlin: Weidmannsche Buchhandlung, 1883)].
>
> Leipzig: M. G. Weidmanns Erben und Reich, 1773-75. 2 vols.
> Biel: Heilmann, 1777. 4 vols. in 2.
> Leipzig: M. G. Weidmanns Erben und Reich, 1778-79. 4 vols. 2nd edition.
> Leipzig: M. G. Weidmanns Erben und Reich, 1786-87. 4 vols. Expanded edition, edited by Christian Friedrich von Blankenburg.
> Leipzig: Weidmann, 1792-94. 4 vols. Expanded edition. [LCPS: S-129a. IDC.]
> Karlsruhe: Christian Gottlieb Schmieder, 1796-97. 4 vols.
> Frankfurt and Leipzig: 1798. 4 vols.

S ● Tonelli, Giorgio, ed. Facsimile of the 1792-94 edition. 5 vols. Hildesheim: Georg Olms, 1967-70.

T ● See Rowen (1979).

T ● Churgin, Bathia. "The Symphony as Described by J. A. P. Schulz (1774): A Commentary and Translation." *CM* 29 (1980):7-16. [*Rilm* 80-530.]

T ● See ● ● ● le Huray and Day (1981).

Die schönen Künste, in ihrem Ursprung, ihrer wahren Natur und besten Anwendung betrachtet [*Rism* B/VI/2, p. 814.]

> Leipzig: M. G. Weidmanns Erben und Reich, 1772.

Register über die in allen vier Theilen der neuen vermehrten zweyten Auflage vorkommenden Schriftsteller, Künstler und Schriften [*Rism* B/VI/2, p. 813.]

> Leipzig: Weidmann, 1799. [LCPS: S-129b.]

S ● Facsimile edition. See (1771-74):(1967-70), above.

LITERATURE:

"Sulzers *Theorie der schönen Kunste*: Artikel Bezifferung." *MagM* 2/2 (1786-87):794-808.

Blankenburg, Christian Friedrich von. *Litterarische Zusätze zu Johann Georg Sulzers Allgemeiner Theorie der schönen Künste . . .* 3 vols. Leipzig: Weidmann, 1796-98; facsimile edition, Frankfurt: Athenäum Verlag, 1972. [*Rism* B/VI/1, p. 153.]

Heym, Ludwig Maximilian. "Darstellung und Kritik der ästhetischen Ansichten J. G. Sulzers." Ph.D. dissertation, The University of Leipzig, 1894.

Groß, Karl Josef. "J. G. Sulzers Allgemeine Theorie der schönen Künste." Ph.D. dissertation, The University of Berlin, 1905.

Leo, Johannes. "Zur Entstehungsgeschichte der *Allgemeine Theorie der schönen Künste* J. G. Sulzers." Ph.D. dissertation, The University of Heidelberg, 1906; published edition (as *Johann Georg Sulzer und die Entstehung seiner "Allgemeinen Theorien der schönen Künste"*), Berlin: Frensdorff, 1907.

Tumarkin, Anna. *Der Ästhetiker Johann Georg Sulzer.* SdG, nos. 79-80. Frauenfeld and Leipzig: Huber, 1933.

Wili, Hans. "Johann Georg Sulzer: Persönlichkeit und Kunstphilosophie." Ph.D. dissertation, The University of Fribourg, Switzerland, 1945; published edition, St. Gallen: Buchdruckerei "Ostschweiz," n.d. Bibliog.

Schnaus, Peter. "Sulzer, Johann Georg." In *MGG* (1949-68). Bibliog.

Serwer, Howard. "Sulzer, Johann Georg." In *NGrove* (1980). Bibliog.

Dahlhaus, Carl. "Zu Schellings Theorie des musikalischen Rhythmus." *PalmFs* (1982):24-31. [*Rilm* 82-3854.]

See also BELLERMANN: (1858); FÉTIS: (1831); (1833-44); KOCH: Seidel (1971), Stevens (1971), Baker (1977), Dahlhaus (1978); SCHEIBE: (1773); SCHULZ: (1799-1800); VIADANA: Haack (1964/ 1974); VOGLER: Stevens (1983); LITERATURE SUPPLEMENT: Abraham and Dahlhaus (1972); Allanbrook (1981); Auhagen (1982/1983); **Barbour (1951/. . ./1972)**; Bauman (1981); Becker (1836-39/1964); Beiche ["Dux"] (1972-), ["Inversio"] (1972-); **Benary (1956/1961**; **Bent**, I. ["Analytical Thinking"] (1980), ["Analysis"] **(1980/1987**, ● ● ● (1984); Bircher (1970); Blumröder (1972-); Boomgaarden (1985/ 1987); Bruck (1928); Cahn ["Retardatio"] (1972-); Cole (1969); Collins (1963), (1966); **Coover (1980)**; Cowart (1987); Dahlhaus (1967), (1985); **Dahlhaus et al. (1987)**; David and Mendel (1945/1966) **Dürr and Gerstenberg (1949-68)**, **(1980)**; Dupont (1933/. . ./1986); Eitner (1900-1904/1959-60); Fischer (1957); Flaherty (1989); Forkel (1792/1962); Frobenius (1972-); Gerber (1790-92/1977), (1812-14/1966); Henneberg (1972/1974); Hosler (1978/

1981); Houle (1960); Kaufmann (1969); Keller (1955/1965); Kelletat [*Temperatur*] (1960); Kramer (1987-88); Krones (1988); Kubota (1986); Laudon (1978); le Huray (1978-79); Levenson (1981); Mahlert and Sunter (1972-); Maier (1984); Mallard (1978); Mann (1987); Mitchell, W. J. (1963); Moyer (1969); Müller-Blattau (1923/. . ./1963); Nelson (1984); Neumann (1979/**1982**), ["Appoggiatura"] (1982); Newman (1963/. . ./1983); Ottenberg (1973/1978); Palisca [*Baroque*] (1968/1981), ["Rezitativ"] (1972-), ["Theory"] (**1980**); Palm (1965); Ratner (1956),

(1980); Reilly (1984-85); Reimer ["Concerto"] (1972-), ["Kammermusik"] (1972-), ["Kenner"] (1972-), (1973); Ritzel (1967/1968); Rosenblum (1988); Rothschild (1961); Schmalzriedt ["Episode"] (1972-), (1985); Schmidt (1979/1981); Seaton (1981); Seidel (1971), (1972-), (1975), (1976); Serauky (1929); Shellhous (1988); Sisman (1978); Smiles (1978); Spitzer and Zaslaw (1986); Stevens (1974); Stowell (1985); Telesco (forthcoming); Tittel (1966); Todd (1983); Vogel (1955/1954); Wirth (1966); **Zaminer (1985)**.

JAN PIETERSZOON SWEELINCK

[1562 – 1621]

Jan Pieterszoon Sweelinck was among the most highly respected teachers of his era and a leading propagator of the theories of Gioseffo ZARLINO. He may have written a composition manual for his students. What survives are various German manuscripts which reveal a direct connection with ZARLINO's *Le istitutioni harmoniche* on matters of counterpoint, as well as some original material (probably by Matthias Weckmann) on double counterpoint. The most complete version, once housed at Hamburg, was lost during World War Two, but fortunately an edition (and comparison with other manuscripts) had been completed at the beginning of the century. This copy had once belonged to J. A. Reincken, who in another now lost manuscript provided an amplified version of much of its contents. Less important manuscript sources are extant in Berlin and Vienna.

"Kompositionsregeln"

> Mss. [Vienna: Minoritenkonvent; Berlin: Deutsche Staatsbibliothek, Musikabteilung.]
>
> > The two "lost" manuscripts perhaps were taken into the Soviet Union in 1945.

S ● Gehrmann, Hermann, ed. *Werken van Jan Pieterszn. Sweelinck*. Vol. 10. The Hague: Martinus Nijhoff; Leipzig: Breitkopf & Härtel, 1901; reprint edition, Farnborough, England: Gregg International Publishers, 1968.

T ● Mathis, Victoria G. "Introduction and Translation of Jan Pieterszn Sweelinck's *Rules of Composition*." M.A. thesis, Memphis State University, 1975.

LITERATURE:

Eitner, Robert. "Ueber die acht, respektive zwölf Tonarten und über den Gebrauch der Versetzungszeichen im XVI. und XVII. Jahrhunderte nach Joh. Peter Sweelinck." *MMg* 3/9 (1871):133-51.

Seiffert, Max. "J. P. Sweelinck und seine direkten deutschen Schüler." Ph.D. dissertation, The University of Leipzig, 1891; published in *VfMw* 7 (1891):145-260.

> Summary in *TvNm* 4/1 (1892-94):1-16.

Vente, Maarten Albert; Vlam, Christiaan; and Annegarn, Alfons. "Sweelinck." Translated by Ursula Aarburg. In *MGG* (1949-68). Bibliog.

Tollefsen, Randall H. "Sweelinck, Jan Pieterszoon." In *NGrove* (1980). Bibliog.

● ● ● Walker, Paul. "From Renaissance 'Fuga' to Baroque Fugue: The Role of the 'Sweelinck Theory Manuscripts'." *SchüJb 1985/86* (1986):93-104. Bibliog.

See also BERNHARD: Braun (1968); FÉTIS: (1833-44); RIEMANN: (1898); WALTHER: (1732); Gehrmann (1891); LITERATURE SUPPLEMENT: Abraham (1968/1969); Apfel [*Beiträge*] (1964); Apfel ["Wandlungen"] (1964); ● ● ● Apfel (1981); Beer (1969); Beiche ["Inversio"] (1972-); Benary (1956/ 1961); Bukofzer (1947); Bullivant (1980); Cazden (1948); Chominski (1962/1981); David and Mendel (1945/1966); Eitner (1900-1904/1959-60); Falck (1965); Federhofer (1944/1950); Ferand (1937/1938); Flindell (1983-84); Gerber (1790-92/1977), (1812-14/1966); Jeppesen (1930/. . ./1974); Mann (1955/. . ./1987); Moser (1936/. . ./1959); Müller-Blattau (1923/. . ./ 1963); Palisca (1949-68); Reese (1954/1959); Robbins (1938); Rogers (1955); Snyder (1980); Soderlund (1980); Subirá (1947/. . ./1958); Troeger (1987); Walker (1987).

SERGEY IVANOVICH TANEEV

[1856–1915]

Whereas his teacher and friend CHAIKOVSKY had concentrated particularly upon harmony in his instruction at the Moscow Conservatory, Sergey Ivanovich Taneev, who succeeded CHAIKOVSKY and for several years served as the Conservatory's director, developed a formidable facility in the art of counterpoint. Taneev noted a decline in the quality of tonal composition towards the end of the nineteenth century and used his influential post as a teacher of some of Russia's finest young composers and theorists (including Rachmaninov, Skryabin, and YAVORSKY) in an attempt to curb it. As a result of his efforts, the Russian school of music theory attained a basis that was both more systematic and more speculative.

Although Taneev taught many subjects during his long tenure at the Conservatory, it was the study of counterpoint — both strict and free — and of form which occupied him most, especially in his later years there. He had planned to write an extensive series of textbooks. Only *Podvizhnoi kontrapunkt strogogo pis'ma* (1909), which has appeared in English as *Convertible Counterpoint in the Strict Style*, was completed, while his student Viktor Mikhailovich Beliaev pieced together his work on canon, *Uchenie o kanone*, for posthumous publication in 1929.

The essence of Taneev's contribution lies in the mathematical rigor with which he described contrapuntal transformations. Whereas vagueness and confusion had once ruled in the art, Taneev's perspective allowed many secrets to come to light with the clarity of algebraic formulas which could represent transformations of both pitch level (a vertical shift) and time (a horizontal shift). By notating interval sizes in accordance with the number of diatonic steps required to pass from one pitch to the other (e.g., a third is "2", an octave is "7"), intervals could be added and subtracted with ease. Special symbols for dissonances alerted practitioners to the special demands of each interval. Taneev's text covers the topic with a rigor and sophistication unmatched by any previous work on counterpoint. Though initially daunting, the system was found to make such types of contrapuntal manipulation much less problematical for his students. One must lament the fact that his pedagogical project did not progress far beyond this stage.

Several shorter documents relating to Taneev's study of Bach, Mozart, and Beethoven, as well as commentary by his pupils, assist in reviving Taneev's perspective on form. Seeking larger-scale relationships within the tonal framework, Taneev developed the conception of a "unifying tonality" into which the various harmonic details of a composition might be subsumed. His prime model for study was the same choice as SCHENKER's: the works of Beethoven. Though his conception is less thoroughly developed than that later advanced by SCHENKER, the assumptions that tonal structure is hierarchical, that structural importance sometimes exceeds an event's duration in time, and that analyses are effectively represented through a careful selection of pitches displayed in staff notation are among the characteristics shared by the two systems.

"O muzyke gorskikh tatar" [On the Music of the Mountain Tatars]

    VE 21/1 (1886):94-98.

    S ● See Protopopov (1947):195-211, below.

Podvizhnoi kontrapunkt strogogo pis'ma [Moveable Counterpoint in the Strict Style]

    Leipzig and Moscow: M. P. Beliaev, 1909. 2 vols. Moscow: Izdatel'stvo akademii nauk SSSR, 1959. Edited by S. S. Bogatyrev.

        Review in *Smuz* /1 (1961):193-95 (Vladimir Vasil'evich Protopopov).

    T ● Brower, G. Ackley, trans. *Convertible Counterpoint in the Strict Style*. Introduction by Serge Koussevitzky. Boston: Bruce Humphries, [1962].

        Reviews in *Composer* 17 (1965):6-7 (John Gardner), *JMT* 8/2 (1964):279-99 (James K. Randall), *MO* 89/1062 (1965-66):351 (H. D.), and *MT* 107/1475 (1966):38 (Gerald Abraham).

"Der Inhalt des Arbeitsheftes von W. A. Mozarts eigenhändig geschriebenen Übungen mit den Unterweisungen durch seinen Vater im strengen Kontrapunkt und reinen Satz (41 Blätter Querquart gebunden)"

    JBISM 1913 33 (1914).

    T ● "Soderzhanie tetradi sobstvennoruchnykh uprazhnenii Motsarta v strogom kontrapunkte." In Protopopov (1947):182-94, below.

Uchenie o kanone [The Doctrine of the Canon]

    Moscow: 1929. Edited by Viktor Mikhailovich Beliaev.

Manuscripts pertaining to music theory

    S ● Kuznetsov, Konstantin Alekseevich, ed. *Sergei Ivanovich Taneev: Lichnost', tvorchestvo i dokumenty ego zhizni: K 10-ti letiiu so dnia ego smerti 1915-1925.* [Sergei Ivanovich Taneev: Personality, Creativity and Documents of His Life: For the 10th Anniversary of His Death 1915-1925.] Moscow: 1925.

S ● Beliaev, Viktor, ed. " 'Analiz moduliatsii v sonatakh Betkhovena' S. I. Taneeva." ['The Analysis of Modulations in Beethoven's Sonatas' by S. I. Taneev.] In *Russkaia kniga o Betkhovene* [The Russian Book on Beethoven], edited by Konstantin Alekseevich Kuznetsov, pp. 191-204. Moscow: Gosudarstvennaia akademiia khudozhestvennikh nauk, 1927.

S ● Kiselev, V. A.; Livanova, T. N.; and Protopopov, Vladimir Vasil'evich. *S. I. Taneev: Materialy i dokumenty: Perepiska i vospominaniia.* [S. I. Taneev: Materials and Documents: Correspondence and Reminiscences.] Vol. 1. Moscow: Izdatel'stvo Akademii Nauk SSSR, 1952.

> Includes "Neskol'ko pisem S. I. Taneeva po muzykal'no-teoreticheskim voprosam" [Several Letters of S. I. Taneev on Music Theory Questions], by Vladimir Vasil'evich Protopopov, pp. 219-249.

S ● Arzamanov, Fedor Georgievich. "S. Taneev: Iz konservatorskikh lektsii." [S. I. Taneev: From Conservatory Lectures.] *Smuz* /1 (1953):44-48.

S ● Arzamanov, Fedor Georgievich. "Zavety S. Taneeva." [Precepts of S. Taneev.] *Smuz* /11 (1956): 27 -39.

S ● Korabel'nikova, Liudmila Zinovevna. "Novye materialy o S. I. Taneeve." [New Material on S. I. Taneev.] *Smuz* /9 (1959):70-73.

S ● Korabel'nikova, L. Z., ed. "Pis'ma S. I. Taneeva k P. N. Renchitskomu." In *Iz arkhivov russkikh muzykantov* [From the Archives of Russian Musicians], pp. 27-48 (Moscow: Gosudarstvennoe muyzkal'noe izdatel'stvo, 1962).

S ● Arzamanov, Fedor Georgievich, and Korabel'nikova, Liudmila Zinovevna, eds. *S. I. Taneev: Iz nauchno-pedagogicheskogo naslediia: Neopublikovannye materialy, vospominaniia uchenikov.* [S. I. Taneev: From the Scientific-Pedagogic Legacy: Unpublished Materials, Recollections of Students.] Moscow: Muzyka, 1967. [*Rilm* 69-2857.]

> A collection of Taneev's essays and analyses, including: "Razbor nachal'nykh nomerov h-moll'noi massy Bakha" [Analysis of the Beginning Numbers of the B-Minor Mass of Bach] (pp. 17-38); "Tezisy lektsii o dvoinoi fuge" [Theses of a Lecture on Double Fugue] (pp. 39-41); "Fragment iz varianta Vstupleniia k knige *Podvizhnoi kontrapunkt strogogo pis'ma*" [A Fragment from a Variant to the Introduction to the Book *Moveable Counterpoint in the Strict Style*] (pp. 49-54); "Zametki o sonatnykh reprisakh Betkhovena"

[Notes on Sonata Recapitulations of Beethoven] (pp. 150-54); "Grafiki tonal'nogo razvitiia fug iz *Khorosho temperiovannogo klavira* I. S. Bakh" [Graphs of the Tonal Development of Fugues from the *Well-Tempered Clavier* of J. S. Bach] (pp. 155-63).

Taneev also translated two works by Ludwig Bußler into Russian: *Uchebnik form instrumental'noi muzyki* (1884), with Nikolai Kashkin, and *Strogii stil'* (1885).

LITERATURE:

Kurdiumov, Yury Vladimirovich. "Novyi metod izucheniia kontrapunkta: Sergei Taneev: *Podvizhnoi kontrapunkt strogogo pis'ma.*" [A New Method of Studying Counterpoint: Sergei Taneev: *Movable Counterpoint in the Strict Style.*] Rmg /14 (1910):381-88.

Beliaev, Viktor Mikhailovich. "*Podvizhnoi kontrapunkt strogogo pis'ma* S. I. Taneeva." [*Moveable Counterpoint in the Strict Style* of S. I. Taneev.] *Muzïka* 125 (1913):259-67.

Beliaev, Viktor Mikhailovich. "Muzykal'no-teoreticheskie eskizy (o *Podvizhnom kontrap unkte strogogo pis'ma* S. I. Taneeva). [Music Theory Sketches (about *Moveable Counterpoint in the Strict Style* of S. I. Taneev).] *Muzïka* 215, 223-24 (1915):187-90, 331-33, 347-48.

Beliaev, Viktor Mikhailovich. "*Podvizhnoi kontrapunkt strogogo pis'ma* S. I. Taneeva." [*Moveable Counterpoint in the Strict Style* of S. I. Taneev.] *Muzsov* /8 (1916):115-29.

Engel, Yuly. "S. I. Taneev, kak uchitel'." [S. I. Taneev as a Teacher.] *Muzsov* /8 (1916):42-73.

> Includes Taneev's "Table of Consonances and Dissonances" opposite page 60.

YAVORSKY, Boleslav Leopol'dovich. "Vospominaniia o S. I. Taneeve." [Recollections about S. I. Taneev.] Ms., [ca. 1938]; published in YAVORSKY: Selected Works (1964-):Vol. 2:1 (1987):241-328.

> An excerpt was published as "Iz vospominanii o S. I. Taneeva" [From Recollections of S. I. Taneev] in *Smuz* /3 (1948):59-62.

Al'shvang, Arnol'd Aleksandrovich. "Perepiska S. I. Taneeva i N. N. Amani." [Correspondence of S. I. Taneev and N. N. Amani.] *Smuz* /7 (1940):75-78.

YAVORSKY, Boleslav Leopol'dovich. "Pis'ma S. I. Taneeva k N. N. Amani." [The Letters of S. I. Taneev to N. N. Amani.] *Smuz* /7 (1940):61-75.

Kotler, N. "Russkaia polifoniia i Taneev." [Russian Polyphony and Taneev.] *Smuz* /5 (1947):53-57.

Protopopov, Vladimir Vasil'evich, ed. *Pamiati Sergeia Ivanovicha Taneeva, 1856-1946: Sbornik statei i materialov k 90-letiiu so dnia rozhdeniia.* [In Memory of Sergei Ivanovich Taneev, 1856-1946: A Collection of Articles and Materials for the 90th Anniversary of His Birth.] Moscow and Leningrad: Muzyka, 1947.

Abraham, Gerald. "Tanejew, Sergei Iwanowitsch." Translated by Margarete Hoffmann-Erbrecht. In *MGG* (1949-68). Bibliog.

Gliere, Reinhold. "Vospominaniia o S. I. Taneeve." [Recollections about S. I. Taneev.] *Smuz* /7 (1955):41-46; reprinted in *R. M. Gliere: Stat'i i vospominaniia* [R. M. Gliere: Articles and Recollections], pp. 68-76 (Moscow: Muzyka, 1975).

Hartmann, Thomas de. "Sergei Ivanovitch Taneieff." *Tempo* 39 (1956):8-15.

Weinberg, Jacob. "Taneev's Audio-Visual Concept of Intervals; Re: Dr. Hugo Norden's 'Toward a Theory of Music'." *BUGJ* 4/10 (1956):176-78.

● ● ●Weinberg, Jacob. "Sergei Ivanovitch Taneiev." *MQ* 44/1 (1958):19-31.

Korabel'nikova, Liudmila Zinovevna. "Taneev o vospitanii kompozitora." [Taneev on the Education of a Composer.] *Smuz* /9 (1960):91-95.

Arzamanov, Fedor Georgievich. *Taneev—Prepodavatel' kursa muzykal'nykh form.* [Taneev—Teacher of a Course on Musical Forms.] Moscow:

Gosudarstvennoe muzykal'noe izdatel'stvo, 1963; revised edition, Moscow: Muzyka, 1984.

Gardner, John. "A Russian Contrapuntist." *Composer* 17 (1965):6-7.

Korabel'nikova, Liudmila Zinovevna. *S. I. Taneev v Moskovskoi konservatorii: Iz istorii russkogo muzykal'nogo obrazovaniia.* [S. I. Taneev in the Moscow Conservatory: From the History of Russian Musical Education.] Moscow: Muzyka, 1974.

Berkov, Viktor Osipovich. "K voprosu o funktsional'noi teorii v Rossii (Stasov, Serov, Larosh, Taneev)." [On the Question of Functional Theory in Russia (Stasov, Serov, Larosh, Taneev).] In his *Izbrannye stat'i i issledovaniia* (Moscow: Sovietskii kompozitor, 1977), pp. 47-53.

Brown, David. "Taneyev, Sergey Ivanovich." In *NGrove* (1980). Bibliog.

> Review in *MQ* 68/2 (1982):161-81 (Allen Forte).

Parker, Beverly Lewis. "Direct Shifting and Mixed Shifting: Important Contrapuntal Techniques or Taneev's Oddities?" *SAJM* 1 (1981):1-29.

Darrell, R. D. "Muscovite Phoenix: The Taneyev Phenomenon." *HFMA* 32/4 (1982):50-51, 80. [*Rilm* 82-954.]

See also LITERATURE SUPPLEMENT: Carpenter (1988); ● ● ●McQuere (1983); Subirá (1947/. . ./1958).

WILLIAM TANS'UR

[1700–1783]

The English country musician of the latter half of the eighteenth century was probably acquanted with the psalm tunes and instruction manuals of William Tans'ur. Though his command of composition and theory was limited, Tans'ur found a ready market for his wares, many of which, such as *A Compleat Melody* [1734], *The Melody of the Heart* (1735), and *The Royal Melody Compleat* (1754-55), included a brief introduction to music fundamentals along with straightforward hymn settings.

A more ambitious development of theoretical topics was offered as *A New Musical Grammar*, first issued in 1746 and repackaged numerous times well into the nineteenth century. The work served the same function as had those by PLAYFORD and SIMPSON in the seventeenth century. In fact, some of Tans'ur's notions are derived directly from SIMPSON, while his dialogue format is similar to MORLEY's, though not nearly so elegant. His perspective commands our attention mainly as a representation of how conservative rural music-making remained, and of what sorts of information someone who served as a teacher among

rural folk thought was important. In addition to routine discussions of clefs, note names, scales, and basic rules of composition, readers confronted pictures of pendulums which could be rigged up (with some inconvenience) to explore the concept of time in music. A brief dictionary of terms was included, making the book a true bargain for interested buyers.

A Compleat Melody; or, The Harmony of Sion . . . Containing a New and Compleat Introduction to the Grounds of Music . . . [*Rism* A/I/8, p. 309; B/VI/2, p. 816.]

> London: James Hodges (W. Pearson), [1734].
> Later editions through 1743.

> S ● *The Works of Mr. William Tans'ur* [*Rism* A/I/8, p. 310.]. Vol. 1. London: James Hodges ([A. and W. Pearson]), [ca. 1735-38]; later editions.

The Melody of the Heart [*Rism* A/I/8, pp. 309-10.]

London: James Hodges (W. Pearson), 1735.

> Later editions. Contains "Compendious Instructions on the Grounds of Musick."

S ● See [1734]:[ca. 1735-38], above.

A New Musical Grammar; or, The Harmonical Spectator, Containing All the Useful Theoretical, Practical, and Technical Parts of Musick . . . [Rism B/VI/2, pp. 817-18.]

> London: for the author (Jacob Robinson), 1746. [LCPS: T-003a. HoM: 1478.]
> London: for the author (Jacob Robinson), 1753.

>> Revised, as *A New Musical Grammar, and Dictionary; or, A General Introduction to the Whole Art of Musick . . .*:

> London: the author and his son; James Hodges (Robert Brown), 1756. [LCPS: T-003b. HoM: 1479.]

>> Revised, as *The Elements of Musick Display'd; or, Its Grammar, or Ground-work Made Easy . . .*:

> London: the author and his son (Stanley Crowder), 1772. [LCPS: T-004.]
> Stokesley: W. Pratt, [ca. 1819].
> London: I. T. Hinton, 1829.

>> Other printings.

S ● Facsimile of the 1772 edition. MMMLF, ser. 2, no. 43. New York: Broude Brothers, forthcoming.

The Royal Melody Compleat; or, The New Harmony of Sion . . . Containing a New and Correct Introduction to the Grounds of Musick . . . [Rism A/I/8, p. 310; B/VI/2, p. 818.]

London: James Hodges (R. Brown), 1754-55. Two vols.

> Several editions. Revised as *The American Harmony; or, Royal Melody Complete . . . [Rism A/I/8, p. 311; B/VI/2, pp. 816-17.]:*

Newburyport: Daniel Bailey, 1769. Two vols. [LCPS: T-002a.]

> Later editions through 1774. LCPS: [T-002c.]

LITERATURE:

Rix, Joseph. "William Tansur." *NQ* ser. 4, no. 2 (1868):257-58.

Rimbault, Edward F. "William Tans'ur." *NQ* ser. 4, no. 2 (1868):401-2.

Williamson, Winifred F. "Tansur, William." Translated by Christa Schimmelpfennig. In *MGG* (1949-68). Bibliog.

Flay, A. L. "An Entrancing Music Primer (William Tans'ur, 1756)." *MO* 92/1093 (1968):29-31.

Temperley, Nicholas. "Tans'ur, William." In *NGrove* (1980). Bibliog.

See also FÉTIS: (1833-44); LITERATURE SUPPLEMENT: Barbour (1952); Becker (1836-39/1964); Burke (1963); Burton (1956); Cazden (1948); **Coover (1980)**; Eitner (1900-1904/1959-60); Forkel (1792/ 1962); Gerber (1790-92/1977), (1812-14/1966); Gillingham (1981); Harding (1938); Harrán (1986); Houle (1987); Jackson (1988); **Kassler** (1971), (1976), ● ● ● **(1979)**; Mendel (1978); **Ritzel (1967/1968)**; **Seidel and Cooper (1986)**; Taddie (1984).

GIUSEPPE TARTINI

[1692 – 1770]

That so eminent a practical musician as Giuseppe Tartini could involve himself in so convoluted a theoretical system as that which he created is among the more curious facts in the history of music. Of course, RAMEAU was also wearing a scientist's hat in his musical speculations, though his influence upon Tartini was not particularly significant. One senses that Tartini purposefully couched his notions in abstruse language and intricate diagrams. But when—or, indeed, if—his perspective is mastered through arduous study, one might be confounded by its arbitrariness, the errors of its execution, and its aloofness from practical considerations.

Tartini divided the study of music into three components which, according to his system, should all produce the same results in order for opinion to attain the status of truth. The first of these involved empirical examination. For this purpose he utilized vibrating strings of various lengths—a reactionary idea, considering how much had been learned about overtones by the middle of the eighteenth century. He also explored the theoretical potential of what he called *terzi suoni* or difference tones—lower-pitched sounds which he had noticed as early as 1714 while playing two notes simultaneously on the violin. They served in Tartini's system as a natural justification for chordal structures. Second, he pursued the mathematical basis of music, focusing upon circles residing inside squares, into which he inserted a plethora of lines each representative of some proportion or relationship. This was his favored topic—one he felt was unjustly neglected by other theorists—and he pursued it vigorously, and defensively, even after receiving the critical evaluations of his contemporaries, including SERRE. From it he derived his major and minor triads, consonances and dissonances, and basic cadence types. Third, Tartini acknowledged the practical component of music, wherein scales are derived from harmony and pitch relationships are enhanced through temperament.

Tartini's perspective was first articulated in his *Trattato di musica secondo la vera scienza dell'armonia* (1754). He offered a simplified and abbreviated version of his ideas in 1767, as *De' principj dell'armonia musicale contenuta nel diatonico genere dissertazione*, and in the same year he defended himself against SERRE with his *Risposta*. Another major work was in progress upon his death: "La scienza platonica fondata sul cerchio." It was published in 1977 as part of a complete works edition, still in progress.

In addition to numerous manuscripts which have yet to be explored in a thorough fashion, Tartini is responsible for a brief yet celebrated text on ornamentation. Though it apparently emerged in the early 1750s and was widely circulated in manuscript (reaching Leopold MOZART before 1756, the year in which his violin method appeared), it was first published in a French translation around 1771. Here, at least, Tartini's artistic sensibilities were utilized, as he specified through numerous music examples the proper execution of the various ornaments used in violin playing. In addition, topics such as the standard non-vibrato tone, techniques of bowing, and cadenzas were addressed. The surviving versions of the work are not identical in content, and each has a somewhat different title. Perhaps Tartini's original (if there indeed was an original exclusive of his students' notes) lacked a title.

Correspondence with MARTINI

S ● See MARTINI: Correspondence: Parisini (1888).

"Regole per arrivare a saper ben suonar il violino . . ."

Ms., [ca. 1752-56]. [Lost.]

> Tartini's original manuscript, now lost, may have had no title. The above title is from a copy made by Tartini's student Giovanni Francesco Nicolai and now housed at the Conservatorio di musica "Benedetto Marcello" in Venice. An incomplete copy, called "Libro de regole, ed esempi necessari per ben suonare," is housed at the University of California, Berkeley. A catalogue of 1818 compiled by Joseph Benzon (and followed by FÉTIS) gave it the title "Trattato delle appoggiature si ascendenti che discendenti per il violino come pure il trillo, tremolo, mordente, ed altro, con dichiarazione delle cadenze naturali e composte." Generations of scholars made reference to the work as "Lezioni pratiche pel violino," derived from a reference to it in Abbé Fanzago's eulogy of Tartini.

T ● Denis, P[ietro], trans. *Traité des agrémens de la musique* . . . [*Rism* B/VI/2, pp. 820-21.] Paris: the translator, [1771] [LCPS: T-010b. SMLMS.]; La Chevardière, [1775].

> Announcement in *MdFr* (March 1771):178.

T ● Babitz, Sol, trans. "Treatise on Ornamentation — Giuseppe Tartini." *JRME* 4/2 (1956):75-102; reprinted as *Treatise on the Ornaments of Music*, Chicago: Music Educators National Conference, 1956; New York: Fischer, [1958]; 2nd edition, (Early Music Laboratory, Bulletin no. 6), Los Angeles: Early Music Laboratory, 1970. [*Rilm* 70-424.]

> Review in *GSJ* 12 (1959):99-100 (Kenneth M. Skeaping).

ST ● ● ● ● Jacobi, Erwin R., trans. and ed. *Traité des agréments de la musique* . . . English translation by Cuthbert Girdlestone. Celle: Hermann Moeck, 1961. Bibliog.

> A printing of the French translation by Denis with parallel texts in English and German, plus a facsimile of the Italian manuscript copy "Regole . . .", with English, German, and French translations of a portion of this manuscript which does not appear in the Denis version. As a supplement, Tartini's letter to Signora Maddalena Lombardini is printed in the original Italian and in English, French, and German translations from the eighteenth century (see below). Reviews in *Consort* 22 (1965):66 (Malcolm Playfoot), *GSJ* 16 (1963):111-12 (Anthony Baines), *JAMS* 15/3 (1962):369 (David Burrows), *JMT* 6/1 (1962): 159-60 (Charles Kent), *Mf* 16/3 (1963):309-11 (Paul Brainard), *ML* 44/2 (1963):166-68 (Robert Donington), *MT* 102/1426 (1961):784-85 (Denis Stevens), *Musica* 16/1 (1962):42 (Werner Bollert), *ÖM* 16/1 (1961):555 (k.), *Orch* 12 (1964):269, *L'organo* 4/2 (1963):224-27 (Luigi Ferdinando Tagliavini), *QdRm* 3 (1965):203-5 (Alfredo Bonaccorsi), *Rdm* 47/2 (1961):216-17 (Marc Pincherle), *SMz* 102/3 (1962):190-91 (mr.), and *Stfm* 44 (1962):116-17 (Ingmar Bengtsson).

Trattato di musica secondo la vera scienza dell'armonia [*Rism* B/VI/2, p. 820.]

> Padua: Stamperia del seminario (Giovanni Manfrè), 1754. [LCPS: T-010a. HoM: 1482. IDC.]
>
> See SERRE: (1763).

T ● Rubeli, Alfred Ulrich. "Giuseppe Tartini: Musiktraktat gemäß der richtigen Wissenschaft der Harmonie, Padua 1754: Übersetzt, mit Einführungen und Erläuterungen versehen." Ph.D. dissertation, The University of Zürich, 1958; published in two separate volumes: *Das Musiktheoretische System Giuseppe Tartinis*, Winterthur: Keller, 1958 [commentary on the treatise]; and *Traktat über die Musik gemäß der wahren Wissenschaft von der Harmonie* [translation and commentary] (OSGM, no. 6), Düsseldorf: Gesellschaft zur Förderung der systematischen Musikwissenschaft e. V., 1966. Bibliog.

> Reviews in *Mf* 22/2 (1969):258-59 (Peter Benary), *MK* 37/4 (1967):170 (Martin Geck), *Musica* 21/5 (1967):256 (Fritz Bose), *Notes* 24/4 (1967-68):718 (Robert Donington), and *NZfM* 132/8 (1971):457 (Heinrich Sievers).

S ● Facsimile edition. MMMLF, ser. 2, no. 8. New York: Broude Brothers, 1966.

> Review in *Mf* 22/2 (1969):258-59 (Peter Benary).

S ● Facsimile edition. See Collected Works: (1973-77):(1973), below.

T ● Johnson, Fredric Bolan. "Tartini's *Trattato di musica secondo la vera scienza dell'armonia*: An Annotated Translation with Commentary." Ph.D. dissertation, Indiana University, 1985. [*DA* 47/06A, pp. 1919-20. UMI 86-17820.]

"Regola per bene accordare il violino"

> Ms., [ca. 1754-67]. [Vienna: Gesellschaft der Musikfreunde.]

T ● Jacobi, Erwin R., trans. "Giuseppe Tartini's *Regola per bene accordare il violino*." In *KaufmannFs* (1981):199-207. Postscript translated by David A. Scrase. [*Rilm* 81-3566.]

"Lettera del defonto signor Giuseppe Tartini alla signora Maddalena Lombardini [later Signora Sirmen], inserviente ad una importante lezione per i suonatori di violino"

> Ms., 1760. [Lost.]

S ● *L'Europa letteraria* 5/2 (1770):75-79.

S ● Venice: Colombani, 1770. [*Rism* B/VI/2, p. 819.]

ST ● Burney, Charles, trans. *Lettera . . ./A Letter from the Late Signor Tartini to Signora Maddalena Lombardini . . .* [*Rism* B/VI/2, p. 820.] London: R. Bremner (George Bigg), 1771; 1779 [LCPS: T-009.]; reprint edition, London: William Reeves, 1913; reprint of the 1779 edition (MPT), New York: Johnson Reprint Corporation, 1967. See [ca. 1752-56]:Jacobi (1961), above.

> Reviews in *Notes* 25/1 (1968-69):46-47 (Robert Donington) and *Rmi* 21/1 (1914):165-66 (B.).

ST ● [Thomas, Antoine-Léonard, trans.] "Lettre de feu Tartini . . ., servant de leçon importante à ceux qui jouent du violon [en Italien & François]." In *Jdm An 1773*, no. 2 (1773):15-29; reprint edition, in Bouvet, Charles, *Une leçon de Giuseppe Tartini et une femme violoniste au XVIIIe siècle*, Paris: Maurice Sénart, 1915; revised edition, 1918. See [ca. 1752-56]:Jacobi (1961), above.

T ● Hiller, Johann Adam, trans. German translation. In Hiller (1784); reprint edition (as *Brief des Joseph Tartini an Magdalena Lombardini, enthaltend eine wichtige Lection für die Violinspieler*, edited by Heinrich Leopold Rohrmann), Hanover: W. Pockwitz jun., 1786. [*Rism* B/VI/2, p. 820.] See [ca. 1752-56]:Jacobi (1961), above.

ST ● See [ca. 1752-56]:Jacobi (1961), above.

"La scienza platonica fondata sul cerchio"

> Ms., [ca. 1764-70]. [Piran, Yugoslavia: Biblioteca del Museo del Mare.]

S ● Todeschini, Cavalla Anna, ed. See Collected Works: (1973-77):(1977), below.

De' principj dell'armonia musicale contenuta nel diatonico genere dissertazione [*Rism* B/VI/2, p. 819.]

> Padua: Stamperia del seminario (Giovanni Manfrè), 1767. [LCPS: T-007. SMLMS.]

S ● Facsimile edition. MMMLF, ser. 2, no. 64. New York: Broude Brothers, 1967.

S ● Facsimile edition. Hildesheim: Georg Olms, 1970.

S ● Facsimile edition. See Collected Works: (1973-77):(1974), below.

Risposta . . . alla critica del di lui trattato di musica di Mons. Le Serre di Ginevra [*Rism* B/VI/2, p. 820.]

> Venice: Antonio Decastro, 1767.

"Libro del contrapunto"

> Ms. [Berlin: Deutsche Staatsbibliothek.]
> The Berlin copy is dated 1774.

"Regola del terzo suono"

> Ms. [London: British Library, Reference Division; Bologna: Conservatorio di musica G. B. Martini.]

"Ricerca del vero principio dell'armonia"

Ms. [Piran, Yugoslavia: Biblioteca del Museo del Mare (?).]

S ● Stefani, Attilio, ed. "Tartini: Dissertazione su la 'Ricerca del vero principio dell'armonia'." *AARov* 160 [ser. 3, vol. 16, no. 2] (1910):107-34.

More complete coverage of Tartini's numerous manuscripts is found in Capri (1945), below, and in Brainard (1949-68), below.

COLLECTED WORKS EDITION:

Le opera di Giuseppe Tartini, ser. 2, nos. 1-3. Padua: Casa editrice dott. Antonio Milani, 1973 (no. 1), 1974 (no. 2), 1977 (no. 3).

> Review in *Notes* 35/2 (1978-79):317-19 (Edward F. Houghton).

LITERATURE:

Anonymous. *Risposta di un anonimo al celebre Signor Rousseau circa al suo sentimento in proposito d'alcune proposizioni del Sig. Giuseppe Tartini.* [*Rism* B/VI/2, p. 980.] Venice: Antonio de Castro, 1769.

> Perhaps written by Tartini himself.

Stillingfleet, Benjamin. *Principles and Power of Harmony.* London: J. and H. Hughs (S. Baker and G. Leigh; B. White; J. Robson; J. Walter), 1771. [*Rism* B/VI/2, p. 809. LCPS: S-126. HoM: 1464.]

Pulver, Jeffrey. "The Literary Works of Giuseppe Tartini." *MMR* 52/621 (1922):215-16.

Capri, Antonio. *Giuseppe Tartini: Con 22 illustrazioni e un catalogo tematico.* IGmis. Milan: Garzanti, 1945. Bibliog.

Brainard, Paul. "Tartini, Giuseppe." In *MGG* (1949-68). Bibliog.

Meyer, Max F. "Subjective Tones: Tartini and Beat-Tone Pitches." *AJP* 70/4 (1957):646-50. Bibliog.

Boyden, David D. "The Missing Italian Manuscript of Tartini's *Traité des Agrémens*." *MQ* 46/3 (1960):315-28.

● ● ● Planchart, Alejandro Enrique. "A Study of the Theories of Giuseppe Tartini." *JMT* 4/1 (1960):32-61. Bibliog.

Jacobi, Erwin R. "G. F. Nicolai's Manuscript of Tartini's *Regole per ben suonar il violino*." Translated by Willis Wager. *MQ* 47/2 (1961):207-23.

Elmer, Minnie. "Tartini's Improvised Ornamentation as Illustrated by Manuscripts from the Berkeley Collection of Eighteenth-Century Italian Instrumental Music." M.A. thesis, The University of California at Berkeley, 1962.

Abbado, Michelangelo. "Presenza e udibilità degli armonici inferiori e conseguente spiegazione del terzo e quarto suono." *Mog* 8/3 (1965):76-78.

Petrobelli, Pierluigi. "Tartini, le sue idee e il suo tempo." *Nrmi* 1/4 (1967):651-75. [*Rilm* 68-384.]

Petrobelli, Pierluigi. *Giuseppe Tartini: Le fonti biografiche.* Smven, no. 1. Florence: Universal Edition (Stiav), 1968. Bibliog.

> Reviews in *Hroz* 23/8 (1970):380-81, *Mf* 24/2 (1971):226-27 (Franz Giegling), *Nrmi* 4/6 (1970):1175-78 (Agostino Ziino), *Rdm* 54/2 (1968):259-60 (Marc Pincherle), and *Ridm* 4 (1970):1175-78.

Petrobelli, Pierluigi. "La scuola di Tartini in Germania e la sua influenza." *Anamu* 5 (1968):1-17. Bibliog. [*Rilm* 69-914.]

Abbado, Michelangelo. "Presenza di Tartini nel nostro secolo." *Rmi* 4/6 (1970):1087-1106. [*Rilm* 72-3070.]

Spodenkiewicz, Wiktor. "Giuseppe Tartini 1692-1770 w 200 rocznice šmierci." *Rmuz* 14/9 (1970):16.

Frasson, Leonardo. "Bibliografia Tartiniana." In *Il Santo Rivista Antoniana di Storia, Dottrina, Arte.* Padua. 2/17/1-2 (1977):283-305.

● ● ● Walker, David Pickering. "The Musical Theory of Tartini." In *Oxford Symposium 1977* (1980):93-111; expanded version in Walker (1978): Chapter 8.

Staehelin, Martin. "Giuseppe Tartini über seine künstlerische Entwicklung: Ein unbekanntes Selbstzeugnis." *AfMw* 35/4 (1978):251-74. Bibliog. [*Rilm* 78-4909.]

Cavallini, Ivano. "Musica e teoria nelle lettere di G. Tartini a padre G. B. Martini." In *AASIB* 68 (1979-80).

Brainard, Paul. "Tartini, Giuseppe." In *NGrove* (1980). Bibliog.

Grimm, Betty Jane. "Treble Choral Acoustics (Tartini's Tone)." *CJ* 21/8 (1981):23-26.

See also d'ALEMBERT: (1752): Elsberry (1984); EXIMENO: [*Dell'origine*] (1774); FÉTIS: (1833-44); (1840); d'INDY: (1903-50); MOMIGNY: (1791-1818); RAMEAU: Pischner (1961/. . ./1967); RIEMANN: (1898); ROUSSEAU, J.-J.: (1768); SERRE: (1763); WALTHER: (1732); LITERATURE SUPPLEMENT: Abbado (1964); Almond (1979); Asselin (1983/1985); Badura-Skoda et al. (1980); Becker (1836-39/1964); Beer (1969); Beyschlag (1907/1953); Bircher (1970); Blood (1979); Burke (1963); Burney (1776-89/. . ./1957); Castellani (1976); Cavallini (1949); Cazden (1948), (1980); Chailley (1967); Chevaillier (1925/1931-32); Cohen (1981); Cohen (1984); **Dahlhaus (1984)**; **Dahlhaus et al. (1987)**; Devore (1987); de Zeeuw (1983); Donington (1963/. . ./1974); Eitner (1900-1904/1959-60); Fellerer (1927/. . ./1972); Fokker (1955); Forkel (1792/1962); Fubini (1971/1983); Gerber (1790-92/1977), (1812-14/1966);

Haase (1969); Hartmann (1923); Heinlein (1927/1928); Hoffman (1953); Houle (1960), (1987); Imig (1969/1970); Jackson (1988); Jacobi (1957-60/1971); Jeppesen ([1951]/1952); Jones (1934); Jorgenson (1957), (1963); Kassler (1971), (1979); Kauko (1958); Krehbiel (1964); La Borde (1780/1978); Lang (1941); **Lindley** ["Just"] **(1980)**, (1982); Lippman (1986); List (1976); Mitchell, J. W. (1963); Mitchell, W. J. (1963); **Neumann**, Frederick (1978), [*Essays*] **(1982)**, (1969), (1986); Newman (1985); Newman (1959/. . ./1983); **Palisca** ["Theory"] **(1980)**; Perinello (1936); Petrobelli (1968); Pole (1879/. . ./1924); Reese (1957/1970); Révész (1946/. . ./1954); Robison (1982); Rohwer (1949-68); Rosenblum (1988); Schoffman ["Descriptive"] (1983); **Seidel and Cooper (1986)**; Sheppard (1978-79); **Shirlaw (1917/. . ./1970)**, (1931); Smiles (1978); Snyder (1980-81); Spender and Shuter-Dyson (1980); Stowell (1985); Subirá (1947/. . ./1958); Truesdell (1960); Vogel (1955/1954), (1962), (1975/1984), **Walker (1978)**; Wellesz and Sternfeld (1973); Whitmore (1988); Wirth (1966); **Zaminer (1985)**; Zaslaw (1979).

GEORG MICHAEL TELEMANN

[1748 – 1831]

As did his grandfather and teacher Georg Philipp TELEMANN, Georg Michael Telemann wrote on figured bass, in a practical treatise called *Unterricht im Generalbaß-Spielen* (1773). Less learned and directed more towards beginners than were the classic treatises of C. P. E. BACH and MARPURG, this brief work was confined to the essentials of the practice and purported to represent a modernization of perspective, as compared with these somewhat older works, of which he was nevertheless (and for good reason) enamored. In a single table, he established what he regarded as the ideal realizations for a large variety of figures. For example, the table reveals that 5 and 8 are to be added when the figure is 3 or a sharp sign; 6 is added when the figure is 4/2 or 4/3. After completing this work, Telemann was more inclined towards promoting his grandfather's music than writing further treatises.

Unterricht im Generalbaß-Spielen, auf der Orgel oder sonst einem Clavier-Instrumente [*Rism* B/VI/2, pp. 822-23.]

Hamburg: Michael Christian Bock, 1773. [LCPS: T-018. IDC.]

Review in *AdB* 22/1 (1774):242-48 [Johann Friedrich AGRICOLA], to which Telemann responded (Riga, 1775).

Über die Wahl der Melodie eines Kirchenliedes . . .

Riga: 1821.

LITERATURE:

Chrysander, F. "Briefe von Karl Philipp Emanuel Bach und G. M. Telemann." *AmZ* new series, 4/23-24 (1869): 177-81, 185-87.

Miesner, Heinrich. "Die Lebensskizze des jüngerer Telemann (1748 – 1831) und seine Werke." *ZVhG* 33 (1933):[143]-56.

Ruhnke, Martin. "Telemann . . . Georg Michael." In *MGG* (1949-68). Bibliog.

Ruhnke, Martin. "Telemann, Georg Michael." In *NGrove* (1980). Bibliog.

See also FÉTIS: (1833-44); QUANTZ: Reilly (1974); LITERATURE SUPPLEMENT: ● ● ● Arnold (1931/. . ./1965); Bauman (1977); Becker (1836-39/ 1964); Eitner (1900-1904/1959-60); Frobenius ["Vollstimmig"] (1972-); Gerber (1790-92/1977); Harich-Schneider ([1939]/. . ./1970); Williams, P. (1970).

GEORG PHILIPP TELEMANN

[1681 – 1767]

The career of Georg Philipp Telemann was marked by extraordinarily successful relations with young musicians, whose lives were enriched by his generosity and by initiatives which resulted in stimulating performance opportunities. This same spirit led Telemann to develop numerous pedagogical plans—including a translation of FUX and a treatise on composition—which, however, never materialized. One project, *Der critische Musikus*, was to be a shared responsibility with SCHEIBE, who, it turns out, wrote the journal himself, though certainly with Telemann's guidance and criticism.

What Telemann completed falls far short of his grand plans: tidbits of perceptive commentary scattered among the prefaces to his compositions, and a demonstration of and comments upon basic figured-bass realization in his *Singe-, Spiel- und General-Baß-Übungen*, individual pieces of which were issued beginning in 1733. In his *Musikalisches Lob Gottes* [1744] Telemann proposed revisions in the notation of figured bass, incorporating horizontal, diagonal, and curved strokes in conjunction with the figures. In his "Neues musikalisches System," written for MIZLER's Sozietät der Musikalischen Wissenschaften, Telemann presented a somewhat muddled account of the distinction between enharmonically equivalent pitches.

Correspondence

> S ● Grosse, Hans, and Jung, Hans Rudolf. *Briefwechsel: Sämtliche erreichbaren Briefe von und an Telemann*. Leipzig: Deutscher Verlag für Musik, 1972. [*Rilm* 73-394.]
>
>> Reviews in *MG* 24/1 (1974):52-53 (Ingeborg Allihn) and *Notes* 30/3 (1973-74):519-21 (Mary Peckham Day).
>
> S ● See QUANTZ: (1753).

Preface to *Fortsetzung des Harmonischen Gottes-Dienstes oder geistliche Cantaten . . .* [*Rism* A/I/8, p. 329.]

> Hamburg: the author (Philipp Ludwig Stromer), 1731-32.

Singe-, Spiel- und General-Baß-Übungen [*Rism* A/I/8, p. 329.]

> [Hamburg: the author, 1733-34.]
>
>> Review in MIZLER: (1736-54):Vol. 2/1 (1740):144-45.
>
> S ● Seiffert, Max, ed. VOBIMg, no. 2. Berlin: Leo Leipmannssohn, 1914; later printings; a Japanese translation (as *Tsuso teion no rensyu*, translated by Mitsugu Yamada and Tsuneo Sunaga), Tokyo: Sinfonia, 1977.
>
>> Review in *Rmi* 28/4 (1921):733 (G. M.).
>
> S ● Facsimile edition. Leipzig: Zentralantiquariat der DDR.

Anleitung, wie man einer General-Baß . . . in alle Tone transponiren könne [*Rism* B/VI/1, p. 393.]

> By Carl Johann Friedrich Haltmeier, edited by Telemann.
>
> Hamburg: Johann Georg Piscator, 1737.

Preface to *Musikalisches Lob Gottes in der Gemeine des Herrn . . .* [*Rism* A/I/8, p. 330.]

> Nuremberg: Balthasar Schmid, [1744].

"Neues musikalisches System"

> In MIZLER: (1736-54):Vol. 3/4 (1752):713-19.

> Review in MIZLER: (1736-54):Vol. 3/4 (1752):720-26 (Christoph Gottlieb SCHRÖTER).

> S ● Revised version, as "Letzte Beschäftigung G. P. Telemanns, im 86sten Lebensjahre, bestehend in einer musikalischen Klang- und Intervallen-Tafel." *UKK* 3 (1767):346-52.

See also KELLNER: (1732):(1737).

See also a collection of Telemann's prefaces, autobiographies, and sundry other documents: *Singen ist das Fundament zur Musik in allen Dingen: Eine Dokumentensammlung*, edited by Werner Rackwitz (RUB, no. 845: Kunstwissenschaften; Leipzig: Philipp Reclam, 1981; TzMw, no. 80; Wilhelmshaven: Heinrichshofen's Verlag, 1981). Bibliog. [*Rilm* 81-212.]

> Reviews in *MB* 14/5 (1982):364-65 (Eckart Kleßmann), *Mf* 37/4 (1984):310-11 (Franz Giegling), *MSch* 32/9 (1981):297-98 (Ingeborg Allihn), *ÖM* 37/7-8 (1982):439 (Manfred Wagner), and *Tibia* 8/1 (1983):293-94 (Reinhold Quandt).

LITERATURE:

Frey, Max W. "Georg Philipp Telemanns *Singe-, Spiel- und Generalbaß-Übungen*: Ein Beitrag zur Geschichte des begleiteten Kunstliedes." Ph.D. dissertation, The University of Zürich, 1921 (1922); published edition, Zürich: G. Lais, 1922.

Ruhnke, Martin. "Telemann, Georg Philipp." In *MGG* (1949-68). Bibliog.

Maertens, Willi. "Georg Philipp Telemann und die Musikerziehung." *MSch* 15/12 (1964):498-502, 515-22. Bibliog.

Pečman, Rudolf. "Der Generalbaß in der Auffassung Georg Philipp Telemanns und František Xaver Brixis." Translated by Jan Gruna. In *Telemann Festtage 1973* (1975):93-99. [*Rilm* 76-9776.]

Allihn, Ingeborg. "Modell oder Anleitung zum Handeln? Bemerkungen zu Telemanns Beiträgen zur Verzierungspraxis in der Instrumentalmusik." In *Konferenzbericht Blankenburg/Harz 1979* (1980):10-14. [*Rilm* 80-1758.]

● ● ● Ruhnke, Martin. "Telemann, Georg Philipp." In *NGrove* (1980). Bibliog.

Bergmann, Walter. "Telemann on the Continuo." *RecMus* 8/1 (1984-86):2-3.

See also FÉTIS: (1833-44); HEINICHEN: (1728):Buelow (1961/. . ./1986); MATTHESON: (1731); (1740); RIEMANN: (1898); SCHRÖTER (1746); SORGE: (1744); [1748]; (1754); [1758]; WALTHER: (1732); LITERATURE SUPPLEMENT: ● ● ● **Arnold (1931/. . ./1965)**; Auhagen (1982/1983); Becker (1836-39/1964); Boomgaarden (1985/1987); Carse (1925/

1964); Chew (1980); **Dahlhaus et al. (1987)**; David and Mendel (1945/1966); Dean (1977); Dreyfus (1987); Eitner (1900-1904/1959-60); Ferand [*Improvisation*] (1956/1961); Forkel (1792/1962); Gerber (1790-92/1977); Hammel (1977-78); Harich-Schneider ([1939]/. . ./1970); Heimann (1970/1973); Jackson (1988); Jung (1969); Keller (1931/. . ./1966); Mann (1987); Mitchell, W. J. (1963); Neumann (1978), ["Appoggiatura"] (1982), (1986); Oberdörffer (1949-68); Reimer ["Kammermusik"] (1972-), ["Kenner"] (1972-); Sachs (1984); Stowell (1985); Subirá (1949/. . ./1958); Tittel (1966); Troeger (1987); Ulrich (1931/1932); Wichmann (1966); Williams, P. (1970); Wirth (1966).

ZACCARIA TEVO

[1651 — ca. 1709-12]

Whereas most theoretical writings propound an individual theorist's views on a specific aspect of music, occasionally there appeared a work which summarized a large body of information, with no pretensions of originality. Zaccaria Tevo's *Musico testore* (1706) borrows profusely from authors both ancient and modern and provides, in under four hundred pages, a rich compendium of the ideas and techniques which formed the basis for early eighteenth-century theory. GALILEI, MERSENNE, and KIRCHER are among the more recent authorities cited, while Boethius, GLAREAN, and especially the early seventeenth-century humanist Gregor Reisch are likewise called upon. Topics ranging from basic aspects of notation and intervals to the complex art of counterpoint mingle between the covers of this useful but now neglected volume.

Il musico testore . . . [*Rism* B/VI/2, pp. 826-27.]

Venice: Antonio Bortoli, 1706. [LCPS: T-030. SMLMS.]

S ● Facsimile edition. BmB, ser. 2, no. 47. Bologna: Forni, 1969.

LITERATURE:

D'Alessi, Giovanni. "Tevo, Zaccaria." Translated by Renate Albrecht. In *MGG* (1949-68). Bibliog.

● ● ● Gallo, Franco Alberto. "Il *Musico testore* di Zaccaria Tevo." *Quad* 8 (1967):101-11. Bibliog.

D'Alessi, Giovanni. "Tevo, Zaccaria." In *NGrove* (1980). Bibliog.

See also FÉTIS: (1833-44); MATTHESON: (1739); WALTHER: (1732); LITERATURE SUPPLEMENT: Becker (1836-39/1964); Blumröder (1972-); Eitner (1900-1904/1959-60); Gerber (1790-92/1977); Ghislanzoni (1949-51); Hawkins (1776/. . ./1969); Lindley (1982); Schmalzriedt ["Coda"] (1972-).

JOACHIM THURINGUS

[b. late sixteenth century]

At a time when books lacked wide distribution, the publication of compendia of others' works served a useful function in making available materials that otherwise would be inaccessible. Joachim Thuringus's *Opusculum bipartitum* (1624) is drawn from a wide array of sources, particularly treatises by GLAREAN, HOFFMANN, and EICHMANN for music fundamentals and modal theory, and by BURMEISTER and especially NUCIUS for their formulations of rhetorical figures used in *musica poetica*.

Thuringus clarified the relationship between improvised and written-out counterpoint, reversing the more normative conception by stating that notated florid counterpoint should emulate the improvised manner. He listed fifteen musical figures, three of which were designated as especially important: *Commissura*, *Fuga*, and *Syncopatio*.

Nucleus musicus de modis seu tonis, ex optimus . . . musicorum abstrusioribus scriptus [*Rism* B/VI/2, p. 831.]

Berlin: Georg Runge, 1622.

Opusculum bipartitum de primordiis musicis . . . [*Rism* B/VI/2, p. 831.]

Revised and expanded version of (1622), above.

Berlin: Georg Runge (Johann Kall), 1624.
Berlin: Georg Runge (Johann Kall), 1625.

LITERATURE:

Federhofer-Königs, Renate. "Thuringus, Joachim." In *MGG* (1949-68). Bibliog.

● ● ●Buelow, George J. "Thuringus, Joachim." In *NGrove* (1980).

See also BURMEISTER: Ruhnke (1955); FÉTIS: (1833-44); GLAREAN: Miller (1961); WALTHER: (1732); Schmitz (1952); LITERATURE SUPPLEMENT: **Apfel (1981)**; Bartel (1982/1985); Becker (1836-39/1964); Brandes (1935); Cahn ["Transitus"] (1972-); Dunning (1980); Eggebrecht (1959); Eitner (1900-1904/1959-60); ● ● ●Feldmann (1958);

Fellerer (1983); Ferand (1951), ["Improvised"] (1956), [*Improvisation*] (1956/1961); Forchert (1986); Forkel (1792/1962); Gerber (1812-14/1966); Gissel (1980/1983), (1986); Gurlitt (1942/1966); Krützfeldt (1961); Lindley (1982); Meier (1949-68); Rauhe (1959-60); Sachs (1972-); Schering (1908); Schmitt (1974-75); Unger (1941/1969); Walker (1987); Warren (1980).

ORAZIO TIGRINI

[ca. 1535 – 1591]

Whereas ZARLINO's conception of music collided with the more progressive developments in compositional theory later in the sixteenth century, it was readily embraced in other circles. The works of several popularizers—including ARTUSI, PONTIO, SWEELINCK, and Orazio Tigrini—made the practical information contained within *Le istitutioni harmoniche* (1558) available to a wider audience. Tigrini's *Compendio della musica* (1588), dedicated to and endorsed by ZARLINO, indicates, via clear marginal annotations, the exact location of the materials from which Tigrini's summary is derived. VICENTINO, Boethius, and various other authors are cited as well. In this way the uninitiated were able to receive instruction on modal theory and counterpoint without entering the domain of speculative theory. Expanding upon ZARLINO, Tigrini listed a variety of cadence formulas for two through six voices. Though MORLEY denied it, some commentators believe that a similar list of cadences in *A Plaine and Easie Introduction* (1597) is derived from Tigrini's work.

Il compendio della musica nel quale brevemente si tratta dell'arte del contrapunto, diviso in quatro libri [*Rism* B/VI/2, pp. 831-32.]

  Venice: Ricciardo Amadino, 1588. [LCPS: T-037a. HoM: 1499. SMLMS.]
  Venice: Ricciardo Amadino, 1602. [LCPS: T-037b.]
  Venice: Amadino, 1638. [Bogus?]

S ● Facsimile of the 1588 edition. MMMLF, ser. 2, no. 25. New York: Broude Brothers, 1966.

Reviews in *Consort* 27 (1971):64 (Lillian M. Ruff), *ML* 48/4 (1967):371-73 (Jack A. Westrup), *MT* 108/1498 (1967):1112 (Charles Cudworth), and ● ● ●*Notes* 24/3 (1967-68):496-97 (Peter Bergquist).

LITERATURE:

Dürr, Walther. "Tigrini, Orazio." In *MGG* (1949-68). Bibliog.

Horsley, Imogene. "Tigrini, Orazio." In *NGrove* (1980).

See also FÉTIS: (1833-44); RIEMANN: (1898); WALTHER: (1732); LITERATURE SUPPLEMENT: Ambros (1878/. . ./1909); **Apfel (1981)**; Becker (1836-39/1964); Beiche ["Dux"] (1972-), ["Inversio"] (1972-); Buelow (1972); Bush (1939), (1946); Cazden (1948); Chomiński (1962/1981); Collins (1964); Eitner (1900-1904/1959-60); Fellerer ["Zur Kontrapunktlehre"] (1972), (1983); Ferand (1937/1938), [*Improvisation*] (1956/1961); Gerber (1790-92/1977); Ghislanzoni (1949-51); Haar (1977); Hannas (1934); Harrán (1973), (1986); Hein (1954); Horsley ["Fugue and Mode"] (1966/1978), [*Fugue: History*] (1966); Isgro (1968); Jeppesen (1922/. . ./1970), (1930/. . ./1974); Luoma (1976); Mahlert and Sunter (1972-); Meier (1974/1988); Neumann (1987); Palisca (1949-68); Robbins (1938); Ruhnke (1949-68); Schmalzriedt ["Reprise"] (1972-); Schwartz (1908); **Seidel and Cooper (1986)**; Walker (1987).

PIER FRANCESCO TOSI

[ca. 1653 – 1732]

The renowned and well-travelled castrato Pier Francesco Tosi addressed the bel canto style of singing in his *Opinioni de' cantori antichi, e moderni* [1723]. At the time newer trends which embraced allegro arias and more virtuosic embellishment were beginning to take hold, putting into question the integrity of cantabile singing. Tosi's work attacks these tendencies for their reliance upon instrumental idioms and for their emphasis of technical skill at the expense of expression. In their place a style enhanced by tasteful embellishment and *tempo rubato* is fostered. Johann Friedrich AGRICOLA transformed the work by adding music examples and liberally annotating the text in his German translation, *Anleitung zur Singkunst* (1757).

Opinioni de' cantori antichi, e moderni; o sieno osservazioni sopra il canto figurato [Rism B/VI/2, pp. 839-40.]

[Bologna: Lelio dalla Volpe, 1723.] [LCPS: T-051a. SMLMS.]

Exists in two nearly identical states.

T ● *Korte aanmerkingen over zangkonst* . . . Leiden: Florus Schouten, 1731.

An abridged translation.

T ● Galliard, [John Ernst], trans. *Observations on the Florid Song; or, Sentiments on the Ancient and Modern Singers*. London: J. Wilcox, 1742 [LCPS: T-051b; HoM: 1503.]; 1743 [LCPS: T-051c.]; facsimile of the 1743 edition, [London: William Reeves, 1926]; [1967]; facsimile of the 1743 edition (with an Introduction by Paul Henry Lang), New York: Johnson Reprint Corporation, 1968; facsimile of the 1743 edition, Geneva: Minkoff Reprints; facsimile edition (edited by Michael Pilkington), London: Stainer & Bell, 1987.

Reviews in *EM* 16/1 (1988):109 (Emma Kirkby) and *MT* 129/1741 (1988):86-87 (Howard Mayer Brown).

T ● AGRICOLA, Johann Friedrich, trans. and ed. *Anleitung zur Singkunst* [LCPS: T-051d. SMLMS.]. Berlin: Georg Ludewig Winter, 1757; facsimile edition (edited by Kurt Wichmann), Leipzig: VEB Deutscher Verlag für Musik, 1966; facsimile edition, see (1723):(1966), below.

Announcements in MARPURG: (1754-78): Vols. 1/4 (1754-55):326-31, 2/3 (1756):269, 3/2 (1757-58):167. Reviews in MARPURG: (1754-78):Vol. 3/4 (1757-58):357-67, *BsW* 2/2 (1757-58):421, *BzMw* 12/1 (1970):76-78 (Robert Schollum), *MG* 21/5 (1971):350-52 (Heinrich

Spieler), *Musica* 22/1 (1968):26 (Lothar Hoffmann-Erbrecht), *Notes* 24/3 (1967-68):482-83 (Owen Jander), and *ÖM* 22/11 (1967):683-84 (H. S.).

T ● Lemaire, Théophile, trans. and ed. *L'art du chant, opinions sur les chanteurs anciens et modernes ou observations sur le chant figuré*. Paris: Rothschild, 1874; facsimile edition, Paris: Éd. d'aujourd'hui, 1978.

S ● Leonesi, Luigi, ed. *La scuola di canto dell'epoca d'oro (secolo XVII): Opinioni de' cantori antichi e moderni*. Naples: F. Di Gennaro and A. Morano, 1904; facsimile edition (BmB, ser. 2, no. 50), Bologna: Forni, 1968.

S ● della Corte, Andrea, ed. *Canto e bel canto*. Bcm, no. 5. Turin: G. B. Paravia, 1933.

ST ● ● ● ● Jacobi, E. R., ed. Facsimile of the 1723 edition and of the 1757 German translation. Celle: Hermann Moeck Verlag, 1966. Bibliog.

Reviews in *BzMw* 12/1 (1970):76-78 (Robert Schollum), *Consort* 24 (1967):328-29 (Lillian M. Ruff), *GSJ* 20 (1967):123-24 (Denis Arnold), *Mens* 23/4 (1968):125 (Gerrit Vellekoop), *Mf* 23/2 (1970):236-37 (Helmut Hucke), *MG* 21/5 (1971):350-52 (Heinrich Spieler), *ML* 48/1 (1967):86-87 (Jack A. Westrup), *MT* 107/1481 (1966):606-7 (Walter Emery), *Muh* 18/7 (1967):370 (D.), *Musica* 22/1 (1968):25-26 (Günther Haußwald), *Musikrevy* 22/6 (1967):286 (Gösta Percy), *Notes* 23/3 (1966-67):507-9 (Owen Jander), *Nrmi* 2/1 (1968):156-57 (Rodolfo Celletti), and *Rdm* 52/2 (1966):247 (Carl de Nys).

S ● Facsimile of the 1723 edition. MMMLF, ser. 2, no. 133. New York: Broude Brothers, 1968.

LITERATURE:

Henderson, W. J. "Tosi on Florid Song." *NMR* 5/57 (1905-6):1073-75.

Ulrich, Bernhard. *Die altitalienische Gesangmethode, die Schule des Belcanto, auf Grund der originalschriften zum ersten Male dargestellt*. Leipzig: F. Kistner & C. F. W. Siegel, 1933.

Tagliavini, Luigi Ferdinando. "Tosi, Pier Francesco." In *MGG* (1949-68). Bibliog.

Tagliavini, Luigi Ferdinando. "Tosi, Pier Francesco." In *EdS* (1954-63). Bibliog.

Celletti, Rodolfo. "La vocalità al tempo del Tosi." *Nrmi* 1/4 (1967):676-84. Bibliog. [*Rilm* 68-3208.]

Casselman, Eugene. "Tosi Reconsidered." *NATSB* 24/4 (1968):8-13. [*Rilm* 68-3205.]

Thomas, Franz. *'Belcanto': Die Lehre des Kunstgesanges nach der alt-italienischen Schule*. Berlin: Georg Achterberg, 1968. [*Rilm* 71-3049.]

> Review in *Muh* 22/2 (1971):102, *Musica* 24/3 (1970):285 (Günther Baum), *NMZ* 18/3 (1969-70):12, *NZfM* 131/9 (1970):460 (Günther Baum) [reprinted in *MB* 2/11 (1970):506], and *OpW* 9 (1968):10.

Beicken, Suzanne Julia. "Johann Adam Hiller's *Anweisung zum musikalisch-zierlichen Gesang*, 1780: A Translation and Commentary." Ph.D. dissertation, Stanford University, 1980. [*Rilm* 80-2764. *DA* 41/05A, p. 1825. UMI 80-24623.]

Boyd, Malcolm. "Tosi, Pier Francesco." In *NGrove* (1980). Bibliog.

Coffin, Berton. "Vocal Pedagogy Classics: *Observations on the Florid Song* by Pier Francesco Tosi." *NATSB* 37/3 (1981):38-39.

Robert, Walter. "Chopin's *Tempo rubato* in Theory and Practice." *PQ* 29/113 (1981):42-44.

Høgel, Sten. "Niels Hansen og det danske syngespils opkomst." *MForsk* 8 (1982):80-129. [*Rilm* 82-2436.]

Peterson, Larry. "Some Observations on Handel's 'He Was Despised' and the Tradition of Laments in Baroque Operas and Oratorios." *NATSB* 45/5 (1989):4-9.

Baird, Julianne. Ph.D. dissertation, Stanford University, forthcoming.

See also FÉTIS: (1833-44); MARPURG: (1763); MOZART: Chesnut (1977); LITERATURE SUPPLEMENT: Babitz (1952), (1967/1969); Babitz and Pont (1973); Badura-Skoda et al. (1980); Barbieri (1983); Barbour (1952); Becker (1836-39/1964); **Benary (1956/1961)**; Beyschlag (1907/1953); Blake (1988); Brown and McKinnon (1980); Bruck (1928); Burney (1776-89/. . ./1957); Castellani (1976); Chesnut (1976); Dean (1977); Donington (1963/. . ./1974); (1980); Eitner (1900-1904/1959-60); Ferand [*Improvisation*] (1956/1961); Geering (1949-68); Gerber (1790-92/1977), (1812-14/1966); Hansell (1968); Harich-Schneider ([1939]/. . ./1970); Hawkins (1776/. . ./1969); Hiller (1768-69); Hoffmann (1974); Jackson (1988); Jander (1980); Kamieński (1918-19); **Lindley** ["Temperaments"] **(1980)**; Mahlert and Sunter (1972-); Mendel (1955); **Neumann** (1981/**1982**), ["Appoggiatura"] (1982), [*Essays*] **(1982)**, (1986); Newman (1985); Palisca ["Rezitativ"] (1972-); Rosenblum (1988); Smiles (1978); Stowell (1985); Subirá (1947/. . ./1958); Sydow-Saak (1972-); Wichmann (1966).

Sir DONALD FRANCIS TOVEY

[1875 – 1940]

In Donald Francis Tovey we meet a distinctive and forceful voice from the waning days of common-practice tonality. Like SCHENKER, Tovey displayed little sympathy for the newer trends that were supplanting the Bach-to-Brahms tradition, but he chose a much different strategy in his confrontations with basic musical issues. His books developed out of other endeavors—editing, lecturing, writing program notes, supplying popular encyclopedias with accessible yet brilliant articles. Together these various projects constitute perhaps the most insightful British writings on music written during this century.

In his own way, Tovey was and remains a controversial figure. Whereas the pedagogues of England (and, to be sure, most other Western nations) stressed rigorous though often uninspired drill in part-writing and model composition, Tovey dispensed with such technical training and focused instead upon what a layman might be capable of perceiving. To be sure, he was for the most part addressing the general reader or concertgoer rather than the conservatory student or professional musician. He held tenaciously to the view

that what his "naive listener" could comprehend through experiencing a musical work should be the focus of serious investigation. There is not a whiff of the notion that artists attain powers of perception and conception residing beyond the reach of most others. And yet Tovey, a distinguished pianist and sometime composer himself, must have possessed insights of greater sophistication than those he chose to share.

One should not look to Tovey for the most perceptive remarks on how tonality, with its wondrous capacity for shifts of local tonal center, works. His charts on key relationships in the "Harmony" article for *Britannica* are clearly inadequate. Nor should one expect to find him supplying procedures for composing a fugue—least of all an academic fugue. When reading Tovey one enters a more genteel, literary realm. Expect to be cajoled, entertained. Expect daring metaphors. And anticipate a keen and unique perspective, dependent upon the standard conceptions of form, thematic development, and key relationships, but never (except perhaps in his *Companion to Beethoven's Pianoforte Sonatas* of

1931) really accounting for every measure or expressing anxiety over not doing so.

Among Tovey's publications the series of articles for the *Encyclopaedia Britannica* (11th edition, 1910-11) attained perhaps the widest circulation. Assembled into one volume after Tovey's death, they address individual forms or genres (aria, cantata, concerto, fugue, opera, rondo, sonata, symphony, variations, etc.) or musical parameters (counterpoint, harmony, instrumentation, rhythm, etc.). Having accepted the Reid Chair of Music at Edinburgh University in 1914, Tovey quickly succeeded in organizing the Reid Orchestra. Selections from his program notes, as well as a few other articles, were published in six volumes as *Essays in Musical Analysis* (1935-39). A separate volume devoted to chamber music appeared posthumously. Another posthumous publication, *Essays and Lectures on Music* (1949), preserves the texts from Tovey's most celebrated public lectures, several of which had been published independently during the 1930s.

The Classical Concerto: Its Nature and Purpose

> London: Joseph Williams, [1903].

S ● See (1935-39):Vol. 3, below.

The Goldberg Variations: An Essay in Musical Analysis

> [London]: Joseph Williams, n.d.

Essays in Musical Analysis

> London: Joseph Williams, [1903].

>> This early work should not be confused with the celebrated set of essays under the same title, below.

"The Vitality of Artistic Counterpoint"

> *ZIMG* 7 (1905-6):365-68.

Articles on music for *Encyclopaedia Britannica*

> 11th edition (1910-11).

>> Reprinted in later editions; revised for the 14th edition.

S ● Foss, Hubert J., ed. *Musical Articles from the "Encyclopaedia Britannica"*. London: Oxford University Press (Humphrey Milford), 1944; later editions; reprint edition, (as *The Forms of Music*), New York: Meridian Books, 1956; London: Oxford University Press, 1957; Cleveland: World, 1961; facsimile of the 1944 edition, St. Clair Shores, Mich.: Scholarly Press, 1977.

>> Reviews in *Etude* 63/7 (1945):371, *KenR* 7/3 (1945):504-7 (Roger Sessions), and *MQ* 31/3 (1945):383-87 (Arthur Mendel).

"Beethoven's Ninth Symphony [in D Minor (Op. 125): An Essay in Musical Analysis]"

> In *Reid Orchestra Concerts (60th Season)*, University of Edinburgh, [1922].
> Edinburgh: James Thin, 1927. Revised edition.
> London: Oxford University Press (Humphrey Milford), [1928].

S ● See (1935-39):Vol. 2, below.

S ● See Rosand (1985):Vol. 14, pp. 279-323.

Forty-Eight Preludes and Fugues by J. S. Bach

> London: The Associated Board of the R. A. M. and the R. C. M.; New York: Oxford University Press, 1924. 2 vols.

>> Review in *ML* 12/4 (1931):378-83 (Ernest Walker).

A Preface: Forty-Eight Preludes and Fugues by J. S. Bach: Critical Explanatory Notes to Each Prelude and Fugue

> London: The Associated Board of the R. A. M. and the R. C. M.; New York: Oxford University Press, 1924. 2 vols. in 1.

"Some Aspects of Beethoven's Art Forms"

> *ML* 8/2 (1927):131-55.

S ● See (1938):(1949/1959), below.

S ● See Rosand (1985):Vol. 7, pp. 169-93.

"Tonality"

> *ML* 9/4 (1928):341-63.

A Companion to Beethoven's Pianoforte Sonatas (Complete Analyses)

> London: The Associated Board of the R. A. M. and the R. C. M., 1931.

>> Numerous printings.

S ● Facsimile of the 1931 edition. New York: AMS Press, 1976.

Ludwig van Beethoven: Sonatas for Pianoforte [with] Commentaries

> London: The Associated Board of the R. A. M. and the R. C. M., 1931. 3 vols.

>> Review in *ML* 13/1 (1932):11-18 (Ernest Walker).

A Companion to "The Art of Fugue" (Die Kunst der Fuge) [by] J. S. Bach

London: Oxford University Press (Humphrey Milford), 1931.

> Later editions. Reviews in *AR* 10/3 (1969):80-81 (Martin Davidson), *ML* 13/2 (1932):224-29 (Isobel Munro), and *MMR* 61/732 (1931):347-48 (Ernest Walker).

Die Kunst der Fuge (The Art of Fugue), by Johann Sebastian Bach, with a Dissertation

London: Oxford University Press, 1931.

> Review in *ML* 13/2 (1932):224-29 (Isobel Munro).

Musical Form and Matter

London: Oxford University Press (Humphrey Milford), 1934.

S ● See (1938):(1949/1959), below.

Essays in Musical Analysis

London: Oxford University Press (Humphrey Milford), 1935-39. 6 vols.

> Later editions, including 1972, 1981, and 1989. Reviews in *Instrumentalist* 27/5 (1972):14, *KenR* 3/2 (1941):243-46 (Henry Woodward), *LQHR* 162/2 (1937):243-46 (Stanley A. Bayliss), *MiE* 37/359 (1973):33, *ML* 16/2 (1935):154-56, 18/1-2 (1935):73-75, 189-91, 19/2 (1938):214-15, 21/2 (1940):184-85 (Ernest Walker), *MO* 112/1337 (1989):176 (Denby Richards), *MR* 45/3-4 (1984):304-10 (A. F. Leighton Thomas), *MT* 124/1679 (1983):35 (Michael Tilmouth), *MuMus* 21 (1973):44, *NatR* 36/6 (1984):61 (Terry Teachout), *PP* 65/4 (1973):18 (Melva Peterson), *QQ* 43/2 (1936):225-28 (H. L. Tracy), *RCMM* 78/2 (1982):198-99 (Anna Barry), *Tempo* 142 (1982):56-57 (Calum MacDonald), *TES* 3469 (1982):23 (Robert Turnbull), and *TLS* 71/3686 (1972):1276.

S ● *Some English Symphonists: A Selection from "Essays in Musical Analysis"*. London: Oxford University Press, 1941.

S ● Kerman, Joseph, ed. *Mozart's C Major Piano Concerto, K 503: The Score of the New Mozart Edition with Historical and Critical Essays*. New York: W. W. Norton, 1970.

> The volume includes, among other essays, a reprint of "K. 503: The Unity of Contrasting Themes and Movements" by Hans Keller, who here and elsewhere offers sharp criticism of Tovey's contributions. [The Keller article was first published in *MR* 17/1-2 (1956):48-58, 120-29.] Reviews in *MR* 31/4 (1970):346-48 (Peter J. Pirie) and *MuMus* 21/1 (1972-73):44 (Jeremy Noble).

S ● See Forbes (1971):143-50.

S ● See Rosand (1985):Vol. 14, pp. 325-41.

Normality and Freedom in Music

Oxford: Clarendon Press, 1936.

S ● See (1938):(1949/1959), below.

"The Training of the Musical Imagination

ML 17/4 (1936):337-56.

"What the Composer Expects from the Listener"

S ● *RS* 1/2 (1961-62):34-39.

> Posthumously published. From a series entitled "Music and the Ordinary Listener" broadcast on the BBC, May 28, 1937.

The Main Stream of Music

London: Humphrey Milford, 1938.

> Review in *ML* 20/2 (1939):196 (Ernest Walker).

S ● British Academy, London. *Proceedings, 1938* 24 (1939):[113]-41.

S ● Foss, Hubert, ed. *Essays and Lectures on Music* [*The Main Stream of Music and Other Essays*]. London: Oxford University Press (Geoffrey Cumberlege), 1949; New York: Meridian Books, 1959; reprint edition, New York: AMS Press.

> Among the major essays of this volume are "Musical Form and Matter," "Normality and Freedom in Music," "The Main Stream of Music," and "The Meaning of Music." Reviews in *HR* 3/3 (1950):438-46 (Joseph Kerman), *JR* 7/1 (1959-60):9 (Richard F. Goldman), *Mf* 4/1 (1951):74-75 (Paul Mies), *ML* 31/2 (1950):151-54 (W. S. Mann), *MSur* 2/4 (1949-50):263 (Hans Keller), *Notes* 7/3 (1949-50):478-80 (Lawrence Norton), and *Rmi* 52/3 (1950):277-78 (Di. Ser.).

S ● See Rosand (1985):Vol. 9, pp. 209-31.

"Words and Music: Some Obiter Dicta"

In *GriersonFs* (1938):341-59.

A Musician Talks

1) *The Integrity of Music*

2) *Musical Textures*

> Posthumously published.

London: Oxford University Press (Geoffrey Cumberlege), 1941. 2 vols. Edited by Hubert J. Foss, with a Preface by Ernest Walker.

> Reviews in *ML* 22/4 (1941):385-89 (Richard Capell), *MR* 2/3 (1941):251-52 (William Saunders), and *Scrutiny* 10/2 (1941-42):106-13 (W. H. Mellers).

S ● Facsimile edition. 2 vols. in 1. St. Clair Shores, Mich.: Scholarly Press, 1977.

Beethoven

Posthumously published.

London: Oxford University Press (Humphrey Milford), 1944. Edited by Hubert J. Foss.

Later editions in 1945 and 1965. Reviews in *Mf* 21/1 (1968):119-20 (Paul Mies), *ML* 26/1 (1945):52-53 (George Sampson), *MQ* 32/2 (1946):296-302 (Paul Henry Lang), and *MR* 6/1 (1945):56-57 (E. H. W. Meyerstein).

Essays in Musical Analysis: Chamber Music

Posthumously published.

London: Oxford University Press (Humphrey Milford), 1944. Edited by Hubert J. Foss.

Reprinted in 1972 and 1989. Reviews in *KenR* 7/3 (1945):504-7 (Roger Sessions), *ML* 26/1 (1945):51 (Ernest Walker), *MQ* 31/3 (1945):383-87 (Arthur Mendel), and *MR* 6/1 (1945):57 (Geoffrey Sharp).

LITERATURE:

Bayliss, Stanley. "Tovey's Wit and Wisdom." *ChMJ* 31/364 (1940):52-53.

Fox Strangways, A. H. "Donald Francis Tovey." *ML* 21/4 (1940):305-11.

Saunders, William. "The Late Sir Donald Francis Tovey, Reid Professor of Music, University of Edinburgh." *MR* 1/4 (1940):300-309.

Bayliss, Stanley. "Tovey as Lecturer." *ChMJ* 32/384 (1941):178-79.

Wordsworth, W. B. "Tovey's Teaching." *ML* 22/1 (1941):60-66.

Dent, Edward T. "Donald Tovey." *MR* 3/1 (1942):1-9.

Fish, Solomon. "The Aesthetics of Sir Donald Francis Tovey." *JAAC* 6/1 (1947-48):60-67.

Redlich, Hans Ferdinand. "Tovey, (Sir) Donald Francis." In *MGG* (1949-68). Bibliog.

Kerman, Joseph. "Counsel for the Defense." *HR* 3/3 (1950-51):438-46.

Grierson, Mary. *Donald Francis Tovey: A Biography Based on Letters*. London: Oxford University Press, 1952; reprint edition, Westport, Ct.: Greenwood Press, [1970].

Reviews in *Canon* 6/2 (1952-53):89 (Kenneth F. Hince), *MAm* 72/16 (1952):33 (Robert Sabin), *MC* 146/7 (1952):30, *ML* 33/3 (1952):198-202 (J. Douglas H. Dickson), *MMR* 82/940 (1952):216 (P. Havard-Williams), *MO* 75/898 (1951-52):601 (H. H.), *MPar* 2/12 (1952):18-19, *MR* 13/2 (1952):154-55, *MT* 93/1311 (1952):210-11 (W. R. A.),

MusT 31 (1952):303, *NMQ* 22/4 (1952):471-73 (Morton Schoenfeld), *Notes* 9/3 (1951-52):407-8 (Ralph Mortiz), *Strad* 63/745 (1952-53):10, and *Tempo* 24 (1952):34-35 (Imogen Holst).

Stevens, George. "Tovey." *HFMA* 11/12 (1961):57-58, 117-19.

Andrews, Ruth P. "Preferred Editions." *AMT* 21/2 (1971-72):30.

Sampson, Peggie. "Tovey and the Student of Today." *JCAUSM* 1/1 (1971):31-37.

Whatley, George Larry. "Donald Francis Tovey and His Contributions to the Study of Harmony and Counterpoint." Ph.D. dissertation, Indiana University, 1974. [*Rilm* 74-3890. *DA* 35/05A, p. 3044. UMI 74-22797.]

Deas, Stewart. "Donald Francis Tovey: The Creative Scholar." *RS* 59 (1975):456-60.

● ● ● Kerman, Joseph. "Tovey's Beethoven." *ASch* 45 (1975-76):795-805; reprinted in *Beethoven Studies 2* (London: Oxford University Press, 1977), edited by Alan Tyson, pp. 172-91.

Whatley, G. Larry. "Donald Francis Tovey: A Survey of His Life and Works." *AMT* 25/5 (1975-76):9-12. Bibliog.

Whitfield, John B. R. "A Noteworthy Centenary (Tovey)." *MusT* 54/12 (1975):22-23.

"Centennial Anniversaries." *PP* 68/3 (1976):18.

Kerman, Joseph. "Viewpoint." *NCM* 2/2 (1978-79):186-91; reprinted in Rosand (1985):Vol. 14, pp. 348-53. [*Rilm* 78-5126.]

Tilmouth, Michael. "Tovey, Sir Donald (Francis)." In *NGrove* (1980). Bibliog.

Review in *NCM* 5/2 (1981-82):168-69 (Joseph Kerman).

● ● ● Wintle, Christopher. " 'Humpty Dumpty's Complaint': Tovey Revalued." *Soun* 11 (1983-84):14-45.

Abstract by the author in *MA* 3/3 (1984):299-300.

Grainger, Percy. "Thoughts about Tone-Art: Tovey Yes-No's Himself about Bach's Continuo Needs." *GrJ* 7/1 (1985):38-41.

See also LITERATURE SUPPLEMENT: Allen ["Philosophies"] (1939); Austin (1966); Beer (1969); ● ● ● **Bent** ["Analysis"] (**1980/1987**); Beswick (1950); Bridges (1984); Broyles (1982-83), (1983); **Dahlhaus** (**1984**); David (1956); Donington (1980); Drabkin (1985); Dunsby and Whittall (1988); Frobenius ["Cantus"] (1972-); Gerboth et al. (1964); Godley (1952); Gwilt (1983-84); Jacobi (1957-60/1971); Jeppesen (1930/. . ./1974); Jorgenson (1957); Kerman (1980-81), (1985); Kinderman (1980-81); Kivy (1980); Lawrence (1978); Lindley (1982); Lloyd (1940-41); Longyear and Covington (1985); McQuere (1983); Newman (1963/. . ./1983), (1969/. . ./1983); Oldroyd (1948); Ratner (1949),

(1980); **Ritzel (1967/1968)**; Rosen (1971/ . . ./1983), (1980/1986); Rosenblum (1988); Rothschild (1953); Schmalzriedt ["Subiectum"] (1972-); Scholes

(1947); Scholz (1981/1983); Shamgar (1978), (1981); Solie (1977); Stevens (1974); Troeger (1987); Whatley (1981).

JOHANN PHILIPP TREIBER

[1675–1727]

Johann Philipp Treiber, an amateur musician whose main occupation was law, created two volumes quite unlike anything else produced within the eighteenth century. His *Sonderbare Invention: Eine Arie in einer einzigen Melodey aus allen Tonen und Accorden, auch jederley Tacten zu componiren* (1702) is, as its title suggests, a composition/conglomeration of disparate chords and meters perpetrated, we must suppose, for pedagogical rather than artistic reasons. *Der accurate Organist im General-Baß* (1704), though not a systematic introduction to figured-bass practice, is especially detailed on the variety of ways in which accidentals might be used by composers and how keyboardists should interpret them. In some cases, the accidentals supplied would seem to modern practitioners to be redundant (e.g., using the natural sign to represent a major third above A-flat in A-flat major); in other cases, his enharmonic equivalents are disconcerting (e.g., using G where we would write F-double-sharp as the leading tone of G-sharp). Instead of enhancing his work with a wide variety of examples, he employed the same two chorales (one in a major mode; one in a minor mode) in most of the keys. A few of these examples include basses with added dissonances in quicker note values, challenging readers to hone their skill in discriminating between notes that require a new chord versus notes that should coexist with a chord previously sounded.

Sonderbare Invention: Eine Arie in einer einzigen Melodey aus allen Tonen und Accorden, auch jederley Tacten zu componiren, so daß sie in dem härtesten Accord anfängt, in dem weichsten auffhöret

und dem Auffmercker dennoch die Abwechselung derer Accorde nicht frembde vorkommet . . . [*Rism* B/VI/2, p. 842.]

Jena: Caspar Junghans, 1702. [LCPS: T-063.]

Der accurate Organist im General-Baß; Das ist, Neue, deutliche und vollständige Anweisung zum General-Baß . . . [*Rism* B/VI/2, p. 842.]

Jena: Caspar Junghans (Arnstadt: Nicolaus Bachmann), 1704.

Reprinted in 1713 and 1715.

LITERATURE:

Kraft, Günther. "Treiber . . . Johann Philipp." In *MGG* (1949-68). Bibliog.

Arnn, John D. "Treiber, Johann Philipp." In *NGrove* (1980). Bibliog.

See also ADLUNG: (1758); FÉTIS: (1833-44); WALTHER: (1732); LITERATURE SUPPLEMENT: ● ● ● **Arnold (1931/. . ./1965)**; Becker (1836-39/1964); Dupont (1933/. . ./1986); Eitner (1900-1904/1959-60); Gerber (1790-92/1977), (1812-14/1966); Heimann (1970/1973); Lester (1978); Williams, P. (1970).

DANIEL GOTTLOB TÜRK

[1756–1813]

Daniel Gottlob Türk's *Klavierschule* (1789) was, for late eighteenth-century readers, an unsurpassed source of practical wisdom concerning the art of playing the clavichord and a repository of useful information of general interest—including discussions of technical terms used in music, summaries of the characteristics which define various categories of composition (overture, serenade, individual dance movements, etc.), and commentary which would enhance the development of musical taste. For modern read-

ers, the work powerfully evokes the standards, practices, and aesthetics of the Classic era. Pianists who perform works of Mozart or Haydn on modern instruments borrowing nineteenth-century legato style and conforming to metronomic exactitude in pacing might find Türk's suggestions concerning non-legato articulation and nuanced rhythmic delivery a revelation. It is upon books such as Türk's that the recent movement towards performance on original instruments depends for sound advice on the use of the keyboard's resources for creating appropriate musical effects.

Türk's design encompasses a broad range of topics, while his format incorporates three categories of material: the text proper (for all readers), indented passages (for teachers), and footnotes (to clarify or expand upon various points, for the most ardent readers). The opening chapter introduces novice keyboardists to the rudiments and notation of music, as well as to the various terms (particularly from the Italian) which mingle with the musical notation in the score. Fingering is carefully assessed in the second chapter. The next three chapters are devoted to various categories of ornamentation, including an assessment of how and when the performer might supplement what the composer has requested explicitly. The sixth chapter addresses execution, with expert commentary on the roles of articulation and accentuation in communicating a work's expressive character. A concluding appendix supplies definitions of numerous terms, as well as individual paragraphs describing prevalent musical genres.

Equally clear and vivid, though less celebrated, is Türk's *Kurze Anweisung zum Generalbaßspielen* (1791), which systematically addresses the declining art of figured-bass realization. Though not on the scale of the *Klavierschule*, the work elucidates the notation of the figures and contains examples of many individual chord types. Of special interest is a three-page chart showing all combinations of figures commonly in use, with indications regarding the pitches which should be included when realizing each chord in textures of three to five voices.

Von den wichtigsten Pflichten eines Organisten: Ein Beytrag zur Verbesserung der musikalischen Liturgie [*Rism* B/VI/2, p. 847.]

> Halle: the author (Halle: Hemmerde; Leipzig: Schwickert), 1787. [LCPS: T-072. HoM: 1512. IDC.]
>
>> Commentary in *AmZ* 16/44 (1814):729-36 (Ma[a]ss.)
>
> Halle: C. A. Schwetschke & Sohn, 1838. Edited by Johann Friedrich Naue.

S ● Billiter, Bernhard, ed. Facsimile of the 1787 edition. Bo, no. 5. Hilversum: Frits Knuf, 1966.

> Review in *ISOI* 3 (1970):237 (Maarten A. Vente).

T ● Woolard, Margot Ann Greenlimb. "Daniel Gottlob Türk's *Concerning the Chief Responsibilities of an Organist*: Translation and Commentary." D.M.A. dissertation, The University of Nebraska, 1987. [*DA* 48/05A, pp. 1053-54. UMI 87-17270.]

Klavierschule; oder, Anweisung zum Klavierspielen für Lehrer und Lernende, mit kritischen Anmerkungen [*Rism* B/VI/2, p. 846.]

> Leipzig and Halle: the author (Leipzig: Schwickert; Halle: Hemmerde & Schwetschke), 1789. [LCPS: T-070. HoM: 1508. IDC.]
>
>> As *Neue Klavier-Schule; oder, Anweisung zum Klavierspielen . . .*:
>
> Vienna: Chr. Gottlob Täubel, 1798. [HoM: 1509.]
>
>> Under the original title:
>
> Leipzig and Halle: the author (Leipzig: Schwickert; Halle: Hemmerde & Schwetschke), 1802.
>
>> Review in *AmZ* 8/13-14 (1805-6):203-7, 209-19.

S ● *Kurze Anweisung zum Klavierspielen: Ein Auszug aus der größern Klavierschule* [*Rism* B/VI/2, p. 847.]. Halle and Leipzig: the author (Leipzig: Schwickert; Halle: Hemmerde & Schwetschke), 1792 [SMLMS.]; enlarged edition, 1805.

T ● [Callcott, John, trans.] "The Clavier-School; or, Instructions for Playing the Harpsichord both for Master and Scholar, with Critical Remarks." Ms., [ca. 1803]. [London: British Library, Reference Division.]

T ● Naumberger, C. G., trans. and ed. *Treatise on the Art of Teaching and Practising the Piano Forte . . .* London: for the proprietor (Preston), [ca. 1804].

T ● Bergsøe, Joh. Frid., trans. *Claveerskole eller Anviisning til at spille paa Claveer*. Copenhagen: S. Sønnichsen, 1818.

S ● Jacobi, Erwin R., ed. Facsimile of the 1789 edition. IGMDm, ser. 1, no. 23. Kassel: Bärenreiter, 1962; 2nd edition, 1967.

> Reviews in *Consort* 21 (1964):327-28 (John Lade), *GSJ* 19 (1966):141-43 (Susi Jeans), *Mf* 18/4 (1965):452-53 (Peter Benary), *ML* 46/2 (1965):153-54 (Howard Ferguson), *MR* 28/2 (1967):151-52 (Henry Raynor), *MR* 33/2 (1972):152 (Henry Raynor), and *L'organo* 4/2 (1963):227-28 (Luigi Ferdinando Tagliavini).

S ● See MacClintock (1979).

S ● See Rowen (1979).

T ● ● ● ● Haggh, Raymond H., trans. and ed. *School of Clavier Playing; or, Instructions in Playing the Clavier for Teachers and Students*. Lincoln: The University of Nebraska Press, 1982. Bibliog.

Reviews in *AR* 24/4 (1983):159-62 (Frederick Neumann), *Choice* 20/10 (1982-83):1468, *JALS* 14 (1983):129 (Maurice Hinson), *JMT* 28/1 (1984):154-57 (Harald Krebs), *ML* 64/3-4 (1983):284-85 (Philip Whitmore), *MusT* 63/5 (1984):24 (John Towse), and *Notes* 40/4 (1983-84):773-75 (Floyd K. Grave).

Kurze Anweisung zum Generalbaßspielen [*Rism* B/VI/2, p. 847.]

> Halle and Leipzig: the author (Leipzig: Schwickert; Halle: Hemmerde & Schwetschke), 1791. [LCPS: T-071a. SMLMS.]
>
> > Review in *AdB* 108/2 (1792):465-73 [Johann Gottlieb PORTMANN].
> >
> > As *Anweisung zum Generalbaßspielen*:
>
> Halle and Leipzig: the author (Leipzig: Schwickert; Halle: Hemmerde & Schwetschke), 1800. [LCPS: T-071b. IDC.]
>
> > Later editions, including some edited by Johann Friedrich Naue. Reviews in *AmZ* 29/51 (1827): 862-64 and *AmZ* 44/3 (1842):55-56.
>
> S ● Billiter, Bernhard, ed. Facsimile of the 1800 edition. Amsterdam: Frits Knuf, 1971. Bibliog.
>
> > Review in *GSJ* 26 (1973):149 (Howard Schott).

Beleuchtung einer Recension des Buches: Kurze Anweisung zum Generalbaßspielen [*Rism* B/VI/2, p. 846.]

> [Halle: 1792.]

"Violinschule"

> Ms., [ca. 1799].

Kleines Lehrbuch für Anfänger im Clavierspielen . . .

> Halle: the author (Hemmerde & Schwetschke), 1802.
>
> > Another edition in 1806.

Anleitung zu Temperaturberechnungen, für diejenigen, welche in dem arithmetischen Theile der Musik keinen mündlichen Unterricht haben können; ins besondere aber für die Besitzer des Kirnbergerschen Werkes: Die Kunst des reinen Satzes etc.

> Halle and Leipzig: the author (Leipzig: Schwickert; Halle: Hemmerde & Schwetschke), 1806.
>
> > Later edition(s?). Review in *AmZ* 11/18 (1808-9):281-86. Commentary in *AmZ* 16/45 (1814):745-54 (Maas[s].) and *AmZ* 38/20 (1836):324-26 (G. W. Fink).

Articles in *AmZ* and other journals, printed anonymously.

LITERATURE:

Lippert, J. Ch. *Verzeichniß der musikalischen und andern Bücher, so wie auch der gedruckten und geschreibenen Musikalien des seligen Professor der Musik und Universitäts-Musikdirektor Dr. Türk, welche . . . versteigert werden sollen.* Halle: 1816; facsimile edition (as *Catalogue of the Music Library of Daniel Gottlob Türk . . .*, edited by A. Hyatt King; ACM, no. 3), Amsterdam: Frits Knuf, 1973.

> Review in *AR* 15/2 (1974):61 (Dale Higbee).

Glenewinkel, Hermann. "Daniel Gottlob Türk nebst einem Überblick über das Hallische Musikleben seiner Zeit." Ph.D. dissertation, The University of Halle, 1909; published edition (incomplete), Halle: Martin Kandler, 1909. Bibliog.

Hedler, Gretchen Emilie. "Daniel Gottlob Türk (1750-1813)." Ph.D dissertation, The University of Leipzig, 1936; published edition, Borna (Leipzig): Großbetrieb für Dissertationsdruck von Robert Noske, 1936.

Hoffmann-Erbrecht, Lothar. "Türk, Daniel Gottlob." In *MGG* (1949-68). Bibliog.

Bittner, Carl. "Daniel Gottlob Türk." *Musica* 17/5 (1963):233.

Vellekoop, Gerrit. "Een oude handleiding voor het klavieronderwijs." *Mens* 18/5 (1963):141-44.

Joseph, John. "Keyboard Comments: Classic Period." *Musart* 21/3 (1968-69):29-35.

Jacobi, Erwin R. "Türk, Daniel Gottlob." In *NGrove* (1980). Bibliog.

Raessler, Daniel M. "Türk, Touch and Slurring: Finding a Rationale." *EM* 17/1 (1989):55-59.

See also CHORON: Simms (1975); FÉTIS: (1833-44); FUX: Federhofer (1988); KIRNBERGER: Beach (1974); LÖHLEIN: (1765-81):Wilson (1979); Glasenapp (1937); LITERATURE SUPPLEMENT: Ahlgrimm (1973); Alekseev (1984); **Arnold (1931/ . . ./1965)**; Auhagen (1982/1983); Babitz (1952); Bauman (1977); Becker (1836-39/1964); Bent et al. (1980); Beyschlag (1907/1953); Bircher (1970); Blake (1988); Broyles (1983); Bruck (1928); Cahn ["Retardatio"] (1972-); Chybiński (1911-12); Cole (1988); Collins (1966); **Dahlhaus et al. (1987)**; Dolmetsch (1915/. . ./1969); Donington (1963/. . ./1974), (1980); Dreyfus (1987); Eitner (1900-1904/1959-60); Forkel (1792/1962); Frobenius ["Vollstimmig"] (1972-); Fuller (1977); Ganz (1972), (1976); Gerber (1790-92/1977), (1812-14/1966); Grave (1985); Hailparn (1981); Harich-Schneider ([1939]/. . ./1970); Houle (1960), (1987); Jackson (1988); **Kassler (1979)**; Keller (1955/1965);

Kelletat [*Temperatur*] (1960); Kretzschmar (1911-12); Krones (1988); Kümmel (1967); Laudon (1978); **Lester (1989)**; **Lindley** ["Temperaments"] **(1980)**; List (1976); Maier (1984); Müller-Blattau (1923/. . ./1963), (1949-68); Nelson (1984); **Neumann**, Frederick (1978), (1979/**1982**), ["Appoggiatura"] (1982), [*Essays*] **(1982)**, (1986); Newman (1985); Newman (1946), (1963/. . ./1983); Oberdörffer (1949-68); Orr (1983); Pikler (1966); Ratner (1980); Reckow (1972-); Reichert (1978); Reimer ["Concerto"] (1972-), ["Kammermusik"] (1972-); **Ritzel (1967/1968)**; Rosen (1971/. . ./1983), (1980/1986); Rosenblum (1988); Rothgeb (1968); Rothschild (1961); Sachs (1972-); Seidel (1971), (1972-); Sheldon (1975), (1981), (1982); Sisman (1978); Smiles (1978); Spitzer and Zaslaw (1986); Stevens (1974); Stowell (1985), (1988); Swain (1988); Telesco (forthcoming); Thomson (1960/1978); Tittel (1966); Todd (1983), (1988-89); Troeger (1987); Vanhulst (1971); Vogel (1976); Wagner (1981); **Wagner (1974)**; **Wason (1981/1985)**; Wessely (1967); Whitmore (1988); Williams, P. ["Harpsichord"] (1968), (1970); Wirth (1966); Wolff (1972-).

FRANCESCO ANTONIO VALLOTTI

[1697–1780]

Like his colleague and fellow Paduan TARTINI — and with greater accuracy and clarity — Francesco Antonio Vallotti used mathematics as a tool in unlocking music's mysteries. Though Vallotti claimed to have developed his theoretical system as early as the 1720s, he saw only a single volume of his comprehensive *Della scienza teorica e pratica della moderna musica* reach its intended audience — in 1779, shortly before his death. The three remaining volumes found their way to MARTINI, who wrote brief commentaries on them, but remained unpublished until the middle of the twentieth century.

Vallotti retained a conservative attitude towards counterpoint, finding even FUX too progressive in his adaptation of sixteenth-century modal practices. His own synthesis of the inversion principle, made independently of RAMEAU's *Traité*, makes his disinclination towards the Frenchman's theory more understandable. His study of temperament (in Book 2 of *Della scienza teorica e pratica*) led him to suggest tempering six fifths by one-sixth comma each, while his pioneering exploration of overtones revealed that harmonics 24, 27, 30, 32, 36, 40, 45, and 48 generate a major scale (but not, unfortunately, the scale whose tonic serves as generator of the harmonics).

"Una memoria di varie decisioni teorico pratiche spettanti al giusto intendimento delle materie musicali"

> Ms., 1725. [Padua: Biblioteca Antoniana, Basilica del Santo.]

"Serie di vari autori greci, latini, italiani e francesi che hanno scritto della musica o antica o moderna con varie erudizioni ed opinioni diversi"

> Ms., 1732. [Padua: Biblioteca Antoniana, Basilica del Santo.]

"Trattato dei tuoni modali, si ecclesiastici corali, che musicali ed armoniali. I: Compendio storico de' tuoni modali della musica greca, del canto ecclesiastico, del canto figurato e della moderna musica; II: Trattato de' tuoni modali, in cui si tratta dei dodici tuoni ecclesiastici e corali"

> Ms., 1733-35. [Padua: Biblioteca Antoniana, Basilica del Santo.]

Correspondence with Count Giordano Riccati di Castelfranco, MARTINI, and others.

> Mss., 1734-79.

> S ● See MARTINI: (1730-84).

>> Mss. [See especially Bologna: Civico museo bibliografico musicale; Padua: Biblioteca Antoniana, Basilica del Santo.]

Della scienza teorica e pratica della moderna musica [*Rism* B/VI/2, p. 854.]

> Padua: Stamperia del seminario (Giovanni Manfrè), 1779. Book 1. [LCPS: V-006.]
> Mss. Books 2-4. [Padua: Biblioteca Antoniana, Basilica del Santo.]

> S ● Bernardino, Rizzi [*sic*], ed., with a Study by Giancarlo Zanon. *Trattato della moderna musica*. Padua: Il messaggero di S. Antonio (Tipografia della provincia Patavina), 1950; Bologna: Forni. Bibliog.

>> Modern edition of all four volumes. Review in *Rmi* 54/1 (1952):74-75 (C.).

"11 bassi del prete Francescantonio Vallotti"

> Ms. [Venice: Biblioteca nazionale Marciana.]

"Contrappunto principii"

> Ms. [Venice: Biblioteca nazionale Marciana.]

"Dell'estensione e carattere dei più communi stromenti"

> Ms. [Venice: Biblioteca nazionale Marciana.]

"Se il tuono minore naturale abbia per base la corda e ottava di D la sol re ovvero quella di A la mi re"

> Ms. [Padua: Biblioteca Antoniana, Basilica del Santo.]

See Hansell (1980), below, for additional information on manuscript materials. See also SABBATINI, L. A.: (1802).

LITERATURE:

SABBATINI, Luigi Antonio. *Notizie sopra la vita e la opere del rev. P. Fr. A. V.* Padua: 1780.

Riccati, Giordano. "Riflessioni . . . sopra il libro primo *Della scienza teorica, e pratica della moderna musica* del P. Francescantonio Vallotti . . ." *NglI* 23 (1787):45-115.

Capanna, Alessandro. "Studio di armonia a quattro parti secondo le teorie dei proff. Vallotti, Asioli, Federici, fatta sotto la direzione del L. Vecchiotti." 2 vols. Ms. [Bologna: Convento de S. Francesco.]

Tebaldini, Giovanni. *L'Archivio musicale della Cappella Antoniana in Padova: Illustrazione storico-critica.* Padua: Tip. e libreria Antoniana, 1895.

Martinotti, Sergio. "Vallotti, Francesco Antonio." Translated by Albert Müry. In *MGG* (1949-68). Bibliog.

● ● ● Hansell, Sven. "Vallotti, Francesco Antonio." In *NGrove* (1980). Bibliog.

Cattin, Giulio, ed. *Francescantonio Vallotti nel II centenario della morte (1780-1980): Biografia, catalogo tematico delle opere e contributi critici*. Csa, no. 3. Padua: Messaggero, 1981; Bologna: Forni.

> Contains "Una 'Nota delli libri di musica' tra le carte del Vallotti" by F. Alberto Gallo and "Il carteggio tra Francescantonio Vallotti e Giambattista Martini" by Vittore Sante Zaccaria, among other studies. Reviews in *Mf* 37/4 (1984):312-14 (Maria Antonella Balsano) and *Nrmi* 17/1 (1983):125-26 (Giuliana Gialdroni).

Lindley, Mark. "La 'Practica ben regolata' di Francescantonio Vallotti." *Ridm* 16/1 (1981):45-95.

See also FÉTIS: (1833-44); SABBATINI, L. A.: (1799), ["Trattato di contrappunto"] (Ms.); TARTINI: (1767); Petrobelli (1967); LITERATURE SUPPLEMENT: Asselin (1983/1985); Becker (1836-39/1964); Blood (1979); Cavallini (1949); Chevaillier (1925/1931-32); **Dahlhaus et al. (1987)**; Eitner (1900-1904/1959-60); Fellerer (1927/. . ./ 1972); Gerber (1790-92/1977), (1812-14/1966); Ghislanzoni (1949-51); Jones (1934); Kauko (1958); **Lindley** (1977), ["Temperaments"] **(1980)**; **Shirlaw (1917/. . ./1970)**; Wessely (1967); Wirth (1966).

LODOVICO VIADANA

[ca. 1560–1627]

The modest comments which Lodovico Viadana supplied for his *Cento concerti ecclesiastici* (1602) describe the initial development of figured-bass practice, and thus they have attained a historical significance which would have astonished their author. In twelve straightforward rules Viadana provided a lucid account of matters such as range on the keyboard, ornamentation, cadences, dynamics, and the tolerable use of parallel fifths and octaves in the accompaniment. His concerti, which are designed for a variety of vocal performance forces, lack true figured basses in the later sense, as no figures are used. Some accidentals are present, however, and the role of the bass in providing a foundation for each work is clearly established.

Preface to *Cento concerti ecclesiastici . . . con il basso continuo per sonar nell'organo, nova inventione commoda per ogni sorte de cantori, & per gli organisti . . .* [*Rism* A/I/9, p. 84.]

> Venice: Giacomo Vincenti, 1602.
>
> Numerous later editions.

ST ● *Opera omnia sacrorum concertuum I. II. III. & IV. vocum . . . cum basso continuo et generali organo adplicato . . .* Frankfurt: Nikolaus Stein, 1613; later editions. [*Rism* A/I/9, p. 86.]

ST ● See Schneider (1917/. . ./1971).

T ● See ● ● ● Arnold (1931/. . ./1965).

T ● See **Strunk (1950)**:419-23.

T ● See Rowen (1979).

LITERATURE:

Mompellio, Federico. "Viadana, Lodovico." Translated by Marianne Damm. In *MGG* (1949-68). Bibliog.

Haack, Helmut. "Anfänge des Generalbaß-Satzes in den *Cento concerti ecclesiastici* (1602) von Ludovico Grossi da Viadana." Ph.D. dissertation, The University of Munich, 1964; published edition (MVM, no. 22), Tutzing: Hans Schneider, 1974. [*Rilm* 75-3489.]

> Abstract in *Mf* 18/3 (1965):320-21. Review in *ÖM* 34/10 (1979):523-24 (Friedrich C. Heller).

Mompellio, Federico. "Ritorno a Lodovico Viadana." *Msac* 90/6 [ser. 2, no. 11] (1966):154-58.

Mompellio, Federico. "Viadana, Lodovico." In *NGrove* (1980). Bibliog.

See also BANCHIERI: (1591):(1609), (1614); FÉTIS: (1833-44); MONTEVERDI: Gallico (1966); PRAETORIUS: (1614-20):Vol. 3 (1618); VOGLER: (1802); WALTHER: (1732); LITERATURE SUPPLEMENT: Ambros (1878/. . ./1909); Baron (1968); Becker (1836-39/1964); Borgir (1971/1987); Braun (1986); Buelow (1972); Bukofzer (1947); Chevaillier (1925/1931-32); **Chomiński** (1962/1981); Dreyfus (1987); Eggebrecht (1957); Eitner (1900-1904/1959-60); Fellerer ["Wesen"] (1982), (1984); Ferand [*Improvisation*] (1956/1961); Gerber (1790-92/1977), (1812-14/1966); Hill (1983); Houle (1987); Jackson (1988); **Kassler (1979)**; Kinkeldey (1910/1968); Neumann, Frederick (1978); North (1987); Oberdörffer (1949-68); Palisca [*Baroque*] (1968/1981); Rauhe (1959-60); Reimer ["Concerto"] (1972-); Schmitt (1974-75); Subirá (1947/. . ./1958); Troeger (1987); Wienpahl (1953); Williams, P. (1970).

NICOLA VICENTINO

(1511 – c. 1576)

Though a contemporary of ZARLINO, Nicola Vicentino formulated ideas which brand him as a musical revolutionary and influential advocate of the revitalization of ancient Greek musical tradition. His understanding of the theoretical sources was (as might be expected) deficient, however, and so he produced, perhaps unwittingly, a unique hybrid sort of music which he propagated throughout Italy both in his treatise *L'antica musica ridotta alla moderna prattica* (1555) and in concerts presented in various cities. As early as 1551 his view that all three genera — diatonic, chromatic, and enharmonic — were to be found in the music of his day was given a public hearing (in debate with Vicente LUSITANO) but was rejected by the two officiating judges, one of whom, Ghiselin DANCKERTS, responded to Vicentino with his own treatise.

If the enharmonic genus was to attain prominence, an instrument which could be used for performance and to rehearse a choir was required. For this purpose Vicentino constructed both an *arcicembalo* and *arciorgano*, two elaborate keyboard instruments with a full complement of chromatic and enharmonic pitches (thirty-one notes per octave). Instead of using the enharmonic pitches as embellishments of the diatonic/chromatic set, Vicentino's practice allowed them to attain an independence of their own, thereby creating startling effects which Vicentino considered a vital tool among the composer's means for expressing the text. Though eight modes and three genera created twenty-four discrete possibilities, more typical was a mixing of the three genera. Vicentino argued that the diatonic genus contained only tones and semitones, the chromatic only semitones and minor thirds, and the enharmonic only dieses and major thirds. This view countered the prevailing notion that major and minor thirds could be generated as the sums of intervals present in the diatonic genus.

In addition to its considerable originality in matters of pitch generation (for which new symbols had to be created) and tuning, Vicentino's treatise includes a useful consideration of compositional structure, with descriptions of the functions of the beginning, middle, and ending sections of a work. The relationships among various modal centers within a work are regarded as hierarchical. Despite the unwieldy nature of Vicentino's system, his reliance upon Greek models adumbrates the emergence of monody, and his innovations provoked an important response by ZARLINO in *Le istitutione harmoniche* (1558).

L'antica musica ridotta alla moderna prattica . . .
[*Rism* B/VI/2, p. 861.]

Rome: Antonio Barre, 1555. [LCPS: V-018. SMLMS.]

Rome: Antonio Barre, 1557.

S ● Lowinsky, Edward E., ed. Facsimile of the 1555 edition. IGMDm, ser. 1, no. 17. Kassel: Bärenreiter, 1959.

Reviews in *Mens* 16/9 (1961):286-87 (Gerrit Vellekoop), *Mf* 14/4 (1961):446-48 (Walter Dürr), and *Rasm* 30/4 (1960):382-84 (Alfredo Bonaccorsi).

T ● See Rowen (1979).

T ● Maniates, Maria Rika, trans. MTTS. New Haven, Ct.: Yale University Press, forthcoming.

Descrizione dell'arciorgano [*Rism* B/VI/2, p. 862.]

Venice: Nicolo Bevil'acqua, 1561.

S ● Catelani, Angelo, ed. "Circolare descrittiva l'arciorgano." *GmdM* 9 (1851):209-10.

ST ● Wolf, J., ed. and trans. "Das Arciorgano des Nicola Vicentino (1561)." *DIB* 35 (1900):299-302.

ST ● Kaufmann, Henry W. "Vicentino's Arciorgano: An Annotated Translation." *JMT* 5/1 (1961):32-53.

T ● See MacClintock (1979).

LITERATURE:

Taisnier, Jean. *Astrologiae ivdiciariae ysagogica . . .* Cologne: A. Birckmannum, 1559.

See Palisca (1959).

Sigonio, Gandolfo. "Discorso intorno a madrigali et a'libri dell'Antica musica . . . da N. Vicentino."

See BOTTRIGARI: (1602).

Zenck, Hermann. "Nicola Vicentinos *L'antica musica* (1555)." In *KroyerFs* (1933):86-101.

Palisca, Claude V. "Vicentino, Don Nicola." Translated by Margarete Hoffmann-Erbrecht. In *MGG* (1949-68). Bibliog.

● ● ● Kaufmann, Henry William. "The Life and Works of Nicola Vicentino (1511-c. 1576)." Ph.D. dissertation, Harvard University, 1960; published edition, MSD, no. 11. [Rome]: American Institute of Musicology, 1966. Bibliog.

Kaufmann, Henry W. "Vicentino and the Greek Genera." *JAMS* 16/3 (1963):325-46.

Brink, Paul Robert. "The Archicembalo of Nicola Vicentino." Ph.D. dissertation, The Ohio State University, 1966. [*DA* 27/09A, p. 3071. UMI 67-02420.]

Nick, Charles. "A Stylistic Analysis of the Music of Nicola Vicentino." Ph.D. dissertation, Indiana University, 1967. [*Rilm* 68-261. *DA* 28/09A, p. 3707. UMI 68-02337.]

Kaufmann, Henry W. "More on the Tuning of the *Archicembalo*." *JAMS* 23/1 (1970):84-94. Bibliog. [*Rilm* 70-2468.]

Harrán, Don. "Vicentino and His Rules of Text Underlay." *MQ* 59/4 (1973):620-32. [*Rilm* 73-3197.]

Schneider, Sigrun. "Mikrotöne in der Musik des 20. Jahrhunderts: Untersuchungen zu Theorie und Gestaltungsprinzipien moderner Kompositionen mit Mikrotönen." Ph.D. dissertation, The University of Mainz, 1973; published edition (OSGM, no. 15), Bonn-Bad Godesberg: Verlag für systematische Musikwissenschaft, 1975. Bibliog.

> Reviews in *LMFI* 11/2 (1978):249-50 (Klaus Schweize), *Me* 29/4 (1975-76):191 (W. Schulze), *Melos/NZfM* 1/6 (1975):505-6 (Christian Möllers), *Musica* 30/1 (1976):59-60 (Wulf Konold), *NMZmJD* 28/6 (1979):56, *ÖM* 31/9 (1976):459 (Werner Schulze), and *Stfm* 59/2 (1977):95-97 (Christina Tobeck).

Maniates, Maria Rika. "Vicentino's *'Incerta et occulta scientia'* Reexamined." *JAMS* 28/2 (1975):335-51.

Tiella, Marco. "The Archicembalo of Nicola Vicentino." *EHM* 1/5 (1975):134-44. [*Rilm* 76-14775.]

Cattin, Giulio. "Nel quarto centenario di Nicola Vicentino teorico e compositore." *Sm* 5 (1976):29-57.

Tiella, Marco. "Settimane di studio sulla musica rinascimentale: Esperienze con l'archicembalo, ricostruito secondo l'originale cinquecentesco; concerti di musica antica." *Nrmi* 10/1 (1976):105-8. [*Rilm* 76-3860.]

● ● ● Kaufmann, Henry W. "Vicentino, Nicola." In *NGrove* (1980). Bibliog.

Rippe, Volker. "Nicola Vicentino—Sein Tonsystem und seine Instrumente: Versuch einer Erklärung." *Mf* 34/4 (1981):393-413. [*Rilm* 82-4561.]

Dahlhaus, Carl. "Musikalischer Humanismus als Manierismus." *Mf* 35/2 (1982):122-29. [*Rilm* 82-2238.]

Maniates, Maria Rika. "What's in a Word? Interpreting Vicentino's Text." In *LangFs* (1984):444-56. Bibliog.

Coates, W. "The Equal Temperament of 31 Notes to the Octave." *Interval* 5/1 (1985-86):23-27.

See also ARTUSI: (1600); (1603); BOTTRIGARI: (1594); (1602); CACCINI: Anfuso and Gianuario (1970); DANCKERTS: (Ms. "Trattato"); DONI: (1635);

(1647); FÉTIS: (1833-44); GALILEI: [Ms. "Discorso . . . enharmonio"]; Chilesotti (1912); LIPPIUS: Rivera (1974/1980); LUSITANO: Barbosa (1970/1977); MOMIGNY: (1791-1818):(1818); MONTEVERDI: Gianuario (1969); Anfuso and Gianuario [1971]; PONTIO: (1588); RIEMANN: (1898); TIGRINI: (1588); ZARLINO: (1558); Lewis (1985-86); LITERATURE SUPPLEMENT: Abraham (1968/1969); Alette (1951); Allen ["Philosophies"] (1939); ● ● ● Apfel (1981); Arnold (1957); Badura-Skoda et al. (1980); Barbieri (1983); Barbour (1932), (1938), (1949-68), (1951/. . ./1972); Becker (1836-39/1964); Beiche ["Dux"] (1972-), ["Inversio"] (1972-); Bent, M. (1984); Bent et al. (1980); Berger ● ● ● (1975/1980), (1980), (1987); Brown (1976); Bullivant (1980); Burney (1776-89/. . ./1957); Cahn ["Retardatio"] (1972-), ["Transitus"] (1972-); Cazden (1948), (1980); Chilesotti (1912); Chominski (1962/1981); Dahlhaus ["Zur Theorie"] (1961), ["Untersuchungen"] (1966/ . . ./1988), (1984); Dahlhaus and Sachs (1980); Dahlhaus et al. (1987); Dürr (1980); Dunning (1980); Dupont (1933/. . ./1986); Eitner (1900-1904/1959-60); Fellerer (1927/. . ./1972), ["Zur Kontrapunktlehre"] (1972), ["Ausdruck"] (1982), (1983); Ferand (1937/1938), (1951), ["Improvised"] (1956), [*Improvisation*] (1956/1961); Fokker (1966); Forkel (1792/ 1962); Frobenius ["Cantus"] (1972-), ["Vollstimmig"] (1972-); Fubini (1971/1983), (1987); Gable (1979); Gerber (1790-92/1977); Ghislanzoni (1949-51); Gianuario (1979); Goldschmidt (1901-4/1967); Grout (1960/. . ./1980); Gut (1976); Haar (1977); Handschin (1948); Hannas (1934); Harrán (1973), (1986); Hawkins (1776/. . ./1969); Horsley (1951), [*Fugue: History*] (1966); Isgro (1968), (1979); Jackson (1988); Jeppesen (1922/. . ./1970), (1930/. . ./1974); Kassler (1979); Keislar (1987); Kinkeldey (1910/1968); Koenigsberger (1979); Kroyer (1901/. . ./1970); Kunze (1979-83); La Fage (1864/1964); Lang (1941); Lange (1899-1900); Leuchtmann (1957/1959); Lindley ["Temperaments"] (1980), (1984); Lockwood (1966/1978); Lowinsky (1946/1967), (1967), ● ● ● (1974); Luoma (1976), (1977); Luper (1938); Mahlert and Sunter (1972-); ● ● ● Maniates (1979); Mann (1955/. . ./1987); McKinnon (1978), (1978); Meer (1980); Meier (1949-68), (1974/1988); Mendel (1978); Nelson (1984); Palisca (1949-68), (1953), (1959), ["Artusi-Monteverdi"] (1968/1985), [*"Ut oratoria musica"*] (1972), (1974/1977), ["Theory"] (1980), (1985); Pole (1879/. . ./1924); Powers ["Mode"] (1980); Reese (1954/1959), (1957/1970); Reichenbach (1948); Reimer ["Concerto"] (1972-), ["Kammermusik"] (1972-); Rogers (1955); Ruhnke (1974); Sachs (1972-); Schmalzriedt ["Subiectum"] (1972-); Seidel (1976),

(1979); **Seidel and Cooper (1986)**; Subirá (1947/. . ./1958); Tilmouth (1980); Todd (1983); Toncitch (1973); Tuksar (1978/1980); Uberti

(1981); Vogel (1975/1984), (1976); **Walker (1941-42/. . ./1985)**, **(1978)**; Walker (1987); Warren (1980); Wienpahl (1953).

GEORG JOSEPH VOGLER

[1749—1814]

Students of the history of harmonic theory have not always appreciated the curious yet influential theorist, Abbé Georg Joseph Vogler. His adoption of Roman numerals for harmonic analysis and penchant for progressive harmonic successions and modulations paved the way for much that was to come in the nineteenth century. Yet his awkward (though self-assured) style, insistence upon reworking the compositions of earlier generations (in particular those of J. S. Bach), and reputation as an organ recitalist who pandered to lowbrow tastes have impeded the scholarly evaluation of his writings.

Living under generally favorable circumstances, Vogler traveled widely. When barely past his youth he ventured to Italy, where he came under the influence of VALLOTTI. Upon his return to Mannheim, he established a music school which was to absorb his theoretical and analytical perspectives and serve as the target for some of his numerous publications.

From his early *Tonwissenschaft und Tonsetzkunst* (1776) onward, Vogler based his theory upon the notion of *Redukzion*, wherein the musical fabric of a composition was condensed into a series of fundamental chords, each a root-position triad without seventh. The identity of the triad could be indicated with a Roman numeral, which established the position of the chord within the prevailing tonal center. The simplicity and elegance of this system, as compared with RAMEAU's, eventually won numerous converts. Later publications, including his *Kuhrpfälzische Tonschule* (1778), the periodical *Betrachtungen der Mannheimer Tonschule* (1778-81), and *Handbuch zur Harmonielehre* (1802), offered refinements and analytical examples which enhanced the system.

As his treatise title specifies, Vogler divided his theory into two components: under *Tonwissenschaft* one finds basic formulations regarding chords, scales, and the concepts of consonance and dissonance; under *Tonsetzkunst* the practical concerns of the composer are addressed. Vogler's notion of modulation, wherein a pivot chord might function in two separate keys and serve as a link between them, was particularly influential. Among the more interesting types of pivots are those involving enharmonic reinterpretation, such as diminished-seventh chords or the dominant seventh/augmented-sixth pairing.

The breadth and ingenuity of Vogler's writings is impressive. He pondered topics ranging from non-European melodic practices (for which he undertook a special tour of exotic places) to a harmonically based contrapuntal theory, and he devised several unusual instruments either for comparing intervals (along the lines of a monochord) or to create unique music. In Vogler one finds the foundation for WEBER's harmonic theory, an important perspective on the concept of inversion, and evidence of the persistence of acoustics as a generator of music's foundations. Certainly, he is more than the charlatan he has sometimes been made out to have been—though also less than the consummate master some of his contemporaries assumed he was.

Tonwissenschaft und Tonsetzkunst [*Rism* B/VI/2, pp. 869-70.]

Mannheim: Kurfürstliche Hofbuchdruckerei, 1776. [LCPS: V-033. SMLMS. IDC.]

A model for [1778], below. Commentary in *AmZ* 20/1, 3, 5-8, 10 (1818):1-10, 41-46, 85-88, 102-6, 121-28, 145-51, 185-90 (Gld.) and 20/32 (1818):565-71.

S ● Facsimile edition. Hildesheim: Georg Olms, 1970.

Stimmbildungskunst [*Rism* B/VI/2, p. 869.]

Mannheim: Kuhrfürstliche Hofbuchdruckerei, 1776. [LCPS: V-032.]

Articles on music in *Deutsche Encyklopädie; oder, Allgemeines Real-Wörterbuch aller Künste und Wissenschaften*

Frankfurt am Main: Varrentrapp Sohn & Wenner, 1778-1807. 23 vols. Edited by Heinrich Gottfried Köster and Johann Friedrich Roos.

Vogler's contributions appear among the letters A through K.

Vogler's Tonschule, Tonwissenschaft und Tonsezkunst . . . [*Rism* B/VI/2, p. 869.]

1) *Kuhrpfälzische Tonschule*

2) *Gründe der kuhrpfälzischen Tonschule in Beyspielen: Als Vorbereitung zur Mannheimer Monat-Schrift und zu den Herausgaben des öffentlichen Tonlehrers*

Mannheim: the author (C. F. Schwan & M. Götz), [1778]. Vol. 1 (in two parts). [LCPS: V-031a. IDC.]

>An expansion of *Tonwissenschaft* (1776), above. Review in *LTZ* 1/35 (August 29, 1778):547-54 [reprinted with supplementary materials in (1778-81):Vol. 1/9-12 (1778-79):202-75, below].

[Mannheim: the author, 1778]. Vol. 2. [LCPS: V-031b.]

Betrachtungen der Mannheimer Tonschule [*Rism* B/VI/2, pp. 867-68.]

Mannheim: 1778-81. 3 vols.

S ● Facsimile edition. Hildesheim: Georg Olms, 1974. 4 vols.

Entwurf eines neuen Wörterbuchs für die Tonschule . . . [*Rism* B/VI/2, p. 868.]

Frankfurt am Main and Leipzig: Varrentrapp Sohn & Wenner, 1780.

Erste musikalische Preisaustheilung für das Jahr 1791 . . . [*Rism* B/VI/2, p. 868.]

Frankfurt am Main: Varrentrapp & Wenner, 1794. [LCPS: V-030.]

Inledning til harmoniens kännedom [*Rism* B/VI/2, p. 869.]

Stockholm: Anders Jacobsson Nordström, 1794. 2 vols.

Clavér Schola . . . [*Rism* B/VI/2, p. 868.]

Stockholm: Anders Jacobsson Nordström, 1798.

Organist-Schola . . . [*Rism* B/VI/2, p. 869.]

Stockholm: Anders Jacobsson Nordström, 1798-99. 2 vols.

Choral-System [*Rism* B/VI/2, p. 868.]

Copenhagen: in Kommission in der Haly'schen Musikhandlung (Niels Christensen) [Stockholm: Kongl. Privilegierende Not-Tryckeriet], 1800. 2 vols.

>Review in *AmZ* 3/16-18 (1800-1801):264-69, 286-89, 315-18.

Offenbach am Main: Johann André, [1800]. 2 vols.

"Data zur Akustik"

AmZ 3/31-34 (1800-1801):517-25, 533-40, 549-54, 565-71.
Leipzig: Breitkopf & Härtel, 1801.

Handbuch zur Harmonielehre und für den Generalbaß, nach den grundsätze der Mannheimer Tonschule . . .

Prague: K. Barth, 1802.

Über die harmonische Akustik und über ihren Einfluß auf alle musikalischen Bildungs-Anstalten

Offenbach am Main: Johann André, [1806].

Zwei und dreisig Präludien für die Orgel und für das Fortepiano, nebst einer Zergliederung in ästhetischer, rhetorischer und harmonischer Rücksicht, mit praktischem Bezug auf das Handbuch der Tonlehre

Munich: Falter, 1806.

S ● Grave, Floyd K., ed. RRMCA, no. 24. Madison, Wisc.: A-R Editions, 1986.

Gründliche Anleitung zum Klavier-Stimmen für die, welche ein gutes Gehör haben

Stuttgart: 1807.

Zwölf Choräle von Sebastian Bach

Leipzig: C. F. Peters, [ca. 1810]. With commentary by Carl Maria von Weber.

System für den Fugenbau als Einleitung zur harmonischen Gesang-Verbindungs-Lehre

Offenbach am Main: Johann André, [ca. 1817].

Published posthumously.

For more comprehensive listings of Vogler's varied publications, see Schweiger (1938), below; Reckziegel (1949-68), below; and Grave (1980), below.

LITERATURE:

Weißbeck, Johann Michael. *Protestationsschrift; oder, Exemplarische Widerlegung einiger Stellen und Perioden der Capellmeister Voglerischen Tonwissenschaft und Tonsetzkunst.* Erlangen: gedruckt mit Kunstmannischen Schriften, [1783]. [*Rism* B/VI/2, p. 882. LCPS: W-017.]

See Knecht (1785).

Verzeichniß der von . . . Vogler nachgelassenen, größtentheils noch nicht bekannten praktischen und theoretischen, im Manuscript vorhandenen Werke, so wie seiner im Druck erschienenen und mehrerer fremden Musikalien . . . Darmstadt: 1814.

Pasqué, Ernst "Abt Vogler als Tonkünstler, Lehrer und Priester." *NhV* (1884).

Schafhäutl, Karl [Franz] Emil von. *Abt Georg Joseph Vogler: Sein Leben, Charakter und musikalisches System, seine Werke, seine Schule, Bildnisse etc.* Augsburg: M. Huttler, 1888.

Schweiger, Hertha. "Abbé Voglers Simplifikationssystem und seine akustischen Studien." *KJb* 29 (1934):72-123.

Schweiger, Hertha. "Abbé G. J. Vogler's Orgellehre: Ein Beitrag zru Klanggeschichte der frühromantischen Orgel." Ph.D. dissertation, The University of

Freiburg im Breisgau, 1938; published edition, Vienna: Kmoch, 1938.

Schweiger, Hertha. "Abt Vogler." *MQ* 25/2 (1939):156-66.

Reckziegel, Walter. "Vogler, Georg Joseph, genannt Abbé." In *MGG* (1949-68). Bibliog.

Sanner, Lars Erik. "Abbé Georg Joseph Vogler som musikteoretiker." *Stfm* 30 (1952):73-102.

Kreitz, Helmut. "Abbé Georg Joseph Vogler als Musiktheoretiker: Ein Beitrag zur Geschichte der Musiktheorie im 18. Jahrhundert." Ph.D. dissertation, The University of Saarbrücken, 1957 (1958).

Jung, K. "Abbé Vogler und sein 'Simplifikationssystem': Abbé Vogler, geb. 15.6.1749, gest. 6.8.1814, Ein Beitrag zum Diskussionstheme 'Das totgeschwiegene Problem des Orgelbauers'." *Mi* 11/4 (1962):344-46.

> This article is missing, curiously, from some copies of *Mi*.

Hamann, Heinz Wolfgang. "Abbé Voglers Simplifikations-System im Urteil der Zeitgenossen." *MK* 33/1 (1963):28-31.

Lenz, Irmgard. "Georg Joseph Vogler, zur 150. Wiederkehr seines Todestages." *NZfM* 125/10 (1964):434-40.

Öijen, Arne. "Fragment ur Josef Voglers liv och gärning." *Musikern* /12 (1966):6.

Grave, Floyd K. "Abbé Vogler's Revision of Pergolesi's *Stabat Mater*." *JAMS* 30/1 (1977):43-71. [*Rilm* 77-539.]

Grave, Floyd K. "Abbé Vogler and the Bach Legacy." *ECenS* 13/2 (1979-80):119-41. Bibliog. [*Rilm* 79-4666.]

Grave, Floyd K. "Abbé Vogler and the Study of Fugue." *MTS* 1 (1979):43-67. [*Rilm* 79-2648.]

Grave, Floyd K. "Abbé Vogler's Theory of Reduction." *CM* 29 (1980):41-69. [*Rilm* 80-548.]

● ● ● Grave, Margaret H. "Vogler, Georg Joseph." In *NGrove* (1980). Bibliog.

Ludvová, Jitka. "Abbé Vogler a Praha." *Hv* 19/2 (1982):99-122. [*Rilm* 82-2623.]

Stevens, Jane R. "Georg Joseph Vogler and the 'Second Theme' in Sonata Form: Some Eighteenth-Century Perceptions of Musical Contrast." *JM* 2/3 (1983):278-304. [*Rilm* 83-2740.]

● ● ● Grave, Floyd K., and Grave, Margaret G. *In Praise of Harmony: The Teachings of Abbé Georg Joseph Vogler*. Lincoln, Nebr.: University of Nebraska Press, 1987. Bibliog.

Jung, Hermann. " 'Der pedantisch geniale Abt Vogler': Musiktheorie und Werkanalyse in der zweiten Hälfte des 18. Jahrhunderts." *Mth* 3/2 (1988):99-115.

Veit [?], Joachim. "Der Einfluß G. J. Voglers und Franz Danzis auf das Schaffen Carl Maria von Webers." Ph.D. dissertation, The University of Detmold, forthcoming.

See also FÉTIS: (1833-44); (1840); MOMIGNY: Chailley (1982); VIADANA: Haack (1964/1974); LITERATURE SUPPLEMENT: Auhagen (1982/1983); Babbitt (1987); Becker (1836-39/1964); Beiche ["Dux"] (1972-); Caplin (1981), (1983); Cavallini (1949); Chew (1980); Cohen and Miller (1979); **Dahlhaus et al. (1987)**; Dunsby and Whittall (1988); Eitner (1900-1904/1959-60); Fellerer (1927/. . ./1972); ["Musikwissenschaft"] (1972); Fischer (1957); Forkel (1792/1962); Grave (1980), (1985); Gut (1972); Heimann (1970/1973); Jacobi (1957-60/1971); Jones (1934); **Kassler (1979)**, (1983-85); Kauko (1958); Knecht (1785); Konecne (1984); Kramer (1975); **Lester** (1979-81), **(1989)**; Lindley (1982); Longyear and Covington (1985); **Mann (1955/. . ./1987)**; Marvin (1987); McCredie (1981); Moyer (1969); Müller-Blattau (1949-68); Nelson (1984); Neumann, Frederick (1978); Newman (1963/. . ./1983); Ratner (1949), (1980); Reichenbach (1948); Reimer ["Concerto"] (1972-); **Ritzel (1967/1968)**; Rosen (1980/1986); Seidel (1971); Sheldon (1982); Shellhous (1988); **Shirlaw (1917/. . ./1970)**; Sondheimer (1925); **Steblin (1981/1983)**; Stege (1927-28); Stevens (1974); Subirá (1947/. . ./1958); Thompson (1980); Thomson (1960/1978); Tittel (1966); Todd (1983); Troeger (1987); Vogel (1955/1954); **Wagner (1974)**; **Wason** ● ● ● **(1981/1985)**, (1988); Wessely (1967); Wichmann (1966); Williams ["Equal"] (1968); Wirth (1966).

GERHARD JOHANN VOSSIUS

[1577 – 1649]

Music's appeal as a subject for humanistic inquiry is seen in several works by the Netherlander Gerhard Johann Vossius. Writing well into the seventeenth century, Vossius adhered to time-honored doctrines stemming from Boethius rather than examining contemporary musical procedures. In fact, the practices of the Greeks and Romans, early Christian and Jewish music, and mythic references to music were among his concerns. Interspersed among other materials in numerous individual volumes are discussions of the creation and transmission of sound; mathematical aspects of music; the position of music among the arts, particularly its relation to poetry, drama, and dance; and its affective nature. MATTHESON erroneously attributed to Gerhard Johann Vossius a work by his son, Isaac VOSSIUS.

De theologia gentili et physiologia Christiana; sive de origine ac progressu idololatriae, deque naturae mirandis quibus homo adducitur ad Deum, libri quatuor . . .

>> Amsterdam: Johann and Cornelius Blaeu, 1641. In 4 books.

>> Later printings.

> S ● See Collected Works (1695-1701):Vol. 5, below.

> S ● Facsimile of the 1641 edition. 3 vols. RG, no. 28. New York: Garland Publishing, 1976.

De artis poeticae natura ac constitutione libri

>> Amsterdam: Ludovicum Elzevirium, 1647.

> S ● See Collected Works (1695-1701):Vol. 3, below.

Poeticarum institutionum libri tres

>> Amsterdam: Ludovicum Elzevirium, 1647.

> S ● See Collected Works (1695-1701):Vol. 3, below.

De quatuor artibus popularibus, de philologia, et scientiis mathematicis, cui operi subjungitur chronologia mathematicorum, libri tres [*Rism* B/VI/2, p. 871.]

>> Amsterdam: Johann Blaeu, 1650. [IDC.]
>> Amsterdam: Johann Blaeu, 1660. [LCPS: V-037.]

> S ● See Collected Works (1695-1701):Vol. 3, below.

Etymologicon linguae latinae. Praefigitur ejusdem de literarum permutatione tractatus

>> Amsterdam: Ludovicum and Danielem Elzevirum, 1662.

>> Edited by Isaac VOSSIUS. Later printings.

> S ● See Collected Works (1695-1701):Vol. 1, below.

See also DONI: Correspondence.

COLLECTED WORKS EDITION:

Gerhardi Johannis Vosssii opera omnia in sex tomos divisa . . . Amsterdam: P. and J. Blaeu, 1695-1701.

LITERATURE:

Hüschen, Heinrich. "Voss, Gerhard Johann." In *MGG* (1949-68). Bibliog.

● ● ● Hüschen, Heinrich. "Der Polyhistor Gerhard Johann Vossius (1577-1649) als Musikschriftsteller." In *WioraFs* (1967):182-90. Bibliog. [*Rilm* 68-116.]

Rademaker, C. S. M. *Gerardus Joannes Vossius (1577-1649)*. Zrvtls, no. 21. Zwolle: W. E. J. Tjeenk Willink, 1967; as *Life and Work of Gerardus Joannes Vossius (1577-1649)* (RlN, no. 5), Assen, The Netherlands: Van Gorcum, 1981.

>> Reviews in *AHR* 87/3 (1982):800 (Frank T. Brechka), *AUMLA* 30 (1968):280-81 (J. Smit), *Choice* 19/7 (1982):900, *HRNB* 10/6 (1981-82):155-56 (John Newell), *JMH* 55/4 (1983):768-70 (Charles B. Schmitt), *RQ* 35/2 (1982):292-93 (Herbert H. Rowen), and *SCN* 27/2 (1969):40 (Joseph IJsewijn).

Hüschen, Heinrich. "Vossius, Gerhard Johann." In *NGrove* (1980). Bibliog.

See also FÉTIS: (1833-44); WALTHER: (1732); LITERATURE SUPPLEMENT: Becker (1836-39/1964); Beiche ["Inversio"] (1972-); Burney (1776-89/. . ./1957); Eitner (1900-1904/1959-60); Forkel (1792/ 1962); Gerber (1790-92/1977); Lippman (1986); Hawkins (1776/. . ./1969); Schäfke (1934/1964).

ISAAC VOSSIUS

[1618 – 1689]

The resurrection of ancient musical practices was, to numerous authors of the late sixteenth and early seventeenth centuries, a desirable goal. The Netherlander Isaac Vossius regarded the poetic meters of the Greeks as the source of their music's reported affective powers. In his *De poematum cantu et viribus rhythmi* (1673), written after he had migrated to England, Vossius presented an extensive account of poetic meters and advocated that they replace the complicated rhythmic characteristics of contemporary practice. Through the unique patterns of pulsations inherent in the various meters, the internal bodily motions of each listener would be churned — sometimes exciting, sometimes calming the passions. The work, though ridiculed by Hawkins (1776) as "an unintelligible rhapsody" written by a "literary coxcomb," was recommended by MATTHESON in his *Vollkommene Kapellmeister* (1739) — though he confused Isaac with his father Gerhard Johann VOSSIUS — and by Forkel, who translated a large segment of it for his *Musikalische-kritische Bibliothek* (1779).

De poematum cantu et viribus rhythmi [*Rism* B/VI/2, p. 872.]

>> Oxford: Theatrum Sheldonianum (London: Robert Scot), 1673. [IDC.]

>> Published anonymously.

T ● Forkel, Johann Nikolaus, trans. "Abhandlung vom Singen der Gedichte, und von der Kraft des Rhythmus." *MkB* 3 (1779):1-107.

See also DONI: Correspondence; MERSENNE: (1617-48).

LITERATURE:

Hüschen, Heinrich. "Voss (Vossius), . . . Isaac." In *MGG* (1949-68). Bibliog.

Serauky, Walter. "Die Affekten-Metrik des Isaac Vossius in ihrem Einfluß auf Joh. Kuhnau und Joh. Seb. Bach." In *SchneiderFsII* (1955):105-13. Bibliog.

● ● ● Hüschen, Heinrich. "Isaac Voss (1618 – 1689) und sein Traktat *De poematum cantu et viribus rhythmi* (Oxford 1673)." In *VötterleFs* (1968):342-64. Bibliog. [*Rilm* 68-1836.]

Blok, F. F. *Contributions to the History of Isaac Vossius's Library*. Amsterdam: North-Holland Publishing, 1974.

>Reviews in *BCol* 23/4 (1974):599 (Michael Hunter) and *Libr* 30/3 (1975):254 (Anna E. C. Simoni).

Hüschen, Heinrich. "Vossius [Voss], Isaac." In *NGrove* (1980). Bibliog.

See also FÉTIS: (1833-44); NORTH, R.: [ca. 1726]; VOSSIUS, G. J.: Hüschen (1967); WALTHER: (1732); LITERATURE SUPPLEMENT: Allen ["Philosophies"] (1939); Becker (1836-39/1964); Burney (1776-89/. . ./1957); Chenette (1967); Donà (1967); Eitner (1900-1904/1959-60); Forkel (1792/1962); Gerber (1790-92/1977); Hawkins (1776/. . ./1969); Houle (1960), (1987); La Fage (1864/1964); ● ● ● Mace (1964/1966); Miller and Cohen (1987); Seidel (1972-); **Seidel and Cooper (1986)**; **Walker (1978)**; **Zaminer (1985)**.

JOHN WALLIS

[1616 – 1703]

Theorists had long been fond of applying their numerical speculations to the experimental context of vibrating strings. By the seventeenth century, when John Wallis, one of England's most brilliant mathematicians before Newton, began to investigate vibration theory, he could draw upon the common knowledge that a string, when plucked exactly in its center, will offer a harsh sound, and that if one of two adjacent strings is plucked, the other might produce sympathetic vibrations if tuned at the unison or an octave below. In 1676 Wallis was told of two independent experiments (by William Noble and by Thomas Pigot) which demonstrated that when two strings are tuned an octave apart and the higher-pitched one is plucked, the other string vibrates sympathetically in two sections, divided at the midpoint, and that each of these vibrations is at twice the frequency of that string's fundamental pitch. A similar relationship existed for other intervals as well.

The following year Wallis published a letter which documents this association between the vibrations of partials and the nodal points on the string. By using lightweight slips one could show that if a string were set in motion (through sympathetic vibration) so as to produce a sound a twelfth above its fundamental pitch, then two points of rest would appear, dividing the string into three equal parts, each of which is related as 1:3, the ratio of the twelfth, to the entire string. In this way physical proof of the potential existence of overtones was established, though Wallis did not claim that the fundamental and overtones sounded *simultaneously* when the string was plucked. He did, however, note that plucking a string at any nodal point, not just its center, would produce an inferior quality of sound. These ideas were later incorporated in his *De algebra* (1693), Chapter 107.

Wallis contributed also to England's awareness of the Greek musical heritage, through translation into Latin of sources by Ptolemy and Bryennius and commentary on Ptolemy by Porphyrius (1682 and 1699), and through his own essays on Greek music and how it compares with contemporary practice (1682, July 1698, August 1698, and 1699). His pronouncements on tuning (March 1698, July 1698) include impractical divisions of the whole step but acknowledge that some organs in England were being tuned in equal temperament, of which he approved in this context.

Operum mathematicorum pars prima

> Contains "Tractatus elenchticus adversus M. Meibomii dialogum de proportionibus."

Oxford: Leon Lichfield (T. Robinson), 1657.

Three letters to Henry Oldenburg on problems of tuning

Mss., May 7, 14, and 25, 1664. [London: Royal Society Manuscript Collection, Early Letters.]

S ● Hall, A. Rupert, and Hall, Marie Boas, eds. and trans. *The Correspondence of Henry Oldenburg*. 11 vols. Madison, Wisc.: The University of Wisconsin Press, 1965-77.

> Reviews in *AS* 23/1 (1967):78-79 (Ronald Sterne Wilkinson), *BHM* 42/5 (1968):476-78 (Donald G. Bates), *Centaurus* 21/3-4 (1977):327 (J. A. Lohne), *EHR* 83/326 (1968):176-77 (Christopher Hill), *History* 52/176 (1967):334-37 (William P. D. Wightman), *HJ* 10/2 (1967):286-93 (Quentin Skinner), *Science* 152/3724 (1966):912-13 (Richard S. Westfall), *SCN* 26/3 (1968):50-51 (J. Max Patrick), and *TLS* 65/3361 (1966):658.

"[Of the Trembling of Consonant Strings:] Dr. Wallis's Letter to the Publisher concerning a New Musical Discovery" (14 March 1677)

> *PTRS* 12/134 (23 April 1677):839-42.

>> Reprinted in abridgments of the *Philosophical Transactions*.

Claudii Ptolemaei harmonicorum libri tres . . . nunc primum graece . . . [*Rism* B/VI/2, p. 674.]

> Oxford: Theatrum Sheldonianum, 1682.

>> Reprinted in abridgments of the *Philosophical Transactions*. Reviews in *PTRS* 13/143 (January 1682/83):20-21 and in Ms. (Robert Hooke) [London: British Library, Reference Division.].

S ● See (1699), below.

De algebra tractatus: Historicus & practicus . . . Operum mathematicorum volumen alterum

> and

Operum mathematicorum volumen tertium. Quo continentur Claudii Ptolemaei, Porphyrii, Manuelis Bryennii harmonica . . . [*Rism* B/VI/2, p. 876.]
Oxford: Theatrum Sheldonianum, 1693, 1699. [LCPS: W-005.]

> Review in *PTRS* 21/254 (July 1699):259-68.

S ● Scriba, Christoph J., ed. Facsimile edition. Hildesheim: Georg Olms, 1972.

"A Question of Musick Lately Proposed to Dr. Wallis, concerning the Division of the Monochord, or Section of the Musical Canon: With His Answer to It" (5 March 1698)

> *PTRS* 20/238 (March 1698):80-84.

>> Reprinted in abridgments of the *Philosophical Transactions*.

"A Letter . . . to Samuel Pepys Esquire, Relating to Some Supposed Imperfections in an Organ."

>   *PTRS* 20/242 (July 1698):249-56.

>>   Reprinted in abridgments of the *Philosophical Transactions*.

"A Letter . . . to Mr. Andrew Fletcher, concerning the Strange Effects Reported of Musick in Former Times, beyond What to Be Found in Later Ages" (18 August 1698)

>   *PTRS* 20/243 (August 1698):297-303.

>>   Reprinted in abridgments of the *Philosophical Transactions*.

[Letter dealing with a Greek manuscript from Budapest]

>   Ms. [London: British Library, Reference Division.]

See also SALMON: (1672); (1688); LITERATURE SUPPLEMENT: Miller and Cohen (1987).

LITERATURE:

Clerke, Agnes Mary. "Wallis, John." In *DNB* (1885-1901). Bibliog.

Scriba, Christoph J. "Wallis, John." In *DSB* (1970-80). Bibliog.

● ● ● Oldham, Guy. "Wallis, John." In *NGrove* (1980). Bibliog.

See also FÉTIS: (1833-44); KEPLER: Dickreiter (1971/1973); MERSENNE: (1617-48); RIEMANN: (1898); WALTHER: (1732); LITERATURE SUPPLEMENT: Archibald (1924); Auda (1930/1979); Auhagen (1982/1983); Becker (1836-39/1964); Bell et al. (1980); Chenette (1967); Crombie (1969); **Dahlhaus et al. (1987)**; ● ● ● Dostrovsky (1969); Eitner (1900-1904/1959-60); Forkel (1792/1962); Gerber (1790-92/1977), (1812-14/1966); Gouk (1980), (1981-82), (1982); Green (1969); Hawkins (1776/. . ./1969); Hunt (1978); Kassler (1979); Koenigsberger (1979); **Lindley** ["Temperaments"] **(1980)**; Lloyd (1940-41); Lottermoser (1949-68); Mace (1964/1966); ● ● ● Miller and Cohen (1987); **Palisca** (1961), ["Theory"] **(1980)**; Truesdell (1960); Vogel (1955/1954), (1969); Williams (1968); **Zaminer (1985)**.

JOHANN GOTTFRIED WALTHER

[1684 — 1748]

As the number of terms and concepts a musician might wish to recall increased, the means by which this knowledge was assembled took on a new dimension. Though seventeenth-century authors such as MERSENNE and KIRCHER wrote profusely and shared abundantly of their knowledge, their readers were required to search out the discussion of each topic, often wading through a lengthy prose exposition to reach the desired information. The dictionary format, in which JANOVKA and BROSSARD had produced pioneering efforts at the beginning of the eighteenth century, offered a more convenient arrangement of materials for quick reference. The first German to assemble a comprehensive music encyclopaedia, Johann Gottfried Walther, was extraordinarily perspicacious in his undertaking and produced a work of considerable fascination.

Terms and names—of musicians both living and dead—are mingled in a single alphabetical compilation in the *Musicalisches Lexicon* (1732), for which Walther painstakingly studied a wide range of books and corresponded with others knowledgeable in the field. Though modern scholarship has surpassed Walther's efforts in reliability and comprehensiveness, his *Lexicon* supplies a vast array of opinions and information that otherwise would have faded with his era. Modern historians of music theory should ponder his selection of terms, the authors he chose to consult (including especially MATTHESON), and the space he devoted to various topics to gain a perspective on the discipline as it existed in the early eighteenth century.

Walther also created a manual called "Praecepta der musicalischen Composition" in conjunction with his teaching in Weimar. Not published until 1955, the work is derived from the best of seventeenth-century treatises, including those by BARYPHONUS, BERNHARD, KIRCHER, and PRINTZ. In addition to the fundamentals of music and standard compositional procedures, the volume addresses the notion of rhetoric in music (incorporating several musical examples) and includes a brief dictionary of terms, antedating his more famous compilation by over twenty years.

Correspondence

Mss., 1702-47.

S ● Beckmann, Klaus, and Schulze, Hans-Joachim, eds. *Johann Gottfried Walther: Briefe*. Leipzig: VEB Deutscher Verlag für Musik, 1987.

Reviews in *MT* 129/1748 (1988):533 (Malcolm Boyd), *Muh* 39/3 (1988):209, and *NZfM* 149/7-8 (1988):102 (Gerhard Schuhmacher).

"Praecepta der musicalischen Composition"

Ms., 1708. [Weimar: Thüringische Landesbibliothek, Musiksammlung.]

S ● Benary, Peter, ed. JBzMf, no. 2. Leipzig: Breitkopf & Härtel, 1955.

Reviews in *Mens* 13/12 (1958):389-90 (Gerrit Vellekoop) and *Mf* 10/4 (1957):565-66 (Martin Ruhnke).

Alte und neue musicalische Bibliothec; oder, Musicalisches Lexicon . . . [*Rism* B/VI/2, pp. 877-78.]

A small part of what became the *Musicalisches Lexicon* (1732), below.

Weimar: the author; Erfurt: D. Limprecht, 1728.

Musicalisches Lexicon; oder, Musicalische Bibliothec, darinnen nicht allein die Musici, welche so wol in alten als neuern Zeiten, ingleichen bey verschiedenen Nationen, durch Theorie und Praxin sich hervor gethan, und was von jedem bekannt worden, oder er in Schrifften hinterlassen, mit allem Fleisse und nach den vornehmsten Umständen angeführet, sondern auch die in greichischer, lateinischer, italiänischer und frantzösischer Sprache gebräuchliche musicalische Kunst- oder sonst dahin gehörige Wörter, nach alphabetischer Ordnung vorgetragen und erkläret, und zugleich die meisten vorkommende Signaturen erläutert werden [*Rism* B/VI/2, p. 878.]

Leipzig: Wolffgang Deer, 1732. [LCPS: W-008. SMLMS. IDC.]

Review in *MonR* 38 (1802):215.

Ms. for a second edition, 1740. [Vienna: Gesellschaft der Musikfreunde.]

S ● Schaal, Richard, ed. Facsimile of the 1732 edition. IGMDm, ser. 1, no. 3. Kassel: Bärenreiter, 1953; reprint editions, 1963; 1967.

Review in *JAMS* 9/1 (1956):40-46 (A. Tillman Merritt).

T ● See **Lester (1989)**.

LITERATURE:

Eitner, Robert. "Johann Gottfried Walther." *MMg* 4/8 (1872):165-67.

Gehrmann, Hermann. "Johann Gottfried Walther als Theoretiker." Ph.D. dissertation, The University of Berlin, 1891; published in *VMw* 7 (1891):468-578; an extract, Leipzig: Breitkopf & Härtel, 1891.

Egel, Hermann Wilhelm. "Johann Gottfried Walthers Leben und Werke." Ph.D. dissertation, The University of Leipzig, 1904.

Schünemann, Georg. "J. G. Walther und H. Bokemeyer: Eine Musikerfreundschaft um Sebastian Bach." *Bach-Jb* 30 (1933): 86-118.

Brodde, Otto. "Johann Gottfried Walther (1684-1748): Leben und Werk." Ph.D. dissertation, The University of Münster, 1935 (1937); published edition (MBzMw, no. 7), Kassel: Bärenreiter, 1937.

Breig, Werner. "Walther, Johann Gottfried." In *MGG* (1949-68). Bibliog.

Godman, Stanley. "English Musicians in Walther's *Musicalisches Lexicon*." *MMR* 81/926-27 (1951):97-100, 125-28.

Schmitz, Arnold. "Die Figurenlehre in den theoretischen Werken Johann Gottfried Walthers." *AfMw* 9/2 (1952):79-100.

Eggebrecht, Hans Heinrich. "Walthers *Musikalisches Lexikon* in seinen terminologischen Partien." *Am* 29/1 (1957):10-27.

Senn, Kurt Wolfgang. "Johann Gottfried Walther und Johann Sebastian Bach: Ursachen und Wirkungen einer Musikerfreundschaft." *MGot* 17/2-3 (1963):27-38, 57-68.

Blount, Gilbert L. "The Use of *Affektenlehre* and the *Figurenlehre* in the Organ Chorales of Johann Gottfried Walther." M.A. thesis, The University of California at Los Angeles, 1964.

Whittaker, James. "As Others Saw It." *Chelys* 3 (1971):19-21. [*Rilm* 73-1838.]

Zakharova, Ol'ga. *K voprusu o muzykal'noi ritorike v tvorchestve Genrikha Shiutsa*. Moscow: Moskovskaia Konservatoriia, 1973. [*Rilm* 74-2227.]

● ● ● Buelow, George J. "Walther, Johann Gottfried." In *NGrove* (1980). Bibliog.

Barber, Graham. "Johann Gottfried Walther (1684-1748): A Tercentenary Tribute." *MT* 125/1702 (1984):721-25.

See also ADLUNG: (1758); BELLERMANN: (1862); BONONCINI: Holler (1955/1963); FÉTIS: (1831); (1833-44); LIPPIUS: Rivera (1974/1980); KEPLER:

Dickreiter (1971/1973); MATTHESON: (1722-25):(1725); (1739); (1740); Becker (1952); Krummacher (1982); Buelow and Marx (1983):Sheldon; RIEMANN: (1898); VIADANA: Haack (1964/1974); LITERATURE SUPPLEMENT: Albrecht (1981); Allen ["Philiosophies"] (1939); Apfel [*Beiträge*] (1964), ["Wandlungen"] (1964); Arlt (1974); Audbourg-Popin (1984); Babitz (1952), (1967/1969); Baron (1968); Bartel (1982/1985); Becker (1836-39/1964); Beiche ["Dux"] (1972-), ["Inversio"] (1972-); **Benary (1956/ 1961)**; Bent, I. (1984); Beyschlag (1907/1953); Blankenburg ["Harmonie"] (1959); Blumröder (1972-); Brandes (1935); Butler (1977); Cahn ["Repercussio"] (1972-); Carse (1925/1964); Collins (1963), (1967); Constantini (1975); ● ● ● **Coover (1980)**; Dahlhaus ["Termini"] (1955), ["Untersuchungen"] (1966/. . ./1988); **Dahlhaus et al. (1987)**; Dammann (1958/1967); David (1956); David and Mendel (1945/1966); Donington (1980); Dreyfus (1987); Dupont (1933/. . ./1986); Eggebrecht (1955); Eitner (1900-1904/1959-60); Federhofer (1969), (1985); Feil (1955); Feldmann (1958); Fellerer (1927/. . ./1972); Fischer (1957), (1978); Flindell (1977), (1983-84); Forchert (1986); Forkel (1792/1962); Frobenius ["Cantus"] (1972-), ["Homophonus"] (1972-), ["Isotonos"] (1972-), ["Polyphon"] (1972-), ["Vollstimmig"] (1972-); Gerber (1790-92/1977); Goldschmidt (1907); Grave (1985); Gurlitt (1942/ 1966), (1954/1966); Gut (1972-); Haase (1969), (1972), (1986); Hartmann (1980); Haw-

kins (1776/. . ./1969); Heimann (1970/1973); Hiller (1768-69); Horsley (1963), [*Fugue: History*] (1966); Houle (1960), (1987); Jackson (1988); **Kassler (1979)**; Katz (1926); Kelletat [*Temperatur*] (1960); Kinkeldey (1910/1968); Kirkendale (1979), (1984); Krützfeldt (1961); Krummacher (1979), (1986); La Fage (1864/1964); **Lester** (1974), **(1989)**; Lindley (1982); Mahlert and Sunter (1972-); Maier (1984); **Mann (1955/. . ./1987)**; Massenkeil (1963); McIntyre (1965); Meier (1974/1988); Mendel (1955), (1978); Moser (1936/. . ./1959); Müller-Blattau (1923/. . ./1963); **Neumann**, Frederick (1967/**1982**), (1978), [*Essays*] **(1982)**; Neumann, Friedrich (1978); Newman (1985); Newman (1946), (1959/. . ./1983), (1963/. . ./ 1983); O'Donnell (1979); Palisca [*Baroque*] (1968/1981), ["Rezitativ"] (1972-); Petrobelli (1968); Pfeiffer (1978); Ratner (1956), (1980); Reckow (1972-); Reese (1957/1970); Reimer ["Concerto"] (1972-), ["Kammermusik"] (1972-); **Ritzel (1967/ 1968)**; Rivera (1978); Rogers (1955); Rosenblum (1988); Ruhnke (1949-68); Sachs (1972-); Schmalzriedt ["Coda"] (1972-), ["Durchführen"] (1972-), ["Reprise"] (1972-); Schmitt (1974-75); Schmitz (1950); Schünemann (1928/1931); Seidel (1972-); Sheldon (1982); Sisman (1978); Sondheimer (1925); Subirá (1947/. . ./1958); Sydow-Saak (1972-); Taddie (1984); Troeger (1987); Tuksar (1978/1980); Walker (1987); Williams, P. ["Equal"] (1968), (1970), (1979); Wirth (1966); Wolff (1972-); **Zaminer (1985)**.

(JACOB) GOTTFRIED WEBER

[1779–1839]

After nearly a century of analytical thought dependent upon a fundamental bass (encompassing RAMEAU's *basse fondamentale* and the analytical endeavors of KIRNBERGER, SCHULZ, and KOLLMANN), the adoption of Roman numerals by VOGLER and wholehearted acceptance of that procedure by Gottfried Weber led the art of analysis in a new direction, one which found few opponents during the nineteenth century and which still influences many harmony texts. Unlike the earlier dependence upon a separate bass pitch written in staff notation, each of Weber's numerals indicates not only the structural root of the pitches under which it resides, but also interprets the chord within a tonal framework, as a step within the prevailing tonal center's scale. In Weber's formulation, the quality of the chord is acknowledged by the relative size of the numeral itself: capital numerals refer to major harmonies, while those in small capitals refer to minor harmonies. Diminished triads are notated using a superscript circle preceding a small-cap numeral, while the presence of a chordal seventh is indicated by a superscript seven (for minor seventh) or slashed seven

(for major seventh) following the numeral, regardless of the inversion of the actual chordal arrangement. Diminished sevenths are regarded as incomplete dominant ninths. Furthermore, a shift of tonal center is accommodated simply by indicating the key in which a group of Roman numerals is to be interpreted. Weber used this technique freely—perhaps too freely for twentieth-century tastes, which have generally inclined more towards the concept of applied, or "secondary," dominants.

Weber's formulations appear in his *Versuch einer geordneten Theorie der Tonsetzkunst*, which was published between 1817 and 1821, and in several derivative works that followed. Weber carefully avoided speculative considerations, allowing his system to respond directly to the music (as he perceived it) without the encumbrances of mathematics or acoustics. Though he held greater respect for the linear origin of suspensions and other embellishing tones than did RAMEAU, his equating of the role of 6/4-position chords with that of their 5/3-position permutations might rankle some modern practitioners of analysis, particularly those influenced by SCHENKER. Following KOCH's lead, Weber remarked on metrical structure, basing his conception upon hierarchical levels both within the context of a given measure (wherein the first, then the third, beats are to be understood as heavier than the second and fourth) and among measures (wherein the first, then the third, measures are to be understood as the heavier parts of a four-measure phrase). A prolific author of articles and reviews for several journals and for Ersch and Gruber's *Enzyklopädie*, he edited *Caecilia: Eine Zeitschrift für das musikalische Welt* for the Schott firm from 1824 until his death.

"Über das sogenannte Generalbass-Spielen bey Aufführung von Kirchen-Musiken, und über würdigere Anwendung der Orgel"

> *AmZ* 15/7 (1813):105-12.

"Erneuerter Versuch einer Begriffsbestimmung von Ton, Tonkunst, und Tonsetz-Kunst: Bruchstück aus einer ungedruckten Theorie der Tonsetzkunst"

> *AmZ* 17/50-51 (1815):829-36, 845-51.

Über chronometrische Tempobezeichnung, welche ohne Chronometer-Maschine überall und jederzeit sogleich verstanden und angewendet werden kann, nebst einer Vergleichungs- und Zurückführungstabelle der Mälzelschen metronomischen Grade auf einfache Pendellängen

> Mainz: B. Schott, 1817.

Versuch einer geordneten Theorie der Tonse[t]zkunst zum Selbstunterricht mit Anmerkungen für Gelehrtere

> Mainz: B. Schott, 1817, 1818, 1821. 3 vols.
>
>> Notice of Vol. 1 in *AmZ* 19/38-39 (1817):637-48, 661-74 (J. G. E. Maass). Review of Vol. 2 in *AmZ* 20/27 (1818):477-87 (J. G. E. Maass). Review of Vol. 3 in *AmZ* 23/36 (1821):609-15. Errors of Vol. 2 listed in *AmZ: Intelligenz-Blatt* [20]/11 (1818):42.
>
> Mainz: B. Schott's Söhne, 1824. 4 vols.
>
>> Notice in *AmZ: Intelligenz-Blatt* [26]/5 (1824):17-18.
>
> Mainz: B. Schott's Söhne, 1830-32. Revised edition. 4 vols.
>
>> Reviews in *AmZ* 34/33 (1832):537-44 (G. W. Fink) and 35/7 (1833):115 and in *Rm*(F) 6/12/15 (1832):116-19 (François-Joseph FÉTIS).

T ● Muth-Rasmussen, trans. *Populair Harmonielære.* Copenhagen: C. C. Lose & Olsen's og C. Schouby's Forlag, 1837.

> Review in (1824-39): 20 (1839):300-302 (J. D. Anton), below.

T ● Warner, James F., trans. (from the 3rd ed.). [*An Attempt at a Systematically Arranged*] *Theory of Musical Composition* [*Treated with a View to a Naturally Consecutive Arrangement of Topics*]. 2 vols. Boston: J. H. Wilkins & R. B. Carter, 1842-46; later editions, including one augmented by John Bishop, London: Robert Cocks, 1851.

Articles on music in *Allgemeine Enzyklopädie der Wissenschaften und Künste . . .*, edited by J. S. Ersch and J. P. Gruber. 167 vols. Leipzig: Joh. Friedr. Gleditsch, 1818-89.

> Weber contributed seventy-three articles under the letters A through C between 1818 and 1832. See Lemke (1968), below, for a complete listing.

Allgemeine Musiklehre zum Selbstunterricht für Lehrer und Lernende

> Darmstadt: Carl Wilhelm Leske, 1822.
> Mainz: B. Schott's Söhne, 1825.
>
>> With an Italian-German dictionary of musical terms:
>
> Mainz: B. Schott's Söhne, 1831.
>
>> Also incorporated within (1817-21):(1830-32), above. Review in *AmZ* 33/41 (1831):669-75 (G. W. Fink).

T ● Dutch translation. Leiden: 1829.

T ● Muth-Rasmussen, trans. *Almindelig Musiklære.* Copenhagen: Udgiverens Forlag, 1836.

T ● Warner, James F., trans. (from the 3rd edition). *General Music Teacher: Adapted to Self-Instruction, Both for Teachers and Learners . . .* Boston: J. H. Wilkins & R. B. Carter, 1842.

> Incorporated within the Warner translation of the *Versuch*, above, and also sold separately.

Caecilia: Eine Zeitschrift für das musikalische Welt

> 1824-39. 20 vols. Edited by Weber.

"Über Tonmalerei"

> Ms., [ca. 1825].

S ● Extract in (1824-39):Vol. 3 (1825):125-72, above.

Die Generalbaßlehre zum Selbstunterricht

> Derived from (1817-21):(1830-32), above.
>
> Mainz: B. Schott's Söhne, 1833.
>
>> Review in *AmZ* 36/9 (1834):138-39.

See Lemke (1968), below, for more exhaustive coverage of Weber's publications, particularly articles and reviews in periodicals.

LITERATURE:

Lemke, Arno. "Weber, Jacob Gottfried." In *MGG* (1949-68). Bibliog.

Fleury, Albert. "Die Musikzeitschrift *Caecilia* (1824-48)." 2 vols. Ph.D. dissertation, The University of Frankfurt, 1952 (1953).

Raeburn, Christopher. "Das Zeitmass in Mozarts Opern." *ÖM* 12/9 (1957):329-33.

Lemke, Arno. *Jacob Gottfried Weber, Leben und Werk: Ein Beitrag zur Musikgeschichte des mittelrheinischen Raumes.* BmrM, no. 9. Mainz: B. Schott's Söhne, 1968. Bibliog. [*Rilm* 68-3484.]

> Reviews in *Mf* 25/1 (1972):112-13 (Arnold Feil), *Muh* 20/2 (1969):88 (G. P.), *NZfM* 130/4 (1969):196 (G. A. Trumpff), and *NZfM* 132/10 (1971):569 (Rudolf Stephan).

Häfner, Roland. "Über Tonmalerei." In *Rheinische Philharmonie (1945-1970): Beiträge zum Musikgeschehen,* pp. 50-60. Koblenz: Rheinische Philharmonie (Mainz: B. Schott's Söhne), 1970. [*Rilm* 70-1481.]

Abraham, Lars Ulrich. "Die *Allgemeine Musiklehre* von Gottfried Weber im Lichte heutiger Musikdidaktik." In *VolkFs* (1974):102-6. [*Rilm* 74-3867.]

Schnaus, Peter. "Gottfried Weber über C. M. v. Webers Ouvertüre zum *Beherrscher der Geister:* Romantik und Pseudo-Romantik einer *AmZ*-Rezension." In *SieversFs* (1978):155-65. [*Rilm* 78-6449.]

Hoffman, Mark. "Weber, (Jacob) Gottfried." In *NGrove* (1980). Bibliog.

Höft, Brigitte. "Gottfried Weber (1779-1839): Ein Porträt." *MAmrM* 42 (1981):45-62.

Saslaw, Janna Karen. "The Theoretical Writings of Gottfried Weber." Ph.D. dissertation, Columbia University, forthcoming.

See also FÉTIS: (1833-44); Groth (1978); HAUPTMANN: Caplin (1984); KOCH: Baker (1976); MARX: Eicke (1966); MOMIGNY: Chailley (1982); RIEMANN: (1898); SCHOENBERG: Rexroth (1969/1971); LITERATURE SUPPLEMENT: Abraham (1966); Auhagen (1982/1983), (1987); Beach (1967), ● ● ● (1974); Becker (1836-39/1964); **Bent** ["Analysis"] **(1980/1987)**; Caplin (1978); Cazden (1948); Chew (1980); Conley (1977); Crocker (1966); **Dahlhaus (1984)**, (1985); DeFotis (1982-83); Dunsby and Whittall (1988); Eitner (1900-1904/1959-60); Federhofer (1944/1950); Fischer (1976); Fox Strangways (1923); Frisius (1969/1970); Frobenius ["Cantus"] (1972-), ["Vollstimmig"] (1972-); Grave (1985); Gut (1972-); Hahn (1960); Henneberg (1972/1974), (1983); Hoffman (1953); Imig (1969/1970); Jacobi (1957-60/1971); Jones (1934); **Kassler (1979)**; Kauko (1958); Levenson (1981), (1983-84); Lindley (1982); ● ● ● Marvin (1987); McQuere (1983); Mitchell, J. W. (1963); Morgan (1978); Moyer (1969); Müller-Blattau (1923/. . ./1963); Nelson (1984); Newman (1969/. . ./1983); Palisca ["Rezitativ"] (1972-); Pole (1879/. . ./1924); Ratner (1949), (1980); Reimer ["Concerto"] (1972-); **Ritzel (1967/1968)**; Rohwer (1949-68); Rothärmel (1963/1968); **Rummenhöller (1967)**; Seidel (1972-), (1975); Serauky (1929); Sheldon (1982); **Shirlaw (1917/. . ./1970)**; Smither (1960); Taddie (1984); Thompson (1980); Thomson (1960/1978); Tittel (1959), (1966); Todd (1983), (1988-89); Vertrees (1974); Vogel (1955/1954), (1976); **Wagner (1974)**; **Wason (1981/1985)**; Werts (1983); Wintle (1982); Wirth (1966); **Zaminer (1985)**.

CARL FRIEDRICH WEITZMANN

[1808 – 1880]

The "Music of the Future" which Liszt and Wagner were composing during the 1850s (and which Brahms and Joachim were to attack in 1860) was ardently defended by the HAUPTMANN pupil and Berlin Conservatory professor Carl Friedrich Weitzmann. Though enamored of Beethoven's music, he added more progressive elements to his theories and reexamined traditional notions concerning consonance and dissonance and the prohibition of parallel fifths. The unexploited resources of the augmented triad and diminished-seventh chord, particularly their enharmonic versatility and capacity for unusual resolutions, were explored in *Der übermäßige Dreiklang* (1853) and *Der verminderte Septimen-Akkord* (1854). His grid showing how every pitch of the octave belonged to exactly one of four augmented triad types and one of three diminished-seventh chord types reflects the practices of the progressives.

Weitzmann acknowledged that the procedures he was demonstrating could be overused and were appropriate more for secular music than for that intended for worship. His perspective reached a wide—though exclusively German-speaking—audience, in part through the fact that what was later published under the title *Harmoniesystem* (1860) was a prizewinning essay printed serially over nine issues of the *Neue Zeitschrift für Musik*.

Der übermäßige Dreiklang

> Berlin: T. Trautwein (J. Guttentag), 1853.

Geschichte des Septimen-Akkordes

> Berlin: T. Trautwein (J. Guttentag), 1854.

Der verminderte Septimen-Akkord

> Berlin: Hermann Peters, 1854.

"Geschichte der Harmonie und ihrer Lehre"

> *NZfM* 51/1-4 (1859):1-3, 9-12, 17-19, 25-27.

"[Harmoniesystem:] Erklärende Erläuterung und musikalisch-theoretische Begründung der durch die neuesten Kunstschöpfungen bewirkten Umgestaltung und Weiterbildung der Harmonik"

> *NZfM* 52/1-9 (1860):2-3, 9-12, 17-20, 29-31, 37-39, 45-46, 53-54, 65-66, 73-75.
> Leipzig: C. F. Kahnt, 1860.
> Liepzig: C. F. Kahnt, 1895.
>
> > Review in *Rmi* 6/4 (1897):756 (Luigi Torchi).

Die neue Harmonielehre im Streit mit der alten . . . mit einer musikalischen Beilage: Albumblätter zur Emancipation der Quinten, und Anthologie klassischer Quintenparallelen

> Leipzig: C. F. Kahnt, 1861.

LITERATURE:

Bowman, Edward Morris, ed. *Bowman's-Weitzmann's Manual of Musical Theory: A Concise, Comprehensive and Practical Text-Book on the Science of Music*. New York: W. A. Pond, 1877; 2nd edition, [1905]; German edition (as *Handbuch der Theorie der Musik*, edited by Felix Schmidt), Berlin: T. C. F. Enslin, 1888.

Catalog der hinterlassenen musikalischen Bibliothek von C. F. Weitzmann. Berlin: 1881.

Eitner, Robert. "Karl Friedrich Weitzmann." *AdBiog* 41 (1896):635-37.

Bekker, Paul "Zum Gedächtnis Karl Friedrich Weitzmanns." *AMuZ* 35/32-33 (1908):577-78.

Flindell, Fred. "Weitzmann, Carl Friedrich." In *MGG* (1949-68). Bibliog.

Gábry, György. "Neuere Liszt-Dokumente." *Stm* 10/3-4 (1968):339-52. Bibliog.

Brinkmann, Reinhold. "Weitzmann, Carl Friedrich." In *NGrove* (1980).

> Review in *MQ* 68/2 (1982):161-81 (Allen Forte).

See also FÉTIS: (1833-44); LITERATURE SUPPLEMENT: Cazden (1948); McCredie (1968); Rea (1978); **Rummenhöller (1967)**; ● ● ●Todd (1988-89); Vogel (1962); ● ● ●Wason (1988); Wirth (1966).

ANDREAS WERCKMEISTER

[1645 – 1706]

Deeply religious and grounded in mediaeval scholarship, Andreas Werckmeister combined mystical and metaphysical speculation with a devotion to God as creator of mathematical order in nature. Yet unlike less musically gifted authors such as KEPLER and FLUDD, Werckmeister, a church musician and expert organ examiner, applied himself to documenting many of the more practical aspects of music, including tuning, composition, and the realization of figured bass. His works were esteemed by eighteenth-century theorists and composers, including certainly J. S. Bach.

Werckmeister is frequently cited for his methods of attaining *ein wohl temperirtes Clavier*, as laid out in his *Musicalische Temperatur* and other treatises. What Werckmeister advocated was not an equalization of all half-steps, but instead various means whereby the inevitable flaw in untempered tuning (in that four ascending pure fifths exceed a pure compound major third) is divided among different intervals in such a way that all keys are tolerable, with greater imperfection residing in the triads utilized less frequently. By this means, a composer could, if he so chose, write in any key or move from one key to any other. J. S. Bach was, of course, among the first to take full advantage of these developments. Since each key retains a specific, though subtle, set of relationships among its pitches, Werckmeister's attribution of affective qualities to various keys (in his *Harmonologia musica* of 1702) depends upon more than the tonal center alone.

Continuing a long tradition among writers on music, Werckmeister displayed an acute interest in numbers and attempted to justify basic components of musical practice with them. Equating the ratios 1:1, 1:2, and 2:3 to the Father, Son, and Holy Spirit might seem a quaint manner of reinforcing the relative perfection of these intervals, but this conceit placed the musical system upon a foundation so steadfast that, Werckmeister supposed, tinkering by later generations of composers would be unthinkable. By similar logic, the major triad (with ratio 4:5:6:8) was seen as more perfect than the minor (with ratio 10:12:15:20). When the major triad's pitches are rearranged (resulting, for example, in a bass pitch E appearing below G and C), the relative size of the numbers needed to display its ratio, as compared with than of C below E and G, attests to its comparative imperfection.

Chorales retained an important position in the Lutheran liturgy, and so Werckmeister supplied the theoretical apparatus of the twelve-mode system to account for them. He acknowledged, however, that few church musicians actually used them correctly and that two modes stood out among these twelve in modern practice. Only in his posthumously published *Musicalische Paradoxal-Discourse* did he use the Aeolian, rather than the Dorian, as the prototype for the minor mode.

Werckmeister's most practical books were intended for those who desired to purchase or test an organ (the *Orgel-Probe*, first issued in 1681) and for performers of basso continuo (particularly *Die nothwendigsten Anmerkungen und Regeln . . .*, which appeared around 1698). Though the technical mechanics of chord construction and voice leading are treated less successfully than can be found in other contemporary treatises, Werckmeister's more general comments on performance display a sensitive artistry. For example, he suggested that the figures need not be followed explicitly when accompanying a dissonant suspension. Instead, the supplied figures represent the total fabric of the piece, and avoiding a dissonance which is being sounded by another performer (and omitting the pitch to which it will eventually resolve) might prove more effective than a mechanical rendering of all the pitches represented by the figures.

Thus in Werckmeister one observes a mixture of speculative and practical elements well suited to an era steeped in theology, confident in new compositional procedures, and respectful of a strong tradition of chorale-based church music.

Orgel-Probe; oder, Kurtze Beschreibung, wie und welcher Gestalt man die Orgel-Wercke von den Orgelmachern annehmen, probiren, untersuchen und den Kirchen liefern könne und solle, benebenst einem . . . Unterricht, wie . . . ein Clavier wohl zu temperiren und zu stimmen sey . . . [Rism B/VI/2, p. 886.]

> Frankfurt am Main and Leipzig: Theodor Philipp Calvisius, 1681.
>
> > As *Erweiterte und verbesserte Orgel-Probe . . .*:

Quedlinburg: Theodor Philipp Calvisius (Johann Heinrich Sievert), 1698. [LCPS: W-026a. SMLMS. IDC.]

Quedlinburg and Aschersleben: Gottlob Ernst Struntz (Waldenburg: Johann Theodor Heinsius), 1716. [LCPS: W-026b.]

> Review in MIZLER: (1736-54):Vol. 1/4 (1738):27-45.

Leipzig: Johann Michael Teubner, 1754. [LCPS: W-026c. IDC.]

Augsburg: Johann Jakob Lotter, 1783. [LCPS: W-026d.]

T ● Lustig, Jacob Wilhelm, trans. *Orgel-proef . . .* Amsterdam: A. Olofsen, [1755] [*Rism* B/VI/2, pp. 886-87. IDC.]; facsimile edition (edited by A. Boumann), Baarn: De Praestantpers, 1968.

> Reviews in *ISOI* 2 (1969):169 (Maarten A. Vente) and *OrganYb 1971* 2 (1972):103 (Peter Williams).

S ● Facsimile of the 1698 edition. Kassel: Bärenreiter, 1927; new edition (IGMDm, ser. 1, no. 30; edited by Dietz-Rüdiger Moser), 1970.

> Reviews in *ArsOr* 19/39 (1971):1609 (Alfred Reichling), *GK* /6 (1971):221 (Hans Schmidt), *ISOI* 8 (1972):602 (Maarten A. Vente), and *OrganYb 1972* 3 (1973):107-8 (Peter Williams).

T ● Sumner, W. L., trans. "Orgelprobe." *OIQ* 6/2-4 (1956):7-15; 25-36; 25-39.

T ● Cellier, Hippolyte, trans. "L'orgelprobe de Werckmeister." *L'orgue* 98, 101, 102 (1961-62):48-50, 19-20, 34-37.

S ● Facsimile of the 1698 edition. See (1697):(1970), below.

T ● Krapf, Gerhard, trans. *Werckmeister's Erweiterte und verbesserte Orgel-Probe in English*. Raleigh, N.C.: Sunbury Press (Bynum Printing Company), 1976.

> Reviews in *AMT* 27/2 (1977):33 (Susan Hegberg), *ChuM* /1 (1977):38-39 (Thomas Gieschen), *Clavier* 16/1 (1977):6-8 (Arthur Birkby), *Diapason* 69/1 [817] (1977):4, *MT* 118/1615 (1977):729 (Peter Williams), *Music* 11/5 (1977):14 (David L. Brattain), *Organ* 62/246 (1983):181-82 (Douglas R. Carrington), *OrganYb 1979* 10 [1979]:164-65 (Peter Williams), and *SacM* 104/1 (1977):25 (William F. Pohl).

Musicae mathematicae Hodegus curiosus; oder, Richtiger musicalischer Weg-Weiser . . . [Rism B/VI/2, p. 884.]

Frankfurt am Main and Leipzig: Theodor Philipp Calvisius (Merseburg: Christian Gottschick), 1686. [SMLMS.]

Frankfurt am Main and Leipzig: Theodor Philipp Calvisius (Merseburg: Christian Gottschick), 1687. [LCPS: W-022. IDC.]

> Perhaps a 1689 edition as well.

S ● Facsimile of the 1687 edition. Hildesheim: Georg Olms, 1972.

Musicalische Temperatur; oder, Deutlicher und warer mathematischer Unterricht, wie man durch Anweisung des Monochordi ein Clavier . . . wol temperirt stimmen könne, damit nach heutiger Manier alle Modi ficti in einer angenehm- und erträglichen Harmonia mögen genommen werden, mit vorhergehender Abhandlung von dem Vorzuge, Vollkommen- und weniger Vollkommenheit der musikalischen Zahlen . . . [*Rism* B/VI/2, pp. 884-85.]

> Frankfurt am Main and Leipzig: [ca. 1686-87]. [Lost.]
>
> Frankfurt am Main and Leipzig: Theodor Philipp Calvisius, 1691.

T ● Hehr, Eliszabeth W., trans. Oberlin, Ohio: Oberlin College, 1974.

S ● Facsimile of the 1691 edition. Amsterdam: Frits Knuf.

S ● Rasch, Rudolf, ed. Facsimile of the 1691 edition. TTL, no. 1. Utrecht: Diapason Press, 1983. [*Rilm* 83-2640.]

> Reviews in *EM* 13/1 (1985):91-93 (Ephraim Segerman), *GSJ* 38 (1985):160-63 (Mark Lindley), *Mi* 33/3 (1984):73, *ML* 69/1 (1988):68-70 (Albert Cohen), and *Rdm* 71/1-2 (1985):184-87 (Herbert Anton Kellner).

Der edlen Music-Kunst Würde, Gebrauch und Miß-brauch, so wohl aus der heiligen Schrift als auch aus etlich alten und neubewährten reinen Kirchen-Lehrern und dann aus den Music-Gründen [*Rism* B/VI/2, p. 883.]

> Frankfurt am Main and Leipzig: Theodor Philipp Calvisius, 1691.
>
>> Review in MIZLER: (1736-54):Vol. 1/1 (1736):45-57.

Hypomnemata musica; oder, Musicalisches Memorial, welches bestehet in kurtzer Erinnerung dessen, so bisshero unter guten Freunden discurs-weise, insonderheit von der Composition und Temperatur möchte vorgangen seyn . . . [*Rism* B/VI/2, p. 884.]

> Quedlinburg: Theodor Philipp Calvisius, 1697. [LCPS: W-021. IDC.]
>
>> Review in MIZLER: (1736-54):Vol. 1/3 (1737):52-59.

S ● Facsimile edition. *Hypomnemaa musica und andere Schriften*. Hildesheim: Georg Olms, 1970.

> Review in *OrganYb 1984* 15 (1985):146-47.

"Nucleus musicus"

> Ms., [ca. 1697]. [Lost.]

Die nothwendigsten Anmerkungen und Regeln, wie der Bassus continuus oder General-Baß wol könne tractiret werden . . . [*Rism* B/VI/2, p. 885.]

> Aschersleben: Gottlob Ernst Struntz, [ca. 1698]. [IDC.]
>
> Aschersleben: Gottlob Ernst Struntz, 1715. [LCPS: W-024b.]
>
>> Review in MIZLER: (1736-54):Vol. 1/2 (1737):49-68. At least one other printing (undated) exists. [LCPS: W-024a.] There may have been another edition, now lost, before that of 1698 (perhaps 1692). An eight-page segment was published separately in 1698.

S ● Thom, Eitelfriedrich, ed. Facsimile of the [ca. 1698] edition. Michaelstein: Kultur- und Forschungsstatte Michaelstein, [1985].

Cribrum musicum; oder, Musicalisches Sieb darinnen einige Mängel eines halb gelehrten Componisten vorgestellet und das Böse von dem Guten gleichsam ausgesiebet und abgesondert worden . . . [*Rism* B/VI/2, p. 883.]

> Quedlinburg and Leipzig: Theodor Philipp Calvisius, 1700. [LCPS: W-019. SMLMS. IDC.]
>
>> Review in MIZLER: (1736-54):Vol. 1/1 (1736):19-25.

S ● Facsimile edition. See (1697):(1970), above.

Harmonologia musica; oder, Kurtze Anleitung zur musicalischen Composition, wie man vermittels der Regeln und Anmerckungen bey den General-Baß einen Contrapunctum simplicem mit sonderbahrem Vortheil durch drey Sätze oder Griffe componiren und ex tempore spielen . . . [*Rism* B/VI/2, p. 883.]

> Frankfurt am Main and Leipzig: Theodor Philipp Calvisius, 1702. [LCPS: W-020. SMLMS. IDC.]

S ● Facsimile edition. See (1697):(1970), above.

J. N. J. Organum Gruningense redivivum; oder, Kurtze Beschreibung des in der Grüningischen Schlos-Kirchen berühmten Orgel-Wercks, wie dasselbe anfangs erbauet und beschaffen gewesen . . . [*Rism* B/VI/2, pp. 885-86.]

> Quedlinburg and Aschersleben: Gottlob Ernst Struntz, [1705]. [LCPS: W-025. SMLMS.]

S ● Smets, Paul, ed. New edition (incomplete). Mainz: Rheingold-Verlag, 1932.

S • Facsimile edition. Bo, no. 22. Amsterdam: Frits Knuf, forthcoming.

Musicalische Paradoxal-Discourse; oder, Ungemeine Vorstellungen, wie die Musica einem hohen und göttlichen Uhrsprung habe, und wie hingegen dieselbe so sehr gemissbrauchet wird . . . [*Rism* B/VI/w, p. 884.]

Quedlinburg: Theodor Philipp Calvisius, 1707. [LCPS: W-023. IDC.]

Published posthumously.

S • Facsimile edition. See (1697):(1970), above.

T • See Godwin (1986).

LITERATURE:

Serauky, Walter. "Andreas Werckmeister als Musiktheoretiker." In *SchneiderFs* (1935):118-25.

Dammann, Rolf. "Werckmeister, Andreas." In *MGG* (1949-68). Bibliog.

Hermann, Ursula. "Andreas Werckmeister (1645-1706)." Ph.D. dissertation, The University of Halle, 1950 (1951).

• • • Dammann, Rolf. "Zur Musiklehre des Andreas Werckmeister." *AfMw* 11/3 (1954):206-37.

Pfrogner, Hermann. "Der Clavis in Andreas Werckmeisters *Nothwendigsten Anmerkungen und Regeln, wie die Bassus continuus oder Generalbaß wol könne tractiret werden* (Aschersleben 1692)." In Osthoff (1954):149-51.

Lucks, F. Wilhelm. "Zu Ehren Andreas Werckmeisters." *Musica* 10/12 (1956):875-76.

Moser, Dietz-Rüdiger. "Andreas Werckmeister: Ein grosser Musiktheoretiker der Barockzeit." *UH* 17/5 (1969):89-91. [*Rilm* 69-903.]

Dekker, Gerard. "Pleidooi voor Werckmeister." *Mens* 25/1 (1970):25-27.

Barnes, John. "Bach's Keyboard Temperament: Internal Evidence from the *Well-Tempered Clavier*." *EM* 7/2 (1979):236-49. [*Rilm* 79-2496.]

• • • Buelow, George J. "Werckmeister, Andreas." In *NGrove* (1980). Bibliog.

Kee, Piet. "Die Geheimnisse von Bachs Passacaglia." Translated by Dirk Harberts. *MK* 52/4-5 (1982):165-75, 235-44; as "The Secrets of Bach's Passacaglia," in *Diap* 74/6-7 [883-84] (1983):10-12, 4-6. [*Rilm* 82-2338.]

Williams, Peter. "J. S. Bach—Orgelsachverständiger unter dem Einfluß Andreas Werckmeisters?" *BachJb 1982* 68 (1983):131-42. [*Rilm* 82-4594.]

Williams, Peter. "Was Johann Sebastian Bach an Organ Expert or an Acquisitive Reader of Andreas Werckmeister?" *JAMIS* 11 (1985):38-54.

Pfeiffer, Rüdiger. "VI. Instrumentenbau Symposium und Kolloquium zu Andreas Werckmeister." *MG* 36/3 (1986):164.

See also ADLUNG: (1758); FÉTIS: (1833-44); HEINICHEN: (1728):Buelow (1961/. . ./1986); KEPLER: Dickreiter (1971/1973); LIPPIUS: Rivera (1974/1980); MATTHESON: (1717); (1721); PRAETORIUS: Gurlitt (1915/1968); RIEMANN: (1898); SORGE: [1748]; WALTHER: (1708); (1732); LITERATURE SUPPLEMENT: Allen ["Philoso-phies"] (1939); **Arnold (1931/. . ./1965)**; Asselin (1983/1985); Badings (1978); **Barbour** (1932), (1947), (1948), (1949-68), **(1951/ . . ./1972)**; Beck (1973); Becker (1836-39/1964); Beiche ["Dux"] (1972-), ["Inversio"] (1972-); **Benary (1956/1961)**; Blackwood (1985); Blankenburg ["Harmonie"] (1959); Blood (1979); Boomgaarden (1985/1987); Braun (1970); Brown and McKinnon (1980); **Buelow** (1972), ["Affections"] (1980), ["Rhetoric"] **(1980)**; Bukofzer (1947); Burke (1963); Burney (1776-89/. . ./1957); Carr (1974); Chafe (1981), (1982); Chomiński (1962/1981); Cohen (1984); **Dahlhaus** ["Untersuchungen"] (1966/. . ./1988), ["Harmony"] **(1980)**; **Dahlhaus et al. (1987)**; Dammann (1958/1967); Dekker (1979); Donington (1963/. . ./1974); Duparcq (1977); Dupont (1933/. . ./1986); Eggebrecht (1955); Eitner (1900-1904/1959-60); Fellerer ["Zur Kontrapunktlehre"] (1972), ["Zur Kontrapunktlehre"] (1973); Flindell (1983-84); Forkel (1792/1962); Gerber (1812-14/1966); Gernhardt (1977); Godwin (1987); Green (1969); Gremion (1974); Hannas (1934); Hartmann (1980); Hawkins (1776/. . ./1969); Heimann (1970/1973); Hiller (1768-69); Horsley [*Fugue: History*] (1966); Hosler (1978/1981); Jackisch (1966); Jackson (1988); Jorgensen (1971); Jorgenson (1957); Katz (1926); Kauko (1958); Kelletat ["Tonordnung"] (1960), (1966); Kretzschmar (1911-12); Lang (1941); **Lester** (1978), **(1989)**; **Lindley** (1977), ["Temperaments"] **(1980)**, (1982), **(1984)**, (1985), (1988); Meer (1980); Mitchell, W. J. (1963); Moser (1967); Moser (1936/. . ./1959); Müller-Blattau (1923/. . ./1963); Nelson (1984); Neumann, Frederick (1978); North (1987); Oberdoerffer (1967); Ottenberg (1973/1978); Rasch (1981), (1983); Reese (1954/1959), (1957/1970); Révész (1946/. . ./1954); Rivera (1978), (1984); Rogers (1955); Rohwer (1949-68); Rothgeb (1968); Ruhnke (1949-68); Schäfke (1934/1964); **Shirlaw (1917/ . . ./1970)**; Snyder (1980); Sydow-Saak (1972-); Taddie (1984); Thieme (1982-83); Troeger (1987); Ulrich (1931/1932); Vogel (1955/1954), (1976); Walker (1987); Wienpahl (1953); Williams, P. ["Harpsichord"] (1968), (1970); Wirth (1966); Zenck (1942); Zimmermann (1976).

RUDOLF WESTPHAL

[1826–1892]

As a lifelong student of ancient Greek writings on metrics, Rudolf Westphal developed a unique perspective on the rhythmic/metric component of eighteenth- and nineteenth-century music. In a career which generated numerous publications relating to Hellenic practices, Westphal documented his interpretation of ancient treatises most comprehensively in *Metrik der griechischen Dramatiker und Lyriker* (which he wrote with August Roßbach and saw into print between 1854 and 1865). He addressed more recent music in works such as *Elemente des musikalischen Rhythmus mit besonderer Rücksicht auf unsere Opem-Musik* (1872) and, especially, *Allgemeine Theorie der musikalischen Rhythmik seit J. S. Bach* (1880), wherein he applied his Aristoxenian bias to music by composers who likely had little if any direct contact with ancient notions concerning time.

Westphal showed how poetic feet and larger segments such as cola, periods, and strophes could correlate to the components of fugues by Bach and sonata movements by Beethoven. Of particular interest is his observation that Bach's fugues tended to be constructed in a three-part form: strophe, antistrophe, epode. Though not all of his analyses convince, and though some of his occasional performance suggestions do not warrant adoption, the novelty and power of Westphal's view had a pronounced influence on the development of rhythmic theory, including recent echoes in the work of Leonard Meyer.

Metrik der griechischen Dramatiker und Lyriker nebst den begleitenden musischen Künsten

1) *Griechische Rhythmik*, by Roßbach.

1a) *Die Fragmente und die Lehrsätze der griechischen Rhythmiker*, by Westphal.

2.1) *Harmonik und Melopöie der Griechen*, by Westphal.

2.2) *Allgemeine griechische Metrik*, by Westphal.

3) *Griechische Metrik nach den einzelnen Strophengattungen und metrischen Stilarten*, by Roßbach and Westphal.

Leipzig: B. G. Teubner, 1854, 1861, 1863, 1865, 1856. 3 vols. (in 5 parts). With August Roßbach.

> The third edition, as *Theorie der musischen Künste der Hellenen*:

Leipzig: B. G. Teubner, 1885-89. With August Roßbach and Hugo Gleditsch.

S ● Facsimile of the 1885-89 edition. Hildesheim: Georg Olms, 1966.

"Die Tradition der alten Metriker"

Philologus 20 (1863):76-108, 238-74.

Plutarch: Über die Musik

> Edited by Westphal. A volume of a larger series (left incomplete by Westphal), *Geschichte der alten und mittelalterlichen Musik*.

Breslau: F. E. C. Leuckart, 1865-66.

System der antiken Rhythmik

Breslau: F. E. C. Leuckart, 1865.

Scriptores metrici graeci

1) *Hephaestionis: De metris enchiridion et De poemate libellus cum scholiis et Trichae Epitomis, adjecta Procli Chrestomathia grammatica* (BsgrT)

Edited by Westphal.

Leipzig: B. G. Teubner, 1866.

Elemente des musikalischen Rhythmus mit besonderer Rücksicht auf unsere Opern-Musik

Jena: Hermann Costenoble, 1872. Part 1.

Sem' fug dlia fortepiano I. S. Bakha v ritmicheskoi redaktsii R. Vestfalia [Seven Fugues for Piano by J. S. Bach, Rhythmic Edition of R. Westphal]

Moscow: 1878.

Allgemeine Theorie der musikalischen Rhythmik seit J. S. Bach: Auf Grundlage der Antiken und unter Bezugnahme auf ihren historischen Anschluß an die Mittelalterliche, mit besonderer Berücksichtigung von Bach's Fugen und Beethoven's Sonaten

Leipzig: Breitkopf & Härtel, 1880.

S ● Facsimile edition. Wiesbaden: Martin Sändig, 1968.

"Iskusstvo i ritm: Greki i Vagner" [Art and Rhythm: The Greeks and Wagner]

Rusves /5 (1880):241-67.

Aristoxenus von Tarent: Melik und Rhythmik des classischen Hellenenthums

Translated and edited by Westphal.

Leipzig: A. Abel, 1883. Vol. 1.
Leipzig: J. A. Barth, 1893. Vol. 2. Edited by Franz Saran.

Posthumously published.

S ● Facsimile edition. Hildesheim: Georg Olms, 1965.

"Beziehungen zwischen moderner Musik und antiker Kunst"

> *MuWb* 14/44-47, 49-52 (1883):537-39, 553-55, 565-66, 577-79, 605-6, 621-22, 633-34, 649-51. With B. Sokolowsky.

Die Musik des griechischen Alterthumes: Nach den alten Quellen neu bearbeiteten

> Leipzig: Veit & Co., 1883.

"Mehrstimmigkeit oder Einstimmigkeit der griechischen Musik"

> *BpW* 4/1-4 (1884):1-6, 33-36, 65-68, 97-103.

"Platos Beziehungen zur Musik"

> *BpW* 4/17-18, 20-22 (1884):513-18, 545-49, 609-11, 641-45, 673-77.

Desiat' fug dlia fortepiano I. S. Bakha v ritmicheskoi redaktsii R. Vestvalia [Ten Fugues for Piano by J. S. Bach, Rhythmic Edition of R. Westphal]

> Moscow: 1890.

>> With Yuly Nikolaevich Mel'gunov, whose "O ritmicheskom ispolnenii fug Bakha" [On the Rhythmic Performance of Bach Fugues] appears as a preface.

"Die Aristoxenische Rhythmuslehre"

> *VMw* 7 (1891):74-107.

Allgemeine Metrik der indogermanischen und semitischen Völker auf Grundlage der vergleichenden sprachwissenschaft (CpaB, nos. 100-104.)

Berlin: S. Calvary & Co., 1892. Edited by Hugo Gleditsch.

> Posthumously published.

LITERATURE:

Sokolowsky, B. von. *Die Musik des griechischen Alterthums und des Orients nach R. Westphals und F. A. Gevaerts neuesten Forschungen*. [Vol. 1 of August Wilhelm Ambros's *Geschichte der Musik*, 3rd edition.] Leipzig: F. E. C. Leuckart, 1887.

Combarieu, Jules. *Théorie du rythme dans la composition moderne d'après la doctrine antique*. Paris: Alphonse Picard et fils, 1897.

Roßbach, August. "Rudolf Westphal." In *AdBiog* 42 (1897):205-16.

Flindell, Fred. "Westphal, Rudolf Georg Hermann." In *MGG* (1949-68). Bibliog.

Winnington-Ingram, R. P. "Westphal, Rudolf (Georg Hermann)." In *NGrove* (1980). Bibliog.

See also GEVAERT: (1875-81); RIEMANN: [*System*] (1903); LITERATURE SUPPLEMENT: Alette (1951); Beiche ["Inversio"] (1972-); **Dürr and Gerstenberg** (1949-68), (**1980**); Henneberg (1972/ 1974); Morgan (1978); Pole (1879/. . ./1924); Reichert (1978); Seidel (1972-), (1975); ● ● ● Smither (1960); Yeston (1974/1976); **Zaminer (1985)**.

BOLESLAV LEOPOL'DOVICH YAVORSKY

[1877 — 1942]

As Russian music was beginning to incorporate a more diverse harmonic vocabulary (in the works of Skryabin, for example), Boleslav Leopol'dovich Yavorsky was developing a complex theory to account for all aspects of music from various periods and styles, including folk music. A rigorous though dogmatic thinker, Yavorsky established logical relationships among such disparate elements as pitch, rhythm, form, and dynamics. The tritone, with its motion- and melody-generating resolution on either a third or sixth, serves as the foundation for the system. Various combinations of pitches are organized into specific modes, or collections of functions—"gravitations"—derived from tritone resolutions and forming an identifiable set of stable and unstable relationships. Each mode might appear at as many as twelve pitch levels, yielding up to twelve "modal tonalities" for each mode. Some modal possibilities depart decisively from the standards of traditional practice, as in his formulations involving stable "tonic" pitch collections such as A C E G or C E G B, as well as his brief discussion of microtonal modes. These unusual collections are the result of—and not the source for—various tritone patterns. A Yavorskian tonic may be dissonant (as in C, E-flat, E, G or B, D, F) yet regarded as functionally stable.

Complete in its basic aspects as early as 1908 (when Yavorsky's *Stroenie muzykal'noi rechi* was published), the system is a blending of abstraction and pertinent analytical observation. Through numerous teaching and editorial positions during the remainder of his career, Yavorsky strongly influenced the direction of modern Soviet theory (including, for example, ASAFIEV's notion of intonation), though his own published works after 1908 are limited to a few attempts at clarification and pedagogical development. It was Protopopov, rather than Yavorsky himself, who formulated the system in its fullest guise (in *Elementy stroeniia muzykal'noi rechi*, published in 1930-31), though not to the satisfaction of some critics (such as Ryzhkin) or of Protopopov's English translator (McQuere), who characterizes the work as "cumbersome and opaque."

Yavorsky's theory of "modal rhythm" (that is, the unfolding of a mode in time) derives from the "auditory gravitation" inherent in the tritone. Various combinations of tritones form carefully defined systems which display a distinctive and hierarchical organization of pitches. The resolutional tendency of the tritone also generates a bipartite rhythmic model, each segment of which may contain multiple pulses. Modal rhythm is realized primarily at the most basic level of a work's creation. As Yavorsky explained in "The Construction of the Melodic Process" (1929): "*Construction* . . . is the basic principle of creative work, which consists of the mastery and harmonious agreement of the forces of gravity for realizing a creative act. *Modal rhythm* is

the unfolding in time of the construction of a musical work. *Composition* . . . is the articulation of the construction of a work of art with a view to disclosing the creative goal. *Formation* . . . is the embodiment . . . of the composition of this construction by means of material standardized for a given art with a view to *expression beyond* the creative goal." [McQuere (1983).]

Though Yavorsky's theory has had little impact outside of Soviet circles, several practitioners of analysis have used its tenets in the study of music by Skryabin, Bartók, and Khachaturian. Those whose scholarly or performance activity embraces Eastern European music might wish to investigate this contemporaneous theory, as it was designed to account for the progressive features which standard analytical methods might prove incapable of addressing.

Stroenie muzykal'noi rechi: Materialy i zametki [The Structure of Musical Speech: Materials and Remarks]

> Moscow: 1908. In three parts.

>> A supplement was issued as "Tekst i muzyka" [Text and Music] in *Muzïka* 163, 166, 169 (1914):8-14, 88-93, 151-56.

Uprazhneniia v golosovedenii [Exercises in Voice Leading]

> Moscow: 1913.

Uprazhneniia v obrazovanii [*skhem*] *ladovogo ritma* [Exercises in the Formation of Schemes of Modal Rhythm]

> Moscow: 1915. Part 1.

>> Review in *Muzïka* 222 (1915):325-26 (Sergei Grigor'evich Kondra).

> Mss. Parts 2 through 5.
> Moscow: Gosudarstvennoe muzykal'noe izdatel'stvo, Muzykal'noe sektor, 1928. 2nd edition of Part 1.

"Osnovnye elementy muzyki" [The Basic Elements of Music]

> *Iskusstvo* [Art] /1 (1923):185-94.

"Vospriiatie ladovykh melodicheskikh postroenii" [The Perception of Modal Melodic Structures]

> With Sofia Nikolaevna Beliaeva-Ekzempliarskaia.

> In *Sbornik eksperimental'no-psikhologicheskikh issledovanii* [A Collection of Experimental Psychological Research], edited by V. M. Ekzempliarsky, Vol. 1, pp. 3-35. Tgakn, no. 1. Leningrad: 1926.

An expanded edition appeared in German as "Die Wirkung des Tonkomplexes bei melodischer Gestaltung" in *AgP* 57/3-4 (1926):489-522.

Struktura melodii [The Structure of Melody]

> With Sofia Nikolaevna Belaieva-Ekzempliarskaia.

Moscow: Gosudarstvennaia akademiia khudozhestvennikh nauk, 1929.

> Contains Yavorsky's "Konstruktsiia melodicheskogo protsessa" [The Construction of the Melodic Process], pp. 7-36, and Beliaeva-Ekzempliarskaia's "Vospriiatie melodicheskogo dvizheniia" [The Perception of Melodic Motion], pp. 37-93.

Elementy stroeniia muzykal'noi rechi [Elements of the Structure of Musical Speech]

> By Sergei Vladimirovich Protopopov, edited by Yavorsky.

Moscow: Gosudarstvennoe muzykal'noe izdatel'stvo, Muzykal'noe sektor, 1930-31. 2 vols.

> T ● McQuere, Gordon Daniel. "*The Elements of the Structure of Musical Speech* by S. V. Protopopov: A Translation and Commentary." Ph.D. dissertation, The University of Iowa, 1978. Bibliog. [*Rilm* 78-1853. *DA* 39/12A, pp. 7047-48. UMI 79-12886.]

Siuity Bakha dlia klaviera [Bach's Suites for the Clavier]

> Published posthumously.

Moscow: 1947. Edited by Sergei Protopopov.

"Betkhoven: Variatsii do minor" [Beethoven's Variations in C Minor]

> Ms.

> S ● In *Iz istorii sovetskoi Betkhoveniany* [From the History of Soviet Beethoven Study], edited by N. L. Fishman, pp. 91-95. Moscow: Sovetskii kompozitor, 1972.

See also TANEEV: [ca. 1938]; (1940).

SELECTED WORKS EDITION:

Shostakovich, Dmitry, ed. *B. Iavorskii: Vospominaniia, stat'i, pis'ma.* [B. Yavorsky: Recollections, Articles, Letters.] Vol. 1. Moscow: Muzyka, 1964; 2nd edition (as *B. Iavorskii: Stat'i, vospominaniia, perepiska* [B. Yavorsky: Articles, Recollections, Correspondence], edited by Isaak Solomonovich Rabinovich), Moscow: Sovetskii kompozitor, 1972. *B. Iavorskii: Izbrannyi trudy* [B. Yavorsky: Selected Works], edited by Isaak Solomonovich Rabinovich, I. A. Sats, and B. I. Rabinovich. Vol. 2:1. Moscow: Sovetskii kompozitor, 1987.

The two editions of the first volume differ in significant respects. Review in *Smuz* (1965):36-38.

LITERATURE:

Briusova, Nadezhda Yakovlevna. *Nauka o muzyke, eia istoricheskie puti i sovremennoe sostoianie.* [The Science of Music, Its Historical Path and Contemporary State.] Moscow: 1910.

Kulakovsky, Lev Vladimirovich. "Nekotorye polozheniia teorii Iavorskogo." [Several Positions of the Theory of Yavorsky.] *Muzyka*(K) /10-12 (1924).

Kulakovsky, Lev Vladimirovich. "Ritmika rechi." [The Rhythmics of Speech.] *Cher* /6-7 (1925):117-225.

Kulakovsky, Lev Vladimirovich. "Razvitie ladovykh elementov." [The Development of Modal Elements.] *Muzyka*(K) /3 (1927).

Sabaneev, Leonid Leonidovich. *Modern Russian Composers.* Translated by Judah A. Joffe. New York: International, 1927; reprint edition (DCPMRS), New York: Da Capo Press, 1975.

Kulakovsky, Lev Vladimirovich. "Kratkie ocherki po teorii ladovogo ritma." [Short Essays on the Theory of Modal Rhythm.] *Muzm* /1-6, 8-9, 12 (1928).

Tsukkerman, Viktor Abramovich. "Teoriia ladovogo ritma i ee primenenie." [The Theory of Modal Rhythm and Its Applications.] *Pmuz* /7-8 (1929):48-52.

"Konferentsiia po teorii ladovogo ritma." [The Conference on the Theory of Modal Rhythm.] *Pmuz* /2 (1930):6-9.

Garbuzov, Nikolai Alexandrovich. "K voprosu ob edinichnoi i dvoinoi sistemakh B. Iavorskogo." [On the Question of the Single and Double Systems of B. Yavorsky.] *Muzo* /1 (1930):18-22.

Garbuzov, Nikolai Alexandrovich. "Zavisit li garmonicheskoe dvizhenie v muzyke ot neustoichivosti tritona." [Does Harmonic Motion in Music Depend on the Instability of the Tritone] *Muzo* /3 (1930):16-21.

Kulakovsky, Lev Vladimirovich. "O teorii ladovogo ritma i ee zadaniiakh." [About the Theory of Modal Rhythm and Its Tasks.] *Muzo* /1 (1930):11-18.

Lunacharsky, Anatoly Vasil'evich. "Neskol'ko zamechanii o teorii ladovogo ritma." [Some Observations on the Theory of Modal Rhythm.] *Pmuz* /2 (1930):10-13.

Kulakovsky, Lev Vladimirovich. "K probleme izucheniia ladovogo stroeniia muzykal'nykh proizvedenii." [On the Problem of the Study of the Modal Construction of Musical Works.] *Smuz* /2 (1933):76-85.

Lunacharsky, Anatoly Vasil'evich. "O rabote B. Iavorskogo *Siuity Bakha dlia klavira.*" [About the Work of B. Yavorsky, *Bach Suites for the Clavier.*] Supplement to the Report No. 6 of the Consultation Commission of NKP. July 9, 1933.

Ryzhkin, Iosif. "Teoriia ladovogo ritma (B. Iavorskii)." [The Theory of Modal Rhythm (B. Yavorsky).] In Ryzhkin and Mazel (1934-39):Vol. 2, pp. 105-205.

Tiulin, Yury Nikolaevich. *Uchenie o garmonii.* [A Study of Harmony.] Leningrad: 1937; 1939; 1966.

Kulakovsky, Lev Vladimirovich, and Tsukkerman, Viktor Abramovich. "Iavorskii—Teoretik." [Yavorsky—A Theorist.] *Smuz* /12 (1959):68-76.

Averbukh, Liya Abramovna, ed. "Daty zhizni i deiatel'nosti." [Dates of Life and Activity.] In Selected Works (1964-):Vol. 1 (1972), above.

Konen, Valentina Dzhozefovna. "Iavorskii i nasha sovremennost'." [Yavorsky and Our Contemporary.] In Selected Works (1964-):Vol. 1 (1972), above.

Kulakovsky, Lev Vladimirovich. "Iavorskii chitaet rukopis." [Yavorsky Reads a Manuscript.] In Selected Works (1964-):Vol. 1 (1964), above.

Lunacharsky, Anatoly Vasil'evich. "Vystuplenie na konferentsii teorii ladovogo ritma 5 Fevralia 1930 g. v Moskve." [Introduction to the Conference of the Theory of Modal Rhythm 5 February 1930 in Moscow.] In Selected Works (1964-):Vol. 1 (1964):151-72, above.

Lunacharsky, Anatoly Vasil'evich. "O teorii ladovogo ritma." [On the Theory of Modal Rhythm.] In Selected Works (1964-):Vol. 1 (1972):36-58, above.

Protopopov, Sergei Vladimirovich. "Boleslav Leopol'dovich Iavorskii (Biograficheskii ocherk)." [Boleslav Leopol'dovich Yavorsky (A Biographical Essay).] In Selected Works (1964-):Vol. 1 (1964):19-42, above.

Tsukkerman, Viktor Abramovich. "Iavorskii—teoretik." [Yavorsky the Theorist.] In Selected Works (1964-): Vol. 1 (1964):173-206, above.

Cukkerman, Viktor. "Bolesław Jaworski jako teoretyk muzyki." [Boleslav Yavorsky as Music Theorist.] In *Polsko-rusyjskie miscellanea muzyczne* [Polish-Russian Music Miscellanea], edited by Zofia Lissa, pp. 353-80. Cracow: Polskie Wyd. Muz., 1967. [*Rilm* 68-2654.]

Dernova, Varvara. *Garmoniia Skriabina.* [The Harmony of Skryabin.] Leningrad: 1968; English translation in Roy James Guenther, "Varvara Dernova's *Garmoniia Skriabina*: A Translation and Critical Commentary," Ph.D. dissertation, Catholic University of America, 1979. [*Rilm* 79-1648. *DA* 40/03A, p. 1142. UMI 79-18573.]

Kholopov, Yury Nikolaevich. "Simmetrichnye lady v teoreticheskikh sistemakh Iavorskogo i Messiana." [Symmetrical Modes in the Theoretical Systems of Yavorsky and Messiaen.] *Muzyka i sovremennost'* [Music and the Contemporary], vol. 7, pp. 247-93. Moscow: Muzyka, 1971.

Tiulin, Yury Nikolaevich. *Natural'nye i al'teratsionnye lady.* [The Natural and Altered Modes.] Leningrad: Muzyka, 1971. [*Rilm* 71-4419.]

Lobanov, Mihail. "Ob izuchenii melodiki russkoi narodnoi pesni v otechestvennom muzykoznanii." [On the Study of the Melody of Russian Folk Song in Russian Musicology.] *Rusf* 14 (1974):263-76. [*Rilm* 74-3424.]

Nabok, I. [The Social Nature of Musical Work in the Theoretical Writing of Boleslav Yavorsky.] In Farbshtein (1977).

Wiłkomirski, Kazimierz. "Bolesław Jaworski twórca teorii myślenia muzycznego." [Boleslav Yavorsky: Originator of the Theory of Musical Thinking.] *Rmuz* 25 (1977):3-6. [*Rilm* 77-5723.]

Baevsky, Vadim Solomonovich. "Iavorskii i nekotorye tendentsii kul'tury ego vremeni." [Yavorsky and Certain Cultural Tendencies of His Time.] *Smuz* /5 (1978):83-89. [*Rilm* 78-4207.]

Daragan, D. " 'Odin iz samykh aktivnykh stroitelei'." ["One of the Very Active Builders."] *Smuz* /5 (1978):81-83.

Kon, Juliia. "Neskol'ko teoreticheskikh parallelei." [Several Theoretical Parallels.] *Smuz* /5 (1978):90-92. [*Rilm* 78-4242.]

Chivinskaia, Nataliia. [Problems of Higher Musical Education Addressed in Works by Boleslav Yavorsky.] In *Psikhologo-pedagogicheskie problemy vysshego muzykal'nogo obrazovaniia* [Psychological and Pedagogical Problems of Higher Musical Education], edited by Vladimir Minin. GMPI, no. 43. Moscow: Gosudarstvennyi muzykal'no-pedagogicheskii institut imeni Gnesinykh, 1979.

Finkel'berg, Natal'ia. [B. L. Yavorsky on Performance Practice.] In *Muzykal'noe ispolnitel'stvo* [Musical Performance Practice], Vol. 10, edited by Vladimir Grigor'ev and Vladimir Natanson. Moscow: Muzyka, 1979.

● ● ● McQuere, Gordon D. "Concepts of Analysis in the Theories of B. L. Yavorsky." *MR* 41/4 (1980):278-88. [*Rilm* 80-5624.]

Belza, Igor. "Yavorsky, Boleslav Leopol'dovich." In *NGrove* (1980).

Gliadeshkina, Z. "Nekotorye osobennosti ladofunktsional'noi organizatsii fortepiannoi muzyki venskikh klassikov (na primere analize odnotonal'nykh periodov v svete teorii B. Iavorskogo)." [Some Features of Modal Functional Organization in Viennese Classic Piano Music (as Illustrated by an Analysis of Non-Modulating Periods According to the Modal Theory of Boleslav Yavorsky).] In *Problemy vysotnoi i ritmicheskoi organizatsii muzyki* [The Problems of Pitch and Rhythmic Organization of Music], edited by Igor' Istomin. Moscow: Gosudarstvennyi muzykal'no-pedagogicheskii institut imeni Gnesinykh, 1980.

Ship, Sergei. "Printsip simmetrii v muzyke i ego proiavlenie v narodnom napeve." [The Principle of Symmetry in Music and Its Manifestation in Folk Melodies.] M.A. thesis, Ryl'skii Institut iskusstva, folk'lora, i etnografiia, 1980. [*Rilm* 80-3664.]

Dernova, Varvara. *Poslednie preliudii Skriabina: Issledovanie.* [The Last Preludes of Scriabin: Research.] Moscow: Muzyka, 1988.

See also RIEMANN: Mazel (1939); LITERATURE SUPPLEMENT: Aranovsky (1980/1983); Barenboim (1970), (1974); Burlas (1974); Carpenter (1988); Dubovsky et al. (1934-36); Jiránek (1967); Kremlev ["Estetika"] (1967), ["O metodologii"] (1967); Mazel (1937), (1940); ● ● ● McQuere (1983); Ryzhkin (1967); Scher (1975); Sochor (1967); Vitányi (1968-69); Yarustovsky (1974).

JEAN YSSANDON

[c. 1555 – 1582]

While much more progressive ideas were being disseminated in Latin and Italian, Jean Yssandon provided in his *Traité de la musique pratique* (1582) a survey of basic materials (derived in part from the treatises of Gaffurio and LISTENIUS) for his countrymen who read only French. Four modal pairs were sufficient for Yssandon, and though he dealt with counterpoint, his music examples inadequately represent polyphonic writing. The work is indicative of the underdeveloped state of theory in France at the time of ZARLINO's achievements in Italy.

Traité de la musique pratique . . . [*Rism* B/VI/2, p. 903.]

Paris: Adrian Le Roy & Robert Ballard, 1582.

S ● Facsimile edition. Geneva: Minkoff Reprint, 1972.

LITERATURE:

Lesure, François. "Yssandon, Jean." Translated by Dorothea Schmidt-Preuß. In *MGG* (1949-68).

● ● ● Seay, Albert. "French Renaissance Theory and Jean Yssandon." *JMT* 15/1-2 (1971):254-73. [*Rilm* 72-287.]

Dobbins, Frank. "Yssandon, Jean." In *NGrove* (1980).

See also FÉTIS: (1833-44); OUVRARD: (1658):Boulay (1984); WALTHER: (1732); LITERATURE SUPPLEMENT: **Apfel (1981)**; Becker (1836-39/1964); Eitner (1900-1904/1959-60); Forkel (1792/1962); Gerber (1812-14/1966); Gut (1972-); Launay (1972); Lindley (1982); **Schneider (1972)**; **Seidel and Cooper (1986)**; Taddie (1984).

LODOVICO ZACCONI

[1555 – 1627]

Lodovico Zacconi viewed sixteenth-century developments in compositional style not as a response to aesthetic theories rummaged from the ancients, but as the reaction of composers to the increasing sophistication of vocal technique. In his *Prattica di musica*, Part 1 (1592), Zacconi contributed to this flowering of vocal artistry with a detailed discussion of improvised vocal ornamentation and performance practice. Improvisation also figures prominently in the second volume (1622), wherein the art of counterpoint is treated systematically. Over a century before FUX's *Gradus ad Parnassum*, a categorization of elementary counterpoint into graduated species is presented, as it is also by DIRUTA and BANCHIERI. Improvisation of a vocal counterpoint either by one individual or by a choir of singers serves as an important pedagogical link between written exercises and actual composition. Zacconi's discussion of counterpoint attains a high level of sophistication through the great variety of canonic strategies demonstrated. In this way he created a quest for technical proficiency not directly related to the demands of the contemporary compositional practice. Not economizing in space or printer's ink, Zacconi included an abundance of examples throughout the two books and allowed himself to comment on numerous secondary issues, such as the classification of instruments and the technique of borrowing from other composers (parody) as a pedagogical tool. Thus the works are a rich mine of information and opinion from a musician who, though he may be viewed as peripheral, nevertheless straightforwardly documented the musical life and techniques of his time.

Prattica di musica utile et necessaria si al compositore per comporre i canti suoi regolatamente, si anco al cantore per assicurarsi in tutte le cose cantabili . . . [*Rism* B/VI/2, pp. 903-4.]

and

Prattica di musica seconda parte . . . [*Rism* B/VI/2, p. 904.]

Venice: Girolamo Polo, 1592. Part 1.
Venice: Bartolomeo Carampello, 1596. Part 1.
[LCPS: Z-009. HoM: 1616. SMLMS. IDC.]

Venice: Alessandro Vincenti, 1622. Part 2.

T ● Chrysander, Friedrich. "Lodovico Zacconi als Lehrer des Kunstgesanges." *VMw* 7 (1891):337-96; 9 (1893):249-310; 10 (1894):531-67.

S ● Facsimile of the 1592 and 1622 editions. 2 vols. BmB, ser. 2, no. 1-2. Bologna: Forni, 1967.

T ● See MacClintock (1979).

S ● Facsimile of the 1596 and 1622 editions. 2 vols. Hildesheim: Georg Olms, 1982.

"Canoni musicali proprii e di diversi autori"

Ms. [Pesaro: Biblioteca Oliveriana.]

S ● Vatielli, Francesco, ed. Pesaro: Stab. tip. Annesio Nobili, 1905; facsimile edition (BmB, ser. 3, no. 15), Bologna: Forni, 1968.

The 1968 edition includes biographical studies by Vatielli as well.

"Paradigma musicale"

Ms. [Pisaro: Biblioteca Oliveriana.]

"Le regole di canto fermo"

[Lost.]

LITERATURE:

Palisca, Claude V. "Zacconi, Lodovico." Translated by Ingeborg Robert. In *MGG* (1949-68).

Singer, Gerhard. "Lodovico Zacconi's Treatment of the 'Suitability and Classification of All Musical Instruments' in the *Prattica di musica* of 1592." Ph.D. dissertation, The University of Southern California, 1968. Bibliog. [*Rilm* 69-3562. *DA* 29/09A, pp. 3174-75. UMI 69-05069.]

Gruber, Gernot. "Lodovico Zacconi als Musiktheoretiker: Studien zur praxisbezogenen Theorie seiner Zeit." Habilitationsschrift, The University of Vienna, 1972. [*Rilm* 75-569.]

Singer, Gerhard. "Zacconi, Lodovico." In *NGrove* (1980). Bibliog.

Haar, James. "A Sixteenth-Century Attempt at Music Criticism." *JAMS* 36/2 (1983):191-209. Bibliog.

See also BONONCINI: Holler (1955/1963); CACCINI: Anfuso and Gianuario (1970); FÉTIS: (1833-44); FUX: Federhofer (1957-58); HERBST: (1643); LIPPIUS: Rivera (1974/1980); MOMIGNY: (1791-1818):(1818); MONTEVERDI: Schrade (1950/ . . ./1981); MORLEY: Stevenson (1952); PENNA: Lederer (1970); RIEMANN: (1898); SCHENKER: Morgan (1978); VIADANA: Haack (1964/1974); WALTHER: (1732); LITERATURE SUPPLEMENT: Abraham (1968/ 1969); Ambros (1878/. . ./1909); **Apfel (1981)**; Arnold (1957); **Barbour (1932)**, **(1951/. . ./1972)**; Becker (1836-39/1964); Beiche ["Dux"] (1972-), ["Inversio"] (1972-); Beyschlag (1907/1953); Blankenburg ["Kanonimprovisationen"] (1959); Brown (1973),

390

(1976); Burney (1776-89/. . ./1957); Cahn ["Retardatio"] (1972-); Chomiński (1962/1981); Collins (1963), (1964); Crocker (1966); Dahlhaus ["Untersuchungen"] (1966/. . ./1988); Dolmetsch (1915/. . ./1969); Donington (1963/. . ./1974); Dürr (1964); Eitner (1900-1904/1959-60); Federhofer (1967); Fellerer (1927/ . . ./1972), ["Zur Kontrapunktlehre"] (1973), ["Ausdruck"] (1982), ["Wesen"] (1982), (1983); Ferand (1937/1938), ["Improvised"] (1956), [Improvisation] (1956/1961); Forkel (1792/1962); Geering (1949-68); Gerber (1790-92/1977), (1812-14/1966); Ghislanzoni (1949-51); Goldschmidt (1890/1892), (1901-4/1967), (1907); Haar (1983), (1986); Harding (1938); Harrán (1973), (1986); Hawkins (1776/. . ./1969); Hein (1954); Horsley (1951), (1963), [Fugue: History] (1966), (1972); Isgro (1968); Jackson (1988); Jander (1980); Jeppesen (1922/. . ./1970), (1930/. . ./1974); Kassler (1979); Kauko (1958); Kinkeldey (1910/1968); Kroyer (1901/. . ./1970); Kuhn (1902); La Fage (1864/1964); Lange (1899-1900); Lawrence (1978); Levitan (1938); Lindley (1982); Lowinsky (1946/1967); Mace (1964/1966); Mahlert and Sunter (1972-); Maniates (1979); Mann (1955/. . ./1987); Meier (1963), (1974/1988); Mendel (1978); Müller-Blattau (1923/. . ./1963); Neumann, Frederick (1978), (1987); Pacchioni (1983); Palisca (1949-68), (1953), (1959), ["Artusi-Monteverdi"] (1968/1985), ["Theory"] (1980); Powers (1974), (1981); Preußner (1939); Reese (1954/1959), ● ● ● (1957/1970); Robbins (1938); Rogers (1955); Sachs (1972-); Schwartz (1908); Seidel and Cooper (1986); Sirch (1981); Taddie (1984); Uberti (1981); Walker (1987); Wichmann (1966).

GIOSEFFO ZARLINO

[1517 – 1590]

At a time when radical experiments in chromatic and enharmonic music and in monody were claiming attention in Italy, Gioseffo Zarlino stood as the chief defender of the polyphonic practice which had evolved over the preceding centuries, culminating, he felt, in the music of his teacher, Adrian Willaert. Another Willaert pupil, Nicola VICENTINO, published L'antica musica ridotta alla moderna prattica, a provocative guide to chromatic and enharmonic composition, in 1555. Zarlino had pursued similar ideas in the 1540s, but by the time of his monumental Le istitutioni harmoniche (1558) he was clearly opposed to such contortions of the contrapuntal art. Though the work's depth and insight reflect decades of thought, the motivation of opposing VICENTINO was present. Later Zarlino found himself battling one of his own pupils, Vincenzo GALILEI, whose study of Greek sources (under MEI's guidance) and experiments with monody led him to detect a variety of faults and errors in his former teacher's work. Zarlino responded to GALILEI's Dialogo della musica antica et della moderna (1581) with Sopplimenti musicali (1589), which, despite its more careful assessment of Greek sources, inadequately countered the powerful forces which were then stirring among more progressive musicians.

Le istitutioni harmoniche develops a strong speculative complement to the study of counterpoint and the modes. Zarlino proposed that the number 6 (numero senario) should serve as the basis for pitch relationships. Though some of his reasons for this decision seem fanciful today (e.g., six planets had been discovered; $1 + 2 + 3 = 1 \times 2 \times 3$), the emergence of a numerical justification for treating thirds as consonances was decisive. Joining the 2:1, 3:2, and 4:3 superparticular ratios of Pythagorean theory were now 5:4 and 6:5. The major sixth (5:3) and minor sixth (8:5) were regarded as the union of a perfect fourth (4:3) and major (5:4) or minor (6:5) third. [In Dimostrationi harmoniche (1571) Zarlino invoked another sonorous number, the ottonario, to justify the 8:5 ratio, but avoided the logical (if empirically unsound) step of classifying the embarrassing 7:5 ratio as consonant.] For choral singing Zarlino advocated the resulting diatonic syntonon tuning, though Giovanni Battista Benedetti soon demonstrated that it would produce unstable pitch during performance and GALILEI bewailed its divergence from Greek prescription and contemporary practice.

Zarlino's conservative treatment of counterpoint both countered VICENTINO and established a standard which other authors, including ARTUSI, TIGRINI, and SWEELINCK, copied. In particular, his insistence that a dissonance must be approached and left by step and must fall within a narrow range of rhythmic possibilities served to ignite the indignation of progressive commentators (GALILEI foremost among them) who noted a freer practice in improvised works and sought to bring new resources to the art of musical expression through daring juxtapositions and uncommon resolutions of pitches.

The most frequent positioning of intervals above the bass was either two thirds or a third surmounted by a fourth (the 5/3 and 6/3 positions of the later figured-bass practice). Zarlino noticed that two arrangements of thirds were common: "Whereas in the first group the major third is often placed beneath the minor, in the second the opposite is true, with a result I can only describe as sad or languid" (Marco

391

and Palisca translation). The consideration of modes bears a strong association with that of GLAREAN, though Zarlino did not acknowledge *Dodecachordon* (1547) as a source. In *Dimostrationi harmoniche* (1571) and later editions of *Le istitutioni harmoniche* a new ordering of the twelve modes, beginning on C, is advanced. As in his discussion of dissonance, Zarlino's restrictive prescriptions regarding the use of the modes, as in the alternation of authentic and plagal modes in adjacent voices of a polyphonic work, imperfectly accord with the music he wished to address. Yet, despite its weaknesses by modern standards, Zarlino's system was readily accepted as the codification of what MONTEVERDI would, a half century later, designate as the *prima prattica* beside which the progressive style was emerging.

Le istitutioni harmoniche . . . [*Rism* B/VI/2, pp. 907-8.]

> Venice: 1558. [LCPS: Z-006a. HoM: 1619. SMLMS.]
> Venice: Francesco de i Franceschi Senese, 1562. [LCPS: Z-006b. HoM: 1620. SMLMS.]
>
> > Revised edition:
>
> Venice: Francesco de i Franceschi Senese, 1573. [LCPS: Z-006c. SMLMS.]

S ● See GALILEI: [ca. 1570-72].

S ● See ARTUSI: (1586).

S ● See Collected Works: (1588-89), below.

S ● See TIGRINI: (1588).

S ● See SWEELINCK: (Mss.).

S ● See Collected Works: (1602 [1622]), below.

T ● Le Fort, Jehan. "Quatre livres ou parties des *Institutions harmoniques*." Ms., [early seventeenth century]. [Paris: Bibliothèque nationale.]

T ● [Hardy, Claude?] A French compendium. Ms., [early seventeenth century]. [Paris: Bibliothèque nationale.]

✳ T ● Trost, Johann Caspar, trans. German translation. [Ms., mid seventeenth century.] [Lost.]

T ● See **Strunk (1950)**:228-61.

T ● ● ● ● Marco, Guy. "Zarlino on Counterpoint: An Indexed Annotated Translation of the *Istitutioni harmoniche*, Book III, with a Glossary and Commentary." Ph.D. dissertation, The University of Chicago, 1956; revised edition (as *The Art of Counterpoint: Part Three of "Le istitutioni har-*

moniche", 1558, with Claude V. Palisca; MTTS, no. 2), New Haven, Ct.: Yale University Press, 1968; reprint edition, New York: W. W. Norton, 1976; reprint edition, New York: Da Capo Press, 1983. Bibliog. [*Rilm* 69/3571.]

> Reviews in *AR* 14/2 (1973):72 (Sabina Teller Ratner), *Choice* 7/3 (1970-71):396, *JAMS* 23/1 (1970):150-54 (Albert Seay), *MEJ* 56/9 (1969-70):91-94 (L. Dean Nuernberger), *Mf* 24/3 (1971):355-56 (Carl Dahlhaus), *MJSMA* 3/5 (1968-69):45, *ML* 50/4 (1969):503-4 (Ian Spink), *MT* 110/1519 (1969):941-42 (Jerome Roche), *Notes* 27/1 (1970-71):41-42 (Peter Bergquist), *Rdm* 56/2 (1970):240-42 (Denise Launay), *SMz* 109/4 (1969):243 (uh.), and *Stm* 13/1-4 (1971):383-84 (K. Csomasz Tóth).

S ● Facsimile of the 1558 edition. MMMLF, ser. 2, no. 1. New York: Broude Brothers, 1965.

> Reviews in *Consort* 26 (1970):459 (Lillian M. Ruff), *Mf* 21/2 (1968):258-61 (Helmut Haack), *ML* 47/1 (1966):67 (H. K. Andrews), *MT* 107/1486 (1966):1062-63 (Denis Arnold), *Notes* 23/3 (1966-67):515-19 (Imogene Horsley), and *Stfm* 49 (1967):222 (Ingmar Bengtsson).

S ● Facsimile of the 1573 edition. Ridgewood, N.J.: Gregg Press, 1966.

> Review in *Mf* 21/2 (1968):258-61 (Helmut Haack).

T ● ● ● ● Cohen, Vered. "Zarlino on Modes: An Annotated, Indexed Translation, with Introduction and Commentary, of Part IV of *Le istitutioni harmoniche*." Ph.D. dissertation, The City University of New York, 1977; published edition (edited and with an Introduction by Claude V. Palisca; MTTS), New Haven, Ct.: Yale University Press, 1983; reprint edition (DCPMRS), New York: Da Capo Press. [*Rilm* 77/5691. *DA* 38/08A, p. 4437.]

> Reviews in *Choice* 21/7 (1983-84):990, *JMT* 29/2 (1985):336-41 (Benito V. Rivera), and *Notes* 41/4 (1984-85):713-15 (Ellen S. Beebe).

T ● See MacClintock (1979).

T ● See Rowen (1979).

T ● See Godwin (1986).

T ● Fendt, Michael. "Das erste Buch der *Istitutione harmoniche* von Gioseffo Zarlino." Ph.D. dissertation, Technical University of Berlin, forthcoming.

✳ T ● Montgomery, Montie Charlene. "A Critical Translation of Book I of the *Istitutione harmoniche* by Gioseffo Zarlino." Ph.D. dissertation, The University of Kentucky, forthcoming.

Dimostrationi harmoniche . . . [*Rism* B/VI/2, p. 907.]

  Venice: Francesco de i Franceschi Senese, 1571.
  [LCPS: Z-005. HoM: 1617. SMLMS. IDC.]
  Venice: Francesco de i Franceschi Senese, 1573.

  S • See Collected Works: (1588-89), below.

  S • See Collected Works: (1602 [1622]), below.

  S • Facsimile of the 1571 edition. MMMLF, ser. 2,
  no. 2. New York: Broude Brothers, 1965.

    Reviews in *Mf* 21/2 (1968):258-61 (Helmut
    Haack), *ML* 47/1 (1966):67 (H. K. Andrews), *MT*
    107/1486 (1966):1062-63 (Denis Arnold), and
    Notes 23/3 (1966-67):519 (Imogene Horsley).

  S • Facsimile of the 1571 edition. Ridgewood, N.J.:
  Gregg Press, 1966.

Sopplimenti musicali . . .

  S • See Collected Works: (1588-89), below.

  S • Facsimile edition. MMMLF, ser. 2, no. 15. New
  York: Broude Brothers, 1966.

  S • Facsimile edition. Ridgewood, N.J.: Gregg Press,
  1966.

    Reviews in *Mf* 21/2 (1968):258-61 (Helmut
    Haack) and *MT* 107/1486 (1966):1062-63 (Denis
    Arnold).

  T • See Rowen (1979):131-33.

  T • Clendinning, Jane Piper. "Zarlino and the Helicon of Ptolemy: A Translation with Commentary
  of Book 3, Chapter 3 of Gioseffo Zarlino's *Sopplimenti musicali*." *Theoria* 2 (1987):39-58.

  T • See **Katz and Dahlhaus (1987-)**:Vol. 2.

COLLECTED WORKS EDITIONS:

De tutte l'opere del R. M. Gioseffo Zarlino . . . [*Rism* B/VI/2,
  pp. 906-7.] Venice: Francesco de' Franceschi
  Senese, 1588-89 [LCPS: Z-004. HoM: 1618, 1621.
  IDC.]; facsimile edition, Hildesheim: Georg Olms,
  1968.

Istitutioni et dimostrationi di musica. [*Rism* B/VI/2, p. 907.]
  Venice: Gio. Antonio & Giacomo de Franceschi,
  1602 [1622].

    In some copies of this edition, "1622" replaces
    the originally printed "1602."

LITERATURE:

Benedetti, Giovanni Battista. *Diversarum speculationum
  mathematicarum et physicarum liber.* Turin: apud

haeredem Nicolai Bevilaque, 1585; reprint edition
(edited by Josef Reiss) in *ZfMw* 7 (1924-25):13-20.

  Contains two letters to Cipriano de Rore (ca.
  1562-64), pp. 277-83. See Palisca (1961).

Abbate, Carlo. *Regulae contrapuncti excerptae ex operibus Zer-
  lini et aljorum ad breviorem tyronum instructionem accommodate.* St. Oslowan: Caspar Haugenhoffer,
  1629; facsimile edition, Leipzig: Zentralantiquariat
  der Deutschen Demokratischen Republik, 1977.

Wiese, Christian Ludwig Gustav, Freiherr von. *Ptolemäus
  und Zarlino, oder wahrer Gesichtskreis der haltbaren
  Universalitäten der Elementar-Tonlehre in den
  sowohl ältern als neuern Zeiten.* Dresden: P. C.
  Hilscher, [1795]. [*Rism* B/VI/2, p. 892.]

Brenet, Michel. "Deux traductions françaises inédites des
  Institutions harmoniques de Zarlino." *Annm* 1
  (1911):125-44.

Högler, Fritz. "Bemerkungen zu Zarlinos Theorie." *ZfMw*
  9/9-10 (1926-27):518-27.

Zenck, Hermann. "Zarlinos *Istitutioni harmoniche* als Quelle
  zur Musikanschauung der italienischen Renaissance." *ZfMw* 12/9-10 (1929-30):540-78. Bibliog.

    Review in *Rmi* 38/2 (1931):299-303 (G. Pannain).

Chiereghin, Salvino. "Zarlino." *Rmi* 37/1-2 (1930):21-37,
  204-18.

    See also *Rmi* 37/3 (1930):401-2.

Zezza, Elvira. "Giuseppe Zarlino." Thesis, The University of
  Pavia, 1948-49.

Palisca, Claude V. "Zarlino, Gioseffo." Translated by Margarete Hoffmann-Erbrecht. In *MGG* (1949-68).
  Bibliog.

Dahlhaus, Carl. "War Zarlino Dualist?" *Mf* 10/2 (1957):286-
  90.

    See also *Mf* 11/1 (1958):89-92 (Jens Rohwer: "In
    eigener Sache: Zu meinen Artikel 'Harmonie-
    lehre' in *MGG* V (Sp. 1614-1665)").

Wienpahl, Robert W. "Zarlino, the Senario, and Tonality."
  JAMS 12/1 (1959):27-41.

Marco, Guy A. "Zarlino's Rules of Counterpoint in the
  Light of Modern Pedagogy." *MR* 22/1 (1961):1-12.
  Bibliog.

Monterosso, Raffaello. "L'estetica di Gioseffo Zarlino."
  Chigiana 24 [new series: no. 4] (1967):13-28. [*Rilm*
  73-280.]

Crocker, Richard L. "Perché Zarlino diede una nuova
  numerazione ai modi?" *Ridm* 3/1 (1968):48-58.
  [*Rilm* 72/3021.]

Haar, James. "Zarlino's Definition of Fugue and Imitation."
  JAMS 24/2 (1971):226-54. Bibliog. [*Rilm* 71/2116.]

Hermelink, Siegfried. "Über Zarlinos Kadenzbegriff." In
  RongaFs (1973):253-73. Bibliog. [*Rilm* 76/15417.]

Reimer, Erich. "Musicus und Cantor: Zur Sozialgeschichte eines musikalischen Lehrstücks." *AfMw* 35/1 (1978):1-32. [*Rilm* 78-2055.]

● ● ● Palisca, Claude V. "Zarlino, Gioseffo." In *NGrove* (1980). Bibliog.

Allard, Joseph C. "Mechanism, Music, and Painting in 17th Century France." *JAAC* 40/3 (1982):269-79. [*Rilm* 82-3826.]

Airoldi, Roberto. "La teoria del temperamento nell'età di Gioseffo Zarlino." Thesis, The University of Pavia (Cremona), 1983-84.

Lewis, Mary S. "Zarlino's Theories of Text Underlay as Illustrated in His Motet Book of 1549." *Notes* 42/2 (1985-86):239-67.

Fico, Lorenzo. "Il concetto di consonanza e dissonanza nelle *Istitutioni harmoniche* di Gioseffo Zarlino." Thesis, The University of Bologna, 1986-87.

Levy, Jim, and Mori, Akane. "The Diatonic Basis of Fugue in Zarlino." *ITO* 9/2-3 (1986-87):33-46.

Blackburn, Bonnie J. "On Compositional Process in the Fifteenth Century." *JAMS* 40/2 (1987):210-84. Bibliog.

> Abstract in *MA* 7/3 (1988):361-62 (Jonathan Wainwright).

See also ARTUSI: (1586); (1590); (1604); BONINI: [ca. 1649-50]; BONONCINI: Holler (1955/1963); BONTEMPI: (1695); CAUS: (1615); CALVISIUS: Rivera (1989); CERONE: (1613); DIRUTA: Soehnlein (1975); FÉTIS (1833-44); (1840); FUX: Sovik (1978); GALILEI: (1581); ["Critica"] [ca. 1589-91]; [*Discorso . . . Zarlino*] (1589); Fano (1934); Walker (1973-74); Rempp (1979); Harrán (1987); GLAREAN: Miller (1961); d'INDY: (1903-50); KEPLER: Dickreiter (1971/1973); LIPPIUS: Rivera (1974/1980); Howard (1985); MERSENNE: (1617-48); Gruber (1970); MOMIGNY: (1791-1818): (1818); MONTEVERDI: Schrade (1950/. . ./1981); Gianuario (1969); Anfuso and Gianuario [1971]; Fabbri (1985); MORLEY: Stevenson (1952); Nutting (1975); OUSELEY: (1882); PENNA: Lederer (1970); PONTIO: (1588); RAMEAU: Chailley (1965); RIEMANN: ["Zarlino"] (1880); (1898); SALINAS: (1577); SOLER: (1765); SWEELINCK: (Mss.); Walker (1986); TIGRINI: (1588); VIADANA: Haack (1964/1974); WALTHER: (1732); WEITZMANN: (1859); ZACCONI: Singer (1968); LITERATURE SUPPLEMENT: Abbado (1964); Abraham (1968/1969); Alekperova (1982); Alette (1951); Allen ["Philosophies"] (1939); Ambros (1878/. . ./1909); **Apfel (1981)**; Armstrong (1978); Arnold (1957); Asselin (1983/1985); Atcherson (1972), (1973); Auhagen (1982/1983); Badura-Skoda et al. (1980); Barbieri (1983); **Barbour** (1932), (1947), **(1951/. . ./1972)**, (1952); Becker (1836-39/1964); Beebe (1976); Beer (1969); Beiche

["Dux"] (1972-), ["Inversio"] (1972-); **Benary (1956/1961)**; **Bent** ["Analysis"] **(1980/1987):(1987)**; Bent, M. (1984); **Berger** ● ● ● **(1975/1980)**, (1980), (1987); Beyer (1958); Bircher (1970); Blankenburg ["Harmonie"] (1959), ["Kanonimprovisationen"] (1959); Blumröder (1972-); Boetticher (1954); Bowen (1984); Brown (1976); Brown and McKinnon (1980); Bryant (1981); **Buelow** (1972), ["Rhetoric"] **(1980)**; **Bullivant (1980)**; Burke (1963); Burney (1776-89/. . ./1957); Bush (1939), (1946); Butler (1977); Cahn ["Transitus"] (1972-); Cavallini (1949); Cazden (1948), (1980); Chailley (1967); Chevaillier (1925/1931-32); Chomiński (1962/1981); Cohen (1966/1978), (1981); Cohen (1984); Čolič (1976); Collins (1963), (1964); **Coover (1980)**; Cowart ["Inventing"] (1989); Crocker (1962), (1966); Dadelsen (1972); **Dahlhaus** ["Konsonanz"] (1949-68), ["Tonsystem"] (1949-68), ["Dreiklang"] (1955), ["Termini"] (1955), ["Untersuchungen"] (1966/. . ./1988), ["Relationes"] (1975), ["Zur Tonartenlehre"] (1976), ["Harmony"] **(1980)**, **(1984)**; **Dahlhaus et al. (1987)**; **Dahlhaus and Sachs (1980)**; Dammann (1958/1967); David and Mendel (1945/1966); Devore (1987); de Zeeuw (1983); Dostrovsky (1969); Drake (1970); Dürr (1980); **Dürr and Gerstenberg** (1949-68), **(1980)**; Dunsby and Whittall (1988); Dupont (1933/. . ./1986); Dyson (1967); Eggebrecht (1955); Eitner (1900-1904/1959-60); Falck (1965); Federhofer (1944/1950), (1969); Fellerer (1927/. . ./1972), ["Zur Kontrapunktlehre"] (1972), ["Zur Kontrapunktlehre"] (1973), ["Ausdruck"] (1982), ["Wesen"] (1982), (1983), (1984); Ferand (1937/1938), ["Improvised"] (1956), [*Improvisation*] (1956/1961); Flindell (1983-84); Fokker (1955); Forchert (1986); Forkel (1792/1962); Frobenius ["Cantus"] (1972-), ["Dauer"] (1972-), ["Isotonos"] (1972-), ["Vollstimmig"] (1972-); Fubini (1971/1983), (1987); Gerber (1790-92/1977), (1812-14/1966); Gerboth et al. (1964); Ghislanzoni (1949-51); Gianuario (1979); Gissel (1986); Goldschmidt (1890/1892), (1901-4/1967); Gouk (1980); Green (1969); Grout (1960/. . ./1980); Gruber (1969); Gut (1976); Haar (1977), (1983), (1986); Haase (1969); Handschin (1948); Hannas (1934); Hanning (1969/1980); Harrán (1973), (1986); Hartmann (1923); Hawkins (1776/. . ./1969); Haydon (1933/1970); Heckmann (1953); Hein (1954); Henderson (1969); Hoffman (1970); Hoffman (1953); Horsley (1951), (1963), ["Fugue and Mode"] (1966/1978), [*Fugue: History*] (1966), (1972); Houle (1987); Hucke (1969); Hüschen (1949-68), (1986); **Hunt (1978)**; Hutchinson and Knopoff (1979-81); Imig (1969/1970); Isgro (1968), ● ● ● (1979); Jackson (1988); Jacobi (1957-60/1971); Jeppesen (1922/. . ./1970), (1930/. . ./1974), ([1951]/1952); Jones (1934); Jorgenson (1957), (1963); **Kassler (1979)**, (1984); Katz (1985); Kauko (1958); Kayser

(1950); Keislar (1987); Kelletat ["Tonordnung"] (1960), (1966); Kinkeldey (1910/1968); Kirkendale (1979), (1984); Koenigsberger (1979); Komma (1972); Kramer (1978); Krantz (1989); Kroyer (1901/. . ./1970); Kunze (1979-83); La Fage (1864/1964); Lang (1941); Lange (1899-1900); Launay (1972); Lawrence (1978); Le Coat (1978); Levarie (1986); **Lester** (1974), ● ● ● (1977), (1978), (1979-81), **(1989)**; Leuchtmann (1957/1959); Levitan (1938); Lewin (1977); Lewis (1975/1978); Lindley ["Just"] (1980), ["Temperaments"] (1980), (1982), (1984); Lippman (1986); Loach (1957); Lockwood (1966/1978); Lowinsky (1946/1967), (1948), (1961/1989); Luoma (1976), (1977); Luper (1938); Mahlert and Sunter (1972-); ● ● ●**Maniates (1979)**; **Mann (1955/. . ./1987)**, (1987); Martin (1932-33); McKinnon (1978); Meer (1980); Meier (1963), (1966), (1969), (1974/1988); Mendel (1978); Mitchell, J. W. (1963); Mitchell, W. J. (1963); Möller (1971); Moyer (1969); Müller (1976); Müller-Blattau (1923/. . ./1963); Nelson (1984); Neumann (1987); Niemöller (1964/1969); Norton (1984); Oberdoerffer (1967); Ortigue (1853/. . ./1971); Pacchioni (1983); **Palisca** (1949-68), (1953), (1959), (1961), ["Artusi-Monteverdi"] (1968/1985), [*Baroque*] (1968/1981), ["Rezitativ"] (1972-), ["Camerata"] (1972), ["*Ut oratoria musica*"] (1972), ["Theory"] **(1980)**, (1981),

(1985), [*Florentine*] (1989); Palisca and Spender (1980); Pikler (1966); Pöhlmann (1969); Pole (1879/. . ./1924); **Powers** (1974), ["Language"] (1980), ["Mode"] ● ● ●**(1980)**, (1981); Rahn (1977); Rasch (1983); Ratner (1980); Reckow (1972-); Reese (1954/1959), (1957/1970); Reichenbach (1948); Reilly (1984-95); Reimer ["Kammermusik"] (1972-); Révész (1946/. . ./1954); Rivera (1978); Robbins (1938); Roberts (1967); Rogers (1955); Rohwer (1949-68); Ruhnke (1949-68), (1973), (1974); Sachs (1972-), (1984); Schäfke (1934/1964); Schenkman (1976); Schmalzriedt ["Reprise"] (1972-), ["Subiectum"] (1972-); **Schneider (1972)**; Schneider (1917/. . ./1971); Schulenberg (1984), (1985-86); Seay (1971); Seidel (1972-), (1976); **Seidel and Cooper (1986)**; **Shirlaw (1917/. . ./1970)**, (1931); Smith (1974); Snyder (1980); Stevenson (1976); Subirá (1947/. . ./1958); Szweykowski (1985); Taddie (1984); Tenney (1988); Thürlings (1877); Tilmouth (1980); Tittel (1959), (1966); Tolkoff (1973); Tuksar (1978/1980); Uberti (1981); Vauclain (1978); Vecchi (1969); Vogel (1955/1954), (1976); Waitzman (1979-81); **Walker (1941-42/. . ./1985)**, (1950/1985), **(1978)**; Walker (1987); Warrack (1945); Warren (1980); Wichmann (1966); Wienpahl (1953), (1955); Wolf (1939); Yates (1947); Yeston (1974/1976); **Zaminer (1985)**; Zenck (1942).

BERNHARD ZIEHN

[1845 – 1912]

Chicago was the venue for the career of Bernhard Ziehn, who had departed Germany for the American Midwest in his early twenties. Though he taught school and performed the duties of an organist for a few years, Ziehn's chief interactions with other musicians were conducted through private lessons, as well as through a variety of publications, including reviews, articles, and the books on music theory for which he is remembered. Despite the distance from his homeland he nevertheless kept in touch with musical developments there and was an irritant to various German scholars whose works had been shipped to Chicago. RIEMANN was a particular target of his criticism.

Unlike HELMHOLTZ, RIEMANN, and other Continental theorists, Ziehn rejected the resonance characteristics of pitch as a basis for his theory. He instead drew upon the precise positioning of the twelve pitches in equal temperament to ensure that enharmonic reinterpretation was possible for all members within the system. Ziehn's *Harmonie- und Modulationslehre* [1887] is a remarkable document of categorization, wherein the minutiae of chord construction are subjected to close scrutiny. Densely packed though somewhat rambling, Ziehn's synthesis of a vast quantity of repertoire is impressive. His use of Roman numerals is unique: instead of denoting the scale degrees of chordal

roots, they indicate chromatic chord structures generated through analogous operations. For example, among his altered triads is I, a major third surmounted by a diminished third; II, a diminished third surmounted by a major third; III, a minor third surmounted by a diminished third; and IV, a diminished third surmounted by a minor third. Of special fascination is the variety of music examples supplied, ranging from Schütz, Bach, and Mozart through standard nineteenth-century repertoire by Berlioz, Wagner, and Liszt, to the music of Richard Strauss and George Chadwick. The work powerfully documents various interactions among adjacent chords and the impact of linear motions. Few of these examples extend beyond two or three measures, which both helps focus the reader's attention upon the issue at hand and camouflages the absence of a long-range perspective.

Somewhat later, Ziehn penetrated the art of musical canons with his *Canonical Studies: A New Technic in Composition* (1912). The examples (which constitute the bulk of the work) extend to nine voices and incorporate a variety of intervallic relationships. Ziehn was particularly fond of his notion of "symmetrical inversion," wherein all pitches are mirrored about the D a step above middle C. Its utilization as a parameter among canonic possibilities made for additional technical challenges and freed the practitioner from some of the ramifications typically associated with tonal practice. (E.g., one example that ends with an ascending arpeggiation of the tonic C, E, G, C below a stable soprano C concludes with a descending arpeggiation of a 6/4-position chord—E, C, A, E above a stable bass pitch E—in its symmetrically inverted version!) While Ziehn enjoyed a dedicated following among his students, Ferruccio Busoni appears to be the one contemporary of international stature who strongly advocated Ziehn's perspective.

Harmonie- und Modulationslehre

> Breslau: Robert Ziehn; Berlin: in Commission bei R. Sulzer (Leipzig: Oscar Brandstetter), [1887]. Berlin and Gross Lichterfelde: Chr. F. Vieweg, [1909].

>> Review in *Rmi* 17/1 (1910):276 (Luigi Torchi).

T ● *Manual of Harmony, Theoretical and Practical*. Vol. 1. Milwaukee: William A. Kaun Music Co.; Leipzig: Carl F. Fleischer, 1907.

>> The second volume survives in manuscript.

"Der Weise von Großmehlra"

> *AMuZ* 17/29-30 (1890):355-63.

>> Response in *AMuZ* 17/31-32 [reads 30-31] (1890):375-76 (Hugo RIEMANN).

Fünf- und sechsstimmige Harmonien und ihre Anwendung (800 Beispiele)/Five- and Six-Part Harmonies: How to Use Them (800 Examples)

> Milwaukee: William A. Kaun Music Co.; Berlin: Richard Kaun Musik Verlag, 1911.

Canonical Studies: A New Technic in Composition/ Canonische Studien, eine neue Compositions-Technik

> Published posthumously.

> Milwaukee: William A. Kaun Music Co.; Berlin: Richard Kaun Musik Verlag, 1912.

S ● Stevenson, Ronald, ed. *Canonic Studies*. London: Kahn & Averill, 1976; New York: Crescendo Publishing, 1977.

>> An abridged edition, including Stevenson's essay, "Bernhard Ziehn's Contribution to the Development of Canon." Reviews in *MiE* 41/385 (1977):144 (Reginald Johnson), *MO* 102/1217 (1979):258-59 (Gwilym Beechey), *MT* 120/1631 (1979):40 (Patric Standford), *MusT* 56/10 (1977):33 (John Morehen), and *Tempo* 121 (1977):30-31 (Edmund Rubbra).

Articles on music

S ● Goebel, Julius, ed. "Gesammelte Aufsätze zur Geschichte und Theorie der Musik." *DAGb* 26-27 (1926-27):5-355.

> A collection of twenty-three articles by Ziehn, plus "Bernhard Ziehn" by Julius Goebel (pp. 7-16), "Personal Recollections of Bernhard Ziehn" by Th. Otterström (pp. 17-25), and "Bernhard Ziehn's Essays on Musical Theory and History" by Th. Otterström (pp. 87-90).

See also RIEMANN: (1898):ZIEHN (1900).

LITERATURE:

Busoni, Ferruccio. "Die 'Gotiker' von Chicago, Illinois." *Signale* 68/5 (1910):163-65; reprinted in Busoni's *Von der Einheit der Musik . . .: Verstreute Aufzeichnungen* (Berlin: Max Hesses Verlag, 1922), pp. 132-36; expanded edition (as *Wesen und Einheit der Musik*, edited by Joachim Herrmann; MHHM, no. 76), 1956.

> Reprinted in Moser (1949-50), below.

Gold, Julius. "Bernhard Ziehn's Contribution to the Science of Music." *MC* 68/26 [1788] (1914):21-22.

Sargeant, Winthrop. "Bernhard Ziehn, Precursor." *MQ* 19/2 (1933):169-77. Bibliog.

Moser, Hans Joachim. "Bernhard Ziehn (1845-1912): Der deutsch-amerikanische Musiktheoretiker." *JMw* 1 (1949-50):208-98; reprinted separately, Bayreuth: Julius Steeger, 1950.

> Reviews in *Mf* 4/1 (1951):79-80 (Willi Kahl) and ●●●*MQ* 37/3 (1951):435-41 (W. J. Mitchell).

Mitchell, William J. "Ziehn, Bernhard." Translated by Leonore Voss-Wunderlich. In *MGG* (1949-68). Bibliog.

Belcher, Euel Hobson, Jr. "The Musical Theories of Bernhard Ziehn." In "The Organ Music of Wilhelm Middelschulte." Ph.D. dissertation, Indiana University, 1975. [*Rilm* 75-2607.]

Smith, Warren Storey. "Ziehn, Bernhard." In *NGrove* (1980). Bibliog.

> Review in *MQ* 68/2 (1982):161-81 (Allen Forte).

Brandse, Wim. "Een canon is iemand die met zijn schaduw wandelt: De theoreticus Bernhard Ziehn en zijn *Canonical Studies*." *Mens* 38/2 (1983):68-72.

Neff, Severine. "Otto Luening (1900-) and the Theories of Bernhard Ziehn (1845-1912)." *CM* 39 (1985):21-41.

Levarie, Siegmund. "Ziehn, Bernhard." In *NGroveAm* (1986).

Neff, Severine. "An American Precursor of Nontonal Theory: Ernst Bacon (1898-). *CM* 44 (1987).

See also LITERATURE SUPPLEMENT: Beiche ["Inversio"] (1972-); Dunsby and Whittall (1988); Haydon (1933/1970); Jeppesen (1922/. . ./1970); Rohwer (1949-68); Weigl (1914-15).

LITERATURE SUPPLEMENT

A

Abbado, Michelangelo. "Sull'esistenza dei suoni armonici inferiori." *Am* 36/4 (1964):234-37.

Abel, Angelika. "Die Zwölftontechnik Weberns und Goethes Methodik der Farbenlehre: Zur Kompositionstheorie und Ästhetik der Neuen Wiener Schule." Ph.D. dissertation, The University of Marburg/Lahn, 1980; published edition (BAfMw, no. 19), Wiesbaden: Steiner, 1982. Bibliog. [*Rilm* 82-3797.]

> Reviews in *Hv* 21/3 (1984):274-75 (vl), *MB* 16/4 (1984):314, and *Mth* 1/2 (1986):186-89 (Ernst-Jürgen Dreyer) [Response in *Mth* 1/3 (1986):283 (Albrecht Riethmüller)].

Abercrombie, J. R. Alexander G. "The Application of Mathematical Techniques to Music Theory." Ph.D. dissertation, King's College, London, forthcoming.

Abraham, Gerald, ed. *The Age of Humanism (1540-1630)*. NOHM, vol. 4. London: Oxford University Press, 1968; Italian edition of Part 2 (as *L'età del rinascimento, 1540-1630*, translated by Francesco Buzzi), Milan: Feltrinelli Editore, 1969. Bibliog. [*Rilm* 79-575.]

> Reviews in *ABBW* 41/6-7 (1968):487, *ARG* 35/9 (1968-69):834-40 (John W. Barker), *ChuMus* 2/25 (1968):20 (Geoffrey Sharp), *Composer* 30 (1968-69):30-31, *Eras* 21/23-24 (1969):750-51 (Walter Kolneder), *GSJ* 22 (1969):102-4 (Denis Arnold), *JAMS* 23/1 (1970):133-36 (Claude V. Palisca), *JCM* 10/8 (1968):20-22 (Donald J. Grout), *Manu* 13/2 (1969):109-13 (Ernst C. Krohn), *MEv* 23/3 (1968):30-32, *Mf* 25/3 (1972): 365-66 (Walther Dürr), *MG* 19/8 (1969):564-66 (Peter Gülke), *MiE* 32/331 (1968):141 (David Epps), *ML* 51/1 (1970):66-69 (Paul Doe), *MR* 30/4 (1969):313-18 (John Boulton), *MT* 109/1504 (1968):539-40 (Jeremy Noble), *Notes* 26/2 (1969-70):254-56 (Howard Mayer Brown), *NZfM* 130/4 (1969):195-96 (Hans Hollander), *ÖM* 23/6-7 (1968):366-67 (R. K.), *PP* 61/1 (1968-69):65 (Melva Peterson), *SchM* 39/8 (1967-68): 29, *Stfm* 52 (1970):112-14 (Hans Eppstein), *Tablet* 222/6664 (Feb. 10, 1968):130-31 (A. Gregory Murray), and *TLS* 67/3472 (1968):990.

Abraham, Lars Ulrich. "Musiktheoretische Unterweisung an einem Lehrerseminar nach 1850." See Vogel (1966):233-55.

Abraham, Lars Ulrich, and Dahlhaus, Carl. *Melodielehre*. MTBT, no. 13. Cologne: Gerig, 1972. Bibliog. [*Rilm* 74-3898.]

> Reviews in *Dmt* 47/5 (1972-73):137-40 (Finn Lykkebo), *GK 1972* 5 (1972):189-90 (Siegmund Helms), *Km* 24/4 (1973):128-29 (Jan Goens), *MB* 6/5 (1974):336-37 (Günther Noll), *Me* 27/4 (1973-74):90 (Friedrich Neumann), *Mens* 28/10 (1973):310-13 (Miep Zijlstra), *Mf* 27/2 (1974): 254-56 (Friedrich Neumann), *MK* 44/3 (1974): 133 (Karlheinz Schlager), *Musica* 27/1 (1973):59-60 (Gerhard Schuhmacher), *NZfM* 135/3 (1974): 210-11 (G. A. Trumpff), *Rdm* 60/1-2 (1974):217-18 (Jean-Jacques Nattiez), *SK* 21/1 (1973-74):41 (Dr. Kundi), and *SMz* 113/1 (1973):53 (Peter Wettstein).

Ahlgrimm, Isolde. "Die Rhetorik in der Barockmusik." *Musica* 22/6 (1968):493-97. [*Rilm* 68-3188.]

Ahlgrimm, Isolde. "De Retoriek in de Barokmuziek." Translated by H. Timmerman. *De Praestant* 18/3-4 (1969):57-60, 92-95; 19/1 (1970):1-3. Bibliog. [*Rilm* 69-3575.]

> Expanded version of Ahlgrimm (1968).

Ahlgrimm, Isolde. "Das vielgestaltige Arpeggio." *Musica* 27/3 (1973):238-44. [*Rilm* 75-2564.]

Albersheim, Gerhard. *Die Tonsprache*. MSzMw, no. 15. Tutzing: Hans Schneider, 1980. [*Rilm* 80-5596.]

Albrecht, Christoph. " 'Jeu inégal' bei Bach? Zu einem aktuellen Interpretationsproblem." *Km* 32/4 (1981):117-20.

Alekperova, Nelli. "Problema muzykal'nogo tvorchestva v istoricheskom aspekte." [The Problem of Musical Creativity in a Historical Context.] In *Izvestiia AN AzSSR: Series on Literature, Language, and Art* 3 (1982):99-106. [*Rilm* 82-3836.]

Alekseev, Aleksandr. *Iz istorii fortepiannoi pedagogiki: Khrestomatiia.* [From the History of Piano Pedagogy: A Reader.] Kiev: Muzychna Ukraina, 1974. [*Rilm* 75-2418.]

Alette, Carl. "Theories of Rhythm." 2 vols. Ph.D. dissertation, The University of Rochester, 1951. Bibliog. [SMLMS.]

Allanbrook, Wye J. "Metric Gesture as a Topic in *Le Nozze di Figaro* and *Don Giovanni*." *MQ* 67/1 (1981):94-112. [*Rilm* 81-498.]

Allard, J. C. "Studies in Theories of Painting and Music in Sixteenth and Seventeenth-Century France." M.Phil. thesis, The University of Essex, 1977.

Allen, Warren Dwight. "Baroque Histories of Music." *MQ* 25/2 (1939):195-209.

Allen, Warren Dwight. "Philosophies of Music History." Ph.D. dissertation, Columbia University, 1939; published edition, New York: American Book Co., 1939. Bibliog.

> Reviews in *Ethics* 50/3 (1939-40):373-74 (Scott Goldthwaite) and *KenR* 2/4 (1940):499-501 (Henry Woodward).

Almond, Clare, ed. "The Developing Violin: Jaap Schröder in Conversation with Christopher Hogwood." *EM* 7/2 (1979):155-65. [*Rilm* 79-1490.]

Ambros, August Wilhelm. *Geschichte der Musik.* Vol. 4, edited by Gustav Nottebohm and C. F. Becker. Leipzig: F. E. C. Leuckart, 1878; 2nd edition, 1881; 3rd edition (edited by Hugo Leichtentritt), 1909.

Anglés, Higinio, and Subirá, José. *Catálogo musical de la Biblioteca nacional de Madrid.* 3 vols. Barcelona: Consejo superior de investigaciones científicas, Instituto español de musicología, 1946-51. Bibliog.

> Reviews in *ML* 29/2 (1948):214-15 (Norman Fraser), *ML* 31/3 (1950):270-71 (A. Hyatt King), and *MQ* 34/1 (1948):121-26.

Apel, Willi. [Appelbaum in 1936 version.] "Accidenten und Tonalität in den Musikdenkmälern des 15. und 16. Jahrhunderts." Ph.D dissertation, The University of Berlin, 1936; published edition (SmA, no. 24), Strasbourg: Heitz, 1937; 2nd edition, Baden-Baden: Valentin Körner, 1972.

> Reviews in *ML* 19/1 (1938):94-95 (J. A. Westrup) and *Rmi* 41/5 (1937):628-29 (Luigi Ronga).

Apel, Willi. *The Notation of Polyphonic Music: 900-1600.* MAA, no. 38. Cambridge, Mass.: Mediaeval Academy of America, 1942; later editions through 1961.

> Reviews in *ML* 24/4 (1943):245-46 (J. A. Westrup), *ML* 27/2 (1946):127-28 (Eric Blom), *MQ* 30/1 (1944):112-18 (M. F. Bukofzer), *MR* 8/1 (1947):47-48 (Gerald Abraham), *Notes* First Series 15 (1942):60-61 (Charles Warren Fox), *Notes*

> 7/2 (1949-50):283-85 (Otto Gombosi), and *Rmi* 48/3 (1946):393-95 (Benvenuto Disertori).

Apfel, Ernst. "Satztechnische Grundlagen der Neuen Musik des 17. Jahrhunderts." *Am* 34/1-2 (1962):67-78. Bibliog.

Apfel, Ernst. *Beiträge zu einer Geschichte der Satztechnik von der frühen Motette bis Bach.* Munich: Eidos, 1964.

> Reviews in *Mens* 24/1 (1969):30-31 (G. V.), *Mf* 19/2 (1966):217-19 (Wolfgang Marggraf), *ML* 48/1 (1967):80-82 (John Bergsagel), and *Notes* 22/3 (1965-66):1031-32 (Ruth Steiner).

Apfel, Ernst. "Wandlungen der Polyphonie von Palestrina zu Bach." *AfMw* 21/1 (1964):60-76.

Apfel, Ernst. "Probleme der theoretischen Harmonik aus geschichtlich-satztechnischer Sicht." In *WioraFs* (1967):140-48. [*Rilm* 68-1196.]

Apfel, Ernst. "Rhythmisch-metrisch und andere Beobachtungen an ostinatobässen." *AfMw* 33/1 (1976): 48-67. [*Rilm* 76-5288.]

Apfel, Ernst. "Musiktheorie, Kompositionslehre und historische Satzlehre." In his *Aufsätze und Vorträge zur Musikgeschichte und historischen Musiktheorie*, pp. 70-84. Saarbrücken: Apfel, 1977. [*Rilm* 77-4314.]

> Reviews in *Melos/NZfM* 4/6 (1978):555-56 (Winfried Kirsch) and *Mens* 34/5 (1979):177.

Apfel, Ernst. *Geschichte der Kompositionslehre: Von den Anfängen bis gegen 1700.* 3 vols. TzMw, nos. 75-77. Wilhelmshaven: Heinrichshofen, 1981. Bibliog. [*Rilm* 81-6093.]

> Reviews in *Adem* 18/5 (1982):283-84 (Y. K.), *Me* 35 (1981-82):80-81 (Cesar Bresgen), *MK* 54/1 (1984):28 (Karlheinz Schlager), *ÖM* 38/3 (1983):197-98 (Herwig Knaus), and *Orch* 30/4 (1982):364 (Diether de la Motte).

Apfel, Ernst, and Dahlhaus, Carl. *Studien zur Theorie und Geschichte der musikalischen Rhythmik und Metrik.* 2 vols. MwS, no. 1. Munich: Katzbichler, 1974. Bibliog. [*Rilm* 76-1633.]

> Reviews in *Mf* 32/2 (1979):212-14 (Wilhelm Seidel) and *Nrmi* 10/2 (1976):312-14 (Gino Stefani).

Arakawa, Tsuneko. "Senritsuron o toshite mita 18 seiki no ongakuyoshiki no hensen." *BYU* 23 (1973):216-21. [*Rilm* 73-4324.]

Aranovsky, Mark. "Intonatsiia, znak i 'novye metody'." [Intonation, Sign, and "New Methods."] *Smuz* /10 (1980):99-109; as "Intonation, Zeichen und neue Methoden," *BzMw* 25/3-4 (1983):238-58. [*Rilm* 80-5598.]

Archibald, R. C. "Mathematicians and Music." *AMMo* 31/1 (1924):1-25. Bibliog.

Arlt, Wulf. "Der Beitrag des 18. Jahrhunderts zum Verständnis der Tonschrift." In *VolkFs* (1974):47-90. [*Rilm* 74-3835.]

Arlt, Wulf. "Natur und Geschichte der Musik in der Anschauung des 18. Jahrhunderts: J.-J. Rousseau and J. N. Forkel." *Melos/NZfM* 2/5 (1976):351-56. [*Rilm* 76-9905.]

Armstrong, James. "How to Compose a Psalm: Ponzio and Cerone Compared." *Sm* 7 (1978):103-39. Bibliog.

Arnold, Denis. " 'Seconda Pratica': A Background to Monteverdi's Madrigals." *ML* 38/4 (1957):341-52.

Arnold, Denis, and Fortune, Nigel. *The Monteverdi Companion*. London: Faber & Faber; New York: W. W. Norton, 1968; revised edition (as *The New Monteverdi Companion*), 1985.

> Reviews in *JAMS* 23/2 (1970):343-49 (Stuart Reiner), *LJ* 93/17 (1968):3563 (Biard Hastings), *MakM* 68 (1968):21-22 (Sidney Twemlow), *MEJ* 55/8 (1968-69):93-94 (Gordon Sandford), *Mf* 34/4 (1971):461-63 (Anna Amalie Abert), *MiE* 32/332 (1968):202 (Mary Ibberson), *ML* 49/4 (1968):389-90 (Jack A. Westrup), *ML* 67/2 (1986):169-72 (Tim Carter), *MO* 93/1107 (1969-70):141-43 (B. R.), *MT* 109/1507 (1968):815-16 (Winton Dean), *Nrmi* 4/1 (1970):142-46 (Federico Mompellio), *NYTBR* 73/36 (1968):22 (D. C. Goddard), *NZfM* 131/1 (1970):41 (Hans Hollander), *Opera* 19/9 (1968):759, *OpN* 33/10 (1968-69):7 (Frank Merkling), *PP* 61/1 (1968-69):65 (Melva Peterson), *PW* 194/2 (1968):163, *TLS* 67/3464 (1968):744, and *TLS* 86/4376 (1987):159 (Warwick Edwards).

Arnold, Franck Thomas. *The Art of Accompaniment from a Thorough-Bass as Practised in the Seventeenth and Eighteenth Centuries*. London: Oxford University Press, Milford, 1931; reprint edition, London: Holland Press, 1961; reprint edition (with a new Introduction by Denis Stevens, AMS/MLARS), New York: Dover Publications, 1965.

> See "The F. T. Arnold Correspondence: A Selection from the Letters from F. T. Arnold to Arnold Dolmetsch" in *Consort* 33 (1977):237-49 (Shelagh Godwin) [*Rilm* 77-3655.]. Reviews in *AmO* 49/4 (1966):6 (Harry W. Gay), *AMT* 16/2 (1966-67):38-39 (Joseph G. Beck), *AR* 9/3 (1968):80 (Martin Davidson), *Clavier* 7/2 (1968):8, *ML* 13/2 (1932):230-33 (R. O. Morris), *ML* 43/2 (1962):164 (James Dalton), *MO* 90/1073 (1966-67):263 (B. R.), *MT* 73/1067-68 (1932):32-34, 123-25 (W. Gillies Whittaker), *MT* 102/1422 (1961):494 (Walter Emery), *MT* 107/1484 (1966):872 (Stanley Sadie), and *MusT* 45/9 (1966):353 (J. R. T.).

Asselin, Pierre-Yves. "Le tempérament en France au 18e siècle." In *Symposium McGill 1981* (1981):45-69. Bibliog. [*Rilm* 82-3556.]

Asselin, Pierre-Yves. "Musique et tempérament: Théorie et pratique de l'accord à l'ancienne." Ph.D. dissertation, The University of Paris VI (Laboratoire d'acoustique musicale), 1983; published edition, Paris: Costallat, 1985. Bibliog.

> Reviews in *Nrmi* 21/1 (1987):120-22 (Elena Ferrari Barassi) and *Rdm* 72/2 (1986):294-96 (Herbert Anton Kellner).

Atcherson, Walter Thomas. "Modal Theory of Sixteenth-Century German Theorists." Ph.D. dissertation, Indiana University, 1960. Bibliog. [*DA* 21/09, p. 2736. UMI 60-06280.]

Atcherson, W. T. "Theory Accommodates Practice: *Confinalis* Theory in Renaissance Music Treatises." *JAMS* 23/2 (1970):326-30. [*Rilm* 70-1589.]

Atcherson, W. T. "Symposium on Seventeenth-Century Music Theory: England." See Cohen ["National Predilections"] (1972):6-15. Bibliog. [*Rilm* 73-1193.]

Atcherson, Walter. "Key and Mode in Seventeenth-Century Music Theory." *JMT* 17/2 (1973):204-32. [*Rilm* 74-1117.]

Auda, Antoine. *Les modes et les tones de la musique et spécialement de la musique medievale*. Brussels: M. Hayez, 1930; reprint edition, New York: Georg Olms, 1979.

Audbourg-Popin, Marie-Danielle. "Éléments d'une sémiotique rationnelle du discours musical: Bach prédicateur." *Rdm* 70/1 (1984):86-94. Bibliog.

Audbourg-Popin, Marie-Danielle. "Bach et le 'gout français'." *Rdm* 72/2 (1986):271-77.

Auhagen, Wolfgang. "Studien zur Tonartencharakteristik in theoretischen Schriften und Kompositionen vom späten 17. bis zum Beginn des 20. Jahrhunderts." Ph.D. dissertation, The University of Göttingen, 1982; published edition (EH, ser. 36, no. 6), Frankfurt am Main: Peter Lang, 1983. Bibliog. [*Rilm* 83-3905.]

Auhagen, Wolfgang. "Chronometrische Tempoangaben im 18. und 19. Jahrhundert." *AfMw* 44/1 (1987):40-57.

Aulabaugh, Alan Richard. "An Analytical Study of Performance Problems in the Keyboard Sonatas of F. J. Haydn." Ph.D. dissertation, The State University of Iowa, 1958. Bibliog. [*DA* 18/06, p. 2160. UMI 58-01602.]

Austin, William W. *Music in the 20th Century from Debussy through Stravinsky*. New York: W. W. Norton, 1966. Bibliog.

> Reviews in *ACR* 9/1 (1966-67):12-13 (Martin Picker), *Booklist* 63/5 (1966-67):294, *Clavier* 6/3 (1967):12, *Composer* 25 (1967):33-34 (Anthony Hedges), *Gram* 45/530 (1967-68):59 (John Westcombe), *Instr* 21/4 (1966-67):30, *JMT* 11/1 (1967):165-69 (Richard Swift), *JRME* 15/2 (1967):174-76 (Henry Leland Clarke), *LJ* 91/4 (1966):950 (Catharine K. Miller), *MCM* 46/3

(1966-67):27 (Quaintance Eaton), *MEJ* 54/3 (1967-68):119-20 (Wayne Barlow), *MiE* 32/331 (1968):141-42 (Peter Dickinson), *MJ* 24/9 (Nov. 1966):60 (Cox), *ML* 49/1 (1968):43-47 (P. A. Evans), *MR* 29/1 (1968):63-64, *MT* 109/1500 (1968):140-41 (Stephen Plaistow), *Notes* 23/2 (1966-67):254-57 (H. Wiley Hitchcock), *NRep* 156/2 (1967):36-37 (Robert Evett), *Numu* 12/2 (1968-69):78 (Göran Fant), *NY* 42/22 (1966):88, *NZfM* 129/1 (1968):44 (Carl Dahlhaus), *OpN* 31/9 (1966-67):37 (Martin Chusid), *Orch* 15/9 (1967):352 (Ma.), *PNM* 5/1 (1966-67):142-47

(Charles Wuorinen) [with Response and Reply in *PNM* 6/1 (1967-68):156-58 (Dale A. Craig, Charles Wuorinen)], *PP* 59/3 (1966-67):19 (Melva Peterson), *RmSr* 20/1 (1967):13-14 (P. M.), *Stfm* 50 (1968):139-42 (Ingmar Bengtsson), and *TLS* 67/3436 (1968):1-3.

Austin, William W. "Martini, Rousseau, Burney and Forkel in Twentieth-Century Perspectives." In *Oxford Symposium 1977* (1980):215-22. Bibliog.

B

Babbitt, Milton. "Past and Present Concepts of the Nature and Limits of Music." In *Report New York 1961* (1961):398-403; reprinted in *Perspectives on Contemporary Music Theory*, edited by Benjamin Boretz and Edward T. Cone, pp. 3-9. New York: W. W. Norton, 1972.

Babbitt, Milton. "Professional Theorists and Their Influence." In *Milton Babbitt: Words About Music*, edited by Stephen Dembski and Joseph N. Straus, pp. 121-62. Madison, Wisc.: The University of Wisconsin Press, 1987.

> Reviews in *ITO* 10/8 (1987-88):15-23 (Jason Gibbs), *JMT* 32/2 (1988):366-79 (Andrew Mead), and *T&P* 12 (1987):67-73 (Eleanor Cory).

Babitz, Sol. "A Problem of Rhythm in Baroque Music." *MQ* 38/4 (1952):533-65.

Babitz, Sol. " 'Concerning the Length of Time That Every Note Must Be Held'." *MR* 28/1 (1967):21-37; as "Anmerkung, welche die Zeit, wie lange jede Note gehalten werden muß, betrifft" (translated by Lenore Wunderlich), *Musica* 23/1 (1969):8-14. [*Rilm* 67-434.]

Babitz, Sol, and Pont, Graham. "Vocal de-Wagnerization and Other Matters." *EMLB* 10 (1973). [*Rilm* 73-4278.]

Badings, Henk. *Over 31-toon-stemming in het algemeen en in het bijzonder gedemonstreerd aan de hand van een eigen compositie*. MKAW, ser. 40, no. 6. Brussels: Paleis der Academiën, 1978. [*Rilm* 78-1750.]

Badura-Skoda, Eva; Collins, Michael; Horsley, Imogene; and Libby, Dennis. "Improvisation." In *NGrove* (1980). Bibliog.

Badura-Skoda, Paul. "Beiträge zu Haydns Ornamentik." *Musica* 36/5 (1982):409-18. [*Rilm* 82-5695.]

Balthazar, Scott L. "Intellectual History and Concepts of the Concerto: Some Parallels from 1750 to 1850." *JAMS* 36/1 (1983):39-72.

Barbieri, Patrizio. "I temperamenti ciclici da Vicentino (1555) a Buliowski (1699): Teoria e pratica 'archicembalistica'." *L'organo* 21 (1983):129-208.

Barbour, James Murray. "Equal Temperament: Its History from Ramis (1482) to Rameau (1737)." Ph.D. dissertation, Cornell University, 1932.

Barbour, J. Murray. "Just Intonation Confuted." *ML* 19/1 (1938):48-60.

Barbour, J. Murray. "Bach and *The Art of Temperament*." *MQ* 33/1 (1947):64-89; reprinted in Rosand (1985): Vol. 6, pp. 2-27.

Barbour, James Murray. "Irregular Systems of Temperament." *JAMS* 1/3 (1948):20-26.

Barbour, J. Murray. "Temperatur und Stimmung." Translated by Wilhelm Stauder. In *MGG* (1949-68). Bibliog.

Barbour, J. Murray. "Violin Intonation in the Eighteenth Century." *JAMS* 5/3 (1952):224-34.

Barbour, James Murray. *Tuning and Temperament: A Historical Survey*. East Lansing, Mich.: Michigan State College Press, 1951; 2nd edition, 1953; reprint edition (DCPMRS), New York: Da Capo Press, 1972. Bibliog.

> Reviews in *Isis* 47/1 (1956):66-67 (W. Paul Gilbert), *JAMS* 6/2 (1953):185-86 (Wayne Barlow), *MN* 44 (1952):18, *MQ* 38/3 (1952):451-57 (David D. Boyden), *MR* 13/4 (1952):320-22 (L. S. Lloyd), *Notes* 9/2 (1951-52):285-86 (Joseph Yasser), *SatR* 34 (December 15, 1951):30, 39 (Peter Yates), and *SwM* 18/7 (1952):8 (H. G. H.).

Barenboim, Lev. "Vydaivshchiesia sovetskie muzykanty-prosvetiteli." [Eminent Soviet Musician-Enlighteners.] *Smuz* /12 (1970):97-102. [*Rilm* 71-3117.]

Barenboim, Lev. *Muzykal'naia pedagogika i ispolnitel'stvo*. [Musical Pedagogy and Performance Practice.] Leningrad: Muzyka, 1974. [*Rilm* 74-3962.]

Barford, Philip. "Music in the Philosophy of Schopenhauer." *Soundings* 5 (1975):29-43. [*Rilm* 75-2945.]

Baron, John H. "Monody: A Study in Terminology." *MQ* 54/4 (1968):462-74. [*Rilm* 68-3192.]

Bartel, Dietrich. "Handbuch der musikalischen Figurenlehre." Ph.D. dissertation, The University of Freiburg im Breisgau, 1982; published edition, Laaber: Laaber-Verlag, 1985. Bibliog.

Reviews in *MB* 19/3 (1987):239 (Hans Bäßler), *Me* 40/1 (1986-87):41-42 (Herwig Knaus), *MiB* 33 (1986):179-81 (Horst Leuchtmann), *Musica* 40/5 (1986):463-64 (Peter Reidemeister), *Notes* 44/1 (1987-88):62-64 (Gregory S. Johnson), *NZfM* 147/12 (1986):78 (Carl Dahlhaus), *ÖM* 41/10 (1986):546-47 (Hartmut Krones), and *Tibia* 13/2 (1988):126-27.

Bartenstein, Hans. "Die frühen Instrumentationslehren bis zu Berlioz." *AfMw* 28/2 (1971):97-118. [*Rilm* 73-1216.]

Bates, Robert Frederick. "From Mode to Key: A Study of Seventeenth-Century French Liturgical Organ Music and Music Theory." Ph.D. dissertation, Stanford University, 1986. [*DA* 47/09A, p. 3228. UMI 87-00725.]

Bauman, Thomas. "The Music Reviews of the *Allgemeine deutsche Bibliothek*." *Am* 49/1 (1977):69-85. [*Rilm* 77-511.]

Bauman, Thomas. "Benda, the Germans, and Simple Recitative." *JAMS* 34/1 (1981):119-31.

Beach, David. "The Functions of the Six-Four Chord in Tonal Music." *JMT* 11/1 (1967):2-31. [*Rilm* 68-1177.]

Beach, David. "The Origins of Harmonic Analysis." *JMT* 18/2 (1974):274-306. [*Rilm* 74-3907.]

Beach, David. "A Recurring Pattern in Mozart's Music." *JMT* 27/1 (1983):1-29.

Beck, Hermann. "Zur Geschichte der musikalischen Werkanalyse." In *FellererFsII* (1973): 35-39. [*Rilm* 74-1758.]

Beck, Hermann. *Methoden der Werkanalyse in Musikgeschichte und Gegenwart*. TzMw, no. 9. Wilhelmshaven: Heinrichshofen, 1974. Bibliog. [*Rilm* 75-2676.]

Reviews in *ArsOr* 24/50 (1976):2385 (A. E.), *Dmt* 49/1 (1974-75):22 (Poul Nielsen), *Hv* 13/2 (1976):187-89 (jl), *Km* 26/4 (1975):106 (Joachim Dorfmüller), *MB* 6/12 (1974):694 (Carl Dahlhaus), *Me* 30/3 (1977):385-87, *Melos/NZfM* 1/1 (1975):63-65 (Arno Forchert), *Mf* 30/3 (1977): 385-87 (Wolfgang Dömling), *Musica* 29/6 (1975):530-31 (Gerd Sievers), *Nrmi* 8/3 (1974): 451-54 (Gino Stefani), and *ÖM* 31/1 (1976):47 (Marion Diederichs-Lafite).

Becker, Carl Ferdinand. *Systematisch-chronologische Darstellung der musikalischen Literatur von der frühesten bis auf die neueste Zeit*. Leipzig: Robert Friese, 1836-39; reprint edition, Amsterdam: Frits A. M. Knuf, 1964. Bibliog.
Derived from Forkel (1792/1962).

Beebe, Ellen Scott. "Mode, Structure, and Text Expression in the Motets of Jacobus Clemens non Papa: A Study of Style in Sacred Music." 2 vols. Ph.D. dissertation, Yale University, 1976. Bibliog. [*Rilm* 76-5163. *DA* 38/01A, pp. 14-15. UMI 77-14280.]

Beer, Anton de. "Die Entwicklung der 31-Tonmusik/The Development of 31-Tone Music." *Sos* 38 (1969):26-41.

Beiche, Michael. "Dux - comes." In *HwmT* (1972-). Bibliog.

Beiche, Michael. "Inversio/Umkehrung." In *HwmT* (1972-). Bibliog.

Bell, James F.; Dostrovsky, Sigalia; and Truesdell, C. "Physics of Music." In *NGrove* (1980). Bibliog.

Bellingham, Bruce Allan. "The *bicinium* in the Lutheran Latin Schools during the Reformation Period." 2 vols. Ph.D. dissertation, The University of Toronto, 1971. Bibliog. [*Rilm* 71-291. *DA* 33/01A, p. 345.]

Bellingham, Bruce A. "Bicinium." In *NGrove* (1980). Bibliog.

Benary, Peter. "Die deutsche Kompositionslehre des 18. Jahrhunderts." Ph.D. dissertation, The University of Jena, 1956; published edition (JBzMf, no. 3), Leipzig: Breitkopf & Härtel, [1961]. Bibliog.

Reviews in *Mens* 16/12 (1961):380, *Mf* 17/3 (1964):318-19 (Arnold Feil), and *Stfm* 44 (1962):78-81 (Ingmar Bengtsson).

Benary, Peter. "Die Stellung der Melodielehre in der Musiktheorie des 18. Jahrhunderts in Deutschland." In *Bericht Kassel 1962* (1963):362-64.

Benjamin, William E. "Pitch-Class Counterpoint in Tonal Music." See Browne (1981):1-32. [*Rilm* 81-1655.]

Bent, Ian. "Analytical Thinking in the First Half of the Nineteenth Century." In *Oxford Symposium 1977* (1980):151-66.

Abstract in *MA* 2/3 (1983):302.

Bent, Ian. "Analysis." In *NGrove* (1980); revised edition (with a Glossary by William Drabkin; NGHM), New York: W. W. Norton, 1987. Bibliog.

Reviews in *CMS* 28 (1988):121-29 (Judith Lochhead), *JMTP* 2/2 (1988):297-310 (Michael R. Rogers), *MA* 2/1 (1983):105-7 (Bryan R. Simms), *ML* 69/4 (1988):503-5 (Arnold Whittall), *MQ* 68/2 (1982):161-81 (Allen Forte), *MT* 129/1741 (1988):81 (Jonathan Dunsby), and *Tempo* 163 (1987):31-33 (Malcolm Miller).

Bent, Ian. "The 'Compositional Process' in Music Theory 1713-1850." *MA* 3/1 (1984):29-55.

Bent, Margaret. "Diatonic *ficta*." *EMH* 4 (1984):1-48.

Bent, Margaret; Lockwood, Lewis; Donington, Robert; and Boorman, Stanley. "Musica ficta." In *NGrove* (1980). Bibliog.

Berger, Karol. "Theories of Chromatic and Enharmonic Music in Italy in the Second Half of the Sixteenth Century." Ph.D. dissertation, Yale University, 1975; published edition (as *Theories of Chromatic and Enharmonic Music in Late Sixteenth-Century Italy*; SiM, no. 10), Ann Arbor, Mich.: UMI Research Press, 1980. Bibliog. [*Rilm* 75-536. *DA* 36/12A, p. 7720.]

Reviews in *ML* 63/1-2 (1982):132-33 (Anthony F. Carver), *MR* 43/3-4 (1982):265-66 (D. S.), *MT* 122/1656 (1981):109-10 (Iain Fenlon), *Notes* 37/3 (1980-81):586-87 (Joel Lester), *OrganYb 1983* 14 (1983):119-20 (Peter Williams), *RQ* 34/3 (1981):432-34 (Mark Lindley), and *Rh* 265/1 (1981):227-28 (Édith Weber).

Berger, Karol. "Tonality and Atonality in the Prologue to Orlando di Lasso's *Prophetiae Sibyllarum*: Some Methodological Problems in Analysis of Sixteenth-Century Music." *MQ* 66/4 (1980):484-504. [*Rilm* 80-5640.]

Berger, Karol. *Musica ficta: Theories of Accidental Inflections in Vocal Polyphony from Marchetto da Padova to Gioseffo Zarlino.* Cambridge: Cambridge University Press, 1987. Bibliog.

Reviews in *EM* 17/1 (1989):92-94 (Gareth Curtis) and *MT* 130/1754 (1989):213 (Daniel Leech-Wilkinson).

Berry, Wallace. "Metric and Rhythmic Articulation in Music." *MTS* 7 (1985):7-33.

Beswick, Delbert Meacham. "The Problem of Tonality in Seventeenth-Century Music." Ph.D. dissertation, The University of North Carolina at Chapel Hill, 1950. [SMLMS.]

Beyer, Paul. *Studien zur Vorgeschichte des Dur-moll.* GMfMA, no. 12. Kassel and Basel: Bärenreiter, 1958. Bibliog.

Review in *Mf* 12/3 (1959):346-48 (Carl Dahlhaus).

Beyschlag, Adolf. *Die Ornamentik der Musik.* Leipzig: Breitkopf & Härtel, 1907; 2nd edition, 1953.

Billeter, Bernhard. "Die Harmonik bei Frank Martin: Untersuchungen zur Analyse neuerer Musik." Ph.D. dissertation, The University of Zürich, 1970; published edition (PSMG, ser. 2, no. 23), Bern and Stuttgart: Haupt, 1971. [*Rilm* 72-1882.]

Reviews in *Mf* 25/4 (1972):498 and *Mf* 28/4 (1975):466-67 (Wolfgang Dömling).

Bircher, Martin. "Von Boethius bis Hindemith: Eine Zürcher Sammlung von Erstausgaben zur Geschichte der Musiktheorie." *Librarium* 13/3 (1970):134-61. [*Rilm* 70-2776.]

Birke, Joachim. *Christian Wolffs Metaphysik und die zeitgenössische Literatur- und Musiktheorie: Gottsched, Scheibe, Mizler. Im Anhang: Neuausgabe zweier musiktheoretischer Traktate aus der Mitte des 18. Jahrhunderts.* QFSKV, ser. 21, no. 145. Berlin: W. de Gruyter, 1966. Bibliog.

Reviews in *GLL* 21/3 (1967-68):243-44, *JAAC* 26/3 (1967-68):418-19 (Herbert M. Schuller), *JEGP* 67/1 (1968):124-26 (Armand Nivelle), *Mf* 21/4 (1968):530-31 (Carl Dahlhaus), and *MLR* 64/1 (1969):220-21 (H. B. Nisbet).

Blackwood, Easley. *The Structure of Recognizable Diatonic Tunings.* Princeton, N.J.: Princeton University Press, 1985.

Reviews in *Choice* 24/5 (1986-87):772 (R. Stahura), *JMT* 32/1 (1988):158-69 (André Barbera), *Mf* 42/1 (1989):99-100 (Wolfgang Voigt), and *ML* 70/2 (1989):238-40 (Mark Lindley and Ronald Turner-Smith).

Blake, Carl LeRoy. "Tempo rubato in the Eighteenth Century." D.M.A. dissertation, Cornell University, 1988. [*DA* 49/02A, p. 163. UMI 88-04554.]

Blankenburg, Walter. "Der Harmonie-Begriff in der lutherisch-barocken Musikanschauung." *AfMw* 16/1-2 (1959):44-56.

Blankenburg, Walter. "Kanonimprovisationen im 16. und Anfang des 17. Jahrhunderts." In *Bericht Köln 1958* (1959):68-69.

Blood, William. " 'Well-Tempering' the Clavier: Five Methods." *EM* 7/4 (1979):491-95. [*Rilm* 79-5495.]

Blume, Jürgen. "Die Tradition der tonalen Beantwortung in der Fuge." *NZfM* 145/12 (1984):7-10.

Blumröder, Christoph von. "Modulatio/Modulation." In *HwmT* (1972-). Bibliog.

Böckl, Rudolf. "Versuch über Metamusik." In *Bericht Musiktheorie* (1972):227-35.

Boetticher, Wolfgang. "Orlando di Lasso als Demonstrationsobjekt in der Kompositionslehre des 16. und 17. Jahrhunderts." See Osthoff (1954):124-27.

Boomgaarden, Donald Roy. "Musical Thought in Britain and Germany during the Early Eighteenth Century." Ph.D. dissertation, The University of Rochester, 1985; published edition (AUS, ser. 5, no. 26), New York: Peter Lang, 1987. Bibliog. [*DA* 46/10A, p. 2848.]

Review in *ML* 70/1 (1989):96-98 (George J. Buelow).

Borgir, Tharald. "The Performance of the Basso Continuo in Seventeenth-Century Italian Music." Ph.D. dissertation, The University of California at Berkeley, 1971; published edition (as *The Performance of the Basso Continuo in Italian Baroque Music*; SiM, no. 90), Ann Arbor, Mich.: UMI Research Press, 1987. Bibliog. [*Rilm* 76-15193. *DA* 38/09A, p. 5112.]

Review in *JVGSA* 25 (1988):57-58 (Julie Ann Sadie).

Borrel, Eugène. "Les indications métronomiques laissées par les auteurs français du XVIIIᵉ siècle." *Rdm* 12/27 (1928):149-52.

Bowen, William Roy. "Music and Number: An Introduction to Renaissance Harmonic Science." Ph.D. dissertation, The University of Toronto, 1984. [*DA* 45/09A, p. 2686.]

402

Brandes, Heinz. "Studien zur musikalischen Figurenlehre im 16. Jahrhundert." Ph.D. dissertation, The University of Berlin, 1935; published edition, Berlin: Triltsch & Huther, 1935. Bibliog.

Braun, Werner. "Musiktheorie im 17./18. Jahrhunderts als 'öffentliche' Angelegenheit." In *Referate Berlin 1970* (1970):37-47. Bibliog. [*Rilm* 72-1063.]

Braun, Werner. "Zur Theorie der Einstimmigkeit im 17./18. Jahrhundert." *Mth* 1/2 (1986):115-22.

Breig, Werner. "Varierender Akkord." In *VwmT* (1972-). Bibliog.

Bremner, Robert. "Some Thoughts on the Performance of Concert Music (1777)." Introduction by Neal Zaslaw. *EM* 7/1 (1979):46-57. [*Rilm* 79-1602.]

Brennecke, Wilfried. *Die Handschrift A. R. 940/941 der Proske-Bibliothek zu Regensburg: Ein Beitrag zur Musikgeschichte im zweiten Drittel des 16. Jahrhunderts.* SLMfK, no. 1. Kassel: Bärenreiter, 1953.

> Reviews in *Mf* 7/2 (1954):228-29 (Hans Joachim Moser), *ML* 36/1 (1955):90-92 (Denis Stevens), *MR* 15/3 (1954):243-44 (Gerald Abraham), and *Notes* 12/1 (1954-55):98-100 (Leo Schrade).

Brewer, Robert Edwin. "Variants in Current Terminology Relating to Modulations." M.M. thesis, Indiana University, 1967. [*Rilm* 68-2653.]

Bridges, Doreen. "*Proceedings* of the Musical Association, 1874-1904: The Historical Significance of British Viewpoints on Music Theory and Education." In *MoyleFs* (1984):290-312. Bibliog.

Britsch, Royden Edwin. "Musical and Poetical Rhetoric in Handel's Setting of Brockes' Passion Oratorio: A Rhetorical Analysis of the Poem with a Study of Handel's Use of the Figurenlehre." Ph.D. dissertation, The Florida State University, 1984. [*DA* 45/06A, p. 1764. UMI 84-19207.]

Bronfin, Elena, ed. "Muzykal'naia éstetika Francii XIX v." Moscow: Muzyka, 1974. [*Rilm* 75-1104.]

Brown, Howard Mayer. *Sixteenth-Century Instrumentation: The Music for the Florentine "Intermedii".* MSD, no. 30. [Rome]: American Institute of Musicology, 1973.

Brown, Howard Mayer. *Embellishing Sixteenth-Century Music.* EMSer, no. 1. London: Oxford University Press, 1976. Bibliog.

> Reviews in *AmO:AGO* 13/5 (1979):20-21 (D. DeWitt Wasson), *AR* 19/1 (1978):42, *EM* 5/1 (1977):93-95 (Denis Arnold), *EM* 5/1 (1977):95-99 (Diana Poulton), *Instr* 32/5 (1977-78):20, 24, *MakM* 92 (1976):18 (Ian Graham-Jones), *Mf* 33/1 (1980):80 (Dietrich Kamper), *MiE* 40/380 (1976):175-76, *ML* 57/4 (1976):425-28 (Bernard Thomas), *MT* 117/1604 (1976):829 (David Fallows), *NACWPIJ* 26/1 (1977):23, 30 (Craig B. Parker), *Notes* 34/4 (1977-78):868-70 (Gilbert L. Blount), *Rdm* 63/1-2 (1977):177-80 (Jean-Pierre Ouvrard), *RecMus* 5/6 (1976):199, *SchM* 48/3

(1976-77):18-19, *Strad* 87/1036 (1976-77):325 (A. D.), and *TLS* 75/3893 (1976):1320 (Robert Donington).

Brown, Howard Mayer, and McKinnon, James W. "Performing practice." In *NGrove* (1980). Bibliog.

Browne, Richmond, ed. "Index of Music Theory in the United States, 1955-70." *ITO* 3/7-11 (1977-78):i-170.

Browne, Richmond, ed. *Music Theory: Special Topics.* New York: Academic Press, 1981.

> Reviews in *JMR* 6/3 (1986):260-67 (Stephen Ehrenkreutz), *JMT* 28/2 (1984):313-20 (Richard Chrisman), *MTS* 4 (1982):125-30 (Wilson Coker), *Nrmi* 21/2 (1987):304-5 (Patrizio Barbieri), and *T&P* 8/1 (1983):43-69 (Jonathan Bernard and William Rothstein).

Broyles, Michael. "Beethoven, Symphony No. 8." *NCM* 6/1 (1982-83):39-46. [*Rilm* 82-2406.]

Broyles, Michael. "The Two Instrumental Styles of Classicism." *JAMS* 36/2 (1983):210-42.

Bruck, Boris. "Wandlungen des Begriffes Tempo rubato." Ph.D. dissertation, The University of Erlangen, 1928; published edition, Berlin: Paul Funk, [1928]. Bibliog.

Bryant, David. "The *Cori Spezzati* of St. Mark's: Myth and Reality." In *EMH* 1 (1981):165-86. [*Rilm* 81-6012.]

Budday, Wolfgang. "Grundlagen musikalischer Formen der Wiener Klassik: An Hand der zeitgenössischen Theorie von Joseph Riepel und Heinrich Christoph Koch dargestellt an Menuetten und Sonatensätzen (1750-1790)." Ph.D. dissertation, The University of Tübingen, 1982; published edition, Kassel: Bärenreiter, 1983. Bibliog. [*Rilm* 83-2667.]

> Reviews in *Hv* 22/1 (1985):92 (J. Buzga), *Mf* 39/1 (1986):621 (Ulrich Mazurowicz), *Muh* 35/1 (1984):43 (F. W. D.), *Musica* 38/4 (1984):368-69 (Christian Möllers), *NZfM* 146/5 (1985):57-58 (Gerhard Schuhmacher), and *ÖM* 40/4 (1985):206 (Elmar Budde).

Budday, Wolfgang. "Über 'Form' und 'Inhalt' in Menuetten Mozarts." *AfMw* 44/1 (1987):58-89.

Buelow, George J. "Symposium on Seventeenth-Century Music: Germany." See Cohen ["National Predilections"] (1972):36-49. Bibliog. [*Rilm* 73-1754.]

Buelow, George J. "Music, Rhetoric, and the Concept of the Affections: A Selective Bibliography." *Notes* 30/2 (1973-74):250-59. Bibliog. [*Rilm* 73-2933.]

Buelow, George J. "The Concept of '*Melodielehre*': A Key to Classic Style." In *Mozart-Jb 1978/79* (1979):182-95. [*Rilm* 79-2621.]

Buelow, George J. "Affections, Doctrine of the." In *NGrove* (1980).

Buelow, George J. "Figures, Doctrine of Musical." In *NGrove* (1980).

Buelow, George J. "Rhetoric and Music." In *NGrove* (1980). Bibliog.

Buelow, George J. "Vocal Ornamentation in the Sacred Music of the Schütz Era." *ACR* 24/2-3 (1982):5-13. [*Rilm* 82-2299.]

Buelow, George J. "Teaching Seventeenth-Century Concepts of Musical Form and Expression: An Aspect of Baroque Music." *CMS* 27 (1987):1-13. Bibliog.

Bujić, Bojan, ed. *Music in European Thought, 1851-1912.* CRLM. Cambridge: Cambridge University Press, 1988.

Bukofzer, Manfred. *Music in the Baroque Era from Monteverdi to Bach.* New York: W. W. Norton, 1947.

> Reviews in *JAAC* 7/3 (1948-49):262-64 (Glen Haydon), *ML* 30/1 (1949):64-66 (Robert Donington), *MQ* 34/3 (1948):435-39 (G. S. Dickinson), *MR* 10/1 (1949):57-59 (Edward J. Dent), *MT* 90/1276 (1949):191-92 (Ivor Keys), *Musica* 4/4 (1950):157-58 (Werner Bollert), *Notes* 5/2 (1947-48):224-25 (Otto Kinkeldey), and *Rmi* 52/3 (1950):276 (A. Della Corte).

Bullivant, Roger. "Fugue." In *NGrove* (1980). Bibliog.

Burde, Wolfgang. "Versuch über Mozart-Interpretation." *ZfMt* 7/1 (1976):22-29. [*Rilm* 77-1477.]

Burdick, Michael Francis. "A Structural Analysis of Melodic Scale-Degree Tendencies in Selected Themes of Haydn, Mozart, Schubert, and Chopin." Ph.D. dissertation, Indiana University, 1977. [*Rilm* 77-1556. *DA* 38/04A, p. 1724. UMI 77-22643.]

Burdick, Michael Francis. "Some Nineteenth-Century Precedents of the *Stufe* Concept." *ITR* 1/1 (1977-78):23-30.

Burke, James Robert. "A Study of Theories of Non-Chord Tones Pertaining to the Music of the Period *c.* 1650 to *c.* 1875." Ph.D. dissertation, Indiana University, 1963. [*DA* 24/12, p. 5347. UMI 64-5443.]

Burlas, Ladislav. "Priekopníci sovietskej estetiky hudby." [Pioneers of the Soviet Aesthetics of Music.] *Rytmus* 6/4, 6, 8 (1974):6, 3-4, 5. [*Rilm* 75-2952.]

Burney, Charles. *A General History of Music, from the Earliest Ages to the Present Period.* 4 vols. London: the author (T. Becket, G. Robinson, J. Robson), 1776-89 [LCPS: B-056a and B-056b. HoM: 280.]; reprint edition (edited by Frank Mercer in 2 vols.), London: G. T. Foulis; New York: Harcourt, Brace, 1935; New York: Dover, 1957; Baden-Baden: Heitz Limited, 1958.

> Reviews in *ChG* 11/9 (1958-59):34, *JR* 6/1 (1958-59):23-24 (Bennet Ludden), *LonM* 33/194 (1935-36):264, *MCM* 37/4 (1957-58):19, 36, *MC* 157/4 (1958):37 (Harold C. Schonberg), *ML* 17/2 (1936):158 (Scott Goddard), *ML* 39/3 (1958):296-97 (Eric Blom), *OpN* 23/15 (1958-59):24 (Douglas A. Mackinnon), *Scrut* 4/4 (1935-36):425-31 (Bruce Pattison), and *VV* 19/2 (1958):77 (Samuel and Sada Applebaum).

Burton, Martin C. "Changing Concepts of Rhythm in English Musical Writings, 1500-1740." Ph.D. dissertation, The University of Rochester, 1956.

Busch, Regina. "Die vergessene Musik: Über nicht-professionelle Komponisten." *Musica* 34/5 (1980):470-73. [*Rilm* 80-5601.]

Bush, Helen Evelyn. "The Emergence of the Chordal Concept in the Polyphonic Period." Ph.D. dissertation, Cornell University, 1939.

Bush, Helen E. "The Recognition of Chordal Formation by Early Music Theorists." *MQ* 32/2 (1946):227-43.

Butler, Gregory Gordon. "The Canonic Sequence in Theory and Practice: A Rhetorical-Musical Study of Its Origins and Development in Keyboard Music to 1750." Ph.D. dissertation, The University of Toronto, 1973. [*Rilm* 75-398. *DA* 35/02A, p. 1140.]

Butler, Gregory G. "Fugue and Rhetoric." *JMT* 21/1 (1977):49-109. [*Rilm* 77-3677.]

Butler, Gregory G. "Music and Rhetoric in Early Seventeenth-Century English Sources." *MQ* 66/1 (1980):53-64. Bibliog. [*Rilm* 80-429.]

Butler, Gregory G. "The Projection of Affect in Baroque Dance Music." *EM* 12/2 (1984):200-207.

Byrt, John. "*Notes Inégales* — Some Misconceptions?" *JAMS* 20/3 (1967):476-80. [*Rilm* 67-2278.]

C

Cahn, Peter. "Repercussio." In *HwmT* (1972-). Bibliog.

Cahn, Peter. "Retardatio, ritardando." In *HwmT* (1972-). Bibliog.

Cahn, Peter. "Transitus." In *HwmT* (1972-). Bibliog.

Cahn, Peter. "Zu einigen Aspekten des Materialdenkens in der Musik des 20. Jahrhunderts." *HindJb 1980* 11 (1982):193-205. [*Rilm* 82-3845.]

Callenberg, Eitel-Friedrich. "Das obersächsische Barocklied: Wort und Ton in der Musiklehre des 17. Jahrhunderts." Ph.D. dissertation, The University of Freiburg im Breisgau, 1952.

Cannon, John T., and Dostrovsky, Sigalia. *The Evolution of Dynamics: Vibration Theory from 1687 to 1742.* SHMPS, no. 6. New York: Springer-Verlag, 1981. Bibliog.

Review in *BJHS* 17/2 (1984):234 (Jeremy Gray).

Caplin, William Earl. "Der Akzent des Anfangs: Zur Theorie des musikalischen Taktes." *ZfMt* 9/1 (1978):17-28. [*Rilm* 78-1759.]

Caplin, William Earl. "Theories of Harmonic-Metric Relationships from Rameau to Riemann." Ph.D. dissertation, The University of Chicago, 1981. Bibliog. [*Rilm* 81-1646. *DA* 42/11A, p. 4638. UMI 05-36664.]

Caplin, William. "Tonal Function and Metrical Accent: A Historical Perspective." *MTS* 5 (1983):1-14.

Carey, C. E. "A Study of Two Theoretical Treatises Published in 1636." Master's thesis, The Ohio State University, 1959.

Carpenter, Ellon DeGrief. "The Theory of Music in Russia and the Soviet Union, ca. 1650-1950." Ph.D. dissertation, The University of Pennsylvania, 1988. [*DA* 49/09A, p. 2441. UMI 88-24722.]

Carpenter, Nan Cooke. "The Study of Music at the University of Oxford in the Renaissance (1450-1600)." *MQ* 41/2 (1955):191-214.

Carr, Dale C. "A Practical Introduction to Unequal Temperament." *Diapason* 65/3 (1974):6-8. [*Rilm* 74-3871.]

Carse, Adam von Ahn. *The History of Orchestration*. London: Kegan Paul, Trench, Trubner & Co.; New York: Dutton, 1925; reprint edition, New York: Dover Publications, [1964].

Reviews in *AMT* 15/1 (1965-66):42 (Joseph G. Beck), *AR* 8/2 (1967):67 (Martin Davidson), *MiE* 29/313 (1965):140-41, *ML* 6/4 (1925):377 (F. Bonavia), *MO* 89/1065 (1965-66):543 (B. R.), *MR* 30/3 (1969):248-49 (Peter J. Pirie), *MuMus* 13/9 (1964-65):52 (Stephen Dodgson), *NZfM* 127/12 (1966):506 (G. A. Trumpff), and *Zvuk* 89 (1968):597-98 (Ivo Supičič).

Castellani, Marcello. "The Italian Sonata for Transverse Flute and Basso Continuo." *GSJ* 29 (1976):2-10.

Cavallini, Edoardo. "Ritorno al dualismo armonico?" *Rmi* 51/2 (1949):162-66.

Cavett-Dunsby, Esther. "Mozart's Codas." *MA* 7/1 (1988): 31-51.

Cazden, Norman. "Musical Consonance and Dissonance." 2 vols. Ph.D. dissertation, Harvard University, 1948. Bibliog.

Cazden, Norman. "Sensory Theories of Musical Consonance." *JAAC* 20/3 (1961-62):301-19.

Comment in *JAAC* 21/2 (1962-63):211-12 (Walter J. Hipple, Jr.) [Reply in *JAAC* 21/2 (1962-63):212-15 (Norman Cazden)].

Cazden, Norman. "The Definition of Consonance and Dissonance." *IRASM* 11/2 (1980):123-68. [*Rilm* 80-5849.]

Černý, Miroslav K. "Předpoklady interpretace sémantických aspektu hudebních forem, jmenovitě formy sonátové." [Premises for Interpreting the Semantic Aspects of Musical Art Forms, with Particular Reference to Sonata Form.] *Estetika* 13/4 (1976):254-70. [*Rilm* 76-7163.]

Chafe, Eric. "Key Structure and Tonal Allegory in the Passions of J. S. Bach: An Introduction." *CM* 31 (1981):39-54. [*Rilm* 81-402.]

Chafe, Eric. "J. S. Bach's *St. Matthew Passion*: Aspects of Planning, Structure, and Chronology." *JAMS* 35/1 (1982): 49-114. [*Rilm* 82-362.]

Chailley, Jacques. *Expliquer l'harmonie?* CHim, no. 16. Lausanne: Éditions rencontre Lausanne et la Guilde du disque, 1967. [*Rilm* 67-1191.]

Reviews in *Jmf* 159-60 (1967):49 (René Dumesnil), *JMT* 12/1 (1968):119-59 (Norman Cazden), *Mf* 21/3 (1968):380 (Ernst Tittel), and *MT* 109/1501 (1968):242 (Peter Williams).

Chenette, Louis Fred. "Music Theory in the British Isles during the Enlightenment." Ph.D. dissertation, The Ohio State University, 1967. Bibliog. [*Rilm* 67-1177. *DA* 28/09A, p. 3696. UMI 68-02965.]

Chernin, Mallorie. "A Practical Application of an Eighteenth-Century Aesthetic: The Development of Pestalozzian Education." *CMS* 26 (1986):53-65. Bibliog.

Chesnut, John. "Mozart as a Teacher of Elementary Musical Theory." Ph.D. dissertation, The University of Chicago, 1976. 2 vols. [*Rilm* 76-9949. *DA* 37/09A, p. 5427.]

Chevaillier, Lucien. "Les théories harmoniques." In *Encyclopédie de la musique et dictionnaire du Conservatoire. Deuxième partie: Technique, esthétique et pédagogie*, edited by A. J. A. Lavignac and L. de La Laurencie, vol. 1, pp. 519-90. Paris: C. Delagrave, 1925; as *Istoriia uchenii o garmonii* [History of the Study of Harmony] (translated by Z. Potagova and V. Taranushchenko, edited by I. V. Ivanov-Boretsky), Moscow: 1931-32.

Review in *Pmuz* /8 (1931):39-43 (Iosif Ryzhkin). See also RAMEAU: Ryzhkin (1933); RIEMANN: Mazel (1934); and LITERATURE SUPPLEMENT: Ryzhkin (1933).

Chew, Geoffrey. "Notation: System or Symbol? Notes on Some Recent Books." *MT* 120/1640 (1979):819-20. [*Rilm* 79-5591.]

Chew, Geoffrey. "Notation [Western, from 1500]." In *NGrove* (1980). Bibliog.

Chew, Geoffrey. "The Spice of Music: Towards a Theory of the Leading Note." *MA* 2/1 (1983):35-53.

Chiba, Junnosuke. "Ju-hachi seiki Deutsch no ensoron kenkyu: J. J. Quantz, E. Bach, Leopold Mozart no chosho no hikakukento." M.A. thesis, Musaschino Academy of Music, 1976. [*Rilm* 76-3958.]

Chilesotti, Oscar. "Di Nicola Vicentino e dei generi greci secondo Vincenzo Galilei." *Rmi* 19/3 (1912):546-65.

Chominski, Józef Michal. *Dějiny [Historia] harmonii i kontrapunktu.* Cracow: Polskie Wydawnictwo Muzyczne, 1958 (Vol. 1); 1962 (Vol. 2; Bibliog.); Vol. 3 forthcoming; as *"History of Harmony and Counterpoint, Volume II: The Renaissance* by Jozef M. Chominski: A Translation, Evaluation, and Critique" (translated by Joseph Martin Krush), Ph.D. dissertation, Michigan State University, 1981. [*Rilm* 81-2415. *DA* 42/12A, p. 4969. UMI 82-12414.]).

> Reviews in *Hroz* 12/22 (1959):937 (Jaroslav Vanicky) and *Rmuz* 7/3 (1963):21-22 (Bohdan Pociej).

Chybinski, Adolf. "Die deutschen Musiktheoretiker im 16.-18. Jahrhundert und die polnische Musik." *ZIMG* 13/2 (1911-12):56-65.

Clermont, Susan J. "A Critical Survey of German Theoretical Concepts of Chromaticism from 1895 to 1915." Ph.D. dissertation, Boston University, forthcoming.

Cobb, Gerard F. "On Certain Principles of Musical Exposition Considered Educationally, and with Special Reference to Current Systems of Musical Theory." *PMA 1883-84* 10 (1884):125-84.

Cohen, Albert. "Survivals of Renaissance Thought in French Theory 1610-1670: A Bibliographical Study." In *ReeseFs* (1966/1978):82-95. Bibliog.

Cohen, Albert. *"La Supposition* and the Changing Concept of Dissonance in Baroque Theory." *JAMS* 24/1 (1971):63-84. Bibliog. [*Rilm* 71-412.]

> See Babitz and Pont (1973).

Cohen, Albert, ed. "National Predilections in Seventeenth-Century Music Theory: A Symposium." *JMT* 16/1-2 (1972):2-71. Bibliog.

Cohen, Albert. "Symposium on Seventeenth-Century Music Theory: France." See Cohen ["National Predilections"] (1972):16-35. Bibliog. [*Rilm* 73-1194.]

Cohen, Albert. "Music in the French Scientific Academy before the Revolution." *SFrR* 1/1 (1977):29-37.

Cohen, Albert. *Music in the French Royal Academy of Sciences: A Study in the Evolution of Musical Thought.* Princeton, N.J.: Princeton University Press, 1981. Bibliog. [*Rilm* 81-2462.]

> Reviews in *AHR* 87/4 (1982):1102-3 (Robert M. Isherwood), *AS* 40/5 (1983):517-18 (Penelope M. Gouk), *JMH* 56/3 (1984):512-15 (Howard Mayer Brown), *JMT* 27/1 (1983):135-40 (Cynthia Verba), *Mf* 38/2 (1985):139-40 (Herbert Schneider), *ML* 63/3-4 (1982):314-16 (Penelope Gouk), *Notes* 39/2 (1982-83):358-59 (Nathan A. Randall), and *Rdm* 69/1 (1983):116-17 (Florence Getreau).

Cohen, Albert. "The Performance of French Baroque Music: A Report on the State of Current Research." *PPrR* 1/1-2 (1988):10-24. Bibliog.

Cohen, Albert, and Miller, Leta E. *Music in the Paris Academy of Sciences, 1666-1793: An Index.* DSMB, no. 43. Detroit: Information Coordinators, 1979. Bibliog.

> Reviews in *ANQ* 18/4 (1979):63, *ARBA* 11 (1980):434 (Robert Skinner), *Fam* 29/3 (1982):149 (Catherine Massip), *MR* 45/2 (1984):149-50 (Leonard Duck), and *MT* 122/1664 (1981):675-76 (Richard Andrews).

Cohen, H. Floris. *Quantifying Music: The Science of Music at the First Stage of the Scientific Revolution, 1580-1650.* UWOSPS, no. 23. Dordrecht, Boston, and Lancaster: D. Reidel, 1984.

> Reviews in *AS* 42/4 (1985):446-47 (Paolo Gozza), *BJHS* 18/3 (1985):369-71 (Penelope M. Gouk), *Isis* 76/283 (1985):444-45 (Albert Cohen), *JMT* 29/2 (1985):328-35 (Jamie C. Kassler), *Mf* 39/3 (1986):290-91 (Helga de la Motte-Haber), *ML* 66/3 (1985):289-92 (Michael Fend), *Rdm* 73/2 (1987):273-77 (Patrice Bailhache), *TLS* 83/4264 (1984):1469 (Brian Pippard), and *TvNm* 34/2 (1984):183-86 (Rudolf Rasch).

Cohen, Henry. "Les traités de contrepoint et de fugue au dix-neuvième siècle." *Chmus* 1/2 (1873):126-33; 2/3 (1874):16-21.

Cole, Malcolm S. "Sonata-Rondo, The Formulation of a Theoretical Concept in the Eighteenth and Nineteenth Centuries." *MQ* 55/2 (1969):180-92. [*Rilm* 69-1036.]

Cole, Malcolm S. " 'Back to the Land': Performance Practice and the Classic Period." *PPrR* 1/1-2 (1988):25-41.

Čolič, Dragutin. *Razvoj teorije harmonskog mišljenja od modalnog višeglasja do proširenog dursko-molskog tonaliteta.* Belgrade: Univerzitet Umetnosti, 1976. [*Rilm* 76-15398.]

Colles, H. C. "Some Musical Instruction Books of the Seventeenth Century." *PMA 1928-29* 55 (1929):31-49.

Collet, Henri. "Contribution à l'étude des théoriciens espagnols de la musique au XVIe siècle." *Annm* 2 (1912):1-63.

Collins, Michael Bruce. "The Performance of Coloration, Sesquialtera, and Hemiola (1450-1750)." Ph.D. dissertation, Stanford University, 1963. Bibliog. [*DA* 24/08, p. 3364. UMI 64-1598.]

> Review in *CM* 5 (1967):123-28 (Arthur Hills) [Reply in *CM* 5 (1967):128-30 (Michael Collins)].

Collins, Michael B. "The Performance of Sesquialtera and Hemiola in the Sixteenth Century." *JAMS* 17/1 (1964):5-28.

Collins, Michael. "The Performance of Triplets in the Seventeenth and Eighteenth Centuries." *JAMS* 19/3 (1966):281-328.

Collins, Michael. "*Notes Inégales*: A Re-examination." *JAMS* 20/3 (1967):481-85. [*Rilm* 67-2280.]

Collins, Michael. "A Reconsideration of French Over-Dotting." *ML* 50/1 (1969):111-23. [*Rilm* 69-2670.]

> Responses in *ML* 50/3 (1969):430-32 (Frederick Neumann and Sol Babitz).

Collins, Michael. "In Defense of the French Trill." *JAMS* 26/3 (1973):405-39. [*Rilm* 73-4279.]

Colucci, Matthew Joseph. "A Comparative Study of Contemporary Musical Theories in Selected Writings of Piston, Krenek and Hindemith." Ph.D. dissertation, The University of Pennsylvania, 1957. Bibliog. [*DA* 17/11, p. 2628. UMI 00-23583.]

Conley, Joyce. "A Comparison of the Theoretical Systems of G. Weber and H. Riemann in Analyses of Chopin's Prelude in E Minor, Op. 28, No. 4." *JGMSOSU* 6 (1977):35-46.

Constantini, Franz-Peter. " 'Hymnentypus' und Kirchentonarten." In *SchenkFs* (1975):132-43. [*Rilm* 76-5323.]

Cook, Nicholas. *A Guide to Musical Analysis*. London: J. M. Dent & Sons; New York: George Brazillier 1987.

> Reviews in *Brio* 24/1 (1987):38-39 (John Wagstaff), *JMT* 32/1 (1988):148-58 (Matthew G. Brown and Douglas J. Dempster), *JMTP* 2/2 (1988):297-310 (Michael R. Rogers), *MEJ* 74/1 (1987):13-14 (Thomas Janson), *ML* 68/4 (1987):375-77 (V. Kofi Agawu), *MR* 47/2 (1986-87):128-30 (Arnold Whittall), *MT* 129/1741 (1988):81-82 (William Drabkin), *Tempo* 163 (1987):31-33 (Malcolm Miller), and *TLS* 87/4425 (1988):89 (Christopher Wintle).

Cooper, Martin, ed. *The Modern Age (1890-1960)*. NOHM, vol. 10. London: Oxford University Press, 1974. Bibliog.

> Reviews in *AJME* 18 (1976):70-71 (David Symons), *ARBA* 6 (1975):500 (Guy A. Marco), *Choice* 12/3 (1975-76):403, *Clavier* 13/8 (1974): 6, *Composer* 56 (1975-76):39 (John Michael East), *Éc* 43/3 (1975):299-300 (J. Legrand), *JAMS* 29/1 (1976):153-56 (Peter S. Odegard), *JMT* 20/1 (1976):138-47 (Joel Mandelbaum), *MEJ* 62/3 (1975-76):77-779 (Truman Bullard), *Melos/NZfM* 2/5 (1976):418-19 (Carl Dahlhaus),

> *Miscm* 9 (1977):212-17 (Andrew D. McCredie), *ML* 56/2 (1975):197-202 (Arnold Whittall), *MT* 116/1583 (1975):38-40 (Paul Griffiths), *NW* 6 (1974):73, *ÖM* 31/4-5 (1976):252-54 (Rudolf Klein), *OpN* 39/5 (1974-75):8 (Ethan C. Mordden), *RmC* 30/133 (1976):72-74, *SchM* 46/2 (1974-75):19-20, *Stfm* 57/2 (1975):76-77 (Gunnar Bucht), *Tempo* 112 (1975):36 (Christopher Norris), *TLS* 73/3796 (1974):1395 (Robin Maconie), and *VQR* 51 (1975):xxvii-xxviii.

Coover, James B. "Music Theory in Translation: A Bibliography." *JMT* 3/1 (1959):70-96; 13/2 (1969):230-48.

Coover, James B. "Dictionaries and Encyclopedias of Music." In *NGrove* (1980). Bibliog.

Cotte, Roger. "La musique dans l'Encyclopédie." *Vmus* 9 (1951):5-6.

Cowart, Georgia. "Critical Language and Musical Thought in the Seventeenth and Eighteenth Centuries." *CMS* 27 (1987):14-29. Bibliog.

Cowart, Georgia, ed. *French Musical Thought, 1600-1800*. SiM, no. 105. Ann Arbor, Mich.: UMI Research Press, 1989. Bibliog.

Cowart, Georgia. "Inventing the Arts: Changing Critical Language in the Ancien Régime." In Cowart [*French*] (1989):211-38. Bibliog.

Crocker, Richard L. "Discant, Counterpoint, and Harmony." *JAMS* 15/1 (1962):1-21. Bibliog.

Crocker, Richard L. *A History of Musical Style*. New York: McGraw-Hill, 1966.

> Reviews in *ACR* 9/1 (1966):12-13 (Martin Picker), *AJME* 4 (1969):69, *Choice* 3/12 (1966-67):1134, *Clavier* 6/6 (1967):8, *Instrumentalist* 21/11 (1966-67):26, *JAMS* 21/1 (1968):103-5 (Henry Leland Clarke), *JMT* 11/1 (1967):144-49 (James Pruett), *JRME* 15/4 (1967):333-36 (Gwynn S. McPeek), *Notes* 23/4 (1966-67):732-33 (Martin Chusid), *PNM* 7/2 (1968-69):36ff. (Leo Treitler), and *Zvuk* 89 (1968):596-97 (Ivo Supičič).

Crombie, A. C. "Mathematics, Music and Medical Science." *Organon* 6 (1969):21-36. Bibliog.

D

Dadelsen, Georg von. "Das Märchen von der grauen Theorie: Retardierende und anregende Kräfte der Musiktheorie in Geschichte und Gegenwart." In *Bericht Musiktheorie* (1972):49-63.

Dahlhaus, Carl. "Konsonanz-Dissonanz [historisch und systematisch]." In *MGG* (1949-68). Bibliog.

Dahlhaus, Carl. "Tonalität [systematik]." In *MGG* (1949-68). Bibliog.

Dahlhaus, Carl. "Tonsysteme." In *MGG* (1949-68). Bibliog.

Dahlhaus, Carl. "Der Dreiklang als Symbol." *MK* 25/5 (1955):251-52.

Dahlhaus, Carl. "Die Termini Dur und Moll." *AfMw* 12/4 (1955):280-96.

Dahlhaus, Carl. "Zur Theory des Tactus im 16. Jahrhundert." *AfMw* 17/1 (1960):22-39.

Dahlhaus, Carl. "Zur Entstehung des modernen Taktsystems im 17. Jahrhundert." *AfMw* 18/3-4 (1961):223-40. Bibliog.

Dahlhaus, Carl. "Zur Theorie des klassischen Kontrapunkts." *KJb* 45 (1961):43-57.

Dahlhaus, Carl. "Über den Begriff der tonalen Funktion." See Vogel (1966):93-102.

Dahlhaus, Carl. "Untersuchungen über die Entstehung der harmonischen Tonalität." Habilitationsschrift, The University of Kiel, 1966; published edition (SSzMw, no. 2), Kassel: Bärenreiter, 1968; reprint edition, 1988; English translation (by Robert Gjerdingen), forthcoming. Bibliog. [*Rilm* 68-1180.]

> Reviews in *MK* 40/2 (1970):124, *Muh* 20/3 (1969):148, and *Musica* 23/3 (1969):283-84 (Lothar Hoffmann-Erbrecht).

Dahlhaus, Carl. "Gefühlsästhetik und musikalische Formenlehre." *DVLG* 41/4 (1967):505-16. [*Rilm* 68-4178.]

Dahlhaus, Carl. *Analyse und Werturteil.* MpFL, no. 8. Mainz: Schott, 1970; as *Analysis and Value Judgment* (translated by Sigmund Levarie; MiM, no. 1), New York: Pendragon Press, 1983. [*Rilm* 70-4112.]

> Reviews in *MB* 6/6 (1974):395-96 (Siegfried Borris), *Mf* 25/3 (1972):379-80 (Gottfried Küntzel), *MT* 125/1702 (1984):704 (William Drabkin), *Muh* 22/2 (1971):100 (F. W. D.), *Musica* 25/3 (1971):294 (Heinz Antholz), *NMZmJD* 20/5 (1971):13 (Norbert Linke), and *Notes* 40/2 (1983-84):281-83 (Eric Werner).

Dahlhaus, Carl. "Über einige theoretische Voraussetzungen der musikalischen Analyse." In *Bericht Musiktheorie* (1972):153-76.

Dahlhaus, Carl. "Relationes harmonicae." *AfMw* 32/3 (1975):208-27. [*Rilm* 76-7135.]

Dahlhaus, Carl. "Some Models of Unity in Musical Form." Translated by Charlotte Carroll Prather. *JMT* 19/1 (1975):2-30; German version (as "Zur Theorie der musikalischen Form") in *AfMw* 34/1 (1977):20-37. [*Rilm* 76-15454 and 77-1576.]

Dahlhaus, Carl. "Neue Musik und 'reine Stimmung'." *Melos/NZfM* 2/2 (1976):115-17.

Dahlhaus, Carl. "Zur Tonartenlehre des 16. Jahrhunderts: Eine Duplik." *Mf* 29/3 (1976):300-303. [*Rilm* 76-5178.]

Dahlhaus, Carl. "Satz und Period: Zur Theorie der musikalischen Syntax." *ZfMt* 9/2 (1978):16-26. [*Rilm* 78-6088.]

Dahlhaus, Carl. "Geschichte als Problem der Musiktheorie: 1600." Über einige Berliner Musiktheoretiker des 19. Jahrhunderts." In Dahlhaus [*Studien*] (1980):405-13. [*Rilm* 80-4682.]

Dahlhaus, Carl. "Harmony." In *NGrove* (1980). Bibliog.

> See Wintle (1982). Review in *MQ* 68/2 (1982):161-81 (Allen Forte).

Dahlhaus, Carl, ed. *Studien zur Musikgeschichte Berlins im frühen 19. Jahrhundert.* SMg, no. 56. Regensburg: Boße, 1980.

Dahlhaus, Carl. "Tonality." In *NGrove* (1980).

> See Wintle (1982). Review in *MQ* 68/2 (1982):161-81 (Allen Forte).

Dahlhaus, Carl. "Über das System der musiktheoretischen Disziplinen im klassisch-romantischen Zeitalter." In *HüschenFs* (1980):76-81. [*Rilm* 80-3748.]

Dahlhaus, Carl. "Studien zur Geschichte der Rhythmustheorie." *JSIM* 1979/80 (1981):133-53. [*Rilm* 81-1648.]

Dahlhaus, Carl. "Hindemiths Theorie des Sekundgangs und das Problem der Melodielehre." *HindJb* 1982 11 (1983):114-25. [*Rilm* 83-1612.]

Dahlhaus, Carl. "Tonalität und Form in Wagners *Ring des Nibelungen*." *AfMw* 40/3 (1983):165-73.

Dahlhaus, Carl. *Die Musiktheorie im 18. und 19. Jahrhundert; Erster Teil: Grundzüge einer Systematik.* GMt, no. 10. Darmstadt: Wissenschaftliche Buchgesellschaft, 1984.

> Reviews in *JMT* 32/1 (1988):133-47 (Lee Rothfarb), *Me* 39/4 (1985-86):173-74 (Elisabeth Haselauer), *Mf* 39/2 (1986):180-81 (Rudolf Flotzinger), *Mth* 1/1 (1986):102-3 (Peter Cahn), *MTS* 10 (1988):127-37 (Thomas Christensen), *Musica* 39/4 (1985):392 (Peter Cahn), *NZfM* 146/1 (1985):41-42 (Rüdiger Weißbach), *ÖM* 41/7-8 (1986):410-11 (Gerold W. Gruber), and *ZfMp* 10/30 (1985):63-65 (Brunhilde Sonntag).

Dahlhaus, Carl. " 'Quantitas intrinseca' und 'Rhythmus'." In *Analytica: Studies in the Description and Analysis of Music*, edited by Anders Lönn and Erik Kjellberg, pp. 17-24. AUU, new series, no. 10. Uppsala: (Motala: Borgströms Tryckeri), 1985.

Dahlhaus, Carl. "Zur Geschichte der musikalischen Figurenlehre." In *RuhnkeFs* (1986):83-93.

Dahlhaus, Carl. "Zum Taktbegriff der Wiener Klassik." *AfMw* 45/1 (1988):1-15.

Dahlhaus, Carl; Dostrovsky, Sigalia; Cannon, John T.; Lindley, Mark; and Walker, Daniel P. *Hören, Messen und Rechnen in der frühen Neuzeit.* GMt, no. 6. Darmstadt: Wissenschaftliche Buchgesellschaft, 1987. Bibliog.

Dahlhaus, Carl, and Sachs, Klaus-Jürgen. "Counterpoint." In *NGrove* (1980). Bibliog.

> See Wintle (1982). Review in *MQ* 68/2 (1982):161-81 (Allen Forte).

Dammann, Rolf. "Die Struktur des Musikbegriffs im deutschen Barock." Habilitationsschrift, The University of Freiburg im Breisgau, 1958; published edition (as *Der Musikbegriff im deutschen Barock*), Cologne: Volk, 1967. Bibliog. [*Rilm* 68-3213.]

Reviews in *Fam* 16/1-2 (1969):74-76 (Dragotin Cvetko), *MB* 3/1 [62] (1971):47 (Carl Dahlhaus), *MK* 58/4 (1988):207-8, *MQ* 55/2 (1969):246-55 (Paul Henry Lang), *Musica* 23/1 (1969):62-63 (Lothar Hoffmann-Erbrecht), *Notes* 26/1 (1969-70):33-34 (Carol MacClintock), and *Rdm* 54/1 (1968):117-19 (D. Launay).

Damschroder, David Allen. "A Bibliography of Fugal Treatises: 1800-1920 (with Emphasis on German Works)." Ms., 1975. [Rochester, N.Y.: Sibley Music Library, Eastman School of Music.] Bibliog.

David, Hans T. "Mozartean Modulations." *MQ* 42/2 (1956):193-212.

David, Hans T., and Mendel, Arthur, eds. *The Bach Reader: A Life of Johann Sebastian Bach in Letters and Documents*. New York: W. W. Norton, 1945; 1966.

Reviews in *AR* 10/3 (1969):83 (Martin Davidson), *CMS* 7 (1967):149 (Martin Chusid), *Composer* 25 (1967):31 (Francis Cameron), *ML* 48/2 (1967):155 (J. A. Westrup), *MR* 29/1 (1968):52-53 (Hans F. Redlich), *MT* 108/1491 (1967):424-25 (Walter Emery), *MCM* 46/5 (1966-67):55 (Quaintance Eaton), *Notes* 3/1 (1945-46):40-41 (Erich Hertzmann), and *PP* 60/1 (1967-68):44-45 (Melva Peterson).

Davidsson, Åke. *Catalogue critique et descriptif des ouvrages théoriques sur la musique imprimés au XVIᵉ et au XVIIᵉ siècles et conservés dans les bibliothèques suédoises.* SmU, no. 2. Upsala: Almquist & Wiksells, 1953.

Reviews in *Mf* 7/4 (1954):480-81 (Hans Albrecht), *ML* 35/1 (1954):67 (A. H. K.), *MQ* 41/1 (1955):107-9 (Dragan Plamenac), *MR* 14/3 (1953):236, *Notes* 11/3 (1953-54):476-77 (Catherine Brooks), and *Stfm* 35 (1953):164 (Åke Vretblad).

Davidsson, Åke. *Bibliographie der musiktheoretischen Drucke des 16. Jahrhunderts.* BbA, no. 9. Baden-Baden: Heitz, 1962.

Reviews in *LQ* 33/2 (1963):221-22 (Guy A. Marco), *Mf* 19/1 (1966):72-74 (Klaus Wolfgang Niemöller), *MR* 26/1 (1965):67-68, *Notes* 20/2 (1962-63):234 (Fred Blum), and *Rdm* 49/[126] (1963):123-24 (F. Lesure).

Dean, Winton. "The Performance of Recitative in Late Baroque Opera." *ML* 58/4 (1977):389-402. [*Rilm* 77-5662.]

DeFotis, William. "Rehearings: Mozart, Quartet in C, K. 465." *NCM* 6/1 (1982-83):31-38. [*Rilm* 82-3593.]

Dekker, Gerard. "Stemmingssystemen voor orgels en andere toetseninstrumenten." *Greg* 103/1 (1979):10-20. [*Rilm* 79-1473.]

Derksen, John Henry. "*De Imitatione*: The Function of Rhetoric in German Musical Theory and Practice (1550-1606)." Ph.D. dissertation, The University of Toronto, 1982. [*DA* 44/03A, p. 606.]

Derr, Ellwood. "Concertante Passages in Keyboard Realizations in Handel: Some Guidelines." *Diapason* 76/9 [910] (1985):9-12.

Deutsch, Diana. "Music Perception." *MQ* 66/2 (1980):165-79. [*Rilm* 80-4042.]

Devore, Richard O. "Theories of Harmony in the United States to 1900." Master's thesis, The University of Iowa, 1982.

Devore, Richard. "Nineteenth-Century Harmonic Dualism in the United States." *Theoria* 2 (1987):85-100.

de Zeeuw, Anne Marie. "Tonality and the Concertos of William Walton." Ph.D. dissertation, The University of Texas at Austin, 1983. [*DA* 45/03A, p. 677. UMI 84-14357.]

Diderot, Denis. *Mémoires sur différens sujets de mathématiques.* Paris: Durand, 1748; later editions, including *Œuvres complètes de Diderot*, Vol. 9, edited by J. Assézat and M. Tourneux (Paris: Garnier, 1875-77).

Review in *Corlit* 1 (1753) (Raynal).

Dill, Charles. "Music, Beauty, and the Paradox of Rationalism." In Cowart [*French*] (1989):197-210.

Dixon, Gail Susan. "Concepts of Pitch Organization from 1900 to 1950: A Summary and Comparison of the Writings of Selected Western Theorists." Ph.D. dissertation, The University of Toronto, 1978. [*Rilm* 78-4011. *DA* 40/02A, p. 524.]

Dolmetsch, Arnold. *The Interpretation of the Music of the Seventeenth and Eighteenth Centuries Revealed by Contemporary Evidence.* Hfm. London: Novello; New York: Gray, 1915; revised edition, London: Novello, 1946; reprint of the 1946 edition (with an Introduction by R. Alec Harman), Seattle: University of Washington Press, 1969.

Reviews in *AR* 10/3 (1969):93 (Dale Higbee), *Instrumentalist* 24/1 (1969-70):16, *ML* 25/4 (1944):246-47 (Dorothy Swainson), *MR* 5/4 (1944):262 (E. J. Wellesz), *MT* 56/874 (1915):724-26, *Rmi* 50/2 (1948):179-83 (Federico Ghisi), and *Scrut* 13/3 (1945-46):238-39 (W. H. Mellers).

Donà, Mariangela. " 'Affetti musicali' nel Seicento." *Stusec* 8 (1967):75-94. Bibliog. [*Rilm* 68-322.]

Donahue, W. H. "The Dissolution of the Celestial Spheres, 1595-1650." Ph.D. dissertation, Cambridge University, forthcoming.

Donington, Robert. *The Interpretation of Early Music.* London: Faber & Faber, 1963; 2nd edition, 1965; 3rd edition, 1974. Bibliog.

Reviews in *AJME* 16 (1975):61 (Margaret Seares), *AMT* 24/5 (1974-75):40-42 (Howard Serwer), *AR* 16/2 (1975):57-58 (Dale Higbee), *ARG* 31/9 (1964-65):907-10 (Igor Kipnis),

Choice 3/5-6 (1966-67):416, *Choice* 11/11 (1974-75):1646, *CLW* 46/7 (1974-75):309, *Composer* 56 (1976-77):38 (Christopher Stembridge), *Consort* 21 (1964):320-22 (Alan Fen-Taylor), *Economist* 252/6837 (1974):115, *JRME* 14/4 (1966):313-15 (R. M. Longyear), *JVGSA* 2 (1965):49-52 (Wendell Margrave), *LJ* 89/4 (1964):870 (Catharine K. Miller), *LJ* 91/5 (1966):1228 (Guy A. Marco), *MEJ* 53/9 (1966-67):110-13 (Donald M. McCorkle), *MEJ* 62/3 (1975-76):101-2 (William Pepper), *Mf* 20/3 (1967):327-28 (Erwin R. Jacobi), *ML* 44/4 (1963):381-85 (J. A. Westrup), *ML* 56/2 (1975):202-4 (J. A. Westrup), *MO* 90/1069 (1966-67):25 (B. R.), *MO* 112/1336 (1989):142 (Phillip Sommerich), *MR* 36/2 (1975):150-52 (Malcolm Boyd), *MT* 107/1475 (1966):40 (Anthony Miller), *MT* 115/1580 (1974):847-48 (Stanley Sadie), *MuMus* 23/6 [270] (1974-75):36-37 (Davitt Moroney), *MusT* 42/11 (1963):455 (John Tobin), *MusT* 54/3 (1975):33 (John Morehen), *Notes* 22/1 (1965-66):711-14 (Albert Cohen), *Notes* 34/2 (1977-78):351-52 (Gilbert L. Blount), *NS* 66/1711 (1963):947 (O. W. Neighbour), *NZfM* 126/1 (1965):49-50 (Bernhard Hansen), *PQ* 13/49 (1964):26-31 (William S. Newman), *PQ* 23/90 (1975):40-42 (William S. Newman), *Spec* 233/7627 (1974):274 (Richard Luckett), *Stfm* 47 (1965):94-99 (Ingmar Bengtsson), *Strad* 86/1018 (1975):655-56, *Tempo* 66-67 (1963):62-63 (F. Ll. Harrison, *TLS* 62/3224 (1963):1024, and *TLS* 74/3809 (1975):259 (John Eliot Gardiner).

Donington, Robert. "String Playing in Baroque Music." *EM* 5/3 (1977):389-93. [*Rilm* 77-3653.]

Donington, Robert. "Ornaments." In *NGrove* (1980). Bibliog.

Dostrovsky, Sigalia. "The Origins of Vibration Theory: The Scientific Revolution and the Nature of Music." Ph.D. dissertation, Princeton University, 1969. [*DA* 30/11A, p. 4895. UMI 70-08361.]

Dostrovsky, Sigalia. "Early Vibration Theory: Physics and Music in the Seventeenth Century." *AHES* 14/3 (1974-75):169-218.

Dotzauer, Wilfried. "Die kirchenmusikalischen Werke Johann Valentin Rathgebers." Ph.D. dissertation, The University of Erlangen-Nürnberg, 1976. [*Rilm* 76-9600.]

Drabkin, William. "The Beethoven Sonatas." *MT* 126/1706 (1985):216-17, 219-20.

Drake, Stillman. "Renaissance Music and Experimental Science." *JHI* 31/4 (1970):483-500. [*Rilm* 71-309.]

Dreyfus, Lawrence. *Bach's Continuo Group: Players and Practices in His Vocal Works*. SHM, no. 3. Cambridge, Mass.: Harvard University Press, 1987.

Reviews in *Choice* 25/4 (1987):632-33 (J. P. Ambrose) and *JAMS* 41/2 (1988):349-55 (Peter Williams).

Dubovsky, Iosef Ignatevich; Yevseev, Sergei Vasilevich; Sposobin, Igor Vladimirovich; and Sokolov, Vladimir. *Prakticheskii kurs garmonii*. [A Practical Course of Harmony.] 2 vols. Moscow: 1934-35. (First edition only.)

Duchez, Marie-Élisabeth. "La représentation spatio-verticale du caractère musical grave-aigu et l'élaboration de la notion de hauteur de son dans la conscience musicale occidentale." *Am* 51/1 (1979):54-73.

Duckles, Vincent. "Johann Adam Hiller's *Critical Prospectus for a Music Library*." In *GeiringerFs* (1970):177-85. Bibliog. [*Rilm* 71-537.]

Dürr, Walther. "Auftakt und Taktschlag in der Musik um 1600." In *GerstenbergFs* (1964):26-36. Bibliog.

Dürr, Walther. "Lingua e musica: Considerazioni sul madrigale di Luca Marenzio *O dolce anima mia*." *Rmus* 18/4 (1980):46-70. [*Rilm* 80-2610.]

Dürr, Walther, and Gerstenberg, Walter. "Rhythmus, Metrum, Takt." In *MGG* (1949-68). Bibliog.

Dürr, Walther, and **Gerstenberg**, Walter. "Rhythm." In *NGrove* (1980). Bibliog.

Review in *MQ* 68/2 (1982):161-81 (Allen Forte).

Dunning, Albert. "Musica reservata (i)." In *NGrove* (1980). Bibliog.

Dunsby, Jonathan, and Whittall, Arnold. *Music Analysis in Theory and Practice*. London: Faber Music; New Haven, Ct.: Yale University Press, 1988. Bibliog.

Reviews in *Brio* 25/2 (1988) (John Wagstaff), *CMS* 28 (1988):121-29 (Judith Lochhead), *JMTP* 2/2 (1988):297-310 (Michael R. Rogers), *ML* 70/1 (1989):76-78 (Anthony Pople), and *MT* 129/1743 (1988):247-48 (William Drabkin).

Duparcq, Jean-Jacques. "Contribution à l'étude des proportions numériques dans l'œuvre de Jean-Sébastian Bach." *Rm* 301-2 (1977):1-59. [*Rilm* 77-423.]

Dupont, Wilhelm. "Geschichte der musikalischen Temperatur." Ph.D. dissertation, The University of Erlangen, 1933 (1935); published edition, Kassel: Bärenreiter, 1935; reprint edition, Lauffen: Orgelbau-Fachverlag, 1986. Bibliog.

Reviews in *AfMf* 1/1 (1936):125-27 (Georg Schünemann) and *MGot* 42/2 (1988):88.

Dyson, Jeanne Manninen. "Aspects of Sixteenth-Century Musical Theory in Italy." M.A. thesis, Tufts University, 1967. [*Rilm* 67-445.]

Dziebowska, Elzbieta. "Instrumentatsia v nauke kompozytsii v XIX veke." *Muzyka* 21/1 (1976):13-33. [*Rilm* 76-1665.]

E

Eggebrecht, Hans Heinrich. "Studien zur musikalischen Terminologie." In *AWLMA* Year 1955, no. 10, pp. 821-947.

Eggebrecht, Hans Heinrich. "Arten des Generalbasses im frühen und mittleren 17. Jahrhundert." *AfMw* 14/2 (1957):61-82.

Eggebrecht, Hans Heinrich. "Zum Figur-Begriff der Musica poetica." *AfMw* 16/1-2 (1959):57-67. Bibliog.

Eggebrecht, Hans Heinrich. "Musicalisches Denken." *AfMw* 32/3 (1975):228-40. [*Rilm* 76-7533.]

Eimert, Herbert. "Bekenntnis und Methode." *ZfMw* 9/2 (1926-27):95-109.

Einstein, Alfred. *Music in the Romantic Era.* New York: W. W. Norton, 1947.

> Reviews in *JAAC* 6/4 (1948):348-49 (Glen Haydon), *ML* 29/1 (1948):73-75 (Richard Capell), *MQ* 33/4 (1947):570-75 (Frederick W. Sternfeld), *MR* 9/3 (1948):209-10 (Alfred Loewenberg), *Notes* 4/4 (1946-47):461-63 (Richard S. Hill), and *YR* 37/1 (1947-48):168-70 (Richard Donovan).

Eitner, Robert. "Der Generalbass des 18. Jahrhunderts." *MMg* 12/10 (1880):151-54, 159-73.

Eitner, Robert. *Biographisch-Bibliographisches Quellen-Lexikon der Musiker und Musikgelehrten der christlichen Zeitrechnung bis zur Mitte der neunzehnten Jahrhunderts.* 10 vols. Leipzig: Breitkopf & Härtel, 1900-1904; 2nd edition (11 vols.), Graz: Akademische Druck- und Verlagsanstalt, 1959-60. Bibliog.

> Review in *Me* 13/2 (1959-60):125 (Othmar Wessely).

Emig, Sandra. "The Musical Circles of Johann David Heinichen and Johann Mattheson." *JGMSOSU* 6 (1977):24-34.

Ensslin, Hermann. "Die Aufbau des Harmoniesystems." Ph.D. dissertation, The University of Tübingen, 1925.

Erpf, Hermann. "Über Bach-Analysen am Beispiel einer Fuge aus dem Wohltemperierten Klavier." *AfMw* 16/1-2 (1959):70-76; reprinted in Schuhmacher [*Zum musikalischen Analyse*] (1974):25-33. [*Rilm* 74-2275.]

F

Falck, Myron Rudolph. "Seventeenth-Century Contrapuntal Theory in Germany. Part One: A Study of Selected Seventeenth-Century German Contrapuntal Treatises. Part Two: Three Treatises of Christoph Bernhard in Translation." 2 vols. Ph.D. dissertation, The University of Rochester, 1965. [*DA* 27/06A, pp. 1849-50. UMI 66-03810.]

Farbshtein, Aleksandr, ed. *Muzykav sotsialisticheskom obshchestve.* [Music in a Socialist Society.] Leningrad: Muzyka, 1977.

Farmer, Henry George. *A History of Music in Scotland.* London: Hinrichsen Edition, 1947; reprint edition (DCPMRS), New York: Da Capo Press, 1970.

> Reviews in *Choice* 8/2 (1971-72):236, *ML* 29/2 (1948):197-98 (Maurice Lindsay), and *Scrut* 15/4 (1947-48):330-31 (W. H. Mellers).

Federhofer, Hellmut. "Musikalische Form als Ganzheit." Habilitationsschrift, The University of Graz, 1944; published edition (as *Beiträge zur musikalischen Gestaltanalyse*), Graz: Akademische Druck- und Verlagsanstalt, 1950.

> Reviews in *Mf* 5/1 (1952):71-72 (Paul Mies), *ML* 32/2 (1951):177-80 (Mosco Carner), *Muzyka* 31/4 [123] (1986):85-91 (Zbigniew Skowron), and *Notes* 8/4 (1950-51):714 (Charles Warren Fox).

Federhofer, Hellmut. "Zur handschriftlichen Überlieferung der Musiktheorie in Österreich in der zweiter Hälfte des 17. Jahrhunderts." *Mf* 11/3 (1958):264-79

Federhofer, Hellmut. "Ein Salzburger Theoretikerkreis." *Am* 36/2-3 (1964):50-79. Bibliog.

Federhofer, Hellmut. *Musikpflege und Musiker am Grazer Habsburgerhof der Erzherzöge Karl und Ferdinand von Innerösterreich (1564-1619).* Mainz: B. Schott's Söhne, 1967. Bibliog. [*Rilm* 68-1813.]

> Reviews in *MdST* 37-38 (1968):1-3 (Wolfgang Suppan), *Me* 22/1 (1968-69):44-45 (Herwig Knaus), *Mens* 24/4 (1969):124 (M. Z.), *Mf* 23/2 (1970):216-17 (Manfred Schuler), *Muh* 19/5 (1968):246 (D.), *Muzsika* 12 (1969):32, *Notes* 26/1 (1969-70):44 (Edward Swenson), *NZfM* 129/10 (1968):454-55 (Heinrich Sievers), *ÖM* 23/11 (1968):640 (O. W.), and *Rdm* 54/2 (1968):256-57 (Simone Wallon).

Federhofer, Hellmut. "Die Dissonanzbehandlung in Monteverdis Kirchenmusikalischen Werken und die Figurenlehre von Christoph Bernhard." In *Congresso Monteverdi 1968* (1969):435-78. Bibliog.

Federhofer, Hellmut. "Johann Joseph Fux und Johann Mattheson im Urteil Lorenz Christoph Mizlers." In *HusmannFs* (1970):111-23. [*Rilm* 70-3138.]

Federhofer, Hellmut. "*Stylus antiquus* und *modernus* im Verhältnis zum strengen und freien Satz." In *HüschenFs* (1980):112-17. [*Rilm* 80-3749.]

Federhofer, Hellmut. *Akkord und Stimmführung in den musiktheoretischen Systemen von Hugo Riemann, Ernst Kurth und Heinrich Schenker.* VdKfM, no. 21. Vienna: Österreichischen Akademie der Wissenschaft, 1981. Bibliog. [*Rilm* 81-1657.]

> Reviews in *JMT* 27/1 (1983):99-110 (David Neumeyer), *MA* 2/1 (1983):102-5 (William Drabkin), *Mf* 39/4 (1986):383-85 (Peter Rummenhöller), *MTS* 4 (1982):131-37 (John Rothgeb), *NMZmJD* 33 (1984):39 (Karl-Otto Plum), *Notes* 38/4 (1981-82):843-44 (Channan Willner), and *Stfm* 64 (1982):84-86 (Ingmar Bengtsson). See also SCHENKER: Dahlhaus (1983).

Federhofer, Hellmut. *Musikwissenschaft und Musikpraxis.* FLV, no. 2. Vienna, Cologne, and Graz: Hermann Böhlaus Nachf., 1985. Bibliog.

> Review in *ÖM* 42/2-3 (1987):132-33 (Hartmut Krones).

Federhofer, Hellmut. "Methoden der Analyse im Vergleich." *Mth* 4/1 (1989):61-69.

Feil, Arnold. "Satztechnische Fragen in den Kompositionslehren von F. E. Niedt, J. Riepel und H. Chr. Koch." Ph.D. dissertation, The University of Heidelberg, 1955; published edition, [Heidelberg: Fehrer & Grosch, 1955]. Bibliog.

Feldmann, Fritz. "Das *Opusculum bipartitum* des Joachim Thuringus (1625) besonders in seinen Beziehungen zu Joh. Nucius (1613)." *AfMw* 15/3 (1958):123-42. Bibliog.

Fellerer, Karl Gustav. "Der Palistrinastil und seine Bedeutung in der vokalen Kirchenmusik des achtzehnten Jahrhunderts: Ein Beitrag zur Geschichte der Kirchenmusik in Italien und Deutschland." Habilitationsschrift, The University of Münster, 1927; published edition, Augsburg: Benno Filser Verlag G.m.b.H., 1929; facsimile of the 1929 edition, Walluf bei Wiesbaden: Dr. Martin Sändig oHG, 1972.

Fellerer, Karl Gustav. "Zur Melodielehre im 18. Jahrhundert." *Stm* 3/1-4 (1962):109-15. Bibliog.

Fellerer, Karl Gustav. "Die Kölner Musiktheoretische Schule des 16. Jahrhunderts." In *LenaertsFs* (1969):121-30. Bibliog. [*Rilm* 71-313.]

Fellerer, Karl Gustav. "Musikwissenschaft in Bayern." In *Musik in Bayern*, vol. 2, edited by Robert Münster, Hans Schmidt, and Folker Göthel, pp. 79-95. Tutzing: H. Schneider, 1972. Bibliog. [*Rilm* 74-1737.]

Fellerer, Karl Gustav. "Zur Kontrapunktlehre im Zeitalter des Humanismus." In *GeeringFs* (1972):139-48. [*Rilm* 73-1202.]

Fellerer, Karl Gustav. "Zum Bild der altklassischen Polyphonie im 18. Jahrhundert." In *MeyerFs* (1973):243-52. [*Rilm* 76-599.]

Fellerer, Karl Gustav. "Zur Kontrapunktlehre im 17. Jahrhundert." In *RongaFs* (1973):179-89. [*Rilm* 76-15409.]

Fellerer, Karl Gustav. "Ausdruck und Klang in der Kirchenmusik um 1600." *KJb 1981* 65 (1982):31-44. [*Rilm* 82-2319.]

Fellerer, Karl Gustav. "Wesen und Werden der italienischen Monody um 1600." In *BeckFs* (1982):57-80. Bibliog. [*Rilm* 82-2321.]

Fellerer, Karl Gustav. "Affectus und Effectus in der italienischen Monodie." *IRASM* 14/1-2 (1983):3-21; 119-46. [*Rilm* 83-6537.]

Fellerer, Karl Gustav. "Monodie und Generalbaß." *Mf* 37/2 (1984):99-110.

Ferand, Ernst. "Die Improvisationspraxis in der Musik." Ph.D. dissertation, The University of Vienna, 1937; published edition (as *Die Improvisation in der Musik: Eine Entwicklungsgeschichtliche und psychologische Untersuchung*), Zürich: Rhein-Verlag, 1938.

> Reviews in *AfMf* 7/4 (1942):244-45 (Herbert Birtner) and *ML* 20/3 (1939):337-38 (Alfred Einstein).

Ferand, Ernest T. " 'Sodaine and Unexpected' Music in the Renaissance." *MQ* 37/1 (1951):10-27.

Ferand, Ernest Thomas. "Improvised Vocal Counterpoint in the Late Renaissance and Early Baroque." *Anm* 4 (1956):129-74. Bibliog.

Ferand, Ernest Thomas. *Die Improvisation: In Beispielen aus neun Jahrhunderten abendländischer Musik.* MwBM, no. 12. Cologne: Arno Volk Verlag, 1956; as *Improvisation in Nine Centuries of Western Music: An Anthology* (AoM, no. 12), Cologne: Arno Volk Verlag, H. Gerig, 1961. Bibliog.

> Review in *MQ* 43/4 (1957):557-61 (Otto Kinkeldey).

Ferran, Dominique. "La technique de clavier en France entre 1650 et 1750." *Omér* 6-7 (1979):33-50. [*Rilm* 79-1474.]

Fillmore, John Comfort. "The Practical Value of Certain Modern Theories Respecting the Science of Harmony." *Etude* 5/2 (1887):23ff.; offprint edition, [Philadelphia: Theodore Presser, 1887].

Fink, Harold J. "The Doctrine of Affections and Handel: The Background, Theory, and Practice of the Doctrine of Affections; With a Comprehensive Analysis of the Oratorios of G. F. Handel." Ph.D. dissertation, Case Western Reserve University, 1953.

Finney, Charles Herbert. "British Theorists of the Nineteenth Century." Ph.D. dissertation, The University of Rochester, 1957.

Fischer, Kurt von. "Zur Theorie der Variation im 18. und beginnenden 19. Jahrhundert." In *Schmidt-GörgFs* (1957):117-30.

Fischer, Kurt von. "Europejska myśl historyczna o muzyce do połowy XVIII wieku." Translated by Zofia Lissa. *Muzyka* 23/3 (1978):55-65. Bibliog. [*Rilm* 78-4689.]

Fischer, Trygve. "Litt om harmonilaerens terminologi." *Nm* 13/2 (1976):63-69. [*Rilm* 76-4034.]

Flaherty, Gloria. "Transport, Ecstasy, and Enthusiasm." In Cowart [*French*] (1989):81-93. Bibliog.

Flechsig, Hartmut. "Studien zu Theorie und Methode musikalischer Analyse." Ph.D. dissertation, The University of Heidelberg, 1974; published edition (BzMf, no. 2), Munich: Katzbichler, 1977. Bibliog. [*Rilm* 76-1621.]

> Review in *Mf* 33/3 (1980):370-71 (Carl Dahlhaus).

Flindell, Edwin Frederick. "Some Notes concerning the Origins of Bach's Inventions." In *GolffingFs* (1977):32-39. [*Rilm* 77-2499.]

Flindell, E. Fred. "Apropos Bach's Inventions." *Bach* 14/4 (1983):3-14; 15/1-2 (1984):3-16, 3-17. Bibliog.

Flotzinger, Rudolf. "Zum Topos von der Völker und Stände verbindenden Wirkung der Musik." *IRASM* 12/2 (1981):91-101. Bibliog. [*Rilm* 81-6656.]

Fokker, A. D. "Equal Temperament with Thirty-One Notes." *OIQ* 5/4 (1955):41-45.

Fokker, Adriaan D. "On the Expansion of the Musician's Realm of Harmony." *Am* 38/2-4 (1966):197-202.

Forbes, Elliott, ed. *Beethoven: Symphony No. 5 in C Minor.* NCS, no. 9. New York: W. W. Norton, 1971. [*Rilm* 71-2283.]

Forchert, Arno. "Musik und Rhetorik im Barock." *SchüJb 1985-86* 7-8 (1986):5-21. Bibliog.

Forkel, Johann Nicolaus. *Allgemeine Litteratur der Musik, oder Anleitung zur Kenntnis musikalischer Bücher welche von den ältesten bis auf die neuesten Zeiten bei den Griechen, Römern und den meisten anderen europäischen Nationen sind geschrieben worden.* Leipzig: Schwickert, 1792; reprint edition, Hildesheim: Georg Olms, 1962. [LCPS: F-043. HoM: 550. SMLMS.]

> This work is a foundation for Lichtenthal (1826) and for Becker (1836-39).

Forkel, Johann Nicolaus. "Über den Zustand der Musik in England." *AmZ* 2/1 (1799-1800):5-9.

Forrester, Donald W. "An Introduction to Seventeenth-Century Spanish Music Theory Books." *JRME* 21/1 (1973):61-67. Bibliog. [*Rilm* 73-1768.]

Forster, Walter V. "Heutige Praktikem im Harmonielehre-unterricht an Musikhochschulen und Konservatorien." See Vogel (1966):257-79.

Fox Strangways, A. H. "The Minor Chord." *ML* 4/1 (1923):26-41.

Frischknecht, Hans Eugen. "Vergleichene Musiktheorie." *SMz* 119/5 (1979):262-68. [*Rilm* 81-1636.]

> Comment in *SMz* 119/6 (1979):370-71 (Max Favre).

Frisius, Rudolf. "Untersuchungen über den Akkordbegriff." Ph.D. dissertation, The University of Göttingen, 1969 (1970). [*Rilm* 70-1140.]

Frobenius, Wolf. "Cantus firmus." In *HwmT* (1972-). Bibliog.

Frobenius, Wolf. "Dauer." In *HwmT* (1972-). Bibliog.

Frobenius, Wolf. "Homophonus/aequisonus." In *HwmT* (1972-). Bibliog.

Frobenius, Wolf. "Isotonos/unisonus/unisono/Einklang." In *HwmT* (1972-). Bibliog.

Frobenius, Wolf. "Monodie." In *HwmT* (1972-). Bibliog.

Frobenius, Wolf. "Polyphon, polyodisch." In *HwmT* (1972-). Bibliog.

Frobenius, Wolf. "Tactus." In *HwmT* (1972-). Bibliog.

Frobenius, Wolf. "Vollstimmig, vielstimmig, mehrstimmig." In *HwmT* (1972-). Bibliog.

Fubini, Enrico, trans. *Gli illuministi e la musica: Scritti scelti.* CfP. Milan: Principato Editore, 1969. Bibliog. [*Rilm* 72-4082.]

> Review in *Nrmi* 4/4 (1970):765-66 (M. Mila).

Fubini, Enrico. *Gli enciclopedisti e la musica.* Turin: Giulio Einaudi, 1971; French translation (as *Les philosophes et la musique*, translated by Danièle Pistone; Mm, no. 13), Paris: Honoré Champion, 1983. Bibliog. [*Rilm* 73-1323.]

> Reviews in *Critique* 41/457-58 (1985):744-46 (Marie-Anne Lescourret), *IRASM* 3/1 (1972): 138 (Ivo Supičič, *Nrmi* 5/5 (1971):889-91 (Massimo Mila), and *Rh* 108/271/550 (1984):481-83 (Édith Weber).

Fubini, Enrico. "Vicentino, Zarlino, Galilei (u zrodel nowozytnei konceptcii muzyki)." *Rmuz* 31/20 (1987):20-23.

Fuchs, Carl Dorius Johann. *Die Freiheit des musikalischen Vortrages im Einklange mit H. Riemann's Phrasierungslehre; nebst einer Kritik der Grundlagen poetischer Metrik des Buches "Le rythme" von Mathis Lussy.* Danzig: A. W. Kafemann, 1885.

Fürstenau, Moritz. *Zur Geschichte der Musik und des Theaters am Hofe der Kurfürsten von Sachsen, Johann Georg II., Johann Georg III. und Johann Georg IV., unter Berücksichtigung der ältesten Theatergeschichte Dresdens.* Dresden: Rudolf Kuntze (E. Blochmann), 1861-62.

Fuller, David. "Dotting, the 'French Style' and Frederick Neumann's Counter-Reformation." *EM* 5/4 (1977): 517-43. [*Rilm* 77-5666.]

> A response to Neumann (1965/. . ./1982) and (1977/1982). Neumann retorted in Neumann (1979/1982).

Fuller, David. "Notes and *inégales* Unjoined: Defending a Definition." *JM* 7/1 (1989):21-28.

> A response to Neumann, F. (1988).

G

Gable, Frederick K. "Possibilities for Mean-Tone Temperament Playing on Viols." *JVGSA* 16 (1979):22-39.

Gaillard, Pierre. "Histoire de la légende palestrinienne." *Rdm* 57/1 (1971):11-22. [*Rilm* 71-318.]

Ganz, Beatrice. "Problems of Articulation in Eighteenth Century Keyboard Music." *Clavier* 11/9 (1972):12-15.

Ganz, Beatrice. "Problems of Articulation in Baroque Keyboard Music (At the Piano or the Organ)." *Bach* 7/2 (1976):3-13. [*Rilm* 76-1582.]

Gardavský, Č. "Liszt und seine tschechischen Lehrer." *Stm* 5/1-4 (1963):69-76.

Gaspari, Gaetano. "Dei musicisti bolognesi al XVI secolo e delle loro opere a stampa: Ragguagli biografici e bibliografici." In *AmR* 2/2 (1876):3-84 and *AmE* new series/1 (1877):125-205; reprinted in Gaspari, *Musica e musicisti a Bologna: Ricerche, documenti e memorie riguardanti la storia dell'arte musicale in Bologna* (BmB, ser. 3, no. 1), Bologna: Forni, [1969], pp. 269-447. Bibliog.

Geering, Arnold. "Gesangspädagogik." In *MGG* (1949-68). Bibliog.

Gerber, Ernst Ludwig. *Historisch-Biographisches Lexicon der Tonkünstler, welches Nachrichten von dem Leben und Werken musikalischer Schriftsteller, berühmter Componisten, Sänger, Meister auf Instrumenten, Dilettanten, Orgel- und Instrumentenmacher, enthält.* Leipzig: J. G. I. Breitkopf, 1790-92; reprint edition (edited by Othmar Wessely), Graz: Akademische Druck- und Verlagsanstalt, 1977. Bibliog. [HoM: 596. SMLMS.]

Gerber, Ernst Ludwig. *Neues historisch-biographisches Lexicon der Tonkünstler, welches Nachrichten von dem Leben und von den Werken musikalischer Schriftsteller, berühmter Komponisten, Sänger, Meister auf Instrumenten, kunstvoller Dilettanten, Musikverleger, Orgel- und Instrumentenmacher, älterer und neuerer Zeit, aus allen Nationen enthält.* Leipzig: A. Kühnel, 1812-14; reprint edition (edited by Othmar Wessely), Graz: Akademische Druck- und Verlagsanstalt, 1966. Bibliog.

Gerboth, Walter; Sanders, Robert L.; Starer, Robert; and Steiner, Frances, eds. *An Introduction to Music: Selected Readings*. New York: W. W. Norton, 1964.

Gernhardt, Klaus. "Die wichtigsten Stimmungsarten der Bach-Zeit, ihre praktische Durchführung und ihr musikalischer Wert — aus der Sicht des Musikinstrumenten-Restaurators." In *Bach-Fest 1975* (1977):355-60. Bibliog. [*Rilm* 77-1376.]

Ghislanzoni, Alberto. "La genesi storica della fuga." *Rmi* 51/1, 3 (1949):1-28, 193-211; 52/1, 3 (1950):25-54, 201-42; 53/1-2 (1951):1-41, 99-141.

Giacotti, D. "Il recupero della tragedia antica a Firenze e la camerata de' Bardi." *CIfm* 3/1 (1968).

Gianuario, Annibale. "La voce umana e la seconda pratica." In *Convegni rinascimento 1976* (1979):13-22.

Gilfoyle, Sandra C. "The Decline of the 'Three Musics' of Boethius in the Sixteenth and Seventeenth Centuries." M.A. thesis, The University of Iowa, 1972. [*Rilm* 73-2573.]

Gillingham, Bryan. "Social and Musical Matters Pertaining to J. C. Bach's Third Set of Keyboard Concertos." *MR* 42/3-4 (1981):225-37. [*Rilm* 81-4756.]

Gissel, Siegfried. "Untersuchungen zur mehrstimmigen protestantischen Hymnenkomposition in Deutschland um 1600." 2 vols. Ph.D. dissertation, The University of Marburg/Lahn, 1980; published edition, Kassel: Bärenreiter, 1983. Bibliog.

> Reviews in *Mf* 40/1 (1987):73 (Bernhard Meier) and *MK* 55/1 (1985):26 (Oswald Bill).

Gissel, Siegfried. "Zur Modusbestimmung deutscher Autoren in der Zeit von 1550-1650: Eine Quellenstudie." *Mf* 39/3 (1986):201-17.

Gjerdingen, Robert O. *A Classic Turn of Phrase: Music and the Psychology of Convention*. SCTM. Philadelphia: University of Pennsylvania Press, 1988. Bibliog.

Gleason, Harold. "A Seventeenth-Century Organ Instruction Book." *Bach* 12/3 (1981):11-20.

Godley, Elizabeth. "The Minor Triad." *ML* 33/4 (1952):285-95.

Godwin, Joscelyn, ed. *Music, Mysticism and Magic: A Sourcebook*. London and New York: Routledge & Kegan Paul, 1986.

> Reviews in *BBN* (1987):503, *MR* 47/2 (1986-87):126-27 (Michael McMullin), and *TLS* 86/4400 (1987):813 (Wilfrid Mellers).

Godwin, Joscelyn. *Harmonies of Heaven and Earth: The Spiritual Dimension of Music from Antiquity to the Avant-Garde*. London: Thames & Hudson; Rochester, Vt.: Inner Traditions International, 1987. Bibliog.

> Reviews in *BBN* (1987):531, *CAY* 9 (1988):5, and *MT* 129 (1988):345.

Göttert, Karl-Heinz. "Streit um Bach." *Concerto* 3/6 (1985-86):4-9.

Goldmann, Alfred. " 'Verzeihen sie mir meine Freyheit': Leopold Mozart und Meinrad Spieß." *AMoz* 34/3 (1987):54-63. Bibliog.

Goldschmidt, Harry, and Brenneis, Clemens. "Aspekte der gegenwärtigen Beethovenforschung." *BzMw* 18/1 (1976):3-38. [*Rilm* 76-9995.]

Goldschmidt, Hugo. *Die italienische Gesangsmethode des XVII. Jahrhunderts und ihre Bedeutung für die Gegenwart.* Breslau: Schlesische Buchdruckerei, Kunst- und Verlags-Anstalt, 1890; revised edition, 1892.

Goldschmidt, Hugo. *Studien zur Geschichte der italienischen Oper im 17. Jahrhundert.* 2 vols. Leipzig: Breitkopf & Härtel, 1901-4; facsimile edition, Hildesheim: Georg Olms, 1967.

Goldschmidt, Hugo. *Die Lehre von der vokalen Ornamentik.* Charlottenburg: Paul Lehsten, 1907.

Goldsmith, Pamela. "Bowing Articulation in the Transitional Period." *Strad* 89/1067 (1978-79):1039-47.

Gouk, Penelope. "The Role of Acoustics and Music Theory in the Scientific Work of Robert Hooke." *AS* 37/5 (1980):573-605. [*Rilm* 80-5943.]

Gouk, Penelope M. "Acoustics in the Early Royal Society, 1660-1680." *NRRSL* 36/2 (1981-82):155-75. Bibliog.

Gouk, Penelope. "Music in the Natural Philosophy of the Early Royal Society." Ph.D. dissertation, The University of London (Warburg Institute), 1982. [*Rilm* 82-3861.]

Grashel, John William. "The Gamut and Solmization in Early British and American Texts." *JRME* 29/1 (1981): 63-70. Bibliog. [*Rilm* 81-1739.]

Grave, Floyd K. " 'Rhythmic Harmony' in Mozart." *MR* 41/2 (1980):87-102. [*Rilm* 80-3768.]

Grave, Floyd K. "Metrical Displacement and the Compound Measure in Eighteenth-Century Theory and Practice." *Theoria* 1 (1985): 25-60.

Green, Burdette Lamar. "The Harmonic Series from Mersenne to Rameau: An Historical Study of Circumstances Leading to Its Recognition and Application to Music." Ph.D. dissertation, The Ohio State University, 1969. Bibliog. [*Rilm* 75-4453. *DA* 30/10A, p. 4478. UMI 70-06786.]

Green, Michael D. "Historical Precedents for Contemporary Theories of Musical Accent: A Study of Rhythmic Theory from Kirnberger to the Present." Ph.D. dissertation, The University of Chicago, forthcoming.

Greenberg, Beth. "Brahms' Rhapsody in G minor, op. 79 no 2: A Study of Analyses by Schenker, Schoenberg, and Jonas." *ITO* 1/9-10 (1975-76):21-29.

> Comment in *ITO* 1/9-10 (1975-76):31-32 (Charles J. Smith).

Greenfield, Jack. "Music, Theory and Tuning in 18th-Century France." *PTJ* 27 (1984):20-23.

Gremion, Claude. "Musique Baroque." *Resth* 27/2 (1974):171-82. [*Rilm* 76-5357.]

Grimes, Calvin Bernard. "American Music Periodicals, 1819-1852: Music Theory and Musical Thought in the United States." Ph.D. dissertation, The University of Iowa, 1974. [*DA* 35/12A, p. 7943. UMI 75-13756.]

Groth, Renate. "Die französische Kompositionslehre des 19. Jahrhunderts." Ph.D. dissertation, The Technical University of Berlin, 1981; published edition (BAfMw, no. 22), Wiesbaden: Steiner, 1983. Bibliog.

> Reviews in *JMT* 30/2 (1986):295-304 (Robert W. Wason), *MB* 19/3 (1987):240 (Peter Rummenhöller), and *Mth* 1/1 (1986):104-6 (Herbert Schneider).

Grout, Donald J. *A History of Western Music.* New York: W. W. Norton, 1960; revised edition, 1973; revised edition (with Claude V. Palisca), 1980; revised edition, 1988.

> Reviews in *AmO* 43/10 (1960):16 (Harry W. Gay), *ARG* 27/6 (1960-61):508-9 (William Kay Archer), *BB* 19/4 [220] (1973-74):81(Eric Fenby), *Choice* 10/4 (1973-74):632, *Choice* 18/3 (1980-81):406, *CLW* 32/8 (1960-61):521 (Frederic Heutte), *Fanfare* 6/6 (1982-83):326-28 (Edward Strickland), *Hroz* 15/23-24 (1962):1008-9 (Ladislav Mokrý), *IME* 2 (1960):84 (Bruce Bray), *Instrumentalist* 14/10 (1959-60):11-12, *JR* 7/3 (1959-60):11 (Richard Franko Goldman), *JRME* 8/2 (1960):124-26 (Warren D. Allen), *JRME* 22/4 (1974):321-23 (Daniel T. Politoske), *LJ* 85/9 (1960):1797 (Catharine K. Miller), *MC* 161/6 (1960):46 (Frederick Werlé), *MC* 163/9 (1961):48 (Frederick Werlé), *MCM* 40/1 (1960):49-50 (Quaintance Eaton), *MCM* 44/3 (1965):28, *MEJ* 46/6 (1959-60):78 (Bruce Bray), *MEJ* 51/4 (1964-65):174, *MEJ* 60/1 (1973-74):88, *MEJ* 67/6 (1980-81):78, *MiE* 26/297 (1962-63):138 (Roger Fiske), *MiE* 37/363 (1973):261 (Michael Hurd), *MJ* 23/3 (1965):16 (Ruth De Cesare), *ML* 43/4 (1962):363-65 (J. A. Westrup), *MO* 86/1025 (1962-63):287 (B. R.), *MT* 103/1438 (1962):845-46 (Alec Harman), *MT* 115/1571 (1974):40-41 (Arthur Jacobs), *Notes* 18/1 (1960-61):47-48 (Albert T. Luper), *NS* 64/1659 (1962):933 (David Drew), *NYHT* 120/41,570/6 (Sept. 25, 1960):15 (Herbert Weinstock), *PP* 53/3 (1961):20 (Melva Peterson), *Response* 6/4 (1965):189 (Gerhard M. Cartford), *Spec* 231/7567 (1973):17-18 (Richard Luckett), and *TLS* 61/3164 (1962):804.

Gruber, Albion. "Evolving Tonal Theory in Seventeenth-Century France." Ph.D. dissertation, The University of Rochester, 1969. Bibliog. [*Rilm* 69-2736. *DA* 30/06A, p. 2559. UMI 69-19779.]

Gruber, Gernot. "Zu Wolfgang Amadeus Mozarts Lehre im *basso fondamentale.*" In *BeckFs* (1982):127-31. [*Rilm* 82-2424.]

Grusnick, Bruno. "Die Dübensammlung: Ein Versuch ihrer chronologischen Ordnung." *Stfm* 46 (1964):27-82; 48 (1966):63-186.

Guion, David. "The Pitch of Baroque Trombones." *JITA* 8 (1980):24-28. Bibliog. [*Rilm* 80-1703.]

Gurlitt, Wilibald. "Der Begriff der Sortisatio in der deutschen Kompositionslehre des 16. Jahrhunderts." *TvNm* 16/3 (1942):194-211; reprinted in Gurlitt (1966):93-104.

Gurlitt, Wilibald. "Musik und Rhetorik: Hinweise auf ihre geschichtliche Grundlageneinheit." *Helicon* 5/1-3 (1944):67-86; reprinted in Gurlitt (1966):62-81. Bibliog.

Gurlitt, Wilibald. "Die Kompositionslehre des deutschen 16. und 17. Jahrhunderts." See Osthoff (1954):103-13; reprinted in Gurlitt (1966):82-92. Bibliog.

Gurlitt, Wilibald. *Musikgeschichte und Gegenwart: Eine Aufsatzfolge.* Edited by Hans Heinrich Eggebrecht. BAfMw, no. 1. Wiesbaden: Franz Steiner, 1966.

Reviews in *Eras* 20/1-2 (1968):30-31 (A. Hyatt King), *Mens* 22/10 (1967):317 (G. V.), *Mf* 21/3 (1968):353-55 (Reinhold Hammerstein), *Musica* 20/6 (1966):302 (Lothar Hoffmann-Erbrecht), *Musica* 21/6 (1967):308 (Lothar Hoffmann-Erbrecht), and *NZfM* 129/4 (1968):189-90 (G. A. Trumpff).

Gut, Serge. "Dominante—Tonika—Subdominante." In *HwmT* (1972-). Bibliog.

Gut, Serge. "La notion de consonance chez les théoriciens du moyen age." *Am* 48/1 (1976):20-44. [*Rilm* 76-1623.]

Gwilt, Richard. "Sonata-Allegro Revisited." *ITO* 7/5-6 (1983-84):3-33.

H

Haar, James. "False Relations and Chromaticism in Sixteenth-Century Music." *JAMS* 30/3 (1977):391-418. Bibliog. [*Rilm* 77-4471.]

Haar, James. "A Sixteenth-Century Attempt at Music Criticism." *JAMS* 36/2 (1983):191-209.

Haar, James. *Essays on Italian Poetry and Music in the Renaissance, 1350—1600.* Berkeley and Los Angeles: University of California Press, 1986. Bibliog.

Review in *Choice* 25/1 (1987-88):140 (M. S. Roy).

Haase, Rudolf. "Kepler und Leibniz als Mittler zwischen Pythagoras und Hindemith." *ZfGf* 7/4 (1963):157-64. Bibliog.

Haase, Rudolf. *Geschichte des harmonikalen Pythagorismus.* PWMa, no. 3. Vienna: Lafite, 1969.

Reviews in *Me* 25/1 (1971-72):46-47 (Eugen Banauch), *MGot* 26/4 (1972):92-96 (Friedrich Zipp), *Musica* 24/1 (1970):67 (Otto Reimer), *Nrmi* 4/5 (1970):954-55 (Gino Stefani), *ÖM* 24/11 (1969):667 (Walter Szmolyan), and *ZfGf* 15/1 (1971):39-41 (W. Heinrich).

Haase, Rudolf. "Die harmonikalen Quellen des klassischen Konsonanzbegriffs." *FÖM* 4 (1972):45-53. [*Rilm* 74-1290.]

Haase, Rudolf. "Harmoniegesetze der Schöpfung bei Swedenborg und in der harmonikalen Forschung der Gegenwart." *OT* 20/1 (1976):7-24. [*Rilm* 76-7544.]

Haase, Rudolf. "Harmonikale Grundlagenforschung." *Am* 58/2 (1986):282-304. Bibliog.

Hahn, Kurt. "Die Anfänge der Allgemeine Musiklehre: Gottfried Weber—Adolf Bernhard Marx." In *Die vielspältige Musik und die allgemeine Musiklehre,* pp. 63-67. MZ, no. 9. Kassel: Bärenreiter, 1960.

Hailparn, Lydia. "Exploring Cadenzas to Beethoven's Piano Concertos." *CMS* 21/1 (1981):48-59. [*Rilm* 81-2584.]

Hall, Robert A., Jr. "How Picard Was the 'Picardy Third'?" *CM* 19 (1975):78-80. Bibliog. [*Rilm* 76-8944.]

Hamilton, James Alexander. *Catechism of Counterpoint, Melody, and Composition, Illustrated with Extracts and Examples from the Theoretical Works of Albrechtsberger, Koch, Reicha . . . &c.* 6th edition, enlarged by John Bishop. London: Cocks, 1854.

Hammel, Marla. "The Figured-Bass Accompaniment in Bach's Time: A Brief Summary of Its Development and an Examination of Its Use, Together with a Sample Realization." *Bach* 8/3 (1977):26-31; 9/1-2 (1978):30-36, 37-39.

Hancock, Wendy. "General Rules for Realising an Unfigured Bass in Seventeenth-Century England." *Chelys* 7 (1977):69-72. [*Rilm* 77-1485.]

Hancock, Wendy E. "The Origins of the Basso Continuo in England, 1585-1625." M.Phil. thesis, The University of Nottingham, 1981.

Handschin, Jacques. *Der Toncharakter: Eine Einführung in die Tonpsychologie.* Zürich: Atlantis, 1948.

Reviews in *Dmt* 25/3 (1950):57 (Herbert Rosenberg), *MQ* 35/3 (1949):485-87 (Carroll C. Pratt), *Musica* 6/10 (1952):443 (Fritz Bose), *Notes* 7/1 (1949-50):117 (Arnold M. Small), and *Rasm* 20/4 (1950):359-60 (Alfredo Bonaccorsi).

Hannas, Ruth. "Evolution of Harmonic Consciousness: A Study of Pre-Eighteenth Century Technics." 4 vols. Ph.D. dissertation, The University of Rochester, 1934. [SMLMS.]

Hanning, Barbara Russano. "The Influence of Humanist Thought and Italian Renaissance Poetry on the Formation of Opera." Ph.D. dissertation, Yale University, 1969; published edition (as *Of Poetry and Music's Power: Humanism and the Creation of Opera*; SiM, no. 13), Ann Arbor, Mich.: UMI Research Press, 1980. [*Rilm* 69-850. *DA* 30/04A, p. 1587.]

Reviews in *OQ* 1/4 (1983-84):195-96 (Efrim Fruchtman) and *RQ* 34/4 (1981):590-93 (Anthony Newcomb).

Hansell, Sven Hostrup. "The Cadence in Eighteenth-Century Recitative." *MQ* 54/2 (1968):228-48. [*Rilm* 68-3243.]

Harburger, Walter. "Musikalische Geometrie: Eine notwendige Neubegründung altbekannter Dinge." *ZfMw* 11/4 (1928-29):193-211.

Harding, Rosamond Evelyn Mary. *Origins of Musical Time and Expression*. London: Oxford University Press, 1938. Bibliog.

Harich-Schneider, Eta. *Die Kunst des Cembalo-spiels, nach den vorhandenen Quellen dargestellt und erläutert.* Kassel: Bärenreiter, [1939]; 1958; 1970; as "The Art of Harpsichord Playing: Demonstrated and Explained According to the Available Sources" (translated by Gordon J. Kinney), typescript [University of Kentucky].

Reviews in *AfMf* 5 (1940):122-24 (Rudolf Steglich) and *OrganYb* 3 (1972):111-12 (Peter Williams).

Harrán, Don. "New Light on the Question of Text Underlay Prior to Zarlino." *Am* 45/1 (1973):24-56. Bibliog. [*Rilm* 73-269.]

Harrán, Don. *Word-Tone Relations in Musical Thought: From Antiquity to the Seventeenth Century.* MSD, no. 40. Neuhausen and Stuttgart: American Institute of Musicology (Hänssler-Verlag), 1986. Bibliog.

Reviews in *JAMS* 42/1 (1989):161-72 (Bonnie J. Blackburn), *JMT* 32/2 (1988):357-66 (Maria Rika Maniates), *ML* 70/1 (1989):78-79 (John Stevens), and *Notes* 44/2 (1987-88):267-69 (Peter Kivy).

Harrán, Don. *In Search of Harmony: Hebrew and Humanist Elements in Sixteenth-Century Musical Thought.* MSD, no. 42. Nauhausen and Stuttgart: American Institute of Musicology (Hänssler-Verlag), 1988.

Harris, John Mackrell. "The Pedagogical Development of College Harmony Textbooks in the United States." D.M.A. dissertation, The University of Texas at Austin, 1969. [*DA* 30/12A, p. 5470. UMI 70-10741.]

Hartig, Linda Bishop. "Johann Georg Tromlitz's *Unterricht die Flöte zu spielen*: A Translation and Comparative Study." Ph.D. dissertation, Michigan State University, 1982. [*Rilm* 82-1463. *DA* 43/06A, p. 1740. UMI 82-24437.]

Hartmann, Andreas. "Affektdarstellung und Naturbeherrschung in der Musik des Barock." *IRASM* 11/1 (1980):25-44. [*Rilm* 80-4002.]

Hartmann, Ernst. "Konsonanz und Dissonanz, zur Geschichte ihres Begriffes und ihrer Theorien." Ph.D. dissertation, The University of Marburg, 1923.

Abstract in *JpFPUM 1922-23* (1924):161-70.

Hawkins, John Isaac. *A General History of the Science and Practice of Music*. 2 vols. London: Payne, 1776 [LCPS: H-014. HoM: 722. SMLMS.]; new edition, London: Novello, 1853; 1875; facsimile of the 1853 edition (with an Introduction by Charles Cudworth; AMS/MLARS), New York: Dover, 1963; facsimile of the 1875 edition (edited by Othmar Wessely; DMBA, no. 5), Graz: Akademische Druck- und Verlagsanstalt, 1969.

Reviews in *ACR* 6/2 (1963-64):14-15 (Martin Picker), *ARG* 31/11 (1964-65):1092-94 (John W. Barker), *Instrumentalist* 18/4 (1963-64):22, *MCM* 44/3 (1965):28 (Quaintance Eaton), *MkB* 2 (1778):166-229 (Johann Nicolaus Forkel), *ML* 45/1 (1964):52-53 (Jack A. Westrup), *MuMus* 12/7 (1963-64):46 (Frank Granville Barker), *MusT* 42/12 (1963):497 (J. R. T.), *Notes* 22/3 (1965-66):1026-27 (Bernard E. Wilson), and *TLS* 63/3227 (1964):4.

Haydon, Glen. *The Evolution of the Six-Four Chord: A Chapter in the History of Dissonance Treatment.* Introduction by Albert I. Elkus. Berkeley, Calif.: University of California Press, 1933; reprint edition (DCPMRS), New York: Da Capo Press, 1971. Bibliog.

Reviews in *ML* 15/1 (1934):102 (Donald Peart), *MO* 96/1143 (1972-73):135 (B. R.), and *MuMus* 21/2 [242] (1972-73):46-47 (Watkins Shaw).

Heckmann, Harald. "Der Takt in der Musiklehre des siebzehnten Jahrhunderts." *AfMw* 10/2 (1953):116-39. Bibliog.

Hedges, Stephen A. "Dice Music in the Eighteenth Century." *ML* 59/2 (1978):180-87. Bibliog. [*Rilm* 78-542.]

Heimann, Walter. "Der Generalbaß-Satz und seine Rolle in Bachs Choral-Satz." Ph.D. dissertation, The University of Freiburg im Breisgau, 1970; published edition (FSMw, no. 5), Munich: Musikverlag Emil Katzbichler, 1973. Bibliog.

Review in *Melos/NZfM* 4/4 (1978):356 (Lars Ulrich Abraham).

Hein, Johannes. "Die Kontrapunktlehre bei den Musiktheoretikern im 17. Jahrhundert." Ph.D. dissertation, The University of Cologne, 1954. Bibliog.

Heinlein, Christian Paul. "The Affective Characters of the Major and Minor Modes in Music." Ph.D. dissertation, The Johns Hopkins University, 1927; published in *JCPs* 8/2 (1928):101-42 and as an offprint, Baltimore: 1928. Bibliog.

Helm, Ernest Eugene. *Music at the Court of Frederick the Great.* Norman, Okla.: University of Oklahoma Press, 1960. Bibliog.

Reviews in *ARG* 27/7 (1961):589-90 (William L. Purcell), *JRME* 10/1 (1962):82-83 (Nan Cooke Carpenter), *LJ* 86/2 (1961):242-43 (Catharine K.

Miller), *Mens* 21/1 (1966):15-18 (Paul van Reijen), *Mf* 15/3 (1962):287 (Willi Kahl), *MR* 23/1 (1962):67-69, *NZfM* 122/7-8 (1961):334-35 (Wolfgang Freitag), and *Rdm* 47 (1961):133 (Pierre Pidoux).

Henderson, Robert Vladimir. "Solmization Syllables in Musical Theory, 1100 to 1600." Ph.D. dissertation, Columbia University, 1969. Bibliog. [*DA* 31/03A, p. 1309. UMI 70-17017.]

Henneberg, Gudrun. "Theorien zur Rhythmik und Metrik in der Musik der Wiener Klassik." Ph.D. dissertation, The University of Mainz, 1972; published edition (as *Theorien zur Rhythmik und Metrik: Möglichkeiten und Grenzen rhythmischer und metrischer Analyse, dargestellt am Beispiel der Wiener Klassik*; MSzMw, no. 6), Tutzing: Hans Schneider, 1974. Bibliog. [*Rilm* 75-2632.]

> Abstract in *Mf* 26/4 (1973):507-9. Reviews in *LMFA* 12/1 (1979):102-3 (Wendelin Müller-Blattau), *Mf* 29/2 (1976):183-86 [("Polemisches zur Theorie der Rhythmik und Metrik", by Carl Dahlhaus [*Rilm* 76-7119]), with Reply in *Mf* 29/4 (1976):465-67 ("Was ist der musikalische Rhythmus?—Eine Entgegnung," by Gudrun Henneberg), Response in *Mf* 29/4 (1976):467-68 (Carl Dahlhaus), Response in *Mf* 29/4 (1977):468-69 ("Zum Verständnis der Akzenttheorie: Eine Antwort auf die Entgegnung von Gudrun Henneberg," by Wilhelm Seidl), and Reply in *Mf* 30/2 (1977):191-93 ("Erwiderung auf Entgegnungen von Carl Dahlhaus und Wilhelm Seidl," by Gudrun Henneberg [*Rilm* 77-1554])], *Notes* 31/4 (1974-75):780-82 (Jürgen Thym), and *Orch* 25/9 (1977):643 (Wolfgang Suppan).

Henneberg, Gudrun. *Idee und Begriff des musikalischen Kunstwerks im Spiegel des deutschsprachigen Schrifttums der ersten Hälfte des 19. Jahrhunderts*. MSzMw, no. 17. Tutzing: Hans Schneider, 1983. Bibliog.

> Review in *Notes* 41/4 (1984-85):727-28 (Thomas S. Grey).

Hill, John Walter. "Realized Continuo Accompaniments from Florence *c* 1600." *EM* 11/2 (1983):194-208. [*Rilm* 83-1582.]

Hiller, Johann Adam. "Kritischer Entwurf einer musikalischen Bibliothek." *WNAMb* 3/1-5, 7-11, 13-14 (1768-69):1-7, 9-12, 17-20, 25-29, 33-36, 49-53, 57-63, 65-68, 73-77, 81-85, 97-99, 103-8.

Hiller, Johann Adam. *Lebensbeschreibungen berühmter Musikgelehrten und Tonkünstler neuer Zeit*. Leipzig: Dyk, 1784. [*Rism* B/VI/1, p. 414. LCPS: H-046.]

Hoag, Barbara Brewster. "A Spanish Clavichord Tuning of the Seventeenth Century." *JAMIS* 2 (1976):86-95.

Hoffman, Donald. "The Chromatic Fourth." *Consort* 26 (1970):445-58. [*Rilm* 70-1143.]

Hoffman, Mark. "A Study of German Theoretical Treatises of the Nineteenth Century." 2 vols. Ph.D. dissertation, The University of Rochester, 1953. Bibliog.

Hoffmann, Niels Frédéric. "Einige Beispiele zum Wechselverhältnis von musiktheoretischer Erkenntnis und musikpraktischer Anweisung." *ZfMt* 5/2 (1974): 11-19. Bibliog. [*Rilm* 76-7108.]

Hoiseth, Gary Thomas. " '*Bases illusoires*': French Theories of Chord Generation and Chord Classification." Ph.D. dissertation, The University of Iowa, forthcoming.

Holtzapple, Jay Charles. "English Theorists, Tonality and the String Fancy, ca. 1590-1680." Master's thesis, The University of Illinois, 1966.

Horsley, Imogene. "Improvised Embellishment in the Performance of Renaissance Polyphonic Music." *JAMS* 4/1 (1951):3-18.

Horsley, Imogene. "The Diminutions in Composition and Theory of Composition." *Am* 35/2-3 (1963):124-53; reprinted in Rosand (1985):Vol. 5, pp. 148-77. Bibliog.

Horsley, Imogene. "Fugue and Mode in Sixteenth-Century Vocal Polyphony." In *ReeseFs* (1966/1978):406-22. Bibliog.

Horsley, Imogene. *Fugue: History and Practice*. New York: Free Press, 1966. Bibliog.

> Reviews in *JMT* 11/1 (1967):152-57 (Gerald Lefkoff), *MT* 108/1488 (1967):138-39 (Paul Steinitz), and *Notes* 24/2 (1967-68):270-72 (Barbara Gordon).

Horsley, Imogene. "Symposium on Seventeenth-Century Music Theory: Italy." See Cohen ["National Predilections"] (1972):50-61. Bibliog.

Horsley, Imogene. "Full and Short Scores in Accompaniment of Italian Church Music in the Early Baroque." *JAMS* 30/3 (1977):466-99.

Hoshino, Hiroshi. "17 seiki Europe no lute to theorbo." In *GakuenFs* (1979):50-64. [*Rilm* 79-3540.]

Hosler, Bellamy Hamilton. "Changing Aesthetic Views of Instrumental Music in Eighteenth-Century Germany." Ph.D. dissertation, The University of Wisconsin at Madison, 1978; published edition (SiM, no. 42), Ann Arbor, Mich.: UMI Research Press, 1981. Bibliog. [*Rilm* 78-4235. *DA* 39/06A, p. 3212.]

> Review in *BJECS* 6/2 (1983):287-90 (J. M. Tudor).

Houle, George Louis. "The Musical Measure as Discussed by Theorists from 1650 to 1800." Ph.D. dissertation, Stanford University, 1960. Bibliog. [*DA* 21/11, p. 3480. UMI 61-01230.]

Houle, George. *Meter in Music, 1600-1800: Performance, Perception, Notation*. MSP. Bloomington, Ind.: Indiana University Press, 1987. Bibliog.

> Reviews in *EM* 16/3 (1988):423-27 (Robert Donington), *ML* 70/1 (1989):93-94 (Erich Schwandt), and *MT* 129/1744 (1988):300-301 (Ellen Teselle Boal).

Howell, Almonte. "Symposium on Seventeenth-Century Music Theory: Spain." See Cohen ["National Predilections"] (1972):62-71. Bibliog. [*Rilm* 73-1779.]

Hucke, Helmut. "Palestrina als Autorität und Vorbild im 17. Jahrhundert." In *Congresso Monteverdi 1968* (1969): 253-61. Bibliog.

> Responses by H. Federhofer, W. Apel, and A. Cavicchi.

Hüschen, Heinrich. "Harmonie." In *MGG* (1949-68). Bibliog.

Hüschen, Heinrich. "Bemerkungen zu den Titeln der Musiktraktate des 15. und 16. Jahrhunderts." In *RuhnkeFs* (1986):158-75.

Hunt, Frederick Vinton. *Origins in Acoustics: The Science of Sound from Antiquity to the Age of Newton*. Foreword by Robert Edmund Apfel. New Haven, Ct.: Yale University Press, 1978.

> Reviews in *AmSc* 67/1 (1979):123 (R. S. Shankland), *AS* 38/3 (1981):367-70 (Erwin Hiebert), *Centaurus* 25/4 (1982):328-29 (D. Ullmann), *Choice* 16/3 (1979-80):411, *Isis* 70/252 (1979): 287-88 (David C. Lindberg), *JASA* 65/2 (1979): 553 (Robert T. Beyer), *JMT* 23/1 (1979):148-50 (Claude V. Palisca), *Leonardo* 13/3 (1980):248-49 (W. Garner), *LJ* 103/15 (1978):1648 (Judith R. Goodstein), *Notes* 36/4 (1979-80):896-97 (Fred Geissler), *SBF* 15/3 (1979-80):144 (Alex F. Burr), and *Ultrasonics* 18/3 (1980):141 (E. A. Neppiras).

Hutchinson, William, and Knopoff, Leon. "The Significance of the Acoustic Component of Consonance in Western Triads." *JMR* 3/1-2 (1979-81):5-22.

I

Ibberson, John B. "A History of Keyboard Theory." Ph.D. dissertation, Indiana University, 1984. [*DA* 44/10A, p. 2921. UMI 84-01522.]

Imig, Renate. "Systeme der Funktionsbezeichnung in den Harmonielehren seit Hugo Riemann." Ph.D. dissertation, The University of Bonn, 1969; published edition (OSGM, no. 9), Düsseldorf: Gesellschaft zur Förderung der systematischen Wissenschaft, 1970. Bibliog. [*Rilm* 70/2548.]

> Reviews in *Mf* 26/1 (1973):132-33 (Carl Dahlhaus), *Ms:CVO* 91/5 (1971):209-10 (Hans-Josef Irmen), and *ZfMt* 1/2 (1970):44-45 ("Riemann und die Funktionstheorie Heute," by Peter Rummenhöller).

Irving, Howard. "Haydn's *Deutscher Tanz* Finales: Style versus Form in Eighteenth-Century Music." *StiM* 20 (1986):12-26.

Isgro, Robert Mario. "The First and Second Practices of Monteverdi: Their Relation to Contemporary Theory." D.M.A. dissertation, The University of Southern California, 1968. Bibliog. [*DA* 29/06A, pp. 1916-17. UMI 68-17029.]

Isgro, Robert Mario. "Sixteenth-Century Conception of Harmony." *CMS* 19/1 (1979):7-52. [*Rilm* 79-3647.]

J

Jackisch, Frederick Frank. "Organ Building in Germany during the Baroque Era According to the Treatises Dating from Praetorius' *Syntagma Musicum* (1619) to Adlung's *Musica mechanica organoedi* (1768)." Ph.D. dissertation, The Ohio State University, 1966. Bibliog. [*DA* 27/11A, p. 3892. UMI 67-06327.]

Jackson, Roland. *Performance Practice, Medieval to Contemporary: A Bibliographic Guide*. MRIG, no. 9; GRLH, no. 790. New York: Garland Publishing, 1988. Bibliog.

> To be updated annually in *PPrR*. Reviews in *Cnv* 125 (1988):17-18 (Ann P. Basart) and *ML* 70/2 (1989):245-47 (Peter Holman).

Jacobi, Erwin R. "Die Entwicklung der Musiktheorie in England nach der Zeit von Jean-Philippe Rameau." Ph.D. dissertation, The University of Zürich, 1957; published edition (SmA, no. 35, 39, and 39a), Strasbourg: Heitz, 1957-60; English translation of Chapter One (as "Harmonic Theory in England After the Time of Rameau") in *JMT* 1/2 (1957):126-46; reprint of the 1957-60 edition, Baden-Baden: Körner, 1971. Bibliog.

> Reviews in *JMT* 5/2 (1961):325-28 (Arthur Hutchings), *JMT* 6/2 (1962):322 (Arthur Hutchings), *Mf* 12/1 (1959):101-2 (Reinhold Sietz), *Mf* 15/1 (1962):94-96 (Reinhold Sietz), *ML* 41/4 (1960):385-86 (Hans F. Redlich), *MQ* 48/2 (1962):254-60 (William J. Mitchell), *Musica* 11/7-8 (1957):472-73 (Hans F. Redlich), *Musica* 14/8 (1960):540 (Hans F. Redlich), *Notes* 17/3 (1959-60):404-5 (Wallace Berry), *NZfM* 119/11 (1958):666 (Arnold Feil), *Rasm* 30/4 (1960):377-

LITERATURE SUPPLEMENT

78 (Alfredo Bonaccorsi), *Rdm* 40 (1957):228-30 (Robert Siohan), *SMz* 98/10 (1958):404, and *SMz* 101/1 (1961):60.

Jacobs, Charles. "Spanish Renaissance Discussion of *musica ficta*." *PAPS* 112/4 (1968):277-98. [*Rilm* 76-9342.]

Jander, Owen. "Solfeggio." In *NGrove* (1980).

Jasinsky, Mark Heber. "A Translation and Commentary on José Harrando's *Arte y puntual explicacion del modo de tocar el violin* (1756)." M.A. thesis, Brigham Young University, 1974. [*Rilm* 74-2306.]

Jenne, Natalie. "Bach's Use of Dance Rhythms in Fugues." *Bach* 4/4 (1973):18-26; 5/1-2 (1974):3-8, 3-21. [*Rilm* 74-313.]

Jeppesen, Knud. "Der Palestrinastil und die Dissonanz." Ph.D. dissertation, The University of Vienna, 1922; published edition, Leipzig: Breitkopf & Härtel, 1925; as *Palestrinastil med særligt henblik paa dissonansbehandlingen*, Copenhagen: Levin & Munksgaard, 1923; as *The Style of Palestrina and the Dissonance* (translated by Margaret N. Hamerik, with an Introduction by Edward J. Dent), London: Oxford University Press, 1927; revised English edition, 1946; reprint of the 1946 edition, New York: Dover, 1970.

> Reviews in *ML* 28/3 (1947):268-69 (Eric Blom), *MR* 8/2 (1947):151-52 (Egon J. Wellesz), *MT* 112/1540 (1971):558-59 (Philip Radcliffe), and *Rmi* 33/2 (1926):272-74 (Ro.).

Jeppesen, Knud. *Kontrapunkt (Vokalpolyfoni)*. Copenhagen: Hansen, 1930; 2nd edition, 1946; revised edition, 1974; as *Kontrapunkt: Lehrbuch der klassischen Vokalpolyphonie* (translated by Julie Schulz), Leipzig: Breitkopf & Härtel, 1935 and later editions to 1970; as *Counterpoint: The Polyphonic Vocal Style of the Sixteenth Century* (translated by Glen Haydon; PHMS), Englewood Cliffs, N.J.: Prentice-Hall, 1939; revised editions through 1960.

> Reviews in *LME* 5/11 (1950):36, *MEur* 1 (1950):17, *ML* 32/1 (1951):59-61 (Peter Latham), *MT* 91/1294 (1950):471-72 (Arthur Hutchings), *Rdm* 42 (1958):235-36 (Félix Raugel), *Rmi* 40/1 (1936):163-64 (C. P.), and *Tempo* 19 (1951):32-33 (John Weissmann).

Jeppesen, Knud. "Zur Kritik der klassichen Harmonielehre." In *Congress Basle 1949* [1951]:23-34; as *Kritiske bemærkninger til den klassiske harmonilære; et foredrang*, Copenhagen: E. Munksgaard, 1952.

Jeppesen, Knud. "On Counterpoint." Translated by Glen Haydon. *MQ* 21/4 (1935):401-7.

Jiránek, Jaroslav. "K otázce tzv. dynamických muzikologických koncepcí poriemannovských (Javorskij, Kurth a Asafjev)." [Concerning the Dynamic Post-Riemann Musicological Concepts (Yavorsky, Kurth, and Asafiev).] *Hv* 4/1 (1967):71-105; 176-78. Bibliog. [*Rilm* 67-1180.]

Johnson, Calvert. "Spanish Renaissance Keyboard Performance Practice: An Introduction." D.M.A. dissertation, Northwestern University, 1973. [*Rilm* 76-2470.]

Johnson, Calvert. "Spanish Keyboard Ornamentation: 1535-1626." *Diapason* 69/2 [818] (1977-78):1, 12-15. [*Rilm* 78-3872.]

Johnstone, H. D. "Tempi in Corelli's 'Christmas Concerto'." *MT* 107/1485 (1966):956-99.

Jonckbloet, Willem Jozef-Andries, and Land, J. P. N., ed. *Musique et musiciens au XVIIe siècle: Correspondance et œuvres musicales de Constantin Huygens*. Shmpb. Leiden: E. J. Brill, 1882.

Jones, John A. " 'Nature Wrought Up to a Higher Pitch': The Influence of Science and Philosophy on the Development of the Heroic Couplet and Baroque Music." *CR* 25/4 (1981):389-416.

Jones, Vincent Lloyd. "The Relation of Harmonic Theory and Practice from Rameau to 1900." Ph.D. dissertation, Harvard University, 1934. Bibliog.

Jorgensen, Owen Henry. "Forgotten Sounds of Music." *PTJ* 14/10 (1971):16-18. [*Rilm* 76-16911.]

Jorgensen, Owen Henry. "In Tune with Old Tunings." *Clavier* 17/8 (1978):26-28. [*Rilm* 78-5865.]

Jorgenson, Dale Alfred. "A History of Theories of the Minor Triad." Ph.D. dissertation, Indiana University, 1957. Bibliog. [*DA* 17/10, p. 2281. UMI 00-22691.]

Jorgenson, Dale. "A Résumé of Harmonic Dualism." *ML* 44/1 (1963):31-42.

Jullien, Adolphe. *La musique et les philosophes au dix-huitième siècle*. Paris: Baur, 1873. [Extract from *RgmdP*.]

Jung, Hans Rudolf. "Telemann und die Mizlerische 'Societät der musikalischen Wissenschaften'." In *Telemann Bericht 1967* (1969):Vol. II:84-97. [*Rilm* 70-3154.]

K

Kähler, Guido. "Studien zur Entstehung der Formenlehre in der Musiktheorie des 18. und 19. Jahrhunderts (von W. C. Printz bis A. B. Marx)." Ph.D. dissertation, The University of Heidelberg, 1958.

Kätzel, Heinrich. "Musikpflege und Musikerziehung in der Stadt Hof im 16. Jahrhundert." Ph.D. dissertation, The University of Erlangen, 1951; published edition (as *Musikpflege und Musikerziehung im Reformations-*

420

jahrhundert, dargestellt am Beispiel der Stadt Hof; VEGL, no. 9), Göttingen: Vandenhoeck & Ruprecht, 1957.

> Reviews in *Mf* 12/4 (1959):513-15 (Ludwig Finscher), *MGot* 16/3 (1962):77, and *Musica* 12/11 (1958):706 (Joseph Müller-Blattau).

Kahl, Willi. *Studien zur Kölner Musikgeschichte des 16. und 17. Jahrhunderts*. BrM, no. 3. Cologne: Staufen-Verlag, 1953.

> Reviews in *Mf* 7/3 (1954):351-53 (Hans F. Redlich), *Rbdm* 10/1-2 (1956):72-75 (Suzanne Clercx), and *Stfm* 35 (1953):165-66 (Åke Davidsson).

Kamieński, Lucian. "Zum 'Tempo rubato'." *AfMw* 1 (1918-19):108-26.

Karube, Yoko. "18 seiki no senritsu ron." M.A. thesis, Tokyo University of Arts, 1969. [*Rilm* 69-3780.]

> Summary in *Og* 15/1 (1969):32-42.

Kassler, Jamie Croy. "British Writings on Music, 1760-1830: A Systematic Essay Toward a Philosophy of Selected Theoretical Writings." 2 vols. Ph.D. dissertation, Columbia University, 1971. Bibliog. [*Rilm* 75-946. *DA* 32/06A, p. 3352. UMI 72-01337.]

Kassler, Jamie Croy. "Music Made Easy to Infant Capacity, 1714-1830: Some Facets of British Music Education." *StiM* 10 (1976):67-78. Bibliog. [*Rilm* 76-15892.]

Kassler, Jamie Croy. "The Science of Music in Transition: The Works of Robert Hooke, William Holder, and Other Seventeenth-Century English Intellectuals." *NN* 1 (1978). [*Rilm* 78-2365.]

Kassler, Jamie Croy. *The Science of Music in Britain, 1714-1830: A Catalogue of Writings, Lectures and Inventions*. 2 vols. GRLH, no. 79. New York: Garland Publishing, 1979. Bibliog. [*Rilm* 79-115.]

> Reviews in *AS* 38/2 (1981):230-32 (Penelope M. Gouk), *ARBA* 11 (1980):423-24 (Frederic Schoettler), *BbF* 26/7 (1981):448-49 (François Lesure), *Cnv* vol. 41, p. 15 (Ann P. Basart), *ML* 63/1-2 (1982):128-30 (Peter le Huray), *MT* 122/1664 (1981):675-76 (Richard Andrewes), *Notes* 37/1 (1980-81):43-44 (Kerry S. Grant), and *TLS* 79/4024 (1980):533.

Kassler, Jamie Croy. "Music as a Model in Early Science." *HSc* 20/2 (1982):103-39. Bibliog. [*Rilm* 82-1726.]

Kassler, Jamie Croy. "The Royal Institution Music Lectures, 1800-1831: A Preliminary Study." *RMARC* 19 (1983-85):1-30. Bibliog.

Kassler, Jamie C. "*Organon*: Musical and Logical Instrument." In *MoyleFs* (1984):122-48. Bibliog.

Kassler, Jamie Croy, and Oldroyd, D. R. "Robert Hooke's Trinity College Musick Scripts, His Music Theory and the Role of Music in His Cosmology." *AS* 40/6 (1983):559-95. [*Rilm* 83-4821.]

Kastner, [Macario] Santiago. "Orígenes y evolución del tiento para instrumentos de tecla: Interpretación de la música hispánica para tecla de los siglos XVI y XVII." *Anmu* 28-29 (1973-74):11-151; as *The Interpretation of 16th- and 17th-Century Iberian Keyboard Music* (translated by Bernard Brauchli; MiM, no. 4), Stuyvesant, N.Y.: Pendragon Press, 1987. Bibliog.

Katz, Erich. "Die musikalischen Stilbegriffe des 17. Jahrhunderts." Ph.D. dissertation, The University of Freiburg im Breisgau, 1926; published edition, Charlottenburg: Wilhelm Flagel, [1926].

Katz, Ruth. *Divining the Powers of Music: Aesthetic Theory and the Origins of Opera*. AiM, no. 3. New York: Pendragon Press, 1985. Bibliog.

> Reviews in *CSoc* 16/5 (1987):721-22 (Rosanne Martorella) and *JAAC* 45/4 (1987):431 (Charles Dyke).

Katz, Ruth, and **Dahlhaus**, Carl, eds. *Contemplating Music: Source Readings in the Aesthetics of Music*. AiM, no. 5. Stuyvesant, N.Y.: Pendragon Press, 1987- .

> Reviews in *Brio* 24/2 (1987):82 (Clifford Bartlett) and *MT* 129/1741 (1988):131-33 (Francis Sparshott).

Kaufmann, Harald. "Zur Problematik der Werkgestalt in der Musik des 18. Jahrhunderts." *NZfM* 130/6 (1969):290-96. [*Rilm* 69-3782.]

Kauko, Väinö Olavi. "The Development of a Phenomenological Approach to Music as Seen in Selected Theories of Tonal Organization." Ph.D. dissertation, The University of Rochester, 1958. Bibliog. [SMLMS.]

Kayser, Hans. *Lehrbuch der Harmonik*. Zürich: Occident-Verlag, 1950.

Keislar, Douglas. "History and Principles of Microtonal Keyboards." *CMJ* 11/1 (1987):18-28. Bibliog.

Keller, Hermann. *Schule des Generalbass-Spiels*. Kassel: Bärenreiter, 1931; various later editions; as *Thoroughbass Method* (translated by Carl Parrish), New York: W. W. Norton, 1965; London: Barrie and Rockliff, 1966. Bibliog.

> Reviews in *ABBW* 36/24 (1965):2282, *ARG* 32 (1965-66):1006 (Igor Kipnis), *Choice* 2/8 (1965-66):491, *Composer* 22 (1966-67):31 (Howard Ferguson), *MakM* 62 (1966):19-20 (Elsie M. Avril), *MiE* 30/322 (1966):307 (Maisie Aldridge), *MK* 26/3 (1956):129 (Walter Blankenburg, *MO* 91/1083 (1967-68):161 (B. R.), *MT* 107/1484 (1966):872 (Stanlie Sadie), *PP* 58/1 (1965-66):58

(Melva Peterson), *Response* 8/2 (1966-67):122 (Newman W. Powell), and *TLS* 65/3370 (1966): 905.

Keller, Hermann. *Phrasierung und Artikulation: Ein Beitrag zu einer Sprachlehre der Musik*. Kassel: Bärenreiter, 1955; as *Phrasing and Articulation: A Contribution to the Rhetoric of Music* (translated by Leigh Gerdine), New York: W. W. Norton, 1965.

> Reviews in *AMT* 15/5 (1965-66):46 (Frederic Schoettler), *Choice* 2/7 (1965-66):395, *Instrumentalist* 20/9 (1965-66):18, *JRME* 14/2 (1966):154-56 (Gordon J. Kinney), *MakM* 62 (1966):19-20 (Elsie M. Avril), *MEJ* 52/6 (1965-66):98-99 (Michael Collins), *MK* 26/4 (1956):188-90 (Werner Bieske), *ML* 37/2 (1956):196-97 (Mosco Carner), *MO* 91/1083 (1967-68):161 (B. R.), *Musica* 11/2 (1957):113-14 (Otto Reimer), *MusT* 45/12 (1966):485 (W. R. A.), *Nmk* 5/2 (1956):57-59 (B. J.), *Notes* 14/2 (1956-57):263-64 (Klaus Speer), *RCMM* 62/3 (1966):100-101, *Response* 8/2 (1966-67):121-22 (Newman W. Powell), *PP* 58/1 (1965-66):58 (Melva Peterson), and *TLS* 65/3373 (1966):965. See also Babitz and Pont (1973).

Kelletat, Herbert. *Zur musikalischen Temperatur insbesondere bei Johann Sebastian Bach*. Kassel: J. G. Oncken, 1960.

> Review in *Mf* 16/1 (1963):82-84 (Carl Dahlhaus).

Kelletat, Herbert. "Zur Tonordnung (Wohltemperierung) im Werke Johann Sebastian Bachs." *US* 9/1 (1960):19-26.

Kelletat, Herbert. *Ein Beitrag zur musikalischen Temperatur der Musikinstrumente vom Mittelalter bis zur Gegenwart*. Reutlingen: Wandel & Goltermann, 1966.

> Review in *Mf* 21/4 (1968):482-97 (Helmut K. H. Lange).

Kerman, Joseph. "How We Got into Analysis, and How to Get Out." *CI* 7/2 (1980-81):311-31; reprinted in Rosand (1985):Vol. 9, pp. 103-23.

> Review in *T&P* 11 (1986):53-74 (Michael Cherlin).

Kerman, Joseph. *Contemplating Music: Challenges to Musicology*. Cambridge, Mass.: Harvard University Press, 1985; as *Musicology*, London: Fontana Press/Collins, 1985.

> Reviews in *BBN* (1985):296 (Peter J. Pirie), *Choice* 23/1 (1985-86):128 (A. K. McNamee), *CM* 39 (1987):66-73 (C. Gibbs), *Dafmf 1985* 16 (1988): 133-37 (Susan Haase Derrett), *EM* 13/4 (1985): 573-75 (David Fallows), *HFMA* 35/11 (1985): MA17-18 (Michael P. Steinberg), *LATBR* (July 21, 1985):10 (David Hamilton), *Listener* 114/2920 (1985):27-28 (Richard Morrison), *LRB* 8/3 (1986): 22-23 (John Deathridge), *MA* 5/1 (1986):97-103 (Peter Evans), *ML* 67/2 (1986):195-96 (Julian Rushton), *MQ* 72/3 (1986):416-18 (John Harbison), *MT* 127/1715 (1986):26-28 (Curtis Price), *NatR* 38/9 (1986):51 (Terry Teachout), *NYRB*

32/12 (1985):23-27 (Robert Winter), *NYTBR* 134/46421 (1985):19 (Erich Leinsdorf), *QQ* 93/1 (1986):209-11 (Margaret Murata), *SHR* 22/1 (1988):86-87 (Renée Cox), *T&P* 11 (1986):53-74 (Michael Cherlin), *TLS* 84/4284 (1985):525-26 (Christopher Wintle), *VdV* 31/5 (1986):77 (Gregory Sandow), and *YR* 75/3 (1985-86):437-44 (William H. Youngren). Comment in *NYRB* 35/4 (1988):19-21 (Philip Gossett).

Kinderman, William. "Dramatic Recapitulation in Wagner's *Götterdämmerung*." *NCM* 4/2 (1980-81):101-12. [*Rilm* 80-4731.]

Kinderman, William. "Das 'Geheimnis der Form' in Wagners *Tristan und Isolde*." Translated by Johannes Maczewski. *AfMw* 40/3 (1983):174-88. [*Rilm* 83-3931.]

Kinkeldey, Otto. *Orgel und Klavier in der Musik des 16. Jahrhunderts: Ein Beitrag zur Geschichte der Instrumentalmusik*. Leipzig: Breitkopf & Härtel, 1910; reprint edition, Hildesheim: Olms; Wiesbaden: Breitkopf & Härtel, 1968.

> Review in *OrganYb 1972* 3 (1972):106-7.

Kirkendale, Warren. "Ciceronians versus Aristotelians on the Ricercar as Exordium, from Bembo to Bach." *JAMS* 32/1 (1979):1-44. Bibliog. [*Rilm* 79-1961.]

Kirkendale, Warren. "*Circulatio*-Tradition, *Maria Lactans*, and Josquin as Musical Orator." *Am* 56/1 (1984):69-92.

Kivy, Peter. *The Corded Shell: Reflections on Musical Expression*. PEA, no. 9. Princeton, N.J.: Princeton University Press, 1980. Bibliog.

> Reviews in *BJA* 22/1 (1982):81-82 (R. A. Sharpe), *Choice* 18/10 (1980-81):1400, *ISP* 15/1 (1983):89-90 (V. A. Howard), *JAAC* 39/4 (1980-81):460-62 (Kingsley Price), *JAE* 16/4 (1982): 105-9 (John Hospers), *JAMS* 39/1 (1986):191-99 (Ruth A. Solie and Elizabeth V. Spelman), *JM* 2/2 (1983):209-14 (Philip A. Alperson), *JMT* 26/1 (1982):166-68 (Paul Wilson), *LJ* 105/20 (1980):2416 (Dika Newlin), *ML* 63/1-2 (1982): 111-12 (J. O. Urmson), *MQ* 68/2 (1982):287-93 (Richard Taruskin), *MR* 44/3-4 (1983):302-4 (Henry Raynor), *MTS* 6 (1984):103-10 (Anne C. Hall), *Notes* 38/2 (1981-82):311-12 (Christopher Hatch), *PRhet* 17/1 (1984):47-55 (Louis E. Auld), *TLS* 80/4083 (1981):762 (Malcolm Budd), and *VQR* 57/2 (1981):67.

Kivy, Peter. *Sound and Semblance: Reflections on Musical Representation*. Princeton, N.J.: Princeton University Press, 1984. Bibliog.

> Reviews in *BJA* 25/4 (1985):398-400 (Malcolm Budd), *Choice* 22/8 (1984-85):1174 (A. W. Hayward), *CRMEB* 88 (1986):90 (Rudolf E. Radocy), *JAAC* 43/4 (1984-85):405-7 (Albert Hayward), *JAE* 21/1 (1987):113-17 (Paul C. L. Tang), *JAMS* 39/1 (1986):191-99 (Ruth A. Solie and Elizabeth V. Spelman), *JMT* 29/2 (1985): 347-58 (Richard Taruskin), *ML* 66/3 (1985):287-89 (J. O. Urmson), *MR* 46/1 (1985):70-71 (R. A. Sharpe), *NCM* 8/3 (1984-85):273-76 (Bruce Ver-

mazen), *Notes* 45/1 (1988):65-66 (Richard D. Burbank), and *PhR* 95/2 [494] (1986):284-88 (Stephanie Ross).

Klein, Rolf. "Die Intervallehre in der deutschen Musiktheorie des 16. Jahrhunderts." Ph.D. dissertation, The University of Cologne, forthcoming.

Kleinman, Sidney. "La solmisation mobile de Jean-Jacques Rousseau à John Curwen." Ph.D. dissertation, The University of Paris (Sorbonne), 1971; published edition, Paris: Heugel, 1974. Bibliog. [*Rilm* 75-2618.]

> Review in *MT* 116/1588 (1975):542 (Bernarr Rainbow).

Knecht, Justin Heinrich. *Erklärung einiger von einem der R. G. B. in Erlangen angetasteten, aber mißverstanden Grundsätze aus der Voglerschen Theorie . . . Nebst angehängten Anmerkungen über Herrn Löhleins Einleitung in den zweyten Theil seiner Clavierschule*. Ulm: Christian Ulrich Wagner, 1785. [*Rism* B/VI/1, p. 456. LCPS: K-024.]

Kob, Walter. "The Smaller Homophonic Forms of Instrumental Music, 1740-1815, in Relation to Theories of Musical Form." Ph.D. dissertation, The University of Rochester, 1965. [*DA* 27/12A, p. 4282. UMI 66-02361.]

Koenigsberger, Dorothy. *Renaissance Man and Creative Thinking: A History of Concepts of Harmony 1400-1700*. Atlantic Highlands, N.J.: Humanities, 1979.

> Reviews in *AHR* 85/2 (1980):381-82 (Donald J. Wilcox), *Apollo* 117/251 (1983):69-70 (E. H. Ramsden), *BBN* (1979):723 (Peter Burke), *Choice* 9/16 (1979-80):1158, *Clio* 10 (1980-81):216-19 (S. K. Heninger, Jr.), *History* 66/217 (1981):293-95 (Letizia A. Panizza), *HRNB* 8/2 (1979-80):26 (Karl H. Dannenfeldt), *Isis* 72/262 (1981):319-20 (Brian Copenhaver), *ISP* 15/1 (1983):92-93 (Richard C. Trexler), *Leonardo* 14/1 (1981):68-69 (S. R. Holtzman), *Mus* 8 (1985):63-65 (Jamie C. Kassler), *NS* 98 (1979): 60 (J. Tambling), *PAA* 11 (1979-80):14-18 (Jamie Croy Kassler), *PolS* 28/3 (1980):492 (Barbara Goodwin), *RQ* 33/3 (1980):424-27 (Marion Leathers Kuntz), *Salesianum* 43/1 (1981):185-86 (L. Toscano), *SCJ* 12/1 (1981):98-99 (E. J. Furcha), and *ZfhF* 10/2 (1983):213-15 (Notker Hammerstein).

Kohlschütter, Bernd. "Die musikalische Ausbildung auf Salzburger Boden im 18. Jahrhundert." In *Mozart-Jb 1978/79* (1979):200-202.

Komma, Karl Michael. "Musikgeschichte und Musiktheorie als pädagogische Disziplin." In *Bericht Musiktheorie* (1972):272-80.

Konecne, Julie Lynn. "Harmonic Reduction Techniques in Music Analysis, c. 1770-1917." Ph.D. dissertation, The University of Iowa, 1984. [*DA* 45/07A, pp. 1910-11. UMI 84-43575.]

Kooiman, Ewald. "Lombardisch ritme in de klassieke Franse muziek: Een vorm van inegalitiet." *Ovt* 3/3-4 (1980):13-22, 29-37. [*Rilm* 80-4516.]

Kooiman, Ewald. "Die *Inégalité* in der französischen Barockmusik." Translated by Hermann J. Busch. *ArsOr* 29/1 (1981):3-15.

Kramer, Gale. "The Prefaces to the Organ-Works of Jean Titelouze." *OrganYb 1978* 9 (1978):2-10.

Kramer, Margarete. "Beiträge zu einer Geschichte des Affektbegriffes in der Musik von 1550-1700." Ph.D. dissertation, The University of Halle/Saale, 1924.

Kramer, Richard. "Notes to Beethoven's Education." *JAMS* 28/1 (1975):72-101. [*Rilm* 75-963.]

Kramer, Richard. "*Gradus ad Parnassum*: Beethoven, Schubert, and the Romance of Counterpoint." *NCM* 11/2 (1987-88):107-20.

Krantz, Steven Charles. "Rhetorical and Structural Functions of Mode in Selected Motets of Josquin des Prez." Ph.D. dissertation, The University of Minnesota, 1989. Bibliog.

Krehbiel, James Woodrow. "Harmonic Principles of Jean-Philippe Rameau and His Contemporaries." Ph.D. dissertation, Indiana University, 1964. Bibliog. [*DA* 25/05, pp. 3019-20. UMI 64-12049.]

Kremlev, Yuri. "Estetika v sovetskom muzykoznanii." [Aesthetics in Soviet Musicology.] *Vtem* 6-7 (1967):18-43.

Kremlev, Yuri. "O metodologii sovetskogo muzykoznaniia." [On the Methodology of Soviet Musicology.] *Vtem* 6-7 (1967):3-17.

Krenek, Ernst. "New Methods in Teaching Counterpoint." *HMYB* 7 (1952):116-28.

Kretzschmar, Hermann. "Allgemeines und Besonderes zur Affektenlehre." *JMbP 1911* 18 (1912):63-77; *JMbP 1912* 19 (1913):65-78. Bibliog.

Krome, Ferdinand. "Die Anfänge des musikalischen Journalismus in Deutschland." Ph.D. dissertation, The University of Leipzig, 1896; published edition, Leipzig: Pöschel & Trepte, 1896.

Krones, Hartmut. "Rhetorik und rhetorische Symbolik in der Musik um 1800: Vom Weiterleben eines Prinzips." *Mth* 3/2 (1988):117-40. Bibliog.

Kroyer, Theodor. "Die Anfänge der Chromatik im italienischen Madrigal des XVI. Jahrhunderts: Ein Beitrag zur Geschichte des Madrigals." Ph.D. dissertation, The University of Munich, 1901; published edition (PIMg, ser. 1, no. 4), Leipzig: Breitkopf & Härtel, 1902; reprint edition, Farnborough, G.B. and Ridgewood, N.J.: Gregg Press, 1968; Wiesbaden: Breitkopf & Härtel, 1970.

Krützfeldt, Werner. "Satztechnische Untersuchungen am Vokalwerk des Michael Praetorius auf der Basis der Musiktheorie seiner Zeit und unter besonderer Berücksichtigung des Wort-Ton-Verhältnisses in den motettischen Sätzen." 2 vols. Ph.D. dissertation, The University of Hamburg, 1961.

Krumhansl, Carol L. "Perceptual Structures for Tonal Music." *MP* 1/1 (1983-84):28-62. [*Rilm* 83-6614.]

Krummacher, Friedhelm. "Die geistliche Aria in Norddeutschland und Skandinavien: Ein gattungsgeschichtlicher Versuch." In *Weltliches und Geistliches Lied des Barock: Studien zur Liedkultur in Deutschland und Skandinavien*, edited by Dieter Lohmeier, pp. 229-64. BzD, no. 2. [Same as *Daphnis* 8/1 (1979). Suasv, no. 7.] Amsterdam: Rodopi, 1979.

Krummacher, Friedhelm. "Heinrich Schütz als 'poetischer Musiker'." *MK* 56/2 (1986):77-83. Bibliog.

Kubota, Keiichi. "Über die musikalische 'Empfindsamkeit'." *Mf* 39/2 (1986):139-48. Bibliog.

Kümmel, Werner Friedrich. "Die Anfänge der Musikgeschichte an den deutschsprachigen Universitäten: Ein Beitrag zur Geschichte der Musikwissenschaft als Hochschuldisziplin." *Mf* 20/3 (1967):262-80. Bibliog. [*Rilm* 68-2082.]

Kümmel, Werner Friedrich. "Musik und Musikgeschichte in biologistischer Interpretation." In *Biologismus im 19. Jahrhundert*, edited by Gunter Mann, pp. 108-46. SMg, no. 5. Stuttgart: Ferdinand Enke, 1973. [*Rilm* 75-2979.]

Kümmerling, Harald. *Almanach für die galante Welt*. SMB, no. 1. Neuss: Peter Päffgen OHG, 1977. [*Rilm* 77-566.]

Kuhn, Max. *Die Verzierungs-Kunst in der Gesang-Musik des 16.-17. Jahrhunderts, (1535-1650)*. PIMg, no. 7. Leipzig: Breitkopf & Härtel, 1902.

Kunze, Stefan. *Wolfgang Amadeus Mozart: Sinfonie g-moll, KV 550*. MdM, no. 6. Munich: Wilhelm Fink, 1968. Bibliog. [*Rilm* 68-3370.]

    Reviews in *Mf* 25/2 (1972):220-22 (Hermann Beck) and *Muh* 19/4 (1968):200.

Kunze, Stefan. "Instrumentalität und Sprachvertonung in der Musik von Heinrich Schütz, I" and "Sprachauslegung und Instrumentalität in der Musik von Schütz: Mit einem Exkurs zur 'Figurenlehre'." *SchüJb* (1979):9-43; 4-5 (1982-83):39-49. [*Rilm* 79-2541.]

L

La Borde, Jean-Benjamin de. *Essai sur la musique ancienne et moderne*. 4 vols. Paris: Eugène Onfroy (impr. Philippe-Denys Pierres), 1780; facsimile edition, (MTFSEC), New York: AMS Press, 1978. [*Rism* B/VI/1, pp. 466-67. LCPS: L-005. SMLMS.]

La Fage, Adrien de. *Essais de diphthérographie musicale, ou notices, descriptions, analyses, extraits et reproductions de manuscrits relatifs à la pratique, à la théorie et à l'histoire de la musique*. 2 vols. 2 vols. Paris: O. Legouix, 1864; reprint edition, Amsterdam: Fritz A. M. Knuf, 1964.

La Motte-Haber, Helga de. "Zum Problem der Klassifikation von Akkorden." *JSIM 1968* (1969):9-28. Bibliog.

La Motte-Haber, Helga de. "Konsonanz und Dissonanz als Kriterien der Beschreibung von Akkorden." *JSIM 1970* (1971):101-27. Bibliog.

La Motte-Haber, Helga de. *Psychologie und Musiktheorie*. SzMp. Frankfurt am Main: Diesterweg, 1976. Bibliog. [*Rilm* 77-1907.]

    Reviews in *Mf* 33/1 (1980):86-87 (Christian Möllers) and *NMZ* 27/3 (1978):18.

Lang, Paul Henry. *Music in Western Civilization*. New York: W. W. Norton, 1941.

    Reviews in *CS* 11 (1942):30 (Frank Knight Dale), *Isis* 34/2 [94] (1942-43):182-86 (George Sarton), *JAAC* 2/6 (1942):70-71 (Edward N. Barnhart), *KenR* 4/2 (1942):240-43 (Henry Woodward), *ML* 24/1 (1943):54-59 (Eric Blom), and *MR* 3/2 (1942):79-80 (Geoffrey Sharp).

Lang, Paul Henry. "The Enlightenment and Music." *ECS* 1/1 (1967-68):93-108. [*Rilm* 68-3371.]

Lange, Georg. "Zur Geschichte der Solmisation." *SIMg* 1 (1899-1900):535-622. Bibliog.

Larosh, Herman. "Istoricheskii metod prepodavaniia teorii muzyki." [The Historical Method of Teaching the Theory of Music.] *Muzl* /2-5 (1873):17-22, 33-40, 47-53, 65-68; reprinted in his *Sobranie muzykal'no-kriticheskikh statei* [A Collection of Musical Critical Articles], Vol. 1, pp. 260-79 (Moscow: 1913).

Larsen, Jens Peter. "Sonatenform-Probleme." In *BlumeFs* (1963):221-30; as "Sonata Form Problems" (translated by Ulrich Krämer), in his *Handel, Haydn, and the Viennese Classical Style* (translated by Ulrich Krämer; SiM, no. 100), Ann Arbor, Mich.: UMI Research Press, 1988, pp. 269-79.

Larsson, Roger Barnett. "The Beautiful, the Sublime and the Picturesque in Eighteenth-Century Musical Thought in Britain." Ph.D. dissertation, The State University of New York at Buffalo, 1980. [*Rilm* 80-4016. *DA* 41/01A, p. 14. UMI 80-16209.]

Laudon, Robert T. "No One Can Possibly Mistake the Genre of This Composition." *CM* 25 (1978):69-82. [*Rilm* 78-248.]

Launay, Denise. "L'art du compositeur de musique: Essai sur la composition musicale en France au temps de

Henri IV et de Louis XIII." In *Musica antiqua III* (1972):209-46. [*Rilm* 73-343.]

Launay, Denise. "L'enseignement de la composition dans les maîtrises, en France, aux XVIᵉ et XVIIᵉ siècles." *Rdm* 68/1-2 (1982):79-90. Bibliog. *Rilm* 82-2349.]

Lawrence, Ian. *Composers and the Nature of Music Education*. London: Scolar, 1978. [*Rilm* 78-1910.]

> Reviews in *AJME* 24 (1979):69, *BBN* (1979):53 (Konstantin Bazarov), *ML* 61/1 (1980):74-76 (Aubrey Hickman), *MT* 120/1631 (1979):39-40 (John Horton), *MuMus* 27/7 [319] (1978-79):43-44 (Kevin Stephens), and *MusT* 58/5 (1979):29 (Brian Brockelhurst).

Lecky, James. "Modern Systems of Harmony." *MT* 21/444 (1880):57-59.

Le Coat, Gerard. "L'art de l'orateur et les techniques d'expression artistique pendant la Renaissance." *RenRef* 2/2 (1978):141-50.

le Huray, Peter. "The Role of Music in Eighteenth- and Early Nineteenth-Century Aesthetics." *PMA 1978-79* 105 (1979):90-99. [*Rilm* 79-1964.]

le Huray, Peter, and Day, James, eds. *Music and Aesthetics in the Eighteenth and Early-Nineteenth Centuries*. CRLM. Cambridge: Cambridge University Press, 1981.

> An abridged edition was issued in 1988. Reviews in *AJME* 31 (1982):65-66 (Michael Kassler), *AR* 23/3 (1982):121 (Jane P. Ambrose), *BBN* (1981):621 (Marjorie E. Rycroft), *BJECS* 6/2 (1983):287-90 (J. M. Tudor), *Choice* 19/6 (1981-82):774, *Composer* 76-77 (1982):36-39 (Francis Routh), *Dmt* 57/1 (1982-83):40-43 (Jørgen I. Jensen), *JAMS* 35/3 (1982):565-77 (Elaine R. Sisman), *KSMBR* 34 (1983):91-94 (Morse Peckham), *Mf* 37/4 (1984):321-22 (Rudolf Flotzinger), *ML* 63/3-4 (1982):316-19 (Howard Serwer), *Mus* 10 (1987):86, *Notes* 38/4 (1981-82):838-39 (Margert Ross Griffel), and *Rdm* 67/2 (1981):256-57 (Philippe A. Autexier).

León Tello, Francisco José. *Estudios de historia de la teoría musical*. Madrid: Consejo superior de investigaciones científicas, Instituto español de musicología, 1962.

> Review in *Rdm* 50 (1964):123-25 (A. Machabey).

León Tello, Francisco José. *La teoría español de la música en los siglos XVII y XVIII*. Madrid: Consejo superior de investigaciones científicas, Instituto español de musicología, 1974.

> Review in *Bhisp* 80/3-4 (1978):355-56 (Guy Bourligueux).

Lerdahl, Fred. "Tonal Pitch Space." *MP* 5/3 (1987-88):315-50.

Lester, Joel. "Root-Position and Inverted Triads in Theory around 1600." *JAMS* 27/1 (1974):110-19. [*Rilm* 74-3914.]

Lester, Joel. "Major-Minor Concepts and Modal Theory in Germany: 1592-1680." *JAMS* 30/2 (1977):208-53. Bibliog. [*Rilm* 77-2522.]

Lester, Joel. "The Recognition of Major and Minor Keys in German Theory: 1680-1730." *JMT* 22/1 (1978):65-103. Bibliog. [*Rilm* 78-4876.]

Lester, Joel. "Simultaneity Structures and Harmonic Functions in Tonal Music." *ITO* 5/5 (1979-81):3-28. [*Rilm* 81-3673.]

Lester, Joel. *Between Modes and Keys: German Theory 1592-1802*. HSMT, no. 3. Stuyvesant, N.Y.: Pendragon Press, 1989.

Lester, Joel. *History of Compositional Theory in the 18th Century*. Cambridge, Mass.: Harvard University Press, forthcoming.

Leuchtmann, Horst. "Die musikalischen Wortausdeutungen in den Motetten des Magnum opus musicum von Orlando di Lasso." Ph.D. dissertation, The University of Munich, 1957 (1960); published edition (Sma, no. 38), Strasbourg and Baden-Baden: P. H. Heitz, 1959.

Levarie, Siegmund. "Harmonic Analysis." *CMS* 26 (1986):66-76.

Levenson, Irene Montefiore. "Motivic-Harmonic Transfer in the Late Works of Schubert: Chromaticism in Large and Small Spans." Ph.D. dissertation, Yale University, 1981. [*Rilm* 81-3716. *DA* 42/05A, p. 1846. UMI 81-24373.]

Levenson, Irene Montefiore. "Smooth Moves: Schubert and Theories of Modulation in the Nineteenth Century." *ITO* 7/5-6 (1983-84):35-53.

Levi, Anthony Herbert Tigar. "Theories of the Passions in French Moralists from du Vair to Descartes." D.Phil. dissertation, Oxford University, 1962-63; published edition (as *French Moralists: The Theory of the Passions, 1585 to 1649*), Oxford: Clarendon Press, 1964. Bibliog.

> Reviews in *AusJP* 43/3 (1965):424-25 (John Passmore), *Choice* 2/12 (1965-66):854, *FrR* 41/3 (1967-68):413-14 (Robert N. Nicolich), *RN* 19/1 (1966):33-36 (Robert E. Hill), and *TLS* 64/3299 (1965):388.

Levitan, Joseph S. "Adrian Willaert's Famous Duo *Quidnam ebrietas*: A Composition Which Closes Apparently with the Interval of a Seventh." *TvNm* 15 (1938):166-233.

Lewin, David. "Forte's Interval Vector, My Interval Function, and Regener's Common-Note Function." *JMT* 21/2 (1977):194-237. [*Rilm* 77-5719.]

Lewin, David. "Some Investigations into Foreground Rhythmic and Metric Patterning." See Browne (1981):101-37. [*Rilm* 81-1650.]

Lewin, David. "A Formal Theory of Generalized Tonal Functions." *JMT* 26/1 (1982):23-60. [*Rilm* 82-1497.]

Lewin, David. "Amfortas's Prayer to Titurel and the Role of D in *Parsifal*: The Tonal Space of the Drama and the Enharmonic C-flat/B." *NCM* 7/3 (1983-84):336-49.

Lewis, Anthony, ed., with Nigel Fortune. *Opera and Church Music*. NOHM, vol. 5. London: Oxford University Press, 1975; as *Storia della musica*, Milan: Feltrinelli, 1978. Bibliog. [*Rilm* 75-828.]

> Reviews in *AJME* 19 (1976):61 (Graham Hardie), *AMT* 26/6 (1976-77):44-45 (Howard Serwer), *CJ* 16/9 (1975-76):34 (Daniel J. Brenner), *CM* 1 (1976):51, *COSB* 18/1 (1975):11, *Éc* 45/1 (1977):70 (J. Legrand), *ECCB 1976* 2 (1979):170-71 (Dennis Libby), *JCM* 21/4 (1979):17-18 (James Boeringer), *MakM* 91 (1976):12 (Lionel Nutley), *Melos/NZfM* 2/3 (1976):243-44 (Hans Hollander), *Mf* 31/1 (1978):104-5 (Werner Braun), *MiE* 40/378 (1976):79-80 (Peter Aston), *Miscm* 11 (1980):267-69 (Andrew D. McCredie), *ML* 57/3 (1976):309-12 (Denis Arnold), *MQ* 62/3 (1976):450-52 (Henry Leland Clarke), *MT* 118/1611 (1977):390-91 (George J. Buelow), *MuMus* 25/2 [290] (1976-77):36-38 (Nicholas Kenyon), *Music* 10/11 (1976):16-17 (Richard French), *MusT* 55/5 (1976):29 (John Morehen), *Nrmi* 10/3 (1976):503-7 (Massimo Mila), *Nrmi* 13 (1979):694-95 (Massimo Mila), *Rh* 101/258 [523] (1977):217-19 (Édith Weber), *Rmuz* 22/17 (1978):7, *Stfm* 61/1 (1979):89-90 (Martin Tegen), and *TLS* 75/3879 (1976):896-97 (Winton Dean).

Lewis, Christopher. "Incipient Tonal Thought in Seventeenth-Century English Theory." *SMUWO* 6 (1981):24-47. [*Rilm* 81-1662.]

Lewis, H. M. "Extra-Harmonic Trumpet Tones in the Baroque Era—Natural Trumpet vs. *Tromba da tirarsi*." *JITG* 5 (1980):39-45.

Lichtenthal, Pietro. *Dizionario e bibliografia della musica*. 4 vols. Milan: Antonio Fontana, 1826.

> Derived from KOCH (1802), Forkel (1792/1962), and Gerber (1790-92).

Lindley, Mark. "Instructions for the Clavier Diversely Tuned." *EM* 5/1 (1977):18-23. [*Rilm* 77-1387.]

Lindley, Mark. "Just Intonation." In *NGrove* (1980). Bibliog.

Lindley, Mark. "Temperaments." In *NGrove* (1980). Bibliog.

Lindley, Mark. "Preface to a Graduate Course in the History of Music Theory." *CMS* 22/2 (1982):83-102. [*Rilm* 82-5897.]

Lindley, Mark. *Lutes, Viols and Temperaments*. New York: Cambridge University Press, 1984.

> Reviews in *Choice* 22/7 (1984-85):1005 (M. D. Grace), *EM* 13/1 (1985):91-93 (Ephraim Segerman), *JVGSA* 22 (1985):65-66 (Linda and John Shortridge), *ML* 67/3 (1986):313-16 (Penelope Gouk), *MT* 126/1710 (1985):465 (David Ledbetter), *RecMus* 8/4 (1984):125, and *TLS* 84/4287 (1985):619 (Ian Woodfield).

Lindley, Mark. "J. S. Bach's Tunings." *MT* 126/1714 (1985):721-26.

Lindley, Mark. "A Suggested Improvement for the Fisk Organ at Stanford." *PPrR* 1/1-2 (1988):107-32.

Lippman, Edward. "The History of Theory." In *Musicology and the Computer, Musicology 1966-2000: A Practial Program; Three Symposia*, edited and with a Preface by Barry S. Brook, pp. 198-203. AMSNYP, no. 2. New York: The City University of New York Press, 1970. [*Rilm* 70-3996.]

Lippman, Edward A. *Musical Aesthetics: A Historical Reader. Volume I: From Antiquity to the Eighteenth Century*. AiM, no. 4. New York: Pendragon Press, 1986.

> Reviews in *Brio* 23/2 (1986):88 (Clifford Bartlett) and *Notes* 44/2 (1987-88):269-70 (Philip Alperson).

List, Erich. "Bemerkungen zur Aufführungspraxis der Musik der Bach-Händel-Zeit." In *Konferenzbericht Blankenburg/Harz 1975* (1976):64-76. [*Rilm* 76-15213.]

Livingstone, Ernest Felix. "The Theory and Practice of Protestant School Music in Germany as Seen through the Collection of Abraham Ursinus (ca. 1600)." Ph.D. dissertation, The University of Rochester, 1962. Bibliog. [*DA* 26/04, p. 2256. UMI 63-07738.]

Livingstone, Ernest F. "The Place of Music in German Education around 1600." *JRME* 19/2 (1971):144-67. [*Rilm* 71-3129.]

Lloyd, Llewelyn Southworth. "Musical Theory in the Early *Philosophical Transactions*." *NRRSL* 3/[2] (1940-41):149-57.

Lloyd, Llewelyn Southworth. "Conflicting Musical Theories of the Nineteenth Century." *MMR* 85/967 (1955):119-22.

Loach, Donald. "A Stylistic Approach to Species Counterpoint." *JMT* 1/2 (1957):181-200.

Lockwood, Lewis. "On 'Parody' as Term and Concept in 16th-Century Music." In *ReeseFs* (1966/1978):560-75. Bibliog.

Longyear, Rey M., and Covington, Kate R. "Tonic Major, Mediant Major: A Variant Tonal Relationship in 19th-Century Sonata Form." *SMUWO* 10 (1985):105-39.

Lonsdale, Roger. "Dr. Burney's 'Dictionary of Music'." *Musicology* 5 (1979):159-71.

Lottermoser, Werner. "Akustik, Geschichte." In *MGG* (1949-68). Bibliog.

Lowinsky, Edward E. *Secret Chromatic Art in the Netherlands Motet*. Translated from the German by Carl Buchman. CUSM, no. 6. New York: Columbia University Press, 1946; reprint edition, New York: Russell & Russell, 1967.

> See also his "Secret Chromatic Art Re-examined" in *Perspectives in Musicology*, edited by Barry S.

Brook, pp. 91-135 (New York: W. W. Norton, 1972 [*Rilm* 72-273.]). Reviews in *Md* 1 (1946):159-67 (Leo Schrade), *ML* 27/4 (1946): 268 (J. A. Westrup), *MQ* 32/3 (1946):471-76 (Willi Apel), *Rmi* 51/4 (1949):328 (a.), *Scrut* 14/3 (1946-47):238 (W. H. Mellers), and *TvNm* 16/4 (1946):253-304 (M. van Crevel).

Lowinsky, Edward E. "On the Use of Scores by Sixteenth-Century Musicians." *JAMS* 1/1 (1948):17-23. Bibliog.

> See also *JAMS* 2/2 (1949):130-34 ["Communication" (Ruth Hannas) and Reply (Lowinsky)].

Lowinsky, Edward Elias. *Tonality and Atonality in Sixteenth-Century Music*. Berkeley, Calif.: University of California Press, 1961; reprint edition, Da Capo Press, 1989.

> Reviews in *JAMS* 16/1 (1963):82-86 (Claude V. Palisca), *JMT* 6/1 (1962):142-53 (Richard L. Crocker), *JRME* 9/2 (1961):171 (Johannes Riedel), *Mf* 17/3 (1964):317-18 (Carl Dahlhaus), *ML* 43/1 (1962):64-66 (H. K. Andrews), *MQ* 48/2 (1962):252-54 (Denis Stevens), *MR* 23/1 (1962):57-58, *MT* 103/1429 (1962):168 (Jeremy Noble), *Notes* 19/2 (1961-62):250-51 (Glen Haydon), *PNM* 2/1 (1963-64):133-36 (Ernst

Krenek), *RN* 15/3 (1962):227 (Imogene Horsley), and *TLS* 62/3193 (1963):339.

Lowinsky, Edward E. "The Musical Avant-Garde of the Renaissance; or, The Peril and Profit of Foresight." In *Art, Science, and History in the Renaissance*, edited by Charles Southward Singleton, pp. 111-62. JHHS. Baltimore: The Johns Hopkins Press, 1967.

Lowinsky, Edward E. "The Problem of Mannerism in Music: An Attempt at a Definition." *Sm* 3 (1974):131-218.

Luoma, Robert Gust. "Aspects of Mode in Sixteenth-Century Magnificats." *MQ* 62/3 (1976):395-408. [*Rilm* 76-2483.]

Luoma, Robert Gust. "Relationships between Music and Poetry (Cipriano de Rore's 'Quando signor lasciaste')." *Md* 31 (1977):135-54. Bibliog. [*Rilm* 77-2420.]

Luper, Albert Thomas. "Portuguese Music Theory in the Early Seventeenth Century: A Critical Study of the *Arte de musica . . .* of Antonio Fernandes." M.M. thesis, The University of Rochester, 1938. Bibliog.

M

MacClintock, Carol, ed. *Readings in the History of Music in Performance*. Bloomington, Ind.: Indiana University Press, 1979.

> Reviews in *AMT* 30/5 (1980-81):48-49 (David Z. Kushner), *Choice* 16/10 (1979-80):1318, *CJ* 22/5 (1981-82):35-38 (Gordon Paine), *Clavier* 19/1 (1980):6 (Christine N. Nagy), *Diapason* 72/11 [864] (1981):11 (Bruce Gustafson), *EM* 8/3 (1980):383-87 (Robert Donington), *JAMS* 35/3 (1982):565-77 (Elaine R. Sisman), *MuMus* 28/5 [329] (1979-80):37-38 (Stephen Pettitt), *NATSB* 36/4 (1979-80):44-45 (Enrique Alberto Arias), and *Notes* 36/4 (1979-80):892-93 (James W. Pruett).

Mace, D. T. "Musical Humanism, the Doctrine of Rhythmus, and the Saint Cecilia Odes of Dryden." *JWCI* 27 (1964):251-92.

> Comment in *JWCI* 29 (1966):282-95 (H. Neville Davies) [Reply in *JWCI* 29 (1966):296-310 (D. T. Mace)].

Mach, Ernst. "Beiträge zur Geschichte der Akustik." *MDMGP* (1892).

> Reprinted in his *Populär-wissenschaftliche Vorlesungen* (Leipzig: Johann Ambrosius Barth, 1896); translated by Thomas J. McCormack in *Popular Scientific Lectures* (Chicago: Open Court Publishing Co., 1898); later editions.

Mackenzie, Alexander Carl Norderstrom. "Keyboard Temperament in England during the Eighteenth and

Nineteenth Centuries." M.Litt. thesis, The University of Bristol, 1980.

Mahlert, Elke, and Sunter, Bernd. "Kadenz." In *HwmT* (1972-). Bibliog.

Maier, Siegfried. *Studien zur Theorie des Taktes in der ersten Hälfte des 18. Jahrhunderts*. FBzMw, no. 16. Tutzing: Hans Schneider, 1984. Bibliog.

Mainka, Jürgen. "Frühe Analysen zweier Stücke aus dem Wohltemperierten Klavier." *BzMw* 7/1 (1965):47-55. Also in *VetterFs* (1969):177-83. [*Rilm* 70-2566.]

Mainke, Dietrich. "Heinrich Schütz als Lehrer." *Sagittarius* 2 (1969):17-28.

Mallard, James Harry. "A Translation of Christian Gottfried Krause's *Von der musikalischen Poesie*, with a Critical Essay on His Sources and the Aesthetic Views of His Time." Ph.D. dissertation, The University of Texas at Austin, 1978. Bibliog. [*Rilm* 78-6428. *DA* 39/11A, pp. 6388-89. UMI 79-10993.]

Maniates, Maria Rika. *Mannerism in Italian Music and Culture, 1530-1630*. Chapel Hill, N.C.: University of North Carolina Press, 1979. Bibliog. [*Rilm* 79-2460.]

> Reviews in *Choice* 17/3 (1980-81):370, *EM* 10/3 (1982):373-75 (Jerome Roche), *JAMS* 34/3 (1981):552-57 (Gary Tomlinson), *LJ* 104/14 (1979):1568 (Allen B. Skei), *ML* 62/3-4 (1981): 400-402 (Denis Arnold), *MQ* 67/1 (1981):125-31 (Jeffrey G. Kurtzman), *MR* 41/4 (1980):309-12 (Denis Stevens), *MT* 122/1658 (1981):243 (Iain Fenlon), *RenRef* 6/4 (1982):284-89 (J. Evan

Kreider), and *RQ* 33/4 (1980):766-69 (James Haar).

Mann, Alfred. "The Theory of Fugue." Ph.D. dissertation, Columbia University, 1955; published edition (as *The Study of Fugue*), New Brunswick, N.J.: Rutgers University Press, 1958; reprint edition, New York: W. W. Norton, 1965; New York: Dover, 1987.

> Reviews in *ABBW* 37/10 (1966):985, *AmO* 41/10 (1958):389-90 (Harry W. Gay), *ChG* 12/5 (1959-60):31, *Clavier* 5/5 (1966):10, *JAMS* 12/1 (1959): 78-80 (Claude V. Palisca), *JMT* 3/2 (1959):316-19 (Donald Loach), *JR* 6/1 (1958-59):23 (Charles Jones), *Mf* 13/2 (1960):242-44 (Carl Dahlhaus), *ML* 41/3 (1960):283-85 (H. K. Andrews), *MMR* 90/1000 (1960):121-23, *MO* 83/993 (1959-60): 619 (H. H.), *MR* 22/1 (1961): 55-61 (Roger Bullivant), *MT* 101/1407 (1960): 300 (Arthur Hutchings), *MuMus* 8/8 (1959-60):33 (Geoffrey Crankshaw), *Notes* 16/1 (1958-59):52-53 (Jan LaRue), *Notes* 23/4 (1966-67): 744-45 (Arthur Daniels), *NYT* 107/36716 (Au-gust 3, 1958): Section 2, p. 7 (John Briggs), *SMz* 100/4 (1960): 267-68, *Tempo* 57 (1961):33 (A. E. F. Dickinson), and *TLS* 59/3027 (1960):140.

Mann, Alfred. "Beethoven's Contrapuntal Studies with Haydn." *MQ* 56/4 (1970):711-26; abridged German version (as "Haydn's Kontrapunktlehre und Beethovens Studien") in *Bericht Bonn 1970* (1971):70-74. [*Rilm* 71-3764; 73-3494.]

Mann, Alfred. "Ist Komponieren lehrbar? Zur klassischen Fugenlehre." *Musica* 35/4 (1981):335-39. [*Rilm* 81-3752.]

Mann, Alfred. *Theory and Practice: The Great Composer as Student and Teacher*. New York: W. W. Norton, 1987.

> Review in *Choice* 25/9 (1988):1413 (J. Rayburn).

Martin, Henriette. "La 'Camerata' du Comte Bardi et la musique florentine du XVIᵉ siècle." *Rdm* 13/42-44 (1932):63-74, 152-61, 227-34; 14/46-47 (1933):92-100, 141-51.

Marvin, Clara. "Two Practices, Three Styles: Typologies of Composition in 17th-Century Italian Writings on Music." Ph.D. dissertation, Yale University, forthcoming.

Marvin, Elizabeth West. "*Tonpsychologie and Musikpsychologie*: Historical Perspectives on the Study of Music Perception." *Theoria* 2 (1987):59-84.

Massenkeil, Günther. "Zur Frage der Dissonanzbehandlung in der Musik des 17. Jahrhunderts." In *Colloques Wégimont 1957* (1963):151-76.

Massera, Giuseppe. "Dalle 'imperfezioni' alle 'perfezioni' della moderna musica." In *Congresso Monteverdi 1968* (1969):397-408.

Mazel, Lev Abramovich. *Fantaziia f-moll Shopena: Opyt analiza*. [The F-Minor Fantasy of Chopin: An Experiment in Analysis.] Moscow: 1937.

Mazel, Lev Abramovich. "O sovetskom teoreticheskom muzykoznanii." [On Soviet Theoretical Musicology.] *Smuz* /12 (1940):15-29.

> See also "K diskussii o sovetskom muzykoznanii" [Toward a Discussion of Soviet Musicology] in *Smuz* /4 (1941):90-98.

McCredie, Andrew D. "The Munich School and Rudi Stephan (1887-1915): Some Forgotten Sources and By-ways of Musical Jugendstil and Expressionism." *MR* 29/3 (1968):197-222. [*Rilm* 68-3490.]

McCredie, Andrew. "La riforma operatistica prima di Gluck e il teatro musicale eroico tedesco dello *Sturm und Drang*." *Rmus* 5 (1981):86-108. [*Rilm* 81-542.]

McIntyre, Ray. "On the Interpretation of Bach's Gigues." *MQ* 51/3 (1965):478-92.

McKinnon, James W. "Jubal vel Pythagoras, quis sit inventor musicae?" *MQ* 64/1 (1978):1-28. [*Rilm* 78-251.]

McQuere, Gordon D., ed. *Russian Theoretical Thought in Music*. RMS, no. 10. Ann Arbor, Mich.: UMI Research Press, 1983. Bibliog. [*Rilm* 83-3886.]

> Contains six studies, including "Russian Music Theory: A Conspectus," by Ellon D. Carpenter; "The Theories of Boleslav Yavorsky," by Gordon D. McQuere; "Varvara Dernova's System of Analysis of the Music of Skryabin," by Roy J. Guenther; "Boris Asafiev and *The Musical Form as a Process*," by Gordon D. McQuere; and "The Contributions of Taneev, Catoire, Conus, Garbuzov, Mazel, and Tiulin," by Ellon D. Carpenter. Review in *MA* 5/1 (1986):103-8 (David Brown).

Meer, John Henry van der. "Saitenklaviere mit enharmonischen Tasten in deutschen Sprachgebiet." In *Bericht Berlin 1974* (1980):592-95. [*Rilm* 80-1642.]

Meier, Bernhard. "Musica reservata." In *MGG* (1949-68). Bibliog.

Meier, Bernhard. "Musiktheorie und Musik im 16. Jahrhundert." In *Bericht Kassel 1962* (1963):356-59.

Meier, Bernhard. "Carl von Winterfeld und die Tonartenlehre des 16. Jahrhunderts." *KJb* 50 (1966):131-63. Bibliog.

Meier, Bernhard. "Alte und neue Tonarten: Wesen und Bedeutung." In *LenaertsFs* (1969):157-68. [*Rilm* 71-1528.]

Meier, Bernhard. *Die Tonarten der klassischen Vokalpolyphonie, nach den Quellen dargestellt*. Utrecht: Oosthoek, Scheltema & Holkema, 1974; as *The Modes of Classical Vocal Polyphony* (translated by Ellen S. Beebe), New York: Broude Brothers, 1988. Bibliog.

> See Dahlhaus ["Zur Tonartenlehre"] (1976). Reviews in *JAMS* 31/1 (1978):136-48 (Leeman L. Perkins), *KJb* 58-59 (1974-75):152 (Karl Gustav Fellerer), *Mf* 29/3 (1976):354-56 (Carl Dahlhaus), *MQ* 62/4 (1976):591-97 (Peter Bergquist), *Ridm* 14/2 (1979):448-57 (Jessie Ann Owens, translated by Lorenzo Bianconi), *Stfm* 58/2

(1976):71-72 (Hans Eppstein), and *TvNm* 26/1 (1976):46-50 (Walter Blankenburg).

Menck, Hans Friedrich. *Der Musiker im Roman: Ein Beitrag zur Geschichte der vorromantischen Erzählungsliteratur.* BnLg, no. 18. Heidelberg: Carl Winters Universitätsbuchhandlung, 1931. Bibliog.

Mendel, Arthur. "Pitch in the Sixteenth and Early Seventeenth Centuries." *MQ* 34/1-4 (1948):28-45, 199-221, 336-57, 575-93.

Mendel, Arthur. "On the Pitches in Use in Bach's Time." *MQ* 41/3-4 (1955):332-54, 466-80.

Mendel, Arthur. "Pitch in Western Music since 1500: A Reexamination." *Am* 50/1-2 (1978):1-92, 328. Bibliog. [*Rilm* 78-1679.]

Miller, Gertrude Brown. "Tonal Materials in Seventeenth-Century English Treatises." Ph.D. dissertation, The University of Rochester, 1960. Bibliog.

Miller, Leta, and Cohen, Albert. *Music in the Royal Society of London, 1660-1806.* DSMB, no. 56. Detroit: Information Coordinators, 1987. Bibliog.

> Reviews in *AMT* 38/2 (1988-89):40-42 (Douglas A. Lee), *ARBA* 19 (1988):508-9 (George Louis Mayer), *Brio* 24/2 (1987):82 (Clifford Bartlett), and *MP* 6/1 (1988-89): 113-14 (Penelope Gouk).

Miller, Poland. "The Augmented Sixth Chord: Its Historical and Theoretical Origin and Development to [the] Era of Key-Feeling." *JMus* 1/1 (1939-40):17-44.

Mitchell, John William. "A History of Theories of Functional Harmonic Progression." Ph.D. dissertation, Indiana University, 1963. [*DA* 25/02, p. 1250. UMI 64-05473.]

Mitchell, William J. "Chord and Context in Eighteenth-Century Theory." *JAMS* 16/2 (1963):221-39.

Möller, Hans-Jürgen. "Aufklärerische Traktate über die 'heilenden Wirkungen' der Musik: Eine Untersuchung über die Beziehungen zwischen Musik-theorie und medizinischen Vorstellungen zur Zeit der Aufklärung." *NZfM* 132/9 (1971):472-77. Bibliog. [*Rilm* 72-1196.]

Möllers, Christian. "Der Einfluß des Konzertsatzes auf die Formentwicklung im 18. Jahrhundert." *ZfMt* 9/2 (1978):34-46. [*Rilm* 78-4987.]

Mongrédien, Jean. "La théorie de l'imitation en musique au début du romanticisme." *RRSer* 8 (1974):86-91.

Moos, Paul. *Moderne Musikästhetik in Deutschland: Historisch-kritische Übersicht.* Berlin and Leipzig: H. Seemann, 1902; revised and enlarged edition (as *Die Philosophie der Musik von Kant bis Eduard von Hartmann: Ein Jahrhundert deutscher Geistesarbeit*), Stuttgart: Deutsche Verlags-Anstalt, 1922.

Morche, Gunther. "Règle de l'octave et basse fondamentale." In *Congress Copenhagen 1972* (1974):556-61. [*Rilm* 76-1625.]

Morel, Fritz. "Organisten und Kapellmeister am Wiener Hof um 1700." *MGot* 21/4 (1967):81-90. [*Rilm* 68-3275.]

Morgan, Robert Porter. "The Delayed Structural Downbeat and Its Effect on the Tonal and Rhythmic Structure of Sonata Form Recapitulation." Ph.D. dissertation, Princeton University, 1969. [*Rilm* 69-4832. *DA* 30/12A, p. 5473. UMI 70-8384.]

Morgan, Robert P. "The Theory and Analysis of Tonal Rhythm." *MQ* 64/4 (1978):435-73. [*Rilm* 78-6023.]

Moser, Dietz-Rüdiger. "Musikgeschichte der Stadt Quedlinburg von Reformation bis zur Auflösung des Stiftes (1539-1802): Beiträge zu einer Musikgeschichte des Herzraumes." Ph.D. dissertation, The University of Göttingen, 1967. [*Rilm* 68-1593.]

Moser, Hans Joachim. *Heinrich Schütz: Sein Leben und Werk.* Kassel: Bärenreiter, 1936; revised edition, 1954; as *Heinrich Schütz: His Life and Work* (translated by Carl F. Pfatteicher), Saint Louis: Concordia, 1959.

> Reviews in *ARG* 26/11 (1959-60):878-80 (Jean Bowen), *Mf* 16/2 (1963):196-97 (Ludwig Finscher), *Notes* 12/1 (1954-55):97-98 (Carl F. Pfatteicher), *Notes* 18/4 (1960-61):579 (Donald L. Mintz), and *PP* 53/1 (1960-61):25 (Melva Peterson).

Moyer, Birgitte Plesner Vinding. "Concepts of Musical Form in the Nineteenth Century with Special Reference to A. B. Marx and Sonata Form." Ph.D. dissertation, Stanford University, 1969. Bibliog. [*Rilm* 69-2747. *DA* 30/08A, p. 3495. UMI 70-01579.]

Müller, István. "Zur Entstehung des harmonischen und des temperierten Tonsystems." *Stm* 18/1-4 (1976):183-258.

Müller-Blattau, Joseph Maria. *Grundzüge einer Geschichte der Fuge.* KSzMw, no. 1. Kaliningrad: Das Musikwissenschaftliche Seminar, K. Jüterbock, 1923; 2nd edition, Kassel: Bärenreiter, 1931; 3rd edition (as *Geschichte der Fuge*), 1963. Bibliog.

> Reviews in *MK* 36/4 (1966):186, *ML* 46/1 (1965):56-59 (Roger Bullivant), *MR* 29/2 (1967):149-50, *Musica* 18/3 (1964):180-81 (Hans Stephan), *Rdm* 50/128 (1964):122 (Pierre Pidoux), *Rmi* 39/3 (1935):601-3 (Luigi Ronga), and *Stfm* 46 (1964):185-87 (Hans Eppstein).

Müller-Blattau, Joseph Maria. "Fuge." In *MGG* (1949-68). Bibliog.

Münnich, Richard. "Von Entwicklung der Riemannschen Harmonielehre und ihrem Verhältnis zu Öttingen und Stumpf." In *RiemannFs* (1909/1965): 60-76.

Munkachy, Louis. "Franz Paul Rigler as Theorist and Composer." Ph.D. dissertation, The University of Pittsburgh, 1968. [*Rilm* 69-1135. *DA* 29/10A, p. 3633. UMI 69-06413.]

Murray, David R. "Major Analytical Approaches to Wagner's Musical Style: A Critique." *MR* 39/3-4 (1978):211-22. [*Rilm* 78-5155.]

Myhill, John. "Musical Theory and Musical Practice." *JAAC* 14/2 (1955-56):191-200.

N

Natale, Marco de. "Questioni metodologiche dell'analisi musicale." *RasmC* 24/2-4 (1971):40-50, 52-62.

Nelson, Richard Bruce. "Theories of Harmonic Modulation in Selected German Treatises of the Eighteenth Century." Ph.D. dissertation, The University of Rochester, 1984. [*DA* 45/01A, p. 13. UMI 84-04570.]

Neumann, Claus. "Die Harmonik der Münchner Schule um 1900." Ph.D. dissertation, The University of Munich, 1939; published edition, Munich: C. Peters Nachf., Kopp & Co. (Würzburg: Konrad Triltsch), 1939. Bibliog.

> Review in *AfMf* 8/1 (1943):60-61 (Ludwig K. Mayer).

Neumann, Frederick. "Misconceptions about the French Trill in the Seventeenth and Eighteenth Centuries." *MQ* 50/2 (1964):188-206; reprinted in Neumann [*Essays*] (1982):183-96.

Neumann, Frederick. "La note pointée et la soi-disant 'maniére française'." *Rdm* 51/1 (1965):66-87; as "The Dotted Note and the So-Called French Style" (translated by Raymond Harris and Edmund Shay), *EM* 5/3 (1977):310-24; reprinted in Neumann [*Essays*] (1982): 73-98.

> See Fuller (1977).

Neumann, Frederick. "The Use of Baroque Treatises on Musical Performance." *ML* 48/4 (1967):315-24 [*Rilm* 67-1167.]; reprinted in Neumann [*Essays*] (1982):1-9.

Neumann, Frederick. "Facts and Fiction about Overdotting." *MQ* 63/2 (1977):155-85; [*Rilm* 77-1495.]; reprinted in Neumann [*Essays*] (1982):111-35.

> See Fuller (1977).

Neumann, Frederick. *Ornamentation in Baroque and Post-Baroque Music: With Special Emphasis on J. S. Bach*. Princeton, N.J.: Princeton University Press, 1978. Bibliog. [*Rilm* 78-5973.]

> An excerpt appears in *MQ* 56/2 (1970):153-61. Reviews in *AmO:AGO* 14/2 (1980):18 (Jane Schatkin Hettrick), *AMT* 34/6 (1984-85):49 (David Z. Kushner), *AR* 21/4 (1980-81):175-77 (Dale Higbee), *AST* 29/4 (1979):45-46 (Harold C. Schonberg), *AST* 30/3 (1980):45 (Alan Grey Branigan and Lois Liebow), *Brio* 16/1 (1979):18-19 (Clifford Bartlett), *Choice* 16/3 (1979-80): 402, *Diapason* 70/9 (1979):6-9 (Bruce Gustafson), *EM* 9/1 (1981):63-68 (Neal Zaslaw), *Fam* 27/3-4 (1980):233-36 (Sven Hansell), *Fanfare* 3/4 (1979-80):218-20 (Mortimer H. Frank), *JAMS* 33/2 (1980):394-402 (David Fuller), *MEJ* 65/7 (1978-79):105, *ML* 63/1-2 (1982):96-101 (Peter Williams), *MQ* 65/4 (1979):597-604 (Lowell Lindgren), *MR* 41/1 (1980):60-62 (Malcolm Boyd), *MT* 120/1638 (1979):625, 638-39 (George J. Buelow), *Notes* 36/4 (1979-80):886-87 (Edward R. Reilly), *NZfM* 141/1 (1980):67 (Klaus Hortschansky), *ÖM* 37/12 (1982):717-18 (Eduard Melkus), *OrganYb* 11 (1980):153-54 (Peter Williams), *Rdm* 69/1 (1983):109-16 (Denis Collins), *SCN* 38/2-3 (1980):52 (Mortimer H. Frank), *StiM* 14 (1980):128-33 (Graham Pont), *Tibia* 5/1 (1980):49-50 (Hans-Peter Schmitz), and *TLS* 78/4002 (1979):72 (Michael Trend).

Neumann, Frederick. "Once More: The 'French Overture Style'." *EM* 7/1 (1979):39-45; reprinted in Neumann [*Essays*] (1982):137-50.

> Reply to Fuller (1977).

Neumann, Frederick. "The Overdotting Syndrome: Anatomy of a Delusion." *MQ* 67/3 (1981):305-47 [*Rilm* 81-3631.]; reprinted in Neumann [*Essays*] (1982):151-82.

Neumann, Frederick. "The Appoggiatura in Mozart's Recitative." *JAMS* 35/1 (1982):115-37 [*Rilm* 82-1466.]; reprinted in Neumann [*Essays*] (1982):251-71.

Neumann, Frederick. *Essays in Performance Practice*. SiM, no. 58. Ann Arbor, Mich.: UMI Research Press, 1982. [*Rilm* 82-3517.]

> Reviews in *AR* 25/4 (1984):147 (Alfred Mann), *Courant* 1/4 (1983):29 (Susan C. Cook), *ML* 65/1 (1984):94-95 (Peter Williams), and *MR* 48/1 (1988):74-75 (C. Malcolm Boyd).

Neumann, Frederick. *Ornamentation and Improvisation in Mozart*. Princeton, N.J.: Princeton University Press, 1986. Bibliog.

> Reviews in *AST* 38/1 (1988):92-93 (Margaret Farish), *Choice* 24/4 (1986-87):635 (C. Isaac), *EM* 16/2 (1988):261-65 (Peter Walls), *JAMS* 41/2 (1988):355-68 (Robert D. Levin), *Mf* 41/1 (1988):81 (Dieter Gutknecht), *MR* 48/1 (1988): 74-75 (C. Malcolm Boyd), *MT* 129/1741 (1988): 128-29 (Stanley Sadie), and *Notes* 45/1 (1988-89):52-57 (Joel Shapiro).

Neumann, Frederick. "Conflicting Binary and Ternary Rhythms: From the Theory of Mensural Notation to the Music of J. S. Bach." *MuF* 6/1 (1987):94-127.

Neumann, Frederick. "The *Notes inégales* Revisited." *JM* 6/2 (1988):137-49.

> Response in Fuller (1989).

Neumann, Friedrich. "Physikalismus in der Musiktheorie." *Am* 41/1-2 (1969):85-106. [*Rilm* 69-5042.]

Neumann, Friedrich. "Zur Krise der Musiktheorie." *Mf* 31/2 (1978): 177-81. [*Rilm* 78-1754.]

Neumann, Friedrich-Heinrich. "Die Theorie des Rezitativs im 17. und 18. Jahrhunderts unter besonderer Berücksichtigung der deutschen Musikschriftums des 18. Jahrhunderts." Ph.D. dissertation, The University of Göttingen, 1955; published edition (as *Die Ästhetik des Rezitativs: Zur Theorie des Rezitativs im 17. und 18. Jahrhundert*; SmwA, no. 41), Strasbourg and Baden-Baden: P. H. Heitz, 1962. Bibliog.

> Reviews in *Mf* 18/3 (1965):341-42 (Helmut Hucke), *ML* 43/4 (1962):359-60 (J. A. Westrup), *Musica* 16/3 (1962):165 (Paul Mies), *NZfM* 123/6 (1962):301-2 (Rudolf Stephan), and *QdRm* 3 (1965):245-47 (Alfredo Bonaccorsi).

Newcomb, Anthony. "The Birth of Music out of the Spirit of Drama: An Essay in Wagnerian Formal Analysis." *NCM* 5/1 (1981-82):38-66. [*Rilm* 81-3726.]

Newman, Anthony. *Bach and the Baroque: A Performing Guide to Baroque Music with Special Emphasis on the Music of J. S. Bach*. New York: Pendragon Press, 1985. Bibliog.

Newman, William S. "The Recognition of Sonata Form by Theorists of the Eighteenth and Nineteenth Centuries." *PAMS 1941* (1946):21-29.

Newman, William S. *The Sonata in the Baroque Era*. Chapel Hill, N.C.: The University of North Carolina Press, 1959; revised editions (New York: W. W. Norton) through 1983. Bibliog.

> Reviews in *AR* 12/2 (1971):58 (Dale Higbee), *Choice* 3/9 (1966-67):781, *HFMA* 9/6 (1959):34, *Hv* 3/3 (1966):484-88 (Tomislav Volek), *Instrumentalist* 13/11 (1958-59):14-16, *JAAC* 18/3 (1959-60):393-94 (Margaret E. Lyon), *JAMS* 12/1 (1959):80-83 (Jan LaRue), *JRME* 7/2 (1959):230-31 (Henry Leland Clarke), *Mf* 14/1 (1961):86-88 (Margarete Reimann), *ML* 41/1 (1960):53-56 (Peter Evans), *MO* 91/1092 (1967-68):665 (B. R.), *MQ* 45/2 (1959):261-65 (Caldwell Titcomb), *MR* 20/3-4 (1959):317-18, *MT* 101/1407 (1960):301 (Wilfrid Dunwell), *Notes* 16/3 (1958-59):390-91 (Putnam Aldrich), *Notes* 23/4 (1966-67):725-26 (Putnam Aldrich), *Rasm* 30/2 (1960):174-75 (Alfredo Bonaccorsi), *Rdm* 44/120 (1959):207-8, *Stfm* 41 (1959):172-75 (Ingmar Bengtsson), *TLS* 59/3027 (1960):140, and *TLS* 67/3453 (1968):453.

Newman, William S. *The Sonata in the Classical Era*. Chapel Hill, N.C.: The University of North Carolina Press, 1963; revised editions (New York: W. W. Norton) through 1983. Bibliog.

> Reviews in *Clavier* 2/4 (1963):9, *Hv* 3/3 (1966): 484-88 (Tomislav Volek), *Jaac* 22/4 (1963-64):478 (Charles W. Hughes), *JMT* 8/1 (1964): 113-17 (Halsey Stevens), *JRME* 12/1 (1964):114-

> 15 (Donald Aird), *LJ* 88/12 (1963):2520 (Elizabeth Muller), *Mf* 18/3 (1965):342-44 (Margarete Reimann), *MJ* 22/3 (1964):112 (Willard Sektberg), *ML* 45/2 (1964):163-65 (Arthur Hutchings), *MO* 87/1039 (1963-64):411-13 (B. R.), *MQ* 50/3 (1964):398-405 (Jan LaRue), *MT* 105/1452 (1964):118-19 (K. W. Dommett), *Notes* 23/2 (1966-67):257-59 (Eugene Helm), *NZfM* 127/12 (1966):506-7 (Carl Dahlhaus), *PP* 56/1 (1963):32 (Melva Peterson), *PQ* 46 (1963-64):31-32 (Alice Levine Mitchell), *Rdm* 50/128 (1964):137-38 (Marc Pincherle), *Stfm* 46 (1964):188-91 (Ingmar Bengtsson), *TLS* 62/3217 (1963):846, and *VQR* 39/4 (1963):clvi.

Newman, William S. *The Sonata Since Beethoven*. Chapel Hill, N.C.: The University of North Carolina Press, 1969; reprint editions (New York: W. W. Norton) through 1983. Bibliog. [*Rilm* 69-3976.]

> Reviews in *Dmt* 46/7-8 (1970-71):215-16 (Gunnar Colding-Jørgensen), *JAMS* 24/1 (1971):133-36 (F. E. Kirby), *ML* 51/4 (1970):442-47 (Michael Tilmouth), *MT* 111/1529 (1970):708-9 (John Warrack), *MuMus* 19/1 [217] (1970-71):79 (Donald James), *Notes* 27/2 (1970-71):263-65 (R. M. Longyear), *Nrmi* 5/6 (1971):1077-80 (Giorgio Pestelli), *NZfM* 132/6 (1971):337-39 (Hans Hollander), *TLS* 69/3576 (1970):1004, and *VQR* 47/1 (1971):xliv.

Newman, William S. "The Performance of Beethoven's Trills." *JAMS* 29/3 (1976):439-62.

Niecks, Fr. "On the Study of Harmony, Counterpoint, and Some Other So-Called Theoretical Branches of the Musical Art." *MMR* 21/244 (1891):77-80.

Nielsen, Poul. *Den musikalske formanalyse: Fra A. B. Marx' "Kompositionslehre" til vore dages strukturanalyse*. KUdMI. Copenhagen: Københavns Universitets Fond til Tilvejebringelse af Laeremidler (Borgens), 1971. [*Rilm* 72-2433.]

Niemöller, Klaus Wolfgang. "Untersuchungen zu Musikpflege und Musikunterricht an den [deutschen] Lateinschulen vom ausgehenden Mittelalter bis um 1600." Habilitationsschrift, The University of Cologne, 1964; published edition (KBzMf, no. 54), Regensburg: Gustav Boße, 1969. Bibliog. [*Rilm* 69-540.]

> Review in *Mf* 28/2 (1975):225-26 (Sigrid Abel-Struth).

Niemöller, Klaus Wolfgang. "Zur Musiktheorie im enzyklopädischen Wissenschaftssystem des 16./17. Jahrhunderts." In *Referate Berlin 1970* (1970):23-35. Bibliog. [*Rilm* 72-1067.]

Noé, Günther von. *Der Vorschlag in Theorie und Praxis: Ein Ratgeber für den Interpreten*. Vienna: Doblinger, 1986.

North, Nigel. *Continuo Playing on the Lute, Archlute and Theorbo*. MSP. Bloomington, Ind.: Indiana University Press, 1987. Bibliog.

Reviews in *BBN* (1987):448, *Choice* 25/5 (1987-88):778 (C. A. Kolczynski), *EM* 16/2 (1988):275-77 (Tim Crawford), and *MEJ* 73 (1988):20.

Norton, Richard. *Tonality in Western Culture: A Critical and Historical Perspective*. University Park, Pa.: The Pennsylvania State University Press, 1984. Bibliog.

Reviews in *Choice* 22/2 (1984-85):280 (R. Stahura), *JMT* 31/1 (1987):134-40 (David Neumeyer), *Mf* 40/4 (1987):382-84 (Hellmut Federhofer), and *MTS* 8 (1986):148-49 (Ellis B. Kohs).

Nowak, Adolf. "Die *numeri judiciales* des Augustinus und ihre musiktheoretische Bedeutung." *AfMw* 32/3 (1975):196-207. [*Rilm* 76-5078.]

Nutting, G. H. "The Solo and Trio Sonata for Violin, 1700-55, Being a Study in Style History Correlated with Contemporary Aesthetic and Theoretical Writings." M.A. thesis, The University of Durham, 1961.

O

Obelkevich, Mary Helen Rowen. "Manifestations of Philosophy and Science in the Music of Seventeenth-Century France." Ph.D. dissertation, Columbia University, 1973. [*DA* 34/06A, pp. 3455-56. UMI 73-28492.]

Oberdörffer, Fritz. "Generalbaß." In *MGG* (1949-68). Bibliog.

Oberdoerffer, Fritz. "Neuere Generalbaßstudien." *Am* 39/3-4 (1967):182-201. [*Rilm* 67-1168.]

Response in *Am* 40/2-3 (1968):178-79 ("Figured Bass as Improvisation," by George J. Buelow and Robert Donington [*Rilm* 68-1136]), with Replies in *Am* 41/3-4 (1969):236-38 ("Again: Figured Bass as Improvisation," by Fritz Oberdoerffer [*Rilm* 69-2683]) and *Am* 41/3-4 (1969):238-39 (Robert Donington [*Rilm* 69-2672]).

O'Donnell, John. "French Style and the Overtures of Bach." *EM* 7/2-3 (1979):190-96, 336-45. [*Rilm* 79-1595.]

Oldroyd, George. *The Technique and Spirit of Fugue: An Historical Study*. Foreword by Sir Stanley Marchant. London: Oxford University Press (Geoffrey Cumberlege), 1948.

Reviews in *ML* 29/3 (1948):287-89 (Arthur Hutchings), *Musicology* 2/4 (1948-49):445-46 (Hans Tischler), and *MR* 9/3 (1948):203-6 (Edward J. Dent).

Oliver, Alfred Richard. "The Encyclopedists as Critics of Music." Ph.D. dissertation, Columbia University, 1949; published edition, New York: Columbia University Press, 1947. Bibliog.

Reviews in *ML* 29/3 (1947):295 (Henry G. Farmer), *MQ* 34/1 (1948):127-29 (Donald Jay Grout), *MT* 91/1283 (1950):19 (David Cherniavsky), *RR* 40/2 (1949):144-45 (George R. Havens), and *ThA* 32/1 (1948):67-68 (Cecil Smith).

Orr, N. Lee. "The Effect of Scoring on the 'Sonata-Form' in Mozart's Mature Instrumental Ensembles." *CMS* 23/2 (1983):46-83.

Ortigue, Joseph Louis d'. "Accompagnement du plain-chant." In his *Dictionnaire liturgique, historique et théorique de plain-chant et de musique d'église*. Paris: L. Potier, 1853; 2nd edition, 1854; reprint of the 1854 edition (DCPMRS), New York: Da Capo Press, 1971.

Ortmann, Otto. "The Fallacy of Harmonic Dualism." *MQ* 10/3 (1924):369-83.

Osthoff, Helmuth, ed. "Die Kompositionslehre des 16. und 17. Jahrhunderts." In *Kongress Bamberg 1953* (1954): 101-55.

Ottenberg, Hans-Günter. "Die Entwicklung des theoretisch-ästhetischen Denkens innerhalb der Berliner Musikkultur von den Anfängen der Aufklärung bis Reichardt." Ph.D. dissertation, Humboldt University (Berlin), 1973; published edition (BzmwF, no. 10), Leipzig: VEB Deutscher Verlag für Musik, 1978. Bibliog. [*Rilm* 74-4129.]

Review in *Mf* 34/2 (1981):221-22 (Walter Salmen).

P

Pacchioni, Giorgio, ed. "Selva de' vari precetti: Aspetti della pratica musicale tra il XVI° e il XVII° secolo in base alle fonti dell'epoca." In *BAIMA: Supplemento* (1983). [*Rilm* 83-1619.]

Packard, Donald Wheeler. "Seven French Theorists of the Nineteenth Century." 2 vols. Ph.D. dissertation, The University of Rochester, 1952. Bibliog. [SMLMS.]

Palisca, Claude V. "Kontrapunkt." Translated by Wilhelm Pfannkuch. In *MGG* (1949-68). Bibliog.

Palisca, Claude Victor. "The Beginnings of Baroque Music; Its Roots in Sixteenth Century Theory and Polemics." Ph.D. dissertation, Harvard University, 1953.

Palisca, Claude V. "A Clarification of 'Musica Reservata' in Jean Taisnier's *Astrologiae*, 1559." *Am* 31/3-4 (1959): 133-61. Bibliog.

Palisca, Claude V. "Scientific Empiricism in Musical Thought." In *Seventeenth-Century Science and the Arts*, edited by Hedley Howell Rhys, pp. 91-137. The William J. Cooper Foundation Lectures, Swarthmore College, 1960. Princeton, N.J.: Princeton University Press, 1961.

Palisca, Claude V. "The Alterati of Florence, Pioneers in the Theory of Dramatic Music." In *GroutFs* (1968):9-38. [*Rilm* 68-1739.]

Palisca, Claude V. "The Artusi-Monteverdi Controversy." In Arnold and Fortune (1968/1985).

Palisca, Claude V. *Baroque Music*. PHHMS. Englewood Cliffs, N.J.: Prentice-Hall, 1968; 2nd edition, 1981. [*Rilm* 68-380.]

> Reviews in *AJME* 4 (1969):69 (Eric Gross), *Choice* 6/1 (1969-70):64, *Clavier* 8/1 (1969):6, *EM* 10/4 (1982):537-39 (Denis Arnold), *Instrumentalist* 23/5 (1968-69):18, *LJ* 93/11 (1968): 2243 (Barbara Henry), *MEJ* 56/2 (1969-70):72-75 (William V. Porter), *Mf* 24/3 (1971):331-32 (Robert L. Marshall), *MiE* 33/335 (1969):35, *ML* 50/3 (1969):411-12 (Ian Spink), *ML* 62/3-4 (1981):432 (Ian Spink), *MR* 32/1 (1971):83-84, *MT* 110/1513 (1969):266 (Stanley Sadie), *Notes* 25/4 (1968-69):717-18 (David Burrows), *Nrmi* 4/3 (1970):566-68 (Lorenzo Bianconi), *OpN* 33/10 (1968-69):7 (Frank Merkling), *PP* 61/4 (1968-69):41 (Melva Peterson), *Stfm* 52 (1970): 114-15 (Erik Kjellberg), *StRev* 22/3 (1969):45-46 (James Goodfriend), and *YR* 58/3 (1968-69): xxviii-xxix.

Palisca, Claude V. "Rezitativ." In *HwmT* (1972-). Bibliog.

Palisca, Claude V. "The 'Camerata Fiorentina': A Reappraisal." *Sm* 1/2 (1972):203-36. Bibliog. [*Rilm* 73-1809.]

Palisca, Claude V. "*Ut oratoria musica*: The Rhetorical Basis of Musical Mannerism." In *The Meaning of Mannerism*, edited by Franklin Westcott Robinson and Stephen G. Nichols, Jr., pp. 37-65. Hanover, N.H.: University Press of New England, 1972. [*Rilm* 72-1580.]

Palisca, Claude V. "Towards an Intrinsically Musical Definition of Mannerism in the Sixteenth Century." *Sm* 3 (1974):313-46; same as *Congresso "Manierismo" 1973* (1977). [*Rilm* 76-9417.]

Palisca, Claude V. "The Musical Humanism of Giovanni Bardi." In *Convegni rinascimento 1976* (1979):45-72.

Palisca, Claude V. "Camerata." In *NGrove* (1980). Bibliog.

Palisca, Claude V. "Theory, Theorists." In *NGrove* (1980). Bibliog.

> Review in *MQ* 68/2 (1982):161-81 (Allen Forte).

Palisca, Claude V. "The Impact of the Revival of Ancient Learning on Music Theory." In *Report Berkeley 1977* (1981):870-78. Bibliog.

> Responses by Thomas Mathiesen, Dietrich Kämper, Don Harrán, and Dean T. Mace, and reply by Claude V. Palisca, ibid., pp. 879-83, 892-93.

Palisca, Claude V. *Humanism in Italian Renaissance Musical Thought*. New Haven, Ct.: Yale University Press, 1985.

> Reviews in *AHR* 91/5 (1986):1232 (Lewis Lockwood), *Choice* 23/10 (1985-86):1550 (A. G. Spiro), *CM* 41 (1986):68-71 (Erik S. Ryding), *EM* 15/1 (1987):89-90 (Ronald Woodley), *HRNB* 15/3 (1986-87):84 (William Weber), *IRASM* 19/1 (1988):127-29 (Ennio Stipčević), *JAMS* 40/2 (1987):337-43 (Barbara R. Hanning), *JMH* 59/4 (1987):873-76 (Gary Tomlinson), *ML* 68/4 (1987):386-89 (Michael Fend), *Notes* 43/3 (1986-87):554-56 (John B. Howard), and *Nrmi* 21/3 (1987):477-79 (Maria Caraci Vela).

Palisca, Claude V. " 'Baroque' as a Music-Critical Term." In Cowart [*French*] (1989):7-21. Bibliog.

Palisca, Claude V. *The Florentine Camerata: Documentary Studies and Translations*. MTTS. New Haven, Ct.: Yale University Press, 1989. Bibliog.

Palisca, Claude V., and Spender, Natasha. "Consonance." In *NGrove* (1980). Bibliog.

Palm, Albert. "Ästhetische Prinzipien in der französischen Musiktheorie des frühen 19. Jahrhunderts." *AfMw* 22/2 (1965):126-39.

Parker, Mark Mason. "Theories of Transposition in French Treatises, ca. 1680 – ca. 1730, with a Critical Translation of Alexandre Frère's *Transpositions de musique* (1706)." Ph.D. dissertation, The University of North Texas, forthcoming.

Parkins, Robert. "Keyboard Fingering in Early Spanish Sources." *EM* 11/3 (1983):323-31.

Parncutt, Richard. "Revision of Terhardt's Psychoacoustical Method of the Root(s) of a Musical Chord." *MP* 6/1 (1988-89):65-93.

Pedrell, Felipe. *Los músicos españoles antiguos y modernos en sus libros ó escritos sobre la música*. Barcelona: Torres y Segui, 1888.

Perinello, Carlo. "I problemi del consonare musicale." *Rmi* 40/1-2, 3-4 (1936):43-56, 286-97.

Pesce, Dolores. *The Affinities and Medieval Transposition*. MSP. Bloomington, Ind.: Indiana University Press, 1987. Bibliog.

Peters, Penelope Miller. "French Harmonic Theory after Rameau." Ph.D. dissertation, The University of Rochester, 1988.

Petrobelli, Pierluigi. "La scuola di Tartini in Germania e la sua influenza." *Anamu* 5 (1968):1-17. Bibliog. [*Rilm* 69-914.]

Pfeiffer, Christel. "Die *Notes inégales*: Ihre Bedeutung und Anwendung aus der Sicht deutscher, musik-geschichtlicher Quellen des 18. Jahrhunderts." *Melos/NZfM* 4/6 (1978):512-15. [*Rilm* 78-5975.]

Pfrogner, Hermann. "Zur Theorieauffassung der Enhar-monik im Zeitalter Mozarts." In *Kongress Wien 1956* (1958):171-76.

Phillips, Leonard Milton, Jr. "The Leipzig Conservatory: 1843-1881." Ph.D. dissertation, Indiana University, 1979. [*Rilm* 79-1842. *DA* 40/02A, p. 531. UMI 79-16957.]

Phipps, Graham H. "Comprehending Twelve-Tone Music As an Extension of the Primary Musical Language of Tonality." *CMS* 24/2 (1984):35-54.

Pietzsch, Gerhard. "Zur Pflege der Musik an den deutschen Universitäten bis zur Mitte des 16. Jahrhunderts." *AfMf* 1/3-4 (1936):257-92, 424-51; 3/3 (1938):302-30; 5/2 (1940):65-83; 6/1 (1941):23-56; 7/2-3 (1942):90-110, 154-69; reprint edition, Hildesheim: Georg Olms, 1971.

Pikler, Andrew G. "History of Experiments on the Musical Interval Sense." *JMT* 10/1 (1966):54-95.

Pincherle, Marc. "On the Rights of the Interpreter in the Performance of Seventeenth- and Eighteenth-Century Music." Translated by Isabelle Cazeaux. *MQ* 44/2 (1958):145-66.

Pinsart, Gérard. "Aspects de l'enseignement musical à Bruxelles sous le régime hollandais (1815-1830)." *Rbdm* 34-35 (1980-81):164-97. [*Rilm* 81-2801.]

Pirrotta, Antonino. "Temperamenti e tendenze nella Came-rata Fiorentina." In *Manifestazioni di attivita' Culturali (Accademia di Santa Cecilia, Rome)*. Rome: Luglio, 1953; as "Temperaments and Tendencies in the Florentine Camerata" (translated by Nigel Fortune), *MQ* 40/2 (1954):169-89; reprinted in his *Music and Culture in Italy from the Middle Ages to the Baroque: A Collection of Essays* (Cambridge, Mass.: Harvard University Press, 1984), pp. 217-34.

> Reviews in *ABBW* 76/24 (1985):4334, *AR* 26/4 (1985):176-77 (Alexander Silbiger), *Choice* 22/3 (1984):436 (W. H. Baxter, Jr.), *EM* 13/4 (1985):578 (David Fallows), *JAMS* 39/2 (1986):389-95 (Ellen Rosand), *Manu* 30/2 (1986):144-45 (Francis J. Guentner), *ML* 66/4 (1985):397-99 (F. W. Sternfeld), *MQ* 70/4 (1984):567-72 (Maria Rika Maniates), *MT* 126/1709 (1985):411 (Iain Fenlon), *Notes* 42/2 (1985-86):281-83 (Janet M. Palumbo), *RQ* 38/3 (1985):529-32 (Leeman L. Perkins), and *SCJ* 16/1 (1985):155-56 (W. T. Atcherson).

Pöhlmann, Egert. "Antikenverständnis und Antikenmißver-ständnis in der Operntheorie der Florentiner Came-rata." *Mf* 22/1 (1969):5-13. [*Rilm* 69-719.]

Pole, William. *The Philosophy of Music*. London: Trübner, 1879; 2nd edition (EFPL, no. 11), 1887; 6th edition (with an Introduction by Edward J. Dent and a sup-plementary essay by Hamilton Hartridge; ILPPSM), London: Kegan Paul, Trench, Trübner & Co.; New York: Harcourt, Brace & Co., 1924.

> Review in *ML* 5/3 (1924):286 (Ernest Walker).

Polezhaev, Aleksandr. "Muzykovedcheskii analiz i ispol-nitel'skaia interpretatsiia." [Music Analysis and the Performer.] *Smuz* 2 (1982):59-63. [*Rilm* 82-1500.]

Powers, Harold S. "The Modality of 'Vestiva i colli'." In *MendelFs* (1974):31-47. [*Rilm* 74-1997.]

Powers, Harold S. "Language Models and Musical Analy-sis." *Eth* 24/1-2 (1980):1-60, 318. Bibliog.

Powers, Harold S. "Mode." In *NGrove* (1980). Bibliog.

Powers, Harold S. "Tonal Types and Modal Categories in Renaissance Polyphony." *JAMS* 34/3 (1981):428-70. Bibliog. [*Rilm* 81-6140.]

Preußner, Eberhard. "Die Methodik im Schulgesang der evangelischen Lateinschulen des 17. Jahrhunderts." Ph.D. dissertation, The University of Berlin, 1924. Ex-cerpt published in *AfMw* 6 (1924):407-49. Bibliog.

Preußner, Eberhard. "Solmisationsmethoden im Schulunter-richt des 16. und 17. Jahrhunderts." *SteinFs* (1939): 112-28.

Prout, Louis B. "Harmonic Analysis." *MMR* 23/265-69 (1893):4-6, 26-30, 50-52, 74-77, 101-3.

Pulver, Jeffrey. *A Biographical Dictionary of Old English Music*. London: Kegan Paul, Trench, Trübner, & Co.; New York: Dutton, 1927; reprint edition (BFBRS, no. 295), New York: Franklin, 1969; reprint edition (DCPMRS, with a new Introduction and Bibliography of the writings of Pulver by Gilbert Blount), New York: Da Capo, 1973.

> Reviews in *ARBA* (1974):396 (Guy A. Marco), *ML* 8/4 (1927):482, and *MT* 114/1565 (1973):705 (David Scott).

R

Rags, Y. N., ed. *Voprosy muzykovedeniia*. [Questions of Musicology.] 2 vols. Moscow: Gosudarstvennyi muzy-kal'no-pedagogicheskii institut imeni Gnesinykh, 1972.

Rahn, Jay. "Text Underlay in French Monophonic Song, ca. 1500." *CM* 24 (1977):63-79. [*Rilm* 77-2435.]

Rainbow, Bernarr. "The Land without Music: Musical Education in England 1800-1860 and its Continental Antecedents." M.Ed. thesis, The University of Leicester, 1964; published edition, London: Novello, 1967. [*Rilm* 74-1207.]

> Reviews in *ChuMus* 2/23 (1968):13 (Winifred Harris), *MakM* 66 (1968):17 (Christopher le Fleming), *MiE* 31/328 (1967):638 (Gordon Reynolds), *ML* 49/2 (1968):178-80 (Margaret Bent), *MO* 91/1085 (1967-68):275 (B. R.), *MR* 29/2 (1968):158-60 (Arnold Whittall), *MT* 109/1502 (1968):337-38 (Nicholas Temperley), and *MusT* 47/2 (1968):33 (I. R.-D.).

Ramírez, Carla J. "A Historical Study of the Doctrine of the Affections as Exemplified in the Theoretical Writings of Johann Mattheson and Jean-Philippe Rameau." Master's thesis, The University of Oregon, 1967.

Randall, D. B. J. "Country Delights for the Gentry: A View from 1669." *SAQ* 80/2 (1981):222-32.

Rasch, Rudolf. "Wohltemperirten gelijkzwevend." *Mens* 36/6 (1981):264-73. [*Rilm* 81-4680.]

Rasch, Rudolf A. "Description of Regular Twelve-Tone Musical Tunings." *JASA* 73/3 (1983):1023-35.

Ratner, Leonard G. "Harmonic Aspects of Classic Form." *JAMS* 2/3 (1949):159-68; reprinted in Rosand (1985):Vol. 7, pp. 101-10. Bibliog.

Ratner, Leonard G. "Eighteenth-Century Theories of Musical Period Structure." *MQ* 42/4 (1956):439-54; reprinted in Rosand (1985):Vol. 7, pp. 85-100.

Ratner, Leonard G. "*Ars Combinatoria*: Chance and Choice in Eighteenth-Century Music." In *GeiringerFs* (1970): 343-63. [*Rilm* 71-612.]

Ratner, Leonard G. *Classic Music: Expression, Form, and Style*. New York: Schirmer; London: Collier Macmillan, 1980. Bibliog.

> Reviews in *Choice* 18/9 (1980-81):1276, *ECS* 17/1 (1983-84):78-82 (John Walter Hill), *JAMS* 35/2 (1982): 351-60 (Bathia Churgin), *JMT* 27/1 (1983):123-27 (Jane Stevens), *Mf* 35/3 (1982):307-9 (Eric Werner), and *Notes* 38/1 (1981-82):64-65 (George R. Hill).

Rauhe, Hermann. "Dichtung und Music im weltlichen Vokalwerk Johann Hermann Scheins: Stilistische und kompositionstechnische Untersuchung zum Wort-Ton-Verhältnis im Lichte der rhetorisch ausgerichteten Sprach- und Musiktheorie des 17. Jahrhunderts." Ph.D. dissertation, The University of Hamburg, 1959 (1960). Bibliog.

Rauschning, Hermann. *Geschichte der Musik und Musikpflege in Danzig*. QDGWp, no. 15. Danzig: Kommissionsverlag der Danziger Verlags-Gesellschaft (Paul Rosenberg), 1931.

Rea, John Rocco. "Franz Liszt's 'New Path of Composition': The Sonata in B Minor as Paradigm." Ph.D. dissertation, Princeton University, 1978. [*Rilm* 78-4016. *DA* 39/06A, p. 3217. UMI 78-23510.]

Reckow, Fritz. "Diapason, diocto, octava." In *HwmT* (1972-). Bibliog.

Reese, Gustave. *Music in the Renaissance*. New York: W. W. Norton, 1954; revised edition, 1959. Bibliog.

> Reviews in *AHR* 60/2 (1954-55):349-50 (Wallace K. Ferguson), *Caecilia* 82/3 (1954-55):109-10 (Rev. Francis J. Guentner), *CCh* 40/3 (1954): 141-42 (J. Vincent Higginson), *Etude* 72/10 (1954):6 (Dale Anderson), *HFMA* 5/1 (1955): 109-11 (Fritz A. Kuttner), *JAMS* 8/2 (1955):123-31 (Charles van den Borren), *JRME* 3/1 (1955): 71-72 (Edith Woodcock), *MAm* 74/12 (1954):20 (Catharine K. Miller), *MC* 150/2 (1954):40 (Harold Schonberg), *MEJ* 41/1 (1954-55):15 (George Bielow), *ML* 36/1 (1955):70-73 (Denis Stevens), *MMR* 85/968 (1955):159-60 (P. T. B.), *MQ* 41/3 (1955):378-91 (Knud Jeppesen), *MT* 96/1352 (1955):531-32 (Gilbert Reaney), *Notes* 11/4 (1953-54):547-48 (J. A. Westrup), *Notes* 17/4 (1959-60):569 (E. H. Sparks), *PP* 47/1 (1954-55):50 (Gladys M. Wilson), *RN* 7/4 (1954):136-40 (Otto Gombosi), and *SatR* 37/27 (1954):16 (Philip L. Miller).

Reese, Gustave. *Fourscore Classics of Music Literature*. New York: The Liberal Arts Press, 1957; reprint edition (DCPMRS), New York: Da Capo Press, 1970.

> Reviews in *Choice* 8/7 (1971-72):845, *Instrumentalist* 12/5 (1957-58):12, *JMT* 2/1 (1958):112-13 (David Kraehenbuehl), *Mf* 11/4 (1958):538-39 (Karl-Werner Gümpel), *ML* 39/3 (1958):286 (Denis Stevens), *MR* 33/2 (1972):148-49, *MT* 99/1382 (1958):197-98 (Denis Stevens), *MT* 111/1534 (1970):1226 (Gerald Abraham), *Notes* 15/3 (1957-58):392-93 (Glen Haydon), and *Stfm* 39 (1957):195-98 (Carl-Allan Moberg).

Reichenbach, Hermann. "History of the Theory of Form in Music." *BAMS* 11-13 (1948):65-67.

Reichert, Peter. "Takt und Akzent: Über den Pulsschlag der Music." *MS:CVO* 98/4-5 (1978):213-23, 310. [*Rilm* 78-3867.]

Reilly, Allyn D. "Modulation and Key Relationships in Eighteenth-Century German Theory." *ITO* 8/4-5 (1984-85): 45-56.

Reimer, Erich. "Concerto/Konzert." In *HwmT* (1972-). Bibliog.

Reimer, Erich. "Kammermusik." In *HwmT* (1972-). Bibliog.

Reimer, Erich. "Kenner—Liebhaber—Dilettant." In *HwmT* (1972-). Bibliog.

Reimer, Erich. "Die Polemik gegen das Virtuosenkonzert im 18. Jahrhundert: Zur Vorgeschichte einer Gattung der Trivialmusik." *AfMw* 30/4 (1973):235-44. [*Rilm* 74-427.]

Reinecke, Hans-Peter. "Über Zusammenhänge zwischen naturwissenschaftlicher und musikalischer Theorien-bildung." In *Referate Berlin 1970* (1970):59-66. Bibliog. [*Rilm* 72-1068.]

Révész, Géza. *Einführung in die Musikpsychologie*. Bern: A. Francke AG, 1946; as *Introduction to the Psychology of Music* (translated by G. I. C. de Courcy), London: Longmanns, Green, 1953; Oklahoma City, Okla.: University of Oklahoma Press, 1954; as *Psicologia della musica* (translated by Bruno Callieri), Florence: Editrice Universitaria, 1954.

> Reviews in *Etude* 72/7 (1954):6 (Dale Anderson), *HFMA* 4/5 (1954-55):20-22, 93 (F. A. Kuttner), *JAAC* 13/1 (1954-55):113 (Paul R. Farnsworth), *JRME* 2/2 (1954):186 (Max Schoen), *LME* 9/7 (1954):32, *MC* 150/2 (1954):40 (Harold Schonberg), *MEJ* 41/1 (1954-55):20 (George Bielow), *MMR* 84/961 (1954):243 (P. T. B.), *MO* 77/921 (1953-54):522-23 (H. H.), *MR* 15/1 (1954):75-76 (Philip E. Vernon), *MT* 95/1332 (1954):78-79 (Colin Mason), *MusT* 32/12 (1953): 593 (H. Lowry), *Notes* 11/3 (1953-54): 465-66 (Carroll C. Pratt), *Rasm* 25/1 (1955):52-54 (M. M.), *Rmi* 50/2 (1948):188-89, and *Tempo* 32 (1954):38 (Hans Keller).

Rex, Walter E. "A propos of the Figure of Music in the Frontispiece of the *Encyclopédie*: Theories of Musical Imitation of d'Alembert, Rousseau and Diderot." In *Report Berkeley 1977* (1981):214-25.

Riedel, Herbert. "Die Darstellung von Musik und Musikerlebnis in der erzählenden deutschen Dichtung." Ph.D. dissertation, The University of Bonn, 1956; published edition (as *Musik und Musikerlebnis . . .* ; AKMLw, no. 12), Bonn: Bouvier, 1959. Bibliog.

> Reviews in *Mf* 15/3 (1962):284-85 (Hans Engel) and *Musica* 14/4 (1960):260-61 (Gottfried Schweizer).

Ritzel, Alfred. "Die Entwicklung der 'Sonatenform' im musiktheoretischen Schrifttum des 18. und 19. Jahrhunderts." Ph.D. dissertation, The University of Frankfurt am Main, 1967; published edition (NmF, no. 1), Wiesbaden: Breitkopf & Härtel, 1968.

> Reviews in *Me* 24/2 (1970-71):94 (Eberhard Würzl), *MT* 109/1506 (1968):731 (Peter Williams), *Stfm* 52 (1970):115-17 (Ingmar Bengtsson), and *Zvuk* 104-5 (1970):231-34 (Petar Stajic).

Rivera, Benito V. "The *Isagoge* (1581) of Johannes Avianius: An Early Formulation of Triadic Theory." *JMT* 22/1 (1978):43-64.

Rivera, Benito V. "The Seventeenth-Century Theory of Triadic Generation and Invertibility and Its Application in Contemporaneous Rules of Composition." *MTS* 6 (1984):63-78.

Robbins, Ralph Harold. "Beiträge zur Geschichte des Kontrapunkts von Zarlino bis Schütz." Ph.D. dissertation, The University of Berlin, 1938; published edition, Berlin: Triltsch & Huther, 1938. Bibliog.

Roberts, Stella. "In Defense of the *Cantus Firmus* and Five Species." *Diapason* 59/1 [697] (1967-68):24-25.

Robison, J. O. "The Messa di voce as an Instrumental Ornament in the Seventeenth and Eighteenth Centuries." *MR* 43/1 (1982):1-14. [*Rilm* 82-3518.]

Rodgers, Julane. "Early Keyboard Fingering, ca. 1520-1620." D.M.A. dissertation, The University of Oregon, 1971. [*DA* 32/09A, p. 5274. UMI 72-8592.]

Rogers, Helen Olive. "The Development of a Concept of Modulation in Theory from the Sixteenth to the Early Eighteenth Century." Ph.D. dissertation, Indiana University, 1955. Bibliog. [*DA* 16/02, pp. 351-52. UMI 00-14665.]

Rohwer, Jens. "Harmonielehre." In *MGG* (1949-68). Bibliog.

Rosand, Ellen, ed. *The Garland Library of the History of Western Music*. 14 vols. New York: Garland Publishing, 1985.

Rosen, Charles. *The Classical Style: Haydn, Mozart, Beethoven*. New York: Viking Press, 1971; New York: W. W. Norton, 1972; as *Le style classique: Haydn, Mozart, Beethoven* (translated by Marc Vignal), Paris: Gallimard, 1978; as *Klasični stil* (translated by Branka Lalič and Ivan Stefanovič), Belgrade: Nolit, 1979; as *Lo stile classico: Haydn, Mozart, Beethoven* (translated by Riccardo Bianchini), Milan: Feltrinelli, 1979; as *Der klassische Stil: Haydn, Mozart, Beethoven* (translated by Traute M. Marshall), Munich: Deutscher Taschenbuch; Kassel: Bärenreiter, 1983.

> Reviews in *AHR* 81/2 (1976):376-77 (R. K. Webb), *BzMw* 28/4 (1986):337 (Jürgen Mainka), *Composer* 50 (1973-74):37-38 (W. R. Pasfield), *CQ* 5/4 (1971):384-89 (Robert Simpson), *Crit* 35/384 (1979):429-44 (Marc Passerieu), *GeoR* 28/2 (1974):366-69 (Edward R. Reilly), *Harmonie* 139 [ca. 1979]:101, *HFMA* 21/9 (1971): MA29-30 (Patrick J. Smith), *HR* 25/4 (1972-73):633-46 (William H. Youngren), *ITR* 1/1 (1977):31-34 (Robert S. Hatten), *Listener* 86/2213 (1971):276 (Paul Hamburger), *LM* 11/4 (1971):114-18 (Ronald Weitzman), *MakM* 77 (1971):23 (Mervyn Buxner), *MakM* 82 (1973):17-19 (Lionel Nutley), *MB* 18/2 (1986):200-201 (Elmar Budde), *Mens* 27/11 (1972):346-49 (Sas Bunge), *Mf* 39/3 (1986):270-72 (Ludwig Finscher), *MiE* 35/349 (1971):495-96 (Michael Hurd), *MISM* 32 (1984):131, *MJ* 29/8 (1971):8 (Ainslee Cox), *ML* 52/3 (1971):327-29 (Roger Fiske), *MO* 96/1147 (1973):361 (B. R.), *Mozart-Jb 1984/85* [1986]:233-36 (Rudolf Kelterborn), *MR* 39/1 (1978):67-69 (Robert L. Jacobs), *MT* 112/1546 (1971):1166-67 (Edward Olleson), *MuMus* 20/2 [230] (1971-72):46-47 (Bayan Northcott), *MusT* 51/1 (1 972):25 (John Standen), *MusT* 57/1 (1978):32 (F. M. Laming), *Nrmi* 15/2 (1981):282-86 (Paolo Gallarati), *NY* 48/13 (1972):123 (Winthrop Sargeant), *NYRB* 18/11 (1972):10-12 (Alan Tyson), *NYTBR* 120/41392 (1971):34-35 (Edward T. Cone), *NZfM* 145/9 (1984):51-52 (Gottfried Eberle),

Öm 39/5 (1984):272 (Rudolf Stephan), *PP* 64/3 (1972):23 (Melva Peterson), *Rh* 529 (1979):277-78 (Édith Weber), *SewR* 81/2 (1973):356-64 (B. W. Haggin), *Stfm* 58/1 (1976):58-59 (Per-Erik Brolinson), *Strad* 82/975 (1971-72):141 (A. D.), *Strad* 88/1050 (1977-78):527 (A. D.), *Tibia* 9/3 (1984):219 (Herbert Höntsch), *TLS* 70/3607 (1971):441, and *Zvuk* 3 (1981):89-92 (Ivan Čavlović).

Rosen, Charles. *Sonata Forms*. New York: W. W. Norton, 1980; revised edition, 1988.

> Reviews in *AMT* 32/1 (1982):38 (G. Larry Whatley), *Clavier* 19/10 (1980):8-9 (Jeffrey Wagner), *Éc* 50/2 (1982):170 (Y. Lenoir), *ECS* 17/2 (1983-84):205-9 (Jane Perry-Camp), *HFMA* 31/1 (1981):MA19, 38 (Patrick J. Smith), *JAMS* 34/3 (1981):557-66 (Jan LaRue), *MA* 1/2 (1982):213-18 (David Osmond-Smith), *MO* 112/1337 (1989):177 (Max Harrison), *MT* 122/1659 (1981):301-4 (James Webster), *Notes* 37/3 (1980-81):576-77 (Christoph Wolff), *NYRB* 27/16 (1980):50-52 (Joseph Kerman), and *NYTBR* 120/44804 (1980):6-7 (Edward Rothstein).

Rosenblum, Sandra P. *Performance Practices in Classic Piano Music: Their Principles and Applications*. Foreword by Malcolm Bilson. MSP. Bloomington, Ind.: Indiana University Press, 1988.

Rothärmel, Marion. "Der musikalische Zeitbegriff seit Moritz Hauptmann." Ph.D. dissertation, The University of Cologne, 1963; published edition (KBzMf, no. 25), Regensburg: Boße, 1963; 2nd edition, 1968. Bibliog.

> Review in *Mf* 18/4 (1965):444-45 (Carl Dahlhaus).

Rothgeb, John. "Harmonizing the Unfigured Bass: A Computational Study." Ph.D. dissertation, Yale University, 1968. [*Rilm* 69-4826. *DA* 30/03A, p. 1197. UMI 69-13799.]

Rothschild, Fritz. *The Lost Tradition in Music*. London: Adam and Charles Black; New York: Oxford University Press, 1953.

> Reviews in *Haus* 23/6 (1959):164-68 (Kurt Rottmann), *MAm* 73/12 (1953):8 (Frances Duncan Barwick), *ML* 34/3 (1953):251-64 (Walter Emery), *MMR* 83/948 (1953):144-48 (Basil Lam), *MO* 76/909 (1953):541-43 (H. H.), *MQ* 39/4 (1953):617-30 (Arthur Mendel), *MR* 14/3 (1953):237-38, *MT* 94/1325 (1953):309-11 (Denis Stevens), *MusT* 32/9 (1953):419 (J. R. T.), *MusT* 35/6 (1956):285 (W. R. A.), *Notes* 11/2 (1953-54):303-6 (Otto Kinkeldey), *PhP* 6/11 (1951-53):132, and *Tempo* 29 (1953):31 (Max Kenyon).

Rothschild, Fritz. *Musical Performance in the Times of Mozart and Beethoven: The Lost Tradition in Music, Part II*. London: Adam and Charles Black; New York: Oxford University Press, 1961; as *Vergessene Traditionen in der Musik: Zur Aufführungspraxis von Bach bis Beethoven*, Freiburg and Zürich: Atlantis, 1964. Bibliog.

> Reviews in *MEJ* 48/1 (1961):120, *MEv* 16/8 (1961):25-26 (Stanley Sadie), *ML* 43/3 (1962): 263-64 (James Dalton), *MO* 84/1003 (1960-61): 405-6, *MT* 102/1421 (1961):434-35 (H. C. Robbins Landon), *MuMus* 9/9 (1960-61):19 (Walter Haydon), *Notes* 18/4 (1960-61):574-75 (Donald W. MacArdle), *NZfM* 126 (1965):133 (G. A. Trumpff), *QdRm* 3 (1965):232-33 (l. a.), *Stm* 8/1-4 (1966):419-22 (L. Somfai), and *TLS* 60/3088 (1961):272.

Rowell, Lewis. *Thinking about Music: An Introduction to the Philosophy of Music*. Amherst, Mass.: University of Massachusetts Press, 1983.

> Reviews in *ABBW* 72/24 (1983):4174, *AmO: AGO* 18/2 (1984):12 (Charles Huddleston Heaton), *BJA* 25/1 (1985):90-91 (Michael Musgrave), *CCen* 100/30 (1983):946, *Choice* 21/3 (1983-84):440, *CME* 12 (1985):51-52 (George N. Heller), *JAAC* 42/4 (1983-84):452-55 (Philip Alperson), *JALS* 15 (1984):212 (John M. Harris), *JMT* 30/1 (1986):141-45 (Roye E. Wates), *LJ* 108/8 (1983):827 (Francisca Goldsmith), *MEJ* 70/5 (1983-84):71-74 (A. David Franklin), *ML* 66/3 (1985):249-50 (J. O. Urmson), *MR* 45/2 (1984): 151-52 (R. A. Sharpe), *MTS* 9 (1987): 195-99 (Judy Lochhead), and *NF* 65/1 (1985):43-44 (Geoffrey Block).

Rowen, Ruth Halle. *Music through Sources and Documents*. Englewood Cliffs, N.J.: Prentice-Hall, 1979. [*Rilm* 79-50.]

> Reviews in *AMT* 29/5 (1979-80):35 (Esther Hoffman Weinstein), *Choice* 16/5-6 (1979-80): 678, *Fam* 26/3 (1979):243-44 (Don L. Hixon), *ITO* 4/3 (1978-79):36-38 (Thomas Riis), *LJ* 104/7 (1979):831 (Allen B. Skei), *MEJ* 65/9 (1978-79):87, *MJ* 37/6 (1979):53 (Bert Wechsler), *MR* 48/1 (1988):71-72 (Henry B. Raynor), *MT* 122/1660 (1981):386 (Iain Fenlon), *Notes* 36/4 (1979-80):892-93 (James W. Pruett), and *SacM* 106/2 (1979):28 (William Tortolano).

Ruf, Wolfgang. "Consort." In *HwmT* (1972-). Bibliog.

Ruff, Lillian M. "The Seventeenth-Century English Music Theorists." Ph.D. dissertation, The University of Nottingham, 1962.

Ruff, Lillian M. "The Social Significance of the Seventeenth-Century English Music Treatises." *Consort* 26 (1970): 412-22. [*Rilm* 70-1753.]

Ruhnke, Martin. "Musica theorica (theoretica), practica, poetica." In *MGG* (1949-68). Bibliog.

Ruhnke, Martin. "Francesco Gasparinis Kanonmesse und der Palestrinastil." In *FellererFsII* (1973):494-511. Bibliog. [*Rilm* 74-2190.]

Ruhnke, Martin. "Lassos Chromatik und die Orgelstimmung." In *BoetticherFs* (1974):291-308. [*Rilm* 74-2005.]

Rummenhöller, Peter. *Musiktheoretisches Denken im 19. Jahrhundert: Versuch einer Interpretation erkenntnistheoretischer Zeugnisse in der Musiktheorie.* SzMg, no. 12. Regensburg: Boße, 1967. Bibliog. [*Rilm* 68-1166.]

> Reviews in *Mens* 24/11 (1969):350 (Gerrit Vellekoop), *ML* 49/2 (1968):189-90 (Hans F. Redlich), and *Muh* 19/3 (1968):144.

Rummenhöller, Peter. "Die philosophischen Grundlagen in der Musiktheorie des 19. Jahrhunderts." In *Beiträge zur Theorie der Künste im 19. Jahrhundert*, edited by Helmut Koopmann and J. Adolf Schmoll gen. Eisenwerth, vol. 1, pp. 44-57. SPL, no. 12/1. Frankfurt am Main: Vittorio Klostermann, 1971. [*Rilm* 71-3075.]

Ryzhkin, Iosef. "Traditsionnaia shkola teorii muzyki." [The Traditional School of Music Theory.] *Smuz /3* (1933):74-98.

Ryzhkin, Iosif. "Traditsionnaia shkola." [Traditional School.] In Ryzhkin and Mazel (1934-39):Vol. 1 (1934):79-121.

Ryzhkin, Iosif. "Sovetskoe teoreticheskoe muzykoznanie (1917-1941)." [Soviet Theoretical Musicology (1917-1941).] *Vtem* 6-7 (1967):147-63. Leningrad: 1967.

Ryzhkin, Iosif, and Mazel, Lev Abramovich. *Ocherki po istorii teoreticheskogo muzykoznaniia.* [Essays on the History of Theoretical Musicology.] 2 vols. Moscow: Gosudarstvennoe muzykal'noe izdatel'stvo, 1934-39.

S

Sachs, Klaus-Jürgen. "Contrapunctus/Kontrapunkt." In *HwmT* (1972-). Bibliog.

Sachs, Klaus-Jürgen. "Aspekte der numerischen und tonartlichen Disposition instrumentalmusikalischer Zyklen des ausgehenden 17. und beginnenden 18. Jahrhunderts." *AfMw* 41/4 (1984):237-56.

Salmen, Walter, ed. *Beiträge zur Geschichte der Musikanschauung im 19. Jahrhundert.* SzMg, no. 1. Regensburg: G. Boße, 1965.

Sanders, Herbert. "Counterpoint Revolutionized." *MQ* 5/3 (1919):338-47.

Sannemann, Friedrich. "Die Musik als Unterrichtsgegenstand in den evangelischen Lateinschulen des 16. Jahrhunderts: Ein Beitrag zur Geschichte des Schulgesanges." Ph.D. dissertation, The University of Berlin, 1903; published edition (MS, no. 4), Berlin: E. Ebering, [1904].

Schäfke, Rudolf. *Geschichte der Musikästhetik in Umrissen.* Berlin and Schöneberg: Max Hesse, 1934; (with a Foreword by Werner Korte) Tutzing: Hans Schneider, 1964.

Schavernoch, Hans. *Die Harmonie des Sphären: Die Geschichte der Idee des Welteneinklangs und der Seeleneinstimmung.* OA, no. 6. Freiburg im Breisgau: Karl Alber, 1981. Bibliog. [*Rilm* 81-3956.]

> Reviews in *ÖM* 38/1 (1983):53 (Rudolf Haase) and *PhH* 17/1 (1984):38-40 (Gerd-Klaus Kaltenbrunner) [Spanish translation by José Antonio Robles-Cahero in *Heterofonia* 18/1 (1985):55-58].

Schellhous, Rosalie Athol. "Voice Leading in Mozart's Figured Basses for Attwood." *JMTP* 2/2 (1988):187-223. Bibliog.

Schenkman, Walter. "The Influence of Hexachordal Thinking in the Organization of Bach's Fugue Subjects." *Bach* 7/3 (1976):7-16. [*Rilm* 76-9813.]

Scher, Steven Paul. " 'O Wort, du Wort, das mir fehlt!': Der Realismusbegriff in der Musik." In *Realismustheorien in Literatur, Malerei, Musik und Politik*, edited by Reinhold Grimm and Jost Hermand, pp. 103-17. UT, ser. 80, no. 871. Stuttgart, Berlin, etc.: W. Kohlhammer, 1975. [*Rilm* 76-4369.]

Schering, Arnold. "Die Lehre von den musikalischen Figuren." *KJb* 21 (1908):106-14. Bibliog.

Schering, Arnold. "Geschichtliches zur 'ars inveniendi' in der Musik." *JMbP 1925* 32 (1926):25-34.

Schering, Arnold. "Musikalische Analyse und Wertidee." In *JMbP 1929* 36 (1930):9-20; reprinted in *Von Wesen der Musik: Ausgewählte Aufsätze*, edited by Karl Michael Komma, pp. 183-200. Stuttgart: K. F. Koehler, 1974.

Schering, Arnold, and Wustmann, Rudolf. *Musikgeschichte Leipzigs III: Das Zeitalter Johann Sebastian Bachs und Johann Adam Hillers (von 1723 bis 1800).* Leipzig: Kistner & Siegel, 1941.

Schmalzriedt, Siegfried. "Coda." In *HwmT* (1972-). Bibliog.

Schmalzriedt, Siegfried. "Durchführen, Durchführung." In *HwmT* (1972-). Bibliog.

Schmalzriedt, Siegfried. "Episode." In *HwmT* (1972-). Bibliog.

Schmalzriedt, Siegfried. "Exposition." In *HwmT* (1972-). Bibliog.

Schmalzriedt, Siegfried. "Reprise/ripresa (nach 1600)." In *HwmT* (1972-). Bibliog.

Schmalzriedt, Siegfried. "Subiectum/soggetto/sujet/Subjekt." In *HwmT* (1972-). Bibliog.

Schmalzriedt, Siegfried. "Charakter und Drama: Zur historischen Analyse von Haydnschen und Beethovenschen Sonatensätzen." *AfMw* 42/1 (1985):37-49.

Schmidt, Harro. *Musikerziehung und Musikwissenschaft im 19. Jahrhundert: Studie zu Lehrplanmaterialien des 19.*

Jahrhunderts. SrzM, no. 16. Hamburg: Karl Dieter Wagner, 1979. Bibliog. [*Rilm* 79-3783.]

> Review in *Musica* 34/3 (1980):292.

Schmidt, Marlene. "Zur Theorie des musikalischen Charakters." Ph.D. dissertation, The University of Heidelberg, 1979; published edition (BzMf, no. 9), Munich and Salzburg: Emil Katzbichler, 1981. Bibliog. [*Rilm* 81-1928.]

> Review in *Mf* 38/1 (1985):52 (Wolfgang Seifert).

Schmitt, Rainer. "Der konzertierende Stil im geistlichen Konzert des frühen 17. Jahrhunderts." *KJb* 58-59 (1974-75):73-84. [*Rilm* 76-5429.]

Schmitz, Arnold. "Die oratorische Kunst J. S. Bachs—Grundfragen und Grundlagen." In *Kongress-Bericht Lüneburg 1950* ([1950]):33-49.

Schneider, Herbert. "Die französische Kompositionslehre in der ersten Hälfte des 17. Jahrhunderts." Ph.D. dissertation, The University of Mainz, 1970; published edition (MSzMw, no. 3), Tutzing: Hans Schneider, 1972. Bibliog. [*Rilm* 72-1681.]

> Reviews in *JAMS* 27/2 (1974):348-52 (Frederick B. Hyde), *Mf* 26/1 (1973):107-8, *Mf* 29/3 (1976):356-57 (Carl Dahlhaus), *ML* 54/4 (1973):463-65 (Howard Mayer Brown), *Muh* 25/4 (1974):206 (Paul Mies), *MQ* 60/1 (1974):132-36 (Albert Cohen), and *Rdm* 60/1-2 (1974):229-30 (Denise Launay).

Schneider, Herbert. "Canevas als Terminus der lyrischen Dichtung." *AfMw* 42/2 (1985):87-101.

Schneider, Max. "Untersuchungen zur Entstehungsgeschichte des Basso continuo und seiner Bezifferung." Ph.D. dissertation, The University of Berlin, 1917; published edition (as *Die Anfänge des Basso continuo und seiner Bezifferung*), Leipzig: Breitkopf & Härtel, 1918; reprint edition, Farnborough: Gregg, 1971.

Schnitzler, Günter, ed. *Musik und Zahl: Interdisziplinäre Beiträge zum Grenzbereich zwischen Musik und Mathematik.* OSGM, no. 17. Bonn and Bad Godesberg: Verlag für systematische Musikwissenschaft GmbH, 1976. Bibliog. [*Rilm* 76-16621.]

> Reviews in *CMJ* 4/3 (1980):59-61 (John Strawn), *Me* 31 (1978):191-92, *Mf* 32/2 (1979):214-16 (Werner W. Reiners), *Musica* 31/4 (1977):354-55 (Dietmar Polaczek), and *Rdm* 64/1 (1978):114-16 (Serge Gut).

Schoffman, Nachum. "Vocal Sonata Forms of Mozart." *CM* 28 (1979):19-29. [*Rilm* 79-3682.]

Schoffman, Nachum. "Descriptive Theory and the Standard Table of Triads." *ISM* 3 (1983):144-55. [*Rilm* 83-1639.]

Schoffman, Nachum. "Pedal Points, Old and New." *JMR* 4/3-4 (1983):369-97. [*Rilm* 83-6284.]

Scholes, Percy A. *The Mirror of Music 1844-1944: A Century of Musical Life in Britain as Reflected in the Pages of the "Musical Times".* 2 vols. London: Novello; Oxford University Press, 1947.

Scholz, Gottfried. "Die Musikanalyse und ihre Grenzen." *ÖM* 36/9 (1981):450-60; as "A zenei analízis és korlátai," *Magyar* 24/1 (1983):58-71. [*Rilm* 81-6110.]

Schünemann, Georg. *Geschichte der deutschen Schulmusik.* HbM. Leipzig: Fr. Kistner & C. F. W. Siegel, 1928; 2nd edition, 1931.

Schuhmacher, Gerhard. "Notwendige Ergänzung: Ein Forschungsbericht." See Schuhmacher [*Zur musikalischen Analyse*] (1974):525-48. [*Rilm* 74-3949.]

Schuhmacher, Gerhard, ed. *Zur musikalischen Analyse.* WdF, no. 257. Darmstadt: Wissenschaftliche Buchgesellschaft, 1974.

> Reviews in *Mf* 31/3 (1978):363-64 (Reinhold Brinkmann), *MK* 45/3 (1975):133-34 (Christiane Bernsdorff-Engelbrecht), *Musica* 29/2 (1975): 163-64 (Diether de La Motte), *ÖM* 30/7 (1975): 387 (Rudolf Klein), *SMz* 114/6 (1974):373, and *ZfMt* 8/1 (1977):54-56 (Hermann Danuser).

Schulenberg, David. "Composition as Variation: Procedures of the Bach Circle of Composers." *CM* 33 (1982):57-87. Bibliog. [*Rilm* 82-2364.]

Schulenberg, David. "Composition Before Rameau: Harmony, Figured Bass, and Style in the Baroque." *CMS* 24/2 (1984):130-48. Bibliog.

Schulenberg, David. "Modes, Prolongations, and Analysis." *JM* 4/3 (1985-86):303-29. Bibliog.

Schwartz, Rudolf. "Zur Geschichte des Taktschlagens." *JMbP 1907* (1908):59-70.

Seaton, Douglass. "A Composition Course with Karl Friedrich Zelter." *CMS* 21/2 (1981):126-38. [*Rilm* 81-5032.]

Seay, Albert. "French Renaissance Theory and Jean Yssandon." *JMT* 15/1-2 (1971):254-72. Bibliog. [*Rilm* 72-287.]

Seidel, Elmar. "Eine Wiener Harmonie- und Generalbaßlehre der Beethoven- und Schubertzeit." In *FederhoferFs* (1971):217-28. [*Rilm* 73-521.]

Seidel, Wilhelm. "Rhythmus/numerus." In *HwmT* (1972-). Bibliog.

Seidel, Wilhelm. *Über Rhythmustheorien der Neuzeit.* NHSzMw, no. 7. Bern and Munich: Francke, 1975. Bibliog. [*Rilm* 76-7124.]

> Reviews in *Notes* 34/3 (1977-78):597-99 (Howard E. Smither), *Mf* 31/2 (1978):220-21 (Carl Dahlhaus), and *Ridm* 13/1 (1978):185-92 (Antonio Serravezza).

Seidel, Wilhelm. *Rhythmus: Eine Begriffsbestimmung.* EdF, no. 46. Darmstadt: Wissenschaftliche Buchgesellschaft, 1976. Bibliog. [*Rilm* 76-7123.]

> Reviews in *JMT* 21/2 (1977):382-87 (Jane R. Stevens), *Mf* 31/1 (1978):107-9 (Carl Dahlhaus),

and *Ridm* 13/1 (1978):185-92 (Antonio Sarravezza).

Seidel, Wilhelm. "Über die Prinzipien der Formtheorie." *JSIM 1978* (1979):7-18. Bibliog. [*Rilm* 79-1660.]

Seidel, Wilhelm. "Über Mozarts Rhythmus." In *Bericht Berlin 1974* (1980):603-5. [*Rilm* 80-1837.]

Seidel, Wilhelm. "Schnell—Langsam—Schnell: Zur 'klassischen' Theorie des instrumentalen Zyklus." *Mth* 1/3 (1986):205-16. Bibliog.

Seidel, Wilhelm, and **Cooper**, Barry. *Entstehung nationaler Traditionen: Frankreich; England.* GMt, no. 9. Darmstadt: Wissenschaftliche Buchgesellschaft, 1986. Bibliog.

    Review in *ML* 69/2 (1988):379-81 (Benito V. Rivera).

Serauky, Walter. *Die musikalische Nachahmungsästhetik im Zeitraum von 1700 bis 1850.* UA, no. 17. Münster: Helios; Westfalen: Lechte, Emsdetten, 1929.

Serwer, Howard. "New Linguistic Theory and Old Music Theory." In *Congress Copenhagen 1972* (1974):652-57. [*Rilm* 76-1627.]

Shamgar, Beth Friedman. "The Retransition in the Piano Sonatas of Haydn, Mozart, and Beethoven." Ph.D. dissertation, New York University, 1978. [*Rilm* 78-6068. *DA* 40/02A, p. 534. UMI 79-12324.]

Shamgar, Beth. "On Locating the Retransition in Classic Sonata Form." *MR* 42/2 (1981):130-43. [*Rilm* 81-3684.]

Shamgar, Beth. "Rhythmic Interplay in the Retransitions of Haydn's Piano Sonatas." *JM* 3/1 (1984):55-68.

Sheldon, David A. "The *Galant* Style Revisited and Re-evaluated." *Am* 47/2 (1975):240-70. Bibliog. [*Rilm* 75-813.]

Sheldon, David A. "Exchange, Anticipation, and Ellipsis: Analytical Definitions of the *Galant* Style." In *KaufmannFs* (1981):225-41. [*Rilm* 81-2634.]

Sheldon, David A. "The Ninth Chord in German Theory." *JMT* 26/1 (1982):61-100. [*Rilm* 82-1520.]

Sheldon, David A. "The Fugue as an Expression of Rationalist Values." *IRASM* 17/1 (1986):29-51.

Sheppard, Leslie. "The Bowed String." *Strad* 86/1024 (1975):335-39.

Sheppard, Leslie. "Vibrato: That Subtle Aural Illusion!" *Strad* 89/1066 (1978-79):939-47.

Shirlaw, Matthew. *The Theory of Harmony: An Inquiry into the Natural Principles of Harmony, with an Examination of the Chief Systems of Harmony from Rameau to the Present Day.* HfM. London: Novello, 1917; reprint edition, DeKalb, Ill.: Coar, 1955; reprint edition (DCPMRS), New York: Da Capo Press, 1969; reprint edition (as *The Theory and Nature of Harmony*, with Shirlaw's monograph "The Nature of Harmony"), Sarasota, Fla.: Coar, 1970.

    Reviews in *JMT* 1/2 (1957):228-29 (Erwin Jacobi) and *Strad* 81/967 (1970-71):331.

Shirlaw, Matthew. "The Nature of the Minor Harmony." *MQ* 17/4 (1931):509-24.

Shirlaw, Matthew. "The Science of Harmony." *MR* 18/4 (1957):265-78.

Shirlaw, Matthew. "The Science of Harmony: The Harmonic Generation of Chords." *JMT* 4/1 (1960):1-18.

Shute, J. D. "The English Musical Theorists of the Seventeenth Century, with Particular Reference to Charles Butler." M.Litt. thesis, The University of Durham, 1972.

Silberman, Israel. "A Comparative Study of Four Theories of Chord Function." Ph.D. dissertation, Columbia University, 1949. [*DA* 10/03, p. 160. UMI 00-01725.]

Sirch, Licia. " 'Violini piccoli alla francese' e 'canto alla francese' nell'*Orfeo* (1607) e negli *Scherzi musicali* di Monteverdi." *Nrmi* 15/1 (1981):50-65. Bibliog. [*Rilm* 81-1612.]

Sisman, Elaine Rochelle. "Haydn's Variations." Ph.D. dissertation, Princeton University, 1978. [*DA* 39/04A, p. 1921. UMI 78-18353.]

Skinner, Olive Ross. *Lessons in Harmony, Designed to Assist the Student in the Study of Richter and Jadassohn.* Bloomington, Ill.: Bulletin Printing Co., 1891.

Skyllstad, Kjell. "Theories of Musical Form as Taught at the Leipzig Conservatory, in Relation to the Musical Training of Edward Grieg." *Smn* 1 (1968):69-77.

Smiles, Joan E. "Directions for Improvised Ornamentation in Italian Method Books of the Late Eighteenth Century." *JAMS* 31/3 (1978):495-509. [*Rilm* 78-5978.]

Smith, F. J. "Traditional Harmony? A Radical Question." *MR* 35/1 (1974):63-75. [*Rilm* 74-3920.]

Smith, Leon R., Jr. "An Investigation of the Inherent Qualities of Musical Intervals as Definers of Melodic Tonality." Ph.D. dissertation, Indiana University, 1967. [*Rilm* 68-2809. *DA* 28/06A, pp. 2284-85.]

Smither, Howard Elbert. "Theories of Rhythm in the Nineteenth and Twentieth Centuries with a Contribution to the Theory of Rhythm for the Study of Twentieth-Century Music." Ph.D. dissertation, Cornell University, 1960. Bibliog. [*DA* 21/08, pp. 2319-20. UMI 61-00018.]

Snyder, John L. "Harmonic Dualism and the Origin of the Minor Triad." *ITR* 4/1 (1980-81):45-78. [*Rilm* 80-5629.]

Snyder, Kerala J. "Dietrich Buxtehude's Studies in Learned Counterpoint." *JAMS* 33/3 (1980):544-64. [*Rilm* 80-4543.]

Sochor, Arnold N. "50 Jahre sowjetische Musik im Spiegel der russisch-sowjetischen Musikwissenschaft." *BzMw* 9 (1967):181-96.

Soderlund, Sandra. *Organ Technique: An Historical Approach.* Chapel Hill, N.C.: Hinshaw Music, 1980.

Solerti, Angelo. *Le origini de melodramma: Testimonianze dei contemporanei.* Pbsm, no. 70. Turin: Fratelli Bocca,

1903; reprint edition (BmB, ser. 3, no. 3), Bologna: Forni, 1969; reprint edition, Hildesheim: Georg Olms, 1969. Bibliog.

Solie, Ruth Ames. "Metaphor and Model in the Analysis of Melody." Ph.D. dissertation, The University of Chicago, 1977. [*Rilm* 77-1558. *DA* 38/03A, p. 1109.]

Sondheimer, Robert. *Die Theorie der Sinfonie und die Beurteilung einzelner Sinfoniekomponisten bei den Musikschriftstellern des 18. Jahrhunderts.* Leipzig: Breitkopf & Härtel, 1925.

Sovík, Thomas Paul. "Music Theorists of the Bohemian Reformation: Translation and Critique of the Treatises of Jan Blahoslav and Jan Josquin." Ph.D. dissertation, The Ohio State University, 1985. [*DA* 46/09A, p. 2611. UMI 85-26255.]

Speak, J. M. "The Circle of Fifths: A Summary History of Its Development as Seen in Some Selected Theoretical Writings from Penna to Rameau." *JGMSOSU* 4 (1973):56-57.

Spender, Natasha, and Shuter-Dyson, Rosamund. "Psychology of Music." In *NGrove* (1980). Bibliog.

Spitzer, John, and Zaslaw, Neal. "Improvised Ornamentation in Eighteenth-Century Orchestras." *JAMS* 39/3 (1986):524-77. Bibliog.

> Comment in *JAMS* 40/2 (1987):368 (Beverly Scheibert).

Sponheuer, Bernd. "Die norddeutsche Orgeltoccata und die 'höchsten Formen der Instrumentalmusik': Beobachtungen an der großen e-moll-Toccata von Nicolaus Bruhns." *SchüJb 1985-86* 7-8 (1986):137-46. Bibliog.

Steblin, Rita Katherine. "Key Characteristics in the Eighteenth and Early Nineteenth Centuries: A Historical Approach." Ph.D. dissertation, The University of Illinois at Urbana-Champaign, 1981; published edition (as *A History of Key Characteristics . . .*; SiM, no. 67), Ann Arbor, Mich.: UMI Research Press, 1983. Bibliog. [*Rilm* 81-3961. *DA* 42/06A, p. 2358.]

> Reviews in *AR* 25/4 (1984):147-48 (Jane P. Ambrose), *ML* 66/4 (1985):388-91 (Karol Berger), *Notes* 40/2 (1983-84):287-89 (John D. Arnn), and *OrganYb 1984* 15 (1985):158-59 (Peter Williams).

Steblin, Rita. "Towards a History of Absolute Pitch Recognition." *CMS* 27 (1987):141-53.

Stege, Fritz. "Die deutsche Musikkritik des 18. Jahrhunderts unter dem Einfluß der Affektenlehre." *ZfMw* 10 (1927-28):23-30.

Stein, Deborah. "The Expansion of the Subdominant in the Late Nineteenth Century." *JMT* 27/2 (1983):153-80.

Steinbeck, Wolfram. " 'Ein wahres Spiel mit musikalischen Formen': Zum Scherzo Ludwig van Beethovens." *AfMw* 38/3 (1981):194-226.

Stevens, Jane R. "Theme, Harmony, and Texture in Classic-Romantic Descriptions of Concerto First-Movement Form." *JAMS* 27/1 (1974):25-60; reprinted in Rosand (1985):Vol. 7, pp. 133-68. [*Rilm* 74-3930.]

Stevenson, Robert. *Spanish Music in the Age of Columbus.* The Hague: Martinus Nijhoff, 1960.

> Reviews in *HispAmR* 14/9 (1961-62):853, *JAMS* 16/1 (1963):88-94 (Isabel Pope), *LJ* 88/10 (1963):2012-13 (Catharine K. Miller), *Mf* 16/3 (1963):295-97 (João de Freitas Branco), *ML* 42/4 (1961):374-75 (Peter Peacock), *MQ* 48/3 (1962):405-8 (Denis Stevens), *MR* 22/4 (1961): 336-37 (Hans Redlich), *Notes* 19/1 (1961-62):64-65 (Gilbert Chase), and *NZfM* 123/12 (1962): 579-80 (G. A. Trumpff).

Stevenson, Robert. "Josquin in the Music of Spain and Portugal." In *Josquin Festival 1971* (1976):217-46. [*Rilm* 76-5265.]

Stoll, Albrecht D. "Figur und Affekt: Zur höfischen Musik und zur bürgerlichen Musiktheorie der Epoch Richelieu." Ph.D. dissertation, The University of Frankfurt am Main, 1978; published edition (FBzMw, no. 4), Tutzing: Schneider, 1978; 2nd edition, 1981. Bibliog. [*Rilm* 78-2690.]

> Review in *ÖM* 34/2 (1979):114-15 (Manfred Wagner).

Stowell, Robin. *Violin Technique and Performance Practice in the Late Eighteenth and Early Nineteenth Centuries.* CMTM. New York: Cambridge University Press, 1985. Bibliog.

> Reviews in *BJECS* 9/2 (1986):307-8 (Robert Jacoby), *Choice* 24/1 (1986-87):140 (D. G. Engelhardt), *EM* 15/4 (1987):531-33 (Roy Goodman), *ML* 68/1 (1987):68-69 (Clive Brown), *Notes* 44/2 (1987-88):261-63 (Sonya Monosoff), and *Strad* 97/1155 (1986):200-201 (Simon McVeigh).

Stowell, Robin. " 'Good Execution and Other Necessary Skills': The Role of the Concertmaster in the Late 18th Century." *EM* 16/1 (1988):21-33.

Straková, Theodora. "Die tschechische Musikwissenschaft in ihrer geschichtlichen Entwicklung." *Stm* 17/1-4 (1975): 257-82. [*Rilm* 77-2334.]

Strizich, Robert. "L'accompagnamento di basso continuo sulla chitarra barocca, II." *Fronimo* 9/34-35 (1981):15-26, 8-27. [*Rilm* 81-1614.]

Strunk, Oliver, ed. and trans. *Source Readings in Music History: From Classical Antiquity through the Romantic Era.* New York: W. W. Norton, 1950; segments issued separately in paperback.

> Reviews in *JAMS* 4/3 (1951):249-51 (Leo Schrade), *MAm* 71/14 (1951):28 (Robert Sabin), *MC* 143/4 (1951):65, *MCM* 30/3 (1950-51):18 (Hazel G. Weaver), *ML* 33/3 (1952):257-58 (Richard Capell), *MQ* 37/3 (1951):430-35 (Erich Hertzmann), *MR* 15/1 (1954):67-68 (J. A. West-

rup), *MT* 93/1316 (1952):450-51 (Wilfrid Mellers), *MusT* 31/6 (1952):303 (J. R. T.), *MWM* 7 (1951):9, *Notes* 8/3 (1950-51):517-18 (Manfred F. Bukofzer), *RN* 4/1 (1951):1-2 (Archibald T. Davison), *SatR* 34 (January 27, 1951):20 (C. G. Burke), *SwM* 18/13 (1951):6, and *TES* (1981):41.

Struthers, Christina. "Old-World Musical Criticism." *MMR* 32/375 (1902):44-45.

Subirá, José. *Historia de la música*. 4 vols. Barcelona: Salvat Editores, 1947; later editions in 1951 and 1958.

Subirá, José. *Historia de la música española e hispanoamericana*. Barcelona: Salvat Editores, 1953.

Sullivan, Anita. *The Seventh Dragon: The Riddle of Equal Temperament*. Lake Oswego, Oregon: Metamorphous Press, 1985. Bibliog.

> Reviews in *Booklist* 82/22 (1986):1650 (Frances Woods), *LATBR* 106/32 (1987):4 (Albert Hayward), *KeyM* 12 (1986):26, *MEJ* 73/5 (1987):61, *NYTBR* 91 [135/46,876] (August 24, 1986):6

(Edward Rothstein), *Parabola* 12/1 (1987):118 (Edward P. Stevenson), *PW* 229/25 (1986):86, and *SPR* 18/9 (1986):14 (Leo Vincent Saint-John).

Swain, Joseph Peter. "Limits of Musical Structure." Ph.D. dissertation, Harvard University, 1983. Bibliog. [*DA* 44/06, p. 1623. UMI 83-22452.]

Swain, Joseph P. "Form and Function of the Classical Cadenza." *JM* 6/1 (1988):27-59.

Swartland, J. "An Examination of Thomas Attwood's Studies with Mozart in the Context of Eighteenth-Century Musical Theory." M.Phil. thesis, The University of York, 1982.

Sydow-Saak, Brigitte. "Intonatio—Intonation/intonare—intonieren." In *HwmT* (1972-). Bibliog.

Szweykowski, Zygmunt M. "Późny renesans w poszukiwaniu ideału muzycznego." *Muzyka* 30/1 [116] (1985):3-36.

T

Taddie, Daniel Lawrence. "*Scale*: An Historical Study of Musical Terminology and Concepts." Ph.D. dissertation, The University of Iowa, 1984. [*DA* 45/07A, pp. 1913-14. UMI 84-23599.]

Tagliavini, Luigi Ferdinando. "L'arte di 'non lasciar vuoto lo strumento': Appunti sulla prassi cembalistica italiana nel Cinque- e Seicento." *Ridm* 10 (1975):360-78; as "The Art of 'Not Leaving the Instrument Empty': Comments on Early Italian Harpsichord Playing" (translated by Barbara Sachs), *EM* 11/3 (1983):299-308. Bibliog. [*Rilm* 75-4434.]

Taylor, Charles. "Sound." In *NGrove* (1980). Bibliog.

Telesco, Paula J. "Enharmonicism in Theory and Practice in Eighteenth-Century Music." Ph.D. dissertation, The Ohio State University, forthcoming.

Tenney, James. *A History of 'Consonance' and 'Dissonance'*. New York: Excelsior Music Publishing Co., 1988. Bibliog.

> Review in *JMR* (1989) (David Damschroder).

Thaler, Lotte. *Organische Form in der Musiktheorie des 19. und beginnenden 20. Jahrhundert*. BmA, no. 25. Munich and Salzburg: Musikverlag Emil Katzbichler, 1984. Bibliog.

> Reviews in *Mf* 39/4 (1986):383 (Diether de la Motte) and *Mth* 2/2 (1987):194 (Wolfgang Dömling).

Thieme, Ulrich. "Die Affektenlehre im philosophischen und musikalischen Denken des Barock—Vorgeschichte, Ästhetik, Physiologie." *Tibia* 7/3 (1982):161-68; 8/1-2 (1983):241-45, 325-34. [*Rilm* 82-6057; 83-1949.]

Thompson, David M. *A History of Harmonic Theory in the United States*. Kent, Ohio: The Kent State University Press, 1980. Bibliog.

> Reviews in *AmM* 1/2 (1983):100 (G. Thaddeus Jones), *AmO:AGO* 15/3 (1981):6 (Charles Huddleston Heaton), *Choice* 18/7 (1980-81):964, *JMT* 25/2 (1981):316-18 (Paul S. Hesselink), *JRME* 29/3 (1980):235-37 (Barton K. Bartle), and *MEJ* 67/7 (1980-81):105.

Thomson, Ulf. "Voraussetzungen und Artungen der österreichischen Generalbasslehre zwischen Albrechtsberger und Sechter." Ph.D. dissertation, The University of Vienna, 1960; published edition (WVzMw, no. 8), Tutzing: Hans Schneider, 1978. Bibliog. [*Rilm* 78-6055.]

> Reviews in *Nrmi* 14/3 (1980):431-32 (Franco Piperno) and *ÖM* 33/10 (1978):560.

Thomson, William Ennis. "A Clarification of the Tonality Concept." Ph.D. dissertation, Indiana University, 1952. [*DA* 12/06, p. 800. UMI 00-04380.]

Thomson, William. "Functional Ambiguity in Musical Structures." *MP* 1/1 (1983-84):3-27.

Thürlings, Adolf. "Die beiden Tongeschlechter und die neuere musikalische Theorie." Ph.D. dissertation, The University of Munich, 1877; published edition, Berlin: Leo Liepmannssohn, 1877.

Tilmouth, Michael. "Parody (i)." In *NGrove* (1980). Bibliog.

Tirabassi, Antonio. "Histoire de l'harmonisation à partir de 1600 á 1750 (Les trois règles)." *Bericht Basel 1924* (1925):328-33.

Tittel, Ernst. *Der neue Gradus: Lehrbuch des strengen Satzes nach Johann Joseph Fux.* 2 vols. Vienna: Doblinger, 1959.

> Reviews in *MG* 10/5 (1960):294-95 (Günter Altmann) and *Notes* 17/4 (1959-60):577-78 (Alfred Mann).

Tittel, Ernst. "Wiener Musiktheorie von Fux bis Schönberg." See Vogel (1966):163-201. Bibliog.

Todd, R. Larry. *Mendelssohn's Musical Education: A Study and Edition of His Exercises in Composition.* CSM. Cambridge: Cambridge University Press, 1983. Bibliog. [*Rilm* 83-850.]

> Reviews in *CM* 37-38 (1984):224-28 (Douglass Seaton), *Composer* 80 (1983):28 (Nigel Burton), *Mf* 38/4 (1985):323-24 (Gerhard Schuhmacher), *ML* 65/3 (1984):288-90 (Jeffrey Hollander), *MT* 125/1693 (1984):153 (William Drabkin), *Notes* 40/4 (1983-84):784-86 (Eric Werner), *Nrmi* 20/1 (1986):110-12 (Pietro Zappala'), *NZfM* 144/7-8 (1983):66 (Hans Christoph Worbs), *Rdm* 71/1-2 (1985):206-8 (Jean-Alexandre Ménétrier), and *T&P* 8/2 (1983):49-52 (Floyd K. Grave).

Todd, R. Larry. "The 'Unwelcome Guest' Regaled: Franz Liszt and the Augmented Triad." *NCM* 12/2 (1988-89):93-115.

Tolkoff, Lyn. "French Modal Theory before Rameau." *JMT* 17/1 (1973):150-63.

Toncitch, Voya. "Dodécaphonie et systèmes de 24 et 31 tons." *SMz* 113/5 (1973):274-78. [*Rilm* 74-2992.]

Traficante, Frank. "Lyra Viol Tunings: 'All Ways Have Been Tryed to Do It'." *Am* 42/3-4 (1970):183-205. [*Rilm* 70-2492.]

Treibitz, C. Howard. "Substance and Function in Concepts of Musical Structure." *MQ* 69/2 (1983):209-26. [*Rilm* 83-1624.]

Troeger, Richard. *Technique and Interpretation on the Harpsichord.* Bloomington, Ind.: Indiana University Press, 1987.

> Reviews in *AMT* 38/3 (1989):57 (Maurice Hinson) and *MR* 48/1 (1988):72-74 (Gregory S. Johnston).

Truesdell, Clifford Ambrose. "The Rational Mechanics of Flexible or Elastic Bodies, 1638-1788 . . ." In *Leonhardi Euleri Opera omnia sub auspiciis Societatis scientiarum naturalium helveticae,* ser. 2, no. 11:2. Zürich: Orell Füssli, 1960.

> For commentary on this work, see Henk Bos, "Mathematics and Rational Mechanics" in *The Ferment of Knowledge: Studies in the Histriography of Eighteenth-Century Science,* edited by G. S. Rousseau and Roy Porter, pp. 327-55. Cambridge: Cambridge University Press, 1980.

Tsuchida, Eizaburo. "*Sonatenform* to *Hauptform* — Sonatenform gainen no seiritsu o megutte." M.A. thesis, The University of Fine Arts and Music (Tokyo), 1979. [*Rilm* 79-1661.]

Tsuchida, Eizaburo. "Shuyokeishiki ni tsuite — 'sonata keishiki' gainen no seiritsu o megutte." *Og* 27/1 (1981):16-34. [*Rilm* 81-1680.]

Tuksar, Stanislav. *Hrvatski renesansni teoretiçari glazbe.* Zagreb: Jugoslavenska akademija znanosti i umjetnosti, 1978; as *Croatian Renaissance Music Theorists* (translated by Sonja Bašiš; SCMC, no. 1), Zagreb: Sveušilišna Naklada (Liburnija) [Music Information Center, Zagreb Concert Management], 1980. Bibliog.

> Reviews in *Armus* 12/1-2 (1981):132-34 (Franjo Bilič), *IRASM* 13/1 (1982):122 (Josip Andreis), and *Zvuk* 1 (1980):114-15 (Darko Grlič).

Turner, Jet E. "*Notes inégales*: Treatises by Bacilly, Loulié, and Démotz: Their Application to the 'Mass for the Convents' by F. Couperin." D.M.A. dissertation, The University of Wisconsin, 1974. [*Rilm* 75-2576. *DA* 35/03A, p. 1692. UMI 74-16234.]

Turrell, Frances Berry. "Modulation: An Outline of Its Prehistory from Aristoxenus to Henry Glarean." Ph.D. dissertation, The University of Southern California, 1956. Bibliog. [SMLMS.]

Turrell, Frances Berry. *The "De Musica" of Boethius: Its Place in the History of Music Theory.* Los Angeles: The University of Southern California Press, 1958.

Tyler, James. "Further Remarks on the Four-Course Guitar." *LSJ* 17 (1975):60-62. [*Rilm* 75-4393.]

U

Uberti, Mauro. "Vocal Techniques in Italy in the Second Half of the 16th Century." Translated by Mark Lindley. *EM* 9/4 (1981):486-95. [*Rilm* 81-6015.]

[Uemura, Kozo. "Musical Invention in the 18th Century: On the *loci topici* of Mattheson and Heinichen."] In *NomuraFs* (1969):40-49. [*Rilm* 70-430.]

> In Japanese.

Ulrich, Ernst. "Studien zur duetschen Generalbaß-Praxis in der ersten Hälfte des 18. Jahrhunderts." Ph.D. dissertation, The University of Münster, 1931 (1932); published edition (MBzMw, no. 2), Kassel: Bärenreiter, 1932. Bibliog.

Unger, Hans-Heinrich. "Die Beziehungen zwischen Musik und Rhetoric im 16.-18. Jahrhundert." Ph.D. dissertation, The University of Berlin, 1941; published edition

(MuG, no. 4), Würzburg: Triltsch, 1941; reprint edition, Hildesheim: Georg Olms, 1969. Bibliog.

Review in *Nrmi* 4/5 (1970):950-54 (Gino Stefani).

V

Vanhulst, Henri. "La pratique de l'improvisation d'après les traités de clavier de l'*empfindsamer Stil*." *Rbdm* 25/1-4 (1971):108-53. [*Rilm* 73-1834.]

Vauclain, Constant. "Some Sonorous Arithmetic." *MR* 39/3-4 (1978):263-72. [*Rilm* 78-6056.]

Vecchi, Giuseppe. "La polemica Artusi-Monteverdi. Bottrigari e Banchieri." In his *Le accademie musicali del primo seicento e Monteverdi a Bologna*, pp. 15-44. Bologna: A. M. I. S., 1969.

Vellekoop, Gerrit. "Twee Spaanse muziektheoretische werken uit de zestiende eeuw." *Mens* 14/7 (1959):222-24.

Vertrees, Julie Anne. "Mozart's String Quartet K. 465: The History of a Controversy." *CM* 17 (1974):96-114. Bibliog. [*Rilm* 74-451.]

Viertel, Karl-Heinz. "Johann Adolph Scheibe und Charles Burney, zwei Musiktheoretiker der Aufklärung." *MG* 26/4 (1976):223-27. [*Rilm* 76-10241.]

Vinquist, Mary, and Zaslaw, Neal, eds. *Performance Practice: A Bibliography*. New York: W. W. Norton, 1971.

> Derived from materials in *CM* 8 (1969):5-96 and 10 (1970):144-72. Supplements in *CM* 12 (1971):129-49 and 15 (1973):126-36. Reviews in *AR* 13/1 (1972):28 (Dale Higbee), *Clavier* 11/4 (1972):5, *Diapason* 64/6 (1973):10 (Lee R. Garrett), *Instrumentalist* 26/6 (1971-72):10, and *PP* 64/4 (1971-72):32 (Melva Peterson).

Vitányi, Iván. "A marxista zeneesztétika uttöröi." [Pioneers of Marxist Music Aesthetics.] *Muzsika* 11/8-10, 12 (1968):22-25, 12-13, 24-27, 29-31; 12/1-4 (1969):36-37, 21-23, 22-23, 20-22. [*Rilm* 70-2674.]

Vogel, Martin. "Die Zahl Sieben in der spekulativen Musiktheorie." Ph.D. dissertation, The University of Bonn, 1955 (1954).

Vogel, Martin. *Der Tristan-Akkord und die Krise der modernen Harmonie-Lehre*. OSGM, no. 2. Düsseldorf: Verlag der Gesellschaft zur Förderung der systematischen Musikwissenschaft, 1962.

> Reviews in *Mf* 17/4 (1964):450-52 (Friedrich Neumann), *Muh* 18/2 (1967):86, and *Notes* 21/1-2 (1963-64):134 (Dika Newlin).

Vogel, Martin, ed. *Beiträge zur Musiktheorie des 19. Jahrhunderts*. SzMg, no. 4. Regensburg: Boße, 1966.

> Reviews in *Mf* 22/3 (1969):401-3 (Friedrich Neumann), *Miscm* 3 (1968):279 (Andrew D. McCredie), *ML* 48/1 (1967):69-70 (Hans Ferdinand Redlich), *Muh* 18/2 (1967):86, and *Stfm* 49 (1967):182-87 (Ingmar Bengtsson).

Vogel, Martin. "Funktionszeichen auf akusticher Grundlage." *ZfMt* 1 (1970).

Vogel, Martin. *Die Lehre von den Tonbeziehungen*. OSGM, no. 16. Bonn: Verlag für systematische Musikwissenschaft, 1975; 2nd edition, 1984. [*Rilm* 76-4448.]

> Reviews in *Me* 29/4 (1975-76):191-92 (W. Schultze), *Mf* 31/4 (1978):498-99 (Jürgen Meyer), *Mi* 33/5 (1984):56, and *ÖM* 33/3 (1978):159 (Werner Schulze).

Vogel, Martin. "Reine Stimmung und Temperierung." In Schnitzler (1976):265-92. Bibliog. [*Rilm* 76-16936.]

W

Wagner, Günther. "Klavierschule im historischen Bezug." *Musica* 35/2 (1981):142-46. [*Rilm* 81-1505.]

Wagner, Manfred. *Die Harmonielehren der ersten Hälfte des 19. Jahrhunderts*. SzMg, no. 38. Regensburg: Boße, 1974. Bibliog. [*Rilm* 76-7158.]

> Reviews in *Me* 31 (1977-78):286-87 (Friedrich Neumann), *Melos/NZfM* 2/2 (1976):157-58 (Carl Dahlhaus), *Mf* 30/3 (1977):387-88 (Peter Rummenhöller), *ÖM* 32/9 (1977):409 (Rudolf Klein), *Rdm* 62/2 (1976):331-33 (Serge Gut), *Stfm* 57/2 (1975):77-78 (Martin Tegen), and *ZfMt* 8/1 (1977):47-48 (Peter Rummenhöller).

Waite, William G. "Bernard Lamy, Rhetorician of the Passions." In *GeiringerFs* (1970):388-96. [*Rilm* 71/505.]

Waitzman, Mimi S. "Meantone Temperament in Theory and Practice." *ITO* 5/4 (1979-81):3-15. Bibliog. [*Rilm* 81-3660.]

Walker, D. P. "Musical Humanism in the Sixteenth and Early Seventeenth Centuries." *MR* 2/1-4 (1941):1-13, 111-21, 220-27, 288-308; 3/1 (1942):55-71; as *Der musikalische Humanismus im 16. und frühen 17. Jahrhunderts* (GMfMA, no. 5), Kassel and Basel: Bärenreiter, 1949; reprint of the 1941-42 edition in Rosand (1985):Vol. 4, pp. 197-267 and in Walker (1985). Bibliog.

> Reviews in *Mens* 6/10 (1951):319, *Mf* 4/1 (1951):88-90 (Georg Reichert), *ML* 31/4 (1950):369 (Hans Gal), *MQ* 37/2 (1951):285-89 (Edward E. Lowinsky), *MR* 12/3 (1951):230

(O. E. Deutsch), *Notes* 7/4 (1949-50):578 (William Klenz), and *Rmi* 56/1 (1954):81-83 (Alfredo Bonaccorsi).

Walker, D. P. "Some Aspects and Problems of *musique mesurée à l'antique*: The Rhythm and Notation of *musique mesurée*." *Md* 4/2-4 (1950):163-86; reprinted in Walker (1985). Bibliog.

Walker, D. P. "La tradition mathématico-musicale du platonisme et les débuts de la science moderne." In *Plato Colloque 1976* (1976):249-60. Bibliog.

Walker, D. P. *Studies in Musical Science in the Late Renaissance*. SWI, no. 37. London: The Warburg Institute, The University of London; Leiden: Brill, 1978. Bibliog.

> Reviews in *AS* 37/6 (1980):706-8 (Sigalia Dostrovsky), *IRASM* 12/1 (1981):75-78 (Stanislav Tuksar), *Isis* 71/257 (1980):347-48 (Stillman Drake), *JMT* 24/1 (1980):107-16 (Joseph Di Giovanni), *ML* 61/2 (1980):190-92 (Claude V. Palisca), and *SCAC* 2 (1981):192-95 (Stephen Gaukroger).

Walker, D. P. *Music, Spirit and Language in the Renaissance*. Edited by Penelope Gouk. London: Variorum Reprints, 1985.

> Review in *TLS* 85/4323 (1986):133 (Anthony Grafton).

Walker, Paul Mark. "Fugue in German Theory from Dressler to Mattheson." Ph.D. dissertation, The State University of New York at Buffalo, 1987. Bibliog. [*DA* 48/02A, p. 247. UMI 87-10763.]

Walsh, Stephen. "Music Analysis: Hearing Is Believing?" *MP* 2/2 (1984-85):237-44.

Warrack, Guy. "Music and Mathematics." *ML* 26/1 (1945):21-27.

Warren, Charles. "Word-painting." In *NGrove* (1980). Bibliog.

Wason, Robert Wesley. "Fundamental-Bass Theory in Nineteenth-Century Vienna." Ph.D. dissertation, Yale University, 1981; published edition (as *Viennese Harmonic Theory from Albrechtsberger to Schenker and Schoenberg*; SiM, no. 80), Ann Arbor, Mich.: UMI Research Press, 1985. [*DA* 43/07A, p. 2152.]

> Reviews in *Mf* 41/4 (1988):381 (Hellmut Federhofer), *Mth* 2/2 (1987):197-98 (Manfred Wagner), and *MTS* 8 (1986):140-43 (William Caplin).

Wason, Robert. "Schenker's Notion of Scale-Step in Historical Perspective: Non-Essential Harmonies in Viennese Fundamental Bass Theory." *JMT* 27/1 (1983):49-73. [*Rilm* 83-1625.]

> Abstract in *MA* 3/3 (1984):297-98 (James Ellis).

Wason, Robert. "Progressive Harmonic Theory in the Mid-Nineteenth Century." *JMR* 8/1-2 (1988):55-90. Bibliog.

Weber, J. G. "Pascal and Music: World Harmony in Early Seventeenth-Century France." *Symposium* 30/1 (1976):75-91.

Weigl, Bruno. "Die alterierten Akkorde." *Musik* 14/8 (1914-15):51-70.

Wellek, Albert. "Konsonanz-Dissonanz [psychologisch]." In *MGG* (1949-68). Bibliog.

Wellesz, Egon, and Sternfeld, Frederick, eds. *The Age of Enlightenment (1745-1790)*. NOHM, vol. 7. London: Oxford University Press, 1973. Bibliog. [*Rilm* 74-1718.]

> Reviews in *AJME* 16 (1975):59 (David Swale), *ARBA* 6 (1975):500 (R.), *AUMLA* 45 (1976):168-69 (David Galliver), *Clavier* 13/4 (1974):6, *Dmt* 49/2 (1974-75):39-40 (Carsten E. Hatting), *HFMA* 24/7 (1974):MA40 (Patrick J. Smith), *JAMS* 28/2 (1975):384-95 (William S. Newman), *MakM* 86 (1974):21 (Janice Holdstock), *MEJ* 61/2 (1974-75):87-88 (Louise Cuyler), *MiE* 38/367 (1974):128 (Clive Unger-Hamilton), *Miscm* 8 (1975):148-52 (Andrew D. McCredie), *MK* 44/4 (1974):183 (Gerhard Schuhmacher), *ML* 55/4 (1974):465-71 (Arthur Hutchings), *MQ* 61/3 (1975):481-85 (Piero Weiss), *MT* 115/1574 (1974):295-301 (Daniel Heartz), *MusT* 54/1 (1975):23 (Frank M. Laming), *Nrmi* 8/2 (1974): 300-303 (Massimo Mila), *NZfM* 135/4 (1974): 268-69 (Hans Hollander), *Rdm* 60/1-2 (1974): 233 (François Lesure), *Stfm* 56/2 (1974):38-39 (Hans Eppstein), and *TLS* 73/3796 (1974):1395 (Denis Matthews).

Werts, Daniel. "A Theory of Scale References." Ph.D. dissertation, Princeton University, 1983. [*DA* 44/06A, p. 1721. UMI 83-22579.]

Wessel, Frederick T. "The Affektenlehre in the Eighteenth Century." Ph.D. dissertation, Indiana University, 1955. [*DA* 16/01, p. 134. UMI 00-14674.]

Wessely, Othmar. *Johann Joseph Fux und Francesco Antonio Vallotti: Jahresgabe 1966 der Johann-Joseph-Fux-Gesellschaft*. Graz: [Johann-Joseph-Fux-Gesellschaft], 1967.

Wessely, Othmar. "Zur ars inveniendi im Zeitalter des Barock." *OmSM* 1/2 (1971-72):113-40. Bibliog.

Whatley, G. Larry. "Music Theory." In *Music in Britain: The Romantic Age, 1800-1914*, edited by Nicholas Temperley, pp. 474-82. AHMB, vol. 5. London: Athlone Press, 1981.

> Reviews in *BBN* (1982):314 (Paul Hindmarsh), *Brio* 19/1 (1982):23-26 (Lewis Foreman), *Composer* 76-77 (1982):36 (Charles Edwards), *CUMR* 5 (1984):333-36 (Kenneth DeLong), *ML* 64/3-4 (1983):237-41 (Arthur Hutchings), *MQ* 69/3 (1983):446-49 (Alan Walker), *MT* 123/1674 (1982):547 (Arthur Jacobs), *NCM* 8/2 (1984-85):164-76 (Richard Swift), *Notes* 39/3 (1982-83):604-5 (Walter Schlesinger), *Tempo* 148 (1984):42-44 (Peter Dickinson), *TLS* 81/4126 (1982):488 (Richard Fairman), and *VS* 27/1 (1983-84):133-35 (William Weber).

Whitmore, P. "Towards an Understanding of the Capriccio." *PMA 1987-88* 113/1 (1988):47-56.

Whittall, Arnold. "Form." In *NGrove* (1980). Bibliog.

Wichmann, Kurt. *Der Ziergesang und die Ausführung der Appoggiatura: Ein Beitrag zur Gesangspädagogik*. Leipzig: VEB Deutscher Verlag für Musik, 1966. Bibliog.

> Review in *MG* 21/5 (1971):350-52 (Heinrich Spieler).

Wienpahl, Robert W. "The Emergence of Tonality." Ph.D. dissertation, The University of California at Los Angeles, 1953. Bibliog. [SMLMS.]

Wienpahl, Robert W. "English Theorists and Evolving Tonality." *ML* 36/4 (1955):377-93.

Wightman, William Persehouse Delisle. *Science in a Renaissance Society*. London: Hutchinson, 1972.

> Reviews in *AS* 30/2 (1973):233-34 (A. J. Meadows), *Choice* 10/3 (1973-74):486, *EHR* 88/349 (1973):891-92 (C. Webster), *RQ* 27/2 (1974):219-21 (Vern L. Bullough), and *TLS* 71/3680 (1972):1057-58.

Williams, David Russell. *A Bibliography of the History of Music Theory*. Fairport, N.Y.: Rochester Music Publishers, 1970; 2nd edition, 1971; Athens, Ohio: Accura Music, 1976. Bibliog.

> Reviews in *AR* 16/2 (1975):61-62 (Sabina Teller Ratner) and *JRME* 21/4 (1973):380-81 (George J. Buelow).

Williams, Peter. "Equal Temperament and the English Organ, 1675-1825." *Am* 40/1 (1968):53-65. [*Rilm* 68-1097.]

Williams, Peter. "The Harpsichord Acciaccatura: Theory and Practice in Harmony, 1650-1750." *MQ* 54/4 (1968):503-23. [*Rilm* 69-2692.]

Williams, Peter. *Figured Bass Accompaniment*. 2 vols. Edinburgh: Edinburgh University Press, 1970. Bibliog.

> Review in *AR* 14/3 (1973):91 (Dale Higbee), *Choice* 10/3 (1973-74):472, *GSJ* 24 (1971):122-23 (James Dalton), *JAMS* 25/3 (1972):476-79 (Tharald Borgir), *ML* 52/3 (1971):321-22 (Jack A. Westrup), *MO* 95/1131 (1971-72):131 (B. R.), *MQ* 58/2 (1972):308-15 (George J. Buelow), *MT* 112/1537 (1971):239-40 (Denis Arnold), *OrganJb* 3 (1972):105 (Gustav Leonhardt), and *TLS* 70/3638 (1971):1457.

Williams, Peter. "*Figurenlehre* from Monteverdi to Wagner." *MT* 120/1636-38, 40 (1979):476-79, 571-73, 648-50, 816-18. [*Rilm* 79-5671.]

Winckel, Fritz. "Konsonanz-Dissonanz [akustisch]." In *MGG* (1949-68). Bibliog.

Winick, Steven David. *Rhythm: An Annotated Bibliography*. Metuchen, N.J.: Scarecrow Press, 1974. [*Rilm* 75-220.]

> Reviews in *AMT* 25/2 (1975-76):37-38 (L. C. Ferguson), *ARBA* 7 (1976):475 (Albert Seay), *Choice* 12/4 (1975-76):516, *Coda* 148 (1976):6 (Barry Tepperman), *GuitP* 9/3 (1975):56 (Barbara Heuman Kriss), *JAAC* 34/1 (1975-76):98-99 (Bruce Archibald), *Musart* 27/3 (1974-75):36 (Sr. Regina Therese Unsinn), *Notes* 32/4 (1975-76):772-74 (Larry Wayne Peterson), *WLB* 49/9 (1974-75):672, and *WWBP* 14/3 (1975):46 (Thomas A. Brown).

Winternitz, Emanuel. "Über Musikinstrumentensammlungen des Frühbarock." In *Smm* (1970):6-18. [*Rilm* 70-3209.]

Wintle, Christopher. "Review Article: Issues in Dahlhaus." *MA* 1/3 (1982):341-55. [*Rilm* 82-6061.]

Wiora, Walter. "*Musica poetica* und musikalisches Kunstwerk." *FellererFsI* (1962):579-89. Bibliog.

Wirth, Franz. "Untersuchungen zur Entstehung der deutschen praktischen Harmonielehre." Ph.D. dissertation, The University of Munich, 1966; published edition, Bamberg: Rudolf Rodenbusch, 1966. Bibliog.

Witkowski, Leon. "Die Musikerziehung im Akademischen Gymnasium zu Torun vom 16. bis 18. Jahrhundert." In *Telemann Festtage 1973* (1975):111-19. Bibliog. [*Rilm* 76-9883.]

Wittwer, Max. "Die Musikpflege im Jesuitenorden unter besonderer Berücksichtigung der Länder deutscher Zunge." Ph.D. dissertation, The University of Greifswald, 1934 (1935); published edition, Greifswald: Grimmer Kreis-Zeitung GmbH, 1934.

Wolf, Hans. "Die musikalischen Bewegungsbegriffe in den Generalbaß- und Kompositionslehren des 18. Jahrhunderts als Fortsetzung der Lehre vom Kontrapunkt." Ph.D. dissertation, The University of Vienna, 1936.

Wolf, Johannes. "Early English Music Theorists: From 1200 to the Death of Purcell." *MQ* 25/4 (1939):420-29.

Wolff, Christoph. "Ricercar." In *HwmT* (1972-). Bibliog.

Wolff, Konrad. "Tonal Relations in Classical Music." *PQ* 26/102 (1978):36-40.

Wunderlich, Henry. "Four Theories of Tonality." *JMus* 2/4 (1940-41):171-80.

Y

Yamaguchi, Hiroko. *"Seconda pratica* — Monteverdi no madrigal ni miru atarashii ongaku nusozo." 2 vols. M.A. thesis, Tokyo Geijutsu Daigaku, 1977. [*Rilm* 77-504.]

Yarustovsky, Boris Mikhailovich, ed. *Intonatsiia i muzykal'nyi obraz.* [Intonation and Musical Imagery.] Moscow: 1965.

Yarustovsky, Boris Mikhailovich. "Soviet Musicology." *Am* 46/1 (1974):50-57.

Yates, Frances Amelia. *The French Academies of the Sixteenth Century.* SWI, no. 15. London: Warburg Institute, University of London, 1947.

> Reviews in *CLit* 3/1 (1951):81-82 (Robert V. Merrill), *JAAC* 8/1 (1949-50):61 (Wolfgang Stechow), *Md* 2/3-4 (1948):259-61 (D. P. Walker), *MLQ* 11/2 (1950):242-43, *MLR* 43/4 (1948):541-42 (M. Dominica Legge), *MR* 9/3 (1948):200-203, *QQ* 56/2 (1949-50):299-301 (J. C. L.), *Rdm* 27 (1948):108-9 (François Lesure), *RES* 25/99 (1949):263-65 (Hardin Craig), and *Speculum* 23/4 (1948):737 (Crane Brinton).

Yates, Frances Amelia. *Giordano Bruno and the Hermetic Tradition.* Chicago: The University of Chicago Press, 1964.

> Reviews in *AHR* 70/2 (1964-65):455-57 (Giorgio de Santillana), *AUMLA* 22 (1964):302-3 (A. W. Rudrum), *CathHR* 51/1 (1965-66):108-9 (Charles R. Meyer), *CJH* 1/2 (1966):82-84 (Dominic Baker-Smith), *CLit* 18/2 (1966):169-72

(Paul E. Memmo, Jr.), *HT* 5/1 (1966):82-87 (George Boas), *IPQ* 4/4 (1964):626-28 (Charles B. Schmitt), *JHP* 3/2 (1965):276-78 (Glennon Anthony Donnelly), *MLR* 61/4 (1966):719-21 (D. P. Walker), *NYRB* 3/2 (1964):8-10 (J. Bronowski), *RMet* 18/2 [70] (1964-65):388 (Kenneth A. Megill), *RN* 18/3 (1965):233-36 (Marjorie Nicholson), and *Tablet* 218/6456 (1964):185 (Renee Haynes).

Yeston, Maury. "The Stratification of Musical Rhythm." Ph.D. dissertation, Yale University, 1974; published edition, New Haven, Ct.: Yale University Press, 1976. [*Rilm* 74-3897. *DA* 38/01A, p. 21.]

> Reviews in *Choice* 13/4 (1976-77):532, *ITO* 2/5 (1976-77):13-26 (Henry Martin), *JAAC* 35/2 (1976-77):244-45 (Roger Solie), *JMT* 21/2 (1977):355-73 (Gary E. Wittlich), *LJ* 101/5 (1976):720 (Dika Newlin), *MEJ* 64/8 (1977-78):19-23 (David Liptak), *Melos/NZfM* 4/2 (1978):168 (Carl Dahlhaus), *Mf* 33/2 (1980):222-24 (Wilhelm Seidel), *MJ* 34/4 (1976):32 (Paul Turok), *MR* 38/3 (1977):224-25 (Peter J. Pirie), *Notes* 34/1 (1977-78):77-80 (Robert G. Hopkins), *PNM* 16/1 (1977-78):144-76 (Charles J. Smith), and *Tempo* 123 (1977):41-43 (Bayan Northcott).

Yeston, Maury. "Rubato and the Middleground." *JMT* 19/2 (1975):286-301.

Z

Zaminer, Frieder, ed. *Ideen zu einer Geschichte der Musiktheorie: Einleitung in das Gesamtwerk.* GMt, no. 1. Darmstadt: Wissenschaftliche Buchgesellschaft, 1985. Bibliog.

Zaslaw, Neal. "The Compleat Orchestral Musician." *EM* 7/1 (1979):46-57.

Zenck, Hermann. "Grundformen deutscher Musikanschauung." *JAWG 1941/42* (1942):15-40.

Ziebler, Karl. "Zur Ästhetik der Lehre von den musikalischen Redefiguren im 18. Jahrhundert." *ZfMw* 15/7 (1933):289-301.

Zimmermann, Jörg. "Wandlungen des philosophischen Musikbegriffs: Über den Gegensatz von mathematisch-harmonikaler und semantisch-ästhetischer Betrachtungsweise." In Schnitzler (1976):81-135. Bibliog.

Zinar, Ruth. "Highlights of Thought in the History of Music Education." *AMT* 33/1-2 (1983):26-28, 44.

Zychowicz, James L. "Transformational Analysis: An Essay toward an Analytical Model." *CM* 37-38 (1984):182-86.

TOPICAL INDEX

Accentuation (see *Rhythm*)

Accidentals (see also *Chromaticism*; *Musica ficta*; *Solmization*)

BANCHIERI; BIANCIARDI; COPRARIO; DANCKERTS; KOLLMANN; ORTIZ; ROUSSIER; TREIBER; VIADANA.

Accompaniment (see also *Continuo*; *Improvisation*)

BACH; BANCHIERI; BIANCIARDI; CAMPION, F.; CHORON; DIRUTA; EBNER; FÉTIS; GASPARINI; GEMINIANI; GEVAERT; HEINICHEN; KELLNER; LÖHLEIN; MANFREDINI; MARTINI; MASSON; MATTHESON; MOMIGNY; PASQUALI; QUANTZ; RAMEAU; REICHA; ROUSSEAU, J.; ROUSSIER; SABBATINI, G.; SAINT-LAMBERT; VIADANA.

Acoustics

Combination Tones; Difference Tones
HELMHOLTZ; HOLDEN; SERRE; TARTINI.

Equal Temperament
ARTUSI; DENIS; GALILEI; HELMHOLTZ; KOLLMANN; LOULIÉ; MATTHESON; NEIDHARDT; SALINAS; SCHRÖTER; SECHTER; SORGE; WALLIS; ZIEHN.

Harmonic Series; Partials
DESCARTES; HELMHOLTZ; HOLDEN; MERSENNE; OUSELEY; OUVRARD; PROUT; RAMEAU; RAVN; SAUVEUR; SORGE; WALLIS.

Microtones
VICENTINO; YAVORSKY.

Physiology of Hearing
DESCARTES; HELMHOLTZ; NORTH, R.; STUMPF.

Pitch Standards
ADLUNG; AGRICOLA, J. F.; DONI; KOCH; KUHNAU; MATTHESON; MERSENNE; MUFFAT; OUSELEY; PRÆTORIUS; QUANTZ; SAUVEUR; TOSI; WALTHER.

Psychology of Hearing
DESCARTES; RIEMANN; STUMPF.

Tuning and Temperament
ADLUNG; ARTUSI; BAN; BANCHIERI; BERMUDO; BOTTRIGARI; CAUS; DAY; DENIS; DONI; GALILEI; GIBELIUS; HAUPTMANN; HEINICHEN; HELMHOLTZ; HOLDEN; HOLDER; HUYGENS; JONES; KELLER; KIRCHER; KIRNBERGER; KOLLMANN; LEIBNIZ; LOULIÉ; MACE; MARPURG; MEI; MERSENNE; NASSARRE; NEIDHARDT; NORTH, R.; OETTINGEN; PRAETORIUS; PRINTZ; QUITSCHREIBER; ROUSSEAU, J.; ROUSSIER; SABBATINI, G.; SALINAS; SALMON; SAUVEUR; SCHNEEGASS; SCHRÖTER; SERRE; SORGE; STAINER; TÜRK; VALLOTTI; VICENTINO; WALLIS; WERCKMEISTER; ZARLINO.

Aesthetics (see also *Style*)

ADLUNG; d'ALEMBERT; BACH; BEER; DAUBE; DESCARTES; DONI; FÉTIS; FINCK; GEMINIANI; GLAREAN; d'INDY; KOCH; LA VOYE-MIGNOT; LEIBNIZ; LUSSY; MARPURG; MARX; MATTHESON; MERSENNE; MORLEY; NORTH, R.; RAMEAU; RIEMANN; ROUSSEAU, J.-J.; SCHEIBE; SCHENKER; SCHOENBERG; SORGE; STAINER; SULZER; TOVEY; TÜRK; VOGLER; YAVORSKY; ZACCONI; ZARLINO.

Affections

d'ALEMBERT; BURMEISTER; DESCARTES; DRESSLER; FUX; GALILEI; HEINICHEN; HERBST; KIRCHER; LIPPIUS; MARPURG; MATTHAEI; MATTHESON; MEI; MERSENNE; NEIDHARDT; NUCIUS; PRINTZ; QUANTZ; SAMBER; SCHEIBE; SORGE; SPIESS; VOSSIUS, G. J.; WALTHER; WERCKMEISTER.

Figures
BACILLY; BERNHARD; BURMEISTER;
HERBST; SAMBER; THURINGUS.

Musical Rhetoric
AHLE; BURMEISTER; HEINICHEN;
HERBST; KIRCHER; KOLLMANN; LIPPIUS;
LISTENIUS; MATTHESON; MERSENNE;
NUCIUS; SAMBER; SCHEIBE; SPIESS;
THURINGUS; VOGLER; WALTHER.

Analysis
Harmonic Analysis
FÉTIS; JADASSOHN; KOLLMANN; LO-
GIER; LOUIS and THUILLE; MOMIGNY;
RICHTER; ROUSSIER; SCHENKER; TAN-
EEV; TOVEY; VOGLER; WEBER; YAVOR-
SKY.

Linear Analysis; Reduction
CZERNY; HALM; KIRNBERGER; KOCH;
KURTH; LA VOYE-MIGNOT; LOGIER;
LOUIS and THUILLE; MOMIGNY; PORT-
MANN; SCHENKER; SECHTER; TANEEV;
VOGLER; ZIEHN.

Melodic Analysis (see also *Melody: Melodic
Composition*)
KOCH; KURTH; SCHENKER; YAVORSKY.

Roman Numerals (see also *Chord Connection*)
RICHTER; SCHRÖTER; SECHTER; VOG-
LER; WEBER; ZIEHN.

Augmented Sixth Chords (see *Chromaticism*)

Basso continuo (see *Continuo*)

Cadences (see also *Chord Connection*)
AHLE; ASAFIEV; BÉTHIZY; BONTEMPI;
CATEL; COPRARIO; DRESSLER; FINCK;
HALM; HERBST; KIRNBERGER;
KOLLMANN; LA VOYE-MIGNOT; LUSI-
TANO; MERSENNE; MORLEY; NIVERS;
NUCIUS; ORTIZ; PARRAN; PENNA;
PEPUSCH; PONTIO; PRINTZ; RAMEAU;
REICHA; SAMBER; SEBASTIANI; SIMPSON;
SOLER; TARTINI; TIGRINI; VIDANA; ZAR-
LINO.

Cadenzas (see *Improvisation*)

Canon (see *Imitation*)

Cantus firmus (see *Counterpoint*)

Chord Connection (see also *Harmony*)
HALM; KOLLMANN; KREHL; LANGLÉ;
MARX; OETTINGEN; RAMEAU; REBER;
ROUSSIER; RIEMANN; RIMSKY- KORSA-
KOV; SCHOENBERG; SCHONSLEDER;
SECHTER; SORGE; VOGLER; WEBER;
ZIEHN.

Chord Construction (see *Harmonic Generation*;
Triadic Theory)

Chromaticism (see also *Affections*; *Musica ficta*)
BÉTHIZY; DAY; DONI; GALILEI; HALM;
HOFFMANN; KOLLMANN; KURTH;
LISTENIUS; LOUIS and THUILLE; LUSI-
TANO; MACFARREN; PROUT; ROUSSIER;
SECHTER; VICENTINO; VOGLER; WEITZ-
MANN.

Augmented Sixth Chords
CHAIKOVSKY; DAY; LOUIS and THUILLE;
REICHA; ROUSSIER; STAINER; VOGLER.

Combination Tones (see *Acoustics*)

Composition
ADLUNG; AHLE; ALBRECHTSBERGER;
BAN; BEER; BONTEMPI; CALVISIUS; CAM-
PION, F.; CHORON; COCLICO; COPRARIO;
CZERNY; DAUBE; FÉTIS; GASPARINI;
GEMINIANI; HEINICHEN; d'INDY; JADAS-
SOHN; JONES; KIRNBERGER; KITSON;
KOCH; KOLLMANN; KREHL; KUHNAU;
LANGLÉ; LA VOYE-MIGNOT; LOBE; LO-
GIER; LORENTE; MARPURG; MARX; MAS-
SON; MATTHESON; MERSENNE;
MOMIGNY; MONTANOS; NASSARRE;
NEIDHARDT; NEIDT; NIVERS; NUCIUS;
OUSELEY; PARRAN; PEPUSCH; PORT-
MANN; PRAETORIUS; PRINTZ; REICHA;
RIEMANN; RIEPEL; ROEL DEL RÍO;
ROUSSIER; SAUVEUR; SCHEIBE;
SCHENKER; SCHOENBERG; SECHTER;
SORGE; SPEER; SPIESS; STAINER;
SWEELINCK; TANS'UR; TIGRINI; VOGLER;
WALTHER; WEBER; WERCKMEISTER;
ZIEHN.

Conducting
FÉTIS; PISA.

Consonance (see also *Consonance vs. Dissonance*)
BURMEISTER; BUTLER; DESCARTES;
EULER; HELMHOLTZ; HUYGENS; KEP-
LER; LEIBNIZ; MATTHESON; MEI; ZAR-
LINO.

Consonance vs. Dissonance (see also *Consonance*; *Dissonance Usage*)

AHLE; ALBRECHTSBERGER; ARTUSI; BAN; BELLERMANN; BONONCINI; BURMEISTER; CAUS; CHERUBINI; DESCARTES; EULER; GALILEI; GLAREAN; HELMHOLTZ; HERBST; HOLDEN; HOLDER; KELLNER; KEPLER; KIRCHER; KOCH; LOBE; LÖHLEIN; LORENTE; MARPURG; MERSENNE; NORTH, F.; NUCIUS; OETTINGEN; PARRAN; PENNA; PEPUSCH; PONTIO; PRINTZ; RAMEAU; SALINAS; SAUVEUR; SCHENKER; STUMPF; TARTINI; VOGLER; WALTHER; WEITZMANN; ZARLINO.

Continuo; Figured Bass

ADLUNG; AGAZZARI; ALBRECHTSBERGER; BACH; BANCHIERI; BÉTHIZY; BIANCIARDI; BROSSARD; CACCINI; CHORON; DAUBE; DEHN; DUBOIS; EBNER; GASPARINI; GEMINIANI; GEVAERT; HEINICHEN; JADASSOHN; JONES; KELLER; KELLNER; KIRNBERGER; KOLLMANN; KUHNAU; LANGLÉ; LOCKE; LÖHLEIN; LOGIER; LOUIS and THUILLE; MANFREDINI; MASSON; MATTHESON; MIZLER; MUFFAT; NIEDT; NIVERS; NORTH, R.; OUVRARD; PAOLUCCI; PASQUALI; PENNA; PEPUSCH; PORTMANN; PRAETORIUS; PRINTZ; QUANTZ; REBER; RIEMANN; SABBATINI, G.; SAINT-LAMBERT; SAMBER; SCACCHI; SCHENKER; SCHRÖTER; SECHTER; SIMPSON; SORGE; SPEER; TELEMANN, G. M.; TELEMANN, G. P.; TOSI; TREIBER; TÜRK; VIADANA; VOGLER; WEBER; WERCKMEISTER.

Continuo Playing

ADLUNG; AGAZZARI; BACH; BANCHIERI; DAUBE; GASPARINI; GEMINIANI; HEINICHEN; KELLER; LIPPIUS; LOCKE; LÖHLEIN; MACE; MATTHESON; NIVERS; NORTH, R.; PASQUALI; PENNA; PRAETORIUS; SABBATINI, G.; SAINT-LAMBERT; SAMBER; SCHRÖTER; SIMPSON; SORGE; TELEMANN, G. P.; TÜRK; VIADANA; WERCKMEISTER.

Unfigured Bass

AGAZZARI; BÉTHIZY; BIANCIARDI; DAY; GASPARINI; GUMPELZHAIMER; HEINICHEN; PENNA; PROUT; SABBATINI, G.; SCHONSLEDER; SPEER.

Counterpoint (see also *Imitation*)

ALBRECHTSBERGER; ARTUSI; BANCHIERI; BELLERMANN; BERARDI; BERMUDO; BERNHARD; BONINI; BONONCINI; BONTEMPI; BRUCKNER; CAMPION, T.; CAUS; CERONE; CERRETO; CHAIKOVSKY; CHERUBINI; CHORON; COCLICO; CZERNY; DANCKERTS; DAUBE; DEHN; DIRUTA; DRESSLER; DUBOIS; DU COUSU; EXIMENO; FABER; FÉTIS; FUX; GALEAZZI; GALILEI; GÉDALGE; HAUPTMANN; HERBST; JADASSOHN; KIRCHER; KIRNBERGER; KITSON; KOCH; KOLLMANN; KREHL; KURTH; LANGLÉ; LA VOYE-MIGNOT; LOBE; LORENTE; LUSITANO; MACFARREN; MANFREDINI; MARPURG; MARTINI; MARX; MASSON; MERSENNE; MOMIGNY; MONTANOS; MORLEY; NASSARRE; NIEDT; NIVERS; NUCIUS; ORNITHOPARCHUS; ORTIZ; OUSELEY; PAOLUCCI; PARRAN; PENNA; PEPUSCH; PLAYFORD; PONTIO; PORTMANN; PRAETORIUS; PRINTZ; PROUT; RAMEAU; RAVN; REBER; REICHA; RICHTER; RIEMANN; RIEPEL; SABBATINI, L. A.; SAMBER; SCHEIBE; SCHENKER; SCHOENBERG; SCHONSLEDER; SEBASTIANI; SECHTER; SIMPSON; SWEELINCK; TANEEV; TARTINI; TEVO; THURINGUS; TIGRINI; VALLOTTI; VICENTINO; VOGLER; WALTHER; WERCKMEISTER; YSANDON; ZACCONI; ZARLINO.

Invertible Counterpint

BACH; BERARDI; BERNHARD; BONONCINI; BRUCKNER; BUTLER; CERRETO; CHERUBINI; FÉTIS; FUX; HAUPTMANN; JADASSOHN; KIRNBERGER; KITSON; KOLLMANN; LOBE; PROUT; PURCELL; REICHA; RICHTER; RIEMANN; SECHTER; SWEELINCK; TANEEV; VICENTINO; ZARLINO.

Species Counterpoint; Cantus firmus

BANCHIERI; BELLERMANN; CERONE; CHAIKOVSKY; CHERUBINI; FABER; FÉTIS; FUX; GALEAZZI; KREHL; LORENTE; LUSITANO; MACFARREN; MARTINI; NASSARRE; PENNA; SCHENKER; ZACCONI; ZARLINO.

Dictionary, Musical (see *Lexicography*)

Difference Tones (see *Acoustics*)

Dissonance (see *Consonance vs. Dissonance*)

Dissonance Usage (see also *Consonance vs. Dissonance*)

> ARTUSI; ASAFIEV; BANCHIERI; BELLER-MANN; BERARDI; BERNHARD; BON-TEMPI; BUTLER; CHORON; DAY; DUBOIS; du COUSU; FUX; GALILEI; GASPARINI; HEINICHEN; KIRNBERGER; KREHL; KURTH; LA VOYE-MIGNOT; LEIBNIZ; LÖHLEIN; LOGIER; LOUIS and THUILLE; MASSON; MATTHESON; NASSARRE; PENNA; PEPUSCH; PLAYFORD; PRINTZ; RAMEAU; REBER; REICHA; SANTA MARÍA; SCHROTER; SIMPSON; SORGE; TANEEV; TARTINI; TREIBER; WERCK-MEISTER; ZARLINO.

Dualism, Harmonic; Undertones

> HAUPTMANN; MARPURG; OETTINGEN; RAMEAU; RIEMANN; TARTINI.

Dynamics

> LUSSY; MACE; MUFFAT; QUANTZ; RIEMANN; VIADANA; YAVORSKY.

Ear-Training

> GÉDALGE; JADASSOHN; RIEMANN.

Enharmonicism (see also *Greek Theory*)

> DONI; FÉTIS; GALILEI; KIRCHER; LOUIS and THUILLE; MERSENNE; MOMIGNY; SABBATINI, G.; SALINAS; TELEMANN, G. P.; TREIBER; VICENTINO; VOGLER; WEITZMANN; ZARLINO; ZIEHN.

Equal Temperament (see *Acoustics*)

Figuration (see *Style*)

Figured Bass (see *Continuo*)

Figures (see *Affections*)

Flute (see *Instruments*)

Form

> ASAFIEV; CZERNY; DESCARTES; DRESS-LER; GALEAZZI; HALM; d'INDY; JADAS-SOHN; KOCH; KOLLMANN; KREHL; LOBE; LÖHLEIN; LORENZ; LUSSY; MACFARREN;

> MARX; MATTHESON; MORLEY; OUSE-LEY; PONTIO; PORTMANN; PRAETORIUS; PRINTZ; PROUT; REICHA; RICHTER; RIEMANN; RIEPEL; ROUSSEAU, J.-J.; SCHENKER; SCHOENBERG; SCHULZ; SULZER; TANEEV; TOVEY; TÜRK; VICEN-TINO; WESTPHAL; YAVORSKY.

> *Phrase Structure*
> > KOCH; PORTMANN; RIEMANN; RIEPEL.

> *Psychology of Form*
> > KURTH; LORENZ; RIEMANN.

Fugue (see *Imitation*)

Fundamental Bass (see *Analysis*; *Inversion, Chordal*)

Genera (see *Greek Theory*)

Greek Theory

> BELLERMANN; BONTEMPI; BOTTRIGARI; BROSSARD; CAUS; DONI; EULER; GALILEI; GEVAERT; GLAREAN; LUSI-TANO; MARTINI; MEI; ROUSSIER; SALI-NAS; SCHRÖTER; VICENTINO; VOSSIUS, G. J.; WALLIS; WESTPHAL.

> *Genera*
> > BOTTRIGARI; DANCKERTS; DONI; GALILEI; KEPLER; LUSITANO; MEI; SALI-NAS; TARTINI; VICENTINO.

Gregorian Chant (see also *Modes*)

> BERMUDO; CHORON; FÉTIS; FINCK; GE-VAERT; GLAREAN; d'INDY; LORENTE; MAILLART; MONTANOS; NASSARRE; NIVERS; ORNITHOPARCHUS; RIEMANN; ROEL DEL RÍO; SAMBER; SEBASTIANI; VALLOTTI.

Guitar (see *Instruments*)

Harmonic Analysis (see *Analysis*)

Harmonic Generation (see also *Inversion, Chordal*; *Triadic Theory*)

> DAY; DESCARTES; FÉTIS; HAUPTMANN; HELMHOLTZ; HOLDEN; HOLDER; HUY-GENS; KIRCHER; KOLLMANN; KURTH; LANGLÉ; LOBE; MACFARREN; MAN-FREDINI; MARPURG; MOMIGNY; NORTH, R.; RAMEAU; SORGE; STAINER; VICEN-TINO; WEBER.

> *Supposition*
> > MARPURG; RAMEAU.

Harmonic Series (see *Acoustics*)

Harmonization of Melodies
> CHAIKOVSKY; d'INDY; KOLLMANN; LOUIS and THUILLE; REBER; RIMSKY-KORSAKOV; SECHTER.

> *Double emploi*
> RAMEAU.

> *Harmonization of Scale*
> CAMPION, F.; RAMEAU; TARTINI.

Harmony (see also *Chord Connection*; *Chromaticism*)
> ALBRECHTSBERGER; BÉTHIZY; BRUCKNER; CATEL; CHAIKOVSKY; CHORON; DAY; DEHN; DUBOIS; FÉTIS; GALEAZZI; GEMINIANI; GEVAERT; HALM; HAUPTMANN; d'INDY; JADASSOHN; KIRNBERGER; KITSON; KOCH; KOLLMANN; KREHL; KURTH; LANGLÉ; LOBE; LOGIER; LOUIS and THUILLE; MACFARREN; MANFREDINI; NORTH, R.; OETTINGEN; OUSELEY; PEPUSCH; PORTMANN; PROUT; REBER; REICHA; RICHTER; RIEMANN; RIMSKY-KORSAKOV; ROUSSIER; SCHENKER; SCHOENBERG; SECHTER; SERRE; STAINER; TANS'UR; TELEMANN, G. P.; VOGLER; WERCKMEISTER; WESTPHAL; ZARLINO; ZIEHN.

Harp (see *Instruments*)

Harpsichord (see *Instruments: Keyboard*)

History of Theory (see also *Greek Theory*)
> ADLUNG; AHLE; BELLERMANN; BONTEMPI; CALVISIUS; CHORON; CZERNY; FÉTIS; GLAREAN; d'INDY; MARTINI; MIZLER; OUSELEY; PEPUSCH; PRINTZ; RIEMANN; ROUSSIER; SALINAS; SCHRÖTER; TEVO; VALLOTTI; VICENTINO; VOSSIUS; G. J.; WALLIS; WEITZMANN; WESTPHAL.

Imitation (see also *Counterpoint*)
> BANCHIERI; BERARDI; BONONCINI; BROSSARD; CHERUBINI; COPRARIO; DRESSLER; FÉTIS; HERBST; MASSON; ORTIZ; PEPUSCH; PONTIO; PURCELL; REICHA; RIEMANN; SIMPSON; ZACCONI; ZARLINO.

Canon
> BERARDI; BERNHARD; BEVIN; BONONCINI; BONTEMPI; CALVISIUS; CERONE; CERRETO; CHORON; DEHN; FÉTIS; FINCK; GALEAZZI; GUMPELZHAIMER; JADASSOHN; KITSON; LOBE; MATTHESON; MORLEY; NIEDT; OUSELEY; PENNA; PEPUSCH; PONTIO; PROUT; PURCELL; REICHA; RICHTER; RIEPEL; SABBATINI, L. A.; SECHTER; SIMPSON; SOLER; TANEEV; ZACCONI; ZIEHN.

> *Fugue*
> ADLUNG; BELLERMANN; BERARDI; BÉTHIZY; BONTEMPI; CHERUBINI; CHORON; DEHN; DUBOIS; FÉTIS; FUX; GALEAZZI; GÉDALGE; JADASSOHN; KELLER; KITSON; KOLLMANN; LANGLÉ; LA VOYE-MIGNOT; LOBE; MARPURG; MARX; MASSON; MOMIGNY; NIVERS; OUSELEY; PEPUSCH; PRAETORIUS; PROUT; REICHA; RICHTER; RIEMANN; RIEPEL; SABBATINI, L. A.; SAMBER; SCACCHI; SECHTER; SORGE; TIGRINI; TOVEY.

Improvisation (see also *Accompaniment*; *Continuo*; *Ornamentation*)
> ADLUNG; AGAZZARI; BACH; BACILLY; BANCHIERI; BIANCIARDI; CERRETO; CZERNY; FABER; GALEAZZI; GEMINIANI; KOLLMANN; MASSON; MATTHESON; NIEDT; ORTIZ; SANTA MARÍA; SEBASTIANI; SIMPSON; SORGE; THURINGUS; ZACCONI.

> *Cadenzas*
> AGRICOLA, J. F.; BACH; CZERNY; QUANTZ; ROUSSEAU, J.-J.; TARTINI; TÜRK.

Instrumentation (see also *Instruments*)
> ADLUNG; AGAZZARI; BERMUDO; BOTTRIGARI; CAMPION, F.; CHORON; CZERNY; GALEAZZI; GEVAERT; GRIMM; JADASSOHN; KIRCHER; KOLLMANN; LOBE; MERSENNE; NASSARRE; PRAETORIUS; PROUT; RAVN; RIEMANN; SCHENKER; SCHOENBERG; SPEER; TOVEY; VOSSIUS, G. J.; ZACCONI.

Instruments
> *Flute*
> GEMINIANI; QUANTZ.

Guitar

CAMPION, F.; GEMINIANI.

Harp

ROUSSIER.

Keyboard

ALBRECHTSBERGER; BACH; BAN; BERMUDO; BONTEMPI; CZERNY; DENIS; DIRUTA; DONI; FÉTIS; GASPARINI; GEMINIANI; HEINICHEN; KIRNBERGER; KOLLMANN; KUHNAU; LÖHLEIN; LOGIER; LUSSY; MACE; MARPURG; MATTHESON; MOMIGNY; NASSARRE; NIVERS; PASQUALI; PENNA; PEPUSCH; RAMEAU; REICHA; ROUSSIER; SABBATINI, G.; SAINT-LAMBERT; SANTA MARÍA; SECHTER; SOLER; SORGE; SPEER; TELEMANN, G. M.; TREIBER; TÜRK; VIADANA; VICENTINO; VOGLER.

Lute

AGAZZARI; CAMPION, F.; GALILEI; MACE; SALMON.

Organ

ADLUNG; AGAZZARI; AGRICOLA, J. F.; BANCHIERI; BERMUDO; CAUS; CERRETO; DENIS; DIRUTA; GASPARINI; GEVAERT; JANOVKA; MACE; MARTINI; MATTHESON; MIZLER; NEIDHARDT; NIEDT; NIVERS; PENNA; PEPUSCH; PRAETORIUS; RAMEAU; RIEPEL; SAINT-LAMBERT; SAMBER; SAUVEUR; SOLER; SORGE; TELEMANN, G. M.; TREIBER; VICENTINO; VOGLER; WALLIS; WEBER; WERCKMEISTER.

Theorbo

CAMPION, F.; MACE.

Viol and *Violin*

BERMUDO; DONI; GALEAZZI; GEMINIANI; KIRNBERGER; KOLLMANN; LÖHLEIN; MACE; MOZART; ORTIZ; PLAYFORD; REICHA; ROUSSEAU, J.; SIMPSON; TARTINI; TÜRK.

Violoncello

GEMINIANI; KIRNBERGER; KOLLMANN; REICHA.

Voice and *Singing*

ADLUNG; AGRICOLA, J. F.; AHLE; BACILLY; BAN; BERNHARD; BONTEMPI; BOTTRIGARI; BUTLER; CACCINI; CAMPION, F.; CRÜGER; DANCKERTS; DEMANTIUS; DENIS; EICHMANN; FABER; FÉTIS; FINCK; FUX; GIBELIUS; HERBST;

HOLDER; JADASSOHN; KINRBERGER; LANGLÉ; LA VOYE-MIGNOT; LISTENIUS; LOULIÉ; MANFREDINI; MARPURG; MARX; MERSENNE; NIVERS; ORNITHOPARCHUS; PLAYFORD; PRINTZ; QUITSCHREIBER; REICHA; RIEPEL; ROUSSEAU, J.; SEBASTIANI; SPEER; TELEMANN, G. P.; TOSI; VOGLER; YAVORSKY; ZARLINO.

Intonation Theory

ASAFIEV.

Inversion, Chordal (see also *Harmonic Generation*)

ALBRECHTSBERGER; BARYPHONUS; CAMPION, T.; COPRARIO; KIRNBERGER; LIPPIUS; NORTH, R.; RAMEAU; RICHTER; TARTINI; VALLOTTI; VOGLER; WERCKMEISTER.

Fundamental Bass

BÉTHIZY; HOLDER; KIRNBERGER; LOGIER; MANFREDINI; MARPURG; RAMEAU; REICHA; ROUSSIER; SABBATINI, L. A.; SCHRÖTER; SECHTER; SERRE; WEBER.

Inversion, Melodic

LIPPIUS; MASSON; ZARLINO.

Just Intonation (see *Acoustics: Tuning and Temperament*)

Keyboard (see *Instruments*)

Lexicography

BELLERMANN; BROSSARD; CHORON; DEMANTIUS; EICHMANN; FÉTIS; GASPARINI; HERBST; JANOVKA; KOCH; LA VOYE-MIGNOT; MARTINI; MERSENNE; MOMIGNY; MOZART; OUVRARD; PEPUSCH; PRAETORIUS; PROUT; RAMEAU; RAVN; RIEMANN; ROUSSEAU, J.-J.; SCHULZ; STAINER; SULZER; TANS'UR; TÜRK; VOGLER; WALTHER.

Lute (see *Instruments*)

Mathematics, Musical (see also *Acoustics*)

ADLUNG; d'ALEMBERT; ALSTED; BARYPHONUS; BURMEISTER; DESCARTES; EULER; EXIMENO; GIBELIUS; HAUPTMANN; HUYGENS; KEPLER; KIRCHER; KOCH; LEIBNIZ; MALCOLM; MARPURG; MARTINI; MATTHAEI; MATTHESON;

MERSENNE; MIZLER; NASSARRE; NEID-
HARDT; RAMEAU; RAVN; RIEPEL; ROEL
DEL RÍO; ROUSSIER; SALMON; SAUVEUR;
SORGE; SPIESS; TANEEV; TARTINI; VAL-
LOTTI; VOSSIUS, G. J.; WALLIS; WERCK-
MEISTER; ZARLINO.

Ratios
CAUS; NASSARRE; PONTIO; WERCKMEIS-
TER.

Senario
CAUS; EULER; GALILEI; LEIBNIZ; MEI;
RAMEAU; ZARLINO.

Meantone Temperament (see *Acoustics: Tuning
and Temperament*)

Melody
AGRICOLA, J. F.; BAN; BÉTHIZY; COP-
RARIO; GALEAZZI; HOLDER; JONES;
KEPLER; KIRNBERGER; KOCH; MARX;
MATTHESON; PONTIO; REICHA;
RIEMANN; RIEPEL; SCHEIBE; SORGE;
TANS'UR; TARTINI; TELEMANN, G. M.;
YAVORSKY.

Melodic Composition (see also *Composition*)
BERMUDO; CHORON; DAUBE; DONI;
JADASSOHN; MATTHESON; MERSENNE;
PONTIO; REICHA; RIEMANN; ROUSSEAU,
J.-J.; TANS'UR.

Melodic Transformation and Motivic Use
GALEAZZI; KOCH; LOBE; PORTMANN;
RIEPEL; SCHENKER; SCHOENBERG;
TOVEY.

Mensuration (see *Rhythm*)

Meter (see *Rhythm*)

Microtones (see *Acoustics*)

Modes (see also *Gregorian Chant*)
AHLE; BANCHIERI; BELLERMANN; BER-
ARDI; BERNHARD; BONONCINI; BUR-
MEISTER; BUTLER; BUTTSTETT;
CALVISIUS; CERRETO; CRÜGER; DANCK-
ERTS; DEHN; DEMANTIUS; DENIS;
DIRUTA; DONI; DRESSLER; EICHMANN;
EULER; FABER; FÉTIS; FUX; GALILEI;
GLAREAN; HERBST; HOFFMANN;
JANOVKA; KEPLER; KUHNAU; LIPPIUS;
LORENTE; MAILLART; MASSON; MAT-
THAEI; MATTHESON; MEI; MERSENNE;
MORLEY; NASSARRE; NIVERS; NUCIUS;

PARRAN; PEPUSCH; PONTIO; PRAE-
TORIUS; PRINTZ; SANTA MARÍA; SERRE;
SPEER; SPIESS; THURINGUS; TIGRINI;
VICENTINO; WERCKMEISTER; YAVOR-
SKY; YSSANDON; ZACCONI; ZARLINO.

Modulation
ALBRECHTSBERGER; BERARDI; CATEL;
CHAIKOVSKY; EULER; FÉTIS; GALEAZZI;
GASPARINI; GEMINIANI; GIBELIUS;
HEINICHEN; JADASSOHN; KELLNER;
KIRNBERGER; KOLLMANN; LANGLÉ;
LOCKE; LÖHLEIN; LOGIER; LOUIS and
THUILLE; MALCOLM; MATTHESON;
MOMIGNY; NEIDHARDT; PEPUSCH;
PRINTZ; REICHA; RIEMANN; RIEPEL;
RIMSKY-KORSAKOV; ROEL DEL RÍO;
SCHENKER; SCHOENBERG; SCHULZ;
SECHTER; SOLER; SORGE; SPEER; TAR-
TINI; TOVEY; VICENTINO; VOGLER;
WEBER; ZIEHN.

Music of the Spheres
BERARDI; FLUDD; KEPLER; KIRCHER;
LEIBNIZ; MERSENNE; WERCKMEISTER.

Musica ficta (see also *Accidentals*; *Chromaticism*;
Modes)
GEMINIANI; LISTENIUS; ORNITHO-
PARCHUS; SIMPSON; TÜRK.

Musica flexanima (see *Text-Music Relationship*)

Musica mundana, humana, instrumentalis (see
Music of the Spheres)

Musica poetica (see *Text-Music Relationship*;
Affections: Musical Rhetoric)

Musica reservata (see *Style*)

Musical Rhetoric (see *Affections*; *Text-Music
Relationship: Musica poetica*)

Non-Harmonic Tones (see *Dissonance Usage*)

Notation
ADLUNG; AGAZZARI; BELLERMANN;
BERMUDO; BURMEISTER; CAUS; CER-
RETO; DANCKERTS; DAY; DONI; DU
COUSU; FABER; FINCK; GUMPELZ-
HAIMER; HOFFMANN; KEPLER; LA VOYE-
MIGNOT; LÖHLEIN; LORENTE; LOULIÉ;
LUSITANO; LUSSY; MACE; MAILLART;

MEI; MERSENNE; MONTANOS; MORLEY; MOZART; ORNITHOPARCHUS; PRAETORIUS; RAVENSCROFT; RAVN; RIEMANN; SALMON; SAUVEUR; SCHENKER; SCHONSLEDER; SCHULZ; SOLER; SPEER; TANEEV; TEVO; TÜRK; WALTHER; WEBER; ZACCONI.

Orchestration
BOTTRIGARI; DAUBE; GEVAERT; MUFFAT; PRAETORIUS; PROUT; REICHA; RIEMANN; RIMSKY-KORSAKOV.

Organ (see *Instruments*)

Ornamentation (see also *Improvisation*)
AGRICOLA, J. F.; BACH; BACILLY; BANCHIERI; CACCINI; COCLICO; COPRARIO; CRÜGER; DIRUTA; DONI; FINCK; GALEAZZI; GASPARINI; GEMINIANI; HEINICHEN; HERBST; LIPPIUS; LOCKE; LOULIÉ; LÖHLEIN; MACE; MANFREDINI; MARPURG; MATTHESON; MERSENNE; MOZART; MUFFAT; NASSARRE; NORTH, R.; ORTIZ; PASQUALI; PENNA; PLAYFORD; PRAETORIUS; PURCELL; QUANTZ; ROUSSEAU, J.; SAINT-LAMBERT; SAMBER; SANTA MARÍA; SCHEIBE; SCHENKER; SIMPSON; TARTINI; TOSI; TÜRK; VIADANA; WALTHER; ZACCONI.

Partials (see *Acoustics*)

Part-Writing (see *Voice-Leading*)

Performance Practice (see also *Continuo: Continuo Playing; Musica ficta*)
ADLUNG; AGRICOLA, J. F.; BACH; BACILLY; BAN; BANCHIERI; BOTTRIGARI; BUTLER; CACCINI; CERRETO; COCLICO; CZERNY; DAUBE; DEMANTIUS; DIRUTA; FINCK; GALEAZZI; GASPARINI; GEMINIANI; KELLER; KIRNBERGER; LUSSY; MARPURG; MEI; MOZART; NASSARRE; NIVERS; NORTH, R.; ORTIZ; PASQUALI; PRAETORIUS; QUANTZ; ROUSSEAU, J.-J.; SAMBER; SANTA MARÍA; SIMPSON; SPEER; TELEMANN, G. M.; TOSI; TÜRK; VIADANA; WERCKMEISTER; ZACCONI; ZARLINO.

Phrase Structure (see *Form*)

Physiology of Hearing Music (see *Acoustics*)

Piano (see *Instruments: Keyboard*)

Pitch Standards (see *Acoustics*)

Psychology of Form (see *Form*)

Psychology of Hearing (see *Acoustics*)

Pythagorean Tuning (see *Acoustics: Tuning and Temperament*)

Ratios (see *Mathematics, Musical*)

Reduction (see *Analysis*)

Rhythm
BAN; FÉTIS; GALEAZZI; GIBELIUS; HAUPTMANN; HOLDEN; JONES; KOLLMANN; LUSSY; MARX; MEI; MERSENNE; MOMIGNY; MOZART; PONTIO; PORTMANN; PRINTZ; RIEMANN; RIEPEL; SCHENKER; SECHTER; TOVEY; VOSSIUS, I.; WESTPHAL; YAVORSKY.
Accentuation
HAUPTMANN; LUSSY; MOMIGNY; ORNITHOPARCHUS; PISA; PRINTZ; TÜRK; WEBER.
Mensuration and Time Signatures
BELLERMANN; CALVISIUS; DANCKERTS; DU COUSU; FABER; FINCK; GLAREAN; HOFFMANN; LORENTE; MAILLART; MONTANOS; MORLEY; NASSARRE; ORNITHOPARCHUS; PENNA; RAVENSCROFT; RIEMANN.
Meter
BANCHIERI; BELLERMANN; HAUPTMANN; LOULIÉ; LUSSY; MOMIGNY; NASSARRE; PONTIO; PORTMANN; PRAETORIUS; PRINTZ; RIEMANN; SALINAS; SCHENKER; SECHTER; SPEER; TARTINI; TREIBER; VOSSIUS, I.; WEBER; WESTPHAL.
Tempo and Tempo Standards
LOULIÉ; LUSSY; MERSENNE; MUFFAT; PISA; QUANTZ; RIEMANN.
Unequal Durations
LOULIÉ.

Roman Numerals (see *Analysis*)

Rudiments (see also *Notation*)
ALBRECHTSBERGER; BERMUDO; BONONCINI; EICHMANN; FABER; FINCK; GUMPELZHAIMER; HERBST; HOLDEN; KITSON; LA VOYE-MIGNOT; LISTENIUS; LUSITANO; MACFARREN; MANFREDINI;

PENNA; PLAYFORD; ROEL DEL RÍO;
SAINT-LAMBERT; SAMBER; SANTA
MARÍA; SIMPSON; TANS'UR; THURINGUS;
TÜRK; WALTHER; YAVORSKY.

Senario (see *Mathematics, Musical*)

Singing (see *Instruments: Voice and Singing*)

Solfege and Solmization
ALSTED; BANCHIERI; BERARDI; BUR-
MEISTER; BUTTSTETT; CALVISIUS;
CRÜGER; DONI; DUBOIS; FINCK; GE-
VAERT; GIBELIUS; GLAREAN; GRIMM;
LANGLÉ; LIPPIUS; LOCKE; LORENTE;
MAILLART; MATTHESON; MEI;
MOMIGNY; PEPUSCH; PRAETORIUS;
QUANTZ; RAVN; SABBATINI, L. A.; SAM-
BER; SAUVEUR; SPEER.

Style
BUTTSTETT; CHORON; DAUBE; DIRUTA;
DONI; FUX; GALILEI; HALM; HEINICHEN;
KIRNBERGER; KOLLMANN; KURTH; LÖH-
LEIN; MANFREDINI; MERSENNE; MONTE-
VERDI; MOZART; NORTH, R.; PROUT;
QUANTZ; SCHEIBE; SCHOENBERG;
SPIESS; TOSI; TÜRK; ZACCONI.
Baroque Classifications
BERARDI; BERNHARD; BONINI; DIRUTA;
DONI; FUX; MATTHESON; MONTEVERDI;
PONTIO; SCACCHI; SEBASTIANI.
Figuration
KOCH; MALCOLM; MERSENNE;
MOMIGNY; NIEDT; PASQUALI; PRINTZ;
RIEMANN.
Musica reservata
COCLICO; HOFFMANN; THURINGUS;
VICENTINO.

Supposition (see *Harmonic Generation*)

Temperament (see *Acoustics: Tuning and
Temperament*)

Tempo and Tempo Standards (see *Rhythm*)

Text-Music Relationship
BAN; CHORON; HEINICHEN; MARPURG;
NUCIUS; PONTIO; RIEMANN; RIEPEL;
SCHONSLEDER.
Musica flexanima
BAN.

Musica poetica
BURMEISTER; CALVISIUS; DRESSLER;
FABER; HERBST; LISTENIUS; NUCIUS;
PRINTZ; VOSSIUS, G. J.; VOSSIUS, I.
Text-Setting
AHLE; BELLERMANN; BERARDI; BUR-
MEISTER; BUTLER; COCLICO; DRESSLER;
FINCK; FUX; GALILEI; GIBELIUS;
HERBST; KIRNBERGER; KOLLMANN;
KUHNAU; LIPPIUS; MEI; MONTEVERDI;
MORLEY; PONTIO; PRINTZ; SCHONS-
LEDER; WALTHER.

Theorbo (see *Instruments*)

Time Signatures (see *Rhythm*; *Notation*)

Tonal Systems
CATEL; KURTH; ROUSSEAU, J.; TANEEV;
WEBER; YAVORSKY.

Tonality
FÉTIS; GEVAERT; d'INDY; KOLLMANN;
MOMIGNY; OETTINGEN; RIEMANN;
SORGE; SPEER; TANEEV; TOVEY; YAVOR-
SKY.

Transposition
CAMPION, F.; DIRUTA; LOULIÉ;
PEPUSCH; PRAETORIUS; PRINTZ; QUIT-
SCHREIBER; ROUSSEAU, J.

Triadic Theory (see also *Harmonic Generation*)
AHLE; ALBRECHTSBERGER; ALSTED;
BARYPHONUS; CRÜGER; KUHNAU;
LIPPIUS; RAVN; SCHNEEGASS; SCHONS-
LEDER; SCHRÖTER; SORGE; VOGLER;
WERCKMEISTER.

Tuning and Temperament (see *Acoustics*)

Undertones (see *Dualism, Harmonic*)

Unequal Durations (see *Rhythm*)

Unfigured Basses (see *Continuo*)

Variation Technique
CZERNY; DAUBE; NIEDT; PRINTZ; PUR-
CELL; REICHA; SCHOENBERG; SECHTER.

Viol and Violin (see *Instruments*)

Violoncello (see *Instruments*)

Voice and Singing (see *Instruments*)

Voice-Leading

> AHLE; BACH; BARYPHONUS; BONTEMPI;
> CAMPION, T.; CATEL; CERONE;
> CHAIKOVSKY; CHORON; DUBOIS;
> EULER; FUX; GASPARINI; HEINICHEN;
> LÖHLEIN; NIVERS; PLAYFORD; PRINTZ;
> REICHA; RICHTER; SCHENKER;
> WERCKMEISTER; YAVORSKY.

Parallel Intervals

> AHLE; BELLERMANN; CAMPION, T.;
> CATEL; CHERUBINI; DIRUTA; FABER;
> HEINICHEN; SCACCHI; SCHENKER;
> VIADANA; WEITZMANN.

CHRONOLOGICAL INDEX

1516 GLAREAN *Isagoge in musicen*
1517 ORNITHOPARCHUS *Musicae activae micrologus*
1533 LISTENIUS *Rudimenta musicae*
1546 GLAREAN *Boethii de musica*
1547 GLAREAN *Dodecachordon*
1548 FABER *Compendiolum musicae*
     FABER *Musica poetica*
1549 BERMUDO *Comiença el libro primero de la declaración*
1550 BERMUDO *Comiença el arte tripharia*
     FABER *Ad musicam practicam*
1551 DANCKERTS *Trattato . . . sopra una differentia musicale*
1552 COCLICO *Compendium musices*
1553 LUSITANO *Introdutione facilissima*
     ORTIZ *Trattado de glosas*
1555 BERMUDO *Comiença el libro llamado declaración*
     VICENTINO *L'antica musica*
1556 FINCK *Practica musica*
1557 GLAREAN *Musicae epitome sive compendium*
1558 ZARLINO *Le istitutioni harmoniche*
1561 DRESSLER *Practica modorum explicatio*
     VICENTINO *Descrizione dell'arciorgano*
1563 DRESSLER *Praecepta musicae poeticae*
     SEBASTIANI *Bellum musicale*
1565 SANTA MARÍA *Libro llamado arte de tañer fantasia*
1566 SALINAS *Musices liber tertius*
1567 MEI *De modis musicis antiquorum*
1568 GALILEI *Fronimo: Dialogo*
1570 GALILEI *Compendio nella theorica della musica*
     MEI *Trattato di musica*
1571 DRESSLER *Musicae practicae elementa*
     ZARLINO *Dimonstrationi harmoniche*
1572 HOFFMANN *Musicae practicae praecepta*
1577 SALINAS *De musica libri septem*
1581 GALILEI *Dialogo . . . della musica antica*
1582 HOFFMANN *Doctrina de tonis seu modis*
     YSSANDON *Traité de la musique pratique*
1586 ARTUSI *L'arte del contraponto*
1588 ARTIUSI *Lettera apologetica del burla*
     GALILEI *Discorso . . . intorno all'uso delle dissonanze*
     GALILEI *Primo libro della prattica del contrapunto*
     PONTIO *Ragionamento di musica*

     TIGRINI *Il compendio della musica*
     ZARLINO *Sopplimenti musicali*
1589 ARTUSI *Seconda parte dell'arte del contraponto*
     GALILEI *Critica fatta . . . intorno ai Supplimenti*
     GALILEI *Discorso intorno a diversi pareri che hebbero*
     GALILEI *Discorso particolare intorno alla diversità*
     GALILEI *Discorso . . . intorno all'opere de . . . Zarlino*
1590 ARTUSI *Trattato apologetica*
     GALILEI *Discorso . . . intorno all'uso dell'enharmonio*
     GALILEI *Discorso particolare intorno all'unisono*
     SCHNEEGASS *Nova et exquisita monochordi dimensio*
1591 BANCHIERI *Conclusioni nel suono dell'organo*
     GALILEI *Dubbi intorno*
     GUMPELZHAIMER *Compendium musicae*
     SCHNEEGASS *Isagoges musicae libri duo*
     SCHNEEGASS *Isagoges musicae, non ita pridem*
1592 CALVISIUS *Melopoiia sive melodiae*
     DEMANTIUS *Forma musices*
     MONTANOS *Arte de musica theorica y pratica*
     SCHNEEGASS *Deutsche Musica für die Kinder*
     ZACCONI *Prattica di musica*
     ZACCONI *Prattica di musica seconda parte*
1593 BOTTRIGARI *Il patricio overo de' tetracordi*
     DIRUTA *Il transilvano*
     DIRUTO *Seconda parte del transilvano*
1594 BOTTRIGARI *Il desiderio overo de' concerti*
     CALVISIUS *Compendium musicae practicae*
     MONTANOS *Arte de canto llano*
1595 PONTIO *Dialogo . . . ove si tratta della theorica*
1596 KEPLER *Prodromus dissertationum cosmographicarum*
1597 MORLEY *A Plaine and Easie Introduction*
1598 QUITSCHREIBER *De canendi elegantia*
1599 BOTTRIGARI *Il Trimerone de' fondamenti armonici*
     BURMEISTER *Hypomnematum musicae poeticae*
1600 ARTUSI *L'Artusi overo delle imperfettioni*
     CALVISIUS *Exercitationes musicae duae*
     EICHMANN *Oratio de divina origine*
1601 BANCHIERI *Cartella, overo regole utilissime*
     BOTTRIGARI *Ant-Artusi*
     BURMEISTER *Musica autoschediastike*
     BURMEISTER *Musicae practicae sive artis canendi*
     CACCINI *Le nuove musiche*

        CERRETO *Della prattica musica*

1602   BOTTRIGARI *Lettera di Federico Verdicelli*

        BOTTRIGARI *Il Melone: Discorso armonico*

        DEMANTIUS *Isagoge artis musicae*

        MEI *Discorso sopra la musica*

        VIADANA *Preface to the Cento concerti*

1603   ARTUSI *Seconda parte dell'Artusi*

1604   ARTUSI *Impresa del molto Rev. G. Zarlino*

        BOTTRIGARI *Aletelogia di Leonardo Gallucio*

        EICHMANN *Praecepta musicae practicae*

1605   ARTUSI *Discorso musicale di Antonio Braccino*

        BANCHIERI *L'organo suonarino*

        HOFFMANN *Brevis synopsis de modis*

        MONTEVERDI *Preface to Il quinto libro*

        MONTEVERDI *Dichiaratione della lettera stampata*

        QUITSCHREIBER *Musicbüchlein für die Jugend*

1606   BURMEISTER *Musica poetica*

1607   AGAZZARI *Sonare sopra'l basso*

        BIANCIARDI *Breve regola per imparar' a sonare*

1608   ARTUSI *Discorso secondo musicale di Antonio Braccino*

        CERRETO *Dell'arbore musicale*

1609   BARYPHONUS *Isagoge musica*

        BURMEISTER *Musica theorica Henrici Brucaei*

        CERONE *Le regole più necessarie*

        LIPPIUS *Disputatio musica prima*

        LIPPIUS *Disputatio musica secunda*

1610   ALSTED *Scientiarum omnium encyclopaediae*

        LIPPIUS *Disputatio musica tertia*

        LIPPIUS *Thematia musica*

        MAILLART *Les tons ou discours*

1611   ALSTED *Elementale mathematicum musica*

        BANCHIERI *La mano et documenti*

        CALVISIUS *Exercitatio musica tertia*

        LIPPIUS *Breviculum errorum musicorum*

        LIPPIUS *Themata fontem omnium erratium musicorum*

        PISA *Breve dichiarazione della battuta musicale*

        QUITSCHREIBER *De parodia tractatus musicalis*

1612   CALVISIUS *Musicae artis praecepta nova*

        CAMPION, T. *A New Way of Making Fowre Parts*

        LIPPIUS *Synopsis musicae novae*

1613   ALSTED *Methodus admirandorum mathematicorum*

        CERONE *El melopeo y maestro*

        NUCIUS *Musices poeticae*

1614   BANCHIERI *Cartellina del canto fermo gregoriano*

        BANCHIERI *Frutto salutifero*

        LIPPIUS *Philosophiae verae ac sincerae synopticae*

        PRAETORIUS *Syntagma musicum*

        RAVENSCROFT *A Briefe Discourse*

1615   BANCHIERI *Al direttorio monastico di canto fermo*

        BARYPHONUS *Pleiades musicae*

        CAUS *Institution harmonique*

        CAUS *Les raisons des forces mouvantes*

1616   FLUDD *Apologia compendiaria fraternitatem*

1617   COPRARIO *Rules How to Compose*

        FLUDD *Tractatus apologeticus integritatem*

        FLUDD *Utriusque cosmi*

1618   DESCARTES *Musicae compendium*

1619   KEPLER *Harmonices mundi*

1620   ALSTED *Cursus philosophici encyclopaedia*

        BARYPHONUS *Ars canendi*

        BARYPHONUS *Institutiones musico-theoricae*

1621   FLUDD *Veritas proscenium*

1622   FLUDD *Monochordum mundi symphoniacum*

        KEPLER *Pro suo opere harmonices mundi*

        THURINGUS *Nucleus musicus de modis*

1623   MERSENNE *Quaestiones celeberrimae in Genesim*

1624   GRIMM *Unterricht, wie ein Knabe*

        THURINGUS *Opusculum bipartitum de primodriis*
             musici

1625   ALSTED *Triumphus bibliorum sacrorum*

        BANCHIERI *Il principiante fanciullo*

        CRÜGER *Kurtzer und verstendlicher Unterricht*

        CRÜGER *Praecepta musicae practicae figuralis*

        MERSENNE *La vérité des sciences*

1626   ALSTED *Compendium philosophium, exhibens*
             methodum

        CERRETO *Dialoghi armonici pel contrapunto*

1627   MERSENNE *Traité de l'harmonie universelle*

1628   BANCHIERI *Lettere armoniche*

        BANCHIERI *La sampogna musicale*

        SABBATINI, G. *Regola facile e breve*

1629   FLUDD *Sophiae cum moria certamen*

        FLUDD *Summum bonum quod est verum*

        GRIMM *Instrumentum instrumentorum*

1630   CRÜGER *Synopsis musica*

1631   BEVIN *A Briefe and Short Instruction*

        CERRETO *Dialogo harmonico*

        SCHONSLEDER *Architectonice musices universalis*

1633   DONI *Trattato della musica scenica*

        FLUDD *Clavis philosophiae et alchymiae*

1634   MERSENNE *Les préludes de l'harmonie universelle*

        MERSENNE *Questions harmoniques*

        MERSENNE *Questions inouyes*

        MERSENNE *Les questions théologiques*

1635   DONI *Compendio del trattato*

        DU COUSU *La musique universelle*

        MERSENNE *Harmonicorum libri*

1636   BUTLER *The Principles of Musik*

        MERSENNE *Harmonicorum instrumentorum libri IV*

        MERSENNE *Harmonie universelle*

1637   BAN *Dissertatio epistolica de musicae natura*

        QUITSCHREIBER *Quarta exercitatio musicalis*

1638   AGAZZARI *La musica ecclesiastica*

1639   PARRAN *Traité de la musique théorique et pratique*

1640   DONI *Annotazioni sopra il compendio*

        DONI *Deux traictez de musique*

1641   KIRCHER *Magnes sive de arte magnetica*

        VOSSIUS, G. J. *De theologia gentili*

1642   BAN *Cort beduydsel vant zingen*

        BAN *Zangh-Bloemzel*

        HERBST *Musica practica*

1643   BAN *Kort sangh-bericht*

DENIS *Traité de l'accord*

HERBST *Musica poëtica*

SCACCHI *Cribrum musicum*

1644 MERSENNE *Cogita physico-mathematica*

RAVN *Brevia et facilia praecepta componendi*

SCACCHI *Lettera per maggiore informatione*

1645 GIBELIUS *Seminarium modulatoriae vocalis*

SCACCHI *An Attack on Roman Micheli's Canoni*

1646 KIRCHER *Ars magna lucis et umbrae*

RAVN *Heptachordum danicum seu nova solsisatio*

1647 DONI *De praestantia musicae veteris*

MERSENNE *Novarum observationum physico-mathematicarum*

VOSSIUS, G. J. *De artis poeticae natura*

VOSSIUS, G. J. *Institutiones poeticae*

VOSSIUS, G. J. *Poeticarum institutionum*

1648 SCACCHI *Epistola ad Excellentissimum*

1649 BERNHARD *Von der Singe-Kunst*

BONINI *Prima parte de' discorsi*

DESCARTES *Les passions de l'âme*

SCACCHI *Breve discorso sopra la musica*

SCACCHI *Judicium cribri musici*

1650 CRÜGER *Quaestiones musicae practicae*

KIRCHER *Musurgia universalis*

VOSSIUS, G. J. *De artium et scientiarum natura*

VOSSIUS, G. J. *De quatuor arbitus popularibus*

1651 GIBELIUS *Compendium modulatoriae*

PLAYFORD *A Musicall Banquet*

1652 HERBST *Compendium musices*

KIRCHER *Oedipus aegyptiacus*

MATTHAEI *Kurtzer, doch ausführlicher Bericht*

1653 HERBST *Arte prattica et poëtica*

1654 PLAYFORD *A Breefe Introduction to the Skill of Musick*

1656 KIRCHER *Itinerarium exstaticum quo mudi*

LA VOYE-MIGNOT *Traité de musique*

1657 BERNHARD *Tractatus compositionis augmentatus*

WALLIS *Operum mathematicorum pars prima*

1658 OUVRARD *Secret pour composer en musique*

1659 GIBELIUS *Kurtzer, jedoch gründlicher Bericht*

SIMPSON *The Division-Violist*

1660 BONTEMPI *Nova quatuor vocibus componendi methodus*

CRÜGER *Musicae practicae praecepta brevia*

GIBELIUS *Introductio musicae theoreticae didacticae*

1661 HUYGENS *Novus cyclus harmonicus*

1662 VOSSIUS, G. J. *Etymologicon linguae latinae praefigitur*

1664 BERNHARD *Ausführlicher Bericht vom Gebrauch*

WALLIS *Three letters to Henry Oldenburg*

1665 NIVERS *Observations sur le toucher*

SIMPSON *The Principles of Practical Music*

1666 GIBELIUS *Propositiones mathematico-musicae*

NIVERS *Méthode facile pour apprendre à chanter*

PRINTZ *Anweisung zur Singe-Kunst*

1667 NIVERS *Traité de la composition de musique*

SIMPSON *A Compendium of Practical Musick*

1668 BACILLY *Remarques curieuses sur l'art de bien chanter*

KIRCHER *Organum mathematicum*

PRINTZ *Compendium musicae*

1669 HOLDER *Elements of Speech*

KIRCHER *Ars magna sciendi*

KIRCHER *Vita admodum reverendi*

1672 LOCKE *Observations upon a Late Book*

LORENTE *El porqué de la música*

PENNA *Li primi albori musicali*

SALMON *An Essay to the Advancement of Musick*

SALMON *A Vindication of an Essay*

1673 BONONCINI *Musico prattico*

KIRCHER *Phonurgia nova*

LOCKE *Melothesia; or, Certain General Rules*

LOCKE *The Present Practice of Music Vindicated*

VOSSIUS, I. *De poematum cantu et viribus rhythmi*

1676 MACE *Musick's Monument*

PRINTZ *Phrynis Mytilenaeus*

1677 NORTH, F. *A Philosophical Essay of Musick*

OUVRARD *L'art et la science des nombres*

WALLIS *Of the Trembling of the Consonant Strings*

1678 PRINTZ *Musica modulatoria vocalis*

PRINTZ *Refutation des Satyrischen Componistens*

ROUSSEAU, J. *Méthode claire, certaine et facile*

1679 KIRCHER *Tariffa Kircheriana*

OUVRARD *Architecture harmonique*

PRINTZ *Declaration oder weitere Erklärung*

1680 KIRCHER *Physiologia Kircheriana experimentalis*

1681 BERARDI *Dicerie musicali*

BERARDI *Ragionamenti musicali*

WERCKMEISTER *Orgel-Probe*

1682 WALLIS *Claudii Ptolemaei harmonicorum*

1683 HUYGENS *Kosmotheoros*

NASSARRE *Fragmentos músicos: Reglas generales*

NIVERS *Dissertation sur le chant grégorien*

1686 WERCKMEISTER *Musicae mathematicae Hodegus curiosus*

WERCKMEISTER *Musicalische Temperatur*

1687 AHLE *Unstruhtinne, oder musicalische Gartenlust*

BERARDI *Documenti armonici*

PRINTZ *Exercitationes musicae theoretico-practicae*

ROUSSEAU, J. *Traité de la viol*

SPEER *Grund-richtiger, kurtz, leicht*

1688 ROUSSEAU, J. *Réponse . . . à la lettre*

SALMON *A Proposal to Perform Musick*

1689 BERARDI *Miscellanea musicale*

NIVERS *L'art d'accompagner sur le basse continue*

PENNA *Direttorio del canto fermo*

PRINTZ *Compendium musicae signatoriae*

1690 AHLE *Kurze doch deutliche Anleitung*

BERARDI *Arcani musicali*

BONTEMPI *Tractatus in quo demonstrantur*

MUFFAT *Preface to Apparatus Musico-Organisticus*

PRINTZ *Historische Beschreibung*

1691 WERCKMEISTER *Der edlen Music-Kunst Würde*

1693 BERARDI *Il perché musicale*

WALLIS *De algebra tractatus*

WALLIS *Operum mathematicorum volumen tertium*

1694 HOLDER *A Treatise of the Natural Grounds*

PURCELL *A Brief Introduction to the Art of Descant*

1695 AHLE *Musikalisches Frühlings-gespräche*

BONTEMPI *Historia musica*

BROSSARD *Élévations et motets à voix seule*

MUFFAT *Preface to Suavioris harmoniae . . . primum*

NORTH, R. *Some Memorandums, concerning Musick*

1696 LOULIÉ *Éléments ou principes de musique*

1697 AHLE *Musikalisches Sommer-gespräche*

BEER *Ursus murmurat*

BEER *Ursus vulpinatur*

MASSON *Nouveau traité des règles*

SAUVEUR *Traité de la théorie de la musique*

WERCKMEISTER *Hypomnemata musica*

WERCKMEISTER *Nucleus musicus*

1698 LOULIÉ *Nouveau système de musique*

MUFFAT *Preface to Suavioris harmoniae . . . secundum*

NIVERS *Méthode certaine pour apprendre le pleinchant*

WALLIS *A Letter . . . to Mr. Andrew Fletcher*

WALLIS *A Letter . . . to Samuel Pepys Esquire*

WALLIS *A Question of Musick*

WERCKMEISTER *Die nothwendigsten Anmerkungen und Regeln*

1699 AHLE *Musikalsiches Herbst-gespräche*

MUFFAT *Regulae concentuum partiturae*

1700 FUX *Exempla dissonantiarum ligatarum*

KUHNAU *Der musicalische Quack-Salber*

KUHNAU *Musicalische Vorstellung*

NIEDT *Musicalische Handleitung*

WERCKMEISTER *Cribrum musicum*

1701 AHLE *Musikalisches Winter-gespräche*

BEER *Bellum musicum oder musikalischer Krieg*

BROSSARD *Dictionaire des termes grecs, latins*

JANOVKA *Clavis ad thesaurum*

MUFFAT *Preface to Außerlesener*

SAUVEUR *Système général des intervalles*

1702 SAINT-LAMBERT *Les principes du clavecin*

SAUVEUR *Application des sons harmoniques*

TREIBER *Sonderbare Invention: Eine Arie*

WERCKMEISTER *Harmonologia musica*

1703 WERCKMEISTER *Harmonologia musica*

KUHNAU *Fundamenta compositionis*

NORTH, R. *Cursory Notes of Musicke*

NORTH, R. *Notes of Me*

NORTH, R. *Some Notes upon an Essay*

1704 SAMBER *Manuductio ad organum*

TREIBER *Der accurate Organist im General-Baß*

1705 KELLER *Rules for Playing a Thorough Bass*

MASSON *Divers traitez sur la composition*

SALMON *The Theory of Musick Reduced*

WERCKMEISTER *Organum Gruningense revidivum*

1706 NEIDHARDT *Beste und leichteste Temperatur*

TEVO *Il musico testore*

1707 SAINT-LAMBERT *Nouveau traité de l'accompagnement*

SAMBER *Continuatio ad manuductionem organicam*

SAUVEUR *Méthode générale pour former les sysêmes*

WERCKMEISTER *Musicalische Paradoxal-Discourse*

1708 GASPARINI *L'armonico pratico al cimbalo*

NIEDT *Musicalisches ABC zum Nutzen*

WALTHER *Praecepta der musikalischen Composition*

1710 NORTH, R. *Annotations to Capt. Prencourt's Short*

SAMBER *Elucidatio musicae choralis*

1711 HEINICHEN *Neu erfundene und gründliche Anweisung*

SAUVEUR *Table générale des sistèmes temperés*

1712 LEIBNIZ *Principes de la nature*

1713 MATTHESON *Das neu-eröffnete Orchestre*

SAUVEUR *Rapport des sons des cordes*

1715 BUTTSTETT *Ut, mi, sol, re, fa, la*

NORTH, R. *An Essay of Musicall Ayre*

NORTH, R. *The Theory of Sounds*

1716 CAMPION, F. *Traité d'accompagnement et de composition*

1717 KUHNAU *Ausspruch über den Orchester-Streit*

MATTHESON *Das beschützte Orchestre*

1719 BEER *Musicalische Discurse*

MATTHESON *Exemplarische Organisten-Probe*

1721 MALCOLM *A Treatise of Musick*

MATTHESON *Das forschende Orchestre*

1722 MATTHESON *Critica musica*

RAMEAU *Traité de l'harmonie*

1723 ADLUNG *Vollständige Anweisung zum Generalbaße*

NASSARRE *Escuela música*

TOSI *Opinioni de' cantori antichi*

1724 BROSSARD *Catalogue des livres de musique*

NEIDHARDT *Sectio canonis harmonici*

PEPUSCH *A Short Explication*

1725 FUX *Gradus ad Parnassum*

VALLOTTI *Una memoria di varie decisioni teorico*

1726 ADLUNG *Musica mechanica organoedi*

EULER *Musices theoreticae systema*

NORTH, R. *The Musicall Gramarian*

RAMEAU *Nouveau système de musique théorique*

1727 ADLUNG *Anweisung zur Fantasie*

ADLUNG *Anweisung zur italienischen Tablatur*

EULER *Dissertatio physica de sono*

1728 HEINICHEN *Der General-Bass in der Composition*

NORTH, R. *Memoires of Musick*

WALTHER *Alte und neue musicalische Bibliothec*

1729 BROSSARD *Lettre en forme de dissertation*

CAMPION, F. *Lettre . . . à un philosophe*

RAMEAU *Polemic with Michel Pignolet de Montéclair*

1730 CAMPION, F. *Addition au traité d'accompagnement*

MALCOLM *A New System of Arithmetick*

PEPUSCH *Rules, or a Short and Compleat Method*

PEPUSCH *A Short Treatise on Harmony*

SCHEIBE *Compendium musices theoretico-practicum*

1731 MATTHESON *Grosse General-Bass-Schule*

TELEMANN, G. P. *Preface to Fortsetzung des Harmonischen*

1732 BEER *Schola phonologica*

KELLNER *Treulicher Unterricht im General-Baß*

NEIDHARDT *Gäntzlich erschöpfte*

RAMEAU *Dissertation sur les différentes métodes*

VALLOTTI *Serie di vari autori Greci*

WALTHER *Musicalisches Lexicon*

1733 TELEMANN, G. P. *Singe-, Spiel- und General-Baß-Übungen*

VALLOTTI *Trattato dei tuoni modali*

1734 MIZLER *Dissertatio, quod musica ars*

NEIDHARDT *Systema generis diatonico-chromatici*

TANS'UR *A Compleat Melody*

1735 MATTHESON *Kleine General-Bass-Schule*

MIZLER *Lusus ingenii de praesenti bello*

TANS'UR *The Melody of the Heart*

1736 MIZLER *Neu eröffnete musikalische Bibliothek*

RAMEAU *Lettre au R. P. Castel*

SCHRÖTER *Der musicalischen Intervallen Anzahl*

TELEMANN, G. P. *Neues musikalisches System*

1737 MATTHESON *Kern melodischer Wissenschaft*

RAMEAU *Génération harmonique*

SCHEIBE *Der critische Musicus*

TELEMANN, G. P. *Anleitung, wie man einer General-Baß*

1738 MATTHESON *Gültige Zeugnisse*

SCHEIBE *Sendschreiben . . . über den Kern*

SCHRÖTER *Sendschreiben an . . . Mizler*

1739 CAMPION, F. *Lettre . . . à Monsieur de Voltaire*

EULER *Tentamen novae theoriae musicae*

GEMINIANI *Rules for Playing in a True Taste*

MATTHESON *Der vollkommene Capellmeister*

MIZLER *Anfangs-Gründe des General-Baßes*

MIZLER *Musikalischer Staarstecher*

RAMEAU *L'art de la basse fondamentale*

SCHEIBE *Abhandlung von den musicalischen Intervallen*

1740 MATTHESON *Grundlage einer Ehren-Pforte*

PEPUSCH *A Short Account of the Thoro Bass*

1741 SORGE *Genealogia allegorica intervallorum*

1742 GEMINIANI *Guida armonica*

MIZLER *Preface to Gespräch von der Musik*

ROUSSEAU, J.-J. *Projet concernant de nouveaux signes*

1743 ROUSSEAU, J.-J. *Dissertation sur la musique moderne*

1744 SORGE *Anweisung zur Stimmung und Temperatur*

TELEMANN, G. P. *Preface to Musikalisches Lob Gottes*

1745 SORGE *Vorgemach der musicalischen Composition*

SPIESS *Tractatus musicus compositorio-practicus*

1746 TANS'UR *A New Musical Grammar*

1747 PEPUSCH *Of the Various Genera and Species of Music*

1748 MATTHESON *Phthongologia systematica*

ROEL DEL RÍO *Institución harmónica*

SORGE *Gespräch zwischen einem Musico theoretico*

1749 d'ALEMBERT *Rapport sur un mémoire*

d'ALEMBERT *Recherches sur la courbe*

GEMINIANI *A Treatise of Good Taste*

MARPURG *Der critische Musicus an der Spree*

RAMEAU *Mémoire ou l'on expose les fondemens*

SORGE *Ausführliche und deutliche Anweisung*

1750 MARPURG *Die Kunst das Clavier zu spielen*

RAMEAU *Démonstration du principe de l'harmonie*

1751 d'ALEMBERT *Articles in the Encyclopédie*

GEMINIANI *The Art of Playing on the Violin*

PEPUSCH *A Short Account of the Twelve Modes*

ROUSSEAU, J.-J. *Articles on Music in the Encyclopédie*

SERRE *Lettre . . . sur la nature d'un mode*

1752 d'ALEMBERT *Élémens de musique*

MARPURG *Vorbericht to J. S. Bach's Die Kunst der Fuge*

QUANTZ *Versuch einer Anweisung*

RAMEAU *Extrait d'une réponse de M. Rameau*

RAMEAU *Nouvelles réflexions de M. Rameau*

RAMEAU *Réflexions sur la manière de former la voix*

RIEPEL *Anfangsgründe zur musicalischen Setzkunst*

SERRE *Réflexions sur la supposition*

TARTINI *Regole per arrivare a saper ben suonar*

1753 BACH *Versuch über die wahre Art, Vol. I*

MARPURG *Abhandlung von der Fuge*

ROUSSEAU, J.-J. *Lettre sur la musique françoise*

SERRE *Essais sur les principes de l'harmonie*

SORGE *Ausweichungs-Tabellen*

1754 BACH *Einfall, einen doppelten Contrapunct*

BÉTHIZY *Exposition de la théorie*

GEMINIANI *The Art of Accompaniament*

MARPURG *Historisch-kritische Beyträge zur Aufnahme*

MATTHESON *Plus ultra, ein Stückwerk*

QUANTZ *Hrn. Johann Joachim Quanzens Antwort*

RAMEAU *Observations sur notre instinct*

ROUSSEAU, J.-J. *Lettre à Monsieur l'Abbé Raynal*

SCHEIBE *Abhandlung vom Ursprunge*

SORGE *Gründliche Untersuchung*

TANS'UR *The Royal Melody Compleat*

TARTINI *Regola per bene accordare il violino*

TARTINI *Trattato di musica secondo*

1755 BACH *Gedanken eines Liebhabers der Tonkunst*

MARPURG *Anleitung zum Clavierspielen*

MARPURG *Handbuch bey dem Generalbasse*

RAMEAU *Erreurs sur la musique dans l'Encyclopédie*

ROUSSEAU, J.-J. *Examen de deux principes*

1756 DAUBE *General-Baß in drey Accorden*

MARTINI *Regola agli organisti per accompagnare*

MOZART *Versuch einer gründlichen Violinschule*

RAMEAU *Suite des erreurs sur la musique*

ROUSSIER *Replies to Labbet's review of Rameau*

1757 KIRNBERGER *Der allezeit fertige*

MARPURG *Anfangsgründe der theoretischen Musik*

MARTINI *Storia della musica*

MOZART *Nachricht von dem gegenwärtigen Zustande*

PASQUALI *The Art of Fingering the Harpsichord*

PASQUALI *Thorough-Bass Made Easy*

RAMEAU *Prospectus, où l'on propose au public*

RAMEAU *Réponse de M. Rameau à MM. les éditeurs*

1758 ADLUNG *Anleitung zu der musikalischen Gelahrtheit*

MARPURG *Anleitung zur Singcomposition*

SORGE *Zuverlässige Anweisung, Claviere und Orgeln*

1759 d'ALEMBERT *De la liberté de la musique*

KIRNBERGER *Allegro für das Clavier alleine*

MARPURG *Kritische Briefe über die Tonkunst*
SCHRÖTER *Bedenken über Herrn Sorges . . . Streit*
SCHRÖTER *Sendschreiben an die Verfasser*
1760 BÉTHIZY *Effets de l'air sur le corps humain*
EULER *Lettres à une princesse d'Allemagne*
GEMINIANI *The Art of Playing the Guitar*
GEMINIANI *L'arte armonica*
KIRNBERGER *Construction der gleichschwebenden Temperatur*
RAMEAU *Code de musique pratique*
RAMEAU *Lettre à M. d'Alembert*
ROEL DEL RÍO *Razón naturel, i científica de la música*
ROUSSEAU, J.-J. *Essai sur l'origine des langues*
SORGE *Compendium harmonicum*
SORGE *Die geheim gehaltene Kunst der Mensuration*
TARTINI *Lettera del defonto signor Giuseppe Tartini*
1761 MARTINI *Report on Rameau's Theoretical Writings*
1762 BACH *Versuch über die wahre Art, Vol. II*
MARPURG *Clavierstücke mit einem practischen*
RAMEAU *Lettre aux Philosophes*
RAMEAU *Observations de M. Rameau*
RAMEAU *Origine des sciences*
SOLER *Llave de la modulación*
1763 DONI *Lyra Barberina*
MARPURG *Anleitung zur Musik überhaupt*
MARTINI *Onomasticum, seu synopsis musicarum*
SERRE *Observations sur les principes de l'harmonie*
SORGE *Kurze Erklärung des Canonis harmonici*
1764 EULER *Conjecture sur la raison*
EULER *Du véritable caractère de la musique*
RAMEAU *Vérité également ignorées et interresantes*
ROEL DEL RÍO *Reparos músicos precisos*
ROUSSIER *Traité des accords*
SCHEIBE *Abhandlung über das Rezitativ*
TARTINI *La scienza platonica*
1765 LÖHLEIN *Clavier-Schule*
LÖHLEIN *Clavier-Schule, zweyter Band*
PAOLUCCI *Arte pratica di contrappunto*
ROUSSIER *Observations sur différens points d'harmonie*
SOLER *Correspondence with Martini*
SOLER *Satisfacción a los reparos precisos*
1766 HOLDEN *A Collection of Church-Music*
SOLER *Carta escrita a un amigo*
1767 MARTINI *Dissertatio de usu progressionis*
SORGE *Anleitung zur Fantasie*
TARTINI *De' principj dell'armonia*
TARTINI *Risposta . . . alla critica*
1768 ADLUNG *Musikalisches Siebengestirn*
ROUSSEAU, J.-J. *Dictionnaire de musique*
1769 MARTINI *Compendio della teoria*
SORGE *Mathematische Beschreibung*
1770 DAUBE *Der musikalische Dilettant*
HOLDEN *An Essay towards a Rational System*
QUANTZ *Anweisung, wie ein Musikus*
ROUSSIER *Lettre . . . touchant la division de zodiaque*
ROUSSIER *Mémoire sur la musique des anciens*
SORGE *Anmerkung über Professor Euler's*

1771 AGRICOLA, J. F. *Beleuchtung von der Frage*
KIRNBERGER *Die Kunst des reinen Satzes*
SULZER *Allgemeine Theorie der schönen Künste*
1772 SCHRÖTER *Deutliche Anweisung zum General-Baß*
SULZER *Die schönen Künste*
1773 EULER *De harmoniae veris principiis*
KIRNBERGER *Die wahren Grundsätze zum Gebrauch*
SCHEIBE *Über die musikalische Composition*
SORGE *Der in der Rechen- und Messkunst*
TELEMANN, G. M. *Unterricht im Generalbaß-Spielen*
1774 EXIMENO *Dell'origine e delle regole della musica*
EXIMENO *Risposta al giudizio delle Efemeridi*
LÖHLEIN *Anweisung zum Violinspielen*
MARTINI *Esemplare o sia saggio fondamentale*
TARTINI *Libro del contrapunto*
1775 EXIMENO *Dubbio . . . sopra il saggio fondamentale*
MANFREDINI *Regole armoniche*
ROUSSIER *L'harmonie pratique*
1776 MARPURG *Versuch über die musikalische Temperatur*
RIEPEL *Harmonisches Syllbenmass*
VOGLER *Stimmbildungskunst*
VOGLER *Tonwissenschaft und Tonsetzkunst*
1777 d'ALEMBERT *Réflexions sur la théorie de la musique*
KIRNBERGER *Recueil d'airs de danse*
1778 VOGLER *Articles on music in Deutsche Encyklopädie*
VOGLER *Betrachtungen der Mannheimer Tonschule*
VOGLER *Vogler's Tonschule*
1779 ROUSSIER *Mémoire sur la musique des chinois*
VALLOTTI *Della scienza teorica*
1780 JONES *Letters from a Tutor to His Pupils*
VOGLER *Entwurf eines neuen Wörterbuchs*
1781 JONES *Physiological disquisitions*
KIRNBERGER *Grundsätze des Generalbasses*
MARTINI *Lettere di un accademico filarmonico*
ROUSSIER *Remarques . . . sur les observations*
1782 KIRNBERGER *Anleitung zur Singekomposition*
KIRNBERGER *Gedanken über die verschiedenen Lehrarten*
KOCH *Versuch einer Anleitung zur Composition*
MARTINI *Intorno alle quinte successive*
ROUSSIER *Mémoire sur la nouvelle harpe*
ROUSSIER *Mémoire sur le noueau clavecin*
SCHRÖTER *Letzte Beschäftigung mit musicalischen Dingen*
1783 KIRNBERGER *Methode, Sonaten aus'm Ermel*
ROUSSIER *Lettre . . . sur l'acception des mots*
1784 JONES *A Treatise on the Art of Music*
1785 PORTMANN *Musikalischer Unterricht*
1786 MANFREDINI *Review of Esteban Arteaga's Le rivoluzioni*
RIEPEL *Baßschlüssel*
SCHULZ *Entwurf einer neuen . . . Musiktablatur*
1787 JONES *The Nature and Excellence of Music*
TÜRK *Von den wichtigsten Pflichten*
1788 MANFREDINI *Difesa della musica moderna*
1789 PORTMANN *Leichtes Lehrbuch der Harmonie*

SABBATINI, L. A. *Elementi teorici della musica*
TÜRK *Klavierschule*
1790 ALBRECHTSBERGER *Gründliche Anweisung zur Composition*
MARPURG *Neue Methode, allerley Arten*
SCHULZ *Gedanken über den Einfluß der Musik*
1791 ALBRECHTSBERGER *Kurzgefaßte Methode den Generalbaß*
GALEAZZI *Elementi teorico-pratici di musica*
MOMIGNY *Encyclopédie méthodique*
TÜRK *Kurze Anweisung zum Generalbaßspielen*
1792 KOLLMANN *An Introduction to the Art of Preluding*
TÜRK *Beleuchtung einer Recension des Buches*
1793 ALBRECHTSBERGER *Ausweichungen von C-dur und C-moll*
1794 VOGLER *Erste musikalische Preisaustheilung*
VOGLER *Inledning til harmoniens kännedon*
1795 KOCH *Journal der Tonkunst*
KOLLMANN *The First Beginning on the Piano Forte*
1796 KOLLMANN *An Essay on Musical Harmony*
1797 DAUBE *Anleitung zur Erfindung der Melodie*
LANGLÉ *Traité d'harmonie et de modulation*
1798 KOLLMANN *Proposals for Publishing by Subscription*
KOLLMANN *A Symphony for the Piano-Forte*
LANGLÉ *Traité de la basse sous les chant*
PORTMANN *Die neuesten und wichtigsten Entdeckungen*
VOGLER *Clavé Schola*
VOGLER *Organist-Schola*
1799 KOLLMANN *An Essay on Practical Musical Composition*
LANGLÉ *Principes élémentaires de musique*
SABBATINI, L. A. *La vera idea delle musicali numeriche*
SCHULZ *Über die in Sulzers Theorie*
SULZER *Register über die in allen vier Theilen*
TÜRK *Violinschule*
1800 REICHA *Études ou exercices pour le piano-forte*
VOGLER *Choral-System*
1801 KOLLMANN *A Practical Guide to Thorough-Bass*
LANGLÉ *Nouvelle méthode pour chiffrer les accords*
LANGLÉ *Solfèges pour servir á l'étude*
VOGLER *Data zur Akustik*
1802 CATEL *Traité d'harmonie*
EXIMENO *Don Lazarillo Vizcardi*
KOCH *Musikalisches Lexikon*
LANGLÉ *Méthode de chant du Conservatoire*
MOMIGNY *Méthode de piano à l'aide*
MOMIGNY *La première anné de leçons de piano-forté*
SABBATINI, L. A. *Trattato sopra le fughe musicali*
TÜRK *Kleines Lehrbuch für Anfänger*
VOGLER *Handbuch zur Harmonielehre*
1803 MOMIGNY *Cours complet d'harmonie et de composition*
REICHA *L'art de varier*
REICHA *Praktische Beispiele: Ein Beitrag*
REICHA *Trente-six fugues pour le pianoforte*
1804 ALBRECHTSBERGER *Kurze Regeln des reinsten Satzes*
CHORON

Principes d'accompagnement des écoles d'Italie
1805 LANGLÉ *Traité de la fugue*
1806 KOLLMANN *A New Theorie of Musical Harmony*
TÜRK *Anleitung zu Temperaturberechnungen*
VOGLER *Über die harmonische Akustik*
VOGLER *Zwei und dreisig Präludien für die Orgel*
1807 KOCH *Über den technischen Ausdruck*
KOLLMANN *An Essay on Earl Stanhope's Principles*
KOLLMANN *Second Practical Guide to Thorough-Bass*
VOGLER *Gründliche Anleitung zum Klavier-Stimmen*
1808 MOMIGNY *Le nouveau solfège avec accompagnement*
1809 CHORON *Principes de composition des écoles d'Italie*
KOLLMANN *The Melody of the Hundredth Psalm*
MOMIGNY *Exposé succinct du seul systême musical*
1810 CHORON *Dictionnaire historique des musiciens*
KOLLMANN *A Series of Twelve Analyzed Fugues*
VOGLER *Zwölf Choräle von Sebastian Bach*
1811 KOCH *Handbuch bey dem Studium der Harmonie*
1812 KOCH *Versuch, aus der harten und weichen Tonart*
KOLLMANN *The Quarterly Musical Register*
1813 LOGIER *A Treatise on Practical Composition*
WEBER *Über das sogenannte Generalbass-Spielen*
1814 LOGIER *An Explanation . . . of the Royal Patent*
REICHA *Petit traité d'harmonie pratique*
REICHA *Sur la musique comme art*
REICHA *Traité de mélodie*
1815 LOGIER *A Companion to the Royal Patent*
REICHA *Études pour le piano-forte*
WEBER *Erneuerter Versuch einer Begriffsbestimmung*
1816 LOGIER *A Syllabus of the Second Examination*
LOGIER *Theoretical and Practical Studies*
REICHA *Cours de composition musicale*
1817 LOGIER *Prospectus of the Musical Academy*
VOGLER *System für den Fugenbau*
WEBER *Über chronometrische Tempobezeichnung*
WEBER *Versuch einer geordneten Theorie*
1818 LOGIER *An Authentic Account of the Examination*
LOGIER *A Refutation of the Fallacies*
LOGIER *Thorough Bass, Being a Second Series*
WEBER *Articles on music in Allgemeine Enzyklopädie*
1820 KOLLMANN *An Introduction to Extemporary Modulation*
SECHTER *Zergliederung des Finale aus Mozarts*
1821 MOMIGNY *La seule vraie théorie de la musique*
TELEMANN, G. M. *Über die Wahl der Melodie*
1822 WEBER *Allgemeine Musiklehre zum Selbstunterricht*
1823 FÉTIS *Méthode élémentaire et abrégée d'harmonie*
1824 FÉTIS *Traité du contrepoint et de la fugue*
LOGIER *A Short Account of the Progress*
MARX *Berliner allgemeine musikalische Zeitung*
REICHA *Traité de haute composition musicale*
SECHTER *Zwölf Variationen im strengen Style*
WEBER *Caecilia: Eine Zeitschrift*
1825 WEBER *Über Tonmalerei*
1826 MARX *Die Kunst des Gesanges, theoretisch-praktisch*
SECHTER *Zwölf neue Variationen im strengen Style*

SECHTER *Zwölf Versetten und eine Fuge*

1827 FÉTIS *Questions sur la diversité d'opinions*

FÉTIS *Des révolutions de l'orchestre*

FÉTIS *Revue musicale*

LOGIER *A System of the Science of Music*

1828 FÉTIS *Introduction à l'étude de l'harmonie*

LOGIER *A Manual Chiefly for the Use of Preceptors*

1829 CZERNY *Systematische Anleitung zum Fantasieren*

LOGIER *Themes . . . for Those Who Are Desirous*

1830 FÉTIS *Curiosité historiques de la musique*

FÉTIS *La musique mise à la portée*

FÉTIS *De la nécessité de résumer les . . . formes*

SECHTER *Practische Generalbaß-Schule*

1831 FÉTIS *Traité élémentaire de musique*

MOMIGNY *À l'Académie des Beaux-Arts*

1832 CHORON *Harmonie.—Systèmes.*

CHORON *Méthode pratique d'harmonie*

FÉTIS *Cours de philosophie musicale*

1833 CHORON *Sur la composition musicale*

FÉTIS *Biographie universelle des musiciens*

REICHA *Art du compositeur dramatique*

WEBER *Die Generalbaßlehre zum Selbstunterricht*

1834 LOGIER *Programme of a Public Examination*

MOMIGNY *Cours général de musique*

SECHTER *Practische und im Zusammenhange*

1835 CHERUBINI *Cours de contre-point et de fugue*

FÉTIS *Résumé philosophique de l'histoire*

SECHTER *Musikalischer Rathgeber*

1836 REICHA *Contrepoint*

1837 FÉTIS *Manuel des compositeurs*

MARX *Die Lehre von der musikalische Komposition*

1839 MARX *Allgemeine Musiklehre: Ein Hülfsbuch*

1840 DEHN *Theoretisch-praktische Harmonielehre*

FÉTIS *Esquisse de l'histoire de l'harmonie*

REICHA *La fugue et le contrepoint*

1841 HAUPTMANN *Erläuterungen zu J. S. Bachs Kunst*

MARX *Die alte Musiklehre im Streit*

1842 LOBE *Andeutungen über meine Lehrmethode*

1844 FÉTIS *Considérations sur l'étude de contre-point*

FÉTIS *Traité complet de la théorie*

LOBE *Compositions-Lehre*

1845 DAY *Treatise on Harmony*

1846 FÉTIS *Système général de la musique*

1849 CZERNY *Die Schule der praktischen Tonsetzkunst*

1850 FÉTIS *Première lettre à M. Halévy*

FÉTIS *Théorie de la musique*

LOBE *Lehrbuch der musikalischen Komposition*

1851 LOBE *Katechismus der Musik*

RICHTER *Die Grundzüge der musikalischen Formen*

1852 FÉTIS *Du développement futur de la musique*

LOBE *Musikalische Briefe: Wahrheit über Tonkunst*

MACFARREN *Analytical Essay on Beethoven's Fidelio*

RICHTER *Die Elementarkenntnisse zur Harmonielehre*

1853 HAUPTMANN *Die Natur der Harmonik und der Metrik*

RICHTER *Lehrbuch der Harmonie*

RICHTER *Die Parktischen Studien zur Theorie*

SECHTER *Die Grundsätze der musikalischen Komposition*

WEITZMANN *Die übermäßige Dreiklang*

1854 WEITZMANN *Geschichte des Septimen-Akkordes*

WEITZMANN *Der verminderte Septimen-Akkord*

WESTPHAL *Metrik der griechischen Dramatiker*

1855 MARX *Die Musik des neunzehnten Jahrhunderts*

1856 GEVAERT *Leerboek van den Gregorianschen zang*

1857 GEVAERT *Leerboek der harmonij en begeleiding*

HELMHOLTZ *Über die physiologischen Ursachen*

MARX *Die Form in der Musik*

1858 BELLERMANN *Die Mensuralnoten und Taktzeichen*

DEHN *Analysen dreier Fugen aus J. S. Bach's*

1859 DEHN *Lehre vom Contrapunkt*

RICHTER *Lehrbuch der Fuge*

WEITZMANN *Geschichte der Harmonie und ihrer Lehre*

1860 MACFARREN *The Rudiments of Harmony*

WEITZMANN *Harmoniesystem: Erklärende Erläuterung*

1861 LOBE *Vereinfachte Harmonielehre*

WEITZMANN *Die neue Harmonielehre im Streit*

1862 BELLERMANN *Der Contrapunct*

LOBE *Katechismus der Compositionslehre*

REBER *Traité d'harmonie*

1863 BELLERMANN *Joannis Tinctoris: Terminorum musicae*

FÉTIS *Effets des circonstances sur la situation*

GEVAERT *Traité général d'instrumentation*

HAUPTMANN *Klang*

HAUPTMANN *Temperatur*

HELMHOLTZ *Die Lehre von den Tonempfindungen*

MARX *Anleitung zum Vortrag Beethovenscher*

WESTPHAL *Die Tradition der alten Metriker*

1865 WESTPHAL *Plutarch: Über die Musik*

WESTPHAL *System der antiken Rhythmik*

1866 FÉTIS *Méthode dans l'enseignement de l'harmonie*

OETTINGEN *Harmoniesystem in dualer Entwickelung*

WESTPHAL *Scriptores metrici graeci*

1867 BELLERMANN *Das Locheimer Liederbuch nebst der Ars*

BELLERMANN *Über die Entwicklung der mehrstimmigen Musik*

GEVAERT *Les origines de la tonalité moderne*

MACFARREN *Six Lectures on Harmony*

1868 BELLERMANN *Das Eilfte Kapitel der Ars Cantus*

BELLERMANN *Einige Bemerkungen über Hucbald'schen*

FÉTIS *Note sur un point de l'histoire*

GEVAERT *Réponse à M. Fétis sur l'origine*

HAUPTMANN *Die Lehre von der Harmonik*

OUSELEY *A Treatise on Harmony*

1869 BELLERMANN *Bemerkungen über den melodischen Gebrauch*

BELLERMANN *Die Wechselnote oder Cambiata*

LOBE *Consonanzen und Dissonanzen*

OUSELEY *A Treatise on Counterpoint, Canon and Fugue*

1870 BELLERMANN *Einige Bemerkungen über die consonirenden*
BELLERMANN *Die Schlüssel im ersten Buche*
BELLERMANN *Über die Eintheilung der Intervalle*
BELLERMANN *Zur Quintenfrage*
1871 GEVAERT *Vade-mecum de l'organiste*
MACFARREN *On the Structure of the Sonata*
STAINER *A Theory of Harmony*
1872 BELLERMANN *Bemerkungen über den Gesangunterricht*
BELLERMANN *Notker Labeo, von der Musik*
CHAIKOVSKY *Rukovodstvo k prakticheskomu*
RICHTER *Lehrbuch des einfachen und doppelten*
RIEMANN *Musikalische Logik: Ein Beitrag*
RIEMANN *Über Tonalität*
WESTPHAL *Elemente des musikalischen Rhythmus*
1873 BELLERMANN *Die Größe der musikalischen Intervalle*
RIEMANN *Über das musikalische Hören*
1874 BELLERMANN *Franconis de Colonia Artis cantus*
HAUPTMANN *Opuscula: Vermischte Aufsätze*
LUSSY *Traité de l'expression musicale*
RIEMANN *Musikalische Grammatik*
RIEMANN *Neue Schule der Harmonik*
1875 CHAIKOVSKY *Kratkii uchebnik garmonii*
GEVAERT *Histoire et théorie de la musique*
MACFARREN *Eighty Musical Sentences*
OUSELEY *A Treatise on Musical Form*
RIEMANN *Die Hilfsmittel der Modulation*
RIEMANN *Die objektive Existenz der Untertöne*
1878 RIEMANN *Studien zur Geschichte der Notenschrift*
WESTPHAL *Sem' fug dlia fortepiano I. S. Bakha*
1879 MACFARREN *Counterpoint: A Practical Course*
OUSELEY *On the Early Italian and Spanish Treatises*
PROUT *Articles in Grove's Dictionary*
1880 RIEMANN *Skizze einer Methode der Harmonielehre*
RIEMANN *Zarlino als harmonischer Dualist*
WESTPHAL *Allgemeine Theorie der musikalischen Rhythmik*
WESTPHAL *Iskusstvo i ritm: Greki i Vagner*
1881 JADASSOHN *Der streng-polyphonische Stil*
1882 HELMHOLTZ *Wissenschaftliche Abhandlungen*
LUSSY *Histoire de la notation musicale*
OUSELEY *On Some Italian and Spanish Treatises*
RIEMANN *Musik-Lexikon: Theorie und Geschichte*
RIEMANN *Die Natur der Harmonik*
1883 JADASSOHN *Musikalische Kompositionslehre*
LUSSY *Le rythme musical: Son origine*
RIEMANN *Elementar-Musiklehre*
RIEMANN *Neue Schule der Melodik*
RIEMANN *Phrasierungsausgabe*
STUMPF *Tonpsychologie*
WESTPHAL *Aristoxenus von Tarent*
WESTPHAL *Beziehungen zwischen moderner Musik*
WESTPHAL *Die Musik des griechischen Alterthums*
1884 RIEMANN *Der Ausdruck in der Musik*
RIEMANN *Musikalische Dynamik und Agogik*
RIMSKY-KORSAKOV *Uchebnik garmonii*
WESTPHAL *Mehrstimmigkeit oder Einstimmigkeit*

WESTPHAL *Platos Beziehungen zur Musik*
1885 LUSSY *Die Correlation zwischen Takt und Rhythmus*
LUSSY *Zur neueren Literatur über die Reform*
STUMPF *Musikpsychologie in England*
1886 JADASSOHN *Aufgaben und Beispiele für . . . Harmonielehre*
JADASSOHN *Erläuternde Anmerkungen . . . der Harmonie*
RIMSKY-KORSAKOV *Prakticheskii uchebnik garmonii*
TANEEV *O muzyke gorskikh tatar*
1887 GEVAERT *Vingt-cinq leçons de solfège*
JADASSOHN *Erläuternde Anmerkungen . . . des Contrapunkts*
JADASSOHN *Erläuterungen zu Ausgewählten Fugen*
PROUT *A Third Book on the Theory of Music*
RIEMANN *Systematische Modulationslehre als Grundlage*
ZIEHN *Harmonie- und Modulationslehre*
1888 MACFARREN *Addresses and Lectures*
RIEMANN *Katechismus der Musik (Allgemeine Musiklehre)*
RIEMANN *Katechismus der Musikinstrumente*
RIEMANN *Lehrbuch des einfachen, doppelten*
RIEMANN *Wie hören wir Musik?*
1889 DUBOIS *Notes et études d'harmonie*
PROUT *Harmony: Its Theory and Practice*
RIEMANN *Katechismus der Kompositionslehre*
RIEMANN *Katechismus des Generalbaß-Spiels*
RIEMANN *Katechismus des Musik-Diktats*
1890 GEVAERT *Les origines du chant liturgique*
JADASSOHN *Die Kunst zu moduliren*
PROUT *Additional Exercises, Melodies*
PROUT *Additional Exercises to Harmony*
PROUT *Counterpoint: Strict and Free*
RIEMANN *Katechismus der Fugen-Komposition*
RIEMANN *Katechismus der Harmonie- und Modulationslehre*
RIEMANN *Katechismus der Phrasierung*
WESTPHAL *Desiat' fug dlia fortepiano I. S. Bakha*
ZIEHN *Der Weise von Großmehlra*
1891 DUBOIS *Quatre-vingt-sept leçons d'harmonie*
DUBOIS *Réalisations des basses et chants*
DUBOIS *Traité d'harmonie théorique et pratique*
JADASSOHN *Gesangschule/Singing Tutor*
PROUT *Double Counterpoint and Canon*
PROUT *Fugue*
PROUT *Key to the Additional Exercises*
PROUT *Key to the Exercises in Harmony*
RIEMANN *Katechismus der Akustik*
RIEMANN *Katechismus der Gesangkomposition*
WESTPHAL *Die Aristoxenische Rhythmuslehre*
1892 d'INDY *Projet d'organisation des études*
JADASSOHN *Allgemeine Musiklehre*
JADASSOHN *Aufgaben und Beispiele für . . . Kontrapunkt*
PROUT *Fugal Analysis: A Companion to Fugue*
RIEMANN *Kurzgefaßte Harmonielehre*

STAINER *Music in Its Relation to the Intellect*

WESTPHAL *Allgemeine Metrik der indogermanischen*

1893 LOUIS *Der Widerspruch in der Musik*

PROUT *Musical Form*

RIEMANN *Vereinfachte Harmonielehre*

1894 JADASSOHN *Anhang zu den hinweisen für die Bearbeitung*

JADASSOHN *Elementar-Harmonielehre für den Schul-*

OETTINGEN *Neue rationelle Gesangschule*

PROUT *Musical Form: A Paper*

1895 GEVAERT *La mélopée antique dans le chant*

JADASSOHN *Schlüssel zu den Aufgaben*

PROUT *Applied Forms: A Sequel*

PROUT *The Relation of Musical Theory to Practice*

RIEMANN *Präludien und Studien*

SCHENKER *Der Geist der musikalischen Technik*

1896 STUMPF *Die pseudo-aristotelischen Probleme*

1897 STUMPF *Geschichte des Konsonanzbegriffes*

1898 JADASSOHN *Methodik des musiktheoretischen Unterrichtes*

PROUT *The Orchestra*

RIEMANN *Geschichte der Musiktheorie*

STUMPF *Beiträge zur Akustik*

1899 GEVAERT *Problèmes musicaux d'Aristote*

JADASSOHN *Zur Einführung in J. S. Bachs Passions-Musik*

JADASSOHN *Melodik und Harmonik bei Richard Wagner*

JADASSOHN *Ratschläge und Hinweise*

JADASSOHN *Das Tonbewußtsein: Die Lehre*

JADASSOHN *Das Wesen der Melodie in der Tonkunst*

1900 d'INDY *Une école de musique*

HALM *Harmonielehre*

RIEMANN *Die Elemente der musikalischen Ästhetik*

RIEMANN *Vademecum der Phrasierung*

1901 DUBOIS *Traité de contrepoint et de fugue*

JADASSOHN *Der Generalbaß: Eine Anleitung*

1902 KREHL *Musikalische Formenlehre (Kompositionslehre)*

OETTINGEN *Das duale System der Harmonie*

RIEMANN *Große Kompositionslehre*

RIEMANN *Katechismus der Orchestrierung*

1903 d'INDY *Cours de composition musicale*

LUSSY *L'anacrouse dans la musique moderne*

PROUT *Analytical Key to the Exercises*

PROUT *Chromatic Harmony*

RIEMANN *Beethoven's Streichquartette*

RIEMANN *System der musikalischen Rhythmik und Metrik*

TOVEY *The Classical Concerto: Its Nature*

TOVEY *Essays in Musical Analysis (1903)*

1904 GÉDALGE *Les rapports de l'harmonie et du contrepoint*

GÉDALGE *Traité de la fugue*

KREHL *Allgemeine Musiklehre*

SCHENKER *Ein Beitrag zur Ornamentik*

1905 DUBOIS *Leçons de solfège à changements*

GEVAERT *Traité d'harmonie théorique et pratique*

PROUT *A Course of Lectures on Orchestration*

RIEMANN *Das Problem des harmonischen Dualismus*

1906 LOUIS and THUILLE *Unsere Harmonielehre*

RIEMANN *Elementar-Schulbuch der Harmonielehre*

SCHENKER *Neue musikalische Theorien und Phantasien*

1907 d'INDY *Cent thèmes d'harmonie*

KITSON *The Art of Counterpoint*

LOUIS and THUILLE *Harmonielehre*

LOUIS and THUILLE *Eine neue Harmonielehre*

1908 KREHL *Beispiele und Aufgaben zum Kontrapunkt*

KREHL *Fuge: Erläuterung und Anleitung*

KREHL *Kontrapunkt: Die Lehre*

KURTH *Die Stil der Oper seria von C. W. Gluck*

RIEMANN *Kleines Handbuch der Musikgeschichte*

SCHENKER *Instrumentations-Tabelle*

YAVORSKY *Stroenie muzykal'noi rechi*

1909 KITSON *Studies in Fugue*

KREHL *Kompositionsunterricht und moderne Musik*

STUMPF *Die Anfänge der Musik*

TANEEV *Podvizhnoi knotrapunkt strogogo pis'ma*

1910 PROUT *Analysis of J. S. Bach's Forty-Eight Fugues*

SCHENKER *J. S. Bach, Chromatische Phantasie und Fuge*

TOVEY *Articles on music for Encyclopaedia Britannica*

1911 LOUIS and THUILLE *Aufgaben für den Unterricht*

SCHOENBERG *Harmonielehre*

SCHOENBERG *Das Komponieren mit selbständigen Stimmen*

ZIEHN *Fünf- und sechsstimmige Harmonien*

1912 LOUIS and THUILLE *Schlüssel zum Harmonielehre*

LUSSY *La sonata pathétique de L. van Beethoven*

SCHENKER *Beethovens neunte Sinfonie: Eine Darstellung*

ZIEHN *Canonical Studies: A New Technic*

1913 DUBOIS *L'enseignement musical*

HALM *Von zwei Kulturen der Musik*

KURTH *Die Voraussetzungen der theoretischen Harmonik*

OETTINGEN *Das duale Harmoniesystem*

RIMSKY-KORSAKOV *Osnovy orkestrovki*

SCHENKER *Die letzten fünf Sonaten Beethovens*

YAVORSKY *Uprazhneniia v golosovedenii*

1914 HALM *Die Symphonie Anton Bruckners*

KITSON *The Evolution of Harmony*

TANEEV *Der Inhalt des Arbeitsheftes*

1915 HALM *Von Grenzen und Ländern der Musik*

YAVORSKY *Uprazhneniia v obrazovanii skhem ladovogo*

1916 KITSON *Applied Strict Counterpoint*

OETTINGEN *Die Grundlage der Musikwissenschaft*

RIEMANN *Ideen zu einer Lehre*

1917 HALM *Heinrich Schenker*

KURTH *Grundlagen des linearen Kontrapunkts*

RIEMANN *Beethovens sämtliche Klavier-Solosonaten*

RIEMANN *Neue Beiträge zu einer Lehre*

SCHOENBERG *Comments on Busoni's Entwurf*

SCHOENBERG *Instrumentationslehre*

1918   DUBOIS *Petit manuel théorique de l'harmonie*
        KREHL *Die Dissonanz als musikalische Ausdrucksmittel*
        KURTH *Zur Motivbildung Bachs: Ein Beitrag*
        RIEMANN *Die Phrasierung im Lichte einer Lehre*
1920   HALM *Heinrich Schenkers Neue musikalische Theorien*
        HALM *Hugo Riemanns Analysen von Beethovens*
        HALM *Über J. S. Bachs Konzertform*
        KITSON *Elementary Harmony*
        KREHL *Theorie der Tonkunst und Kompositionslehre*
        KURTH *Romantische Harmonik und ihre Krise*
1921   GÉDALGE *L'enseignement de la musique par l'éeducation*
        KREHL *Harmonielehre [Tonalitätslehre]*
        SCHENKER *L. van Beethoven: Sonata, Op. 27, Nr. 2*
        SCHENKER *Der Tonwille: Flugblätter zum Zeugnis*
1922   LORENZ *Die formale Gestaltung des Vorspiels*
        LORENZ *Gedanken und Studien*
        STUMPF *Sammelbände für . . . Musikwissenschaft*
        TOVEY *Beethoven's Ninth Symphony*
1923   YAVORSKY *Osnovnye elementy muzyki*
1924   HALM *Chromatik und Tonalität*
        LORENZ *Betrachtungen über Beethovens Eroica-Skizzen*
        LORENZ *Der formale Schwung in R. Strauss' Till*
        LORENZ *Das Geheimnis der Form bei Richard Wagner*
        TOVEY *Forty-Eight Preludes and Fugues by J. S. Bach*
        TOVEY *A Preface: Forty-Eight Preludes and Fugues*
1925   KITSON *Modern Harmony from the Standpoint*
        KURTH *Bruckner*
        SCHENKER *Beethoven V. Sinfonie: Darstellung*
        SCHENKER *Das Meisterwerk in der Musik*
1926   HALM *Beethoven*
        HALM *Einführung in die Musik*
        KITSON *Additional Exercises to Elementary Harmony*
        LORENZ *Das Finale in Mozarts Meisteropern*
        SCHOENBERG *Die Lehre von Kontrapunkt*
        STUMPF *Die Sprachlaute*
        YAVORSKY *Vospriiatie ladovykh melodicheskikh*
        ZIEHN *Articles on music*
1927   KITSON *Counterpoint for Beginners*
        KITSON *Invertible Counterpoint and Canon*
        KITSON *Rudiments of Music*
        SCHOENBERG *Probleme der Harmonie*
        TOVEY *Some Aspects of Beethoven's Art Forms*
1928   HALM *Über den Wert musikalischen Analysen*
        LORENZ *Abendländische Musikgeschichte im Rhythmus*
        TOVEY *Tonality*
1929   ASAFIEV *Kniga o Stravinskom*
        KITSON *The Elements of Fugal Construction*
        LORENZ *Homophone Großrhythmik in Bachs Polyphonie*
        TANEEV *Uchenie o kanone*
        YAVORSKY *Struktura melodii*
1930   ASAFIEV *Muzykal'naia forma kak protsess*
        KITSON *Six Lectures on Accompanied Vocal Writing*
        LORENZ *Das Relativitätsprinzip in den . . . Formen*
        YAVORSKY *Elementy stroeniia muzykal'noi rechi*
1931   KITSON *Contrapuntal Harmony for Beginners*

        KITSON *Rudiments of Music for Junior Classes*
        KURTH *Musikpsychologie*
        TOVEY *A Companion to Beethoven's Pianoforte Sonatas*
        TOVEY *A Companion to The Art of Fugue*
        TOVEY *Die Kunst der Fuge*
        TOVEY *Ludwig van Beethoven: Sonatas for Pianoforte*
1932   SCHENKER *Fünf Urlinie-Tafeln*
1933   SCHENKER *Johannes Brahms, Oktaven und Quinten*
1934   SCHOENBERG *Der musikalische Gedanke und die Logik*
        TOVEY *Musical Form and Matter*
1935   SCHENKER *Der freie Satz*
        TOVEY *Essays in Musical Analysis*
1936   KITSON *The Elements of Musical Composition*
        LORENZ *Klangmischung in Anton Bruckners Orchester*
        LORENZ *Neue Formerkenntnisse*
        TOVEY *Normality and Freedom in Music*
        TOVEY *The Training of the Musical Imagination*
1937   LORENZ *Neue Gedanken zur Klangspaltung*
        TOVEY *What the Composer Expects from the Listener*
1938   TOVEY *The Main Stream of Music*
        TOVEY *Words and Music: Some Obiter Dicta*
1941   TOVEY *A Musician Talks*
1942   SCHOENBERG *Models for Beginners in Composition*
1944   ASAFIEV *Eugenii Onigen*
        TOVEY *Beethoven*
        TOVEY *Essays in Musical Analysis: Chamber Music*
1947   ASAFIEV *Charodeika*
        ASAFIEV *Muzykal'naia forma kak protsess, kn. 2-aia*
        YAVORSKY *Siuity Bakha dlia klaviera*
1950   SCHOENBERG *Style and Idea*
1954   SCHOENBERG *Structural Functions of Harmony*
1963   SCHOENBERG *Preliminary Exercises in Counterpoint*
1967   SCHOENBERG *Fundamentals of Musical Composition*
n.d.   ALBRECHTRSBERGER *Clavierschule für Anfänger*
        ALBRECHTSBERGER *Generalbass- und Harmonielehre*
        BAN *Zangh-bericht*
        BROSSARD *Fragments d'une méthode de violon*
        BROSSARD *Meslanges et extraits relatifs à l'histoire*
        BROSSARD *Recueil d'extraits d'ouvrages imprimés*
        BRUCKNER *Teaching materials concerning music theory*
        CHERUBINI *Marches d'harmonie pratiquées*
        CHORON *Introduction à l'étude générale et raisonnée*
        CZERNY *Briefe über den Unterricht*
        CZERNY *Die Kunst des Präludirens*
        CZERNY *Die Kunst des Vortrags*
        CZERNY *Vollständige theoretisch-practische*
        DU COUSU *Système royale*
        EBNER *Rules on figured bass*
        FUX *Singfundament*
        GALILEI *Traduzione d'un discorso latino*
        GALILEI *Trattato di musica di Plutarco*
        GASPARINI *Guida ossia dizionario armonico*
        GASPARINI *Li principii della composizione*

HAUPTMANN *Aufgaben für den einfachen und doppelten*

JADASSOHN *Erläuterungen der in Joh. Seb. Bachs Kunst*

KOCH *Über die physischen . . . Gegenstände*

KOCH *Vergleichung der verschiedenen Systeme*

LOULIÉ *Élémens ou principes de musique*

LOULIÉ *Supplément des principes ou éléments de musique*

LUSITANO *Un tratado de canto organo*

MARTINI *Nomenclatura musicale*

MEI *De nomi delle corde del monochordo*

MERSENNE *Livre de la nature des sons*

MUFFAT *Nothwendige Anmerkung bey der Musik*

NEIDHARDT *Compositio harmonica problematice tradita*

OUVRARD *La musique rétablie depuis son origine*

PASQUALI *Theory*

PEPUSCH *Rules for to Play a Thorough Bass*

PEPUSCH *Various Papers . . . Relating to Harmony*

PEPUSCH *Writings on scales, clefs, thoroughbass, etc.*

PRAETORIUS *Kurzer Bericht waß bey uberliefferung*

QUANTZ *Solfeggi*

RAVENSCROFT *A Treatise of Musick*

REICHA *Cours de Mélodie*

REICHA *Fragments harmoniques*

REICHA *Die Grundsätze der praktischen Harmonie*

REICHA *Haute composition musicale*

REICHA *Kunst der praktischen Harmonie*

REICHA *Notes et exemples musicaux sur la permutation*

RIEPEL *Eine Abhandlung vom Kanon*

RIEPEL *Der Fugen-Betrachtung*

RIEPEL *Silva rerum, ein Notiz-exzerptenbuch*

RIMSKY-KORSAKOV *Razbor Snegurochki*

ROUSSEAU, J.-J. *Leçons de musique*

SABBATINI, L. A. *Canoni sui principi elementare*

SABBATINI, L. A. *Esame d'uno scolaro del Padre L. A. Sabbatini*

SABBATINI, L. A. *Studi di contrappunto*

SABBATINI, L. A. *Trattato di contrappunto*

SALINAS *De musica quatuor priores libri*

SCHENKER *Kommentar zu Ph. E. Bach's Versuch*

SCHENKER *Die Kunst des Vortrags*

SCHENKER *Von dem Stimmführung des Generalbasses*

SCHRÖTER *Euclides von der Harmonie*

SCHRÖTER *Historie der Harmonie und Melodie*

SCHRÖTER *Von vollstimmigen und unbezifferten*

SECHTER *Abhandlung über die musikalisch-akustischen*

SECHTER *Vom Canon*

SECHTER *Miscellanea*

SOLER *Theórica, y práctica del temple*

SORGE *Die Melodie aus der Harmonie*

SWEELINCK *Kompositionsregeln*

TARTINI *Regola del terzo suono*

TARTINI *Ricerca del vero principio dell'armonia*

TOVEY *The Goldberg Variations: An Essay*

VALLOTTI *Contrappunto principii*

VALLOTTI *Dell'estensione e carattere*

VALLOTTI *Se il tuono minore naturale*

VALLOTTI *Undici bassi del prete Francescantonio Vallotti*

WALLIS *Letter dealing with a Greek manuscript*

YAVORSKY *Betkhoven: Variatsii do minor*

ZACCONI *Canoni musicali proprii*

ZACCONI *Paradigma musicale*

ZACCONI *Le regole di canto fermo*

TITLE INDEX

Abendländische Musikgeschichte im Rhythmus	LORENZ	*Allgemeine Theorie der schönen Künste*	SULZER
Abhandlung über das Rezitativ	SCHEIBE	*Die alte Musiklehre im Streit*	MARX
Abhandlung über die musikalisch-akustischen	SECHTER	*Alte und neue musicalischen Bibliothec*	WALTHER
Eine Abhandlung vom Kanon	RIEPEL	*L'anacrouse dans la musique moderne*	LUSSY
Abhandlung vom Ursprunge	SCHEIBE	*Analysen dreier Fugen aus J. S. Bach's*	DEHN
Abhandlung von den musicalischen Intervallen	SCHEIBE	*Analysis of J. S. Bach's Forty-Eight Fugues*	PROUT
Abhandlung von der Fuge	MARPURG	*Analytical Essay on Beethoven's Fidelio*	MACFARREN
À l'Académie des Beaux Arts	MOMIGNY	*Analytical Key to the Exercises*	PROUT
Académie royale des sciences	GEVAERT	*Andeutungen über meine Lehrmethode*	LOBE
Der accurate Organist im General-Baß	TREIBER	*Die Anfänge der Musik*	STUMPF
Addition au traité d'accompagnement	CAMPION, F.	*Anfangsgründe der theoretischen Musik*	MARPURG
Additional Exercises, Melodies	PROUT	*Anfangs-Gründe des General-Baßes*	MIZLER
Additional Exercises to Elementary Harmony	KITSON	*Anfangsgründe zur musicalischen Setz-kunst*	RIEPEL
Additional Exercises to Harmony	PROUT	*Anhang zu den hinweisen für die Bear-beitung*	JADASSOHN
Addresses and Lectures	MACFARREN	*Anleitung, wie man einer General-Baß*	TELEMANN, G. P.
Aletelogia di Leonardo Gallucio	BOTTRIGARI	*Anleitung zu der musikalischen Gelahrtheit*	ADLUNG
De algebra tractatus	WALLIS	*Anleitung zu Temperaturberechnung*	TÜRK
Allegro für das Clavier alleine	KIRNBERGER	*Anleitung zum Clavierspielen*	MARPURG
Der allezeit fertige	KIRNBERGER	*Anleitung zum Vortrag Beethovenscher*	MARX
Allgemeine Metrik der indoger-manischen	WESTPHAL	*Anleitung zur Erfindung der Melodie*	DAUBE
Allgemeine Musiklehre	JADASSOHN	*Anleitung zur Fantasie*	SORGE
Allgemeine Musiklehre	KREHL	*Anleitung zur Musik überhaupt*	MARPURG
Allgemeine Musiklehre: Ein Hülfsbuch	MARX	*Anleitung zur Singcomposition*	MARPURG
Allgemeine Musiklehre zum Selbst-unterricht	WEBER	*Anleitung zur Singekomposition*	KIRNBERGER
Allgemeine Theorie der musikalischen Rhythmik	WESTPHAL	*Anmerkung über Professor Euler's*	SORGE
		Annotation to Capt. Prencourt's Short	NORTH, R.
		Annotazioni sopra il compendio	DONI

Title	Author
L'antica musica ridotta	VICENTINO
Ant-Artusi	BOTTRIGARI
Anweisung, wie ein Musikus	QUANTZ
Anweisung zum Violinspielen	LÖHLEIN
Anweisung zur Fantasie	ADLUNG
Anweisung zur italienischen Tablatur	ADLUNG
Anweisung zur Singe-Kunst	PRINTZ
Anweisung zur Stimmung und Temperatur	SORGE
Apologia compendiaria fraternitatem	FLUDD
Application des sons harmoniques	SAUVEUR
Applied Forms: A Sequel	PROUT
Applied Strict Counterpoint	KITSON
Dell'arbore musicale	CERRETO
Arcani musicali	BERARDI
Architectonice musices universalis	SCHONSLEDER
Architecture harmonique	OUVRARD
Die Aristoxenische Rhythmuslehre	WESTPHAL
Aristoxenus von Tarent	WESTPHAL
L'armonico pratico al cimbalo	GASPARINI
Ars canendi	BARYPHONUS
Ars magna lucis et umbrae	KIRCHER
Ars magna sciendi	KIRCHER
L'art d'accompagner sur le basse continue	NIVERS
L'art de varier	REICHA
L'art de la basse fondamentale	RAMEAU
Art du compositeur dramatique	REICHA
L'art et la science des nombres	OUVRARD
The Art of Accompaniament	GEMINIANI
The Art of Counterpoint	KITSON
The Art of Fingering the Harpsichord	PASQUALI
The Art of Playing on the Violin	GEMINIANI
The Art of Playing the Guitar	GEMINIANI
L'arte armonica	GEMINIANI
Arte de canto llano	MONTANOS
Arte de musica theorica y pratica	MONTANOS
L'arte del contraponto	ARTUSI
Arte pratica di contrappunto	PAOLUCCI
Arte prattica et poëtica	HERBST
Articles in Grove's Dictionary	PROUT
Articles in the Encyclopédie	d'ALEMBERT
Articles on music	ZIEHN
Articles on music for Encyclopaedia Britannica	TOVEY
Articles on music in Allgemeine Enzyklopädia	WEBER
Articles on music in Deutsche Encyklopädie	VOGLER
Articles on music in the Encyclopédie	ROUSSEAU, J.-J.
De artis poeticae natura	VOSSIUS, G. J.
De artium et scientiarum natura	VOSSIUS, G. J.
L'Artusi overo delle imperfettioni	ARTUSI
An Attack on Romano Micheli's Canoni	SCACCHI
Aufgaben für den einfachen und doppelten	HAUPTMANN
Aufgaben für den Unterricht	LOUIS and THUILLE
Aufgaben und Beispiele für . . . Harmonielehre	JADASSOHN
Aufgaben und Beispiele für . . . Kontrapunkt	JADASSOHN
Der Ausdruck in der Musik	RIEMANN
Ausführliche und deutliche Anweisung	SORGE
Ausführlicher Bericht vom Gebrauch	BERNHARD
Ausspruch über den Orchester-Streit	KUHNAU
Ausweichungen von C-dur und C-moll	ALBRECHTSBERGER
Ausweichungs-Tabellen	SORGE
An Authentic Account of the Examination	LOGIER
J. S. Bach, Chromatische Phantasie und Fuge	SCHENKER
Baßschlüssel	RIEPEL
Bedenken über Herrn Sorges . . . Streit	SCHRÖTER
Beethoven	HALM
Beethoven	TOVEY
Beethoven Fünfte Sinfonie: Darstellung	SCHENKER
L. van Beethoven: Sonate, Op. 27, Nr. 2	SCHENKER.
Beethovens neunte Sinfonie: Eine Darstellung	SCHENKER

Beethoven's Ninth Symphony	TOVEY
Beethovens sämtliche Klavier-Solosonaten	RIEMANN
Beethoven's Streichquartette	RIEMANN
Beispiele und Aufgaben zum Kontrapunkt	KREHL
Beiträge zur Akustik	STUMPF
Ein Beitrag zur Ornamentik	SCHENKER
Beleuchtung einer Recension des Buches	TÜRK
Beleuchtung von der Frage	AGRICOLA, J. F.
Bellum musicale	SEBASTIANI
Bellum musicum oder musikalischer Krieg	BEER
Bemerkungen über den Gesangunterricht	BELLERMANN
Bemerkungen über den melodischen Gebrauch	BELLERMANN
Berliner allgemeine musikalische Zeitung	MARX
Das beschützte Orchestre	MATTHESON
Beste und leichteste Temperatur	NEIDHARDT
Betkhoven: Variatsii do minor	YAVORSKY
Betrachtungen der Mannheimer Tonschule	VOGLER
Betrachtungen über Beethovens Eroica-Skizzen	LORENZ
Beziehungen zwischen moderner Musik	WESTPHAL
Biographie universelle des musiciens	FÉTIS
Boethii de musica	GLAREAN
A Breefe Introduction to the Skill of Musick	PLAYFORD
Breve dichiarazione della battuta musicale	PISA
Breve discorso sopra la musica	SCACCHI
Breve regola per imparar' a sonare	BIANCIARDI
Brevia et facilia praecepta componendi	RAVN
Breviculum errorum musicorum	LIPPIUS
Brevis synopsis de modis	HOFFMANN
A Brief Introduction to the Art of Descant	PURCELL
A Briefe and Short Instruction	BEVIN
A Briefe Discourse	RAVENSCROFT
Briefe über den Unterricht	CZERNY
Bruckner	KURTH
Caecilia: Eine Zeitschrift	WEBER
De canendi elegantia, octodecim praecepta	QUITSCHREIBER
Vom Canon	SECHTER
Canoni musicali proprii	ZACCONI
Canoni sui principi elementare	SABBATINI, L. A.
Canonical Studies: A New Technic	ZIEHN
Carta escrita a un amigo	SOLER
Cartella, overo regole utilissime	BANCHIERI
Cartellina del canto fermo gregoriano	BANCHIERI
Catalogue des livres de musique	BROSSARD
Cent thèmes d'harmonie	d'INDY
Charodeika	ASAFIEV
Choral-System	VOGLER
Chromatic Harmony	PROUT
Chromatik und Tonalität	HALM
The Classical Concerto: Its Nature	TOVEY
Claudii Ptolemaei harmonicorum	WALLIS
Clavér Schola	VOGLER
Clavier-Schule	LÖHLEIN
Clavierschule für Anfänger	ALBRECHTSBERGER
Clavier-Schule, zweyter Band	LÖHLEIN
Clavierstücke mit einem practischen	MARPURG
Clavis ad thesaurum	JANOVKA
Clavis philosophiae et alchymiae	FLUDD
Code de musique pratique	RAMEAU
Cogita physico-mathematica	MERSENNE
A Collection of Church-Music	HOLDEN
Comiença el arte tripharia	BERMUDO
Comiença el libro llamado declaración	BERMUDO
Comiença el libro primero de la declaración	BERMUDO
Comments on Busoni's Entwurf	SCHOENBERG
A Companion to Beethoven's Pianoforte Sonatas	TOVEY
A Companion to The Art of Fugue	TOVEY
A Companion to the Royal Patent	LOGIER

Compendio del trattato	DONI
Il compendio della musica	TIGRINI
Compendio della teoria	MARTINI
Compendio nella theorica della musica	GALILEI
Compendiolum musicae	FABER
Compendium harmonicum	SORGE
Compendium modulatoriae	GIBELIUS
Compendium musicae	GUMPELZ-HAIMER
Compendium musicae	PRINTZ
Compendium musicae practicae	CALVISIUS
Compendium musicae signatoriae	PRINTZ
Compendium musices	COCLICO
Compendium musices	HERBST
Compendium musices theoretico-practicum	SCHEIBE
A Compendium of Practical Musick	SIMPSON
Compendium philosophium, exhibens methodum	ALSTED
A Compleat Melody	TANS'UR
Compositio harmonica problematice tradita	NEIDHARDT
Compositions-Lehre	LOBE
Conclusioni nel suono dell'organo	BANCHIERI
Conjecture sur la raison	EULER
Considérations sur l'étude de contre-point	FÉTIS
Consonanzen und Dissonanzen	LOBE
Construction der gleichschwebenden Temperatur	KIRNBERGER
Continuatio ad manuductionem organi-cam	SAMBER
Contrappunto principii	VALLOTTI
Der Contrapunct	BELLERMANN
Contrapuntal Harmony for Beginners	KITSON
Contrepoint	REICHA
Die Correlation zwischen Takt und Rhythmus	LUSSY
Correspondence with Martini	SOLER
Cort beduydsel vant zingen	BAN
Counterpoint: A Practical Course	MACFARREN
Counterpoint for Beginners	KITSON
Counterpoint: Strict and Free	PROUT
Cours complet d'harmonie et de com-position	MOMIGNY
Cours de composition musicale	d'INDY
Cours de composition musicale	REICHA
Cours de contre-point et de fugue	CHERUBINI
Cours de mélodie	REICHA
Cours de philosophie musicale	FÉTIS
Cours général de musique	MOMIGNY
A Course of Lectures on Orchestration	PROUT
Cribrum musicum	SCACCHI
Cribrum musicum	WERCKMEISTER
Critica fatta . . . intorno ai Supplimenti	GALILEI
Critica musica	MATTHESON
Der critische Musicus an der Spree	MARPURG
Der critische Musicus	SCHEIBE
Curiosités historiques de la musique	FÉTIS
Cursory Notes of Musicke	NORTH, R.
Cursus philosophici encyclopaedia	ALSTED
Data zur Akustik	VOGLER
Declaration oder weitere Erklärung	PRINTZ
Démonstration du principe de l'har-monie	RAMEAU
Der in der Rechen- und Meßkunst	SORGE
Descrizione dell'arciorgano	VICENTINO
Desiat' fug dlia fortepiano I. S. Bakha	WESTPHAL
Il desiderio, overo de' concerti	BOTTRIGARI
Deutliche Anweisung zum General-Baß	SCHRÖTER
Deutsche Musica für die Kinder	SCHNEEGASS
Deux traictez de musique	DONI
Du développement futur de la musique	FÉTIS
Dialoghi armonici pel contrapunto	CERRETO
Dialogo . . . della musica antica	GALILEI
Dialogo harmonico	CERRETO
Dialogo . . . ove si tratta della theorica	PONTIO
Dicerie musicali	BERARDI
Dichiaratione della lettera stampata	MONTEVERDI
Dictionaire des termes grecs, latine	BROSSARD
A Dictionary of Musical Terms	STAINER

Dictionnaire de musique	ROUSSEAU, J.-J.
Dictionnaire historique des musiciens	CHORON
Difesa della musica moderna	MANFREDINI
Dimostrationi harmoniche	ZARLINO
Direttorio del canto fermo	PENNA
Al direttorio monastico di canto fermo	BANCHIERI
Discorso intorno a diversi pareri che hebbero	GALILEI
Discorso . . . intorno all'opere di m. G. Zarlino	GALILEI
Discorso . . . intorno all'uso delle dissonanze	GALILEI
Discorso . . . intorno all'uso dell'enharmonio	GALILEI
Discorso musicale di Antonio Braccino	ARTUSI
Discorso particolare intorno alla diversita	GALILEI
Discorso particolare intorno all'unisono	GALILEI
Discorso secondo musicale di Antonio Braccino	ARTUSI
Discorso sopra la musica	MEI
Disputatio musica prima	LIPPIUS
Disputatio musica secunda	LIPPIUS
Disputatio musica tertia	LIPPIUS
Dissertatio de usu progressionis	MARTINI
Dissertatio epistolica de musicae natura	BAN
Dissertatio physica de sono	EULER
Dissertation sur la musique moderne	ROUSSEAU, J.-J.
Dissertation sur la chant grégorien	NIVERS
Dissertation sur le différentes métodes	RAMEAU
Dissertatio, quod musica ars	MIZLER
Die Dissonanz als musikalisiche Ausdrucksmittel	KREHL
Divers traitez sur la composition	MASSON
The Division-Violist	SIMPSON
Doctrina de tonis seu modis	HOFFMANN
Documenti armonici	BERARDI
Dodecachordon	GLAREAN
Don Lazarillo Vizcardi	EXIMENO
Double Counterpoint and Canon	PROUT
Das duale Harmoniesystem	OETTINGEN
Das duale System der Harmonie	OETTINGEN
Dubbi intorno	GALILEI
Dubbio . . . sopra il saggio fondamentale	EXIMENO
Un école de musique	d'INDY
Der edlen Music-Kunst Würde	WERCKMEISTER
Effets de l'air sur le corps humain	BÉTHIZY
Effets des circonstances sur la situation	FÉTIS
Eighty Musical Sentences	MACFARREN
Das eilfte Kapitel der Ars Cantus	BELLERMANN
Einfall, einer doppelten Contrapunct	BACH
Einführung in die Musik	HALM
Zur Einführung in J. S. Bachs Passions-Musik	JADASSOHN
Einige Bemerkungen über die consonirende	BELLERMANN
Einige Bemerkungen über Hucbald'schen	BELLERMANN
Élémens de musique	d'ALEMBERT
Élémens ou principes de musique	LOULIÉ
Elementale mathematicum musica	ALSTED
Elementar-Harmonielehre für den Schul-	JADASSOHN
Elementar-Musiklehre	RIEMANN
Elementar-Schulbuch der Harmonielehre	RIEMANN
Die Elementarkenntnisse zur Harmonielehre	RICHTER
Elementary Harmony	KITSON
Die Elemente der muiskalischen Aesthetik	RIEMANN
Elemente des musikalischen Rhythmus	WESTPHAL
Elementi teorici della musica	SABBATINI, L. A.
Elementi teorico-pratici di musica	GALEAZZI
The Elements of Fugal Construction	KITSON
The Elements of Musical Composition	KITSON
Elements of Speech	HOLDER
Éléments ou principes de musique	LOULIÉ
Elementy stroeniia muzykal'noi rechi	YAVORSKY
Élévations et motets à voix seule	BROSSARD
Elucidatio musicae choralis	SAMBER
Encyclopaedia septem tonus distincta	ALSTED

Encyclopédie méthodique	MOMIGNY
L'enseignement de la musique par l'éducation	GÉDALGE
L'enseignement musical	DUBOIS
Entwurf einer neuen . . . Musiktablatur	SCHULZ
Entwurf eines neuen Wörterbuchs	VOGLER
Epistola ad Excellentissimum	SCACCHI
Erläuternde Anmerkungen . . . der Harmonie	JADASSOHN
Erläuternde Anmerkungen . . . des Contrapunkts	JADASSOHN
Erläuterungen der in Joh. Seb. Bachs Kunst	JADASSOHN
Erläuterungen zu Ausgewählten Fugen	JADASSOHN
Erläuterungen zu J. S. Bachs Kunst	HAUPTMANN
Erneuerter Versuch einer Begriffsbestimmung	WEBER
Erreurs sur la musique dans l'Encyclopédie	RAMEAU
Erste musikalische Preisaustheilung	VOGLER
Esame d'uno scolaro del Padre L. A. Sabbatini	SABBATINI, L. A.
Escuela música	NASSARRE
Esemplare o sia saggio fondamentale	MARTINI
Esquisse de l'histoire de l'harmonie	FÉTIS
Essai sur l'origine des langues	ROUSSEAU, J.-J.
Essais sur les principes de l'harmonie	SERRE
An Essay of Musicall Ayre	NORTH, R.
An Essay on Earl Stanhope's Principles	KOLLMANN
An Essay on Musical Harmony	KOLLMANN
An Essay on Practical Musical Composition	KOLLMANN
An Essay to the Advancement of Musick	SALMON
An Essay towards a Rational System	HOLDEN
Essays in Musical Analysis (1903)	TOVEY
Essays in Musical Analysis	TOVEY
Essays in Musical Analysis: Chamber Music	REICHA
Dell'estensione e carattere	VALLOTTI
Études ou exercises pour le piano-forte	REICHA
Études pour le piano-forte	REICHA
Etymologicon linguae latinae praefigitur	VOSSIUS, G. J.
Euclides von der Harmonie	SCHRÖTER
Eugenii Onegin	ASAFIEV
The Evolution of Harmony	KITSON
Examen de deux principes	ROUSSEAU, J.-J.
Exempla dissonantiarum ligatarum	FUX
Exemplarische Organisten-Probe	MATTHESON
Exercitatio musica tertia	CALVISIUS
Exercitationes musicae duae	CALVISIUS
Exercitationes musicae theoretico-practicae	PRINTZ
An Explanation . . . of the Royal Patent	LOGIER
Exposé succinct de seul systême musical	MOMIGNY
Exposition de la théorie	BÉTHIZY
Extrait d'une réponse de M. Rameau	RAMEAU
Das Finale in Mozarts Meisteropern	LORENZ
The First Beginning on the Piano Forte	KOLLMANN
Forma musices	DEMANTIUS
Die formale Gestaltung des Vorspiels	LORENZ
Der formale Schwung in R. Strauss' Till	LORENZ
Die Form in der Musik	MARX
Das forschende Orchestre	MATTHESON
Forty-Eight Preludes and Fugues by J. S. Bach	TOVEY
Fragmentos musicos: Reglas generales	NASSARRE
Fragments d'une méthode de violon	BROSSARD
Fragments harmoniques	REICHA
Franconis de Colonia Artis cantus	BELLERMANN
Der freie Satz	SCHENKER
Fronimo: Dialogo	GALILEI
Frutto salutifero	BANCHIERI
Fünf- und sechsstimmige Harmonien	ZIEHN
Fünf Urlinie-Tafeln	SCHENKER
Fugal Analysis: A Companion to Fugue	PROUT
Fuge: Erläuterung und Anleitung	KREHL
Der Fugen-Betrachtung	RIEPEL
Fugue	PROUT
La fugue et la contrepoint	REICHA
Fundamenta compositionis	KUHNAU

Fundamentals of Musical Composition	SCHOENBERG
Gäntzlich erschöpfte	NEIDHARDT
Gedanken eines Liebhabers der Tonkunst	BACH
Gedanken über den Einfluß der Musik	SCHULZ
Gedanken über die verschiedenen Lehrarten	KIRNBERGER
Gedanken und Studien	LORENZ
Die geheim gehaltene Kunst der Mensuration	SORGE
Das Geheimnis der Form bei Richard Wagner	LORENZ
Der Geist der musikalischen Technik	SCHENKER
Genealogia allegorica intervallorum	SORGE
Der Generalbaß: Eine Anleitung	JADASSOHN
Der General-Bass in der Composition	HEINICHEN
General-Baß in drey Accorden	DAUBE
Generalbass- und Harmonielehre	ALBRECHTS-BERGER
Die Generalbaßlehre zum Selbstunterricht	WEBER
Génération harmonique	RAMEAU
Gesangschule/Singing Tutor	JADASSOHN
Geschichte der Harmonie und ihrer Lehre	WEITZMANN
Geschichte der Musiktheorie	RIEMANN
Geschichte des Konsonanzbegriffes	STUMPF
Geschichte des Septimen-Akkordes	WEITZMANN
Gespräch zwischen einem Musico theoretico	SORGE
The Goldberg Variations: An Essay	TOVEY
Gradus ad Parnassum	FUX
Von Grenzen und Ländern der Musik	HALM
Die Größe der musikalischen Intervalle	BELLERMANN
Grosse General-Bass-Schule	MATTHESON
Große Kompositionslehre	RIEMANN
Gründliche Anleitung zum Klavier-Stimmen	VOGLER
Gründliche Anweisung zur Composition	ALBRECHTS-BERGER
Gründliche Untersuchung	SORGE
Die Grundlage der Musikwissenschaft	OETTINGEN
Grundlage einer Ehren-Pforte	MATTHESON
Grundlagen des linearen Kontrapunkts	KURTH
Grund-richtiger, kurtz, leicht	SPEER
Die Grundsätze der musikalischen Komposition	SECHTER
Die Grundsätze der praktischen Harmonie	REICHA
Grundsätze des Generalbaäes	KIRNBERGER
Die Grundzüge der musikalischen Formen	RICHTER
Gültige Zeugnisse	MATTHESON
Guida armonica	GEMINIANI
Guida ossia dizionario armonico	GASPARINI
Handbuch bey dem Generalbasse	MARPURG
Handbuch bey dem Studium der Harmonie	KOCH
Handbuch zur Harmonielehre	VOGLER
De harmoniae veris principiis	EULER
Harmonices mundi	KEPLER
Harmonicorum instrumentorum libri IV	MERSENNE
Harmonicorum libri	MERSENNE
L'harmonie pratique	ROUSSIER
Harmonie. — Systèmes.	CHORON
Harmonie- und Modulationslehre	ZIEHN
Harmonie universelle	MERSENNE
Harmonielehre	HALM
Harmonielehre	LOUIS and THUILLE
Harmonielehre	SCHOENBERG
Harmonielehre [Tonalitätslehre]	KREHL
Harmoniesystem: Erklärende Erläuterung	WEITZMANN
Harmoniesystem in dualer Entwickelung	OETTINGEN
Harmonisches Syllbenmaß	RIEPEL
Harmonologia musica	WERCKMEISTER
Harmony: Its Theory and Practice	PROUT
Haute composition musicale	REICHA
Heinrich Schenker	HALM
Heinrich Schenkers Neue musikalische Theorien	HALM

Heptachordum danicum seu nova solsisatio	RAVN
Die Hilfsmittel der Modulation	RIEMANN
Histoire de la notation musicale	LUSSY
Histoire et théorie de la musique	GEVAERT
Historia musica	BONTEMPI
Historie der Harmonie und Melodie	SCHRÖTER
Historische Beschreibung	PRINTZ
Historisch-kritische Beyträge zur Aufnahme	MARPURG
Homophone Großrhythmik in Bachs Polyphonie	LORENZ
Hrn. Johann Joachim Quanzens Antwort	QUANTZ
Hypomnemata musica	WERCKMEISTER
Hypomnematum musicae poeticae	BURMEISTER
Hugo Riemanns Analysen von Beethovens	HALM
Ideen zu einer Lehre	RIEMANN
Impresa del molto Rev. G. Zarlino	ARTUSI
Der Inhalt des Arbeitsheftes	TANEEV
Inledning til harmoniens kännedom	VOGLER
Institución harmónica	ROEL DEL RÍO
Institution harmonique	CAUS
Institutiones musico-theoricae	BARYPHONUS
Institutiones poeticae	VOSSIUS, G. J.
Instrumentation	PROUT
Instrumentationslehre	SCHOENBERG
Instrumentations-Tabelle	SCHENKER
Instrumentum instrumentorum	GRIMM
Intorno alle quinte successive	MARTINI
Introductio musicae theoreticae didacticae	GIBELIUS
Introduction à l'étude de l'harmonie	FÉTIS
Introduction à l'étude générale et raisonnée	CHORON
An Introduction to Extemporary Modulation	KOLLMANN
An Introduction to the Art of Preluding	KOLLMANN
Introductione facilissima	LUSITANO
Invertible Counterpoint and Canon	KITSON
Isagoge artis musicae	DEMANTIUS
Isagoge in musicen	GLAREAN
Isagoge musica	BARYPHONUS
Isagoges musicae libri duo	SCHNEEGASS
Isagoges musicae, non ita pridem	SCHNEEGASS
Iskusstvo i ritm: Greki i Vagner	WESTPHAL
Le istituzioni harmoniche	ZARLINO
Itinerarium exstaticum quo mundi	KIRCHER
Joannis Tinctoris: Terminorum musicae	BELLERMANN
Johannes Brahms, Oktaven und Quinten	SCHENKER
Journal der Tonkunst	KOCH
Judicium cribri musici	SCACCHI
Katechismus der Akustik	RIEMANN
Katechismus der Compositionslehre	LOBE
Katechismus der Fugen-Komposition	RIEMANN
Katechismus der Gesangkomposition	RIEMANN
Katechismus der Harmonie- und Modulationslehre	RIEMANN
Katechismus der Kompositionslehre	RIEMANN
Katechismus der Musik	LOBE
Katechismus der Musik (Allgemeine Musiklehre)	RIEMANN
Katechismus der Musikinstrumente	RIEMANN
Katechismus der Orchestrierung	RIEMANN
Katechismus der Phrasierung	RIEMANN
Katechismus des Generalbaß-Spiele	RIEMANN
Katechismus des Musik-Diktats	RIEMANN
Kern melodischer Wissenschaft	MATTHESON
Key to the Additional Exercises	PROUT
Key to the Exercises in "Harmony"	PROUT
Klang	HAUPTMANN
Klangmischung in Anton Bruckners Orchester	LORENZ
Klavierschule	TÜRK
Kleine General-Bass-Schule	MATTHESON
Kleines Handbuch der Musikgeschichte	RIEMANN
Kleines Lehrbuch für Anfänger	TÜRK
Kniga o Stravinskom	ASAFIEV
Kommentar zu Ph. E. Bach's Versuch	SCHENKER

Das Komponieren mit selbständigen Stimmen	SCHOENBERG
Kompositionsregeln	SWEELINCK
Kompositionsunterricht und moderne Musik	KREHL
Kontrapunkt: Die Lehre	KREHL
Kort sangh-bericht	BAN
Kosmothoros	HUYGENS
Kratkii uchebnik garmonii	CHAIKOVSKY
Kritische Briefe über die Tonkunst	MARPURG
Die Kunst des Clavier zu spielen	MARPURG
Die Kunst der Fuge	TOVEY
Kunst der praktischen Harmonie	REICHA
Kunst des Gesanges, theoretisch-praktisch	MARX
Die Kunst des Präludirens	CZERNY
Die Kunst des reinen Satzes	KIRNBERGER
Die Kunst des Vortrags	CZERNY
Die Kunst des Vortrags	SCHENKER
Die Kunst zu moduliren	JADASSOHN
Kurtzer, doch ausführlicher Bericht	MATTHAEI
Kurtzer, jedoch gründlicher Bericht	GIBELIUS
Kurtzer und verstendtlicher Unterricht	CRÜGER
Kurze Anweisung zum Generalbaß-spielen	TÜRK
Kurze doch deutliche Anleitung	AHLE
Kurze Erklärung des Canonis harmonici	SORGE
Kurze Regeln des reinsten Satzes	ALBRECHTS-BERGER
Kurzer Bericht waß bey uberliefferung	PRAETORIUS
Kurzgefaßte Harmonielehre	RIEMANN
Kurzgefaßte Methode den Generalbaß	ALBRECHTS-BERGER
Leçons de musique	ROUSSEAU, J.-J.
Leçons de solfège à changements	DUBOIS
Leerboek der harmonij en begeleiding	GEVAERT
Leerboek van den Gregoriaenschen zang	GEVAERT
Lehrbuch der Fuge	RICHTER
Lehrbuch der Harmonie	RICHTER
Lehrbuch der musikalischen Komposition	LOBE
Lehrbuch des einfachen, doppelten	RIEMANN
Lehrbuch des einfachen und doppelten	RICHTER
Lehre vom Contrapunkt	DEHN
Die Lehre von den Tonempfindungen	HELMHOLTZ
Die Lehre von der Harmonik	HAUPTMANN
Die Lehre von der musikalische Komposition	MARX
Die Lehre von Kontrapunkt	SCHOENBERG
Leichtes Lehrbuch der Harmonie	PORTMANN
Letter dealing with a Greek manuscript	WALLIS
A Letter . . . to Mr. Andrew Fletcher	WALLIS
A Letter . . . to Samuel Pepys Esquire	WALLIS
Lettera apologetica del burla	ARTUSI
Lettera del defonto signor Giuseppe Tartini	TARTINI
Lettera di Federico Verdicelli	BOTTRIGARI
Lettera per maggiore informazione	SCACCHI
Lettere armoniche	BANCHIERI
Lettere di un accademico filarmonico	MARTINI
Letters from a Tutor to His Pupils	JONES
Lettre à M. d'Alembert	RAMEAU
Lettre . . . à Monsieur de Voltaire	CAMPION, F.
Lettre à Monsieur l'Abbé Raynal	ROUSSEAU, J.-J.
Lettre . . . à un philosophe	CAMPION, F.
Lettre au R. P. Castel	RAMEAU
Lettre aux Philosophes	RAMEAU
Lettre en forme de dissertation	BROSSARD
Lettre . . . sur l'acception des mots	ROUSSIER
Lettre sur la musique françoise	ROUSSEAU, J.-J.
Lettre . . . sur la nature d'un mode	SERRE
Lettre . . . touchant la division du zodiaque	ROUSSIER
Lettres à une princesse d'Allemagne	EULER
Die letzten fünf Sonaten Beethovens	SCHENKER
Letzte Beschäftigung mit musicalischen Dingen	SCHRÖTER
De la liberté de la musique	d'ALEMBERT
Libro del contrapunto	TARTINI
Libro llamado arte de tañer fantasia	SANTA MARÍA
Livre de la nature des sons	MERSENNE

Llave de la modulación	SOLER	*Méthode dans l'enseignement de l'harmonie*	FÉTIS
Das Locheimer Liederbuch nebst der Art	BELLERMANN	*Méthode de chant du Conservatoire*	LANGLÉ
Ludwig van Beethoven: Sonatas for Pianoforte	TOVEY	*Méthode de piano à l'aide*	MOMIGNY
Lusus ingenii de praesenti bello	MIZLER	*Méthode élémentaire et abregée d'harmonie*	FÉTIS
Lyra Barberina	DONI	*Méthode facile pour apprendre à chanter*	NIVERS
Magnes sive de arte magnetica	KIRCHER	*Méthode générale pour former les systêmes*	SAUVEUR
The Main Stream of Music	TOVEY		
La mano et documenti	BANCHIERI	*Méthode pratique d'harmonie*	CHORON
A Manual Chiefly for the Use of Preceptors	LOGIER	*Methode, Sonaten aus'm Ermel*	KIRNBERGER
Manuductio ad organum	SAMBER	*Methodik und Harmonik bei Richard Wagner*	JADASSOHN
Manuel des compositeurs	FÉTIS	*Methodus admirandorum mathematicorum*	ALSTED
Marches d'harmonie pratiquées	CHERUBINI		
Mathematische Beschreibung	SORGE	*Metrik der griechischen Dramatiker*	WESTPHAL
Mehrstimmigkeit oder Einstimmigkeit	WESTPHAL	*Miscellanea*	SECHTER
Das Meisterwerk in der Musik	SCHENKER	*Miscellanea musicale*	BERARDI
Die Melodie aus der Harmonie	SORGE	*Models for Beginners in Composition*	SCHOENBERG
Melodik und Harmonik bei Richard Wagner	JADASSOHN	*Modern Harmony from the Standpoint*	KITSON
		De modis musicis antiquorum	MEI
The Melody of the Heart	TANS'UR	*Monochordum mundi symphoniacum*	FLUDD
The Melody of the Hundredth Psalm	KOLLMANN	*Zur Motivbildung Bachs: Ein Beitrag*	KURTH
Il Melone: Discorso armonico	BOTTRIGARI	*Music in Its Relation to the Intellect*	STAINER
La mélopée antique dans la chant	GEVAERT	*Musica autoschediastike*	BURMEISTER
El melopeo y maestro	CERONE	*La musica ecclesiastica*	AGAZZARI
Melopoiia sive melodiae	CALVISIUS	*De musica libri septem*	SALINAS
Melothesia; or, Certain General Rules	LOCKE	*Musica mechanica organoedi*	ADLUNG
Mémoire ou l'on expose les fondemens	RAMEAU	*Musica modulatoria vocalis*	PRINTZ
Mémoire sur la musique des anciens	ROUSSIER	*Musica poetica*	BURMEISTER
Mémoire sur la musique des chinois	ROUSSIER	*Musica poetica*	FABER
Mémoire sur la nouvelle harpe	ROUSSIER	*Musica poëtica*	HERBST
Mémoire sur le nouveau clavecin	ROUSSIER	*Musica practica*	HERBST
Memoires of Musick	NORTH, R.	*De musica quatuor prioes libri*	SALINAS
Una memoria di varie decisioni teorico	VALLOTTI	*Musica theorica Henrici Brucaei*	BURMEISTER
Die Mensuralnoten und Taktzeichen	BELLERMANN	*Musicae activae micrologus*	ORNITHOPARCHUS
Meslanges et extraits relatifs à l'histoire	BROSSARD		
Méthode certaine pour apprendre le pleinchant	NIVERS	*Musicae artis praecepta nova*	CALVISIUS
		Musicae compendium	DESCARTES
Méthode claire, certaine et facile	ROUSSEAU, J.	*Musicae epitome sive compendium*	GLAREAN

Musicae mathematicae Hodegus curiosus	WERCKMEISTER
Musicae practicae elementa	DRESSLER
Musicae practicae praecepta	HOFFMANN
Musicae practicae praecepta brevia	CRÜGER
Musicae practicae sive artis canendi	BURMEISTER
Musical Form	PROUT
Musical Form: A Paper	PROUT
Musical Form and Matter	TOVEY
Musicalische Discurse	BEER
Musicalische Handleitung	NIEDT
Musicalische Paradoxal-Discourse	WERCKMEISTER
Der musicalische Quack-Salber	KUHNAU
Musicalische Temperatur	WERCKMEISTER
Musicalische Vorstellung	KUHNAU
Musicalisches ABC zum Nutzen	NIEDT
Musicalisches Lexicon	WALTHER
A Musicall Banquet	PLAYFORD
The Musicall Gramarian	NORTH, R.
Ad musicam practicam	FABER
Musicbüchlein für die Jugend	QUITSCHREIBER
Musices liber tertius	SALINAS
Musices poeticae	NUCIUS
Musices theoreticae systema	EULER
A Musican Talks	TOVEY
Musick's Monument	MACE
Musico prattico	BONONCINI
Il musico testore	TEVO
Musikalische Briefe: Wahrheit über Tonkunst	LOBE
Der musikalische Dilettant	DAUBE
Musikalische Dynamik und Agogik	RIEMANN
Musikalische Formenlehre (Kompositionslehre)	KREHL
Der musikalische Gedanke und die Logik	SCHOENBERG
Musikalische Grammatik	RIEMANN
Musikalische Kompositionslehre	JADASSOHN
Musikalische Logik: Ein Beitrag	RIEMANN
Musikalische Syntaxis	RIEMANN
Der musikalischen Intervallen Anzahl	SCHRÖTER
Musikalischer Rathgeber	SECHTER
Musikalischer Staarstecher	MIZLER
Musikalischer Unterricht	PORTMANN
Musikalisches Frühlings-gespräche	AHLE
Musikalisches Herbst-gespräche	AHLE
Musikalisches Lexikon	KOCH
Musikalisches Siebengestirn	ADLUNG
Musikalisches Sommer-gespräche	AHLE
Musikalisches Winter-gespräche	AHLE
Musikpsychologie	KURTH
Musikpsychologie in England	STUMPF
Die Musik des griechischen Alterthums	WESTPHAL
Die Musik des neunzehnten Jahrhunderts	MARX
Musik-Lexikon: Theorie und Geschichte	RIEMANN
La musique mise à la portée	FÉTIS
La musique rétablie depuis son origine	OUVRARD
La musique universelle	DU COUSU
Musurgia universalis	KIRCHER
Muzykal'naia forma kak protsess	ASAFIEV
Muzykal'naia forma kak protsess, kn. 2-aia	ASAFIEV
Nachricht von dem gegenwärtigen Zustande	MOZART
Die Natur der Harmonik	RIEMANN
Die Natur der Harmonik und der Metrik	HAUPTMANN
The Nature and Excellence of Music	JONES
De la nécessité de résumer les ... formes	FÉTIS
Neu erfundene und gründliche Anweisung	HEINICHEN
Neu eröffnete musikalische Bibliothek	MIZLER
Neue Beiträge zu einer Lehre	RIEMANN
Neue Formerkenntnisse	LORENZ
Neue Gedanken zur Klangspaltung	LORENZ
Eine neue Harmonielehre	LOUIS and THUILLE
Die neue Harmonielehre im Streit	WEITZMANN
Neue Methode, allerley Arten	MARPURG

Neue musikalische Theorien und Phantasien	SCHENKER
Neue rationelle Gesangschule	OETTINGEN
Neue Schule der Harmonik	RIEMANN
Neue Schule der Melodik	RIEMANN
Zur neueren literatur über die Reform	LUSSY
Das neu-eröffnete Orchestre	MATTHESON
Neues musikalisches System	TELEMANN, G. P.
Die neuesten und wichtigsten Entdeckungen	PORTMANN
A New Musical Grammar	TANS'UR
A New System of Arithmetick	MALCOLM
A New Theory of Musical Harmony	KOLLMANN
A New Way of Making Fowre Parts	CAMPION, T.
Nomenclatura musicale	MARTINI
De nomi delle corde del monochordo	MEI
Normality and Freedom in Music	TOVEY
Note sur un point de l'histoire	FÉTIS
Notes et études d'harmonie	DUBOIS
Notes et exemples musicaux sur la permutation	REICHA
Notes of Me	NORTH, R.
Nothwendige Anmerkung bey der Musik	MUFFAT
Die nothwendigsten Anmerkungen und Regeln	WERCKMEISTER
Notker Labeo, von der Musik	BELLERMANN
Nouveau manuel complet de musique vocale	CHORON
Nouveau sistème de musique	LOULIÉ
Le nouveau solfège avec accompagnement	MOMIGNY
Nouveau système de musique théorique	RAMEAU
Nouveau traité de l'accompagnement	SAINT-LAMBERT
Nouveau traité des regles	MASSON
Nouvelle méthode pour chiffrer les accords	LANGLÉ
Nouvelles réflexions de M. Rameau	RAMEAU
Nova et exquisita monochordi dimensio	SCHNEEGASS
Nova quatuor vocibus componendi methodus	BONTEMPI
Novarum observationum physico-mathematicarum	MERSENNE
Novus cyclus harmonicus	HUYGENS
Nucleus musicus	WERCKMEISTER
Nucleus musicus de modi	THURINGUS
Le nuove musiche	CACCINI
O muzyke gorskikh tatar	TANEEV
Die objektive Existenz der Untertöne	RIEMANN
Observations de M. Rameau	RAMEAU
Observations sur différens points d'harmonie	ROUSSIER
Observations sur le toucher	NIVERS
Observations sur les principes de l'harmonie	SERRE
Observations sur notre instinct	RAMEAU
Observations upon a Late Book	LOCKE
Oedipus aegyptiacus	KIRCHER
On Some Italian and Spanish Treatises	OUSELEY
On the Early Italian and Spanish Treatises	OUSELEY
Onomasticum, seu synopsis musicarum	MARTINI
Operum mathematicorum pars prima	WALLIS
Operum mathematicorum volumen tertium	WALLIS
Opinioni de' cantori antichi	TOSI
Opuscula: Vermischte Aufsätze	HAUPTMANN
Opusculum bipartitum de primordriis musicis	THURINGUS
Oratio de divina origine	EICHMANN
The Orchestra	PROUT
Organist-Schola	VOGLER
L'organo suonarino	BANCHIERI
Organum Gruningense redivivum	WERCKMEISTER
Organum mathematicum	KIRCHER
Orgel-Probe	WERCKMEISTER
Origine des sciences	RAMEAU
Dell'origine e delle regole della musica	EXIMENO
Les origines de la tonalité moderne	GEVAERT
Les origines du chant liturgique	GEVAERT
Osnovnye elementy muzyki	YAVORSKY
Osnovy orkestrovki	RIMSKY-KORSAKOV
Paradigma musicale	ZACCONI

De parodia tractatus musicalis	QUITSCHREIBER	*Prakticheskii uchebnik garmonii*	RIMSKY-KORSAKOV
Les passions de l'âme	DESCARTES	*Praktische Beispiele: Ein Beitrag*	REICHA
Il Patricio overo de' tetracordi	BOTTRIGARI	*Die praktischen Studien zur Theorie*	RICHTER
Il perché musicale	BERARDI	*Prattica di musica*	ZACCONI
Petit manuel théorique de l'harmonie	DUBOIS	*Prattica di musica seconda parte*	ZACCONI
Petit traité d'harmonie pratique	REICHA	*Della prattica musica*	CERRETO
Philosophiae verae ac sincerae synop-ticae	LIPPIUS	*A Preface: Forty-Eight Preludes and Fugues*	TOVEY
A Philosophical Essay of Musick	NORTH, F.	*Preface to Apparatus Musico-Organisti-cus*	MUFFAT
Phonurgia nova	KIRCHER	*Preface to Außerlesener*	MUFFAT
Die Phrasierung im Lichte einer Lehre	RIEMANN	*Preface to Fortsetzung des Har-monischen*	TELEMANN, G. P.
Phrasierungsausgabe	RIEMANN	*Preface to Gespräch von der Musik*	MIZLER
Phrynis Mytilenaeus	PRINTZ	*Preface to Il quinto libro*	MONTEVERDI
Phthongologia systematica	MATTHESON	*Preface to Musikalisches Lob Gottes*	TELEMANN, G. P.
Physiologia Kircheriana experimentalis	KIRCHER	*Preface to Suavioris harmoniae . . . primum*	MUFFAT
Physiological disquisitions	JONES	*Preface to Suavioris harmoniae . . . secundum*	MUFFAT
A Plaine and Easie Introduction	MORLEY	*Preface to the Cento concerti*	VIADANA
Platos Beziehungen zur Musik	WESTPHAL	*Preliminary Exercises in Counterpoint*	SCHOENBERG
Pleiades musicae	BARYPHONUS	*Les préludes de l'harmonie universelle*	MERSENNE
Plus ultra, ein Stückwerk	MATTHESON	*La première année de leçons de piano-forte*	MOMIGNY
Plutarch: Über die Musik	WESTPHAL	*Première lettre à M. Halévy*	FÉTIS
Podvizhnoi kontrapunkt strogogo pis'ma	TANEEV	*The Present Practice of Music Vindi-cated*	LOCKE
De poematum cantu et viribus rhythmi	VOSSIUS, I.	*Prima parte de' discorsi*	BONINI
Poeticarum institutionum	VOSSIUS, G. J.	*Li primi albori musicali*	PENNA
Polemic with Michel Pignolet de Monté-clair	RAMEAU	*Primo libro della prattica del con-trapunto*	GALILEI
El porqué de la música	LORENTE	*Principes d'accompagnement des écoles d'Italie*	CHORON
Practica modorum explicatio	DRESSLER	*Principes de composition des écoles d'Italie*	CHORON
Practica musica	FINCK	*Principes de la nature*	LEIBNIZ
A Practical Guide to Thorough-Bass	KOLLMANN	*Les principes du clavecin*	SAINT-LAMBERT
Practische Generalbaß-Schule	SECHTER	*Principes élémentaires de musique*	LANGLÉ
Practische und im Zusammenhange	SECHTER	*Il principiante fanciullo*	BANCHIERI
Praecepta der musikalischen Composi-tion	WALTHER	*Li principii della composizione*	GASPARINI
Praecepta musicae poeticae	DRESSLER	*De' principj dell'armonia*	TARTINI
Praecepta musicae practicae	EICHMANN		
Praecepta musicae practicae figuralis	CRÜGER		
Präludien und Studien	RIEMANN		
De praestantia musicae veteris	DONI		

The Principles of Musik	BUTLER
The Principles of Practical Music	SIMPSON
Pro suo opere harmonice mundi	KEPLER
Das Problem des harmonischen Dualismus	RIEMANN
Probleme der Harmonie	SCHOENBERG
Problèmes musicaux d'Aristote	GEVAERT
Prodromus dissertationum cosmographicarum	KEPLER
Programme of a Public Examination	LOGIER
Projet concernant de nouveaux signes	ROUSSEAU, J.-J.
Projet d'organisation des études	d'INDY
A Proposal to Perform Musick	SALMON
Proposals for Publishing by Subscription	KOLLMANN
Propositiones mathematico-musicae	GIBELIUS
Prospectus of the Musical Academy	LOGIER
Prospectus, où l'on propose au public	RAMEAU
Die pseudo-aristotelischen Probleme	STUMPF
Quaestiones celeberrimae in Genesim	MERSENNE
Quaestiones musicae practicae	CRÜGER
Quarta exercitatio musicalis	QUITSCHREIBER
The Quarterly Musical Register	KOLLMANN
Quatre-vingt-sept leçons d'harmonie	DUBOIS
De quatuor artibus popularibus	VOSSIUS, G. J.
A Question of Musick	WALLIS
Questions harmoniques	MERSENNE
Questions inouyes	MERSENNE
Questions sur la diversité d'opinions	FÉTIS
Les questions théologiques	MERSENNE
Ragionamenti musicali	BERARDI
Ragionamento di musica	PONTIO
Les raisons des forces mouvantes	CAUS
Rapport des sons des cordes	SAUVEUR
Rapport sur un mémoire	d'ALEMBERT
Les rapports de l'harmonie et du contrepoint	GÉDALGE
Ratschläge und Hinweise	JADASSOHN
Razbor Snegurochki	RIMSKY-KORSAKOV
Razón naturel, i científica de la música	ROEL DEL RÍO
Réalisations des basses et chants	DUBOIS
Recherches sur la courbe	d'ALEMBERT
Recueil d'airs de danse	KIRNBERGER
Recueil d'extraits d'ouvrages imprimés	BROSSARD
Réflexions sur la manière de former la voix	RAMEAU
Réflexions sur la supposition	SERRE
Réflexions sur la théorie de la musique	d'ALEMBERT
Refutation des Satyrischen Componistens	PRINTZ
A Refutation of the Fallacies	LOGIER
Register über die in allen vier Theilen	SULZER
Regola agli organisti per accompagnare	MARTINI
Regola del terzo suono	TARTINI
Regola facile e breve	SABBATINI, G.
Regola per bene accordare il violino	TARTINI
Regole armoniche	MANFREDINI
Le regole di canto fermo	ZACCONI
Regole per arrivare a saper ben suonar	TARTINI
Le regole più necessarie	CERONE
Regulae concentuum partiturae	MUFFAT
The Relation of Musical Theory to Practice	PROUT
Das Relativitätsprinzip in den . . . Formen	LORENZ
Remarques curieuses sur l'art de bien chanter	BACILLY
Remarques . . . sur les observations	ROUSSIER
Reparos musicos precisos	ROEL DEL RÍO
Replies to Labbat's review of Rameau	ROUSSIER
Réponse . . . à la lettre	ROUSSEAU, J.
Réponse à M. Fétis sur l'origine	GEVAERT
Réponse de M. Rameau à MM. les éditeurs	RAMEAU
Report on Rameau's Theoretical Writings	MARTINI
Résumé philosophique de l'histoire	FÉTIS
Review of Esteban Arteaga's Le rivoluzioni	MANFREDINI
Des révolutions de l'orchestre	FÉTIS
Revue musicale	FÉTIS

Ricerca del vero principio dell'armonia	TARTINI
Risposta al giudizio delle Efemeridi	EXIMENO
Risposta . . . alla critica	TARTINI
Romantische Harmonik und ihre Krise	KURTH
The Royal Melody Compleat	TANS'UR
Rudimenta musicae	LISTENIUS
The Rudiments of Harmony	MACFARREN
Rudiments of Music	KITSON
Rudiments of Music for Junior Classes	KITSON
Rukovodstvo k praticheskomu	CHAIKOVSKY
Rules for Playing a Thorough Bass	KELLER
Rules for Playing in a True Taste	GEMINIANI
Rules for to Play a Thorough Bass	PEPUSCH
Rules How to Compose	COPRARIO
Rules on figured bass	EBNER
Rules, or a Short and Compleat Method	PEPUSCH
Le rythme musical: Son origine	LUSSY
Sammelbände für . . . Musikwissen-schaft	STUMPF
La sampogna musicale	BANCHIERI
Satisfacción a los reparos precisos	SOLER
Die Schlüssel im ersten Buche	BELLERMANN
Schlüssel zu den Aufgaben	JADASSOHN
Schlüssel zum Harmonielehre	LOUIS and THUILLE
Die schönen Künste	SULZER
Schola phonologica	BEER
Die Schule der praktischen Tonsetz-kunst	CZERNY
Scientiarum omnium encyclopaediae	ALSTED
La scienza platonica	TARTINI
Della scienza teorica	VALLOTTI
Scriptores metrici graeci	WESTPHAL
Se il tuono minore naturale	VALLOTTI
Seconda parte del transilvano	DIRUTA
Seconda parte dell'arte del contraponto	ARTUSI
Seconda parte dell'Artusi	ARTUSI
Second Practical Guide to Thorough-Bass	KOLLMANN
Secret pour composer en musique	OUVRARD
Sectio canonis harmonici	NEIDHARDT
Seminarium modulatoriae vocalis	GIBELIUS
Sem' fug dlia fortepiano I. S. Bakha	WESTPHAL
Sendschreiben an die Verfasser	SCHRÖTER
Sendschreiben an . . . Mizler	SCHRÖTER
Sendschreiben . . . über den Kern	SCHEIBE
Serie di vari autori Greci	VALLOTTI
A Series of Twelve Analyzed Fugues	KOLLMANN
La seule vraie théorie de la musique	MOMIGNY
A Short Account of the Progress	LOGIER
A Short Account of the Thoro Bass	PEPUSCH
A Short Account of the Twelve Modes	PEPUSCH
A Short Explication	PEPUSCH
A Short Treatise on Harmony	PEPUSCH
Silva rerum, ein Notiz-exzerptenbuch	RIEPEL
Singe-, Spiel- und General-Baß-Übungen	TELEMANN, G. P.
Singfundament	FUX
Siuity Bakha dlia klaviera	YAVORSKY
Six Lectures on Accompanied Vocal Writing	KITSON
Six Lectures on Harmony	MACFARREN
Skizze einer Methode der Har-monielehre	RIEMANN
Solfèges pour servir à l'étude	LANGLÉ
Solfeggi	QUANTZ
Some Aspects of Beethoven's Art Forms	TOVEY
Some Memorandums, concerning Musick	NORTH, R.
Some Notes upon an Essay	NORTH, R.
Sonare sopra'l basso	AGAZZARI
La sonata pathétique de L. van Beethoven	LUSSY
Sonderbare Invention: Eine Arie	TREIBER
Sophiae com moria certamen	FLUDD
Sopplimenti musicali	ZARLINO
Die Sprachlaute	STUMPF
Die Stil der Oper seria von C. W. Gluck	KURTH
Stimmbildungskunst	VOGLER
Storia della musica	MARTINI
Der streng-polyphonische Stil	JADASSOHN

Stroenie muzykal'noi rechi	YAVORSKY
Structural Functions of Harmony	SCHOENBERG
On the Structure of a Sonata	MACFARREN
Struktura melodii	YAVORSKY
Studi di contrappunto	SABBATINI, L. A.
Studien zur Geschichte der Notenschrift	RIEMANN
Studies in Fugue	KITSON
Style and Idea	SCHOENBERG
Suite des erreurs sur la musique	RAMEAU
Summum bonum quod est verum	FLUDD
Supplément des principes ou éléments de musique	LOULIÉ
Sur la composition musicale	CHORON
Sur la musique comme art	REICHA
A Syllabus of the Second Examination	LOGIER
Die Symphonie Anton Bruckners	HALM
A Symphony for the Piano-Forte	KOLLMANN
Synopsis musica	CRÜGER
Synopsis musicae novae	LIPPIUS
Syntagma musicum	PRAETORIUS
System der antiken Rhythmik	WESTPHAL
System der musikalischen Rhythmik und Metrik	RIEMANN
System für den Fugenbau	VOGLER
A System of the Science of Music	LOGIER
Systema generis diatonico-chromatici	NEIDHARDT
Systematische Anleitung zum Fantasieren	CZERNY
Systematische Modulationslehre als Grundlage	RIEMANN
Système général de la musique	FÉTIS
Systême général des intervalles	SAUVEUR
Système royale	DU COUSU
Table générale des sistèmes temperés	SAUVEUR
Tariffa Kircheriana	KIRCHER
Teaching materials concerning music theory	BRUCKNER
Temperatur	HAUPTMANN
Tentamen novae theoriae musicae	EULER
Themata fontem omnium errantium musicorum	LIPPIUS
Thematia musica	LIPPIUS
Themes . . . for Those Who Are Desirous	LOGIER
De theologia gentili	VOSSIUS, G. J.
Theoretical and Practical Studies	LOGIER
Theoretisch-praktische Harmonielehre	DEHN
Theòrica, y práctica del temple	SOLER
Théorie de la musique	FÉTIS
Theorie der Tonkunst und Kompositionslehre	KREHL
Theory	PASQUALI
A Theory of Harmony	STAINER
The Theory of Musick Reduced	SALMON
The Theory of Sounds	NORTH, R.
A Third Book on the Theory of Music	PROUT
Thorough Bass, Being a Second Series	LOGIER
Thorough-Bass Made Easy	PASQUALI
Three letters to Henry Oldenburg	WALLIS
Tonality	TOVEY
Das Tonbewußtsein: Die Lehre	JADASSOHN
Tonpsychologie	STUMPF
Les tons ou discours	MAILLART
Der Tonwille: Flugblätter zum Zeugnis	SCHENKER
Tonwissenschaft und Tonsetzkunst	VOGLER
Tractatus apologeticus integritatem	FLUDD
Tractatus compositionis augmentatus	BERNHARD
Tractatus in quo demonstrantur	BONTEMPI
Tractatus musicus compositorio-practicus	SPIESS
Die Tradition der alten Metriker	WESTPHAL
Traduzione d'un discorso latino	GALILEI
The Training of the Musical Imagination	TOVEY
Traité complet de la théorie	FÉTIS
Traité d'accompagnement et de composition	CAMPION, F.
Traité de contrepoint et de fugue	DUBOIS
Traité de haute composition musicale	REICHA
Traité de la basse sous le chant	LANGLÉ
Traité de la composition de musique	NIVERS
Traité de la fugue	GÉDALGE

Traité de la fugue	LANGLÉ
Traité de la musique théorique et pratique	PARRAN
Traité de la musique pratique	YSSANDON
Traité de la théorie de la musique	SAUVEUR
Traité de la viol	ROUSSEAU, J.
Traité de l'accord	DENIS
Traité de l'expression musicale	LUSSY
Traité de l'harmonie	RAMEAU
Traité de l'harmonie universelle	MERSENNE
Traité de mélodie	REICHA
Traité de musique	LA VOYE-MIGNOT
Traité des accords	ROUSSIER
Traité d'harmonie	CATEL
Traité d'harmonie	REBER
Traité d'harmonie et de modulation	LANGLÉ
Traité d'harmonie théorique et pratique	DUBOIS
Traité d'harmonie théorique et pratique	GEVAERT
Traité du contrepoint et de la fugue	FÉTIS
Traité élémentaire de musique	FÉTIS
Traité général d'instrumentation	GEVAERT
Il transilvano	DIRUTA
Un tratado de canto organo	LUSITANO
Trattado de glosas	ORTIZ
Trattato apologetica	ARTUSI
Trattato dei tuoni modali	VALLOTTI
Trattato della musica scenica	DONI
Trattato di contrappunto	SABBATINI, L. A.
Trattato di musica	MEI
Trattato di musica di Plutarco	GALILEI
Trattato di musica secondo	TARTINI
Trattato sopra le fughe musicali	SABBATINI, L. A.
Trattato . . . sopra una differentia musicale	DANCKERTS
A Treatise of Good Taste	GEMINIANI
A Treatise of Musick	MALCOLM
A Treatise of Musick	RAVENSCROFT
A Treatise of the Natural Grounds	HOLDER
A Treatise on Counterpoint, Canon and Fugue	OUSELEY
Treatise on Harmony	DAY
A Treatise on Harmony	OUSELEY
A Treatise on Musical Form	OUSELEY
A Treatise on Practical Composition	LOGIER
A Treatise on the Art of Music	JONES
Of the Trembling of the Consonant Strings	WALLIS
Trente-six fugues pour le pianoforte	REICHA
Treulicher Unterricht im General-Baß	KELLNER
Il Trimerone de' fondamenti armonici	BOTTRIGARI
Triumphus bibliorum sacrorum	ALSTED
Uchebnik garmonii	RIMSKY-KORSAKOV
Uchenie o kanone	TANEEV
Über chronometrische Tempobezeichnung	WEBER
Über das musikalische Hören	RIEMANN
Über das sogenannte Generalbass-Spielen	WEBER
Über den technischen Ausdruck	KOCH
Über den Wert musikalischen Analysen	HALM
Über die Eintheilung der Intervalle	BELLERMANN
Über die Entwicklung der mehrstimmigen Musik	BELLERMANN
Über die harmonische Akustik	VOGLER
Über die in Sulzers Theorie	SCHULZ
Über die musikalische Composition	SCHEIBE
Über die physiologischen Ursachen	HELMHOLTZ
Über die physischen . . . Gegenstände	KOCH
Über die Wahl der Melodie	TELEMANN, G. M.
Über J. S. Bachs Konzertform	HALM
Über Tonalität	RIEMANN
Über Tonmalerei	WEBER
Der übermäßige Dreiklang	WEITZMANN
Undici bassi del prete Francescantonio Vallotti	VALLOTTI
Unsere Harmonielehre	LOUIS and THUILLE
Unstruhtinne, oder musicalische Gartenlust	AHLE

Unterricht im Generalbaß-Spielen	TELEMANN, G. M.
Unterricht, wie ein Knabe	GRIMM
Uprazhneniia v golosovedenii	YAVORSKY
Uprazhneniia v obrazovanii skhem ladovogo	YAVORSKY
Ursus murmurat	BEER
Ursus vulpinatur	BEER
Ut, mi, sol, re, fa, la	BUTTSTETT
Utriusque cosmi	FLUDD
Vade-mecum de l'organiste	GEVAERT
Vademecum der Phrasierung	RIEMANN
Of the Various Genera and Species of Music	PEPUSCH
Various Papers . . . Relating to Harmony	PEPUSCH
La vera idea delle musicali numeriche	SABBATINI, L. A.
Vereinfachte Harmonielehre	LOBE
Vereinfachte Harmonielehre	RIEMANN
Vergleichung der verschiedenen Systeme	KOCH
Du véritable caractère de la musique	EULER
Veritas proscenium	FLUDD
La vérité des sciences	MERSENNE
Vérités également ignorées et interresantes	RAMEAU
Der verminderte Septimen-Akkord	WEITZMANN
Versuch, aus der harten und weichen Tonart	KOCH
Versuch einer Anleitung zur Composition	KOCH
Versuch einer Anweisung	QUANTZ
Versuch einer Geordneten Theorie	WEBER
Versuch einer gründlichen Violinschule	MOZART
Versuch über die musikalische Temperatur	MARPURG
Versuch über die wahre Art, Vol. I	BACH
Versuch über die wahre Art, Vol. II	BACH
A Vindication of an Essay	SALMON
Vingt-cinq leçons de solfège	GEVAERT
Violinschule	TÜRK
Vita admodum reverendi	KIRCHER
Vogler's Tonschule	VOGLER
Der vollkommene Capellmeister	MATTHESON
Vollständige Anweisung zum Generalbaße	ADLUNG
Vollständige theoretisch-practische	CZERNY
Vom vollstimmigen und unbezifferten	SCHRÖTER
Von dem Stimmführung des Generalbasses	SCHENKER
Von den wichtigsten Pflichten	TÜRK
Von der Singe-Kunst	BERNHARD
Die Voraussetzungen der theoretischen Harmonik	KURTH
Vorbericht to J. S. Bach's Die Kunst der Fuge	MARPURG
Vorgemach der musicalischen Composition	SORGE
Vospriiatie ladovykh melodicheskikh	YAVORSKY
Die wahren Grundsätze zum Gebrauch	KIRNBERGER
Die Wechselnote oder Cambiata	BELLERMANN
Der Weise von Großmehlra	ZIEHN
Das Wesen der Melodie in der Tonkunst	JADASSOHN
What the Composer Expects from the Listener	TOVEY
Der Widerspruch in der Musik	LOUIS
Wie hören wir Musik?	RIEMANN
Der wieder das beschützte Orchestre	BUTTSTETT
Wissenschaftliche Abhandlungen	HELMHOLTZ
Words and Music: Some Obiter Dicta	TOVEY
Writings on scales, clefs, thoroughbass, etc.	PEPUSCH
Zangh-bericht	BAN
Zangh-Bloemzel	BAN
Zarlino als harmonischer Dualist	RIEMANN
Zergliederung des Finale aus Mozarts	SECHTER
Zur Quintenfrage	BELLERMANN
Zuverlässige Anweisung, Claviere und Orgeln	SORGE
Von zwei Kulturen der Musik	HALM
Zwei und dreisig Präludien für die Orgel	VOGLER
Zwölf Choräle von Sebastian Bach	VOGLER
Zwölf neue Variationen im strengen Style	SECHTER
Zwölf Variationen im strengen Style	SECHTER
Zwölf Versetten und eine Fuge	SECHTER

NAME INDEX

Aarburg, Ursula: 344
Abbado, Michelangelo: 351, 397
Abbate, Carlo: 393
Abbate, Carolyn: 316
Abel, Angelika: 397
Abel-Struth, Sigrid: xxviii, 431
Abercrombie, J. R. Alexander G.: 397
Abert, Anna Amalie: xli, 36, 45, 74, 75, 97, 209, 399
Abert, H.: 37
Abetti, Giorgio: 138
Abraham, Gerald: xxxviii, 17, 56, 95, 171, 223, 280, 323, 345, 347, 397, 398, 403, 435
Abraham, Lars Ulrich: 239, 379, 397, 417
Achron, Joseph: 279
Adam, Charles: 69, 70
Adams, F. John, Jr.: 307
Adams, Robert D. W.: 319
Adelung, Wolfgang: 52
Adkins, Cecil: 218
Adler, Guido: xli, 154
Adler, Irving: 99
ADLUNG, Jakob: **1-2**, 3, 419
Adorno, Theodor W.: 148, 313, 325
Adrian, John Stanley: 312
Adrio, Adam: xviii, xliii, 2, 4, 25, 47, 68, 111
Aeschbacher, Gerhard: 1
Agate, Edward: 279
Agawu, V. Kofi: 313, 325, 407
AGAZZARI, Agostino: **2-3**, 237
AGRICOLA, Johann Friedrich: 1, **3**, 4, 352, 356
AHLE, Johann Georg: **4**, 5
Ahle, Johann Rudolf: 4
Ahlgrimm, Isolde: 338, 397
Ahnell, Emil Gustave: 257
Ahonen, Kathleen: 92
Aimé-Martin, L.: 70
Aird, Donald: 431
Airoldi, Roberto: 394
Airy, Osmund: 222

Aiton, Eric J.: 99, 135, 139
Akimov, P. V.: 155
Alain, Émile Chartier: see Chartier, Émile
Albersheim, Gerhard: 308, 397
Albert, Heinrich: xli
Alberti, Domenico: 231
Albrecht, Christoph: 397
Albrecht, Hans: xl, xli, 39, 48, 51, 56, 58, 64, 69, 73, 76, 78, 84, 89, 109, 409
Albrecht, Johann Lorenz: 1, 337
Albrecht, Renate: 102, 106, 354
Albrecht, Theodore: xlii
ALBRECHTSBERGER, Johann Georg: **5-7**, 57, 87, 93, 237, 262, 416, 442, 445
Alderman, Pauline: 324
Aldrich, Putnam: 17, 144, 431
Aldridge, Maisie: 421
Alekperova, Nelli: 397
Alekseev, Aleksandr: 398
d'ALEMBERT, Jean le Rond: **7-10**, 32, 57, 80, 182, 185, 250, 251, 253, 254, 255, 258, 283, 284, 285, 332, 342, 436
Alette, Carl: 398
Alewyn, Richard: 26
Alexander, Ian W.: 70
Alexander, Josef: 167
Alexitch, Antonietta: 141
Alfieri, Pietro: 50
Allanbrook, Wye J.: 398
Allard, Joseph C.: 394, 398
Allen, Warren Dwight: 398, 415
Allerup, Albert: 121
Allihn, Ingeborg: 248, 353
Almeida, D. de: 71
Almond, Clare: 398
Alperson, Philip A.: 422, 426, 437
Alquié, Ferdinand: 70
Al'shvang, Arnol'd Aleksandrovich: 346

ALSTED, Johann Heinrich: **10-11**, 121, 160
Alstedius, Johannes Henricus: see ALSTED, Johann Heinrich
Alston, R. C.: xxi
Altenburg, Detlef: xlii
Altmann, Günter: 443
Altmann, Wilhelm: 274
Altwein, Erich F. W.: 112, 137
Alvin, L.: 87
Ambros, August Wilhelm: 398
Ambrose, Jane P.: 246, 247, 410, 425, 441
Ameln, Konrad: 224
Amiot, Joseph-Marie: 288
Ammann, Peter: 91
Amory, A. H.: 265
Anderson, Dale; 321, 435, 436
Anderson, Gene Henry: 258
Anderson, Owen: 35
Andraschke, Peter: 321
Andreis, Josip: 195, 213, 443
Andrewes, Richard: 421
Andrews, Hilda: 222
Andrews, H. K.: 305, 322, 392, 393, 427, 428
Andrews, Richard: 168, 406
Andrews, Ruth P. 360
Anfuso, Nella: 46, 210
Angerer, Manfred: xliii
Anglés, Higinio: 398
Anglès, Higino: 29, 53
Annegarn, Alfons: 21, 344
Anonymous (BOTTRIGARI chapter): 37
Anonymous (LOGIER chapter): 168
Anonymous (ROEL-DEL-RÍO chapter): 281
Antcliffe, Herbert: 127
Antholz, Heinz: 408
Anthony, James M.: 202
Anthony, James R.: 39
Anton, J. D.: 378
Antonicek, Theophil: xliii

Antoniotto, Giorgio: 103, 104

Apelt, Ernst Friedrich: 136

Apel, Willi: 17, 398, 419, 427

Apfel, Ernst: 196, 398

Apfel, Robert Edmund: 419

Appel, Bernhard R.: 333, 334

Applebaum, Sada: 102, 404

Applebaum, Samuel: 102, 404

Apps, Howard Llewellyn: 213

Arakawa, Tsuneko: 144, 247, 398

Aranguren, Julia: 296

Aranovsky, Mark: 16, 398

Archer, William Kay: 415

Archibald, Bruce: 446

Archibald, R. C.: 398

Arias, Enrique Alberto: 313, 427

Ariga, Noyuri: 196

Aristotle: xl, 106, 199, 216, 422

Aristoxeni iunior: see
    MATTHESON, Johann

Aristoxenus: 199, 384, 443

Arlin, Mary Irene: 86, 88, 105

Arlt, Wulf: 197, 399

Armitage, A.: 125, 137

Armitage, Merle: 322

Armstrong, James: 399

Arnaud, Abbé François: 256

Arnn, John D.: 79, 361, 441

Arnold, Denis: 94, 209, 210, 227, 356,
    392, 393, 397, 399, 403, 426,
    427, 433, 446

Arnold, Donna: 331

Arnold, Elsie M.: 210

Arnold, Franck Thomas: 164, 366,
    399

Arnold, Friedrich Wilhelm: 26

Arnold, Samuel: 132

Arteaga, Esteban: 181

Artega, S.: 83

Artelt, W.: xxxiv

ARTUSI, Giovanni Maria: **11-12**, 36,
    37, 208, 209, 210, 355, 391,
    392, 433, 444

Arzamanov, Fedor Georgievich: 346,
    347

ASAFIEV, Boris Vladimirovich:
    12-16, 51, 154, 386, 420, 428

Aschmann, Rudolf: 109

Ashbee, Andrew: 92

Asselin, Pierre-Yves: 399

Assézat, J.: 409

Aston, Peter: 426

Atcherson, Walter Thomas: 399, 434

Atkinson, Edmund: 118

Attali, Jacques: 286

Atteln, Horst: 10, 138

Attwood, Thomas: 168, 442

Auda, Antoine: 399

Audbourg-Popin, Marie-Danielle: 399

Auger, Léon: 298

Augst, Bertrand: 71

Auhagen, Wolfgang: 399

Aulabaugh, Alan Richard: 399

Auld, Louis E.: 422

Ausbach, Horst: 246

Austin, John Charles: 311

Austin, William W.: xli, 399

Autexier, Philippe A.: 252, 425

Averanio, Nicolao: 91

Averbukh, Liya Abramovna: 388

Avianius, Johannes: 436

Avril, Elsie M.: 421, 422

Ayrey, Craig: 306, 314

Ayrton, William: 168

Azopardi, Francesco: 57

Baake, Friedrich: 99

Baas, Bernard: 159

Babbitt, Milton: 309, 400

Babitz, Sol: 247, 248, 349, 400, 406,
    407, 422

Bache, Constance: 163

Bachur, Bernhard: 243

BACH, Carl Philipp Emanuel: **17-19**,
    149, 165, 176, 212, 213, 246,
    247, 303, 305, 352, 405

Bach, J. C.: 186, 414

Bach, Johann Sebastian: xvii, xxxviii,
    3, 17, 66, 67, 77, 85, 95, 102,
    112, 114, 128, 129, 130, 142,
    144, 146, 150, 151, 153, 154,
    155, 162, 170, 182, 183, 196,
    197, 204, 205, 217, 218, 219,
    228, 243, 244, 256, 257, 271,
    275, 300, 301, 302, 303, 305,
    306, 307, 309, 315, 318, 324,
    327, 328, 345, 346, 357, 358,
    359, 360, 369, 370, 371, 373,
    376, 380, 383, 384, 385, 387,
    395, 397, 398, 399, 400, 404,
    405, 409, 410, 411, 413, 414,
    416, 417, 420, 422, 426, 428,
    429, 430, 431, 432, 437, 438,
    439

BACILLY, Bénigne de: **20**, 443

Bacon, Ernst: 396

Bacon, R. M.: 168, 206

Bacon, Sir Francis: 202

Baddam: 294

Badings, Henk: 400

Badura-Skoda, Eva: 400

Badura-Skoda, Paul: 62, 400

Baehr, Johann: See BEER, Johann

Bäßler, Hans: 401

Baevsky, Vadim Solomonovich: 388

Bagge, Selmar: 331

Bailey, Walter B.: 320, 322, 324

Bailhache, Patrice: 120, 406

Baines, Anthony: 349

Baird, Julianne: 182, 357

Baker, David: 43

Baker, James: 314

Baker, Jennifer: 43

Baker, Keith M.: 9

Baker, Nancy Kovaleff: 148, 149

Baker, Theodore: 6, 128, 129, 163,
    267

Baker-Smith, Dominic: 447

Balbi, Melchiorre: 291

Baldwin, Olive: 295

Ballan, Harry Reuben: 325

Balsano, Maria Antonella: 366

Balthazar, Scott L.: 400

Balz, Albert G. A.: 70

Balzano, Gerald J.: 315

Bamberger, Carl: 309

BAN, Joan Albert: **21-22**

Banauch, Eugen: 137, 416

BANCHIERI, Adriano: 2, **22-24**, 93,
    121, 390, 444

Bandini, Angelo Maria: 75

Banister, Henry Charles: 66, 179

Banks, Paul: 41

Bannius, Ioan Albert: see BAN, Joan
    Albert

Barassi, Elena Ferrari: 399

Barattieri, Gian Francesco: 8

Barber, Elinore L.: 39, 286, 302

Barber, E. M.: 128

Barber, Graham: 376

Barbera, André: 402

Barbieri, Francisco Asenjo: 83

Barbieri, Patrizio: 400, 403

Barblan, Guglielmo: 2, 97

Barbosa, Maria Augusta: 175

Barbour, James Murray: 251, 252,
    253, 255, 256, 317, 400

Barce, Ramon: 320

Bardez, Jean-Michel: 8

Bardi, Giovanni de' (Count): 45, 97,
    199, 428, 433

Barenboim, Lev: 400

Baresel, A.: xxvi

Barford, Philip: 18, 400

Baridon, Michel: 259

Barini, Giorgio: 45

Barker, Frank Granville: 67, 417

Barker, John W.: 397, 417

Barlay, O. Szabolcs: 73

Barlay, Szabolcs Ö.: 73

Barlow, Wayne: 400

Barnes, John: 383

Barnhart, Edward N.: 424

Baroffio, Bonifacio: 52

Baron, John H.: 400

Baróti, Dezsö: 258
Barraclough, Geoffrey: 137
Barras, Vincent: 325
Barrell, Bernard: 257
Barrett, William Alexander: 340
Barr, Raymond A.: 329
Barry, Anna: 359
Barry, Malcolm: 312, 313
Barsky, V.: 315
Barsova, I.: 155
Bartel, Dietrich: 400
Bartenstein, Hans: 401
Bartle, Barton K.: 442
Bartlett, Clifford: 68, 283, 306, 421,
    426, 429, 430
Bartley, S. Howard: 120
Bartók, Béla: 386
Barton, Todd: 92
Barwick, Frances Duncan: 437
BARYPHONUS, Henricus: **24-25**,
    47, 110, 121, 160, 237, 375
Barzun, Jacques: 88
Basalla, George: 99, 136
Basart, Ann P.: 419, 421
Bašiš, Sonja: 443
Basso, Alberto: 256
Bates, Donald G.: 374
Bates, Robert Frederick: 401
Bauducco, F. M.: 24
Bauer, Glen Alan: 325
Bauer, Izabella: 258
Baum, Richard: xliii
Bauman, Thomas: 401
Baumgardt, Carola: 135
Baxter, W. H., Jr.: 434
Bayliss, Stanley A.: 359, 360
Baynard, John: 123
Bazarov, Konstantin: 425
Beach, David Williams: 143, 144, 308,
    311, 313, 314, 315, 316, 401
Beaudoin, Russell Martin: 210
Beaulieu, Armand: 200
Beaussant, Philippe: 258
Beccari, J. P.: 255
Bêche: 58
Beck, Hermann: xxxii, xli, 277, 401,
    424
Beck, Joseph G.: 399, 405
Beck, L. J.: 70
Beck, R. T.: 322
Becker, Carl Ferdinand: 398, 401, 413
Becker, Heinz: xli, xlii, 169, 171, 196
Becker, Peter: 302
Becking, Gustav Wilhelm: 272, 274
Beckmann, Klaus: 376
Becquart, Paul: 88
Beebe, Ellen Scott: 392, 401, 428
Beechey, Gwilym: 104, 220, 396

Beer, Anton de: 401
Beer, Arthur: 136, 138
BEER, Johann: **25-26**
Beer, Peter: 136,138
Beeson, Roger A.: 311
Beethoven, Ludwig van: 6, 13, 61, 62,
    85, 93, 112, 113, 162, 170, 179,
    243, 251, 262, 270, 273, 303,
    304, 305, 306, 307, 308, 309,
    310, 312, 313, 314, 315, 316,
    345, 346, 358, 360, 379, 384,
    387, 403, 410, 413, 416, 423,
    428, 431, 436, 437, 438, 439,
    440, 441
Behn, Siegfried: xxxvi
Behncke, Gustav: 190
Behne, Klaus-Ernst: 298
Beiche, Michael: 323, 401
Beicken, Suzanne Julia: 357
Beier, Hans-Joachim: 235, 244
Bekker, Paul: 154, 380
Belaikov, P.: 86
Belcher, Euel Hobson, Jr.: 396
Beliaev, Viktor Mikhailovich: 244,
    345, 346
Beliaeva-Ekzempliarskaia, Sofia
    Nikolaevna: 386
Bell, Arthur E.: 125
Bell, Clara: 219
Bell, James F.: 81, 120, 401
Bellasis, Edward: 56
BELLERMANN, (J. G.) Heinrich:
    26-27, 93, 144
Bellermann, Ludwig: 26
Bellingham, Bruce Allan: 84, 401
Belt, Philip R.: 328
Belza, Igor: 388
Bembo, Pietro: 422
Benary, Peter: 30, 300, 301, 350, 362,
    376, 401
Benda, Georg: 401
Benedetti, Giovanni Battista: 391, 393
Benedetto, Renato di: 97
Benelli, Alemanno: see Melone,
    Annibale
Bengtsson, Ingmar: 35, 115, 201, 349,
    392, 400, 401, 410, 412, 431,
    436, 444
Benjamin, William E.: 306, 313, 401
Benndorf, Kurt: 47, 153
Bennett, Joseph: 56
Bennett, Lawrence E.: 35
Bent, Ian D.: 307, 311, 315, 401
Bent, Margaret: 401, 435
Benzon, Joseph: 349
BERARDI, Angelo: **27-28**, 299
Berg, Alban: 15, 318, 324, 326
Berg, Alfred: 129

Berg, Darrell M.: 19
Berg, Sigurd: 213
Berger, Karol: 401, 402, 441
Bergmann, Walter: 196, 353
Bergner, Caroline: 301
Bergquist, Peter: 293, 294, 311, 314,
    355, 392, 428
Bergsagel, John: 261, 398
Bergsøe, Joh. Frid.: 362
Bergson, Henri: 154
Berkov, Viktor Osipovich: 280, 347
Berlioz, Hector: 167, 172, 256, 262,
    303, 395, 401
Berman, Laurence: xlii
Bermúdez, Gregorio Santiso: 281
BERMUDO, Juan: **29-30**, 59, 175,
    226
Bernard, Jonathan W.: 258, 403
Bernardi, Steffano: 121
Bernardino, Rizzi: 365
BERNHARD, Christoph: **30-31**,
    153, 194, 295, 299, 375, 411
Bernick, Thomas: 24, 31
Bernoulli, Daniel: 250, 256
Bernoulli, Eduard: 238, 81
Bernoulli, Rudolf: 81
Bernsdorff-Engelbrecht, Christiane:
    439
Bernstein, David: 314
Bernt, H. H.: 49
Berry, Lloyd E.: 49
Berry, Wallace: 310, 402, 419
Berselli, Raffaella: 71
Berthier, Annie: 202
Berthier, Paul: 257
Besseler, Heinrich: xxiv, xli, 120, 275,
    342
Beswick, Delbert Meacham: 402
Béthisy de Mézières, Eugène-Eléonor
    de: see
    BÉTHIZY, Jean Laurent de
BÉTHIZY, Jean Laurent de: 8, 32
Betti, Adolfo: 104
Beuval, Basnage de: 124
BEVIN, Elway: **32-33**
Bewerunge, Henry: 271, 272
Beyer, Ferdinand: 62
Beyer, Paul: 402
Beyer, Robert T.: 419
Beyschlag, Adolf: 402
Bianchi, Lino: xix
Bianchini, Riccardo: 436
BIANCIARDI, Francesco: **33**
Bianconi, Lorenzo: 428, 433
Bieder, Eugen: 185
Bielow, George: 435, 436
Bieri, Georg: 40
Biermann, David: 319

Bieske, Werner: 422
Bignami, Giovanni: 99
Bilič, Franjo: 443
Bill, Oswald: 414
Billeter, Bernhard: 33, 257, 258, 362,
    363, 402
Bilson, Malcolm: 437
Bimberg, Siegfried: 13
Bindel, Ernst: 137
Binkley, Thomas: xxviii
Birchensha, John: 10, 11
Bircher, Martin: 402
Birkby, Arthur: 381
Birke, Joachim: 402
Birkholz, Adam Michael: see Booz,
    Ada Mah
Birkner, Günter: 288
Birnbaum, Johann Abraham: 300,
    301, 302
Birtner, Herbert: 108, 412
Bishop, John: 63, 85, 264, 378
Bister, Heribert: 125
Bittner, Carl: 213, 363
Black, Leo: 321
Blackburn, Bonnie J.: xxxix, 394, 417
Blacklock, Thomas: 8, 284
Blackwood, Easley: 402
Blahoslav, Jan: 441
Blainville, Charles-Henri de: 284, 332
Blake, Carl LeRoy: 402
Blanchard, H. D.: 145, 337
Bland, D. S.: 92
Blankenburg, Christian Friedrich: 343
Blankenburg, Walter: 1, 43, 44, 61,
    68, 76, 239, 339, 402, 421, 429
Blaserna, Pietro: 119
Blaze, François Henri Joseph: see
    Castil-Blaze
Blessinger, Karl: 173
Blewitt, Jonathan: 168
Bleyle, Carl O.: 337
Bloch, Robert: 305
Bloch, Suzanne: 227
Block, Geoffrey: 437
Blok, F. F.: xxxii, 373
Blom, Eric: 1, 42, 94, 144, 275, 398,
    404, 420, 424
Blondel, François: 229
Blood, William: 402
Bloom, Peter Anthony: 86, 87, 88
Blount, Gilbert L.: 376, 403, 410, 434
Blow, John: 60
Blum, Carl: 86
Blum, Fred: 409
Blum, Klaus: 265
Blum, Stephen: 287
Blume, Christel: 29, 53, 83
Blume, Christiane: 245, 257, 280

Blume, Friedrich: xxvii, xli, 3, 28, 40,
    43, 44, 91, 196, 204, 238, 239
Blume, Jürgen: 402
Blume, Ruth: 291, 334
Blumenfeld, Harold: 238
Blumröder, Christoph von: 325, 402
Boadella, Ricard: 296
Boal, Ellen Teselle: 418
Boas, George: 70, 447
Boatwright, Howard: 310
Bobango, Gerald J.: 141
Bobillier, Marie: see Brenet, Michel
Bobrovsky, Viktor: 13
Bodemann, Eduard: 158
Böckl, Rudolf; 402
Boeringer, James: 426
Boësset, Antoine: 21
Boethius, Anicius Manlius Severinus:
    42, 79, 107, 108, 199, 226, 402,
    414, 443
Boetticher, Wolfgang: xli, 402
Boganova, Tat'iana Vasil'evna: 55
Böhmer, Jan: 21
Bohn, Peter: 108
Bokemeyer, H.: 376
Bolis, Luciano: 188
Bollert, Werner: 34, 349, 404
Bonaccorsi, Alfredo: 30, 35, 120, 239,
    257, 274, 349, 367, 416, 420,
    431, 445
Bonavia, F.: 98, 99, 126, 405
Bonavia, M. R.: 127
Bond, Ann: 214
Bond, Timothy: 322
Bondesen, J. D.: 267
Bonge, Dale Jay: 162
Bonham, Gillian: 286
BONINI, Severo: 33-34
Bonino, Mary Ann Teresa: 34, 210
BONONCINI, Giovanni Maria: 34-35
Bonte, Hans Georg: 339
BONTEMPI, Giovanni Andrea:
    35-36
Boomgaarden, Donald Roy: 144, 295,
    402
Boorman, Stanley: 401
Booth, Mark: 49
Booz, Ada Mah: 90
Bordonaro, Adriana Viola: 292
Boretz, Benjamin: 400
Borgese, Elisabeth Mann: 305
Borghini, Vincenzo: 199
Borgir, Tharald: 402, 446
Boring, Edwin Garrigues: 119
Bormann, Renate: xxxix
Borrel, Eugène: 18, 48, 58, 257, 402
Borren, Charles van den: 64, 435
Borris, Siegfried: 144, 324, 408

Borroff, Edith: xli
Bos, Henk: 443
Bos, H. J. M.: xxxix, 125
Bose, Fritz: 144, 171, 195, 207, 247,
    350, 416
Bose, Madelon: 155
Boskey, James B.: 209
Bosse, Gustav: xxi
Bosshart, Beatrice: 82
Boßler, Heinrich Philipp Karl: 237
Bossuyt, Ignace: 109
Bottrigari, Enrico: 37
BOTTRIGARI, Ercole: 11, 12,
    36-37, 367, 444
Boulay, Jean-Michel: 229
Boulton, John: 397
Bourligueux, Guy: 48, 425
Bourreau, Louis: 39
Boutroux, Léon: 274
Bouvet, Charles: 350
Bouws, Jan: 169
Bouyer, Raymond: 176
Bowen, Jean: 429
Bowen, William Roy: 402
Bowman, Edward Morris: 380
Bowman, Elsa McPhee: 301
Boyd, C. Malcolm: 143, 234, 357, 376,
    410, 430
Boyd, George R.: 114
Boyden, David D.: 103, 104, 211, 212,
    351, 400
Braccino da Todi, Antonio: 11, 12,
    208
Bradshaw, Murray C.: 73
Brahms, Johannes: 115, 303, 307,
    312, 315, 316, 325, 357, 379,
    415
Brahy, Edouard: 128
Brainard, Paul: 239, 349, 351
Branco, João de Freitas: 441
Brandenburg, Seighard: 312
Brandes, Heinz: 403
Brandse, Wim: 396
Branigan, Alan Grey: 430
Bran-Ricci, J.: 20
Branzoli, G.: 267, 270
Brashovanova, L.: 141
Brattain, David L.: 381
Brauchli, Bernard: 421
Brauen, Fred: 141
Braun, Werner: 31, 195, 196, 197,
    249, 261, 403, 426
Bray, Bruce: 415
Bray, Roger: 59
Brechka, Frank T.: 372
Breig, Werner: 171, 323, 376, 403
Breitkopf, Johann Gottlob
    Immanuel: 18

Bremner, Robert: 403
Brenet, Michel: 39, 48, 256, 393
Brennan, Juan Arturo: 91
Brennecke, Wilfried: xl, xli, 157, 403
Brenneis, Clemens: 414
Brenner, Daniel J.: 426
Brentnall, Ernest: 128, 130
Bresciano, Carlo Valgulio: 99
Bresgen, Cesar: 398
Breslauer, Peter: 334
Bresnan, Joan: xxvii
Brett, Philip: 178, 211
Breuer, János: 321, 322, 324
Brewer, Robert Edwin: 403
Brewster, David: 81
Brewster, J.: 81
Bridge, J. Frederick: 66, 223, 228
Bridges, Doreen: 403
Bridgman, Nanie: 20
Bridoux, André: 70
Briganti, Francesco: 36, 73
Briggs, Asa: 92
Briggs, J. Morton, Jr.: 9
Briggs, John: 428
Briggs, Robin: 92
Briner, Andres: 321
Brink, Paul Robert: 368
Brinkmann, Reinhold: 321, 322, 380, 439
Brinton, Crane: 447
Briscoe, Roger Lee: 253, 254
Britsch, Royden Edwin: 403
Briusova, Nadezhda Yakovlevna: 387
Brixel, Eugen: 248
Brixis, František Xaver: 353
Broadwood, Evelyn: 146
Brockelhurst, Brian: 425
Brockt, Johannes: 69
Brodde, Otto: 61, 376
Broder, Nathan: 309
Brody, Elaine: 88
Brofsky, Howard: 187, 188, 230
Brolinson, Per-Erik: 437
Bromander, Lennart: 99
Bronarski, Ludwik: 56
Bronfin, Elena: 403
Bronowski, J.: 447
Bronson, Bertrand H.: 49
Brook, Barry S.: 426, 427
Brooks, Catherine: 409
Brosche, Günter: 265
BROSSARD, Sébastien de: **38-39,** 284, 375
Brouncker, William Lord: 69
Brower, G. Ackley: 345
Brown, Clive: 441
Brown, Daniel: 311
Brown, David C.: 49, 55, 67, 347, 428

Brown, Howard Mayer: xix, 46, 247, 356, 397, 403, 406, 439
Brown, John Russell: 91
Brown, Malcolm Hamrick: xxxiii, 14
Brown, Matthew G.: 315, 407
Brown, Maurice J. E.: 331
Brown, Theodore M.: 132
Brown, Thomas A.: 446
Browne, Richmond: 258, 311, 403
Browning, James: 171
Broyles, Michael: 403
Brucaeus, Henricus: 42
Bruck, Boris: 403
BRUCKNER, (Joseph) Anton: xv, **39-41,** 112, 154, 155, 156, 170, 172, 182, 308, 314, 318, 330, 331
Brüggen, Frans: 38, 194, 246
Bruehl, C. M.: xxxii
Bruguera y Morreras, Juan Bautista: 334, 335
Bruhns, Nicolaus: 441
Bruins, E. M.: 9
Bruno, Giordano: 447
Brunold, P.: 285
Brusatti, Otto: xl, 324
Brush, Stephen G.: 82
Bryant, Carolyn: 226
Bryant, David: 403
Bryennius, Manuel: 374
Bryk, Otto J.: 135
Bucchi, G. F.: 279
Buchenau, Artur: 70
Buchman, Carl: 426
Buchner, Max: xliii
Bucht, Gunnar: 407
Budday, Wolfgang: 403
Budd, Malcolm: 422
Budde, Elmar: 24, 403, 436
Budde, Gudrun: 321
Bücken, Ernst: 155, 265
Buelow, George J.: xxxiv, 1, 4, 25, 26, 44, 61, 65, 107, 116, 117, 134, 141, 153, 161, 196, 197, 205, 219, 224, 242, 295, 302, 327, 328, 338, 339, 355, 376, 383, 402, 403, 404, 426, 430, 432, 446
Bugg, Eugene G.: 159
Bujić, Bojan: 119, 271, 306, 341, 342, 404
Bukofzer, Manfred F.: 59, 60, 398, 404, 442
Bulichius: 121
Buliowski: 400
Bullard, Truman: 407
Bulley, Michael: 265
Bullivant, Roger: 404, 428, 429

Bullough, Vern L.: 99, 446
Bunge, Sas: 436
Burbank, Richard D.: 423
Burchill, James Frederick: 292
Burckhardt, Felix: 338, 339
Burckhardt, J. J.: 82
Burda, Antonin: 131
Burde, Wolfgang: 148, 404
Burdick, Michael Francis: 404
Burgess, Anthony: 49, 247
Burgess, Henry Thacker: 81
Burke, C. G.: 442
Burke, James Robert: 404
Burke, Peter: 423
Burkhart, Charles: 311, 312, 314
Burlas, Ladislav: 404
BURMEISTER, Joachim: **41-42,** 160, 161, 224, 354
Burney, Charles: 132, 150, 151, 181, 234, 284, 285, 350, 400, 404, 426, 444
Burnham, Scott Gordon: 191
Burr, Alex F.: 419
Burrows, David L.: 101, 349, 433
Burton, Arthur: 211
Burton, Martin C.: 223, 404
Burton, Nigel: 443
Burtt, Edwin A.: 70
Busby, Thomas: 150, 151, 167
Busch, Hermann J.: 214, 423
Busch, Hermann Richard: 82
Busch, Regina: 113, 325, 404
Bush, Helen Evelyn: 404
Bushnell, Vinson Clair: 29
Busi, Leonida: 188
Busoni, Ferruccio: 320, 396
Bußler, Ludwig: 346
Buszin, Walter E.: 61
BUTLER, Charles: **42-43,** 47, 440
Butler, David: 315
Butler, Gregory Gordon: 35, 197, 404
Buttstädt, Johann Heinrich: see BUTTSTETT, Johann Heinrich
BUTTSTETT, Johann Heinrich: **43-44,** 193
Buxner, Mervyn: 436
Buxtehude, Dietrich: 440
Bužga, Jaroslav: 265, 403
Buzon, Frédéric de: 69, 71
Buzzi, Francesco: 397
Bychkov, Jurii: 16
Bychkov, Yury: 55
Byrt, John Clare: 18, 248, 275, 404
Cabezón, Antonio de: 296
CACCINI, Giulio: 33, **45-46,** 106
Cadwallader, Allen: 315, 316, 317
Cady, Henry L.: 314

Cafiero, Luca: 91
Cagianelli, Floriana: 323
Cahn, Peter: 63, 101, 197, 315, 404, 408
Cahn-Speyer, Rudolf: 301
Cairola, Giovanni: 70
Caldwell, John A.: 101, 162
Calegari, Antonio: 291
Callcott, John Wall: 123, 150, 151, 362
Callenberg, Eitel-Friedrich: 404
CALVISIUS, Sethus: 24, 42, **46-48**, 60, 110, 121, 261
Calvocoressi, Michel D.: 256, 269, 274, 279
Cameron, Francis: 409
Campbell, Bruce B.: 308
Campbell, Le Roy B.: 130
CAMPION, François: **48-49**
CAMPION, Thomas: 47, **49-50**, 234, 245, 334
Candaux, Jean-Daniel: 286
Cannon, Beekman Cox: 196, 197
Cannon, John T.: 404, 408
Cantarella, Marie-Paule: 88
Cantrell, Byron: 54
Cantrick, Robert B.: 314
Capaccioli, Enrico: 23
Capanna, Alessandro: 365
Capell, Richard: 88, 359, 411, 441
Capellen, Georg: 274, 331
Caplin, William Earl: 115, 143, 275, 312, 331, 405, 445
Capri, Antonio: 351
Caputo, Maria Carmela: 232
Caraci, Maria: 209
Carapetyan, Armen: xxviii, xxxi
Carapetyan, Leon: 235
Carbasus, Abbé: see CAMPION, François
Cardno, J. A.: 118
Carey, C. E.: 405
Carlez, Jules Alexis: 50, 58
Carner, Mosco: 207, 309, 319, 320, 321, 324, 411, 422
Carpenter, Ellon DeGrief: 405, 428
Carpenter, Nan Cooke: 405, 417
Carpenter, Patricia: 320, 325
Carr, Dale C.: 405
Carrière, Paul: 308
Carrington, Douglas R.: 381
Carroll, Frank Morris: 334, 335
Carroll, Malcolm: 286
Carse, Adam von Ahn: 209, 405
Carter, Roy Everett: 319, 325
Carter, Tim: 46, 399
Cartford, Gerhard M.: 415
Carver, Anthony F.: 402

Caspar, Max: 135,136
Casselman, Eugene; 357
Castel, Louis Bertrand: 250, 251, 252, 253, 256
Castelfranco, Count Giordano Riccati di: see Riccati, Giordano
Castellani, Marcello: 405
Castéra, René de: 126
Castil-Blaze (Blaze, François Henri Joseph): 284
Castilon, F. D.: 247
Caswell, Austin Baldwin: 20, 265
CATEL, Charles-Simon: 13, **50-51**, 55, 56, 85, 157, 261, 262
Catelani, Angelo: 367
Catoire, Georgii Lvovich: 106, 428
Cattell, J. McKeen: 119
Cattin, Giulio: 23, 366, 368
Caus, Isaac de: 52
CAUS, Salomon de: **51-52**, 230
Cavallini, Edoardo: 405
Cavallini, Ivano: 351
Cavallotti, Enrico: 257
Cavett-Dunsby, Esther: 148, 315, 405
Cavicchi, A.: 419
Čavlovič, Ivan: 437
Caylus, le Comte de: 256
Cazden, Norman: 405
Cazeaux, Isabelle: 434
Celletti, Rodolfo: 356, 357
Cellier, Hippolyte: 381
Cerasoli, Giorgio: 292
Černý, Miroslav K.: 15, 40
CERONE, Pietro: **52-53**, 83, 169, 200, 207, 216, 229, 280, 296, 334, 399
CERRETO, Scipione: **53-54**
Cervelli, Luisa: 72
Cesare, Ruth de: 272
Chabanon, de: 256
Chadwick, George: 395
Chafe, Eric: 405
CHAIKOVSKY, Petr Il'ich: 13, **54-55**, 105, 163, 278, 280, 345
Chailley, Jacques: 87, 207, 256, 257, 258, 405
Chambers, J. K.: 314
Chan, Mary: 222, 223
Chandler, B. Glenn: 252, 258
Chantavoine, Jean: 255
Chapman, Roger E.: xli, 201, 325
Chappell, William: 66, 228
Charlton, David: 169, 268
Charlton, Peter: 340
Charnassé, Hélène: 48
Charnova, Anna Ivanovna: 274
Chartier, Émile: 70
Chase, Gilbert: 29, 441

Chavarri, Eduardo L.: 83
Chechott, V. A.: 176
Cheliapov, N. I.: 155
Chenette, Louis Fred: 405
Chenevert, James: 331
Cheong, Wai-Ling: 145
Cherednichenko, T.: 15
Cherlin, Michael: 317, 422
Cherniavsky, David: 432
Chernin, Mallorie: 405
CHERUBINI, Luigi: 50, **55-56**, 85, 93, 102, 157
Cherubini, Ralph: 213
Chesnut, John Hind: 213, 405
Chevaillier, Lucien: 405
Chevalier, A. Le: 281
Chew, Geoffrey: 161, 405
Chiba, Junnosuke: 405
Chiereghin, Salvino: 393
Child, Peter: 314
Childe, Timothy: 124
Chilesotti, Oscar: 99, 177, 285, 406
Chilmead, Edmund: 202
Chiodino, Giovanni Battista: 121
Chiti, Girolamo: 188
Chittum, Donald: 312
Chivinskaia, Nataliia: 388
Chmaj, Ludwik: 70
Chmelar, Rudolf: 113
Chomiński, Józef Michał: 406
Chopin, Fryderyk Franciszek: xv, xix, xxxix, 56, 303, 307, 310, 315, 325, 404, 407, 428
CHORON, Alexandre-Étienne: 5, 6, **57-58**, 87, 94, 147, 148, 183, 184, 291
Chouillet, Anne-Marie: 259
Chrisman, Richard: 403
Christensen, Jean: 322, 325, 326
Christensen, Jesper: 326
Christensen, Thomas Street: 9, 19, 124, 222, 223, 253, 255, 258, 259, 275, 408
Christman, Arthur H.: 246
Chrysander, Friedrich: xxiv, 219, 352, 390
Churchill, John: 231
Churgin, Bathia: 97, 116, 343, 435
Chusid, Martin: 400, 407, 409
Chybiński, Adolf: 406
Cicero: 422
Cígler, Radovan: 131
Citkowitz, Israel: 308, 320
Clapham, John: 131
Clark, Edward: 309
Clark, J. Bunker: xxi
Clark, Michael: 6
Clark, Stephen L.: 19

Clark, William: 313
Clarke, Desmond M.: 71
Clarke, Eric: 315
Clarke, Henry Leland: 223, 399, 407, 426, 431
Clarke, James: 190
Clarke, Mary Cowden: 50, 56
Claro, Samuel: 210
Clemens non Papa, Jacobus: 401
Clendinning, Jane Piper: 393
Clercx, Suzanne: 18, 236, 421
Clercx-Lejeune, Suzanne: xxxviii
Clerke, Agnes Mary: 375
Clermont, Susan J.: 406
Closson, Ernest: 106
Clymer, W.: xli
Coates, W.: 368
Cobb, Gerard F.: 406
COCLICO, Adrianus Petit: **59**
Coffee, Curtis: 247
Coffin, Berton: 357
Cogan, Robert: 120
Cohausz, Alfred: 202
Cohen, Albert: 20, 32, 52, 71, 78, 116, 124, 158, 174, 180, 202, 220, 229, 230, 255, 258, 259, 289, 298, 333, 375, 382, 399, 403, 406, 410, 418, 419, 429, 439
Cohen, Annabel: 312
Cohen, Henry: 406
Cohen, H. Floris: 125, 406
Cohen, H. Robert: xxvii
Cohen, I. Bernard: 135, 138
Cohen, Peter: 18
Cohen, Vered: 392
Cohn, Richard: 314
Coker, Wilson: 403
Colding-Jørgensen, Gunnar: 431
Cole, Malcolm Stanley: 63, 151, 207, 406
Cole, Percival Richard: 10
Coleridge, Arthur Duke: 114, 228
Colhardt, Johann: 84
Čolić, Dragutin: 406
Colles, H. C.: 406
Collet, Henri: 175, 406
Collier, Joel: 168
Collins, Denis: 430
Collins, Dennis: 18
Collins, James: 70
Collins, Michael Bruce: 248, 400, 406, 407, 422
Colucci, Matthew Joseph: 407
Columbus, Christopher: 299
Combarieu, Jules: 385
Combe, Edouard: 177
Compenius, Esaias: 238
Comploi, Franz: 197

Cone, Edward T.: 323, 400, 436
Confalonieri, Giulio: 56
Conley, Joyce: 407
Conlon, Pierre M.: 285, 286
Connelly, Kenneth: 310
Conrat, Friedrich: 119
Constantini, Franz-Peter: 407
Conus, Georgy Eduardovich: 428
Cook, D. F.: 234
Cook, Frederick: 201
Cook, Martha: 251
Cook, Nicholas: 316, 407
Cook, Susan C.: 430
Cooke, Deryck: 41
Coon, Oscar: 163, 267
Cooper, Barry: 101, 222, 231, 440
Cooper, Grosvenor: 310
Cooper, John: See COPRARIO, John
Cooper, Kenneth: 214
Cooper, Martin: 407
Coopersmith, J. M.: 196
Coover, James B.: 407
Copenhaver, Brian: 423
Coprario, Giovanni: see COPRARIO, John
COPRARIO, John: **60**
Corbin, P. F.: 92
Corelli, Arcangelo: 102, 214, 420
Cornell, J. H.: 163, 268
Cort van den Linden, R.: 322
Corvinus, Johann Michael: see RAVN, Hans Mikkelsen
Cory, Eleanor: 400
Cosma, Viorel: 10, 339
Cotte, Roger: 56, 285, 286, 407
Cottingham, John: 71
Couperin, F.: 443
Courvoisier, Antoine: 325
Courvoisier, Walter: 173
Cousin, Victor: 70
Cousineau, M.: 288
Cousu, Antoine du: see DU COUSU, Antoine
Covington, Kate R.: 426
Cowart, Georgia: 197, 259, 407, 409, 413, 433
Cowen, David C.: 91
Cox, Ainslee: 400, 436
Cox, Reneé: 422
Coxon, Carolyn: 334
Craddock, Peter: 17
Craft, Robert: 13
Craig, Dale A.: 400
Craig, Hardin: 447
Cramer, Carl Friedrich: xxvi
Crane, Frederick Baron: 140, 239
Crankshaw, Geoffrey: 428

Cranna, Clifford Alan, Jr.: 23
Craven, James Brown: 91
Crawford, Tim: 432
Crevel, Marcus van: 59, 109, 427
Crocker, Richard L.: 393, 407, 427
Crockett, Charlotte Gwen: 248
Crombie, A. C.: 407
Cronin, Vincent: 91
Crookes, David Z.: 238
Cross, Charlotte M.: 324
Crotch, William: 168
Crouch, Margaret Long: 335
Crozier, Catharine Pearl: 73
CRÜGER, Johannes **60-61**, 160
Cube, Felix-Eberhard von: 314, 315
Cudworth, Charles L.: 94, 101, 108, 123, 132, 141, 178, 231, 234, 294, 355, 417
Cukkerman, Viktor: 388
Cummings, W. H.: 228
Cummins, Charles: 168
Curtis, Alan: 68
Curtis, Gareth: 402
Curwen, John: 423
Cushing, Luther Stearns: 86
Cutts, John P.: 49
Cuyler, Louise: xli, 111, 445
Cvetko, Dragotin: 409
Cyr, Mary: 258
CZERNY, Carl: **61-63**, 165, 262, 263, 264
Dabrowski, Florian: 323
d'Accone, Frank: xx
Dadelsen, Georg von: xli, 144, 239, 275, 407
Dahlhaus, Carl: xviii, xxxviii, xxxix, xl, xliii, 13, 18, 30, 31, 42, 56, 69, 94, 98, 99, 113, 115, 118, 120, 136, 137, 138, 140, 149, 154, 155, 170, 171, 175, 191, 195, 202, 207, 223, 225, 239, 248, 252, 258, 275, 299, 301, 305, 306, 307, 308, 314, 318, 321, 322, 323, 325, 326, 329, 331, 343, 368, 392, 393, 397, 398, 400, 401, 402, 407, 408, 409, 412, 413, 418, 419, 422, 427, 428, 431, 437, 439, 444, 446, 447
Dale, Catherine: 127
Dale, Frank Knight: 309, 424
Dale, Kathleen: 209
Dale, Sir Henry H.: 221
D'Alessi, Giovanni: 354
Dallery, Carleton: 71
Dalton, James: 399, 437, 446
Damerini, Adelmo: xxxviii, 12, 56
Damm, Marianne: 366

Dammann, Rolf: 383, 408
Damp, Georg Edward: 215
Damschroder, David Allen: 314, 315, 409, 442
DANCKERTS, Ghiselin: **64**, 175, 367
Daniels, Arthur Michael: 94, 293, 428
Daniskas, John: 309
Dannenberg, Peter: 321
Dannenfeldt, Karl H.: 423
da Nova, Giovanni: xxxv
Danuser, Hermann: 439
Danzi, Franz: 371
Daragan, D.: 388
Darbellay, Etienne: 19
Darrell, R. D.: 310, 347
Dart, R. Thurston: xxxi, 29, 49, 60, 104, 209, 211, 249, 293
Dati, Carlo Roberto: 74
DAUBE, Johann Friedrich: **64-65**
David, Ernest: 176
David, Hans T.: 60, 103, 183, 301, 409
Davidson, Martin: 359, 399, 405, 409
Davidsson, Åke: 409, 421
Davies, H. Neville: 427
Davies, John: 315
Davis, Ferdinand: 102
Davis, Shelley: 149
Davis, Walter R.: 49, 50
Davison, Archibald T.: 442
DAY, Alfred: **65-66**, 179, 228, 243, 244, 340
Day, James: 8, 255, 343
Day, Mary Peckham: 353
Dean, Winton: 56, 320, 399, 409, 426
Deane, Basil: 56
Dean-Smith, Margaret: 235
Dear, Peter Robert: 202
Deas, Stewart: 360
Deathridge, John: 18, 19, 422
de Bruyn, P. J.: 64
Debus, Allen G.: xxxi, 91, 92
Debussy, Claude: 126, 256, 303, 324
De Cesare, Ruth: 415
Dechant, Hermann: xli
Dechevrens, A.: 177
Decker, C. V.: 190
de Courcy, G. I. C.: 436
de Cousu, Antoine: see DU COUSU, Antoine
Decsey, Ernst: 40, 173
DeFotis, William: 409
Degtiarev, Stepan: 181
de' Guarinoni, Eugenio: 77
DEHN, Siegfried (Wilhelm): **66-67**, 183, 189, 190
Dekker, Gerard: 383, 409
Dekker, Wil: 111
de La Borde, Jean-Benjamin: 287, 288

Delaere, Mark: 325
Delaire, Jacques Auguste: 265
de la Voye Mignot: see LA VOYE-MIGNOT, de
Delezenne, Charles Edouard Joseph: 87
Delfini, Carlo: 93
Deliège, Célestin: 314, 315
della Corte, Andrea: 196, 356, 404
Della Seta, Fabrizio: xxxix
del Nero, Piero: 199
DeLong, Kenneth: 445
De Luccia, Paolo: 202
Del Villar, Mary: 91
Demachy: 281, 282
DEMANTIUS, Johannes Christoph: **67-68**
Dembski, Stephen: 400
de Monti, Henry: 168
Démotz: 443
Demoz de la Salle: 38
Dempster, Douglas J.: 407
Demuth, Norman: 127, 265
Denecke, Heinz Ludwig: 274
DENIS, Jean: **68-69**
Denis, Pietro: 93, 349
Dent, Edward J.: 404, 420, 432, 434
Dent, Edward T.: 360
Derksen, John Henry: 409
Dernova, Varvara: 388, 389, 428
Derode, Victor: 86
Derr, Ellwood: 409
Derrett, Susan Haase: 422
DESCARTES, René: xxi, xxxiii, 21, **69-72**, 193, 194, 240, 250, 425
Desgraves, Louis: 286
Deshayes, Thérèse: 253
Desmarets, Henri: 70
Dessau, Princess d'Anhalt: 80
Deutsch, Diana: 409
Deutsch, Otto Erich: 211, 444, 445
Devore, Richard O.: 409
DeVoto, Mark: 319
de Waard, Cornélis: 200
Dewhirst, David W.: 138
de Zeeuw, Anne Marie: 409
Díaz, Gregorio: 334, 335
Dibelius, Ulrich: 305
Dickinson, A. E. F.: 428
Dickinson, G. S.: 404
Dickinson, Peter: 400, 445
Dickreiter, Michael: 82, 138, 139
Dickson, J. Douglas H.: 360
Diderot, Denis: xx, 7, 8, 9, 251, 257, 283, 342, 409, 436
Diederich, Susanne: 32
Diederichs-Lafite, Marion: 401
Diettrich, Eva: xliii

Di Giovanni, Joseph: 445
Dijk, Jan van: 82
Dill, Charles: 409
d'Indy, Vincent: see Indy, Vincent d'
Dineen, P. Murray: 326
DIRUTA, Girolamo: 22, **72-73**, 93, 121, 390
Disertori, Benvenuto: 227, 246, 296, 398
Di Toma, Gabriele: 188
Dittersdorf, Karl Ditters von: 328
Dittler, L. A.: 59
Dixon, Gail Susan: 409
Dixon, Graham: 2
Dmitrieva-Mei, T. P.: 14
Dmitriyev, A. N.: 279
Dobbins, Frank: 389
Dobbs, Bettyjo Teeter: 92
Dodgson, Stephen: 279, 405
Doe, Paul: 397
Dömling, Wolfgang: 320, 401, 402, 442
Dörffel, A.: 108
Dolmetsch, Arnold: 45, 399, 409
Dolmetsch, Nathalie: 282, 333
Dombois, Eugen: 82
Dommel, Hermann: 91
Dommer, Arrey von: 148
Dommett, K. W.: 431
Don, Gary W.: 316
Donà, Mariangela: 56, 409
Donahue, W. H.: 409
Donatoni, Franco: 92
DONI, Giovanni Battista: 21, **74-75**, 180, 187, 199, 201, 372, 373
Donington, Robert: 17, 18, 103, 104, 116, 178, 192, 231, 247, 248, 292, 349, 350, 401, 403, 404, 409, 410, 418, 427, 432
Donnelly, Glennon Anthony: 447
Donohue, H. E. F.: 137
Donovan, Arthur: 132
Donovan, Richard: 411
Doolittle, James: 257
Dopheide, Bernhard: 273
Dorfmann, Félix: 279
Dorfmüller, Kurt: 178
Dorian, Frederick: 209
Dortmüller, Joachim: 401
Dortous de Mairan, Jean-Jacques: 7
Dostrovsky, Sigalia: 81, 298, 401, 404, 408, 410, 445
Dotzauer, Wilfried: 410
Douel, Martial: 51
Dowland, John: 226
Dowling, W. Jay: 315
Downes, Olin: 320

Drabkin, William: 27, 167, 305, 306, 312, 313, 314, 315, 316, 401, 407, 408, 410, 412, 443
Dräger, Hans-Heinz: 202
Draheim, H.: 138
Drake, Stillman, 99, 137, 410, 445
DREßLER, Gallus: **76**, 161, 317, 445
Drew, David: 323, 415
Dreyer, Ernst-Jürgen: 397
Dreyfus, Kay: 312
Dreyfus, Lawrence: 410
Drillon, Jacques: 209
Droysen, Dagmar: xxxvi
Druilhe, Paule: 157
Drummond, Pippa: 248
Dryden, John: 427
Dubiel, Joseph: 314
DUBOIS, Théodore: **76-77**, 261
Dubos, Jean-Baptiste Abbé: 20, 71
Dubovsky, Iosef Ignatevich: 410
Du Caurroy, François-Eustache, Sieur de St.-Frémin: 230
Ducharger: 256
Duchez, Marie-Élisabeth: 9, 258, 259, 284, 286, 410
Duck, Leonard: 406
Duckles, Vincent: 20, 38, 188, 410
DU COUSU, Antoine: **77-78**
Dünkelfeind, Caspar: see BACH, Carl Philipp Emanuel
Dürr, Gerda: 208, 230
Dürr, Walter: 367
Dürr, Walther: 236, 355, 397, 410
Dürrnberger, Johann August: 39
Duffy, Celia: 156, 314, 326
Dufour, I: 125
Dufour, Théophile: 283, 285
Dufourcq, Norbert: xxxvi, 69, 220, 256
Duggan, Joseph F.: 5
Dumesnil, René: 405
Dumling, Albrecht: 322
Dun, Finlay: 265
Duncan, Alistair M.: 71, 135
Duncan, David Allen: 202, 203
Dunlap, Rhodes: 49
Dunn, John Petrie: 305
Dunn, Leslie: 49
Dunning, Albert: 21, 59, 410
Dunsby, Jonathan M.: 305, 306, 312, 313, 315, 316, 324, 325, 401, 410
Dunwell, Wilfrid: 431
Duparc, Henri: 126
Duparcq, Jean-Jacques: 257, 410
Du Pasquier, Louis Gustave: 81
Dupont, Wilhelm: 410
Durante, Francesco: 57
Du Reneau: see OUVRARD, René

Durrant, J.: 209
Dutoit, E.: 176
du Vair: 425
Dyke, Charles: 421
Dyson, Jeanne Manninen: 410
Dziebowska, Elzbieta: 410
Eager, J. A.: 168
Eaglefield-Hall, A.: xxi
Eamon, William: 92
Earhart, A. Louise Hall: 32
Earhart, Will: 146
East, John Michael: 407
Eaton, Quaintance: 400, 409, 415, 417
Ebcioglu, Kemal: 316
Eberhard, Otto: 242
Eberle, Gottfried: 436
Ebersbach, Günther W.: 338
Ebert, Hermann: 119
Ebisawa, Bin: 286
EBNER, Wolfgang: **79**, 121
Eckhart-Bäcker, Ursula: 127
Eckstein, Friedrich: 40, 338
Edler, Arnfried: 155
Edwards, Charles: 319, 445
Edwards, Warwick: 399
Egan, John Bernard: 201
Egel, Hermann Wilhelm: 376
Eggebrecht, Hans Heinrich: xvii, xxiii, xxxviii, 68, 121, 148, 184, 275, 301, 376, 411, 416
Eggers, Wolfgang: 178, 333
Egk, W.: 213
Ehrenkreutz, Stephen: 403
Ehrichs, Alfred: 45
Eibner, Franz: 305, 310
EICHMANN, Peter: **79**, 354
Eicke, Kurt-Erich: 191
Eimert, Herbert: 411
Einstein, Albert: 135
Einstein, Alfred: 112, 212, 274, 411, 412
Eitner, Robert: 84, 89, 202, 238, 247, 344, 376, 380, 411
Ekzempliarsky, V. M.: 386
Elders, Willem: xlii
Eliot, Samuel Atkins: 86
Elkus, Albert I.: 417
Elliott, Gilbert: 102
Elliott, J. H.: 92
Elliott, Richard M.: xx
Ellis, Alexander J.: 66, 118, 119
Ellis, James: 445
Ellis: 235
Ellison, Ross Wesley: 1
Elmer, Minnie: 351
Elsässer, H.: 138
Elsässer, Thomas: 106

Elsberry, Kristie Beverly: 8
Elsberry, Thomas Norman: 265
Elschek, Oskár: 13, 14
Elsner, Jürgen: 15
Elukhen, Alexander: 279
Elvers, Rudolf: 174
Emerson, Jan: 309
Emery, Walter: 356, 399, 409, 437
Emig, Sandra: 411
Emmanuel, Maurice: 265
Emmerig, Thomas: 277, 278
Engel, Hans: xli, 436
Engel, J. J.: 81
Engel, Yuly Dmitrievich: 270, 272, 274, 346
Engelbach, G. L.: 151, 167
Engelfred, A.: 130
Engelhardt, D. G.: 441
Engelhardt, Ruth: 144
Engelke, Bernhard: 76
Ensslin, Hermann: 411
Entzenmueller, Jodoc: 111
Eppelsheim, Jürgen: 339
Epps, David: 397
Eppstein, Hans: 397, 429, 445
Epstein, David Mayer: 306, 313, 323
Erasmus, Desiderius: 107
Erckmann, Fritz: 285
Erdmann, Benno: xvii
Erdmann: see Élie Häseler
Erhard, Albert: 282
Erig, Richard: 248
Erpf, Hermann: 40, 411
Erpff, Hermann: 321
Ersch, J. S.: 378
Erwin, Charlotte E.: 308, 319
Erzakovich, B.: 15
Escal, Françoise: 9
Eschenburg, Johann Joachim: xxxvi
Eschweiler, Franz: 163
Espinosa, Alma: 219
Esser, Heribert: 308
Esteban, Julio: 63
Esteve, Juan J.: 320
Estève, Pierre: 253, 256
Etinger, M.: 155
Ettelson, Trudy Gottlieb: 286
Euclid: 327
EULER, Leonhard: **80-82**, 204, 250, 254, 332, 443
Eval'd, Z.: 154
Evans, Jeffrey: 133
Evans, P. A.: 400
Evans, Peter: 94, 310, 422, 431
Evans, Richard: 306
Evans, R. J. W.: 92
Evett, Robert: 400
Evidon, Richard: 40

EXIMENO (y Pujades), Antonio: **83**, 188, 216

Fabbri, Mario: xxxviii

Fabbri, Paolo: 210

FABER, Heinrich: **84**, 110, 161, 317

Fabris, Dinko: 227

Fagerberg, Erling: 67

Fairman, Richard: 445

Falck, Myron Rudolph: 30, 411

Falck, Robert: 325

Falenciak, Joanna: 205

Falle, George: 223

Fallon, David: 238

Fallows, David: 238, 403, 422, 434

Falvy, Z.: 73

Famintsyn, A. S.: 190, 267

Fano, Fabio: 98, 99, 210

Fant, Göran: 400

Fanti, Napoleone: 188

Fanzago, Abbé: 349

Farbshtein, Aleksandr: 14, 411

Fargas y Soler, Antonio: 86

Farish, Margaret: 430

Farmer, Henry George: 58, 123, 257, 411, 432

Farnsworth, Paul R.: 436

Farrar, Lloyd P.: 125

Farrell, Peter: 227

Fassmann, Kurt: 82

Faulkner, Helen: 324

Faulkner, Quentin: 1

Faulkner, Thomas: 209, 298

Favre, Georges: 51, 157

Favre, Max: 413

Fay, Laurel: 67

Fayolle, François Joseph: 57

Feder, Georg: 130

Federhofer, Hellmut: xxviii, xxxviii, xli, xlii, 31, 94, 95, 214, 215, 275, 295, 306, 308, 309, 310, 312, 314, 315, 316, 323, 325, 411, 412, 419, 432, 445

Federhofer-Königs, Renate: 354

Federl, Ekkehard: 339

Federmann, Maria: 59

Federoff, Yvette: 58

Fédorov, Vladimir: 14

Feerst, Robin Nan: 46

Feil, Arnold: 94, 379, 401, 412, 419

Feingold, Mordechai: 202

Feld, Steven: 314

Feldman, Martha: 50

Feldmann, Fritz: 196, 224, 412

Felix, Werner: xxxviii

Feller, Marilyn: 46

Fellerer, Karl Gustav: xxv, xxvi, xli, 34, 35, 53, 56, 75, 109, 120, 190, 329, 412, 428

Fellmann, Emil Alfred: 82

Fellowes, Edmund H.: 211

Fenaroli, Fedele: 57

Fenby, Eric: 415

Fend, Michael: 406, 433

Fendt, Michael: 392

Fenlon, Iain: xxi, 402, 427, 434, 437

Fen-Taylor, Alan: 410

Fenton, John: 314, 321, 324

Fenwick, Richard D.: 341

Ferand, Ernest T.: 84

Ferand, Ernst: 412

Ferchault, Guy: 126, 127, 262

Ferdinand, Henning: 175

Ferdinand, King of inner Austria: 411

Ferguson, Howard: 164, 292, 362, 421

Ferguson, L. C.: 446

Ferguson, Wallace K.: 435

Fernandes, Antonio: 427

Ferracin, Gianni: 83

Ferran, Dominique: 412

Ferraris, Giorgio: 239

Ferris, Joan: 257

Féruselle, Pierre: 51

FÉTIS, François-Joseph: xxxii, 5, 6, 52, 55, 57, 58, 66, **85-89**, 102, 105, 157, 167, 189, 202, 263, 349, 378

Fetter, David: 339

Fiala, J.: 265

Ficher, Jacobo: 279

Fico, Lorenzo: 394

Fiebig, Folkert: 31

Fiechtner, H. A.: 40

Field, Christopher D. S.: 60, 334

Field, J. V.: 139

Field, Michael Greet: 320

Fillmore, John Comfort: 270, 412

FINCK, Hermann: 57, 59, **89-90**

Findeisen, Wilhelm: 285

Fink, Gottfried Wilhelm: 62, 67, 167, 189, 190, 191, 363, 378

Fink, Harold J.: 412

Finkel'berg, Natal'ia: 388

Finney, Charles Herbert: 412

Finney, Oliver John: 49

Finney, Ross Lee: 103

Finscher, Ludwig: xliii, 187, 421, 429, 436

Fiocchi, Vincenzo: 57

Fischer, Hans: 144

Fischer, Kurt von: 155, 156, 213, 412, 413

Fischer, Trygve: 413

Fischer-Krückeberg, Elisabeth: 61

Fisenden, Owen: 247

Fish, Solomon: 360

Fishman, N. L.: 387

Fiske, Roger: 415, 436

Fisk, Eliot: 227

Fitzlyon, April: 67

Flaherty, Gloria: 413

Flay, A. L.: 348

Flechsig, Hartmut: 413

Fleischhauer, Günter: xxxix, xl

Fleissner, Otto: 99

Fleming, Christopher le: 435

Fleming, Michael David: 238

Fletcher, Andrew: 375

Fletcher, John: 141

Fleury, Albert: 379

Flindell, Edwin Frederick: 318, 380, 385, 413

Fling, Robert Michael: 144

Floros, Constantin: xxiii

Flotzinger, Rudolf: xliii, 40, 95, 408, 413, 425

FLUDD, Robert: **90-92**, 134, 135, 136, 380

Fludd, W. H. Grattan: 32

Förster, Kasper: 299

Förster, Wilhelm: 136

Fokker, Adriaan Daniël: 82, 125, 413

Folkerts, Menso: 137

Fontenelle, Bernard le Bouvier de: 298

Foote, Arthur W.: 267

Forbes, Elliott: 307, 359, 413

Forbes, Eric G.: 9, 137

Forchert, Arno: 191, 193, 197, 218, 238, 239, 401, 413

Foreman, Lewis: 445

Forkel, Johann Nikolaus: xxvii, 18, 110, 143, 148, 372, 373, 399, 400, 401, 413, 417, 426

Forrester, Donald Williams: 216, 413

Forschner, Hermann: 149

Forster, Walter V.: 413

Forte, Allen: 219, 304, 306, 310, 311, 313, 314, 316, 347, 380, 396, 401, 408, 410, 425, 433

Fortner, Wolfgang: 194

Fortune, Nigel: 210, 399, 426, 434

Foss, Hubert J.: 358, 359

Fowles, Ernest: 176

Fox, Charles Warren: 88, 185, 196, 209, 398, 411

Fox Strangways, A. H.: 211, 360, 413

Fraguier, Marguerite-Marie de: 127

Fral'kin, Viktor: 29, 296

Framery, Nicolas-Étienne: 206

Franck, César: 126, 262

Franco of Cologne: 26, 27

Françon, Marecel: 285

Frank, Jonathan: 244

Frank, Mortimer H.: 227, 430

Frankel, Robert E.: 312
Franklin, A. David: 437
Franklin, Peter: 325
Frascarelli, Angelo: 97
Fraser, Norman: 398
Frasson, Leonardo: 351
Frederick, King II: 80 (see also Frederick the Great)
Frederick, Kurt: 185
Frederick the Great: 17, 19, 246, 417 (see also Frederick, King II)
Freedman, Frederick: xx
Freeman, Robert N.: 7
Frei, Walter: 109
Freiherr von Waldberg, Max: see Waldberg, Max Freiherr von
Freitag, Wolfgang: 418
French, Richard F.: 13, 426
Frère, Alexandre: 433
Frerichs, Elli: 185
Fréron, Elie-Catherine: 253, 254, 256
Frescobaldi, Girolamo: 326
Frese, Anna: 229, 262
Freud, Sigmund: 154
Freudenberger, Berthold: 342
Frey, Martin: 274
Frey, Max W.: 353
Frickhinger, H. W.: xxii
Friedberg, Gertrude: 321
Friedland, Bea: xx
Friedmann, Martin George: 104
Frisch, Christian: 135,136
Frisch, Manfred: 337
Frisch, Walter Miller: 325
Frischknecht, Hans Eugen: 413
Frisius, Rudolf: 305, 413
Fritzsche, Otto Fridolin: 108
Frizius, Joachim: see FLUDD, Robert
Frobenius, Wolf: 109, 413
Fröström, Nils: 9
Froger, Jacques: 297
Fruchtman, Efrim: 417
Fryčer, Jaroslav: 265
Fryer, W. R.: 202
Fryklund, Daniel: 88
Fubini, Enrico: 8, 284, 413
Fuchs, Carl Dorius Johann: 176, 271, 413
Fuchss, W.: 109
Fürstenau, Moritz: 36, 413
Füssl, Karl Heinz: xxxvi
Fujioka, Yumiko: 15
Fulcher, Jane: 286
Fulda, Adam von: 224
Fuller, David: 18, 174, 292, 413, 430
Fuller-Maitland, J. A.: 219
Furcha, E. J.: 423

Furtwängler, Wilhelm: 309
Fuß, Nicolaus: 81
FUX, Johann Joseph: 5, 26, 27, 35, 57, **93-96**, 152, 186, 188, 193, 194, 196, 204, 232, 299, 303, 339, 352, 365, 390, 411, 443, 445
Gabeau, A.: 127
Gable, Frederick K.: 414
Gablitst, Fedor: 165
Gábry, György: 380
Gaffurio, Franchino: 107, 226, 230, 389
Gaillard, Pierre: 414
Gal, Hans: 444
Galand, Joel: 317
GALEAZZI, Francesco: **97**
Galeffi, Romano: 159
Galilei, Galileo: 100
GALILEI, Vincenzo: 11, 12, 33, 74, **97-100**, 199, 354, 391, 392, 413
Galladol: 112
Gallarati, Paolo: 436
Gallardo, Bartolomé José: 208
Gallet, Anne: 292
Galliard, John Ernst: 356
Gallico, Claudio: 74, 210
Gallimard, Jean-Edme: 256
Galliver, David: 46, 445
Gallo, Franco Alberto: 52, 53, 354, 366
Gallon, Jean: 262
Gallon, Noël: 262
Gallucio, Leonardo: 37
Galushko, M.: 15
Gambale, Emanuele: 87
Gandillot, Maurice: 71
Ganse, Albrecht: 107
Ganz, Beatrice: 414
Garbuzov, Nikolai Alexandrovich: 387, 428
García, Francisco: 53
García Matos, M.: 293
Gardavský, Č.: 265, 414
Garden, Edward: 67
Gardiner, John Eliot: 410
Gardner, John: 94, 95, 345, 347
Garner, W.: 419
Garrett, Lee Raymond: 22, 444
Garros, Madeleine: 220
Gary, Charles L.: 310
Gaspari, Gaetano: 188, 414
GASPARINI, Francesco: xxxix, **100-101**, 116, 437
Gassendi, Pierre: 90, 91
Gatens, William J.: 115, 341
Gatti, Carlo: xxiii
Gaudibert, Eric: 325

Gaukroger, Stephen: 445
Gaum, Günther: 357
Gauthier, L.-E.: 58
Gay, Harry W.: 102, 116, 279, 399, 415, 428
Gebauer, Joh. Chr.: 267
Gebuhr, Ann Karen: 314
Geck, Karl: 333
Geck, Martin: 30, 350
GÉDALGE, André: 77, **101-2**
Gedge, David: 228
Geering, Arnold: xli, 414
Gehring, Franz: 268
Gehrmann, Hermann: 344, 376
Geierhaas, Gustav: 173
Geiringer, Karl: xli, 238
Geissler, Fred: 419
Gelrud, Paul G.: 103, 212
GEMINIANI, Francesco: **102-4**, 332
Geoffrey-Dechaume, Antoine: 246
George, David Neal: 51
George, Graham: 311
George, Jonathan: 283
Georgiades, Thrasybulos G.: xxix
Gérard, C.: 315
Gérard, Yves: xxvii
Gerber, Ernst Ludwig: 414, 426
Gerbert, Martin: 188
Gerboth, Walter: 18, 209, 251, 414
Gerdine, Leigh: 422
Gerhard, Roberto: 323
Gerhartz, Karl: 213
Gerlach, Reinhard: xlii
Gerlach, Walther: 119, 137, 138
Gernhardt, Klaus: 414
Gersmann, Friedrich: 248
Gerson-Kiwi, Edith: 227
Gerstenberg, Walter: xxxviii, xli, xlii, 207, 219, 410
Getreau, Florence: 406
GEVAERT, François-Auguste: 45, 54, 55, 87, **105-6**, 273, 385
Gewirth, Alan: 70
Gherzfeld, Gherzoff: 129
Ghisi, Federico: 45, 409
Ghislanzoni, Alberto: 414
Giacotti, D.: 414
Gialdroni, Giuliana: 175, 366
Gianuario, Annibale: 46, 210, 414
Giazotto, Remo: 37, 213
Gibbons, Henry: 49
Gibbs, C.: 422
Gibbs, Jason: 400
GIBELIUS, Otto: **107**, 110
Gibson, Louisa: 243
Giegling, Franz: 104, 182, 197, 351, 353
Gieschen, Thomas: 381

Gil, François d'Assise: 87
Gilbert, J.: 70
Gilbert, Steven E.: 314
Gilbert, W. Paul: 400
Gilfoyle, Sandra C.: 414
Gillespie, G. C.: xxi
Gilliland, Esther Goetz: 310
Gillingham, Bryan: 414
Gillio, Pier Giuseppe: 323
Gil-Marchex, Henri: 256
Gilson, Paul: 265
Gingerich, Owen: 135, 136, 138
Ginguené, Pierre-Louis: 206
Ginzburg, Semyon L'vovich: 280
Giorgi, Cecilia: 200
Girac, Emilius: 190
Girdlestone, Cuthbert Morton: 257, 258, 349
Girschner, Christian Friedrich Johann: 168
Gissel, Siegfried: 414
Gjerdingen, Robert O.: 408, 414
Glahn, Henrik: xxxix
GLAREAN, Heinrich: 42, 57, 74, 76, **107-110**, 122, 193, 198, 199, 226, 260, 261, 354, 392, 443
Glasenapp, Franzgeorg von: 166
Glazemaker, J. H.: 69, 70
Gleason, Harold: 260, 301, 414
Glebov, Igor: see ASAFIEV, Boris Vladimirovich
Gleditsch, Hugo: 385
Glehn, M. E. von: 176
Gleitman, Lila: xxvii
Glenewinkel, Hermann: 363
Gliadeshkina, Z.: 388
Gliere, Reinhold: 347
Glinka, Mikhail: 51, 66, 67
Gloede, Wilhelm: 171
Gluck, Christoph Willibald von: 3, 154, 285
Gnesin, Mikhail Fabianovich: 279, 280
Gnorimus, Master: see MORLEY, Thomas
Goddard, D. C.: 399
Goddard, Scott: 146, 404
Gode, Alexander: 284
Godley, Elizabeth: 298, 414
Godman, Stanley: 376
Godwin, Joscelyn: 90, 92, 136, 140, 141, 383, 392, 414
Goebel, Julius: 272, 396
Goebels, Franzpeter: 63
Göhler, Georg: 155
Goehlinger, F.-A.: 39
Goehr, Alexander: 322, 323, 324
Goens, Jan: 397
Görner, Rüdiger: xlii, 207

Goethe, Johann Wolfgang von: 133, 159, 248, 343, 397
Göthel, Folker; 412
Göttert, Karl-Heinz: 302, 414
Götze, Heinz: xl
Gojowy, Detlef: 67
Gołab, Maciej: 316
Gold, Julius: 396
Goldbach, Christian: 80
Goldbach, Christoph: 158
Goldhan, Wolfgang: 140
Goldman, Richard Franko: 359, 415
Goldmann, Alfred: 339, 414
Goldschmidt, Harry: 15, 414
Goldschmidt, Hugo: 45, 415
Goldsmith, Francisca: 437
Goldsmith, Pamela: 415
Goldthwaite, Scott: 298, 398
Golffing, Francis: xli
Gollmick, Karl: 87
Gombosi, Otto: 398, 435
Goodfriend, James: 433
Goodman, Alfred Grant: 113, 152, 173
Goodman, Roy: 441
Goodstein, Judith R.: 419
Goodwin, Barbara: 423
Goos, Herta: 6, 34, 66
Gorce, Jérôme de la: 258
Gordon, Barbara: 418
Gorenstein, N.: 220
Gori, Antonio Francisco: 74, 75
Gossett, Philip: 251, 254, 422
Gossman, Lionel: 286
Gottfried, Clemens: 306
Gottsched, Johann Christoph: 301, 302, 402
Gottwaldt, Heinz: 329
Gouk, Penelope M.: 202, 222, 223, 406, 415, 421, 426, 429, 445
Gould, Murray J.: 311, 312
Gozza, Paolo: 406
Grabner, Hermann: 274
Grace, M. D.: 426
Graebner, Eric: 315
Grafton, Anthony T.: 92, 445
Graham, George Farquhar: 168
Graham-Jones, Ian: 227, 403
Grainger, Percy: 360
Grandi, Cesare A.: 323
Grandi, Walter: 323
Grant, Cecil Powell: 144
Grant, Kerry S.: 421
Grasberger, Franz: xxxvi, 40, 171
Grasberger, Renate: 41
Grashel, John William: 415
Grassineau, James: 38, 39
Graubard, Mark: 125

Graubart, Michael: 324, 325
Graun, Karl Heinrich: 328
Grave, Floyd K.: 363, 370, 371, 415, 443
Grave, Marget Grubb: 371
Grave, Margaret H.: 371
Gray, Jeremy: 405
Graybill, Roger: 316
Grebe, Karl: 41
Green, Burdette Lamar: 415
Green, James: 106
Green, Michael D.: 415
Green, Robert Anthony: 281, 282
Greenberg, Beth: 415
Greenfield, Jack: 145, 202, 218, 415
Greer, David C.: 49, 227
Gregory, Pope I: 105
Gregory, Tullio: 91
Gremion, Claude: 415
Grey, John: 120
Grey, Thomas S.: 418
Grieg, Edward: 440
Grierson, Mary: 360
Grierson, Sir Herbert: xli
Gries, Peter: 312
Griesbach, Karl-Rudi: 323
Griffel, Margert Ross: 425
Griffin, Julia Ann: 227
Griffiths, Paul: 324, 325, 407
Griffiths, Ralph: 81
Grigor'ev, Vladimir: 296, 388
Grimarest, Jean-Leonor de: 20
Grimes, Calvin Bernard: 415
Grimm, Betty Jane: 351
Grimm, Friedrich Melchior, Baron von: xx, 254
GRIMM, Heinrich: 24, 47, **110**, 193
Grimm, Reinhold: 438
Grimm: xx
Grimsley, Ronald: 9
Grlič, Darko: 443
Gross, Eric: 433
Groß, Karl Josef: 343
Grosse, Hans: 353
Grossman, Margaret Rosso: 75
Grossman, Orin: 307
Groth, Renate: 88, 157, 255, 415
Grotius, Hugo: 21
Grout, Donald Jay: xli, 397, 415, 432
Grove, George: xxi, 130, 242
Gruber, Albion: 38, 51, 158, 202, 415
Gruber, Gernot: 40, 390, 415
Gruber, Gerold W.: 41, 408
Gruber, J. P.: 378
Grues, H.: 18
Grüß, Hans: 239
Grunsky, Hans Alfred: 170
Grusnick, Bruno: 31, 415

G'schrey, Richard: 173
Gubisch, Gérard: 320
Gudel, Joachim: 196, 300
Gudewill, Kurt: xlii
Gülke, Dorothea: 283
Gülke, Peter: 26, 265, 283, 286, 397
Gümpel, Karl-Werner: 435
Guenther, Ralph Russell: 127
Guenther, Roy James: 388, 428
Guentner, Francis J.: 434, 435
Guernsey, Wellington: 86
Guéroult, M. Georges: 118
Guerrero, Luis Juan: 71
Gugo Riman: see RIEMANN, Hugo
Guido: 193, 232
Guilford, Baron: see NORTH, Francis
Guion, David: 415
GUMPELZHAIMER, Adam: 84, **110-11**
Gunn, Anne: 123
Gurlitt, Wilibald: 238, 274, 416
Gushee, Lawrence A.: 272
Gustafson, Bruce: 73, 427, 430
Gut, Serge: 416, 439, 444
Guterman, Norbert: 311
Gutheil, Crystal H.: 104
Gutiérrez, Francisco Antonio: 83
Gutknecht, Dieter: 430
Gutmann, Joseph: 141
Gutmann, Veronika: 239, 282
Guzmán, Jorge de: 52
Gwilt, Richard: 416
Gwinner, Fannie Louise: 190
Gymnicus, I.: 226
Gysi, Fritz: 285
Haack, Helmut: 251, 252, 253, 256, 275, 366, 392, 393
Haar, James: 390, 393, 416, 428
Haas, Robert: 33
Haase, Hans: xli, 134, 221, 223, 227, 231
Haase, Rudolf: xvii, xxxix, 136, 137, 138, 139, 158, 159, 416, 438
Haase, Ursula: 139
Haberl, Ferdinand: xlii, 188
Habicht, Walter: 81, 82
Häfner, Roland: 379
Händel, Georg F.: 197, 207, 426 see also Handel, George Frideric
Haensel, Uwe: xlii
Häseler, Élie: 169
Haflich, Steven: 312
Haggh, Raymond Herbert: 143, 272, 362
Haggin, B. W.: 437
Hagmann, Peter: 286
Hagstroem, G.: 136

Hahn, Grete: 213
Hahn, H. G.: 92
Hahn, Kurt: 153, 190, 416
Hahn, Roger: 9
Hahne, Gerhard: 261, 329
Hailparn, Lydia: 416
Haimo, Ethan: 325
Halbfass, Wilhelm: 71
Halbreich, Harry: 323
Haldane, Elizabeth S.: 70
Halévy, Fromental: 55, 87
Halfpenny, Eric: 248
Hall, Anne C.: 422
Hall, A. Rupert: 374
Hall, Marie Boas: 374
Hall, Robert A., Jr.: 416
Hallman, Gordon: 265
Hallnäs, Lars: 311
HALM, August Otto: **112-13**
Haltmeier, Carl Johann Friedrich: 353
Hamann, Heinz Wolfgang: 371
Hambræus, Bengt: 29, 35, 323
Hamburger, Paul: 436
Hamel, Peter Michael: 139
Hamerik, Margaret N.: 420
Hamilton, A.: 231
Hamilton, David: 422
Hamilton, James Alexander: 56, 62, 233, 264, 416
Hammel, Marla: 416
Hammelmann, H. A.: 171
Hammer, Franz: 136
Hammerstein, Notker: 423
Hammerstein, Reinhold: xvii, xxix, 416
Hancock, Wendy: 282, 416
Handel, George Frideric: 77, 132, 228, 233, 243, 353, 357, 403, 409, 412, 424 see also Händel, Georg F.
Handman, Dorel: xix
Handschin, Jacques: 416
Hankins, Thomas Leroy: 9
Hanna, Lyle: 161
Hannas, Ruth: 52, 53, 138, 416, 427
Hannaway, Owen: 92
Hanning, Barbara Russano: 34, 209, 416, 433
Hansell, Sven Hostrup: 291, 365, 366, 417, 430
Hansen, Bernhard: 239, 274, 339, 410
Hansen, Mathias: 322
Hansen, Niels: 357
Hansen, Peter: 285
Hanslick, Eduard: 275, 325
Hantz, Edwin Charlton: 314
Haraszti, Emile: 73
Harberts, Dirk: 383
Harbison, John: 422

Harburger, Walter: 135, 417
Hardie, Graham: 426
Harding, Rosamond Evelyn Mary: 417
Hardy, Claude: 392
Harich-Schneider, Eta: 296, 417
Harley, John: 294
Harman, Richard Alexander: 66, 179, 211, 229, 244, 294, 340, 409, 415
Harnisch, Otto Siegfried: 121
Harnisch, W.: 168
Harper, Gwendoline: 67
Harrán, Don: 100, 368, 417, 433
Harrando, José: 420
Harré, R.: 137
Harris, Donald: 324
Harris, John Mackrell: 417, 437
Harris, Raymond: 430
Harris, S.: 311
Harris, Winifred: 435
Harrison, Frank Lloyd: 272, 410
Harrison, Max: 321, 322, 437
Harrison, W. H. John: 229
Harriss, Ernest Charles: 3, 195, 197
Harris-Warrick, Rebecca: 292
Hartig, Linda Bishop: 417
Hartman, James B.: 68
Hartmann, Andreas: 417
Hartmann, Eduard von: 429
Hartmann, Ernst: 417
Hartmann, Heinrich: 309
Hartmann, Thomas de: 347
Hartner, Willy: 82
Hartog, Jacques: 129, 267
Hartridge, Hamilton: 434
Harvey, David: 314
Harvey, Jonathan: 313, 324
Harwood, Gregory W.: 97
Harwood, Ian: 238
Haselauer, Elisabeth: 408
Haselböck, Hans: 138
Hasenclever, Richard: 136
Haspeslagh, Jan: 286
Hastings, Biard: 399
Hatch, Christopher: 311, 314, 422
Hattaway, Michael: 227
Hatten, Robert S.: 312, 436
Hatting, Carsten E.: 445
Hauk, Ingrid: 163
Hauptmann, Ernst: 114
HAUPTMANN, Moritz: **113-15**, 152, 189, 225, 266, 268, 317, 379, 437
Hausdorff, Otto: 112
Haußwald, Günter: 116, 356
Havard-Williams, P.: 360
Havelaar, Charles: 246

Havens, George R.: 432
Havingha, Gerhardus: 134
Hawkins, John Isaac: 372, 417
Hayashi, Mikinori: 275
Haydn, Franz Joseph: xxiii, xxxix, xl, 63, 93, 94, 95, 132, 145, 149, 205, 207, 262, 263, 303, 305, 307, 312, 325, 331, 361, 399, 400, 404, 419, 424, 428, 436, 438, 440
Haydon, Glen: xlii, 60, 66, 101, 404, 411, 417, 420, 427, 435
Haydon, Walter: 437
Hayes, Deborah: 125, 252, 253, 258
Hayes, Elizabeth Loretta: 184
Hayes, Gerald F.: 238, 294
Haynes, Renee: 447
Hayward, Albert: 422, 442
Heard, J. F.: 137
Heartz, Daniel: xl, 285, 286, 445
Heathcote, William Edward: 114
Heaton, Charles Huddleston: 81, 312, 437, 442
Heck, Johann Caspar: 93, 195, 246, 248
Heckenbach, Willibrord: 109
Heckmann, Harald: xxxviii, 38, 196, 238, 242, 417
Hedges, Anthony: 399
Hedges, Stephen A.: 417
Hedler, Gretchen Emilie: 363
Hefling, Stephen E.: 248
Hegberg, Susan: 381
Hehr, Eliszabeth W.: 382
Heije, J. P.: 21
Heimann, P. M.: 118, 132
Heimann, Walter: 417
Hein, Johannes: 417
HEINICHEN, Johann David: 100, **116-17**, 133, 165, 193, 194, 291, 336, 339, 411, 443
Heinlein, Christian Paul: 417
Heinrich, W.: 416
Heintze, H.: 285
Heintze, James R.: 180, 181
Helianus: see AHLE, Georg Johann
Heller, Friedrich C.: 40, 366
Heller, George N.: 437
Hellman, C. Doris: 136, 137, 138
Hellouin, Frédéric: 50, 51
Helm, Ernest Eugene: 3, 18, 321, 417, 431
Helm, Everett: 323, 327
Helman, Zofia: 314, 315, 316
HELMHOLTZ, Hermann von: 113, **117-21**, 225, 341, 342, 395
Helmore, Thomas: 228
Helms, Siegmund: 397

Henberger, Richard: 56
Henderson, Robert Vladimir: 418
Henderson, W. J.: 356
Henfling, Conrad: 158, 159
Heninger, S. K., Jr.: 136, 423
Henke, Käthe: 340
Henke, Matthias: 197
Henneberg, Gudrun: 149, 418
Henriot, Patrice: 258
Henry, Barbara: 433
Henry, Charles: 9, 256
Henry IV: 425
Hentschel, Ernst Julius: 168, 190
HERBST, Johann Andreas: 23, 79, **121-22**, 161, 338
Herbst, Kurt: 155
Herder, Johann Gottfried: 343
Herivel, J. W.: 137
Herlin, Théodore: 87
Hermand, Jost: 438
Herman, Robert Henry: 98
Hermann, Ursula: 383
Hermelink, Siegfried: xviii, 393
Hermosillo, Carmen: 29
Herrmann, Joachim: 396
Herschel, J. F. W.: 169
Herschkel, E.: xxxiv
Hertzmann, Erich: 409, 441
Herzfeld, Friedrich: 171
Hesse, Max: xxvii
Hesselink, Paul S.: 442
Hest, Jeffrey: 311
Hetsch, Gustav: 115
Hettrick, Jane Schatkin: 430
Hettrick, William E.: 111
Heughebaert, H.: 207
Heussner, Horst: xli
Heutte, Frederic: 415
Heym, Ludwig Maximilian: 343
Hickman, Aubrey: 425
Hickman, Roger: 104
Hickmann, Ellen: 200, 239
Hiebert, Erwin: 419
Hiekel, Hans Otto: 239
Higbee, Dale: 68, 103, 246, 248, 363, 409, 430, 431, 444, 446
Higginson, J. Vincent: 209, 435
Hill, Christopher: 92, 374
Hill, George R.: 435
Hill, John Walter: 188, 418, 435
Hill, Richard S.: 310, 320, 411
Hill, Robert E.: 425
Hiller, Ferdinand: 114, 115
Hiller, Johann Adam: xxxvi, 1, 3, 116, 288, 332, 350, 357, 410, 418, 438
Hills, Arthur: 406
Hillsman, Walter: 341
Hilmar, Ernst: 323

Hilse, Walter: 31
Hilton, Wendy: 202
Himelfar, H.: 91
Hince, Kenneth F.: 360
Hindemith, Paul: xxiii, 137, 139, 315, 323, 402, 407, 408, 416
Hindle, Brooke: 132
Hindmarsh, Paul: 445
Hine, Janet: 223
Hinson, Maurice: 63, 363, 443
Hipple, Walter J., Jr.: 405
Hirsch, Andreas: 140
Hirsch, Guy: 82
Hirsch, Paul: xxxvi
Hita, Rodríguez de: 281
Hitchcock, H. Wiley: xxix, 45, 46, 400
Hixon, Don L.: 437
Hławiczka, Karol: 144
Hoag, Barbara Brewster: 418
Hobohm, Wolf: 134
Hoboken, Anthony von: xlii
Höft, Brigitte: 379
Högel, Sten: 357
Högler, Fritz: 393
Hoelty-Nickel, Theodore: xlii
Höntsch, Herbert: 437
Höpfner, Thomas M.: 32, 43
Hövker, R.: 190
Hoffman, Donald: 418
Hoffman, Mark: 177, 225, 275, 379, 418
Hoffmann, Arthur: xxxvi
HOFFMANN, Eucharius: **122**, 354
Hoffmann, Hans: xliii
Hoffmann, Mark: 115
Hoffmann, Niels Frédéric: 418
Hoffmann, P.: 80
Hoffmann, Richard: 325, 326
Hoffmann, Winfried: xxxviii
Hoffmann, W. L.: 67
Hoffmann-Erbrecht, Lothar: xxix, 18, 166, 188, 194, 356, 363, 408, 409, 416
Hoffmann-Erbrecht, Margarete: 55, 347, 367, 393
Hofmann, J. E.: 137, 138, 159
Hofmann, Richard: 163
Hofmiller, Josef: 213
Hogg, Helen Sawyer: 138
Hogwood, Christopher: 164, 398
Hohenemser, Richard Heinrich: 56
Hoiseth, Gary Thomas: 192, 418
Hoke, Hans Gunter: 185, 204, 205, 277, 301
Holcomb, Margaret Ann: 315
HOLDEN, John: **122-23**, 231
Holden, Stephen S.: 295

HOLDER, William: **123-24**, 133, 221, 421
Holdstock, Janice: 445
Hollander, Hans: 67, 397, 399, 426, 431, 445
Hollander, Jeffrey: 443
Holle, Hugo: 154
Holler, Karl Heinz: 34
Holm, Theodora: 37, 49, 54, 60, 123
Holman, Peter: 227, 419
Holschneider, Andreas: xli
Holst, Imogen: 360
Holton, Gerald: 136, 137
Holtzapple, Jay Charles: 418
Holtzman, S. R.: 423
Home, R. W.: xvii
Honegger, Arthur: 127
Hooke, Robert: 123, 374, 415, 421
Hooper, Joseph Graham: 32
Hoover, Kathleen O'Donnell: 209
Hopkins, George William: 322
Hopkins, Robert G.: 447
Hornbostel, Erich Moritz von: 341, 342
Hornby, Richard: 92
Horský, Zdeněk: 138
Horsley, Imogene: 54, 150, 192, 227, 355, 392, 393, 400, 418, 427
Horton, John: 425
Hortschansky, Klaus: 293, 299, 430
Hoshino, Hiroshi: 418
Hosler, Bellamy Hamilton: 418
Hospers, John: 422
Houghton, Edward F.: 108, 351
Houle, George Louis: 418
Howard, John Brooks: 161, 433
Howard, Samuel: 211
Howard, V. A.: 422
Howell, Almonte C., Jr.: 169, 174, 216, 220, 281, 296, 419
Howes, F.: 310
Howey, Henry Eugene: 338
Hoyt, Reed J.: 315
Hsu, Dolores Menstell: 155
Hucbald: 27, 322
Huck, Rainer: 260
Hucke, Helmut: 106, 356, 419, 431
Hudson, Barton: 53
Hübsch-Pfleger, Lini: 239
Hüschen, Heinrich: xli, xlii, 372, 373, 419
Huffman, William H.: 92
Hughes, Charles W.: 234, 247, 431
Hughes, Rosemary: 56,95
Huglo, Michel: 88, 162
Hullah, John: 66
Hullfish, William R.: 334
Hulse, Stewart H.: 315

Hultberg, Warren Earl: 296
Humbert, Georges: 270, 272
Hunt, Frederick Vinton: 419
Hunt, Thomas Webb: 286
Hunter, Henry: 81
Hunter, Michael: 373
Hunter, Richard: 132
Hurd, Michael: 49, 67, 415, 436
Hurlbut, Ira D.: 274
Hurstfield, Joel: 92
Husmann, Heinrich: xxxviii, xlii, 26, 119
Hutchings, Arthur: 35, 58, 310, 419, 420, 428, 431, 432, 445
Hutchins, Robert Maynard: xxii
Hutchinson, William: 419
HUYGENS, Christiaan: xxxix, **124-25**, 233, 420
Huygens, Constantijn: 124
Huys, Bernard: 88
Hyde, Frederick Bill: 202, 439
Ibberson, John B.: 419
Ibberson, Mary: 399
Ichikawa, Schinichiro: 4
Iiranek, Ya: 16
Ijsewijn, Joseph: 372
Ilgner, C. F.: 168
Imig, Renate: 419
Imoto, Shoji: 247
Inada, Hiroko: 195
d'INDY, Vincent: **126-27**
Ingen, F. J. van: 153
Ionta, Sylvester John: 188
Irmen, Hans-Josef: 56, 339, 419
Irving, Howard: 419
Isaac, C.: 430
Isaac, Heinrich: 26
Isgro, Robert Mario: 419
Isherwood, Robert M.: 9, 406
Ishibashi, Hiro: xli
Ishihala, Toshinori: 247
Isoyama, Tadashi: 196
Istel, Edgar: 173, 285
Istomin, Igor': 388
Ivanov-Boretsky, I. V.: 405
Jack, Adrian: 324
Jackendoff, Ray: 314
Jackisch, Frederick Frank: 419
Jackman, James L.: 101
Jackson, Barbara: 212
Jackson, Roland: xx, 12, 171, 236, 419
Jacobi, Erwin R.: 66, 151, 187, 251, 255, 256, 257, 333, 349, 350, 351, 356, 362, 363, 410, 419, 440
Jacobs, Arthur: 415, 445
Jacobs, Charles: 296, 420
Jacobs, Eduard: 25

Jacobs, Robert L.: 436
Jacoby, Robert: 441
Jacquot, Jean: 178
JADASSOHN, Salomon: **128-30**, 152, 440
Jakoby, Richard: xxxv, xliii
Jalowetz, Heinrich: 322
James, Donald: 431
Jameux, Dominique: 321
Janáček, Leoš: xxxix
Jander, Owen: 20, 356, 420
Janetzky, Kurt: 140
JANOVKA, Tomáš Baltazar: 38, **131**, 375
Jansen, Albert: 285
Janson, Thomas: 407
Jardine, Lisa: 92
Jardine, N.: 135
Jasinsky, Mark Heber: 420
Javorsky, Boleslav: see YAVORSKY, Boleslav Leopol'dovich
Jeans, Susi: 139, 362
Jeanson, Gunnar: 112
Jenkins, Newell: 35
Jenne, Natalie: 420
Jensen, Gustav: 56
Jensen, Jørgen I.: 425
Jeppesen, Knud: 94, 420, 435
Jessopp, Augustus: 221, 222
Jičinsky, B.: 13
Jiránek, Jaroslav: 13, 14, 15, 420
Joachim, Joseph: 379
Jodin, Mathieu: 128
Jöde, Fritz: 112
Joffe, Judah A.: 387
Johann Georg II, King: 413
Johann Georg III, King: 413
Johann Georg IV, King: 413
Johns, Donald: 315
Johnson, Calvert: 420
Johnson, David: 231
Johnson, Douglas: 312
Johnson, Fredric Bolan: 350
Johnson, Gregory S.: 401
Johnson, J. E.: 306
Johnson, Reginald: 396
Johnsson, Bengt: 209, 261
Johnston, Gregory S.: 443
Johnstone, H. D.: 420
Jonas, Oswald: 304, 305, 306, 307, 308, 309, 310, 311, 313, 315, 317, 415
Jonckbloet, Willem Jozef-Andries: 21, 420
Jones, Charles: 428
Jones, Edward Huws: 178
Jones, Frank N.: 9, 118
Jones, Gregory Paul: 149

Jones, Griffith: 251
Jones, G. Thaddeus: 442
Jones, Harold Spencer: 136
Jones, John A.: 420
Jones, Patricia Collins: 66
Jones, Vincent Lloyd: 420
JONES, William: **131-32**
Joppig, G.: 306
Jorgens, Elise Bickford: 49
Jorgensen, Owen Henry: 420
Jorgenson, Dale Alfred: 115, 420
Joseph, John: 363
Josquin des Prez: xxxix, 26, 59, 314,
    422, 423, 441
Josquin, Jan: 441
Josten, C. H.: 91, 92
Jourdain, Philip E. B.: 70
Jousse, John: 6, 231
Joyce, Frederick Wayland: 228
Jozzi, Giuseppe: 231
Jubal: 428
Jullien, Adolphe: 420
Jumilhac, Pierre-Benoît de: 78
Jung, Carl Gustav: 137
Jung, Hans Rudolf: 212, 353, 420
Jung, Hermann: 371
Jung, K: 371
Jung, Karl: 145
Juon, Paul: 54, 55
Jurafsky, A.: 279
Juškevič, Adolf P.: 80, 81 (see
    Youschkevitch, A. P.)
Just, Martin: xxxviii
Kabalevsky, D. B.: 14
Kade, O.: 59
Kade, Reinhard: 68
Kähler, Guido: 420
Kämper, Dietrich: 209, 433
Kätzel, Heinrich: 420
Kahl, Russell: 118
Kahl, Willi: xl, 13, 58, 63, 396, 418,
    421
Kahn, Lina: 70
Kalff, S.: 21,125
Kalib, Sylvan Sol: 307
Kalkbrenner, Friedrich Wilhelm
    Michael: 167
Kallen, Gerhard: xxxvi
Kaltenbrunner, Gerd-Klaus: 438
Kamien, Roger: 306, 314
Kamieński, Lucian: 421
Kamper, Dietrich: 403
Kandinsky, Wassily: 325
Kangro, Hans: 141
Kant, Immanuel: 308, 325, 429
Kapp, Reinhard: 113
Karajan, Herbert von: xl
Karbaum, Michael: 65

Karbusicky, Vladimir: 13
Kargon, Robert H.: 132
Karkoschka, Erhard: 305, 306
Karl, King of inner Austria: 411
Karube, Yoko: 421
Kashkin, Nikolai Dmitrievich: 163,
    346
Kassler, Jamie Croy: xlii, 123, 132,
    222, 223, 314, 406, 421, 423
Kassler, Michael: 150, 151, 310, 311,
    425
Kastner, Macario Santiago: 29, 293,
    296, 335, 421
Kataoka, Gido: 54
Kattsoff, Louis O.: 135
Katz, Adele T.: 309
Katz, Erich: 247, 421
Katz, Ruth: 30, 69, 98, 99, 118, 136,
    140, 195, 202, 252, 301, 306,
    307, 321, 322, 393
Katzenberger, Günter: xliii
Kauffmann, Paul: 84
Kaufmann, Harald: 310, 421
Kaufmann, Helen L.: 104
Kaufmann, Henry William: 175, 367,
    368
Kaufmann, Walter: xlii
Kauko, Väinö Olavi: 421
Kaul, Oskar: 141, 173
Kayser, Hans: 136, 421
Kealey, Edward J.: 202
Keane, Sister Michaela Marie: 257
Kearns, William: 125
Keats, John: xxv
Kee, Piet: 383
Keferstein, Dr.: 189
Keiler, Allan R.: 258, 312, 314, 317
Keislar, Douglas: 421
KELLER, Gottfried: 123, **133**
Keller, Hans: 298, 310, 323, 359, 436
Keller, Hermann: 302, 421, 422
Keller, Wilhelm: 225, 310
Kelletat, Herbert: 422
KELLNER, David: **133-34**, 353
Kellner, Herbert Anton: 382, 399
Kellner, Johann Peter: 218
Kelterborn, Rudolf: 436
Kelvin, Lord: 119
Kennig, Albert: see GEVAERT,
    François-Auguste
Kent, Charles: 69, 349
Kenyon, John: 92
Kenyon, Max: 437
Kenyon, Nicholas: 426
KEPLER, Johannes: xxxix, 47, 90, 91,
    134-39, 230, 380
Kerman, Joseph: 171, 209, 310, 359,
    360, 422, 437

Kermode, Frank: 92
Kernan, Alvin: 92
Kerr, David Wallis: 213
Kerridge, W. H.: 322
Kessler, Hubert: 310
Keys, Ivor: 404
Keyser, Samuel Jay: xxvii
Khachaturian, Aram: 386
Kholopov, Yury Nikolaevich: 313, 388
Kidson, Frank: 235
Kier, Herfrid: 331
Kiesewetter, Raphael Georg: 45,83
Kimmel, Walter S.: 102
Kinderman, William: 422
King, A. Hyatt: 398, 416
King, Judith D.: 312
King, Matthew Peter: 150, 151
Kingdon, Robert K.: 202
King-Hele, D. G.: 138
Kinkeldey, Otto: 2, 178, 211, 296,
    404, 412, 422, 437
Kinney, Gordon J.: 29, 282, 417, 422
Kintzler, Catherine: 80, 251, 253, 254,
    255, 258, 259, 286
Kinzel, Hugo Jos: 113
Kipnis, Igor: 101, 409, 421
Kirakowska, Susan: 104
Kirby, Frank Eugene: 89, 431
KIRCHER, Athanasius: xxxiv,
    139-42, 93, 229, 240, 280, 290,
    354, 375
Kirchmann, J. H.: 70
Kirk, Elise K.: 188
Kirkby, Emma: 356
Kirkendale, Warren: 422
Kirkpatrick, Ralph: 17, 18
KIRNBERGER, Johann Philipp: 27,
    85, **142-45**, 150, 182, 183, 185,
    328, 330, 342, 377, 415
Kirsch, Ernst: 108
Kirsch, Winfried: 41, 227, 398
Kirschkorn, Kurt: 310
Kisch, Eve: 285
Kiselev, V. A.: 346
KITSON, Charles Herbert: **146-47**
Kivy, Peter: 196, 197, 417, 422
Kjellberg, Erik: 408, 433
Klare, Johannes: 285
Klare, Waltraud: 285
Klauwell, Otto: 56, 163
Kleffel, Arno: 173
Klein, Rolf: 423
Klein, Rudolf: 306, 407, 439, 444
Klein, Ulrich: 138
Kleinman, Sidney: 286, 423
Klemm, Eberhardt: 319
Klenin, Emily: 314
Klenz, William: 35, 445

Klerk, Jos de: 21
Kleßmann, Eckart: 353
Kling, H.: 285
Kloocke, Kurt: 286
Kloppenburg, W. C. M.: 144
Klose, Friedrich: 40
Kluge, Reiner: xl
Kmicic-Mieleszyński, Wacław: 299, 300
Knapp, M.: 81
Knaus, Herwig: 41, 398, 401, 411
Knecht, Justin Heinrich: 370, 423
Kneif, Tibor: 13, 59
Knepler, Georg: xlii, 15
Knocker, Editha: 212
Knöfel, E.: 136
Knopoff, Leon: 419
Knorr, F.: 165
Knouse, Nola Reed: 148, 178 See Reed, Nola
Knowles, C. H. G.: 244
Kob, Walter: 423
KOCH, Heinrich Christoph: 57, **147-49**, 176, 182, 205, 206, 262, 269, 276, 328, 342, 378, 403, 412, 416, 426
Koch, Walter Albert: 137
Köchel, Ludwig Ritter von: 94
Koechlin, Charles: 102
Köhler, Louis: 114, 115
Köhler, Wolfgang: 202
Koenigsberger, Dorothy: 423
Koenigsberger, Leo: 119
Köster, Heinrich Gottfried: 369
Koestler, Arthur: 137
Kohlschütter, Bernd: 423
Kohs, Ellis B.: 310, 432
Kolczynski, C. A.: 432
Kolisch, Rudolf: 322
KOLLMANN, Augustus Frederic Christopher: **150-51**, 168, 377
Kolneder, Walter: xxxv, 214, 215, 248, 302, 310, 397
Kolof, Mizler von: see MIZLER von Kolof, Lorenz Christoph
Komar, Arthur J.: 305, 309, 310, 311, 316
Komma, Karl Michael: 423, 438
Kon, Juliia: 388
Kondra, Sergei Grigor'evich: 386
Konecne, Julie Lynn: 423
Konen, Valentina Dzhozefovna: 388
Konold, Wulf: 321, 368
Kooiker, Anthony: 164
Kooiman, Ewald: 423
Koopmann, Helmut: 438
Korabel'nikova, Liudmila Zinovevna: 346, 347

Kornauth, Egon: 321
Korsten, F. J. M.: 223
Korsyn, Kevin: 316
Korte, Werner: xxvi, 438
Kortholt, Christian: 158
Kosar, Anthony Jay: 87, 88, 306
Kotler, N.: 346
Kotov, Petr Aleksandrovich: 280
Koyré, Alexandre: 137
Krabbe, Wilhelm: 67
Kraehenbuehl, David: 310, 435
Krämer, Ulrich: 326, 424
Krafft, Fritz: 118, 137, 138
Kraft, Günther: xli, 361
Kraft, Leo: 95
Krall, Emil: 54
Kramer, Gale: 423
Kramer, Margarete: 423
Kramer, Richard: 17, 19, 423
Krantz, Steven Charles: 423
Krapf, Gerhard: 381
Krassowski, Janusz: 73, 300
Kratochwil, Heinz: 306
Kraus, Egon: 323
Kraus, Hedwig: 144
Krause, Christian Gottfried: 427
Krause, Ernst: 324
Krause, Heinz: 26
Krause-Graumnitz, Heinz: 26
Kravitt, Edward F.: 173
Krebs, Carl: 73
Krebs, Harald: 312, 316, 363
Krehbiel, James Woodrow: 423
KREHL, Stephan: 115, **152**
Kreichgauer: 82
Kreider, J. Evan: 427, 428
Kreidler, Walter: 155
Kreitz, Helmut: 371
Kremer, Joseph-François: xix, 251, 252
Kremer-Marietti, Angele: 284
Kremlev, Yuri: 423
Krenek, Ernst: 407, 423, 427
Kretzschmar, Hermann: xxv, 75, 162, 423
Kriss, Barbara Heuman: 446
Kriukov, Andrei Nikolaevich: 16
Kröner, Gisela: 159
Krohn, Ernst C.: 274, 275, 397
Krome, Ferdinand: 423
Krones, Hartmut: 4, 401, 412, 423
Kross, Siegfried: xliii, 18, 19
Kroyer, Theodor: xlii, 423
Krüger, E.: 118
Krueger, Theodore Howard: 305
Krützfeldt, Werner: 239, 424
Kruglikov, S. N.: 280
Krumhansl, Carol L.: 424

Krummacher, C.: 197
Krummacher, Friedhelm: xxxix, 424
Krush, Joseph Martin: 406
Kruttge, E.: 18
Kubota, Keiichi: 424
Kučera, Václav: 14
Kudlawiec, Dennis Paul: 311
Kühn, Clemens: 309, 320
Kühn, Hellmut: xxxviii
Kühn, Walter: 274
Kümmel, Werner Friedrich: 187, 424
Kümmerling, Harald: 424
Küntzel, Gottfried: 408
Kuhn, August: 206
Kuhn, Ernst: 13
Kuhn, Max: 424
Kuhn, Thomas S.: 70
KUHNAU, Johann: **153-54**, 210, 242, 373
Kulakovsky, Lev Vladimirovich: 387, 388
Kundi, Dr.: 188, 397
Kunisch, Hermann: xxxii
Kunselman, Joan D.: 312, 313, 317
Kuntz, Marion Leathers: 423
Kunze, Gerhard: xxxvi
Kunze, Stefan: 265, 424
Kurdiumov, Yury Vladimirovich: 272, 346
Kuronen, Darcy: 292
Kurpinski, Karol: 264
KURTH, Ernst: 13, **154-56**, 170, 273, 412, 420
Kurtzman, Jeffrey G.: 427
Kushner, David Zakeri: 311, 325, 427, 430
Kuttner, Fritz A.: 435, 436
Kuznetsov, Konstantin Alekseevich: 345, 346
Kwasnik, Walter: 337
Labbet de Morambert, Antoine-Jacques: 254, 288
Labeo, Notker: 27
La Borde, Jean-Benjamin de: 8, 424
La Cuesta, Ismael Fernández de: 293
Lade, John: 362
Ladewig, James: 104
Ladukhin, A.: 271
Läusimpeltz, Charis: see PRINTZ, Wolfgang Caspar
La Fage, Juste Adrien Lenoir de: 58, 94, 424
La Fond, Jean François de: 294
Lagas, Roelof: xlii
Laing, Millard Myron: 265
La Laurencie, L. de: 405
Lalič, Branka: 436
Laloy, Louis: 126, 256

Lam, Basil: 437
Lamb, James Boyd: 313
Lambert, J. Philip: 151
Lambert, Michel: 291
Lamblin, André: 316
Laming, Frank M.: 436, 445
La Motte, Diether de: 305, 322, 398, 439, 442
La Motte-Haber, Helga de: 156, 315, 342, 406, 424
Lampadius: 59
Lampe, John Frederick: 233
Lampl, Hans: 238
Lamy, Bernard: 444
Land, J. P. N.: 21, 125, 420
Landon, Christa: 331
Landon, H. C. Robbins: see Robbins Landon, H. C.
Landormy, Paul: 274
Lang, Paul Henry: xlii, 6, 60, 196, 256, 309, 356, 360, 409, 424
Lang, Robert: 317
Lange, Georg: 424
Lange, Helmut K. H.: 296, 337, 422
Langenmantel, Hieronymus Ambrosius: 140, 141
Langham, Ian: 314
Langhorne, John: 123
LANGLÉ, Honoré François Marie: 50, 56, **157**
Langlie, Warren M.: 323
Lantier, Pierre: 261, 262
La Porte, Claude-Nicolas de: 256
Larosh, Herman: 347, 424
Larsen, Arved Martin, III: 28
Larsen, Holger: 319
Larsen, Jens Peter: xl, 424
Larson, Steve: 307, 316
Larsson, Roger Barnett: 424
LaRue, Jan: xl, xlii, 88, 312, 428, 431, 437
Laski, Jean: 109
Laskowski, Larry: 312, 314
Lasocki, David: 248
Lassen, H. C. F.: 148
Lasserre, Pierre: 256
Lasso, Orlando di: 26, 41, 42, 66, 67, 109, 402, 425, 437
Latham, Peter: 420
Laudon, Robert T.: 424
Laufer, Edward: 306
Laugel, Antoine Auguste: 119
Launay, Denise: 30, 116, 138, 229, 339, 392, 409, 424, 425, 439
Laurencie, Lionel de la: xlii, 77
Lavignac, Albert J. A.: 77, 405
LA VOYE-MIGNOT, DE: **157-58**
Lawrence, Ian: 425

Lawrence, Merle: 120
Lawrenson, Tom: 92
Layer, Adolf: 213
Lazzari, Maria Grazia: 286
Leak, John: 52
Lebeau, Elisabeth: 39, 257
Lebedeva, Elena: 15
Leborne, Ambroise: 50
Lecky, James: 425
Le Clercq, Alexandre: 78
Le Coat, Gérard: 315, 425
Ledbetter, David: 292, 426
Ledbetter, Steven: 226
Ledda, Primarosa: 75
Lederer, Josef-Horst: 33, 232, 324
Lee, Douglas A.: 429
Lee, Sir Sidney: xxi
Leech-Wilkinson, Daniel: 402
Lefkoff, Gerald: 418
Lefkowitz, Murray: 164
Le Fort, Jehan: 392
Legge, M. Dominica: 447
Legrand, J.: 67, 407, 426
Lehmann, Dieter: 13, 14, 15
le Huray, Peter: xix, xx, 8, 164, 255, 343, 421, 425
LEIBNIZ, Gottfried Wilhelm: xl, **158-59**, 204, 298
Leibowitz, René: 321
Leicester, Henry M.: 91
Leichtentritt, Hugo: 163, 309, 398
Leigh, R. A.: xl
Leinsdorf, Erich: 422
Leipp, E.: 257
Le Jeune, Claude: 230
Lek, Robbert van der: 171
Lekai, Louis J.: 202
Le Maire, Charles: 220
Le Maire, Jean: 202
Lemaire, Théophile: 356
Lemke, Arno: 378, 379
Lemokh, Vikenti Osipovich: 190
Lenaerts, René Bernard: xlii
Lenneberg, Hans: 195, 197, 201
Lenoble, Robert: 202
Lenoir, Yves: 209, 437
Lenz, Irmgard: 371
Leo, Johannes: 343
Leo, Leonardo: 57
Leonesi, Luigi: 356
Leonhardt, Gustav: 446
León Tello, Francisco José: 425
Leprade, Paul A.: 69
Lerdahl, Fred: 314, 316, 425
Leroy, Edmund Walter: 201
Lescat, Philippe: 259
Lescourret, Marie-Anne: 413
Lesemann, Heidi: 326

Leslie, John Kenneth: 208
Lesser, Elisabeth: 253
Lessing, Gotthold Ephraim: 185
Lessman, Otto: 173
Lester, Joel: xxiii, 82, 93, 94, 131, 160, 161, 194, 313, 376, 402, 425
Lesure, François: 69, 88, 201, 202, 327, 389, 409, 421, 445, 447
Leuchtmann, Horst: 401, 425
Levarie, Siegmund: 396, 408, 425
Levenson, Boris: 280
Levenson, Irene Montefiore: 425
Leverkühn, Adrian: 325
Levi, Anthony Herbert Tigar: 425
Levi, Josef: 130
Levi, Vito: 40
Levin, A.: 102
Levin, Robert D.: 430
Levin, Saul: 15
Levitan, Joseph S.: 108, 425
Levy, Edward: 311
Levy, Jim: 394
Levy, Morton: 309, 311
Lévy-Schoen, A.: 118
Lewin, David: 323, 425, 426
Lewis, Anthony: 426
Lewis, Christopher: 326, 426
Lewis, David: 88, 115, 258, 314
Lewis, H. M.: 426
Lewis, Mary S.: 394
Liadov, A. K.: 280
Libavius, Andreas: 90
Libby, Dennis: 101, 182, 400, 426
Libin, Laurence: 238
Lichtenhahn, Ernst: 109
Lichtenthal, Pietro: 413, 426
Lidke, Wolfgang: 213
Lieberman, Ira: 155
Liebermann, Marc L.: 298
Liebling, James: 54
Liebow, Lois: 430
Liess, Andreas: 94
Limmert, Erich: 324
Lindberg, David C.: 419
Lindgren, Lowell: 430
Lindley, Mark: 202, 366, 382, 402, 408, 426, 443
Lindsay, Maurice: 411
Lindsey, David Ray: 258
Link, John W., Jr.: 185
Linke, Norbert: 322, 408
Lioncourt, Guy de: 126
Lippert, J.: 363
LIPPIUS, Johannes: 10, 24, 60, 110, **160-61**, 193, 240, 261, 317
Lippman, Edward Arthur: 195, 199, 202, 254, 284, 310, 311, 426
Lippmann, Friedrich: xxxix

Lippold, Eberhard: 13, 15
Liptak, David: 447
Lisle, Christiane: 321
Lissa, Zofia: xxxix, 14, 388, 413
List, Erich: 426
List, Martha: 136, 137, 138
Listen: see LISTENIUS, Nikolaus
LISTENIUS, Nikolaus: **161-62**, 389
Liszt, Franz: xxiv, 61, 126, 172, 262, 303, 326, 379, 380, 395, 414, 435, 443
Livanova, T. N.: 346
Livingston, Herbert: 310
Livingstone, Ernest Felix: 84, 426
Ljungar-Chapelon, A.: 248
Lloyd, Llewelyn Southworth: 119, 400, 426
Lloyd, Norman: 309
Lloyd-Jones, David: 55
Loach, Donald Glenn: 109, 426, 428
Lobanov, Mihail: 388
LOBE, Johann Christian: 54, 55, **162-63**
Lochhead, Judith: 401, 410, 437
Locke, Arthur W.: 71
LOCKE, Matthew: **164**, 235, 294
Lockspeiser, Edward: 56, 95, 256, 308, 309
Lockwood, Lewis: xxxiv, 64, 401, 426, 433
LÖHLEIN, Georg Simon: 63, **165-66**, 423
Lönn, Anders: 408
Loeschmann, Horst B.: 305
Loewe, K.: 168
Loewenberg, Alfred: 411
LOGIER, Johann Bernhard: **166-69**, 150, 151, 189, 190, 228
Lohmann, Johannes: 71
Lohmeier, Dieter: 424
Lohne, J. A.: 137, 138, 374
Loidol, Rafael: 40
Lombardini, Maddalena: 349, 350
Lonardi, Massimo: 33
Londée, Jonas: 134
London, S. J.: 120
Long, John H.: 227
Longuet-Higgins, Christopher: 314, 315
Longyear, Rey M.: 410, 426, 431
Lonsdale, Roger: 132, 426
Loquin, Anatole: 87
Lord, Phillip J.: 334
LORENTE, Andrés: **169**, 296
LORENZ, Alfred (Ottokar): **170-71**, 155
Lorenzen, Hermann: 110
Lorenzoni, Antonio: 247

Loriti, Henricus: see GLAREAN, Heinrich
Lossius, Lucas: 41
Lott, Walter: xliii
Lotter, Johann Jakob: 213
Lottermoser, Werner: 119, 426
Lotze, Hermann: 119
LOUIS, Rudolf, and THUILLE, Ludwig: **172-73**, 273
Louis XIII: 425
LOULIÉ, Étienne: **173-74**, 443
Louvier, Alain: 102
Lovewell, S. Harrison: 270, 273
Lowbury, Edward Joseph Lister: 49
Lowinsky, Edward E.: xxxix, 64, 209, 286, 293, 367, 426, 427, 444
Lowry, H.: 436
Luciani, S. A.: 2
Luckett, Richard: 227, 410, 415
Lucks, F. Wilhelm: 383
Lucktenberg, George H.: 292
Ludden, Bennet: 404
Ludvová, Jitka: 371
Ludwig, Hellmut: 202
Lübenau, L.: 128
Lück, Hartmut: 320, 324
Lück, Rudolf: 323
Luening, Otto: 396
Luisi, Francesco: 34, 53
Luisi, Leila Galleni: 34
Luk'ianov, V.: 15
Lully, Jean Baptiste: 214
Lunacharsky, Anatoly Vasil'evich: 387, 388
Lundin, Robert W.: 315
Luntz, Erwin: 215
Luoma, Robert Gust: 427
Luper, Albert Thomas: 415, 427
Luppi, Andrea: 159
LUSITANO, Vicente: 64, 74, **175**, 367
LUSSY, Mathis: **176-77**, 205, 274, 413
Lustig, Jacob Wilhelm: 184, 246, 381 see also Lustig, Jaques Guillaume
Lustig, Jaques Guillaume: 183, 231 see also Lustig, Jacob Wilhelm
Lustig, Roger L.: 148, 197
Luten, C. J.: 171
Luther, Wilhelm Martin: 76
Lvoff, Alexis de: 88
Lykkebo, Finn: 397
Lynn, Michael: 285
Lyon, Margaret E.: 431
Lyra, Justin Wilhelm: 226
Lysten: see LISTENIUS, Nikolaus
M. D. *** de Dijon: 9

Maar, Gerold: 138
Maas, Chris: 21
Maasih, Camelia: 138
Maass, J. G. E.: 362, 363, 378
MacArdle, Donald W.: 437
Macarry, P.: 85
MacClintock, Carol: 2, 18, 22, 37, 46, 73, 75, 89, 98, 103, 202, 211, 213, 214, 222, 223, 238, 247, 292, 362, 367, 390, 392, 409, 427
MacDonald, Calum: 359
Mace, Dean T.: 202, 427, 433
MACE, Thomas: **178**
MacFarren, C. Natalia: 190
MACFARREN, Sir George Alexander: 66, **179**, 228
MacGillivray, James A.: 223
Mach, Ernst: 119, 427
Machabey, Armand: 91, 257, 425
Macirone, George: 190
Mack, Dietrich: 171
Mackensen, Ludolf v.: 159
Mackenzie, Alexander Carl Norderstrom: 427
Mackerness, E. D.: 178, 223
Mackey, Donald: xl
Mackinnon, Douglas A.: 404
Maclean, Charles: 223
Maconie, Robin: 407
Maczewski, Johannes: 422
Maddison, R. E. W.: 137
Madou, Jean-Pol: 286
Maecklenburg, Albert: 274
Maedel, Rolf: 82
Maegaard, Jan: 321
Maertens, Willi: 353
Magee, Noel Howard: 265
Magnus, F. C.: see Haydn, Franz Joseph
Mahlert, Elke: 427
Mahling, Christoph-Hellmut: xlii, xliii
Mahnke, Dietrich: 159
Mahrenholz, Christhard: 1
Maier, Elisabeth: 41
Maier, Siegfried: 427
MAILLART, Pierre: **180**
Mainka, Jürgen: 302, 329, 427, 436
Mainke, Dietrich: 427
Mairan, Jean-Jacques Dortous de: 7
Maitland, J. A. Fuller: 169
Maks, Christina Sandrina: 52
MALCOLM, Alexander: **180-81**, 233
Maleden, Pierre: 207
Malgoire, Jean-Claude: 80, 251, 253, 254, 255, 258
Malignon, Jean: 258
Malipiero, Gian Francesco: 209

Mallard, James Harry: 427
Malloch, William: 63
Mancini, Giambattista: 181, 182
Mandelbaum, Joel: 407
Manfredi, Alessandro: 93
MANFREDINI, Vincenzo: **181-82**
Mangeot, André: 103
Manget, Jean Jacques: 91
Maniates, Maria Rika: xlii, 367, 368, 417, 427, 434
Manion, Mark Martin: 155
Mann, Alfred: 35, 94, 95, 183, 187, 188, 197, 212, 331, 332, 428, 430, 443
Mann, Gunter: xxxiv, 424
Mann, Michael: 309
Mann, Thomas: 325
Mann, William S.: 298, 323, 359
Mannes, Leopold: 309
Mantica, Francesco: xxxi, 45
Manz, Gustav: 119
Manzoni, Giacomo: 37, 319, 321, 322
Maragliano Mori, Rachele: 45
Marcase, Donald Earl: 23, 24
Marcello, Benedetto: 67
Marcello, H.: 176
Marchant, Sir Stanley: 432
Marchetto da Padova: 402
Marco, Guy A.: 310, 391, 392, 393, 407, 409, 410, 434
Marcozzi, Rudy T.: 314
Marenzio, Luca: 410
Margenau, Henry: 118
Marggraf, Wolfgang: 398
Margrave, Wendell: 322, 410
Maria, Tomas de Santa: see SANTA MARIA, Tomas de
Marin, Oscar S. M.: 314
Marion, Jean-Luc: xxi
Marion, M. C.: 36
Marnold, Jean: 274
Maróthy, J.: 14
MARPURG, Friedrich Wilhelm: 3, 7, 8, 17, 18, 57, 64, 66, 67, 116, 142, 143, 144, **182-86**, 196, 213, 242, 246, 247, 277, 327, 328, 330, 331, 336, 337, 352, 356
Marra, James: 314
Marsh, William: 333
Marshall, Christopher: 314
Marshall, Robert L.: xlii, 433
Marshall, Traute M.: 436
Marshall, W. A.: 287
Marston, Nicholas: 316
Martin, Frank: 402
Martin, Henriette: 428
Martin, Henry: 311, 312, 316, 447
Martin, James M. II: 337

Martin, Serge: 258
MARTINI, Giovanni Battista: 57, 83, **186-89**, 230, 251, 252, 253, 254, 255, 257, 290, 335, 349, 351, 365, 366, 400
Martín Moreno, Antonio: 281
Martinotto, Sergio: 365
Martorella, Rosanne: 421
Marvin, Clara: 24, 428
Marvin, Elizabeth West: 273, 315, 428
MARX, Adolf Bernhard: 66, 67, 87, 167, **189-91**, 190, 273, 416, 420, 429, 431
Marx, Hans Joachim: xxxviii, 19, 197
Marx, Karl: 309
Marx-Weber, Magda: xxxviii
Mason, Colin: 321, 436
Mason, Kevin: 48
Mason, Lowell: 50
Massenkeil, Günther: xxxviii, 71, 428
Massera, Giuseppe: 12, 71, 200, 428
Massip, Catherine: 258, 406
MASSON, Charles: **192**
Masson, Paul-Marie: xlii, 256, 285
Massumi, Brian: 286
Mast, Paul: 307
Mateer, David G.: 260
Materassi, Marco: 2
Mathews, William Smythe Babcock: 151
Mathiesen, Thomas: 433
Mathis, Victoria G.: 344
MATTHAEI, Conrad: **192-93**
MATTHESON, Johann: 1, 32, 34, 38, 43, 93, 147, 153, 183, **193-98**, 204, 218, 242, 251, 254, 299, 300, 301, 339, 372, 375, 411, 435, 443, 445
Matthews, Denis: 445
Matveeva, Susanna: 257
Matzdorf, Paul: 89
Maurer, Maurer: 181
Maurice, Paule: 261, 262
Maxham, Robert Eugene: 297, 298
May, William S.: 24
Mayer, George Louis: 429
Mayer, Ludwig K.: 430
Mayer, William: 102
Maync, Harry: xxxiii
Mayr, Otto: 111
Maze, Nancy: 45
Mazel, Lev Abramovich: 14, 15, 16, 155, 256, 274, 388, 428, 438
Mazurowicz, Ulrich: 403
Mazzola, Guerino: 95
Mazzucato, Alberto: 87
McArtor, Marion E.: 104
McBride, Jerry: 322, 324, 325

McCachren, Renee: 266
McCalla, James: 312
McCorkle, Donald M.: 116, 312, 410
McCormack, Thomas J.: 427
McCracken, D. J.: 70
McCredie, Andrew D.: 67, 311, 407, 426, 428, 444, 445
McCreless, Patrick: 156, 171, 314, 316, 317
McCune, Mark P.: 115, 269
McGeary, Thomas: 68, 69, 325
McGuire, J. E.: 132
McIntyre, Ray: 428
McKeon, Richard: 70
McKinnon, James W.: 403, 428
McMullin, Michael: 414
McNamee, A. K.: 422
McPeek, Gwynn S.: 407
McQuere, Gordon Daniel: 386, 387, 388, 428
McRoe, Donald: 101
McVeigh, Simon: 441
Mead, Andrew: 400
Meadows, A. J.: 446
Mealand, Anna Mary: 102
Meath, Gerard: 49
Medushevsky, Viacheslav: 15
Medvedeva, Marie: 265
Meer, John Henry van der: 428
Meerens, Charles: 106
Meeùs, Nicolas: 29
Meggett, Joan: 323
Megill, Kenneth A.: 447
MEI, Girolamo: 74, 97, 98, **198-200**, 293, 391
Meibom, M.: 374
Meier, Bernhard: 59, 84, 89, 109, 122, 180, 414, 428
Meinardus, Ludwig: 196
Meinong, Alexius: 341
Meisel, Maribel: 328
Meister: xx
Mekeel, Joyce: 144
Melkus, Eduard: 430
Mellers, Wilfrid: 49, 227, 257, 298, 309, 359, 409, 411, 414, 427, 442
Melone, Annibale: 36, 37
Mel'gunov, Yuly Nikolaevich: 385
Memmo, Paul E., Jr.: 447
Menck, Hans Friedrich: 429
Mendel, Arthur: xlii, 17, 183, 301, 358, 360, 409, 429, 437
Mendelssohn, Felix: 443
Mendelssohn, J.: 190
Menéndez y Pelayo, Marcelino: 208
Ménétrier, Jean-Alexandre: 443
Mengozzi, Bernardo: 157

Mercadier, E.: 71
Mercer, Frank: 404
Mercier, André: 70
Merck, J. H.: 343
Meredith, Henry: 248
Merkley, Lora L.: 153
Merkling, Frank: 399, 433
Merrick, Arnold: 5, 263, 264
Merrill, Robert V.: 447
Merritt, A. Tillman: xlii, 1, 42, 59, 195, 247, 376
MERSENNE, Marin: 21, 69, 74, 77, 90, 91, 123, 124, 134, 135, 180, **200-203**, 206, 217, 229, 230, 354, 373, 375, 415
Mesnard, Pierre: 70
Metcalf, Edwin Styles: 264
Meyer, Charles R.: 447
Meyer, Ernst Hermann: xl, xlii
Meyer, Jürgen: 444
Meyer, Kathi: 37
Meyer, Leonard B.: xxxiii, 310, 384
Meyer, Max F.: 351
Meyer, Ramon E.: 235
Meyer, Reinhart: xxi
Meyerstein, E. H. W.: 127, 320, 360
Meylan, Pierre: 126, 257
Meyvalian, Hagop: xxxix
Miasoedov, Andrei Nikolaevich: 55
Michaelis, Christian Friedrich: 168, 169
Michajlov, G. K.: 82
Michel, Winfried: 246, 248
Micheli, Romano: 299
Michels, L. C.: 226
Mickelsen, William Cooper: 272
Middendorf, John H.: 82
Middleton, Alain Henri: 254
Middleton, Richard: 311
Mies, Paul: 170, 263, 359, 360, 411, 431, 439
Miesner, Heinrich: 352
Mikhailov, M. K.: 280
Miklaszewski, Kacper: 315
Miklin, J.: 184
Mila, Massimo: 413, 426, 445
Milhaud, Darius: 102
Milhaud, Gérard: 70
Millard, Peter: 223
Miller, Anthony: 410
Miller, Catharine K.: 35, 171, 323, 399, 410, 415, 417, 418, 435, 441
Miller, Clement Albin: 84, 108, 109
Miller, Gertrude Brown: 429
Miller, Leta E.: 258, 375, 406, 429
Miller, Malcolm: 316, 401, 407
Miller, Patrick: 316

Miller, Philip L.: 435
Miller, Poland: 256, 429
Millet, Jean: 20
Milne, John: 247
Milner, Anthony: 18
Milton, John: xxvii, 75
Minim, Dr.: 168
Minin, Vladimir: 388
Mintz, Donald L.: 429
Mischiati, Oscar: xxxv, 24, 188, 230, 234
Mitchell, Alice Levine: 62, 63, 431
Mitchell, John William: 429
Mitchell, M.: 171
Mitchell, William J.: xxviii, 17, 18, 101, 305, 309, 310, 311, 321, 396, 419, 429
Mitchells, K.: 311
Miuller, Teodor: 280
MIZLER von Kolof, Lorenz Christoph: 80, 93, 107, 133, 195, **204-5**, 241, 300, 301, 327, 336, 339, 353, 381, 382, 402, 411, 420
Moberg, Carl-Allan: 257, 435
Mocqauereau, André: 207
Moelich, Gabriel: 31
Möller, Dietlind: 239
Möller, Hans-Jürgen: 429
Möllers, Christian: 154, 322, 368, 403, 424, 429
Moesgaard, K. P.: 135
Mohr, Wilhelm: 113
Mokrý, Ladislav: 415
Moldenit, von: 247
MOMIGNY, Jérôme-Joseph de: 8, 87, 148, 176, **205-7**, 273, 284
Mompellio, Federico: 109, 366, 399
Mongrédien, Jean: 77, 207, 429
Monici, A.: 182
Monod, Edmond: 177
Monosoff, Sonya: 441
Montagu-Nathan, M.: 14
Montalenti, G.: 132
MONTANOS, Francisco de: 52, **207-8**
Montéclair, Michel Pignolet de: 252
Monterosso, Raffaello: xxxix, 210, 393
MONTEVERDI, Claudio, and MONTEVERDI, Giulio Cesare: xxxix, 11, 12, 27, 30, 33, 36, 105, **208-10**, 236, 326, 392, 399, 404, 411, 419, 433, 440, 444, 446, 447
Montgomery, Merle: 126
Montgomery, Montie Charlene: 392
Montillet, William: 129
Montparker, Carol: 62

Mooney, Kevin: 316
Moore, Douglas: xxxi
Moorer, James A.: 120
Moormann, Ludwig: 308
Moos, Paul: 429
Moran, John H.: 284
Morche, Gunther: 429
Mordden, Ethan C.: 407
Moreau, Marie-Germaine: 254
Morehen, John: 231, 396, 410, 426
Morel, Alexander-Jean: 206
Morel, Fritz: 429
Morelli, Giovanni: 138
Moretti, Maria Giovanna: 321
Morgan, John P.: 267, 268
Morgan, Robert Potter: 312, 429
Mori, Akane: 394
Morin, Germain: 106
Moritz, Ralph: 323
Morland, Sir Samuel: 140
MORLEY, Thomas: 42, 60, **210-11**, 226, 260, 340, 347, 355
Moroney, Davitt: 410
Morris, Mellasenah Young: 265
Morris, R. O.: 399
Morrison, Philip: 118
Morrison, Richard: 422
Morsch, Anna: 18
Mortiz, Ralph: 360
Morton, Bruce N.: 311
Moscheles, Ignaz: 176
Moser, Dietz-Rüdiger: xli, 381, 383, 429
Moser, Hans Joachim: 1, 25, 152, 153, 212, 339, 396, 403, 429
Moses, Gavriel Josef: 210
Motte, Benj.: 294
Moyer, Birgitte Plesner Vinding: 191, 429
Moyle, Alice M.: xlii
MOZART, Leopold: 103, 165, 176, **212-13**, 246, 349, 405, 414
Mozart, Wolfgang Amadeus: xxiv, xxviii, xxxviii, 63, 93, 148, 170, 186, 205, 207, 213, 225, 248, 263, 270, 303, 305, 307, 309, 330, 331, 345, 361, 379, 395, 401, 403, 404, 405, 409, 415, 424, 430, 432, 434, 436, 437, 438, 439, 440, 442, 444
Mraz, Gerda: xxxix
Mraz, Gottfried: xxxix
Müller, August Eberhard: 165
Müller, C. F.: 168
Müller, Carl Christian: 331
Mueller, Conrad G.: 118
Müller, Günther: xxxvi
Müller, István: 429

Müller, Kurt: 159
Müller, Robert: 9
Müller-Blattau, Joseph Maria: xlii, 30, 339, 421, 429
Müller-Blattau, Wendelin: 418
Münnich, Richard: xlii, 153, 429
Münster, Robert: 412
Müry, Albert: 236, 365
MUFFAT, Georg: 94, **214-15**
Muller, Elizabeth: 431
Muller, Jean-Pierre: 18
Muller, Maurice: 9
Multhauf, Robert P.: 91
Munkachy, Louis: 429
Munro, Isobel: 359
Munstedt, Peter Alan: 235
Munter, Friedrich: 173
Murata, Margaret: 422
Murcia, Santiago de: 48
Murdoch, Dugald: 71
Murphy, Richard Miller: 296
Murray, A. Gregory: 397
Murray, David R.: 430
Murray, Russell Eugene, Jr.: 236
Musgrave, Michael: 306, 324, 325, 437
Musicus [pseud.]: 244
Muth-Rasmussen: 378
Mutli, Andrei Fedorovich: 280
Myers, Herbert W.: 239
Myhill, John: 430
Nabok, I.: 388
Nadel, Siegfried: 274
Nádor, Georg: 137
Nagy, Christine N.: 427
Nallin, Walter E.: 279
Narmour, Eugene: 305, 311, 312, 314
Nasarre, Pablo: see NASSARRE, Pablo
Nash, Peter Paul: 319, 324
NASSARRE, Pablo: **216**
Natale, Marco de: 430
Natanson, Vladimir: 296, 388
Nattiez, Jean-Jacques: 127, 397
Naue, Johann Friedrich: 362, 363
Nauert, Charles G., Jr.: 92
Naumann, Carl Ernst: 115
Naumberger, C. G.: 362
Navarro, Francisco: 86
Nazaikinskii, Evgenii Vladimirovich: 15, 16
Nedbal, Miroslav: 265
Nef, Albert: 133
Neff, Severine: 320, 325, 396
NEIDHARDT, Johann Georg: **216-18**
Neighbour, Oliver W.: 324, 326, 410
Nejedlý: 15
Nelson, Richard Bruce: 144, 295, 430

Nemirovskaya, I.: 55
Neologos: see QUANTZ, Johann Joachim
Neppiras, E. A.: 419
Nest'ev, I. V.: 16
Neumann, Claus: 430
Neumann, Frederick: 248, 363, 407, 413, 430
Neumann, Friedrich: 321, 397, 431, 444
Neumann, Friedrich-Heinrich: 431
Neumann, Hans: 310
Neumann, Werner: 163, 301
Neumeyer, David: 314, 316, 412, 432
Neuparth, Júlio Cândido: 105
Newcomb, Anthony: 417, 431
Newdigate, B. H.: 211
Newell, John: 372
Newlin, Dika: xlii, 40, 320, 322, 323, 324, 422, 444, 447
Newman, Anthony: 431
Newman, Ernest: xxiii
Newman, Joel: 37
Newman, William S.: 62, 63, 144, 410, 431, 445
Newton, George: 45
Newton, Isaac: 221, 374
Nicaise, Abbé: 229
Nichelmann, Christoph: 19
Nichihara, Minoru: 141
Nichols, Robert Shelton: 87, 88
Nichols, Stephen G., Jr.: 433
Nicholson, Marjorie: 447
Nick, Charles: 368
Nicolai, Giovanni Francesco: 349, 351
Nicole, François: 7
Nicolich, Robert N.: 425
Niecks, Frederick: 88, 163, 176, 243, 270, 274, 431
NIEDT, Friedrich Erhard: **218-19**, 196, 412
Nielsen, Poul: 401, 431
Niemann, Walter: 17
Niemöller, Klaus Wolfgang: 89, 162, 227, 409, 431
Niggli, A.: 133
Nikitis, O.: 244
Niloff, Artur: see SCHENKER, Heinrich
Nisard, Théodore: 78
Nisbet, H. B.: 402
Nishihara, Minoru: 155, 224
Nislen, Tobias: 140
Nitsche, Peter: xxxviii, 113
Nivelle, Armand: 402
NIVERS, Guillaume Gabriel: **219-20**
Noack, Elisabeth: 237

Noble, Jeremy: 209, 227, 359, 397, 427
Noble, Richard D. C.: 18, 56, 226
Noble, William: 374
Noblitt, Thomas: xlii
Noé, Günther: 431
Noiray, Michel: 258
Noll, Günther: 285, 286, 397
Nomura, Yosio: xlii
Norden, Hugo: 347
Norman, Buford: 258
Normann, Theodore F.: 102
Noro, Aiko: 305
Norris, Christopher: 407
Norris, Geoffrey: 15, 54, 67
Northcott, Bayan: 67, 257, 321, 436, 447
NORTH, Francis (1st Baron Guilford): 123, **220-21**, 223
North, Nigel: 431
NORTH, Roger: 220, **221-23**
Norton, Lawrence: 359
Norton, Richard: 432
Noske, Fritz R.: xxi, 21
Noss, Luther: 319
Notker Labeo: see Labeo, Notker
Nottebohm, Gustav: 6, 398
Novak, Saul: 309, 314
Novello, Sabilla: 5
Nowak, Adolf: 432
Nowak, Leopold: 40, 41, 331
NUCIUS, Johannes: **223-24**, 326, 354, 412
Nuernberger, L. Dean: 392
Nutley, Lionel: 426, 436
Nutting, Geoffrey: 211
Nutting, G. H.: 432
Nux, Johannes: see NUCIUS, Johannes
Nys, Carl de: 356
Obelkevich, Mary Helen Rowen: 432
Oberdörffer, Fritz: 219, 232, 290, 292, 328, 337, 432
Ochse, Orpha: 296
Ockeghem, Johannes: 26, 108
Odegard, Peter S.: 407
Odlozilik, Otakar: 92
O'Donnell, John: 432
Öijen, Arne: 371
Oesch, Hans: xliii, 322
OETTINGEN, Arthur Joachim von: 113, **225-26**, 268, 429
Ogolevets, Aleksei Stepanovich: 55
Ohm, Georg Simon: 120
Oistrach, David: 212
Oldenburg, Henry: 374
Oldham, Guy: 375
Oldroyd, David: 314

Oldroyd, George: 432
Oliver, Alfred Richard: 432
Oliveri, Giuseppe: 323
Olleson, Edward: xl, 436
Oppel, Reinhard: 6
Ordshonikidse, Givi: 15
Ord-Hume, Arthur W. J. G.: 19
Orel, Alfred: xlii, 40, 79
Orgel, Stephen: xxxii, 92
Orledge, Robert: 127
Orlova, Elena Mikhailovna: 13, 14, 15, 16, 280
ORNITHOPARCHUS, Andreas: **226-27**, 329
Orr, N. Lee: 432
Orrey, Leslie: 311, 321
Orrilard: 71
Ortigue, Joseph Louis d': 432
ORTIZ, Diego: 59, **227-28**
Ortmann, Otto: 432
Osborne, George Alexander: 228
Osborne, Richard Dale: 288
Oshibuchi, Takako: 104
Osmond-Smith, David: 437
Osmont, Robert: 286
Oster, Ernst: 304, 306, 310, 314
Osthoff, Helmuth: xl, xliii, 416, 432
Otaño, Nemesio: 83
Otero, Francisco: 83
Ottenberg, Hans-Günter: 18, 432
Otterström, Th.: 396
Ottlová, Marta: 191
OUSELEY, Sir Frederick Arthur Gore: 56, 66, 87, **228-29**, 340
Ouvrard, Jean-Pierre: 403
OUVRARD, René: 173, **229**
Ovenden, Michael W.: 138
Owens, Jessie Ann: 428
Pacchioni, Giorgio: 432
Packard, Donald Wheeler: 432
Paddison, Max: 313
Pagliaro, Harold E.: 82
Paine, Gordon: 427
Paisov, Yu I. : 16
Palau y Dulcet, Antonio: 208
Palestrina, Giovanni Pierluigi da: 26, 27, 28, 33, 52, 66, 67, 94, 95, 207, 299, 398, 412, 419, 420, 437
Palisca, Claude V.: xxviii, 12, 34, 42, 54, 73, 74, 75, 99, 100, 197, 199, 200, 293, 299, 300, 367, 390, 391, 392, 393, 394, 397, 415, 419, 427, 428, 432, 433, 445
Palm, Albert: xlii, 206, 207, 433
Palmer, Horatio Richmond: 62
Palmer, Peter: 67

Palumbo, Janet M.: 434
Pamuła, Maria: 227
Pancharoen, Natchar: 315
Panetta, Vincent J., Jr.: 68
Panizza, Letizia A.: 423
Pannain, G.: 30, 393
Paoli, Domenico de': 209
PAOLUCCI, Giuseppe: **230**
Papakhian, Arsen Ralph: 253, 256
Pappas, John: 9
Paquette, Daniel: 32, 286
Parish, George D.: 313
Parisini, Federico: 187, 188
Parkany, Stephen: 156
Parker, Beverly Lewis: 347
Parker, Craig B.: 403
Parker, C. Gerald: 67
Parker, James Cutler Dunn: 267
Parker, Mark Mason: 433
Parker, Roger: 316
Parkins, Robert: 433
Parkinson, G. H. R.: 159
Parks, Richard S.: 95
Parmentola, Carl: 323
Parncutt, Richard: 433
Parodi, Renato: 102
PARRAN, Antoine: **230**
Parrini, Paolo: 159
Parrish, Carl: 272, 421
Parry, Sir C. Hubert H.: 66, 243
Pascal, Blaise: 445
Pasfield, W. R.: 231, 321, 436
Pasmore, H. B.: 128
PASQUALI, Niccolo: **231**
Pasqué, Ernst: 370
Pass, Walter: 320
Passeri, Giovanni Battista: 75
Passerieu, Marc: 436
Passmore, John: 425
Pastille, William Alfred: 305, 306, 307, 315, 317
Patrick, J. Max: 374
Patrizi, Francesco: 36
Pattison, Bruce: 211, 404
Pauchard, P. Anselm: 188
Paul, Bernhard: 7
Paul, Charles Bennett: 251, 256, 257
Paul, Ernst: 6
Paul, Oscar: 114,115
Pauli, Wolfgang: 137
Pauls, Karlheinz: 282
Paumann, Conrad: 26
Paumgartner, Bernhard: 212, 308
Pavlov-Arbenin, A.: 15
Payne, Anthony: 322
Payne, Ian: 260
Payzant, Geoffrey B.: 310
Peacock, Peter E.: 29, 441

Pearce, Charles William: 66, 243, 244, 270
Peart, Donald: 417
Pechefsky, Rebecca R.: 325
Peckham, Morse: 425
Pečman, Rudolf: xxxix, 149, 353
Pedrell, Felipe P.: 83, 267, 433
Peel, John: 314
Pelliot, Alice: 102
Pelseneer, Jean: 70, 80, 201
PENNA, Lorenzo: 34, **232**, 441
Pennequin, Louis: 340
Pepper, William: 410
PEPUSCH, Johann Christoph: 180, **233-34**
Pepys, Samuel: 375
Percy, Gösta: 356
Perels, Kurt: xxxvi
Pereyra, Marie Louise: 209
Pergolesi, Giovanni Battista: 328, 371
Perinello, Carlo: 129, 433
Perkins, Leeman L.: 428, 434
Perkins, Robert L.: 71
Perle, George: 321
Perlinger, Joseph: 212
Pernye, András: 73
Perry-Camp, Jane: 437
Persky, Stanley: 311
Persoons, Guido: xlii
Pesce, Dolores: 433
Pestalozza, Luigi: 321
Pestelli, Giorgio: 431
Petermann, Kurt: 338
Peters, Penelope Miller: 433
Peterson, Larry Wayne: 357, 446
Peterson, Melva: 56, 94, 95, 171, 211, 359, 397, 399, 400, 409, 415, 422, 429, 431, 433, 437, 444
Pétrarque: xxi
Petrobelli, Pierluigi: 188, 351, 434
Pettitt, Stephen: 427
Petty, Wayne: 307
Petukhov, Mikhail: 118
Pfaff, J. W.: 136
Pfannkuch, Wilhelm: xxxviii, xli, 123, 132, 133, 147, 164, 178, 179, 257, 432
Pfatteicher, Carl F.: 429
Pfeiffer, Christel: 434
Pfeiffer, Rüdiger: 383
Pfitzner, Hans Erich: 324
Pfrogner, Hermann: 383, 434
Philaetius: see SERRE, Jean-Adam
Philarmonikos: see HOLDEN, John
Philipps, John: 164
Phillips, Joel A.: 306
Phillips, Leonard Milton, Jr.: 434
Phillips, R. C.: 115

Phillips, William J.: 146
Phipps, Graham H.: 325, 331, 434
Picard, Joseph: 50, 51
Pick, Richard: 91
Picker, Martin: 399, 407, 417
Picot, C.: 70
Pidoux, Pierre: 418, 429
Pierson, Henry Hugh: 6
Pietzsch, Gerhard: 47, 434
Pigot, Thomas: 374
Pikler, Andrew G.: 434
Pilkington, Michael: 356
Pilotto, Ornella: 324
Pincherle, Marc: 349, 351, 431, 434
Pinegar, Sandra: 205
Pinsart, Gérard: 434
Pintard, René: 200
Pipegrop, Heinrich: see
        BARYPHONUS, Henricus
Piperno, Franco: xxxix, 442
Pippard, Brian: 406
Pirie, Peter J.: 272, 359, 405, 422, 447
Pirrotta, Antonino: 434
Pirro, André: 71
PISA, Agostino: **234**
Pischner, Hans: 257
Pisk, Paul A.: 323, 324
Piston, Walter: 54, 321, 407
Pistone, Danièle: xxvii, 413
Pittman, Josiah: 50, 190
Plaistow, Stephen: 400
Plamenac, Dragan: 18, 409
Planchart, Alejandro Enrique: 351
Platen, Emil: 154
Plath, Wolfgang: 213
Plato: xl, 209
Playfoot, Malcolm: 349
PLAYFORD, John: 32, 45, 46, 49,
        164, **234-35**, 245, 334, 347
Plettner, Arthur: 309
Plum, Karl-Otto: 312, 314, 316, 412
Plutarch: 99
Poch Blasco, Serafina: 53
Pochon, Alfred: 285
Pociej, Bohdan: 406
Pöhlmann, Egert: 434
Pohl, William F.: 381
Pokorny, Joel: 120
Polaczek, Dietmar: 439
Pole, William: 66, 228, 434
Polezhaev, Aleksandr: 434
Poli, Marie-Hélène: 210
Politoske, Daniel T.: 415
Pollack, Hans: 163
Pollens, Stewart: 68
Pollin, Alice M.: 53,83
Pond, Celia: 282

Pont, Graham: 247, 248, 400, 406,
        422, 430
PONTIO, Pietro: 52, **236**, 355, 399
Ponzio, Pietro: see PONTIO, Pietro
Poole, H. Edmund: 123
Pope, Isabel: 29, 441
Pople, Anthony: 410
Porphyrios: 138, 374
Porset, Charles: 284, 286
Porter, Roy: 443
Porter, William V.: 45, 433
PORTMANN, Johann Gottlieb: 5,
        236-37, 363
Portnoy, Julius: 310
Potagova, Z.: 405
Potashnikova, M: 257
Poth, Adolphe: 212
Potiron, Henri: 106
Potter, Jean A.: 71
Potter, S. B.: 102
Pottier, R.-J.: 78
Pougin, Arthur: 86, 285
Poulin, Pamela L.: 219
Poulton, Diana: 49, 226, 296, 403
Powell, Anthony: 92
Powell, Newman Wilson: xlii, 143, 422
Powers, Harold S.: 434
PRAETORIUS, Michael: 2, 24, 25,
        67, 84, 110, 121, 193, **237-40**,
        240, 261, 419, 424
Prather, Charlotte Carroll: 408
Pratt, Carroll C.: 416, 436
Pratt, George: 315, 321
Predari, Erberto: 86
Prelleur, Peter: 133
Prenant, Lucie: 71
Prencourt, Captain (Mr.): 222, 223
Prendergast, A. H. D.: 223
Preuß, Ekkehard: 138
Preußen, Anna Amalie von: 144
Preußner, Eberhard: 434
Prévost, Abbé: 253
Price, Curtis: 422
Price, Kingsley: 422
Pringsheim, Klaus: 120
PRINTZ, Wolfgang Caspar: 1, 69,
        194, 204, 218, **240-42**, 375, 420
Prior, Susan: 248
Procházka, Jaroslav: 265
Proctor, Gregory: 306, 316
Prota-Giurleo, Ulisse: 291
Protopopov, Sergei Vladimirovich:
        386, 387, 388
Protopopov, Vladimir Vasil'evich: 55,
        279, 280, 345, 346, 347
PROUT, Ebenezer: 17, 66, 228,
        242-45, 246, 271
Prout, Louis B.: 244, 434

Pruett, James W.: xlii, 43, 407, 427,
        437
Pruitt, William: 220
Prunières, Henry: 20
Prynne, Michael W.: 178
Psellus, Michael: 205
Ptolemy: 138, 199, 374
Pügner, Georg: 169
Puffett, Derrick: 171, 305, 319
Puig, Jose Subirá: 335
Pujades, Antonio Eximeno y: see
        EXIMENO y Pujades, Antonio
Pulver, Jeffrey: 49, 60, 178, 185, 211,
        223, 235, 260, 334, 351, 434
PURCELL, Henry: 32, 49, 228, 235,
        245, 446
Purcell, William L.: 417
Pushchin, B.: 14
Pythagoras: 71, 204, 287, 288, 416,
        428
Quandt, Reinhold: xli, 140, 353
QUANTZ, Johann Joachim: 17, 104,
        176, 212, **246-49**, 353, 405
Querol, Miguel: 169, 208, 216, 281
QUITSCHREIBER, Georg: **249**
Quittard, Henri: 126
Rabich, Ernst: 173, 301
Rabinovich, B. I.: 387
Rabinovich, Isaak Solomonovich: 387
Racek, Jan: 71, 263
Rachmaninov, Sergei: 345
Rackwitz, Werner: 353
Radcliffe, Philip: 420
Rademaker, C. S. M.: xxxii, 372
Radice, Mark A.: 197
Radocy, Rudolf E.: 422
Radulescu, Michael: 214, 215
Raeburn, Christopher: 379
Raessler, Daniel M.: 363
Rags, Y. N.: 434
Raguenet, François: 197
Rahn, Jay: 434
Rahn, John: 313
Rainbow, Bernarr: xx, 283, 286, 423,
        435
Rakijaš, Branko: 163
Rameau, Claude: 256
RAMEAU, Jean-Philippe: 7, 8, 9, 17,
        32, 50, 57, 64, 65, 80, 85, 114,
        117, 142, 145, 182, 183, 186,
        187, 192, 193, 194, 206, 221,
        225, 229, **250-60**, 282, 283, 284,
        286, 287, 288, 291, 303, 307,
        316, 327, 330, 332, 336, 340,
        348, 369, 377, 400, 405, 415,
        419, 420, 423, 433, 435, 439,
        441, 443
Ramírez, Carla J.: 435

Ramis, Bartolomeo: 400
Ramsden, E. H.: 423
Ramsey, Basil: 67
Randall, D. B. J.: 435
Randall, James K.: 345
Randall, Nathan A.: 406
Rapp, Rolf: 98
Rasch, Rudolf A.: 22, 120, 124, 297, 298, 338, 382, 406, 435
Raskin, Marcus G.: 310
Rasmussen, Mary: 248
Rast, Nicholas: 308, 316
Ratcliffe, Stephen: 49
Rathgeber, Johann Valentin: 410
Ratner, Leonard G.: 149, 277, 435
Ratner, Sabina Teller: 101, 392, 446
Rattansi, P. M.: 92
Raugel, Félix: 77, 420
Rauhe, Hermann: 435
Rauhut, Franz: 91
Rauschning, Hermann: 435
RAVENSCROFT, Thomas: **260**
Ravetz, J. R.: 9,99
Ravizza, Victor: xli
RAVN, Hans Mikkelsen: **261**
Rayburn, J.: 428
Raynal, Abbé: xx, 254, 284
Raynor, Henry B.: 310, 311, 362, 422, 437
Rayón, J. Sancho: 208
Rea, John Rocco: 435
Reaney, Gilbert: 43, 435
Reardon, Colleen Ann: 2
REBER, Henry: 76, 77, **261-62**
Rebikov, Vladimir Ivanovich: 105
Reckow, Fritz: 435
Reckziegel, Walter: 116, 370, 371
Reddick, Harvey Phillips: 195
Redepenning, Dorothea: 248
Redlich, Hans Ferdinand: 12, 23, 88, 151, 209, 231, 298, 360, 409, 419, 421, 438, 441, 444
Reed, Nola Jane: 277 See Knouse, Nola Jane
Reese, Gustave: xlii, 226, 435
Regener, Eric: 311, 425
Reger, Max: 225, 275, 303, 307
Rehm, Wolfgang: xliii
Reich, Wilhelm: 188
Reich, Willi: 163, 188, 308, 321, 323, 331
Reich, Wolfgang: 36
REICHA, Antoine-Joseph: 55, 61, 62, 87, 102, 176, 205, 228, **262-66**, 416
Reichardt, Johann Friedrich: xviii, 165, 328, 432
Reiche, Jens Peter: 324

Reichel, Eugen: 301
Reichenbach, Herman: 309, 435
Reichert, Georg: xxxviii, 65, 444
Reichert, Peter: 435
Reichling, Alfred: 195, 381
Reichling, Matthias: 337
Reid, Michael Alan: 20
Reidemeister, Peter: 239, 401
Reif, Jo-Ann: 325
Reiff, Alfred: 52
Reijen, Paul van: 418
Reilly, Allyn Dixon: 336, 435
Reilly, Edward Randolph: 104, 247, 248, 430, 436
Reilly, P. Conor: 141
Reimann, Margarete: 29, 195, 201, 257, 431
Reimer, Erich: 394, 435
Reimer, Otto: 110, 416, 422
Reincken, J. A.: 344
Reinecke, Hans-Peter: xxxvi, 435
Reiner, Stuart: 399
Reiners, Werner W.: 439
Reininghaus, Friedrich Christoph: xxxviii
Reisch, Gregor: 354
Rejchova: see REICHA, Antoine-Joseph
Rejchy, Antonín: see REICHA, Antoine-Joseph
Rempp, Frieder: 99,100
Rensch, Richard: 145
Renwick, William: 316
Répaci, Francesco A.: 19
Requeno, V.: 83
Reti, Rudolph: 298
Réty, Hippolyte: 58
Retzel, Frank: 314
Reuter, Fritz: 152
Révész, Géza: 436
Rex, Walter E.: 8, 436
Rexroth, Dieter: 323
Reymann, Rita Marie: 87
Reynolds, Gordon: 435
Reynolds, William H.: 313
Rhau, Georg: 161
Rheinberger, Josef: 56
Rhys, Hedley Howell: 433
Ribera y Maneja, Antonio: 152, 270, 271
Riccati, Giordano: 365
Ricci, Vittorio: 243
Richard, August: 18
Richards, Denby: 359
Richelieu, Armand Jean du Plessis: 441
Richter, Alfred: 267

RICHTER, Ernst Friedrich: **266-68**, 440
Richter, Julius: 226
Richter, Lukas: 205, 323
Rid, Christoph: 84, 110
Riedel, Friedrich Wilhelm: xli, 94, 153
Riedel, Herbert: 436
Riedel, Johannes: 272, 427
RIEMANN, (Karl Wilhelm Julius) Hugo: xliii, 105, 106, 112, 113, 114, 146, 152, 172, 173, 176, 189, 205, 207, 225, 243, **268-76**, 303, 330, 341, 395, 396, 405, 407, 412, 413, 419, 429
Riemer, Otto: 47, 195
RIEPEL, Joseph: 147 **276-78**, 403, 412
Riesemann, O. von: 279
Ries, Hugibert: see RIEMANN, Hugo
Rieß, Otto: 328
Riessauw, Anne-Marie: 106
Riethmüller, Albrecht: 138, 309, 397
Rietsch, Heinrich: 176, 214
Riezler, Walter: 308
Rifkin, Joshua: 31
Riggins, Herbert Lee: 313, 316
Rigler, Franz Paul: 429
Riis, Thomas: 437
Rimbault, Edward Francis: 222, 348
Rimskogo-Korsakova: see RIMSKY-KORSAKOV, Nikolai Andreevich
Rimsky-Korsakov, Georgii Mikhailovich: 14
Rimsky-Korsakov, Nadezhda Nikolaevna: 279
Rimsky-Korsakov, Nikolai Andreevich: 14, 55, **278-80**
Rimsky-Korsakov, Vladimir Nikolaevich: 280
Ringer, Alexander L.: 209, 309, 324
Ringo, James: 192
Rink, John: 306
Rio, Antonio Ventura Roel del: see ROEL DEL RIO, Antonio Ventura
Ripin, Edwin M.: 82
Rippe, Volker: 368
Rishton, Timothy J.: 181
Ritchie, A. M.: 71
Ritter, Fanny Raymond: 163
Ritzel, Alfred: 436
Rivera, Benito V.: 42, 47, 160, 163, 227, 392, 436, 440
Rix, Joseph: 348
Riza, Bayram: 14
Robbins Landon, H. C.: xxxvi, xli, 437

Robbins, Ralph Harold: 436
Robert, Frédéric: 262
Robert, Ingeborg: 390
Robert, Walter: 357
Roberts, Linda: 120
Roberts, Rosemary: 338, 339
Roberts, Stella: 436
Robijns, Jozef: xlii
Robinet, André: 158
Robinson, Franklin Westcott: 433
Robinson, Philip E. J.: 286
Robison, J. O.: 436
Robledo, Luis: 91
Robles-Cahero, José Antonio: 438
Robrieux, Jean-Jacques: 258
Roche, Daniel: 9
Roche, Jerome: 210, 290, 392, 427
Rochester, Marc: 324
Rochot, Bernard: 200
Rodgers, Julane: 436
Rodis-Lewis, Geneviève: 70
Roeder, Michael T.: 325
Röder, Thomas: 278
ROEL DEL RÍO, Antonio Ventura: **280-81**, 334, 335
Roeser, Valentin: 183, 212
Rösing, Helmut; 309
Roger, Estienne: 220
Rogers, Helen Olive: 436
Rogers, John: 139
Rogers, Michael R.: 401, 407, 410
Roggius, Nicolaus: 67, 68
Rognoni, Luigi: 293, 319, 321
Rohrmann, Heinrich Leopold: 350
Rohwer, Jens: 393, 436
Roig-Francolí, Miguel A.: 296
Rokseth, Yvonne: 227
Roland-Manuel, M.: 71
Rollinson, T. H.: 267
Romano, Giulio: see CACCINI, Giulio
Romijn, C.: 19
Ronan, Colin A.: 92,118
Roncaglia, Gino: xxxviii
Ronga, Luigi: xliii, 209, 398, 429
Roos, Johann Friedrich: 369
Roquet, Antoine Ernest: 78
Rore, Cipriano de: 393, 427
Rosand, Ellen: 97, 214, 258, 307, 312, 358, 360, 395, 400, 418, 422, 434, 435, 436, 441, 444
Rose, Adrian P.: 282
Rose, Bernard W. G.: 116
Rose, Gloria: 2, 101
Rose, Marilyn Gaddis: 315
Rosecrance, Barbara: 49
Rosen, Charles: 307, 436, 437
Rosen, Edward: 99, 136, 137

Rosenberg, Herbert: 416
Rosenblum, Sandra P. 437
Rosenfeld, L.: 82
Rosenkaimer, Eugen: 301
Rosenschein, Stanley J.: 312
Roske, Michael: 191
Rosner, Burton R.: 314
Ross, G. R. T.: 70
Ross, Stephanie: 423
Roßbach, August: 384, 385
Rossi, Luigi Felice: 56, 264
Roth, Hermann: 308
Roth, Leon: 21, 69
Roth, Lynette: 145
Rothärmel, Marion: 437
Rothfarb, Lee Allen: 154, 155, 156, 408
Rothgeb, John: 304, 306, 307, 308, 311, 312, 313, 314, 315, 325, 412, 437
Rothschild, Fritz: 437
Rothstein, Edward: 437, 442
Rothstein, William Nathan: 306, 308, 313, 315, 316, 317, 325, 403
Rottmann, Kurt: 437
Rousseau, G. S.: 443
ROUSSEAU, Jean: **281-82**
ROUSSEAU, Jean-Jacques: xvii, xl, 7, 38, 39, 206, 251, 254, 257, **282-87**, 341, 351, 399, 400, 423, 436
Roussel, Albert: 126
ROUSSIER, Pierre-Joseph: 57, 254, **287-89**
Routh, Francis: 425
Rouxel, Mathurin: 106
Rowell, Lewis: 272, 437
Rowen, Herbert H.: 372
Rowen, Ruth Halle: 11, 28, 38, 45, 63, 108, 143, 148, 195, 209, 211, 238, 252, 285, 293, 343, 362, 366, 367, 392, 393, 437
Rowse, A. L.: 227
Roy, M. S.: 416
Rozin, Vadim: 16
Rubbra, Edmund: 322, 396
Rubeli, Alfred Ulrich: 139, 349
Rubio, Samuel: 335
Rubsamen, Walter H.: 224
Ruchevskaia, Ekaterina: 15
Ruddick, James D.: 213
Rudio, Ferdinand: 81
Rudolphus, C.: 264
Rudorff, Friedrich Karl: 115
Rudrum, A. W.: 447
Rudwick, M. J. S.: xxxix
Rühlmann, Franz: xliii
Ruf, Wolfgang: 437

Rufer, Josef: 319, 322, 323
Ruff, Lillian M.: 21, 39, 60, 94, 101, 108, 141, 180, 192, 235, 254, 256, 295, 355, 356, 392, 437
Ruff, Willie: 139
Ruhnke, Martin: xliii, 31, 42, 59, 79, 101, 107, 115, 122, 131, 160, 239, 249, 329, 352, 353, 376, 437
Rukavishnikov, V.: 280
Rummenhöller, Peter: xxxviii, 115, 412, 415, 419, 438, 444
Rushton, Julian: 9, 206, 422
Russell, Craig H.: 48
Russell, William F.: 202
Russo, Paolo: 258
Rycroft, Marjorie E.: 425
Ryding, Erik S.: 433
Ryhming, Gudrun Kristina: 20
Ryom, Peter: xxxix
Ryzhkin, Iosif Yakovlevich: 256, 274, 280, 386, 387, 388, 405, 438
Saathen, Friedrich: 322
Sabaneev, Leonid Leonidovich: 387
SABBATINI, Galeazzo: **290**
SABBATINI, Luigi Antonio: 57, **290-91**, 365
Sabin, Robert: 209, 360, 441
Sabine, W. C.: 119
Sachs, Barbara: 442
Sachs, Harvey: 316
Sachs, Klaus-Jürgen: 219, 408, 438
Sádecký, Zdeněk: 14
Sadie, Julie Ann: 402
Sadie, Stanley: xxix, 18, 39, 56, 94, 95, 247, 257, 270, 399, 410, 421, 430, 433, 437
Sadowsky, Reah: 335
Sadowsky, Rosalie D. Landres: 71
St. Evremond: 197
Saint-John, Leo Vincent: 442
SAINT-LAMBERT, de: 133, **291-92**
Saint Lambert, Michel de: 292
Saint-Saëns, Camille: 127, 262
Sajak, Rainer: 39
Sala, Niccolò: 57
Salazar, Adolfo: 71
Salieri, Antonio: 262
SALINAS, Francisco de: 175, 216, **293-94**
Salmen, Walter: xl, 432, 438
SALMON, Thomas: 164, 235, **294-95**, 375
Salter, Lionel: 17, 322
Salter, Timothy: 49
Salzer, Felix: xxviii, 304, 305, 307, 308, 309, 311, 314
SAMBER, Johann Baptist: **295**

Sampayo Ribeiro, Mário de: 175
Sampson, George: 360
Sampson, Peggie: 360
Sams, Eric: 307, 311
Samuel, Harold E.: 121
Samuels, Robert: 315
Sanders, Herbert: 438
Sanders, Robert L.: 209, 251, 414
Sandford, Gordon: 399
Sandon, Nicholas: 227
Sandow, Gregory: 422
Sandré, Gustave: 129, 162, 163, 267, 268
Sannemann, Friedrich: 438
Sanner, Lars Erik: 371
SANTA MARÍA, Tomás de: 52, 175, **296-97**
Santerre, E. M. E.: 206
Santillana, Giorgio de: 137, 447
Saran, Franz: 384
Sargeant, Winthrop: 310, 396, 436
Sargenti, Simonetta: 342
Saroni, Hermann S.: 189
Sarravezza, Antonio: 440
Sarton, George: 201, 424
Sartori, Claudio: 236
Saslaw, Janna Karen: 379
Sasse, Dietrich: 27
Satoh, Tetsuo: 324
Sats, I. A.: 387
Saunders, William: 359, 360
SAUVEUR, Joseph: 69, 117, 200, 250, **297-99**
Saxl, F.: xxxv
SCACCHI, Marco: 27, 30, 31, 33, **299-300**
Scarlatti, Americo: 141
Scarlatti, Domenico: 315
Schaal, Richard: xxxvi, 75, 152, 170, 171, 257, 309, 322, 328, 376
Schachter, Carl E.: 305, 306, 311, 312, 313, 314, 316
Schaedlich, Hans-Werner: 113
Schäfer, Wilhelm: 112
Schäfke, Rudolf: 247, 438
Schaffer, John William: 192
Schafhäutl, Karl Franz Emil von: 370
Schanzlin, Hans Peter: 177
Scharlau, Ulf: 140, 141
Scharnagl, A.: 94, 278
Scharwenka, Xaver: xxiii
Schavernoch, Hans: 438
Scheck, Gustav: 247
Schedl, Claus: 138
SCHEIBE, Johann Adolph: 204, **300-302**, 327, 328, 352, 402, 444
Scheibert, Beverly: 441

Schein, Johann Hermann: 435
Schellhous, Rosalie Athol: 438
Schemann, Ludwig: 56
Schenk, Erich: xl, xliii, 40, 153
SCHENKER, Heinrich: 17, 93, 95, 112, 142, 172, 251, 266, 275, **303-17**, 318, 319, 323, 324, 330, 345, 357, 378, 412, 415, 445
Schenkman, Walter: 194, 196, 197, 438
Scher, Steven Paul: 438
Scherchen, Hermann: 298
Schering, Arnold: xxviii, xliii, 108, 215, 246, 311, 438
Scheurleer, D. F.: xliii
Schick, Joseph: 136
Schiebler, D.: xxxvi
Schiedermayr, Joh. Bapt.: 212
Schiffer, Brigitte: 324
Schilling, Gustav: 17
Schilling, Rudolf: 113
Schimmelpfennig, Christa: 348
Schinelli, Achille: 129
Schläder, Jürgen: xli
Schlag, Gerald: xxxix
Schlager, Karlheinz: 397, 398
Schlecht, Raymund: 89, 329
Schlegel, Franz Anton: 247
Schleiner, Louise: 75
Schlesinger, Walter: 445
Schleuning, Peter: 294
Schmalzriedt, Siegfried: 20, 31, 113, 438
Schmedler: 138
Schmid, Alois: 278
Schmid, Edmund: 310
Schmid, Ernst Fritz: 18
Schmid, Theodor Karl: 112, 113
Schmidt, Christian Martin: 324
Schmidt, Ernst Fritz: 213
Schmidt, Felix: 380
Schmidt, Hans: xliii, 195, 238, 279, 381, 412
Schmidt, Harro: 438
Schmidt, Heinrich: 196
Schmidt, Lothar: 191
Schmidt, Marlene: 439
Schmidt-Görg, Joseph: xlii, xliii
Schmidt-Preuß, Dorothea: 127, 158, 216, 220, 230, 234, 235, 389
Schmidt-Preuß, Reinhard: 281
Schmiedecke, Adolf: 26
Schmitt, Charles B.: 372, 447
Schmitt, Rainer: 439
Schmitz, Arnold: 376, 439
Schmitz, Eugen: 45, 190, 242
Schmitz, Hans-Peter: 246, 248, 430

Schmoll gen. Eisenwerth, J. Adolf: 438
Schnapper, Edith B.: 156
Schnath, Georg: 159
SCHNEEGASS, Cyriacus: **317-18**
Schneider, Frank: 213, 320
Schneider, Herbert: 192, 255, 258, 283, 406, 415, 439
Schneider, Max: xviii, xliii, 195, 227, 366, 439
Schneider, Otto: 27
Schneider, Sigrun: 368
Schneiderheinze, Armin: xxxviii
Schneider-Klement, Albrecht: 125
Schnitzler, Günter: 439, 444, 447
Schnoebelen, Anne: 187, 188
Schnürmann, Leo: 256
Schoen, Max: 436
SCHOENBERG, Arnold: xxiv, xxxi, xxxvi, 40, 120, 225, 303, 308, **318-26**, 415, 443, 445
Schöne, Alfred: 114
Schoenfeld, Morton: 360
Schönfeld, Tobias: 239
Schoettler, Frederic: 421, 422
Schoffman, Nachum: 439
Schofield, Robert E.: 132
Schole, Heinrich: 155
Scholes, Percy A.: 439
Schollum, Robert: 356
Scholz, Bernhard: 67
Scholz, Gottfried: 322, 439
Scholz-Michelitsch, Helga: 19
Schonberg, Harold C.: 321, 404, 430, 435, 436
SCHONSLEDER, Wolfgang: **326-27**
Schopenhauer, Arthur: 112, 154, 400
Schott, Gaspar: 140
Schott, Howard: 68, 292, 363
Schouten, Hennie: 321
Schrade, Leo: xxxvii, 209, 403, 427, 441
Schreiber, Ulrich: 321, 324
Schreiber, Wolfgang: 324
Schröder, Jaap: 398
Schröder-Auerbach, Cornelia: 212
SCHRÖTER, Christoph Gottlieb: 85, 300, 301, **327-28**, 353
Schubarth, Johann Kaspar: 277
Schubert, Franz: xl, 93, 155, 303, 310, 314, 330, 331, 332, 404, 423, 425, 439
Schubert, Giselher: 225
Schubert, Peter N.: 109
Schünemann, Georg: 161, 234, 342, 376, 410, 439

Schütz, Heinrich: xxxiii, 24, 25, 30, 31, 299, 395, 404, 424, 427, 429, 436
Schuh, Willi: 207
Schuhmacher, Gerhard: 4, 137, 170, 239, 271, 273, 307, 338, 376, 397, 403, 439, 443, 445
Schulenberg, David: 439
Schuler, Manfred: 411
Schuller, Herbert M.: 402
Schultz, Helmut: xlii
Schultz, Howard: 91
Schultz, Ingo: 10
Schultze, W.: 444
SCHULZ, Johann Abraham Peter: 142, 143, **328-29**, 342, 377
Schulz, Julie: 420
Schulze, Hans-Joachim: 18, 301, 376
Schulze, Werner; 159, 368, 444
Schulz-Euler, Sophie: 81
Schumann, Erich: 342
Schumann, Robert: 303
Schumann, Wolfgang: 112
Schuneman, Robert: 247
Schutte, Sabine: 13
Schwab, Heinrich W.: xxxix
Schwab, Richard N.: 8
Schwandt, Erich: 418
Schwanzara, Ernst: 40
Schwartz, Judith L.: 247
Schwartz, Nathan: 263
Schwartz, Richard Isadore: 173
Schwartz, Rudolf: 439
Schwarz, Boris: 321
Schwarz, Viktor: 155
Schwarzmaier, Ernst: 277
Schweiger, Hertha: 370, 371
Schweize, Klaus: 368
Schweizer, Gottfried: 436
Schwering, Julius: xxxvi
Schwinger, Wolfram: 144, 301, 324
Schytte, Henrik Vissing: 270
Scott, David: 235, 434
Scott, Irene Schreier: 308
Scott, J. F.: 71
Scrase, David A.: 350
Scriba, Christoph J.: 374, 375
Seares, Margaret: 409
Searle, Humphrey: 320, 321, 323
Seaton, Douglass: 439, 443
Seay, Albert: xix, 59, 161, 389, 392, 439, 446
SEBASTIANI, Claudius: 226, **329**
Sebba, Gregor: 70, 71
Sechet, Pierre: 246
SECHTER, Simon: 39, 40, 142, 182, 183, 189, 318, **330-32**, 442
Seck, Friedrich: 138

Seebeck, August: 120
Seeger, Charles: xlii, 305
Seelig, Wolfgang: 171
Seelkopf, Martin: 24
Sefferi, O.: 225
Segerman, Ephraim: 239, 382, 426
Sehnal, Jiří: 131
Seidel, Elmar: 275, 312, 439
Seidel, Wilhelm: xviii, 71, 115, 149, 398, 418, 439, 440, 447
Seifert, Wolfgang: 439
Seiffert, Max: 144, 299, 344, 353
Sektberg, Willard: 431
Selle, Gustav F.: 190
Semmens, Richard Templar: 174, 297
Sénelier, Jean: 285
Seng, Nikolaus: 141
Seng, Peter J.: 49
Senn, Kurt Wolfgang: 376
Senn, Walter: 7
Serauky, Walter: xliii, 9, 373, 383, 440
Sérieyx, Auguste: 126
Sérieyx, Marie Louise: 126
Serov, Alexander Nikolaevich: 347
Serravezza, Antonio: 439
SERRE, Jean-Adam: 8, 103, **332-33**, 349
Serres, Louis de: 127
Serres, Michel: 159
Serwer, Howard Jay: xl, 145, 185, 343, 409, 425, 426, 440
Sesini, Ugo: 37
Sessions, Roger: 305, 309, 358, 360
Setaccioli, Giacomo: 270
Šetková, Dana: 263
Seuss, John G.: 35
Sevier, Zay V. David: 4
Sewall, Maud G.: 322
Seyfried, Ignaz Ritter von: 5, 6, 57, 87
'sGravesande, G. J.: 124, 125
Shaffer, Henry: 315
Shakespeare, William: xxxiii
Shaknazarova, Nonna G.: 14, 15, 16
Shamgar, Beth Friedman: 440
Shankland, R. S.: 419
Shapiro, Joel: 430
Sharp, Geoffrey: 360, 397, 424
Sharpe, R. A.: 422, 437
Shattuck, Charles H.: 92
Shaw, Marilyn L.: 120
Shaw, Watkins: 147, 244, 257, 283, 311, 417
Shay, Edmund: 430
Shea, William R.: 201
Shedlock, James S.: 223
Shedlock, John South: 270, 271
Sheldon, David A.: 184, 197, 440
Shelkov, N. V.: 279

Shelley, Percy Bysshe: xxv
Sheppard, Leslie: 440
Sherbon, James W.: 315
Sherman, Stuart P.: 49
Shields, Allan: 315
Shifrin, Seymour; 321
Shigehara, Shinichi: 322
Shiloah, Amnon: 202
Ship, Sergei: 389
Shipley, Linda Patricia: 335
Shirinian, Ruzanna K.: 29
Shirlaw, Matthew: 228, 440
Sholund, Edgar Roy: 59
Shortridge, John: 426
Shortridge, Linda: 426
Shosktakovich, Dmitry: 387
Shurtz, H. Paul: 331
Shute, J. D.: 440
Shuter-Dyson, Rosamund: 441
Sieber, Wolfgang: xli
Siefert, Paul: 299, 300
Siegel, Hedi: 272, 305, 306, 307, 308, 317
Siegele, Ulrich: 286
Siegmund-Schultze, Walther: xxxix, xl, 196, 275
Sietz, Reinhold: 163, 219, 419
Sievers, Gerd: 274, 275, 401
Sievers, Heinrich: xliii, 350, 411
Sigonio, Gandolfo: 37, 367
Silantien, John: 341
Silbermann, Gottfried: 337
Silberman, Israel: 310, 440
Silbiger, Alexander: 434
Silliman, Robert H.: 9
Silz, Priscilla Manton Kramer: 137
Simcox, Edith: 118
Simms, Bryan R.: 58, 308, 319, 324, 401
Simon, Jules: 70
Simonds, Bruce: 256
Simoni, Anna E. C.: 373
Simpson, Adrienne: 263, 265
SIMPSON, Christopher: 32, 49, 178, 234, **333-34**, 347
Simpson, Kenneth: 116, 286
Simpson, Robert: 436
Singer, Gerhard: 390
Singleton, Charles Southward: 427
Siohan, Robert: 158, 420
Sirch, Licia: 440
Sirinjan, Ruzanna K.: see Shirinian, Ruzanna K.
Sirker, Udo: 298
Sirmen, Maddalena Lombardini: 350
Sisman, Elaine Rochelle: 148, 149, 425, 427, 440
Sjöqvist, Gunnar: 259

Skapski, George J.: 301
Skeaping, Kenneth M.: 349
Skei, Allen B.: 427, 437
Skinner, Olive Ross: 440
Skinner, Quentin: 374
Skinner, Robert: 406
Skowron, Zbigniew: 258, 411
Skrebkov, Sergei: 14
Skryabin, Alexander Nikolaevich: 345, 386
Skrzypczak, Mirosława: 135
Skyllstad, Kjell: 440
Slatin, Sonia: 311
Slavická-Hachová, Eva: 191
Slavický, Milan: 191
Slavinsky, Y.: 244
Slawson, Wayne: 314
Sloboda, John A.: 314, 315
Small, Arnold M.: 416
Smallman, Basil: 197
Smart, H. R.: 70
Smart: 168
Smets, Paul: 382
Smiles, Joan E.: 440
Smirnov, Vladimir I.: 81
Smit, J.: 372
Smith, Anne: 239
Smith, Arthur Timothy: 43
Smith, Cecil: 320, 432
Smith, Charles J.: 312, 316, 415, 447
Smith, Charles Samuel: 81
Smith, F. J.: 71, 440
Smith, Jo Ann La Torra: 62
Smith, Joan Allen: 324
Smith, Leon R., Jr.: 440
Smith, Martin Dennis: 265
Smith, Norman Kemp: 70
Smith, Patrick J.: 247, 436, 437, 445
Smith, Warren Storey: 396
Smither, Howard Elbert: 45, 439, 440
Smoliar, Stephen W.: 151, 312, 313
Snelders, H. A. M.: xxxix, 138
Snook, Susan Pauline: 65
Snyder, John L.: 440
Snyder, Kerala Johnson: 31, 440
Sochor, Arnold N.: 440
Soderlund, Sandra: 440
Söhngen, Oskar: xxxvi
Soehnlein, Edward John: 72, 73
Sokolov, Vladimir: 410
Sokolowsky, B. von: 385
Solander, Daniel: 134
SOLER, Antonio: 187, 281, **334-35**
Soler Ramos, Antonio Francisco Javier José: see SOLER, Antonio
Solerti, Angelo: 34, 45, 74, 75, 440
Solie, Roger: 447

Solie, Ruth Ames: 272, 312, 313, 422, 441
Somer, Avo: 95
Somerset, H. V. F.: 285
Somfai, L.: 437
Sommerich, Phillip: 410
Sommerset, H. V. F.: 223
Sommervogel, Carlos: 141
Sondheimer, Robert: 441
Sonnenkalb, Fried. Wilhelm: 64
Sonntag, Brunhilde: 408
Sørensen, Søren: xxxix
SORGE, Georg Andreas: 81, 85, 165, 182, 184, 185, 327, **336-38**
Šotolová, Olga: 265
Souberbielle, Léon: 297
Souris, André: 178, 257
Southgate, Thomas Lea: 66, 211, 223, 229
Sovik, Thomas Jon: 95
Sovík, Thomas Paul: 441
Spada da Faenza, D. Vincentio: 12
Spanyi, M.: 145
Sparks, E. H.: 327, 435
Sparshott, Francis: 315, 421
Spazier, Karl: 328
Speak, J. M.: 441
Specht, R. John: 324
SPEER, Daniel: **338-39**
Speer, Klaus: 422
Speiser, Andreas: 81, 136
Spelman, Elizabeth V.: 422
Spena, Rosa: 28
Spender, Natasha: 433, 441
Spieler, Heinrich: 356, 446
Spies, Claudio: 319, 321
SPIESS, Meinrad: **339-40**, 414
Spieß, Otto: 82, 212
Spink, Ian: xv, 43, 46, 235, 392, 433
Spink, J. S.: 286
Spiro, A. G.: 433
Spitta, Philipp: 108, 218, 219
Spitzer, John: 441
Spivak, Samuel: 331
Spodenkiewicz, Wiktor: 351
Spohr, Louis: xliii, 168, 213
Sponheuer, Bernd: 441
Sposobin, Igor Vladimirovich: 410
Spratt, John Fenton: 272, 323
Squire, W. Barclay: 245
Stäblein, Bruno: xliii
Staehelin, Martin: 351
Stahlman, William D.: 136
Stahura, R.: 306, 402, 432
STAINER, Sir John: xxx, 211, 228, 243, **340-41**
Stajić, Petar: 436
Stampfl, Inka: 215

Standen, John: 257, 436
Standford, Patric: 54, 396
Stang, Fredda L.: 247
Stanhope, Earl: 151
Stanley, Jerome Merlin: 123
Starer, Robert: 209, 251, 414
Stark, James Arthur: 46
Starke, Reinhold: 224
Starobinski, Jean: 284
Starowolski, Szymon: 226
Stasov, Vladimir Vasilevich: 347
Stauder, Wilhelm: 120, 121, 141, 400
Stauffer, George: 337
Steblin, Rita Katherine: 441
Stechow, Wolfgang: 447
Steele, John: 227
Stefan, Paul: 40
Stefani, Attilio: 351
Stefani, Gino: 92, 141, 188, 195, 398, 401, 416, 444
Stefanovič, Ivan: 436
Stege, Fritz: 196, 441
Steger, Hillmuth: 63
Steglich, Rudolf: xl, 274, 417
Steil, Anneli: 302
Stein, Carl: 167
Stein, Deborah: 441
Stein, Erwin: 321, 322
Stein, Franz A.: xlii
Stein, Fritz: xliii
Stein, Herbert von: 171
Stein, Leonard: 320, 321, 322, 324, 325
Steinbeck, Wolfram: 31, 441
Steinberg, Maximilian: 279
Steinberg, Michael P.: 422
Steiner, Ena: 321, 324
Steiner, Frances: 251, 414
Steiner, Ruth: 398
Steinhardt, Milton: 213
Steinitzer, Max: 173
Steinitz, Paul: 418
Stellfeld, Bent: 261
Stembridge, Christopher: 409
Stempel, Larry: 313
Stepanov, Aleksei Alekseevich: 55, 280
Stephan, Hans: 429
Stephan, Rudolf: xviii, xxxviii, 70, 71, 113, 171, 306, 315, 320, 321, 322, 324, 325, 379, 428, 431, 437
Stephen, Sir Leslie: xxi
Stephens, Charles Edward: 66, 228
Stephens, Kevin: 425
Sterl, Raimund W.: 337
Stern, David: 314

Sternfeld, Frederick W.: 254, 411, 434, 445
Steuermann, Clara: 324
Stevens, Denis W.: 26, 35, 59, 209, 238, 296, 349, 399, 403, 427, 435, 437, 441
Stevens, George: 360
Stevens, Halsey: 431
Stevens, Jane R.: 149, 371, 435, 439, 441
Stevens, John: xix, xx, 417
Stevens, William: 132
Stevenson, Edward P. 442
Stevenson, Robert: 29, 52, 83, 175, 208, 211, 227, 293, 335, 441
Stevenson, Ronald: 396
Stewart, James: 306
Stiefel, Eberhard: 327
Stier, Ernst: 102
Stillingfleet, Benjamin: 351
Stillings, Frank S.: 101
Stillings, Kemp: 103
Stinson, John: 222
Stipčevič, Ennio: 433
Stockhammer, Robert: 153
Stockmann, Bernhard: 31, 268
Stockton, Constant Noble: 92
Stoddard, Hope: 320
Stöckl, Rudolf: 278
Stöpel, Franz David Christoph: 55, 168
Stöpfgeshoff, Susanne: 242
Stoffer, Thomas H.: 156
Stokowski, Leopold: 322
Stoll, Albrecht D.: 441
Stollbrock, Ludwig: 214, 215
Stone, Kurt: 153
Stone, Peter Eliot: 265
Stone, Reppard: 181
Stoothoff, Robert: 71
Stopford, John: 313
Storch, Karl Arno: 301
Stowell, Robin: 441
Straeten, Edmund vander: 64
Strainchamps, Edmond: xlii
Straková, Theodora: 441
Strang, Gerald: 321, 322
Straus, Joseph N.: 400
Strauss, John F. 286
Strauss, Richard: 170, 172, 303, 325, 395
Stravinsky, Igor: 13
Strawn, John: 120, 439
Streetman, Richard David: 31
Strickland, Edward: 415
Střítecký, Jaroslav: 14
Strizich, Robert: 441
Strong, E. W.: 99

Strong, Roy: 92
Stroux, Christoph: 84
Strunk, Oliver: 2, 11, 18, 45, 52, 94, 98, 108, 209, 211, 212, 214, 215, 219, 246, 251, 283, 366, 392, 441
Strunz, Franz: xxv
Struthers, Christina: 442
Stubington, Jill: xlii
Stuckenschmidt, Hans Heinz: 320, 322, 323
Stucky, Steven: 324
STUMPF, Carl: 119, 274, **341-42**, 429
Suaudeau, René: 257
Subirá, José: 83, 398, 442
Suchalla, Ernst: 17
Suck, Friedrich: 169
Suddard, E. F. E.: 105
Suess, John G.: 35
Sullivan, Anita: 442
Sulz, Josef: 41
SULZER, Johann Georg: 143, 144, 147, 328, **342-44**
Sumner, Floyd G.: 145
Sumner, W. L.: 52, 381
Sunaga, Tsuneo: 353
Sunderman, F. William: 120
Sunter, Bernd: 427
Suphan, Bernhard: 343
Supičič, Ivo: 405, 407, 413
Suppan, Wolfgang: 411, 418
Suskin, Sylvan: 51
Sutkowski, Adam: 214
Sutter, Albert de: 106
Sutter, Berthold: xxii, 138
Sutter, Milton: 97
Swackhamer, John: 308
Swainson, Dorothy: 409
Swain, Joseph Peter: 314, 315, 442
Swale, David: 445
Swanston, R. B.: 306
Swarowsky, Hans: 324
Swartland, J.: 442
SWEELINCK, Jan Pieterszoon: 60, 299, **344**, 355, 391, 392
Swenson, Edward: 411
Swift, Richard: 62, 308, 314, 322, 399, 445
Swinburne, J.: 146
Sydow-Saak, Brigitte: 442
Syfert: See Siefert, Paul
Sýkora, Václav Jan: 263
Symons, David: 322, 407
Synge, J. L.: 82
Sypher, Wylie: 92
Szegö, Júlia: 213

Szmolyan, Walter: 137, 138, 321, 324, 325, 326, 416
Szweykowski, Zygmunt Marian: 46, 100, 300, 442
Tacconi, Massimo: 54
Taddie, Daniel Lawrence: 442
Tagliavini, Luigi Ferdinando: xxxv, 21, 101, 188, 349, 356, 362, 442
Taisnier, Jean: 367, 433
Talbot, Michael: 188
Tallián, Tibor: 322
Talma, Louise: 209
Tambling, J.: 423
Tamemoto, Akiko: 305
TANEEV, Sergey Ivanovich: **345-47**, 387, 428
Tang, Paul C. L.: 422
Tannenberg, David: 337
Tannery, Paul: 70
TANS'UR, William: 133, **347-48**
Tanzer, William: see TANS'UR, William
Tapia, Martín de: 29
Tapinsmus, Matz: see PRINTZ, Wolfgang Caspar
Taranushchenko, V.: 405
Tarr, Edward H.: 140
TARTINI, Giuseppe: 66, 83, 118, 290, 332, **348-52**, 365, 434
Taruskin, Richard: 67, 316, 422
Taylor, A. E.: 70
Taylor, Charles: 442
Taylor, Eric: 285, 322
Taylor, Franklin: 267
Taylor, Irmgard C.: 219
Taylor, Sedley: 119
Tchaikovsky, Petr Il'ich: see CHAIKOVSKII, Petr Il'ich
Teachout, Terry: 359, 422
Tebaldini, Giovanni: 188, 365
Tegen, Martin: 20, 426, 444
TELEMANN, Georg Michael: **352**
TELEMANN, Georg Philipp: xxviii, xl, 133, 247, 248, 300, 328, **352-54**, 420
Telesco, Paula J.: 442
Tempelhof, Georg Friedrich: 144
Temperley, Nicholas: 179, 229, 341, 348, 435, 445
Tenney, James: 442
Tenschert, Roland: 6
Tepperman, Barry: 446
Tepping, Susan: 314
Terhardt, Ernst: 120
Termini, Olga: 324
Terry, Sir Richard: 222
Teske, Hermien: 246
Tessier, André: 209, 292

Tetenburg, Gerrit J.: 21
Tetley-Kardos, Richard: 18
TEVO, Zaccaria: **354**
Textor, K. A.: 63
Thaler, Lotte: 442
Thalheimer, E.: 18
Theile, Johann: 31
Thieme, Carl August: 218
Thieme, Ulrich: 442
Thimus, Albert, Freiherr von: 136
Thoinan, Er.: see Roquet, Antoine
    Ernest
Thom, Eitelfriedrich: xxxix, xl, 196,
    382
Thomas, Antoine-Léonard: 350
Thomas, A. F. Leighton: 17, 56, 321,
    359
Thomas, Bernard: 403
Thomas, Ernst: 323
Thomas, Franz: 357
Thompson, Clyde H: 282
Thompson, David M.: 442
Thomson, Arthur: 9
Thomson, John M.: xxi
Thomson, Ulf: 442
Thomson, William Ennis: 442
Thoor, Alf: 275
Thorne, Adrian: 324
Thürlings, Adolf: 442
Thuille, Ludwig: see LOUIS, Rudolf,
    and THUILLE, Ludwig
THURINGUS, Joachim: 224, 275,
    354-55, 412
Thym, Jürgen: 143, 306, 418
Tiella, Marco: 368
Tiersot, Julien: 51, 256, 285
TIGRINI, Orazio: 210, **355**, 391, 392
Tilesio, Balthasar Heinrich: 70
Tilmouth, Michael: 56, 95, 123, 133,
    164, 178, 180, 260, 295, 334,
    359, 360, 431, 442
Timmerman, H.: 397
Timms, Colin: 36
Tinctoris, Joannis: 26, 226
Tirabassi, Antonio: 442
Tischler, Hans: 209, 310, 432
Titcomb, Caldwell: 431
Titelouze, Jean: 423
Tittel, Ernst: 34, 40, 94, 331, 405, 443
Tiulin, Yury Nikolaevich: 280, 388,
    428
Tobeck, Christina: 368
Tobin, John: 410
Todd, R. Larry: 443
Todeschini, Cavalla Anna: 350
Tokawa, Seicchi: 18, 225
Tolkoff, Lyn: 443
Tollefsen, Randall H.: 21, 125, 344

Tolstoi, S. L.: 244
Tomas de Santa Maria: see SANTA
    MARIA, Tomas de
Tomlinson, Gary: 427, 433
Tonassi, Pietro: 264
Tonazzi, Bruno: 104
Toncitch, Voya: 443
Tonelli, Giorgio: 343
Torchi, Luigi: 26, 128, 129, 130, 190,
    243, 244, 267, 268, 269, 270,
    271, 272, 273, 279, 305, 342,
    396
Torek, Paul: 128
Tornifore, Tonino: 141
Torrefranca, Fausto: 270, 271, 273
Torres, Joseph de: 208, 216
Tortolano, William: 437
Toscano, L.: 423
TOSI, Pier Francesco: 3, **356-57**
Tóth, K. Csomasz: 392
Touchet, J.: 70
Toulmin, Stephen: 135, 137
Tourneux, M.: xx, xxix, 409
TOVEY, Sir Donald Francis: **357-61**
Towse, John: 363
Traber, Jürgen Habakuk: xxxviii
Tracy, H. L.: 359
Traficante, Frank: 443
Trapp, J. B.: xxxv
Travis, Roy: 310
Trede, Hilmar: 135
Treder, H.-J.: 99
TREIBER, Johann Philipp: **361**
Treibitz, C. Howard: 443
Treitler, Leo: 310, 313, 407
Trend, J. B.: 293
Trend, Michael: 209, 341, 430
Trevor-Roper, Hugh: 92
Trexler, Richard C.: 423
Troccoli, Gaetano: 100
Troeger, Richard: 443
Tromlitz, Johann Georg: 417
Trost, Johann Caspar: 11, 51, 72, 238,
    290, 392
Trotter, T. H. Yorke: 146
Truesdell, Clifford Ambrose: 9, 80,
    81, 82, 298, 401, 443
Trummer, Johann: 95
Trumpff, G. A.: 29, 171, 279, 379,
    397, 405, 416, 437, 441
Trunz, Erich: 136
Truscott, Harold: 127
Tschaikovsky, Petr Il'ich: see
    CHAIKOVSKII, Petr Il'ich
Tschudi, Aegidius: 109
Tsuchida, Eizaburo: 443
Tsukahara, Tetsuo: 213

Tsukkerman, Viktor Abramovich:
    387, 388
Tuchowski, Andrzej: 314
Tudor, J. M.: 418, 425
TÜRK, Daniel Gottlob: 237, **361-64**
Tuksar, Stanislav: 443, 445
Tull, James Robert: 13
Tumarkin, Anna: 343
Tureck, Rosalyn: 247
Turnbull, Robert: 359
Turner, A. J.: 92
Turner, Denis: 256
Turner, Jet E.: 443
Turner, R. Steven: 120
Turner-Smith, Ronald: 402
Turnow, Hans: 196
Turok, Paul H.: 321, 322, 447
Turrell, Frances Berry: 108, 443
Tutenberg, Fritz: 141
Tuynman, P.: xxxii
Tveit, S.: 275
Twemlow, Sidney: 399
Twittenhoff, Wilhelm: 277
Tyler, James: 443
Tyndall, John: 118
Tyrrell, John: 131
Tyson, Alan: 436
Uberti, Mauro: 443
Übele, Gerhard: 6
Ueda, Akira: 321
Uemura, Kozo: 443
Ugolini, M.: 275
Ulanov, Barry: 17, 319
Ullmann, D.: 419
Ulrich, Bernhard: 108, 356
Ulrich, Ernst: 443
Unger, Hans-Heinrich: 443
Unger, Johann Friedrich: 80
Unger-Hamilton, Clive: 445
Unsinn, Sr. Regina Therese: 446
Untersteiner, A.: 270
Unverricht, Hubert: xli, 36
Urban, Paul: 82, 138
Urquhart, Dan Murdock: 208
Urmson, J. O.: 422, 437
Ursinus, Abraham: 426
Uspensky, V. V.: 67
Utendal, Alexander: 109
Valentin, Erich: xliii, 1, 213
Valentini, Pier Francesco: 234
Valle, Pietro della: 75
VALLOTTI, Francesco Antonio:
    290, 291, **365-66**, 369, 445
Vanderdoodt, Jean-Baptiste: 87
Van der Linden, Albert: 88, 106, 275
Vander Linden, Albert: see Van der
    Linden, Albert
Vandermonde, M.: 288

Vanhulst, Henri: 444
Vanický, Jaroslav: 406
Varda, Maria Paola de: 182
Vasina-Grossman, V.: 14, 15
Vatielli, Francesco: 45, 75, 390
Vauclain, Constant: 444
Vaudou, François: xix
Vaught, Raymond: 202
Vauthier, Gabriel: 58
Vecchi, Giuseppe: xviii, 11, 23, 24, 36, 37, 187, 444
Veit, Joachim: 371
Vela, Maria Caraci: 433
Velasco, Sebastián López de: 208
Velimirović, Miloš: 205
Vellekoop, Gerrit: 239, 257, 334, 356, 363, 367, 376, 438, 444
Vendrova, T.: 15
Venn, Lyn: 223
Vente, Maarten Albert: 22, 23, 201, 219, 337, 344, 362, 381
Verba, E. Cynthia: 258, 287, 406
Verchaly, André: 20, 78, 158, 174, 178, 180, 201, 230
Verdicelli, Federico: 37
Vermazen, Bruce: 422, 423
Vernon, Philip E.: 436
Verona, Gabriella Gentili: 18
Verrall, John: 310, 321
Vertrees, Julie Anne: 444
Veselovskii, I. N.: 82
Vetter, Isolde: 41
Vetter, Walther: xxxvi, xliii, 274
Vettori, Piero: 199
VIADANA, Lodovico: 210, 237, **366**
Vianna da Motta, J.: 274
Viano, C. Augusto: xix
VICENTINO, Nicola: 36, 37, 64, 74, 99, 175, 206, 290, 293, 355, **367-69**, 391, 400, 406, 413
Vickers, Brian: 92
Vickess, S. E.: 179
Victoria, Marcos: 71
Vidal, Paul: 56
Viertel, Karl-Heinz: 26, 36, 444
Vignal, Marc: 436
Vila, José: 335
Villoteau, Guillaume André: 285
Vilmar, Irmgard: 229
Vinquist, Mary: 444
Visser, Piet: 213
Visser, R. P. W.: xxxix
Vitányi, Iván: 444
Vivian, Percival: 49
Vizcardi, Don Lazarillo: 83
Vlad, Roman: 321
Vlam, Christiaan: 344
Vockerodt, Gottfried: 25

Vockner, Josef: 40
Vötterle, Karl: xliii
Vogel, Emil: 209
Vogel, Martin: xxxi, 81, 144, 225, 443, 444
Vogelsang, Konrad: 321
Vogelsanger, Siegfried: 239
Vogler, Abbé: see VOGLER, Georg Joseph
VOGLER, Georg Joseph: 143, **369-71**, 377, 423
Vogt, Felix: 176
Vogt, M.: 131
Voigt, Johann Carl: 204
Voigt, Wolfgang: 402
Voisé, Waldemar: 109
Vojtěch, Ivan: 320, 321
Volek, Tomislav: 131, 275, 431
Volk, Arno: xliii
Voltaire, François Marie Arouet de: xxxv, 48, 256, 258
Volupius Decorus, Musagetes: see SCHONSLEDER, Wolfgang
von Dyck, Walther: 135, 136
Vonessen, Franz: 159
Voss, Egon: 171
VOSSIUS, Gerhard Johann: 21, **371-72**
VOSSIUS, Isaac: **372-73**
Voss-Wunderlich, Leonore: 396
Voye Mignot, de la: see LA VOYE-MIGNOT, de
Vregille, Camille de: 70
Vretblad, Åke: 409
Vrieslander, Otto: 18, 308
Vrin, J.: 70
Vulpius, Melchior: 84
Vysloužil, Jiří: 265
Waack, Karl-Friedrich: 28
Wachsmuth, R.: 118
Wade, Bonnie: xl
Waelrant, Hubert: 47
Waeltner, Ernst Ludwig: xxvi
Wagenseil, Georg Christoph: 19
Wager, Willis: 351
Wagner, Aleksandra: 313, 315
Wagner, Günther: 149, 302, 444
Wagner, Hans: 9
Wagner, Jeffrey: 437
Wagner, J. K.: 237
Wagner, Karl Friedrich: 215
Wagner, Manfred: 19, 41, 353, 441, 444, 445
Wagner, Richard: 105, 112, 126, 128, 130, 154, 155, 170, 171, 172, 256, 303, 379, 384, 395, 400, 408, 422, 430, 431, 446
Wagstaff, John: 313, 321, 407, 410

Wahsner, Renate: 139
Wainwright, Jonathan: 394
Waite, Russell T.: 214
Waite, William G.: 444
Waitzman, Mimi S.: 444
Waldberg, Max Freiherr von: xviii
Waldeck, Arthur: 309
Waldersee, Paul Graf: xxxiv
Waldmann, Guido: 13, 14
Waldstein, Wilhelm: 40
Walker, Alan: 311, 445
Walker, Daniel P.: 408
Walker, David Pickering: 21, 37, 100, 137, 351, 444, 445, 447
Walker, Ernest: 358, 359, 360, 434
Walker, Geoffrey J.: 197
Walker, John A.: 314
Walker, Paul Mark: 344, 445
Wallace, Barbara K.: 64
Wallis, Charles Glenn: 135
WALLIS, John: 221, 294, **374-75**
Wallon, Simone: 58, 411
Walls, Peter: 104, 430
Walsh, Stephen: 445
Walter, Horst: 95
Walter, Rudolf: 214, 215
WALTHER, Johann Gottfried: 34, 38, 153, 196, 197, 204, **375-77**
Walton, William: 409
Waltz, Hermann: 331
Wang, Richard: 227
Wangermée, Robert: 88
Ward, John M.: 296
Warfield, Gerald: xxvi
Waring, William: 284
Warner, James F.: 378
Warner, Thomas: 35
Warrack, Guy: 445
Warrack, John: 67, 163, 197, 431
Warrain, Francis: 136
Warren, Charles: 445
Warren, Richard M.: 118,120
Warren, Roslyn P.: 118
Wason, Robert Wesley: 273, 319, 415, 445
Wasson, D. DeWitt: 403
Watanabe, Ruth: 239
Waters, Edward N.: 40
Wates, Roye E.: 437
Watson, Henry: 178
Watt, Henry J.: 119
Weaver, Hazel G.: 209, 441
Weaver, William: 67
Webb, R. K.: 436
Webbe: 167
Webber, Geoffrey: 197
Webber, W. S. Lloyd: 147
Weber: xxxvi

Weber, Carl Maria von: 370, 371
Weber, Christoph Maria von: 379
Weber, Édith: 161, 188, 402, 413, 426, 437
WEBER, (Jacob) Gottfried: 87, 266, 369, **377-79**, 407, 416
Weber, J. G.: 445
Weber, William: 433, 445
Webern, Anton: 318, 397
Webster, C.: 446
Webster, Charles.: 92
Webster, James: xl, 437
Webster, William: 313
Wechsler, Bert: 437
Wegele, Ludwig: 213
Wehmeyer, Grete: 63
Wehrhan, August Heinrich: 190
Wehrli, Werner: 136
Weightman, J. G.: 137
Weigl, Bruno: 445
Weiland, Frits: 312
Weinberg, Jacob: 347
Weinmann, Alexander: 7, 263
Weinstein, Esther Hoffman: 437
Weinstock, Herbert: 415
Weise, Dagmar: xliii
Weiss, Adolph: 320, 322
Weiß, Günter: xliii
Weiss, Piero: 63, 257, 265, 445
Weißbach, Rüdiger: 408
Weißbeck, Johann Michael: 370
Weisse, Hans: 307, 309
Weissmann, John: 420
Weitzman, Ronald: 436
WEITZMANN, Carl Friedrich: **379-80**
Welby, Frances A.: 119
Wellek, Albert: 342, 445
Wellesz, Egon J.: 95, 309, 322, 323, 409, 420, 445
Wells, Alan: 325
Wells, Robin Headlam: 50
Wen, Eric: 317
Wenig, Peter: 25
WERCKMEISTER, Andreas: 25, 43, 124, 217, **380-83**
Werlé, Frederick: 310, 415
Wermbter, Paul: 274
Werner, Arno: 26
Werner, Christoph: 299
Werner, Eric: 137, 408, 435, 443
Werner, Krzysztof: 300 (see Werner, Christoph)
Werner, L.-G.: 262
Wernli, Andreas: 24
Werts, Daniel: 197, 445
Wesendonk, K. von: 119
Wesley, Samuel: 167

Wesołowski, F.: 73
Wessel, Frederick T.: 445
Wessely, Helene: 211, 224
Wessely, Othmar: xxi, xxii, xxxvi, xliii, 40, 94, 95, 111, 141, 187, 196, 242, 411, 414, 417, 445
Westcombe, John: 399
Westendorf, Craig J.: 109
Westfall, Richard S.: 374
Westphal, Kurt: 40
WESTPHAL, Rudolf: **384-85**
Westrup, Jack Allan: 29, 43, 94, 101, 108, 141, 171, 178, 180, 187, 196, 201, 206, 209, 223, 231, 235, 236, 238, 244, 245, 251, 252, 253, 255, 256, 286, 293, 294, 334, 355, 356, 398, 399, 409, 410, 415, 417, 427, 431, 435, 441, 442, 446
Wettstein, Peter: 397
Wetzel, Hermann: 154, 173, 273
Wever, Ernest Glen: 120
Weyer, Rolf-Dieter: 120
Whatley, George Larry: 360, 437, 445
Whelden, Roy M. III: 297
Whiteman, Michael: 275
Whiteside, D. T.: 138
Whitfield, John B. R.: 360
Whitmore, Philip: 18, 143, 148, 363, 446
Whitmore, P. J. S.: 202
Whitrow, G. J.: 135
Whittaker, James: 376
Whittaker, W. Gillies: 399
Whittall, Arnold: 306, 312, 313, 319, 322, 401, 407, 410, 435, 446
Wichmann, Hermann: 106
Wichmann, Kurt: 356, 446
Wicklein, Gerald: 82
Widmann, Bernhard: 224
Wiechens, Bernward: 188
Wiehmayer, Theodor: 274
Wienke, Gerhard: 13, 275
Wienpahl, Robert W.: 393, 446
Wiese, Christian Ludwig Gustav, Freiherr von: 393
Wieser, Heinz-Gregor: 95
Wightman, William Persehouse Delisle: 91, 374, 446
Wihtol, Austris A.: 130
Wilbrandt, Jürgen: 311
Wilcox, Donald J.: 423
Wildgruber, Jens: 171
Wili, Hans: 343
Wilkins, Harry P.: 128
Wilkinson, Cathryn: 47
Wilkinson, Christopher: 110, 193
Wilkinson, Ronald Sterne: 374

Wiłkomirski, Mazimierz: 388
Will, Roy T.: 257
Willaert, Adrian: 391, 425
Wille, Günther: 42
Wille, Rudolf: xl
Willfort, E. St.: 108
Willheim, Imanuel: 301
Williams, David Russell: 446
Williams, J. G.: 234
Williams, Kathleen: 49
Williams, Peter: 22, 24, 30, 93, 195, 231, 239, 292, 296, 381, 383, 402, 405, 410, 417, 430, 436, 441, 446
Williams, Robert Fortson: 201
Williamson, Winifred F.: 147, 348
Willier, Stephen: 46
Willner, Channan: 314, 315, 412
Wills, Harold Edward: 292
Wilson, Bernard E.: 417
Wilson, Christopher Robert: 49, 227
Wilson, Colin: 92, 137
Wilson, Dora Jean: 165, 166
Wilson, Gladys M.: 209, 435
Wilson, John: 221, 223
Wilson, Margaret D.: 71
Wilson, Paul: 422
Wilson, Peter Niklas: 18, 19
Wilson, Thelma: 295
Winckel, Fritz: 82, 298, 446
Wingell, Richard: 226
Wingert, Hans: 309
Winick, Steven David: 446
Winnington-Ingram, R. P.: 385
Winter, E.: 80
Winter, Eduard: 82
Winter, Marion O: 335
Winter, Robert: 422
Winterfeld, Carl von: 428
Winternitz, Emanuel: 201, 446
Wintle, Christopher W.: 306, 308, 314, 315, 324, 360, 407, 408, 422, 446
Winzenburger, Janet: 39, 286, 302
Winzenburger, Walter: 143, 195
Wiora, Walter: xxxix, xxxv, xxxix, xl, xliii, 40, 191, 283, 386, 329, 446
Wirth, Franz: 446
Wisdom, J. O.: 70
Wiśniowski, Jerzy: xl
Withol, Joseph: 279
Witkowski, Leon: 446
Witthauer, Johann Georg: 165
Witting, C.: 177
Wittlich, Gary E.: 447
Wittwer, Max: 446
Wöhlke, Franz: 204
Wörner, Karl H.: 137

Wohlfahrt, Frank: 155
Wokler, Robert: 284, 286
Woldemar, Michel: 212
Woldt, John William: 29
Wolf, Edward: 5
Wolf, E. W.: 19
Wolf, Hans: 309, 446
Wolf, J.: 367
Wolf, Johannes: xxxii, xliii, 446
Wolf, R. E.: 2
Wolff, Chr.: 82
Wolff, Christian: 402
Wolff, Christoph: xxxiv, 437, 446
Wolff, Conrad: 324
Wolff, Gustav (Tyson-): 128, 130
Wolff, Hellmuth Christian: 20, 209, 274, 275, 327
Wolff, Konrad: 302, 446
Wolffheim, Werner: xliii
Wollenberg, Susan: 18, 95, 197, 214, 215, 338
Wonderlich, Elvera: 94
Wonnegger, Johannes Litavicus: 108
Wood, Charles: 146
Wood, David A.: xxiii
Wood, Godfrey: 104
Wood, Ross: 73
Woodcock, Edith: 435
Woodfield, Ian: 426
Woodley, Ronald: 160, 433
Woods, Frances: 442
Woodward, Henry: 359, 398, 424
Woolard, Margot Ann Greenlimb: 362
Woolf, Harry: 99
Worbs, Hans Christian: 443
Worbs, Hans Christoph: 283, 286
Wordsworth, W. B.: 360
Wordsworth, William: 56
Wožna, Małgorzata; 177
Wucherpfennig, Hermann: 3
Wuensch, Gerhard: 275
Würze, Anton: 137
Würzl, Eberhard: 7, 436
Wunderlich, Henry: 446
Wunderlich, Lenore: 400
Wuorinen, Charles: 400
Wussing, H.: 82

Wustmann, Rudolf: 438
Wutta, Eva Renate: 188
Wyneken, Gustav: 112
Yamada, Mitsugu: 353
Yamagata, Shigetaro: 322
Yamaguchi, Hiroko: 447
Yarustovsky, Boris Mikhailovich: 14, 447
Yasser, Joseph: 320, 400
Yasuda, Hiroshi: 155
Yates, Frances Amelia: 91, 92, 447
Yates, Peter: 400
YAVORSKY, Boleslav Leopol'dovich: 345, 346, **386-89**, 420
Yeston, Maury: 307, 310, 311, 312, 447
Yevseev, Sergei Vasilevich: 410
Yokota, Erisa: 314
Yoshida, Kazuko: 258
Young, Alison: 49
Young, Percy M.: 32, 309
Youngren, William H.: 422, 436
Youschkevitch, A. P.: 80, 82 (see Juškevič, Adolf P.)
YSSANDON, Jean: **389**, 439
Zaccaria, Vittore Sante: 188, 366
ZACCONI, Lodovico: 53, 59, 121, **390-91**
Zahn, Dana: 263
Zak, Vladimir: 15
Zakharova, Ol'ga: 376
Zakrzewska-Gebka, Elzbieta: 135
Zam, Maurice: 324
Zamazal, Franz: 41
Zaminer, Frieder: xl, 106, 269, 447
Zamorski, A.: 279
Zanden, Jos van der: 7
Zanetti, Emilia: 36
Zanon, Giancarlo: 365
Zanoncelli, Luisa: 69, 71
Zanotti, Francesco Maria: 187, 188
Zappala', Pietro: 443
Zarco del Valle, M. R.: 208
ZARLINO, Gioseffo: 10, 11, 28, 33, 34, 46, 47, 51, 52, 59, 64, 77, 80, 97, 98, 99, 100, 108, 117, 135, 139, 158, 198, 199, 200,

206, 208, 210, 226, 229, 236, 240, 250, 261, 269, 293, 329, 344, 355, 367, 389, **391-95**, 402, 413, 417, 436
Zaslaw, Neal: 251, 252, 253, 254, 255, 256, 403, 430, 441, 444, 447
Zaszkaliczky, Tamás: 73
Zawadzki, Jerzy: 300
Zayas, Rodrigo de: 293
Zejfas, Natalija: 197
Zeleny, Walter: 331
Zelter, Karl Friedrich: 439
Zemtsovsky, Izalii: 14, 15
Zenck, Hermann: xxii, xlii, 59, 367, 393, 447
Zenck, Martin: 302
Zenetti, Leopold von: 41
Zenkl, Luděk: 120, 265
Zentner, Wilhelm: 173
Zezza, Elvira: 393
Zhitomirsky, D. V.: 16
Zich, Jaroslav: 14
Ziebler, Karl: 447
ZIEHN, Bernhard: 272, **395-96**
Ziggelaar, Aug.: 135
Ziino, Agostino: 188, 234, 351
Zijlstra, Miep: 286, 397
Ziller, Ernst: 43
Zillig, Winfried: 323
Zimmerl, Hanns: 171
Zimmerman, Franklin B.: 223, 235
Zimmermann, Jörg: 447
Zimmermann, Michael: 258
Zinar, Ruth: 447
Zingel, Hans Joachim: xliii
Zingerle, Francesco G.: 267
Zipp, Friedrich: 416
Zorina, A. P.: 280
Zsako, Julius: 214
Zubrilov, I: 134
Zuckerkandl, Victor: 309, 311
Zuckerman, Elliott: 171
Zurmühl, Georg: 119
Zychowicz, James L.: 447
Żymalkowski, Ulrich: 159